...blatt is a writer, editor, and educational consultant who has ...ively in Asia, Africa, and Latin America. During the past 30 ...contributed to more than 50 elementary, junior high, and high ...udies texts and ancillaries, and has written almost a dozen his... ...teenagers. A graduate of Hunter College of the City of New ...niversity of Chicago, Greenblatt is a former teacher and a mem... ...onal Association of Scholars and the Illinois Council for Social ...listed in *Who's Who in America 2003* and *Who's Who in the World*

...o is a high school teacher in the New York City school system, ...taught since 1970. A graduate of the City College of New York ...niversity of New York, he has trained student teachers and con... ...veral books. Lemmo has been instrumental in developing pilot ...programs and curricula and was rated an exemplary teacher by ...cation Department of New York. He is also a member of the ...ncil for the Social Studies, the Association for Supervision and ...Development, and other professional organizations, and he has ...sively in more than 55 countries.

...encoe

The McGraw-Hill Companies

...ited States of America

...s to:
...-Hill
...e
...3240-4027

...40-1 (Student Edition)

...24-X (Teacher Wraparound Edition)

.../043 08 07 06 05 04 03

ACADEMIC CONSULTANTS

Jerrold Green, Ph.D.
Director
Middle East Studies Center
University of Arizona
Tucson, Arizona

Al Naklowycz, Ph.D.
President
Ukrainian-American Academic Association of California
Carmichael, California

Joseph R. Rosenbloom, Ph.D.
Professor of Classics
Washington University
St. Louis, Missouri

FOLDABLES **Dinah Zike**
Educational Consultant
Dinah-Might Activities, Inc.
San Antonio, Texas

TEACHER REVIEWERS

Richard Ammentorp
Schaumburg School District
Schaumburg, Illinois

Rick Boeglin
Richardson North Junior High School
Richardson, Texas

Margaret Gray, Ph.D.
Vigo County School Corporation
Terre Haute, Indiana

Kathleen A. Grotto
West Orange Senior High School
West Orange, New Jersey

Dianne Hill
Muskogee Public Schools
Muskogee, Oklahoma

Joseph Scheideler
Canton Junior/Senior High School
Collinsville, Connecticut

Janice H. Suddith
Paul Laurence Dunbar Middle School for Innovation
Lynchburg, Virginia

Teacher Wraparound Edition

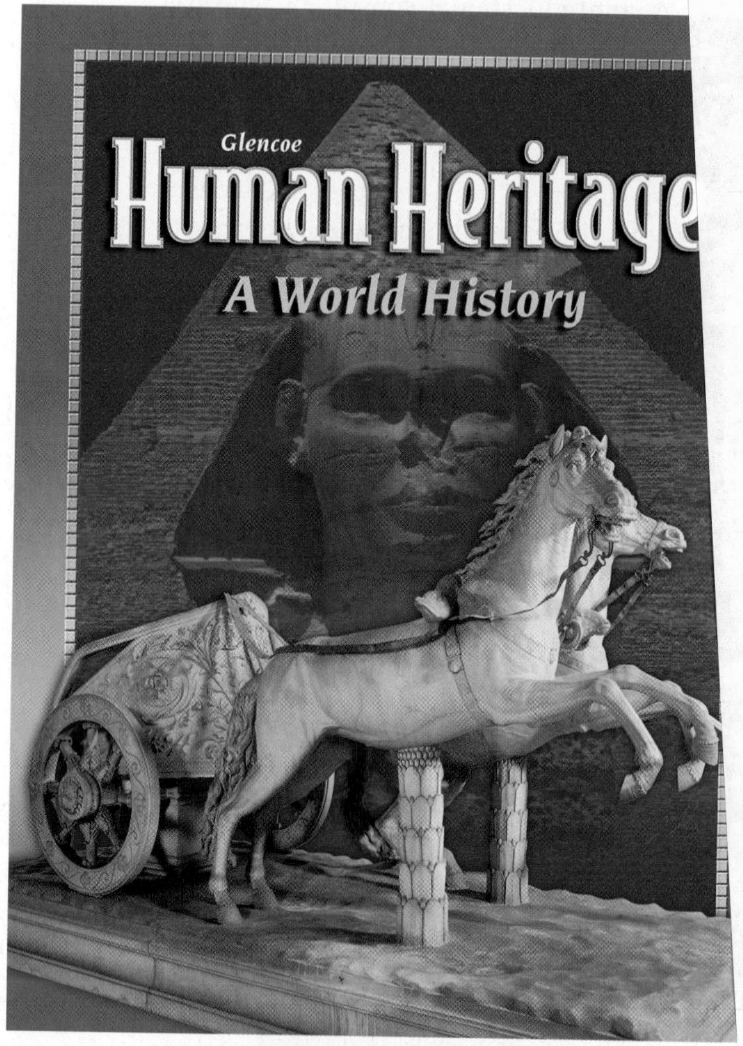

Miriam Greenblatt
Peter S. Lemmo

McGraw Hill Glencoe

New York, New York Columbus, Ohio Chicago, Illinois Peoria, Illinois Woodland H

AUTHORS

Miriam Green
traveled extens
years, she has
school social st
tory books for
York and the U
ber of the Nati
Studies. She is
2003.

Peter S. Lemm
where he has
and the City U
tributed to se
instructional
the State Edu
National Cou
Curriculum D
traveled exte

McGraw Hill Gl

Printed in the Un

Send all inquirie
Glencoe/McGra
8787 Orion Pla
Columbus, OH

ISBN 0-07-8462

ISBN 0-07-8462

1 2 3 4 5 6 07

gift

Contents

Contents

Contents

Unit 12 The Twentieth Century

PRIMARY SOURCES Library

NATIONAL GEOGRAPHIC

Features

Map Skills

Critical Thinking Skills

Technology Skills

People in History

Charts, Diagrams, and Illustrations

Map Study

NCSS Correlation

Theme	1	2	3	4	5
Culture and Traditions	4, 5	1, 2	1, 2, 3	2, 3, 4	1, 2
Continuity and Change	1, 2, 5	1, 2	1	2	1, 2
Geography and History	1, 2, 3, 4, 5	1, 2	1, 2	1, 2, 4	1, 2
Individual Action	5	1, 2	1, 2	1, 2, 4	1, 2
Groups and Institutions		1, 2	1, 2	2, 3, 4	1, 2
Government and Democracy		2	1, 2	2, 3	2
Economic Factors	3	2	1, 2	3, 4	
Science and Technology			3	5	
Global Connections	1		2, 3	3, 5	
Civic Rights and Responsibilities					
Skill Category/ Specific Skill	**Map Skills/** Understanding a Mercator Projection **Critical Thinking Skills/** Understanding Cause and Effect	**Map Skills/** Determining Relative Location	**Critical Thinking Skills/** Distinguishing Fact from Opinion **Map Skills/** Identifying Physical Features	**Map Skills/** Reading Map Legends	

Theme	11	12	13	14	15
Culture and Traditions	1, 2	1, 2	1, 2, 3	4	1, 2, 3
Continuity and Change	1	2	2	2, 5	2, 4
Geography and History			1	2, 3, 4, 5	1, 4
Individual Action	1, 2	1, 2	2	1, 3, 5	1, 2, 3, 4
Groups and Institutions	1	1	2	2, 5	3, 4
Government and Democracy	2	1, 2	3	1, 3, 5	1, 2, 4
Economic Factors		2	1, 2	3, 4	2, 4
Science and Technology	2				
Global Connections		2	3	3, 4	2
Civic Rights and Responsibilities	2			1	1
Skill Category/ Specific Skill			**Map Skills/** Reading a Political Map		**Critical Thinking Skills/** Identifying the Main Idea

*The section numbers set in red indicate the central theme of the section.

Theme	6	7	8	9	10
Culture and Traditions	1, 2	1, 2, 3	1, 2, 3, 5, 6	1, 2	1, 2, 3, 4
Continuity and Change	1, 2	3	5, 6	2	3, 4
Geography and History	1, 2	1, 3	4, 5, 6	1, 2	1, 3
Individual Action	1, 2	1, 2, 3	1, 2, 5, 6	1, 2	1, 2, 3
Groups and Institutions	1, 2	3	1, 5	1, 2	1, 3
Government and Democracy		1, 3			1, 3
Economic Factors	1	2, 3	1, 2, 3, 5, 6	1, 2	2, 3
Science and Technology		2	2, 5		
Global Connections	1, 2		1, 2, 3		
Civic Rights and Responsibilities					1, 2, 3
Skill Category/ Specific Skill	Map Skills/ Reading a Map Scale Critical Thinking Skills/Making Comparisons		Map Skills/ Reading Latitude	Map Skills/ Reading Longitude	Map Skills/Reading Physical Maps Crtitcal Thinking Skills/ Recognizing Bias

Theme	16	17	18	19	20
Culture and Traditions	1, 2, 3	1	1, 3	1, 2	1, 2
Continuity and Change	2, 3	1	3	1, 2	1, 2
Geography and History	2, 3	2	2	1, 2	1, 3
Individual Action	1, 2	1	1, 2, 3	2	1, 2
Groups and Institutions	1, 2, 3	1, 2	1, 2, 3	1, 2	2, 3
Government and Democracy		1, 2		2	
Economic Factors		2	3	2	1
Science and Technology					
Global Connections	1, 2	2	3	1, 2	3
Civic Rights and Responsibilities					
Skill Category/ Specific Skill			Technology Skills/ Developing Multimedia Presentations Map Skills/ Understanding Inset Maps		Map Skills/ Tracing Historical Routes

NCSS Correlation

Theme	21	22	23	24	25
Culture and Traditions	1, 2, 3	1, 2, 3	1, 2, 3, 4	1, 2, 3, 4	1, 2, 3, 4
Continuity and Change	1, 2, 3, 4	1, 2	1, 2, 3, 4	2	2
Geography and History	1, 2, 4	1, 2	1, 2, 4	1, 4	4
Individual Action	2, 3	1, 2	2, 3, 4	1, 2, 4	2, 3, 4
Groups and Institutions	1, 2, 3, 4	1, 2	1, 2, 3, 4	2, 3, 4	1, 2, 3, 4
Government and Democracy	1, 2	1	2, 4	1, 2	1, 2
Economic Factors	1, 4	2	1, 2	1, 4	4
Science and Technology		3			4
Global Connections	3, 4	1, 3			4
Civic Rights and Responsibilities				1, 4	
Skill Category/ Specific Skill	Critical Thinking Skills/Making Generalizations		Map Skills/ Analyzing Historical Maps		Technology Skills/ Evaluating a Web Site Map Skills/ Determining Exact Location

Theme	31	32	33	34	35
Culture and Traditions	1, 2, 3	1, 2, 3	2, 4	1	1, 2, 3
Continuity and Change	1, 2, 3	1, 2, 3	3, 4, 5	1, 2	1, 2, 3
Geography and History	1, 2, 3, 4, 5	1, 2	2, 4	1, 2	1, 2
Individual Action	1, 3	1, 2, 3	1, 3, 4, 5	1, 2	1, 2, 3
Groups and Institutions	2, 3, 4	1, 2, 3	1, 3, 4	1, 2	2, 3
Government and Democracy	1, 2, 3, 4, 5, 6	1, 2, 3	4	1, 2	1, 2, 3
Economic Factors	1, 2, 3, 4, 5, 6	1, 2, 3	2, 3, 4, 5	1, 2	1, 2, 3
Science and Technology		3	1, 2, 3, 4, 5	1	
Global Connections	1, 2, 3, 4, 5, 6	1, 3	1, 2, 3, 4, 5	2	1, 2
Civic Rights and Responsibilities	3	1, 2, 3	4	1	1, 2
Skill Category/ Specific Skill		Map Skills/ Reading a Military Map Technology Skills/ Building a Database			Map Skills/ Comparing Historical Maps Critical Thinking Skills/Predicting Consquences

*The section numbers set in red indicate the central theme of the section.

Theme	26	27	28	29	30
Culture and Traditions	1, 2, 3, 4, 5	1, 2, 3, 4, 5	1, 2, 3, 4, 5	1, 2, 3, 4, 5	
Continuity and Change	2, 3, 5	2, 4, 5	1	2, 3	1, 2
Geography and History	1, 2, 3	1, 2, 4, 5	1	5, 6	1, 2, 3
Individual Action	3, 4, 5	1, 2, 3, 4	1, 2, 3, 4, 5	1, 2, 3, 4, 5	1, 2, 3
Groups and Institutions	2, 3, 4	2, 5	1, 4	1, 2, 3, 4, 5, 6	2
Government and Democracy	3	1, 2, 3, 4, 5	1, 4, 5	4, 5, 6	1, 2, 3
Economic Factors	1, 2, 3, 4	1, 3	1, 3		1, 2, 3
Science and Technology		3, 4	1, 3		1
Global Connections	1		3	2, 3	1, 2, 3
Civic Rights and Responsibilities			1		
Skill Category/ Specific Skill				Critical Thinking Skills/Drawing Conclusions	Map Skills/ Reviewing Map Legends

Theme	36	37	38	39
Culture and Traditions	1, 2, 3, 5	1, 2, 3	2, 3	1, 2, 3
Continuity and Change	2, 3	1, 2, 3	1, 3	1, 2, 3
Geography and History	1, 2, 3, 4	1, 2, 3	1	1, 2
Individual Action	2, 3, 4	1, 2, 3	1, 2, 3	1, 2, 3
Groups and Institutions	3	2, 3	2, 3	1, 2, 3
Government and Democracy	1, 2, 3, 4, 5	1, 2	1, 2, 3	1, 2, 3
Economic Factors	1, 2, 3, 4, 5	1, 2, 3	1, 2, 3	1, 2, 3
Science and Technology	1, 3	1	1	3
Global Connections	2, 3, 4, 5	1, 2, 3	1, 3	1, 2, 3
Civic Rights and Responsibilities	5	2	1, 3	1, 2, 3
Skill Category/ Specific Skill			Technology Skills/ Using an Electronic Spreadsheet	Map Skills/ Reading a Demographic Map

Classroom Solutions

Reading Strategies

How Can I Help My Students Read and Understand the Textbook?

Social studies teachers do not have to be reading teachers to help students read and understand their textbooks. Often poor readers lack interest in the topic, have trouble concentrating, cannot understand a word or sentence, or are confused as to how the information fits together. These problems can frustrate the student and the teacher, but there are strategies that can be used to improve comprehension and retention of information. Using these reading strategies not only helps poor readers, but also strengthens the reading skills of strong readers.

Activate Prior Knowledge

Activating prior knowledge provides opportunities for students to discover and articulate what they already know about key concepts and ideas. It stimulates student interest and prepares students to incorporate new information into a larger picture. In addition, it helps the teacher to determine a starting place for instruction.

George Lee White/CORBIS

- ✔ Write the topic on the board and have students brainstorm what they know about it. Record their responses on the board.
- ✔ Ask general or specific questions about the topic and see how students respond to them.
- ✔ Present an anticipation guide. An anticipation guide provides a series of statements about an idea or topic. Students read each statement and tell whether they agree or disagree, based on their prior understandings and experiences.
- ✔ Use a K-W-L-H or K-W-L chart to activate prior knowledge and set reading purposes. Students identify what they already **know** (or think they know) and what they **want** to find out about the topic. After reading, students complete the chart.

K	W	L	H
What I **Know**	What I **Want** to Find Out	What I **Learned**	**How** I Can Learn More

Set Reading Purposes

Reading is a purposeful activity. We read to find answers to specific questions, to satisfy curiosity, and to be entertained.

- ✔ Have students preview the reading selection. Tell students to read the title, headings, and subheadings. Draw students' attention to diagrams, tables, and other visuals and their captions. Discuss how these will help comprehension.
- ✔ Prompt students to predict what they might learn in the selection, based on their preview. Invite them to list additional questions they hope to answer through the reading. Have them identify possible problems, such as unfamiliar words or ideas, to watch for as they read.
- ✔ Discuss the need to "shift gears" in reading speed and attention when reading. Support students as they plan how best to read a selection—slowly to watch for new vocabulary and ideas or quickly to review previously learned ideas. They can also discuss new information with a buddy as they read.

Vocabulary Development

Vocabulary knowledge and reading comprehension are closely related.

- ✔ Before students read, preteach vocabulary that is crucial for understanding key topics and concepts.
- ✔ Relate new vocabulary to known words and ideas. After introducing a word and its definition, have students name synonyms or related words they know.
- ✔ If a student encounters an unfamiliar word while reading, have him or her try to pronounce it aloud. Sometimes saying the word will trigger one's memory of its meaning.
- ✔ As students read, help them use prefixes (word parts added to the beginning of base words), suffixes (word parts added to the end of base words), and roots (word elements from which other words are formed) as clues to decipher the meaning of words.
- ✔ Encourage students to use the context of surrounding words and sentences to determine a word's meaning.
- ✔ If context clues and structural analysis fail to help a student understand an important word as

Common Prefixes	Meanings	Examples
un-, dis-, non-, im- and il-	"not" or "the opposite of"	unwrapped, dishonest, nonprofit, immortal, illogical
re-	"again" or "back"	reheat
post-	"after"	postwar
uni-	"one"	unicycle

Common Suffixes	Meanings	Examples
-ship, -hood	"state of" or "condition of"	friendship, neighborhood
-ment	"act of" or "state of"	management
-ish	"like"	childish
-ous	"full of" or "like"	joyous

they read, have students find the definition in a glossary or dictionary. If the word is not critical for understanding, have students note the word and read on. Later, have students reread the word in context. If the meaning is still unclear, have students consult the dictionary.

Taking Notes

Taking notes challenges readers to determine what is most important and to organize information in a way that makes sense. Note-taking can also help students stay focused as they read. Reviewing notes can build students' retention of important information.

✔ Have students take notes after they have read long paragraphs in the section rather than the entire chapter. This helps them focus on important ideas and details and prevents them from losing track of the flow of information.

✔ Remind students that as they take notes on the section, they should not take a long time to do it. Students should read, think, write, and move on.

✔ Have students take notes using note cards. Notes should be recorded in the students' own words and labeled with the page number where the entire text appears.

✔ To use notes to review a passage, have students read through the notes, highlighting the most important information. As they review, encourage students to annotate their notes, making connections between related ideas and clarifying difficult concepts.

Summarizing

Summarizing demands that students identify the most important ideas and details to create a streamlined version of the text.

✔ After reading the section, have students recall as much of the information as possible. If the main idea and its supporting details are presented in a certain order, make sure students can recall that organization.

✔ As they summarize, students should try to answer as many of the following questions as possible: *who, what, where, when, why,* and *how.*

✔ If the section does not have a main idea that is clearly stated, have students create one that is concise but comprehensive. Have students state the main idea in a topic sentence at the beginning of their summaries.

✔ Sometimes summaries seem disconnected when details are left out. Students should use connector words such as "and" or "because," along with introductory or closing statements, to make ideas more connected.✦

Reading Comprehension: Be Aware, Reread, and Connect (BARC)

Advice from Dr. Elizabeth Pryor, Ph.D.
Research Center for Educational Technology
Kent State University, Kent, Ohio

Many students think silent reading means just looking at words and saying them in their heads. They do not make the connection that reading is supposed to make sense! Have you ever read a paragraph or a page and then said to yourself, "What was that?" As a good reader, you were aware of your lack of understanding. Poor readers, on the other hand, just keep on reading the words, unaware that they do not understand them.

What strategies do good readers use when this happens? Most reread the text they did not understand. Before rereading I study key words I might have missed. When I reread, sometimes I "whisper read" so I can hear the text as well as read it. As I reread, I try to connect what I am reading with something I already know. If I reread and still don't understand, I read it a third (or fourth) time. Each rereading increases comprehension.

In summary, **Be aware** of understanding as you read, **reread,** and **connect** the reading to what you already know. **BARC!**

Classroom Solutions

Test-Taking Strategies

How Can I Help My Students Succeed on Tests?

It's not enough for students to learn social studies facts and concepts—they must be able to show what they know in a variety of test-taking situations.

How Can I Help My Students Do Well On Objective Tests?

Objective tests may include multiple choice, true/false, and matching questions. Applying the following strategies can help students do their best on objective tests.

Multiple Choice Questions

- ✔ Students should read the directions carefully to learn what answer the test requires—the best answer or the right answer. This is especially important when answer choices include "all of the above" or "none of the above."
- ✔ Advise students to watch for negative words in the questions, such as *not, except, unless, never,* and so forth. If the question contains a negative, the correct answer choice is the one that does not fit.
- ✔ Students should try to mentally answer the question before reading the answer choices.
- ✔ Students should read all the answer choices and cross out those that are obviously wrong. Then they should choose an answer from those that remain.

True/False Questions

- ✔ It is important that students read the entire question before answering. For an answer to be true, the entire statement must be true. If one part of a statement is false, the answer should be marked *False.*
- ✔ Remind students to watch for words like *all, never, every,* and *always.* Statements containing these words are often false.

Matching Questions

- ✔ Students should read through both lists before they mark any answers.
- ✔ Unless an answer can be used more than once, students should cross out each choice as they use it.
- ✔ Using what they know about grammar can help students find the right answer. For instance, when matching a word with its definition, the definition is often the same part of speech (noun, verb, adjective, and so forth) as the word.

How Can I Help My Students Do Well On Essay Tests?

Essay tests require students to provide thorough and well-organized written responses, in addition to telling what they know. Help students use the following strategies on essay tests.

Analyze:	To **analyze** means to systematically and critically examine all parts of an issue or event.
Classify or Categorize:	To **classify** or **categorize** means to put people, things, or ideas into groups, based on a common set of characteristics.
Compare and Contrast:	To **compare** is to show how things are similar, or alike. To **contrast** is to show how things are different.
Describe:	To **describe** means to present a sketch or impression. Rich details, especially details that appeal to the senses, flesh out a description.
Discuss:	To **discuss** means to systematically write about all sides of an issue or event.
Evaluate:	To **evaluate** means to make a judgment and support it with evidence.
Explain:	To **explain** means to clarify or make plain.
Illustrate:	To **illustrate** means to provide examples or to show with a picture or other graphic.
Infer:	To **infer** means to read between the lines or to use knowledge and experience to draw conclusions, make a generalization, or form a prediction.
Justify:	To **justify** means to prove or to support a position with specific facts and reasons.
Predict:	To **predict** means to tell what will happen in the future, based on an understanding of prior events and behaviors.
State:	To **state** means to briefly and concisely present information.
Summarize:	To **summarize** means to give a brief overview of the main points of an issue or event.
Trace:	To **trace** means to present the steps or stages in a process or event in sequential or chronological order.

Read the Question

The key to writing successful essay responses lies in reading and interpreting questions correctly. Teach students to identify and underline key words in the questions, and to use these words to guide them in understanding what the question asks. Help students understand the meaning of some of the most common key words, listed in the chart on page T20.

Plan and Write the Essay

After students understand the question, they should follow the writing process to develop their answer. Encourage students to follow the steps below to plan and write their essays.

1. Map out an answer. Make lists, webs, or an outline to plan the response.

↓

2. Decide on an order in which to present the main points.

↓

3. Write an opening statement that directly responds to the essay question.

↓

4. Write the essay. Expand on the opening statement. Support key points with specific facts, details, and reasons.

↓

5. Write a closing statement that brings the main points together.

↓

6. Proofread to check for spelling, grammar, and punctuation.

How Can I Help My Students Prepare for Standardized Tests?

Students can follow the steps below to prepare for a test.

Bill Aron/PhotoEdit

✔ **Read About the Test** Students can familiarize themselves with the format of the test, the types of questions that will be asked, and the amount of time they will have to complete the test.

✔ **Review the Content** Consistent study throughout the school year will help students build social studies knowledge and understanding. If there are specific objectives or standards that are tested on the exam, help students review these facts or skills to be sure they are proficient.

✔ **Practice** Provide practice, ideally with real released tests, to build students' familiarity with the content, format, and timing of the real exam. Students should practice all the types of questions they will encounter on the test—multiple choice, short answer, and extended response.

✔ **Analyze Practice Results** Help students improve test-taking performance by analyzing their test-taking strengths and weaknesses. Spend time discussing students' completed practice tests, explaining why particular answers are right or wrong. Help students identify what kinds of questions they had the most difficulty with. Look for patterns in errors and then tailor instruction to review the appropriate test-taking skills or social studies content.✦

Help Students Learn by Reviewing Graded Tests

Advice from Tara Musslewhite
Humble Independent School District
Humble, Texas

Frequently reviewing graded tests is a great way for students to assess their test-taking skills. It also gives teachers the opportunity to teach test-taking strategies and review content. As the class rereads each test question, guide students to think logically about their answer choices. Show students how to:

1. Read each question carefully to determine its meaning.
2. Look for key words in the question to support their answers.
3. Recognize synonyms in the answer choices that may match phrases in the question.
4. Narrow down answer choices by eliminating ones that don't make sense.
5. Anticipate the answer before looking at the answer choices.
6. Circle questions of which they are unsure and go back to them later. Sometimes a clue will be found in another question on the test.

Classroom Solutions

Alternative Assessment Strategies

How Can I Go Beyond Tests to Assess Students' Understanding of Social Studies Facts and Concepts?

In response to the growing demand for accountability in the classroom, educators must use multiple assessment measures to accurately gauge student performance. In addition to quizzes, tests, essay exams, and standardized tests, assessment today incorporates a variety of performance-based measures and portfolio opportunities.

What Are Some Typical Performance-Based Assessments?

There are many kinds of performance-based assessments. They all share one common characteristic—they challenge students to create products that demonstrate what they know. One good way to present a performance assessment is in the form of an open-ended question.

Writing

Performance-based writing assessments challenge students to apply their knowledge of social studies concepts and information in a variety of written ways. Writing activities are most often completed by one student, rather than by a group.

- ✔ **Journals** Students write from the perspective of a historical character or a citizen of a particular historical era.
- ✔ **Letters** Students write a letter from one historical figure to another or from a historical figure to a family member or other audience.
- ✔ **Position Paper or Editorial** Students explain a controversial issue and present their own opinion and recommendations, supported with strong evidence and convincing reasons.
- ✔ **Newspaper** Students write a variety of stories from the perspective of a reporter living in a particular historical time period.
- ✔ **Biographies and Autobiographies** Students write about historical figures either from the third person point of view (biography) or from the first person (autobiography).
- ✔ **Creative Stories** Students integrate historical events into a piece of fiction, incorporating the customs, language, and geography of the period.
- ✔ **Poems and Songs** Students follow the conventions of a particular type of song or poem as they tell about a historical event or person.
- ✔ **Research Reports** Students synthesize information from a variety of sources into a well-developed research report.

Oral Presentations

Oral presentations allow students to demonstrate their social studies literacy before an audience. Oral presentations are often group efforts, although this need not be the case.

- ✔ **Simulations** Students hold simulations, or reenactments, of actual events, such as trials, acts of civil disobedience, battles, speeches, and so forth.
- ✔ **Debates** Students debate two or more sides to a historical policy or issue. Students can debate from a contemporary perspective or in a role play in which they assume a viewpoint held by a historical character.
- ✔ **Interview** Students conduct a mock interview of an historical character or bystander.
- ✔ **Oral Reports** Students present the results of research efforts in a lively oral report.
- ✔ **Skits and Plays** Students use historical events as the basis for a play or skit. Details should accurately reflect customs, language, and the setting of the period.

Visual Presentations

Visual presentations allow students to demonstrate their social studies understandings in a variety of visual formats. Visual presentations can be either group or individual projects.

- ✔ **Model** Students make a model to demonstrate or represent a process, place, event, battle, artifact, or custom.
- ✔ **Museum Exhibit** Students create a rich display of materials around a topic. Typical displays might include models, illustrations, photographs, videos, writings, and audiotaped explanations.
- ✔ **Graph or Chart** Students analyze and represent historical data in a line graph, bar graph, table, or other chart format.
- ✔ **Drawing** Students represent or interpret a historical event or period through illustration, including political cartoons.
- ✔ **Posters and Murals** Posters and murals may include maps, time lines, diagrams, illustrations, photographs, and written explanations that reflect students' understandings of historical information.

- ✔ **Quilt** Students sew or draw a design for a patchwork quilt that shows a variety of perspectives, events, or issues related to a key topic.
- ✔ **Videotapes** Students film a video to show historical fiction or to preserve a simulation of a historical event.
- ✔ **Multimedia Presentation or Slide Show** Students create a computer-generated multimedia presentation containing historical information and analysis.

How Are Performance Assessments Scored?

There are a variety of means used to evaluate performance tasks. Some or all of the following methods may be used.

- ✔ **Scoring Rubrics** A scoring rubric is a set of guidelines for assessing the quality of a process and/or product. It sets out criteria used to distinguish acceptable responses from unacceptable ones, generally along a scale from excellent to poor.
- ✔ **Models of Excellent Work** Teacher-selected models of excellent work concretely illustrate expectations and help students set goals for their own projects.
- ✔ **Student Self-Assessment** Common methods of self-assessment include ranking work in relation to the model, using a scoring rubric, and writing their own goals and then evaluating how well they have met the goals they set for themselves. Regardless of which method or methods students use, they should be encouraged to evaluate their behaviors and processes, as well as the finished product.
- ✔ **Peer or Audience Assessment** Many of the performance tasks target an audience other than the classroom teacher. If possible, the audience of peers should give the student feedback. Have the class create rubrics for specific projects together.
- ✔ **Observation** As students carry out their performance tasks, you may want to formally observe students at work. Start by developing a checklist, identifying all the specific behaviors and understandings you expect students to demonstrate. Then observe students as they carry out performance tasks and check off the behaviors as you observe them.
- ✔ **Interviews** As a form of ongoing assessment, you may want to conduct interviews with students, asking them to analyze, explain, and assess their participation in performance tasks. When projects take place over an extended period of time, you can hold periodic interviews as well as exit interviews. In this way the interview process allows you to gauge the status of the project and to guide students' efforts along the way.✦

Targeting Multiple Intelligences

Advice from John Cartaina
Consultant, New Jersey Council of Social Studies

Authentic performance assessment provides students with different learning styles opportunities to demonstrate their successful learning. The table below lists types of learning styles.

Learning Style	Characteristics of Students
Linguistic	Read regularly, write clearly, and easily understand the written word
Logical-Mathematical	Use numbers, logic, and critical thinking skills
Visual-Spatial	Think in terms of pictures and images
Auditory-Musical	Remember spoken words and produce rhythms and melodies
Kinesthetic	Learn from touch, movement, and manipulating objects
Interpersonal	Understand and work well with other people
Intrapersonal	Have a realistic understanding of their strengths and weaknesses
Naturalist	Can distinguish among, classify, and use features of the environment

You may want to assign activities to students that accommodate their strongest learning styles, but frequently ask them to use their weakest learning styles.

Classroom Solutions

Cooperative Group Strategies

How Can I Use Cooperative Learning to Teach Social Studies?

Today's social and economic climate requires flexibility. Workers must be able to function independently, work well with groups, and engage in fair-minded competition. For this reason, most educators recommend a healthy balance of instructional strategies to foster cooperative, competitive, and individualistic styles of problem solving and learning. Cooperative learning requires students to work together—each with a specific task—to pursue a common goal. Because part of each student's evaluation is determined by the overall quality of the group's work, students help one another accomplish the group goal.

How Do I Form Cooperative Groups?

- ✔ **Composition** Most experts recommend that cooperative groups be heterogeneous, reflecting a range of student abilities, backgrounds, and learning styles. However, this does not necessarily mean that students should be assigned to groups on a random basis.
- ✔ **Group Size** The size of cooperative groups can change, depending upon the task. Some cooperative tasks are best accomplished in pairs. For most projects, groups of three to five students are ideal.
- ✔ **Abilities** Consider the tasks and projects the groups will undertake as you make group assignments. You may want to make sure each group has a strong manager, a strong writer, a strong artist, a good listener, and so forth.
- ✔ **Balance** Some teachers use a "family-of-five" approach to grouping. A strong leader heads each group. Two pairs of students with opposing styles or strengths complete the "family." Paired students might exhibit traits such as outgoing and shy, creative and conventional, spontaneous and methodical, and so on. Each group continues to work together throughout the semester or year, with the goal that students develop greater flexibility in their own problem-solving abilities and greater respect for the contributions of others.
- ✔ **Roles** In most instances, you will want to assign a specific role for each student to play in a group, such as designer, moderator, recorder, researcher, presenter, graphic artist, actor, and so forth. Roles should be interdependent, requiring students to rely upon one another in order to successfully carry out their individual responsibilities. As students gain experience in working in cooperative groups, turn over more of the responsibility for establishing individual roles and responsibilities to the group.

How Do I Help Groups Run Smoothly?

- ✔ **Seating Arrangements** Explain how and where groups should sit. Pairs can sit with desks or chairs face-to-face. Larger groups do well with desks or chairs gathered in a circle or with students seated around a table.
- ✔ **Warm-Ups** Provide an introductory activity for new groups. Even when students know one another, they can benefit by making formal introductions and sharing their thoughts on a sentence starter, such as "If I could go anywhere in the world, I would go to . . ." or "If I could have lived at any period in history, I would choose. . ."
- ✔ **Rules** Set clear expectations and rules for groups. Typical rules include addressing group members by name, making eye contact, listening politely, expressing disagreement with respect, welcoming others' questions, valuing others' contributions, providing positive feedback, and assisting others when asked.

How Do I Use Cooperative Groups in My Classroom?

- ✔ **Share and Tell** Have students form groups of four. Assign each group member a number between one and four. Ask a factual recall question. Have group members discuss the question and come up with an answer. Call out a number between one and four. The student with that number who is first to raise his or her hand answers the question. The group earns a point for a correct answer.
- ✔ **Circle Partners** Have the class separate into two equal groups and form two circles, with one circle inside the other. Each student faces a partner in the opposing circle. Ask a question and

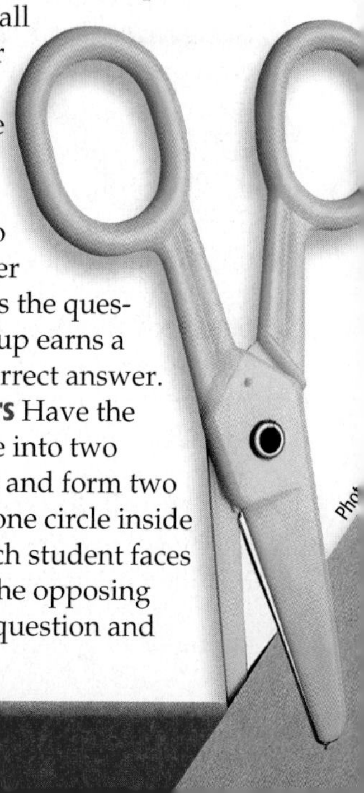

LWA-Dann Tardif/CORBIS STOCK MARKET

have partners discuss the answer. If partners do not know the answer they can ask another pair for help. Then, call on students in the inside circle, the outside circle, or all students to say the answer aloud together.

✔ **In the Know** Provide students with a set of end-of-chapter questions or other questions covering content you want students to master. Tell students to circulate around the room to find someone who can answer a question on the worksheet. After listening to the answer, the student paraphrases it, writes the answer on the worksheet, and asks the "expert" to read and sign off on the answer if it is correct. Students move on to find a student to answer the next question. The process continues until students have completed their worksheets.

✔ **Open-Ended Projects** The best long-term projects for cooperative groups are those that are open-ended and multidimensional. That is, the task or question should have many possible answers and should lend itself to many different presentation possibilities.

Multiple intelligences Appropriate projects should challenge students and allow students of various abilities and backgrounds to contribute significantly to solving the problem and executing the project. One way to assess the validity of a potential project is to see whether it requires the use of many different strengths or "intelligences."

Assigning roles Because of the complexity of long-term projects, it is essential that students have clearly assigned roles and responsibilities. Once cooperative groups are established and successful in your classroom, be sure to vary the assignments given to each student from project to project.

Deadlines Define interim and final deadlines to encourage students to pace their efforts appropriately.

How Do I Assess Group and Individual Efforts?

✔ **Expectations** As with any assignment, set clear guidelines and high expectations for projects. Show models of excellent past projects, if possible, and define what criteria projects must meet to earn the highest grade.

✔ **Group and Individual Grades** Before students begin, define what percentage of the grade will be based on group work and how much will be based on individual effort. Many teachers give two equally weighted grades: a group grade—the same for each team member—and an individual grade.

✔ **Self-Assessment** Provide a checklist or rating scale for each group member. Have students evaluate their own contribution to the group, as well as the contributions of other group members. In addition to assessing the quality of the finished product, have students evaluate the processes they used within the group, such as showing respect for others' ideas. Provide space on the evaluation sheet for students to explain why they rated themselves and group members as they did.✦

Troubleshooting

Advice from Carey Boswell, M.Ed.
Humble Independent School District
Humble, Texas

Modern research overwhelmingly suggests that student learning is enhanced when cooperative groups are used in the classroom. Like many other teachers, I was uncertain of how much learning was taking place when I set up cooperative groups. I struggled with noise and control issues and off-task behavior by some students. I found a solution, though.

A cooperative group activity occurs whenever a student works with another student. Cooperative groups do not have to be large groups. Smaller groups ensure that all students are engaged and contribute to the group effort. Smaller groups also guarantee that members perform multiple tasks so that real learning occurs. I often combine two or more small groups into a larger group for short comparative tasks. After making this small adjustment, I am able to assign cooperative group tasks to students at least once a week and student performance, comprehension, and learning has increased in my classroom.

Classroom Solutions

Web Strategies

How Can I Use the Internet to Teach Social Studies?

Aaron Haupt

From the Internet to round-the-clock live newscasts, teachers and students have never before had so much information at their fingertips. Yet never before has it been so confusing to determine where to turn for reliable content and what to do with it once you have found it. In today's world, social studies teachers must not only use the Internet as a source of up-to-the-minute information for students; they must teach students how to find and evaluate sources on their own.

What's Available On the Internet?

- ✔ **Teacher-Focused Web Sites** These Web sites provide teaching tips, detailed lesson plans, and links to other sites of interest to teachers and students.
- ✔ **Historical Documents** Thousands of primary source documents have now been cataloged and placed on the Web. Some sites provide text-only versions. Others provide photographs of actual documents and artifacts as well as insightful commentary and analysis.
- ✔ **Geographical Information** The Web holds a variety of geographical resources, from historical, physical, and political maps; to interactive mapping programs; to information about people and places around the world.
- ✔ **Statistics** Government Web sites are rich depositories for statistics of all kinds, including census data and information about climate, education, the economy, and political processes and patterns.
- ✔ **Reference Sources** Students can access full-text versions of encyclopedias, dictionaries, atlases, and other reference books, as well as databases containing millions of journal and newspaper articles.
- ✔ **News** Traditional media sources, including television, radio, newspapers, and newsmagazines, sponsor Internet sites that provide almost instantaneous news updates, as well as in-depth news coverage and analysis. Extensive archives facilitate research on past news stories.
- ✔ **Topical Information** Among the most numerous Web sites are those organized around a particular topic or issue, such as the Civil War or the stock market. These Internet pages may contain essays, analyses, and other commentaries, as well as primary source documents, maps, photographs, video and audio clips, bibliographies, and links to related online resources.
- ✔ **Organizations** Many organizations such as museums post Web pages that provide online exhibits, archives, and other information.

Glencoe Online

Glencoe provides an integrated Web curriculum for your textbook. The **Chapter Overview** Web link provides previews and reviews to help students better understand each chapter's organization and content. Engaging **Student Web Activities** challenge students to apply what they've learned. **Self-Check Quizzes** at the end of each chapter let you and your students assess their knowledge. You can also access additional resources, including links relevant to your state.

Finding Things on the Internet

The greatest asset of the Internet—its vast array of materials—is also its greatest deterrent. Many excellent social studies-specific sites provide links to relevant content. Using Internet search engines can also help you find what you need.

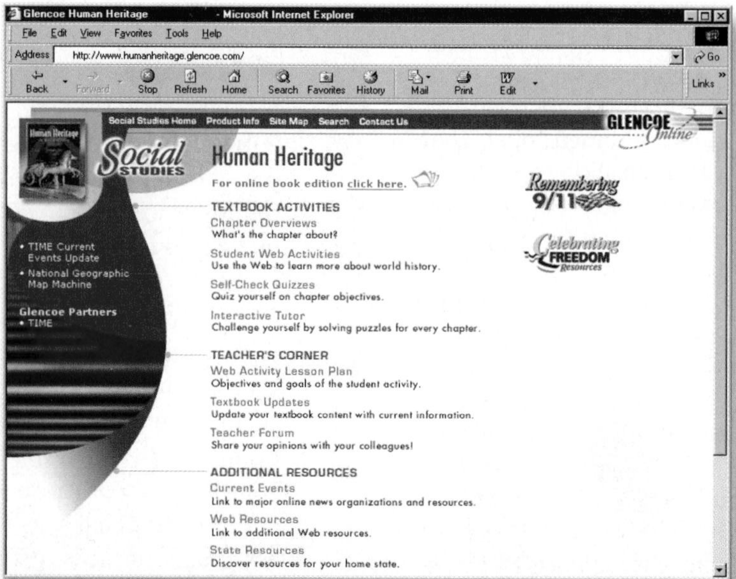

✔ A search engine is an Internet search tool. You type in a keyword, name, or phrase, and the search engine lists the URLs for Web sites that match your search. However, a search engine may find things that are not at all related or may miss sites that you would consider of interest. The key is to find ways to define your search.

✔ Not all search engines are the same. Each seeks out information a little bit differently. Different search engines use different criteria to determine what constitutes a "match" for your search topic. The Internet holds numerous articles that compare search engines and offer guidelines for choosing those that best meet your needs.

✔ An advanced search allows you to refine the search by using a phrase or a combination of words. The way to conduct an advanced search varies from search engine to engine; check the search engine's Help feature for information. Encourage students to review this information regularly for each of the search engines they use.

How Do I Teach Students to Evaluate Web Sites?

Anyone can put up a Web site. Web content is easy to change, too, so Webmasters constantly update their Web sites by adding, modifying, and removing content. These characteristics make evaluating Web sites both more challenging and more important than traditional print resources. Teach students to critically evaluate Web resources, using the questions and criteria below.

1 **Purpose:** What is the purpose of the Web site or Web page? Is it an informational Web page, a news site, a business site, an advocacy site, or a personal Web page? Many sites serve more than one purpose. For instance, a news site may provide current events accompanied by banner ads that market the products advertisers think readers might want.

2 **URL:** What is the URL, or Web address? Where does the site originate? That can sometimes tell you about the group or business behind the Web page. For example, URLs with .edu and .gov domain names indicate that the site is connected to an educational institution or a government agency, respectively. A .com suffix usually means that a commercial or business interest hosts the Web site, but may also indicate a personal Web page. A nonprofit organization's Web address may end with .org.

3 **Authority:** Who wrote the material or created the Web site? What qualifications does this person or group have? Who has ultimate responsibility for the site? If the site is sponsored by an organization, are the organization's goals clearly stated?

4 **Accuracy:** How reliable is the information? Are sources listed so that they can be verified? Is the Web page free from surface errors in spelling and grammar? How does it compare with other sources you've found on the Web and in print?

5 **Objectivity:** If the site presents itself as an informational site, is the material free from bias? If there is advertising, is it easy to tell the difference between the ads and other features? If the site mixes factual information with opinion, can you spot the difference between the two? If the site advocates an opinion or viewpoint, is the opinion clearly stated and logically defended?

6 **Currency:** When was the information first placed on the Web? Is the site updated on a regular basis? When was the last revision? If the information is time-sensitive, are the updates frequent enough?

7 **Coverage:** What topics are covered on the Web site? What is the depth of coverage? Are all sides of an issue presented? How does the coverage compare with other Web and print sources? ✦

See the *Glencoe Social Studies Guide to Using the Internet* for additional information and teaching strategies.

Make a Classroom Web Page

Advice from Mary Trichel
Atascocita Middle School
Humble Independent School District
Humble, Texas

Set up a classroom Web page with student-friendly access to useful links for class lessons. The Web page can be used by students at school or from their own homes. An easy teacher Web site source can be found at www.quia.com

To preview my Web page, visit the following link: www.quia.com/pages/trichel.html

In addition to quia.com, there are many other teacher-friendly Web page makers available on the Internet free of charge for teacher use. Use a search engine to access these pages and actively involve students in the design, layout, and construction of a class Web page.

Classroom Solutions

Primary Source Strategies

How Do I Use Primary Sources in My Classroom?

PhotoDisc

Anthony Redpath/CORBIS STOCK MARKET

A primary source is direct evidence of an event, idea, period, or development. It is an oral or written account obtained from actual participants in an event. Examples of primary sources include the following:

- ✔ official documents (records, statistics)
- ✔ political declarations, laws, and rules for governance
- ✔ speeches and interviews
- ✔ diaries, memoirs, and oral histories
- ✔ autobiographies
- ✔ recipes and cookbooks
- ✔ advertisements and posters
- ✔ letters

Physical objects, such as tools and dishes, can be primary sources; so can visual evidence in the form of fine art, photographs, maps, films, and videotapes. Primary sources can also include songs and audio recordings.

Why Use Primary Sources in Your Classroom?

Using primary sources to teach transforms the study of social studies from a passive process to an active one. Students become investigators—finding clues, formulating hypotheses and drawing inferences, making judgments, and reaching conclusions. Bringing primary sources into the classroom stimulates students to think critically about events, issues, and concepts rather than just memorizing dates, names, and generalizations reached by others.

Choosing Primary Sources

- ✔ Provide exposure to a variety of source types, including historic photographs, folk or popular music, financial records or household accounts, as well as letters, journals, and historic documents.
- ✔ When choosing print sources, consider the interests and reading levels of your students. Many texts contain challenging vocabulary and unfamiliar sentence structure. You may need to create a reader's guide that defines key vocabulary and paraphrases the main points of the reading.
- ✔ Some documents may be too long. Decide whether using an excerpt will provide enough information for students to draw conclusions.
- ✔ Depending upon the topic and your instructional objectives, you may need to provide several different primary sources to expose students to a variety of perspectives.
- ✔ Decide how students will access the primary sources: through the Internet, the library, a museum, or other print resources. Consider the possibility of an Internet virtual field trip for students. Moving from URL to URL, students can visit museum sites and other Web pages to view artifacts; interpret economic or census data; and read journals, letters, and official documents.

How Do I Introduce Students to Primary Sources?

Carefully explain the nature of primary sources when you introduce them to students. Although primary sources contain valuable clues, be sure to alert students that primary sources contain biases and prejudices, and must be approached with caution. Every primary source reflects the creator's point of view to some degree.

Using Primary Sources in the Classroom

Primary sources provide a rich source of inspiration for a variety of instructional strategies. They can be used to spark interest in a new topic, foster deeper exploration into a historical era, or assess students' understanding of social studies concepts and facts.

- ✔ **Pre-Reading Activities** Present a primary source for students to study at the beginning of a new chapter or topic. Have students analyze the source, using the questions and guidelines presented on the next page. Then have students make

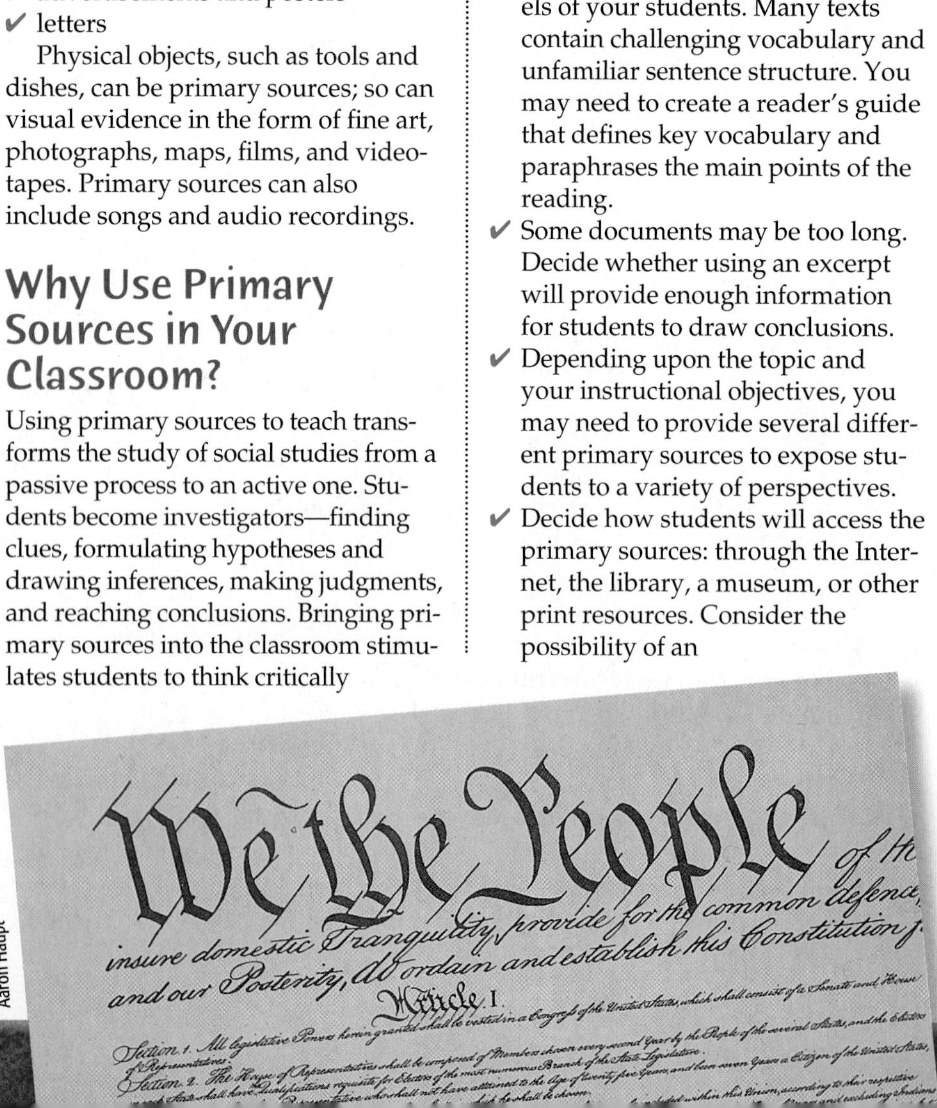

Aaron Haupt

Interpreting a Primary Source

Before students interpret a primary source, they need to know the context into which the source fits. Then they can use questions and guidelines, such as those below, to help them analyze and interpret the primary source.

Print Sources

- Who created the source, and what was the purpose for doing so?
- Did the writer personally experience or witness the event(s)?
- At what point did the writer record the information—as it happened or afterward? How long after?
- Who was the intended audience?
- Was the writer trying to record facts, express an opinion, or persuade others to take action?
- What is the author's main message?
- What values does the document convey?
- What bias does it reflect?
- What information about the topic can you gather from this document?
- Compare this document with what you know about the topic. Does it confirm those ideas or introduce a new perspective?
- How might other accounts about this topic support or modify the message this source delivers?

Visual Sources

- Who created the source, and what was the purpose for doing so?
- What does the image show?
- What mood does the image convey?
- Who or what dominates the image or catches your eye?
- How does the view impact the message?
- What details can you learn from the image?
- What is excluded from view?
- What bias does the visual reflect?
- What information about the topic can you gather from this visual?
- How might other visuals about this topic support or modify the message this one delivers?

Audio Sources

- Who created the source? What was the purpose for creating this source?
- What is the main idea of the audio?
- What mood does the recorder's voice convey?
- What bias does the audio text reflect?
- What information about the topic can you gather from this audio source?
- Compare the information in this source with what you already know about the topic. Does it confirm those ideas or introduce a new perspective?
- How might other sources about this topic support or modify the message that this one delivers?

predictions about what they might learn in the upcoming lessons.

✔ **Exploring Information** Provide a variety of primary sources related to a topic or time period. Have students compare and contrast the items, analyzing the information, making inferences, and drawing conclusions about the period.

✔ **Evaluation Activities** Have students evaluate a primary source and tell how it supports or refutes what they learned in the textbook or have students read a primary source document that provides one perspective on a topic, and have students write their own account, presenting another perspective or opinion.✦

Classroom Activity: Reading and Understanding Primary Sources

Advice from Leslie Espinosa
Humble Independent School District
Humble, Texas

1. Before class make a list of student reading partners. Make sure one of the two is a good reader.
2. Have students read a primary source document (or part of a primary source document), taking turns as they go. They should "mark" any words that they do not understand.
3. After each paragraph, the student pair should stop and paraphrase what it says in their own words.
4. Students should look up unfamiliar words they've marked and create an illustrated dictionary entry for each term (over the course of the year or semester).
5. Ask student pairs to present their paraphrased primary source to the rest of the class.

Classroom Solutions

Addressing the Needs of Special Students

How Can I Help ALL My Students Learn Social Studies?

Today's classroom contains students from a variety of backgrounds and with a variety of learning styles, strengths, and challenges. With careful planning, you can address the needs of all students in the social studies classroom. The following tips for instruction can assist your efforts to help all students reach their maximum potential.

Richard Hutchings/PhotoEdit

- ✔ Survey students to discover their individual differences. Use interest inventories of their unique talents so you can encourage contributions in the classroom.
- ✔ Model respect of others. Adolescents crave social acceptance. The student with learning differences is especially sensitive to correction and criticism—particularly when it comes from a teacher. Your behavior will set the tone for how students treat one another.
- ✔ Expand opportunities for success. Provide a variety of instructional activities that reinforce skills and concepts.
- ✔ Establish measurable objectives and decide how you can best help students meet them.
- ✔ Celebrate successes and praise "work in progress."
- ✔ Keep it simple. Point out problem areas—if doing so can help a student affect change. Avoid overwhelming students with too many goals at one time.
- ✔ Assign cooperative group projects that challenge all students to contribute to solving a problem or creating a product.

How Do I Reach Students with Learning Disabilities?

- ✔ Provide support and structure. Clearly specify rules, assignments, and responsibilities.
- ✔ Practice skills frequently. Use games and drills to help maintain student interest.
- ✔ Incorporate many modalities into the learning process. Provide opportunities to say, hear, write, read, and act out important concepts and information.
- ✔ Link new skills and concepts to those already mastered.
- ✔ Allow students to record answers on audiotape.
- ✔ Allow extra time to complete tests and assignments.
- ✔ Let students demonstrate proficiency with alternative presentations, including oral reports, role plays, art projects, and with music.
- ✔ Provide outlines, notes, or tape recordings of lecture material.
- ✔ Pair students with peer helpers, and provide class time for pair interaction.

How Do I Reach Students with Behavioral Disorders?

- ✔ Provide a structured environment with clear-cut schedules, rules, seat assignments, and safety procedures.
- ✔ Reinforce appropriate behavior and model it for students.
- ✔ Cue distracted students back to the task through verbal signals and teacher proximity.
- ✔ Set very small goals that can be achieved in the short term. Work for long-term improvement in the big areas.

How Do I Reach Students with Physical Challenges?

- ✔ Openly discuss with the student any uncertainties you have about when to offer aid.

- ✔ Ask parents or therapists and students what special devices or procedures are needed, and whether any special safety precautions need to be taken.
- ✔ Welcome students with physical challenges into all activities, including field trips, special events, and projects.
- ✔ Provide information to help able-bodied students and adults understand other students' physical challenges.

How Do I Reach Students with Visual Impairments?

- ✔ Facilitate independence. Modify assignments as needed.
- ✔ Teach classmates how and when to serve as guides.
- ✔ Limit unnecessary noise in the classroom, if it distracts the student with visual impairments.
- ✔ Provide tactile models whenever possible.
- ✔ Foster a spirit of inclusion. Describe people and events as they occur in the classroom. Remind classmates that students with visual impairments cannot interpret gestures and other forms of nonverbal communication.
- ✔ Provide taped lectures and reading assignments.
- ✔ Team the student with a sighted peer for written work.

How Do I Reach Students with Hearing Impairments?

- ✔ Seat students where they can see your lip movements easily and where they can avoid visual distractions.
- ✔ Avoid standing with your back to the window or light source.
- ✔ Use an overhead projector to maintain eye contact while writing.
- ✔ Seat students where they can see speakers.

Mug Shots/CORBIS STOCK MARKET

- ✔ Write all assignments on the board, or hand out written instructions.
- ✔ If the student has a manual interpreter, allow both student and interpreter to select the most favorable seating arrangements.
- ✔ Teach students to look directly at each other when they speak.

How Do I Reach English Language Learners?

- ✔ Remember, students' ability to speak English does not reflect their academic abilities.
- ✔ Try to incorporate the students' cultural experience into your instruction. The help of a bilingual aide may be effective.
- ✔ Avoid cultural stereotypes.
- ✔ Pre-teach important vocabulary and concepts.
- ✔ Encourage students to preview text before they begin reading, noting headings, graphic organizers, photographs, and maps.

How Do I Reach Gifted Students?

- ✔ Make arrangements for students to take selected subjects early and to work on independent projects.
- ✔ Ask "what if" questions to develop high-level thinking skills. Establish an environment safe for risk taking.
- ✔ Emphasize concepts, theories, ideas, relationships, and generalizations.
- ✔ Promote interest in the past by inviting students to make connections to the present.
- ✔ Let students express themselves in alternate ways, such as creative writing, acting, debate, simulations, drawing, or music.
- ✔ Provide students with a catalog of helpful resources, listing such things as agencies that provide free and inexpensive materials, appropriate community services and programs, and community experts.
- ✔ Assign extension projects that allow students to solve real-life problems related to their communities.✦

Customize Your Classroom!

Advice from Marilyn Gerken
Pickerington Local Schools
Pickerington, Ohio

Provide individualized activities and assignments for a variety of student ability levels. Develop learning packets for chapters and units of study with varying formats, levels, and types of assignments. Assign points and contract students based on their selection of activities to be completed. The activities in the Student Edition can be used for many of the learning activities and assignments.

Reading Strategies

Helping students become active readers is only the first step in training students for success. The second step is helping students retain and use the knowledge they have gained through reading.

How Can You Help Students Retain What They Read? The better students understand what they read, the more they will remember—so teaching students to use the reading strategies on these pages aids retention. In addition, you can help students use formal study systems such as working with graphic organizers.

Graphic Organizers That Help Students Read and Comprehend Graphic organizers provide a visual format that requires students to restructure information as they analyze and interpret it. In addition, presenting information graphically helps students remember facts and concepts more easily, since they can "picture" it in their mind's eye. Students can productively use graphic organizers prior to reading to activate prior knowledge, during reading to process and analyze information, and after instruction to summarize and draw conclusions. Encourage students to use graphic organizers in the following ways. *(See page 1.)*

Be an Active Reader!

How Should I Read My Textbook? Reading your social studies book is different than other reading you might do. Your textbook has a great amount of information in it. It is an example of nonfiction writing—it describes real-life events, people, ideas, and places.

Here are some reading strategies that will help you become an active textbook reader. Choose the strategies that work best for you. If you have trouble as you read your textbook, look back at these strategies for help.

✓ Before You Read

Set a Purpose

- Why are you reading the textbook?
- How might you be able to use what you learn in your own life?

Preview

- Read the chapter title to find out what the topic will be.
- Read the subtitles to see what you will learn about the topic.
- Skim the photos, charts, graphs, or maps.
- Look for vocabulary words that are boldfaced. How are they defined?

Draw From Your Own Background

- What do you already know about the topic?
- How is the new information different from what you already know?

If You Don't Know What A Word Means...

- think about the setting, or *context,* in which the word is used.
- check if prefixes such as *un, non,* or *pre* can help you break down the word.

viii

Good Study Habits for Successful Students

As you work with students on reading strategies, keep in mind and share the following tips for helping students retain what they read and prepare for all types of tests.

- **Keep Up:** Frequent review will help students build long-term memory and understanding.
- **Visualize and Recite Information:** Visual images are powerful ones. Students should try to associate a name, event, or idea with a picture. They can visualize the steps in a process or a sequence of events. Students should repeat important information aloud, whenever possible.

As You Read

Question

- What is the main idea?
- How well do the details support the main idea?
- How do the photos, charts, graphs, and maps support the main idea?

Connect

- Think about people, places, and events in your own life. Are there any similarities with those in your textbook?

Predict

- Predict events or outcomes by using clues and information that you already know.
- Change your predictions as you read and gather new information.

Visualize

- Use your imagination to picture the settings, actions, and people that are described.
- Create graphic organizers to help you see relationships found in the information.

Reading Do's

Do ...

- ✔ establish a purpose for reading
- ✔ think about how your own experiences relate to the topic
- ✔ try different reading strategies

Reading Don'ts

Don't...

- ⦸ ignore how the textbook is organized
- ⦸ allow yourself to be easily distracted
- ⦸ hurry to finish the material

After You Read

Summarize

- Describe the main idea and how the details support it.
- Use your own words to explain what you have read.

Assess

- What was the main idea?
- Did the text clearly support the main idea?
- Did you learn anything new from the material?
- Can you use this new information in other school subjects or at home?

Reading Strategies

- Use a web to show connections between related ideas, to describe the characteristics of a place or group, or to list examples.
- Use a tree to show a hierarchy of ideas or the structure of an organization or group.
- Use a flowchart to explain steps in a process. Use a time line or chain-of-events diagram to show a chronology or the order of events.
- Analyze causal relationships with a cause-and-effect chart or a problem-and-solution diagram.
- Use a Venn diagram to compare and contrast attributes or characteristics.

Use Writing to Help Students Understand What They Read

Writing provides a way for students to demonstrate what they have learned. More significantly, writing can facilitate greater understanding and richer learning by encouraging writers to transform knowledge into something new. Appropriate writing assignments can help students build social studies concepts in the following ways.

- Writing challenges students to analyze, evaluate, and interpret events.
- Writing invites students to synthesize information from a variety of sources, including students' own prior knowledge and experiences.
- Writing requires students to make connections, draw conclusions, and support their judgments with facts and details.
- The writing process promotes a systematic approach to content analysis by teaching students to focus their thoughts, expand and refine their ideas, and express their viewpoints precisely.

Good Study Habits for Successful Students

- **Use the Body:** Incorporate movement into study routines, if possible. Students can march in place or pace while reciting a sequence of events or saying a list of items.
- **Study Groups:** Encourage students to work with others to review for a test. They can discuss important topics and take turns asking and answering questions.
- **The Big Picture:** Essay tests often ask "big picture" questions. To help students get the big picture, have them identify main ideas in reading selections; develop summaries of important topics; and create webs, maps, or other graphic organizers to draw conclusions and analyze relationships.

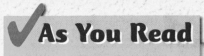

Introducing **UNIT 1**

OVERVIEW

Unit 1 serves as an introduction to the study of world history and geography and sets the stage for the development of civilization.

- **Chapter 1** acquaints the students with the six essential elements of geography, and with geographical features. It also discusses how scientists uncover clues that help them piece together what happened in the distant past.
- **Chapter 2** deals with prehistory and the various stages of development people went through before civilization evolved.

UNIT OBJECTIVES

After reading Unit 1, students will be able to:

1. identify important geographic elements.
2. explain ways in which geography has influenced the course of history.
3. specify how scientists work together to learn about the past.
4. describe how hunters and food gatherers and food producers lived during prehistoric times.

UNIT PROJECT

Have students select five major achievements of prehistoric people that have been most important to humankind. Ask them to rank the achievements, listing the most important first. Then, working in groups, have them create a display of these achievements, bringing prehistoric life into the classroom. Finally, have them write a paragraph explaining the achievement and how important it was to the development of civilization.

UNIT 1

Place and Time

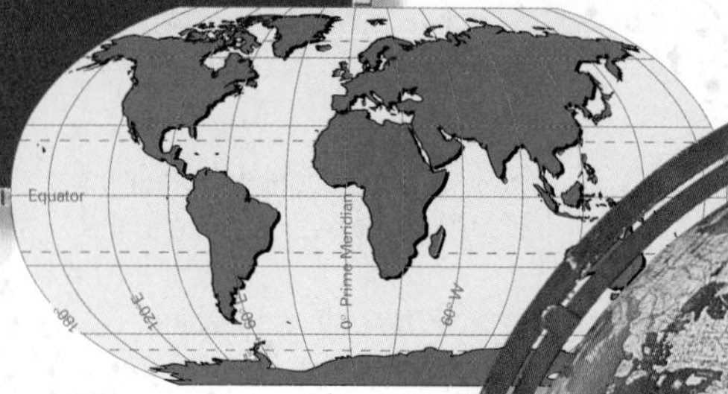

▲ An early globe

Egyptian water clock ▼

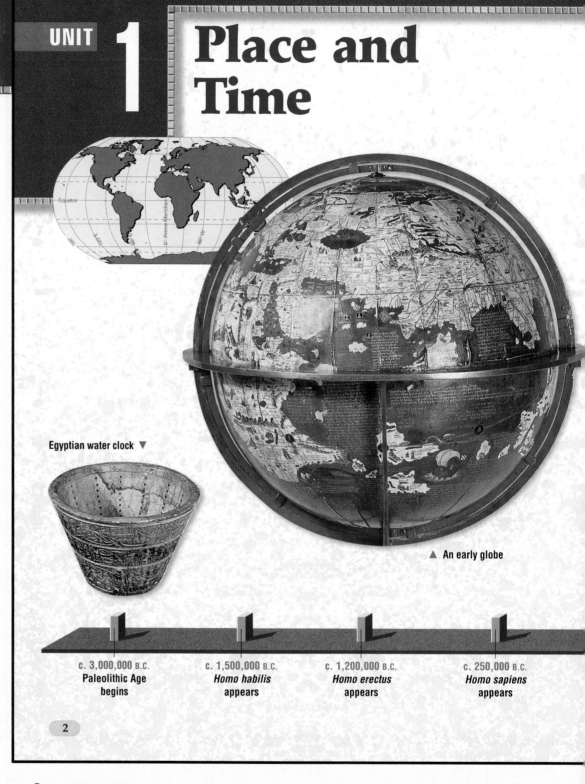

c. 3,000,000 B.C. Paleolithic Age begins

c. 1,500,000 B.C. *Homo habilis* appears

c. 1,200,000 B.C. *Homo erectus* appears

c. 250,000 B.C. *Homo sapiens* appears

About the Unit Opening

Examining Artifacts

Ask students how these two artifacts illustrate the Unit title. *(The globe shows places on the earth; the water clock shows a way of keeping time.)* Tell students that historians use two words—*where* and *when*—to study place and time. Have students use these words to form questions about early humans, the start of farming, and the first cities.

Global Chronology

Refer students to the unit time line above. Explain that *c.* means "about" and that B.C. means "before Christ." Ask students to explain what the time line covers. *(major events in prehistory)* About how long did the Paleolithic Age last? *(about 2,992,000 years)*

FOLDABLES™ Study Organizer

Summarizing Information Study Foldable *Make this foldable journal about geography and how it influenced history, and use it as a study guide.*

Step 1 *Fold a sheet of paper in half from top to bottom.*

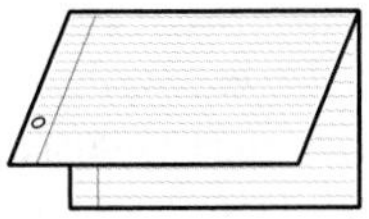

Step 2 *Fold it in half again from side to side and label as shown.*

Place
and
Time

Reading and Writing *As you read the unit, use your "place and time journal" to describe how geography has affected early civilization settlements.*

PRIMARY SOURCES Library

See pages 674–675 for another primary source reading to accompany Unit 1.

GO TO Read "The Iceman" from the **World History Primary Source Document Library CD-ROM.**

c. 100,000 B.C.
Cro-Magnons appear

c. 8000 B.C.
Neolithic Age begins

c. 6500 B.C.
Catal Hüyük established

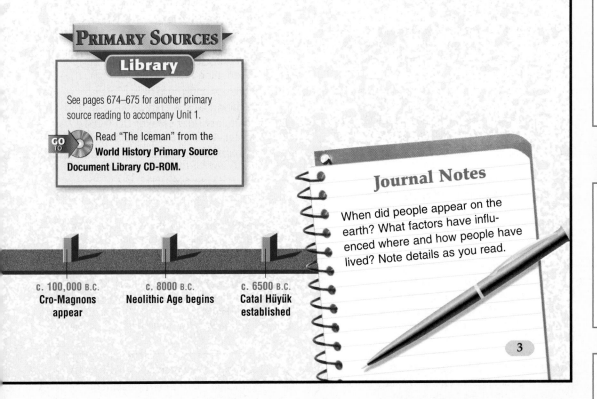

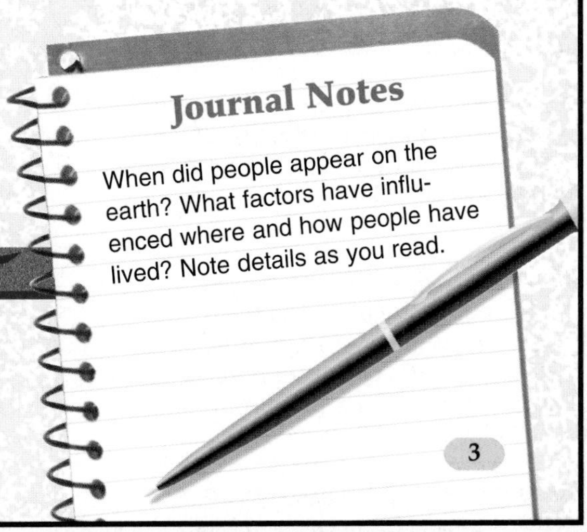
Journal Notes
When did people appear on the earth? What factors have influenced where and how people have lived? Note details as you read.
3

Geographic Location

Unit 1 focuses mainly on the continents of Africa, Europe, and Asia, where archaeologists have found the remains and artifacts of prehistoric people. However, developments here impacted the whole world.

GLENCOE TECHNOLOGY

MindJogger Videoquiz

Use **MindJogger Videoquiz** to preview the unit content.

Available in DVD and VHS

FOLDABLES™ Study Organizer

Purpose Students make and use this foldable to help them record and learn information about how geography has influenced history. As students read the unit, they should write main ideas and key terms in their foldables. Students can use this journal study guide when preparing for quizzes and tests in this unit.

Have students complete **Reading and Study Skills Foldables** Activity 1.

RECORDING JOURNAL NOTES

Ask students to name the factors that have influenced where people have lived. Tell students to note details about these factors in their journals as they read this unit.

PRIMARY SOURCES Library

Additional primary sources from the **World History Primary Source Document Library CD-ROM** can be used during the study of Unit 1, including:

- "The Discovery of 1470," by Richard E. Leakey

A primary source about African origins can be found on pages 674–675.

Chapter 1 Planning Guide

Timesaving Tools

TeacherWorks™ All-In-One Planner and Resource Center

- **Interactive Teacher Edition** Access your Teacher Wraparound Edition and your classroom resources with a few easy clicks.
- **Interactive Lesson Planner** Planning has never been easier! Organize your week, month, semester, or year with all the lesson helps you need to make teaching creative, timely, and relevant.

Use Glencoe's **Presentation Plus!** multimedia teacher tool to easily present dynamic lessons that visually excite your students. Using Microsoft PowerPoint® you can customize the presentations to create your own personalized lessons.

Objectives	Reproducible Resources	Multimedia Resources
Section 1 **Elements of Geography** Describe how the six essential elements of geography help explain what a place is like and why it is like that.	Reproducible Lesson Plan Chapter 1 Vocabulary and Guided Reading Activity Reading Essentials and Study Guide 1-1 Chapter 1 Cooperative Learning Activity Chapter 1 Chart and Graph Skill Activity Section 1 Quiz	Interactive Student Edition CD-ROM Graphic Organizer Transparency 1 Vocabulary PuzzleMaker CD-ROM ExamView® Pro Testmaker CD-ROM Glencoe Skillbuilder Interactive Workbook CD-ROM, Level 1 Presentation Plus! CD-ROM
Section 2 **Land, Water, and Climate** Explain how landforms, waterways, and climate have shaped history.	Reproducible Lesson Plan Reading Essentials and Study Guide 1-2 Chapter 1 Geography and Map Activity Section 2 Quiz	Teaching Transparency and Activity 1B Vocabulary PuzzleMaker CD-ROM Interactive Tutor Self-Assessment CD-ROM ExamView® Pro Testmaker CD-ROM
Section 3 **Natural Resources** Describe how natural resources have shaped history.	Reproducible Lesson Plan Reading Essentials and Study Guide 1-3 Section 3 Quiz	Interactive Tutor Self-Assessment CD-ROM ExamView® Pro Testmaker CD-ROM Glencoe Skillbuilder Interactive Workbook CD-ROM, Level 1
Section 4 **Legends** Analyze the importance of legends in the study of history.	Reproducible Lesson Plan Reading Essentials and Study Guide 1-4 Unit 1 World Literature Readings 1 & 2 Section 4 Quiz	Vocabulary PuzzleMaker CD-ROM Interactive Tutor Self-Assessment CD-ROM ExamView® Pro Testmaker CD-ROM
Section 5 **Archaeology** Summarize how archaeology helps scientists learn about ancient civilizations	Reproducible Lesson Plan Reading Essentials and Study Guide 1-5 Chapter 1 Enrichment Activity Unit 1 Primary Source Readings Section 5 Quiz	Teaching Transparency and Activity 1A Interactive Tutor Self-Assessment CD-ROM Glencoe Skillbuilder Interactive Workbook CD-ROM, Level 1
Chapter 1 **Review and Evaluation**	Chapter 1 Reteaching Activity Chapter 1 Performance Assessment Activity Spanish Chapter Summary and Glossary Chapter 1 Test	Interactive Tutor Self-Assessment CD-ROM Glencoe Skillbuilder Interactive Workbook CD-ROM, Level 1 Audiocassettes* ExamView® Pro Testmaker CD-ROM

*Also available in Spanish.

Chapter 1 Planning Guide

Performance Assessment Activities

Climate Maps Tell students to create a simple outline map of the world showing the continents. Ask them to add major climate zones to their maps and to create a key. As students read the chapter, have them locate and mark each place as they read. Discuss differences between climate zones, and identify places with climates similar to where students live.

CHAPTER RESOURCES

LITERATURE ABOUT THE PERIOD

Courlander, Harold. *The King's Drum, and Other African Tales.* Harcourt, 1962. Folktales from Africa south of the Sahara

READINGS FOR THE STUDENT

Demko, George, Jerome Agel, and Eugene Boe. *Why in the World: Adventures in Geography.* Anchor, 1992. Multifaceted look at geography through the relationship of people and the earth.

READINGS FOR THE TEACHER

Natoli, Salvatore J., ed. *Strengthening Geography in the Social Studies: National Council for the Social Studies, Bulletin 81.* NCSS/SSSS. Ideas for teaching geographic concepts.

KEY TO ABILITY LEVELS

Teaching strategies have been coded for varying learning styles and abilities.

L1 Level 1 activities are **basic** activities and should be within the ability range of all students.

L2 Level 2 activities are **average** activities and should be within the ability range of the average to above-average student.

L3 Level 3 activities are **challenging** activities designed for the ability range of above-average students.

ELL ELL activities should be within the ability range of English Language Learning students.

NATIONAL GEOGRAPHIC Teacher's Corner

INDEX TO NATIONAL GEOGRAPHIC MAGAZINE

The following articles relate to this chapter:

Note: Since many of the magazine's articles emphasize the broad geographical themes mentioned in this chapter, students are encouraged to explore its back issues (see magazine CD-Rom listing under Additional National Geographic Society Products). For instance, see:

- "Inca Rescue," by Guillermo A. Cook, May 2002.
- "Life at the Bottom of the World," by Roff Martin Smith, December 2001.
- "Once and Future Fury: California's Volcanic North," by Priit Vesilind, October 2001.
- "The Rise of Life on Earth—When Life Nearly Came to an End: The Permian Extinction," by Hillel Hoffmann, September 2000.
- "Celebrations of Earth," by Stuart Franklin, January 2000.
- "Journey to the Heart of the Sahara," by Donovan Webster, March 1999.

NATIONAL GEOGRAPHIC SOCIETY PRODUCTS AVAILABLE FROM GLENCOE

To order the following, call Glencoe at 1-800-334-7344:

- *PicturePack: Physical Geography of the World (Transparencies)*
- *Picture Atlas of the World (CD-ROM)*
- *PicturePack: World Geography Library (Transparencies)*

ADDITIONAL NATIONAL GEOGRAPHIC SOCIETY PRODUCTS

To order the following, call National Geographic at 1-800-368-2728:

- *The Complete National Geographic: 108 Years of National Geographic Magazine on CD-ROM (CD-ROMs)*
- *Exploring Your World: The Adventure of Geography (Book)*
- *World (Laminated Desk Maps)*
- *National Geographic World Atlas for Young Explorers (Book)*

Access *National Geographic's* new dynamic MapMachine Web site and other geography resources at:

www.nationalgeographic.com

www.nationalgeographic.com/maps

OVERVIEW

Chapter 1 links the six essential elements of geography to the study of the earth. It also shows how legends and archaeology help historians learn about the past.

➤ **Section 1** describes the six essential elements of geography.
➤ **Section 2** discusses the kinds of landforms, waterways, and climates found on the earth.
➤ **Section 3** describes the natural resources on the earth.
➤ **Section 4** explains how legends have been used to obtain clues to the past.
➤ **Section 5** examines the importance of archaeology.

CHAPTER OBJECTIVES

After reading Chapter 1, students will be able to:

1. describe how the six essential elements of geography help explain what a place is like and why.
2. explain how landforms, waterways, climate, and natural resources have shaped history.
3. discuss why legends are important to the study of history.
4. summarize how archaeology helps scientists learn about ancient civilizations.

EXAMINING ARTIFACTS

Point out that history is more than written words. Ask students what the bronze plaque and Stonehenge tell them about the early people who designed them. What other sources of information on the past can they name?

PERFORMANCE ASSESSMENT ✓

Use the Performance Assessment activities on page 4B to help you evaluate students as they complete the chapter.

CHAPTER 1

Geography and History
3,000,000 B.C.–Present

▼ Celtic bronze plaque

Stonehenge ▶

c. 1500 A.D.	1719 A.D.	1799 A.D.	1832 A.D.	1946 A.D.
Archaeology begins	**Archaeologists uncover Pompeii**	**Rosetta Stone discovered**	**Prehistory organized into periods**	**Carbon 14 method of dating developed**

4 UNIT 1 PLACE AND TIME

TEACHING RESOURCES

TEACHER PLANNING AND SUPPORT

🗁 Reproducible Lesson Plan 1-1, 1-2, 1-3, 1-4, 1-5
🗁 Teaching Strategies for the World History Classroom (Including Block Scheduling Pacing Guides)
💿 Presentation Plus! CD-ROM

REVIEW AND REINFORCEMENT

🗁 Reading Essentials and Study Guide 1-1, 1-2, 1-3, 1-4, 1-5
🗁 Chapter 1 Vocabulary and Guided Reading Activity
💿 Vocabulary PuzzleMaker CD-ROM
📠 Teaching Transparencies 1A & 1B
🗁 Chapter 1 Reteaching Activity

🗁 Chapter 1 Cooperative Learning Activity
🗁 Chapter 1 Activity Book Activity
🗁 Chapter 1 Chart and Graph Skill Activity
🗁 Reading and Study Skills Foldables
💿 Interactive Tutor Self-Assessment CD-ROM
📼 Unit 1 MindJogger VideoQuiz

APPLICATION AND HANDS-ON ACTIVITIES

📑 Daily Questions in Social Studies
💿 Student Presentation Builder CD-ROM

Section 1 Assessment

1. **Define:** geography, absolute location, relative location, place, region.
2. What six essential elements do geographers use to study the earth?
3. Why do geographers organize the world into regions?

Critical Thinking

4. **Making Comparisons** How does the element of the world in spatial terms differ from the element of places and regions?

Graphic Organizer Activity

5. Draw a diagram like this one, and use it to summarize information about each of the six essential elements of geography.

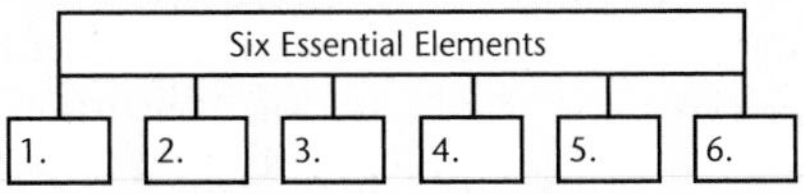

SECTION 2 Land, Water, and Climate

Photographs of the earth taken from space show a contrast of water and land beneath huge swirls of white clouds. These photographs reflect three of the things geographers study: land, water, and climate.

Landforms Land covers about 30 percent of the surface of the earth. Land is made up of four main kinds of **landforms,** or natural features of the earth's land surface. These landforms are mountains, hills, plateaus, and plains. Geographers describe each landform by its **elevation,** or height above sea level, and its **relief,** or changes in height.

Mountains are the highest of the world's landforms. They rise at least 2,000 feet, or 610 meters, above sea level. One of the peaks in the Himalaya (him uh lā' uh) Mountains in central Asia is Mount Everest, the world's highest mountain. It towers 29,035 feet, or 8,852 meters, above sea level. Other mountain ranges, like the Appalachians (ap uh lā' chunz) in the eastern United States, are not as high. Mountains generally have high relief.

Hills are lower than mountains. They rise from 500 to 2,000 feet, or 152 to 610 meters, above sea level. They generally have moderate relief. Plateaus are raised areas of flat or almost flat land. Plateaus can vary in elevation from 300 to 3,000 feet, or 91 to 914 meters, above sea level. Most of them have low relief.

Plains are large areas of flat or gently rolling land. They generally rise less than 1,000 feet, or 305 meters, above sea level and have low relief. The world's largest plain is the North European Plain, which stretches for more than 1,000 miles, or 1,609 kilometers, from the western coast of France to the Ural Mountains in Russia.

Reading Check What are the four main kinds of **landforms?** How do geographers use **elevation** and **relief** to describe landforms?

Fun Facts . . .

Island Tips Some of the world's islands are really mountain summits—the tips of volcanoes that have risen from the sea. The highest summit in Hawaii, Mauna Kea, rises 13,796 feet, or 4,205 meters, above sea level. However, when measured from its base, Mauna Kea stands 32,000 feet, or 9,750 meters—taller than Mount Everest.

Use the **Interactive Tutor Self-Assessment CD-ROM** to review Section 1.

L2 **Art** Have students work in small groups to create clay relief diagrams showing the four kinds of landforms. Have them label these landforms and add other geographic features if they choose. ELL

Reading Check Answer
The four kinds of **landforms** include mountains, hills, plateaus, and plains. **Elevation** describes height above sea level, and **relief** describes changes in height.

GEOGRAPHY AND HISTORY

Mountain ranges vary in age as well as height. The Himalayas are young mountains, having been formed about 25 million years ago. The Appalachians, which were formed about 225 million years ago, are among the oldest mountains in the world.

Use the **Vocabulary PuzzleMaker CD-ROM** to create crossword and word search puzzles.

Section 1 Assessment Answers

1. geography, study of the earth and the ways people live and work on it (p. 5); absolute location, the exact location of a place on the earth's surface (p. 5); relative location, the position of a place in relation to other places (p. 6); place, features that give an area its own identity (p. 6); region, area that has common characteristics (p. 7)
2. the world in spatial terms, places and regions, physical systems, human systems, environment and society, the uses of geography
3. to make it easier to study the world
4. Students might indicate that the world in spatial terms gives more specific details about a place, whereas places and regions describes a place's relation to other places.
5. Summaries should reflect information about the six essential elements of geography.

Assign the Chapter 1 **Section 1 Quiz** in the TCR. Testmaker available.

L2 **Geography: Physical Systems** Have students work in pairs to write a brief description of a natural disaster and explain how it changed the earth. *(Students may describe the aftereffects of an earthquake, floods, and volcanic eruptions.)* ELL

Reading Check Answer
The inner **core** is solid rock, and the outer part is melted rock. The **mantle** is mostly hot, solid rock, while the **crust** is composed of a thin layer of rock, sand, and soil.

Reading Check Answer
Continental drift results from the movement of **tectonic plates.**

L1 **Critical Thinking** Ask students to explain the main characteristics of each layer of the earth's structure shown in the diagram on this page. *(The inner core is solid rock; the outer core is melted rock; the mantle is hot, solid rock; the crust is rock, sand, and soil.)*

MAKING CONNECTIONS

➤➤ **Geography** The idea of continental drift was first proposed in 1912 by Alfred Wegener. Evidence in support of his theory was found in the 1950s and 1960s, when scientists discovered a worldwide system of mountainlike ridges on the ocean floor.

Surface Changes From Inside the Earth

The land surface of the earth is constantly changing. Most changes are caused by forces from deep within the earth, usually heat and pressure.

Reading Check What is the composition of the earth's **core, mantle,** and **crust?**

Heat and pressure are caused by the structure of the earth itself. The inside of the earth is made up of three separate layers. At the center of the earth is the **core.** The inner part of the core is solid rock, and the outer part of the core is made up of melted rock. Around the core is the **mantle,** which is made up mostly of hot, solid rock. Floating on the melted outer part of the mantle is a thin layer of rock, sand, and soil called the **crust.** The crust may be from 3 to 30 miles, or 5 to 49 kilometers, thick.

Reading Check What is the connection between **tectonic plates** and **continental drift?**

Heat from the core—the hottest part of the earth—causes the rock in the mantle to rise. This puts pressure on the crust and causes it to move. In recent years, scientists have come to believe that the crust does not move in one piece but in separate sections called **tectonic** (tek ton′ ik) **plates.** These plates move very slowly, about 0.8 to 2 inches, or 2 to 5 centimeters, a year. Plates can move together, move apart, or slide past one another.

This movement of the plates explains what geographers call **continental drift.** Most geographers believe that about 220 million years ago, all the continents of the world formed one huge land mass named Pangaea (pan jē′ uh). Over time, the plates

Major Landforms

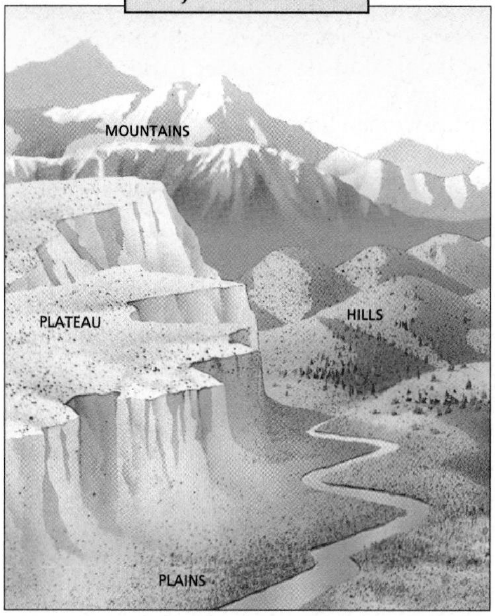

The Earth's Structure

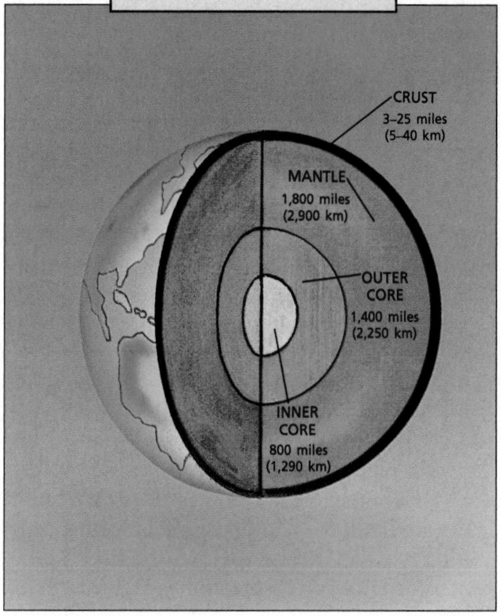

MEETING SPECIAL NEEDS

Provide students who are visual learners with an outline map of the world. Have them label the continents. Then have them cut out the continents and piece them together as they may have looked as one huge land mass named Pangaea. Use this activity as a lead-in to a discussion of continental drift.

Refer to *Inclusion for the Middle School Social Studies Classroom: Strategies and Activities* for additional resources.

Tectonic Plates

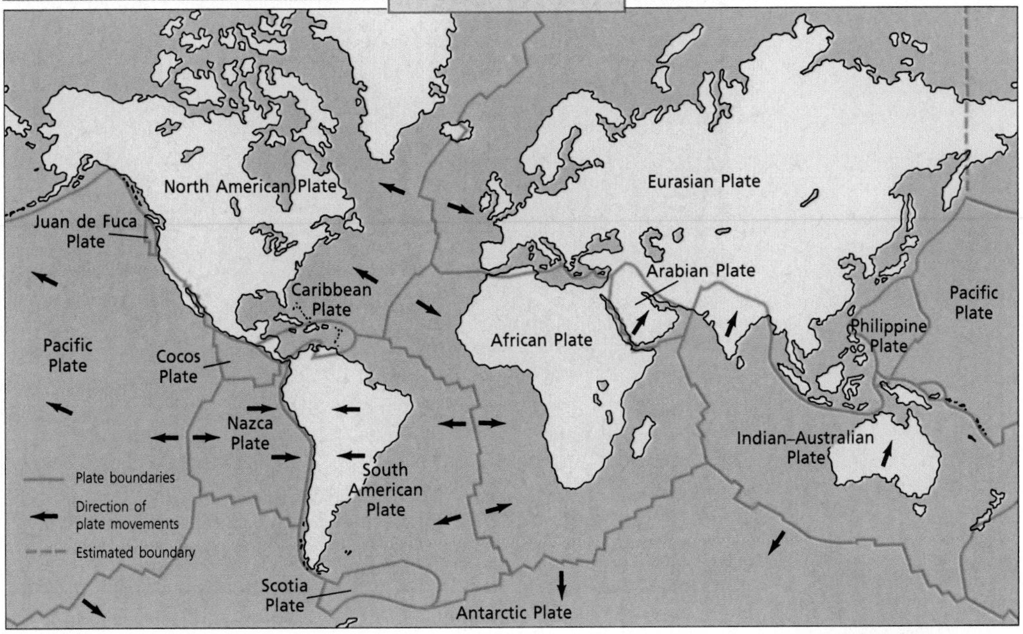

moved and Pangaea split into seven continents. Some plates, such as the ones on which Africa and South America are located, moved apart. Other plates, such as the plates on which India and most of Asia are located, collided. The crust where these two plates met was squeezed upward to form the Himalayas.

Plate movement also creates **volcanoes.** These are cone-shaped mountains made when melted rock called magma flows up from the earth's mantle through cracks in the crust and then cools into solid rock. The Hawaiian Islands, for example, were formed by volcanoes that thrust up from the ocean floor.

Plate movements can also cause **earthquakes**, or sudden shifts in the earth's crust. These often happen when tectonic plates slide past one another. About 800,000 earthquakes occur each year with only about 50,000 of them strong enough for people to even feel them. A strong earthquake, however, can cause loss of life and serious property damage.

Both volcanoes and earthquakes are generally found along the edges of the earth's tectonic plates. They are so common around the Pacific Ocean that geographers call this area the "Ring of Fire."

The tectonic plates are still moving. Most geographers believe that thousands of years from now, California, which is on

MAP STUDY

PHYSICAL SYSTEMS
The idea that the continents were once joined and then slowly drifted apart is called the continental drift theory.
Which plate is colliding with the South American plate along the west coast of South America?

Reading Check How are **volcanoes** formed? What is a common cause of **earthquakes?**

DID YOU KNOW ??

Hawaii is the second largest volcanic island; Iceland is the largest. Hualalai and Mauna Loa, two of Hawaii's three active volcanoes, are among the world's highest mountains, if measured from the ocean floor.

MAP STUDY

Answer

Nazca Plate

Reading Check Answer Plate movements create **volcanoes** and are a common cause of **earthquakes.**

LINKING PAST TO PRESENT

There have been several serious earthquakes in the United States. In 1906, an earthquake that caused a great fire in San Francisco left more than 500 dead or missing. A 1989 earthquake in the same location killed dozens. Although this earthquake was quite strong, buildings have been constructed to withstand strong earthquakes and fireproof materials have been used in construction.

COOPERATIVE LEARNING

Organize the class into two groups. Assign volcanic eruptions to one group and earthquakes to the other group. Tell each group to make a list of natural disasters caused by these surface changes from inside the earth. Then have members work together to research information about the natural disasters on their list and to prepare an oral report and bulletin-board display of their subject.

CAPTION ANSWER

sudden shifts in the earth that happen when tectonic plates slide past one another

L3 Critical Thinking Have students contrast the surface changes of forces from inside the earth with the surface changes of forces from outside the earth. *(Students should note that forces from inside the earth cause sudden, drastic changes in the earth's surface and are usually destructive. Forces from outside the earth are more gradual in nature and can either help or hurt people.)*

L2 Geography: Environment and Society Have a volunteer read aloud a description of the Dust Bowl in the 1930s from an encyclopedia or history book. Discuss the way society affected the environment in this disaster and vice versa as a volunteer writes the causes on the board. Have students create a graphic organizer that shows the results of your discussion.

EARTHQUAKE DISASTERS Mexico has experienced many earthquakes that have caused terrible loss of life and property. These earthquakes most often occur without warning. **What causes an earthquake?**

a different plate from most of the United States, will be located far off the west coast of Canada.

Surface Changes From Outside the Earth Forces from outside the earth also cause changes on its surface. Three main forces are wind, water, and ice. All three reshape the land by a process called erosion (i rō′ zhuhn), in which rock and soil are moved from one place on the earth's surface to another. These forces can either help or hurt people.

An example of helpful wind erosion can be found in the plains of northern China, where large amounts of wheat and other food crops are grown. The plains are covered with a thick, rich, yellowish soil called *loess* (les) which was carried there by winds blowing from deserts to the west. During the 1930s, however, winds blew away so much of the soil in the central part of the United States that the area became known as the Dust Bowl.

Water erosion that is helpful can be seen in the Mekong (may′ kawng) River of Southeast Asia. This river carries rich soil down from the mountains and spreads it over the lowlands, creating one of the most fertile areas in the world. Harmful water erosion occurs when the Huang Ho (hwong huh) in northern China overflows its banks and floods farms and homes.

Ice erosion has also caused changes on the earth's surface and in people's lives. Four times in the last 500,000 years, during

EXTENDING THE CONTENT

The edges of the Pacific Ocean basin (which are generally the same as the borders of the Pacific plate plus some smaller plates) have come to be called the "Ring of Fire" because most of today's active volcanoes are located here. In North America, the Ring includes Alaska's Aleutians, the Cascade Range (where Mount St. Helens erupted), and Mexico's Popocatepetl. It continues southward through Central America and down the western edge of South America into Antarctica. On the other side of the Pacific are Japan's Fujiyama, the Southern Alps of New Zealand, and mountains in the Philippines and Indonesia.

what are called the Ice Ages, great ice sheets called **glaciers** spread out from the North and South poles. The ice drove people and animals away, smoothed hills into plains, created lakes, and dug new channels for rivers.

Reading Check How did **glaciers** affect human and physical geography?

Landforms in History Throughout history, landforms have played an important part in helping people decide where to live. People stayed away from mountainous areas where travel was difficult or where the air was so thin that it was hard to breathe. Instead, people settled mostly in plains and hilly areas where the soil was rich enough for crops to grow.

Landforms also have made a big difference in the political relationships of people. In ancient times the Greeks lived in many different city-states. One reason the Greeks did not join together to form a nation was that their communities were separated from one another by a landform—mountains.

Waterways About 70 percent of the earth's surface is covered with water. The largest waterways in the world are the four oceans—the Atlantic, the Pacific, the Indian, and the Arctic.

MAP STUDY

PHYSICAL SYSTEMS
Scientists believe that glaciers covered large areas of the earth's surface during the Ice Ages. **What continents were affected the most by the Ice Ages?**

Ice Ages

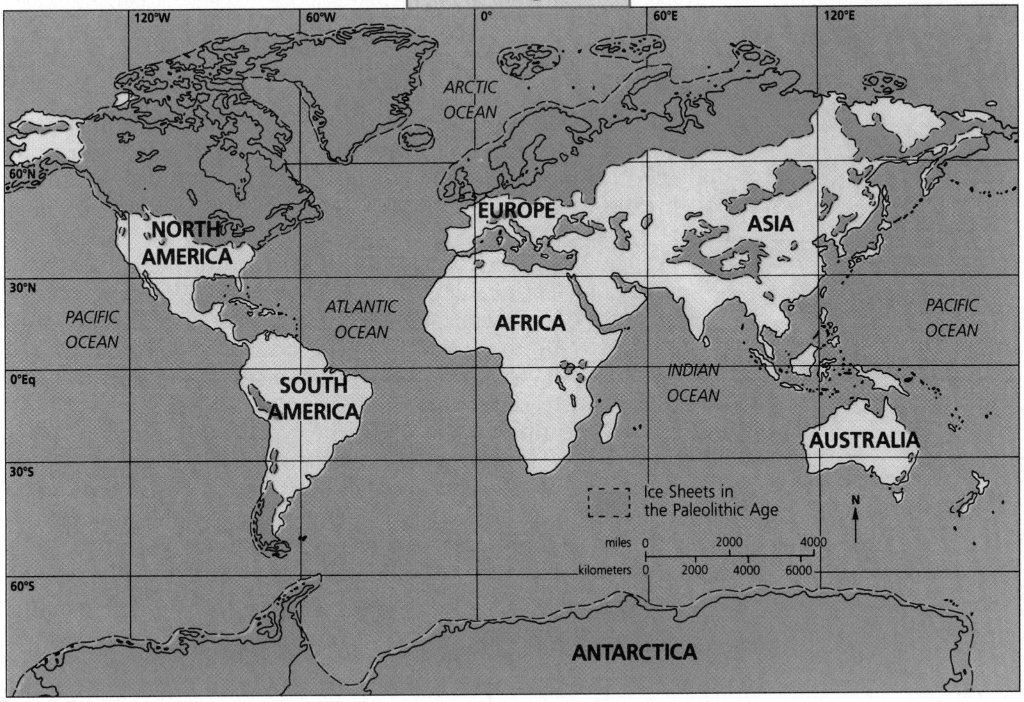

Reading Check Answer
Glaciers drove people and animals away, smoothed hills into plains, created lakes, and dug new channels for rivers.

L3 **Critical Thinking** Ask students to explain the duality of the Mississippi River in bringing both prosperity and devastation to the people who live along it. Have some students research the flood of 1993 and create a graph or chart showing loss of acres of farmland, lives, and destroyed property. Have other students research the economic prosperity enjoyed by those who earn their living from the river, creating a chart or graph of dollars earned and jobs generated. Have the two groups share their charts.

DID YOU KNOW ??

The Atlantic Ocean was named by the Romans after the Atlas Mountains that rose at the western end of the Mediterranean Sea. The Mediterranean got its name from two Latin words meaning "in the middle of the land." The Pacific Ocean was named by Spanish explorer Ferdinand Magellan, who found it calm and peaceful after his stormy voyage around Cape Horn.

MEETING SPECIAL NEEDS

Help English Language Learning students learn the geographical terms that are discussed in this chapter. Have the class use their textbook and geographical reference materials to create a list of geographical features. Next, ask students to group related terms into the following categories: landforms and waterways. Organize students into two groups and assign one category to each group. Have each student in the group define and illustrate one or more terms. When all the students have finished their assignments, compile the definitions and illustrations into an illustrated dictionary to use as a class reference.

Refer to ***Inclusion for the Middle School Social Studies Classroom: Strategies and Activities*** for additional resources.

MAP STUDY Answer

North America, Europe, Asia, and Antarctica

L3 **Critical Thinking** Have students research to make a list of the ten largest cities, based on population, in the United States. Using their text Atlas, have students locate each city to determine if it is near a waterway. Ask students to give reasons why so many cities are located near waterways.

Reading Check Answer The longest **river system** is the Nile.

Reading Check Answer Movements of the earth affect **climate** through changes in a place's distance and angle from the sun.

Reading Check Answer A place's **latitude** determines the amount of heat it receives from the sun.

L1 **Critical Thinking** Ask students to explain the differences between weather and climate. *(Weather is the conditions in the earth's atmosphere at a certain place and time. Climate is the pattern of weather over many years.)*

Smaller bodies of salt water are known as seas. They are usually partly surrounded by land. Bodies of water that are completely surrounded by land are known as lakes. The world's largest freshwater lake is Lake Superior in North America. It is about 350 miles, or 563 kilometers, long and 160 miles, or 257 kilometers, wide.

Waterways that empty into another body of water are known as rivers. Most rivers begin high in mountains or hills. A river and all the streams that flow into it make up a **river system.** The longest river system in the world is the Nile, which flows about 4,160 miles, or 6,693 kilometers, from its source in the highlands of central Africa to its mouth on the Mediterranean Sea.

Reading Check What is the longest **river system** in the world?

Waterways in History Like landforms, waterways have played an important part in helping people decide where to live. People's earliest homes were along the banks of rivers and other waterways. These bodies of water provided them with a means for travel and trade, drinking water, and irrigation for crops as farming developed. Thus, river valleys were often sites for villages and cities. Animals also used waterways for food and drinking water, so the riverbanks were good hunting grounds.

Climate and the Sun The pattern of the weather of a place over many years is **climate.** The most important thing that shapes climate is the sun. The sun provides the earth with heat and light. All parts of the earth, however, do not receive the same amount of sunlight.

Reading Check How is **climate** shaped by movements of the earth?

As the earth moves through space, it *rotates,* or spins like a top. Geographers say that it spins on its *axis,* an imaginary line that runs through the earth's center from the North Pole to the South Pole. It takes one day of 24 hours for the earth to spin around completely.

Besides rotating, the earth moves around the sun in an almost circular path called an *orbit.* This motion, known as a *revolution,* takes one year of 365¼ days to complete. It is the earth's revolution around the sun that causes the seasons.

Seasons vary from one part of the world to another. The earth's axis, instead of being straight up and down, is tilted at an angle. This means that places in the Northern Hemisphere are tilted toward the sun from March to September. As a result, these places have spring and summer at that time. During these same months, however, the Southern Hemisphere is tilted away from the sun. There it is fall and winter. Six months later, from September to March, conditions reverse, and the seasons are the opposite.

Reading Check How can a place's **latitude** help you predict temperatures in the area?

Climate Zones The amount of heat from the sun a place receives depends on its **latitude,** or distance north or south of the

EXTENDING THE CONTENT

Making a list of the world's longest rivers is not an easy task. Some references use only the length of the river itself, while others use the length of the entire river system. For example, the Mississippi River itself is 2,348 miles (or 3,779 km) long and ranks twelfth in length in the world. Some sources will rank the Mississippi the third longest river because they consider the combined Mississippi-Missouri rivers for length—3,880 miles (or 6,240 km).

The Earth's Revolution

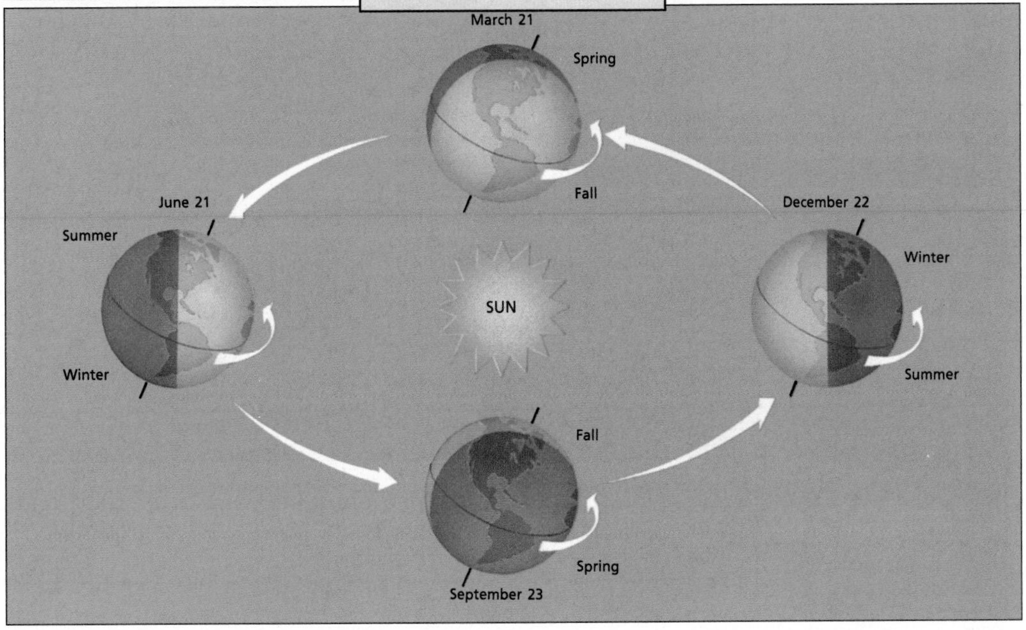

Equator. Rays from the sun are most direct at the Equator. Geographers often organize the earth into three climate zones based on latitude.

The **tropical zone,** also called the tropics, is the area between the Tropic of Cancer and the Tropic of Capricorn. The tropical zone always receives the most direct rays of the sun. Most places in the tropics are hot year-round.

Reading Check Where is the **tropical zone** located?

The **temperate** (tem'puh ruht) **zone** is found in both the area between the Tropic of Cancer and the Arctic Circle in the Northern Hemisphere, and the area between the Tropic of Capricorn and the Antarctic Circle in the Southern Hemisphere. The sun's rays reach the temperate zone at a slant for part of the year and almost directly for the rest of the year. As a result, the weather in this zone is generally cold in winter and warm in summer.

Reading Check What type of weather is found in each **temperate zone?**

The **polar zone** is the area north of the Arctic Circle and south of the Antarctic Circle. This area receives no sunlight at all during part of the year and only slanting rays during the rest of the year. As a result, the climate in the polar zone is very cold, and few people live there.

Reading Check Why is the **polar zone** very cold?

Climate, Water, and Wind

In addition to the sun, climate is shaped by large bodies of water, which keep the temperature of a place from getting too hot or too cold. Water gains or

MAKING CONNECTIONS

>> Science Climate closely affects plant life. Hot, dry places have plants that are able to remove moisture from the air and store water in their stems. Forests flourish in areas with warm temperatures and at least moderate rainfall. When rainfall is light, vegetation consists of tall grasses. Some mosses survive in very cold places.

Reading Check Answer The **tropical zone** is located between the Tropic of Cancer and the Tropic of Capricorn.

Reading Check Answer Weather in the **temperate zone** is generally cold in winter and warm in summer.

Reading Check Answer The **polar zone** receives little or no sunlight. (It is tilted away from the sun.)

DID YOU KNOW ??

The sun's surface temperature is several thousand degrees and at its center, the temperature is between 10 to 20 million degrees. An object on the sun would weigh about 28 times its weight on the earth.

MEETING SPECIAL NEEDS

Help tactile/kinesthetic learners understand the earth's revolution by having them demonstrate the movement of the earth on its axis, its rotation around the sun, and its orbit around the sun. They may use a globe for the earth and a flashlight to represent the sun. Discuss how the earth's axis is always tilted in the same direction. This affects the temperature of places. Demonstrate how the earth's rotation around the sun causes day and night. Finally, demonstrate how the earth's revolution and the earth's tilt cause the changing seasons.

Refer to ***Inclusion for the Middle School Social Studies Classroom: Strategies and Activities*** for additional resources.

CAPTION ANSWER

Prevailing winds blow from a certain direction most of the time. Monsoon winds change direction depending on the season of the year.

Reading Check Answer
Prevailing winds blow from a certain ("prevailing") direction most of the year. **Ocean currents** are steady streams of either hot or cold water.

Reading Check Answer
As the air rises over mountains, it cools and drops its moisture, or **precipitation.**

MAKING CONNECTIONS

>> **Science** In the days of sailing ships, experienced sea captains and navigators took advantage of their knowledge of the winds to make long voyages that seem almost unbelievable today.

NATIONAL GEOGRAPHIC

NGS PICTURESHOW CD-ROM
Picture Atlas of the World
You and your students can see the challenges and solutions involved in making maps by viewing the Mapping Our World animation "Round Earth on Flat Paper."

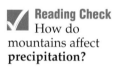

MONSOON Monsoons are very important to the agriculture of southern Asia. The wet, or summer, monsoons bring moisture necessary for farming to the area. Here, an Indian farmer struggles to plow his fields in the midst of monsoon winds and rain. **How do monsoons differ from prevailing winds?**

Fun Facts . . . .

Record Rain Cherrapunji, India, holds the world's record for annual rainfall. From August 1860 to August 1861, monsoons dumped 1,042 inches, or 2,647 centimeters, on the town. That's a downpour!

loses heat more slowly than land. Also, air over a lake is cooler than air over the land.

Climate is also shaped by the movement of air and ocean water. Air that moves is called wind. Some winds are known as **prevailing** (pri vā′ lĕng) **winds** because they blow from a certain direction almost all the time. Other winds are called monsoons because they change direction according to the season of the year. Monsoons often bring heavy rainfall. Ocean water that flows in a steady stream is called an **ocean current.** Both winds and ocean currents carry heat or cold and moisture all over the world. Ocean currents that flow from the Equator toward the poles warm the lands they pass. Currents that flow from the poles to the Equator cool the land they pass.

Reading Check How did **prevailing winds** get their name? What are **ocean currents?**

Climate and Altitude

Climate is also shaped by altitude. The higher the altitude, the colder the climate. In the tropical zone, people often prefer living in highlands rather than lowlands because the highland temperatures are more comfortable. The ancient Incas settled in the Andes Mountains of Peru instead of along the Pacific coast for that reason. Mountains also affect **precipitation**—the falling of moisture such as rain or snow. As the air rises over mountains, it cools and drops its moisture.

Reading Check How do mountains affect **precipitation?**

EXTENDING THE CONTENT

The pattern of prevailing winds worldwide is due to temperature differences and to the earth's rotation, which deflects winds from a straight-line path. At the Equator, for instance, rising warm air causes clouds and uncertain breezes where a ship might be motionless for days. Immediately to the north and south are two bands of trade winds, cool easterly winds that blow slightly toward the Equator. In the middle latitudes, the earth's rotation makes the prevailing winds westerlies. These winds are stormier and more erratic than the trade winds. For early European explorers, though, they provided a dependable route homeward from the Americas across the Atlantic.

Understanding a Mercator Projection

Because Earth is a sphere, no flat map can show its whole surface. Mapmakers use different **projections** (pruh jek´ shuhns), or ways of representing Earth on a flat surface.

One projection used often is a Mercator (muhr kāt´ uhr) projection. Named after Gerardus Mercator, a Flemish mapmaker of the 1500s, it is made by wrapping paper around a globe. A light shining from the center of the globe projects Earth's features onto the paper. This allows the map to be traced.

The parts of the map that are most like the earth are where the paper touches the globe, such as at the Equator. The parts that are most *distorted* (dis tort´ ed), or twisted out of shape, are where the paper does not touch the globe, such as near the poles.

Map Practice

1. **Which of the earth's climate zones is shown most accurately?**
2. **Which is most distorted?**
3. **Is the shape of North America more accurate on this map or on a globe? Why?**

World Climate Zones

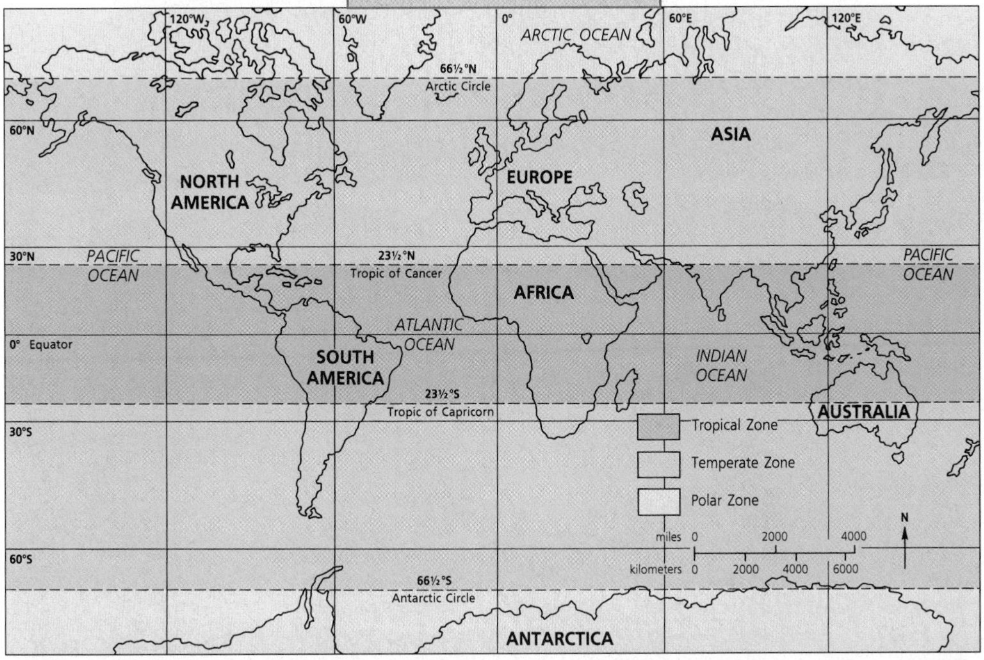

SPOTLIGHT ON: WORLD CLIMATE

Factors of climate can change as has been shown in recent years all over the world. Much of Africa north of the Equator receives very little rainfall. In this area is the world's largest tropical desert—the Sahara. However, at one time the Sahara was a fertile region that supported a thriving civilization. Because of a gradual lack of rainfall, most of this area is now uninhabitable. On the southern border of this desert is the Sahel, which in Arabic means *coastal land.* Between 1968 and 1980 a drought in the Sahel destroyed livestock and caused the starvation of many West Africans.

MAP SKILLS

TEACH

Understanding a Mercator Projection

Instruct students to read the instructional part of the feature. Ask: Why can't a flat map show the whole surface of the earth? *(because the earth is a sphere)* Which parts of the Mercator projection are most like the earth? *(parts where the paper touches the globe, such as at the Equator)* Direct students to study the map. Ask: Which continent is more accurate on a Mercator projection, South America or Asia? Why? *(South America, because it is located closer to the Equator than Asia.)*

Next, have students work in small groups to study other projections. Assign each group one of the following projections: conic, sinusoidal, polar, Lambert azimuthal equal-area projection, or Winkel Tripel. Have students find an example of their projection, explain how it is made, and describe its inaccuracies. Have each group present their findings.

Assign the Chapter 1 **Geography and Map Activity.**

Answers to Map Practice

1. Tropical Zone
2. Polar Zone
3. The globe representation is more accurate because no flat map can accurately represent a sphere.

Use the **Glencoe Skillbuilder Interactive Workbook CD-ROM, Level 1,** to provide instruction and practice in key social studies skills.

L3 **Critical Thinking** Ask students if they think one kind of climate is more beneficial economically to a country than another. Have students explain their answers and give examples that support it.

CAPTION ANSWER

Russia has often gone to war with other countries in order to capture land for warm water ports and harbors.

Fun Facts . . .

Climate Early Greeks classified climates based on what they knew about Greece and areas to the south and north. They called their own climate *temperate* because it posed few problems of shelter and clothing. They believed the area south of the Mediterranean Sea became hotter, so they called these lands *torrid.* Cold winds from the north led them to call that area *frigid.*

Climate in History Climate, like land and waterways, plays an important part in shaping history. It helps determine where people live, what kind of clothes they wear, what kind of houses they build, and what crops they grow. It also affects the speed with which they work and the kinds of things they do for entertainment. Since climate is something humans cannot control, it has affected civilizations since prehistoric times.

Sometimes climate affects the way a country behaves towards its neighbors. Climate has also helped decide the outcomes of wars. For example, many of Russia's harbors stay frozen during much of the year. In the past, Russia has often gone to war with other countries in order to capture land for warm water ports. Climate was also one reason the Russians were able to stop the invasions of French ruler Napoleon Bonaparte (nuh pō′ lē uhn bō′ nuh part) in the 1800s and German ruler Adolf Hitler in the 1940s. The Russians were used to the bitter cold and snow of their country's winter, whereas the invaders were not.

COLD CLIMATE This buoy has become frozen in the St. Petersburg Harbor during the cold Russian winter. Such waterways have been important many times in Russia's history. **What has the lack of warm water ports and harbors caused Russia to do in the past?**

MEETING SPECIAL NEEDS

Have interested students research the affects of climate on the soldiers who fought in such wars as Vietnam and the Persian Gulf War. Encourage them to interview any participants in these wars that they happen to know. Have them explain their findings in an oral report to the class.

Refer to ***Inclusion for the Middle School Social Studies Classroom: Strategies and Activities*** for additional resources.

Section 2 Assessment

1. **Define:** landforms, elevation, relief, core, mantle, crust, tectonic plates, continental drift, volcanoes, earthquakes, erosion, glaciers, river system, climate, latitude, tropical zone, temperate zone, polar zone, prevailing winds, ocean current, precipitation.
2. What are some of the ways landforms and waterways have been important to history?
3. Into what climate zones do geographers often organize the earth?

Critical Thinking

4. **Making Generalizations** How does climate affect the way that you live?

Graphic Organizer Activity

5. Draw a diagram like this one, label it with the four kinds of landforms, and list examples of each landform in your community, state, or region.

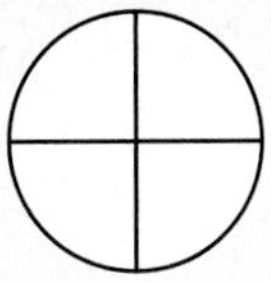

SECTION 3 Natural Resources

Natural resources are materials found in nature. Some, such as air, are found everywhere. Others, such as oil, are found only in certain areas. Some places have many natural resources, while others have few.

Reading Check What are some examples of **natural resources?**

Kinds of Natural Resources There are different kinds of natural resources. Some resources helpful to people include air, water, soil, sunlight, minerals, fossil fuels, forests, and animal life. Some of these—air, water, soil, and sunlight—are essential for any kind of life to exist. They are the most important natural resources.

Other natural resources, while not essential for life, are important because they enable people to live better. One such resource is **minerals,** or nonliving substances found beneath the earth's surface. Throughout history, people have used such minerals as iron, copper, tin, gold, and silver to make tools, weapons, jewelry, and money. Fossil fuels, such as coal, oil, and natural gas, provide the energy needed to heat homes and power machines.

Reading Check Why have **minerals** been important to people throughout history?

Natural resources become valuable only when people learn how to use them. For example, during the 1200s Marco Polo left his native city of Venice, in present-day Italy, and traveled to

Use the **Interactive Tutor Self-Assessment CD-ROM** to review Section 2.

L2 **Geography: Places and Regions** Organize students into seven groups to make natural resource maps of the continents. Assign each group one of the continents. Have a member of each group present its map to the class. Discuss which continent appears to be most abundant in resources and what implications could exist as a result. ELL

L3 **Critical Thinking** Ask students to consider why some countries think of their people as their most important natural resource. What countries would be most likely to think this way? *(China, India)* Why?

Reading Check Answer
Examples of **natural resources** include air, water, soil, sunlight, minerals, fossil fuels, forests, and animal life.

Reading Check Answer
People have used **minerals** to make tools, weapons, jewelry, and money.

Use the **Vocabulary Puzzlemaker CD-ROM** to create crossword and word search puzzles.

Section 2 Assessment Answers

1. All terms are defined in the text Glossary.
2. Landforms and waterways played an important part in where people lived and their political relationships.
3. the tropical, temperate, and polar zones
4. Answers will vary but should give examples of the way climate affects the way they live.
5. The diagrams should include examples of the mountains, hills, plateaus, and plains in your community or state. (You might use the presence and/or absence of these landforms to discuss the unique features of your region, as would be the case in states on the Great Plains, along the Rockies, and so on.)

Assign the Chapter 1 **Section 2 Quiz** in the TCR. Testmaker available.

CAPTION ANSWER

iron, copper, tin, gold, silver

L1 **Art** Have students find pictures in newspapers and magazines or draw illustrations of renewable resources and nonrenewable resources. Then divide a bulletin board in half. Title one side "Renewable Resources" and the other side "Nonrenewable Resources." Display pictures and illustrations on the bulletin board. Use the bulletin board to start a discussion of how students can conserve their use of nonrenewable resources.

L3 **Geography: Environment and Society** Have students research laws passed in their state to control the pollution of the air, soil, and water. Ask them to present their findings in an oral report to the class. Have the class decide if any additional laws are needed.

Reading Check Answer

Renewable resources can be replaced; **nonrenewable resources** cannot.

MINERALS Some natural resources are found beneath the ground and are called minerals. Oil and coal are two minerals for which people drill and mine underground. The oil well shown here (left) is in the jungles of Nigeria. Coal mining in North Dakota is also shown (right). **What are other examples of minerals?**

China. A few years after returning home, he wrote a book about the wonderful things he had seen on his journey. One of these was a black rock, now known as coal, which the Chinese dug out of the ground and burned to keep themselves warm. The Venetians (vi nē′ shuhnz) doubted Marco Polo. They had not used coal as the Chinese had. People later changed their minds about coal when they began using it as a fuel to power steam engines and to process steel.

Reading Check How do **renewable resources** and **nonrenewable resources** differ from each other?

Some resources can be replaced as they are used. These are **renewable resources.** For example, American farmers who lived in the Dust Bowl of the 1930s were able to get back their once-rich soil. To do this they used better ways of farming and planted trees to keep the soil from being blown away. Other natural resources cannot be replaced as they are used. These are **nonrenewable resources.** For example, once fossil fuels and most minerals are used up, they will be gone forever.

In recent years, people have become more and more concerned about making better use of the world's natural resources. Some countries have passed laws to slow down the pollution of the air, water, and soil. Scientists also are trying to develop new sources of energy.

COOPERATIVE LEARNING

Ask the class to name important resources that need to be conserved, as you write responses on the board. Organize students into as many groups as there are items on the list. Have each group investigate efforts being made to conserve its resource. Have each group also brainstorm other ways in which their resource might be conserved. After each group has completed its work, ask each to participate in a round-table discussion in which group members take turns suggesting ways to conserve their assigned resource.

Natural Resources in History Natural resources affected the location and growth of settlements throughout history. The sharing of these resources has also been important. Rich soil and plenty of water made farming possible and led to the rise of cities. Asians and Europeans came into contact with one another partly because Europeans wanted the silks and spices of Asia. Modern industry started in countries that had large amounts of coal and iron ore for making steel. During the 1800s, the discovery of gold in California, South Africa, Australia, and Alaska caused hundreds of thousands of people to move to those areas.

Section 3 Assessment

1. **Define:** natural resources, minerals, renewable resources, nonrenewable resources.
2. What resources are needed for life?

Critical Thinking

3. **Demonstrating Reasoned Judgment** Why do you think people have become more interested in making better use of the world's natural resources?

Graphic Organizer Activity

4. Create a diagram such as this one, and use it to show examples of how natural resources have helped shape history.

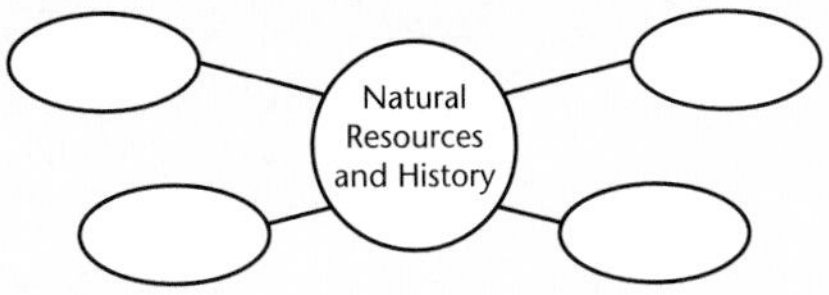

RENEWABLE RESOURCES Soil is considered a renewable resource. Some human activities, like the strip mining of coal (left), use up the land. With careful management, however, such areas can be reclaimed, or made productive again (right). **What are some examples of nonrenewable resources?**

Use the **Interactive Tutor Self-Assessment CD-ROM** to review Section 3.

CAPTION ANSWER

fossil fuels and most minerals such as copper, tin, and gold

DID YOU KNOW ??

Oil takes millions of years to form, and the earth's supply is limited. Industrialized countries like the United States consume far more oil than they produce and must import large amounts. Many experts believe that the world's fossil fuels will be used up if steps are not taken to limit their consumption and to find alternative energy sources.

L2 **Science** Have students research to find out about alternative energy sources. Then have them make a diorama showing one of the alternative energy sources being used or applied.

Section 3 Assessment Answers

1. natural resources, materials found in nature (p. 19); minerals, nonliving substances found beneath the earth's surface (p. 19); renewable resources, resources that can be replaced (p. 20); nonrenewable resources, resources that cannot be replaced (p. 20)
2. air, water, soil, and sunlight
3. Answers will vary but might include that people are afraid resources will be used up, and they want to stop pollution of these resources.
4. Examples should come from the subsection "Natural Resources in History" on this page. Encourage students to add more than four examples, either from Section 3 or from their own knowledge of history.

Assign the Chapter 1 **Section 3 Quiz** in the TCR. Testmaker available.

DID YOU KNOW ??

The drawing on this page of the student text depicts the Chinese legend of P'an Gu.

L2 **Critical Thinking** Ask students why they think people developed legends to explain their past.

L3 **Writing** Have students imagine that they were living long ago, when there were no scientific explanations for natural occurrences. Have students write a legend explaining thunder and lightning.

Use the **Vocabulary PuzzleMaker CD-ROM** to create crossword and word search puzzles.

Reading Check Answer
Legends help explain the past.

SECTION 4 Legends

Reading Check What are the purposes of **legends?**

People have always been interested in learning about the past. Every group of people on the earth has **legends,** or folktales, that help to explain the past. These legends began as stories that were spoken or sung. People passed them down from generation to generation.

A Chinese Legend The Chinese have a legend about the beginnings of China. It says that the universe was a huge egg. When the egg split open, the upper half became the sky, and the lower half became the earth. Out of the split egg came P'an Gu (pan gū), the first man. Each day for 18,000 years P'an Gu grew taller, the sky grew higher, and the earth grew thicker. Then P'an Gu died. His head split and became the sun and the moon. His blood filled the rivers and the seas. His hair became the forests and the meadows. His perspiration became the rain. His breath became the wind and his voice, the thunder.

MULTICULTURAL PERSPECTIVES

Every culture has at least one creation myth or legend. The following is a Norse myth as told in Bulfinch's classic *Mythology: The Age of Fable.*

"There was once no heaven above nor earth beneath, but only bottomless deep, and a world of mist in which flowed a fountain. Twelve rivers flowed from this fountain, and when they had flowed far from their source, they froze into ice . . ."

"Southward from the world of mist was the world of light. From this flowed a warm wind upon the ice and melted it. The vapours rose in the air and formed clouds, from which sprang Ymir, the Frost giant, and his progeny [children] and the cow Audhumbla, whose milk afforded nourishment and food to the giant . . . While she [the cow] was one day licking the salt stones there appear at first the hair of a man, on

An African Legend The Africans have a legend about why the sun shines more brightly than the moon. It says that God created the Moon and then the Sun. Because the Moon was bigger and brighter, the Sun became jealous and attacked the Moon. They fought and wrestled until the Sun begged for mercy. Then they wrestled again. This time the Sun threw the Moon into the mud. Dirt splashed all over the Moon, and it was no longer as bright as before. To stop the fighting, God stepped in. He told the Sun that from then on it would be brighter than the Moon and would shine during the day for kings and workers. He told the Moon that from then on it would shine only at night for thieves and witches.

A Rumanian Legend The Rumanians have a legend about the creation of mountains and valleys. It says that when God finished making the heavens, He measured them with a little ball of thread. Then He started to create the earth to fit under them. A mole came along and offered to help. So God let the mole hold the ball of thread while He created the earth.

STONEHENGE Many legends have been told about the ancient ruins of Stonehenge in Great Britain, shown here. These stones are arranged in an unusual formation believed to date back to prehistoric times. **How do modern people learn about ancient legends such as the stories about Stonehenge?**

Independent Practice

L2 **Language Arts** Have students research legends about a group of people they are interested in. Ask students to prepare a reading of one legend for the class. Have them write the name of the legend and its topic on a notecard and attach it to a wall map of the world showing where the culture it represents exists, or did exist.

DID YOU KNOW

It is believed that Stonehenge was built in three phases from 2800 to 1500 B.C. Besides being used for tribal gatherings and religious ceremonies, the stones were probably used to find out when major astronomical happenings would occur.

CAPTION ANSWER

People passed them down from generation to generation. After people developed writing, they wrote down their legends.

MULTICULTURAL PERSPECTIVES

the second day the whole head, and on the entire form endowed with beauty, agility, and power. This new being was a god, from whom and his wife, a daughter of the giant race sprang the three brothers Odin, Vili, and Ve."

"They slew the giant Ymir, and out of his body formed the earth, of his blood the seas, of his bones the mountains, of his hair the trees, of his skull the heavens, and of his brain clouds, charged with hail and snow. Of Ymir's eyebrows, the gods formed Midgard (middle earth), destined to become the abode of man. "

L1 **Art** Discuss how legends are very descriptive and help people form pictures in their minds while they listen to the legends or while they read the legends. Ask how this might help archaeologists and anthropologists learn about early people. Have students illustrate one of the legends they read in this section.

L2 **Language Arts** Read to the students legends about the beginning of the world from the book written by Virginia Hamilton, *In the Beginning: Creation Stories from Around the World*; Harcourt, 1988. Have students compare and contrast legends from different parts of the world. What elements are similar? What seems dissimilar about these legends?

Reading Check Answer
Archaeologists study the remains of past human life. **Anthropologists** study the origin and development of humans.

Use the **Interactive Tutor Self-Assessment CD-ROM** to review Section 4.

While God was weaving and shaping the earth, the mole let out the thread little by little. God was too busy to notice that, at times, the mole let out more thread than it should have. When God was finished, He was amazed to find that the earth was too big to fit under the heavens.

The mole, seeing what it had done, was afraid. It ran off and buried itself. God sent the bee to find the mole and ask it what should be done. But when the bee found the mole, it would not answer the question.

The bee hid in a flower, hoping the mole would think it was alone and start talking to itself. Soon, the mole thought out loud. It said that it would squeeze the earth so that the mountains would stick up and the valleys would sink down. Then the earth would be small enough to fit under the heavens. Upon hearing this, the bee buzzed off. The mole heard the buzzing and became angry. It put a curse on the bee, saying, "Henceforth, feed on yourself."

The bee told God what the mole had said. God squeezed the flat earth so that the mountains rose up, the valleys sank down, and the earth fit under the heavens. God then turned the mole's curse into a blessing. Ever since, the bee makes its own honey, while the mole lives underground and is afraid to come out.

Other Legends

These Chinese, African, and Rumanian legends are about the creation of the world. This is not true of all legends. Many are about the deeds of godlike men and women or about strange and wonderful lands. Other legends explain natural elements such as the placement of stars or why a maple tree has red leaves. Some even explain geographic features such as mountains and rivers.

After people developed writing more than 5,000 years ago, they wrote down their legends. Many came to be thought of as fact. In recent years, **archaeologists,** or scientists who study the remains of past human life, and **anthropologists,** or scientists who study the origin and development of humans, became curious about how much of certain legends was fiction and how much was fact. This led them to search out the truth of some of the legends.

Reading Check What type of work is done by **archaeologists?** What do **anthropologists** study?

Section 4 Assessment

1. **Define:** legends, archaeologists, anthropologists.
2. How did people learn legends?

Critical Thinking

3. **Analyzing Information** What legends do you know? What do they try to explain?

Graphic Organizer Activity

4. Draw a diagram like this one, and use it to show the order of events in one of the legends in this section.

Section 4 Assessment Answers

1. legends, folktales that help explain the past (p. 22); archaeologists, scientists who study human remains (p. 24); anthropologists, scientists who study human origins (p. 24)
2. They were stories that were spoken or sung and passed down from generation to generation.
3. Answers will vary but students should name legends they know and their themes.
4. Events should highlight the main points in the legend and be placed in the correct sequence.

Assign the Chapter 1 **Section 4 Quiz** in the TCR. Testmaker available.

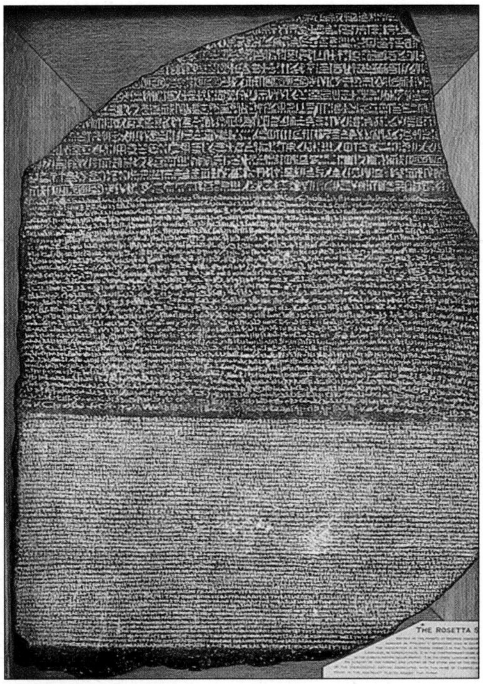

EGYPTIAN ARTIFACTS Archaeologists have uncovered many artifacts in Egypt. This spearhead (left), from about 15,000 B.C., is one of the oldest objects found in the region. The Rosetta Stone (right), from around 200 B.C., is one of the most famous archaeological finds. On it is carved a decree issued by Egyptian priests to honor a leader. **What kinds of objects can be considered artifacts?**

SECTION 5 Archaeology

Archaeology, or the study of the remains of past human life and cultures, began about 500 years ago. At that time, some Europeans dug up old marble statues and ornaments made by the ancient Greeks and Romans and sold them for a great deal of money. Scientists began to study these **artifacts,** or things made by people. They found they could learn from the artifacts how people lived long ago. People who lived in ancient times did not leave many written records.

Artifacts do not have to be works of art. They can be anything made by people such as weapons, tools, or pottery. The earliest artifacts are pieces of hard rock that were chipped into cutting or digging tools or into weapons.

Reading Check How did **archaeology** get its start?

Reading Check What information did scientists discover from the study of **artifacts?**

CAPTION ANSWER

things made by people

DID YOU KNOW

In recognition of the earth's diverse religions, some people use the letters C.E. (Common Era) instead of A.D. (*anno Domini*, or "in the year of our Lord," referring to the birth of Christ) and B.C.E. (Before the Common Era) instead of B.C. (before Christ).

Use the **Vocabulary PuzzleMaker CD-ROM** to create crossword and word search puzzles.

Reading Check Answer
Archaeology got its start when some Europeans dug up old marble statues and ornaments made by the ancient Greeks and Romans and sold them for a lot of money.

Reading Check Answer
Artifacts show scientists how people lived in ancient times.

PRIMARY SOURCES Library

You might assign "African Origins," from pages 674–675 of the Primary Sources Library.

MULTICULTURAL PERSPECTIVES

In today's world, dolls are considered toys, but archaeological evidence suggests that in ancient times, dolls played an important part in adult life as well. Ritual dolls, probably used in fertility rites, have been found in Europe from France to Russia, from the Aurignacian culture that existed there some 40,000 years ago.

DID YOU KNOW ??

In the summer of A.D. 79, Pompeii was a prosperous town of about 20,000. The mild, sunny climate attracted wealthy Romans to vacation there and live in the comfortable villas. Thriving vineyards (in soil rich from volcanic ash) surrounded the city. Nearby Mount Vesuvius, though unknown to be a volcano, had not erupted for centuries. Its sudden eruption one August afternoon rained hot ashes, stones, and cinders on Pompeii for a day and a half, and choked the town with deadly fumes. Only those who left the city quickly survived.

MAKING CONNECTIONS

➤➤ **History** The Rosetta Stone records a law written in 196 B.C. praising Egyptian King Ptolemy V. The Rosetta Stone is made of basalt. It was found by Jean-Francois Champollion in 1799 near Rosetta, a town 34 miles, or 54 km, east of Alexandria, Egypt.

CAPTION ANSWER

Herculaneum

People in History

Mary Nicol Leakey
1913–1996

Paleoanthropologist

At age 11, Mary Nicol Leakey visited a cave filled with prehistoric paintings. The cave inspired her to become a paleoanthropologist—a person who studies prehistoric humans and prehumans. She later left England for East Africa. Here she discovered prehuman footprints more than 3.6 million years old! For more on this discovery, see pages 674–675.

Archaeological Finds About 1700, some Italian farmers discovered they were living on top of an ancient Roman city named Herculaneum (huhr kyul lā′ nē uhm) that had been buried for more than 1,000 years. In 1719 archaeologists began uncovering the city. After more than 50 years, they uncovered not only Herculaneum but also another Roman city called Pompeii (pom pā′). These cities contained, among other things, fine houses, theaters, streets, and temples. More importantly, from what they found, the archaeologists learned exactly how ancient Romans lived.

The discovery of Herculaneum and Pompeii was followed in 1799 by one of the greatest of all archaeological discoveries. This was the finding in Egypt of the Rosetta Stone, a slab of stone on which are carved ancient Egyptian picture-writing and its Greek translation. Although scholars knew the Greek language well, they had not been able to *decipher,* or explain the meaning of, the ancient Egyptian language. The Rosetta Stone was a two-

POMPEII The Roman city of Pompeii was buried under the mud and lava from a volcanic eruption in 79 A.D. Discovered in the 1700s, the site has provided much information about Roman life and art, such as this wall painting from a home. **What other ancient Roman city was discovered in the 1700s?**

EXTENDING THE CONTENT

When archaeologists excavated Pompeii, they found restaurants with games and wine on the table, bakeries with bread in the oven, and family pets in the houses. They found comfortable townhouses with colorful tiled floors, paintings on the walls, and elegant furnishings. Many had central gardens with pools, fountains, benches, and statues. In Pompeii's warm climate, people spent much time outside in the family garden. Less wealthy people often lived in small rooms over shops or in apartments.

When people first began to investigate the past, many saw it as a "treasure house" of statues, paintings, and jewelry to be

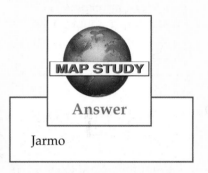

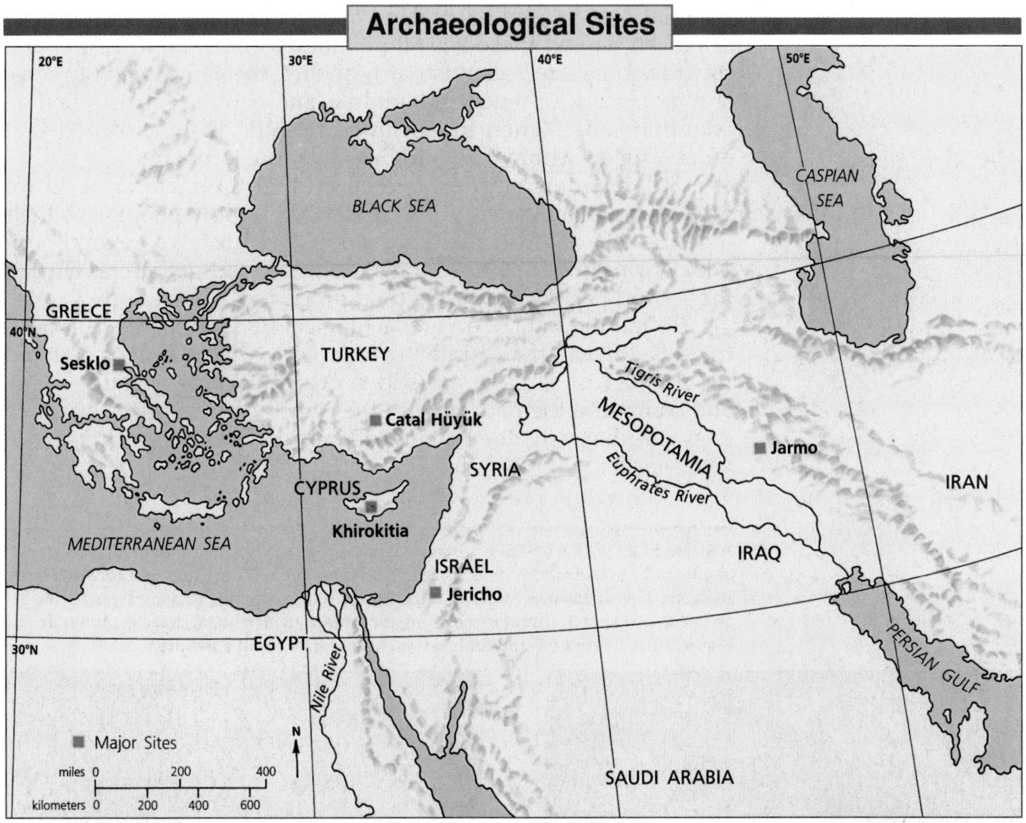

language dictionary that gave them the key to the meaning of Egyptian picture-writing. Now they could learn much more about the history of Egypt and its people.

A great many archaeological finds have been made since the discovery of the Rosetta Stone. For example, between 1850 and 1950 archaeologists uncovered five lost civilizations. In 1988 they discovered the oldest known piece of cloth, woven 9,000 years ago. Archaeologists continue to make discoveries in many parts of the world. This can be especially difficult because often only small pieces of artifacts are found. Thus, archaeologists have only hints or clues about people of past civilizations.

Dating Archaeological Remains After archaeologists *excavate,* or dig into the earth, to uncover remains of the past, they have to *date,* or find the age of, the remains. In 1832 Christian J. Thomsen, a Danish archaeologist, divided early human history into three *ages,* or periods. These ages were based on the

MAP STUDY

PLACES AND REGIONS Archaeologists carefully piece together information gathered at archaeological sites. **What archaeological site is found near the Tigris and Euphrates rivers?**

L2 **History** Have students research the five lost civilizations uncovered by archaeologists between 1850 and 1950 and write reports about their findings to share with the class.

L2 **Daily Life** Ask students what they think archaeologists thousands of years from now would learn if life were frozen in your town today, as it was in Pompeii. What would they be able to excavate from the twentieth century? ELL

MAP STUDY

Answer

Jarmo

L3 **Critical Thinking** Have students draw at least four conclusions about the locations of the archaeological sites shown on the map on this page. Have students write their conclusions in statement form. For example: All the archaeological sites are located between 30° N and 40° N. Have students share their statements.

EXTENDING THE CONTENT

collected and sold. During this period of history, tombs were looted, temples were destroyed, and gold objects melted down. Wealthy private collectors took home objects they could find. Victorious generals systematically cleaned out the tombs and temples of conquered lands. With the development of archaeology as a science came more responsibility and more public interest in historical findings.

material people used for making tools and weapons during them. Thomsen named these ages the Stone Age, the Bronze Age, and the Iron Age. Later, scientists also divided the Stone Age into three shorter periods of time—old, middle, and new. Scientists relied on common sense when unearthing artifacts. They assumed that older artifacts would be found beneath more recent ones.

Still later, archaeologists realized that the material used for tools and weapons was not as important as how people got their food. So they divided early human history into two general periods. During the first period, people were food gatherers. During the second period, they were food producers.

To tell the date of an archaeological find, scientists first used trees. Each year, trees form a new growth ring. Scientists counted the number of rings in a wooden object, such as a house beam, and compared the pattern with the rings of a tree whose age they knew. In that way, they could identify dates as far back as 3,000 years earlier.

ARCHAEOLOGICAL SITES Archaeological research is a major method of learning about ancient civilizations. Specialized techniques and tools are required for successful research. This archaeological excavation (left) is at the Agora in Athens, Greece. The archaeologist shown (right) is searching for artifacts with a metal detector. **What do bones, animal remains, and tools tell archaeologists about a people?**

DID YOU KNOW ??

Archaeologists are concerned about preserving archaeological sites that have not yet been excavated. Some of these sites are threatened by development of the land. Also, archaeologists are concerned about the illegal sale of artifacts. They are trying to create and enforce international laws to end the import of artifacts that do not have an export certificate from the country where the artifacts were discovered.

LINKING PAST TO PRESENT

Emperor Napoleon of France took scholars and scientists with him on an expedition to Egypt in 1798 to study its ancient culture. Napoleon brought boatloads of Egyptian artifacts home to Paris, but he did not keep them for himself. Instead he had a new wing built on the royal palace known as the Louvre—one of the largest art museums in the world today.

CAPTION ANSWER

Their tools tell how people got their food, what they ate, and in what time period they lived.

SPOTLIGHT ON: WILLARD FRANK LIBBY

Willard Frank Libby was born in 1908 in Grand Valley, Colorado. He taught chemistry at the University of California at Berkeley from 1933 until 1945. From 1945 until 1959, he was a member of the Institute for Nuclear Studies and the chemistry department at the University of Chicago. It was during this period that he made his famous discovery about carbon 14 dating. In 1960, in large part for this discovery, he was awarded the Nobel Prize for chemistry.

Understanding Cause and Effect

CRITICAL THINKING SKILLS

You know that if you watch television instead of completing your homework, you will receive poor grades. This is an example of a cause-and-effect relationship. This cause—watching television instead of doing homework—leads to an effect—poor grades.

When you look for why or how an event or chain of events took place, you are developing the skill of understanding causes and effects.

CAUSES AND EFFECTS

CAUSES
- Europeans dig up artifacts for sale.
- Scientists study these artifacts.
- Artifacts provide information on the past.

↓

Start of Archaeology

↓

EFFECTS
- Lost civilizations are uncovered.
- Early human history is divided into periods.
- New methods of dating are devised.

GO TO Glencoe's **Skillbuilder Interactive Workbook CD-ROM, Level 1,** provides instruction and practice in key social studies skills.

Learning the Skill A *cause* is any person, event, or condition that makes something happen. What happens as a result is known as an *effect*. These guidelines will help you identify cause and effect:

- Look for "clue words" that alert you to cause and effect, such as *because, led to, brought about, produced,* and *therefore.*
- Look for logical relationships between events, such as "She did this and then that happened."

In a chain of historical events, one effect often becomes the cause of other effects. The chart on this page shows such a chain of events.

Skill Practice

Study the cause-and-effect chart on this page. Then answer the questions below.

1. **What were some of the causes of the start of archaeology?**
2. **What were some of the effects of archaeology upon history?**
3. **What effect do you think the discovery of lost civilizations has had upon our view of the past?**

CRITICAL THINKING SKILLS

TEACH

Understanding Cause and Effect

You might introduce this lesson by asking students to write down one good thing that happened to them in the past week. Call on a volunteer to share his or her experience. Ask the student these questions: "What caused this event to happen?" "What was the effect of the event on your life?"

Use the following diagram to display the student's responses.

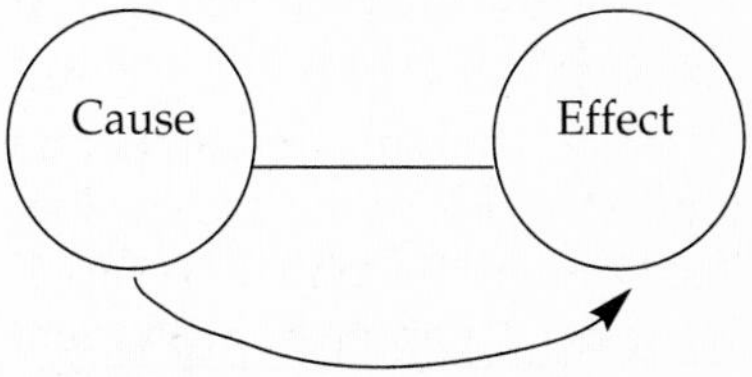

Ask the rest of the class to create similar diagrams showing the cause and effect of the experiences that they wrote down. Use this exercise to introduce the skill lesson and questions on this page.

Answers to Skill Practice

1. Europeans dug up artifacts for sale. The scientists who studied these artifacts discovered important information about the past.

2. Lost civilizations were uncovered. Early human history was divided into periods, and new methods of dating were developed.

3. Answers will vary, but encourage students to appreciate the effect of the past on our present-day lives. (For example, you might refer students to the "Linking Across Time" feature in each chapter of this book.)

TEAM TEACHING STRATEGIES

Science Working with a science teacher, distribute pictures of tree stumps with differing sizes of rings to small groups of students. Have them speculate on the cause of these differences. *(Abundant rainfall produces wide rings; dry years produce narrow rings.)* Explore the effects of differing rainfall patterns on the way people live.

Next, review with students how scientists have used trees to help date archaeological objects. *(Answers should reflect information on page 28.)* Then, ask students what additional information a tree stump or wooden object might provide to archaeologists. *(information on the weather or climate at an ancient site, reasons people may or may not have farmed, reasons people abandoned a site, and so on)*

ASSESS

Check for Understanding

Ask students to summarize the main points of the chapter, orally or in writing. Discuss the answers to the Section and Chapter Review questions.

Evaluate

Assign the Chapter 1 **Performance Assessment Activity** in the TCR.

Administer the **Chapter 1 Test** found in the TCR. Testmaker available.

Reteach

Have students work in small groups to explain what they discovered about the four "Chapter Focus" objectives on page 5.

Assign the Chapter 1 **Reteaching Activity** in the TCR.

Enrich

Have students research and report on one of the archaeological sites on the map on page 27.

Assign Chapter 1 **Enrichment Activity** in the TCR.

CLOSE

Have the students prepare a time capsule that would include artifacts that best represent their lives and cultures today.

Use **Interactive Tutor Self-Assessment CD-ROM** to review Section 5.

HISTORY Online

Self-Check Quiz gives students an interactive chapter tutorial. Have them access ***Chapter 1 Quiz*** at humanheritage.glencoe.com

In 1946 an American scientist named Willard Frank Libby discovered that all living things contain a radioactive element called carbon 14. After plants, animals, and humans die, the carbon 14 gradually disappears. By measuring how much carbon 14 a skeleton or the remains of a wooden boat contain today, scientists can figure out about how old the object is as far back as about 30,000 years.

Section 5 Assessment

1. **Define:** archaeology, artifacts.
2. Why did scientists begin to study artifacts?
3. Why was the discovery of the Rosetta Stone important?

Critical Thinking

4. **Predicting Consequences** What would you like about being an archaeologist? What would you dislike?

Graphic Organizer Activity

5. Draw a diagram like the one below, and use it to show the three major periods in early human history.

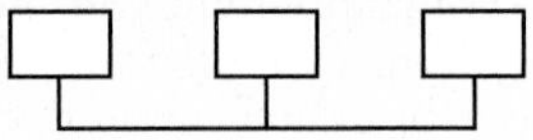

Chapter Summary & Study Guide

1. Geographers use six essential elements to study the earth: the world in spatial terms, places and regions, physical systems, human systems, environment and society, and the uses of geography.
2. Mountains, hills, plateaus, and plains make up 30 percent of the surface of the earth.
3. The surface of the earth is constantly undergoing change.
4. About 70 percent of the earth's surface is covered by water.
5. Climate is shaped by many factors, including winds, ocean currents, and altitude.
6. Geographers divide the earth into climate zones based on latitude.
7. Examples of natural resources include air, water, sunlight, minerals, fossil fuels, forests, and animal life.
8. Renewable resources can be replaced. Nonrenewable resources are gone forever when used up.
9. Legends have helped people explain the past.
10. Archaeologists study artifacts to learn how people lived long ago.
11. Since 1946, scientists have used the carbon 14 method of dating to identify the age of artifacts.

HISTORY Online

Self-Check Quiz

Visit the *Human Heritage* Web site at humanheritage.glencoe.com and click on ***Chapter 1—Self-Check Quiz*** to assess your understanding of this chapter.

Section 5 Assessment Answers

1. archaeology, the study of human remains (p. 25); artifacts, things made by people (p. 25)
2. to learn how people lived long ago
3. It gave scholars the key to the meaning of Egyptian picture-writing.
4. Answers will vary, but students should give specific examples that relate to an archaeologist's job.
5. The periods include the Stone Age, Bronze Age, and Iron Age.

Assign the Chapter 1 **Section 5 Quiz** in the TCR. Testmaker available.

CHAPTER 1 Assessment

Using Key Terms

Imagine you are writing an explanation for a younger student of how geography has shaped history. Use the following words to describe in a simple way how landforms, waterways, and climate have influenced history.

landforms	tectonic plates	glaciers
climate	elevation	river system
natural resources	archaeology	artifacts
	erosion	

Understanding Main Ideas

1. What are the four major kinds of landforms?
2. What do geographers believe caused Pangaea to split into seven continents?
3. How has erosion both helped and hurt people?
4. Why did early people settle along the banks of waterways?
5. Why are air, water, soil, and sunlight important natural resources?
6. How have people's views about natural resources changed in recent years?
7. How is the carbon 14 test used as a dating tool?

Critical Thinking

1. In what climate zone would you prefer to live? Why?
2. "It is important to plan the use of the world's natural resources." What is your opinion of this statement? Explain.
3. Why is it important to identify the date of artifacts as exactly as possible?
4. How do ideas about the past change as more knowledge becomes available?

Graphic Organizer Activity

History Create a diagram like this one, and use it to show some of the archaeological finds that have changed history.

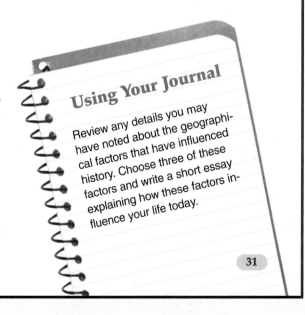

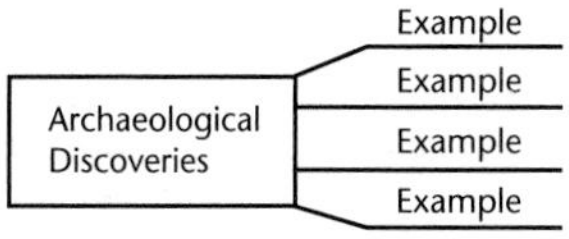

Geography in History

Physical Systems Look at the map on page 13 that shows how far ice sheets moved during the Ice Ages. What descriptive statements could you make about the movement of ice north of the Equator compared to south of the Equator?

Using Your Journal

Review any details you may have noted about the geographical factors that have influenced history. Choose three of these factors and write a short essay explaining how these factors influence your life today.

31

CHAPTER 1 Assessment Answers

Using Key Terms

Explanations will vary but should include all the key terms to describe how these have influenced history.

Understanding Main Ideas

1. mountains, hills, plateaus, and plains
2. continental drift
3. Sometimes wind erosion contributes to making land rich for farming, as in China. Erosion can also destroy people's way of life, as evidenced by the Dust Bowl.
4. because they provided drinking water, fish and other food, good hunting grounds, rich soil for farming, water for irrigation, and easier trade and travel
5. because they are needed for any kind of life to exist
6. Now there are laws to slow down pollution and new sources of energy are being developed.
7. dates artifacts older than those that can be dated by using trees

Critical Thinking

1. Answers will vary, but students should provide reasons.
2. Answers will vary but should include that natural resources are necessary to maintain life.
3. Answers will vary but should include that exact dating helps reconstruct history.
4. Answers will vary.

Graphic Organizer Activity

examples include: Herculaneum, Pompeii, Rosetta Stone, lost civilizations discovered since 1850, 9,000-year old piece of cloth discovered in 1988, any of the sites on the map on page 27

Bonus Test Question

For Chapter 1 Test

You are living in an area where you receive no sunlight for part of the year and slanted rays the rest of the year. You see a bear. What color is it? *(white—polar bear)*

Using Your Journal

Essays will vary but should include concrete references to modern examples. You might call on volunteers to read their essays and discuss them with the class.

Geography in History

There was greater movement of ice north of the Equator than south of the Equator.

Chapter 2 Planning Guide

Timesaving Tools

TeacherWorks™ All-In-One Planner and Resource Center

- **Interactive Teacher Edition** Access your Teacher Wraparound Edition and your classroom resources with a few easy clicks.
- **Interactive Lesson Planner** Planning has never been easier! Organize your week, month, semester, or year with all the lesson helps you need to make teaching creative, timely, and relevant.

PRESENTATION Plus!

Use Glencoe's **Presentation Plus!** multimedia teacher tool to easily present dynamic lessons that visually excite your students. Using Microsoft PowerPoint® you can customize the presentations to create your own personalized lessons.

Objectives	Reproducible Resources	Multimedia Resources
Section 1 **The Paleolithic Age** Explain how tools, language, clothing, and the discovery of fire helped early people advance, and describe what Neanderthals and Cro-Magnons were like.	Reproducible Lesson Plan Chapter 2 Vocabulary and Guided Reading Activity Reading Essentials and Study Guide 2-1 Chapter 2 Geography and Map Activity Chapter 2 Chart and Graph Skill Activity Unit 1 Primary Source Readings Chapter 2 Enrichment Activity Section 1 Quiz	Interactive Student Edition CD-ROM Graphic Organizer Transparency 9 Vocabulary PuzzleMaker CD-ROM Interactive Tutor Self-Assessment CD-ROM ExamView® Pro Testmaker CD-ROM Glencoe Skillbuilder Interactive Workbook CD-ROM, Level 1 Presentation Plus! CD-ROM
Section 2 **The Neolithic Age** Discuss how people changed from food gatherers to food producers and why specialization, government, and religion were important in Neolithic societies.	Reproducible Lesson Plan Reading Essentials and Study Guide 2-2 Chapter 2 Cooperative Learning Activity Section 2 Quiz	Teaching Transparencies and Activities 2A & 2B Vocabulary PuzzleMaker CD-ROM Interactive Tutor Self-Assessment CD-ROM ExamView® Pro Testmaker CD-ROM Glencoe Skillbuilder Interactive Workbook CD-ROM, Level 1
Chapter 2 **Review and Evaluation**	Chapter 2 Reteaching Activity Chapter 2 Performance Assessment Activity Unit 1 Standardized Test Practice Spanish Chapter Summary and Glossary Chapter 2 Test	Vocabulary PuzzleMaker CD-ROM Interactive Tutor Self-Assessment CD-ROM Glencoe Skillbuilder Interactive Workbook CD-ROM, Level 1 Audiocassettes* ExamView® Pro Testmaker CD-ROM

*Also available in Spanish.

✓ Performance Assessment Activities

Time Line Have students create an illustrated time line tracing the progression of early people from prehistory to the establishment of the first cities. The time line should depict how early people may have looked, what they wore, where they lived, and the tools they used.

CHAPTER RESOURCES

LITERATURE ABOUT THE PERIOD

Auel, Jean M. *The Clan of the Cave Bear.* Bantam, 1984. A Cro-Magnon girl is adopted by a Neanderthal tribe.

READINGS FOR THE STUDENT

Johanson, Donald and James Shreece. *Lucy's Child: The Discovery of a Human Ancestor.* William Morrow and Company, Inc., 1989. An account of Johanson's return to Africa in 1986.

READINGS FOR THE TEACHER

Gowlett, John. *Ascent to Civilization: The Archaeology of Early Man.* Knopf, 1984. The rise and development of human culture revealed by archaeological finds.

Pfeiffer, John. *The Emergence of Humankind.* Harper & Row, 1985. The unfolding story of human evolution and the human condition.

KEY TO ABILITY LEVELS

Teaching strategies have been coded for varying learning styles and abilities.

L1 Level 1 activities are **basic** activities and should be within the ability range of all students.

L2 Level 2 activities are **average** activities and should be within the ability range of the average to above-average student.

L3 Level 3 activities are **challenging** activities designed for the ability range of above-average students.

ELL ELL activities should be within the ability range of English Language Learning students.

NATIONAL GEOGRAPHIC Teacher's Corner

INDEX TO NATIONAL GEOGRAPHIC MAGAZINE

The following articles relate to this chapter:

- "Meet Kenya Man," by Karen E. Lange, October 2001.
- "France's Magical Ice Age Art: Chauvet Cave," by Jean Clottes, August 2001.
- "The Dawn of Humans: New Finds in South Africa," by Andre W. Keyser, May 2000.
- "Saharan Rock Art," by David Coulson, June 1999.
- "The Dawn of Humans," by Lee Berger, August 1998.

NATIONAL GEOGRAPHIC SOCIETY PRODUCTS AVAILABLE FROM GLENCOE

To order the following, call Glencoe at 1-800-334-7344:

- *PicturePack: Physical Geography of the World (Transparencies)*
- *Picture Atlas of the World (CD-ROM)*
- *PicturePack:World Geography Library (Transparencies)*

ADDITIONAL NATIONAL GEOGRAPHIC SOCIETY PRODUCTS

To order the following, call National Geographic at 1-800-368-2728:

- *Wonders of the Ancient World: National Geographic Atlas of Archaeology (Book)*
- *Read & Explore: Painters of the Cave, by Patricia Lauber (Literature Kit)*

Access *National Geographic's* new dynamic MapMachine Web site and other geography resources at:

www.nationalgeographic.com

www.nationalgeographic.com/maps

Introducing **CHAPTER 2**

OVERVIEW

Chapter 2 deals with the Paleolithic and Neolithic ages.

- **Section 1** focuses on the lifestyle of the earliest humans—the food gatherers of the Paleolithic, or Old Stone, Age.
- **Section 2** describes the developments of the Neolithic, or New Stone, Age—the beginning of farming, the domestication of animals, and the formation of villages.

CHAPTER OBJECTIVES

After reading Chapter 2, students will be able to:

1. explain how tools, language, clothing, and the discovery of fire helped early people advance.
2. summarize what Neanderthals and Cro-Magnons were like.
3. describe how people changed from food gatherers to food producers.
4. discuss why specialization, government, and religion were important in Neolithic societies.

EXAMINING ARTIFACTS

These artifacts show the skills and talents of early humans. The Paleolithic ivory carving—barely one and a half inches high—depicts the face of a *Homo sapien* crafted sometime between 30,000 and 20,000 B.C. By this time, early humans had spread out of Africa and into the more temperate zones of the world. Explore how these artifacts help dispel stereotypes about prehistoric "cave people."

PERFORMANCE ASSESSMENT ✓

Use the Performance Assessment Activities on page 32B to help you evaluate students as they complete the chapter.

CHAPTER 2

Prehistoric People

8000 B.C.–3000 B.C.

▲ Neolithic pottery

Paleolithic carving ▶

TEACHING RESOURCES

TEACHER PLANNING AND SUPPORT

- Reproducible Lesson Plan 2-1, 2-2
- Teaching Strategies for the World History Classroom (Including Block Scheduling Pacing Guides)
- Presentation Plus! CD-ROM

REVIEW AND REINFORCEMENT

- Reading Essentials and Study Guide 2-1, 2-2
- Chapter 2 Vocabulary and Guided Reading Activity
- Vocabulary PuzzleMaker CD-ROM
- Teaching Transparencies 2A & 2B
- Chapter 2 Reteaching Activity
- Chapter 2 Cooperative Learning Activity
- Chapter 2 Activity Book Activity
- Chapter 2 Chart and Graph Skill Activity
- Reading and Study Skills Foldables
- Interactive Tutor Self-Assessment CD-ROM
- Unit 1 MindJogger VideoQuiz

APPLICATION AND HANDS-ON ACTIVITIES

- Daily Questions in Social Studies
- Unit 1 Hands-On History Lab Activity
- Student Presentation Builder CD-ROM

Chapter Focus

Read to Discover

- How tools, language, clothing, and the discovery of fire helped early people advance.
- What Neanderthals and Cro-Magnons were like.
- How people changed from food gatherers to food producers.
- Why specialization, government, and religion were important in Neolithic societies.

HISTORY Online

Chapter Overview

Visit the *Human Heritage* Web site at **humanheritage.glencoe.com** and click on ***Chapter 2—Chapter Overviews*** to preview this chapter.

Terms to Learn	People to Know	Places to Locate
prehistory	Lucy	Olduvai Gorge
civilization	Neanderthals	Jericho
migrate	Cro-Magnons	Catal Hüyük
specialization		

Why It's Important Most archaeologists believe people have lived on the earth for millions of years. The period of time before the invention of writing is called **prehistory**. It lasted until about five thousand years ago, when people learned how to write. Through the use of artifacts, archaeologists have traced the milestones that paved the way from prehistory to the rise of **civilization**—a time when people progressed culturally and began to live in cities.

Reading Check When did **prehistory** end? What helped bring about the rise of **civilization?**

SECTION 1 The Paleolithic Age

Although there were no written records during prehistory, scientists have learned a great deal about prehistoric people. They have learned how early human beings lived and what important discoveries were made. Scientists also think they know why people moved out of Africa to other parts of the world.

Many scientists believe that until about 1.75 million years ago, people lived only on the grasslands of eastern and southern Africa. Then the earth's climate changed—it became colder. Ocean water froze into huge glaciers that spread out from the North and South poles. As the ice sheets grew, the sea level fell and uncovered land that had been under water. Land bridges then connected Africa to both southern Europe and southwestern Asia.

HISTORY Online

Chapter Overview introduces students to chapter content and key terms. Have them access ***Chapter 2 Overview*** at **humanheritage.glencoe.com**

FOCUS

Bellringer

Write the following question on the board: If you were marooned on a desert island, what tools would you need to survive?

Motivational Activity

Ask students to list the tools they would need to survive on a desert island. Have a volunteer write them on the board. Discuss how studying the tools of prehistoric people can help us to understand our past.

GUIDE TO READING

Reading Strategy

Ask students to read "Why It's Important" and summarize the chapter's main theme. *(Developments during prehistory paved the way for the rise of civilization.)* L1

Vocabulary Precheck

Ask students to define each of the "Terms to Know." Have a volunteer consult the dictionary for any unfamiliar words. L1 ELL

Use the Vocabulary PuzzleMaker CD-ROM for Chapter 2 to create a crossword puzzle. L1

Assign Chapter 2 Vocabulary and Guided Reading Activity.

Assign Reading Essentials and Study Guide 2-1.

Reading Check Answer

Prehistory ended about five thousand years ago. The invention of writing and the rise of cities helped bring about the rise of **civilization.**

GEOGRAPHY ACTIVITIES

- Chapter 2 Geography and Map Activity
- Outline Map Resource Book

INTERDISCIPLINARY CONNECTIONS

- World Music: A Cultural Legacy
- Unit 1 World Literature Reading 1

ENRICHMENT AND EXTENSION

- World History Primary Source Document Library CD-ROM
- Chapter 2 Enrichment Activity
- Foods Around the World

ASSESSMENT AND EVALUATION

- Chapter 2 Performance Assessment Activity
- Chapter 2 Section Quizzes 2-1, 2-2
- Chapter 2 Test
- Unit 1 Standardized Test Practice
- Chapter 2 ExamView® Pro Testmaker CD-ROM
- Chapter 2 Digests Audiocassettes Activities and Tests

SPANISH RESOURCES

- Chapter 2 Spanish Chapter Summary and Glossary
- Chapter 2 Spanish Digests Audiocassettes Activities and Tests

TEACH

Guided Practice

L1 **Daily Life** Ask students to write a short essay explaining how tools, language, clothing, and the discovery of fire helped early people advance. Have students share their essays with the class. Then ask students to rank the innovations in the order of importance. Have students draw conclusions about the importance of tools, language, clothing, and the discovery of fire in the advancement of early people. ELL

Reading Check Answer Early people were able to **migrate** out of Africa by making their way around the northern deserts and across land bridges.

Reading Check Answer People shared their food with each other and took care of those who were sick or injured.

CAPTION ANSWER

to keep warm and dry, to protect themselves from animals, to clear out brush and undergrowth, and to cook food

Reading Check How did early people **migrate** out of Africa?

People were able to **migrate**, or make their way, around the desert of northern Africa and across the land bridges. Between about 1.75 million and 700,000 years ago, people made their way into Europe and Asia. Much later, between about 40,000 and 15,000 years ago, they also migrated to the Americas.

Scientists call the first age in which people lived the Paleolithic (pā lē uh lith' ik) Age, or Old Stone Age. It lasted from about 2.3 million years ago until 10,000 years ago. During this period, people obtained their food by hunting and gathering.

Reading Check How did living in **bands** help people survive?

Obtaining Food

Paleolithic people lived in small **bands**, or groups, of about 30 members. When the food supply was good, the bands grew to about 40 or 50 members. Most of the group members lived to be no more than 20 or 25 years old. More than half of the children died from illnesses or were killed by animals before their first birthdays.

The people within a group lived and worked together and shared their food. They fed and cared for people who became injured or sick.

GROUP LIFE Experts believe that most early people lived in groups made up of several families. Here, a group of hunters use stones to sharpen tools. Two men carry a large animal killed in a hunt, as a few women tend fires near their tents. **How did Paleolithic people use fire?**

COOPERATIVE LEARNING

Organize the class into small groups to prepare a bulletin-board display showing the history of crops such as wheat, barley, corn, rice, potatoes, yams, and cotton. Each group's contribution should graphically portray the crop, when and where it originated, and where it is grown now. Below the graphics, students should include information about the cultivation of the crop then and now, and the economic importance of the crop then and now. Each group member should have a specific task. Have each group discuss its contribution before posting it on the bulletin board.

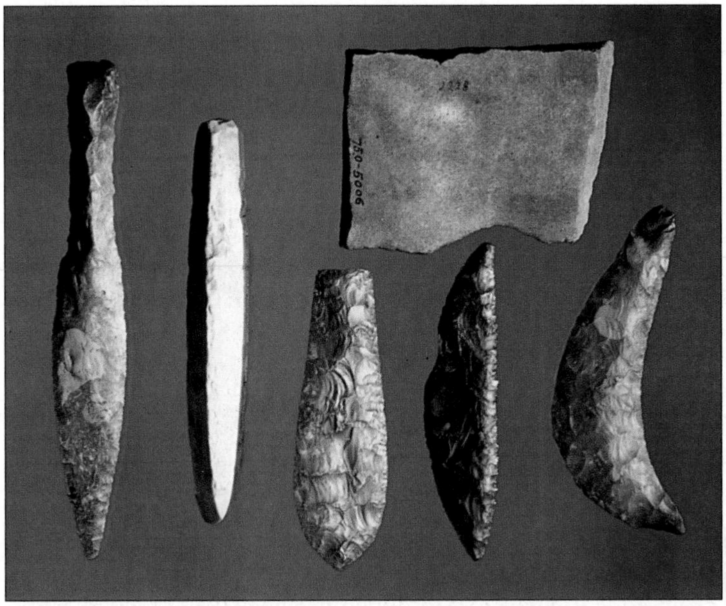

EARLY TOOLS For more than 2 million years, prehistoric people lived by hunting animals and gathering plants. They used tools made of wood and stone. The wooden tools have decayed. Archaeologists, however, have found many stone tools. **For what purposes did prehistoric people use stone tools?**

Each band searched for food within an area known as its **home territory.** This usually covered about two square miles, or five square kilometers, for every band member. There were campsites at various places throughout the home territory. The band stayed at a campsite until the available food supply was used up and then moved.

Women and children gathered berries, nuts, fruit, and eggs out of bird and turtle nests. They poked sticks into bee nests to get honey and into the ground to dig roots.

Men of the group obtained meat. They caught fish using their bare hands and hunted small animals with sticks and stones. Occasionally, they were able to kill a large animal that was too young, too old, or too badly hurt to run away. A good kill meant that the group would have enough meat to last for several days.

Reading Check What were some of the features of a band's **home territory**?

Then & Now

Oldest Tools In 1995, archaeologists working in Ethiopia found stone spear points more than 2.6 million years old, making them the earliest tools found on Earth.

Making Tools

Life for hunters and gatherers became easier when they learned to make tools. At first the only tools people had were sticks and stones they found on the ground. Soon they learned to shape stones to make them more useful.

CAPTION ANSWER

to cut the meat off animals' bones, split animal bones, and chop up plants

GEOGRAPHY AND HISTORY

People in Europe, Africa, and western Asia usually made their tools out of flint, a stone found on the surface of Earth. In eastern Asia, where there was not much flint, people made their tools out of quartz.

Reading Check Answer

A band's **home territory** usually covered about two square miles (five square kilometers) and included campsites at various places.

EXTENDING THE CONTENT

Some scientists are predicting global warming, an increase in global average temperatures. Unlike the natural forming and melting of glaciers in prehistory, human activities are responsible for much global warming. Trapping of heat by gases in the atmosphere, such as carbon dioxide, results in a greenhouse effect. Burning fossil fuels is one human activity that releases carbon dioxide in the air.

L1 **Language Arts** Have students write a simple step-by-step set of directions for starting a fire as it was done in Paleolithic times, as if they were writing it to be used by someone who lived at that time. Have them share their directions, asking other students to judge if they were accurate. **ELL**

L2 **Critical Thinking** Have each student decide which advance they think was more important in the development of civilization: toolmaking or language. Have them discuss their positions.

People in History

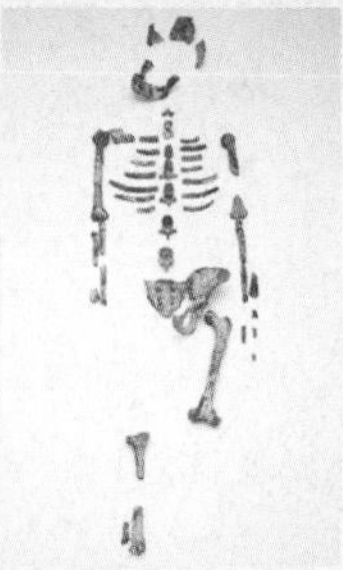

Lucy
c. 3,200,000 B.C.

Hominid Skeleton

Lucy made headlines in 1974 when two scientists—Donald C. Johanson and Tom Gray—discovered her skeleton in the deserts of Ethiopia. They named her after a popular Beatles song, "Lucy in the Sky with Diamonds." Although Lucy walked the earth 3.2 million years ago, her skeleton was nearly complete. She gave the world its first look at an early prehuman.

Among the earliest shaped stones are the *Olduvan pebble tools,* named after the Olduvai Gorge in eastern Africa where they were first discovered. Pebble tools were made from pebbles or stones about the size of a fist. The toolmaker hit one pebble with another, removing chips and creating a jagged cutting edge. This edge was sharp enough to cut the meat off of small animals' bones, split animal bones, and chop up plants.

Later people learned to knock long, sharp-edged chips, called flakes, from stones and use them as tools. Using flakes for knives, they could butcher, or cut up, animals as big as elephants quickly and efficiently. People also used flakes to scrape one end of a wooden branch into a sharp point for a digging stick or a meat skewer.

Making Fire

People also learned to make fire during the Paleolithic Age. The first fires they knew about were made by nature, such as those started by lightning. Eventually, people discovered how to make fire themselves. They created sparks by rubbing two sticks or stones together, or rapidly turning a stick in a hole in a dry log.

People used fire to keep themselves warm and dry. They also used it as a weapon, throwing burning sticks of wood at animals to drive them away. Sometimes they used fire to drive big animals into mudholes. The heavy animals would sink in the mud and people could then kill them.

People also used fire to clear out brush and undergrowth. Finally, people used fire to cook food. Cooked food was much easier to chew and digest than raw food. As a result, people spent less time eating and more time doing other things.

Seeking Shelter

Early people usually camped out in the open. They protected themselves from the wind by digging pits in the ground or by crouching in dry river beds. They also took shelter under an overhanging rock or piled up brush.

At first, early people used caves only for such emergencies as escaping from a sudden storm or a large animal. By about 100,000 years ago, however, people in China, western Europe, and southwestern Asia were living in caves most of the time.

Making Clothing

After hunters began killing large animals, they found that the animal skins could be used for protection and warmth. They scraped the skins clean and then laid them out in the sun to dry. Later, people discovered that pounding fat into the skin while it was drying would make it softer.

At first people wrapped the skins around themselves. Later, they learned how to fasten the skins together. Clothing made a big difference in where people lived. Before they had clothing, most people stayed in areas that were warm and dry. Once they

EXTENDING THE CONTENT

A ravine 295 feet (or 90 m) deep in northern Tanzania, known as Olduvai Gorge, is part of the Great Rift Valley, a series of valleys that extends all the way north to Syria. The sides of the ravine resemble a layer cake of different strata laid bare by the cutting action of ancient rivers. A prehistoric lake had swamped old bones with sediment and later disappeared. Through millennia, nearby volcanoes spewed ash over Olduvai, creating the distinct strata. In 1959, the Leakeys made major discoveries in the deepest and oldest layers at Olduvai.

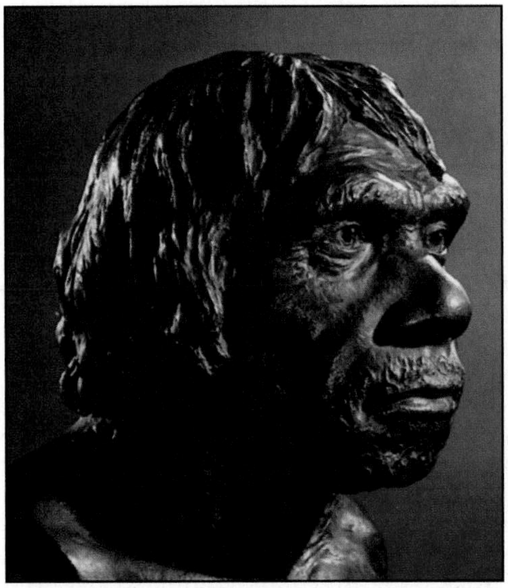 

PREHISTORIC PEOPLE There were two types of early *Homo sapiens,* Neanderthals and Cro-Magnons. From the remains of these two peoples, scientists have tried to reconstruct how they might have looked. These models show the facial features of the Neanderthal (left) and a Cro-Magnon (right). **In what areas of the world did the first people most likely live?**

had clothing to protect them from the weather, they were able to move into areas that were cooler and wetter.

Developing Language

In addition to learning to make tools, fire, and clothing, early people developed language. Before they learned to talk, early people simply made sounds or pointed to objects to express meaning. Hand signals were probably used for common things such as water, food, animals, and weapons. Gradually, because of new social needs, sounds and hand signals were no longer enough. The development of language was a great human achievement. It made it possible for people to work together, share ideas, and pass on their beliefs and stories. The younger generations could learn more easily from older generations, and greater progress was made in all areas of civilization.

The Neanderthals

The first people on Earth are known as *Homo habilis* (hō mō huh bil′ uhs), or "skillful man." Next came *Homo erectus* (hō′ mō ē rekt′ uhs), or "man who walks upright." Then, between about 300,000 and 200,000 years ago, came *Homo sapiens* (hō′ mō sāp′ ē uhnz), or "man who thinks."

Then... & Now

Languages There may be 2,000 to 10,000 languages in the world today. Dialects, or variations within a language, range from about 20,000 to more than 50,000. The largest native language in the world is Chinese, but among the many dialects are Mandarin, Cantonese, Wu, Min, Xiang, Kan, and Hakka.

CAPTION ANSWER

throughout Europe and in parts of Asia and Africa

LINKING PAST TO PRESENT

In 1992, a skull fragment that had been sitting in a tray at the National Museum of Kenya for 25 years was given a closer look. New dating methods reveal the fragment to be 2.4 million years old, which makes it the earliest known remains of the genus *Homo* by 500,000 years.

MULTICULTURAL PERSPECTIVES

Hadar in Ethiopia is part of the Great Rift Valley. At Hadar, sediments along shores of ancient lakes are reappearing because of earth movements and erosion. In the 1970s, Dr. Donald Johanson and a French geologist, Maurice Taieb, mounted an expedition into the area. The now world-famous fossilized skeleton "Lucy" was found in 1974. Later, other spectacular hominid finds at Hadar were made at just one site. The remains of at least 13 individuals were found jumbled together. Johanson dubbed this collection of more than 200 bones the "First Family."

L2 **Culture** Help students create a chart about what Neanderthals and Cro-Magnons were like. Divide the board into two columns, one labeled "Neanderthals" the other labeled "Cro-Magnons." Have students complete the chart with the following information: where each lived, how each got their food, kinds of tools each used, and other interesting facts. ELL

DID YOU KNOW ??

Neanderthal faces were somewhat oddly shaped, with a low, forward-sloping forehead and projecting nose and jaws. This shape of face, called a muzzle shape, and the compact body was a useful adaptation to keeping warm in the cold climate of Germany. Richard Leakey points out that people began to look "modern" in Africa at an earlier time, perhaps because they had no need to adapt to cold.

Linking Across Time

Answers will vary, but students should understand that traditional cultures have kept alive customs and practices passed down through the generations.

There are two kinds of *Homo sapiens*. The first is the Neanderthal (nē an′ der tahl), named after the Neander River in Germany, where their remains were first discovered in 1856. Since then, other Neanderthal remains have been found throughout Europe and in parts of Asia and Africa. Scientists estimate that about 1 million Neanderthals were living at any one time.

Neanderthal people were good hunters. They used traps to catch birds and small animals. They used *pitfalls* to catch large animals like the rhinoceros and the elephant. A pitfall was a large hole that was covered with branches, leaves, and earth. As an animal ran across this hole, it crashed through the covering and fell into the pit. The hunters would then kill the animal with spears.

Neanderthals were also builders. In northern areas, for example, they made houses by covering a framework of mammoth bones with animal skins. More bones piled on the bottoms of the skins prevented them from being blown away. As many as 30 people lived in such a house during the cold months of the year. They improved cave dwellings by digging drainage ditches in caves and designing rock protection for entrances.

According to experts, Neanderthals were also the first people to bury their dead. Archaeologists have found graves of people from this time in which they discovered the remains of flowers, tools, and food.

Linking Across Time

The Aborigines Archaeologists have found spearheads and cave paintings showing that hunters traveled to Australia more than 40,000 years ago. Their descendants call themselves the Aborigines (ab uh rij′ uh nēz) and live much as their ancestors did (far right). **Why does the study of traditional cultures provide valuable information about the past?**

MULTICULTURAL PERSPECTIVES

Most people still imagine Neanderthal people as looking like the stereotype—stooping and gorilla-like. Actually, according to anthropologist Richard Leakey, the people of Neanderthal times could probably (with the right clothes) pass unnoticed in a modern crowd. They were fairly short, stocky, muscular, with powerful shoulders and arms, but were taller than earlier *Homo erectus* and *Homo habilis*, and walked about as upright as we do.

PREHISTORIC HORSE This prehistoric painting of a horse was found on the wall of a cave in Lascaux, France. Early art such as this always showed the animal's profile. **What can scientists learn about Cro-Magnon people from looking at their art?**

The Cro-Magnons

The second kind of *Homo sapiens* is the Cro-Magnon (krō mag′ nahn), named after a rock shelter in France where their remains were first discovered in 1868. Cro-Magnons appeared in North Africa, Asia, and Europe about 100,000 years ago. Archaeologists consider them the first modern human beings.

Cro-Magnons were very skillful toolmakers. They invented the *burin,* which resembles a chisel. By using the burin, people could make other tools and objects from antler, bone, ivory, and shell, as well as stone and wood.

Using new tools made Cro-Magnons better hunters, thus increasing their food supply. Points of antler or bone fastened to the end of wooden sticks could penetrate the hides of larger animals. People fashioned antler and bone into *spear throwers,* or devices that made spears fly through the air faster and farther. This allowed hunters to stay a greater distance from animals, making hunting less dangerous.

Fun Facts . . .

First Razors Cro-Magnons may have invented the first razors. Some Cro-Magnon cave paintings portray beardless men, and Cro-Magnon graves contain sharpened shells—the first razors. Later peoples hammered razors out of bronze or iron.

LINKING PAST TO PRESENT

Ask students to name groups of people in recent history, or contemporary life, who have used bone, antler, and ivory to fashion needles, fishing hooks, combs, tools, and other items.

CAPTION ANSWER

about their ceremonies, traditions, and history

SPOTLIGHT ON: CRO-MAGNONS

Archaeologists have unearthed evidence that prehistoric men were shaving as early as 18,000 B.C. Some Cro-Magnon cave paintings portray beardless men, and early Cro-Magnon gravesites contain sharpened shells that were the first razors. Later, people hammered razors out of bronze, and eventually, out of iron. Mirrors were first water ponds, and then highly polished metal.

DID YOU KNOW ??

The evidence for Cro-Magnon leaders consists of high-status burials. Archaeologists have discovered certain Cro-Magnons buried with ivory daggers, amber beads, and other signs of high rank.

LINKING PAST TO PRESENT

A hunter-gatherer society today lives on in Africa. The Khoisan people, who live in the Kalahari Desert region of Botswana and Namibia, hunt animals and gather wild plants, much as early peoples did.

Use the **Interactive Tutor Self-Assessment CD-ROM** to review Section 1.

Fun Facts . . .

The Flute The first musical instrument invented by early humans was the flute. Carved bone flutes date back more than 30,000 years.

Another important tool that Cro-Magnons invented was the axe, which they used to cut down trees and hollow out the logs to make canoes. In southeastern Asia, they cut down stalks of bamboo and tied them together with vines to make rafts. Winds or ocean currents then carried the rafts to other lands. It is likely that this is how people reached Australia about 40,000 years ago.

Cro-Magnons also fashioned bone, ivory, and shell into body ornaments, such as necklaces and rings. They decorated their clothing with bone or ivory beads. They played music on flutes carved from long, hollow bones.

Cro-Magnons were artists as well as toolmakers. They carved statues out of ivory and bone or molded them out of clay. They covered the walls of some caves in western Europe, Africa, and South America with pictures painted brightly with paints made from minerals. The pictures show mostly animals, such as horses, bulls, and deer, but also show outlines and patterns of lines, dots, and curves.

Many anthropologists think cave paintings may have had religious significance. Cro-Magnons believed that animals had spirits. They thought that painting an animal's picture gave people power over its spirit and would help them find and kill the animal. Anthropologists think the cave paintings may have been a kind of textbook about Cro-Magnon ceremonies, traditions, or history.

Cro-Magnon bands cooperated, often hunting large animals together. This required them to jointly agree on rules and the first true leaders. Every year or so, they held social gatherings where they exchanged information about the movement of animal herds. They also traded materials such as amber and shells.

Section 1 Assessment

1. **Define:** prehistory, civilization, migrate, bands, home territory.
2. Why did early people begin to move out of Africa and into other parts of the world about 1 million years ago?
3. How did tools change in the Paleolithic Age?

Critical Thinking

4. **Analyzing Information** What do you think was the most important advancement made by early people? Explain.

Graphic Organizer Activity

5. Draw a diagram like this one, and use it to compare ways of life followed by the Neanderthals and Cro-Magnons. Be sure to include the accomplishments of each.

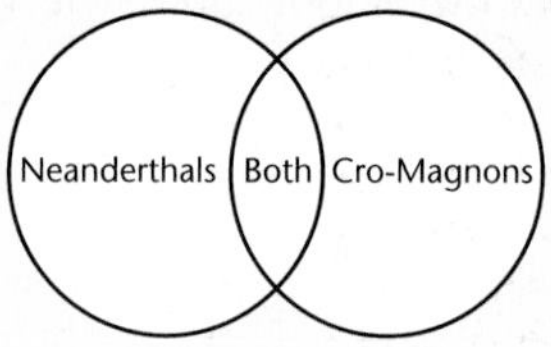

Section 1 Assessment Answers

1. prehistory, began when people appeared and ended when writing developed (p. 33); civilization, advanced society (p. 33); migrate, move (p. 34); bands, groups of about 30 members (p. 34); home territory, area where bands gathered food (p. 35)
2. Climate became colder, ice sheets grew, and land bridges were created.
3. from sticks and stones to shaped tools
4. Answers will vary, but students should provide reasons for their choices.
5. Student answers should reflect the unique contributions of both the Neanderthals and Cro-Magnons, as well as shared traits such as a hunting way of life, practice of religion, social cooperation, and so on.

Assign the Chapter 2 **Section 1 Quiz** in the TCR. Testmaker available.

DOMESTICATING ANIMALS Early people painted scenes of their hunting and food-producing activities. Here, a cave painting from North Africa shows cattle being herded. Some cattle are tied to a rope, while women and children do chores. **What was the importance of learning to herd animals?**

Then . . . & Now

Early Art Paleolithic artists used three basic colors: black, red, and yellow. The pigments came from natural sources such as charcoal, clay, and minerals such as iron. They used these materials so skillfully that when Pablo Picasso, one of the masters of modern art, saw cave paintings in France, he reportedly exclaimed: "We have invented nothing!"

SECTION 2 The Neolithic Age

In the Neolithic (nē uh lith' ik), or New Stone Age, about 8000 B.C., people changed from food gatherers to food producers. Over several thousand years they began to obtain most of their food from farming. This brought about such great changes in the way they lived that experts call the beginning of farming the Neolithic Revolution.

HISTORY Online

Student Web Activity
Visit the *Human Heritage* Web site at humanheritage.glencoe.com and click on ***Chapter 2—Student Web Activities*** to find out more about the Neolithic Age.

Farmers and Herders

Two important discoveries brought on the Neolithic Revolution. One was learning to grow food. The other was learning to herd animals.

Experts believe that people discovered that seed from wild grains, such as wheat and barley, could be planted and harvested. This probably came about when they noticed that new shoots had grown from spilled grain. Scientists believe agriculture developed independently in different parts of the world. In southwestern Asia, early people grew wheat and barley, and in

CAPTION ANSWER

It helped people change from food gatherers to food producers.

DID YOU KNOW ??

The expanded food supply increased the average life expectancy to 30 years.

Use the **Vocabulary PuzzleMaker CD-ROM** to create crossword and word search puzzles.

HISTORY Online

Student Web Activity objectives and answers can be found at the ***Chapter 2 Web Activity Lesson Plan*** at humanheritage.glencoe.com

MAKING CONNECTIONS

➤➤ **History** It is believed that women remained the farmers until Neolithic people learned to hitch an animal to a plow and the animal became the beast of burden on the farm. Then, men took over the farming.

MEETING SPECIAL NEEDS

For students who need additional reinforcement, play a "What's My Meaning?" word game. Organize the class into teams. Have each team survey the chapter and list 15 terms to be defined by another team. (These can include key terms as well as terms like *Paleolithic* and *Homo habilis.*) The first team gives a term for the second team to define or explain. The moderator assigns points—from one to five—for the answer given. The team with the most points is declared the winner.

Refer to ***Inclusion for the Middle School Social Studies Classroom: Strategies and Activities*** for additional resources.

Reading Check Answer **Domesticated** animals turned some hunters into herders.

Reading Check Answer The increase in the food supply—through farming and herding—caused the world's **population** to grow.

CAPTION ANSWER

for carrying and storing food, and for cooking

DID YOU KNOW ??

Dogs were domesticated and used to help hunt small game. Cattle, pigs, goats, and sheep were domesticated and used for meat. Chickens provided Neolithic people with eggs and meat.

Economics at a Glance

The Traditional Economy

Economic decisions are based on three questions: What should be produced? How should it be produced? and For whom should it be produced? In a *traditional economy,* these questions are answered based on customs or habits. People are generally not free to make decisions about what they want or would like to have. Their roles are defined by customs passed down from their ancestors. Have students identify the advantages and disadvantages of a *traditional economy.* *(Advantages may include: there is little uncertainty over what one will do for a living; life is generally the same since it is based on customs or habits. Disadvantages may include: new ideas or ways of doing things are not encouraged; people are expected to stay in certain roles.)*

eastern Asia, they grew millet, rice, and soy beans. In Mexico, they grew corn, squash, and potatoes, and they grew peanuts and a grain called sorghum in Africa.

People probably learned they could herd animals when a hunting band built fences to enclose a herd of wild animals they had chased into a ravine. The hunters killed one animal at a time, saving the rest for later. Soon captured animals began to lose their fear of people and became **domesticated,** or tamed, and the hunters became herders. In time, Neolithic people were breeding animals to improve the animals' qualities. People also began using certain animals such as donkeys, camels, and llamas as pack animals.

Reading Check How did **domesticated** animals change the way some hunters lived?

The Neolithic Revolution greatly increased people's food supplies. With more food available, the **population,** or number of people, began to grow. Experts think there were about 5 million people in the world in 8000 B.C. Within 4,000 years the population grew to about 90 million. People were also living longer.

Reading Check What caused the world's **population** to grow?

Early Villages Once people began to produce food, they were able to settle in one place. They built permanent shelters and formed villages of about 150 to 200 people in areas with a good soil and water supply.

POTTERY MAKING Neolithic people learned the art of baking clay pottery. Baked clay, unlike sun-dried clay, will not disintegrate in water. In this picture, men are covering the oven so that the pots inside will bake. **How did Neolithic people use pottery?**

EXTENDING THE CONTENT

Farming in the Neolithic period began at different times in different parts of the world—and the influence of crops and animals that were raised in those first centuries still can be seen in the traditional diet and cuisine in various parts of the world. In the Fertile Crescent, Mesopotamians began farming about 8,000 B.C. As in every early farming culture, the basic crop was a cereal grain. In the Middle East, the original crops were wheat, barley, and other cereal grains, along with garden crops such as peas, beans, squash, and yams.

CHAPTER 2 Assessment

Using Key Terms

Write a short description of a day in the life of a person who lived during the Paleolithic or Neolithic ages. Use the following words in your description.

prehistory	civilization	migrate
bands	home territory	domesticated
population	specialization	

Understanding Main Ideas

1. What is the main difference between the Paleolithic and Neolithic ages?
2. Why did Paleolithic people move from place to place?
3. How did early men and women share the work of getting food?
4. How did the discovery of fire affect people's lives?
5. What difference did clothing make in the way people lived?
6. Why did the Cro-Magnons produce cave paintings?
7. How did increased food supplies cause increased population?
8. Why did people in the Neolithic Age begin to take up different occupations?
9. How did people in the Neolithic Age change their form of government?

Critical Thinking

1. Do you think the development of farming should be called a revolution? Explain.
2. What would you have liked about living in Catal Hüyük? What would you have disliked?
3. How would you have organized work activities if you had been a village chief?

Graphic Organizer Activity

Economics Draw a diagram like this one, and use it to show the steps leading up to the rise of villages in the Neolithic Age. (Add steps as necessary.)

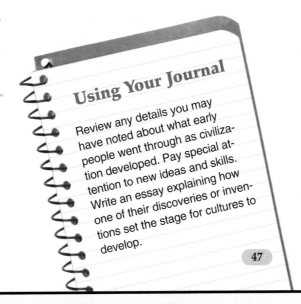

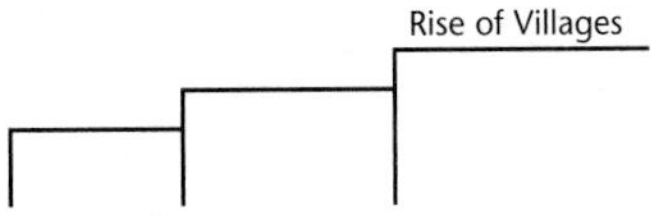

Geography in History

Environment and Society When early people began to build shelters, they used some geographic features to decide where they would build their homes. What features affected their choice of building sites? How might geography affect their choice of building materials?

Using Your Journal

Review any details you may have noted about what early people went through as civilization developed. Pay special attention to new ideas and skills. Write an essay explaining how one of their discoveries or inventions set the stage for cultures to develop.

CHAPTER 2 Assessment Answers

Using Key Terms

Descriptions will vary but should include all the key terms.

Understanding Main Ideas

1. the way people got food
2. to search for food
3. Women gathered berries, nuts, eggs, roots; men hunted.
4. It enabled early people to cook food, keep warm, frighten animals, and refine weapons.
5. It protected early people from the weather, enabling them to move to cooler and wetter regions.
6. They thought that creating an animal in paint gave them a kind of magic power over its spirit.
7. More food was available to support larger numbers of people, and people lived longer.
8. When fewer people were needed to produce food, they began to take up jobs that had nothing to do with food production.
9. They chose a chief to settle disputes and direct village activities.

Critical Thinking

1. Answers will vary but should indicate that farming was a momentous development.
2. Answers will vary but should include specific examples.
3. Answers will vary but should reflect Neolithic work and tools.

Graphic Organizer Activity

Steps might include: rise of farming and domestication of animals, increased population, construction of permanent shelters, specialization, and so on.

Bonus Test Question

For Chapter 2 Test

Imagine you are a Neolithic person who has just survived an avalanche. How might this natural disaster make life harder? How might it make life easier? *(Answers will vary.)*

Using Your Journal

Essays will vary but should include specifics about one development. You might call on volunteers to read their essays to the class.

Geography in History

Answers may vary but should include consideration of mountains, rivers and streams, valleys, and swamps.

UNIT 1 Around the World

FOCUS

Objectives

After reading the Around the World for Unit 1, your students will be able to:

1. locate parts of Africa where prehistoric art is found.
2. identify types of animals herded by prehistoric peoples in Africa.
3. appreciate prehistoric art as a form of historic evidence.

Bellringer

Ask students to describe the Sahara. *(Most students will focus on its qualities as a desert, using adjectives such as hot, dry, sandy, and so on.)*

Motivational Activity

Refer students to the Around the World feature, pointing out that the Sahara was once a vast, wet grassland. Ask: Which of the animals in the pictures on pages 48–49 probably would not survive in the Sahara today? *(crocodile, giraffe, cattle)*

TEACH

Geography: The World in Spatial Terms Refer students to the map on page 48. Tell them that prehistoric art has been found on every continent except Antarctica. Africa has some of the world's oldest art, including paintings that may reach back more than 40,000 years. Ask: In what parts of Africa are most prehistoric paintings found? *(southern and southeastern Africa)* Where are most engravings found? *(northern Africa, particularly the Sahara, Morocco, and Egypt's Nile Valley)*

UNIT 1 Around

PREHISTORIC PEOPLES OF THE SAHARA

During the prehistoric era, the Sahara—the world's largest desert—looked nothing like it does today. Vast grasslands stretched across a broad open plain. Rivers and shallow lakes shimmered in the sun. The land was wet and green enough to support bands of hunters and some of the earth's earliest communities of herders.

Between 10,000 and 4,000 years ago, the area's climate changed. The rains stopped falling and the temperatures rose. The grasslands, rivers, and lakes disappeared. So did the prehistoric peoples who once lived there. However, they left behind a rich legacy of rock art that has kept their stories alive.

Prehistoric Art in Africa

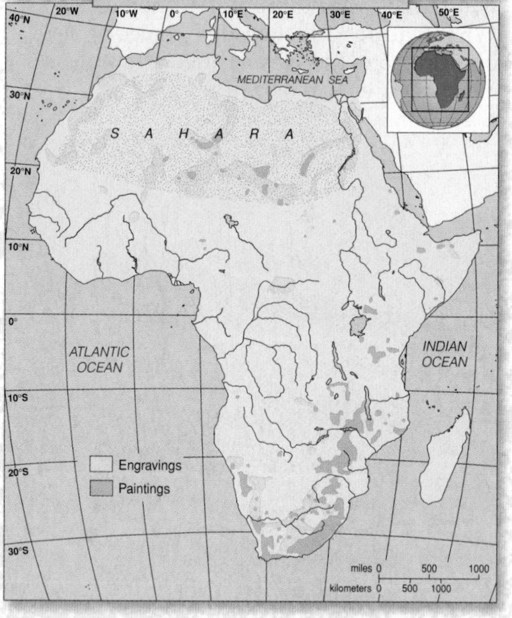

▲ Africa has more prehistoric rock art sites than any other continent.

▲ In the dry desert of modern Libya, a life-size crocodile stretches across a rock. The engraving, carved about 9,000 years ago, captures a time when these giant reptiles soaked up the sun on the banks of ancient rivers.

SPOTLIGHT ON: THE SAHARA

During the Ice Age, temperatures had been too cold for evaporation, and rainfall declined around the world. At this time, the Sahara was a vast, uninhabitable desert, much like today. When the Ice Age ended, however, clouds heavy with rain blew in from the Atlantic Ocean. As the clouds dropped their water, the desert shrank to a narrow strip and new rivers and lakes appeared. Lake Chad, which did not exist in 12,000 B.C., swelled to nearly 400,000 acres—an area nearly ten times its present-day size.

Evidence of the well-watered Sahara was discovered by astronauts in the late 20th century. Staring down at the earth from space shuttles, they saw the remains of ancient river beds beneath the shifting sands of the desert—glimpsing what the land may have looked like more than 4,000 years ago.

the World

▲ The camel arrived on the Sahara from Asia about 2,200 years ago. By then the grasslands of the past had nearly vanished. Today the Sahara is a vast sea of sand and rock, covering more than 3.5 million square miles.

◄ Starting about 7,500 ▲ years ago, herding and farming emerged on the grassy northern plains of Africa. Paintings and carvings show the kinds of cattle raised by prehistoric peoples in this region.

Carved more than 7,000 years ago, this pair of giraffes grazed on the tall grasses that once covered the Sahara. Prehistoric people may have tried to domesticate, or tame, these animals. ▼

Taking Another Look

1. In what parts of Africa is ancient rock art found?
2. What types of animals did prehistoric peoples of the region herd?

Hands-On Activity

Creating Art Design a postage stamp that one of the modern nations in the Sahara might create to celebrate its rock art.

ANSWERS TO TAKING ANOTHER LOOK

1. Answers should reflect information on the map on page 48. You might point out that much of the art has been found in the cliffs and caves of Africa's most mountainous regions. Encourage students to suggest reasons for this. *(Sample response: Prehistoric peoples found shelter and protection in these areas.)*

2. different kinds of cattle, camels

Hands-On Activity
Postage stamps should reflect information about prehistoric peoples in the feature and in Chapter 2.

LINKING PAST TO PRESENT

The prehistoric rock art of the Sahara has stood the test of time. Working with stone chisels, artists chipped grooves so deep that even the scouring winds and sands of the Sahara have not worn them away. In some places, grooves still sink more than two inches into the stone faces where they were carved.

The biggest threat facing the prehistoric art is not the environment, but humans. Tourists wet the paintings to make colors more brilliant for photos. People retouch the art, thinking they will keep its magic alive. Worst of all, thieves chisel out engravings or paintings to sell them.

Discuss with students why many historians and archaeologists fear the loss of this art. *(The art is a link with vanished cultures.)*

ASSESS

Check for Understanding

Have students answer the questions in **Taking Another Look** on page 49.

Enrich

Encourage students to create an illustrated version of the map on page 48. To find examples of rock art in each of the regions on the map, have students visit the Web site for the Trust for African Rock Art (TARA). Photographs by TARA's founder David Coulson can be found at: www.tara.org.uk

CLOSE

Ask students to speculate on why prehistoric peoples may have created rock art. *(for religious purposes, for decoration, to record important events, and so on)*

Answers and Analyses

1C Culture/Environment

On page 11, volcanoes and earthquakes are attributed to plate movement, and not to human habitation. Therefore, choices A and B can be eliminated. From the discussion of glaciers on pages 12–13, it is unreasonable to assume that humans could cause glaciers to advance. The way that people build their homes might affect wind and water, which are said on page 12 to cause erosion.

2J Economics

The difference between renewable and non-renewable resources is discussed on pages 20–21. There it states that coal and minerals are nonrenewable, so choices F and G can be eliminated. Plastic is not a resource; it is a product that is made from resources. Therefore, choice H can be eliminated.

THE PRINCETON REVIEW **TEST-TAKING TIP**

A great number of standardized test questions are constructed to test essential vocabulary or concepts. Encourage students to learn specialized vocabulary by keeping a list of words with definitions on the side of the board.

3A Culture/Environment

The first paragraph on page 22 states that legends are stories that help to *explain the past*. This information makes A the best choice.

THE PRINCETON REVIEW

Standardized Test Practice

Directions: Choose the *best* answer to each of the following multiple choice questions. If you have trouble answering a question, use the process of elimination to narrow your choices. Write your answers on a separate piece of paper.

1. The ways that people build their homes can cause which of the following surface changes to the earth?

A Earthquakes
B Volcanic eruptions
C Erosion
D Advancement of glaciers

Test-Taking Tip: Always read the question and *all* of the answer choices carefully. Avoid answers that seem extreme. For example, it is very unlikely that the way people build their homes could *cause* the *advancement of glaciers.* Therefore, you can eliminate answer D.

2. Some resources are nonrenewable, while others are renewable. Which of the following is an example of a renewable resource?

F Coal
G Minerals
H Plastic
J Timber

Test-Taking Tip: Think about the meaning of these terms. *Resources,* often referred to as "*natural resources,*" are materials found in nature. Renewable resources can be replaced as they are used. *Nonrenewable resources* CANNOT be replaced. It is a good idea to keep a vocabulary list of new words as you read each new chapter. The **glossary** of your textbook can help you define these unfamiliar words.

3. Many early legends were created as ways to

A explain the creation of Earth
B explain where archaeological remains came from
C compare different societies
D introduce children to a tribe's language

Test-Taking Tip: Think of familiar examples to double-check your understanding of the question. Remember, sometimes more than one answer seems correct. For instance, though the telling of legends certainly helped children learn a tribe's language, that was not the primary reason they were created. Always choose the *best* answer.

4. The discovery of the Rosetta Stone allowed scientists to

F understand the fall of the Roman Empire
G understand the ancient Egyptian language
H understand how Pompeii was destroyed
J translate the ancient Greek language into English

Test-Taking Tip: This question asks you to remember a *fact* about the Rosetta Stone. The Rosetta Stone served as a *language* dictionary. Only two answer choices discuss *languages,* so you can easily eliminate the others.

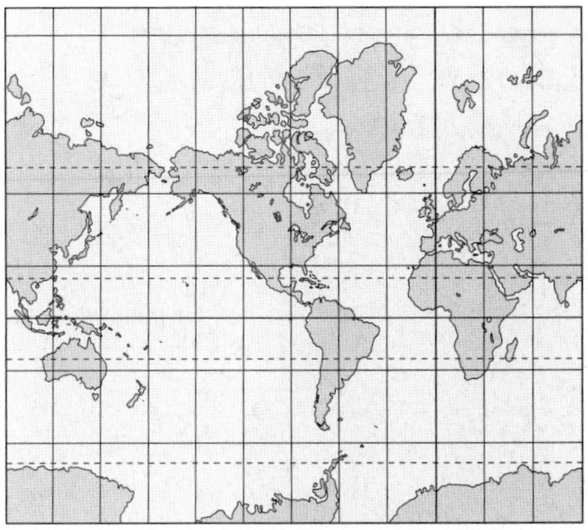

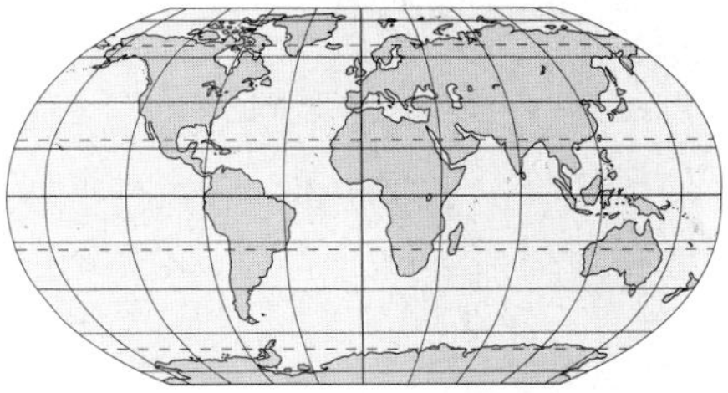

5. Which of the following CANNOT be shown on the map on the top?

A True direction
B Latitude and longitude
C Bodies of water
D The exact size of all continents

> ***Test-Taking Tip:*** The map on the top is called a *Mercator projection.* Remember, a *map projection* is a way of representing a *round* earth on a *flat* piece of paper. What becomes distorted in a Mercator projection?

6. Which of the following is NOT considered an artifact?

F A spearhead from ancient Egypt
G A fossil of an extinct fish from the Paleolithic era
H A clay water pitcher from the Shang dynasty
J A silver bracelet from Pompeii

> ***Test-Taking Tip:*** Another important term to remember is *artifact.* Artifacts are *things made by people.* Be careful when a question uses the words NOT or EXCEPT—overlooking these words is a common error. Look for the answer choice that does NOT fit.

7. During the Paleolithic Age, people lived in groups of 20 to 30 people. Increases in population within these bands were usually caused by

A low average birth weight
B discovery of safe migration routes
C a stable food supply
D frequent natural disasters

> ***Test-Taking Tip:*** Eliminate answers that do not make sense. For example, answers A and D probably would probably cause a *drop* in population rather than an increase.

STOP

51

Tested Objectives

Questions	Reading Objective
1	Perceive relationships and recognize outcomes
2	Analyze information
3, 4	Identify central issues
5	Make comparisons
6, 7	Make inferences and generalizations

Answers and Analyses

4G History

A description of the Rosetta Stone can be found on pages 26–27. There it states that the Rosetta stone gave scholars *the key to the meaning of Egyptian picture-writing.*

THE PRINCETON REVIEW TEST-TAKING TIP

Encourage students to use the process of elimination. They probably recall that the Rosetta Stone has to do with ancient languages, which will allow students to narrow the choices down to G and J, and then they can make a good guess.

5D Geography

According to page 17, a Mercator projection *distorts* the shape and size of continents, especially in the areas farther away from the equator.

6G Culture/Environment

On page 25, an artifact is defined as something *made by people.* Each of these is an example of something made by humans except for G.

7C Culture/Environment

According to page 34, *when the food supply was good, the bands grew to about 40 or 50 members.*

THE PRINCETON REVIEW TEST-TAKING TIP

Remind students to read the question very carefully, because often one or more answer choices will be the exact opposite of the desired reponse. Choices A and D would *decrease,* not increase, the population.

Introducing **UNIT 2**

OVERVIEW

Unit 2 describes the emergence and development of civilization in the river valleys of the Middle East, South Asia, and China.

- **Chapter 3** discusses the rise of civilization in the Tigris-Euphrates valley of Mesopotamia, focusing on Sumer as well as later Mesopotamian empires.
- **Chapter 4** summarizes how civilization developed in the Nile Valley of Egypt and highlights the Old, Middle, and New Kingdoms.
- **Chapter 5** deals with the Harappan civilization of the Indus River valley in India and Pakistan, and the Shang civilization of the Huang Ho River valley in China.

UNIT OBJECTIVES

After reading Unit 2, your students will be able to:

1. give examples of how the environment influenced the ways in which people of the river valleys lived.

2. discuss the early civilizations of Mesopotamia, Egypt, and the eastern river valleys in terms of their similarities and differences.

3. summarize the contributions made by the river valley civilizations to other civilizations.

UNIT PROJECT

Have students create a "You Are There" display to represent what they learn about these early civilizations. After dividing them into groups, have each group choose among the Sumerians, Babylonians, Egyptians, Harappans, and Shang to display. Students can decide what and how to present their material, in written, visual, or interactive formats.

UNIT 2 River Valley Civilizations

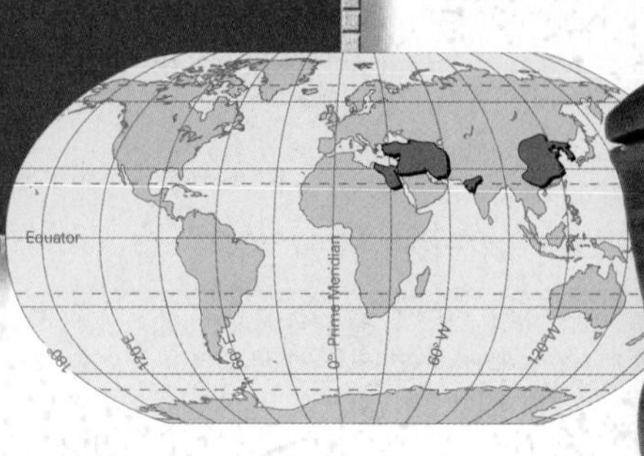

◄ Egyptian wood carving

Blue Nile hippopotamus ▼

5000 B.C. Groups of people begin migrating

3500 B.C. Sumeria established

2600 B.C. Old Kingdom begins in Egypt

2300 B.C. Sargon I establishes world's first empire

ABOUT THE UNIT OPENING

Examining Artifacts

Tell students that plants, animals, and scenes associated with the Nile River played an important role in Egyptian art. Use the carvings of the Egyptian water bearer and the river hippo as examples. Encourage students to speculate on reasons ancient peoples such as the Egyptians built the world's earliest civilizations along the banks of rivers.

Global Chronology

Refer students to the unit time line. Ask students to recall the meaning of B.C. and A.D. *(B.C. means "before Christ" and A.D. stands for* anno Domini *which means "in the year of the Lord.")* Ask students to explain what the time line covers. *(some major events in the early river valley civilizations in the Middle East, South Asia, and China)*

FOLDABLES
Study Organizer

Compare and Contrast Study Foldable *Make this foldable to help you compare and contrast the river valley civilizations that developed in the Middle East, South Asia, and China.*

Step 1 *Fold a sheet of paper in half from side to side.*

Fold it so the left edge is about ½ inch from the right edge.

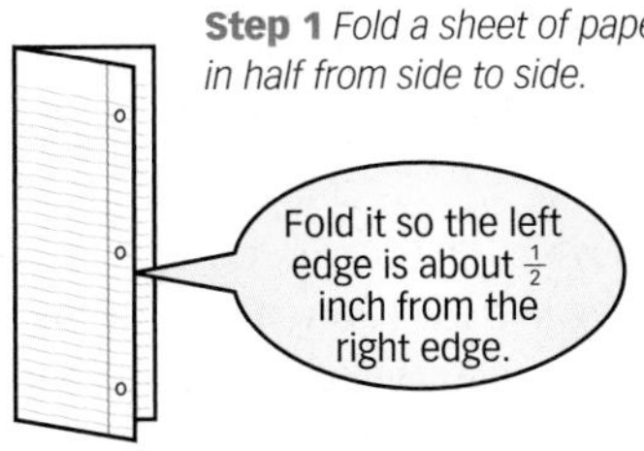

Step 2 *Turn the paper and fold it into thirds.*

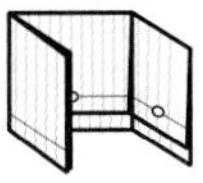

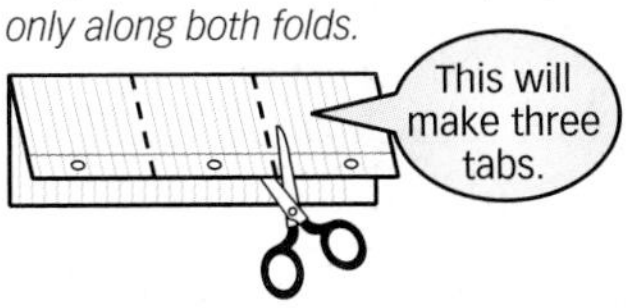

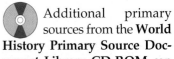

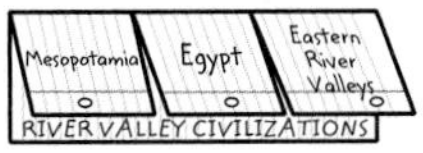

Reading and Writing *As you read the unit, write notes under each appropriate tab of your foldable. Keep in mind that you are trying to compare these civilizations.*

Step 3 *Unfold and cut the top layer only along both folds.*

This will make three tabs.

Step 4 *Label as shown.*

Mesopotamia | Egypt | Eastern River Valleys
RIVER VALLEY CIVILIZATIONS

PRIMARY SOURCES
Library

See pages 676–677 for another primary source reading to accompany Unit 2.

GO TO Read "The Epic of Gilgamesh" from the **World History Primary Source Document Library CD-ROM.**

1800 B.C.
Hammurabi establishes Babylonian Empire

1766 B.C.
Shang Dynasty begins in China

1600 B.C.
New Kingdom begins in Egypt

Journal Notes

What was daily life like more than 5,000 years ago? Note details about it as you read.

 53

Geographic Location

The civilizations discussed in this unit arose along the Tigris-Euphrates, Nile, Indus, and Huang Ho river valleys. Have students locate these rivers on the appropriate maps in their text Atlas. Then have volunteers locate them on a wall map of the world.

ABCNEWS INTERACTIVE™

VIDEOCASSETTE
Turning Points in World History

Have students view **Tape 1 Chapter 3** to learn more about the Sumerians.

GLENCOE TECHNOLOGY

MindJogger Videoquiz
Use **MindJogger Videoquiz** to preview the unit content.

Available in DVD and VHS

FOLDABLES
Study Organizer

Purpose Use this foldable to determine what students understand about the river valley civilizations in the Middle East, South Asia, and China. Students should compare these civilizations which were alike in many ways. To get students started, point out that these civilizations all developed ways of controlling floods and producing a surplus of food.

Have students complete **Reading and Study Skills Foldables** Activity 2.

RECORDING JOURNAL NOTES

Have students write a description of a typical day in their lives. Then have volunteers read their descriptions, and write some details on the board. Explain to students that they could note these kinds of details as they read about early civilizations.

PRIMARY SOURCES
Library

Additional primary sources from the **World History Primary Source Document Library CD-ROM** can be used during the study of Unit 2, including:
• "Hymn to Osiris"

Primary sources about the pursuit of justice can be found on pages 676–677.

Chapter 3 Planning Guide

Timesaving Tools

TeacherWorks™ All-In-One Planner and Resource Center

- **Interactive Teacher Edition** Access your Teacher Wraparound Edition and your classroom resources with a few easy clicks.
- **Interactive Lesson Planner** Planning has never been easier! Organize your week, month, semester, or year with all the lesson helps you need to make teaching creative, timely, and relevant.

Use Glencoe's **Presentation Plus!** multimedia teacher tool to easily present dynamic lessons that visually excite your students. Using Microsoft PowerPoint® you can customize the presentations to create your own personalized lessons.

Objectives	Reproducible Resources	Multimedia Resources
Section 1 The Rise of Sumer Describe how religion, family life, and government influenced Sumerian civilization.	Reproducible Lesson Plan Chapter 3 Vocabulary and Guided Reading Activity Reading Essentials and Study Guide 3-1 Chapter 3 Cooperative Learning Activity Chapter 3 Chart and Graph Skill Activity Chapter 3 Enrichment Activity Unit 2 Primary Source Readings Unit 2 World Literature Reading 1 Section 1 Quiz Unit 2 Hands-On History Lab	Interactive Student Edition CD-ROM Teaching Transparencies and Activities 3A & 3B Graphic Organizer Transparency 6 Vocabulary PuzzleMaker CD-ROM Interactive Tutor Self-Assessment CD-ROM ExamView® Pro Testmaker CD-ROM Glencoe Skillbuilder Interactive Workbook CD-ROM, Level 1 Presentation Plus! CD-ROM
Section 2 Later Mesopotamian Empires Explain why Hammurabi and his reforms were important.	Reproducible Lesson Plan Reading Essentials and Study Guide 3-2 Chapter 3 Geography and Map Activity Section 2 Quiz	Vocabulary PuzzleMaker CD-ROM Interactive Tutor Self-Assessment CD-ROM ExamView® Pro Testmaker CD-ROM Glencoe Skillbuilder Interactive Workbook CD-ROM, Level 1
Section 3 Contributions Describe how the Mesopotamian civilization contributed to other civilizations.	Reproducible Lesson Plan Reading Essentials and Study Guide 3-3 Section 3 Quiz	Vocabulary PuzzleMaker CD-ROM Interactive Tutor Self-Assessment CD-ROM ExamView® Pro Testmaker CD-ROM Glencoe Skillbuilder Interactive Workbook CD-ROM, Level 1
Chapter 3 Review and Evaluation	Chapter 3 Reteaching Activity Chapter 3 Performance Assessment Activity Spanish Chapter Summary and Glossary Chapter 3 Test	Vocabulary PuzzleMaker CD-ROM Interactive Tutor Self-Assessment CD-ROM Glencoe Skillbuilder Interactive Workbook CD-ROM, Level 1 Audiocassettes* ExamView® Pro Testmaker CD-ROM

*Also available in Spanish.

✓ Performance Assessment Activities

Newspaper Articles Remind students that the elements of a newspaper article include *who, what, where, when, why,* and *how.* Have students choose an event from the chapter to write about in newspaper style. When the articles are completed, students can share them with the class.

CHAPTER RESOURCES

LITERATURE ABOUT THE PERIOD

Oppenheim, A. Leo. *Letters from Mesopotamia.* University of Chicago Press, 1967. A translation of business and personal letters found in cuneiform.

READINGS FOR THE STUDENT

Foster, Leila Merrell. *The Sumerians.* Watts, 1990. Discusses the rise and fall of the Sumerian civilization and includes several photographs of Sumerian artifacts.

Wetwood, Jennifer. *Gilgamesh, and Other Babylonian Tales.* Coward, McCann & Geoghegan, 1970. Retells ancient tales of Sumer and Babylon.

READINGS FOR THE TEACHER

Gailey, Harry A. *History of Africa Volume I: Earliest times to 1800.* Krieger, 1980. An overview of this period in African history.

Hawkes, Jacquetta, ed. *Atlas of Ancient Archaeology.* McGraw-Hill, 1974. Traces the patterns of ancient cultures and civilizations around the world.

KEY TO ABILITY LEVELS

Teaching strategies have been coded for varying learning styles and abilities.

L1 Level 1 activities are **basic** activities and should be within the ability range of all students.

L2 Level 2 activities are **average** activities and should be within the ability range of the average to above-average student.

L3 Level 3 activities are **challenging** activities designed for the ability range of above-average students.

ELL ELL activities should be within the ability range of English Language Learning students.

NATIONAL GEOGRAPHIC Teacher's Corner

INDEX TO NATIONAL GEOGRAPHIC MAGAZINE

The following articles relate to this chapter:

- "Journey to the Copper Age," by Katherine Ozment, April 1999.
- "The Power of Writing," by Joel L. Swerdlow, August 1999.
- "Iraq: Crucible of Civilization," by Merle Severy, May 1991.

NATIONAL GEOGRAPHIC SOCIETY PRODUCTS AVAILABLE FROM GLENCOE

To order the following, call Glencoe at 1-800-334-7344:

- *PicturePack: Physical Geography of the World (Transparencies)*
- *PictureShow: Ancient Civilizations: Egypt and the Fertile Crescent (CD-ROM)*
- *PicturePack: Fertile Crescent (Transparencies)*
- *The Fertile Crescent (Poster Set)*
- *PictureShow: Ancient Civilizations Library (CD-ROMs)*
- *PicturePack: Ancient Civilizations Library, Part II (Transparencies)*

ADDITIONAL NATIONAL GEOGRAPHIC SOCIETY PRODUCTS

To order the following, call National Geographic at 1-800-368-2728:

- *National Geographic Atlas of World History (Book)*
- *Wonders of the Ancient World: National Geographic Atlas of Archaeology (Book)*

Access *National Geographic*'s new dynamic MapMachine Web site and other geography resources at:
www.nationalgeographic.com
www.nationalgeographic.com/maps

Introducing **CHAPTER 3**

OVERVIEW

Chapter 3 focuses on the development of civilization in Mesopotamia from around 3500 B.C. to 1800 B.C.

- **Section 1** describes the rise of Sumer and the development of city-states.
- **Section 2** discusses the effects of conquest on the development of Mesopotamia.
- **Section 3** presents the contributions of Mesopotamia.

CHAPTER OBJECTIVES

After reading Chapter 3, your students will be able to:

1. describe how religion, family life, and government influenced Sumerian civilizations.
2. explain why Hammurabi and his reforms were important.
3. name Mesopotamian contributions.

EXAMINING ARTIFACTS

Introduce Chapter 3 by asking students what the helmet suggests about how Sumer rose to power. *(through conquest)* What does it tell them about Sumer's wealth? *(that it possessed riches such as gold)* Explain that the carving is a portrait of a man and woman found at a Sumerian temple. What can students infer about family relationships from this carving? *(that they were close)*

PERFORMANCE ASSESSMENT ✓

Use the Performance Assessment Activities on page 54B to help you evaluate students as they complete the chapter.

CHAPTER 3

Mesopotamia

3500 B.C.–1700 B.C.

▲ Gold Sumerian warrior's helmet

Sumerian man and woman ▼

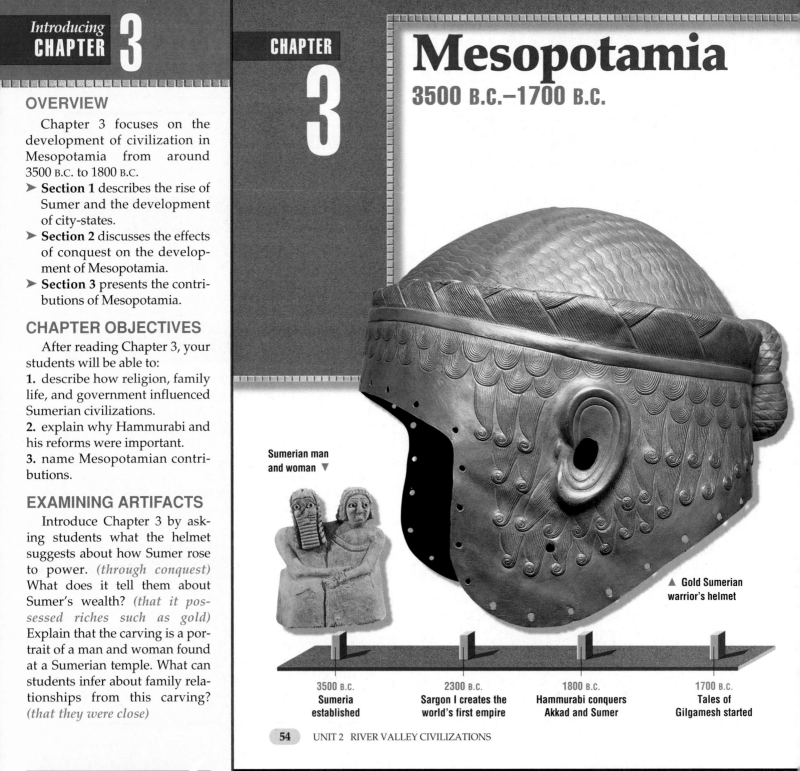

3500 B.C. Sumeria established

2300 B.C. Sargon I creates the world's first empire

1800 B.C. Hammurabi conquers Akkad and Sumer

1700 B.C. Tales of Gilgamesh started

TEACHING RESOURCES

TEACHER PLANNING AND SUPPORT

- Reproducible Lesson Plan 3-1, 3-2, 3-3
- Teaching Strategies for the World History Classroom (Including Block Scheduling Pacing Guides)
- Presentation Plus! CD-ROM

REVIEW AND REINFORCEMENT

- Reading Essentials and Study Guide 3-1, 3-2, 3-3
- Chapter 3 Vocabulary and Guided Reading Activity
- Vocabulary PuzzleMaker CD-ROM
- Teaching Transparencies 3A & 3B
- Chapter 3 Reteaching Activity
- Chapter 3 Cooperative Learning Activity
- Chapter 3 Activity Book Activity
- Chapter 3 Chart and Graph Skill Activity
- Reading and Study Skills Foldables
- Interactive Tutor Self-Assessment CD-ROM
- Unit 2 MindJogger VideoQuiz

APPLICATION AND HANDS-ON ACTIVITIES

- Daily Questions in Social Studies
- Unit 2 Hands-On History Lab Activity
- Student Presentation Builder CD-ROM

Chapter Focus

Read to Discover

- How religion, family life, and government influenced the civilization of Sumer.
- Why Hammurabi and his reforms were important.
- How the developments of Mesopotamia contributed to other civilizations.

HISTORY Online

Chapter Overview

Visit the *Human Heritage* Web site at **humanheritage.glencoe.com** and click on ***Chapter 3—Chapter Overviews*** to preview this chapter.

Terms to Learn

city-state
artisans
ziggurat
cuneiform
scribe
priest-kings
empire
culture
reform
reign

People to Know

Gilgamesh
Sargon I
Hammurabi

Places to Locate

Mesopotamia
Sumer
Ur
Babylon

Why It's Important The earliest known civilizations developed along the Tigris and Euphrates rivers, which begin in the mountains of eastern Turkey. The twin rivers each flow more than 1,000 miles, or 1,600 kilometers, southeast across a great plain in an area known as the Middle East. Then, the waters join and empty into the Persian Gulf. Today, the land between the two rivers is part of the country of Iraq. In ancient times, the area was called Mesopotamia (mes uh puh tay′ me uh), "the land between the rivers."

Around 4000 B.C., groups of people began migrating, or moving, into Mesopotamia. They developed so many new ideas that the area has been called the "cradle of civilization." The influence of Mesopotamia left a lasting impact on the ancient world.

SECTION 1 The Rise of Sumer

The people who settled in southern Mesopotamia about 3500 B.C. were a short, stocky, black-haired people called Sumerians (sū mer′ ē uhnz). Their area of Mesopotamia was known as Sumer (sū′ mŭhr).

HISTORY Online

Chapter Overview introduces students to chapter content and key terms. Have them access ***Chapter 3 Overview*** at **humanheritage.glencoe.com**

FOCUS

Bellringer

Write the following question on the chalkboard: *What is a cradle of civilization?* Have students write their responses.

Motivational Activity

Ask volunteers to share their explanations of a cradle of civilization. Ask: *What features would an area need in order to give birth to and encourage the growth of a civilization?* Suggest that students consider this question as they study the section.

GUIDE TO READING

Reading Strategy

Ask students to read "Why It's Important" and summarize the chapter's main theme. *(The people of Mesopotamia developed many new ideas and left a lasting impact on world civilization.)*

Vocabulary Precheck

Ask students to define each of the "Terms to Learn." Have a volunteer consult the dictionary for any unfamiliar words. L1 ELL

Use the Vocabulary PuzzleMaker CD-ROM for Chapter 3 to create a crossword puzzle. L1

Assign Chapter 3 Vocabulary and Guided Reading Activity.

Assign Reading Essentials and Study Guide 3-1.

GEOGRAPHY ACTIVITIES

- Chapter 3 Geography and Map Activity
- Building Geography Skills for Life
- Outline Map Resource Book

INTERDISCIPLINARY CONNECTIONS

- Unit 2 World Literature Reading 1
- World Art & Architecture Transparency 2, *Standard of Ur: Peace*
- World Music: A Cultural Legacy

ENRICHMENT AND EXTENSION

- Unit 2 Primary Source Readings
- World History Primary Source Document Library CD-ROM
- Chapter 3 Enrichment Activity
- Foods Around the World

ASSESSMENT AND EVALUATION

- Chapter 3 Performance Assessment Activity
- Chapter 3 Section Quizzes 3-1, 3-2, 3-3
- Chapter 3 Test
- Chapter 3 ExamView® Pro Testmaker CD-ROM
- Chapter 3 Digests Audiocassettes Activities and Tests

SPANISH RESOURCES

- Chapter 3 Spanish Chapter Summary and Glossary
- Chapter 3 Spanish Digests Audiocassettes Activities and Tests

TEACH

Guided Practice

L2 **Daily Life** Write the following question on the board: *"How did religion, family life, and government influence Sumerian civilization?"* Ask volunteers to write a script about daily life in Sumer that includes the following members of Sumerian society: a priest, a student, a scribe, and a woman. Explain that the script should answer the question on the board.

Direct the remaining members of the class to act as anthropologists whose job it is to answer the original question by observing the role-play.

HISTORY Online

Student Web Activity objectives and answers can be found at the ***Chapter 3 Web Activity Lesson Plan*** at humanheritage.glencoe.com

Linking Across Time

sample responses: to prevent forgery, as proof of authority, and so on

NATIONAL GEOGRAPHIC

Use these materials to enrich student understanding of Mesopotamian civilizations.

NGS PICTURESHOW CD-ROM
Egypt and the Fertile Crescent

NGS PICTURPACK TRANSPARENCY SET
Fertile Crescent

HISTORY Online

Student Web Activity
Visit the *Human Heritage* Web site at humanheritage.glencoe.com and click on ***Chapter 3—Student Web Activities*** to find out more about the Sumerian civilization.

Sumerian civilization is the earliest known on Earth. For the first time, people began to control their physical environment. The Sumerians knew they had to control the twin rivers. The rivers flooded each spring. When the waters went down, natural *levees* (lev′ ēz), or raised areas of soil, remained behind. The Sumerians built the levees even higher and used them to keep back the floodwaters. During summer when the land became dry, they poked holes in the levees. The river water that ran through the holes made channels in the soil. The Sumerians made the channels larger until they became canals. They used the water in the canals to irrigate their crops. The chief crop of the Sumerians was barley. The Sumerians also grew wheat, sesame, flax, fruit trees, date palms, and many different kinds of vegetables.

A system of irrigation canals took much planning. People had to learn to work together. In time, they became more organized. They set up governments to make laws so they would know what was expected of them. As the population grew, they began to build cities.

There was no building stone and little timber in Sumer. The Sumerians had to find other materials to use for their houses and public buildings. They mixed mud from the river with crushed reeds to make bricks. They left the bricks out in the sun to bake and then used them to build their cities. One of the great cities of

Linking Across Time

Official Seals Around 3500 to 3400 B.C., officials in Mesopotamia started using cylinder seals (below) to mark goods and verify documents written in cuneiform on clay. Today governments around the world continue to use seals to mark documents such as the passports carried by United States citizens (right). **Why do you think governments stamp important documents with seals?**

COOPERATIVE LEARNING

Organize the class into three groups. Have each group research information about one aspect of life in ancient Sumer, Akkad, or Babylon. Have groups prepare a class presentation, the subject and format of which they determine cooperatively. Subjects could include lifestyles, occupations, religious practices, or achievements. Formats could include role plays, lectures, and skits. Direct group members to decide what role each team member will play in gathering and presenting the material. Allow time after each presentation for discussion and questions.

Assign Chapter 3 *Cooperative Learning Activity* in the TCR.

Sumer was Ur (uhr). The Sumerians were the first city-builders in this area of the world.

City-States Each Sumerian city was considered a state in itself, with its own god and government. Each **city-state** was made up of the city and the farmland around it. Each city was surrounded by a wall of sun-dried brick. The wall had bronze gates that were opened during the day and closed at night to keep out lions and bandits.

Narrow, winding streets led from the gates to the center of the city. Near the center were the houses of the upper class—priests and merchants. These houses were two stories high with wooden balconies. The balconies looked out over courtyards around which the living quarters were built. The courtyards provided light and air for rooms. Outside walls were windowless to keep out heat from the sun and smells of the streets.

Behind the houses of the rich were the houses of the middle class—government officials, shopkeepers, and **artisans** (art′ uh zuhnz), or skilled workers. These houses also were built around open courtyards but were only one story high. Farther out were the houses of the lower class—farmers, unskilled workers, and people who made their living by fishing.

The Sumerians were very proud of their cities. Often, one city-state would go to war with another city-state. They fought over boundary lines and to prove which city-state was stronger.

Reading Check What areas made up each Sumerian **city-state?**

Reading Check What are **artisans?**

Religious and Family Life At the center of each Sumerian city was a temple, called a **ziggurat** (zig′ uh rat). The word "ziggurat" means "mountain of god" or "hill of heaven." Each ziggurat was made up of a series of square levels. Each level was smaller than the one below it. Great stairways led to the top of a ziggurat, which was believed to be the home of the city's chief god. Only priests could enter the home of the god.

Around the ziggurat were courts. The courts and the ziggurat were the center of Sumerian life. Artisans worked there. Children went to school there. Farmers, artisans, and traders stored their goods there. The poor were fed there. All great events were celebrated in this area.

The Sumerians believed that all the forces of nature, such as wind, rain, and flood, were alive. Because they could not control these forces, they viewed them as gods. In all, there were more than 3,000 Sumerian gods.

The Sumerians believed that at first there were only male gods. Then female gods appeared. The male gods found they had to work very hard to please the female gods. The male gods decided that they needed servants to do their work. So, from the mud of the rivers, they made humans who would be their servants. The Sumerians believed that they were on Earth only to

Reading Check What was the purpose of a **ziggurat?**

Reading Check Answer Each **city-state** was made up of a city and the farmland around it.

L2 **Critical Thinking** Ask students to give possible reasons why the Sumerians had more than 3,000 gods who represented the forces of nature.

Reading Check Answer **Artisans** are skilled workers.

Reading Check Answer A **ziggurat** served as a temple and center of religious life.

MEETING SPECIAL NEEDS

Encourage students who are tactile/kinesthetic learners to work in small groups to create models of a Sumerian city using materials of their choice. Direct students to use the information in the text and in historical reference books to help them construct the models. Display the models in the classroom.

Refer to ***Inclusion for the Middle School Social Studies Classroom: Strategies and Activities*** for additional resources.

CAPTION ANSWER

Sumerians believed in more than 3,000 gods.

MAKING CONNECTIONS

➤➤ **Language Arts** Cuneiform was used by heterogeneous groups who spoke different languages. It served as the writing system for diverse cultures for some 3,000 years. Sumerians, Akkadians, Babylonians, Assyrians, Hittites, and Ancient Persians are among the peoples whose language was written in cuneiform.

Reading Check Answer
Cuneiform was the Sumerian system of writing made up of hundreds of wedge-shaped markings.

DID YOU KNOW ??

Sumerian students had to memorize a list of about 600 word signs. They copied and recopied their lessons until they mastered them.

Reading Check Answer
A **scribe** might work for the temple, the palace, the government, the army, a merchant, or in his own business.

SUMERIAN PRAYING STATUES To honor their gods, Sumerians left statues of themselves within their temple. These statues, standing with their hands clasped, were meant to offer prayers when the people were not present. **In how many gods did the Sumerians believe?**

serve the gods. If the gods were unhappy with them, their crops would not grow and they would not live happy lives. Therefore, the goal of each Sumerian was to please the gods.

Only priests, however, could know the will of the gods. This made Sumerian priests very powerful. For example, all land was owned by a city's god. But priests controlled and administered the land in the god's name. The priests also ran schools.

Schools were only for the sons of the rich. Poorer boys worked in the fields or learned a trade. Schools were made up of rooms off the temple courtyards. They were known as tablet houses because their main purpose was to teach students how to write. Students sat in rows on brick benches. They wrote with sharp-ended reeds on clay tablets about the size of a postcard. Sumerian writing was called **cuneiform** (kyū nē′ uh form). It was made up of hundreds of markings shaped like wedges.

Reading Check What was **cuneiform?**

Writing developed because people had to keep track of business deals. When people lived in villages, they knew everyone and could remember what goods they exchanged with whom. When cities arose, there were too many people and goods to remember. At first, the Sumerians used pictures to represent objects. Later, they used pictures to represent ideas. Still later, they used pictures to represent syllables.

When a student graduated from school, he became a **scribe,** or writer. He worked for the temple, the palace, the government, or the army. Some scribes went to work for a merchant or set up their own businesses as public writers.

Reading Check What were some of the places a **scribe** might work?

MULTICULTURAL PERSPECTIVES

Learning to write the hundreds of cuneiform symbols in ancient times was a long, difficult process. One clay tablet found in Sumer seems to be a composition that teachers gave their students for practice. Students wrote once, found their mistakes, scraped off the surface of the clay tablet, and wrote again. The following is an excerpt from a clay tablet. "First I had to recite my homework. Then I prepared my new tablet. I copied out the text that the supervisor gave me. Then I ate my lunch. After 'Break', the father of the tablet house asked me questions. Last of all, I was given a written task that I had to do in the tablet house. After my lessons I went straight home. My father heard me recite..."

Although only Sumerian males went to school, women did have rights. They could buy and sell property. They could run businesses and own and sell enslaved persons.

Although a woman handled her husband's affairs when he was away, the husband was the head of a household. He could divorce his wife by saying, "You're not my wife." If he needed money, he had the right to sell or rent his wife and children as enslaved persons for up to three years. He also arranged the marriages of his children.

Children were expected to support their parents when the parents became old and were also expected to obey older family members. All family members were to obey the gods and the priests.

Priests and Kings At first, Sumerian priests were also kings of city-states. One of the most famous **priest-kings** was Gilgamesh (gil' ga mesh) of Uruk (ū' rūk). Tales told about Gilgamesh made him seem more like a god than a person. One tale, written about 1700 B.C., is the oldest known story in the world.

In the story, Gilgamesh and his friend Enkidu (en' ki dū) travel the world performing great acts of courage. When Enkidu dies, Gilgamesh searches for a way to live forever. He learns that only the gods can live forever. Part of the Gilgamesh story tells of a great flood that covered the whole world. The account of the flood is very much like the biblical story of Noah and the ark.

The Sumerian priest-kings received advice from an assembly made up of free men. When war broke out with another city-state, the assembly would choose one of its members to serve as military leader until the war was over. As time went on, these leaders stayed in charge even after peace returned. By about 3000 B.C., they took the place of priests as permanent kings. At the same time, kingship became *hereditary* (huh red' uh ter ē), or passed down from parent to child.

Then & Now

Cuneiform Today only about 250 people know how to read the more than 1 million cuneiform signs that make up the written Sumerian language. To change this, a team of language experts at the University of Pennsylvania is working on an 18-volume Sumerian dictionary. The team expects the work to be done sometime in the 2000s.

Reading Check Who was one of the most famous Sumerian **priest-kings?**

Section 1 Assessment

1. **Define:** city-state, artisans, ziggurat, cuneiform, scribe, priest-kings.
2. How did the Sumerians gain control of the twin rivers?
3. What was the center of Sumerian life?

Critical Thinking

4. **Making Comparisons** How would you compare the lives of women in the time of Sumer to the lives of women in the modern world?

Graphic Organizer Activity

5. Draw a diagram like this one, and use it to show accomplishments of the Sumerians.

MAKING CONNECTIONS

>> **Literature** Gilgamesh is the first known hero figure in literature. His story was the prototype for later epic poetry and may have influenced Homer's epics, the *Iliad* and the *Odyssey*.

Reading Check Answer One of the most famous Sumerian **priest-kings** was Gilgamesh.

GEOGRAPHY AND HISTORY

By 3000 B.C. the Sumerians had established 12 city-states in the Tigris-Euphrates valley, including Ur, Uruk, and Eridu. The Fertile Crescent, as the area is often called because of its relatively rich topsoil and its curved shape, was able to support city-state populations ranging from 20,000 to 250,000.

Use the **Interactive Tutor Self-Assessment CD-ROM** to review Section 1.

Section 1 Assessment Answers

1. city-state, self-governing city (p. 57); artisans, skilled workers (p. 57); ziggurat, Sumerian temple (p. 57); cuneiform, Sumerian writing (p. 58); scribe, Sumerian writer (p. 58); priest-kings, Sumerian priests who were also kings (p. 59)
2. by building natural levees even higher
3. the courts and the ziggurat
4. Answers will vary. Students may point out that like Sumerian women, modern women can buy property and businesses. Modern women, however, also can get an education, divorce, and cannot be enslaved.
5. Accomplishments might include: levees to control flooding, a system of irrigation canals, construction of brick cities, organization of city-states, development of a writing system, creation of literature such as the story of Gilgamesh.

Assign Chapter 3 **Section 1 Quiz** in the TCR. Testmaker available.

CRITICAL THINKING SKILLS

TEACH

Distinguishing Fact From Opinion

You might introduce this activity by asking students to complete these sentences on a sheet of paper:

The best song ever written is: ________________.

The best food ever created is: ________________.

Record student answers on the board under two heads: Best Song and Best Food. On top of these two columns, write the words "Differences in Opinion." Ask students to define the word "opinion." Use their answers to introduce the skills lesson and the accompanying questions.

Answers to Skill Practice

1. Fact. It can be proven by existing archaeological finds.
2. Opinion. Some people might think other accomplishments are more important. The sentence also includes the judgment word "greatest."
3. Fact. It can be proven by evidence found at the sites of ancient city-states such as Sumer.
4. Opinion. Women at the time might have seen their lives differently. The sentence also includes the judgment word "terrible."
5. Opinion. The statement cannot be proven. The sentence also includes the judgment word "better."

CRITICAL THINKING SKILLS

Distinguishing Fact From Opinion

Suppose a friend says, "Our school's basketball team is awesome. That's a fact." Actually, it is not a fact; it is an opinion. Are you able to tell the difference?

Learning the Skill A **fact** answers a specific question such as: What happened? Who did it? When and where did it happen? Why did it happen? Statements of fact can be checked for accuracy and proven. If your friend had said, "We have the highest-ranking team in the state," that could be a fact. We can look up the rankings of state teams and determine whether the statement is a fact.

An **opinion,** on the other hand, expresses beliefs, feelings, and judgments. Although it may reflect someone's thoughts, we cannot prove or disprove it.

An **opinion** often begins with phrases such as *I believe, I think, probably, it seems to me,* or *in my opinion.* It often contains words such as *might, could, should,* and *ought,* and superlatives such as *best, worst,* and *greatest.* Judgment words that express approval or disapproval—such as *good, bad, poor,* and *satisfactory*—also usually indicate an opinion.

To distinguish between facts and opinions, ask yourself these questions:

- Does this statement give specific information about an event?
- Can I check the accuracy of this statement?
- Does this statement express someone's feelings, beliefs, or judgment?
- Does it include phrases such as *I believe,* superlatives, or judgment words?

Skill Practice

Read each numbered statement. Then tell whether each is a fact or an opinion, and explain how you arrived at your answer.

1. **Sumerian civilization is the earliest known on Earth.**
2. **The greatest accomplishment of the Sumerians was their system of irrigation.**
3. **A temple called a ziggurat formed the center of Sumerian life.**
4. **Women in Sumeria had terrible lives.**
5. **The priest-kings were better rulers than the military leaders who came into power.**

GO TO Glencoe's **Skillbuilder Interactive Workbook CD-ROM, Level 1,** provides instruction and practice in key social studies skills.

60

TEAM-TEACHING STRATEGY

Language Arts Work with a language arts teacher to develop a lesson on persuasive writing. Explain to students that people sometimes use facts to support an opinion. Illustrate this by distributing copies of letters to the editor from your local newspaper. Have students identify the main opinion expressed in each letter and the facts used to support that opinion.

Next, tell students to imagine that they are scribes working for Hammurabi. As they read Section 2, have students record his achievements. Assign groups of students to use these facts to write letters persuading conquered peoples to accept this opinion: "Hammurabi is the best ruler you could possibly have."

SECTION 2 Later Mesopotamian Empires

About 2400 B.C., the power of Sumer started to fade. New civilizations began to develop in Mesopotamia as conquerors moved in from nearby areas.

Sargon I Sargon I (sar′ gon) was a ruler from an area in northern Mesopotamia known as Akkad (ak′ ad). About 2300 B.C., he moved his armies south and began to conquer the city-states of Sumer one by one. He united the conquered city-states with Akkad and became known as king of Sumer and Akkad. Thus, Sargon I created the world's first **empire** (em′ pīr), or group of states under one ruler. He extended this empire to include all of Mesopotamia.

Under Sargon I, Akkadian became the language of the people. Sumerian was used only for religious purposes. The Akkadians, however, worshiped the Sumerian gods. They also wrote their language in Sumerian cuneiform. Sargon I ruled his empire for more than 50 years. Shortly after his death, the empire fell.

Hammurabi of Babylon Following the death of Sargon I, the separate city-states again rose to power. Then, about 1800 B.C., a new group of people called Amorites (am′ uh rīts) entered the Tigris-Euphrates valley and built cities of their own. One of these cities was Babylon (bab′ uh luhn). The king of Babylon, Hammurabi (ham uh rob′ ē), conquered Akkad and Sumer and became ruler of a great new empire.

The people of Babylon took as their own many parts of the **culture,** or way of life, of the people they had conquered. For example, they took over the language of the city-states. They also worshiped the same Sumerian gods that the Akkadians had worshiped, but they gave those gods Babylonian names.

Hammurabi was a great conqueror. He extended his rule to the Mediterranean Sea. As ruler, he brought about many changes. He improved irrigation systems by building and repairing canals. He changed religion by raising the god of Babylon above all other gods. When the people began to worship this god as well as their own local god, they became more united. Hammurabi also reorganized the tax system and began a government housing program.

The **reform,** or improvement, for which Hammurabi became best known was a code of law. Each city-state had its own code. Hammurabi took what he believed were the best laws from each code. He put these together and then issued one code by which everyone in the empire was to live. Hammurabi wanted to make sure that his code was carried out fairly and justly. To do this, he

Reading Check How did Sargon I build his **empire?** From what **culture** did the people of Babylon borrow? For what **reform** is Hammurabi best known?

People in History

Hammurabi
c.1750 B.C.

Babylonian King

Hammurabi built an empire that stretched north from the Persian Gulf through the Tigris and Euphrates valleys and west to the Mediterranean Sea. He turned Babylon into one of the most powerful capitals of the ancient world.

Reading Check Answer Sargon I built the world's first **empire** by conquering city-states and uniting them. Babylonians borrowed from the **culture** of other people by adopting the language of city-states and worshiping some of the same gods. Hammurabi is best known for his **reform** of law.

PRIMARY SOURCES Library

You might assign "The Pursuit of Justice," from pages 676–677 of the Primary Sources Library.

Use the **Vocabulary PuzzleMaker CD-ROM** to create crossword and word search puzzles.

SPOTLIGHT ON: SARGON I

Sargon I tells his own story in an account found carved on a block of diorite. The story is similar to the biblical story of Moses.

"Of my father I know only his name . . . My mother was a priestess . . . She brought me into the world secretly . . . She took a basket of reeds, placed me inside it, covered it with pitch [tar], and placed me in the Euphrates. And the river, without which the land cannot live, carried me through part of my future kingdom . . . and bore me along to Akki, who fetched water to irrigate the fields. Akki made a gardener of me. In the garden that I cultivated Inanna [chief goddess] saw me. And she turned her favor toward me and promised to make me great."

MAP SKILLS

TEACH

Identifying Physical Features

Instruct the students to study the map on page 62 to answer the following questions:

What empire was located partly in the mountains? *(Hammurabi's empire)*

What seas border Asia Minor? *(Mediterranean Sea, Black Sea)*

Have the students look at the physical map of the Middle East on pages 714–715 in the textbook Atlas. Point out to students that this map uses many colors and grades of shading to show physical features. Ask the students to identify and locate physical features of the Middle East shown on this map.

Assign Chapter 3 **Geography and Map Activity** in the TCR.

Answers to Map Practice

1. Bodies of water shown on the map in addition to the Mediterranean Sea are the Persian Gulf, the Caspian Sea, the Black Sea, and the Red Sea.

2. Besides the Nile, the rivers shown on the map are the Tigris River and the Euphrates River.

3. The map and the map key indicate that there was an ancient coastline of the Persian Gulf.

Identifying Physical Features

Different physical features making up Earth's surface are often shown on maps. They include landforms, such as mountains, hills, plateaus, and plains. Physical features also include bodies of water, such as oceans, seas, lakes, and rivers.

Most maps use black boundary lines and color to point out water and land areas. Blue is generally used to show the size and shape of large bodies of water. For example, notice the Mediterranean Sea located west of Syria on the map below. Rivers, such as the Nile River in Egypt, are often shown by black lines. To distinguish rivers from boundaries, which are also shown by black lines, rivers are usually labeled.

Maps in this textbook use earth tone colors to point out land areas. Mountains are shown by shades of black. For example, there are mountains located where the Euphrates River begins but not where the river empties into the Persian Gulf.

Look at the map below, and answer the following questions.

Map Practice

1. **In addition to the Mediterranean, what seas are shown?**
2. **Besides the Nile, what rivers are shown?**
3. **How can you tell that the Persian Gulf coastline has changed over the years?**

Mesopotamia

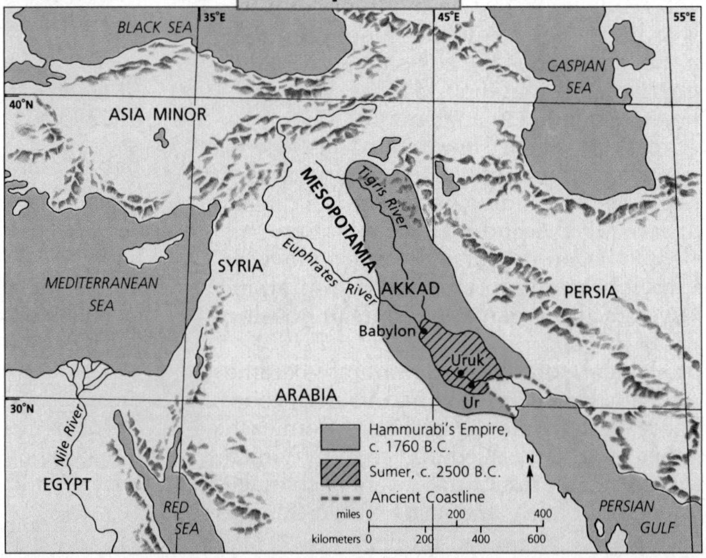

GO TO

Glencoe's **Skillbuilder Interactive Workbook CD-ROM, Level 1,** provides instruction and practice in key social studies skills.

SPOTLIGHT ON: MESOPOTAMIA

The area of Mesopotamia, in addition to being known as "the cradle of civilization," was also known as "the fertile crescent." It was given this name because the actual area was shaped like a crescent and the land was extremely fertile. Both the climate and the silt from the Tigris and Euphrates rivers added to its richness and productivity.

appointed royal judges. Judges who were not honest and witnesses who did not tell the truth were punished.

Hammurabi's code covered almost everything in daily life. A person was believed innocent until proven guilty. Once proven guilty, a person was punished. Punishments ranged from fines to death. There were no prison sentences. Members of the upper class generally were punished more severely than members of the middle or lower classes.

During Hammurabi's rule, Babylon became an important trade center. Babylonians exchanged their *surplus,* or extra, products for money or for goods. People from other parts of the world came to trade, some from as far away as India and China. These traders paid gold and silver for the goods made by Babylonians.

Hammurabi ruled for more than 40 years. His **reign** (rān), or period of power, is known as the Golden Age of Babylon. After his death, however, the Babylonian Empire declined, and Mesopotamia was again divided into a number of small city-states.

Sculpture of a Sumerian Chariot

Reading Check What did people call the **reign** of Hammurabi?

Section 2 Assessment

1. **Define:** empire, culture, reform, reign.
2. What happened to Sumer under Sargon I's rule?
3. How did Hammurabi come to power?

Critical Thinking

4. **Using Reasoned Judgment** What do you think Hammurabi would say about the court system in the United States today?

Graphic Organizer Activity

5. Draw a diagram like this one, and use it to show key events in the life of Hammurabi.

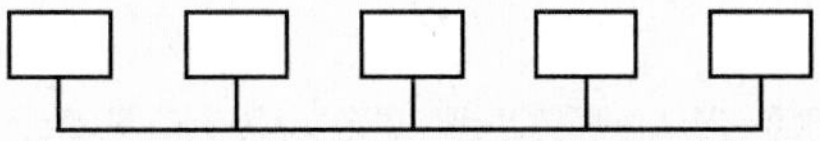

SECTION 3 Contributions

From the beginnings of Sumer until the death of Hammurabi, the influence of Mesopotamia on other civilizations was felt in many ways. Inventions, customs, and ideas of the Sumerian and Babylonian cultures were copied and improved upon by other peoples.

The Sumerians developed the earliest known civilization in the world. Mesopotamia has been called "the cradle of civilization." The oldest written records known are Sumerian. The Sumerians were the first people to write down their laws. Sumerian cuneiform became the model for other people's writing.

The Sumerians also invented many things such as the wheel, which helped transportation. Another was the plow, which made

Section 2 Assessment Answers

1. empire, states under one ruler (p. 61); culture, way of life (p. 61); reform, improvement (p. 61); reign, period of power (p. 63)
2. It was conquered and united with Akkad.
3. by conquering Akkad and Sumer
4. Answers will vary, but note that he agreed that a person is believed innocent until proven guilty.
5. Events might include: birth c. 1750 B.C., conquest of Akkad and Sumer, expansion of rule to the Mediterranean, institution of many reforms, organization of laws into a single code, and so on.

Assign Chapter 3 **Section 2 Quiz** in the TCR. Testmaker available.

Independent Practice

L3 **Mathematics** Have students create illustrated time lines of Mesopotamian history from 5000 B.C. (people migrate to Mesopotamia) to 1750 B.C. (end of Hammurabi's empire). Suggest that they create several mathematically based questions about their time lines for other students to answer.

Reading Check Answer People called the **reign** of Hammurabi the Golden Age of Babylonia.

Use the **Interactive Tutor Self-Assessment CD-ROM** to review Section 2.

LINKING PAST TO PRESENT

Government officials in ancient civilizations directed and organized large construction projects that employed many people. How do the roles of these officials compare to the roles of modern government officials who oversee the expansion of cities?

ASSESS

Check for Understanding

Ask students to summarize the main points of the chapter, orally or in writing. Discuss the answers to the Section and Chapter Assessment questions.

Use the **Vocabulary PuzzleMaker CD-ROM** to create crossword and word search puzzles.

Evaluate

Assign Chapter 3 **Performance Assessment Activity** in the TCR.

Administer **Chapter 3 Test** found in the TCR. Testmaker available.

Reteach

Organize students in small groups. Have pairs or individuals in each group outline a different section of the chapter. Have students regroup and compile the outlines into a chapter outline. Then have group members use the outline to quiz one another.

Assign Chapter 3 **Reteaching Activity** in the TCR.

Enrich

Assign Chapter 3 **Enrichment Activity** in the TCR.

CLOSE

Ask students to evaluate the following statement: *"The Golden Age of Babylon" is an appropriate name for Hammurabi's reign.*

Use the **Interactive Tutor Self-Assessment CD-ROM** to review Section 3.

HISTORY Online

Self-Check Quiz gives students an interactive chapter tutorial. Have them access ***Chapter 3 Quiz*** at humanheritage.glencoe.com

it possible for farmers to grow more food with less effort. Still another was the sailboat, which replaced muscle power with wind power.

The people of Mesopotamia developed a 12-month calendar based on the cycles of the moon. The calendar marked the times for religious festivals and planting.

From Mesopotamia also came contributions in the field of mathematics. The people developed a number system based on 60. From that came the 60-minute hour, 60-second minute, and 360-degree circle. The people of Mesopotamia also used a clock that was operated by controlled drops of water.

Section 3 Assessment

1. Why was Mesopotamia called "the cradle of civilization"?
2. What did the people of Mesopotamia contribute to the field of mathematics?

Critical Thinking

3. **Determining Cause and Effect** How have inventions by the people of Mesopotamia helped shape present-day life?

Graphic Organizer Activity

4. Draw a diagram like this one, and use it to show facts that support this statement: Mesopotamia was "the cradle of civilization."

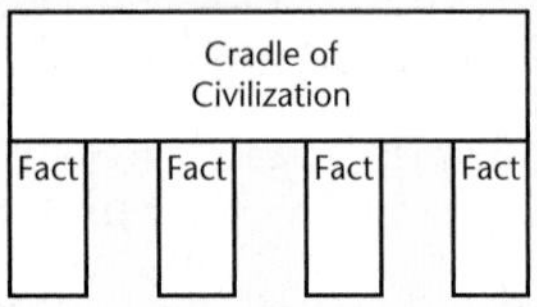

Chapter Summary & Study Guide

1. Civilization began in an area known as Mesopotamia, located between the Tigris and Euphrates rivers.
2. Sumer was the first known civilization in the world.
3. Sumerian civilization consisted of a series of city-states, the most important of which was Ur.
4. Each Sumerian city-state had its own chief god and government.
5. Sargon I of Akkad created the world's first empire in 2300 B.C.
6. About 1800 B.C., Hammurabi conquered Akkad and Sumer and established the Babylonian Empire.
7. Hammurabi unified the Babylonian Empire by setting up a single code of law and by raising the god of Babylon above all others.
8. Major contributions of the Mesopotamian civilizations include writing, the wheel, the plow, the sailboat, and a number system based on 60.

HISTORY Online

Self-Check Quiz

Visit the *Human Heritage* Web site at humanheritage.glencoe.com and click on ***Chapter 3—Self-Check Quiz*** to assess your understanding of this chapter.

Section 3 Assessment Answers

1. because the earliest known civilization developed there

2. a number system based on 60, which led to the 60-minute hour, 60-minute second, and 360-degree circle

3. Answers will vary, but might note that there would not be bicycles if the wheel had not been invented.

4. Facts might include any of the many accomplishments and inventions mentioned in this section, particularly those that influenced later civilizations such as our own.

Assign Chapter 3 **Section 3 Quiz** in the TCR. Testmaker available.

CHAPTER 3 Assessment

Using Key Terms

Imagine that you are a visitor to ancient Mesopotamia. Use the following words in a letter home in which you describe what you have seen and experienced during your visit.

artisans	culture	empire
ziggurat	priest-kings	scribe
reform	cuneiform	city-state
reign		

Understanding Main Ideas

1. Why were the twin rivers important to Sumerian life?
2. Why was the ziggurat important to the Sumerians?
3. Who was Gilgamesh, and why was he important?
4. What did Sargon I accomplish?
5. What trading system did the people of Babylonia use?
6. What changes did Hammurabi bring to Mesopotamia?
7. What happened to people who broke Hammurabi's laws?
8. Why was the sailboat an important invention?

Critical Thinking

1. In what ways do you think your school is similar to or different from the schools in Sumeria?
2. What do you think would have happened to Sumer if it had suffered ten years of drought? How would the kingdom be affected?
3. Why do you think religion played such an important part in Sumerian life?

Graphic Organizer Activity

History Create a chart like this one, and use it to write newspaper headlines that tell the importance of each date to the history of Mesopotamia.

Date	Headline
3500 B.C.	
2300 B.C.	
1800 B.C.	
1700 B.C.	

Geography in History

Human Systems Babylon became a major trading center. Refer to the map on page 62 and imagine that you are King Hammurabi. You must select the location for another settlement that you hope will also become a trading center. Where would you locate this settlement? Explain.

Using Your Journal

Compare any details you may have noted about life in early Sumeria with details of your daily life. Write a paragraph explaining things that are similar and different as if you were explaining them to someone who lived in 2000 B.C.

Bonus Test Question

For Chapter 3 Test

The Sumerians developed ways of telling time and counting. What elements of that system remain today, and what parts have disappeared? *(the 60-minute hour, 360° circle; modern numbers are based on 10.)*

Using Your Journal

Journal entries will vary, but students should compare their way of life with that of Sumerians. You might call on volunteers to read their entries to the class.

Geography in History

Answers will vary but could mention a location with access to transportation, closeness to bodies of water, and proximity to Babylon.

CHAPTER 3 Assessment Answers

Using Key Terms

Letters will vary. Students should include the terms in a letter home describing their visit to ancient Mesopotamia.

Understanding Main Ideas

1. They used water to irrigate crops, mud from the rivers to make bricks, and fish and waterfowl for food.
2. because they were the center of Sumerian life—all great events were celebrated there
3. a famous priest-king; in a tale about him he learned that only the gods can live forever, and that people should take pride in what they do
4. He created the world's first empire.
5. They exchanged their surplus products for money or goods.
6. extended Babylonian rule, improved irrigation systems, raised god of Babylon above all other gods, reorganized tax system, began government housing program, codified laws
7. They were punished.
8. because it replaced muscle power with wind power

Critical Thinking

1. Answers will vary, but should show a knowledge of Sumerian education.
2. Answers will vary, but could note 10 years of drought could cause food and water shortages and cause Sumerians to migrate.
3. Answers will vary, but could note that Sumerians believed all forces of nature were gods to serve.

Graphic Organizer Activity

Headlines will vary, but should reflect the importance of each of the events on the time line on page 54.

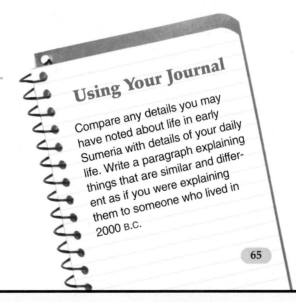

Chapter 4 Planning Guide

Timesaving Tools

TeacherWorks™ All-In-One Planner and Resource Center

- **Interactive Teacher Edition** Access your Teacher Wraparound Edition and your classroom resources with a few easy clicks.
- **Interactive Lesson Planner** Planning has never been easier! Organize your week, month, semester, or year with all the lesson helps you need to make teaching creative, timely, and relevant.

Presentation Plus! Use Glencoe's **Presentation Plus!** multimedia teacher tool to easily present dynamic lessons that visually excite your students. Using Microsoft PowerPoint® you can customize the presentations to create your own personalized lessons.

Objectives	Reproducible Resources	Multimedia Resources
Section 1 **The Nile** Analyze why the Nile River was so important to the growth of Egypt.	Reproducible Lesson Plan Chapter 4 Vocabulary and Guided Reading Activity Reading Essentials and Study Guide 4-1 Chapter 4 Geography and Map Activity Unit 2 World Literature Reading 2 Section 1 Quiz	Interactive Student Edition CD-ROM Graphic Organizer Transparency 2 Vocabulary PuzzleMaker CD-ROM Interactive Tutor Self-Assessment CD-ROM ExamView® Pro Testmaker CD-ROM Glencoe Skillbuilder Interactive Workbook CD-ROM, Level 1 Presentation Plus! CD-ROM
Section 2 **The Old Kingdom** Discuss how pharaohs, pyramids, and religious beliefs influenced the Old Kingdom of Egypt.	Reproducible Lesson Plan Reading Essentials and Study Guide 4-2 Chapter 4 Enrichment Activity Section 2 Quiz	Vocabulary PuzzleMaker CD-ROM Interactive Tutor Self-Assessment CD-ROM ExamView® Pro Testmaker CD-ROM Glencoe Skillbuilder Interactive Workbook CD-ROM, Level 1
Section 3 **The Middle Kingdom** Describe what happened during Egypt's Middle Kingdom.	Reproducible Lesson Plan Reading Essentials and Study Guide 4-3 Section 3 Quiz	Vocabulary PuzzleMaker CD-ROM Interactive Tutor Self-Assessment CD-ROM ExamView® Pro Testmaker CD-ROM Glencoe Skillbuilder Interactive Workbook CD-ROM, Level 1
Section 4 **The New Kingdom** Explain why Egyptian civilization grew and then declined during the New Kingdom.	Reproducible Lesson Plan Reading Essentials and Study Guide 4-4 Chapter 4 Cooperative Learning Activity Section 4 Quiz	Teaching Transparencies and Activities 4A & 4B Vocabulary PuzzleMaker CD-ROM Interactive Tutor Self-Assessment CD-ROM ExamView® Pro Testmaker CD-ROM
Section 5 **Contributions** Summarize what the Egyptians contributed to other civilizations.	Reproducible Lesson Plan Reading Essentials and Study Guide 4-5 Chapter 4 Chart and Graph Skill Activity Section 5 Quiz	Vocabulary PuzzleMaker CD-ROM Interactive Tutor Self-Assessment CD-ROM Glencoe Skillbuilder Interactive Workbook CD-ROM, Level 1
Chapter 4 **Review and Evaluation**	Chapter 4 Reteaching Activity Chapter 4 Performance Assessment Activity Spanish Chapter Summary and Glossary Chapter 4 Test	Vocabulary PuzzleMaker CD-ROM Interactive Tutor Self-Assessment CD-ROM ExamView® Pro Testmaker CD-ROM Glencoe Skillbuilder Interactive Workbook CD-ROM, Level 1 Audiocassettes*

*Also available in Spanish.

Chapter 4 Planning Guide

Performance Assessment Activities

Television Newscast Have students imagine they are television journalists carried back in time to ancient Egypt. Have them write and present a newscast-style report on an object or structure to be shown on the evening news.

Chapter Resources

LITERATURE ABOUT THE PERIOD

Perl, Lila. *Mummies, Tombs, and Treasure: Secrets of Ancient Egypt.* Clarion Books, 1990. An account of ancient Egyptian beliefs about death and the afterlife.

READINGS FOR THE STUDENT

Morley, Jaquelin, Mark Bergin, and John James. *An Egyptian Pyramid.* Peter Bedrick, 1991. Explains how the pyramids were built and their purpose.

Rossini, Stephane. *Egyptian Hieroglyphics: How to Read and Write Them.* Dover, 1989. Describes the principles of Egyptian reading and writing.

READINGS FOR THE TEACHER

Bowman, Alan K. *Egypt after the Pharaohs.* Berkeley: University of California Press, 1986. History of Egypt 332 B.C.-642 A.D., portraying daily life, government, economy, architecture, and culture.

THE HISTORY CHANNEL. A&E HOME VIDEO. Biography

The following videotape programs are available from Glencoe:

- **Cleopatra: Destiny's Queen**
  1-56501-454-5
- **King Tut: The Face of Tutankhamen**
  1-56501-159-7
- **Mummies and the Wonders of Ancient Egypt**
  1-56501-773-0

To order, call Glencoe at 1-800-334-7344. To find resources to accompany many of these, check:

A&E Television: www.aande.com
The History Channel: www.historychannel.com

National Geographic Teacher's Corner

INDEX TO NATIONAL GEOGRAPHIC MAGAZINE

The following articles relate to this chapter:

- "The Pyramid Builders," by Virginia Morell, November 2001.
- "Egypt's Hidden Tombs," by Zahi Hawass, September 2001.
- "Pharaohs of the Sun," by Rick Gore, April 2001.
- "Valley of the Mummies," by Donovan Webster, October 1999.

NATIONAL GEOGRAPHIC SOCIETY PRODUCTS AVAILABLE FROM GLENCOE

To order the following, call Glencoe at 1-800-334-7344:

- *PicturePack: Ancient Egypt (Transparencies)*
- *PictureShow: Ancient Civilizations: Egypt and the Fertile Crescent (CD-ROM)*
- *PictureShow: Ancient Civilizations Library (CD-ROMs)*

ADDITIONAL NATIONAL GEOGRAPHIC SOCIETY PRODUCTS

To order the following, call National Geographic at 1-800-368-2728:

- *Egypt: Quest for Eternity (Video or Videodisc)*
- *GeoKit: Ancient Egypt (Multimedia Teaching Module)*
- *Mr. Mummy (Video)*
- *Pharaoh's Voyage for Eternity (Video)*
- *Who Built the Pyramids? (Video)*

Access *National Geographic's* new dynamic MapMachine Web site and other geography resources at:
www.nationalgeographic.com
www.nationalgeographic.com/maps

KEY TO ABILITY LEVELS

Teaching strategies have been coded for varying learning styles and abilities.

L1 Level 1 activities are **basic** activities and should be within the ability range of all students.

L2 Level 2 activities are **average** activities and should be within the ability range of the average to above-average student.

L3 Level 3 activities are **challenging** activities designed for the ability range of above-average students.

ELL ELL activities should be within the ability range of English Language Learning students.

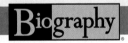

OVERVIEW

Chapter 4 focuses on the changes in society during the Old, Middle, and New Kingdoms.

➤ **Section 1** explains the importance of the Nile River to the Egyptian civilization.
➤ **Section 2** discusses Egypt's Old Kingdom.
➤ **Section 3** describes Egypt's Middle Kingdom.
➤ **Section 4** traces the New Kingdom.
➤ **Section 5** presents Egyptian contributions.

CHAPTER OBJECTIVES

After reading Chapter 4, students will be able to:

1. analyze why the Nile River was so important to the growth of Egyptian civilization.
2. discuss how pharaohs, pyramids, and religious beliefs influenced the Old Kingdom.
3. describe what happened during Egypt's Middle Kingdom.
4. explain why Egyptian civilization grew then declined during the New Kingdom.
5. list Egyptian contributions.

EXAMINING ARTIFACTS

Tell students that the elaborate gold mask and intricately painted sandals were found in Egyptian tombs. Ask: What does the location of these artifacts tell you about the Egyptian people? *(that they held strong beliefs about death and the afterlife)*

PERFORMANCE ASSESSMENT ✓

Use the Performance Assessment activities on page 66B to help you evaluate students as they complete the chapter.

CHAPTER 4

Egypt

3100 B.C.–671 B.C.

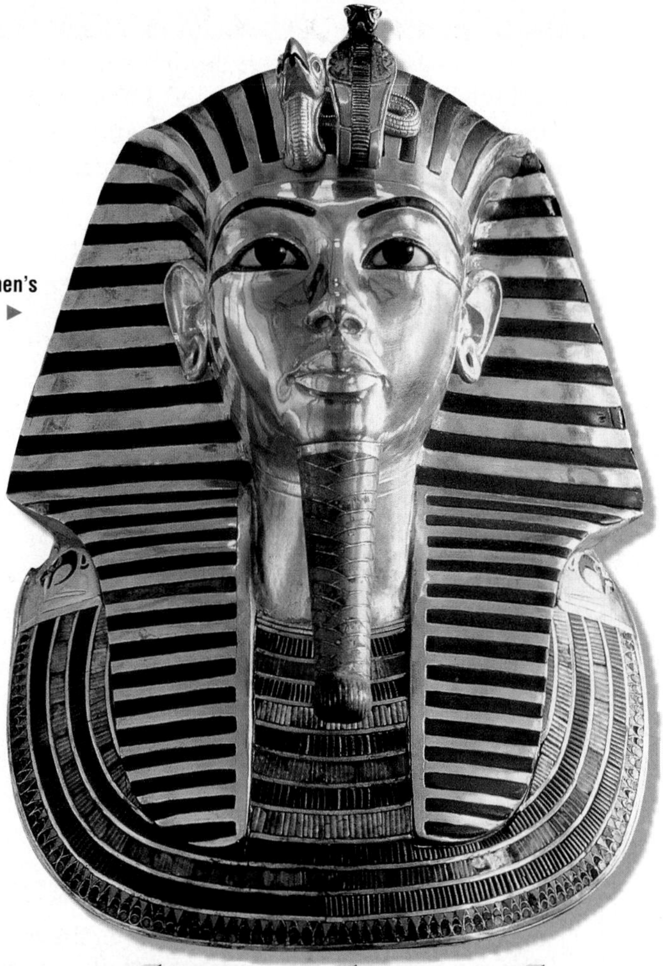

Tutankhamen's gold mask ►

▲ Wooden Egyptian sandals

TEACHING RESOURCES

TEACHER PLANNING AND SUPPORT

- Reproducible Lesson Plan 4-1, 4-2, 4-3, 4-4, 4-5
- Teaching Strategies for the World History Classroom (Including Block Scheduling Pacing Guides)
- Presentation Plus! CD-ROM

REVIEW AND REINFORCEMENT

- Reading Essentials and Study Guide 4-1, 4-2, 4-3, 4-4, 4-5
- Chapter 4 Vocabulary and Guided Reading Activity
- Vocabulary PuzzleMaker CD-ROM
- Teaching Transparencies 4A & 4B
- Chapter 4 Reteaching Activity
- Chapter 4 Cooperative Learning Activity
- Chapter 4 Activity Book Activity
- Chapter 4 Chart and Graph Skill Activity
- Reading and Study Skills Foldables
- Interactive Tutor Self-Assessment CD-ROM

APPLICATION AND HANDS-ON ACTIVITIES

- Daily Questions in Social Studies
- World Games Activity Card 10
- Unit 2 Hands-On History Lab Activity
- Student Presentation Builder CD-ROM

Chapter Focus

Read to Discover

- Why the Nile River was so important to the growth of Egyptian civilization.
- How Egyptian religious beliefs influenced the Old Kingdom.
- What happened during Egypt's Middle Kingdom.
- Why Egyptian civilization grew and then declined during the New Kingdom.
- What the Egyptians contributed to other civilizations.

HISTORY Online

Chapter Overview

Visit the *Human Heritage* Web site at **humanheritage.glencoe.com** and click on ***Chapter 4—Chapter Overviews*** to preview this chapter.

Terms to Learn	People to Know	Places to Locate
shadoof	Narmer	Nile River
pharaoh	Ahmose	Punt
pyramids	Thutmose III	Thebes
embalming	Hatshepsut	
mummy	Amenhotep IV	
legend		
hieroglyphic		
papyrus		

Why It's Important The Egyptians settled in the Nile River valley of northeast Africa. They most likely borrowed ideas such as writing from the Sumerians. However, the Egyptian civilization lasted far longer than the city-states and empires of Mesopotamia. While the people of Mesopotamia fought among themselves, Egypt grew into a rich, powerful, and unified kingdom. The Egyptians built a civilization that lasted for more than 2,000 years and left a lasting influence on the world.

SECTION 1 The Nile

The Nile River flows north 4,145 miles, or 6,671 kilometers, from the mountains of central Africa to the Mediterranean Sea. The last 600 miles, or 960 kilometers, is in Egypt. There, the river cuts a narrow, green valley through the desert. Shortly before the Nile reaches the sea, it branches to form a fan-shaped area of fertile land called a *delta.* Most ancient Egyptians lived in this area. For a long time, they were protected from foreign invasions by the desert, the sea, and waterfalls called *cataracts* (kat' uh rakts).

HISTORY Online

Chapter Overview introduces students to chapter content and key terms. Have them access ***Chapter 4 Overview*** at **humanheritage.glencoe.com**

FOCUS

Bellringer

Have students write the words *ancient Egypt* on their papers. Ask them to write words or phrases that come to mind when they think of ancient Egypt.

Motivational Activity

Call on volunteers to share their ideas about ancient Egypt. Write these on the chalkboard and have students notice the words and phrases that appear most often. *(Nile River, pharaohs, pyramids, fertile lands, mummies)* Have students copy any words or phrases that were not on their papers. Then tell them that they will learn the historical significance of these terms as they study the section.

GUIDE TO READING

Reading Strategy

Ask students to read "Why It's Important" and summarize the chapter's main theme. *(Egyptian civilization lasted a long time and left a lasting impression on world civilization.)*

Vocabulary Precheck

Ask students to define each of the "Terms to Learn." Have a volunteer consult the dictionary for any unfamiliar words. L1 ELL

Use the Vocabulary PuzzleMaker CD-ROM for Chapter 4 to create a crossword puzzle. L1

Assign Chapter 4 Vocabulary and Guided Reading Activity.

Assign Reading Essentials and Study Guide 4-1.

GEOGRAPHY ACTIVITIES

- Chapter 4 Geography and Map Activity
- Outline Map Resource Book

INTERDISCIPLINARY CONNECTIONS

- Unit 2 World Literature Reading 2
- World Art & Architecture Transparency 3, *Tutankhamen's Throne*
- World Art Print 1, *Mask of Pharaoh Tutankhamen*
- World Music: A Cultural Legacy

ENRICHMENT AND EXTENSION

- World History Primary Source Document Library CD-ROM
- Chapter 4 Enrichment Activity
- Foods Around the World

ASSESSMENT AND EVALUATION

- Chapter 4 Performance Assessment Activity
- Chapter 4 Section Quizzes 4-1, 4-2, 4-3, 4-4, 4-5
- Chapter 4 Test
- Chapter 4 ExamView® Pro Testmaker CD-ROM
- Chapter 4 Digests Audiocassettes Activities and Tests

SPANISH RESOURCES

- Chapter 4 Spanish Chapter Summary and Glossary
- Chapter 4 Spanish Digests Audiocassettes Activities and Tests

TEACH

Guided Practice

L1 **Geography: Environment and Society** Have students locate the Nile River on the map of Africa on page 716 in the text Atlas. Point out the Delta of the Nile. Next, write the following phrase on the board: *Egypt: the gift of the Nile.* Inform students that this is a phrase coined by the historian Herodotus, and elicit from them the possible meanings of the phrase. Ask students how the Egyptians made use of the Nile River.

CAPTION ANSWER

the desert, the sea, and waterfalls called cataracts

Reading Check Answer

A **shadoof** was used to lift water from the Nile to basins or bowl-shaped holes.

LINKING PAST TO PRESENT

The Aswan High Dam in southeastern Egypt was built in the 1960s partly to protect crops and people against seasonal flooding. The lack of this flooding, however, means that fertile soil is no longer deposited annually. Instead, farmers in the area rely on chemical fertilizers to make the soil fertile. Ask students to describe how the dam has changed the environment around the Nile.

Use **Interactive Tutor Self-Assessment CD-ROM** to review Section 1.

NILE RIVER Over thousands of years, the flooding of the Nile River has left rich soil all along its banks. The Nile River valley is only 3 percent of Egypt's land, yet most Egyptians live and work in this area. **What geographical features protected the Egyptians in the Nile River delta?**

The Egyptians had an advantage over the people of the other river valley civilizations. Every year, about the middle of July, the Nile overflowed its banks. The flood waters went down but left behind large amounts of rich soil good for growing crops.

Egyptian farmers planted their fields while the soil was still wet. To water their crops during the dry season, the Egyptians dug out *basins,* or bowl-shaped holes. They used a machine called a **shadoof** (shuh dūf') to lift water from the Nile to the basins. The Egyptians raised flax, wheat, barley, and grapes.

Reading Check How was a **shadoof** used?

Section 1 Assessment

1. **Define:** shadoof.
2. Where did most Egyptians live?
3. How did the Egyptians control the Nile?

Critical Thinking

4. **Making Comparisons** How did the Egyptians' use of the Nile River compare with the Sumerians' use of the Tigris and Euphrates rivers?

Graphic Organizer Activity

5. Draw a diagram like this one, and use it to show how the Nile River influenced Egyptian civilization. (Add more lines as needed.)

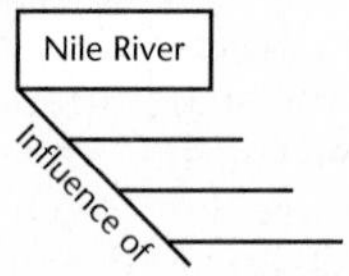

Section 1 Assessment Answers

1. shadoof, machine used to lift water (p. 68)
2. in the Nile delta
3. by building a system of basins and irrigation canals
4. Answers will vary, but could note both Egyptians and Sumerians depended on the rivers for living, and both civilizations controlled their environment. The Egyptians dug out basins and built irrigation canals to the fields. The Sumerians also built irrigation canals. The Egyptians raised flax, wheat, barley, and grapes. The Sumerians grew barley, wheat, sesame, flax, fruit trees, date palms, and vegetables.
5. Sample responses: cataracts served as protection, flooding left behind good soil, provided water to grow crops in dry season.

Assign the Chapter 4 **Section 1 Quiz** in the TCR. Testmaker available.

SECTION 2 The Old Kingdom

At first, Egypt was made up of two kingdoms. One was Upper Egypt, which lay in the southern part of the Nile River valley. The other was Lower Egypt, which lay in the north delta.

Narmer, also known as Menes (mē′ nēz), was a king of Upper Egypt. About 3100 B.C., he led his armies from the valley north into the delta. He conquered Lower Egypt and married one of its princesses, uniting the two kingdoms. He wore a double crown, the high white one of the south and the shallow red one of the north. Narmer had many titles. He was called "Lord of Upper and Lower Egypt," "Wearer of Both Crowns," and "Lord of the Two Lands." He set up a new capital at Memphis, a city on the border between Upper and Lower Egypt.

About 2600 B.C., the Old Kingdom started in Egypt. It lasted for nearly 500 years. During the period of the Old Kingdom, Egyptian cities became centers of religion and government. Kings, priests, government officials, and artisans lived there.

Most Egyptians, however, did not live in cities. They lived on large estates along the banks of the Nile. The rich Egyptians who owned these estates lived in wood and brick houses with beautiful gardens and pools. Walls were decorated with brightly

Then & Now

Diets Change The diet of poor laborers and farmers in ancient Egypt consisted largely of bread, made of wheat and a grain called emmer. Today most villagers and poor city dwellers in Egypt eat a simple diet based on bread and fool, or broad beans. For a typical evening meal, each person dips bread into a large communal bowl of vegetable stew.

EGYPTIAN LIFE Paintings from tombs offer much information about everyday life in ancient Egypt. Here, a wall painting shows a man and woman plowing and planting their fields. **How did the lives of the rich differ from those of the poor in Egypt?**

GEOGRAPHY AND HISTORY

Direct students to the map of ancient Egypt on page 75. Explain that because the Nile River flows from central Africa into the Mediterranean Sea, or from south to north, the southern part of Egypt is actually Upper Egypt, and the northern half is actually Lower Egypt.

CAPTION ANSWER

The rich owned large estates and lived in elegant houses, while the poor farmed the land and lived in small mud-brick houses.

MAKING CONNECTIONS

➤➤ **Geography: The World in Spatial Terms** The Nile is the longest river in the world. Its two branches are the Blue Nile, which begins in the Ethiopian highlands, and the White Nile, which rises in Uganda and meets the Blue Nile at present-day Khartoum.

Use the **Vocabulary Puzzle-Maker CD-ROM** to create crossword and word search puzzles.

EXTENDING THE CONTENT

One reason we know a great deal about homes in ancient Egypt is that small models—called soul houses—often were included in the things buried with a person to assure him or her of a pleasant afterlife. The houses of both rich and poor were comfortable in the dry, hot climate. With almost no rain, it was practical to build mud-brick walls and flat roofs with vents to catch the breeze. Egyptians had less furniture in their homes than people today have—a few brightly colored chairs and stools, small tables, oil lamps, and chests for storing clothes. Beds were like cots, with tightly stretched cord springs.

DID YOU KNOW ??

The Egyptians wore loincloths or slips of linen made from flax. The linen was strong, did not soil easily, and kept the wearer cool. On their feet, the Egyptians wore reed or leather sandals with curled-up toes, although they usually walked barefoot.

Linking Across Time

The flood water left behind good soil for growing crops.

Reading Check Answer Egyptians viewed the **pharaoh** as a ruler, a priest, and a god.

NATIONAL GEOGRAPHIC

Use these materials to enrich student understanding of ancient Egyptian culture.

NGS PICTURESHOW CD-ROM
Egypt and the Fertile Crescent

NGS PICTUREPACK TRANSPARENCY SET
Ancient Egypt

Linking Across Time

Harvesting Wheat Both men and women harvested the wheat crops that helped fuel the growth of ancient Egypt (left). Today some Egyptian farmers still harvest this crop by hand with a sickle (right), much as their ancestors did more than 3,000 years ago. **What is the connection between the flooding of the Nile and the production of wheat?**

colored paintings that showed scenes of daily life. A household was made up of an owner's family, servants, and artisans. The artisans were hired to build boats, weave linen, and make tools and pottery.

Most Egyptians, however, were farmers who lived in villages on the estates. At first, their houses were made of reeds and mud. Later, they were made of sun-baked mud-brick. These houses generally had only one room with a roof made of palm leaves. They were built on high ground so that they would be safe from the yearly flood. Egyptian farmers worked in the fields and took care of the cattle. When they were not farming, they built monuments, dug ditches, and repaired roads.

Reading Check How did the Egyptians view the **pharaoh?**

The Pharaoh

The Egyptians believed that the strength and unity of their country came from having a strong ruler. At first, Egyptian rulers were called kings. Later, they were called **pharaoh** (fār′ ō), meaning "great house." To Egyptians, the pharaoh was a ruler, a priest, and a god. He was the center of Egyptian life and ruled on Earth the way other gods ruled in heaven.

The pharaoh owned all the land in Egypt, but he gave gifts of land to rich Egyptians and priests. To make sure the land produced well, the pharaoh saw to it that dams and irrigation canals were built and repaired. The pharaoh also ordered the building of brick *granaries,* or buildings for storing grain. These were used to store grain from good harvests so people would not starve in times of bad harvests.

MULTICULTURAL PERSPECTIVES

One thing that made the position of women strong in Egypt was the economic power of inheritance. Custom dictated that property descend from mother to daughter. Thus, to keep property in the family, pharaohs often married relatives.

The pharaoh also chose all government officials. They made certain that taxes were gathered and building permits were given out. Trade with other lands was in the pharaoh's hands. The word of a pharaoh was law.

The Egyptians believed that what happened to Egypt depended on the pharaoh's actions. As chief priest, the pharaoh carried out certain rituals. For example, he made the first break in the irrigation dikes each year to open the land to the water. When the water went down, he drove a sacred bull around the capital city. The Egyptians believed this ritual would make the soil rich so they could grow good crops. The pharaoh was the first to cut the ripe grain. Egyptians believed this would bring a good harvest.

Pharaohs were treated with great respect. Whenever they appeared in public, people played music on flutes and cymbals. They also bowed and "smelled the earth," or touched their heads to the ground.

Fun Facts. . . .

A Big Pyramid
The Pyramid of Khufu (see photo) contains more than 2 million stone blocks that average 2 1/2 short tons, or 2.3 metric tons, each. The pyramid originally stood 481 feet, or 147 meters, high. Today its base covers about 13 acres, or 5 hectares.

The Pyramids

Another way the people of the Old Kingdom showed how they felt about the pharaohs was by building them great tombs called **pyramids** (pir' uh midz). Because the sun sank in the west, these "Houses of Eternity" were built on the west bank of the Nile. They were designed to protect the pharaohs' bodies from floods, wild animals, and robbers. The Egyptians believed the pharaohs would be happy after death if they had their personal belongings. Therefore, they placed a pharaoh's clothing, weapons, furniture, and jewelry in the pyramids.

Reading Check What was the purpose of the **pyramids?**

PYRAMIDS AT GIZA The pyramids were built at Giza on the Nile River. The largest pyramid once enshrined the body of King Khufu. **What items were probably buried with the King?**

Reading Check Answer The **pyramids** were tombs for the pharaohs.

L3 **Critical Thinking** Write the following criteria of a civilization on the board: *a writing system, a well-organized government, art and literature, and specialization of labor.* Ask students to write a brief explanation of how ancient Egypt met these criteria.

CAPTION ANSWER

Egyptians buried personal items, items of wealth, and any utilitarian and comfort items the pharaoh might need in the afterlife.

A&E HOME VIDEO.

The following videotape program is available from Glencoe to enrich Chapter 4:

- **Pyramids of Giza**

To find classroom resources to accompany this video, check the following home page:

A&E Television:
www.aande.com

COOPERATIVE LEARNING

Encourage students to study the illustrations in this chapter. Point out that ancient Egyptian paintings presented the human face and limbs in profile, while the upper torso, shoulders, and eyes were presented in front view. Suggest that they find more examples of ancient Egyptian art such as in *The Atlas of Ancient Egypt* by John Baines and Jaromír Málek. Once they are familiar with this art style, have students plan and create a mural using the Egyptian style of art to illustrate a scene from Egyptian daily life.

L1 **Daily Life** Inform students that the organization of Egyptian society was like the structure of a pyramid. Draw a pyramid on the chalkboard and label it with Egyptian social positions as students relate them, starting with royalty at the top. Discuss the lifestyle of each.

DID YOU KNOW ??

Enslaved persons were not employed in building the pyramids. Enslavement did not become common in Egypt until the New Kingdom, when conquests in Syria and Palestine brought in prisoners of war. Then enslaved persons built monuments and temples for the pharaohs in the New Kingdom.

MAKING CONNECTIONS

➤➤ **Language Arts** The term *underworld* had a different meaning for the ancient Egyptians than it has for most people today. To the Egyptians, it meant the cool, tree-shaded land of Osiris, where even the poor could rest.

CAPTION ANSWER

They tried to lead a good life and learn certain magic spells.

It took many people and much work to build the pyramids. Farmers worked on them during the three summer months that their fields were flooded. The workers used copper tools to cut huge granite and limestone blocks from quarries across the Nile valley or in Upper Egypt. The blocks of rock were tied with ropes onto wooden sleds, pulled to the Nile, placed on barges filled with sand, and floated across the river. Other workers then unloaded the blocks and pulled them to the place where the pyramids were being built. Huge mud and brick ramps were built beside each of the pyramids. The workers dragged the blocks up the ramps to each new layer of the pyramid.

Then & Now

Mummies Today scientists are able to perform CAT scans on mummy cases, allowing the scientists to see inside without opening the mummy case. Using computers, they turn the two-dimensional CAT-scan pictures into three-dimensional images of the mummies.

Religious Beliefs The Egyptians believed in many gods. Two of the most important gods were the river god Hapi (hop' ē) and the sun god Re (rā). The Egyptians depended on the river and the sun. The river brought them water and fertile soil, while the sun helped their crops to grow.

Another important god was Osiris (ō sī ris), god of the harvest and of eternal life. According to Egyptian legend, Osiris was an early pharaoh who gave his people laws and taught them farming. He and his wife Isis (ī'sis) ruled over the dead. The Egyptians believed that the souls of the dead went to the underworld. There, they were weighed on a scale. If a person had led a good life and knew certain magic spells, the scales balanced. Then, Osiris would grant the person life after death. To learn the correct magic spells, Egyptians studied a special book called the *Book of the Dead.*

EGYPTIAN GODS The god Osiris ruled over the Egyptian underworld. Here, he sits in judgment as other animal-headed gods weigh a dead man's soul and record the results. The scales have balanced, so the dead man may enter the underworld. **How did Egyptians prepare for life after death?**

MEETING SPECIAL NEEDS

Encourage students who are tactile/kinesthetic learners to make dioramas, models, or diagrams of a pyramid under construction as described in the subsection titled "The Pyramids." Display the students' creations in the classroom.

Refer to ***Inclusion for the Middle School Social Studies Classroom: Strategies and Activities*** for additional resources.

The Egyptians also used a process called **embalming** (em balm' ēng) to preserve the bodies of the dead. At first, they used the process to preserve the body of the pharaoh because they believed the soul could not live without the body. It was important for a pharaoh's soul to live after death. In that way, the pharaoh would continue to take care of Egypt.

Later, embalming was used to preserve other people as well as the pharaoh. To embalm a body, the Egyptians placed it in a wooden box and covered it with a chemical called natron. Natron dried up the water in the body, causing it to shrink. After the shrunken body had dried, it was wrapped with long strips of linen. The wrapped body was known as a **mummy.** The mummy of a poor person was often buried in a cave or in the sand. The mummy of a rich person was placed inside a special case or coffin. The coffin was then placed in a tomb.

Reading Check Why did the Egyptians develop the practice of **embalming?**

Reading Check What is a **mummy?**

Section 2 Assessment

1. **Define:** pharaoh, pyramids, embalming, mummy.
2. How did most Egyptians live during the Old Kingdom?
3. What did the Egyptians believe happened to a person after death?

Critical Thinking

4. **Making Comparisons** How were the pharaohs similar to and different from government leaders of the United States today?

Graphic Organizer Activity

5. Draw this diagram, and use it to compare the Egyptian burial practices for the rich and the poor.

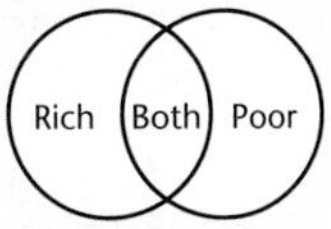

SECTION 3 The Middle Kingdom

About 2300 B.C., government officials, jealous of the pharaoh's power, took control of Egypt. Almost 200 years of confusion followed. Finally, new pharaohs brought peace and a new period called the Middle Kingdom.

Pharaohs had less power in the Middle Kingdom. After death, they were no longer buried in pyramids but in tombs cut into cliffs. Then the Egyptians began to trade with countries beyond the Nile valley.

The Middle Kingdom came to an end in 1786 B.C., when Egypt was invaded by the Hyksos (hik' sōs), a people from western Asia. The Hyksos crossed the desert in horse-drawn chariots and used weapons made of bronze and iron. Egyptians had always fought on foot with weapons made of copper and stone and were defeated.

Egyptian Bronze Art

Reading Check Answer Egyptians developed **embalming** to preserve the bodies of the dead and to protect the soul.

Reading Check Answer A **mummy** is the wrapped body of an embalmed dead person.

Use **Interactive Tutor Self-Assessment CD-ROM** to review Section 2.

L3 **Critical Thinking** Have students locate Egypt on the map of the Middle East on pages 714–715 in the text Atlas. Ask students how Egypt's location provided opportunities for the exchange of ideas, knowledge, skills, and customs between Africa, Asia, and other civilizations.

A&E HOME VIDEO.

The following videotape program is available from Glencoe to enrich Chapter 4:

- **Mummies and the Wonders of Ancient Egypt**

To find classroom resources to accompany this video, check the following home page:

A&E Television:
www.aande.com

Use the **Vocabulary PuzzleMaker CD-ROM** to create crossword and word search puzzles.

Section 2 Assessment Answers

1. pharaoh, Egyptian king (p. 70); pyramids, tombs for pharaohs (p. 71); embalming, process to preserve bodies (p. 73); mummy, body wrapped with linen (p. 73)
2. Most Egyptians lived as farmers in villages on large estates along the Nile.
3. Their souls went to the underworld and were weighed on a scale. If the scales balanced, Osiris granted life after death.
4. Sample responses: Both provide for citizens and deal with foreign policy/trade. U.S. leaders are not considered gods.
5. Both were embalmed. The poor were buried in a cave or in the sand; the rich were placed in special coffins inside a tomb.

Assign the Chapter 4 **Section 2 Quiz** in the TCR. Testmaker available.

GEOGRAPHY AND HISTORY

The term *Hyksos* is believed to have come from the Egyptian words meaning "Princes from Foreign Uplands." These rulers were most likely desert warriors from the Semitic tribes of nomadic herders in nearby Palestine and Syria.

Use **Interactive Tutor Self-Assessment CD-ROM** to review Section 3.

Use the **Vocabulary PuzzleMaker CD-ROM** to create crossword and word search puzzles.

DID YOU KNOW ??

In order to show her authority and keep her name alive, Hatshepsut wore male clothes and a ceremonial false beard and built a huge temple amid the cliffs at Deir el Bahri.

The Hyksos ruled Egypt for about 150 years. They copied some Egyptian customs but most Egyptians hated them. Around 1550 B.C., an Egyptian prince named Ahmose (ah mo' suh), using Hyksos weapons, led an uprising and drove the Hyksos out of Egypt.

Section 3 Assessment

1. How did the Middle Kingdom come about?
2. What ended Hyksos rule?

Critical Thinking

3. **Demonstrating Reasoned Judgment** Do you think the decrease in the pharaohs' power had a positive or negative effect on Egypt? Explain.

Graphic Organizer Activity

4. Draw a diagram like this one, and use it to compare the power of the pharaohs in the Old Kingdom and the Middle Kingdom.

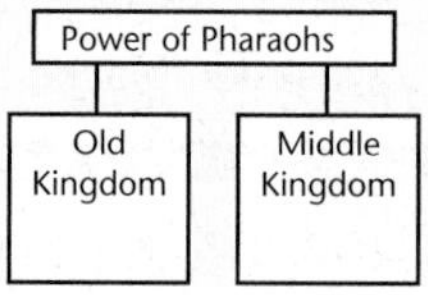

SECTION 4 The New Kingdom

Ahmose founded another line of pharaohs and began the period known as the New Kingdom. During this time, Egypt became richer and its cities grew larger.

During the New Kingdom, most pharaohs were no longer content to remain within the Nile valley but marched their armies into lands to the east. It was during this period that the Egyptian empire was founded. One warrior-pharaoh, Thutmose III (thūt mō' suh), with an army of 20,000 archers, spear throwers, and charioteers, extended Egyptian control into Syria (sir' ē uh) and Palestine (pal' uh stīn).

One of the few pharaohs who was not interested in war and conquest was Hatshepsut (hat shep' sūt), Thutmose III's stepmother, who had ruled Egypt before her stepson. Her chief interests were trade and the building of temples. During her rule, Egyptian traders sailed along the coast of east Africa to the land of Punt. In the land of Punt, the Egyptians traded beads and metal tools and weapons for such things as ivory, a black wood called *ebony* (eb' uh nē), monkeys, hunting dogs, leopard skins, and *incense,* or material burned for its pleasant smell. The Egyptians had never seen most of these things. They welcomed the returning traders with a huge reception.

Statue of Hatshepsut

Religion The Egyptians of the New Kingdom began to worship a new god. As the god of the city of Thebes, he had been called Amon. When Thebes became the capital of Egypt,

Section 3 Assessment Answers

1. A new line of pharaohs unified Egypt after a period of confusion.
2. Ahmose led an uprising and drove the Hyksos out of Egypt.
3. Answers will vary, but should include why the pharaoh had either a positive or a negative effect on Egypt.
4. Sample responses: *Old Kingdom*—considered a ruler, priest, and god; owned all the land and chose all the officials; treated with great respect; buried in pyramids; *Middle Kingdom*—had less power, buried in tombs cut into cliffs.

Assign the Chapter 4 **Section 3 Quiz** in the TCR. Testmaker available.

Reading Map Legends

In order to show information on maps, mapmakers use symbols. These are marks that stand for such things as places, directions, and features. Symbols include lines, dots, stars, and small pictures.

A list of symbols and what they stand for is called a **legend.** By reading legends, it is possible to identify empires, nations, religions, climates, and any other information that can be shown on a map.

For example, on the "Ancient Egypt" map below, notice that there are three symbols in the legend. Each symbol stands for the boundary of one of the Egyptian kingdoms. The broken line stands for the southern boundary of the Old Kingdom. The Middle Kingdom's boundary is shown by the dotted line. The area of the New Kingdom is shown in green.

MAP SKILLS

Map Practice

1. **Which Egyptian kingdom included only the first cataract?**
2. **Which kingdom extended to the second cataract?**
3. **In which kingdom was Thebes located?**

Ancient Egypt

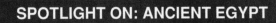

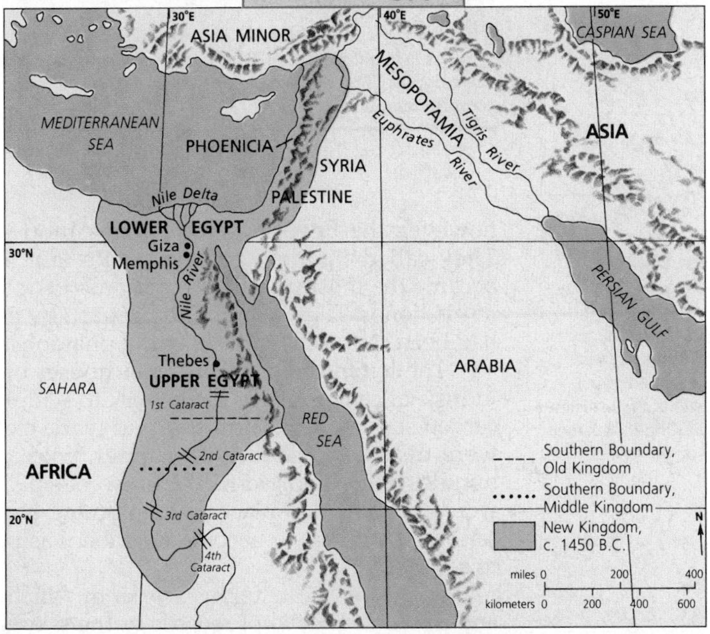

GO TO

Glencoe's **Skillbuilder Interactive Workbook CD-ROM, Level 1,** provides instruction and practice in key social studies skills.

75

MAP SKILLS

TEACH

READING MAP LEGENDS

Instruct the students to study the map on page 75 to answer the following questions:

What symbol should be added to the legend for cataracts? *(two short parallel lines)*

What symbol should be added to the legend for cities? *(a black dot)*

Next, have the students refer to the map of Mesopotamia on page 62 to answer the following questions:

What symbol is used to show Hammurabi's Empire? *(the color brown)*

What symbol is used to show an ancient coastline? *(a dashed line)*

Assign Chapter 4 **Geography and Map Activity** in the TCR.

Answers to Map Practice

1. Old Kingdom
2. Middle Kingdom
3. all three kingdoms

SPOTLIGHT ON: ANCIENT EGYPT

Although Egypt's desert land is often thought of in connection with the camel, this animal was not actually brought to Egypt until 525 B.C. The most common beast of burden in ancient Egypt was the donkey. Lions also prowled the deserts of ancient Egypt, and cats, who were often mummified after they died, were a favorite house pet.

TEACH

GUIDED PRACTICE

L3 **Critical Thinking** Have students write letters to the editor of a newspaper explaining their position on this question: Did religion play a greater role in Egyptian society than it does in our society today? Ask students to support their response with reasons.

CAPTION ANSWER

The temples were built by enslaved persons.

MAKING CONNECTIONS

➤➤ **Language Arts** It was difficult to become a scribe. A student enrolled in school at age 5 and attended classes from sunup to sundown until age 17. Scribes, associated with the ruling class, did not have to work in the fields and were paid more than most Egyptians.

TEMPLE AT KOM OMBO Warring pharaohs of the New Kingdom built large temples to honor their gods. The stone block in front of this temple shows Egyptian hieroglyphs. This temple has many statues and monuments. **Who provided the labor to build temples?**

Fun Facts . . . .

The Best Dentist
Egyptians could have benefited from regular trips to the dentist. Everyone, rich and poor, suffered from cavities, inflamed gums, and infections. A physician in the Old Kingdom named Hesire won the title of "Chief of the Tooth-doctors."

however, the Egyptians combined Amon with the sun god Re. They called the new god Amon-Re (ah′ muhn rā′). Amon-Re became the most powerful god of all. People built many temples in his honor. These were built, in part, by enslaved persons who had been captured by the warring pharaohs.

The temples were more than houses of worship. They were industrial centers. They gave work to sculptors and artisans who carved statues, built furniture, and made clothes for priests. They were treasuries, filled with copper, gold jewelry, glass bottles, bundles of grain, dried fish, and sweet-smelling oils. The temples were also schools—places where young boys were trained to be scribes. The right to become a scribe was passed on from father to son.

Scribes wrote religious works in which were spells, charms, and prayers. They kept records of the pharaohs' laws and lists of

MULTICULTURAL PERSPECTIVES

The wigs, cosmetics, and jewelry worn by the ancient Egyptians present a vivid image of these people. Generally, both men and women wore simply cut tunics and sheaths of draped, pleated, natural linen. Egyptian men and women's jewelry, wigs, and makeup, however, were elaborate and striking. They wore wigs or hairpieces with curls. Some Egyptians shaved their heads. Bold green (from powdered malachite) and black eyeliners were often worn. Red ocher was applied as lipstick and blusher. Henna colored their hair. Many Egyptians wore large necklaces that covered their chests. Earrings first became popular in the New Kingdom.

the grain and animals paid as taxes. They copied fairy tales and adventure stories and wrote down medical prescriptions.

There were several kinds of Egyptian writing. One was **hieroglyphic** (hī uhr uh glif′ ik), or a kind of writing in which pictures stand for words or sounds. The Egyptians carved and painted hieroglyphs, or picture symbols, on their monuments. However, scribes needed an easier form of writing to keep records. So, they developed two other kinds of writing in which hieroglyphs were rounded off and connected.

Decline of Egypt Over time, the priests of Amon-Re gained much power and wealth. They owned one third of Egypt's land and began to play a major role in the government. As time passed, the pharaohs' power declined.

Then, about 1370 B.C., a new pharaoh named Amenhotep IV (ah muhn hō′ tep) came to the throne. He did not like the priests. He did not agree with them on what was good for Egypt. He wanted to return power to the pharaohs. Amenhotep IV closed the temples of Amon-Re and fired all temple workers. He set up a new religion that was different from the old religion because only one god was worshiped. This god was called Aton (ah′ tuhn). Amenhotep IV changed his name to Akhenaton (ahk nah′ tuhn), which means "Spirit of Aton." Only his family and close advisers, however, accepted the new religion.

HIEROGLYPHS Ancient Egyptians viewed hieroglyphs as gifts from the gods. The pictures were first used as a way of keeping records. Later, they represented the sounds of spoken language. Here, hieroglyphs are painted on a coffin lid. **How did hieroglyphs differ from cuneiform?**

Reading Check What was **hieroglyphic** writing?

People in History

Tutankhamen
c. 1369 B.C.–1351 B.C.

Egyptian Pharaoh

Nicknamed the "boy king," Tutankhamen came to power at age 9. He pleased the priests by rejecting Akhenaton's religion. Although frail, he loved to race chariots and hunt animals. When he died at age 18, officials placed him in a treasure-filled tomb. The tomb's beautiful contents, discovered in 1922, made "King Tut" one of Egypt's most famous pharaohs.

Reading Check Answer
Hieroglyphic writing used pictures to stand for words or sounds.

Independent Practice

L1 **Writing** Instruct students to devise a rebus writing system and to write a sample sentence or phrase. Call on volunteers to write their samples and keys on the chalkboard. Discuss similarities and differences in the rebuses used. ELL

L2 **Language Arts** Write the following scenarios on the chalkboard:

1. You are a historian studying the New Kingdom of Egypt before the reign of Amenhotep IV. Describe the main events in the growth of Egyptian civilization.

2. You are a historian studying the New Kingdom of Egypt after the reign of Amenhotep IV. Describe the most important events in the decline of Egyptian civilization.

Tell students to choose one scenario and write the description of events. Have volunteers read their histories to the class.

CAPTION ANSWER

Hieroglyphs were picture symbols, while cuneiform was made up of hundreds of markings shaped like wedges.

COOPERATIVE LEARNING

Have the students write and perform a play about one of the people listed in the section. Divide the class into small groups. Have each group be responsible for researching the person chosen. Group members can volunteer for a specific task in the project, such as writing the script, acting, making costumes, finding props, writing and designing programs, and designing sets. At each stage of the project, all students should be given an opportunity to react to the group task. Then have the students present the play to other classes.

Assign Chapter 4 *Cooperative Learning Activity* in the TCR.

After Amenhotep IV died, about 1360 B.C., his son-in-law Tutankhamen (tū tahng kah′ muhn) became pharaoh. He was only nine years old. The priests made Tutankhamen return to the old religion. He died after ruling for only nine years.

Little by little, Egypt lost its power. One reason was the struggle between the priests and the pharaohs. Another was the pharaohs' attempts to keep neighboring countries under Egyptian control. Much energy and money was spent on war. Then, too, other peoples of the eastern Mediterranean were using iron weapons. Since Egypt had no iron ore, money was spent to bring in small amounts to make weapons.

By 1150 B.C., Egypt's empire was gone. Egyptian civilization kept growing weaker until Egypt was taken over by a people known as the Assyrians (uh sē′ rē uhnz) in 671 B.C.

Section 4 Assessment

1. **Define:** hieroglyphic.
2. How did rulers of the New Kingdom expand trade?
3. Why did Egypt grow weak?

Critical Thinking

4. **Drawing Conclusions** In your opinion, which of the following pharaohs contributed the most to Egyptian civilization: Thutmose III, Hatshepsut, Amenhotep IV, or Tutankhamen? Explain.

Graphic Organizer Activity

5. Draw this diagram, and use it to show important events in the history of the New Kingdom. (Add boxes as needed.)

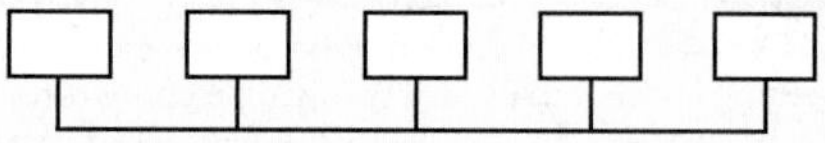

SECTION 5 Contributions

Reading Check How was **papyrus** made?

The Egyptians made many contributions to other civilizations. One was a paper called **papyrus** (puh pī′ ruhs). It was made from a reed also called papyrus. In order to write on papyrus, the Egyptians invented ink. The dry climate of Egypt preserved some writings so well that they can still be read today.

Papyrus had other uses. It was made into baskets and sandals. It was also tied in bundles to make columns for houses. Even rafts and riverboats were made of papyrus.

Other contributions of the Egyptians lay in the field of mathematics. They used a number system based on ten. They also

LINKING PAST TO PRESENT

Popular interest in ancient Egypt soared with the discovery in 1922 of the sealed tomb of the ruler Tutankhamen. Though "King Tut" was a minor figure in history, the discovery influenced fashion, jewelry, home decoration, and even popular music. Sensational newspapers warned of a curse on those who had opened the tomb.

The treasures of Tutankhamen, now mostly exhibited in the Egyptian Museum in Cairo, are still visited by thousands of people every year.

Use **Interactive Tutor Self-Assessment CD-ROM** to review Section 4.

Reading Check Answer
Papyrus was made from a reed also called papyrus.

A&E HOME VIDEO.

The following videotape program is available from Glencoe to enrich Chapter 4:

- **King Tut: The Face of Tutankhamen**

To find classroom resources to accompany this video, check the following home page:

A&E Television:
www.aande.com

Use the **Vocabulary PuzzleMaker CD-ROM** to create crossword and word search puzzles.

Section 4 Assessment Answers

1. hieroglyphic, a kind of writing in which pictures stand for words or sounds (p. 77)
2. through conquest and by expanding contacts with other people
3. struggles between priests and pharaohs, costly wars, lack of iron for weapons
4. Answers will vary, but could note one of the pharaohs and explain how he or she contributed to the New Kingdom.
5. Answers will vary, but will probably center around the achievements of pharaohs of the New Kingdom. Suggest that students begin with the founding of a new line of pharaohs by Ahmose.

Assign the Chapter 4 **Section 4 Quiz** in the TCR. Testmaker available.

used fractions and whole numbers. They used geometry to *survey,* or measure, land. When floods washed away the boundary markers that separated one field from the next, the Egyptians surveyed the fields to see where one began and the other ended.

The Egyptians knew the Nile flooded about the same time every year. They used this knowledge to make a calendar. The calendar had three seasons of 120 days each, and 5 special feast days for the gods.

The Egyptians also made contributions in the field of medicine. As dentists, eye doctors, animal doctors, and surgeons, Egyptian doctors were the first specialists in medicine. They were

HISTORY Online

Student Web Activity

Visit the *Human Heritage* Web site at humanheritage.glencoe.com and click on ***Chapter 4—Student Web Activities*** to find out more about Egyptian contributions.

MEDICAL PRACTICE IN ANCIENT EGYPT Egyptian skill in medicine was highly valued in the Mediterranean area for 2,500 years. Here, an Egyptian doctor gives medicine to a patient. The doctor's assistant holds a scroll listing directions for treating the illness. **What kind of medical help did Egyptian doctors give their patients?**

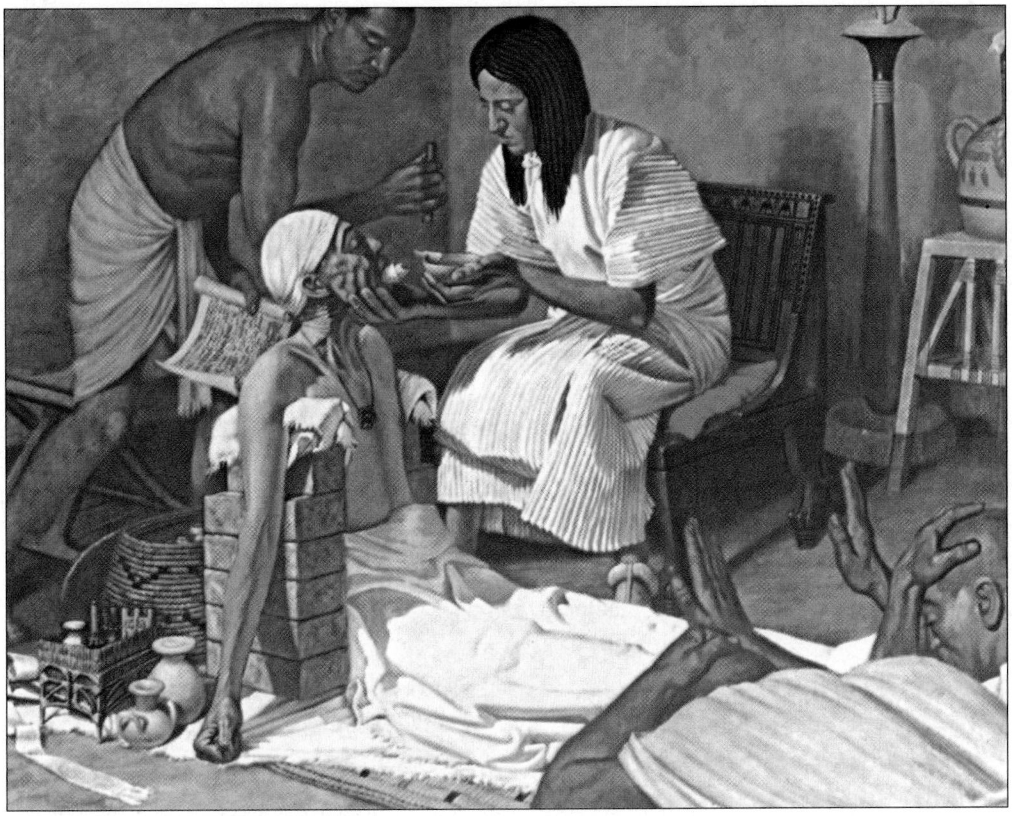

HISTORY Online

Student Web Activity objectives and answers can be found at the ***Chapter 4 Web Activity Lesson Plan*** at humanheritage.glencoe.com

CAPTION ANSWER

Egyptians had dentists, eye doctors, animal doctors, and surgeons. Their physicians were the first to use splints, bandages, and compresses. They also treated such problems as indigestion and hair loss.

ASSESS

Check for Understanding

Ask students to summarize the main points of the chapter, orally or in writing. Discuss the answers to the Section and Chapter Assessments.

Evaluate

Assign the Chapter 4 **Performance Assessment Activity** in the TCR.

Administer the **Chapter 4 Test** in the TCR. Testmaker available.

MEETING SPECIAL NEEDS

If possible, obtain a copy of the book *Ancient Lives: Daily Life in Egypt of the Pharaohs* by John Romer. Gather students who are auditory learners and read excerpts from the book to help the students understand the social customs and daily lives of Egyptians. Involve students in a discussion about how their way of life compares to the lives of ancient Egyptians.

Refer to ***Inclusion for the Middle School Social Studies Classroom: Strategies and Activities*** for additional resources.

Reteach

For each section, have students write a sentence that summarizes the main concept. Call on volunteers to read their sentences. Have the class choose the best summary sentences for each section.

Assign Chapter 4 **Reteaching Activity** in the TCR.

Enrich

Have students research one of the people mentioned in the chapter and write a biographical sketch about them.

Assign Chapter 4 **Enrichment Activity** in the TCR.

CLOSE

Have students discuss the following question: Which contribution of the Egyptians to other civilizations was the most important? Why?

Use **Interactive Tutor Self-Assessment CD-ROM** to review Section 5.

HISTORY Online

Self-Check Quiz gives students an interactive chapter tutorial. Have them access ***Chapter 4 Quiz*** at humanheritage.glencoe.com

the first to use splints, bandages, and compresses. They were masters at sewing up cuts and at setting broken bones. The Egyptians also treated such problems as indigestion and hair loss. For indigestion, they used castor oil. For hair loss, they used a mixture of dog toes, dates, and a donkey hoof.

Section 5 Assessment

1. **Define:** papyrus.
2. What mathematical contributions did the Egyptians make to civilization?
3. What medical contributions did the Egyptians make to other civilizations?

Critical Thinking

4. **Demonstrating Reasoned Judgment** Which Egyptian contribution do you think has had the greatest impact on life in the United States today?

Graphic Organizer Activity

5. Draw a diagram like this one, and use it to rate Egyptian contributions from most important to least important. (Add lines as needed.)

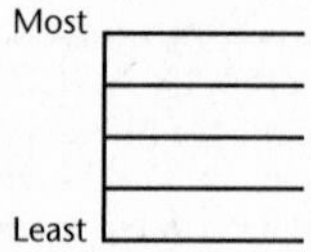

Chapter Summary & Study Guide

1. Egyptian civilization began in the Nile River valley over 5,000 years ago.
2. About 3100 B.C., Narmer united Upper and Lower Egypt.
3. The Old Kingdom began about 2600 B.C. and lasted for nearly 650 years.
4. Kings of Egypt became known as pharaohs and were viewed by Egyptians as rulers, priests, and gods.
5. During the Old Kingdom, pyramids were built as tombs for pharaohs.
6. The Egyptians worshiped many gods.
7. The Egyptians placed great importance on life after death and created a process to preserve bodies as mummies.
8. The Middle Kingdom began about 1950 B.C. and lasted until the Hyksos invasion of Egypt in 1786 B.C.
9. The New Kingdom began after Ahmose drove the Hyksos out of Egypt about 1550 B.C.
10. During the New Kingdom, most pharaohs were interested in conquest.
11. During the New Kingdom, priests became very powerful.
12. Amenhotep IV tried to establish a religion based on one god, but he failed.
13. Toward the end of the New Kingdom, Egypt began to decline.
14. Egyptian contributions to later civilizations included the use of geometry, surveying, and papyrus.

HISTORY Online

Self-Check Quiz

Visit the *Human Heritage* Web site at humanheritage.glencoe.com and click on ***Chapter 4—Self-Check Quiz*** to assess your understanding of this chapter.

Section 5 Assessment Answers

1. papyrus, Egyptian paper (p. 78)
2. They used a number system based on 10, fractions and whole numbers, and geometry to survey the land.
3. They were the first to use splints, bandages, compresses, setting of broken bones, and treatment of indigestion and hair loss.
4. Answers will vary but could include the mention of any modern conveniences that were made possible by Egyptian ingenuity.
5. Answers will vary, but encourage students to name their choice for most important contribution and reasons for their selection.

Assign Chapter 4 **Section 5 Quiz** in the TCR. Testmaker available.

CHAPTER 4 Assessment

Using Key Terms

Use the following list of words to write a newspaper article describing the contributions of the Egyptians.

sadoof	pharaoh	pyramids
embalming	mummy	legend
hieroglyphic	papyrus	

Understanding Main Ideas

1. What did the Egyptians borrow from the Sumerians?
2. What did the Nile River give to the Egyptian people?
3. Why did the Egyptians show such great respect for the pharaoh?
4. What role did the Hyksos play in the development of Egyptian civilization?
5. What role did religion play in Egypt during the Old Kingdom? During the New Kingdom?
6. What kinds of writing did the Egyptians have, and why were they used?
7. What problems did flooding of the Nile River create, and how did the Egyptians try to solve them?
8. How did the Egyptians use the papyrus reed?

Critical Thinking

1. Do you agree with experts who call Egypt "the gift of the Nile"? Explain.
2. How was the government of Egypt similar to that of Babylonia? How was it different?
3. Do you think Amenhotep IV was wise in opposing the priests of Amon-Re? Explain.
4. Would you have liked living in ancient Egypt? Why or why not?

Graphic Organizer Activity

History Create a chart like this one, and use it to compare characteristics of the Old Kingdom, Middle Kingdom, and New Kingdom of Egypt.

Old Kingdom	Middle Kingdom	New Kingdom

Geography in History

Environment and Society Note the area covered by ancient Egypt on the map on page 75. Why do you think the empire developed where it did, rather than expanding to the west or only to the south? Explain your answer.

Using Your Journal

Compare the effect of government on the lives of Egyptians with the effect of government on your daily life. Write a few short paragraphs explaining elements that are similar and those that are different.

81

CHAPTER 4 Assessment Answers

Using Key Terms

Newspaper articles will vary but should use the vocabulary words listed.

Understanding Main Ideas

1. farming, seeds for wheat and barley, and writing
2. water and rich soil
3. because the pharaoh was considered a ruler, priest, and god
4. They introduced iron and bronze weapons and a new style of fighting.
5. During both the Old and New Kingdoms, religious rituals were carried out by the pharaoh and brought unity. Religion during Akhenaton's rule divided the people.
6. Hieroglyphic writing used on monuments; other writing to write religious works and records.
7. The floods washed away boundary markers, so the Egyptians surveyed fields. They also developed calendars to predict the floods.
8. for paper, baskets, sandals, columns for houses, rafts, and riverboats

Critical Thinking

1. Answers will vary, but note that Egypt needed the Nile .
2. Both held complete power. The ruler of Egypt was considered a god-king; the ruler of Babylon was not.
3. Answers will vary, but could say that this helped the decline of Egypt.
4. Answers will vary, but students should give explanations.

Graphic Organizer Activity

Entries will vary, but should show knowledge of the unique accomplishments of each kingdom.

Bonus Test Question

For Chapter 4 Test

The Old Kingdom began about 2600 B.C., the Middle Kingdom about 2060 B.C., and the New Kingdom about 1600 B.C. If the New Kingdom ended about 1500 years after the Old Kingdom began, in what year did it end? *(1100 B.C.)*

Using Your Journal

Journal entries will vary, but students should compare the effects of Egyptian government on the lives of Egyptians with the effect of government on their own daily lives.

Geography in History

Answers will vary, but should include reliance on the Nile River and Mediterranean; proximity to people; and natural barriers.

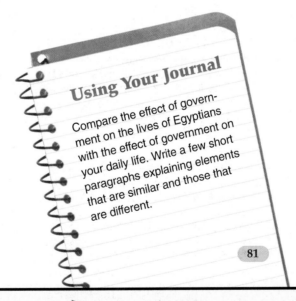

Chapter 5 Planning Guide

Timesaving Tools

TeacherWorks™ All-In-One Planner and Resource Center

- **Interactive Teacher Edition** Access your Teacher Wraparound Edition and your classroom resources with a few easy clicks.
- **Interactive Lesson Planner** Planning has never been easier! Organize your week, month, semester, or year with all the lesson helps you need to make teaching creative, timely, and relevant.

Presentation Plus! Use Glencoe's **Presentation Plus!** multimedia teacher tool to easily present dynamic lessons that visually excite your students. Using Microsoft PowerPoint® you can customize the presentations to create your own personalized lessons.

Objectives	Reproducible Resources	Multimedia Resources
Section 1 **The Indus River Valley** Discuss how the Indus River valley civilization developed. Summarize what is known from the ruins of the ancient cities of Harappa and Mohenjo-daro.	Reproducible Lesson Plan Chapter 5 Vocabulary and Guided Reading Activity Reading Essentials and Study Guide 5-1 Chapter 5 Cooperative Learning Activity Section 1 Quiz	Interactive Student Edition CD-ROM Teaching Transparency and Activity 5A Graphic Organizer Transparency 5 Vocabulary PuzzleMaker CD-ROM Interactive Tutor Self-Assessment CD-ROM ExamView® Pro Testmaker CD-ROM Glencoe Skillbuilder Interactive Workbook CD-ROM, Level 1 Presentation Plus! CD-ROM
Section 2 **The Huang Ho Valley** Explain how religion influenced the Shang dynasty. Analyze why the Shang dynasty declined.	Reproducible Lesson Plan Reading Essentials and Study Guide 5-2 Chapter 5 Chart and Graph Skill Activity Chapter 5 Geography and Map Activity Chapter 5 Enrichment Activity Section 2 Quiz	Teaching Transparency and Activity 5B Vocabulary PuzzleMaker CD-ROM Interactive Tutor Self-Assessment CD-ROM ExamView® Pro Testmaker CD-ROM Glencoe Skillbuilder Interactive Workbook CD-ROM, Level 1
Chapter 5 Review and Evaluation	Chapter 5 Reteaching Activity Chapter 5 Performance Assessment Activity Unit 2 Standardized Test Practice Spanish Chapter Summary and Glossary Chapter 5 Test	Vocabulary PuzzleMaker CD-ROM Interactive Tutor Self-Assessment CD-ROM Glencoe Skillbuilder Interactive Workbook CD-ROM, Level 1 Audiocassettes* ExamView® Pro Testmaker CD-ROM

*Also available in Spanish.

Performance Assessment Activities

Daily Life Organize students into groups of four. Suggest that students imagine that they are living during the time of the Shang dynasty. Have students in each group choose one of the following roles: a Shang ruler, a noble, a farmer, or a married woman. Tell the group members to describe their daily lives. Then ask students to make a chart comparing each person's way of life.

Chapter Resources

Literature About the Period

Chang, Richard F. *Chinese Mythical Stories*. Yale Far Eastern Publications, 1990. Legends and myths of China.

Readings for the Student

National Geographic Society (Special Publications Division). *Mysteries of the Ancient World.* National Geographic Society, 1979. A collection of articles with photographs of ancient sites, including Harappa and Mohenjo-daro.

Oliphant, Margaret. *Atlas of the Ancient World.* Simon and Schuster, 1992. Survey of the ancient world cultures including those of India and China.

Readings for the Teacher

Basham, A.L. *The Wonder That Was India.* Taplinger, 1967. A survey of the history of ancient India.

National Geographic Teacher's Corner

Index to National Geographic Magazine

The following articles relate to this chapter:

- "Indus Civilization: Clues to an Ancient Puzzle," by Mike Edwards, June 2000.
- "Black Dragon River: On the Edge of Empires," by Simon Winchester, February 2000.

National Geographic Society Products Available from Glencoe

To order the following, call Glencoe at 1-800-334-7344:

- *PicturePack: Physical Geography of the World (Transparencies)*
- *PicturePack: Ancient India*
- *PictureShow: Ancient Civilizations: India and China (CD-ROM)*
- *PictureShow: Ancient Civilizations Library (CD-ROMs)*
- *PicturePack: Ancient Civilizations Library, Part I (Transparencies)*

Additional National Geographic Society Products

To order the following, call National Geographic at 1-800-368-2728:

- *National Geographic Atlas of World History (Book)*
- *Wonders of the Ancient World: National Geographic Atlas of Archaeology (Book)*

Access *National Geographic*'s new dynamic MapMachine Web site and other geography resources at:
www.nationalgeographic.com
www.nationalgeographic.com/maps

Key to Ability Levels

Teaching strategies have been coded for varying learning styles and abilities.

L1 Level 1 activities are **basic** activities and should be within the ability range of all students.

L2 Level 2 activities are **average** activities and should be within the ability range of the average to above-average student.

L3 Level 3 activities are **challenging** activities designed for the ability range of above-average students.

ELL ELL activities should be within the ability range of English Language Learning students.

Introducing CHAPTER 5

OVERVIEW

Chapter 5 focuses on the development of the Harappan and Shang civilizations in South Asia and China.

- **Section 1** describes the Harappan civilization in the Indus River valley.
- **Section 2** explains the development of the Shang civilization in the Huang Ho valley.

CHAPTER OBJECTIVES

After reading Chapter 5, students will be able to:

1. discuss how the Indus River valley civilization developed.
2. summarize what is known from the ruins at Harappa and Mohenjo-daro.
3. explain how religion influenced the Shang dynasty.
4. analyze why the Shang dynasty declined.

EXAMINING ARTIFACTS

Have students study the two objects on this page—a toy horse and a necklace. Based on what they have learned in earlier chapters, what would they assume about the level of the culture that produced these goods? *(Sample responses: people stayed in one place and could accumulate goods; probably had enough food to support a class of artisans; valued children and gave them toys)*

PERFORMANCE ASSESSMENT ✓

Use the Performance Assessment Activities on page 82B to help you evaluate students as they complete the chapter.

CHAPTER 5 Eastern River Valleys

2500 B.C.–1000 B.C.

▼ Terra-cotta toy horse

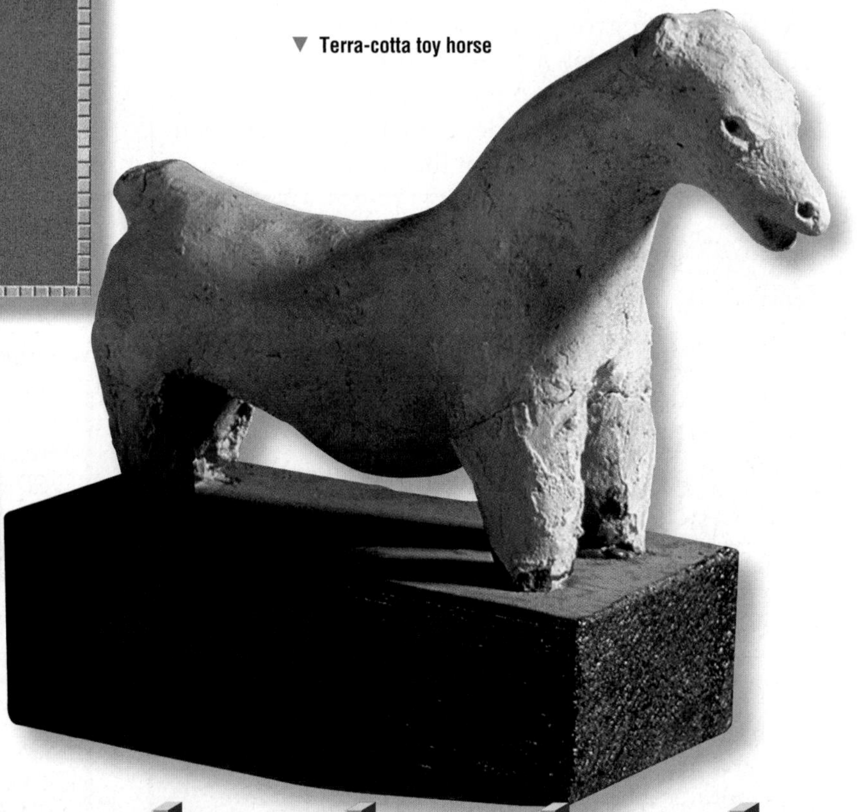

▲ A Harappan necklace

- **2500 B.C.** Cities appear in Indus River valley
- **2000 B.C.** Cities appear in Huang Ho valley
- **1766 B.C.** Shang come to power in China
- **1200 B.C.** Aryans arrive in Indus River valley
- **1122 B.C.** Zhou invade Shang kingdom

TEACHING RESOURCES

TEACHER PLANNING AND SUPPORT

- Reproducible Lesson Plan 5-1, 5-2
- Teaching Strategies for the World History Classroom (Including Block Scheduling Pacing Guides)
- Presentation Plus! CD-ROM

REVIEW AND REINFORCEMENT

- Reading Essentials and Study Guide 5-1, 5-2
- Chapter 5 Vocabulary and Guided Reading Activity
- Vocabulary PuzzleMaker CD-ROM
- Teaching Transparencies 5A & 5B
- Chapter 5 Reteaching Activity
- Chapter 5 Cooperative Learning Activity
- Chapter 5 Activity Book Activity
- Chapter 5 Chart and Graph Skill Activity
- Reading and Study Skills Foldables
- Interactive Tutor Self-Assessment CD-ROM
- Unit 2 MindJogger VideoQuiz

APPLICATION AND HANDS-ON ACTIVITIES

- Daily Questions in Social Studies
- Unit 2 Hands-On History Lab Activity
- Student Presentation Builder CD-ROM

Chapter Focus

Read to Discover

- How the Indus River valley civilization developed.
- What has been learned from the ruins of Harappa and Mohenjo-daro.
- How religion influenced the Shang dynasty.
- Why the Shang dynasty declined.

HISTORY Online

Chapter Overview

Visit the *Human Heritage* Web site at **humanheritage.glencoe.com** and click on ***Chapter 5—Chapter Overviews*** to preview this chapter.

Terms to Learn

planned communities
citadel
dynasty
ancestors
oracle bones
nobles

People to Know

Harappans
Aryans
Yü the Great
Wu

Places to Locate

Indus River
Harappa
Mohenjo-daro
Huang Ho valley

Why It's Important By 2500 B.C., cities started to appear in the Indus valley of South Asia. By 2000 B.C., they were being established in the Huang Ho (Yellow River) valley of China.

More isolated than the people of Mesopotamia or Egypt, the people of the eastern river valley civilizations were cut off from other parts of the world by high mountains, broad deserts, and large bodies of water. As a result, they became *self-sufficient*, or able to take care of nearly all their own needs. Compared to the Sumerians and the Egyptians, they did little trading with other parts of the world.

Because few artifacts have been found, much of what is known about the ancient eastern river valley civilizations comes from legends. Even so, available evidence points to unique and rich cultures that continue to interest archaeologists.

SECTION 1 The Indus River Valley

The Indus River flows through the countries known today as Pakistan and India. About 2500 B.C., a group of people called Harappans (huh rap' uhnz) settled in the valley of the Indus River. Although others had lived there before, the Harappans

GEOGRAPHY ACTIVITIES

- Chapter 5 Geography and Map Activity
- Building Geography Skills for Life
- Outline Map Resource Book

INTERDISCIPLINARY CONNECTIONS

- World Music: A Cultural Legacy

ENRICHMENT AND EXTENSION

- World History Primary Source Document Library CD-ROM
- Chapter 5 Enrichment Activity
- Foods Around the World

ASSESSMENT AND EVALUATION

- Chapter 5 Performance Assessment Activity
- Chapter 5 Section Quizzes 5-1, 5-2
- Chapter 5 Test
- Chapter 5 Standardized Test Practice Workbook
- Chapter 5 ExamView® Pro Testmaker CD-ROM
- Chapter 5 Digests Audiocassettes Activities and Tests

SPANISH RESOURCES

- Chapter 5 Spanish Chapter Summary and Glossary
- Chapter 5 Spanish Chapter Digests Audiocassettes Activities and Tests

HISTORY Online

Chapter Overview introduces students to chapter content and key terms. Have them access ***Chapter 5 Overview*** at **humanheritage.glencoe.com**

FOCUS

Bellringer

Write on the board: *How do you think mountains affected the lives of people in early civilizations?* Have students write a brief answer.

Motivational Activity

Have students read their thoughts about how mountains have affected civilizations. Then tell students that the early Indus River and Huang Ho valley civilizations were isolated from other civilizations by natural barriers such as high mountains. Ask students how isolation might affect a civilization. *(It forced them to take care of all their needs. They were unable to exchange ideas with other people.)*

GUIDE TO READING

Reading Strategy

Ask students to read "Why It's Important" and summarize the chapter's main theme. *(Because of geographic barriers, the eastern river valley civilizations developed self-sufficient and unique cultures known largely through artifacts and legends.)*

Vocabulary Precheck

Ask students to define each of the "Terms to Learn." Have a volunteer consult the dictionary for any unfamiliar words. L1 ELL

Use the Vocabulary PuzzleMaker CD-ROM for Chapter 5 to create a crossword puzzle. L1

Assign Chapter 5 Vocabulary and Guided Reading Activity.

TEACH

Guided Practice

L2 **Critical Thinking** Ask students to discuss how the Harappans controlled their environment in order to survive in the Indus valley.

MAP STUDY

Answer

Hindu Kush Mountains, Himalaya Mountains, Thar Desert, and the Arabian Sea.

Economics at a Glance

Economics

Economics is the study of how people make choices about ways to use scarce resources to fulfill their needs and wants. In order to do this, people must make economic choices to balance needs and wants. Have students describe two different types of wants for a business, a government, and a society. *(Answers may include: better technology and more educated employees; improved roads and better schools; and defense weapons and affordable health care.)* Then ask students to identify the arguments for choosing one over the other. *(For example, students may note that by hiring more educated people, better quality products will be produced. Increased profits from the products could then be invested in new technology.)*

were the first to create a civilization. Harappan civilization extended about 1,000 miles, or 1,600 kilometers, from the foothills of the Himalayas to the Indian Ocean. This area was more than twice the size of either Mesopotamia or Egypt.

The lives of the Harappan people were shaped by the Indus River. The river fertilized the land and made its soil rich. When the river flooded, however, it swept away everything in its path. People had to control the Indus in order to settle near it. To do this, they built dikes and dams. They cleared land for farming and built irrigation systems to bring water to dry areas. They grew barley, wheat, peas, melons, and dates and fished in the river.

The Harappans were the earliest known people to grow cotton. They spun the cotton, wove it into cloth, and dyed it bright colors. They produced cotton cloth hundreds of years before anyone else.

The Indus River influenced the way the Harappans built their cities. To protect cities from floods, the Harappans built them on raised mounds. They used river mud to make bricks, which they baked in the sun. Then they went one step further. They *fired,* or baked, some bricks in *kilns,* or ovens. They used these kiln-dried bricks as a covering over the mud bricks. The fired bricks were stronger and lasted much longer than sun-dried ones. The Harappans used fired bricks for houses and public buildings.

Early India

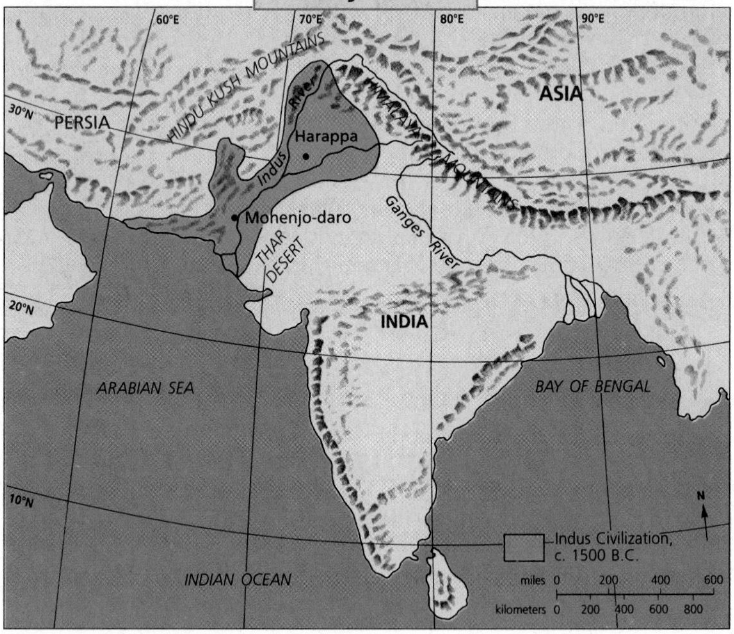

MAP STUDY

PLACES AND REGIONS India is part of the triangle-shaped peninsula that forms the southern part of the continent of Asia. **What geographic features would have helped to protect the people of the Indus River valley from enemies?**

MEETING SPECIAL NEEDS

Students who benefit from auditory instruction can retain the lesson better if they participate in partner reading. Pair students and have partners take turns reading paragraphs or sections of the text aloud. The partner not reading should follow the text as it is being read. At the end of each paragraph or section, students should quiz each other on the content. Discuss the main ideas as a class.

Refer to ***Inclusion for the Middle School Social Studies Classroom: Strategies and Activities*** for additional resources.

Shang China

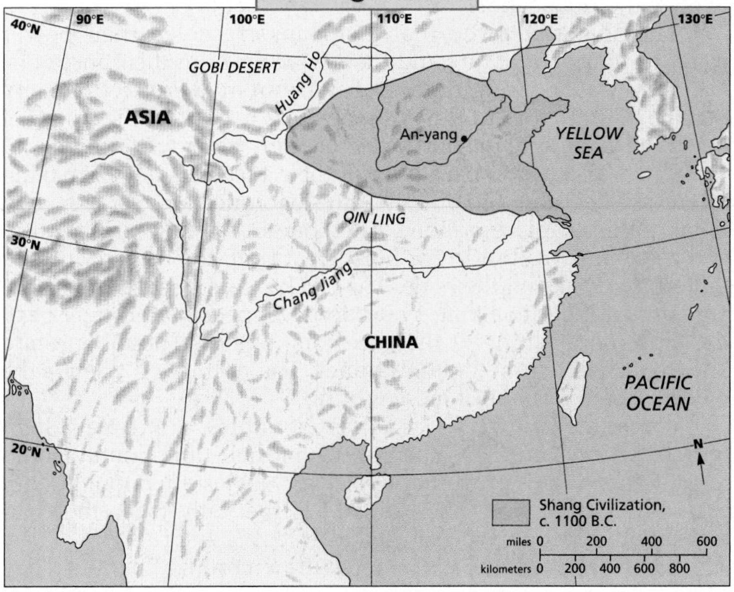

cities. Most were designed in the same way. At the center stood a palace and a temple. Public buildings and the homes of high government officials were built around the palace. Within an outer district were workshops, burial grounds, and the homes of the workers.

Most of the Shang people, however, did not live in the city. The city was the home of the rich, the educated, and the skilled. Poorer people lived in the countryside. They were farmers who grew such grains as millet, wheat, and rice and raised cattle, sheep, and chickens. The farmers also produced silk, which was used to make clothes for the very rich. The Chinese produced silk hundreds of years before anyone else.

Spirits, Ancestors, and Kings

The Shang worshiped **spirits,** or supernatural beings, which they believed lived in mountains, rivers, and seas. The people believed they had to please the spirits. If the spirits became angry or unhappy, the people might suffer a poor harvest or lose a battle.

The Shang believed that **ancestors,** or those from whom one is descended, also influenced people's fortunes. So, they offered their ancestors food, wine, and special prayers. They hoped their ancestors would help them in time of need and bring them good fortune. Because of this respect for ancestors, family ties were very important to the Shang. They had rules about how family members should act toward one another. Children were taught to

MAP STUDY

PLACES AND REGIONS The landforms of China contributed to the early isolation of the Chinese. **What geographical features would have discouraged the Shang people from movement to other lands or their contact with other people?**

Reading Check What role did **spirits** play in Shang religion?

Reading Check Why did the Shang respect their **ancestors?**

MAP STUDY Answer

The geographical features that would have stopped the Shang people from movement to other lands include the mountains to the west, the Gobi Desert, the Yellow Sea, and the Pacific Ocean.

DID YOU KNOW ??

The buildings of the Shang people faced south to get as much sun as possible during the cold winter months.

Reading Check Answer The Shang believed the **spirits** lived in the mountains, rivers, and seas, and that people needed to please the spirits to avoid misfortune.

Reading Check Answer The Shang believed that **ancestors** influenced people's fortunes.

MEETING SPECIAL NEEDS

Encourage students who are tactile/kinesthetic learners to prepare a bulletin board depicting the early history of China. Have the students discuss what should be included in the display. Some suggestions are maps showing what crops were grown, drawings of artifacts, and illustrations of the layout of an excavated city. Assign small groups to research and prepare each topic with each student assuming responsibility for a specific task. Have the class design and assemble the bulletin-board display.

Refer to ***Inclusion for the Middle School Social Studies Classroom: Strategies and Activities*** for additional resources.

MAKING CONNECTIONS

>> **Language Arts** The Chinese writing system helped to hold the Chinese people together through the centuries. Although spoken language changed from place to place, the written language stayed the same.

Reading Check Answer

Oracle bones were pieces of polished bone with patterns of cracks. Shang kings used the oracle bones to get answers to questions from their ancestors. The **nobles** were people of high rank who spent much time hunting and battling each other or enemies of the Shang.

CAPTION ANSWER

They used oracle bones before making important decisions.

DID YOU KNOW ??

The Shang oracle bones carry between 2,500 and 3,000 different syllabic characters. In order to write in Chinese, a writer had to memorize each character. Because it was so difficult to master all the characters, only a few people in ancient China could read and write.

Reading Check

What were **oracle bones?** Who were the **nobles,** and what role did they play in the Shang dynasty?

People in History

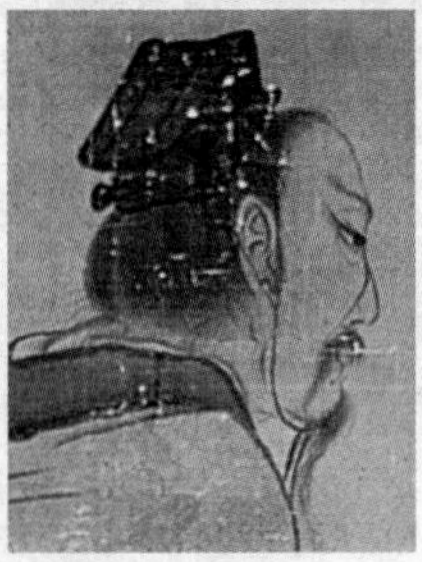

Wu
c. 1000 B.C.

Zhou King

Wu, the ruler of a former Shang territory, led the attack against the last Shang emperor. The emperor was so cruel that many soldiers gave up without a fight. Wu, known as "the Military King," believed the gods wanted the Zhou dynasty to rule China, and he became the first Zhou ruler.

obey their parents and to honor older people. Wives were trained to obey their husbands.

The Shang believed that their kings received their power from the spirits of nature and their wisdom from their ancestors. For this reason, religion and government were tied closely together. An important duty of kings was to contact the spirits of nature to make sure they provided enough water for farming.

Kings also asked the advice of their ancestors before making important decisions. To do this, kings had questions scratched on a flat, polished piece of bone. The bone had a hole drilled in it, and a hot bar was put in the hole. Heat from the bar produced a pattern of cracks on the bone. The cracks were believed to be the ancestors' replies to a king's questions. A special interpreter gave the king the meaning of the ancestors' replies. These bones are known as **oracle** (ōr′ uh kuhl) **bones.** The writing on them is the oldest known form of Chinese writing.

Under the king was a large class of **nobles,** or people of high rank in a kingdom. They spent much of their time hunting, both for pleasure and as preparation for war. Nobles often fought with each other about land. They joined together only when they had to fight other people who refused to accept Shang rule.

Nobles rode into battle in horse-drawn bronze chariots. They wore bronze helmets and armor made of buffalo or rhinoceros hide. They were skilled in the use of the bow and arrow. Their

ORACLE BONES Shang rulers tried to learn the future by using oracle bones. Here, a turtle shell used for this purpose shows an early form of Chinese writing. **When did Shang rulers use oracle bones?**

EXTENDING THE CONTENT

In addition to producing fine bronze objects, the people of the Shang dynasty carved beautiful ivory and jade statues. They wove silk into elegantly colored cloth for the upper class and fashioned pottery from kaolin, a fine white clay.

arrows had sharp points of bone or bronze. Soldiers marched on foot behind nobles' chariots. These soldiers generally were poor peasants whom the nobles had forced to leave their farms and join the army.

Decline of the Shang

There was a great gap between rich and poor during the rule of the Shang. Rich Shang lived in the cities in wooden houses. They owned bronze weapons and ornaments and wore linen, wool, fur, and silk clothes. Poor Shang lived in the countryside and worked with wooden or stone tools. Their houses were thatched or mud huts or caves scooped out of the ground. Neither group felt any loyalty toward the other.

Many experts believe that this gap between rich and poor weakened the Shang civilization. In 1122 B.C., a people known as Zhou (jō) invaded the Shang kingdom. The Shang were not united enough to hold off the invaders, and their civilization came to an end.

Linking Across Time

Metal Casting Shang metalsmiths perfected a form of casting to create some of the finest bronze works the world has ever known (below). Metalsmiths still use molds to create everything from artworks to machine parts (right). **What conclusions can you draw about Shang technology?**

L1 **Daily Life** Ask students to imagine themselves as a king, noble, soldier, or farmer during the Shang dynasty in ancient China. Have students write a diary entry describing a day in the life of the person they have chosen. Call on volunteers to read their diary entries to the class.

Linking Across Time

Conclusions will vary, but most students will conclude that the Shang excelled at bronze metalwork and turned metal casting into an art.

Check for Understanding

Ask students to summarize the main points of the chapter, orally or in writing. Discuss the answers to the Section and Chapter Assessment questions.

Evaluate

Assign Chapter 5 **Performance Assessment Activity** in the TCR.

Administer **Chapter 5 Test** in the TCR. Testmaker available.

Reteach

Have students survey the chapter and make a list of questions to test their knowledge of the chapter. Working in pairs, students can quiz each other.

Assign Chapter 5 **Reteaching Activity** in the TCR.

MULTICULTURAL PERSPECTIVES

The people of the Chinese dynasties believed that their rulers governed according to a principle known as a Mandate from Heaven. If rulers were just and effective, they received a mandate. If rulers did not govern properly—as indicated by poor crops or losses in battle—they lost the mandate to someone else who then started a new dynasty. This principle started with the Zhou dynasty.

Enrich

Ask students to bring to class illustrations of bronze objects made by the Shang and other dynasties. Allow students to discuss and list similarities and differences in the art.

Assign Chapter 5 **Enrichment Activity** in the TCR.

CLOSE

Have students write a paragraph describing the features of the Harappan civilization or the Shang dynasty that made them attractive to invaders.

Use **Interactive Tutor Self-Assessment CD-ROM** to review Section 2.

HISTORY Online

Self-Check Quiz gives students an interactive chapter tutorial. Have them access ***Chapter 5 Quiz*** at humanheritage.glencoe.com

GLENCOE TECHNOLOGY

MindJogger Videoquiz

Use **MindJogger Videoquiz** to review students' knowledge of the unit.

Available in DVD and VHS

The Shang left behind a great gift to the rest of the world in their works of bronze. These include sculptures, cups, vases, fancy vessels, and a variety of other items used for religious purposes. Many art experts believe these are among the finest works of bronze ever made.

Section 2 Assessment

1. **Define:** dynasty, spirits, ancestors, oracle bones, nobles.
2. What were some of the Shang religious beliefs?
3. What may have been the reason for the decline of the Shang civilization?

Critical Thinking

4. **Formulating Questions** If world leaders today could use oracle bones, what questions might they want answered before making decisions?

Graphic Organizer Activity

5. Draw a diagram like this one, and use it to show the structure of a typical Shang city.

Chapter Summary & Study Guide

1. The eastern river valley civilizations began in the Indus River valley about 2500 B.C. and in the Huang Ho valley about 2000 B.C.
2. The first people to build a civilization in the Indus River valley were the Harappans.
3. The Harappans are believed to have been the first people to produce cotton cloth, bake bricks in ovens, and build sanitation systems.
4. The Harappan cities of Harappa and Mohenjo-daro are the oldest known planned communities.
5. No one knows for sure how the Harappan civilization ended, but the Aryans moved into and took over the valley about 1200 B.C.
6. The legendary kingdom of Xia probably was established in China about 2000 B.C.
7. The Shang started the first recorded Chinese dynasty around 1766 B.C.
8. The Shang believed spirits and ancestors influenced their lives.
9. The Shang developed the form of writing found on oracle bones and a method of making beautiful bronze artworks.
10. Shang civilization ended with the Zhou invasion of 1122 B.C.

HISTORY Online

Self-Check Quiz

Visit the *Human Heritage* Web site at humanheritage.glencoe.com and click on ***Chapter 5—Self-Check Quiz*** to assess your understanding of this chapter.

Section 2 Assessment Answers

1. dynasty, ruling family in China (p. 88); spirits, supernatural beings (p. 89); ancestors, those from whom one is descended (p. 89); oracle bones, bones to receive messages from ancestors (p. 90); nobles, people of high rank (p. 90)
2. Sample beliefs: worship of spirits, worship of departed ancestors, spiritual powers and duties of kings
3. the distance between the rich and poor
4. Answers will vary but should include questions about current affairs.
5. center—palace and temple; around the palace/temple—public buildings and homes of high government officials; outer district—workshops, burial grounds, homes of workers

Assign Chapter 5 **Section 2 Quiz** in the TCR. Testmaker available.

5. **The Mesopotamian, Egyptian, and Indus River valley civilizations arose where they did because**

A of advice from their religious leaders about where to settle

B there were so many hunting grounds in North Africa

C the rivers they settled near provided a means of transportation

D of the many renewable resources available nearby

Test-Taking Tip: Think about what these three civilizations had in common (they all settled in river valleys). Why was this geographical feature so important to the development of these societies?

6. **The Egyptians made many contributions to other civilizations. Which of the following was NOT developed by the Egyptians?**

F papyrus

G a number system based on ten

H medical splints and bandages

J city-states

Test-Taking Tip: Be careful—overlooking the words NOT or EXCEPT is a common error. Look for the answer that does NOT fit. Since the Egyptians *did* develop papyrus (a type of paper made from reeds), answer F is not the correct choice.

Ancient Egypt

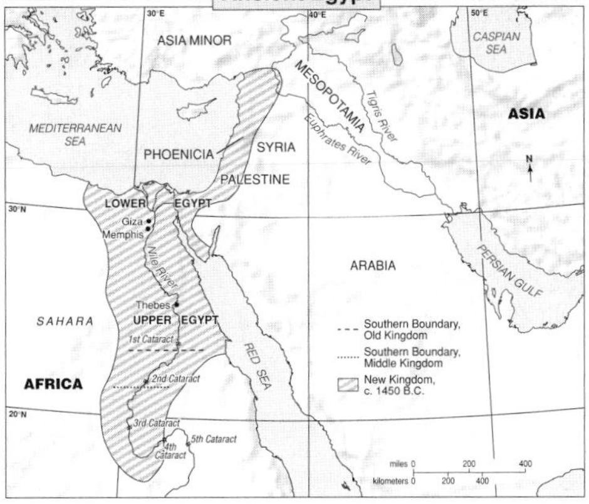

7. **According to the map above,**

A ancient Egypt did not include Thebes

B the New Kingdom of Egypt included the Sahara

C the southern boundary of the Old Kingdom was near the 1st Cataract of the Nile

D Phoenicia was not part of the New Kingdom of Egypt

Test-Taking Tip: Use the map's *legend,* or *key,* to help you understand what the map's symbols represent. Make sure your answer is supported by information *on the map.* Do not rely on your memory.

STOP

97

Tested Objectives

Questions	Reading Objective
1	Identify supporting ideas
2, 7	Analyze information
3, 4	Identify central issues
5	Draw conclusions
6	Make inferences and generalizations

STANDARDIZED TEST PRACTICE

4H Culture/Environment

While the Egyptians built pyramids, the Mesopotamians did not; the Mesopotamians developed the 60-minute hour, but nothing is said about how the Egyptians kept time. Therefore, choices F and J can be eliminated. It is unreasonable to think that they taught English to students. Evidence for H can be found on pages 56 and 70.

THE PRINCETON REVIEW **TEST-TAKING TIP**

Remind students that when a question asks for something true of *both* civilizations, any choice that they know does not apply to one or the other can be eliminated.

5D Culture/Environment

Since the origin of villages and cities is tied to the possibility of agriculture, and farming requires irrigation, the best answer is the availability of natural resources such as water.

6J History

Since the Mesopotamians had city-states (according to page 61), they were not invented by the Egyptians.

7C Geography

According to the map, the southern boundary of the Old Kingdom is just south of the first cataract.

OVERVIEW

Unit 3 surveys the rise and fall of important kingdoms and empires in the ancient Middle East, Africa, and the Americas to 1500 A.D.

- **Chapter 6** describes the Phoenicians and the Hebrews and their interest in trade and religion, and their contributions to later civilizations.
- **Chapter 7** discusses the contributions of the Assyrians, Chaldeans, and Persians and examines how their empires were forged and maintained and how their ideas spread.
- **Chapter 8** explains the development of civilization in sub-Saharan Africa and the Americas, and how ideas spread through trade and through conquest of these civilizations.

UNIT OBJECTIVES

After reading Unit 3, your students will be able to:

1. give examples of the important cultural and religious contributions of the Phoenicians and the Hebrews.

2. explain how the rise of empires affected the early peoples of the Middle East.

3. characterize the kinds of empires that developed in Africa and the Americas.

UNIT PROJECT

Have students create a monument to one of the kingdoms and civilizations studied in Unit 3. Their goal is to research their civilization and devise and create a monument that represents the people and/or their achievements. Monuments can take any form students choose, such as an object, videotape, or story.

UNIT 3

Ideas and Armies

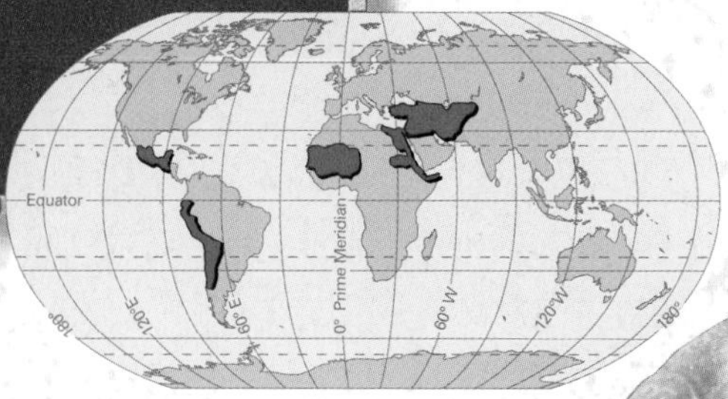

Mayan sculpture of a serpent ▼

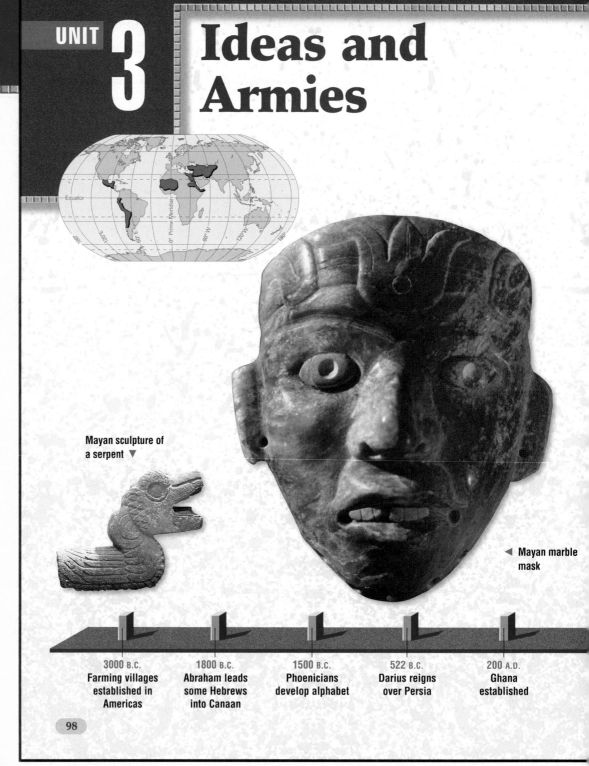

◀ Mayan marble mask

- 3000 B.C. Farming villages established in Americas
- 1800 B.C. Abraham leads some Hebrews into Canaan
- 1500 B.C. Phoenicians develop alphabet
- 522 B.C. Darius reigns over Persia
- 200 A.D. Ghana established

98

ABOUT THE UNIT OPENING

Examining Artifacts

Remind students that historians sometimes have to obtain information and draw conclusions about past civilizations based on artifacts alone. Refer students to the Mayan sculpture and mask on this page. Brainstorm with students what these artifacts tell them about the Maya, a people from Mesoamerica.

Global Chronology

Refer students to the unit time line above. Ask students about what year farming villages were established throughout the Americas. *(3000 B.C.)* Ask students what contribution the Phoenicians made to civilization in 1500 B.C. *(developed the alphabet)*

FOLDABLES™ Study Organizer

Comparing Information Study Foldable *Make this foldable to help you compare and contrast Middle Eastern and African and American civilizations.*

Step 1 *Fold one sheet of paper in half from side to side.*

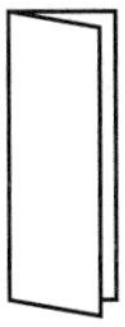

Step 2 *Turn the paper and fold it into thirds.*

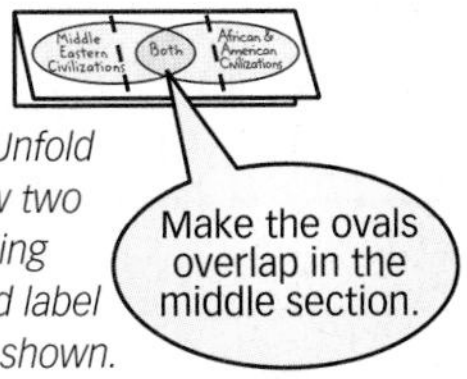

Step 3 *Unfold and draw two overlapping ovals and label them as shown.*

Step 4 *Cut the top layer only along both fold lines.*

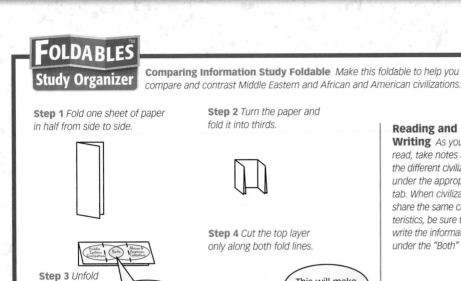

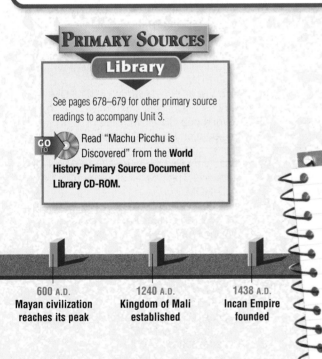

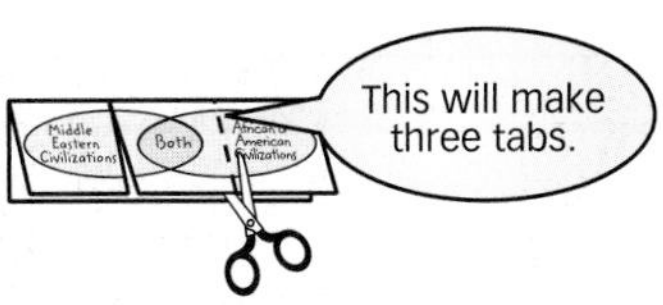

Reading and Writing *As you read, take notes about the different civilizations under the appropriate tab. When civilizations share the same characteristics, be sure to write the information under the "Both" tab.*

PRIMARY SOURCES Library

See pages 678–679 for other primary source readings to accompany Unit 3.

GO TO Read "Machu Picchu is Discovered" from the **World History Primary Source Document Library CD-ROM.**

600 A.D. Mayan civilization reaches its peak

1240 A.D. Kingdom of Mali established

1438 A.D. Incan Empire founded

Journal Notes

What contributions to the modern world were made by civilizations more than 3,000 years ago? Note details about these contributions as you read.

99

Geographic Location

The civilizations discussed in this unit were located in the Middle East; in northeastern, eastern, and western Africa; and in Central America and South America along the Andes Mountains. Have students locate these places in their text Atlas. Then have volunteers locate them on a wall map of the world.

GLENCOE TECHNOLOGY

MindJogger Videoquiz

Use **MindJogger Videoquiz** to preview the unit content.

Available in DVD and VHS

FOLDABLES™ Study Organizer

Purpose Students use this foldable to organize similarities and differences between Middle Eastern and African & American Civilizations. As students read this unit, they should list features of these civilizations under the appropriate tabs, placing shared features under the middle tab. When students have completed their foldables, they should have a description of the main characteristics of these civilizations.

Have students complete **Reading and Study Skills Foldables** Activity 3.

RECORDING JOURNAL NOTES

Have students make a list of recent inventions that 3,000 years from now might be important. Tell students to note details about the contributions to the modern world made by civilizations more than 3,000 years ago.

PRIMARY SOURCES Library

Additional primary sources from the **World History Primary Source Document Library CD-ROM** can be used during the study of Unit 3, including:

- "Popul Vuh: The Mayan Book of the Dawn of Life"

Primary sources about the empire of Mali can be found on pages 678–679.

Chapter 6 Planning Guide

Timesaving Tools

TeacherWorks™ All-In-One Planner and Resource Center

- **Interactive Teacher Edition** Access your Teacher Wraparound Edition and your classroom resources with a few easy clicks.
- **Interactive Lesson Planner** Planning has never been easier! Organize your week, month, semester, or year with all the lesson helps you need to make teaching creative, timely, and relevant.

Use Glencoe's **Presentation Plus!** multimedia teacher tool to easily present dynamic lessons that visually excite your students. Using Microsoft PowerPoint® you can customize the presentations to create your own personalized lessons.

Objectives	Reproducible Resources	Multimedia Resources
Section 1 **The Phoenicians** Discuss the Phoenicians and their role in the growth of Mediterranean commerce and the development of the alphabet	Reproducible Lesson Plan Chapter 6 Vocabulary and Guided Reading Activity Reading Essentials and Study Guide 6-1 Chapter 6 Chart and Graph Skill Activity Chapter 6 Geography and Map Activity Section 1 Quiz Unit 3 Hands-On History Lab	Interactive Student Edition CD-ROM Graphic Organizer Transparency 3 Teaching Transparencies and Activities 6A & 6B Vocabulary PuzzleMaker CD-ROM Interactive Tutor Self-Assessment CD-ROM ExamView® Pro Testmaker CD-ROM Glencoe Skillbuilder Interactive Workbook CD-ROM, Level 1 Presentation Plus! CD-ROM
Section 2 **The Hebrews** Summarize the Hebrews and their development of new ideas, such as the belief in one god and social justice.	Reproducible Lesson Plan Reading Essentials and Study Guide 6-2 Chapter 6 Cooperative Learning Activity Chapter 6 Enrichment Activity Unit 3 World Literature Reading 1 Section 2 Quiz	Vocabulary PuzzleMaker CD-ROM Interactive Tutor Self-Assessment CD-ROM ExamView® Pro Testmaker CD-ROM Glencoe Skillbuilder Interactive Workbook CD-ROM, Level 1
Chapter 6 **Review and Evaluation**	Chapter 6 Reteaching Activity Chapter 6 Performance Assessment Activity Spanish Chapter Summary and Glossary Chapter 6 Test	Vocabulary PuzzleMaker CD-ROM Interactive Tutor Self-Assessment CD-ROM Glencoe Skillbuilder Interactive Workbook CD-ROM, Level 1 Audiocassettes* ExamView® Pro Testmaker CD-ROM

*Also available in Spanish.

MOSES According to the Bible, Yahweh allowed Moses and the Hebrews to pass through the Red Sea. The waters then closed again, drowning the pharaoh and his army. **What important set of laws did God give Moses on Mount Sinai?**

Moses and the Ten Commandments After the Hebrews settled in Egypt, they were enslaved. About 600 years later, Moses, the Hebrew leader at the time, appeared before the pharaoh and told him to end Hebrew enslavement and let the Hebrews leave Egypt. The pharaoh at first refused but later agreed. Moses then led the Hebrews out of Egypt. The pharaoh again changed his mind and led his army in pursuit. According to the Bible, Yahweh parted the Red Sea to allow the Hebrews to cross and they escaped into the Sinai (sī′ nī) Desert. They called their escape the *Exodus* (ek′ suh duhs).

Life in the desert was hard, but Moses told the Hebrews not to give up. Moses led them to Mount Sinai. There, he climbed to the top of the mountain to receive a message from God. The Bible states that Yahweh told Moses that He would protect the Hebrews and lead them back to Canaan. In return, they were to renew the *covenant* (kuv′ uh nuhnt), or agreement, with Him. They were to promise to obey certain laws, the most important of which became the Ten Commandments.

The Ten Commandments stated that the Hebrews were to give their loyalty only to Yahweh. They were not to worship other gods or idols (ī′ dls). The Ten Commandments also taught that it was wrong to lie, steal, or murder, and that people should honor their parents and respect other people's property.

The Hebrews believed God was just, and they too should be just. They used laws to influence the way people behaved. Their

Fun Facts . . .

Ramses II No one knows for sure, but many scholars believe that Ramses II was the pharaoh who tried to stop the flight of Moses and the Hebrews out of Egypt. Ramses ruled Egypt for nearly 70 years and outlived a dozen of his sons.

CAPTION ANSWER

the Ten Commandments

GEOGRAPHY AND HISTORY

Explain to the students that present-day Jews commemorate the Exodus from Egypt and rededicate themselves to freedom each year during an eight-day celebration called Passover. Ask volunteers to research and trace the Hebrew's Exodus on a map of the Middle East for the rest of the class.

Independent Practice

L3 **Critical Thinking** Ask students to respond to the following: Many people accept the Bible as a collection of sacred writings. How might it also be a historical document?

EXTENDING THE CONTENT

According to Exodus 20:2-14, in one version of the Bible, the Ten Commandments are:

You shall have no other gods beside me.

You shall not make for yourself a sculptured image. . . .

You shall not swear falsely by the name of the Lord your God. . . .

Remember the sabbath day and keep it holy. . . .

Honor your father and your mother. . . .

You shall not murder.

You shall not commit adultery.

You shall not steal.

You shall not bear false witness against your neighbor.

You shall not covet . . . anything that is your neighbor's.

Reading Check Answer
Social justice means that everyone has a right to be treated fairly.

DID YOU KNOW ??

For the Hebrews, Canaan was the Promised Land, a land they thought was flowing with milk and honey. To give thanks for the richness of the land, they celebrated the festival of Savouth, which began with a pilgrimage in the early spring and continued for seven weeks.

CAPTION ANSWER

olives, flax, barley, wheat, and grapes

Reading Check What does **social justice** mean?

laws affected not only individuals but the whole community. The Hebrews believed in **social justice.** Everyone had a right to be treated fairly.

The Promised Land Moses died shortly before the Hebrews reached Canaan. The Hebrews were afraid that without a strong leader they would not be able to enter Canaan. The people who already lived there had built many walled cities on hilltops. Soldiers in lookout towers guarded the cities against enemy attack. However, Joshua, a new leader and a good general, brought the Hebrews safely into the promised land.

Once they had settled in Canaan, the Hebrews became farmers and shepherds. They copied the Canaanites' tools and borrowed their alphabet. Canaan was rocky and dry. There was little water. So, during the two months of the rainy season, farmers collected and stored water in small caves or underground basins. During the dry season, they used what they had stored to irrigate their crops of olives, flax, barley, wheat, and grapes.

Most Hebrews lived in one-room houses. The room was divided in two, with one section slightly higher than the other. During the day, people cooked and did other household chores in the lower level. At night, donkeys and goats bedded down there, while the family slept on the upper level. The walls of the houses

People in History

Moses
c. 1300 B.C.–1200 B.C

Hebrew Prophet

During the Hebrew enslavement, the pharoah ordered the death of all Hebrew male infants. To save her son, Moses' mother put him in a papyrus basket and floated him down the Nile. Pharoah's daughter rescued the baby and raised him as her own. Moses later fled Egypt and worked as a shepherd until about age 80, when according to the Bible, Yahweh instructed him to free his people.

HARVEST IN ANCIENT ISRAEL Hebrew writers called Canaan "a land flowing with milk and honey." This area, however, had a dry climate and little water. The Hebrews had to work hard to farm the land. Hebrew farmers and their workers gathering the harvest are shown in this painting. **What crops did the Hebrews grow in Canaan?**

COOPERATIVE LEARNING

Organize the class into small groups. Suggest to each group that they are members of a school (or city) "commandment committee." It is their task to write a list of commandments to guide school behavior that they think will cover all necessary considerations and possibilities. Encourage groups to list commandments by priority.

Regroup the students and allow each group to share their commandments and poll their consensus.

Assign Chapter 6 *Cooperative Learning Activity* in the TCR.

Making Comparisons

CRITICAL THINKING SKILLS

Suppose you want to buy a portable compact disc (CD) player, and you must choose among three models. You would probably compare characteristics of the three models, such as price, sound quality, and size to figure out which model is best for you. In the study of world history, you often compare people from different cultures or regions. You might also compare people and events from one time period with those from a different time period.

Learning the Skill When making comparisons, you examine two or more groups, situations, events, or documents. Then you identify any similarities and differences. For example, the chart on this page compares the characteristics of two ancient civilizations.

When making comparisons, you first decide what items will be compared and determine which characteristics you will use to compare them. Then you identify similarities and differences in these characteristics.

PHOENICIAN AND HEBREW CIVILIZATIONS

CULTURAL CHARACTERISTIC	PHOENICIANS	HEBREWS
Homeland	*Canaan*	Canaan
Political organization	*city-states*	12 tribes
Method of rule	*kings/merchant councils*	kings/council of elders
Main occupations	*artisans, merchants, shippers*	herders, farmers, traders
Religion	*belief in many gods closely tied to nature*	belief in one all-powerful god
Main contribution	*spread of an alphabet*	idea of a single, just god

Skill Practice

Analyze the information on the chart on this page. Then answer these questions.

1. **What items are being compared?**
2. **What characteristics are being used to compare them?**
3. **In what ways were the Phoenicians and the Hebrews similar?**
4. **In what ways were the two groups different?**
5. **Suppose you wanted to compare the Phoenician and Hebrew religions in more detail. What are some of the characteristics you might compare?**

GO TO Glencoe's **Skillbuilder Interactive Workbook CD-ROM, Level 1,** provides instruction and practice in key social studies skills.

CRITICAL THINKING SKILLS

TEACH

Making Comparisons

Introduce this lesson by writing the words "cat" and "dog" on the chalkboard. Ask students to name ways these two animals are alike. *(Both are mammals. They each have four legs, are covered with fur, and so on.)* Then have students identify differences. *(Cats meow, dogs bark. Cats can climb trees, most dogs cannot. Cats belong to the feline family, dogs belong to the canine family.)*

Point out to students that they have just practiced the skill of making comparisons. Explain that comparing means looking for similarities and differences. Brainstorm some of the things that historians might compare. *(nations, regions, leaders, important events, cultures, and so on)* Then assign the skills lesson and accompanying questions.

Answers to Skill Practice

1. Phoenicians and Hebrews
2. items under "Cultural Characteristics"
3. Similarities might include: both lived in Canaan, both had kings, both traded.
4. Phoenicians were organized into city-states, the Hebrews into tribes. Phoenician occupations centered around trade, while many Hebrews worked as farmers and herders. The Phoenicians had many gods, the Hebrews had one. The Phoenicians contributed the alphabet, the Hebrews contributed the idea of one just god.
5. Sample response: number of gods, characteristics of the gods/god, worship practices, attitudes toward death, and so on.

TEAM TEACHING STRATEGIES

Language Arts Invite the language arts teacher to explain the use of a Venn diagram in making comparisons. Then organize the class into groups, and have each group use a Venn diagram to compare the lives of David and Solomon. In an information-sharing session, compile a master diagram on the chalkboard. Ask students to note similarities and differences between the lives of these two leaders.

Next, instruct students to use the Venn diagram to create two "People in History" features like the one on page 110. Have them research missing information, such as estimated dates of birth and death, as well as other interesting details about David and Solomon. Also encourage students to illustrate their features, either with a photocopy of a painting or their own drawing.

L3 **Language Arts** Have students write a paragraph explaining the importance of prophets in Hebrew history. Students may wish to read the writings of the prophets in the Jewish Bible or Old Testament to gain more insight.

Reading Check Answer A Hebrew **judge** settled disputes and led troops into battle.

Reading Check Answer David wrote many of the **psalms** in the Bible.

Reading Check Answer The **prophets** were persons claiming to have received messages from God. They criticized the way many Hebrews were living and reminded them of their duty to God and to one another.

Biography®

The following videotape program is available from Glencoe to enrich chapter 6:

- **King David**

To find classroom resources to accompany this video, check the following home page:

A&E Television: www.aande.com

were made of mud-brick or stone plastered with mud and whitewashed. Floors were made of beaten clay. Wooden beams supported a flat, thatched roof, which was covered with clay.

Reading Check What was the role of a Hebrew **judge**?

Kings

After Joshua died the 12 Hebrew tribes split apart. Each tribe was led by a council of elders. In times of crisis, a temporary leader called a **judge** settled disputes and led troops into battle.

In time, the Hebrews decided they needed a king to unite them. A warrior-farmer named Saul became their first king. He ruled well for several years. Toward the end of his reign, however, he lost the people's support. When Saul died in battle, David became the new king.

David reunited the Hebrews and defeated the Canaanites. He captured a Canaanite fortress and on that site established Jerusalem (juh rū′ suh luhm), the capital of the Hebrew kingdom. A fine musician, David wrote many of the **psalms** (sahms), or sacred songs, found in the Bible.

Reading Check Who wrote many of the **psalms** found in the Bible?

After David died, his son Solomon (sahl′ uh muhn) became king. Through trade and treaties with other lands, Solomon brought peace and made the Hebrew kingdom more powerful. He built a huge temple in Jerusalem out of limestone, cedar wood, and gold. It was designed and built by artisans from Phoenicia.

Solomon's wealth and wisdom became known all through the Middle East. Many Hebrews, however, were not happy with Solomon. They did not like working on his building projects or paying the high taxes he demanded. After Solomon died, the Hebrews in the northern part of the country set up their own separate kingdom called Israel. A southern kingdom, which was ruled from Jerusalem, became known as Judah. For nearly 200 years, the two kingdoms fought each other off and on. Gradually, both became weak enough for others to conquer.

Reading Check Who were the **prophets**, and what message did they deliver?

The Prophets

Prophets, or persons claiming to have messages from God, appeared in the Hebrew kingdoms. They came from cities and villages. They were teachers, farmers, and shepherds. They criticized the way the Hebrews were living. The rich were mistreating the poor, and government officials were accepting bribes. The prophets reminded the Hebrews of their duty to God and to one another. They warned the Hebrews that Yahweh would punish them if they did not return to His ways.

Some prophets added a new meaning to the laws of Moses. They taught that Yahweh was the god not only of Hebrews, but of everyone.

The people refused to listen to the prophets' warnings. Then, it was too late. Powerful neighbors took over the Hebrew kingdoms. After 722 B.C., the Israelites, the people of the northern kingdom, disappeared. Although the Judeans survived, most were forced to move to Babylonia in 586 B.C.

EXTENDING THE CONTENT

Solomon's Temple, though destroyed more than 2,500 years ago, is one of the best-known buildings of ancient times. From the description given in the First Book of Kings, we know even the names of artisans who worked on it. The temple had three rooms in a row, all 33 feet (11 m) wide; the outer porch, 16 feet (5 m) wide; the central hall or holy place, 66 feet (21 m) long; and steps leading up to the square inner chamber, or holy of holies, which was kept totally dark. The Ark of the Covenant was in the center of the holy of holies.

While in Babylonia, the Judeans, or Jews, made changes in their religion. Having lost the great temple at Jerusalem, they had to find some other way to worship God. They began meeting in small groups on the **sabbath,** or day of rest. The groups would pray and talk about their religion and history. The Jews wrote down their laws, sayings, and stories of the past on scrolls. The study of these writings led the Jews to value learning, and their teachers became important leaders.

The Jews spent 70 years in Babylonia before they were allowed to return to their homeland. They rebuilt Jerusalem and the temple. Under a scribe named Ezra, they wrote down the laws of Moses in five books called the *Torah* (tor' uh). Other writings were added later to make the Old Testament of the Bible.

Reading Check What did Jews do on the **sabbath**?

HEBREW PROPHETS

Name	Teachings
Elijah *c. 850 B.C.*	Everyone should behave in a moral way.
Amos *c. 755 B.C.*	Prayers and sacrifices do not make up for bad deeds. Behaving justly is much more important than ritual.
Hosea *745-730 B.C.*	God is a god of love and compassion who loves His people the way a father loves his children. God suffers when people turn from Him and do not follow His commandments.
Isaiah of Jerusalem *740-701 B.C.*	People can have peace and prosperity only if they carry out God's will. The future depends on how justly one behaves in the present.
Micah *714-700 B.C.*	Both rich and poor have to obey God's laws. It is important to "do justly, love mercy, and walk humbly with thy God."
Jeremiah *626-587 B.C.*	Suffering is the result of wickedness. God will make a new covenant with the Jews in the future.
Ezekiel *593-571 B.C.*	People are responsible for their own behavior.
Isaiah of Babylon *c. 545 B.C.*	God is the god of all people. God will free Israel and lead it back to the promised land.

Reading Check Answer

The Jews met in small groups on the **sabbath** to pray and talk about their religion and history.

L1 Critical Thinking Direct students to choose one of the teachings by a Hebrew prophet on the chart on page 113. Then have them explain the teaching in their own words.

ASSESS

Check for Understanding

Ask students to summarize the main points of the chapter, orally or in writing. Discuss the answers to the Section and Chapter Assessment questions.

Evaluate

Assign Chapter 6 **Performance Assessment Activity** in the TCR.

Administer **Chapter 6 Test** in the TCR. Testmaker available.

MEETING SPECIAL NEEDS

Discuss with students who are auditory learners what questions they would ask a rabbi about Judaism, if they had the opportunity. Ask a volunteer to record the questions.

If possible, arrange for a rabbi or religious resource person to speak to students, answering their questions in person. If a personal visit is not possible, ask the speaker to record the answers to the questions on tape. Play the recording for students.

Refer to ***Inclusion for the Middle School Social Studies Classroom: Strategies and Activities*** for additional resources.

Reteach

Have students work in groups to outline different subsections. Then have groups exchange their outlines and use them to quiz other members of their group.

Assign Chapter 6 **Reteaching Activity** in the TCR.

Enrich

Suggest students compare a psalm from the Book of Psalms to the lyrics of a modern song they know that also has a theme or message. Which is more understandable?

Assign Chapter 6 **Enrichment Activity** in the TCR.

CLOSE

Ask students to list places where people have historically practiced their religion, such as temples and churches. Then have them describe how Jews changed their rituals when they no longer had the Jerusalem Temple.

Use **Interactive Tutor Self-Assessment CD-ROM** to review Section 2.

HISTORY Online

Self-Check Quiz gives students an interactive chapter tutorial. Have them access ***Chapter 6 Quiz*** at humanheritage.glencoe.com

Major Contributions The Hebrews were the first people to believe in one god. At first, they believed God was concerned only about them. They expected other people to worship many gods. Later, some prophets said God cared about all peoples and all nations.

The Hebrews were the first to believe in a just god. They believed individuals and society should likewise be just. Their laws were designed to teach people to treat one another fairly.

Section 2 Assessment

1. **Define:** descendants, social justice, judge, psalms, prophets, sabbath.
2. Where did the Hebrews trade? What goods did they trade?
3. What new ideas did the Hebrews develop and contribute to later civilizations?

Critical Thinking

4. **Demonstrating Reasoned Judgment** How was the Hebrew belief in one god important to civilization?

Graphic Organizer Activity

5. Draw a diagram like this one, and use it to show milestones in the history of the Hebrews. (Add boxes as needed.)

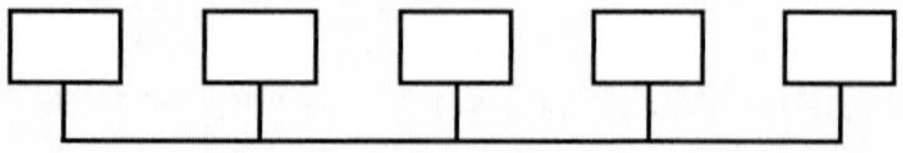

Chapter Summary & Study Guide

1. Phoenician civilization began to develop about 1830 B.C.
2. Phoenicians earned a living from the sea and from trade items such as cedar and purple dye.
3. One of the most important Phoenician contributions was the spread of an alphabet.
4. The Phoenicians set up colonies along the North African coast, including Carthage, founded in 814 B.C.
5. According to the Bible, God made an agreement with Abraham whereby the Hebrews could always live in Canaan if they would worship Him alone.
6. About 1200 B.C., the Hebrews escaped Egyptian bondage and, under Moses' leadership, made a new covenant with God, promising to obey the Ten Commandments.
7. An important Hebrew contribution was the belief in a single just god and a just society.

HISTORY Online

Self-Check Quiz

Visit the *Human Heritage* Web site at humanheritage.glencoe.com and click on ***Chapter 6—Self-Check Quiz*** to assess your understanding of this chapter.

Section 2 Assessment Answers

1. descendants, offspring (p. 107); social justice, equal treatment (p. 110); judge, settled disputes (p. 112); psalms, sacred songs (p. 112); prophets, had messages from God (p. 112); sabbath, day of rest (p. 113)
2. from Ur to Harran and along the Mediterranean coast; gold, copper, and ivory goods
3. the belief in a single god and a just society
4. Answers will vary.
5. Milestones will vary, but should reflect the chronological order of events in this section, starting with Yahweh's agreement with Abraham.

Assign Chapter 6 **Section 2 Quiz** in the TCR. Testmaker available.

CHAPTER 6 Assessment

Using Key Terms

Imagine that you are a traveler to Canaan. Use the following words to write a letter home explaining the new ideas that you have learned about during your visit.

treaties	holy of holies	colonies
descendants	social justice	judge
psalms	prophets	sabbath

Understanding Main Ideas

1. Why were the Phoenicians successful long-distance sailors?
2. What were some of the features of a Phoenician city-state?
3. According to the Bible, what agreement did Yahweh make with Abraham?
4. Why did the Hebrews believe in social justice?
5. Why did the Hebrews make changes in their religion while living in Babylonia?

Critical Thinking

1. How can people who have very limited natural resources still manage to earn a living?
2. Why were language and religion by themselves not enough to unify the Phoenician people?
3. How does the idea that God is just affect the way people behave?
4. Explain the phrase, "Do justly, love mercy, and walk humbly with thy God."
5. Why do you think many people during this time believed that people should listen to prophets?

Graphic Organizer Activity

Culture Create a diagram like this one, and use it to compare Phoenician and Hebrew religious beliefs and practices.

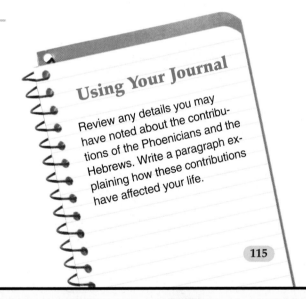

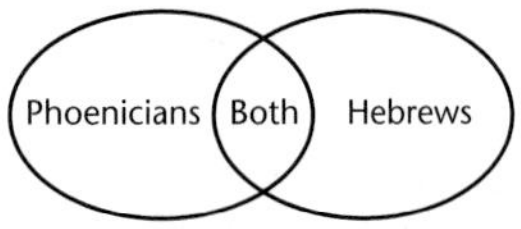

Geography in History

Places and Regions The Hebrews moved from place to place within the same region along the Mediterranean Sea. Choose one of their migrations and describe the geography and features of the land through which they passed. Then make a map showing the route and the geographic features of their migration.

Using Your Journal

Review any details you may have noted about the contributions of the Phoenicians and the Hebrews. Write a paragraph explaining how these contributions have affected your life.

Bonus Test Question

For Chapter 6 Test

Who would be more likely to win achievement awards in the following (Canaanites, Aegeans, or both): agriculture, mathematics, wool weaving, map making, desert survival, astronomy? *(probable answers: Canaanites, Aegeans, Canaanites, both, Canaanites, Aegeans)*

Using Your Journal

Paragraphs will vary but students might include the ways that the alphabet, the idea of treaties, the idea of one god, and the idea of social justice affect them.

Geography in History

Depending upon which migration students choose to describe, they should include arid, dry land; sand, mountains; little vegetation; rivers and/or Mediterranean Sea.

CHAPTER 6 Assessment Answers

Using Key Terms

Letters will vary but should include that these are new ideas they have learned in Canaan.

Understanding Main Ideas

1. because of strong, fast ships, and plotted courses
2. Most were crowded, had stone walls around them for protection, with shops behind. The port lay outside the walls.
3. that if Abraham and his followers were to go to Canaan and obey Yahweh they could always live there
4. because they should be like God who was just
5. because they had lost the great temple at Jerusalem

Critical Thinking

1. Answers will vary but should include through trade.
2. because mountains separated groups of Phoenicians
3. Answers will vary but should include that if people believe God is just, they will behave justly.
4. Answers will vary but should include that justice should be tempered with love and mercy.
5. Answers will vary but could refer to the power the prophets had to incite the people.

Graphic Organizer Activity

Sample responses: both—worshiped in temples; Phoenicians—believed in many gods closely tied to nature, embalmed bodies, believed in life after death, practiced sacrifice; Hebrews—believed in one just god, worshiped on the sabbath, compiled sacred writings into the Torah and Old Testament.

Chapter 7 Planning Guide

Timesaving Tools

TeacherWorks™ All-In-One Planner and Resource Center

- **Interactive Teacher Edition** Access your Teacher Wraparound Edition and your classroom resources with a few easy clicks.
- **Interactive Lesson Planner** Planning has never been easier! Organize your week, month, semester, or year with all the lesson helps you need to make teaching creative, timely, and relevant.

PRESENTATION Plus! Use Glencoe's **Presentation Plus!** multimedia teacher tool to easily present dynamic lessons that visually excite your students. Using Microsoft PowerPoint® you can customize the presentations to create your own personalized lessons.

Objectives	Reproducible Resources	Multimedia Resources
Section 1 **The Assyrians** Discuss how the Assyrian civilization rose in Mesopotamia and expanded into neighboring lands.	Reproducible Lesson Plan Chapter 7 Vocabulary and Guided Reading Activity Reading Essentials and Study Guide 7-1 Chapter 7 Cooperative Learning Activity Chapter 7 Chart and Graph Skill Activity Section 1 Quiz	Interactive Student Edition CD-ROM Graphic Organizer Transparency 4 Vocabulary PuzzleMaker CD-ROM Interactive Tutor Self-Assessment CD-ROM ExamView® Pro Testmaker CD-ROM Glencoe Skillbuilder Interactive Workbook CD-ROM, Level 1 Presentation Plus! CD-ROM
Section 2 **The Chaldeans** Summarize the Chaldeans and their methods of ruling and increasing trade.	Reproducible Lesson Plan Reading Essentials and Study Guide 7-2 Section 2 Quiz	Vocabulary PuzzleMaker CD-ROM Interactive Tutor Self-Assessment CD-ROM ExamView® Pro Testmaker CD-ROM Glencoe Skillbuilder Interactive Workbook CD-ROM, Level 1
Section 3 **The Persians** Explain how Persian ideas spread through the forging of large empires, and how their social and religious life helped create a stable society.	Reproducible Lesson Plan Reading Essentials and Study Guide 7-3 Chapter 7 Geography and Map Activity Chapter 7 Enrichment Activity Section 3 Quiz	Teaching Transparencies and Activities 7A & 7B Vocabulary PuzzleMaker CD-ROM Interactive Tutor Self-Assessment CD-ROM ExamView® Pro Testmaker CD-ROM Glencoe Skillbuilder Interactive Workbook CD-ROM, Level 1
Chapter 7 **Review and** **Evaluation**	Chapter 7 Reteaching Activity Chapter 7 Performance Assessment Activity Spanish Chapter Summary and Glossary Chapter 7 Test	Vocabulary PuzzleMaker CD-ROM Interactive Tutor Self-Assessment CD-ROM Glencoe Skillbuilder Interactive Workbook CD-ROM, Level 1 Audiocassettes* ExamView® Pro Testmaker CD-ROM

*Also available in Spanish.

✓ Performance Assessment Activities

Friendly Letters Instruct students to imagine that they are teenagers living in one of the civilizations described in the chapter. Tell them to write a letter to a friend in a neighboring city describing a day in their lives. Ask volunteers to share their letters with the class.

CHAPTER RESOURCES

READINGS FOR THE STUDENT

Jameson, Cynthia. *The Secret of the Royal Mounds: Henry Layard and the First Cities of Assyria*. Coward, McCann & Geoghegan, 1980. An illustrated account of the career of Layard, the discoverer of ancient Nineveh and one of the first scientific archaeologists.

Saggs, H.W. *Everyday Life in Babylonia and Assyria.* Dorset Press, 1987. Describes the life and customs of ancient Babylonians and Assyrians.

READINGS FOR THE TEACHER

Collins, Robert. *The Medes and the Persians: Conquerors and Diplomats.* McGraw-Hill, 1975. Recounts the daily lives, beliefs, and government of the ancient Persians.

Editors of Time-Life Books. *Lost Civilizations: Mesopotamia—The Mighty Kings.* Time-Life Books, 1995. A vividly illustrated look at civilizations in the Fertile Crescent.

KEY TO ABILITY LEVELS

Teaching strategies have been coded for varying learning styles and abilities.

L1 Level 1 activities are **basic** activities and should be within the ability range of all students.

L2 Level 2 activities are **average** activities and should be within the ability range of the average to above-average student.

L3 Level 3 activities are **challenging** activities designed for the ability range of above-average students.

ELL ELL activities should be within the ability range of English Language Learning students.

NATIONAL GEOGRAPHIC Teacher's Corner

INDEX TO NATIONAL GEOGRAPHIC MAGAZINE

The following article relates to this chapter:

- "Iraq: Crucible of Civilization," by Merle Severy, May 1991.

NATIONAL GEOGRAPHIC SOCIETY PRODUCTS AVAILABLE FROM GLENCOE

To order the following, call Glencoe at 1-800-334-7344:

- *PicturePack: Physical Geography of the World (Transparencies)*
- *Picture Atlas of the World (CD-ROM)*

ADDITIONAL NATIONAL GEOGRAPHIC SOCIETY PRODUCTS

To order the following, call National Geographic at 1-800-368-2728:

- *Arabia: Sand, Sea, and Sky (Video)*
- *Families of the World Series: Israel (Video)*
- *National Geographic Atlas of World History (Book)*
- *Wonders of the Ancient World: National Geographic Atlas of Archaeology (Book)*

Access *National Geographic*'s new dynamic MapMachine Web site and other geography resources at:
www.nationalgeographic.com
www.nationalgeographic.com/maps

Introducing **CHAPTER 7**

OVERVIEW

Chapter 7 focuses on the Assyrian, Chaldean, and Persian empires and their contributions to the ancient Middle East.

- **Section 1** discusses the Assyrian civilization and its empire in Mesopotamia.
- **Section 2** explains the features of the Chaldean civilization and its city of Babylon.
- **Section 3** describes the contributions made by Persians to other civilizations.

CHAPTER OBJECTIVES

After reading Chapter 7, your students will be able to:

1. explain how the Assyrians established and maintained an empire in Mesopotamia.

2. describe what the Chaldean city of Babylon was like.

3. discuss how the Persians were able to rule an empire that stretched from Egypt to India.

EXAMINING ARTIFACTS

Ask students what these artifacts reveal about the Assyrians. *(Sample response: They possessed wealth and saw themselves—or their ruler—as strong as a lion.)* As students read through the chapter, direct them to decide whether a winged lion accurately represents the Assyrian people.

PERFORMANCE ASSESSMENT

Use the Performance Assessment Activities on page 116B to help you evaluate students as they complete the chapter.

CHAPTER 7

Military Empires

1400 B.C.–570 B.C.

▲ Gold Assyrian jewelry

◀ Assyrian winged lion

- **1400 B.C.** Hittites develop iron making
- **800 B.C.** Assyrians establish empire
- **612 B.C.** Chaldeans capture Nineveh
- **570 B.C.** Zoroaster introduces new religion
- **539 B.C.** Persians seize Mesopotamia

TEACHING RESOURCES

TEACHER PLANNING AND SUPPORT

- Reproducible Lesson Plan 7-1, 7-2, 7-3
- Teaching Strategies for the World History Classroom (Including Block Scheduling Pacing Guides)
- Presentation Plus! CD-ROM

REVIEW AND REINFORCEMENT

- Reading Essentials and Study Guide 7-1, 7-2, 7-3
- Chapter 7 Vocabulary and Guided Reading Activity
- Vocabulary PuzzleMaker CD-ROM
- Teaching Transparencies 7A & 7B
- Chapter 7 Reteaching Activity
- Chapter 7 Cooperative Learning Activity
- Chapter 7 Activity Book Activity
- Chapter 7 Chart and Graph Skill Activity
- Reading and Study Skills Foldables
- Interactive Tutor Self-Assessment CD-ROM

APPLICATION AND HANDS-ON ACTIVITIES

- Daily Questions in Social Studies
- Unit 3 Hands-On History Lab Activity
- Student Presentation Builder CD-ROM

GEOGRAPHY ACTIVITIES

- Chapter 7 Geography and Map Activity
- Outline Map Resource Book

Chapter Focus

Read to Discover

- How the Assyrians established and maintained an empire in Mesopotamia.
- What the Chaldean city of Babylon was like.
- How the Persians were able to rule an empire that stretched from Egypt to India.

HISTORY Online

Chapter Overview

Visit the *Human Heritage* Web site at **humanheritage.glencoe.com** and click on ***Chapter 7—Chapter Overviews*** to preview this chapter.

Terms to Learn	**People to Know**	**Places to Locate**
empires	Ashurbanipal	Nineveh
smelting	Nebuchadnezzar	Babylon
provinces	Cyrus	Persepolis
caravans	Darius	Lydia
astronomers	Zoroaster	

Why It's Important While the Phoenicians and the Hebrews were developing their civilizations, powerful kingdoms rose and fell in Mesopotamia. Built by the Assyrians, the Chaldeans (kal dē´ uhns), and the Persians, these kingdoms were not content to stay where their civilizations began. Rulers raised large armies and expanded into neighboring lands. They developed new ways of organizing their **empires**—territories governed by a single ruler or nation. They also increased trade. Through conquest and trade, these three empire-builders spread their ideas and customs over a wide area.

Reading Check Which people used large armies to build powerful **empires** in Mesopotamia?

SECTION 1 The Assyrians

About 1,000 years after Hammurabi ruled, a people called Assyrians rose to power in Mesopotamia. Their country, Assyria, lay in the upper part of the Tigris River valley. The Assyrians spoke the same language and used the same writing system as the Babylonians.

The Assyrians were warriors. Experts believe their liking for war was influenced by geography. Assyria's rolling hills and rain-watered valleys did not provide protection against invaders. Assyrian shepherds and farmers had to learn to fight to survive. In time, fighting became a way of life.

The Assyrians built a powerful army. By 1100 B.C., they had defeated their neighboring enemies. By 800 B.C., they were strong enough to take over cities, trading routes, and fortresses throughout Mesopotamia.

INTERDISCIPLINARY CONNECTIONS

- World Music: A Cultural Legacy
- World Art Print 2, Lion—from the *Ishtar Gate*

ENRICHMENT AND EXTENSION

- World History Primary Source Document Library CD-ROM
- Chapter 7 Enrichment Activity
- Foods Around the World

ASSESSMENT AND EVALUATION

- Chapter 7 Performance Assessment Activity
- Chapter 7 Section Quizzes 7-1, 7-2, 7-3
- Chapter 7 Test
- Chapter 7 ExamView® Pro Testmaker CD-ROM
- Chapter 7 Digests Audiocassettes Activities and Tests

SPANISH RESOURCES

- Chapter 7 Spanish Chapter Summary and Glossary
- Chapter 7 Spanish Chapter Digests Audiocassettes Activities and Tests

HISTORY Online

Chapter Overview introduces students to chapter content and key terms. Have them access ***Chapter 7 Overview*** at **humanheritage.glencoe.com**

FOCUS

Bellringer

Write this saying on the chalkboard: *So passes away the glory of the world.* Ask students to write a sentence that explains the meaning of the word *glory* in this statement.

Motivational Activity

Discuss students' explanations of *glory*. Then ask the students to think about the world today and find examples of countries that are declining from a position of earlier glory.

Reading Check Answer the Assyrians, Chaldeans, and Persians

GUIDE TO READING

Reading Strategy

Ask students to read "Why It's Important" and summarize the chapter's main theme. *(Through trade and conquest, the Assyrians, Chaldeans, and Persians spread ideas and customs throughout Mesopotamia.)*

Vocabulary Precheck

Ask students to define each of the "Terms to Learn." Have a volunteer consult the dictionary for any unfamiliar words. L1 ELL

Use the Vocabulary PuzzleMaker CD-ROM for Chapter 7 to create a crossword puzzle. L1

Assign Chapter 7 Vocabulary and Guided Reading Activity.

Assign Reading Essentials and Study Guide 7-1.

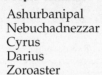

CAPTION ANSWER

into units of foot soldiers, charioteers, cavalry, and archers

MAKING CONNECTIONS

>> **Daily Life** Many Assyrians lived in small villages in the midst of fields. Traders, government officers, and artisans lived in the cities in flat-roofed brick houses, some of which had bathrooms with asphalt floors and drains to carry away water. Most clothing was made of wool.

Reading Check Answer
In **smelting,** metalworkers hammer impurities out of heated iron ore and rapidly cool it.

NATIONAL GEOGRAPHIC

Use these materials to enrich student understanding of the Middle Eastern civilizations.

NGS PICTURESHOW CD-ROM
Egypt and the Fertile Crescent

NGS PICTUREPACK TRANSPARENCY SET
Fertile Crescent

ANCIENT CIVILIZATIONS POSTER SET
The Fertile Crescent

Fun Facts . . .

New Model The Hittites developed a chariot that could carry two soldiers *and* a driver. Other peoples, including the Egyptians, used a two-person chariot. With their three-person chariot, Hittites could field twice as many soldiers as their foes.

ASSYRIAN SOLDIERS Assyrian kings often celebrated their victories by decorating palaces and temples with scenes of warfare. Here, a wall sculpture shows Assyrian soldiers. **How was the Assyrian army organized?**

The Assyrian Army

The Assyrian army was well-organized. It was divided into groups of foot soldiers armed with shields, helmets, spears, and daggers. It also had units of charioteers, cavalry, and archers.

At first, the Assyrians fought only during summer when they did not have to be concerned about planting or harvesting crops. Later, as they took over more land, soldiering became a year-round job. When the Assyrians needed more soldiers, they hired them from other places or forced the people they had conquered to serve.

Assyrian power was due partly to their weapons, which were made of iron. Iron weapons are harder and stronger than weapons made of copper or tin. Iron had been used in the Middle East for many centuries. Until about 1400 B.C., however, it was too soft to be made into weapons. Then, a people called Hittites (hi′ tītz) developed a process of **smelting.** They heated iron ore, hammered out its impurities, and rapidly cooled it. The Assyrians borrowed the skill of smelting from the Hittites.

Reading Check How did the process of **smelting** work?

The Assyrians were cruel warriors. For several hundred years, their armies spread death and destruction throughout the Middle East. They were especially skilled in attacking cities. They tunneled under walls or climbed over them on ladders. They used beams mounted on movable platforms to ram holes through city gates. Once they captured a city, they set fire to its buildings and carried away its citizens and goods.

Anyone who resisted Assyrian rule was punished. Those who did not resist had to pay heavy taxes. The Assyrians also

MULTICULTURAL PERSPECTIVES

Assyrians were the first hairstylists. They refined this styling so much that hairstyles became a major part of the culture. Assyrians even had laws specifying the hairstyles of people in certain jobs. They cut short hair into graduated tiers and arranged long hair in ringlets and curls. They oiled, perfumed, and tinted hair. They even curled hair with a fire-heated iron bar, the first known curling iron.

found a way to conquer people without fighting. They spread stories of their cruelty. Other people were so frightened by the stories that they would simply surrender.

Kings and Government Assyria's kings were strong leaders. They had to be to rule an empire that extended from the Persian Gulf in the east to the Nile valley in the west. Assyrian kings spent much of their time fighting battles and punishing enemies. However, they were also involved in peaceful activities. A great Assyrian king, Ashurbanipal (osh uhr bon' uh pol), started one of the world's first libraries. It held 25,000 tablets of hymns, stories, and biographies.

Assyrian kings had to control many peoples spread over a large area. To do this, they divided their empire into **provinces,** or political districts. They then chose officials to govern each province. The officials collected taxes and made certain the king's laws were obeyed.

All provinces were connected by a system of roads. Although only roads near major cities were paved, all were level enough for carts and chariots to travel on. Over the roads moved the trade of the empire. Government soldiers were posted at stations along the

Reading Check Why did the Assyrians divide their empire into **provinces**?

The Assyrian and Chaldean Empires

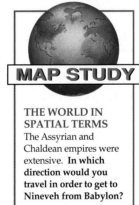

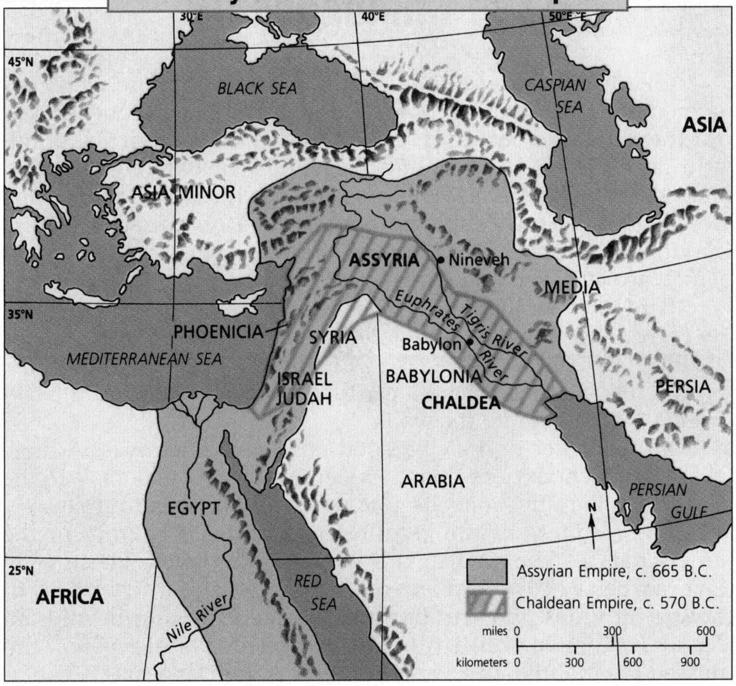

MAP STUDY

THE WORLD IN SPATIAL TERMS

The Assyrian and Chaldean empires were extensive. **In which direction would you travel in order to get to Nineveh from Babylon?**

TEACH

L1 **Map Reading** Ask students to study the map on page 119 to answer the following questions: Which empire was larger, Chaldean or Assyrian? *(Assyrian Empire)* Which empire was located in the Tigris-Euphrates valley? *(both)* What part of the Chaldean Empire was not part of the Assyrian Empire? How can you tell? *(area in Arabia, between the Euphrates River and the Mediterranean Sea; has a yellow background)*

Reading Check Answer The Assyrians divided their empire into **provinces** so they could collect taxes and enforce laws over a large area.

MAP STUDY Answer

north

Economics at a Glance

Movement of Goods

Roads and waterways help move goods from one region to another. Communication systems, including the Internet, are also important for moving goods. Roads, waterways, and communication systems help communities grow and prosper. Have students look at the map on page 119. Ask them to identify the waterways and bodies of water that helped the Assyrian and Chaldean empires with the transportation of goods. *(Assyrian empire: Red Sea, Nile River, Mediterranean Sea, Tigris River, Euphrates River, Persian Gulf; Chaldean empire: Mediterranean Sea, Tigris River, Euphrates River, Persian Gulf)*

SPOTLIGHT ON: ASHURBANIPAL

Ashurbanipal was both a brutal Assyrian king and a scholar. Since he was able to read and write Assyria's cuneiform writing, he collected every cuneiform tablet in the kingdom that he felt was worth saving. His collection was stored in his library at Nineveh. The collection included 22,000 tablets written in Sumerian, Babylonian, and Assyrian. These tablets represented 2,500 years of Mesopotamian written history and included letters, official documents, and dictionaries and studies of mathematics, astronomy, and botany.

Guided Practice

L2 **Geography: Human Systems** Have students make travel plans for an ancient Greek who is planning to visit one of the empires discussed in this chapter. In a letter to the traveler, have students give detailed information, including a travel route and list of sites to visit.

Use the **Interactive Tutor Self-Assessment CD-ROM** to review Section 1.

DID YOU KNOW ??

The ziggurat in Babylon is thought to be the Tower of Babel mentioned in the Book of Genesis, Chapter 11 of the Old Testament.

Use the **Vocabulary PuzzleMaker CD-ROM** to create crossword and word search puzzles.

roads to protect traders from bandits. Messengers on government business used the stations to rest and to change horses.

In time, the empire became too large to govern. After Ashurbanipal died, various conquered peoples worked to end Assyrian rule. One group was the Chaldeans. In 612 B.C., they captured Nineveh (nin′ uh vuh), the Assyrian capital. The Assyrian Empire crumbled shortly after.

Section 1 Assessment

1. **Define:** empire, smelting, provinces.
2. How was Assyria governed?
3. Why did the Assyrian Empire fall?

Critical Thinking

4. **Forming Conclusions** Do you think ruling by fear is an effective way to govern? Why or why not?

Graphic Organizer Activity

5. Draw a diagram like this one, and use it to show the cause and effects of the Assyrian warrior way of life.

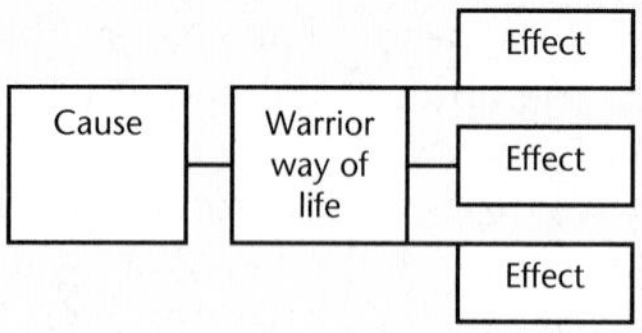

SECTION 2 The Chaldeans

Like the Assyrians, the Chaldeans were warriors who conquered many different peoples. Under their king Nebuchadnezzar (neb uh kuhd nez′ uhr), they extended their empire's boundaries as far west as Syria and Palestine. The Chaldeans called themselves Babylonians. This was because most Chaldeans were descendants of the people who made up Hammurabi's empire about 1,200 years earlier. They built a new capital at Babylon in which nearly 1 million people lived.

Babylon was the world's richest city up to that time. It had its own police force and postal system. Huge brick walls encircled the city. The walls were so wide that two chariots could pass on the road on top. Archers guarded the approaches to the city from towers built into the walls.

In the center of the city stood palaces and temples. A huge ziggurat reached more than 300 feet, or over 90 meters, into the sky. When the sun shone, its gold roof could be seen for miles.

The richness of the ziggurat was equaled by that of the king's palace. The palace had "hanging gardens." These were layered beds of earth planted with large trees and masses of flowering vines and shrubs. They seemed to hang in mid-air. Nebuchadnezzar built the gardens to please his wife, who missed the mountains and plants of her native land.

Fun Facts . . . .

Seven Wonders Historians of the time counted the Hanging Gardens of Babylon among the Seven Wonders of the World. Other wonders included: the pyramids of Egypt, the statue of Zeus at Olympia, the temple of Artemis (Diana) at Ephesus, the mausoleum at Halicarnassus, the Colossus of Rhodes, and the lighthouse at Pharos.

Section 1 Assessment Answers

1. empires, territories governed by a single ruler or nation (p. 117); smelting, process of heating iron ore, hammering it, and rapidly cooling it (p. 118); provinces, political districts (p. 119)
2. Assyrian kings divided their empire into provinces and then chose officials to govern each. The officials collected taxes and enforced laws.
3. because it became too large to govern and had many enemies
4. Answers will vary but students must give reasons to support their opinions. Characteristics of good leadership may be added.
5. Cause—a geography that did not provide protection against invaders; Effects—built a strong army; defeated neighboring enemies; took over cities, trading routes, and fortresses throughout Mesopotamia

Assign Chapter 7 **Section 1 Quiz** in the TCR. Testmaker available.

made all evil things in the world. Ahura Mazda and Ahriman were at war with each other all of the time.

Zoroaster said human beings had to decide which god they would support. Zoroaster then listed the good and bad deeds a person performed. Good deeds were keeping one's word, giving to the poor, working the land, obeying the king, and treating others well. Bad deeds included being lazy, proud, or greedy. Zoroaster could tell from the list which god a person had chosen. He believed that in the end Ahura Mazda would defeat Ahriman. People who supported Ahura Mazda would enjoy happiness after death. Those who supported Ahriman would be punished.

Trade The Persians thought they should be warriors, farmers, or shepherds. They refused to become traders. They believed that trade forced people to lie, cheat, and be greedy. They did, however, encourage trade among all peoples they conquered.

The Persians improved and expanded the system of roads begun by the Assyrians. One road, the Royal Road, ran more than 1,600 miles, or more than 2,560 kilometers. A journey that took three months before the Royal Road was built took only 15 days after it was completed. The Persians also opened a caravan route to China. Silk was first brought west along this route.

MAP STUDY

THE WORLD IN SPATIAL TERMS
The Persian Empire stretched from the Nile River to the Indus River, a distance of 3,000 miles, or 4,800 kilometers. Within this empire, the Persians ruled more than 50 million people. **Into what continents did the Persian Empire extend?**

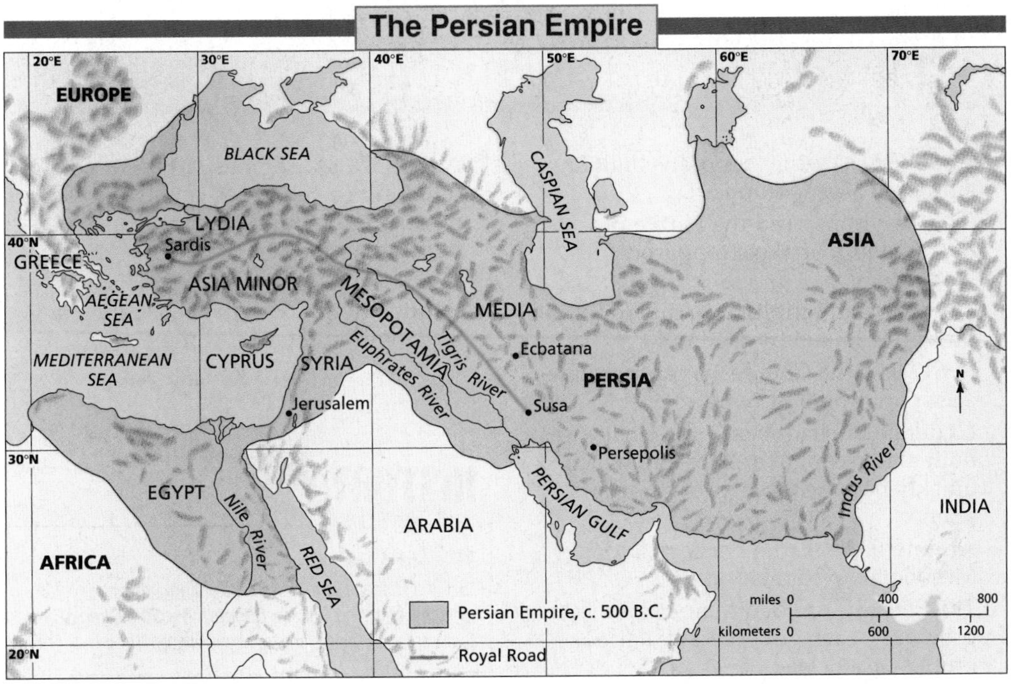

L2 **Map Scale** Have students use the map of the Persian Empire to find the distances between the following places: Susa and Sardis along the Royal Road *(approximately 1,600 miles or 2,574 km)*, Susa and Jerusalem *(approximately 1,000 miles or 1,609 km)*, Ecbatana and Jerusalem *(approximately 900 miles or 1,448 km)*, Persepolis and Sardis *(approximately 1,900 miles or 3,057 km)*. ELL

MAP STUDY

Answer

Europe, Asia, and Africa

ASSESS

Check for Understanding

Ask students to summarize the main points of the chapter, orally or in writing. Discuss the answers to the Section and Chapter Review questions.

Evaluate

Assign Chapter 7 **Performance Assessment Activity** in the TCR.

Administer **Chapter 7 Test** in the TCR. Testmaker available.

MEETING SPECIAL NEEDS

Divide students with limited English proficiency into three groups. Have each group prepare a travel poster on one of the empires discussed in the chapter. Explain that their poster should try to sell their assigned empire as a vacation destination. Have students work together on a format for presenting the information on the poster. Encourage students to include points of interest. Display completed posters around the classroom.

Refer to ***Inclusion for the Middle School Social Studies Classroom: Strategies and Activities*** for additional resources.

Reteach

Organize students into small groups to write a poem or short story that expresses the main ideas of one section in the chapter.

Assign Chapter 7 **Reteaching Activity** in the TCR.

Enrich

Have students investigate one of the people discussed in the chapter and write a biographical sketch of the person. Suggest authors present the biographical sketch to the class as if they are that person.

Assign Chapter 7 **Enrichment Activity** in the TCR.

CLOSE

Have students discuss this question: *Based on your reading of the chapter—which is more likely to bring about change in a culture—an idea brought to people through peaceful means or an idea forced on them?*

Use **Interactive Tutor Self-Assessment CD-ROM** to review Section 3.

HISTORY Online

Self-Check Quiz gives students an interactive chapter tutorial. Have them access ***Chapter 7 Quiz*** at humanheritage.glencoe.com

The Persians spread the idea of using coins for money. The first known coins had been made in Lydia (lid′ ē uh), a tiny kingdom in Asia Minor bordering on the Aegean Sea. After conquering Lydia, the Persian king decided to use gold coins in his empire. This helped to increase trade. It also changed the nature of trade. Merchants who had sold only costly goods began to sell everyday, cheaper things as well. They sold chickens, dried fish, furniture, clothing, and pots and pans. Since people could get more goods, they began to live better than they had before.

Section 3 Assessment

1. How did the Persians treat people they conquered?
2. What religious ideas did Zoroaster introduce to Persia?
3. In what ways did the Persians contribute to the growth of trade within their empire?

Critical Thinking

4. **Making Comparisons** How do the roles of government officials in the United States compare with the roles of government officials in Persia?

Graphic Organizer Activity

5. Draw a diagram like this one, and use it to describe the government, economy, and religion of the Persian Empire.

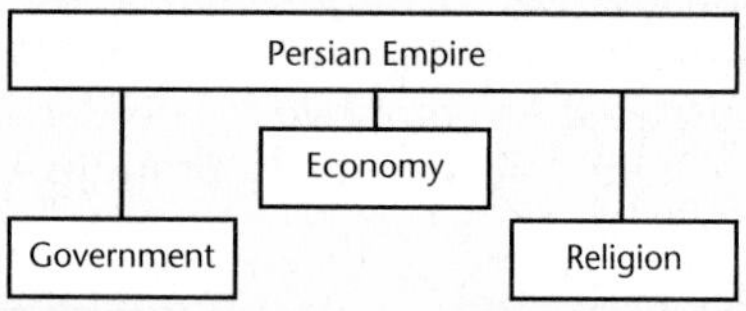

Chapter Summary & Study Guide

1. About 800 B.C., the Assyrians built an empire in Mesopotamia.
2. The Assyrians used the Hittite process of smelting to make strong iron weapons.
3. The Assyrian Empire was divided into provinces linked by roads.
4. In 612 B.C., the Chaldeans captured the Assyrian capital of Nineveh.
5. Under Nebuchadnezzar, the Chaldeans built a new capital at Babylon, which quickly became a center of trade and science.
6. Around 539 B.C., the Persians added Mesopotamia to their empire.
7. The Persians divided their empire into provinces, each governed by various groups of officials.
8. About 570 B.C., Zoroaster taught a new religion in which good and evil took the form of two gods who were constantly fighting each other.
9. Though the Persians did not become traders themselves, they encouraged trade within their far-flung empire.

HISTORY Online

Self-Check Quiz

Visit the *Human Heritage* Web site at humanheritage.glencoe.com and click on ***Chapter 7—Self-Check Quiz*** to assess your understanding of this chapter.

Section 3 Assessment Answers

1. The Persians let them keep their own language, religion, and laws.
2. one good and one bad god, choosing a god, and punishment after death
3. They improved the system of Assyrian roads, opened a caravan route to China, and spread coins.
4. Answers will vary but may include Persian officials were appointed, whereas U.S. officials are elected; both officials dealt with taxation and in providing protection.
5. government: should reflect mild rule toward conquered peoples and descriptions on page 124; economy: should emphasize importance of trade and descriptions on pages 125–126; religion: should highlight Zoroaster and descriptions on pages 124–125

Assign Chapter 7 **Section 3 Quiz** in the TCR. Testmaker available.

CHAPTER 7 Assessment

Using Key Terms

Imagine you are writing a feature magazine article about the Assyrian and Chaldean empires. Use the following words in your article to describe some of the achievements made in these two empires.

empires	smelting	provinces
caravans	astronomers	

Understanding Main Ideas

1. What do experts believe influenced the Assyrians to become warriors?
2. What made the Assyrians such feared fighters?
3. Why did the Chaldeans call themselves Babylonians?
4. What was the importance of the god Marduk to the Babylonians?
5. What was the relationship between the Persians and the Aryans?
6. In Persian government, who were "the Eyes and Ears of the King," and what did they do?
7. How was family life in Persia alike for both the rich and poor?
8. Why did the Persians refuse to become traders?

Critical Thinking

1. How can the reputation of a group like the Assyrians affect how others act toward that group?
2. How did the introduction of coins affect trade?
3. How would you describe the Persian attitude toward trade, and how wise was this policy?
4. In which of the empires discussed in this chapter would you have chosen to live? Explain.

Graphic Organizer Activity

Citizenship Create a diagram like this one, and use it to compare the governments of the Assyrian and Persian Empires.

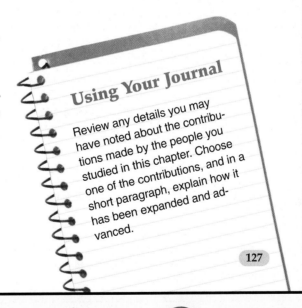

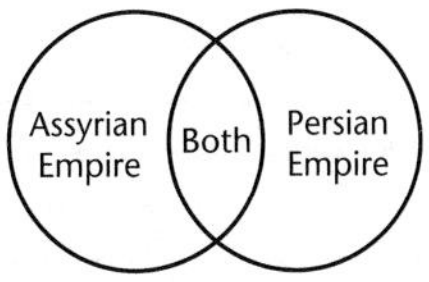

Geography in History

Environment and Society What changes in their environment did the Persians make that extended ideas started by the Assyrians and Chaldeans? Explain your answer.

Using Your Journal

Review any details you may have noted about the contributions made by the people you studied in this chapter. Choose one of the contributions, and in a short paragraph, explain how it has been expanded and advanced.

CHAPTER 7 Assessment Answers

Using Key Terms

Articles will vary but students should use the words to describe these empires' achievements.

Understanding Main Ideas

1. Assyria's geography
2. They were cruel warriors who burned cities and carried away its citizens and goods.
3. Most were descendants of the people who had made up Hammurabi's empire.
4. They believed Marduk would make their crops grow and help keep peace.
5. The Persians were originally part of the Aryan people.
6. They were government officials who traveled throughout the empire to assess taxes and check on rumors of rebellion.
7. Both lived in houses with pointed roofs and porches that faced the sun, and both had large families ruled by the father.
8. because they believed that trade forced people to lie and cheat

Critical Thinking

1. Students should note that a reputation of strength or cruelty will cause fear.
2. It increased trade and the types of goods sold.
3. Answers will vary but should include Persians' aversion to trade that later changed.
4. Answers will vary.

Graphic Organizer Activity

Sample responses: both—ruled by kings, divided empire into provinces, used officials to collect taxes and enforce laws; Assyria—relied on fear, harsh punishment of resisters, levied heavy taxes; Persia—relied on fairness instead of force, used inspectors to keep king informed, appointed judges to control law

Bonus Test Question

For Chapter 7 Test

What is smelting and why was this technology important to the development of a system of roads by the Assyrians? *(Smelting, the process of heating and cooling metal to form it, allowed the Assyrians to make weapons that made them successful conquerors.)*

Using Your Journal

Paragraphs will vary but should explain how the contribution has been expanded and advanced. You might call on volunteers to share their paragraphs with the class.

Geography in History

The Persians extended roads started by the Assyrians and maintained the division into provinces. Farming methods including irrigation canals were borrowed from the Chaldeans.

Chapter 8 Planning Guide

Timesaving Tools

TeacherWorks™ All-In-One Planner and Resource Center

- **Interactive Teacher Edition** Access your Teacher Wraparound Edition and your classroom resources with a few easy clicks.
- **Interactive Lesson Planner** Planning has never been easier! Organize your week, month, semester, or year with all the lesson helps you need to make teaching creative, timely, and relevant.

Use Glencoe's **Presentation Plus!** multimedia teacher tool to easily present dynamic lessons that visually excite your students. Using Microsoft PowerPoint® you can customize the presentations to create your own personalized lessons.

Objectives	Reproducible Resources	Multimedia Resources
Section 1 **Ancient African Kingdoms** Discuss how the ancient African civilizations of Kush and Aksum passed along elements of their culture to the world.	Reproducible Lesson Plan Chapter 8 Vocabulary and Guided Reading Activity Reading Essentials and Study Guide 8-1 Section 1 Quiz	Interactive Student Edition CD-ROM Graphic Organizer Transparency 1 Vocabulary PuzzleMaker CD-ROM Interactive Tutor Self-Assessment CD-ROM ExamView® Pro Testmaker CD-ROM Presentation Plus! CD-ROM
Section 2 **The Middle Kingdoms** Identify how West African kingdoms grew and developed.	Reproducible Lesson Plan Reading Essentials and Study Guide 8-2 Chapter 8 Cooperative Learning Activity Chapter 8 Chart and Graph Skill Activity Chapter 8 Geography and Map Activity Section 2 Quiz	Vocabulary PuzzleMaker CD-ROM Interactive Tutor Self-Assessment CD-ROM Glencoe Skillbuilder Interactive Workbook CD-ROM, Level 1
Section 3 **East African Civilizations** Summarize how East African civilizations developed as trading regions.	Reproducible Lesson Plan Reading Essentials and Study Guide 8-3 Chapter 8 Enrichment Activity Unit 3 Primary Source Readings Section 3 Quiz	Vocabulary PuzzleMaker CD-ROM ExamView® Pro Testmaker CD-ROM Glencoe Skillbuilder Interactive Workbook CD-ROM, Level 1
Section 4 **Path to the Americas** Explain why people crossed into the Americas.	Reproducible Lesson Plan Reading Essentials and Study Guide 8-4 Section 4 Quiz	Vocabulary PuzzleMaker CD-ROM Interactive Tutor Self-Assessment CD-ROM
Section 5 **Mesoamerica** Describe the civilizations in Mesoamerica.	Reproducible Lesson Plan Reading Essentials and Study Guide 8-5 Section 5 Quiz	Vocabulary PuzzleMaker CD-ROM ExamView® Pro Testmaker CD-ROM
Section 6 **The Incas** Characterize what life was like for the Incas.	Reproducible Lesson Plan Reading Essentials and Study Guide 8-6 Section 6 Quiz	Teaching Transparencies and Activities 8A & 8B Vocabulary PuzzleMaker CD-ROM ExamView® Pro Testmaker CD-ROM
Chapter 8 **Review and Evaluation**	Chapter 8 Reteaching Activity Chapter 8 Performance Assessment Activity Unit 3 Standardized Test Practice Spanish Chapter 8 Summary and Glossary Chapter 8 Test	Vocabulary PuzzleMaker CD-ROM Interactive Tutor Self-Assessment CD-ROM Glencoe Skillbuilder Interactive Workbook CD-ROM, Level 1 Audiocassettes* ExamView® Pro Testmaker CD-ROM

*Also available in Spanish.

Performance Assessment Activities

A Geographical Journal Have students keep a geographical journal of the continents they will study in this chapter (Africa, North America, South America). Instruct them to sketch an outline map of each continent and to locate each empire or civilization as it is studied, along with any other information they choose.

CHAPTER RESOURCES

LITERATURE ABOUT THE PERIOD

Courlander, Harold. *A Treasury of African Folklore.* Crown Publishers, 1975. Collection of the oral literature, traditions, myths, and legends of Africa.

READINGS FOR THE STUDENT

Chu, Daniel, and Elliot Skinner. *A Glorious Age in Africa; the Story of Three Great African Empires.* Doubleday (Zenith Books), 1990. Illustrated account of Ghana, Mali, and Songhai.

Stuart, Gene S. *America's Ancient Cities.* National Geographic Society, 1988. Illustrated collection of essays on cultures of North America and Mesoamerica.

READINGS FOR THE TEACHER

Gallenkamp, Charles. *Maya: The Riddle and Rediscovery of a Lost Civilization.* Viking, 1985. Detailed account of the Mayas.

KEY TO ABILITY LEVELS

Teaching strategies have been coded for varying learning styles and abilities.

L1 Level 1 activities are **basic** activities and should be within the ability range of all students.

L2 Level 2 activities are **average** activities and should be within the ability range of the average to above-average student.

L3 Level 3 activities are **challenging** activities designed for the ability range of above-average students.

ELL ELL activities should be within the ability range of English Language Learning students.

NATIONAL GEOGRAPHIC Teacher's Corner

INDEX TO NATIONAL GEOGRAPHIC MAGAZINE

The following articles relate to this chapter:

- "Uncovering a Mural: Early Date of Wall Art Stuns Experts," by Tom O'Neill, April 2002.
- "Bushmen: Last Stand for Southern Africa's First People," by Peter Godwin, February 2001 .
- "Paintings of the Spirt," by David Lewis-Williams, February 2001.
- "The Dawn of Humans: Hunt for the First Americans," by Michael Parfit, December 2000.
- "Rediscovering America," by Tom Brooks, January 2000.

NATIONAL GEOGRAPHIC SOCIETY PRODUCTS AVAILABLE FROM GLENCOE

To order the following, call Glencoe at 1-800-334-7344:

- *PicturePack: Ancient Civilizations: Middle America (Transparencies)*
- *PicturePack: Ancient Civilizations: South America (Transparencies)*
- *PictureShow: Ancient Civilizations: Middle and South America (CD-ROM)*
- *PictureShow: Ancient Civilizations: Africa (CD-ROM)*
- *PicturePack: Ancient Civilizations: Africa (Transparencies)*

ADDITIONAL NATIONAL GEOGRAPHIC SOCIETY PRODUCTS

To order the following, call National Geographic at 1-800-368-2728:

- *Read & Explore: Discovering the Inca Ice Maiden, by Johan Reinhard (Literature Kit)*

Access *National Geographic*'s new dynamic MapMachine Web site and other geography resources at:
www.nationalgeographic.com
www.nationalgeographic.com/maps

THE HISTORY CHANNEL. A&E HOME VIDEO. Biography

The following videotape programs are available from Glencoe:

- **Machu Picchu: City in the Sky**
  0-7670-0143-5
- **Peru: Warriors and Treasure**
  0-7670-1861-3

To order, call Glencoe at 1-800-334-7344. To find resources to accompany these videos, check:

A&E Television: www.aande.com
The History Channel: www.historychannel.com

Introducing **CHAPTER 8**

OVERVIEW

Chapter 8 focuses on the development of civilization in Africa and the Americas.

- ➤ **Section 1** discusses the Kush and Aksum civilizations.
- ➤ **Section 2** describes West African kingdoms.
- ➤ **Section 3** describes the contributions of the East African civilizations.
- ➤ **Section 4** explains why people migrated to the Americas.
- ➤ **Section 5** summarizes the civilizations of Mesoamerica.
- ➤ **Section 6** analyzes the Inca civilization of South America.

CHAPTER OBJECTIVES

After reading Chapter 8, students will be able to:

1. discuss how the ancient civilizations of Kush and Aksum passed along their culture.
2. summarize how West African and East African kingdoms developed because of trade.
3. explain how bands of people crossed into the Americas.
4. describe the civilizations that developed in Mesoamerica.
5. discuss Inca culture.

EXAMINING ARTIFACTS

Ask students what occupation they think the terra cotta figure holds. *(soldier)* Why? *(because both the figure and the horse are wearing armor)* Point to the gold disc, and have students speculate on the connection between the disc and rider. Have students review and revise their theories as they read the chapter.

PERFORMANCE ASSESSMENT ✓

Use the Performance Assessment Activities on page 128B to help you evaluate students as they complete the chapter.

CHAPTER 8

Africa & the Americas

2000 B.C.–1500 A.D.

◀ Terra-cotta hors[e] and rider from Mal[i]

▲ Gold Ashanti disc from Mali

TEACHING RESOURCES

TEACHER PLANNING AND SUPPORT

- Reproducible Lesson Plan 8-1, 8-2, 8-3, 8-4, 8-5, 8-6
- Teaching Strategies for the World History Classroom (Including Block Scheduling Pacing Guides)
- Presentation Plus! CD-ROM

REVIEW AND REINFORCEMENT

- Reading Essentials and Study Guide 8-1, 8-2, 8-3, 8-4, 8-5, 8-6
- Chapter 8 Vocabulary and Guided Reading Activity
- Vocabulary PuzzleMaker CD-ROM
- Teaching Transparencies 8A & 8B
- Chapter 8 Reteaching Activity
- Chapter 8 Cooperative Learning Activity
- Chapter 8 Activity Book Activity
- Chapter 8 Chart and Graph Skill Activity
- Reading and Study Skills Foldables
- Interactive Tutor Self-Assessment CD-ROM
- Unit 3 MindJogger VideoQuiz

APPLICATION AND HANDS-ON ACTIVITIES

- Daily Questions in Social Studies
- Unit 3 Hands-On History Lab Activity
- World Games Activity Card 3
- World Crafts Activity Cards 9, 10
- Student Presentation Builder CD-ROM

Chapter Focus

Read to Discover

- How the ancient African civilizations of Kush and Aksum passed along elements of their culture.
- How West African kingdoms and East African civilizations grew because of trade.
- How Native Americans developed farming and other skills.
- What kinds of civilizations developed in Mesoamerica.
- What life was like for the Inca of South America.

HISTORY Online

Chapter Overview
Visit the *Human Heritage* Web site at **humanheritage.glencoe.com** and click on ***Chapter 8—Chapter Overviews*** to preview this chapter.

Terms to Learn
- silent barter
- pilgrimage
- population explosion
- quipus

People to Know
- Kashta
- Piankhi
- Ezana
- Sundiata Keita
- Mansa Musa
- Sunni Ali
- Askia Muhammad
- Montezuma II
- Pachacuti

Places to Locate
- Meroë
- Timbuktu
- Zimbabwe
- Bering Strait
- Tenochtitlán
- Kilwa

Why It's Important While armies carved out empires in the Middle East, civilizations developed in Africa south of the Sahara and in the Americas. Through conquest and trade, Africans and early Americans built great kingdoms and empires that rivaled civilizations elsewhere in the world.

SECTION 1 Ancient African Kingdoms

Other civilizations besides Egypt flourished in ancient Africa. Archaeologists have discovered enough remains to know what these African civilizations were like.

Kush The first of these African civilizations was Kush. It lay south of Egypt on the Nile River in present-day Sudan (sū dan'). Its history began about 2000 B.C. At that time, the Kushites were nomadic cattle herders. They grazed long-horned cattle on a *savannah* (suh van' uh), or grassy plain.

During the New Kingdom, Egyptian armies conquered Kush. Kush remained part of Egypt for almost 500 years. Over

HISTORY Online

Chapter Overview introduces students to chapter content and key terms. Have them access ***Chapter 8 Overview*** at **humanheritage.glencoe.com**

FOCUS

Bellringer

Ask students to estimate what percentage of time they spend each day eating and sleeping—the basic functions of living.

Motivational Activity

Ask students to share their time estimates. Discuss how the ability to take care of basic needs influences the kind of life people can lead. Suggest that students recall this discussion as they study the empires and civilizations in this chapter.

GUIDE TO READING

Reading Strategy

Ask students to read "Why It's Important" and summarize the chapter's main theme. *(Through conquest and trade, peoples in Africa and the Americas built civilizations that rivaled those elsewhere in the world.)*

Vocabulary Precheck

Ask students to define each of the "Terms to Learn." Have a volunteer consult the dictionary for any unfamiliar words. L1 ELL

Use the Vocabulary PuzzleMaker CD-ROM for Chapter 8 to create a crossword puzzle. L1

Assign Chapter 8 Vocabulary and Guided Reading Activity.

Assign Reading Essentials and Study Guide 8-1.

GEOGRAPHY ACTIVITIES
- Chapter 8 Geography and Map Activity
- Outline Map Resource Book

INTERDISCIPLINARY CONNECTIONS
- World Art & Architecture Transparency 10, *Gold Pendant Mask*
- World Music: A Cultural Legacy

ENRICHMENT AND EXTENSION
- Unit 3 Primary Source Readings
- World History Primary Source Document Library CD-ROM
- Chapter 8 Enrichment Activity
- Foods Around the World

ASSESSMENT AND EVALUATION
- Chapter 8 Performance Assessment Activity
- Chapter 8 Section Quizzes 8-1, 8-2, 8-3, 8-4, 8-5, 8-6
- Chapter 8 Test
- Unit 3 Standardized Test Practice
- Chapter 8 ExamView® Pro Testmaker CD-ROM
- Chapter 8 Digests Audiocassettes Activities and Tests

SPANISH RESOURCES
- Chapter 8 Spanish Chapter Summary and Glossary
- Chapter 8 Spanish Digests Audiocassettes Activities and Tests

TEACH

Guided Practice

L3 **Critical Thinking** Ask students to consider the significance of the Assyrian invasion of Kush. How did the inhabitants of Kush benefit from the invasion? How or what did they lose by the invasion? *(Benefits: learned iron-smelting, which helped them grow large amounts of grain and make iron goods for trade, which helped make Meroë a major trading center; Losses: forced to give up territory in Egypt)*

CAPTION ANSWER

Aksumite armies burned Meroë to the ground.

Economics at a Glance

Economic Interdependence
The economies of Kush, India, Arabia, and China were economically interdependent during this time. *Economic interdependence* means that a country relies on others as they rely on it, to provide the goods and services it uses. Events in one part of the country or world can have an impact elsewhere as a result of economic interdependence. Today, for example, bad weather in countries where sugar cane is grown can influence sugar prices in the United States, which can affect the price of snack foods. Economic interdependence is not bad, however, because countries still benefit from relying on other countries that produce goods more efficiently. Have students write a one-page report about an event that has occurred within the past five years and how it affected a specific region of the world. Ask students to describe the event and its economic impact.

time, the Kushites learned many things from the Egyptians. They learned to worship the god Amon-Re. They learned how to work copper and bronze. They changed Egyptian hieroglyphs to fit their own language.

About 1160 B.C., Egypt's power declined. In time, the Kushites won back their independence. They set up a capital at Napata (nap' uht uh). From Napata, they sent caravans into Egypt. These caravans carried gold, ivory, ebony, and other goods to trade.

About 750 B.C., the Kushite king Kashta (kahsh' tuh) set out to conquer Egypt. He led his cavalry into Egypt and took some territory. His son Piankhi (pyahng' kē) completed the conquest and founded a dynasty that ruled Egypt for 70 years. However, during the 600s B.C., the Assyrians invaded Egypt. Armed with iron weapons, they drove the Kushites back to the south.

Despite their losses, the Kushites gained something from the Assyrians. They learned the secret of iron-smelting. Soon, Kushite farmers, using iron hoes, were growing large amounts of grain. Kushite blacksmiths were making iron knives and spears, which they exchanged for cotton textiles and other goods from India, Arabia, and China. Kush became a great trading nation.

Around 540 B.C., the Kushites moved their capital to Meroë (mār' ō ē). The city was on the Nile, which provided an avenue

Fun Facts . . .

A Brave Queen One warrior-queen of Meroë, Amanirenas, challenged the Romans who seized Egypt after the death of Cleopatra. The Romans eventually drove Amanirenas back into Meroë, but she fought valiantly and her deeds are recorded in Greek and Roman histories of the time.

KUSHITE PYRAMIDS The Kushites copied many elements of Egyptian art, language, and religion. The pyramids near the cities of Meroë and Napata are imitations of Egyptian pyramids. The Kushite pyramids are smaller, however, and have more steeply sloped sides. **What happened to the city of Meroë?**

COOPERATIVE LEARNING

Organize the class into groups of three or four. Have each group select one culture studied in this chapter for further investigation. Each group should write a journal of an imagined archaeologist who has discovered artifacts from the selected culture. Every member of the group is responsible for researching the culture by using the text and library resources, taking notes during a group discussion about which artifacts to include, drawing pictures of artifacts, and drawing the location of the cultural group on a map.

for trade and transportation. Nearby were large deposits of iron ore and trees to fuel smelting furnaces. Meroë also lay in the center of good grazing land.

In Meroë, there was a huge temple dedicated to Amon-Re, with a long avenue of stone rams leading to its entrance. Sandstone palaces and houses of red brick filled the city. Walls of buildings were tiled in blue and yellow or covered with paintings. Small pyramids stood in the royal cemetery. Smelting furnaces poured forth huge columns of smoke, and around the furnaces lay heaps of shiny black *slag,* or waste from smelting.

Kush remained a great trading country for some 600 years, and then began to decline. As it declined, another kingdom rose to take its place. This was Aksum in present-day Ethiopia. About 350 A.D., Aksumite armies burned Meroë to the ground.

Aksumite Stone Monument

Aksum Like Kush, Aksum was a trading country. Through ports on the Red Sea, Aksumite merchants served as middlemen for countries on the Mediterranean and in the Far East. They imported silks, spices, and elephants from India. They exported gold, ivory, and enslaved people from Africa. Jewish, Greek, and Arab merchants settled in Aksum.

It was most likely the Greeks who brought Christianity to Aksum. Emperor Ezana (ex zah' nuh), whose armies had destroyed Meroë, converted to Christianity in 324 A.D. This heritage was passed down to the present day.

Aksumites achieved many things. They developed a writing system. They learned to farm on *terraces* (ter' is uhz), or raised levels of land. They minted gold coins and built stone monuments 60 feet, or 18 meters, tall.

Over time, Aksum's power as a trading country began to decline. This was because other kingdoms began to interfere with Aksum's trade. After Arab armies swept across North Africa in the 600s A.D., the Aksumites retreated toward the *interior,* or inland areas, of their country. There, they lived in isolation for more than 1,000 years.

Section 1 Assessment

1. How did the Kushites and Egyptians influence each other?
2. Why did the Kushites choose Meroë as their capital?

Critical Thinking

3. **Making Generalizations** How were the kingdoms of Kush and Aksum influenced by other cultures?

Graphic Organizer Activity

4. Draw a diagram like this one, and use it to show the effects of iron-smelting on Kush. (Add boxes as needed.)

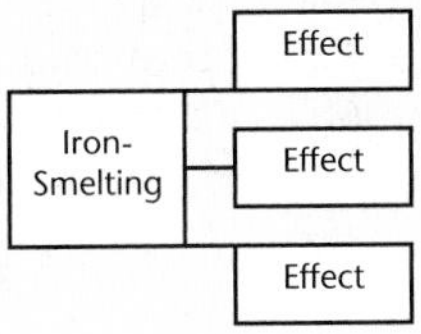

DID YOU KNOW

The most common Kushite symbols found on their pottery are the snake, the lion, and the lotus.

GEOGRAPHY AND HISTORY

Ethiopia is situated where Aksum once stood. As Aksum, it exerted a wide influence in the Horn of Africa, southern Arabia, the Red Sea, and as far west as Kush. With the spread of Islam, Aksum's foreign trade ended. Aksum was a small Christian area in the larger, Muslim East Africa. Its geographical isolation and being located on high plateaus helped the country keep its religious and cultural individuality.

Use **Interactive Tutor Self Assessment CD-ROM** to review Section 1.

Section 1 Assessment Answers

1. Kushites learned to worship the god Amon-Re, how to work in copper and bronze, and to adopt hieroglyphs to fit their language. Egypt was ruled for a time by Kush and was also influenced through trade.

2. It was on the Nile, it was near large deposits of iron ore and trees to fuel smelting furnaces, and it had good grazing land.

3. Answers will vary but Kushites learned iron-smelting from the Assyrians; they worshiped the same god and built pyramids like the Egyptians; Aksumites took Christianity from the Greeks.

4. possible effects: made iron hoes, which increased grain production; made iron knives and spears for trade; moved capital to Meroë, where large deposits of iron ore and trees to fuel smelting could be found; grew into a great trading nation

Assign the Chapter 8 **Section 1 Quiz** in the TCR. Testmaker available.

TEACH

L2 **Communication** Have two students act out a silent barter using modern objects and ask why this technique was used in Africa. *(to eliminate language problems, to show trust and good will)* Ask students how difficult or simple their simulated barter was. Would this be successful in modern times? Have the class discuss why effective trade was important to the growth of African kingdoms.

Reading Check Answer
In **silent barter,** Ghanian merchants and gold miners would exchange goods and gold without saying a word or even seeing each other.

LINKING PAST TO PRESENT

The present nation of Ghana is not located in the same area of West Africa as the empire of Ghana was located in the mid-1000s. The early empire of Ghana is now occupied by the countries of Mauritania and Mali.

DID YOU KNOW

Ancient Ghana's capital consisted of two cities connected by a road lined with houses. The king and soldiers lived in one city; Arab traders lived in the second city.

Use the **Vocabulary PuzzleMaker CD-ROM** to create crossword and word search puzzles.

SECTION 2 The Middle Kingdoms

Several large trading kingdoms arose in West Africa after 400 A.D. Their rise was aided by the knowledge of iron-smelting. This was most likely brought to West Africa by *refugees,* or people who flee for safety, from Kush.

Ghana The first of these trading kingdoms was Ghana (gah' nuh). Legend has it that Ghana was founded about 200 A.D. Around 350 A.D., the Ghanians learned how to smelt iron. With iron swords and lances, Ghanian warriors expanded the boundaries of their country. They also gained control over West Africa's major trade routes.

Along these trade routes, goods were carried by caravans of camels or donkeys. The most important goods were salt and gold. Caravans carried salt south from Taghaza (tuh gah' zuh) in present-day Algeria (al jir' ē uh). They returned north with gold from Wangara (wahn gar' uh), an area southwest of Ghana.

Reading Check How did **silent barter** work?

Ghanian merchants and Wangara gold miners used a trading technique called **silent barter.** Ghanian merchants would travel to a trading site along a river in Wangara. They would place salt and other goods on the ground and beat drums to signal the gold miners. Then, they would withdraw. Next, the gold miners would appear, look at the goods, and leave some gold. Then, they would withdraw. If the Ghanians thought they had received enough gold, they would take it and leave. If not, they would withdraw and wait for the miners to leave more gold. When the exchange was over, the Ghanians would trade the gold to merchants from North Africa. Often, the gold was shipped to Europe and Asia for sale.

Photograph of Camel Caravan

Only gold dust could be used in trade. Nuggets became the property of the king, who controlled the economy. Legend has it that one nugget was so heavy that it served as a hitching post for the king's horses.

In 1042 A.D., Arabs from North Africa started a war against Ghana. They destroyed the capital and made the Ghanians give them tribute. Ghana managed to regain its independence but was not strong enough to survive.

Mali By 1240 A.D., Ghana was a part of Mali (mah' lē), a large trading kingdom in West Africa. The king of Mali, whose army had conquered Ghana, was Sundiata Keita (sūn dē ah' tuh kī' tuh), or "Hungering Lion."

COOPERATIVE LEARNING

Divide students into three groups, and ask them to pretend they are members of Arab caravans visiting each of the three empires described in this section. Direct them to record their impressions of the journey, including the trip across the Sahara, in the form of journal entries. Call on members from each group to read the entries aloud.

You might use this exercise to introduce the primary source reading, *The Sultan of Mali,* by Arab scholar Ibn Fadl Allah al Omari on pages 678–679 of the **Primary Sources Library.**

Assign Chapter 8 ***Cooperative Learning Activity*** in the TCR.

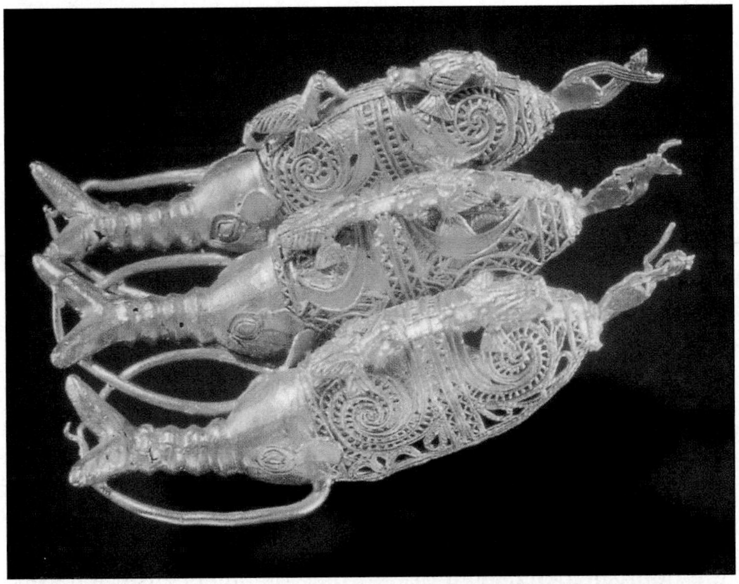

GOLD DESIGNS The gold mined in ancient Africa was often formed into intricate designs on jewelry and ceremonial ornaments. These pieces are elephant charms. **Who controlled most of the gold supply in ancient Ghana?**

Sundiata Keita did several things to make his kingdom strong. He reestablished the salt-gold trade, which the Arabs had disrupted. He organized a permanent army. He divided the kingdom into provinces, each headed by a general. The generals kept the peace and saw that there was enough food for the people. To strengthen ties with different groups in the kingdom, Sundiata Keita moved his capital from place to place.

Sundiata Keita wanted to impress the people with his power. When he appeared in public, trumpeters announced his arrival. He sat on an ebony throne under an arch made from large elephant tusks. He never spoke directly to people. Instead, requests were answered by servants standing at the foot of the stairs leading to the throne.

One of the most famous kings of Mali was Mansa Musa I (mahn′ sah mū′ sah), or King Moses I. One reason Mansa Musa was famous was because of a **pilgrimage** (pil′ gruh mij), or religious journey, he made to Arabia in 1324–25. It took more than 14 months to cover the 3,000 miles, or 4,800 kilometers. Some 12,000 servants traveled with the king. Each carried a 4-pound, or 1.8-kilogram, gold bar. Mansa Musa gave many of these bars to poor

People in History

Mansa Musa I
c. 1337 A.D.

West African Emperor

A grandson or grand-nephew of the warrior king Sundiata Keita, Mansa Musa guided Mali to its height of power. Under his rule, Mali grew to the size of western Europe and, in terms of gold, it outdid the wealth of Egypt. Mansa Musa used his large army to secure safe passage of travelers and traders through his empire and to keep order for nearly 25 years.

Reading Check What is a **pilgrimage?**

L1 **Daily Life** Have students imagine they are Arab traders traveling to Ghana, Mali, or Songhai. Ask the "traders" to make a list of the goods they are bringing to trade and the goods they will be trading for. Suggest that students also include the means by which they are traveling. Ask students which kingdom they would most like to trade with and why.

MAKING CONNECTIONS

>> **Agriculture** The people of Mali grew such crops as sorghum, rice, yams, beans, and onions. They also grew cotton which they made into cloth.

CAPTION ANSWER

The kings or rulers controlled the gold in ancient Ghana.

Reading Check Answer
A **pilgrimage** is a religious journey.

PRIMARY SOURCES Library

You might assign "The Empire of Mali" from pages 678–679 of the Primary Sources Library.

SPOTLIGHT ON: MANSA MUSA I

One of the most celebrated travelers of the Middle Ages was Mansa Musa I, ruler of Mali in the 1300s. Europeans who learned of his *hajj* included pictures of him holding a gold nugget on their maps of Africa. On his holy pilgrimage to Makkah, Musa stopped in Cairo where he visited the local sultan. Mansa Musa, who had brought a great deal of gold with him, gave it freely to needy people in Egypt and other places he traveled. When Mansa Musa and his entourage returned to Mali, he brought with him some of the brightest and most talented scholars and architects. His dream was to build great cities in Mali to be centers of learning. Mansa Musa's sharing of wealth affected the Egyptian economy negatively. So much gold was in circulation that it was devalued.

people he met along the way. As a result of this trip, news of Mansa Musa and Mali reached as far as Europe.

In Arabia, Mansa Musa met a Spanish architect whom he brought back to Mali. There, the architect built a university in the trading city of Timbuktu (tim buhk tū'). It became a great center of learning and drew students from Europe, Asia, and Africa.

After 25 years, Mansa Musa's reign ended. The rulers who followed him were weak. Within 100 years after Mansa Musa's death, Mali lost its land to others.

Songhai The kingdom that replaced Mali as the most powerful in West Africa was Songhai (song' hī). By the late 1400s, it controlled almost all the land that had been part of Mali. Songhai also conquered other lands and became the largest of the three trading kingdoms.

The Sultan Sunni Ali, in 1464, ruled Songhai from the city of Gao. He maintained a huge army equipped with armor, camels and horses. He also had a large navy that patrolled the Niger River. Following Sunni Ali's death, Askia Muhammad came to power in Songhai. He extended the empire even more and culture flourished. Sultan Askia welcomed teachers, doctors, poets, students, and religious leaders from Asia and Europe.

Songhai was more organized than the other two kingdoms. It was divided into provinces, with a governor for each. Everyone used the same weights and measures and the same legal system. Only members of the ruling Songhai could become political leaders or join the cavalry. Other groups had special jobs, such as caring for the army's horses or serving at the royal court. Most enslaved people, often prisoners of war, worked as farmers.

Despite its power, Songhai lasted only 100 years. In 1591 A.D., the ruler of Morocco sent an army across the Sahara to seize Songhai's gold mines. Though only half of the Moroccan soldiers survived the trip, they had guns. They defeated Songhai's soldiers, who were armed only with swords and spears.

Section 2 Assessment

1. **Define:** silent barter, pilgrimage.
2. What were two important trade goods in West Africa?
3. How was the kingdom of Songhai organized?

Critical Thinking

4. **Making Inferences** Why do you think Ghanian merchants set up a system called silent barter?

Graphic Organizer Activity

5. Draw a diagram like this one, and use it to summarize the accomplishments of the three great West African kingdoms.

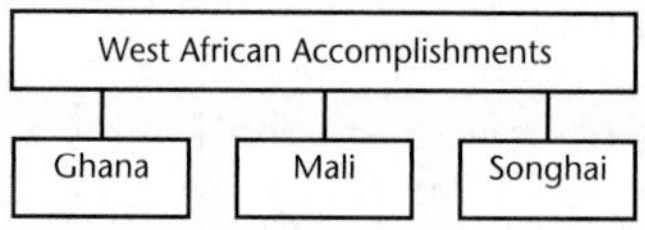

LINKING PAST TO PRESENT

During the Songhai Empire, Timbuktu was a major center for trade in gold, enslaved people, and salt. Merchants, religious divines, and scholars mingled in this Muslim city. Today Timbuktu is a smaller city but retains visible remnants of its past in mosques and monuments.

GEOGRAPHY AND HISTORY

The people of Songhai used the Niger River for military transportation and trade. They also built dikes and canals along the river.

L2 **Economics** Africa's early kingdoms became wealthy from the development of trade of natural resources. Ask students to read and report on current newspaper or magazine articles about how African nations today are working to increase trade or development of their natural resources.

Use **Interactive Tutor Self-Assessment CD-ROM** to review Section 2.

Section 2 Assessment Answers

1. silent barter, system of trade in ancient Ghana (p. 132); pilgrimage, a religious journey (p. 133)
2. salt and gold
3. It was divided into provinces, each with a governor. Everyone used the same weights, measures, and legal system.
4. Answers will vary but might include that Ghanian merchants might have been dealing with people who did not speak their language.
5. Accomplishments should reflect the policies established by the rulers of each kingdom, particularly the growth of trade and the encouragement of learning.

Assign Chapter 8 **Section 2 Quiz** in the TCR. Testmaker available.

Reading Latitude

To measure distances north and south, mapmakers use imaginary lines on maps and globes. These are called lines of latitude and they run east and west around Earth. Lines of latitude are often called parallels because they never meet and remain the same distance from each other all the way around Earth.

Latitude is measured in degrees, as shown by the symbol °. The Equator, which is a line of latitude, is marked 0° because all other lines of latitude are measured from it. One degree of latitude equals about 69 miles, or 110 kilometers.

There are 90 lines of latitude from the Equator to each pole. Those lines north of the Equator are marked with an **N**. Those lines south of the Equator are marked with an **S**.

Map Practice

1. **Which civilization was located closest to the Equator?**
2. **Which city, Timbuktu or Napata, was located closest to the 20°N line of latitude?**
3. **Which line of latitude runs through the center of the great trading civilization of Zimbabwe?**

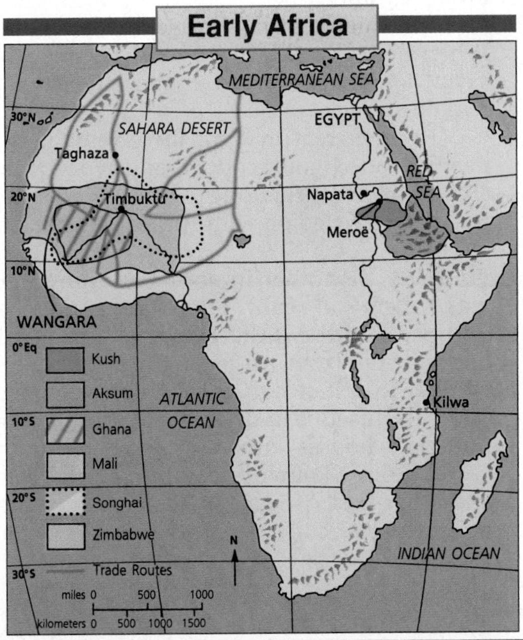

GO TO

Glencoe's **Skillbuilder Interactive Workbook CD-ROM, Level 1,** provides instruction and practice in key social studies skills.

135

MAP SKILLS

TEACH

Reading Latitude

Instruct students to study the map on page 135 to answer the following questions:

Which city was located close to the 10° S line of latitude? *(Kilwa)*

Which city lies almost halfway between 20° N and 30° N lines of latitude? *(Taghaza)*

Between what two lines of latitude do most of the early empires and civilizations of Africa lie? *(10° N and 20° N)*

Ask students to make a generalization about early civilizations of Africa based on their latitude. *(Students' generalizations might include that the climate between 10° N and 20° N was conducive to farming and trade for early African civilizations.)*

Answers to Map Practice

1. Mali
2. Napata
3. 20° S

SPOTLIGHT ON: EARLY AFRICA

As trading grew in ancient Africa, so did the need for some form of currency or money. Paper currency and coins did not yet exist. Until the mid-fifteenth century, cowrie shells and trading beads were used as currency. Among some West African people, iron chains and spearheads were also used as money. Then, in the mid-1400s, while the Songhai Empire was rising, coins became popular. As always, gold nuggets were considered to be of great value by almost all peoples.

Reading Check Answer A **population explosion** caused the Shona to leave their home because the land could not support the increased number of people.

L1 **Geography: Human Systems** Ask students to brainstorm the reasons why people today move from one geographic area to another. *(better climate, education, job opportunities, and religious or political freedom)* Ask students to compare these reasons for migration with those of early peoples.

Use the **Vocabulary PuzzleMaker CD-ROM** to create crossword and word search puzzles.

SECTION 3 East African Civilizations

The growth of trading kingdoms in West Africa was matched by the rise of trading kingdoms and city-states in East Africa. Goods moved from the interior of East Africa to coastal markets, which, in time, became large city-states. Each of these had its own ruler and government.

Reading Check How did a **population explosion** cause the Shona to leave their homeland?

Zimbabwe

One of the best-known trading kingdoms was Zimbabwe (zim bah' bwā). The people of Zimbabwe speak a language known as Bantu (ban' tū). Their ancestors, the Shona (shō' nuh), once lived in present-day Nigeria (nū jir' ē uh) in West Africa. About 100 A.D., a **population explosion,** or a large and sudden growth in population, took place. Since the land could not support the increased number of people, many Shona began to leave their homeland to look for new homes.

The Shona settled in Zimbabwe in East Africa about 700 A.D. There, they built towns using stones that were cut in such a way that they fit together without mortar. The capital had houses, a fort, and a temple. The fort stood on top of a hill and was surrounded by a huge wall. Besides the temple, the enclosed area contained the houses of the chief and his officials.

The people of Zimbabwe viewed their chief as a god-king. They approached him by crawling on their stomachs. Officials imitated him. If he coughed, they coughed. When he ate, they ate. The chief kept his throne as long as he was in good health. When he grew old, however, he was expected to take poison. Then, a younger man would become chief, and Zimbabwe could remain strong.

Zimbabwe Ruins

Another reason Zimbabwe remained strong was trade. Its people traded gold, copper, and ivory from the interior to merchants from cities along Africa's east coast. From these cities, trade was carried on with Arabia, Persia, India, and China.

Kilwa

Another important trading city-state in East Africa was Kilwa (kil' wuh). From Kilwa, merchants sailed across the Red Sea and the Indian Ocean. The people of Kilwa collected heavy taxes from traders of other countries. They used their wealth to extend their power over neighboring city-states. They also used it to dress in fine cotton and silk and to fill their four-story houses with vases and hangings from India and China.

A culture known as Swahili (swah hē' lē) developed in Kilwa and other East African city-states. Many Arab traders had settled in the coastal cities. For this reason, Swahili culture is a mix of

EXTENDING THE CONTENT

Bantu is a group of over 500 languages spoken by over 150 million people in central, eastern, and southern Africa . A subgroup of the Benue-Congo group of Niger-Congo language family, Bantu includes the languages of Rwanda, Makua, Xhosa, and Zulu. Most Bantu languages are tonal, which means they use pitch to differentiate words that might be pronounced in the same way.

Arabic and African cultures. The Swahili language is a combination of Bantu and Arabic.

Section 3 Assessment

1. **Define:** population explosion.
2. How did the people of Zimbabwe view their leader?
3. How did the people at Kilwa use their wealth?

Critical Thinking

4. **Understanding Cause and Effect** A population explosion among the Shona caused many of these people to leave their homeland. What are some of the events or conditions that might cause people to leave their homelands today?

Graphic Organizer Activity

5. Draw a diagram like this one, and use it to show features of Swahili culture.

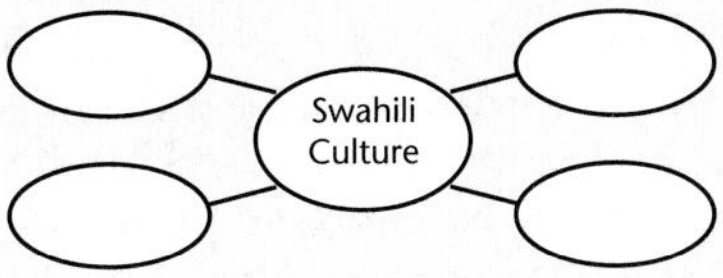

SECTION 4 Path to the Americas

Until about 25,000 years ago, there were no people in the Americas. Then, hunting-and-food-gathering bands began to cross into the Americas from Asia over a land bridge. This land bridge was formed during the last Ice Age. At that time, large amounts of ocean water were frozen into huge glaciers, and sea levels dropped. Today, this bridge is covered by the waters of the Bering Strait.

The bands came in search of food, following grass-grazing animals that had crossed earlier. The bands lived off their kill and also gathered wild plants. Over time, they spread all through the Americas. Experts believe people reached the southern tip of South America by about 9000 B.C.

About 7000 B.C., the last Ice Age ended. The climate became hotter and drier, and in many areas deserts took the place of grasslands. Large game almost disappeared. So, people had to find other ways of getting food.

By 6000 B.C., people in the Tehuacán (tā wah kahn') Valley south of present-day Mexico City had developed farming. By 3000 B.C., there were thousands of small farming villages all through the Americas. The most important crop was *maize* (māz), or corn.

Between 3000 B.C. and 1000 B.C., people developed such skills as weaving and pottery making. They grew peanuts, tomatoes, and potatoes. In a few areas, they built irrigation systems that helped support a growing population.

Section 3 Assessment Answers

1. population explosion, large and sudden growth in population (p. 136)
2. as a god-king
3. to extend their power over neighboring city-states, to dress in fine cotton and silk, and to fill their houses with riches from India and China
4. Answers will vary but might include that people leave their homes because of war, famine, disease, religious persecution, or simply hope of a better life.
5. sample features: made up of city-states, traded with people across the Red Sea and Indian Ocean, mix of Arabic and African cultures, spoke a language made up of Arabic and Bantu

Assign Chapter 8 **Section 3 Quiz** in the TCR. Testmaker available.

DID YOU KNOW

The earliest hunting-and-food-gathering bands had fire and cooked their food, but had not domesticated the dog. The people wore hides and furs. Their weapons were wooden spears tipped with sharpened stones.

L2 **Culture** Organize tactile/kinesthetic learners into three groups. Assign each group one of the following Mesoamerican groups: the Olmecs, the Mayas, or the Aztecs. Each group should create a simple board game involving the history and people of their chosen civilization. Suggest they design a gameboard and basic rules for playing the game. Suggest each group invite other students to play their game.

Use **Interactive Tutor Self Assessment CD-ROM** to review Section 3.

NATIONAL GEOGRAPHIC

TRANSPARENCIES
Physical Geography of the World
Display the following to enrich student appreciation of the diverse environments settled by Native Americans.
2. Sonoran Desert, U.S.
3. Rocky Mountains, Canada
4. Grand Canyon, U.S.
6. Mississippi River, U.S.
8. Baffin Island, Canada
9. Appalachian Mountains, U.S.

Use the **Vocabulary PuzzleMaker CD-ROM** to create crossword and word search puzzles.

DID YOU KNOW ??

The Mayan counting system based on 20 included concepts of zero and place value. A stylized shell was the symbol for zero, a dot stood for each unit 1-4, and the symbol for 5 was a bar.

Use **Interactive Tutor Self-Assessment CD-ROM** to review Section 4.

Independent Practice

L3 **Critical Thinking** Ask students to name the characteristics of a centralized government, as you write responses on the chalkboard. Have students form groups to describe what must happen in a civilization before a centralized government can form. *(division of labor—one group producing enough food, housing, and other necessities for the community; establishment of military or political force to maintain peace)*

A&E HOME VIDEO.

The following videotape program is available from Glencoe to enrich Chapter 8:

- **The Maya**

To find classroom resources to accompany this video, check the following home page:

A&E Television:
www.aande.com

Use the **Vocabulary Puzzle-Maker CD-ROM** to create crossword and word search puzzles.

Section 4 Assessment

1. How did hunting-and-gathering bands travel to the Americas?
2. How long may it have taken for people to spread out over North and South America?
3. When and where did farming first appear?

Critical Thinking

4. **Understanding Cause and Effect** What do you think caused hunting-and-gathering bands to push farther south into the Americas?

Graphic Organizer Activity

5. Draw a diagram like this one, and use it to show the cause and effects of the invention of farming in the Americas.

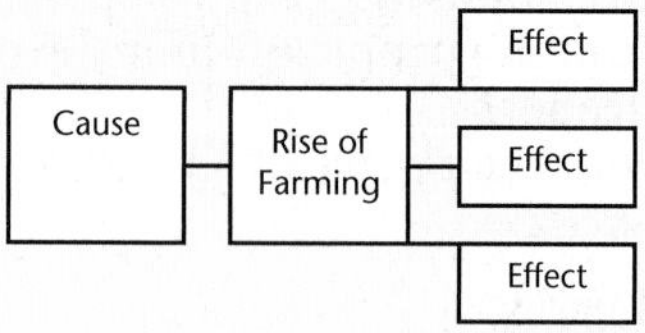

SECTION 5 Mesoamerica

As the number of people grew, societies became more complex. Several great civilizations rose in Mesoamerica, or Middle America, before 900 A.D. and others later.

The Olmecs One of the earliest civilizations in Mesoamerica was that of the Olmecs (ōl' meks). It came into being around 1000 B.C. About 900 years later, it disappeared mysteriously. The Olmecs had a great influence on other peoples of the area and was called the "mother culture." They developed planned cities, hieroglyphic writing, and a calendar.

The Olmecs lived along the southern coast of the Gulf of Mexico. Part of the year, the people farmed. The rest of the year they built stone cities, which were chiefly religious centers. The cities stood on top of huge hills. They had temples; sacred pools; and houses for priests, artists, and architects. The people lived in nearby villages. They visited the cities on festival and market days.

Mayan Figure

The Mayas Another great civilization, that of the Mayas (mī' uhz), began in Mesoamerica about 500 B.C. It reached its peak between 300 and 900 A.D. The Mayas lived in present-day southeast Mexico, Belize (buh lēz'), and Guatemala (gwah tuh mah' luh). Like the Olmecs, the Mayas lived in farming villages that surrounded religious cities. Mayan cities had temples and houses for priests and nobles.

The Mayas were great traders. Their cities, linked by roads paved with white cement, had busy marketplaces. Canoes handled local trade along the coasts.

Section 4 Assessment Answers

1. perhaps across a land bridge over the Bering Strait
2. from 23,000 B.C. to 9000 B.C., or about 14,000 years
3. By 6,000 B.C., people in the Tehuacán Valley south of present-day Mexico City had developed farming.
4. Answers will vary but could include the need for food, safety from attack, weather, or curiosity.
5. sample responses: cause—end of last Ice Age and disappearance of most large game; effects—rise of farming villages, development of weaving and pottery making, construction of irrigation ditches, population growth

Assign Chapter 8 **Section 4 Quiz** in the TCR. Testmaker available.

Linking Across Time

Tortillas Mayan women rose at dawn to boil and grind corn for making the dough for tortillas—thin, round, flat breads. They then worked the dough by hand (left) before baking. Tortillas remain a basic part of the Mayan diet today (right), with women making tortillas in much the same way as their ancestors. **Why was maize (corn) important to the development of civilization in the Americas?**

The Maya adapted their own hieroglyphs from the Olmecs. Mayan mathematicians came up with the idea of zero and a counting system based on 20. Mayan astronomers were able to predict when eclipses of the sun and the moon would take place. They developed a calendar, based on that of the Olmecs, with a year of 365 days. They also made cotton cloth and paper.

About 900 A.D., most Mayas abandoned their cities and disappeared. No one knows why. A plague may have broken out. Perhaps the soil could no longer produce enough food. War may have interfered with trade.

The Aztecs Later, a third great civilization, that of the Aztecs, rose in Mesoamerica. About 1200 A.D., the Aztecs began moving south into the central valley of Mexico. Through military conquest, they expanded their empire to include all of central Mexico. By 1400 A.D., the Aztec Empire had 5 million people.

The Aztecs made the people they conquered pay tribute. This took the form of corn, clothing, rubber, and wood. It is believed that each year 2 million cotton cloaks alone were sent to the capital, Tenochtitlán (tā noch tē tláhn').

Tenochtitlán was built on an island in Lake Texcoco (teks kō' kō). *Causeways,* or paved roads, connected the island to the mainland. The city had pyramid-temples, palaces, gardens, zoos, schools, and markets. About 300,000 people lived there. Some dressed in feathered capes and cloaks of many colors. Women wore flowers and feathers in their hair.

Fun Facts . . .

Busy Markets Markets played an important part in the economic and social life of the Aztec. The market at Tlateloco was the largest in the ancient Americas. About 60,000 people may have visited the market each day.

Linking Across Time

Sample response: Maize was one of the first crops grown in the Americas and allowed for later cultural development.

LINKING PAST TO PRESENT

Tenochtitlán means "near the cactus." Legend has it that Huitzilopochli, the god of sun and war, told the Aztecs to build their city in the place where they found an eagle with a snake in its beak perched on a cactus. The eagle-snake cactus symbol appears on the modern Mexican flag.

MULTICULTURAL PERSPECTIVES

Olmec priests wore jaguar skins, bright red robes, bird feathers, and flower-topped headdresses. They also filed their teeth and put semi-precious stones in them. Some nobles placed splint-like boards on their children's heads and wrapped them with cloth to create elongated skulls, which they thought were beautiful.

Painting of Aztec Farmer

To feed the people, the Aztecs had to create more farmland. They filled in parts of the lake and dug drainage canals. They planted crops in soil-filled reed baskets anchored in the lake. They also built *aqueducts* (ak' wuh dukts), or water channels, to bring fresh water to the city's reservoirs from mainland springs. Canoes delivered the water from the reservoirs to people's houses.

The Aztecs were a warlike people. War and religion were closely connected. The people worshiped two major gods. One was the rain god who stood for the peaceful life of farming. The other was the sun god who stood for war and expanding empire. The Aztecs believed that the sun god needed human sacrifices. The Aztecs felt that if they did not make them, the sun would not rise in the morning. Victims were generally prisoners of war.

The Aztec Empire reached its height in the early 1500s under Montezuma II (mahn tuh zū' muh). During his reign, however, Spaniards, who had guns and horses, attacked the Aztecs. Easily defeated by the Spaniards, the Aztecs lost their empire.

Section 5 Assessment

1. What were some of the accomplishments of the Maya?
2. How did the Aztec Empire come to an end?

Critical Thinking

3. **Drawing Conclusions** Why do you think Mayan civilization ended?

Graphic Organizer Activity

4. Draw a diagram like this one, and use it to summarize the accomplishments of the three great Mesoamerican civilizations.

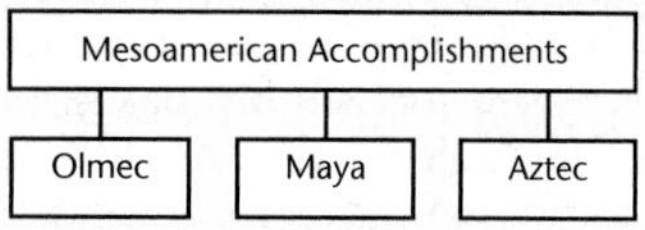

SECTION 6 The Incas

About the same time the Aztecs moved south into central Mexico, the Incas moved out from Peru. They established an empire that stretched along the west coast of South America for about 2,500 miles, or 4,000 kilometers. By the 1500s, there were 12 million people in the Inca Empire.

HISTORY Online

Student Web Activity

Visit the *Human Heritage* Web site at humanheritage.glencoe.com and click on ***Chapter 8—Student Web Activities*** to find out more about the ancient civilizations of the Americas.

History The Incas started out as farmers and shepherds. They built villages on the rocky slopes of the Andes Mountains. In the fertile valley below, they grew corn, potatoes, and other crops. On pastures above, they grazed alpacas (al pak' uhz) and llamas (lah' muhs).

In 1438, the Inca ruler Pachacuti (pah chuh kū' tē) conquered several neighboring peoples and founded the Inca Empire. He used several techniques to hold it together. He ordered

Section 5 Assessment Answers

1. farming and building stone cities
2. The Spaniards, who had guns and horses, defeated the Aztecs.
3. Answers will vary but could include disease, conquering army, poor farming, and bad weather conditions.
4. sample responses: Olmec—planned cities, hieroglyphic writing, calendar; Maya—religious cities, cement roads for trade, hieroglyphic writing, idea of zero and counting system based on 20, ability to predict eclipses, 365-day calendar, production of cotton cloth and paper; Aztec—construction of huge empire, monumental architecture of Tenochtitlán, use of drainage canals and aqueducts

Assign Chapter 8 **Section 5 Quiz** in the TCR. Testmaker available.

Use **Interactive Tutor Self-Assessment CD-ROM** to review Section 5.

HISTORY Online

Student Web Activity objectives and answers can be found at the ***Chapter 8 Web Activity Lesson Plan*** at humanheritage.glencoe.com

MAKING CONNECTIONS

>> **Religion** Religion was central to Inca life. The Incas had many gods. The most important was Inti, the sun god. Because of this, the Incas called themselves the "Children of the Sun."

A&E HOME VIDEO.

The following videotape programs are available from Glencoe to enrich Chapter 8:

- **Machu Picchu: City in the Sky**
- **Peru: Warriors and Treasure**

To find classroom resources to accompany these videos, check the following home page:

A&E Television: www.aande.com

Use the **Vocabulary PuzzleMaker CD-ROM** to create crossword and word search puzzles.

conquered peoples to worship the Inca sun god in addition to their own gods. He made the Inca language of Quechua (kech' wuh) the official language. He moved people who had been living under Inca rule into newly conquered lands. They helped spread Inca culture and watched for signs of rebellion.

Pachacuti also had a huge system of stone-paved roads built. Rope suspension bridges crossed canyons and rivers. Way stations with food, weapons, and other supplies needed by the Inca army were set up on the roads. Only soldiers and government officials were allowed to use the roads.

Inca Way of Life A ruler, known as the Inca, determined the way of life. Land belonged to the ruler and not to the people who worked it. Villagers paid taxes to the empire in two ways.

Then & Now

Growing Grains The Aztecs and Incas grew high-protein grains called amaranth and quinoa. Today these grains, native to the Americas, have become important in parts of India, Pakistan, Nepal, and China. Amaranth and quinoa, in the form of flour and cereals, have become common in U.S. health-food stores.

Early American Empires

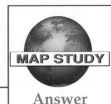

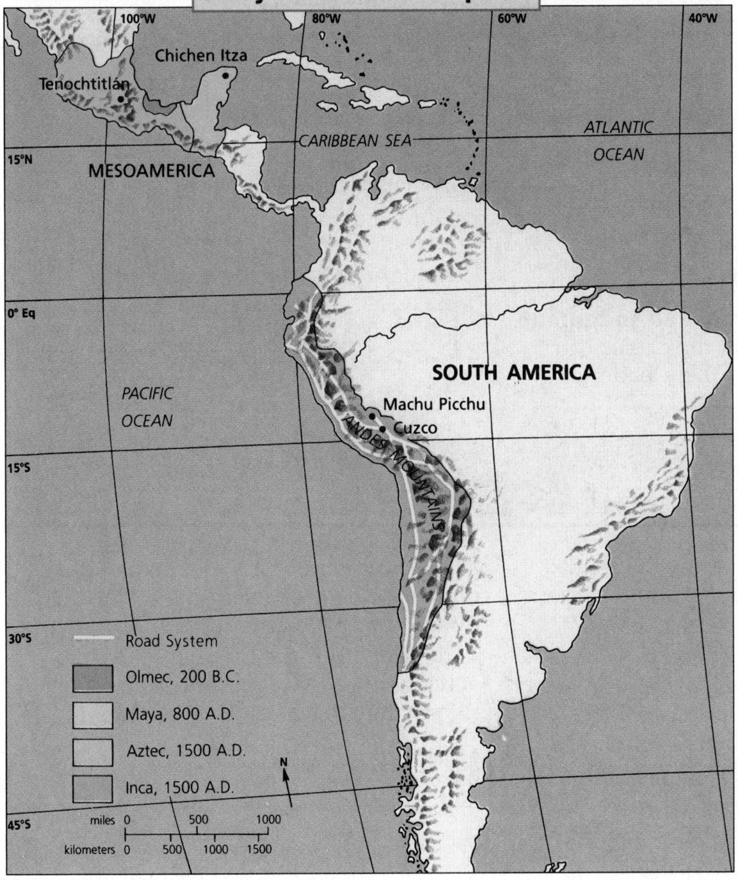

MAP STUDY

ENVIRONMENT AND SOCIETY The Inca developed engineering skills that enabled them to build a large network of roads. **How did the environment of the Inca make road building more difficult?**

MAP STUDY

Answer

The Incas had to build roads through mountainous areas.

L1 **Geography: The World in Spatial Terms** Have students write five questions about the locations and relationships of places shown on the map of early American empires. Have students ask their questions to the class. ELL

ASSESS

Check for Understanding

Ask students to summarize the main points of the chapter, orally or in writing. Discuss the answers to the Section and Chapter Assessment questions.

Evaluate

Assign Chapter 8 **Performance Assessment Activity** in the TCR.

Administer **Chapter 8 Test** in the TCR. Testmaker available.

EXTENDING THE CONTENT

Sometimes called the "lost city of the Andes," the Incas' startling mountain fortress of Machu Picchu had never been seen except by local Native Americans until 1911. It was discovered by a Yale University expedition led by Hiram Bingham. The ruined city perches 8,000 feet (2,438 m), high in the mountains on a lush green ridge between two steep rocky peaks, about 50 miles (80 km) from Cuzco, Peru. It has a temple and citadel, as well as the ruins of many small stone houses. Thousands of worn stone steps connect the remains of farming terraces, squares, fountains, and aqueducts.

Reading Check Answer
Quipus were counting devices of knotted strings of different colors, with each color, knot, and space representng something.

GLENCOE TECHNOLOGY

MindJogger Videoquiz

Use **MindJogger Videoquiz** to review students' knowledge of the unit.

Available in DVD and VHS

Reteach

Assign Chapter 8 **Reteaching Activity** in the TCR.

Enrich

Have students investigate the way in which the Mayas and Aztecs processed and prepared chocolate. If possible, encourage students to demonstrate the methods for the class.

Assign Chapter 8 **Enrichment Activity** in the TCR.

CLOSE

Hold a class discussion about why the kingdoms and civilizations described in this chapter declined.

Use **Interactive Tutor Self-Assessment CD-ROM** to review Section 6.

HISTORY Online

Self-Check Quiz gives students an interactive chapter tutorial. Have them access ***Chapter 8 Quiz*** at **humanheritage.glencoe.com**

They paid through their labor. This involved not only farming land, but also building roads and mining gold. In addition, they paid taxes in kind.

The Inca had to keep track of people and goods. Because there was no written language, special accountants used **quipus** (kē′ pūz), or counting devices, to do this. Quipus were made up of knotted strings of different colors. Each color represented a different item. The knots in each string stood for tens, hundreds, and so on. The spaces between the knots stood for zero.

Reading Check What were **quipus,** and how did the Inca use them?

The wealth of the Inca Empire was shown in the way the ruler lived. His palace was the size of a town. There were hundreds of rooms and thousands of servants. The Inca's bodyguards wore gold armor. The poles of the litter in which he was carried were covered with gold. A desire for this wealth was part of the reason the Spaniards destroyed the Inca Empire in the early 1500s.

Section 6 Assessment

1. **Define:** quipus.
2. How big was the Inca Empire at its peak?
3. How did Pachacuti hold the Inca Empire together?

Critical Thinking

4. **Demonstrating Reasoned Judgment** Suppose the Inca had the choice of keeping Pachacuti as their leader or electing a new one. Which choice do you think they would have taken? Explain.

Graphic Organizer Activity

5. Draw a diagram like this one, and use it to show the changes that Pachacuti brought to the Incan way of life.

Before → Rise of Pachacuti → After

Chapter Summary & Study Guide

1. The Kushites and Egyptians influenced each other through conquest and trade.
2. The Aksumites destroyed Kush and later converted to Christianity.
3. The kingdoms of Ghana, Mali, and Songhai built West African empires based on a trade in salt and gold.
4. A population explosion led the Shona to build Zimbabwe in East Africa.
5. Kilwa and other coastal cities handled trade between Africa and Arabia, Persia, India, and China.
6. The Olmec and the Maya invented many new ideas, including forms of writing and a calendar.
7. The Aztec and the Inca built complex civilizations that lasted until the time of European arrival in the Americas.

HISTORY Online

Self-Check Quiz

Visit the *Human Heritage* Web site at **humanheritage.glencoe.com** and click on ***Chapter 8—Self-Check Quiz*** to assess your understanding of this chapter.

Section 6 Assessment Answers

1. quipus, Inca counting devices (p. 142)
2. 12 million people
3. He ordered conquered peoples to worship the Inca sun god, made Quechua the official language, and moved people who had been living under Inca rule into newly conquered lands.
4. Answers will vary but should include that some people would rather replace him with a less strict, less dictatorial leader. Others may want to keep him as a leader since he provided well for them.
5. sample responses: *before*—made up of farmers and shepherds living in scattered villages; *after*—a large unified empire connected by roads and customs (Also, see answer to question 3.)

Assign Chapter 8 **Section 6 Quiz** in the TCR. Testmaker available.

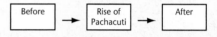

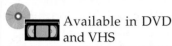

CHAPTER 8 Assessment

Using Key Terms

Imagine that you are putting together a photo display about ancient civilizations. You have found a photo that illustrates each of these terms:

silent barter
population explosion
pilgrimage
quipus

Use each term in a one-sentence caption describing what the photo shows.

Understanding Main Ideas

1. How did Ghana gain control of West African trade routes?
2. What was the effect of Mansa Musa's pilgrimage?
3. What was the main difference between the Mesoamerican civilizations that developed before and after 900 A.D.?
4. What did the Olmec contribute to other civilizations?
5. How did the Aztec treat the people they conquered?
6. Who directed and controlled the Incan way of life?

Critical Thinking

1. How do you think the development of African civilization might have been different if the Kushites did not develop iron-smelting?
2. Why was trade important to the growth of African civilization?
3. Which Mesoamerican civilization would you choose to live in? Why?
4. What contributions did early American civilizations make to present-day life in the United States?

Graphic Organizer Activity

History Draw two parallel time lines like the ones shown, and use them to compare important events in the early civilizations of Africa and the Americas. Sample events are provided to help you get started.

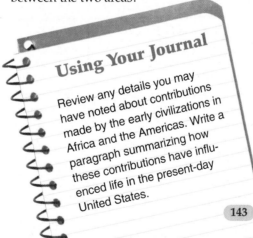

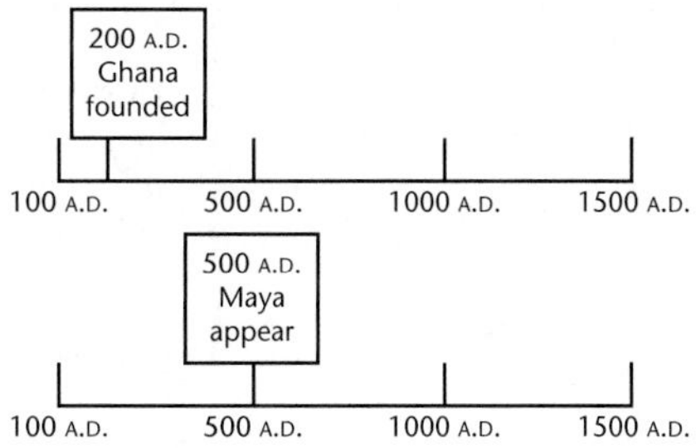

Geography in History

The World in Spatial Terms Compare the maps of early empires found on pages 135 and 141. What similarities in locations of these civilizations can you find? What differences in locations are there between the two areas?

Using Your Journal

Review any details you may have noted about contributions made by the early civilizations in Africa and the Americas. Write a paragraph summarizing how these contributions have influenced life in the present-day United States.

CHAPTER 8 Assessment Answers

Using Key Terms

Captions will vary but should include a descriptive sentence for the scene.

Understanding Main Ideas

1. by the use of iron swords and lances
2. News of Mansa Musa and Mali spread as far as Europe. Mansa Musa also met a Spanish architect while in Arabia and convinced him to help build a university in Timbuktu.
3. The earlier civilizations were peaceful, had rulers interested in learning, religion and trade; later civilizations were warlike, with religions marked by human sacrifice.
4. planned cities, hieroglyphic writing, a calendar
5. The Aztecs made them pay tribute and sacrificed some of them to the sun god.
6. the ruler

Critical Thinking

1. Answers will vary but should include lack of progress.
2. Answers will vary but should include that without trade, African civilizations would not have interacted and shared ideas.
3. Answers will vary but should include specific reasons.
4. Answers will vary.

Graphic Organizer Activity

Students should pick important dates highlighted in the chapter and arrange them at correct intervals on the time line.

Bonus Test Question

For Chapter 8 Test

You dig up pottery from a past civilization and know that it was made by the Olmec. What evidence helped you reach your conclusion? *(The pottery is adobe clay, was found near the ruins of a city, contains kernels of corn, and so on.)*

Using Your Journal

Diary entries will vary. You might call on volunteers to read their entries to the class.

Geography in History

Similarities: both are contiguous, close to the Equator, and coastal; differences: Mesoamerican empires stretched north and bordered the Pacific Ocean; African kingdoms stretched east and bordered the Atlantic and Indian oceans.

FOCUS

Objectives

After reading the Around the World for Unit 3, your students will be able to:

1. state the length of time the Zhou held power.

2. discuss how the Zhou changed farming in the China.

3. recognize the artistic and musical accomplishments of the Zhou.

Bellringer

Starting with the drafting of the Constitution in 1787, ask students how long the United States government has been in existence. *(Students should subtract 1787 from the present year.)*

Motivational Activity

Refer students to the Around the World feature, pointing out that the Zhou dynasty ruled China for more than 800 years. Ask: What do the pictures on pages 144–145 reveal about what the Zhou achieved during this time span? *(sample responses: built a great empire, used irrigation channels to grow rice, created artistic and musical works, developed a tradition of strong family ties)*

TEACH

Geography: Places and Regions Have students examine the map on page 144. Ask: What geographic features helped isolate China from the outside world? *(the mountains to the west and the Yellow Sea to the east)* Link this geographic isolation to the Zhou kings who considered the outside world as "uncivilized."

Next, divide the class into groups, and assign each group

UNIT 3 Around

THE ZHOU

The Zhou dynasty ruled for more than 800 years—the longest ruling dynasty in Chinese history. Zhou kings claimed they ruled according to a "mandate from heaven." However, this claim did not stop ambitious nobles from challenging their power. For the last 500 years of their rule, Zhou kings watched their empire crumble as warring states tried to seize control of China.

Despite the constant warfare, the Zhou dynasty oversaw many advancements. Achievements ranged from the development of new philosophies to the invention of new weapons.

▲ The Zhou ruled from 1028 B.C. to about 256 B.C. Boundaries changed constantly throughout this period. This map shows the Zhou Empire around the height of its power.

The Zhou introduced many advances in farming, including the irrigation channels used by Chinese farmers today. These channels allowed farmers to flood the fields used to grow rice. Production of rice became increasingly important as the Zhou extended their power into China's great river basins. ▼

SPOTLIGHT ON: THE ZHOU

The following are some details about daily life in China during the Zhou dynasty.

- Most people were poor farmers living in rural homes of mud and straw.
- Meals of peasants were mostly rice and vegetables, and rarely, meat.
- As many as 100 family members lived together under the rule of the oldest male relative.
- Males were more valued as family members than females.
- Peasant women made all of the clothing out of rough fabric. The wealthy wore silk.
- It was unusual for a peasant to travel outside of the village. Languages were not the same from region to region.
- Art objects and ornate furniture filled the homes of the wealthy.

the World

▲ The Zhou created ornate metal statues, such as this winged dragon.

The Zhou kings considered the outside world uncivilized. They prided themselves on their cultural accomplishments. These chimes come from a Zhou orchestra, which included flutes, drums, wooden clappers, and more. The chimes consist of 64 bronze bells ranging in size from 8 inches to 5 feet. ▼

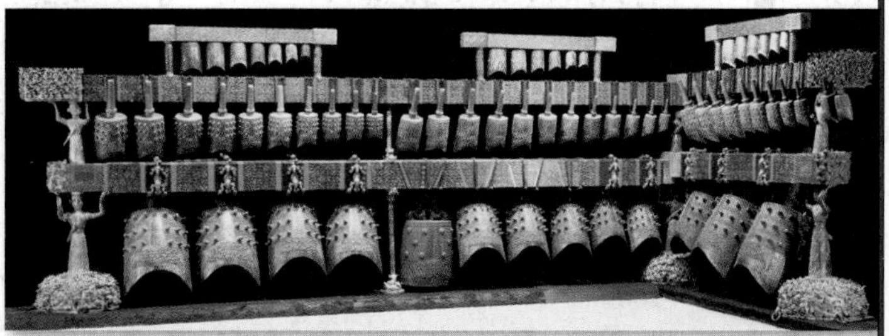

The Zhou had strong family ties and traditions. These mourning figures honor a family member who has died. ►

Bronze work, such as this three-legged bowl and ladle, were crafted by the Zhou. ▼

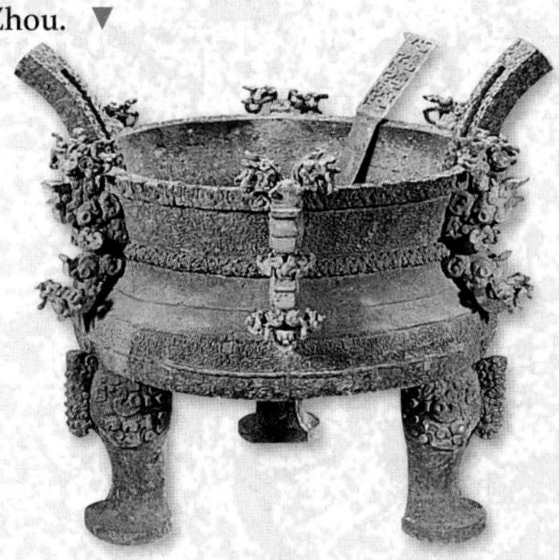

Taking Another Look

1. When did the Zhou dynasty begin and end?
2. What advancement in farming did Zhou rulers introduce?

Hands-On Activity

Writing an Announcement Write an announcement for a CD of music played on the bronze chimes created during the Zhou dynasty.

ANSWERS TO TAKING ANOTHER LOOK

1. The Zhou ruled from 1028 B.C. to about 256 B.C.
2. The Zhou introduced the irrigation channels used by Chinese farmers today. These channels helped control flooding and increased rice production.

Hands-On Activity

Announcements will vary, but students should place the chimes in the context of world history, noting the great age of Chinese civilization and the region's early cultural development.

one of the cultures, kingdoms, or city-states studied in Unit 3. Tell students to imagine that they are representatives sent to visit the Zhou emperor. What will they take to prove the accomplishments of their homeland? L1

LINKING PAST TO PRESENT

Confucius, one of the greatest Chinese philosophers, lived during the Zhou dynasty. He believed in a peaceful world and respect for the family. His philosophy, Confucianism, set up a code of ethics still followed today. One of his teachings included:

Do not do to others what you would not want others to do to you.

Encourage interested students to find other Confucian ethical teachings and share them with the class.

ASSESS

Check for Understanding

Have students answer the questions in **Taking Another Look** on page 145.

Enrich

Developments under the Zhou, such as the invention of iron plows and flood-control systems, increased food and helped make Zhou China the most densely populated country. Assign interested students to find out China's population rank today.

CLOSE

Assign students to review the accomplishments of the Shang on pages 88–92, and ask them to explore how the Zhou built on Shang achievements.

STANDARDIZED TEST PRACTICE

Answers and Analyses

1B History

According to page 103, the Phoenicians were not unified under a single government, nor did they conquer distant lands (though they traded widely). Choices C and D can therefore be eliminated. Nothing is said about a system of numbers. On pages 105–106, however, it states that the Phoenicians took the alphabet and *carried it to Europe.*

2H History

The top of page 103 states that the Phoenicians signed *treaties* according to which *they promised to supply free shipments of goods* in exchange for their independence.

3B History

According to page 114, *the Hebrews were the first people to believe in one god.*

THE PRINCETON REVIEW **TEST-TAKING TIP**

When several choices seem possible, students should reread the question and look for a key word in the question that will help make one choice better than others. In this case, the key word is *first*. This information should help students eliminate several choices.

4F Civics

The Ten Commandments mention neither an exchange system nor punishments for crimes; choices G and H can be eliminated. The Code of Hammurabi does not mention one god, so choice J can be eliminated. Therefore, F is the best choice.

THE PRINCETON REVIEW

Standardized Test Practice

Directions: Choose the *best* answer to each of the following multiple choice questions. If you have trouble answering a question, use the process of elimination to narrow your choices. Write your answers on a separate piece of paper.

1. Which of the following statements about the Phoenicians is true?

- **A** The Phoenicians invented the system of numbers we use today.
- **B** The Phoenicians introduced a written alphabet to Europe.
- **C** The Phoenicians lived under a single, unified government.
- **D** The Phoenicians used their navy to conquer and settle many distant lands.

Test-Taking Tip: This question requires you to remember an important *fact* about the Phoenicians. Since the Phoenicians did not have a *single, unified government,* you can eliminate answer C.

2. In what unique way did the Phoenicians protect themselves from being conquered by other nations?

- **F** They built a strong army that other nations feared.
- **G** They conquered other countries and took over foreign governments.
- **H** They signed peace treaties with neighboring countries.
- **J** They created a strong, unified central government in their country.

Test-Taking Tip: The important word in this question is *unique.* The Phoenicians certainly did not invent the idea of having a strong army (answer F). What *new idea* did they try?

3. The Hebrews are thought to be the first people to

- **A** devise a moral code
- **B** worship one god
- **C** live in the desert area known as Canaan
- **D** write down their religious legends

Test-Taking Tip: Make sure that you read the question and *all* the answer choices carefully. Think back to the other cultures and civilizations you have studied. Do you remember if, for instance, the Egyptians wrote down their religious legends? They did so in hieroglyphics. Though the Hebrews *did* write down their religious legends, they were not the *first* people to do so. Therefore, you can eliminate answer D.

4. The Ten Commandments and the Code of Hammurabi are similar because they both

- **F** say that people should respect each other and each other's property
- **G** established a regulated exchange system
- **H** lay out the proper punishments for different crimes
- **J** instruct people to worship only one god

Test-Taking Tip: This question asks you to make a *comparison.* Choose the answer that is true for *both* sets of laws. Eliminate any choice that is not true of either the Ten Commandments or the Code of Hammurabi.

The Assyrian and Chaldean Empires

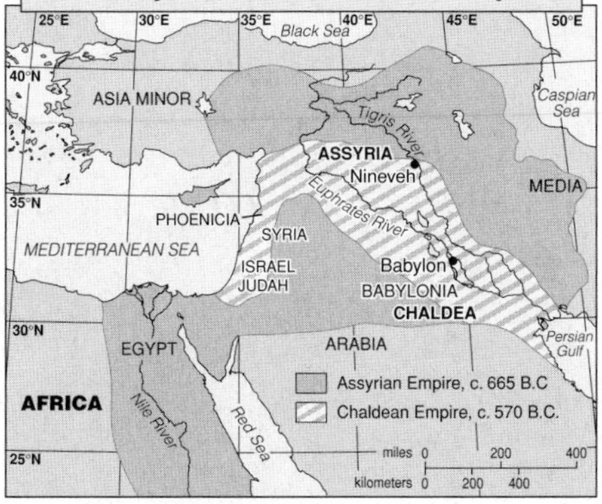

Use the map above to answer questions 5 and 6.

5. Approximately how far is it from Babylon to Nineveh?

A 100 miles
B 150 miles
C 300 miles
D 450 miles

Test-Taking Tip: Use the *map scale* to determine the distance from one point to another. If you do not have a ruler, you can use a small piece of paper to copy the length of the scale. Hold the paper next to the area you want to measure to help you estimate the distance.

6. Which of the following is east of Assyria?

F The Black Sea
G Media
H Phoenicia
J Israel

Test-Taking Tip: Study the map carefully before you choose an answer. Which way is *east* on a map?

7. What was something new and different about how the Persians traded?

A They kept track of trades using a written alphabet.
B They traded pots and pans in exchange for cloth.
C They only traded within their own country.
D They did business by using coins for money.

Test-Taking Tip: Notice that the question asks you to identify what was *new and different* about the Persians' method of trading. Was trading pots and pans for cloth a *new and different* idea?

STOP

Tested Objectives

Questions	Reading Objective
1, 5, 6	Analyze information
2, 3	Identify supporting ideas
4	Make comparisons
7	Evaluate information

Answers and Analyses

5C Geography

The scale on the bottom of the map indicates that the distance from Babylon to Nineveh is roughly 300 miles.

THE PRINCETON REVIEW **TEST-TAKING TIP**

All of the information needed to answer the question is on the map, but students need to read very carefully to avoid mistakes. In this case, students need to make sure that they do not confuse miles and kilometers on the scale.

6G Geography

According to the map, Phoenicia and Israel are west of Assyria, and the Black Sea is north of Assyria. The one choice that is east of Assyria is Media.

7D Economics

According to page 126, the Persians *spread the idea of using coins for money.*

THE PRINCETON REVIEW **TEST-TAKING TIP**

Students should scrutinize the language of the question to make sure they understand it thoroughly. The Phoenicians used an alphabet, so choice A cannot be right. Choice C is unlikely to be *new and different.*

Introducing
UNIT 4

OVERVIEW

Unit 4 examines the history of the ancient Greeks from the rise of the Aegean civilizations to the conquest of Greece by the Romans.

- ➤ **Chapter 9** describes the Minoan and Mycenaean civilizations out of which Hellenic civilization grew.
- ➤ **Chapter 10** discusses the evolution of the polis as the political and geographic center of Greek life and examines in detail the city-states of Athens and Sparta.
- ➤ **Chapter 11** explains the major contributions made to western civilization by the Greeks of the Classical Age.
- ➤ **Chapter 12** summarizes the Hellenistic period from the Macedonian conquest to the coming of the Romans.

UNIT OBJECTIVES

After reading Unit 4, students will be able to:

1. discuss how the Greek culture developed.

2. describe how Greek culture spread.

3. summarize Greek contributions to western civilizations.

UNIT PROJECT

Have students imagine that they are one of the following: a Minoan priest-king, a Mycenaean seafarer, a Spartan warrior, an Athenian citizen, an Olympic athlete, Socrates, Plato, Aristotle, a Greek wife of Philip of Macedonia, or Alexander the Great. Tell students that in these roles they maintained diaries. Have them write several diary entries describing special events in their lives. Ask students to make an oral presentation of their entries to the class.

UNIT 4

The Greeks

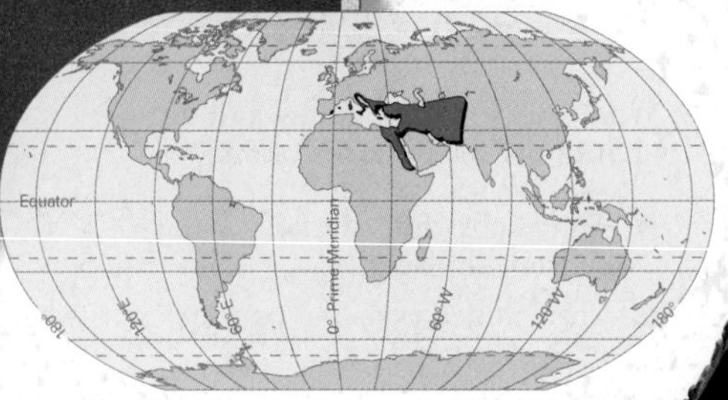

The Erectheum ►

▲ A Greek urn

2800 B.C.	2000 B.C.	1250 B.C.	750 B.C.
Minoan civilization begins	Mycenaeans move into Balkan Peninsula	Trojan War	Homer writes the *Iliad* and the *Odyssey*

ABOUT THE UNIT OPENING

Examining Artifacts

Ask students what two Greek accomplishments these artifacts show. *(architecture/sculpture and trial by jury)* Based on these artifacts, ask students to infer, or guess, some of the things the Greeks may have valued. *(sample responses: art, beauty, justice, and so on)* Tell students that this unit will highlight Greek contributions to world civilization.

Global Chronology

Ask students to name time line entries that indicate this time period was turbulent. *(Trojan War, Persian Wars begin, Peloponnesian War)* Ask students to name time line entries that indicate culture flourished during this time. *(Homer writes* Iliad *and* Odyssey*, Golden Age of Athens begins)*

FOLDABLES
Study Organizer

Organizing Information Study Foldable *Make this foldable to help you organize information about the history and culture of Greece.*

Step 1 *Mark the midpoint of the side edge of a sheet of paper.*

Draw a line along the midpoint.

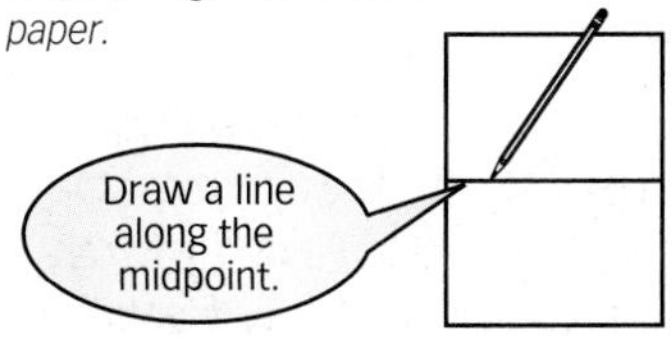

Step 2 *Turn the paper and fold the outside edges in to touch at the midpoint. Label as shown.*

Greece

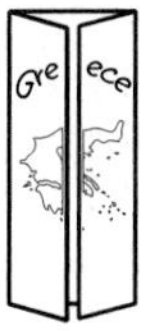

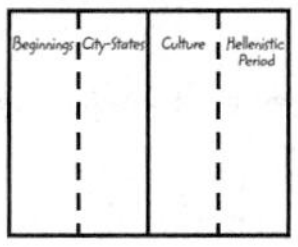

Reading and Writing *As you read the unit, organize your notes by writing the main ideas with supporting details under the appropriate tab.*

Step 3 *Open and label your foldable as shown.*

Beginnings | City-States | Culture | Hellenistic Period

PRIMARY SOURCES
Library

See pages 680–681 for another primary source reading to accompany Unit 4.

 GO TO Read "The Death of Socrates" from the **World History Primary Source Document Library CD-ROM.**

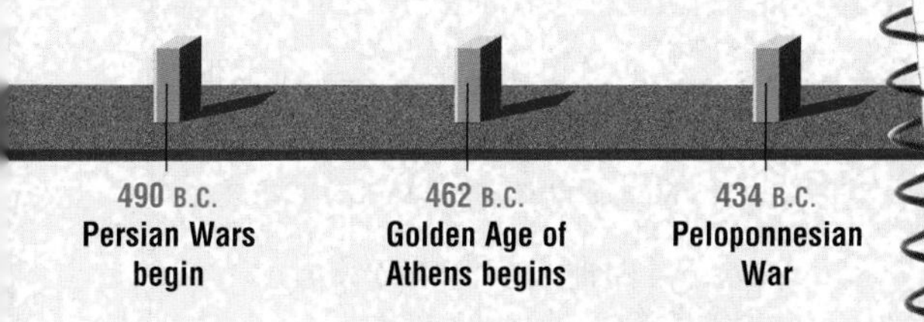

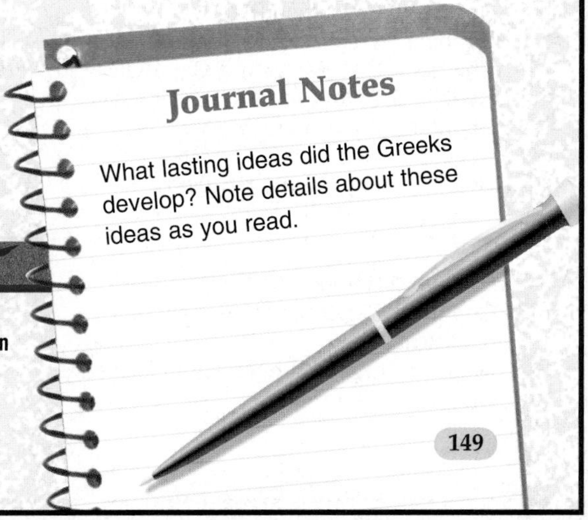

Journal Notes

What lasting ideas did the Greeks develop? Note details about these ideas as you read.

 149

490 B.C.
Persian Wars begin

462 B.C.
Golden Age of Athens begins

434 B.C.
Peloponnesian War

Geographic Location

The Greek civilizations discussed in this unit were located from the Mediterranean Sea eastward to the Indus Valley. Have students locate these places in their text Atlas and name the continents that this area includes. *(Europe, Africa, and Asia)*

ABCNEWS
INTERACTIVE

 VIDEOCASSETTE
Turning Points in World History

Have students view **Tape 1 Chapter 5** to learn about the origins of democracy.

MindJogger Videoquiz

Use **MindJogger Videoquiz** to preview the unit content.

 Available in DVD and VHS

FOLDABLES
Study Organizer

Purpose Students will create and use this foldable to organize information about Greece. Encourage students to include information on the geography, culture, important people, and contributions of Greece. Students will group information from the unit into four categories and determine relevent factual information.

Have students complete **Reading and Study Skills Foldables** Activity 4.

RECORDING JOURNAL NOTES

Help students begin writing in their journals by brainstorming ideas they think were developed by the Greeks. Write responses on the board. Have students note in their journal details about the contributions to the modern world that were developed by the Greeks.

PRIMARY SOURCES
Library

Additional primary sources from the **World History Primary Source Document Library CD-ROM** can be used during the study of Unit 4, including:

● The "Odyssey," by Homer

Primary sources about Greek society can be found on pages 680–681.

Chapter 9 Planning Guide

Timesaving Tools

TeacherWorks™ All-In-One Planner and Resource Center

- **Interactive Teacher Edition** Access your Teacher Wraparound Edition and your classroom resources with a few easy clicks.
- **Interactive Lesson Planner** Planning has never been easier! Organize your week, month, semester, or year with all the lesson helps you need to make teaching creative, timely, and relevant.

PRESENTATION Plus!

Use Glencoe's **Presentation Plus!** multimedia teacher tool to easily present dynamic lessons that visually excite your students. Using Microsoft PowerPoint® you can customize the presentations to create your own personalized lessons.

Objectives	Reproducible Resources	Multimedia Resources
Section 1 **The Minoans** Discuss the way of life of the Minoans and how geography influenced the early peoples who lived on Crete and the Balkan Peninsula.	Reproducible Lesson Plan Chapter 9 Vocabulary and Guided Reading Activity Reading Essentials and Study Guide 9-1 Chapter 9 Cooperative Learning Activity Section 1 Quiz Unit 4 Hands-On History Lab	Interactive Student Edition CD-ROM Graphic Organizer Transparency 7 Vocabulary PuzzleMaker CD-ROM Interactive Tutor Self-Assessment CD-ROM ExamView® Pro Testmaker CD-ROM Glencoe Skillbuilder Interactive Workbook CD-ROM, Level 1 Presentation Plus! CD-ROM
Section 2 **The Mycenaeans** Summarize the Mycenaean way of life and how the Dark Age affected the Aegean world.	Reproducible Lesson Plan Reading Essentials and Study Guide 9-2 Chapter 9 Geography and Map Activity Chapter 9 Chart and Graph Skill Activity Chapter 9 Enrichment Activity Section 2 Quiz Unit 4 Primary Source Readings	Teaching Transparencies and Activities 9A & 9B Vocabulary PuzzleMaker CD-ROM Interactive Tutor Self-Assessment CD-ROM ExamView® Pro Testmaker CD-ROM Glencoe Skillbuilder Interactive Workbook CD-ROM, Level 1
Chapter 9 **Review and Evaluation**	Chapter 9 Reteaching Activity Chapter 9 Performance Assessment Activity Spanish Chapter Summary and Glossary Chapter 9 Test	Vocabulary PuzzleMaker CD-ROM Interactive Tutor Self-Assessment CD-ROM Glencoe Skillbuilder Interactive Workbook CD-ROM, Level 1 Audiocassettes* ExamView® Pro Testmaker CD-ROM

*Also available in Spanish.

Performance Assessment Activities

Writing Have students write their own version of the *Iliad* using prose or poetry. Tell them to imagine they are one of the soldiers hidden inside the Trojan horse. They should describe their feelings as the horse is pulled into Troy by the Trojans, the ensuing battle, their escape from Troy, and their adventures on their way home.

CHAPTER RESOURCES

LITERATURE ABOUT THE PERIOD

Renault, *The King Must Die.* Random House, 1988. Retells the legend of Theseus's struggle with the Minotaur.

READINGS FOR THE STUDENT

Evslin, Bernard. *Heroes and Monsters of Greek Myth.* Scholastic, 1988. Retells many Greek myths.

READINGS FOR THE TEACHER

Cotterell, Arthur. *The Minoan World.* Charles Scribner's Sons, 1979. Surveys Minoan civilization.

Fine, John V. A. *The Ancient Greeks.* Belknap Press, 1983. Surveys the Greek world up to the accession of Alexander the Great.

KEY TO ABILITY LEVELS

Teaching strategies have been coded for varying learning styles and abilities.

L1 Level 1 activities are **basic** activities and should be within the ability range of all students.

L2 Level 2 activities are **average** activities and should be within the ability range of the average to above-average student.

L3 Level 3 activities are **challenging** activities designed for the ability range of above-average students.

ELL ELL activities should be within the ability range of English Language Learning students.

NATIONAL GEOGRAPHIC Teacher's Corner

INDEX TO NATIONAL GEOGRAPHIC MAGAZINE

The following article relates to this chapter:

- "Echoes of the Heroic Age: Ancient Greece, Part I," by Caroline Alexander, December 1999.

NATIONAL GEOGRAPHIC SOCIETY PRODUCTS AVAILABLE FROM GLENCOE

To order the following, call Glencoe at 1-800-334-7344:

- *PicturePack: Physical Geography of the World (Transparencies)*
- *PictureShow: Ancient Civilizations: Greece and Rome (CD-ROMs)*
- *PicturePack: Ancient Greece (Transparencies)*
- *PicturePack: Ancient Civilizations Library, Part I (Transparencies)*

Access *National Geographic's* new dynamic MapMachine Web site and other geography resources at:
www.nationalgeographic.com
www.nationalgeographic.com/maps

THE HISTORY CHANNEL. A&E HOME VIDEO. Biography

The following videotape program is available from Glencoe:

- **The Trojan City**
  0-7670-0647-X

To order, call Glencoe at 1-800-334-7344. To find classroom resources to accompany many of these videos, check the following home pages:

A&E Television: www.aande.com
The History Channel: www.historychannel.com

OVERVIEW

Chapter 9 introduces Minoan and Mycenaean cultures as forerunners of Greek civilization.

- **Section 1** discusses the way of life of the Minoans.
- **Section 2** explains the culture of the Mycenaeans.

CHAPTER OBJECTIVES

After reading Chapter 9, students will be able to:

1. describe what life was like for the Minoans.
2. discuss how geography influenced the people who lived on Crete and the Balkan Peninsula.
3. summarize what life was like for the Mycenaeans.
4. explain how the Dark Age affected the Aegean world.

EXAMINING ARTIFACTS

Have students identify the vehicle in the fresco. *(chariot)* Based on prior knowledge, call on a volunteer to name the chariot's most common use. *(as a weapon of war)* Direct students to find items in the time line that prove that the Mycenaeans engaged in warlike activities. Ask: What else can you infer about Mycenaean culture based on these artifacts? Tell students to evaluate their inferences as they read through the chapter.

PERFORMANCE ASSESSMENT ✓

Use the Performance Assessment activities on page 150B to help you evaluate students as they complete the chapter.

CHAPTER 9

Beginnings

2800 B.C.–750 B.C.

Mycenaean fresco of women driving a chariot ▼

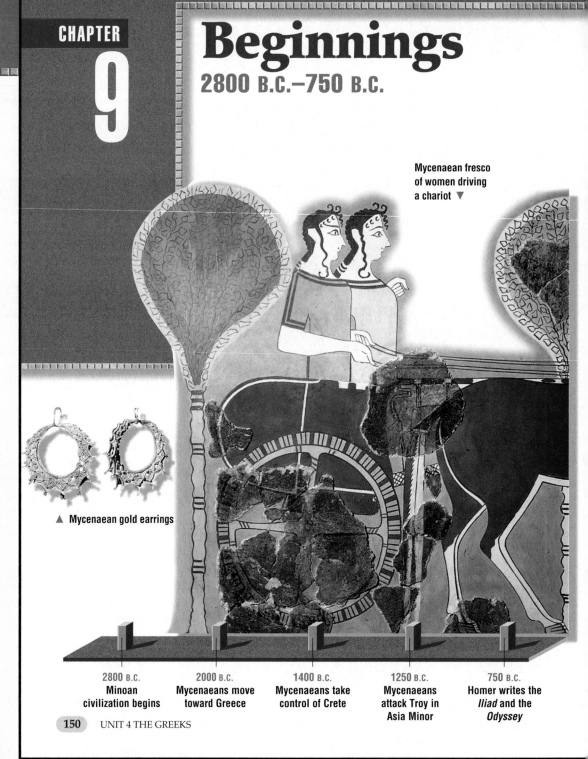

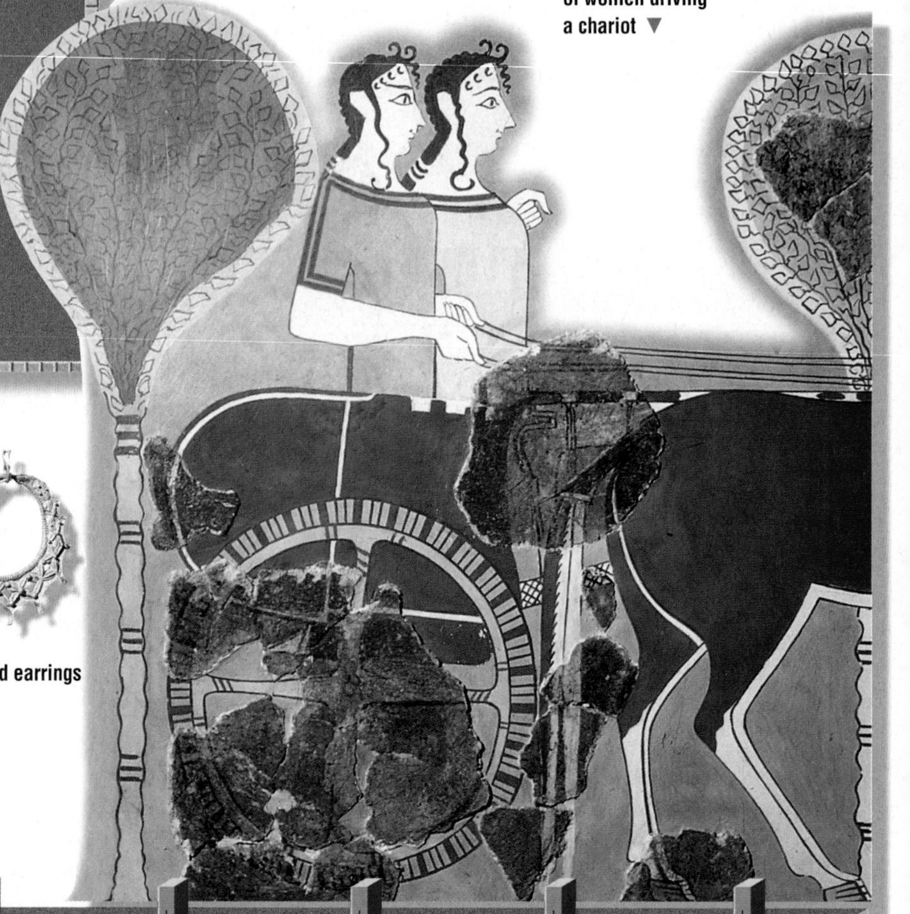

▲ Mycenaean gold earrings

2800 B.C.	2000 B.C.	1400 B.C.	1250 B.C.	750 B.C.
Minoan civilization begins	Mycenaeans move toward Greece	Mycenaeans take control of Crete	Mycenaeans attack Troy in Asia Minor	Homer writes the *Iliad* and the *Odyssey*

TEACHING RESOURCES

TEACHER PLANNING AND SUPPORT

- Reproducible Lesson Plan 9-1, 9-2
- Teaching Strategies for the World History Classroom (Including Block Scheduling Pacing Guides)
- Presentation Plus! CD-ROM

REVIEW AND REINFORCEMENT

- Reading Essentials and Study Guide 9-1, 9-2
- Chapter 9 Vocabulary and Guided Reading Activity
- Vocabulary PuzzleMaker CD-ROM
- Teaching Transparencies 9A & 9B
- Chapter 9 Reteaching Activity
- Chapter 9 Cooperative Learning Activity
- Chapter 9 Activity Book Activity
- Chapter 9 Chart and Graph Skill Activity
- Reading and Study Skills Foldables
- Interactive Tutor Self-Assessment CD-ROM
- Unit 4 MindJogger VideoQuiz

APPLICATION AND HANDS-ON ACTIVITIES

- Daily Questions in Social Studies
- Unit 4 Hands-On History Lab Activity
- Student Presentation Builder CD-ROM

Chapter Focus

Read to Discover

- What life was like for the Minoans.
- How geography influenced the early peoples who lived on Crete and the Balkan Peninsula.
- What life was like for the Mycenaeans.
- How the "Dark Age" affected the Aegean world.

HISTORY Online

Chapter Overview

Visit the *Human Heritage* Web site at **humanheritage.glencoe.com** and click on ***Chapter 9—Chapter Overviews*** to preview this chapter.

Terms to Learn	People to Know	Places to Locate
bull leaping	Theseus	Crete
labyrinth	Homer	Balkan Peninsula
parchment	Odysseus	Troy
shrines	Helen	Asia Minor
megaron		Ionia
tenants		
civil wars		

Why It's Important Greek civilization grew out of a combination of two earlier civilizations, Minoan (muh nō′ uhn) and Mycenaean (mīsuh nē′ uhn). Due to the geography of the land, both became great sea powers. Although their power was eventually destroyed, the Minoans and the Mycenaeans left an important *legacy* (leg′ uh sē), or gift from the past, to the Greeks.

SECTION 1 The Minoans

Minoan civilization rose around 2800 B.C. on Crete (krēt), an island in the Mediterranean Sea. The Minoans, who were also known as Cretans, grew wheat, barley, grapes, and olives. When the olive groves and vineyards produced more than was needed, the Minoans traded the surplus for goods they could not grow or make on Crete.

Since there were many forests on Crete, the Minoans learned to work with wood and became good carpenters. They also learned to work with metal. They used their metalworking and carpentry skills to build ships and began to earn a living from trade instead of farming.

When pirates threatened them, the Minoans changed the way they built their ships so the ships could go faster. They made them slimmer, with two or three masts instead of one. The Minoans also put a deck over the heads of rowers to protect them.

HISTORY Online

Chapter Overview introduces students to chapter content and key terms. Have them access ***Chapter 9 Overview*** at **humanheritage.glencoe.com**

FOCUS

Bellringer

Ask students to write their favorite commercial jingle or slogan.

Motivational Activity

Discuss students' favorite jingles and ask volunteers to recite them. Ask students why some commercials are remembered. *(People usually remember things they hear, especially if it rhymes or is put to music.)* Tell students that in this chapter they will learn about a world-famous poet who wrote about the songs and legends that he had heard.

GUIDE TO READING

Reading Strategy

Ask students to read "Why It's Important" and summarize the chapter's main theme. *(The Minoan and Mycenaean cultures paved the way for the rise of Greek civilization.)*

Vocabulary Precheck

Ask students to define each of the "Terms to Learn." Have a volunteer consult the dictionary for any unfamiliar words. L1 ELL

Use the Vocabulary PuzzleMaker CD-ROM for Chapter 9 to create a crossword puzzle. L1

Assign Chapter 9 Vocabulary and Guided Reading Activity.

Assign Reading Essentials and Study Guide 9-1.

GEOGRAPHY ACTIVITIES
- Chapter 9 Geography and Map Activity
- Outline Map Resource Book

INTERDISCIPLINARY CONNECTIONS
- World Music: A Cultural Legacy

ENRICHMENT AND EXTENSION
- World History Primary Source Document Library CD-ROM
- Chapter 9 Enrichment Activity
- Foods Around the World

ASSESSMENT AND EVALUATION
- Chapter 9 Performance Assessment Activity
- Chapter 9 Section Quizzes 9-1, 9-2
- Chapter 9 Test
- Chapter 9 ExamView® Pro Testmaker CD-ROM
- Chapter 9 Digests Audiocassettes Activities and Tests

SPANISH RESOURCES
- Chapter 9 Spanish Chapter Summary and Glossary
- Chapter 9 Spanish Chapter Digests Audiocassettes Activities and Tests

TEACH

Guided Practice

L1 **Geography: Places and Regions** Ask students to locate Crete on the map of Western Europe in the text Atlas. Ask students to describe geographical features that offered protection to Minoan cities. *(seas and mountains)* ELL

Reading Check Answer

Bull leaping was a form of bullfighting in which a young man grabbed a bull's horns, somersaulted onto its back, and did a back flip into a female partner's arms.

DID YOU KNOW ??

Minoan toilets did not flush in the modern sense. Waste material was deposited into a drain pipe through which water ran.

HISTORY Online

Student Web Activity objectives and answers can be found at the ***Chapter 9 Web Activity Lesson Plan*** at humanheritage.glencoe.com

MAKING CONNECTIONS

>> **Legends** A legend of ancient Crete tells about the world's first robot. A huge bronze figure with the body of a man and the head of a bull guarded the island's coast. If enemies landed, it would heat its body in fire, grab the invaders, and burn them to ashes.

Minoan Jar

They placed a wooden beam in the *prow,* or front part of the ship. This was used to smash a hole in enemy ships to sink them.

Over time, the Minoans drove off the pirates. By about 2000 B.C., Crete was the world's first important seafaring civilization. Minoan merchant ships traveled far to trade pottery, leather and bronze armor, and metal jewelry.

The People The Minoans were a small people with bronzed skin and long dark hair. Men wore striped loincloths, long robes embroidered with flowers, or trousers that bagged at the knees. Women wore full skirts and short-sleeved jackets that laced in front. The Minoans had small waists and wore tight belts to show them off. They also wore jewelry, such as gold and silver earrings, necklaces, bracelets, and rings.

The Minoans spent their time in a variety of ways. Men farmed and fished. They raised cattle, long-horned sheep, and goats. They also served in the navy and the royal guard. Women performed household duties, attended sporting events, and went hunting in chariots.

The people of Crete loved sports. They built what was probably the world's first arena. It stood in the open air. Stone steps formed grandstands, where about 500 people could sit and watch the action. The king and the royal party had their own special box seats.

Reading Check What was **bull leaping?**

Boxing matches were held in the arena. **Bull leaping,** a form of bullfighting, was also held there. A young man and woman "fought" the bull together. The man would grab the bull's horns. As the bull raised its head to toss him, the man would do a somersault, landing on his feet on the bull's back. He would then do a back flip. Standing behind the bull, the woman would catch her partner as he landed. Many experts believe bull leaping was a religious ceremony as well as a sport.

Cities and Palaces The Minoans built many cities, which were different from those of other ancient civilizations in two ways. At the heart of each Minoan city stood a palace rather than a temple. Also, Minoan cities did not have walls around them. Instead, people depended on the sea and navy for protection.

One of the largest cities of Crete was Knossos (kuh nahs' uhs). It covered about 28 acres, or 11.2 hectares. About one-fifth of the area was taken up by a five-story palace that served as a government building, temple, factory, and warehouse. Its walls were built of stone and sun-dried brick framed with wooden beams. The Minoans decorated the inside walls with brightly colored *frescoes* (fres' kōs), or watercolor paintings made on damp plaster. The palace had bathrooms with bathtubs and flush toilets. It also had hot and cold running water and portable fireboxes to heat rooms.

HISTORY Online

Student Web Activity

Visit the *Human Heritage* Web site at humanheritage.glencoe.com and click on ***Chapter 9—Student Web Activities*** to find out more about the Minoans.

MEETING SPECIAL NEEDS

Have visual learners study the Minoan frescoes found in this chapter and in other reference books. Point out to students the various shades and colors used in the frescoes. Have students work in small groups to create a fresco with small scraps of torn paper, colored with markers or crayons in the Minoan style. Topics from the Minoan culture could include: daily life, sports, city design, or religion. Provide each group with a large sheet of newsprint to use for the fresco. Display frescoes in the classroom.

Refer to ***Inclusion for the Middle School Social Studies Classroom: Strategies and Activities*** for additional resources.

The palace had several entrances. Passageways and rooms formed a **labyrinth** (lab' uh rinth), or a network of paths through which it is difficult to find one's way. Because labyrinth means "double ax," the palace was called the "House of the Double Ax." The palace was also called by that name because it was filled with pictures, carvings, and bronze models of a double ax.

Sea captains, merchants, and shipbuilders lived in houses around the palace. Past their houses stood those of artisans who made beautiful cups and vases and designed delicate jewelry.

Houses were built side by side around courtyards. Most were two stories high. Lower walls were made of stone, and the upper walls were made of sun-dried brick. The inside walls were painted with scenes from daily life. Each house also had its own well and drains.

Many early Minoan houses had no entrance from the street. A person went in or out through the roof and lowered a ladder over the side of the house. Later, wooden doors and windows made of oiled and tinted **parchment** (parch' muhnt), or thin animal skin, were added.

Reading Check What is a **labyrinth?**

Reading Check How did Minoans use **parchment** in building their homes?

BULL LEAPING This painting from Knossos shows Minoans bull leaping. In the center, a man leaps over the bull's back. Another man grips the bull's horns so that it will lift its head and toss him. The woman behind the bull prepares to catch the leapers. **What other sporting event was held in a Minoan arena?**

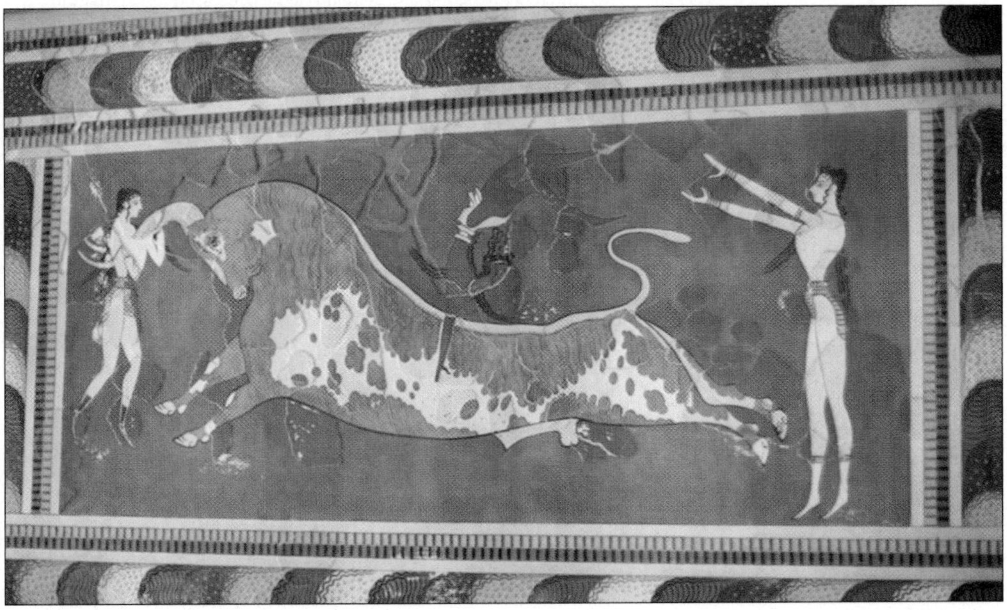

Reading Check Answer A **labyrinth** is a complicated network of paths.

Reading Check Answer Minoans used **parchment** for windows in their homes.

CAPTION ANSWER

boxing matches

L1 **Geography: Environment and Society** Have students list occupations of Minoans. *(farmers, fishers, shepherds, sea captains, merchants, shipbuilders, artisans)* What did most of the occupations have in common? *(a connection with the sea)* Why would occupations related to the sea be plentiful in Minoan society? *(Crete is a small island surrounded by the sea.)*

DID YOU KNOW

The palace at Knossos was built around 2000 B.C. It was discovered in 1900 by Sir Arthur Evans, a British archaeologist.

COOPERATIVE LEARNING

Call on volunteers to research the story of Theseus and the Minotaur—a half bull, half human monster that lived inside a labyrinth at the Palace of Knossos. Meet with the volunteers to practice a retelling of the story to the class as a whole.

After students have presented the story, divide the rest of the class into groups, and have each group design murals depicting scenes from the myth. Assign the storytellers to coordinate the scenes prepared by each group. When students are done, display the murals, which might be drawn on poster board, on a wall of the classroom.

Assign Chapter 9 *Cooperative Learning Activity* in the TCR.

Reading Check Answer The Minoans built **shrines** to worship their gods.

DID YOU KNOW

Minoan writing, which is known as Linear A, has not been deciphered.

CAPTION ANSWER

They believed she made plants grow and brought children into the world.

MAKING CONNECTIONS

➤➤ **Daily Life** Minoan women enjoyed a higher status than women in other civilizations. For example, they were permitted to attend sporting events. Also, Minoan religion had more goddesses than gods.

Reading Check Why did the Minoans build **shrines?**

Rulers and Religion The rulers of Crete were priest-kings. They made the laws and represented the gods on Earth. The priest-kings would climb to the top of Mount Juktas (yūk′ tuhs) to look for a sign from heaven that would tell them the will of the gods. Then, they would tell their people what the gods wanted them to do.

The Minoans had many gods. The main god was the Great Goddess, Mother Earth. She made plants grow and brought children into the world. To honor her, the Minoans built **shrines,** or sacred places to worship, in palaces, on housetops, on hilltops, and in caves. The people believed that hilltops led to heaven, and caves led to the underworld.

Sacred horns made of clay and covered with stucco rested against the back wall of each shrine. A hole between the horns held a bronze double ax. Around the horns were clay models of animals. People left offerings of human hair, fruit, flowers, jewels, and gold at the shrines.

The Minoans believed that certain things were sacred. The lily was their sacred flower. The king wore a plumed crown of lilies and a lily necklace. The double ax was sacred. It stood for the power of Mother Earth and the authority of the king. The dove was sacred because it flew to the heavens.

MINOAN RELIGION This Minoan fresco shows a religious ceremony. As a musician plays the harp, two women and a man carry offerings to a shrine. The double axes with birds sitting on them (left) are symbols of the Great Goddess. **What did Minoans believe about the Great Goddess?**

MEETING SPECIAL NEEDS

Have auditory learners listen to the audiocassette for this chapter. Then hold a discussion about the possible reasons for the decline of early civilizations including the Minoans and the Mycenaeans.

Refer to *Inclusion for the Middle School Social Studies Classroom: Strategies and Activities* for additional resources.

The Fall of the Minoans No one is certain why Minoan civilization came to an end. What is certain is that about 1400 B.C., control of the sea and of Crete passed to the Mycenaeans.

Legend explains the fall of the Minoans with the story of Theseus (thee' see uhs) and the Minotaur (min' uh tauhr). A young Greek prince named Theseus was brought to Knossos. He was to be sacrificed to the Minotaur, a huge monster the king kept in the palace labyrinth. The Minotaur had the body of a man and the head of a bull and lived on human flesh. Theseus was put into the labyrinth. He fought the monster with a magical sword and killed it. When the Minotaur died, the power of the Minoans died too.

Section 1 Assessment

1. **Define:** bull leaping, labyrinth, parchment, shrines.
2. What kind of government did the Minoans have?
3. How did cities in Crete differ from cities in other ancient civilizations?

Critical Thinking

4. **Making Generalizations** How did geography influence the development of the Minoan civilization?

Graphic Organizer Activity

5. Draw a chart like this one, and use it to fill in details on Minoan civilization.

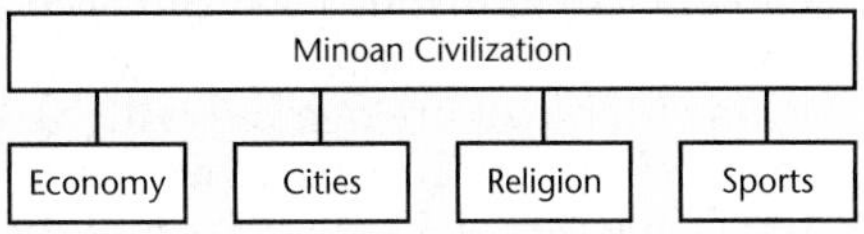

SECTION 2 The Mycenaeans

The Mycenaeans came from the grasslands of southern Russia. Around 2000 B.C., small groups started making their way west into Europe and then south through the Balkan (bol' kuhn) Peninsula. Finally, they settled in the lowlands of Greece.

The Mycenaean kings built fortress-palaces on hilltops. In times of danger or attack, the people in the villages outside the palace walls took shelter within the palace. Its chief feature was the **megaron** (meg' uh ron), or a square room with a fireplace in its center. The king held council meetings and entertained in the megaron.

Land was divided into estates that were farmed either by enslaved people or by **tenants,** or people who live on and work another person's land. Landowners gave the king horses, chariots, weapons, wheat, farm animals, honey, and hides in exchange for protection. Tenants labored to supply many of these items.

Reading Check How did Mycenaean kings use the **megaron?** How did **tenants** earn a living?

Use the **Interactive Tutor Self-Assessment CD-ROM** to review Section 1.

L3 **Critical Thinking** Ask students to explain what purpose myths and legends about monsters might have served the Minoans. *(They might have provided supernatural explanations of actual events.)*

MAKING CONNECTIONS

>> **Folklore** According to legend, Ariadne, the Minoan king's daughter, gave Theseus the clue of unwinding a ball of thread to help him find his way out of the labyrinth. After killing the Minotaur, Theseus escaped from Crete with Ariadne.

Reading Check Answer
Mycenaean kings used the **megaron** to hold council meetings and to entertain people. **Tenants** earned a living by working on another person's land.

DID YOU KNOW

The Mycenaeans got their name from their chief fortress-palace of Mycenae, which was excavated in 1876–1877 by a German amateur archaeologist named Heinrich Schliemann.

Use the **Vocabulary PuzzleMaker CD-ROM** to create crossword and word search puzzles.

Section 1 Assessment Answers

1. bull leaping, form of bullfighting (p. 152); labyrinth, path network (p. 153); parchment, thin animal skin (p. 153); shrines, sacred places (p. 154)
2. They were ruled by priest-kings, who represented the gods.
3. At the heart of each city stood a palace, and cities did not have walls around them.
4. Answers will vary, but due to geography the Minoans became a sea power. Because of forests on Crete, the Minoans worked with wood. Because Minoan cities were near the sea, they did not have walls.
5. Items in each box should reflect innovations and achievements mentioned in the text. You might use these responses as examples: economy—world's first important seafaring nation; cities—palace at the center instead of a temple, no walls; religion—Great Goddess, Mother Earth, main deity; sports—bull leaping.

Assign Chapter 9 **Section 1 Quiz** in the TCR. Testmaker available.

MAP SKILLS

TEACH

Reading Longitude

Ask students to study the map to answer the following questions:

Along which line of longitude is Mount Juktas located? *(25 °E)*

Between which two lines of longitude is Cyprus located? *(30 °E and 35 °E)*

Along what approximate line of longitude is Mycenae located? *(23 °E)*

Between which lines of longitude was the Minoan culture located? *(20 °E and 35 °E)*

Have students use the map of Western Europe in the text Atlas to create questions about the locations of places based on longitude. Have students ask a partner their questions.

Answers to Map Practice

1. 25° E
2. Mycenae

Use the **Glencoe Skillbuilder Interactive Workbook CD-ROM, Level 1,** to provide instruction and practice in key social studies skills.

MAP SKILLS

Reading Longitude

To measure distances east and west on Earth, mapmakers use imaginary lines on maps and globes. These are called lines of **longitude,** or **meridians** (muh rid′ ē uhnz), and they run from the North Pole to the South Pole.

Like lines of latitude, meridians are measured in degrees. All meridians are measured from the Prime Meridian, a line of longitude that runs through Greenwich, England. The Prime Meridian is marked 0°. Those lines east of the Prime Meridian are marked with an E, from 1°E to 180°E. Those lines west of the Prime Meridian are marked with a W, from 1°W to 180°W. Unlike lines of latitude, meridians are not always the same distance from one another. They are farthest apart at the Equator, and closest together at the poles.

Lines of longitude are often used to help specify location. For example, it is much easier to find Troy on the map below if one knows that it is located at about 26°E.

Look at the map below, and answer the following questions.

Map Practice

1. **Along which line of longitude was Knossos located?**
2. **Which early Aegean city was located closest to 20°E?**

The Early Aegean World

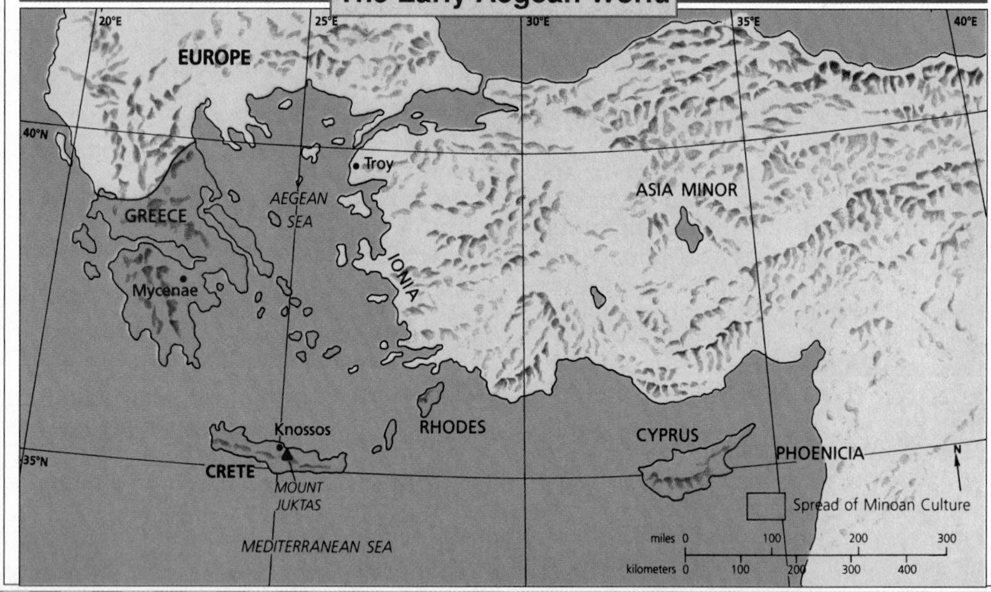

156

SPOTLIGHT ON: THE AEGEAN WORLD

Archaeologists have unearthed relics of the Greek civilization by digging throughout the Aegean area. Artifacts have also been found in another treasury of sorts—the Mediterranean Sea. Many important and interesting relics have been found in the waters near Crete and Cyprus. Students may enjoy reading more about these discoveries in *Diving to the Past: Recovering Ancient Wrecks* by W. John Hackwell.

Linking Across Time

Greek Shipping The seafaring tradition has continued from Mycenaean times (below) into the present. Today Greece is among the top ten shipping nations in the world (right). **What does the size of this modern Greek ship tell you about Greek trade today?**

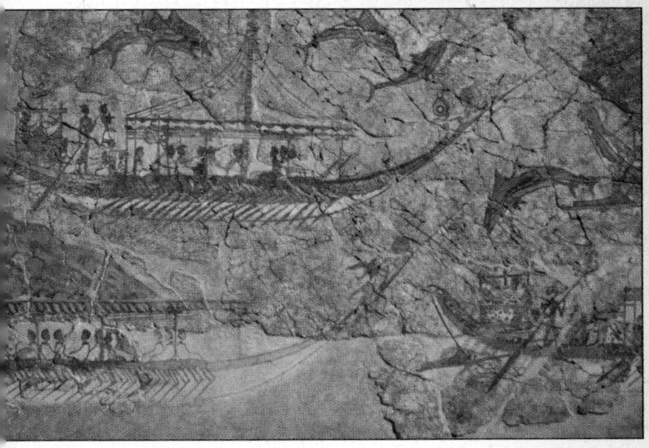

Although they kept large herds of cattle, the Mycenaeans relied on hunting to get more meat. They hunted rabbit, deer, boar, wild bulls, and game birds. Women rode with the men in chariots during the hunt. When hunters were after big game, they used greyhounds. The game was captured with nets or killed with spears, slings, or bows and arrows.

Traders and Pirates Shortly after the Mycenaeans settled in the lowlands of Greece, they were visited by Minoan traders from Crete. The Mycenaeans began to imitate Minoan gold and bronze work. They adapted Cretan script to their own language. They copied Minoan fashions. Most important of all, they learned how to build ships and how to navigate.

The Mycenaeans also began to grow olives. They made presses to squeeze oil from the olives. They used the oil for cooking, as fuel for lamps, and to rub on their bodies. They sold plain oil in large clay jars and perfumed oil in painted vases. Sale of the oil made the Mycenaeans rich. It also led to the founding of trading stations and settlements on nearby islands.

EXTENDING THE CONTENT

Gold was not a metal native to Mycenaean lands, but has been found in Mycenaean tombs and shaft graves. Historians believe that Mycenaean rulers either traded or fought to acquire gold and other riches. During this period, Egypt was the leading source of gold in the Mediterranean. It seems possible that mercenaries, or paid warriors, from Mycenae may have fought for the Egyptians and were paid in gold.

Linking Across Time

sample answers: that Greeks still transport much of their goods by sea; that shipping still plays an important part in the Greek economy

Independent Practice

L2 **Daily Life** Ask students to research and make a chart comparing the chief agricultural crops and occupations of the Mycenaeans to those of present-day Greeks.

DID YOU KNOW ??

Troy was discovered and excavated by Heinrich Schliemann in 1870. As he dug, Schliemann found nine cities at the site. The seventh city down is presumed to be Troy of the Trojan War period.

Economics at a Glance

Needs and Wants

The choices that individuals and countries make are based on their *needs* and *wants*. Needs are items that are necessary for survival, such as food, shelter, and clothing. Wants are things that people desire to have. The growth of the olive oil industry helped the Mycenaeans satisfy their cooking and fuel needs. Olive oil also satisfied their wants since it could be used as a moisturizer and perfume. Write the following statements on the board for students to complete: "Things I need to live include. . ." "Things I want to have include. . ." Call on volunteers to read their completed lists to the class. Then have students discuss how they distinguished between what they need and what they want.

L1 **Writing** Have students imagine that they are traders who come to do business with the Mycenaeans. Tell them to write letters home describing Mycenaean fortress-palaces, land, occupations, and lifestyles. Have students share their letters.

LINKING PAST TO PRESENT

The events and heroes of the Trojan War, along with their later fates, became the subjects of the greatest Greek tragedies. For example, Euripedes' *Trojan Women* looks at the human aftermath of war in the fallen city. Aeschylus's *Oresteia*, a trilogy of poetic dramas about the ill-fated House of Atreus, begins with Agamemnon's homecoming from victory at Troy. Later writers throughout the world have also drawn on this famous story.

CAPTION ANSWER

from songs and legends that had been handed down by word of mouth

A&E HOME VIDEO.

The following videotape program is available from Glencoe to enrich Chapter 9:

- **The Trojan City**

To find classroom resources to accompany this video, check the following home page:

A&E Television:
www.aande.com

People in History

Homer
c. 700s B.C.

Greek Poet

Homer remains a mystery. Nobody knows what he looked like or exactly when he lived. Ancient Greek *bards*, or poets, called him the "Ionian bard," so maybe Homer came from Ionia. Tradition says Homer was blind, but he was not blind to history. Archaeologists have proven that many of the stories told by Homer actually took place. That means his poems are more than good literature—they are also good history.

Despite their success in trade, the Mycenaeans were warriors at heart. In battle, they used large hide shields with wooden frames and fought with spears and swords. Their leaders wore fancy bronze armor. At first, the Mycenaeans fought one another. After they learned about shipbuilding and navigation, they outfitted pirate fleets and began to raid nearby lands. By about 1400 B.C., they had replaced the Minoans as the chief power of the Aegean world.

The Trojan War The Mycenaeans are famous for their attack on Troy, a major trading city in Asia Minor. This attack probably took place during the middle 1200s B.C. At the time, the Trojans (trō′ juhns) controlled the trade routes to the Black Sea. They made money by taxing the ships that carried grain and gold from southern Russia to Greece.

About 500 years after the Mycenaeans attacked Troy, a blind Greek poet named Homer (hō′ muhr) composed a long poem about the event. He called his poem the *Iliad* (il′ ē uhd). Homer also composed a poem called the *Odyssey* (ahd′ uh sē), which tells about the wanderings of Odysseus (ō dis′ ē uhs), a Mycenaean hero of the Trojan War. Homer drew his material for the two

THE TROJAN HORSE The first Greek myths came from the Mycenaeans. Later, the poet Homer gathered these legends and used them to write his works. Here, a painting of the Trojan horse from Homer's poem the *Iliad* is shown. **Where did Homer get his material for the *Iliad* and the *Odyssey*?**

MULTICULTURAL PERSPECTIVES

Literature, sculpture, music, and even everyday speech still reflect the incidents and characters of the Trojan War. People who have read a line of Homer's *Iliad* or Virgil's *Aeneid,* which finishes the story of Troy, are familiar with the story of the Trojan Horse. Some quotes from the story are familiar phrases, such as the reference to Helen: "Was this the face that launched a thousand ships?"

poems from songs and legends that had been handed down by word of mouth. He then added his own descriptions and details of everyday life.

According to Homer's account in the *Iliad*, the Trojan War was fought over a woman. The king of Troy had a son named Paris, who fell in love with Helen, the wife of a Mycenaean king. When Paris took Helen to Troy, her husband became angry. He formed an army and sailed after them. However, the walls of Troy were so tall, thick, and strong that the Mycenaeans could not get into the city. They had to camp on the plain outside the city walls.

After ten years of fighting, the Mycenaeans still had not taken Troy. Then, Odysseus suggested a way they could capture the city. He had the soldiers build a huge, hollow wooden horse. The best soldiers hid inside the horse, while the rest boarded their ships and sailed away.

The Trojans saw the ships leave and thought they had won the war. They did not know the Mycenaean ships would return after dark. The Trojans tied ropes to the wooden horse and pulled it into the city as a victory prize. When they fell asleep, the Mycenaean soldiers hidden inside the horse came out. They opened the city gates and let in the rest of the Mycenaean army. The Mycenaeans killed the king of Troy and burned the city. Then, with Helen, they returned to their homes.

Mycenaean Goldwork

A "Dark Age"

The Mycenaeans did not return to peaceful ways after crushing Troy. Instead, a series of **civil wars,** or wars between opposing groups of citizens, broke out. Within 100 years after the end of the Trojan War, almost no Mycenaean fortress-palaces were left. Soon after, a people called Dorians (dōr′ ē uhns) entered Greece and conquered the Mycenaeans. Their iron swords were not as well made as Mycenaean bronze swords. Nevertheless, Dorian swords were stronger. Thousands of Mycenaeans fled the Greek mainland and settled on Aegean islands and on the western shore of Asia Minor. These settlements later became known as Ionia (ī ō′ nē uh).

Reading Check How did **civil wars** weaken the Mycenaeans?

As a result of the civil wars and the Dorian invasion, the Aegean world entered a "Dark Age," which lasted until about 800 B.C. It was a time of wandering and killing. Overseas trade stopped. The people of the Aegean region forgot how to write and keep records. The skills of fresco painting and working with ivory and gold disappeared. The Aegean world was cut off from the Middle East, and the people had to create a new civilization on their own.

The people started over. Once again, herding and farming became the main ways of life. Local leaders ruled small areas. These leaders called themselves kings, but they were little more than chiefs. At first, the borders of the areas they ruled kept changing. In time, however, the borders became fixed, and each area became an independent community. The people of these

DID YOU KNOW ??

Odysseus was later called Ulysses by the Romans.

L1 History Have students imagine they were Mycenaeans who lived before and after the Dorian invasion. Tell them that they are responsible for writing two journal entries. In the first entry, they should describe Mycenaean life before the Dorian invasion. In the second entry, they should describe how their lives have changed.

Reading Check Answer After the **civil wars**, almost no Mycenaean fortress-palaces were left, making it easy for the Dorians to conquer Greece.

ASSESS

Check for Understanding

Ask students to summarize orally or in writing the main points of the chapter. Discuss the answers to the Section and Chapter Assessment questions.

Evaluate

Assign Chapter 9 **Performance Assessment Activity** in the TCR.

Administer **Chapter 9 Test** in the TCR. Testmaker available.

COOPERATIVE LEARNING

Organize the class into small groups and have each group find additional information about a Greek hero or heroine—either from the *Iliad* or *Odyssey* or from Greek myths. Each group should then write their own adventure involving their subject, and decide how it will be presented to the class. Some suggestions include acting out a myth, making a videotape, or presenting it on decorated poster board.

Reteach

Have students use the key terms to describe the main concepts of the chapter.

Assign Chapter 9 **Reteaching Activity** in the TCR.

Enrich

Have students take turns reading aloud passages from the *Iliad* and the *Odyssey.* What do they like most and least about what they hear?

Assign Chapter 9 **Enrichment Activity** in the TCR.

CLOSE

Ask students to discuss which of the following statements is most true: *The early Greek people shaped their environment* OR *The early Greek people were shaped by their environment.*

Use **Interactive Tutor Self-Assessment CD-ROM** to review Section 2.

HISTORY Online

Self-Check Quiz gives students an interactive chapter tutorial. Have them access ***Chapter 9 Quiz*** at **humanheritage.glencoe.com**

communities began calling themselves Hellenes (hel' ēns), or Greeks. They worked hard to redevelop their culture and to learn new crafts and skills. The civilization they created flourished from about the 700s B.C. until 336 B.C.

Section 2 Assessment

1. **Define:** megaron, tenants, civil wars.
2. In what ways were the Mycenaeans influenced by Minoan culture?
3. According to Homer, how did the Mycenaeans finally win the Trojan War?
4. What happened in the Aegean world during the "Dark Age"?

Critical Thinking

5. **Demonstrating Reasoned Judgment** Why was the growing of olives such an important development for the Aegean world?

Graphic Organizer Activity

6. Draw a diagram like this one, and use it to show the causes and effects of the Trojan War on the Mycenaeans.

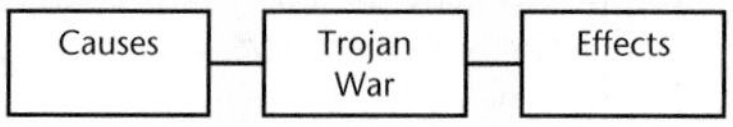

Chapter Summary & Study Guide

1. Minoan civilization began to develop on the Mediterranean island of Crete around 2800 B.C.
2. The Minoans started as farmers but eventually turned to trade.
3. Since the Minoans depended on the sea and their ships for protection, their cities were not walled.
4. The Minoans worshiped many gods, the most important of which was the Great Goddess, Mother Earth.
5. Around 1400 B.C., the Mycenaeans took control of the Mediterranean.
6. Instead of cities, the Mycenaeans built fortress-palaces on hilltops.
7. The Mycenaeans learned many things from the Minoans, including a writing script and the skills of shipbuilding and navigation.
8. The Mycenaeans fought a lengthy war against Troy, described in two long poems, the *Iliad* and the *Odyssey.*
9. After years of civil war, the Mycenaeans were conquered by the Dorians.
10. During the 300 years of the "Dark Age," the people of the Aegean area lost many of their skills and had to create a new civilization.

HISTORY Online

Self-Check Quiz

Visit the *Human Heritage* Web site at **humanheritage.glencoe.com** and click on ***Chapter 9—Self-Check Quiz*** to assess your understanding of this chapter.

Section 2 Assessment Answers

1. megaron, palace room with a center fireplace (p. 155); tenants, people who work another person's land (p. 155); civil wars, wars between opposing groups within one nation (p. 159)
2. They copied Minoan metalwork, adapted Cretan script, copied Minoan fashions, and learned how to build and navigate ships.
3. by hiding soldiers in a wooden horse and tricking the Trojans into dragging it inside their city
4. It was a time of wandering and killing, overseas trade stopped, people forgot how to write, and artistic skills disappeared.
5. Oil was squeezed from olives and used for many things, which led to riches.
6. sample responses: *causes*—Trojan control of trade routes to Black Sea; according to Homer, capture of Helen by Trojan king; *effects*—eruption of a series of civil wars, conquest by the Dorians, "Dark Age" for the Aegean world

Assign Chapter 9 **Section 2 Quiz** in the TCR. Testmaker available.

CHAPTER 9 Assessment

Using Key Terms

Imagine that you are living among the early Greeks. Use the following words to write a paragraph describing the life of the Minoans and the Mycenaeans.

bull leaping	labyrinth	parchment
shrines	megaron	tenants
civil wars		

Understanding Main Ideas

1. What civilizations combined to form Greek civilization?
2. In what ways were the Minoan people able to gain control of the Mediterranean Sea?
3. What do experts believe about the sport of bull leaping?
4. Why didn't Minoan cities have walls around them?
5. What were some of the features of the palace at Knossos?
6. What did the Mycenaeans build instead of cities?
7. How was the Trojan War described in the *Iliad?*
8. Why did the people of Greece have to create a new civilization?

Critical Thinking

1. How well did the Minoans use their natural resources? Explain your answer.
2. What effect did being an island civilization have on the Minoans?
3. What role did religion play in Minoan daily life?
4. In what ways would the Mycenaean civilization have been different if the people had not learned to build and sail ships?

Graphic Organizer Activity

Culture Create a before-and-after chart like the one shown, and use it to show what the Mycenaean civilization was like before and after contact with the Minoans.

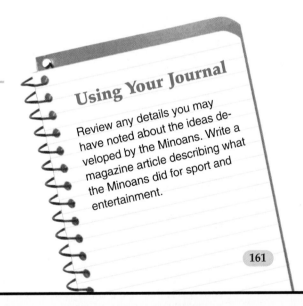

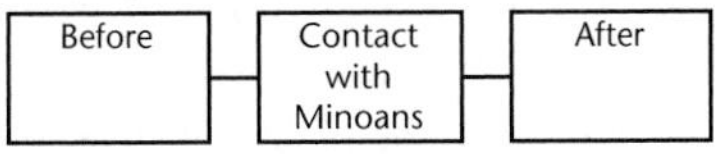

Geography in History

Places and Regions Refer to the map on page 156 as you think about the "Dark Age" of the Aegean region. What human actions and geographic factors made it possible for this period of history to last for 300 years?

Create a poster warning people about the events and geographic factors that led to the "Dark Age."

Using Your Journal

Review any details you may have noted about the ideas developed by the Minoans. Write a magazine article describing what the Minoans did for sport and entertainment.

CHAPTER 9 Assessment Answers

Using Key Terms

Paragraphs will vary but should include comparisons.

Understanding Main Ideas

1. Minoan and Mycenaean
2. They built faster ships with a large wooden beam in the prow to smash and sink enemy ships.
3. that it was a religious ceremony as well as a sport
4. the people depended on the sea and navy for protection
5. It was five stories high, built of stone, framed with wood, and decorated with frescoes. It had bathrooms, several entrances, and labyrinths.
6. fortress-palaces
7. Paris took Helen to Troy. The Mycenaeans attacked Troy; they later built a huge wooden horse with soldiers hidden inside which was pulled into Troy. The Mycenaeans burned the city.
8. because their civilization was destroyed during the Dark Age

Critical Thinking

1. Answers will vary, but the Minoans used resources wisely.
2. It provided natural protection and also made travel and trade easier.
3. Answers will vary, but religion gave kings power.
4. Answers will vary but could include lack of development.

Graphic Organizer Activity

Answers should reflect information on pages 157–158. The most important change shown will be knowledge of shipbuilding and navigation, which allowed the Mycenaeans to expand their influence in the Aegean world.

Bonus Test Question

For Chapter 9 Test

Imagine you are an archaeologist who has dug up artifacts you believe are Mycenaean. Describe two artifacts you have found and what each was used for. *(Answers will vary but should be supported by explanation.)*

Using Your Journal

Magazine articles will vary but should include the fact that Minoans changed the way ships were made so that they could go faster. The Minoans loved sports and built what was probably the world's first arena.

Geography in History

Answers will vary but should include references to the isolation caused by the sea, mountains, migrations, and civil wars.

Chapter 10 Planning Guide

Timesaving Tools

TeacherWorks™ All-In-One Planner and Resource Center

- **Interactive Teacher Edition** Access your Teacher Wraparound Edition and your classroom resources with a few easy clicks.
- **Interactive Lesson Planner** Planning has never been easier! Organize your week, month, semester, or year with all the lesson helps you need to make teaching creative, timely, and relevant.

Use Glencoe's **Presentation Plus!** multimedia teacher tool to easily present dynamic lessons that visually excite your students. Using Microsoft PowerPoint® you can customize the presentations to create your own personalized lessons.

Objectives	Reproducible Resources	Multimedia Resources
Section 1 **The Polis** Explain why the polis was the geographic and political center of Greek life.	Reproducible Lesson Plan Chapter 10 Vocabulary and Guided Reading Activity Reading Essentials and Study Guide 10-1 Section 1 Quiz Unit 4 Hands-On History Lab	Interactive Student Edition CD-ROM Graphic Organizer Transparency 12 Vocabulary PuzzleMaker CD-ROM Interactive Tutor Self-Assessment CD-ROM ExamView® Pro Testmaker CD-ROM Glencoe Skillbuilder Interactive Workbook CD-ROM, Level 1 Presentation Plus! CD-ROM
Section 2 **Sparta** Describe life in Sparta, noting how Sparta was different from other Greek city-states, especially in regard to the role of women.	Reproducible Lesson Plan Reading Essentials and Study Guide 10-2 Section 2 Quiz	Vocabulary PuzzleMaker CD-ROM Interactive Tutor Self-Assessment CD-ROM ExamView® Pro Testmaker CD-ROM Glencoe Skillbuilder Interactive Workbook CD-ROM, Level 1
Section 3 **Athens** Discuss life in Athens, summarizing how the Persian War affected Greece, and describe how Athens controlled other city-states.	Reproducible Lesson Plan Reading Essentials and Study Guide 10-3 Chapter 10 Chart and Graph Skill Activity Chapter 10 Geography and Map Activity Unit 4 World Literature Reading 2 Chapter 10 Cooperative Learning Activity Section 3 Quiz	Teaching Transparencies and Activities 10A & 10B Vocabulary PuzzleMaker CD-ROM Interactive Tutor Self-Assessment CD-ROM ExamView® Pro Testmaker CD-ROM Glencoe Skillbuilder Interactive Workbook CD-ROM, Level 1
Section 4 **Decline of the City-States** Explain why Athens and the other Greek city-states declined.	Reproducible Lesson Plan Reading Essentials and Study Guide 10-4 Chapter 10 Enrichment Activity Section 4 Quiz	Vocabulary PuzzleMaker CD-ROM Interactive Tutor Self-Assessment CD-ROM ExamView® Pro Testmaker CD-ROM Glencoe Skillbuilder Interactive Workbook CD-ROM, Level 1
Chapter 10 **Review and Evaluation**	Chapter 10 Reteaching Activity Chapter 10 Performance Assessment Activity Spanish Chapter Summary and Glossary Chapter 10 Test	Vocabulary PuzzleMaker CD-ROM Interactive Tutor Self-Assessment CD-ROM Glencoe Skillbuilder Interactive Workbook CD-ROM, Level 1 Audiocassettes* ExamView® Pro Testmaker CD-ROM

*Also available in Spanish.

Chapter 10 Planning Guide

Performance Assessment Activities

Model Have students work in small groups to create a model of a Greek city-state. Tell students to use the information from their textbook or from other reference books. The models should include: farming villages, fields, orchards, acropolis and its temple, and an agora. Display models in the classroom.

CHAPTER RESOURCES

LITERATURE ABOUT THE PERIOD

Renault, Mary. *The Last of the Wine.* Random House, 1975. A novel about Athens during the Peloponnesian War.

READINGS FOR THE STUDENT

Burrell, Roy. *The Greeks: Rebuilding the Past Series.* Oxford University Press, 1990.

Hamilton, Edith. *The Greek Way.* Norton, 1983. Story of the Greek spirit and mind told by great writers.

READINGS FOR THE TEACHER

Editors of Time-Life Books. *What Life Was Like at the Dawn of Democracy.* Time-Life Books, 1997. A look at classical Athens during the years 525 B.C.–322 B.C.

Editors of Time-Life Books. *Greece—Temples, Tombs, and Treasures.* Time-Life Books, 1994. A colorful look at the history and art of Ancient Greece.

KEY TO ABILITY LEVELS

Teaching strategies have been coded for varying learning styles and abilities.

L1 Level 1 activities are **basic** activities and should be within the ability range of all students.

L2 Level 2 activities are **average** activities and should be within the ability range of the average to above-average student.

L3 Level 3 activities are **challenging** activities designed for the ability range of above-average students.

ELL ELL activities should be within the ability range of English Language Learning students.

NATIONAL GEOGRAPHIC Teacher's Corner

INDEX TO NATIONAL GEOGRAPHIC MAGAZINE

The following articles relate to this chapter:

- "Ascent to Glory: Ancient Greece, Part II," by Caroline Alexander, February 2000.
- "Iran: Testing the Waters of Reform," by Fen Montaigne, July 1999.

NATIONAL GEOGRAPHIC SOCIETY PRODUCTS AVAILABLE FROM GLENCOE

To order the following, call Glencoe at 1-800-334-7344:

- *PictureShow: Ancient Civilizations: Greece and Rome (CD-ROM)*
- *PicturePack: Ancient Greece (Transparencies)*
- *PicturePack: Ancient Civilizations Library, Part I (Transparencies)*

ADDITIONAL NATIONAL GEOGRAPHIC SOCIETY PRODUCTS

To order the following, call National Geographic at 1-800-368-2728:

- *Wonders of the Ancient World: National Geographic Atlas of Archaeology (Book)*

Access *National Geographic's* new dynamic MapMachine Web site and other geography resources at:
www.nationalgeographic.com
www.nationalgeographic.com/maps

THE HISTORY CHANNEL. A&E HOME VIDEO. Biography

The following videotape program is available from Glencoe to enrich Chapter 10:

- **Mystical Monuments of Ancient Greece**
  0-7670-0012-9

To order, call Glencoe at 1-800-334-7344. To find classroom resources to accompany this video, check the following home pages:

A&E Television: www.aande.com
The History Channel: www.historychannel.com

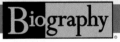

Introducing **CHAPTER 10**

OVERVIEW

Chapter 10 discusses Greek city-states, particularly Sparta and Athens.

- **Section 1** discusses the development of the Greek polis.
- **Section 2** summarizes the way of life in Sparta.
- **Section 3** describes the growth of democracy in Athens and its dominance in the Delian League.
- **Section 4** analyzes the decline of the Greek city-states.

CHAPTER OBJECTIVES

After reading Chapter 10, students will be able to:

1. explain why the polis was the geographic and political center of Greek life.
2. describe what life was like in Sparta and Athens.
3. summarize how the Persian Wars affected Greece.
4. discuss how Athens controlled the other city-states.
5. explain why Athens and the other city-states declined.

EXAMINING ARTIFACTS

Tell students that Sparta and Athens were the two leading city-states in ancient Greece. Explain that the woman on the coin is the goddess Athena. Ask: What do these artifacts tell you about each city-state? *(Sample responses: Spartans had a strong army; the Athenians worshiped Athena and used coins for trade.)* Record answers for review at the end of the chapter.

PERFORMANCE ASSESSMENT ✓

Use the Performance Assessment activities on page 162B to help you evaluate students as they complete the chapter.

CHAPTER 10

The City-States

700 B.C.–335 B.C.

▲ Athenian silver coin

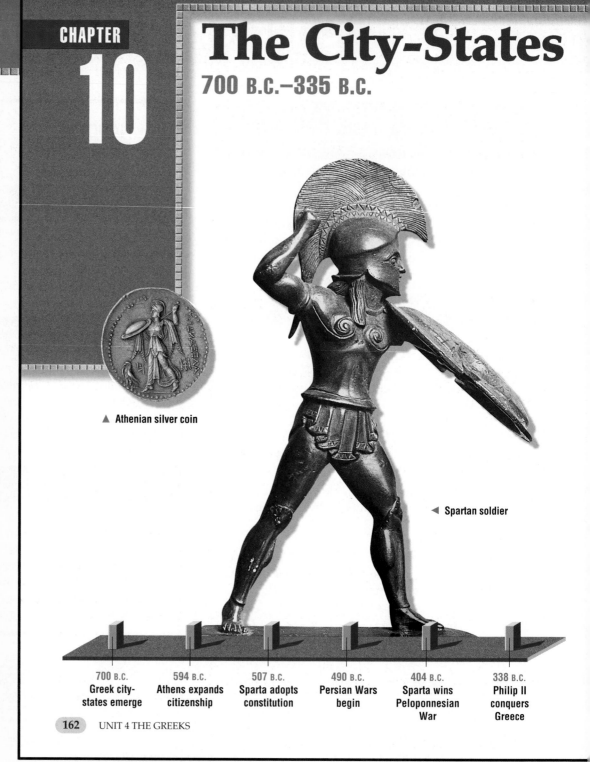

◄ Spartan soldier

- 700 B.C. Greek city-states emerge
- 594 B.C. Athens expands citizenship
- 507 B.C. Sparta adopts constitution
- 490 B.C. Persian Wars begin
- 404 B.C. Sparta wins Peloponnesian War
- 338 B.C. Philip II conquers Greece

TEACHING RESOURCES

TEACHER PLANNING AND SUPPORT

- Reproducible Lesson Plan 10-1, 10-2, 10-3, 10-4
- Teaching Strategies for the World History Classroom (Including Block Scheduling Pacing Guides)
- Presentation Plus! CD-ROM

REVIEW AND REINFORCEMENT

- Reading Essentials and Study Guide 10-1, 10-2, 10-3, 10-4
- Chapter 10 Vocabulary and Guided Reading Activity
- Vocabulary PuzzleMaker CD-ROM
- Teaching Transparencies 10A & 10B
- Chapter 10 Reteaching Activity
- Chapter 10 Cooperative Learning Activity
- Chapter 10 Activity Book Activity
- Chapter 10 Chart and Graph Skill Activity
- Reading and Study Skills Foldables
- Interactive Tutor Self-Assessment CD-ROM

APPLICATION AND HANDS-ON ACTIVITIES

- Daily Questions in Social Studies
- Unit 4 Hands-On History Lab Activity
- Student Presentation Builder CD-ROM

The Council of Five Hundred handled the daily business of Athens. Members were chosen each year by lot. The names of 500 citizens were drawn from a large pot. No one could serve on the Council for more than two terms. Thus, every citizen had a chance to be a Council member.

There were two reasons why the Athenians preferred choosing council members by lot rather than by voting. First, they believed that in an election, people who had money or who could speak well would have an unfair advantage. Second, the Athenians believed that every citizen was smart enough to hold public office. The only exception was in times of war. Then, a skillful general was needed on the Council.

Greek Helmet

Under Cleisthenes, citizens were required to educate their sons. Since there were no public schools, boys either had a tutor or attended a private school. Starting when they were seven years old, boys studied writing, mathematics, and music. They also practiced sports and memorized the works of Homer and other noted Greek poets.

When they turned 18 years old, Athenian males became citizens. They went to the temple of the god Zeus (zūs) and took an oath of citizenship in front of their family and friends. In the oath, they promised to help make Athens a better place in which to live. They also promised to be honorable in battle, follow the constitution, and respect their religion.

The Persian Wars About the time Athens was going through government changes, the Persians ruled the largest and most powerful empire in the western world. In 545 B.C., the Persians conquered Ionia—the Greek city-states in Asia Minor and on the Aegean islands. About 20 years later, the Ionians revolted. They asked the city-states on the Greek mainland for help. Athens and another polis responded by sending a few warships. After five years of fighting, however, the Persians put down the revolt. Although the Ionians were defeated, Darius, the Persian king, was not satisfied. He wanted to punish the mainland Greeks for helping the Ionians.

In 490 B.C., Darius sent a fleet of 600 ships and a well-equipped army to Greece. The Persians landed on the plain of Marathon about 26 miles, or 41 kilometers, northeast of Athens. After several days, the Persians decided to sail directly to Athens and attack it by sea. They began loading their ships. As soon as most of the Persian soldiers were aboard, Greek soldiers ran down in close order from the hills around Marathon. The remaining Persian troops were not prepared to meet this kind of attack and were defeated. A runner set off for Athens with news of the victory. Upon reaching Athens, he cried out *Nike!*, the Greek goddess of victory, and then died of exhaustion. Winning the Battle of Marathon gave the Greeks a great sense of confidence.

Then & Now

The Marathon The runner Pheidippides (fi dip′ uh dez) carried the news of the victory at Marathon back to Athens, about 26 miles away. He delivered his message and fell dead of exhaustion. Today, a *marathon* is a footrace of 26 miles, 385 yards. The term may describe any long-distance race.

L1 **Chronology** As a class, develop a time line depicting the historical events of Greece dating from 545 B.C., the defeat of the Ionians, to 404 B.C., the defeat of the Athenians. Lead the class in a discussion of the causes of the events listed on the time line and what effect each event had on the Greek city-states. ELL

LINKING PAST TO PRESENT

The present-day marathon is a race named after the Athenian victory over the Persians. The Greek runner who died bringing the victory news from Marathon to Athens was a well-known professional athlete named Pheidippides. His run from Marathon to the agora in Athens—about 26 miles, or 42 km—was the inspiration for the modern marathon race. This race was part of the first modern Olympic Games in 1896.

PRIMARY SOURCES Library

You might assign "Greek Society," from pages 680–681 of the Primary Sources Library.

MULTICULTURAL PERSPECTIVES

Have interested students research information about Greek city-states other than Athens and Sparta and report their findings to the class. The city-states of Argos, Corinth, Sicyon, Olympia, Delphi, Thessaly, Thebes, Miletus, and Ephesus are possible choices. Have students discuss the similarities and differences among the city-states.

Reading Check Answer The **triremes** were warships with three levels of rowers on each side.

DID YOU KNOW ??

A Greek trireme was about 125 feet (or 38 m) long and 20 feet (or 6 m) wide with a square sail on its mast. In battle, all three levels of 174 oarsmen rowed while a flutist piped the stroke.

CAPTION ANSWER

Xerxes returned to Asia; the remaining Persian troops were defeated by the Greeks in the Battle of Plataea; then the Persian navy was destroyed, ending the Persian War.

L2 Writing Have students imagine they witnessed the Battle of Salamis. Have them write a letter to the editor of an Athenian newspaper describing the battle.

Reading Check What did Athenian **triremes** look like?

Shortly after the Battle of Marathon, rich silver mines were found near Athens. The Athenians spent their new wealth on **triremes** (trī′ rēmz), or warships that had three levels of rowers on each side, one above the other. Soon, Athens had the largest navy in Greece. The Athenians planned to be prepared if the Persians returned.

The Persians did return. In 480 B.C., Darius's son Xerxes (zerk′ sēz) sent 250,000 soldiers across the Aegean and conquered northern Greece. In order to stop the Persians from taking all of Greece, 20 Greek city-states banded together. The Spartans led the army, while the Athenians led the navy.

First, 7,000 Greek soldiers headed for the narrow pass of Thermopylae (ther mop′ uh lē), about 100 miles, or 160 kilometers, from Athens. There, they held off the Persian army for three days. This gave the people of Athens time to flee to the island of Salamis (sal′ uh muhs). Meanwhile, all but 300 Spartans and 700 other Greeks withdrew from Thermopylae. The Persians, helped by a traitor, found a way around the pass. They killed every soldier guarding the pass and then marched on Athens. Finding the city almost deserted, they set it on fire.

BATTLE OF SALAMIS The Greek fleet, led by the Athenians, defeated the Persian navy in the Bay of Salamis. The faster Greek triremes were able to sail close to the Persian ships and attack with spears and arrows. **What happened to the Persians after the Battle of Salamis?**

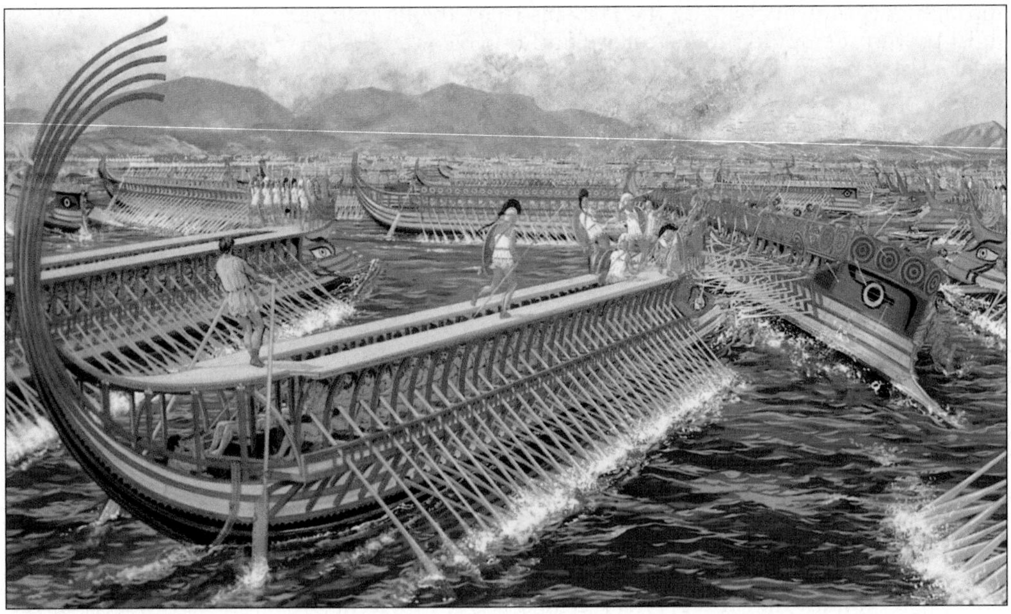

SPOTLIGHT ON: LEONIDAS

King Leonidas of Sparta stayed with the 300 Spartans at the narrow pass of Thermopylae to stand against the Persian army. He wanted to remain obedient to the law of Sparta—never surrender on the battlefield but fight until victory or death.

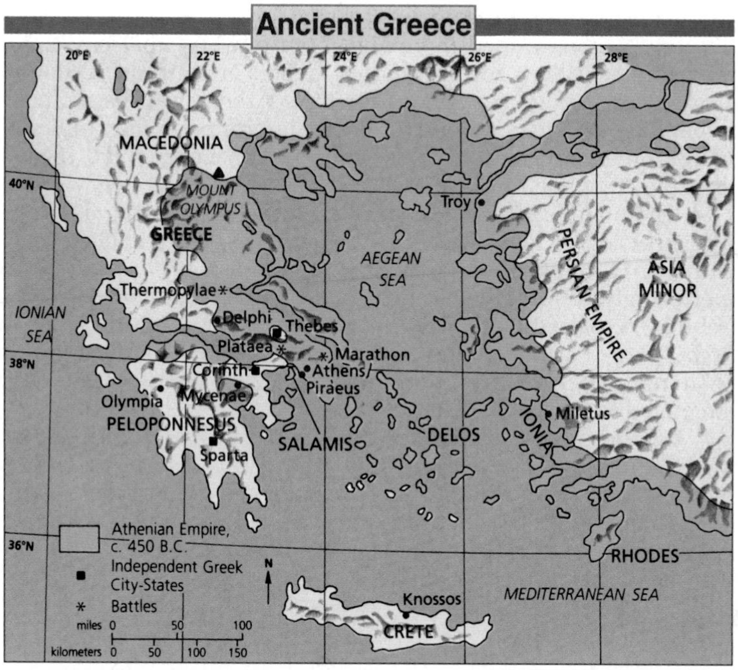

MAP STUDY

THE WORLD IN SPATIAL TERMS
The Persians wanted to extend their empire into Europe. **How did the location of Greece make it a likely place for a Persian attack?**

Then, the Greeks tricked the Persian fleet into sailing into the strait between Athens and Salamis. Since the strait was too narrow for all the Persian ships to enter at once, the Greeks could take them on a few at a time. Also, once the Persian ships were in the strait, their large size made them difficult to handle. With their lighter, faster ships, the Greeks defeated the Persian fleet.

Following the defeat, Xerxes returned to Asia. However, he left some troops behind. In 479 B.C., they were defeated by the Greeks in the Battle of Plataea (pluh tē′ uh). A few days later, Greek ships destroyed what was left of the Persian navy. The Persian Wars were over.

The Delian League and the Athenian Empire

The Persians had been driven from Greece, but they still ruled Ionia. Because of this, the Athenians suggested that the Greek city-states form a **defensive league,** or protective group. Since the league had its headquarters on the island of Delos, it was called the Delian (dē′ lē uhn) League. Sparta was one of the few Greek city-states that did not join the League.

Once a city-state became a League member, it could not withdraw unless all the other members agreed. The League had a common navy. Its ships were usually built and crewed by Athenians, but the other city-states paid the costs.

Reading Check
What is a **defensive league**?

MAP STUDY
Answer

because Persia would have needed to conquer Greece in order to reach the European mainland

GEOGRAPHY AND HISTORY

Direct the students to use the map on this page. Have them locate the battle sites of the Persian War. Ask students what the location of the battle sites suggests about the probable outcome of the Persian War. *(The battles were fought on territory of Greek city-states instead of territory on the Persian Empire; therefore, the Greek soldiers knew the geography of the area better than the Persian soldiers, which gave them a great advantage toward winning.)*

Reading Check Answer
A **defensive league** is a group organized for the purpose of protection.

MULTICULTURAL PERSPECTIVES

Pericles expressed his ideas about the importance of democracy in a funeral speech when he said democracy must be controlled by many and not a few people. He also said:

When it is a question of putting one person before another in positions of public responsibility, what counts is not membership of a particular class, but the actual ability which the man possesses.

LINKING PAST TO PRESENT

Male citizens were expected to participate in government and to defend the polis in time of war. As Pericles said, "We do not say that a man who takes no interest in politics minds his own business. We say he has no business here at all."

Many countries today expect the same participation from their citizens, both male and female.

MAKING CONNECTIONS

>> **Geography: Places and Regions** At the beginning of the Peloponnesian War, Pericles planned Athenian strategy. To avoid a direct battle with the well-trained Spartan troops, he moved the rural population of Athens behind the city walls. He ordered the Athenian navy to attack the Spartan coast and to keep the sea lanes open for supplies.

Linking Across Time

because olives were an important food and trade item for the Athenians

People in History

Pericles
c. 495 B.C.–429 B.C.

Athenian General

As leader of Athens, Pericles turned the city-state into a center of learning. His influence was so great that historians call the period of his power the "Age of Pericles."

The League worked well for a while. As time passed, though, Athens gained more and more power. Other city-states had to ask Athens for permission to sail or to trade. Criminal cases were brought to Athens for trial. Athenian coins replaced other Greek money. Athenian soldiers interfered in the politics of other Greek city-states. In short, the Delian League had turned into the Athenian Empire.

The main leader of Athens at the time was a general named Pericles (per′ uh klēz). Pericles was known as the "first citizen" of Athens. He had a dream of Athens as the most beautiful and perfect city of the time. To help make this dream come true, he rebuilt the palaces and temples on the Acropolis. It took 11 years to build the Parthenon (par′ thuh non), the temple of the goddess Athena. Much of this building was done with money that belonged to the Delian League.

Pericles also built the Long Walls. These were two parallel, fortified walls with tile roofs. The Long Walls connected Athens with its seaport of Piraeus (pī rē′ uhs) some five miles, or eight kilometers, away. Having the Long Walls meant Athens could get supplies even in times of war.

Linking Across Time

The Olive Tree According to Greek legend, the goddess Athena created the olive tree as her gift to human beings. Greek farmers have harvested olives for food and oil (below) for thousands of years. The olive tree continues to play an important part in the Greek economy today (right). **Why do you think Sparta burned the olive groves around Athens when it declared war on the city-state in 434 B.C.?**

174

COOPERATIVE LEARNING

Organize the class into two groups. Assign one group the Persian Wars and the other group the Peloponnesian War. Each group should prepare an oral and visual presentation about their assigned war. Divide each group into subgroups to research facets of the topic, such as the impact of geography on the battles and the leaders involved. Visuals might include drawings of soldiers, weapons, battle formations, fortifications, and ships. Each group should prepare a large time line of the events.

Pericles led Athens for almost 30 years. During this period, art, philosophy, and literature reached new heights. Many people who came to Athens from other city-states settled there.

Decline of Athens The more powerful Athens became, the more resentful other Greek city-states grew. Anti-Athenian feelings soon spread throughout Greece. When the Athenians attacked one of Sparta's allies, a group of city-states led by Sparta declared war on Athens. The war, which was called the Peloponnesian (pel uh puh nē′ zhuhn) War, lasted almost 30 years. It ended in 404 B.C. when Athens surrendered to Sparta.

Between the war and a plague that struck during the war, Athens also lost more than one quarter of its people. Much of its land was ruined. Thousands of young Athenian men left home and became **mercenaries** (mer′ suh nār ēz), or hired soldiers, in the Persian army.

When the Spartans took control of Athens in 404 B.C., they set up an oligarchy and chose 30 Athenian aristocrats to rule there. Not long after that, the Athenians successfully revolted and once more set up a democracy. However, Athens was never again as powerful as it had been before the Peloponnesian War.

Sculpture of Pericles

Reading Check What type of jobs did Greek **mercenaries** seek in Persia?

Section 3 Assessment

1. **Define:** oligarchy, constitution, democratic, triremes, mercenaries.
2. What political reforms did Cleisthenes introduce?
3. What changes did Pericles bring to Athens?

Critical Thinking

4. **Understanding Cause and Effect** What were some of the causes and effects of the Peloponnesian War?

Graphic Organizer Activity

5. Draw a diagram like this, and use it to show how the Delian League affected both Athens and other city-states.

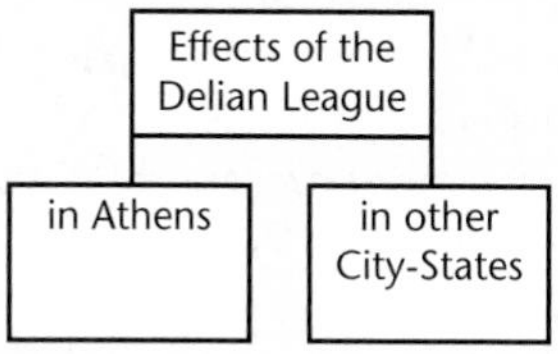

SECTION 4 Decline of the City-States

After the Peloponnesian War, most Greeks began to lose their sense of community. The war had lasted a long time and had cost a great deal of money. People became more interested in making money and having a good time. Soon, bitterness developed between the upper and lower classes within each polis.

INDEPENDENT PRACTICE

L2 Critical Thinking Ask students to brainstorm measures that could have been taken to help prevent the decline of Athens and other Greek city-states. Ask students to share their ideas.

Reading Check Answer Greek **mercenaries** sought jobs as hired soldiers in the Persian army.

DID YOU KNOW ??

It is generally believed that the plague was either typhus or a highly malignant form of scarlet fever, which appeared in the Mediterranean area for the first time. Among those who died in the plague were Pericles and his family.

Use **Interactive Tutor Self-Assessment CD-ROM** to review Section 3.

Use the **Vocabulary PuzzleMaker CD-ROM** to create crossword and word search puzzles.

ASSESS

Check for Understanding

Ask students to summarize orally or in writing the main points of the chapter. Discuss the answers to the Section and Chapter Assessment questions.

Section 3 Assessment Answers

1. oligarchy, rule by a few (p. 169); constitution, principles for governing (p. 169); democratic, favors equality of all people (p. 169); triremes, warships (p. 172); mercenaries, hired soldiers (p. 175)
2. set up the first democratic constitution, opened the Assembly to males over 20 and the council to all citizens.
3. rebuilt the palaces and temples on the Acropolis, including the Parthenon; built the Long Walls; encouraged philosophy and learning
4. sample responses: *causes*—Greek aid to Ionians, Persian expansion; *effects*—buildup of Athenian navy, formation of Delian League
5. sample responses: *Athens*—dominated Greece, gained wealth to beautify the acropolis; *other city-states*—lost power; forced to use Athenian money, courts, and ships; grew resentful

Assign the Chapter 10 **Section 3 Quiz** in the TCR. Testmaker available.

Evaluate

Assign Chapter 10 **Performance Assessment Activity** in the TCR.

Administer **Chapter 10 Test** in the TCR. Testmaker available.

Reteach

Help students chart the main ideas and events described in the chapter.

Assign Chapter 10 **Reteaching Activity** in the TCR.

Enrich

Have students present to the class illustrations of Greek vase painting, and describe the details shown on the paintings.

Assign Chapter 10 **Enrichment Activity** in the TCR.

CLOSE

Ask students to compare the advantages and disadvantages of living in a Greek-city state with those they listed for modern city life in the Bellringer activity.

Use **Interactive Tutor Self-Assessment CD-ROM** to review Section 4.

HISTORY Online

Self-Check Quiz gives students an interactive chapter tutorial. Have them access ***Chapter 10 Quiz*** at humanheritage.glencoe.com

After the war, Sparta ruled Greece. The Spartans were harsh rulers who angered the other Greeks. As a result, in 371 B.C., a group of city-states led by Thebes (thēbz) overthrew Spartan rule. The rule of Thebes, however, was no better than that of Sparta. It weakened the city-states even more. The Greeks were no longer strong enough or united enough to fight off invaders. In 338 B.C., Philip II of Macedonia (mas uh dō′ nē uh) conquered Greece.

Section 4 Assessment

1. How did the Peloponnesian War help destroy the sense of community in most Greek city-states?
2. What were some of the reasons for the decline of the Greek city-states?

Critical Thinking

3. **Drawing Conclusions** Why might the Greeks have become more interested in making money for themselves rather than for the city-state after the Peloponnesian War?

Graphic Organizer Activity

4. Draw a flow chart like this one, and use it to trace the decline of the Greek city-states after the Peloponnesian War.

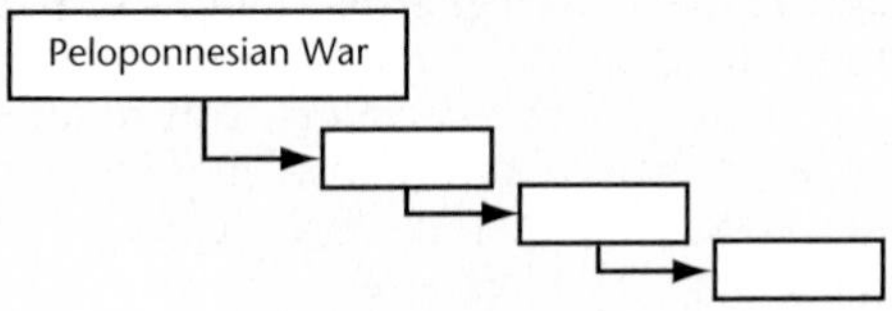

Chapter Summary & Study Guide

1. Around 700 B.C., city-states became the center of Greek life.
2. The two greatest city-states were Sparta and Athens.
3. Sparta spent most of its time training its citizens for war.
4. Spartan women had more freedom than women in other city-states.
5. Spartans believed new ideas would weaken their way of life, so they tried to prevent change.
6. Between 750 and 507 B.C., Athens went through a series of reforms to broaden democracy.
7. In 507 B.C., Cleisthenes put into effect the first democratic constitution.
8. After several wars with Persia, Athens became Greece's leading polis.
9. Sparta defeated Athens in the Peloponnesian War, which was fought between 431 and 404 B.C.
10. The Peloponnesian War weakened the Greek city-states, leading to the conquest of Greece by Philip II of Macedonia in 338 B.C.

HISTORY Online

Self-Check Quiz

Visit the *Human Heritage* Web site at humanheritage.glencoe.com and click on ***Chapter 10—Self-Check Quiz*** to assess your understanding of this chapter.

Section 4 Assessment Answers

1. The war lasted a long time and was costly; people were discouraged and they began to lose interest in what was good for their city-state.
2. Bitterness developed between the upper and lower classes within each polis, the rule of Thebes weakened the city-states, and the Greeks could no longer fight off invaders.
3. Answers will vary but might include the idea that they were tired of being involved in war and decided to pay attention to themselves.
4. sample responses: lost sense of community, increased interest in money-making, increased bitterness between upper and lower classes in each polis, harsh rule by Sparta, rebellion and rule by Thebes, lack of strength to resist invaders

Assign Chapter 10 **Section 4 Quiz** in the TCR. Testmaker available.

CHAPTER 10 Assessment

Using Key Terms

Imagine you are living in Greece during the time of the Persian Wars. Use the following words to write a letter to a friend describing the organization and government of Sparta and Athens at that time.

polis	acropolis	agora
aristocrats	perioeci	oligarchy
helots	democratic	constitution
triremes	mercenaries	defensive league

Understanding Main Ideas

1. Why did Greek communities have little contact with one another?
2. What did the citizens of a polis consider most important?
3. Why was it important for Spartan women to be physically fit?
4. Why did Sparta remain a poor farming society?
5. Why was the Battle of Marathon important for the Greeks?
6. How did Athenians use the Delian League to build an empire?

Critical Thinking

1. Do you think that the Spartan emphasis on military training benefited Sparta? Why or why not?
2. What method of choosing members of the Athenian Council of Five Hundred would you have suggested? Explain your answer.
3. Why do you think some people in Athens might have objected to the title of "first citizen" for Pericles? Explain your answer.
4. What may happen to a community as a result of a long war? Why?

Graphic Organizer Activity

Culture Draw a Venn diagram like this one, and use it to compare Sparta and Athens at their height of power.

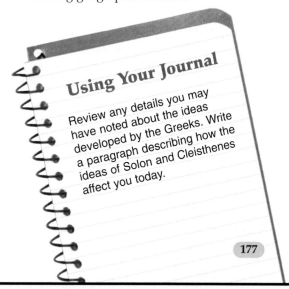

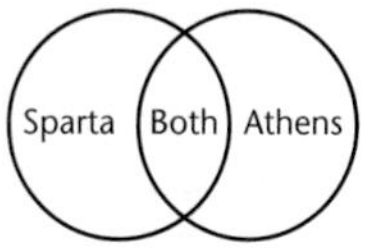

Geography in History

Places and Regions Note the location of the Greek city-states on the map on page 173. Why do you think these city-states developed in the places that they did, and what geographic features might have affected this development? Write a paragraph explaining the relationship between a city's location and the surrounding geographic features.

Using Your Journal

Review any details you may have noted about the ideas developed by the Greeks. Write a paragraph describing how the ideas of Solon and Cleisthenes affect you today.

CHAPTER 10 Assessment Answers

Using Key Terms

Letters will vary but should include several comparisons.

Understanding Main Ideas

1. because they were separated by mountains and by the sea
2. the good of the polis
3. so they would bear healthy male warriors
4. because it spent its time and energy only on the art of war
5. because it gave the Greeks a great sense of confidence
6. Athens gained more power, controlled sailing and trade, and interfered in the politics of other city-states.

Critical Thinking

1. Answers will vary.
2. Answers will vary but could include the blind drawing being more fair but less qualitative than an election.
3. Answers will vary but could include reference to his good and bad qualities.
4. Answers will vary but should include that people may become discouraged, fight among themselves, and lose their sense of community.

Graphic Organizer Activity

Venn diagrams should reflect unique features of each city-state. Shared characteristics might include such items as: spoke the Greek language, created its own government and laws, valued a strong military, worshiped same gods and goddesses, and so on.

Bonus Test Question

For Chapter 10 Test

What would Cleisthenes say about a city-state ruled by one woman who served for life, a council elected by voting, no organized army, and public schools for all citizens?

Using Your Journal

Paragraphs should include the idea that democratic constitutions are part of the U.S. and many local governments. The House of Representatives, like the Assembly, has the power to make laws.

Geography in History

Answers may vary but could include references to good farming land, optimum location for trade and/or sea access, the safety of highlands or islands, and heritage.

Chapter 11 Planning Guide

Timesaving Tools

TeacherWorks™ All-In-One Planner and Resource Center

- **Interactive Teacher Edition** Access your Teacher Wraparound Edition and your classroom resources with a few easy clicks.
- **Interactive Lesson Planner** Planning has never been easier! Organize your week, month, semester, or year with all the lesson helps you need to make teaching creative, timely, and relevant.

Presentation Plus!

Use Glencoe's **Presentation Plus!** multimedia teacher tool to easily present dynamic lessons that visually excite your students. Using Microsoft PowerPoint® you can customize the presentations to create your own personalized lessons.

Objectives	Reproducible Resources	Multimedia Resources
Section 1 **Religious Practices** Describe how the Greeks honored their gods and goddesses, and summarize what contributions were made in athletics and the arts during the Golden Age of Greek culture.	Reproducible Lesson Plan Chapter 11 Vocabulary and Guided Reading Activity Reading Essentials and Study Guide 11-1 Chapter 11 Cooperative Learning Activity Unit 4 World Literature Reading 1 Section 1 Quiz	Interactive Student Edition CD-ROM Graphic Organizer Transparency 9 Teaching Transparency and Activity 11A Vocabulary PuzzleMaker CD-ROM Interactive Tutor Self-Assessment CD-ROM ExamView® Pro Testmaker CD-ROM Glencoe Skillbuilder Interactive Workbook CD-ROM, Level 1 Presentation Plus! CD-ROM
Section 2 **Science** Discuss how Socrates, Plato, Aristotle, and other Greek thinkers influenced the development of western civilization.	Reproducible Lesson Plan Reading Essentials and Study Guide 11-2 Chapter 11 Chart and Graph Skill Activity Chapter 11 Geography and Map Activity Chapter 11 Enrichment Activity Section 2 Quiz	Teaching Transparency and Activity 11B Vocabulary PuzzleMaker CD-ROM Interactive Tutor Self-Assessment CD-ROM ExamView® Pro Testmaker CD-ROM Glencoe Skillbuilder Interactive Workbook CD-ROM, Level 1
Chapter 11 **Review and Evaluation**	Chapter 11 Reteaching Activity Chapter 11 Performance Assessment Activity Spanish Chapter Summary and Glossary Chapter 11 Test	Vocabulary PuzzleMaker CD-ROM Interactive Tutor Self-Assessment CD-ROM Glencoe Skillbuilder Interactive Workbook CD-ROM, Level 1 Audiocassettes* ExamView® Pro Testmaker CD-ROM

*Also available in Spanish.

✓ Performance Assessment Activities

Time Capsules Have students contribute to a "Golden Age of Greece" time capsule. Ask each student to research and write about one of the following aspects of Greek culture: architecture, art, history, literature, science, mathematics, philosophy, or law. Encourage students to create a visual representation of their subject to post with their writing.

CHAPTER RESOURCES

LITERATURE ABOUT THE PERIOD

Hamilton, Edith, trans. *Three Greek Plays*. Norton, 1958. Included are the *Trojan Woman* of Euripedes, *Prometheus Bound*, and *Agamemnon* of Aeschylus.

Jowett, Benjamin, trans. *The Dialogues of Plato*. Random House, 1920. The definitive translation, including *The Republic*.

READINGS FOR THE STUDENT

Boyer, Sophia A., and Winifred Lubell. *Gifts from the Greeks, Alpha to Omega*. Rand McNally, 1970. Descriptions of areas of Greek life illustrated with drawings of Greek art.

READINGS FOR THE TEACHER

Grant, Michael. *The Classical Greeks*. Scribner, 1989. Connects culture with historical events. Spans art, architecture, philosophy, and drama.

KEY TO ABILITY LEVELS

Teaching strategies have been coded for varying learning styles and abilities.

L1 Level 1 activities are **basic** activities and should be within the ability range of all students.

L2 Level 2 activities are **average** activities and should be within the ability range of the average to above-average student.

L3 Level 3 activities are **challenging** activities designed for the ability range of above-average students.

ELL ELL activities should be within the ability range of English Language Learning students.

NATIONAL GEOGRAPHIC Teacher's Corner

INDEX TO NATIONAL GEOGRAPHIC MAGAZINE

The following article relates to this chapter:

- "Golden Age Treasures," by George F. Bass, March 2002.

NATIONAL GEOGRAPHIC SOCIETY PRODUCTS AVAILABLE FROM GLENCOE

To order the following, call Glencoe at 1-800-334-7344:

- *PicturePack: Physical Geography of the World (Transparencies)*
- *PicturePack: Ancient Greece (Transparencies)*
- *PictureShow: Ancient Civilizations: Greece and Rome (CD-ROMs)*
- *Ancient Civilizations: Ancient Greece (Poster Set)*
- *PicturePack: Ancient Civilizations Library, Part I (Transparencies)*

Access *National Geographic*'s new dynamic MapMachine Web site and other geography resources at:
www.nationalgeographic.com
www.nationalgeographic.com/maps

THE HISTORY CHANNEL. A&E HOME VIDEO. Biography

The following videotape program is available from Glencoe:

- **Powerful Gods of Mount Olympus**
  1-56501-927-X

To order, call Glencoe at 1-800-334-7344. To find classroom resources to accompany this video, check the following home pages:

A&E Television: www.aande.com
The History Channel: www.historychannel.com

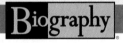

Introducing **CHAPTER 11**

OVERVIEW

Chapter 11 describes the many cultural contributions made by the Greeks during the Golden Age.

- **Section 1** discusses Greek creativity and the people's attempt to honor their gods and goddesses especially in athletics and theater.
- **Section 2** identifies Socrates, Plato, and Aristotle and the development of Greek science.

CHAPTER OBJECTIVES

After reading Chapter 11, students will be able to:

1. describe how the Greeks honored their gods and goddesses.
2. summarize Greek contributions to athletics and the arts.
3. discuss how Greek thinkers influenced the development of world civilization.

EXAMINING ARTIFACTS

Refer students to the chapter title, and ask: What cultural contributions are represented by the artifacts on this page? *(Most students will probably say sculpture and pottery.)* Ask students to think of other culteral contributions that can be traced back to the Greeks. Have students return to their list at the end of the chapter to make additional notes.

PERFORMANCE ASSESSMENT ✓

Use the Performance Assessment activities on page 178B to help you evaluate students as they complete the chapter.

CHAPTER 11

Cultural Contributions

775 B.C.–338 B.C.

▲ Greek vase with women runners

◀ Statue of an Athenian girl

TEACHING RESOURCES

TEACHER PLANNING AND SUPPORT

- Reproducible Lesson Plan 11-1, 11-2
- Teaching Strategies for the World History Classroom (Including Block Scheduling Pacing Guides)
- Presentation Plus! CD-ROM

REVIEW AND REINFORCEMENT

- Reading Essentials and Study Guide 11-1, 11-2
- Chapter 11 Vocabulary and Guided Reading Activity
- Vocabulary PuzzleMaker CD-ROM
- Teaching Transparencies 11A & 11B
- Chapter 11 Reteaching Activity
- Chapter 11 Cooperative Learning Activity
- Chapter 11 Activity Book Activity
- Chapter 11 Chart and Graph Skill Activity
- Reading and Study Skills Foldables
- Interactive Tutor Self-Assessment CD-ROM

APPLICATION AND HANDS-ON ACTIVITIES

- Daily Questions in Social Studies
- Unit 4 Hands-On History Lab Activity
- Student Presentation Builder CD-ROM

Chapter Focus

Read to Discover

- How the Greeks honored their gods and goddesses.
- What contributions in athletics and the arts were made during the "Golden Age" of Greek culture.
- How Greek thinkers influenced the development of world civilization.

HISTORY Online

Chapter Overview

Visit the *Human Heritage* Web site at **humanheritage.glencoe.com** and click on ***Chapter 11—Chapter Overviews*** to preview this chapter.

Terms to Learn

oracles
prophecy
pancratium
pentathlon
philosophia
Socratic method
hypothesis
syllogism

People to Know

Herodotus
Socrates
Plato
Aristotle

Places to Locate

Mount Olympus
Olympia

Why It's Important The Greeks made many contributions to world civilization. Their accomplishments resulted, in part, because of an important religious belief. The Greeks felt their gods were honored if people tried to imitate them. The greater the skill the Greeks showed in thinking, athletic games, or the arts, the more the gods were honored. Greek efforts to do their best produced a "Golden Age" of learning. Many historians call this period the "Classical Age of Greece."

SECTION 1 Religious Practices

Although most Greeks held similar religious beliefs, there was no single Greek religion. Each city-state worshiped its own gods. Officials in each polis were in charge of public feasts and sacrifices. In their own homes, heads of families prayed and offered sacrifices to the gods.

Greek priests and priestesses often served as **oracles,** or persons who, it was believed, could speak with the gods. Many Greeks went to oracles for advice. The advice was generally given in the form of a **prophecy** (prof' uh sē), or a statement of what might

Reading Check Why did many Greeks go to the **oracles?** What is a **prophecy?**

GEOGRAPHY ACTIVITIES

- Chapter 11 Geography and Map Activity
- Outline Map Resource Book

INTERDISCIPLINARY CONNECTIONS

- Unit 4 World Literature Reading 1
- World Music: A Cultural Legacy

ENRICHMENT AND EXTENSION

- Unit 4 Primary Sources Reading
- World History Primary Source Document Library CD-ROM
- Chapter 11 Enrichment Activity
- Foods Around the World

ASSESSMENT AND EVALUATION

- Chapter 11 Performance Assessment Activity
- Chapter 11 Section Quizzes 11-1, 11-2
- Chapter 11 Test
- Chapter 11 ExamView® Pro Testmaker CD-ROM
- Chapter 11 Digests Audiocassettes Activities and Tests

SPANISH RESOURCES

- Chapter 11 Spanish Chapter Summary and Glossary
- Chapter 11 Spanish Digests Audiocassettes Activities and Tests

HISTORY Online

Chapter Overview introduces students to chapter content and key terms. Have them access ***Chapter 11 Overview*** at **humanheritage.glencoe.com**

FOCUS

Bellringer

Write this quotation from John Keats on the board: *A thing of beauty is a joy forever.* Have students write a few sentences telling whether they agree.

Motivational Activity

Discuss students' opinions of Keats's quotation and what might constitute a "thing of beauty" in modern times. Ask students what things from more than 2,000 years ago might be considered "a joy forever."

GUIDE TO READING

Reading Strategy

Ask students to read "Why It's Important" and summarize the chapter's main theme. *(Greek accomplishments, growing out of efforts to honor the gods, helped shape world civilization.)*

Vocabulary Precheck

Ask students to define each of the "Terms to Learn." Have a volunteer consult the dictionary for any unfamiliar words. L1 ELL

Use the Vocabulary PuzzleMaker CD-ROM for Chapter 11 to create a crossword puzzle. L1

Assign Chapter 11 Vocabulary and Guided Reading Activity.

Assign Reading Essentials and Study Guide 11-1.

Reading Check Answer

Greeks went to **oracles** to seek advice from the gods.
A **prophecy** is a statement of what might happen in the future.

TEACH

Guided Practice

L2 **Religion** Write the following scenario on the board: *You are a scholar with an interest in religions, living across the sea from the Greeks during the Classical Age. Your society has heard rumors that the Greeks approach their gods and goddesses differently than people have in the past. Your superiors have expressed great interest in these new religious beliefs, and have sent you to gather information on the Greek gods and goddesses.* Then tell students to write an account of their findings to be presented to their superiors upon their return home.

CAPTION ANSWER

Often a prophecy could mean more than one thing. People seeking advice had to decide what they believed to be the true meaning of the prophecy.

A&E HOME VIDEO.

The following videotape program is available from Glencoe to enrich Chapter 11:

- **Powerful Gods of Mount Olympus**

To find classroom resources to accompany this video, check the following home page:

A&E Television:
www.aande.com

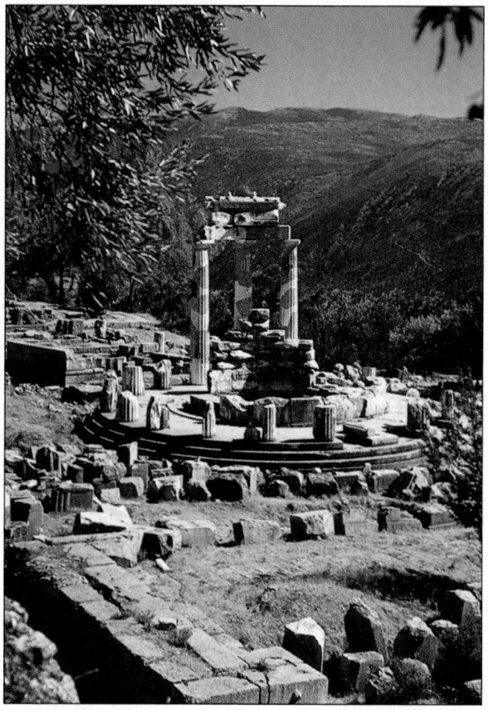

THE DELPHIC ORACLE The most popular oracle was a priestess in the temple at Delphi. The Greeks believed that Delphi was the center of the world, and they built many temples and other public buildings there (right). The painting of the Delphic oracle (left) shows her offering a prophecy to a Greek man. **Why was a prophecy from an oracle often confusing?**

Fun Facts . . . .

The Oracle at Delphi
Pilgrims to the oracle at Delphi descended a staircase into an underground vault in the Temple of Apollo, where a priestess sat. Sulfurous gases bubbled up from the crack in the earth beneath her chair, swirling around her as the pilgrim asked a question. Priests then translated the answer into a verse for the pilgrim to recite and try to understand.

happen in the future. Often, a prophecy could mean more than one thing. The person seeking advice had to decide what he or she believed to be the true meaning of the prophecy.

Gods and Goddesses of Mount Olympus

During the Golden Age, the Greeks worshiped the gods of Mount Olympus (ō lim' puhs). There were 12 major gods and goddesses. Each had specific duties to carry out.

Most ancient peoples feared their gods. They believed that people were put on Earth only to obey and serve the gods. The Greeks were the first people to feel differently. They placed importance on the worth of the individual. Because they believed in their own value, the Greeks had a great deal of self-respect. This allowed them to approach their gods with dignity.

The Greeks built temples to honor their gods. Inside each temple stood a statue of the god being honored. In front of the

EXTENDING THE CONTENT

The architects of the Parthenon—the temple to Athena—understood perspective and optical illusions. Thus they made the temple's columns thicker in the middle and thinner at the top so that the columns appeared straight when viewed from a distance. The steps leading up to the Parthenon, actually lower in the center than at either end, likewise appear straight.

statue was an altar. Because the Greeks believed the temple was the god's home, they did not enter it. They worshiped outside, as a sign of respect.

Another way the Greeks honored their gods was with different kinds of festivals. Each showed the power of the god in whose honor it was given. Out of the festivals came two important contributions to western culture. These were the Olympic Games and the theater.

The Olympic Games Every four years, in the middle of summer, a festival was held in Olympia (ō lim′ pē uh) to honor the god Zeus. Olympia was not really a town. It was a group of

HISTORY Online

Student Web Activity
Visit the *Human Heritage* Web site at humanheritage.glencoe.com and click on ***Chapter 11—Student Web Activities*** to find out more about Greek contributions.

OLYMPIAN GODS AND GODDESSES

Name	Realm
Zeus	ruler of Mount Olympus; king of the gods; god of the weather
Aphrodite	goddess of love and beauty
Apollo	god of the sun; patron of truth, archery, music, medicine, and prophecy
Ares	god of war
Artemis	goddess of the moon; mighty huntress and "rainer of arrows"; guardian of cities, young animals, and women; twin sister of Apollo
Athena	goddess of wisdom; city god of Athens; patron of household crafts; protectress in war of those who worshiped her; daughter of Zeus
Demeter	goddess of crops, giver of grain and fruit
Dionysus	god of fertility, of joyous life and hospitality, and of wild things
Hephaestus	god of fire and artisans; maker of Pandora, the first mortal woman; husband of Aphrodite
Hera	protectress of marriage, children, and the home; wife of Zeus
Hermes	god of orators, writers, and commerce; protector of thieves and mischief-makers; guardian of wayfarers; messenger to mortals; son of Zeus
Poseidon	god of the sea and earthquakes; giver of horses to mortals

HISTORY Online

Student Web Activity objectives and answers can be found at the ***Chapter 11 Web Activity Lesson Plan*** at humanheritage.glencoe.com

L2 **Language Arts** Have students choose a god or goddess from the chart on this page and read a myth about them. Students might refer to *Book of Greek Myths* by Ingri and Edgar D'Aulaire. Then have students give oral reviews of the myths and their opinion of the worthiness of their deity.

NATIONAL GEOGRAPHIC

Use these materials to enrich student understanding of ancient Greek culture.

NGS PICTURESHOW CD-ROM
Greece and Rome

NGS PICTUREPACK TRANSPARENCY SET
Ancient Greece

ANCIENT CIVILIZATIONS POSTER SET
Ancient Greece

MEETING SPECIAL NEEDS

Help students who need to review the vocabulary and concepts in this chapter by having them create a crossword puzzle on a large sheet of butcher paper or on the board. Have a volunteer find a word or term in the chapter and write it on the paper horizontally or vertically. Have another student write a clue that defines that word, and then add a word to the paper crossing the previous word in crossword puzzle fashion. Have students continue composing the puzzle as long as they can fit words, adding numbered clues as they go. After compiling 10 words or more, have students create a blank puzzle, using squares or blanks for each letter, and the list of numbered clues to challenge another class.

Refer to ***Inclusion for the Middle School Social Studies Classroom: Strategies and Activities*** for additional resources.

L1 History Ask students to compare the events of the ancient Olympic Games with those of the present-day Olympics. Have interested students investigate when and where the next modern summer and winter Olympics will be held. ELL

DID YOU KNOW ??

Although women were not allowed to take part in the Olympics, they could own the chariot teams that competed in the races.

CAPTION ANSWER

chariot race, boxing, the pancratium, and the pentathlon

Fun Facts...

The Olympics
According to legend, King Pelops founded the Olympics to repay Zeus for helping him win a chariot race and gain Hippodameia, a rival king's daughter. Hippodameia then began the Heraia, a festival honoring Zeus's wife Hera. The Heraia, held at the same time as the Olympics, gave women a chance to compete in foot races.

temples and arenas built in fields. A 40-foot, or 12-meter, gold and ivory statue of Zeus stood in one of the temples.

The festival was known as the Olympic Games. It was the most important sporting event in Greece. While the games were going on, the Greeks would stop fighting any war in which they were involved. When the Spartans refused to call a truce during the Peloponnesian War to compete in the games, they had to pay a fine.

Athletes came from all over Greece and from Greek colonies in Africa, Italy, and Asia Minor to take part in the games. Individuals, rather than teams, competed. Only men were allowed to take part. Women were not even allowed to watch. Each athlete had to swear on the sacred boar of Zeus that he would follow the rules of the games. Those who broke the rules were fined.

The Olympics were made up of many events. One of the most exciting was the chariot race. It was held in the Hippodrome (hip' uh drōm), which was an oval track with grandstands around it. The chariots had small wheels and were open in the back. At first, they were pulled by four horses. Later, only two horses were used. About 40 chariots started the race, but only a few could finish the 9 miles, or 14.4 kilometers. The driver of the winning chariot received a crown made from olive leaves.

WARRIOR'S RACE The first Olympic Games were mainly simple foot races. Later, other events were added. One of these additions was the warrior's race. In it, runners competed wearing full armor and carrying a shield. **What were some other events in the early Olympics?**

MULTICULTURAL PERSPECTIVES

Though the Olympic Games were the oldest and most prestigious athletic event in Greece, they were not unique. There were three other major sports festivals held at two- or four-year intervals: the Pythian Games honoring Apollo at Delphi, the Nemean Games for Zeus, and the Isthmian Games held at Corinth to honor Poseidon. Games alternated so there was at least one major event a year. All of these games were "Panhellenic," drawing from all of Greece and its colonies.

Another major event was boxing. Boxers did not use their fists. They wrapped their hands with strips of ox hide and slapped one another with the flat of the hand. There were no set rounds or points. A match between two boxers went on until one raised a finger in the air as a sign of defeat.

Another fighting event was the **pancratium** (pan krā' shē uhm). This was a combination of boxing and wrestling in which no holds were barred between the two fighters. The only two things a fighter could not do were gouge an opponent's eyes or bite.

The winner of the **pentathlon** (pen tath' luhn) was considered the best all-around athlete. The pentathlon itself was made up of five events. Those who took part had to run, jump, throw the discus (dis' kuhs), wrestle, and hurl the javelin (jav' luhn). Like other winners, the winner of the pentathlon was crowned with an olive-leaf wreath.

Olympic winners were heroes. Poets wrote about them. City-states held parades for them. Some city-states even gave them free meals for a year.

Between the different events at the games, poets read their works aloud. Herodotus (hi rahd' uh tuhs), the "Father of History," first read his account of the Persian Wars at the Olympics. Greek historians even dated events by Olympiads (ō lim' pē ads), or the four-year periods between games. The first recorded date in Greek history is the date of the first Olympic Games, which occurred in 776 B.C.

Reading Check How did athletes compete in the **pancratium?** What five events made up the **pentathlon?**

The Theater

The theater grew out of festivals given in honor of the god Dionysus (dī uh nī' suhs). About 600 B.C., the Ionians began telling stories about Dionysus at festivals. A chorus chanted and danced each story to the music of a flute. At certain points, the chorus fell silent. The chorus leader then gave a *soliloquy* (suh lil' uh kwē), or talk in which personal thoughts and feelings are expressed to the audience.

In time, the chorus became shorter and the soliloquies longer. Stories were then told about other gods and heroes. About the time of the Persian Wars, a Greek poet named Aeschylus (es' kuh luhs) added an additional character to each story. Now, instead of singing or telling a story, it was acted out. Thus, Aeschylus created what came to be known as a play.

The first Greek plays were *tragedies* (traj' uh dēz), or stories about suffering. All dealt with the past and with the relationships between people and gods. Not all of them had unhappy endings. Still, they all pointed out that though people suffered, most individuals were able to carry on despite their suffering.

Three of the great writers of tragedy were Aeschylus, Sophocles (sahf' uh klēz), and Euripides (yū rip' uh dēz). All three lived in Athens during its Golden Age. Aeschylus wrote about power and its effect on people. Sophocles showed that people

Then... & Now

Orchestra *Orchestra* is a Greek word from the verb "to dance." At first, it meant the space between the stage and the audience where the chorus performed. In modern times, the term designates both the area in front of the stage and the group of musicians who plays there.

Reading Check Answer

In the **pancratium,** athletes competed in a no-holds barred fighting event that combined wrestling and boxing. In a **pentathlon,** athletes had to run, jump, throw the discus, wrestle, and hurl the javelin.

MAKING CONNECTIONS

>> **Drama** The Greek playwrights differed with each other on important issues. For example, Aeschylus, who had fought at Marathon and Salamis, was proud of Athens' military accomplishments and said so in his plays. Euripedes, on the other hand, condemned the suffering caused by war.

DID YOU KNOW ??

Sophocles's most famous play, *Oedipus Rex,* deals with the plight of Oedipus, a king who unknowingly kills his father and marries his mother. Oedipus uses all his powers to solve the crime of murder, only to discover that he is the murderer.

COOPERATIVE LEARNING

Have students plan and execute a Greek Heritage Day. Divide the class into groups. Assign each group an ancient Greek achievement to demonstrate to the class, such as drama, painting, sculpture, and architecture. The groups should decide what form their demonstration will take. Make sure that each member of the group has a specific assignment. The demonstrations could include a performance of part of a drama, a model of a vase, or a model of a building.

Assign Chapter 11 *Cooperative Learning Activity* in the TCR.

L2 **Critical Thinking** Ask students why they suppose women were not permitted to perform in Greek plays. Have them brainstorm a list of reasons they could use to argue for a change in this practice.

DID YOU KNOW ??

Because of their frank treatment of issues, the plays of Euripedes shocked many Athenians. As a result, Euripedes was a controversial figure during his lifetime.

Linking Across Time

Rows of stone benches were cut into the side of a hill so that large audiences could look down upon a central stage.

Comedy and Tragedy Masks

suffered because of their sins and mistakes and that suffering could make someone a better person. Euripides tried to show that people suffered because they did bad things.

Soon after the development of tragedy, a second kind of play came into being. It was *comedy,* or a play with a happy ending. Unlike tragedies, Greek comedies were about the present. At first, they poked fun at certain politicians and other polis leaders, who often were in the audience. Later, comedies did away with the chorus. They also stopped poking fun at specific people. Instead, they poked fun at a certain kind of person, such as a son who wastes money or an enslaved person who plots against a master. One of the greatest writers of Greek comedy was Aristophanes (ar uh stahf' uh nēz). He found something funny about everyone.

Greek plays were performed only at community festivals. They began at sunrise and went on all day. Tragedies were presented in the morning and comedies in the afternoon. All the performers were men. Women were allowed to watch plays but could not act in them.

Each actor wore a huge canvas and plaster mask that showed the gender, age, and mood of the character. The mouth of the mask was shaped like a funnel. This helped carry the sound of the actor's voice to the entire audience. Actors also wore heavy padding under their robes and boots with thick soles. This made them seem larger than they really were.

Linking Across Time

Greek Theaters The idea of having audiences sit around a stage to watch a play started with the Greeks (left). Today people go to theaters to watch everything from plays to movies to rock concerts (below). **How did the design of Greek theaters allow many people to attend a performance?**

EXTENDING THE CONTENT

The earliest Greek plays took place around 600 B.C. at festivals honoring Dionysus, the Greek god of wine and fertility. The audience sat on a hillside around an open space, where a chorus chanted a story about Dionysus and danced to the sound of a flute. Eventually cities began building permanent amphitheaters, carving into a hillside, adding rows of stone seats, and paving the stage area. A low building erected behind the stage served as a dressing room and backstage area.

Plays were given in open-air theaters. Anyone who did not have enough money to buy a ticket was admitted free. The audience sat on rows of stone benches set on the side of a hill. The benches were arranged in a semicircle around a stage that was level with the ground.

The Greeks believed support of the theater was a public responsibility. An official of each polis chose the plays to be performed. This official then assigned each play to a wealthy citizen to stage. A panel of citizens judged the plays at each festival.

Section 1 Assessment

1. **Define:** oracles, prophecy, pancratium, pentathlon.
2. How did the Greeks honor their gods and goddesses?
3. Who took part in the Olympics?

Critical Thinking

4. **Demonstrating Reasoned Judgment** Do you think support of the theater should be the responsibility of government or private groups? Explain.

Graphic Organizer Activity

5. Draw a diagram like this one, and use it to list events at the Greek Olympics. (Add additional answer lines as needed.)

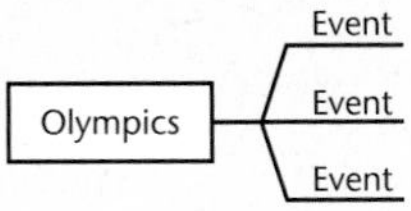

SECTION 2 Science

Among the things on which the Greeks placed great importance was *intellect* (in′ tuh lekt), or the ability to learn and reason. The Greeks thought intellect should be used to its fullest. Because of this, they asked questions about many things and studied the laws of nature. To the Greeks, studying the laws of nature and loving wisdom were the same thing. They called it ***philosophia*** (fi la sō fē′ ya). Today, people who search for such knowledge and wisdom are known as scientists and *philosophers.* Much of what they know is based on the thoughts of the Greeks.

Reading Check What did ***philosophia*** mean to the ancient Greeks?

Socrates In 399 B.C., a trial was held in Athens. The person on trial was Socrates (sok′ ruh tēz), a 70-year-old Athenian philosopher who was interested in the thinking process. Socrates gave up private business so he could spend his time searching for truth. He believed people could discover truth if they knew how to think.

In his search for truth, Socrates walked throughout Athens trying to teach people how to think. He did this by asking questions. Each question was designed to make a person arrive

L3 Writing Have students imagine they are playwrights who have a temporary writer's block. Suggest they look through the daily newspaper for an event or story that would make a good play. If time allows, suggest they outline the major characters and plot line of their play.

Use **Interactive Tutor Self-Assessment CD-ROM** to review Section 1.

Reading Check Answer To the Greeks, ***philosophia*** meant a love of wisdom and studying the laws of nature.

DID YOU KNOW ??

Socrates's wife, Zantippe, was known to be a disgruntled person who was constantly nagging her husband for not earning more money. Socrates, instead of becoming upset, merely said that living with such a person was good training for learning how to get along with other people.

Use the **Vocabulary PuzzleMaker CD-ROM** to create crossword and word search puzzles.

Section 1 Assessment Answers

1. oracles, those able to speak to gods (p. 179); prophecy, a statement of what might happen in the future (p. 179); pancratium, boxing and wrestling contest (p. 183); pentathlon, five-event contest (p. 183)

2. They built temples, held festivals, and tried to imitate the gods by excelling in everything they did.

3. athletes from all over Greece and from Greek colonies in Africa, Italy, and Asia Minor

4. Answers will vary but issues of financing and control could be included.

5. sample events: chariot racing, boxing, pancratium (boxing and wrestling), pentathlon (running, jumping, discus throwing, wrestling, hurling the javelin)

Assign Chapter 11 **Section 1 Quiz** in the TCR. Testmaker available.

Reading Check Answer The **Socratic method** encouraged people to think by asking questions in an effort to reach a conclusion or to find the truth.

Independent Practice

L3 **Critical Thinking** Have students debate this resolution: *The trial of Socrates was not justified.* Have students draw folded slips of paper on which you have written "pro" or "con." Tell students they must defend whatever side of the question they draw. Have them research the background of the trial and the arguments presented. Conduct the debate so that students with opposing arguments alternate with each other. Have the audience decide the debate's winner.

CAPTION ANSWER

They regretted executing Socrates and put up a bronze statue in his honor.

DID YOU KNOW ??

Socrates could have easily escaped death with the help of friends, but he refused. He argued that a state is doomed when individuals start flouting the laws that do not suit them.

Reading Check How did the **Socratic method** encourage people to think?

step-by-step at a final conclusion, or truth. This form of questioning is known as the **Socratic** (sō krat' ik) **method.**

All Athenians did not react in the same way to Socrates's teachings. Some were pleased because they learned how to examine their own beliefs and to think things out. Others saw Socrates's ideas as dangerous. They did not like self-examination, particularly when it pointed out their own mistakes. In time, they began to consider Socrates a threat to Athens. Finally, they accused him of denying the gods, corrupting the young, and trying to overthrow the government.

Socrates was tried before a jury of some 500 citizens. He defended himself by speaking about truth and goodness. He said, "Wealth does not bring goodness. But goodness brings wealth and every blessing, both to the citizen and to the polis." He also said he would not change his beliefs even to save his life.

The jury found Socrates guilty and sentenced him to death. The sentence was carried out by making Socrates drink poisonous hemlock juice. Later, the Athenians regretted having executed Socrates, so they put up a bronze statue in his honor.

Fun Facts...

Rules for Life
Many quotes about ethical, or morally correct, living have been attributed to Socrates. These are two of the best known:

- "The unexamined life is not worth living."
- "I am a citizen, not of Athens or Greece, but of the world."

DEATH OF SOCRATES Socrates faced death with self-control and dignity. Here, in an eighteenth-century painting, he is surrounded by his sorrowing friends as he prepares to drink poisonous hemlock juice. **How did the Athenians regard Socrates after his death?**

SPOTLIGHT ON: SOCRATES

An example of the Socratic method:

Socrates: Does falsehood then exist among men?

Euthydemus: It does assuredly.

Socrates: Under which head [justice or injustice] *shall we place it?*

Euthydemus: Under injustice, certainly.

Socrates: Well then . . . if a father, when his son requires medicine, and refuses to take it, should deceive him, and give him the medicine as ordinary food, and, by adopting such deception, should restore him to health, under which head must we place such an act of deceit?

Euthydemus: We must place it under [justice].

—Xenophon, from *Memorabilia*

GREEK PHILOSOPHERS The ideas of Greek thinkers influenced the development of world civilization. Here, in a sixteenth-century European painting, Plato and Aristotle discuss the meaning of human achievement with their pupils. **What was the subject of Plato's *The Republic*?**

CAPTION ANSWER

political science, or the study of government

MAKING CONNECTIONS

>> **Government** Plato's dislike of democracy probably came from his personal experience. As a young man, he had witnessed much political turmoil in Athens during the Peloponnesian Wars. He had also been shocked by the Athenian treatment of Socrates.

Plato Socrates left no writings. All that is known about him comes from one of his pupils, an Athenian aristocrat named Plato (plā′ tō). Plato recorded the speeches Socrates made at his trial and just before his death.

Plato was 30 years old when Socrates died. Until then, Plato had wanted to become a politician. In 399 B.C., he changed his mind. He left Greece and traveled in Egypt and Italy for the next 12 years. When he returned, he set up a school outside Athens in the sacred grove of the hero Academus (ak uh dē′ muhs). The school, where Plato hoped to train government leaders, was called the Academy. Plato taught there almost 40 years. The Academy itself lasted almost 900 years after Plato's death.

Plato's beliefs were contrary to the ideas that had made Athens great. Plato believed in order. He thought political liberty was disorder and did not approve of it. He thought only the wise and good should rule.

Plato set down his ideas about an ideal state in a book called *The Republic.* It is the first book ever written on **political science,** or the study of government. In it, Plato examined different kinds of government and explained how to avoid political errors.

Like Socrates, Plato believed in truth. He thought it could be found only after a long, hard search. In a work called *The Dialogues*

Reading Check What is the subject of **political science?**

Reading Check Answer **Political science** studies the subject of government.

SPOTLIGHT ON: PLATO

Plato distrusted the lower classes and wanted only the best-educated citizens to participate in government. As he explained in the *Republic,*

Until philosophers are kings, or the kings and princes of the world have the spirit and power of philosophy, and those commoner natures who pursue either to the exclusion of the other are compelled to stand aside, cities will never have rest from their evils, no, nor the human race.

MAKING CONNECTIONS

➤➤ **Ideas** Plato rejected the reliability of the senses (seeing, hearing, touch, smell, and taste), believing that the many things that could be perceived by these senses were only "appearances." Reality, the "real" world, was constructed from ideas, or ideal "forms," which could be understood through logical thought and reasoning.

Reading Check Answer

The **scientific method** is a series of steps to help scientists study something.
A **hypothesis** is a possible explanation.
A **syllogism** uses reasoning to reach a conclusion based on information in related statements.

DID YOU KNOW ??

Aristotle's school was called the Lyceum. Because he taught while walking with his students, he and his followers were called "peripatetic," which comes from a Greek word meaning "to walk around."

Sculpture of Aristotle

Reading Check What is the purpose of the **scientific method?** What is a **hypothesis?** How does a **syllogism** work?

People in History

Aristotle
384 B.C.–322 B.C.

Greek Scientist

After studying in Greece, Aristotle returned to Macedonia to teach the son of King Philip II. This boy, later known as Alexander the Great, would one day conquer many lands, including Greece. Thus, Aristotle's ideas came to influence an entire empire.

(dī′ uh logs), he showed how difficult it is to discover truth. *The Dialogues* consists of a series of discussions in which different people talk about such things as truth and loyalty. Socrates is the leading speaker in many discussions. Through these discussions, Plato brings out the self-questioning that goes on within a person troubled by such issues.

Aristotle One of Plato's brightest pupils was Aristotle (ā r′ uh stot l). Aristotle came to the Academy when he was 17 years old and stayed for 20 years. Before he died in 322 B.C., he founded his own school in Athens and wrote more than 200 books.

Aristotle was known as "the master of them that know." He believed in using one's senses to discover the laws that govern the physical world. He was the first to *classify,* or group together, plants and animals that resemble each other. His system, with some changes, is still used today. It has helped scientists handle a great amount of information in an orderly way.

Aristotle also added to the ideas of an earlier Greek scientist named Thales (thā′ lēz) of Miletus (mi let′ uhs). Thales developed the first two steps of what is known today as the **scientific method.** This is the process used by scientists to study something. First, Thales collected information. Then, based on what he observed, he formed a **hypothesis** (hī poth′ uh sis), or possible explanation. Aristotle provided a third step in the scientific method when he said that a hypothesis must be tested to see if it is correct.

Another important contribution Aristotle made was in *logic* (loj′ ik), or the science of reasoning. He developed the **syllogism** (sil′ uh jiz uhm). This is a method of reasoning that uses three related statements. The third statement is a conclusion based on the information given in the first two. For example:

Athenians are Greeks.
Socrates is an Athenian.
Therefore, Socrates is Greek.

Discoveries and Inventions Greek scientists were not looking for ways to make life easier or better. They were trying to add to their store of knowledge. They had none of the tools scientists have today. There were no telescopes, microscopes, or scales that weigh small amounts. Even without these, however, the Greeks made important discoveries.

Their curiosity led Greek scientists to discover that natural events are not caused by the way gods behave. They also learned that the world is governed by natural laws that people can discover and understand.

There were many Greek scientists. The first was Thales of Miletus, who came from Ionia. Thales not only developed the first two steps of the scientific method, but he also correctly predicted

SPOTLIGHT ON: ARISTOTLE

To extend People in History, provide these additional details on Aristotle:

If the term *Renaissance man* had been coined 1800 years earlier, it would have been the perfect description of Aristotle—an inventive, curious thinker who succeeded brilliantly in every field he explored. Aristotle set standards and methods for analyzing areas of study—politics, rhetoric, drama, poetry, aesthetics, ethics, and logic. He was one of the few Classical authors whose works affected every subsequent era. Even today, we use his terms for kinds of government and apply some of his ideas of structure to plays and poetry.

GREEK SCIENTISTS

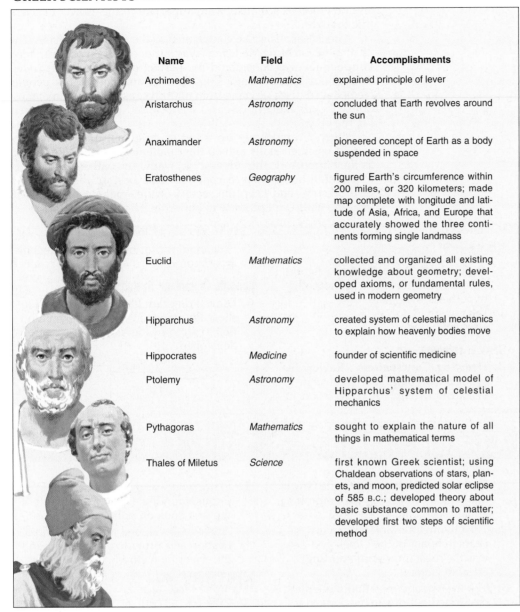

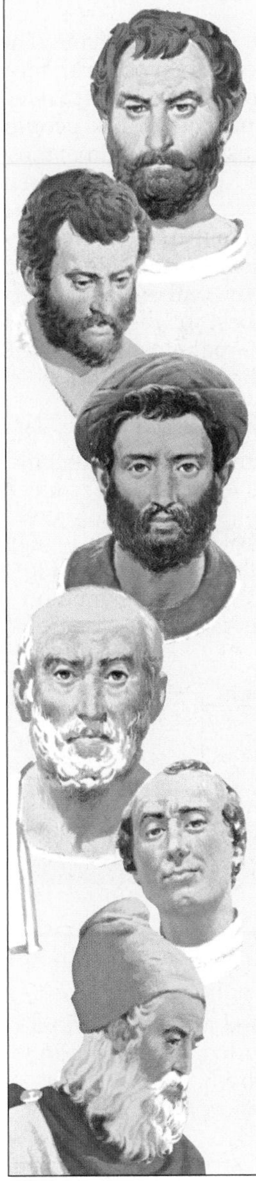

Name	Field	Accomplishments
Archimedes	*Mathematics*	explained principle of lever
Aristarchus	*Astronomy*	concluded that Earth revolves around the sun
Anaximander	*Astronomy*	pioneered concept of Earth as a body suspended in space
Eratosthenes	*Geography*	figured Earth's circumference within 200 miles, or 320 kilometers; made map complete with longitude and latitude of Asia, Africa, and Europe that accurately showed the three continents forming single landmass
Euclid	*Mathematics*	collected and organized all existing knowledge about geometry; developed axioms, or fundamental rules, used in modern geometry
Hipparchus	*Astronomy*	created system of celestial mechanics to explain how heavenly bodies move
Hippocrates	*Medicine*	founder of scientific medicine
Ptolemy	*Astronomy*	developed mathematical model of Hipparchus' system of celestial mechanics
Pythagoras	*Mathematics*	sought to explain the nature of all things in mathematical terms
Thales of Miletus	*Science*	first known Greek scientist; using Chaldean observations of stars, planets, and moon, predicted solar eclipse of 585 B.C.; developed theory about basic substance common to matter; developed first two steps of scientific method

L2 **Science** Have students research the accomplishments of a Greek scientist listed in the chart. Then hold a science fair and have students role-play their chosen scientist and explain accomplishments or discoveries using visuals or other means.

DID YOU KNOW ??

Being a doctor in Greece was often an occupation that was passed from father to son. Many doctors ran clinics near the marketplace where they bandaged wounds or bled patients to draw out diseases.

ASSESS

Check for Understanding

Ask students to summarize orally or in writing the main points of the chapter. Discuss the answers to the Section and Chapter Assessment questions.

Evaluate

Assign Chapter 11 **Performance Assessment Activity** in the TCR.

Administer **Chapter 11 Test** in the TCR. Testmaker available.

EXTENDING THE CONTENT

The ancient Greeks were heir to all the mathematical knowledge of the Mesopotamian and Egyptian civilizations. They built upon that inheritance by using their sense of reason to pursue the "Why?" and "What does it mean?" questions of mathematics. Thales of Miletus began the mathematical revolution. He laid the foundation that is still part of introductory courses in geometry. The followers of Pythagoras advanced mathematics into a quasi-religion. Euclid simplified and organized the new knowledge. Apollonius explored the aspects of conic sections. Archimedes is the father of scientific notation.

Reteach

Divide the class into teams to try and guess a term defined in the chapter or the name of a person described in the chapter from clues given by other team members.

Assign Chapter 11 **Reteaching Activity** in the TCR.

Enrich

Have students write syllogisms and share them with one another.

Assign Chapter 11 **Enrichment Activity** in the TCR.

CLOSE

Ask students to compare the role religion played in the lives of ancient Greeks to the role it plays in modern American society. Encourage them to note both similarities and differences.

Use **Interactive Tutor Self-Assessment CD-ROM** to review Section 2.

HISTORY Online

Self-Check Quiz gives students an interactive chapter tutorial. Have them access ***Chapter 11 Quiz*** at **humanheritage.glencoe.com**

an eclipse of the sun in 585 B.C. The contributions made by Thales and other Greek scientists were important to the growth of scientific thought.

Greek scientists also contributed to the field of medicine. The "Father of Scientific Medicine" was Hippocrates (hi pok' ruh tēz). Hippocrates was considered the perfect physician. He traveled throughout Greece diagnosing illnesses and curing sick people. He believed diseases came from natural causes. At the time, most other doctors thought diseases were caused by evil spirits entering the body.

Hippocrates drew up a list of rules about how doctors should use their skills to help their patients. His rules are known as the Hippocratic (hip uh krat' ik) Oath. The oath says that doctors should honor their teachers, do their best for the sick, never give poisons, and keep the secrets of their patients. Doctors all over the world still promise to honor the Hippocratic Oath.

Section 2 Assessment

1. **Define:** *philosophia*, Socratic method, political science, scientific method, hypothesis, syllogism.
2. What were Plato's beliefs about government?

Critical Thinking

3. **Drawing Conclusions** Review the syllogism on page 188. Then write a syllogism to help you draw a conclusion about one of the Greek thinkers in this chapter.

Graphic Organizer Activity

4. Draw a diagram like this one. Use it to show the steps in the scientific method that Thales of Miletus and Aristotle developed.

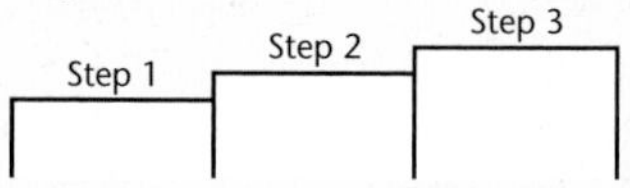

Chapter Summary & Study Guide

1. During the "Golden Age," the Greeks made many contributions in thinking, athletics, and the arts.
2. The Olympic Games, held every four years in honor of the Greek god Zeus, was the most important sporting event in Greece.
3. The theater, and eventually the play, developed out of a festival given in honor of the Greek god Dionysus.
4. Socrates, in his search for truth, developed a form of questioning known as the Socratic method.
5. Plato, who was one of Socrates's pupils, founded a school and wrote the first book on political science.
6. Aristotle developed a system of classification and provided a third step in the scientific method.

HISTORY Online

Self-Check Quiz

Visit the *Human Heritage* Web site at **humanheritage.glencoe.com** and click on ***Chapter 11—Self-Check Quiz*** to assess your understanding of this chapter.

Section 2 Assessment Answers

1. *philosophia*, studying nature and loving wisdom (p. 185); Socratic method, way of questioning (p. 186); political science, study of government (p. 187); scientific method, studying science (p. 188); hypothesis, possible explanation (p. 188); syllogism, three-statement reasoning (p. 188)

2. order, no political liberty, and wise and good rulers

3. Syllogisms will vary but should show an understanding of the way in which a syllogism works. The conclusion reached in each syllogism should accurately reflect the thinking of the philosophers chosen.

4. Step 1: collect information; Step 2: form a hypothesis; Step 3: test the hypothesis

Assign Chapter 11 **Section 2 Quiz** in the TCR. Testmaker available.

CHAPTER 11 Assessment

Using Key Terms

Use the following words to make a chart that explains the ideas and contributions of the Greeks.

oracles	prophecy
pancratium	pentathlon
philosophia	Socratic method
political science	scientific method
hypothesis	syllogism

Understanding Main Ideas

1. What was the role of oracles in Greek religion?
2. What role did women play in the Olympic Games?
3. What was the relationship between Greek historians and the Olympic Games?
4. How did tragedies differ from comedies?
5. How did Athenians react to the teachings of Socrates?
6. Why did Plato set up the Academy?
7. How does the scientific method work?
8. In what subjects were Greek scientists most interested?
9. What was Euclid's most famous achievement?

Critical Thinking

1. What would you have done if it had been your decision whether or not to put Socrates on trial?
2. Why is the scientific method important to modern science?
3. How important was religion in ancient Greek civilization? Explain your answer.
4. Would you like being taught through the Socratic method? Why or why not?

Graphic Organizer Activity

History Draw a chart like this one, and use it to list four Greek ideas or inventions and to explain the effect each has had on your life.

Idea/Invention	Effect on My Life
1.	
2.	
3.	
4.	

Geography in History

Human Systems The Olympic Games drew contestants from all the areas under Greek control. What different methods of travel would athletes have used to reach Olympia where the games were held? Create a poster advertising transportation to the games.

Using Your Journal

Review any details you may have noted about the ideas developed by the Greeks. Imagine that you have a chance to interview an important Greek thinker. Write a list of questions you might like to ask this person.

Bonus Test Question

For Chapter 11 Test

The Greek oracles often spoke in riddles. Solve this riddle: Your mother has heard sad news. Your mother's father's daughter has called to say your brother's grandfather's son's wife's son has died. Who called? *(your aunt)* Who died? *(your cousin)*

Using Your Journal

Questions will vary but should include major points significant to the person's achievement. You could have students role-play the interview, one assuming the part of the Greek historical figure.

Geography in History

Answers may vary but should include major forms of transportation such as by foot, cart, and horse, and the proximity of the sea.

CHAPTER 11 Assessment Answers

Using Key Terms

Charts will vary but should explain the contributions made by ancient Greeks.

Understanding Main Ideas

1. They spoke to the gods and gave advice and prophecies to the Greek people.
2. They were not allowed to take part in or watch the games.
3. Historians read their works aloud at the games and dated historical events by the Olympiads.
4. Tragedies told about suffering and relationships between people and the gods. Comedies were humorous and poked fun at people.
5. Some were pleased but others saw Socrates' ideas as very dangerous.
6. because he hoped to train government leaders
7. collecting information and forming and testing a hypothesis
8. political science, medicine, mathematics, and so on
9. advances in mathematics

Critical Thinking

1. Answers will vary but could include the reasons for and against this decision.
2. Answers will vary but include that it provides a consistent way for scientists to do research.
3. Answers will vary but should include that religion and the gods were very important.
4. Answers will vary.

Graphic Organizer Activity

Ideas or inventions will vary, but should include realistic examples of how each item can be linked to their lives. (As an extension, have students illustrate some of these connections in Linking Across Time features such as the one on page 184.)

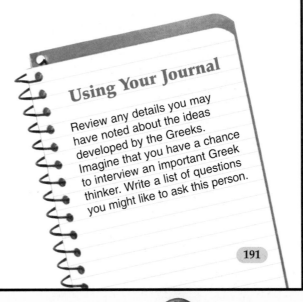

Chapter 12 Planning Guide

Timesaving Tools

TeacherWorks™ All-In-One Planner and Resource Center

- **Interactive Teacher Edition** Access your Teacher Wraparound Edition and your classroom resources with a few easy clicks.
- **Interactive Lesson Planner** Planning has never been easier! Organize your week, month, semester, or year with all the lesson helps you need to make teaching creative, timely, and relevant.

Use Glencoe's **Presentation Plus!** multimedia teacher tool to easily present dynamic lessons that visually excite your students. Using Microsoft PowerPoint® you can customize the presentations to create your own personalized lessons.

Objectives	Reproducible Resources	Multimedia Resources
Section 1 **Philip II of Macedonia** Summarize how the spread of Greek culture influenced people from Gibraltar to India, and explain how Philip II of Macedonia gained control of Greece.	Reproducible Lesson Plan Chapter 12 Vocabulary and Guided Reading Activity Reading Essentials and Study Guide 12-1 Section 1 Quiz	Interactive Student Edition CD-ROM Graphic Organizer Transparency 15 Vocabulary PuzzleMaker CD-ROM Interactive Tutor Self-Assessment CD-ROM ExamView® Pro Testmaker CD-ROM Glencoe Skillbuilder Interactive Workbook CD-ROM, Level 1 Presentation Plus! CD-ROM
Section 2 **Alexander the Great** Discuss how Alexander attempted to bring unity to his empire, and describe how Alexander's empire changed after his death.	Reproducible Lesson Plan Reading Essentials and Study Guide 12-2 Chapter 12 Cooperative Learning Activity Chapter 12 Chart and Graph Skill Activity Chapter 12 Geography and Map Activity Chapter 12 Enrichment Activity Section 2 Quiz	Teaching Transparencies and Activities 12A & 12B Vocabulary PuzzleMaker CD-ROM Interactive Tutor Self-Assessment CD-ROM ExamView® Pro Testmaker CD-ROM Glencoe Skillbuilder Interactive Workbook CD-ROM, Level 1
Chapter 12 **Review and Evaluation**	Chapter 12 Reteaching Activity Chapter 12 Performance Assessment Activity Unit 4 Standardized Test Practice Spanish Chapter Summary and Glossary Chapter 12 Test	Vocabulary PuzzleMaker CD-ROM Interactive Tutor Self-Assessment CD-ROM Glencoe Skillbuilder Interactive Workbook CD-ROM, Level 1 Audiocassettes* ExamView® Pro Testmaker CD-ROM

*Also available in Spanish.

Chapter 12 Planning Guide

Performance Assessment Activities

Geography Have students draw a base map showing the empire of Alexander the Great and the growth of the Greek influence. (See the map on page 196.) Then have students research to find the route of Alexander's conquest and add the route to the base map of the empire.

CHAPTER RESOURCES

LITERATURE ABOUT THE PERIOD

Easterling, P.E. and B. M. W. Knox, eds. *The Cambridge History of Classical Literature, Vol. 1, Greek Literature.* Cambridge, 1985. Collection of ancient Greek literature.

READINGS FOR THE STUDENT

Harris, Nathaniel. *Alexander the Great and the Greeks.* Bookwright Press, 1986. Details about the contributions Alexander made to the Greeks.

Renault, Mary. *The Persian Boy.* Bantam, 1988. The second of three novels about Alexander the Great.

READINGS FOR THE TEACHER

Editors of Time-Life Books. *Empires Ascendent.* Time-Life Books, 1987. Includes a chapter tracing Alexander's triumphant military campaign.

Nichols, Roger and Kenneth McLeish. *Through Greek Eyes.* Cambridge University Press, 1991. Integrates excerpts from primary sources in discussions of ancient Greek history.

KEY TO ABILITY LEVELS

Teaching strategies have been coded for varying learning styles and abilities.

L1 Level 1 activities are **basic** activities and should be within the ability range of all students.

L2 Level 2 activities are **average** activities and should be within the ability range of the average to above-average student.

L3 Level 3 activities are **challenging** activities designed for the ability range of above-average students.

ELL ELL activities should be within the ability range of English Language Learning students.

NATIONAL GEOGRAPHIC Teacher's Corner

INDEX TO NATIONAL GEOGRAPHIC MAGAZINE

The following articles relate to this chapter:

- "Alexander the Conquerer: Ancient Greece, Part III," by Caroline Alexander, March 2000.
- "Tale of Three Cities: Alexandria,Cordoba, and New York," by Joel L. Swerdlow, August 1999.

NATIONAL GEOGRAPHIC SOCIETY PRODUCTS AVAILABLE FROM GLENCOE

To order the following products, call Glencoe at 1-800-334-7344:

- *PicturePack: Physical Geography of the World (Transparencies)*
- *Picture Atlas of the World (CD-ROM)*

ADDITIONAL NATIONAL GEOGRAPHIC SOCIETY PRODUCTS

To order the following, call National Geographic at 1-800-368-2728:

- *National Geographic Atlas of World History (Book)*
- *Wonders of the Ancient World: National Geographic Atlas of Archaeology (Book)*

Access *National Geographic*'s new dynamic MapMachine Web site and other geography resources at:
www.nationalgeographic.com
www.nationalgeographic.com/maps

THE HISTORY CHANNEL. A&E HOME VIDEO. Biography

The following videotape program is available from Glencoe:

- **Mystical Monuments of Ancient Greece**
  0-7670-0012-9

To order, call Glencoe at 1-800-334-7344. To find classroom resources to accompany this video, check:
A&E Television: www.aande.com
The History Channel: www.historychannel.com

OVERVIEW

Chapter 12 describes the accomplishments of Philip of Macedonia and Alexander the Great in spreading Greek civilization.

➤ **Section 1** analyzes the political and military strategies that enabled Philip to conquer the Greek city-states.

➤ **Section 2** describes the personality, military conquests, and political objectives of Alexander the Great.

CHAPTER OBJECTIVES

After reading Chapter 12, students will be able to:

1. summarize how the spread of Greek culture influenced people from Gibraltar to India.

2. explain how Philip II of Macedonia gained control of Greece.

3. discuss how Alexander tried to unify his empire.

4. describe how Alexander's empire changed after his death.

EXAMINING ARTIFACTS

Point out the relationship between the two figures in the artifacts—i.e., father and son. Ask students what they can infer from the fact that Alexander is known as Alexander the Great rather than his real name, which was Alexander III. Tell students that they will learn how Alexander greatly extended his father's empire.

PERFORMANCE ASSESSMENT ✓

Use the Performance Assessment Activities on page 192B to help you evaluate students as they complete the chapter.

CHAPTER 12

The Hellenistic Period

335 B.C.–145 B.C.

A gold coin showing Philip II of
◀ Macedonia

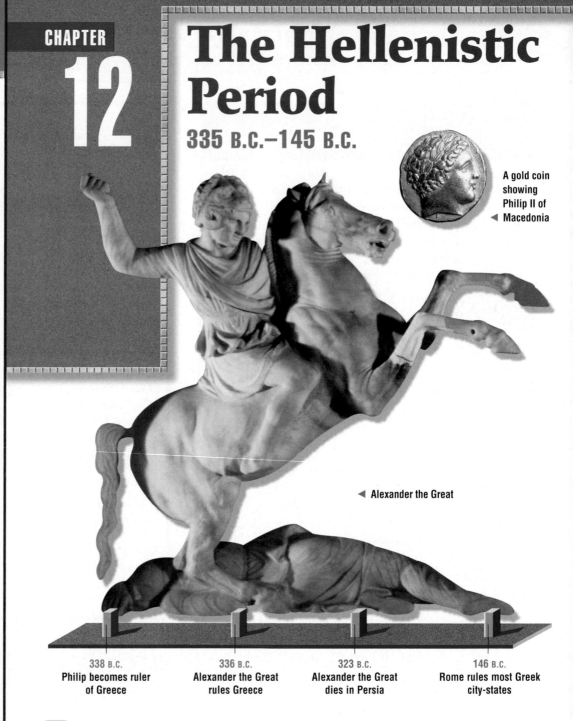

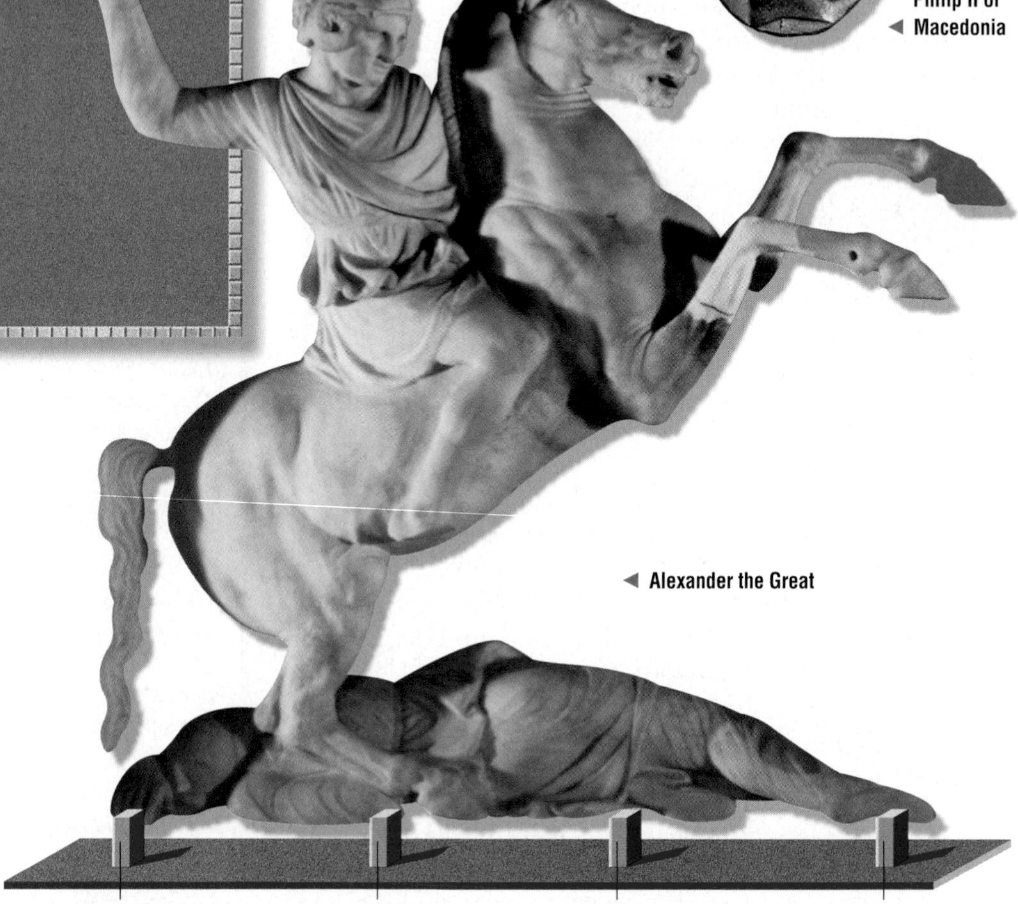

◀ Alexander the Great

338 B.C.	336 B.C.	323 B.C.	146 B.C.
Philip becomes ruler of Greece	**Alexander the Great rules Greece**	**Alexander the Great dies in Persia**	**Rome rules most Greek city-states**

TEACHING RESOURCES

TEACHER PLANNING AND SUPPORT

📁 Reproducible Lesson Plan 12-1, 12-2
📁 Teaching Strategies for the World History Classroom (Including Block Scheduling Pacing Guides)
💿 Presentation Plus! CD-ROM

REVIEW AND REINFORCEMENT

📁 Reading Essentials and Study Guide 12-1, 12-2
📁 Chapter 12 Vocabulary and Guided Reading Activity
💿 Vocabulary PuzzleMaker CD-ROM
📄 Teaching Transparencies 12A & 12B

📁 Chapter 12 Reteaching Activity
📁 Chapter 12 Cooperative Learning Activity
📁 Chapter 12 Activity Book Activity
📁 Chapter 12 Chart and Graph Skill Activity
📁 Reading and Study Skills Foldables
💿 Interactive Tutor Self-Assessment CD-ROM
📼 Unit 4 MindJogger VideoQuiz

APPLICATION AND HANDS-ON ACTIVITIES

📁 Daily Questions in Social Studies
💿 Student Presentation Builder CD-ROM

Chapter Focus

Read to Discover

- How the spread of Greek culture influenced people from Gibraltar to India.
- How Philip II of Macedonia gained control of Greece.
- How Alexander attempted to bring unity to his empire.
- How Alexander's empire changed after his death.

HISTORY Online

Chapter Overview

Visit the *Human Heritage* Web site at **humanheritage.glencoe.com** and click on ***Chapter 12—Chapter Overviews*** to preview this chapter.

Terms to Learn

hostage
phalanx
alliances
orator
barbaroi
factories
emigrated

People to Know

Philip of Macedonia
Demosthenes
Alexander the Great

Places to Locate

Macedonia
Persia
Alexandria

Why It's Important After the Greek city-states lost their independence, many changes took place. The new rulers of Greece built empires and increased trade. At the same time, they spread Greek culture and customs. Before long, Greek ideas were influencing people from Gibraltar (juh brol' tuhr) to India.

The Greek language came to be spoken by many people. Greek architecture was copied for new buildings. Students studied Greek literature in school. People used Greek furniture in their homes. Greek plays became a popular form of entertainment. Business people took up Greek ways of banking.

The period in which all this took place has come to be called the Hellenistic (hel uh nis' tik) Age. The term "Hellenistic" means "like the Hellenes, or the Greeks."

SECTION 1 Philip II of Macedonia

By 338 B.C., Greece had a new ruler, Philip II of Macedonia. Macedonia was a small, mountainous country north of Greece. Most Macedonians were farmers. They cared little for the Greeks and had fought them in the Persian Wars. Macedonian kings, however, were of Greek descent and admired Greek culture.

Philip became ruler of Macedonia in 359 B.C. During his youth, he was a **hostage** (hos' tij), or a person held by an enemy until certain promises are carried out, for three years in Thebes. In those

Reading Check What is a **hostage**?

HISTORY Online

Chapter Overview introduces students to chapter content and key terms. Have them access ***Chapter 12 Overview*** at **humanheritage.glencoe.com**

FOCUS

Bellringer

Have each student list three accomplishments of the ancient Greeks that they have learned thus far.

Motivational Activity

Discuss students' lists and write accomplishments on the board. Have students copy the list and then survey the chapter to add Hellenistic accomplishments.

GUIDE TO READING

Reading Strategy

Ask students to read "Why It's Important" and summarize the chapter's main theme. *(The new Greek rulers built empires, increased trade, and spread Greek culture.)*

Vocabulary Precheck

Ask students to define each of the "Terms to Learn." Have a volunteer consult the dictionary for any unfamiliar words. L1 ELL

Use the Vocabulary PuzzleMaker CD-ROM for Chapter 12 to create a crossword puzzle. L1

Assign Chapter 12 Vocabulary and Guided Reading Activity.

Assign Reading Essentials and Study Guide 12-1.

Reading Check Answer

A **hostage** is a person held by an enemy until certain promises are carried out.

GEOGRAPHY ACTIVITIES

- Chapter 12 Geography and Map Activity
- Outline Map Resource Book

INTERDISCIPLINARY CONNECTIONS

- World Art & Architecture Transparency 7, *Nike of Samothrace*
- World Music: A Cultural Legacy

ENRICHMENT AND EXTENSION

- World History Primary Source Document Library CD-ROM
- Chapter 12 Enrichment Activity
- Foods Around the World

ASSESSMENT AND EVALUATION

- Chapter 12 Performance Assessment Activity
- Chapter 12 Section Quizzes 12-1, 12-2
- Chapter 12 Test
- Unit 4 Standardized Test Practice
- Chapter 12 ExamView® Pro Testmaker CD-ROM
- Chapter 12 Digests Audiocassettes Activities and Tests

SPANISH RESOURCES

- Chapter 12 Spanish Chapter Summary and Glossary
- Chapter 12 Spanish Digests Audiocassettes Activities and Tests

TEACH

Guided Practice

L2 **History** Have students work in pairs to create a dialogue for an interview between Philip of Macedonia and a newspaper reporter from the *Macedonian Times.* Tell students to focus the dialogue on Philip's campaign to unify the Greek city-states and spread the Greek culture. Have pairs read the dialogue to the class, with one student playing the role of the reporter and the other, the role of Philip.

Reading Check Answer
A **phalanx** was powerful because soldiers charged as a group.

CAPTION ANSWER

He tried to warn them that Philip was dangerous.

years, he learned to love Greek culture. However, he learned to dislike the weaknesses of the Greek form of government.

Philip believed it was his destiny to unify the Greek city-states and spread Greek culture. As soon as he became ruler of Macedonia, he set out to fulfill that destiny. It took him a little over 20 years.

Philip went about reaching his goal in many ways. For example, until his time, the Macedonian army was made up of volunteers, who fought only in the summer. Philip turned this part-time volunteer army into a year-round, well-organized, professional one.

Reading Check Why was a **phalanx** powerful?

Philip developed an infantry formation called a **phalanx** (fā' langks). Foot soldiers formed a solid body some 16 rows deep. Those in each line stayed so close together that their shields overlapped. This gave them added protection. The phalanx charged as a group, which gave it more striking power.

Philip also armed his soldiers with spears that were 14 feet, or over 4 meters, long. This was twice as long as ordinary spears. He

People in History

Demosthenes
383 B.C.–322 B.C.

Greek Orator

Demosthenes, born into a wealthy Athenian family, was a great speaker and politician. He is most famous for a series of speeches called "Philippics," in which he warned the Greek people about King Philip of Macedonia. By 338 B.C., however, Philip had conquered Greece, and the city-states had lost their independence.

DEMOSTHENES Demosthenes worked to preserve the freedom of the Greek city-states. He was known for his ability as a public speaker. It is said he trained himself by shouting above the roar of the ocean waves with his mouth full of pebbles. **What did Demosthenes try to tell the Greeks about Philip of Macedonia?**

SPOTLIGHT ON: DEMOSTHENES

To extend People in History, provide these additional details on Demosthenes.

Demosthenes, born in 384 B.C., was the son of the owner of a sword-making factory. He was orphaned at age 7, and his guardians squandered his inheritance so that he could not have a good education. At age 22, he sued them and won, which encouraged his driving ambition to be a great orator. According to Plutarch, a first-century Greek biographer and essayist, Demosthenes studied with a well-known actor for help with gestures and expression. He practiced his gestures in front of a large mirror. Demosthenes' fervor and skill won admiration from Philip, even though Demosthenes angrily spoke against Philip.

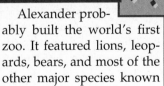

LIGHTHOUSE OF ALEXANDRIA The lighthouse of Alexandria was one of the Seven Wonders of the Ancient World. It towered over Alexandria's two excellent harbors. A fire on top provided light to guide ships into port. **Why was Alexandria also considered a center for learning?**

follow Greek customs. They called such people ***barbaroi*** (bar' buh roi), from which the word "barbarians" comes. Because of such feelings, Alexander's attempt to achieve unity among the people in his empire was not successful.

Reading Check What English word is derived from ***barbaroi?***

Alexandria During his rule, Alexander founded about 70 cities, 16 of which were named Alexandria (al ig zan' drē uh) after himself. He encouraged Greeks and Macedonians to settle in the new cities, which were scattered throughout the empire.

The most noted Alexandria was in Egypt. Within 70 years after its founding, it had become a center of trade and learning. Greeks from throughout the eastern Mediterranean came there. They wanted to make the most of its economic opportunities and to be a part of its intellectual and social life.

Alexandria had two great harbors. They were protected by *breakwaters,* or barriers that break the force of waves. A lighthouse 400 feet, or about 122 meters, tall dominated the harbors. It is considered one of the Seven Wonders of the Ancient World.

Looking out over the chief harbor was a palace and a school with a library. The school was known as the Museum. It became a center for poets, writers, philosophers, and scientists. The library had the largest collection of books in ancient times. There, Euclid (ū' kluhd) wrote his geometry book. There, Eratosthenes (er uh

HISTORY Online

Student Web Activity
Visit the *Human Heritage* Web site at **humanheritage.glencoe.com** and click on ***Chapter 12—Student Web Activities*** to find out more about Alexandria.

CAPTION ANSWER

because of its school and library

L1 **The Arts** Prepare the class to view the film *Alexander the Great & the Greeks.* (See Chapter Resources in the Chapter 12 Planning Guide.) After viewing the film ask: *What are some examples of how Alexander tried to bring unity to his empire? Was Alexander successful in achieving this goal? Was his goal realistic? Why or why not? Could such a goal be realized today? Is such a goal desirable?*

Reading Check Answer
"Barbarians" comes from ***barbaroi.***

HISTORY Online

Student Web Activity objectives and answers can be found at the ***Chapter 12 Web Activity Lesson Plan*** at **humanheritage.glencoe.com**

L2 **Geography: The World in Spatial Terms** Have students research the other 15 cities named after Alexander the Great and locate them on a map. **ELL**

DID YOU KNOW ??

Alexander probably built the world's first zoo. It featured lions, leopards, bears, and most of the other major species known to the world at the time.

COOPERATIVE LEARNING

Divide the class into groups to prepare a class book that illustrates the exploits of Alexander. Assign each group an area of conquest to work on including Thebes, Granicus River, Issus, Egypt, Guagamela, and Indus River valley. Each group's contribution should include a description of the geographic area, what happened there and when, and a map of the region. Groups could include drawings such as costumes, weapons, and buildings. Have members agree upon individual tasks and manner of presentation.

Assign Chapter 12 ***Cooperative Learning Activity*** in the TCR.

Independent Practice

L1 **Daily Life** Show students examples of advertisements for cities or regions from business or travel magazines. Have them write advertisement copy for a magazine to be distributed throughout the Hellenistic world that extols the virtues of living in Alexandria, Egypt.

L1 **History** Have students use the map on page 196 to identify and locate the three divisions of Alexander's empire following his death. **ELL**

CAPTION ANSWER

because his troops refused to go any farther

MAKING CONNECTIONS

>> **The Arts** Arrian, a Roman general, used the eyewitness accounts of Alexander's generals to write a thorough, unbiased biography of Alexander the Great. In describing the retreat from India, Arrian told the story of Alexander that reveals his leadership qualities. Marching through the hot sands toward water, Alexander led his men on foot. A party he had sent ahead to search for water returned with a helmet full. Although thirsty, Alexander took the water and poured it on the ground. This action, and that of walking when he could ride, showed the soldiers that he did not expect them to endure hardships that he wasn't willing to endure himself.

Fun Facts . . .

Alexander's Hero The mother of Alexander the Great told her son that Achilles, a hero of the Trojan War, was his ancestor. He learned Homer's *Iliad*—which tells Achilles' story—by heart and always carried a copy of it with him.

ALEXANDER THE GREAT Alexander conquered tremendous amounts of territory. His empire stretched from Greece to northern India. This painting of Alexander shows him leading his army ashore in Asia Minor and claiming all lands to the east as his own. **Why was Alexander unable to continue his conquests beyond India?**

tahs' thuh nēz) reasoned that a ship could reach India by sailing west from Spain. There, Archimedes (ar kuh mēd' ēz) and Hero (hē' rō) invented several machines.

Then & Now

Greek Translation In about 250 B.C., Jewish scholars in Alexandria translated the Hebrew Bible into Greek, a version known as the Septuagint. The Eastern Orthodox Church still uses the Septuagint version of the Old Testament.

End of the Empire In 323 B.C., when Alexander was in Babylon, he became ill and died. He was 33 years old and had ruled for 13 years. His body was wrapped in gold and placed in a glass coffin in the Royal Tombs of Alexandria, Egypt. After his death, Alexander became a romantic legend. More than 80 versions of his life have been written in more than 20 languages.

After Alexander's death, fights broke out over who was to rule the empire. The areas Alexander had conquered in India returned to their original rulers. Three of Alexander's generals divided the rest of the empire among themselves. Antigonus (an tig' uh nuhs) became king of Macedonia. Ptolemy (tahl' uh mē) established the dynasty of the Ptolemies in Egypt. Seleucus (suh lū' kuhs) formed the Seleucid Empire in Persia. Athens and

EXTENDING THE CONTENT

People in the Hellenistic world admired the Hellenic style of art and architecture and enthusiastically imitated it in temples and other public buildings that adorned their thriving cities. Greek style inspired architects and sculptors in Roman times, and later, during the Renaissance, European humanists revived the Classical style of art and architecture. The Greek Revival, or neoclassical, style of architecture arose in the late 1700s and lasted into the early 1800s. Buildings in the Greek style are still being built.

Sparta again became independent city-states. Most other Greek city-states banded together into one of two leagues, but neither league had much power or importance.

Greek cultural influence, however, became stronger than ever after Alexander's death. The rulers who took Alexander's place adopted Greek as their language and used Alexander's titles. They even used his portrait on their coins.

Trade grew. From Africa and Asia came spices, ivory, incense, pearls, and rare woods. From Syria and Egypt came glass, metals, and linen. From Greece came olive oil, wine, and pottery. From Sicily and Egypt came wheat.

The cities that had been part of Alexander's empire now existed chiefly for trade and grew along with it. City officials made their laws, language, calendar, and coins Greek. Teachers brought Greek customs and ideas into schools. Merchants and bankers used Greek methods to run their businesses.

Fun Facts . . . .

Greek Discoveries
Greek scientists at Alexandria made several key discoveries. Eratosthenes calculated the earth's circumference to within 1 percent of its actual size. Archimedes invented a watering tool that Egyptian farmers used for nearly 2,000 years.

Linking Across Time

Hellenistic Influence The columns of an ancient Greek temple (left) influenced the style of this United States government building (right). **Why do you think the Hellenistic style of art and architecture is often used on present-day government buildings?**

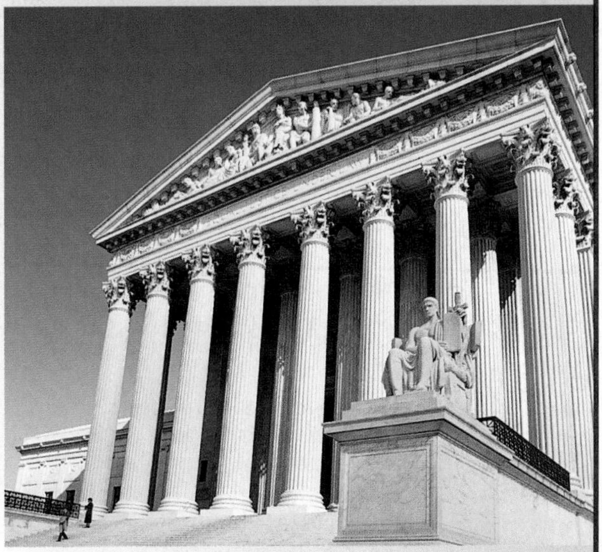

Economics at a Glance

Trade
Sometimes it may be better for a country to trade with another country for a good rather than make that good itself. A county has an *absolute advantage* when it is able to produce more of a given product than another country can. A country has a *comparative advantage* when it is able to make a product more efficiently than another country. Point out that geography can influence whether or not a country has an absolute or comparative advantage. Climate, landforms, and natural resources all affect what a nation is able to produce and trade. Have students select a product that a particular nation trades and write a paragraph explaining how geography influences the production of that item.

Linking Across Time

Answers will vary, but Greek architectural styles are used for buildings where democratic governments such as the United States conduct business.

ASSESS

Check for Understanding

Ask students to summarize the main points of the chapter, orally or in writing. Discuss the answers to the Section and Chapter Assessment questions.

Evaluate

Assign Chapter 12 **Performance Assessment Activity** in the TCR.

Administer **Chapter 12 Test** in the TCR. Testmaker available.

MEETING SPECIAL NEEDS

Arrange for visual or tactile/kinesthetic learners to visit an art or history museum and view examples of ancient Greek art and architecture. If this is not possible, enlist the help of an art teacher or local artist to bring examples of sculptures to class, and to speak to the students about the influence of Greek art on other societies. Encourage student participation by helping students prepare questions ahead of time.

Refer to ***Inclusion for the Middle School Social Studies Classroom: Strategies and Activities*** for additional resources.

GLENCOE TECHNOLOGY

MindJogger Videoquiz

Use **MindJogger Videoquiz** to review students' knowledge of the unit.

Available in DVD and VHS

Reading Check Answer

Factories are places where goods are made. Population fell when many young Greeks **emigrated.**

Reteach

Have volunteers tell the main ideas under each chapter heading.

Assign Chapter 12 **Reteaching Activity** in the TCR.

Enrich

Assign Chapter 12 **Enrichment Activity** in the TCR.

CLOSE

Ask students to discuss whether they agree or disagree with the following statement: *Might makes right.*

Use **Interactive Tutor Self-Assessment CD-ROM** to review Section 2.

HISTORY Online

Self-Check Quiz gives students an interactive chapter tutorial. Have them access ***Chapter 12 Quiz*** at humanheritage.glencoe.com

Reading Check What are **factories?** What happened to city-states when many young Greeks **emigrated?**

The Greek city-states, however, were never the same again. Although they kept their political independence, they could not gain back the power of the past. In time, economic conditions grew worse. Great **factories,** or places where goods are made, had been built in the new Hellenistic cities. Greek manufacturers now found they could not compete with these factories. Because of this, more and more young Greeks **emigrated** (em′ uh grāt ed), or left one place to settle in another. Population in the Greek city-states fell. There were not enough people to work the land, and many farms once again became wilderness. By 146 B.C., most of the Greek city-states were under Roman control.

Section 2 Assessment

1. **Define:** *barbaroi*, factories, emigrated.
2. Who was Alexander the Great?
3. What conquests did Alexander make?
4. How did Greek influence continue to grow and spread after Alexander's death?

Critical Thinking

5. **Forming Conclusions** How successful would Alexander's dream of uniting the world in peace be today? Explain.

Graphic Organizer Activity

6. Draw a time line like this one, and use it to show the major events in the life of Alexander the Great.

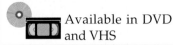

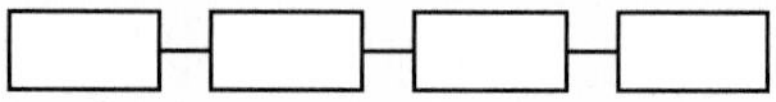

Chapter Summary & Study Guide

1. Philip II believed it was his destiny to unify the Greek city-states and spread Greek culture.
2. Philip II was able to conquer Greece in 338 B.C.
3. When Philip II died in 336 B.C., his son Alexander took over power.
4. Alexander was a great general whose conquests stretched from the Nile to the Indus.
5. Alexander tried without success to unite the Macedonians, the Greeks, and the Persians.
6. The most famous city founded by Alexander was Alexandria, Egypt.
7. After Alexander died in 323 B.C., his empire was divided among three of his generals.
8. Despite Alexander's death, Greek cultural influence became stronger.
9. Although the Greek city-states again became independent following Alexander's death, economic conditions in Greece grew worse.
10. Most Greek city-states were under Roman control by 146 B.C.

HISTORY Online

Self-Check Quiz

Visit the *Human Heritage* Web site at humanheritage.glencoe.com and click on ***Chapter 12—Self-Check Quiz*** to assess your understanding of this chapter.

Section 2 Assessment Answers

1. *barbaroi*, non-Greeks (p. 197); factories, places where goods were made (p. 200); emigrated, left one place to settle in another (p. 200)
2. emperor who spread Greek culture
3. the Persian Empire to northern India
4. later rulers adopted Greek language, titles, law, language, calendar, and coins; teachers used Greek ideas in schools; and merchants used Greek methods.
5. Answers will vary but could include the difficulty of ending world conflicts and efforts by the United Nations.
6. sample events: studies with Aristotle, comes to throne at age 20, builds empire, builds 70 cities, dies at age 33

Assign Chapter 12 **Section 2 Quiz** in the TCR. Testmaker available.

CHAPTER 12 Assessment

Using Key Terms

Use the following words to write a short paragraph about how Philip II gained control of Greece. Then write a paragraph about what helped cause the end of the city-states.

hostage	phalanx	alliances
orator	*barbaroi*	factories
emigrated		

Understanding Main Ideas

1. What changes did Philip II make in his army?
2. How did Philip II view marriage?
3. Why did the Greeks refuse to listen to Demosthenes' warnings?
4. What did Aristotle teach Alexander?
5. Why was Alexander unable to achieve unity among the people of his empire?
6. Why did many Greeks go to Alexandria, Egypt?
7. How did the physical features of Alexandria, Egypt, help trade?
8. What had happened to the Greek city-states by 146 B.C.?

Critical Thinking

1. Do you think Philip II was a successful military leader? Explain.
2. What other names might historians have given Alexander besides "the Great"?
3. What do you think Alexander could have done differently to achieve unity among the people in his empire? Explain.
4. In what ways can customs be spread without conquest?

Graphic Organizer Activity

Economics Create a cause-and-effect chart like this one, and use it to show reasons why the Greek city-states declined and the effects of their decline.

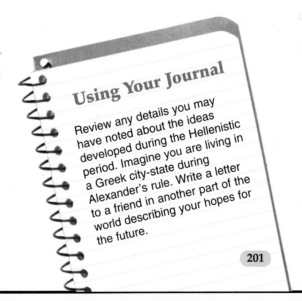

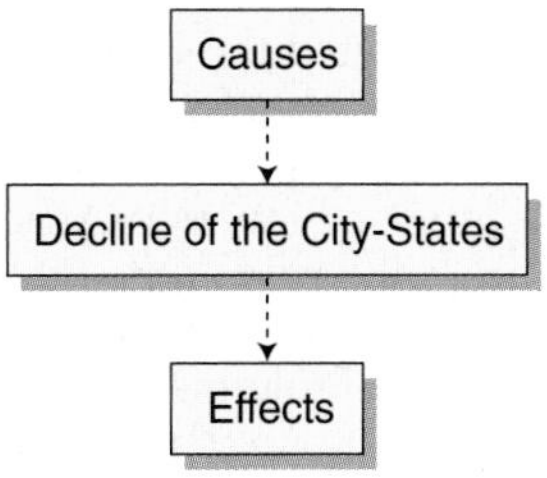

Geography in History

Environment and Society What geographical features had an impact on the Greek economy? Note especially the development of manufacturing over farming and the Greeks' constant travel and trade.

Using Your Journal

Review any details you may have noted about the ideas developed during the Hellenistic period. Imagine you are living in a Greek city-state during Alexander's rule. Write a letter to a friend in another part of the world describing your hopes for the future.

201

CHAPTER 12 Assessment Answers

Using Key Terms

Paragraphs will vary but should include specific references to Philip's methods.

Understanding Main Ideas

1. armed a professional army with long spears, slingshots, and bows and arrows; developed the phalanx
2. as a way of forming political alliances
3. because they were unhappy with their local governments
4. literature, political science, geography, and biology
5. They refused to treat Alexander as a god; Greeks looked down on all non-Greeks.
6. its economic opportunities and intellectual and social life
7. It had two great harbors that were protected by breakwaters.
8. fell under Roman control

Critical Thinking

1. Answers will vary. Students may note that Philip II organized a professional army and developed new military strategies and weapons.
2. Answers will vary but could include aspects of Alexander's character.
3. Answers will vary. Students may say Alexander should not have tried to force a new way of life on the people.
4. Answers will vary but might include through trade, learning, traveling missionaries and merchants, marriage, and alliances.

Graphic Organizer Activity

sample causes: rise of factories in new Hellenistic cities, emigration of Greek youth; sample effects: declining population, land/farms became wilderness, fell to Romans

Bonus Test Question

For Chapter 12 Test

Alexander was a very practical, clear-thinking leader. If he were to write a handbook of rules on how to organize an army, what do you think would be the first three suggestions in his book? *(Answers will vary.)*

Using Your Journal

Letters will vary but might include the idea that Greek culture and people would flourish and leaders would settle disagreements among Greek city-states, and form political alliances.

Geography in History

Answers will vary but should include the accessibility of the sea for trade and for obtaining raw materials, lack of good farmland, and mountains.

FOCUS

Objectives

After reading the Around the World for Unit 4, your students will be able to:

1. locate Nubia and cite geographic factors that protected it from invasion.

2. cite some of Nubia's accomplishments.

3. compare the civilizations of Nubia and ancient Greece.

Bellringer

Ask students to name the earliest ancient African civilization that they can think of. *(Many students will probably say Egypt. If any students say Kush [Chapter 8], hold a class vote on which civilization students think is the oldest.)*

Motivational Activity

Refer students to the Around the World feature, pointing out that many archaeologists today think that Nubia preceded the development of Egypt. Ask: What works of art on pages 202–203 show contact between Nubia and Egypt? *(sample responses: style of Nubian pendant, silver mask, figures from Egyptian grave, and so on)*

TEACH

Geography: The World in Spatial Terms Have students study the map on page 202. Ask: What geographic obstacles made it difficult for the ancient Greeks to reach Nubia? *(cataracts, deserts, and perhaps, depending upon political relations, passage through Egypt itself)*

UNIT 4 Around

THE NUBIANS

Tales of Nubia—the vast land south of Egypt—fascinated the Greeks. They learned of its existence from stories told by the Egyptians or by the Nubians who lived in Egypt. However, few non-Africans visited Nubia until the rule of the Ptolemies, the Greek rulers of Egypt from 332 B.C. to 30 B.C. Under the Ptolemies, the Greeks got a firsthand look at one of the oldest civilizations in the ancient world.

Today, many archaeologists believe the Nubians may have developed their first culture around 8000 B.C. The Nubians also established a series of kingdoms in the area, such as Kush, that challenged the power of Egypt, Greece, and Rome. By the time Kush fell in 350 A.D., the Greek city-states had been under Roman rule for almost 500 years.

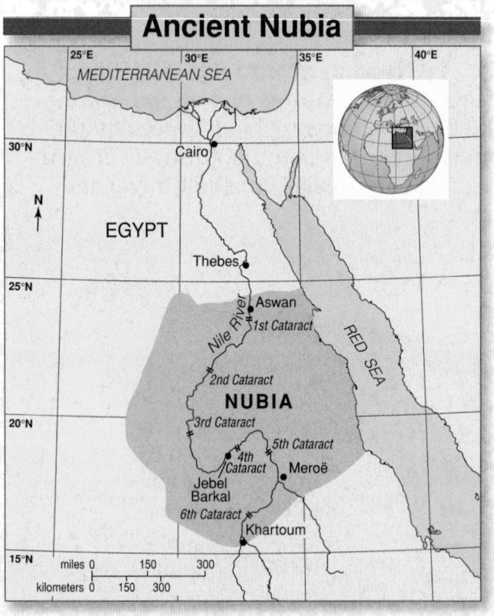

▲ Geographical features, such as strong rapids and blazing deserts, protected the Nubians from unwanted visitors.

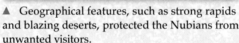

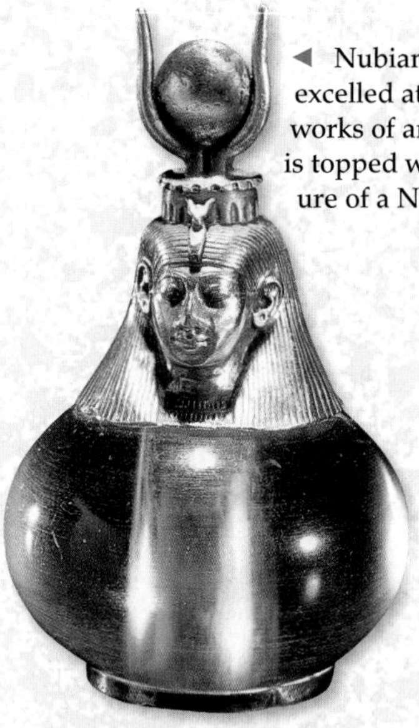

◄ Nubian craftworkers excelled at creating fine works of art. This pendant is topped with a gold figure of a Nubian ruler.

SPOTLIGHT ON: NUBIA

European knowledge of Nubia came mostly from legend. No European knew whether or not cities such as Meroë actually existed. In 1772, Scottish explorer James Bruce rightly guessed that he had sighted the ruins of Meroë on his search for the source of the Blue Nile. Final proof came when a French expedition found the fabled city in the early 1800s. Read aloud this account from a diary written by one of the explorers, and ask students how the discovery might have changed European views of history.

Imagine my joy when I saw the tops of a crowd of pyramids raised a little on the horizon, and tipped by the rays of the sun. . . . Looking round, I saw a second group of pyramids to the west, and, not far from the river, a huge field of ruins . . . indicating the site of an ancient city.

the World

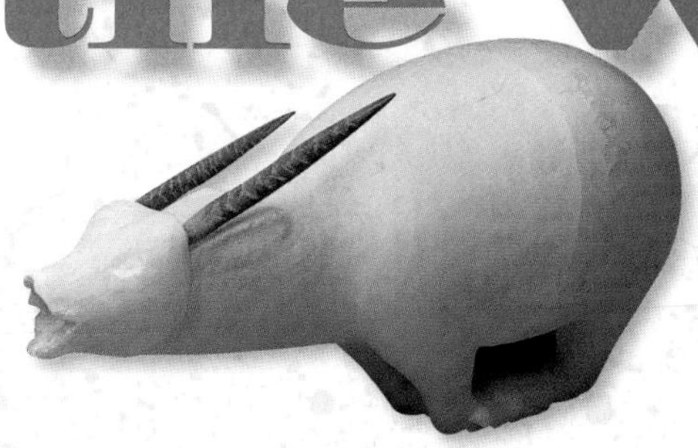

▲ The animals of inland Africa, such as lions, elephants, and giraffes, inspired Nubian artists. This bottle shows a bound oryx—a large African antelope prized by the Nubians for their beautiful long straight horns.

These figures of Nubian bowmen were found in the grave of a wealthy Egyptian buried around 2000 B.C. The Nubians were such skilled archers that the Egyptians called Nubia the "Land of the Bow." In times of peace, the Egyptians hired the Nubians as bodyguards. ▲

This bronze statue of a ▶ Nubian king, dating from about 700 B.C., was found in Cairo, Egypt, in 1929.

The Nubians learned to work in bronze thousands of years ago. This statue of a Nubian king shows the skullcap and headband worn by the rulers of Kush. ▼

Taking Another Look

1. Where was Nubia located?
2. How did Nubia's location prevent the ancient non-African world from knowing much about its accomplishments?

Hands-On Activity

Creating an Advertisement Create a newspaper advertisement announcing a tour of Nubian artworks around the United States.

203

DID YOU KNOW ??

Long after the Romans took over the Greek city–states, the Nubians resisted Roman expansion. Conflicts resulted in an agreement that established a permanent frontier between Roman Egypt and Meroë. Thereafter Meroë enjoyed a profitable trade with the Romans—a fact proven by the Roman shoes, statues, coins, and other artifacts found at Meroë. It seems the Nubians knew more about the classical Mediterranean world than people in that region knew about the Nubians.

ASSESS

Check for Understanding

Have students answer the questions in **Taking Another Look** on page 203.

Enrich

Have students imagine they are Greek geographers in the 400s B.C. After a long and dangerous journey, they have finally reached Meroë, the center of Nubian power at this time. Have students write an account of the journey and the wonderful sights that they have seen. (For more on Meroë, refer students to pages 130–131.)

CLOSE

Have students compare the geography of Greece with the geography of Nubia. Encourage them to suggest reasons Nubia was able to achieve greater unity than the Greek city-states. *(Sample response: Greek communities were separated by the mountains and the sea, while Nubians lived along the band of fertile soil that stretched along the banks of the Nile River south of the first cataract.)*

ANSWERS TO TAKING ANOTHER LOOK

1. At its height, Nubia stretched along both banks of the Nile from an area just above the first cataract to the area where the Nile River forks into the White Nile and the Blue Nile. It covered lands in southern Egypt and parts of the Sudan.

2. The cataracts and deserts served as obstacles to contact.

Hands-On Activity

The advertisements should accurately describe artworks shown in this feature and the uniqueness of the culture that created them.

Answers and Analyses

1B Geography

According to the map, Athens is located at 24°E (24 degrees east) longitude.

2G Civics

There is no provision in the American Constitution for choosing by lottery. Remind students to be very careful when they see the words NOT or EXCEPT in a question. Overlooking these words is a common source of error on multiple-choice tests.

THE PRINCETON REVIEW **TEST-TAKING TIP**

Students can often answer EXCEPT and NOT questions by association. Choices F, H and J are all associated with the Constitution of the United States, but G is not. Therefore G is the best guess.

3C History

The Delian League is discussed on pages 173–175. There it states that *Athens gained more and more power,* and eventually *Athenian soldiers interfered in the politics of other Greek city-states.* This power imbalance led to anti-Athenian sentiment.

THE PRINCETON REVIEW **TEST-TAKING TIP**

Encourage students to use what they know, even if their knowledge is incomplete. Even if all they recall is that Athens was the driving force behind the Delian League, they will realize that choices A and D are unlikely.

THE PRINCETON REVIEW

Standardized Test Practice

Directions: Choose the *best* answer to each of the following multiple choice questions. If you have trouble answering a question, use the process of elimination to narrow your choices. Write your answers on a separate piece of paper.

Greece and Persia

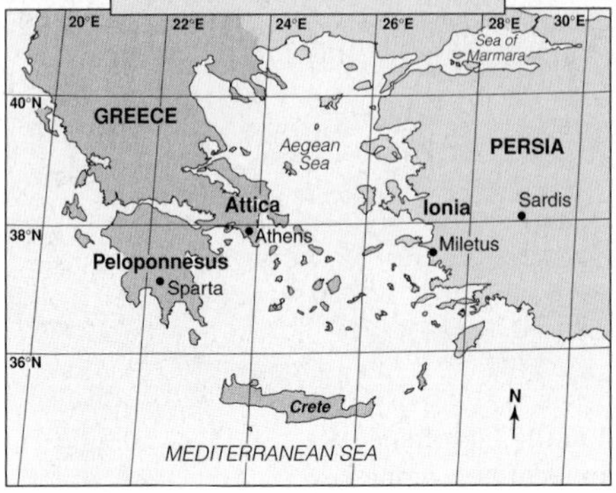

1. Along which line of longitude is Athens located?

A 22°E

B 24°E

C 38°N

D 36°N

Test-Taking Tip: *Lines of longitude*, or *meridians*, are used to measure distances east and west. They run from the North Pole to the South Pole. Be careful not to confuse *longitude* and *latitude*.

2. The Constitution of the United States has much in common with the constitution of ancient Athens. Which of the following provisions of the Athenian constitution is NOT part of the United States Constitution?

F Freedom of speech

G Choosing members of government by lottery

H Limits on the terms of elected officials

J Two separate bodies of government

Test-Taking Tip: Remember that the correct answer is true of the Athenian constitution but not true of the U.S. Constitution. Therefore, you can eliminate any answer that you know to be true of the U.S. Constitution. For instance, the United States Constitution *does* provide for freedom of speech, and so answer F cannot be the correct choice.

3. To protect themselves from attacks by the Persians, many Greek city-states joined the Delian League. This alliance allowed them to work together to defend themselves. Why did the Delian League eventually fall apart?

A The League suspended the voting rights of the Athenians.

B Most city-states decided that they would rather defend themselves alone.

C Athens took over the League, which made Athens too powerful.

D Athens stopped giving money to the League, so the League went bankrupt.

Test-Taking Tip: This question requires you to remember a *fact* about the Delian League. Make sure that you read the question and *all* of the answer choices carefully before selecting the *best* answer.

4. Socrates made several contributions to the fields of philosophy and science. Why was he sentenced to death in 399 B.C.?

F Many people thought that he gave the rulers of Athens bad advice.

G He designed a plan to overthrow the government of Greece.

H He encouraged all people to leave their jobs and go in search of truth.

J Many Athenians felt threatened by him because he pointed out their mistakes.

> ***Test-Taking Tip:*** Eliminate answers that do not make sense. Socrates was not interested in overthrowing the government; therefore, you can eliminate answer G.

5. The goal of early Greek philosophers was

A to create new inventions to improve Greek society

B to look for truths by using logic

C to find ways to spread Christianity throughout the world

D to redesign the military to be more effective

> ***Test-Taking Tip:*** It is important to remember what *philosophers* are. Although they are a type of scientist, their goal is not to *create new inventions* (answer A). The word *philosopher* means "lover of knowledge." Which answer choice fits best with this information?

6. Socrates' method of reaching a conclusion came to be called the Socratic method. However, this technique is not the only way to reach a conclusion. The scientific method is another way. How are the Socratic method and the scientific method similar?

F Both require performing experiments with chemicals in a laboratory.

G Both rely on following a step-by-step process to come to a conclusion.

H Both place an emphasis on trusting instincts and ideas over physical evidence.

J Both have been replaced by more advanced methods today.

> ***Test-Taking Tip:*** This question requires you to make a *comparison.* That means you must choose the answer that is true for *both* methods. Since the Socratic method does *not* use chemicals, and the scientific method *does* rely on physical evidence, you can rule out answers F and H.

7. Which of the following contributed to the end of the Greek empire?

A Alexander the Great, a powerful and well-liked ruler, died.

B People started moving out of Greek city-states, creating a shortage of workers.

C There were conflicts about who would rule over the empire.

D All of the above.

> ***Test-Taking Tip:*** Do not choose the first answer that "makes sense." Always read *all* of the answer choices before choosing the *best* one, especially when one of your choices is "all of the above" or "none of the above."

STOP

4J History

Socrates is discussed on pages 185–186. There it states that some Athenians *did not like self-examination, particularly when it pointed out their own mistakes,* and that for this reason they began to see Socrates as a threat.

5B History

No mention is made of Christianity or of the military, so choices C and D can be eliminated. While choice A is tempting, since modern scientists often create new inventions, no inventions are discussed on the pages about philosophers. On page 185, Socrates is said to have been *searching for truth.*

6G History

At the top of page 186, the Socratic method is described as a step-by-step approach to arrive at a final conclusion. On page 188, the scientific method developed by Thales and completed by Aristotle is described as having three steps: collecting information, making a hypothesis, and testing the hypothesis.

7D History

The demise of the Greek empire is discussed on pages 198–200. Among the reasons cited were Alexander's death; a drop in population and subsequent shortage of workers; and fights over control of the empire.

Tested Objectives

Questions	Reading Objective
1	Analyze information
2	Make comparisons
3	Draw conclusions
4, 7	Perceive relationships and recognize outcomes
5	Identify central issues
6	Make comparisons

OVERVIEW

Unit 5 surveys the history of Rome from its beginnings as a small city-state to the decline of its powerful empire.

- **Chapter 13** discusses the settlement of Italy, focusing on the Etruscans.
- **Chapter 14** analyzes the history of the Roman Republic from the sixth century B.C. to the establishment of the Roman Empire and its decline.
- **Chapter 15** explains the development of the Roman Empire from its founding in 31 B.C. to its fall in 476 A.D., focusing on the *Pax Romana*.
- **Chapter 16** summarizes the rise of Christianity to become a major influence on Western civilization.

UNIT OBJECTIVES

After reading Unit 5, students will be able to:

1. explain how the city of Rome became a great empire.

2. summarize what contributions the Romans made to Western civilization.

3. discuss the relationship between the Roman Empire and Christianity.

UNIT PROJECT

Organize students into three groups. Assign each group one of the following topics: Etruria, the Roman Republic, or the Roman Empire. Tell groups to create a chart about their topic using the following headings: *Government, Religion, Daily Life, Contributions, Famous Rulers.* Compile the three charts into a master chart titled *The Romans.*

UNIT 5

The Romans

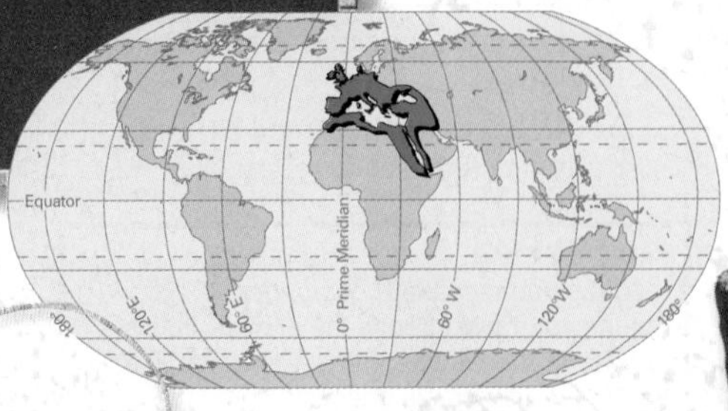

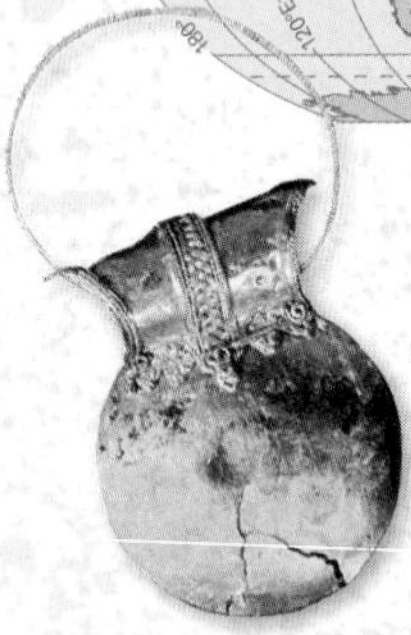

▲ A Roman charm, or *bulla*

▼ A Roman family at the dinner table

- **1000 B.C.** Latins settle on Palatine Hill
- **600 B.C.** Etruscans rule the central Italian Peninsula
- **509 B.C.** Romans set up republic
- **264 B.C.** Punic Wars begin

206

ABOUT THE UNIT OPENING

Examining Artifacts

Tell students that a *bulla* was a good-luck charm commonly given to Roman children by adults. Based on this information and the scene of a Roman family, what can students infer about how the Romans viewed children? *(They valued children.)* Explain that Rome built one of the greatest empires in the ancient world. Ask: What do you think it would be like to grow up as a citizen of a huge empire?

Global Chronology

Ask students to explain what the time line covers. *(major events in the history of Rome)* Ask students to name the time line entry that indicates that Rome had an organized government. *(Romans set up republic)*

FOLDABLES™ Study Organizer

Categorizing Information Study Foldable *Make this foldable to help you organize your notes about the history of Rome.*

Step 1 *Fold a sheet of paper in half from side to side, leaving ½ inch tab along the side.*

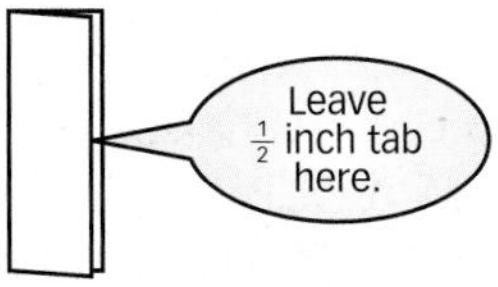

Step 2 *Turn the paper and fold it into fourths.*

Step 3 *Unfold and cut along the three fold lines.*

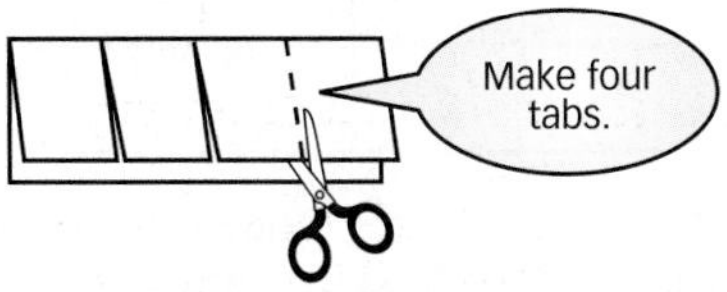

Step 4 *Label as shown.*

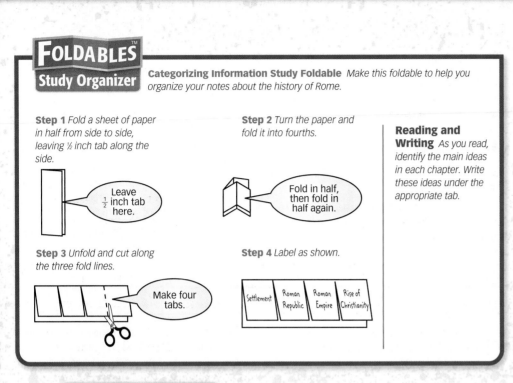

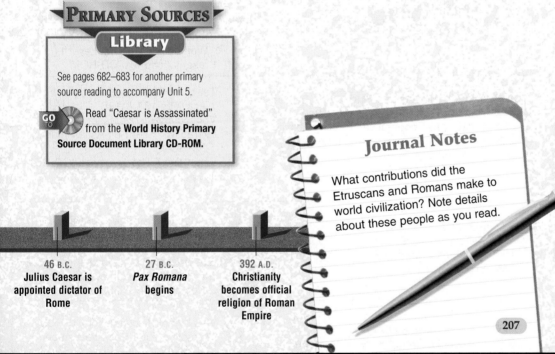

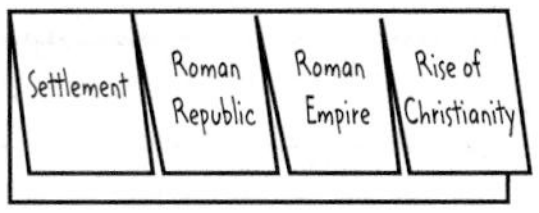

Reading and Writing *As you read, identify the main ideas in each chapter. Write these ideas under the appropriate tab.*

PRIMARY SOURCES Library

See pages 682–683 for another primary source reading to accompany Unit 5.

GO TO Read "Caesar is Assassinated" from the **World History Primary Source Document Library CD-ROM.**

Journal Notes

What contributions did the Etruscans and Romans make to world civilization? Note details about these people as you read.

46 B.C. Julius Caesar is appointed dictator of Rome

27 B.C. *Pax Romana* begins

392 A.D. Christianity becomes official religion of Roman Empire

Geographic Location

At its peak, the Roman Empire extended into the following regions: the Mediterranean, North Africa, and the Middle East. Have students locate these places in their text Atlas and name the continents that this area includes. *(Europe, Africa, and Asia)* Ask students what problems might arise in governing such a vast area. *(delays in communication, need to provide defense against invaders and rebellions, tax collection, law enforcement)*

GLENCOE TECHNOLOGY

MindJogger Videoquiz

Use **MindJogger Videoquiz** to preview the unit content.

Available in DVD and VHS

FOLDABLES Study Organizer

Purpose As students are reading the chapters in this unit, they will have to identify main ideas and important concepts and write these on their foldables. By grouping information from the unit into categories, students will in effect describe the history of Rome.

Have students complete **Reading and Study Skills Foldables** Activity 5.

RECORDING JOURNAL NOTES

Have students make a list of Roman contributions. Write responses on the board. Have students note in their journals details about the contributions of the Etruscans and Romans to the modern world.

PRIMARY SOURCES Library

Additional primary sources from the **World History Primary Source Document Library CD-ROM** can be used during the study of Unit 5, including:

- "The Gauls Sack Rome," by Livy
- "The Edict of Milan," by Constantine and Licinius

Primary sources about the eruption of Mount Vesuvius can be found on pages 682–683.

Chapter 13 Planning Guide

Timesaving Tools

TeacherWorks™ All-In-One Planner and Resource Center

- **Interactive Teacher Edition** Access your Teacher Wraparound Edition and your classroom resources with a few easy clicks.
- **Interactive Lesson Planner** Planning has never been easier! Organize your week, month, semester, or year with all the lesson helps you need to make teaching creative, timely, and relevant.

Use Glencoe's **Presentation Plus!** multimedia teacher tool to easily present dynamic lessons that visually excite your students. Using Microsoft PowerPoint® you can customize the presentations to create your ow personalized lessons.

Objectives	Reproducible Resources	Multimedia Resources
Section 1 **Founding of Rome** Describe how Rome was founded.	Reproducible Lesson Plan Chapter 13 Vocabulary and Guided Reading Activity Reading Essentials and Study Guide 13-1 Section 1 Quiz Unit 5 Hands-On History Lab	Interactive Student Edition CD-ROM Graphic Organizer Transparency 1 Vocabulary PuzzleMaker CD-ROM Interactive Tutor Self-Assessment CD-ROM ExamView® Pro Testmaker CD-ROM Glencoe Skillbuilder Interactive Workbook CD-ROM, Level 1 Presentation Plus! CD-ROM
Section 2 **The Etruscans** Describe what daily life was like for the Etruscans and identify their religious beliefs.	Reproducible Lesson Plan Reading Essentials and Study Guide 13-2 Chapter 13 Cooperative Learning Activity Chapter 13 Geography and Map Activity Section 2 Quiz	Teaching Transparencies and Activities 13A & 13B Vocabulary PuzzleMaker CD-ROM Interactive Tutor Self-Assessment CD-ROM ExamView® Pro Testmaker CD-ROM Glencoe Skillbuilder Interactive Workbook CD-ROM, Level 1
Section 3 **Etruscans and Romans** Identify how the Etruscans contributed to Roman civilization.	Reproducible Lesson Plan Reading Essentials and Study Guide 13-3 Chapter 13 Chart and Graph Skill Activity Section 3 Quiz	Vocabulary PuzzleMaker CD-ROM Interactive Tutor Self-Assessment CD-ROM ExamView® Pro Testmaker CD-ROM Glencoe Skillbuilder Interactive Workbook CD-ROM, Level 1
Chapter 13 **Review and Evaluation**	Chapter 13 Reteaching Activity Chapter 13 Performance Assessment Activity Spanish Chapter Summary and Glossary Chapter 13 Test	Vocabulary PuzzleMaker CD-ROM Interactive Tutor Self-Assessment CD-ROM Glencoe Skillbuilder Interactive Workbook CD-ROM, Level 1 Audiocassettes* ExamView® Pro Testmaker CD-ROM

*Also available in Spanish.

Performance Assessment Activities

Legends Have students create legends about the founding of their community. Students might use the name of their community, its geographic location, or its main economic activity as inspiration.

CHAPTER RESOURCES

LITERATURE ABOUT THE PERIOD

Virgil. *Aeneid.* Translated by John Dryden. Heritage, 1944. The national epic of Rome.

READINGS FOR THE STUDENT

Hamblin, Dora Jane. *The Etruscans* (Emergence of Man series). Time-Life Books, 1975. History of Etruscan people.

READINGS FOR THE TEACHER

Editors of Time-Life Books. *Lost Civilizations: Etruscans—Italy's Lovers of Life.* Time-Life Books, 1995. Provides a close-up look at a little-known people.

Sprenger, Maja and Gilda Bartolini. *The Etruscans: Their History, Art, and Architecture.* Abrams, 1983. Analyzes the history of the Etruscans through their art and architecture.

KEY TO ABILITY LEVELS

Teaching strategies have been coded for varying learning styles and abilities.

L1 Level 1 activities are **basic** activities and should be within the ability range of all students.

L2 Level 2 activities are **average** activities and should be within the ability range of the average to above-average student.

L3 Level 3 activities are **challenging** activities designed for the ability range of above-average students.

ELL ELL activities should be within the ability range of English Language Learning students.

NATIONAL GEOGRAPHIC Teacher's Corner

INDEX TO NATIONAL GEOGRAPHIC MAGAZINE

The following articles relate to this chapter:

- "Roman Legacy," by T.R. Reid, August 1997.
- "Roman Empire," by T.R. Reid, July 1997.

NATIONAL GEOGRAPHIC SOCIETY PRODUCTS AVAILABLE FROM GLENCOE

To order the following, call Glencoe at 1-800-334-7344:

- *PicturePack: Physical Geography of the World (Transparencies)*
- *PicturePack: Ancient Rome (Transparencies)*
- *PictureShow: Ancient Civilizations: Greece and Rome (CD-ROM)*
- *Ancient Civilizations: Ancient Rome (Poster Set)*

ADDITIONAL NATIONAL GEOGRAPHIC SOCIETY PRODUCTS

To order the following, call National Geographic at 1-800-368-2728:

- *National Geographic Atlas of World History (Book)*
- *Wonders of the Ancient World: National Geographic Atlas of Archaeology (Book)*
- *Romans (Map)*

Access *National Geographic*'s new dynamic MapMachine Web site and other geography resources at:
www.nationalgeographic.com
www.nationalgeographic.com/maps

THE HISTORY CHANNEL. A&E HOME VIDEO. Biography

The following videotape program is available from Glencoe:

- **Hidden City of the Etruscans**
  1-56501-972-5

To order, call Glencoe at 1-800-334-7344. To find classroom resources to accompany this video, check the following home pages:

A&E Television: www.aande.com
The History Channel: www.historychannel.com

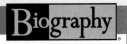

OVERVIEW

Chapter 13 describes the beginnings of civilization in Italy.

- **Section 1** describes the founding of Rome.
- **Section 2** discusses the rise of the Etruscans, their daily life, and their religious beliefs.
- **Section 3** summarizes the contributions the Etruscans made to Roman civilization.

CHAPTER OBJECTIVES

After reading Chapter 13, students will be able to:

1. explain how Rome was founded.
2. describe what daily life was like for the Etruscans.
3. identify the religious beliefs held by the Etruscans.
4. cite Etruscan contributions to Roman civilization.

EXAMINING ARTIFACTS

Refer students to the artifacts, and challenge them to brainstorm a list of skills that the Etruscans may have possessed. *(painting, dancing, pottery-making, use of an alphabet)* Encourage students to add to this list as they read the chapter.

PERFORMANCE ASSESSMENT ✓

Use the Performance Assessment Activities on page 208B to help you evaluate students as they complete the chapter.

CHAPTER 13

Beginnings

1000 B.C.–500 B.C.

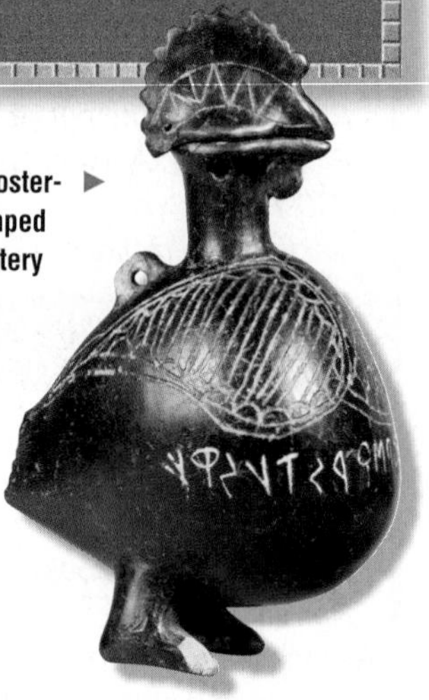

Rooster-shaped pottery

Painting of an Etruscan woman

1000 B.C.	800 B.C.	616 B.C.	600 B.C.
Latins settle on Palatine Hill	Rome is founded	Etruscans conquer Rome	Etruscans dominate all of northern Italy

TEACHING RESOURCES

TEACHER PLANNING AND SUPPORT

- Reproducible Lesson Plan 13-1, 13-2, 13-3
- Teaching Strategies for the World History Classroom (Including Block Scheduling Pacing Guides)
- Presentation Plus! CD-ROM

REVIEW AND REINFORCEMENT

- Reading Essentials and Study Guide 13-1,13-2, 13-3
- Chapter 13 Vocabulary and Guided Reading Activity
- Vocabulary PuzzleMaker CD-ROM
- Teaching Transparencies 13A & 13B
- Chapter 13 Reteaching Activity
- Chapter 13 Cooperative Learning Activity
- Chapter 13 Activity Book Activity
- Chapter 13 Chart and Graph Skill Activity
- Reading and Study Skills Foldables
- Interactive Tutor Self-Assessment CD-ROM
- Unit 5 MindJogger VideoQuiz

APPLICATION AND HANDS-ON ACTIVITIES

- Daily Questions in Social Studies
- Unit 5 Hands-On History Lab Activity
- Student Presentation Builder CD-ROM

Chapter Focus

Read to Discover

- How Rome was founded.
- What daily life was like for the Etruscans.
- What religious beliefs were held by the Etruscans.
- How Etruscans contributed to Roman civilization.

HISTORY Online

Chapter Overview

Visit the *Human Heritage* Web site at **humanheritage.glencoe.com** and click on ***Chapter 13—Chapter Overviews*** to preview this chapter.

Terms to Learn	People to Know	Places to Locate
soothsayers	Aeneas	Rome
omens	Romulus	Palatine
catacombs	Remus	Etruria
Forum		Lydia
fasces		
mundus		

Why It's Important Italy extends south from Europe into the Mediterranean Sea. On the west coast is the mouth of the Tiber (ti´ buhr) River. Fifteen miles upstream is a group of seven hills. On the hill known as the Palatine (pal´ uh tīn), an early people founded a settlement later known as Rome. This settlement would become the center of a great empire, whose achievements still influence life today.

SECTION 1 Founding of Rome

Romans have a legend about the founding of their city. After the fall of Troy, the gods ordered a Trojan prince called Aeneas (uh nē´ uhs) to lead his people to a promised land in the West. When Aeneas's group reached Italy, they joined forces with a people known as Latins (lat´ nz).

About 800 B.C., a Latin princess gave birth to twin sons fathered by the god Mars. The princess had taken an oath never to have children. Because she broke her word, she was punished. Her sons, Romulus (rom´ ū luhs) and Remus (rē´ muhs), were taken from her and left to die on the bank of the flooding Tiber.

Romulus and Remus were found by a she-wolf, which fed and cared for them. One day a shepherd killed the she-wolf and discovered the babies. He took them to his home.

When the boys grew older, they decided to build a city on the Tiber. They decided to let the gods choose which brother should rule the city.

HISTORY Online

Chapter Overview introduces students to chapter content and key terms. Have them access ***Chapter 13 Overview*** at **humanheritage.glencoe.com**

FOCUS

Bellringer

Have students complete the following statement: *People made up legends to ________.*

Motivational Activity

Call on students to read their completed statements. *(Students' statements should include that legends often were created to explain mysterious or unknown happenings.)* Tell students that in this chapter they will learn about a legend that explains the founding of Rome.

GUIDE TO READING

Reading Strategy

Ask students to read "Why It's Important" and summarize the chapter's main theme. *(The Latin settlement of Rome would one day become the center of an empire that still influences life today.)*

Vocabulary Precheck

Ask students to define each of the "Terms to Learn." Have a volunteer consult the dictionary for any unfamiliar words. L1 ELL

Use the Vocabulary PuzzleMaker CD-ROM for Chapter 13 to create a crossword puzzle. L1

Assign Chapter 13 Vocabulary and Guided Reading Activity.

Assign Reading Essentials and Study Guide 13-1.

GEOGRAPHY ACTIVITIES

- Chapter 13 Geography and Map Activity
- Outline Map Resource Book

INTERDISCIPLINARY CONNECTIONS

- World Music: A Cultural Legacy

ENRICHMENT AND EXTENSION

- World History Primary Source Document Library CD-ROM
- Chapter 13 Enrichment Activity
- Foods Around the World

ASSESSMENT AND EVALUATION

- Chapter 13 Performance Assessment Activity
- Chapter 13 Section Quizzes 13-1, 13-2, 13-3
- Chapter 13 Test
- Chapter 13 ExamView® Pro Testmaker CD-ROM
- Chapter 13 Digests Audiocassettes Activities and Tests

SPANISH RESOURCES

- Chapter 13 Spanish Chapter Summary and Glossary
- Chapter 13 Spanish Digests Audiocassettes Activities and Tests

TEACH

Guided Practice

L2 **Language Arts** Have students work in small groups to write a script for the legend about the founding of Rome. Encourage them to include a list of characters and a setting description. Have groups present their scripts to the class.

L1 **Geography: The World in Spatial Terms** Have a student locate Italy on a wall map. Note its location in relation to the Mediterranean world. Discuss why Italy was a good place for an important civilization to develop. *(The country's central location helped the Romans assert their control over the Mediterranean world.)* ELL

LINKING PAST TO PRESENT

Scholars are still trying to translate the inscriptions found in Etruscan tombs and temple ruins.

Use **Interactive Tutor Self-Assessment CD-ROM** to review Section 1.

NATIONAL GEOGRAPHIC

Use these materials to enrich student understanding of ancient Rome.

ANCIENT CIVILIZATIONS POSTER SET
Ancient Rome

Use the **Vocabulary PuzzleMaker CD-ROM** to create crossword and word search puzzles.

Each brother climbed to the top of a different hill to watch for a sign from the gods. Then 12 vultures flew over the Palatine. Since Romulus stood atop the Palatine, he claimed to be king. He and Remus then fought, and Remus was killed. Romulus became king of the city, which he named Rome.

Experts have learned that about 1000 B.C, groups of people with iron weapons began invading the lands around the Mediterranean. One group invaded Egypt and brought down the New Kingdom. Another group moved into the Balkan Peninsula. A third group, the Latins, settled on the Palatine. Romans belonged to this group.

The area where the Latins settled had a pleasant climate and fertile soil. Nearby were dense forests that supplied the Latins with timber. They built gravel roads to bring salt and other items from the coast.

By 776 B.C., the settlement on the Palatine had become a village of about 1,000 people. Most of the people were farmers who lived in wooden huts and worked the land. Their main crops were wheat and barley.

Section 1 Assessment

1. According to legend, how was Rome founded?
2. What natural resources existed in the area settled by the Latins?
3. How did the Latins live?

Critical Thinking

4. **Evaluating Information** How true do you think the legend of Rome's founding is? Explain your answer.

Graphic Organizer Activity

5. Draw a diagram like this one, and use it to show the main events in the legend of Romulus and Remus. (Add more boxes, if necessary.)

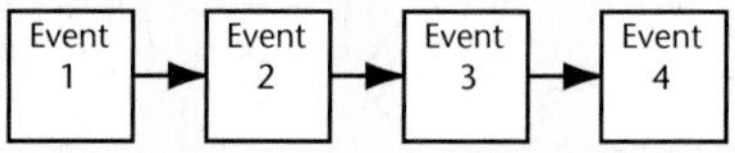

SECTION 2 The Etruscans

Etruscan Jewelry

Around 800 B.C., a people called Etruscans (ē truhs' kuhnz) settled in Etruria (ē trur' ē uh), the rolling hill country north of the Latin village on the Palatine. The Etruscans wrote in an alphabet borrowed from the Greeks. They spoke a language different from any other in the ancient world. Many historians believe they came from the kingdom of Lydia in Asia Minor.

The Etruscans dug tunnels and built dams to drain their marshy fields. High on hilltops, they built a number of cities, each surrounded by a thick wall.

The Etruscans were Italy's first highly civilized people. They were known as "the people of the sea." As pirates, they were

Section 1 Assessment Answers

1. About 800 B.C., a Latin princess gave birth to twin sons fathered by a god. As punishment, her sons, Romulus and Remus, were taken from her and raised by a she-wolf and then a shepherd and his wife. Later the brothers built a city on the Tiber and let the gods choose the city's ruler. The two fought, Remus was killed, and Romulus became king of Rome.
2. pleasant climate, fertile soil, dense forests, salt and fish carried from the coast
3. Most were farmers who lived in wooden huts.
4. Answers will vary. Students should give reasons why they think the legend does or does not have some validity.
5. Events should follow the chronological order in the story. You might expand on this activity by having students turn their graphic organizers into storyboards.

Assign Chapter 13 **Section 1 Quiz** in the TCR. Testmaker available.

Reading A Political Map

In all parts of the world, people have created governments in order to live together. Maps that show areas ruled by particular governments are called **political maps.** Most people use political maps to find cities and countries.

Political maps use symbols to show the location of capitals and other cities. A star is usually used to show the capital of a country or state, and a dot is used to show other cities. Boundary lines mark where a country or state begins and ends. Boundaries may be shown by solid, dashed, or dotted lines. Colors often show the size and shape of countries and states. All these symbols, lines, and colors are not really on Earth's surface, but what they show exists.

On the map of "Early Italy" below, the three colors show the particular areas ruled by three peoples.

Map Practice

1. **Who controlled the southernmost part of Italy?**
2. **What two cities are shown?**
3. **What people controlled the smallest area?**

Early Italy

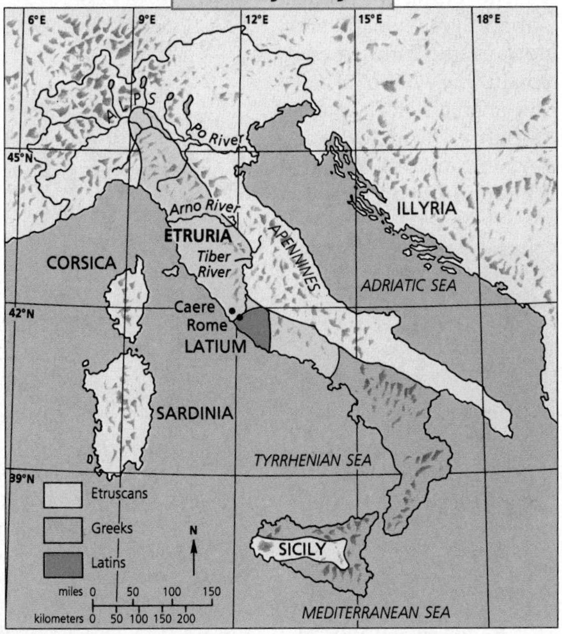

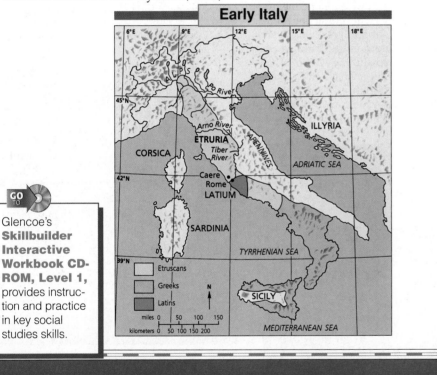

GO TO

Glencoe's **Skillbuilder Interactive Workbook CD-ROM, Level 1,** provides instruction and practice in key social studies skills.

MAP SKILLS

TEACH

Reading a Political Map

Have students read the introductory section of the skill on page 211. Ask students what they think most people use political maps for. *(to find cities and countries)* What are three ways boundaries may be shown on maps? *(by solid, dashed, or dotted lines)* What are often used on political maps to show the size and shape of countries and states? *(colors)* Direct students' attention to the map on the skill page. Ask them what is used to show boundary lines on this map of early Italy. *(solid lines)* What people controlled the Arno River? *(Etruscans)* What city was ruled by the Etruscans? *(Caere)*

Answers to Map Practice

1. Greeks
2. Caere and Rome
3. Latins

GEOGRAPHY AND HISTORY

Why do you think the Etruscans became "the people of the sea?" *(Their extensive coastline would have encouraged the people to become dependent on the sea for their livelihood.)*

Assign Chapter 13 **Geography and Map Activity** in the TCR.

SPOTLIGHT ON: EARLY ITALY

The Tiber River was a dominant influence on Etruria. Some historians believe this 252-mile (405 km) river was known originally as Albulla—referring to the whiteness of its waters—and was later changed to the name Tiber for Tiberius, a king of Alba Lunga (an area south of Rome) who drowned in it.

HISTORY Online

Student Web Activity objectives and answers can be found at the ***Chapter 13 Web Activity Lesson Plan*** at humanheritage.glencoe.com

Linking Across Time

Buildings might include one-story homes with central courtyards, temples, and so on. (Students might also name some of the public buildings in the Forum, described on page 215.)

L3 **Critical Thinking** Point out that most civilizations borrow from other culture groups. For example, the Etruscans borrowed the Greek alphabet and some Greek gods. Have students brainstorm a list of some things American culture has borrowed from other cultures. *(examples: words from Latin, French, Greek, or Spanish; foods from Italy, China, or Mexico; holiday traditions such as the Christmas tree from Germany)*

HISTORY Online

Student Web Activity

Visit the *Human Heritage* Web site at **humanheritage.glencoe.com** and click on ***Chapter 13—Student Web Activities*** to find out more about the historical roots of Rome.

feared and envied throughout the Mediterranean. As traders, they were admired and respected.

Etruscan farmers used mostly iron tools to grow barley, millet, wheat, grapes, and other fruits. They raised pigs, goats, sheep, ducks, chickens, and cattle. The farmers used cattle for food and to pull plows and wagons.

Etruscan miners dug copper, lead, iron, and tin. Etruscan metalworkers and sculptors turned these metals into weapons, utensils, and jewelry. Etruscan merchants exchanged both metals and finished goods for luxury items of gold, silver, and ivory from Syria, Greece, and other eastern Mediterranean countries.

The Etruscans had a strong army. The soldiers learned much about weapons and battle techniques from the Greeks. Their infantry formed a phalanx much like the one used by the Greeks. However, the Etruscans had one "weapon" no one else

Linking Across Time

Arches Etruscan engineers were among the first to use arches widely in their architecture. The semicircular stone arches could support great weight and allowed them to build gateways into fortified cities (below). Today the arch remains the symbol of a gateway, as illustrated by the stainless steel Gateway Arch in St. Louis, Missouri (right). The arch acts as a symbol of the door to the American West. **What types of buildings might be found in an Etruscan city?**

212

COOPERATIVE LEARNING

The Romans borrowed extensively from other cultures. Provide students with a wall-sized sheet of paper on which to show a composite of what Romans borrowed with a graphic organizer of their own design. Assign students to small groups. Have each group research one major topic and then complete one portion of the wall diagram. *(Romans adapted Etruscan rituals, Etruscan and Greek gods, Greek styles of architecture and sculpture, Greek medicine and science, and Egyptian astronomy.)* Each group should divide among its members the tasks of researching, obtaining pictures, drawing illustrations, and writing captions.

Assign Chapter 13 *Cooperative Learning Activity* in the TCR.

CHAPTER 13 Assessment

Using Key Terms

Imagine you are an archaeologist studying the ruins of an Etruscan city for the first time. Use the following words to write a letter describing some of the exciting things that you have discovered.

social order	soothsayers	omens
catacombs	necropolis	Forum
gladiatorial games	triumph	fasces
municipal	mundus	

Understanding Main Ideas

1. What part of Italy did the Etruscans dominate?
2. How did the kind of shoes the Etruscans wore help them in battle?
3. What group of people owned most of the land in Etruria?
4. Why did the Etruscans build their temples to face east?
5. How have experts learned much of what they know about Etruscan life?
6. Who was the first Etruscan ruler of Rome?
7. What customs did the Romans borrow from the Etruscans?
8. What religious beliefs did the Etruscans intoduce to the Romans?

Critical Thinking

1. Compare the role of women in Etruria with their role in Greek civilization.
2. What role did religion play in Etruscan life? How did Etruscan religious ideas differ from those of the Greeks?
3. What would you have enjoyed the most about living in Etruria? Explain.
4. Was the Etruscan conquest of Rome good for the Romans? Explain.

Graphic Organizer Activity

Culture Draw a diagram like the one shown, and use it to compare the role of women in Etruria with the role of women in most Greek city-states.

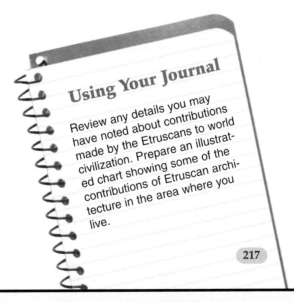

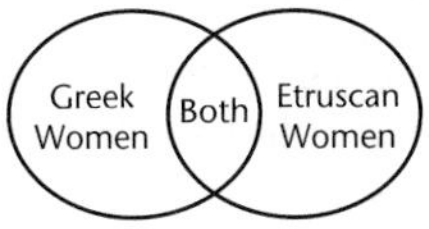

Geography in History

The World in Spatial Terms Look at the map on page 211. If the people of Etruria were attacked by another empire, from what direction and by what means would the attack come? What geographic feature might protect Etruria? Draw a map showing the most likely routes of a possible attack.

Using Your Journal

Review any details you may have noted about contributions made by the Etruscans to world civilization. Prepare an illustrated chart showing some of the contributions of Etruscan architecture in the area where you live.

Bonus Test Question

For Chapter 13 Test

You are a stranger leaving an Etruscan city with one of its citizens. Outside the city, the citizen tells you that you are looking at a *necropolis*. Describe what you see. *(rows of mounds of earth piled above tombs, wide streets that open into plazas)*

Using Your Journal

Charts will vary, but students might include the arch, bridges, sewer systems, and the public square.

Geography in History

Answers will vary but should include attacks coming from the sea, down rivers, or overland from north or south. Protection came from two mountain ranges.

CHAPTER 13 Assessment Answers

Using Key Terms

Letters will vary but should include all the key terms.

Understanding Main Ideas

1. Etruria and eventually all of northern Italy, including the Latin village on the Palatine
2. They gave them better footing on rough or hilly ground.
3. a few wealthy families
4. because the Etruscans believed the east and the left were lucky
5. from Etruscan tombs
6. Lucius Tarquinius
7. gladiatorial games, the triumph, and the fasces
8. soothsayers and gods with human forms

Critical Thinking

1. Etruscan women danced, took part in public celebrations, and could own property. Greek women could not attend the Olympic Games or go out without a chaperone.
2. Religion influenced Etruscan building of temples and cities, and ceremonies, songs, and dances. The Greeks were not afraid of their gods, as Etruscans were.
3. Answers will vary but students should provide reasons for their conclusions.
4. Answers will vary but Etruscans made contributions to many Roman achievements.

Graphic Organizer Activity

Answers will vary, but comparisons should reveal that Etruscan women had greater personal freedom than Greek women. As a variation, you might assign students to compare women in specific city-states (such as Sparta or Athens) with Etruscan women.

Chapter 14 Planning Guide

Timesaving Tools

TeacherWorks™ All-In-One Planner and Resource Center

- **Interactive Teacher Edition** Access your Teacher Wraparound Edition and your classroom resources with a few easy clicks.
- **Interactive Lesson Planner** Planning has never been easier! Organize your week, month, semester, or year with all the lesson helps you need to make teaching creative, timely, and relevant.

Use Glencoe's **Presentation Plus!** multimedia teacher tool to easily present dynamic lessons that visually excite your students. Using Microsoft PowerPoint® you can customize the presentations to create your own personalized lessons.

Objectives	Reproducible Resources	Multimedia Resources
Section 1 The Government Describe how the government of the Roman Republic was formed.	Reproducible Lesson Plan Chapter 14 Vocabulary and Guided Reading Activity Reading Essentials and Study Guide 14-1 Chapter 14 Chart and Graph Skill Activity Chapter 14 Enrichment Activity Section 1 Quiz	Interactive Student Edition CD-ROM Graphic Organizer Transparency 11 Vocabulary PuzzleMaker CD-ROM Interactive Tutor Self-Assessment CD-ROM ExamView® Pro Testmaker CD-ROM Glencoe Skillbuilder Interactive Workbook CD-ROM, Level 1 Presentation Plus! CD-ROM
Section 2 Roman Expansion Explain how the Roman Republic was able to expand and protect its territory.	Reproducible Lesson Plan Reading Essentials and Study Guide 14-2 Chapter 14 Cooperative Learning Activity Chapter 14 Geography and Map Activity Section 2 Quiz	Vocabulary PuzzleMaker CD-ROM Interactive Tutor Self-Assessment CD-ROM ExamView® Pro Testmaker CD-ROM Glencoe Skillbuilder Interactive Workbook CD-ROM, Level 1
Section 3 The Punic Wars Describe the Punic Wars and their effect on the Roman Republic.	Reproducible Lesson Plan Reading Essentials and Study Guide 14-3 Section 3 Quiz	Vocabulary PuzzleMaker CD-ROM Interactive Tutor Self-Assessment CD-ROM ExamView® Pro Testmaker CD-ROM Glencoe Skillbuilder Interactive Workbook CD-ROM, Level 1
Section 4 Effects of Conquest Discuss how the effects of conquest changed the Roman economy and government.	Reproducible Lesson Plan Reading Essentials and Study Guide 14-4 Section 4 Quiz	Vocabulary PuzzleMaker CD-ROM Interactive Tutor Self-Assessment CD-ROM ExamView® Pro Testmaker CD-ROM Glencoe Skillbuilder Interactive Workbook CD-ROM, Level 1
Section 5 Roman Leadership Analyze how reformers and generals attempted to save the Roman Republic.	Reproducible Lesson Plan Reading Essentials and Study Guide 14-5 Unit 5 Primary Source Readings Section 5 Quiz	Teaching Transparencies and Activities 14A & 14B Vocabulary PuzzleMaker CD-ROM ExamView® Pro Testmaker CD-ROM Glencoe Skillbuilder Interactive Workbook CD-ROM, Level 1
Chapter 14 Review and Evaluation	Chapter 14 Reteaching Activity Chapter 14 Performance Assessment Activity Spanish Chapter Summary and Glossary Chapter 14 Test	Vocabulary PuzzleMaker CD-ROM Interactive Tutor Self-Assessment CD-ROM Glencoe Skillbuilder Interactive Workbook CD-ROM, Level 1 Audiocassettes* ExamView® Pro Testmaker CD-ROM

*Also available in Spanish.

Performance Assessment Activities

The Arts Have students prepare a visual "tour" of modern Rome and the remnants of the ancient Roman civilization. They should present illustrations, diagrams, and pictures while providing information as "tour guides."

CHAPTER RESOURCES

READINGS FOR THE STUDENT

Burrell, Roy. *The Romans: Rebuilding the Past*. Oxford University Press, 1991. Historical outline of ancient Rome.

Tingay, Graham. *Julius Caesar*. Cambridge University Press, 1991. Account of the life and achievements of Julius Caesar.

Windrow, Martin. *The Roman Legionary*. Franklin Watts, 1984. Historical background and detailed information on the Roman soldier's training and duties, weapons, armor, equipment, and daily life.

READINGS FOR THE TEACHER

Asimov, Isaac. *The Roman Republic*. Houghton Mifflin, 1966. Focuses on Rome's rise to power from the founding of the city.

THE HISTORY CHANNEL. A&E HOME VIDEO. Biography

The following videotape programs are available from Glencoe to enrich Chapter 14:

- **Ancient Rome**
  0-7670-1263-1
- **Julius Caesar: Master of the Romans**
  0-7670-0572-4
- **The Lost Legions of Rome**
  1-56501-952-0

To order, call Glencoe at 1-800-334-7344. To find classroom resources to accompany many of these videos, check the following home pages:

A&E Television: www.aande.com
The History Channel: www.historychannel.com

NATIONAL GEOGRAPHIC Teacher's Corner

INDEX TO NATIONAL GEOGRAPHIC MAGAZINE

The following articles relate to this chapter:

- "Roman Shipwrecks," by Robert D. Ballard, April 1998.
- "Roman Legacy," by T.R. Reid, August 1997.
- "Roman Empire," by T.R. Reid, July 1997.
- "Brindisi Bronzes," by O. Louis Mazzatenta, April 1995.

NATIONAL GEOGRAPHIC SOCIETY PRODUCTS AVAILABLE FROM GLENCOE

To order the following, call Glencoe at 1-800-334-7344:

- *PicturePack: Ancient Rome (Transparencies)*
- *PictureShow: Ancient Civilizations: Greece and Rome (CD-ROM)*
- *Ancient Civilizations: Ancient Rome (Poster Set)*
- *PicturePack: Ancient Civilizations Library, Part I (Transparencies)*

ADDITIONAL NATIONAL GEOGRAPHIC SOCIETY PRODUCTS

To order the following, call National Geographic at 1-800-368-2728:

- *In the Shadow of Vesuvius (Video or Videodisc)*
- *Romans (Map)*

Access *National Geographic's* new dynamic MapMachine Web site and other geography resources at:
www.nationalgeographic.com
www.nationalgeographic.com/maps

KEY TO ABILITY LEVELS

Teaching strategies have been coded for varying learning styles and abilities.

L1 Level 1 activities are **basic** activities and should be within the ability range of all students.

L2 Level 2 activities are **average** activities and should be within the ability range of the average to above-average student.

L3 Level 3 activities are **challenging** activities designed for the ability range of above-average students.

ELL ELL activities should be within the ability range of English Language Learning students.

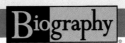

OVERVIEW

Chapter 14 traces Rome's development as a republic.

- **Section 1** summarizes the rise of Roman democracy.
- **Section 2** describes the army's role in the Roman Republic.
- **Section 3** discusses Rome's rise to power in the Mediterranean region.
- **Section 4** analyzes the effects of foreign conquests.
- **Section 5** examines the attempts to solve the Republic's problems.

CHAPTER OBJECTIVES

After reading Chapter 14, students will be able to:

1. describe how the Roman government was organized.
2. explain how the Roman Republic was able to expand.
3. summarize how the effects of conquest changed the Roman economy and government.
4. discuss efforts to save the Roman Republic.

EXAMINING ARTIFACTS

Have students study the artifacts. Then ask: What do you think was one of the reasons the Roman Republic grew so strong? *(the power and/or loyalty of legionaries)* Call on students to describe what the eagle symbolizes to them. Tell them to think about whether this was an accurate symbol for the Roman Republic as they read through the chapter.

PERFORMANCE ASSESSMENT

Use the Performance Assessment Activities on page 218B to help you evaluate students as they complete the chapter.

CHAPTER 14

The Roman Republic

509 B.C.–30 B.C.

▲ The Roman eagle on an onyx cameo

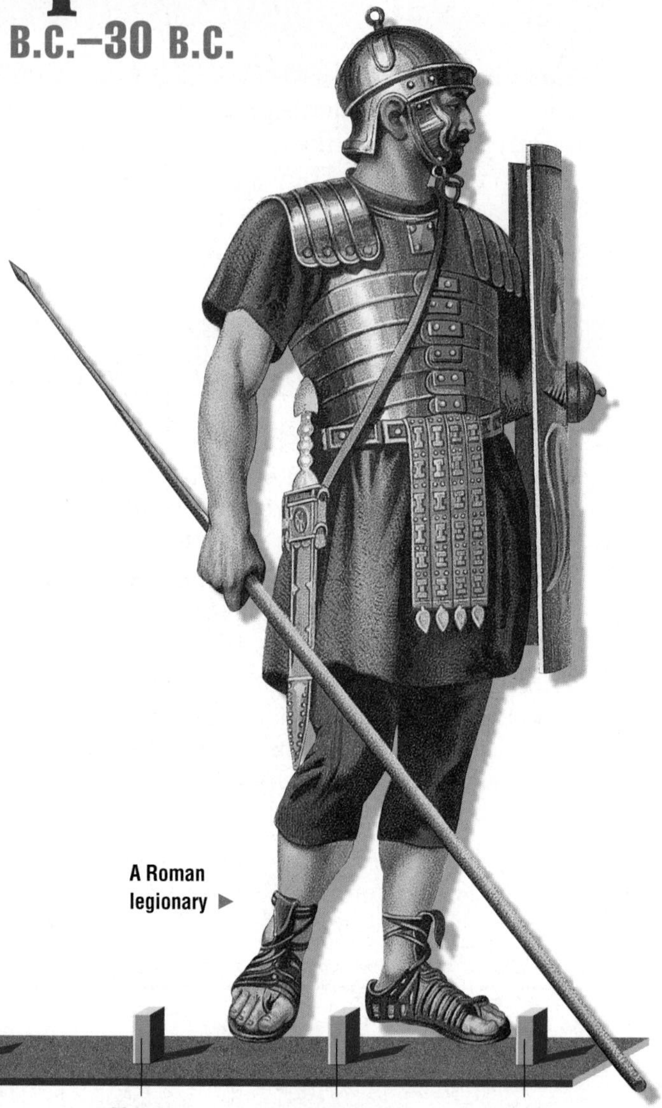

A Roman legionary ▶

- **509 B.C.** Romans set up republic
- **450 B.C.** Twelve Tables are written
- **264 B.C.** Punic Wars begin
- **46 B.C.** Julius Caesar appointed dictator of Rome
- **31 B.C.** Octavian becomes sole ruler of Roman Empire

TEACHING RESOURCES

TEACHER PLANNING AND SUPPORT

- Reproducible Lesson Plan 14-1, 14-2, 14-3, 14-4, 14-5
- Teaching Strategies for the World History Classroom (Including Block Scheduling Pacing Guides)
- Presentation Plus! CD-ROM

REVIEW AND REINFORCEMENT

- Reading Essentials and Study Guide 14-1, 14-2, 14-3, 14-4, 14-5
- Chapter 14 Vocabulary and Guided Reading Activity
- Vocabulary PuzzleMaker CD-ROM
- Teaching Transparencies 14A & 14B
- Chapter 14 Reteaching Activity
- Chapter 14 Cooperative Learning Activity
- Chapter 14 Activity Book Activity
- Chapter 14 Chart and Graph Skill Activity
- Reading and Study Skills Foldables
- Interactive Tutor Self-Assessment CD-ROM

APPLICATION AND HANDS-ON ACTIVITIES

- Daily Questions in Social Studies
- Unit 5 Hands-On History Lab Activity
- Student Presentation Builder CD-ROM

Chapter Focus

Read to Discover

- How the government of the Roman Republic was organized.
- How the Roman Republic was able to expand its territory.
- How the effects of conquest changed the Roman economy and government.
- How reformers attempted to save the Roman Republic.

HISTORY Online

Chapter Overview
Visit the *Human Heritage* Web site at **humanheritage.glencoe.com** and click on ***Chapter 14—Chapter Overviews*** to preview this chapter.

Terms to Learn	People to Know	Places to Locate
republic	Tarquin the Proud	Carthage
patricians	Hannibal Barca	Sicily
plebeians	Tiberius Gracchus	Gaul
consuls	Julius Caesar	Corinth
legionaries	Mark Antony	
dictator	Octavian	
triumvirate		

Why It's Important In 509 B.C., the Romans overthrew Tarquin (tar' kwin) the Proud, their Etruscan king, and set up a **republic.** Under this form of government, people choose their rulers. However, not everyone had an equal say in the Roman Republic. The **patricians** (puh trish' uhnz)—members of the oldest and richest families—were the only ones who could hold public office or perform certain religious rituals. Poorer citizens, known as **plebeians** (pli bē' uhnz), paid taxes and served in the army. Yet they could not marry patricians or hold office. If they fell into debt, they could be sold into slavery.

In later years, reformers would take steps to make the Roman Republic more democratic. The idea of a government chosen by the people would serve as a model for future generations, including the founders of the United States.

Reading Check What is a **republic?** Who were the **patricians** and the **plebeians?**

SECTION 1 The Government

At the head of the Roman Republic were two **consuls** (kon' suhlz) who were chosen each year. They were administrators and military leaders. Each had the power to **veto,** or say no to, the acts of the other. Both had to agree before any law was passed.

Next in importance was the Senate. It was made up of 300 men called senators who were chosen for life. The Senate handled the daily problems of government. It advised the consuls.

Reading Check How long did the **consuls** hold power? How did the **veto** prevent a consul from becoming too powerful?

HISTORY Online

Chapter Overview introduces students to chapter content and key terms. Have them access ***Chapter 14 Overview*** at humanheritage.glencoe.com

FOCUS

Bellringer

Ask students to write what first comes to their minds when they hear this phrase: *fields upon fields of Roman legions.*

Motivational Activity

Ask: What are the implications of keeping a standing army? *(Students may mention the need for defense or the use of armies for conquest.)*

GUIDE TO READING

Reading Strategy

Ask students to read "Why It's Important" and summarize the chapter's main theme. *(Efforts to make the Roman Republic more democratic became the model for future generations.)*

Vocabulary Precheck

Ask students to define each of the "Terms to Learn." L1 ELL

Use the Vocabulary PuzzleMaker CD-ROM for Chapter 14. L1

Assign Chapter 14 Vocabulary and Guided Reading Activity.

Assign Reading Essentials and Study Guide 14-1.

Reading Check Answer
In a **republic,** people choose their rulers. **Patricians** were members of the oldest and richest families and **plebeians** were poorer citizens.

Reading Check Answer
The **consuls** held power for one year. The **veto** allowed one consul to negate the other.

GEOGRAPHY ACTIVITIES
- Chapter 14 Geography and Map Activity
- Outline Map Resource Book

INTERDISCIPLINARY CONNECTIONS
- World Music: A Cultural Legacy

ENRICHMENT AND EXTENSION
- World History Primary Source Document Library CD-ROM
- Chapter 14 Enrichment Activity
- Foods Around the World

ASSESSMENT AND EVALUATION
- Chapter 14 Performance Assessment Activity
- Chapter 14 Section Quizzes 14-1, 14-2, 14-3, 14-4, 14-5
- Chapter 14 Test
- Chapter 14 ExamView® Pro Testmaker CD-ROM
- Chapter 14 Digests Audiocassettes Activities and Tests

SPANISH RESOURCES
- Chapter 14 Spanish Chapter Summary and Glossary
- Chapter 14 Spanish Digests Audiocassettes Activities and Tests

TEACH

Guided Practice

L3 **Language Arts** Have students imagine they are well-educated plebeians in the early days of the Roman Republic. Have them write letters to the Roman Senate demanding representation and written laws.

Reading Check Answer

Tribunes protected the rights of the plebeians.

Use **Interactive Tutor Self-Assessment CD-ROM** to review Section 1.

CAPTION ANSWER

The Senate handled the daily problems of government. It advised the consuls, discussed ways to deal with other countries, proposed laws, and approved public contracts for building roads and temples.

DID YOU KNOW ??

The consuls were in charge of the state treasury, were judges in all law cases, and were commanders in chief of the army during wars.

MAKING CONNECTIONS

➤➤ **Citizenship** The Twelve Tables outlined how Roman citizens were to act in public. The Roman people considered knowledge of the law so important that Roman students had to learn the laws of the Twelve Tables by heart.

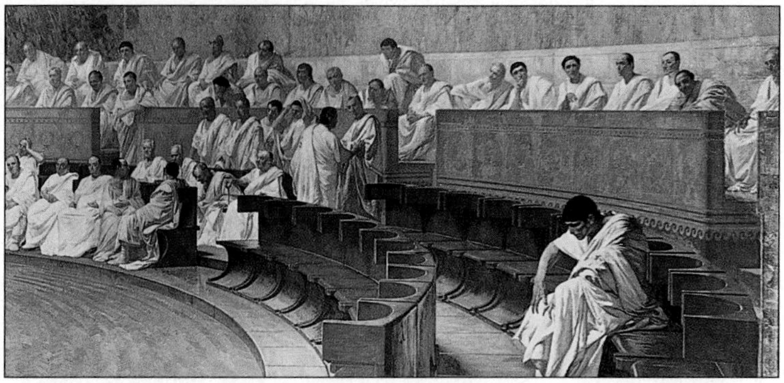

ROMAN SENATE This painting shows the famous orator Cicero making a speech attacking a political opponent. **What duties did the Senate perform in the Roman Republic?**

It discussed ways to deal with other countries, proposed laws, and approved public contracts for building roads and temples.

Reading Check What role did the **tribunes** play in Roman government?

Judges, assemblies, and **tribunes** (trib′ yūnz), or government officials who protected the rights of plebeians, were also part of the Roman government. All Roman citizens belonged to the assemblies, which could declare war or agree to peace terms.

Until about 450 B.C., Roman laws were not written down. In that year, laws were carved on 12 bronze tablets known as the Twelve Tables. These were placed in the Forum. The laws applied to both patricians and plebeians. Most were about wills, property rights, and court actions. The laws on the Twelve Tables became the foundation for all future Roman laws.

The election of tribunes and recording of laws were the first steps to a more democratic government. Later, more plebeian demands were met. By about 250 B.C., no one could be sold into slavery because of debt. Plebeians could hold public office.

Section 1 Assessment

1. **Define:** republic, patricians, plebeians, consuls, veto, tribunes.
2. What were some restrictions placed on the plebeians during the early years of the Roman Republic?

Critical Thinking

3. **Demonstrating Reasoned Judgment** Why do you think it was important for the Romans to have laws written down?

Graphic Organizer Activity

4. Draw this diagram, and use it to describe each part of Roman government.

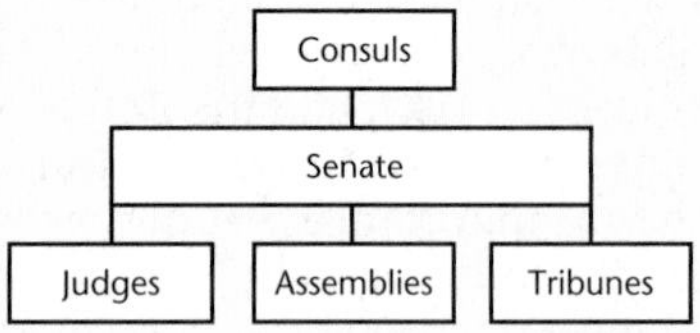

Section 1 Assessment Answers

1. republic, government where people choose their rulers (p. 219); patricians, the oldest and richest Roman families (p. 219); plebeians, poorer people of Rome (p. 219); consuls, heads of the Roman Republic (p. 219); veto, to say no to (p. 219); tribunes, Roman officials elected to protect the lower class (p. 220)
2. They could not marry patricians or serve in the government, and if they got into debt, they could be enslaved.
3. Answers will vary, but students could note that recording laws makes them enforceable.
4. Descriptions should match each of the parts of Roman government discussed in Section 1.

Assign the Chapter 14 **Section 1 Quiz** in the TCR. Testmaker available.

SECTION 2 Roman Expansion

Once the Romans had set up a republic, they worked to protect it. They were afraid that the Etruscans would try to regain control of Rome. To prevent this, the Romans crossed the Tiber River and conquered several Etruscan cities. Roman land now bordered that of other Italian people. To protect their new boundaries, the Romans either conquered their neighbors or made alliances with them. By 290 B.C., Rome was the leading power in central Italy. By 275 B.C., it ruled the whole peninsula. By 146 B.C., Rome ruled most of the Mediterranean world.

The Romans were able to gain territory because they had a strong army that was organized into **legions** (lē′ juhnz). Each legion contained some 5,000 soldiers called **legionaries** (lē′ juh ner ēz) and was divided into groups of 60 to 120 soldiers.

The legion had several advantages over the phalanx. The legion was smaller and could move faster. Soldiers in a phalanx fought as a group and attacked from only one direction. Each legionary depended on his own fighting ability. The groups within a legion could split off from the main body and attack from the sides and the rear as well as the front.

Then & Now

Rank and File The basic unit of the Roman legion was the *maniple*—120 soldiers standing side by side in ranks of 10 and lined up one behind another in files of 12. The term *rank and file,* which refers to the ordinary members of an organization, comes from this military system.

Reading Check How did Roman **legions** differ from the phalanx? How many **legionaries** were in each legion?

Linking Across Time

Citizen-Soldiers During the early years of the Roman republic, all male citizens were required to serve in the army (below). Today military service continues to be an important responsibility of citizenship in democratic nations such as the United States (right). **Why did the use of citizen-soldiers help ensure the loyalty of legionaries to Rome?**

Reading Check Answer Roman **legions** were smaller and could move faster than the phalanx. There were some 5,000 **legionaries** in each legion.

Use the **Vocabulary PuzzleMaker CD-ROM** to create crossword and word search puzzles.

Linking Across Time

Answers will vary, but most students will focus on the desire of citizens to protect both their rights and their homeland.

GEOGRAPHY AND HISTORY

The Romans established military settlements—called *coloniae*—throughout Italy to defend strategic heights over river crossings. To link these *coloniae,* the legions forged a chain of roads up and down the Italian peninsula. As war yielded gradually to peace, some of these roads became major trade routes.

A&E HOME VIDEO.

The following videotape programs are available from Glencoe to enrich Chapter 14:

- **Ancient Rome**
- **The Lost Legions of Rome**

To find classroom resources to accompany these videos, check the following home page:

A&E Television:
www.aande.com

COOPERATIVE LEARNING

Review information on Roman legions in Section 2. Then divide the class into groups, and tell each group of students to imagine that they are army recruiters for the Roman republic. Their job is to enlist citizen-soldiers in the military. Assign them to design recruitment posters that might be hung in the Forum or other public place. You might ask volunteers to call a local recruitment office for one of the military services and request contemporary posters. These can be hung in the classroom as models. When students are done, have them present their posters to the class.

Assign Chapter 14 *Cooperative Learning Activity* in the TCR.

MAKING CONNECTIONS

➤➤ **Language Arts** *Punic* is the Latin word for *Phoenician*. The Punic Wars were so named because Carthage was a colony founded by the Phoenicians.

DID YOU KNOW ??

To frighten their enemies, Roman legionnaires often carried dragon flags—said to have originated in China. Dragon flags were long pieces of cloth that, when attached to a pole and held in the wind, gave the terrifying appearance of a writhing dragon.

Use **Interactive Tutor Self-Assessment CD-ROM** to review Section 2.

Use the **Vocabulary PuzzleMaker CD-ROM** to create crossword and word search puzzles.

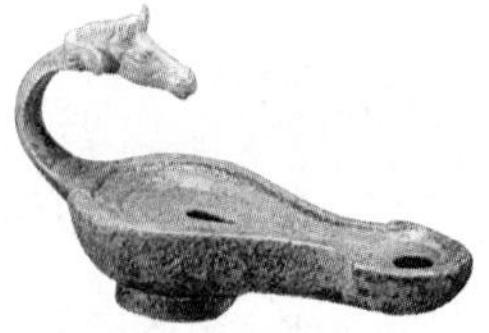

Roman Bronze Lamp

Legionaries were well trained. They spent hours practicing with their double-edged iron swords. They went on long marches every day. Before going to sleep, they had to build complete fortified camps, even when the legion would stay in an area only one night. They built roads out of lava blocks so soldiers and supplies could move forward more rapidly.

The Romans were mild rulers. At first, they did not tax the people they conquered. They let the conquered people keep their own governments and take care of their own affairs. Some were even allowed to become Roman citizens. In return, the conquered people were expected to serve in the Roman army and to support Rome's foreign policy. As a result, many enemies of Rome became loyal Roman allies.

Section 2 Assessment

1. **Define:** legions, legionaries.
2. Why were the Romans able to gain territory?
3. What was life like for a Roman legionary?

Critical Thinking

4. **Drawing Conclusions** How would you describe the way the Romans treated people they conquered, and do you think this was wise? Explain.

Graphic Organizer Activity

5. Draw a chart like this one, and use it to show the cause and effects of Roman conquest of Etruscan cities.

SECTION 3 The Punic Wars

By 264 B.C., the Romans had conquered some Greek city-states in southern Italy. This brought them into contact with the Phoenician city of Carthage. Carthage controlled most of North and West Africa, most of what is now Spain, and some islands off the coast of Italy. Carthage also ruled the western half of Sicily (sis' uh lē), a large island at the toe of the Italian "boot." The Romans felt threatened by the Carthaginians (kar thuh jin' ē uhnz). They also wanted Sicily's granaries.

The First Punic War In 264 B.C., the Romans and Carthaginians clashed. The war that broke out lasted for 23 years. It was the first of three wars between Rome and Carthage that came to be known as the Punic (pyū' nik) Wars.

Carthage's military strength lay in its navy, while Rome's lay in its army. At first, the Romans had no navy. They built

Section 2 Assessment Answers

1. legions, divisions of Roman soldiers (p. 221); legionaries, Roman soldiers (p. 221)
2. because they had a strong army that was organized into legions
3. Student answers should reflect the information in paragraph one at the top of this page.
4. Answers will vary, but students could note that by treating the people mildly Romans gained their loyalty.
5. sample responses: *causes*—wanted to protect the republic, feared Etruscans might try to retake Rome; *effects*—Roman land now bordered that of other Italian peoples, conquered or made alliances with their neighbors, eventually secured control of the whole peninsula

Assign Chapter 14 **Section 2 Quiz** in the TCR. Testmaker available.

their first fleet to fight the Carthaginians. The Romans modeled their ships after a Carthaginian warship they found abandoned on a beach. They made one improvement on the Carthaginian model. They added a *corvus* (kor' vuhs), or a kind of movable bridge, to the front of each ship. The Romans knew they could not outsail the Carthaginians, but believed they could outfight them. The corvus allowed soldiers to board an enemy ship and fight hand-to-hand on its decks. In a sense, it changed a sea war into a land war.

The Romans lost many ships and men in storms during the First Punic War. Yet, in the end, they defeated the Carthaginians. In 241 B.C., the Carthaginians agreed to make peace and left Sicily.

Fun Facts . . .

Carthage Marcus Portius Cato, a prominent statesman and writer, believed that Carthage posed a great threat to Rome. He reportedly ended every speech—no matter what the subject—with "Carthage must be destroyed!"

Hannibal and the Second Punic War In 218 B.C., the Second Punic War began. At that time, the Carthaginians, led by General Hannibal Barca (han' uh buhl bar' ka), attacked the Roman army by land from the north. Hannibal and his troops surprised the Roman army by marching from Spain through southern Gaul (gol), or present-day France, and then crossing the Alps into Italy. They brought elephants with them across the snow-covered mountains to help break through the Roman lines.

Winning victory after victory, Hannibal's army fought its way to the gates of Rome. When the Carthaginian army got to Rome, however, it did not have the heavy equipment needed to

HANNIBAL Hannibal's army, with elephants, faced many dangers in its attack on Rome. The elephants had to be floated on barges across rivers and brought over the snow-capped Alps. **Why did Hannibal's attack on the city of Rome fail?**

HISTORY Online

Student Web Activity

Visit the *Human Heritage* Web site at **humanheritage.glencoe.com** and click on ***Chapter 14—Student Web Activities*** to find out more about the Punic Wars.

L1 Geography: The World in Spatial Terms Suggest students work together to develop a chart on the chalkboard or poster board summarizing the three Punic Wars. For each war, students should include the dates, the areas where the war was fought, the locations of major battles, and the final outcome. ELL

MAKING CONNECTIONS

➤➤ **History** Hannibal's father was a Carthaginian general during the first Punic War. He made Hannibal take an oath to never be friends with the Romans. Hannibal was commander in chief of the Carthaginian army by age 26.

CAPTION ANSWER

because Hannibal's army did not have the heavy equipment needed to break down Rome's walls, and it was short on supplies and soldiers

HISTORY Online

Student Web Activity objectives and answers can be found at the ***Chapter 14 Web Activity Lesson Plan*** at **humanheritage.glencoe.com**

MEETING SPECIAL NEEDS

Have gifted learners debate the following topic: *The wars between Rome and Carthage were worth the short-term and long-term costs for Rome.* Half of the group should defend the statement, the other half should argue against the statement. The rest of the class can act as the audience and decide which side presented the most persuasive arguments.

Refer to ***Inclusion for the Middle School Social Studies Classroom: Strategies and Activities*** for additional resources.

DID YOU KNOW ??

Under the terms of surrender, the Carthaginians also had to destroy all but 10 of their warships and promise not to start war again without Rome's permission.

LINKING PAST TO PRESENT

Speakers of English are often speakers of Latin without knowing it. Everyday terms like "A.M." and "P.M." are short for the Latin *ante meridiem* and *post meridiem*—"before noon" and "after noon." The *Exit* sign over a door is Latin for "he (she, it) goes out." Anyone who has joined an *ad hoc* committee, gone to an *alumni* reunion, figured something *per capita,* or added *P.S. (post scriptum)* to a letter, has used Latin.

Use **Interactive Tutor Self-Assessment CD-ROM** to review Section 3.

MAKING CONNECTIONS

>> **History** One of Rome's opponents, King Pyrrhus of Epirus, won two difficult victories over the Romans in 280 and 279 B.C. He sustained such great losses, however, that he reportedly exclaimed, "Another such victory and we are lost."

Use the **Vocabulary PuzzleMaker CD-ROM** to create crossword and word search puzzles.

Fun Facts. . . .

Hannibal's Strength
Hannibal began crossing the Alps with about 46,000 troops and 37 elephants. He emerged with 26,000 troops and almost no elephants. A Roman general proclaimed: "They are ghosts and shadows of men already half dead. All their strength has been crushed and beaten out of them by the Alpine crags." The general was wrong. The Gauls, who were enemies of the Romans, joined Hannibal and boosted his army to almost 50,000.

batter down the city's walls. It could not get more supplies because the Roman navy controlled the sea.

Unable to capture Rome, Hannibal and his troops roamed the countryside of southern Italy for 15 years. They raided and burned towns and destroyed crops. Then, the Romans attacked Carthage, and Hannibal was called home to defend it. Hannibal lost his first battle—and the war—at the town of Zama (zā' muh). The power of Carthage was broken.

In 201 B.C., Carthage agreed to pay Rome a huge sum of money and to give up all its territories, including Spain. The Spanish resources of copper, gold, lead, and iron now belonged to the Romans.

The Third Punic War Following the Second Punic War, there was peace for about 50 years. Then, Carthage began to show signs of regaining power. To prevent this, the Romans attacked in 149 B.C., the Third Punic War. They burned Carthage and plowed salt into its fields so nothing would grow. They killed the Carthaginians or sold them into slavery.

That same year, 146 B.C., the Greek city-state of Corinth (kor' inth) and some of its allies refused to obey a Roman order. The Romans attacked Corinth and burned it to the ground. Rome already controlled Macedonia and Syria. Now, it added Greece to the areas under its rule. Thus, Rome became the leading power of the Mediterranean world.

Section 3 Assessment

1. What territory did Carthage control in 264 B.C.?
2. What happened to Carthage in the Third Punic War?
3. How did Rome become the leading power of the Mediterranean world?

Critical Thinking

4. **Predicting Consequences** What might have happened to Rome if it had lost the Punic Wars?

Graphic Organizer Activity

5. Draw a chart like this one, and use it to summarize the outcome of each of the Punic Wars.

Punic Wars	Outcome
First	
Second	
Third	

SECTION 4 Effects of Conquest

The conquests and the wealth that came with them changed Rome's economy and government. Among the changes were the replacement of small farms with large estates, the use of enslaved people, a movement from farms to cities, and the decline of the Roman Republic.

Section 3 Assessment Answers

1. all of North Africa, most of Spain, some islands off the coast of Italy, and the western half of Sicily
2. The city was burned, its land was destroyed by plowing salt into the fields, and its people were killed or sold into enslavement.
3. by destroying Corinth and adding Greece to the areas under its rule
4. Answers will vary, but students might indicate that Rome would not have been able to expand its republic or might have been taken over by the Carthaginians.
5. *First*—Rome lost many ships and soldiers, but defeated the Carthaginians and forced them to leave Sicily. *Second*—Carthage agreed to pay Rome a huge sum of money and gave up all its territories, including Spain. *Third*—Rome added Greece to its empire and became the leading power in the Mediterranean world.

Assign Chapter 14 **Section 3 Quiz** in the TCR. Testmaker available.

Agricultural Changes Rome's conquests brought changes in agriculture. One change was in the size and purpose of farms. Most Romans had been small farmers who believed in hard work and service to Rome. Now, the small farms were replaced by large estates called **latifundias** (lat uh fuhn' dē uhs). The small farms had grown wheat for food. Latifundias, on the other hand, produced crops, sheep, and cattle for sale at market. Some contained olive groves and vineyards. Because they no longer grew their own wheat, the Romans began to import wheat from such conquered areas as Sicily and North Africa.

The main reason for this change in Roman agriculture was Hannibal's invasion. While his soldiers were in Italy, they lived off the land. To prevent them from getting food, Roman farmers burned their fields and crops. By the time the Second Punic War was over, much of the land was ruined. Most Roman farmers did not have money to fix up their farms or restore the land. Only patricians and rich business people had that kind of money. They bought the small farms and combined them to make latifundias.

Another change in agriculture was in who worked the land. When Rome first began expanding, the Romans did not enslave the people they conquered. By 146 B.C., that was no longer true. The Romans were impressed by the wealth of Greece, Syria, and Carthage. Since those areas had widespread slavery, the Romans sent thousands of prisoners to Rome as enslaved people. Most lived and worked on latifundias.

From Farm to City The farmers who had sold their land had few choices. They could stay and work the land for the new owners or move to the city. Almost all of them moved to Rome.

There the farmers crowded into wooden apartment buildings six or more stories high. Living conditions were terrible. The aqueducts that brought water to the city were not connected to apartment buildings. Neither were the sewers that carried away waste. Buildings often caught fire or collapsed. Diseases such as typhus (tī' fuhs) were common.

Most farmers could not earn a living in the city. Except for construction, Rome had almost no industry. Most businesses were staffed by enslaved people from Greece. About the only way the farmers could get money was by selling their votes to politicians.

Decline of the Roman Republic As Rome's rule spread beyond Italy, the Romans began to demand taxes, as well as enslaved people, from the areas they conquered. Tax contracts were sold to people called **publicans** (pub' luh kuhnz). They paid Rome ahead of time for the contracts. Then, they collected taxes from the conquered people. The amount of taxes collected was supposed to be no more than 10 percent above the price paid for the contract. Most publicans, however, made extra money.

Reading Check What was the purpose of the **latifundias?**

Sculpture of Roman Consul

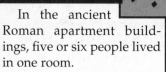

Reading Check Why did Rome sell tax contracts to the **publicans?**

Reading Check Answer The **latifundias** produced crops, sheep, and cattle for sale at market.

GEOGRAPHY AND HISTORY

The technique of people burning their own fields and crops in the path of an invading army is known as a scorched-earth policy. It has been used for centuries by many societies.

DID YOU KNOW ??

In the ancient Roman apartment buildings, five or six people lived in one room.

Reading Check Answer Rome sold tax contracts because the **publicans** paid Rome ahead of time for the contracts.

NATIONAL GEOGRAPHIC

Use these materials to enrich student understanding of ancient Rome.

NGS PICTUREPACK TRANSPARENCY SET
Ancient Rome

EXTENDING THE CONTENT

Enslaved persons' lives varied dramatically in the Roman Republic.

Those who worked in mines or quarries, or who rowed in the galleys of the navy, lived under brutal conditions. In contrast, educated Greeks taken prisoner might become tutors or stewards in wealthy households, leading lives more comfortable than those of free peasants. One estimate places the number of enslaved persons at one-fourth of the Italian population during Augustus's time.

CAPTION ANSWER

in wooden apartment buildings six or more stories high

MAKING CONNECTIONS

➤➤ **Economics** The provinces rebelled against high taxes causing Roman legions to be permanently stationed in most provinces. Because putting down revolts cost Rome troops and money, the provinces began to strain Rome's resources.

DID YOU KNOW ??

Roman camps were almost always rectangular with an entrance gate on each of the four sides. Tents were set up in street-like rows that were laid out in straight lines and crossed each other at right angles. At the signal of a trumpet, the camps could be broken up quickly.

Use **Interactive Tutor Self-Assessment CD-ROM** to review Section 4.

ROMAN APARTMENTS Wealthy Romans built brick and stone apartments. They decorated the floors with mosaics and the walls with paintings. These apartment dwellers owned only a few pieces of furniture, most of which were simple in design. **What sort of buildings did poor Romans live in during the Republic?**

By about 135 B.C., Rome was in a great deal of trouble. Because farmers had lost their land, they had also lost their economic and political independence. Merchants had become poorer because rich Romans could get luxuries elsewhere. Artisans had lost business because rich Romans wanted goods from Greece and Syria. Government officials were too busy getting rich to worry about solving the republic's problems.

The gap between rich and poor grew greater. The poor hated the rich for what the rich had done to them. The rich hated and feared the poor. Rome was no longer politically stable.

Section 4 Assessment

1. **Define:** latifundias, publicans.
2. How was Roman agriculture influenced by Hannibal?
3. What was life like in Rome during the decline of the republic?

Critical Thinking

4. **Identifying Central Issues** Why might a large gap between rich and poor present problems for an empire?

Graphic Organizer Activity

5. Draw this diagram, and use it to compare Roman agriculture before and after the rise of the latifundias.

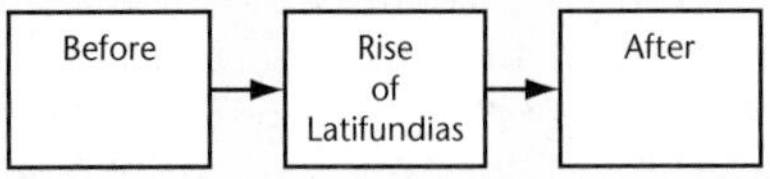

Section 4 Assessment Answers

1. latifundias, large estates (p. 225); publicans, Roman tax collectors (p. 225)
2. Roman farmers burned their fields and crops. After the Second Punic War, most farmers did not have money to restore the land, so latifundias appeared, which produced cash crops. Farmers were replaced by enslaved people.
3. Life was hard for most farmers, merchants, and artisans. Government officials became rich and the gap between rich and poor increased.
4. Answers will vary, but students might indicate risk of rebellion.
5. Answers should show the shift from hard-working farmers loyal to Rome to large estates where enslaved people produced cash crops for sale. Problems that led to the decline of the republic should also appear in the "After" box.

Assign Chapter 14 **Section 4 Quiz** in the TCR. Testmaker available.

SECTION 5 Roman Leadership

Over the next 100 years, many different popular leaders tried to improve conditions in Rome. Some were reformers, while others were generals.

Sculpture of Tiberius Gracchus

The Reformers Tiberius Sempronius Gracchus (tī bir′ ē uhs sem prō nē uhs grak′ uhs) was the first reformer. He thought making small farmers leave their land had caused Rome's troubles.

When he became a tribune in 133 B.C., Tiberius Gracchus wanted to limit the amount of land a person could own. He wanted to divide up public lands and give them to the poor. Another tribune vetoed his idea. Tiberius Gracchus then talked the assembly into putting his idea into effect and getting rid of that tribune.

Tiberius Gracchus ran for a second term as tribune, although it was against the law. To stop him, the Senate staged a riot and had him and hundreds of his followers killed.

In 123 B.C., Tiberius Gracchus's younger brother Gaius (gī′ yuhs) Sempronius Gracchus was elected tribune. He thought moving the poor from the city back to the countryside was the answer to Rome's troubles.

Gaius Gracchus improved and extended the reforms of his brother. He had the government take over the sale of wheat and sell it to the poor below market price. Soon, however, wheat was being given away rather than sold. Nearly one out of every three Romans was receiving free wheat. Meanwhile, the Senate began to feel threatened by some of Gaius Gracchus's ideas and in 121 B.C. had him killed.

The Generals After the reformers came the generals. In 107 B.C., General Gaius Marius (mar′ ē uhs), a military hero, became consul. The son of a day laborer, Marius was the first lower-class Roman to be elected to such a high office. He was supported by many ex-soldiers who felt the rich and the government had taken advantage of them. Many of the ex-soldiers had been farmers who had lost their farms when they left to serve in the army.

Marius thought he could end Rome's troubles by setting up a professional army. Until this time, only property owners could become legionaries. Marius opened the army to everyone. He convinced the poor to join by offering them pay, land, pensions, and *booty,* or things taken from the enemy in war. Marius's plan helped Rome by providing jobs for many out-of-work Romans. At the same time, it hurt the Roman Republic. Instead of giving loyalty to the government, the soldiers gave it to the general who hired and paid them.

L1 **Critical Thinking** Help students create cause-event-effects graphic organizers on the chalkboard showing the attempts made by reformers and generals to improve conditions in Rome. Create an organizer for each reformer or general. ELL

DID YOU KNOW ??

During their terms of office, tribunes could not be away from the city for even one night. They also had to always keep their doors open so that citizens could come to them for help.

Use the **Vocabulary PuzzleMaker CD-ROM** to create crossword and word search puzzles.

COOPERATIVE LEARNING

Organize the class into eight groups. Assign each group one of the following Roman leaders: Tiberius Gracchus, Gaius Marius, Lucius Cornelius Sulla, Pompey, Julius Caesar, Mark Antony, and Octavian.

Tell each group to research its assigned leader and write a list of five or six questions, along with the leader's responses, to be used in an interview for a talk show titled "Roman Forum." Then have two members of each group role-play the part of their group's leader and the part of the talk show host of "Roman Forum."

Reteach

Have students explain briefly, in their own words, the importance of each of the following: the government of the Roman Republic, the Punic Wars, Hannibal, latifundia, Gracchus, Marius, Sulla, Julius Caesar, and Octavian.

Assign Chapter 14 **Reteaching Activity** in the TCR.

Enrich

Have students prepare a report on the Roman legions. Encourage students to illustrate their reports. Display the reports in the classroom.

Assign Chapter 14 **Enrichment Activity** in the TCR.

CLOSE

Work with students to prepare a chronology of events and issues that led to the fall of the republic. Have students choose two or three events or issues that they think were the most significant and explain their choices.

Use **Interactive Tutor Self-Assessment CD-ROM** to review Section 5.

HISTORY Online

Self-Check Quiz gives students an interactive chapter tutorial. Have them access ***Chapter 14 Quiz*** at **humanheritage.glencoe.com**

For a while, the triumvirate worked. Then, fights broke out among the three leaders. When the fighting ended in 31 B.C., Octavian had won. Within four years, he became sole ruler of the Roman Empire.

Section 5 Assessment

1. **Define:** dictator, triumvirate.
2. Why did civil war break out in Rome?
3. Why did a group of Roman senators murder Julius Caesar?

Critical Thinking

4. **Demonstrating Reasoned Judgment** How effective do you think a triumvirate is as a form of government? Explain.

Graphic Organizer Activity

5. Draw this chart, and use it to summarize the reforms supported by popular leaders during the closing years of the Roman Republic.

Leader	Reform	Effect

Chapter Summary & Study Guide

1. In 509 B.C., the Romans overthrew the Etruscans and set up a republic.
2. About 450 B.C., leaders wrote down Roman laws in the Twelve Tables.
3. By 275 B.C., well-trained Roman legions had taken control of Italy.
4. Between 264 and 146 B.C., Rome and Carthage fought three wars known as the Punic Wars.
5. The organization of Roman lands into large estates forced many small farmers off the land and into the cities.
6. By 135 B.C., Rome faced many serious political and economic problems.
7. A series of reform-minded leaders tried various ways to improve conditions in Rome, but political rivalries prevented any leader from holding power for long.
8. After Julius Caesar was killed by Romans who feared he might become king, power was divided among three leaders.
9. Fights among the three-way rule of Mark Antony, Octavian, and Marcus Lepidus led to the collapse of the Roman Republic.
10. In 31 B.C., Octavian became the sole ruler of the Roman Empire.

HISTORY Online

Self-Check Quiz

Visit the *Human Heritage* Web site at **humanheritage.glencoe.com** and click on ***Chapter 14—Self-Check Quiz*** to assess your understanding of this chapter.

Section 5 Assessment Answers

1. dictator, absolute ruler (p. 228); triumvirate, three-person rule (p. 228)
2. sample responses: conflicts between Marius and Sulla over a military command; rise of a professional army more loyal to its commanders than to Rome
3. because they feared Caesar planned to make himself king
4. Answers will vary. Some students might see a triumvirate as a way to check executive power. Others might see it as divisive and an invitation to conspiracy.
5. Charts should correctly show the changes brought about by each reform.

Assign Chapter 14 **Section 5 Quiz** in the TCR. Testmaker available.

Using Key Terms

Imagine that you are writing a "Citizenship Handbook" for the new Roman citizens of 46 B.C. Write one sentence explaining the importance of each of the following terms.

republic patricians plebeians
consuls veto tribunes
legions legionaries latifundias
publicans dictator triumvirate

Understanding Main Ideas

1. What changes were made in Rome's government as a result of demands by the plebeians?
2. Why was the Roman legion so effective in battle?
3. Why did Rome decide to fight three wars against Carthage?
4. How were the Romans able to overcome the navy of Carthage?
5. What effect did latifundias have on Rome's small farmers?
6. Who won the struggle for political power after the death of Julius Caesar?
7. What effect did Marius's reforms have on the loyalty of the legionaries?
8. Why did the Senate order Julius Caesar to break up his legions?

Critical Thinking

1. How wise do you think the Romans were to enslave the people they conquered? Explain.
2. Do you think the Romans were wise or foolish to start taxing the people they conquered? Explain.
3. If you had lived in Rome after 135 B.C., what would you have done to solve its problems?
4. If you had lived when Caesar was killed, how would you have felt about his murder? Explain.

Graphic Organizer Activity

History Create a chart like this one, and use it to show steps in the decline of the Roman Republic.

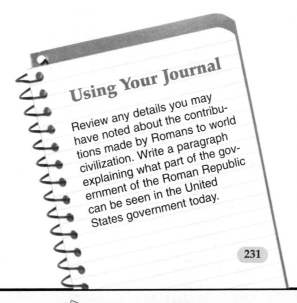

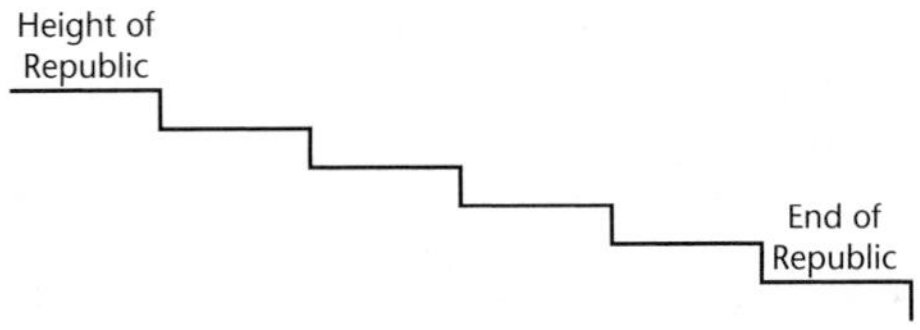

Height of Republic

End of Republic

Geography in History

Human Systems Refer to the map on page 228. Imagine you are a government representative who must travel from Rome to Cyprus. Describe how you would travel and what route you would take. Then draw a map showing your route.

Using Your Journal

Review any details you may have noted about the contributions made by Romans to world civilization. Write a paragraph explaining what part of the government of the Roman Republic can be seen in the United States government today.

231

Using Key Terms

Handbooks will vary but students should use all the words and include explanations.

Understanding Main Ideas

1. No one could be enslaved because of debt, and plebeians could marry patricians and hold public office.
2. because it was small and fast and could split off and attack from all sides
3. because Rome felt threatened by Carthage and wanted the Carthaginian granaries in Sicily
4. They added a corvus to the front of their ships, thus changing a sea war into a land war.
5. They forced many farmers to move to the city.
6. Octavian
7. shifted the loyalty of legionaries from the government to the general who hired them
8. because they feared he was growing too strong

Critical Thinking

1. Answers will vary, but students could note that enslaving conquered people caused dissension.
2. Answers will vary, but taxing coincided with the republic's decline.
3. Answers will vary.
4. Answers will vary, but students should give reasons.

Graphic Organizer Activity

Steps chosen by students will vary somewhat but should include important factors in chronological order, such as Roman expansion and rise of latifundias, forced movement of small farmers into cities, enslavement of conquered peoples, sale of tax contracts to publicans, and so on.

Bonus Test Question

For Chapter 14 Test
Predict what will happen: Julius Caesar was not murdered in 44 B.C. He continued as ruler of Rome, but was advised to share ruling with Mark Anthony. The Senate has resigned in protest against Caesar's laws. Caesar must do something—what?

Using Your Journal

Paragraphs will vary, but students might make their comparisons with the Roman Senate, tribunes, veto, and the Twelve Tables.

Geography in History

Answers will vary and may include a sea route by ship or a land-sea route involving horses, carts, and ships.

Chapter 15 Planning Guide

Timesaving Tools

TeacherWorks™ All-In-One Planner and Resource Center

- **Interactive Teacher Edition** Access your Teacher Wraparound Edition and your classroom resources with a few easy clicks.
- **Interactive Lesson Planner** Planning has never been easier! Organize your week, month, semester, or year with all the lesson helps you need to make teaching creative, timely, and relevant.

Use Glencoe's **Presentation Plus!** multimedia teacher tool to easily present dynamic lessons that visually excite your students. Using Microsoft PowerPoint® you can customize the presentations to create your own personalized lessons.

Objectives	Reproducible Resources	Multimedia Resources
Section 1 The Rule of Augustus Explain how Augustus ruled the Roman Empire.	Reproducible Lesson Plan Chapter 15 Vocabulary and Guided Reading Activity Reading Essentials and Study Guide 15-1 Unit 5 World Literature Reading 2 Chapter 15 Enrichment Activity Section 1 Quiz	Interactive Student Edition CD-ROM Graphic Organizer Transparency 15 Teaching Transparency and Activity 15A Vocabulary PuzzleMaker CD-ROM Interactive Tutor Self-Assessment CD-ROM ExamView® Pro Testmaker CD-ROM Glencoe Skillbuilder Interactive Workbook CD-ROM, Level 1 Presentation Plus! CD-ROM
Section 2 *Pax Romana* Analyze what happened to trade and law during the *Pax Romana.*	Reproducible Lesson Plan Reading Essentials and Study Guide 15-2 Section 2 Quiz	Teaching Transparency and Activity 15B Vocabulary PuzzleMaker CD-ROM Interactive Tutor Self-Assessment CD-ROM ExamView® Pro Testmaker CD-ROM Glencoe Skillbuilder Interactive Workbook CD-ROM, Level 1
Section 3 Daily Life Describe what daily life was like during the *Pax Romana.*	Reproducible Lesson Plan Reading Essentials and Study Guide 15-3 Chapter 15 Cooperative Learning Activity Unit 5 World Literature Reading 1 Section 3 Quiz	Vocabulary PuzzleMaker CD-ROM Interactive Tutor Self-Assessment CD-ROM ExamView® Pro Testmaker CD-ROM Glencoe Skillbuilder Interactive Workbook CD-ROM, Level 1
Section 4 Fall of the Empire Summarize why the Roman Empire declined and what attempts were made to save the empire from collapse.	Reproducible Lesson Plan Reading Essentials and Study Guide 15-4 Chapter 15 Chart and Graph Skill Activity Chapter 15 Geography and Map Activity Section 4 Quiz	Vocabulary PuzzleMaker CD-ROM Interactive Tutor Self-Assessment CD-ROM ExamView® Pro Testmaker CD-ROM Glencoe Skillbuilder Interactive Workbook CD-ROM, Level 1
Chapter 15 Review and Evaluation	Chapter 15 Reteaching Activity Chapter 15 Performance Assessment Activity Spanish Chapter Summary and Glossary Chapter 15 Test	Vocabulary PuzzleMaker CD-ROM Interactive Tutor Self-Assessment CD-ROM Glencoe Skillbuilder Interactive Workbook CD-ROM, Level 1 Audiocassettes* ExamView® Pro Testmaker CD-ROM

*Also available in Spanish.

✓ Performance Assessment Activities

Mathematics Have students prepare a chart of Arabic numerals (1 through 15, then 20, 30, 40, 50, 60, 70, 80, 90, 100, 500, and 1,000), the corresponding Roman numerals, and the Latin names for the numerals. Ask them to research how Romans performed mathematical calculations and to write a few problems for other students to solve.

CHAPTER RESOURCES

LITERATURE ABOUT THE PERIOD

Grant, Michael. *Greek and Latin Authors, 800 B.C.-A.D. 1000.* H.W. Wilson Co., 1980. Sketches of Greek and Latin authors and their works.

READINGS FOR THE STUDENT

Dillon, Eilis. *Rome Under the Emperors.* Thomas Nelson, 1975. Views of Roman society and family life in the time of Trajan, as seen by young people of four different families and social classes.

Foster, Genevieve. *Augustus Caesar's World.* Scribner's Sons, 1947. Classic history of Augustus's time.

READINGS FOR THE TEACHER

Fagg, Christopher. *Ancient Rome.* Warwick Press, 1978. Examines the Roman Empire from its beginnings through its decline.

Gibbon, Edward. *The Portable Gibbon: The Decline and Fall of the Roman Empire.* Viking, 1965. Summary of the classic historical study.

KEY TO ABILITY LEVELS

Teaching strategies have been coded for varying learning styles and abilities.

L1 Level 1 activities are **basic** activities and should be within the ability range of all students.

L2 Level 2 activities are **average** activities and should be within the ability range of the average to above-average student.

L3 Level 3 activities are **challenging** activities designed for the ability range of above-average students.

ELL ELL activities should be within the ability range of English Language Learning students.

NATIONAL GEOGRAPHIC Teacher's Corner

INDEX TO NATIONAL GEOGRAPHIC MAGAZINE

The following articles relate to this chapter:

- "Roman Shipwrecks" by Robert D. Ballard, April 1998.
- "Roman Legacy," by T.R. Reid, August 1997.
- "Roman Empire," by T.R. Reid, July 1997.
- "Brindisi Bronzes," by O. Louis Mazzatenta, April 1995.

NATIONAL GEOGRAPHIC SOCIETY PRODUCTS AVAILABLE FROM GLENCOE

To order the following, call Glencoe at 1-800-334-7344:

- *PicturePack: Ancient Rome (Transparencies)*
- *PictureShow: Greece and Rome (CD-ROM)*
- *Ancient Civilizations: Ancient Rome (Poster Set)*

ADDITIONAL NATIONAL GEOGRAPHIC SOCIETY PRODUCTS

To order the following, call National Geographic at 1-800-368-2728:

- *National Geographic Atlas of World History (Book)*
- *Wonders of the Ancient World: National Geographic Atlas of Archaeology (Book)*
- *The Builders: Marvels of Engineering (Book)*

Access *National Geographic's* new dynamic MapMachine Web site and other geography resources at:
www.nationalgeographic.com
www.nationalgeographic.com/maps

THE HISTORY CHANNEL. A&E HOME VIDEO. Biography

The following videotape programs are available from Glencoe to enrich Chapter 15:

- **Augustus: First of the Emperors**
  0-7670-0573-2
- **The Incredible Monuments of Rome**
  1-56501-870-2
- **Rome's Glorious Cities**
  0-7670-0611-9

To order, call Glencoe at 1-800-334-7344. To find classroom resources to accompany many of these videos, check:

A&E Television: www.aande.com
The History Channel: www.historychannel.com

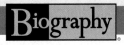

OVERVIEW

Chapter 15 traces the Roman Empire from the rule of Augustus to the fall of Rome.

- **Section 1** summarizes the rule of Augustus.
- **Section 2** describes Roman contributions to trade and law during the *Pax Romana*.
- **Section 3** discusses the daily life of Romans.
- **Section 4** analyzes the causes of the fall of the Roman Empire.

CHAPTER OBJECTIVES

After reading Chapter 15, your students will be able to:

1. explain how Augustus ruled the Roman Empire.
2. analyze what happened to trade and law during the *Pax Romana.*
3. describe daily life during the *Pax Romana.*
4. summarize why the Roman Empire declined.
5. discuss efforts to save the Roman Empire.

EXAMINING ARTIFACTS

Ask students to describe ways the education of Romans—and the tools for learning—differed from their own. *(Students may note the one-on-one instruction, the informal [home] setting, use of a scroll instead of a book, use of inkpot and pen instead of a ballpoint or computer.)* Call on students to guess some of the subjects a Roman student might study. Have them check their answers as they read Chapter 15.

PERFORMANCE ASSESSMENT ✓

Use the Performance Assessment Activities on page 232B to help you evaluate students as they complete the chapter.

CHAPTER 15

The Roman Empire

27 B.C.–410 A.D.

Sculptures of a Roman teacher and student ▼

▲ Roman inkpot and pen

- 27 B.C. Octavian becomes first Roman emperor
- 125 A.D. Roman law is standardized
- 330 A.D. Constantine I moves Roman capital to Constantinople
- 378 A.D. Battle of Adrianople
- 410 A.D. Rome falls to Germanic invaders

TEACHING RESOURCES

TEACHER PLANNING AND SUPPORT

- Reproducible Lesson Plan 15-1, 15-2, 15-3, 15-4
- Teaching Strategies for the World History Classroom (Including Block Scheduling Pacing Guides)
- Presentation Plus! CD-ROM

REVIEW AND REINFORCEMENT

- Reading Essentials and Study Guide 15-1, 15-2, 15-3, 15-4
- Chapter 15 Vocabulary and Guided Reading Activity
- Vocabulary PuzzleMaker CD-ROM
- Teaching Transparencies 15A & 15B
- Chapter 15 Reteaching Activity
- Chapter 15 Cooperative Learning Activity
- Chapter 15 Activity Book Activity
- Chapter 15 Chart and Graph Skill Activity
- Reading and Study Skills Foldables
- Interactive Tutor Self-Assessment Software

APPLICATION AND HANDS-ON ACTIVITIES

- Daily Questions In Social Studies
- Unit 5 Hands-On History Lab Activity
- Student Presentation Builder CD-ROM

Chapter Focus

Read to Discover

- How Augustus ruled the Roman Empire.
- What happened to trade and law during the *Pax Romana.*
- What daily life was like during the *Pax Romana.*
- Why the Roman Empire declined.

HISTORY Online

Chapter Overview

Visit the *Human Heritage* Web site at **humanheritage.glencoe.com** and click on ***Chapter 15—Chapter Overviews*** to preview this chapter.

Terms to Learn	People to Know	Places to Locate
emperor	Augustus	Circus Maximus
census	Marcus Aurelius	Constantinople
tariffs	Diocletian	Adrianople
gladiators	Constantine I	Danube River
	Alaric	

Why It's Important In 27 B.C., Octavian told the Senate that he had restored the republic, and he offered to resign as sole ruler of Rome. The Senate turned down the offer and gave him several titles. In the end, Octavian took for himself the title of Augustus (ah guhs' tuhs), or "revered one." That is what he is generally called in history books.

In practice, Octavian became the first Roman **emperor,** or absolute ruler of an empire. His policies paved the way for more than 200 years of peace. Even after the empire collapsed, Roman influence would survive in much of the world.

Reading Check What is an **emperor?**

SECTION 1 The Rule of Augustus

Augustus was a clever politician. He held the offices of consul, tribune, high priest, and senator all at the same time. However, he refused to be crowned emperor. Augustus knew that most Romans would not accept one-person rule unless it took the form of a republic.

Augustus kept the assemblies and government officials of the republic. He was careful to make senators feel honored. He talked of tradition and the need to bring back "old Roman virtues."

At the same time, Augustus strengthened his authority in two ways. First, he had every soldier swear allegiance to him personally. This gave him control of the armies. Second, he built up his imperial household to take charge of the daily business of

GEOGRAPHY ACTIVITIES

- Chapter 15 Geography and Map Activity
- Outline Map Resource Book

INTERDISCIPLINARY CONNECTIONS

- Unit 5 World Literature Readings 1 & 2
- World Art & Architecture Transparency 9, *Pantheon*
- World Music: A Cultural Legacy

ENRICHMENT AND EXTENSION

- Unit 5 Primary Source Readings
- World History Primary Source Document Library CD-ROM
- Chapter 15 Enrichment Activity
- Foods Around the World

ASSESSMENT AND EVALUATION

- Chapter 15 Performance Assessment Activity
- Chapter 15 Section Quizzes 15-1, 15-2, 15-3, 15-4
- Chapter 15 Test
- Chapter 15 ExamView® Pro Testmaker CD-ROM
- Chapter 15 Digests Audiocassettes Activities and Tests

SPANISH RESOURCES

- Chapter 15 Spanish Chapter Summary and Glossary
- Chapter 15 Spanish Digests Audiocassettes Activities and Tests

HISTORY Online

Chapter Overview introduces students to chapter content and key terms. Have them access ***Chapter 15 Overview*** at **humanheritage.glencoe.com**

FOCUS

Bellringer

Write the following on the board: *"All roads lead to Rome."* Have students write about what they think the quote means.

Motivational Activity

Discuss students' responses. Then read the following quotation from Latin author Tertullian. *"Everywhere roads are built . . . Wherever there is a trace of life, there are houses and human inhabitants, well-ordered governments, and civilized life."* Focus discussion on what kind of empire the quote describes.

GUIDE TO READING

Reading Strategy

Ask students to read "Why It's Important" and summarize the chapter's main theme. *(The policies of Octavian ensured a long peace and the enduring influence of Roman culture).*

Vocabulary Precheck

Ask students to define each of the "Terms to Learn." L1 ELL

Use the Vocabulary PuzzleMaker CD-ROM for Chapter 15 to create a crossword puzzle. L1

Assign Chapter 15 Vocabulary and Guided Reading Activity.

Assign Reading Essentials and Study Guide 15-1.

Reading Check Answer An **emperor** is the absolute ruler of an empire.

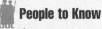

TEACH

Guided Practice

L1 **Geography: Places and Regions** Display a wall map of Western Europe and North Africa. Point out the natural barriers that Augustus used to round out the Roman Empire—the Rhine and Danube rivers, the Atlantic Ocean, and the Sahara. Discuss why these barriers made the empire easy to defend. ELL

Reading Check Answer
The **freedmen** were former enslaved people.

Reading Check Answer
Augustus ordered a **census** to make sure people were not paying too little or too much tax.

Use **Interactive Tutor Self Assessment CD-ROM** to review Section 1.

A&E HOME VIDEO.

The following videotape programs are available from Glencoe to enrich Chapter 15:

- **Augustus: First of the Emperors**
- **Rome's Glorious Cities**

To find classroom resources to accompany these videos, check the following home page:

A&E Television:
www.aande.com

Reading Check Who were the **freedmen?**

government. He chose people because of their talent rather than their birth. This gave enslaved people and **freedmen**, or former enslaved people, a chance to be part of the government.

Augustus wanted boundaries that would be easy to defend. So, he rounded out the empire to natural frontiers—the Rhine (rīn) and Danube (dan′ yūb) rivers in the north, the Atlantic Ocean in the west, and the Sahara in the south—and stationed soldiers there.

Augustus was not interested in gaining new territory for Rome. Instead, he worked on governing the existing empire. He gave provincial governors long terms of office. This allowed them to gain experience in their jobs. He also paid them large salaries. In this way, they would not feel the need to overtax the people or keep public money for themselves. To make sure that people did not pay too little or too much tax, Augustus ordered a **census** (sen′ suhs), or population count, to be taken from time to time.

Reading Check Why did Augustus order a **census?**

Augustus also made Rome more beautiful. He wrote strict laws to govern the way people behaved in public. He protected the city by setting up a fire brigade and a police force. He encouraged learning by building Rome's first library.

Augustus ruled for 41 years. During that time, he brought peace to Rome. He also gave the Romans a new sense of patriotism and pride. He made Roman citizenship available to people in the provinces. Most important, however, he reorganized the government of Rome so that it ran well for more than 200 years.

Section 1 Assessment

1. **Define:** emperor, freedmen, census.
2. Why did Augustus refuse to be crowned emperor?
3. How did Augustus try to make the Roman Empire like a republic?

Critical Thinking

4. **Demonstrating Reasoned Judgment** Which of Augustus's improvements do you think was the most important? Explain.

Graphic Organizer Activity

5. Draw this diagram, and use it to show the achievements of Augustus.

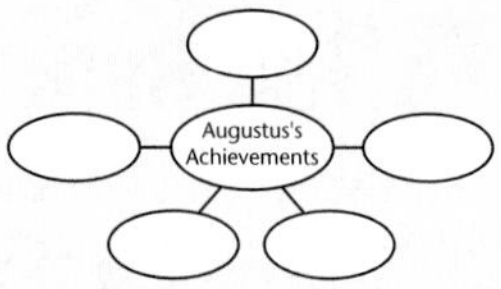

SECTION 2 Pax Romana

The peace that Augustus brought to Rome was called the *Pax Romana* (pahks rō mah′ nah). It lasted for 200 years. Of course, revolts and other problems were not unknown during this time. For the most part, however, Rome and its people prospered. Civilization spread, and cultures mixed.

Section 1 Assessment Answers

1. emperor, absolute ruler (p. 233); freedmen, former enslaved people (p. 234); census, population count (p. 234)
2. He knew most Romans would not accept one-person rule unless it was in a republic.
3. He kept the assemblies and government officials, made senators feel honored, talked of tradition and the need to bring back "old Roman virtues," and made the official religion important again.
4. Answers will vary, but students should explain their choices.
5. Sample achievements: won the loyalty of soldiers, gave enslaved people and freedmen a chance to be part of government, rounded out the empire to its natural frontiers, reformed provincial government, ordered a census, wrote strict laws to control public behavior, set up a fire brigade and police force, built Rome's first library, and so on.

Assign Chapter 15 **Section 1 Quiz** in the TCR. Testmaker available.

Trade With peace came increased trade. The same coins were used throughout the empire. There were no **tariffs** (tar′ ifz), or taxes placed on goods brought into the country. Goods and money moved freely along the trade routes. The Mediterranean was cleared of pirates, making it safe for trade and travel. Shipping became a big business. Every summer, hundreds of ships carried grain from North Africa to Italy. Other ships bound for Rome were loaded with cargoes of brick, marble, granite, and wood to be used for building. Luxury items, such as amber from the north and silk from China, passed overland across Roman roads.

Increased trade meant more business for Romans. The city hummed. Shopkeepers grew richer. Wine and olive oil were the main items bought by other countries. Italy became a manufacturing center for pottery, bronze, and woolen cloth.

Law During the *Pax Romana*, Roman law went through major changes. Because the times were different, the laws first set down

Reading Check
What are **tariffs?**

MAP STUDY

PLACES AND REGIONS The Roman Empire had been divided into two parts. **What empire did Greece belong to?**

The Expansion of the Roman Empire

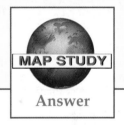

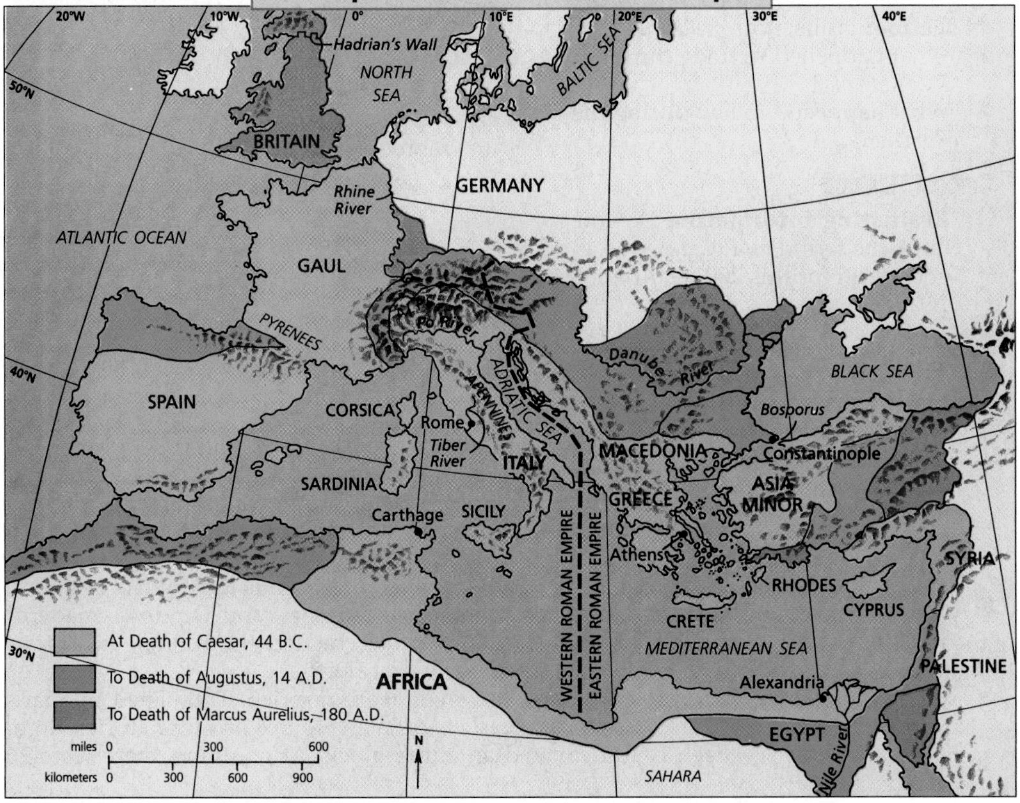

Reading Check Answer
Tariffs are taxes placed on goods brought into a country.

Use the **Vocabulary Puzzle-Maker CD-ROM** to create crossword and word search puzzles.

L2 **Map Skills** Have students refer to the map on this page to identify the regions in which the empire expanded. *(Western Europe, Middle East, North Africa)* What sea did most Roman land border? *(Mediterranean)* Have students use the map scale to calculate the distance of the farthest point of the empire from the city of Rome. *(about 1,800 miles, or 2,896 km)*

Assign the Chapter 15 **Geography and Map Activity** in the TCR.

MAP STUDY
Answer
Eastern Roman Empire

NATIONAL GEOGRAPHIC

Use these materials to enrich student understanding of everyday life in ancient Rome.

NGS PICTURESHOW CD-ROM
Greece and Rome

COOPERATIVE LEARNING

Assign students to groups to research specific areas of culture during the *Pax Romana.* Divide each topic into smaller areas to be covered by individuals in each group. Groups should decide how to organize their reports into coordinated presentations. The following topics might be suggested: Roman daily life (food, housing, amusements, household duties, women's lives, education); philosophy (ideas of citizenship, justice, religion); language and literature (Romance languages, specific poets or historians); or architecture (Roman roads, the arch in architecture).

L1 **Economics** During the *Pax Romana* many changes took place in trade in the Roman Empire. This affected more people than those who actually carried goods to other markets. Using student volunteers, ask students to list on the board all people and/or occupations that were affected by the increase in Roman trade.

Reading Check Answer The *juris prudentes* were special lawyers and legal writers who helped Roman judges write new laws.

Use **Interactive Tutor Self-Assessment CD-ROM** to review Section 2.

PRIMARY SOURCES Library

You might assign "Eruption of Mount Vesuvius" from pages 682–683 of the Primary Sources Library.

Reading Check Answer A Roman **domus** had marble walls, colored stone floors, glass windows, a furnace to heat rooms, and pipes to carry water to upper floors.

Use the **Vocabulary PuzzleMaker CD-ROM** to create crossword and word search puzzles.

on the Twelve Tables were changed. When Rome conquered a new territory, Roman merchants had to do business with non-Romans. Roman judges had to write new laws that would be as fair to non-Romans as to Romans. The Roman judges were helped by special lawyers and legal writers called ***juris prudentes*** (jū′ ruhs prū′ duhntz).

Reading Check Who were the ***juris prudentes,*** and what were they supposed to do?

After a while, the judges and their helpers developed certain principles of law that were fair to everyone. A law was believed to be just because it was reasonable, not because the government had the power to make people obey it. Everyone was considered equal before the law. A person was innocent until proven guilty.

By about 125 A.D., Roman law was *standardized.* This meant that legal procedures were the same in all parts of the empire. This helped Rome govern a large area successfully. In later years, Roman legal principles formed the basis for the laws of most western countries and of the Christian church.

Section 2 Assessment

1. **Define:** tariffs, *juris prudentes*.
2. What happened to trade during the *Pax Romana*?
3. What happened to law during the *Pax Romana*?

Critical Thinking

4. **Evaluating Information** Do you think the term *Pax Romana* was a good term for this 200-year period in Roman history, or would you describe it with another term? Explain.

Graphic Organizer Activity

5. Draw this diagram, and use it to show the effects of the *Pax Romana*. (Add more lines as needed.)

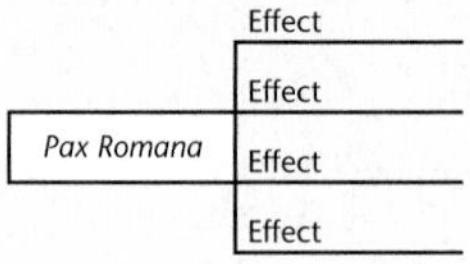

SECTION 3 Daily Life

In the early years of the empire, about 1 million people lived in Rome. It suffered from many of the same problems as cities of today. There was too little housing. The air was polluted. There was crime in the streets. The cost of living was high. Many Romans could not find jobs and had to pay taxes on almost everything.

Reading Check What were some of the features of a Roman **domus?**

A rich person in Rome lived in a **domus** (dō′ muhs), or house, with marble walls, colored stone floors, and windows made of small panes of glass. A furnace heated the rooms, and pipes brought water even to the upper floors.

Most Romans, however, were not rich. They lived in apartment houses called *islands* that were six or more stories high. Each island covered an entire block. At one time, there were 26

Section 2 Assessment Answers

1. tariffs, taxes placed on goods brought into the country (p. 235), *juris prudentes*, special lawyers and legal writers (p. 236)
2. It increased.
3. Certain principles of fairness were developed, including the ideas that everyone is equal before the law and that a person is considered innocent until proven guilty. By about 125 A.D., the law was standardized.
4. Answers will vary, but students could note because it was a time that Rome prospered, few battles took place, civilization spread, and cultures mixed.
5. Sample effects: Rome prospered, civilization spread, cultures mixed, trade increased, pirates cleared from the Mediterranean, shipping became big business, Roman businesses grew, new laws were written and old ones revised, laws became standardized, and so on.

Assign Chapter 15 **Section 2 Quiz** in the TCR. Testmaker available.

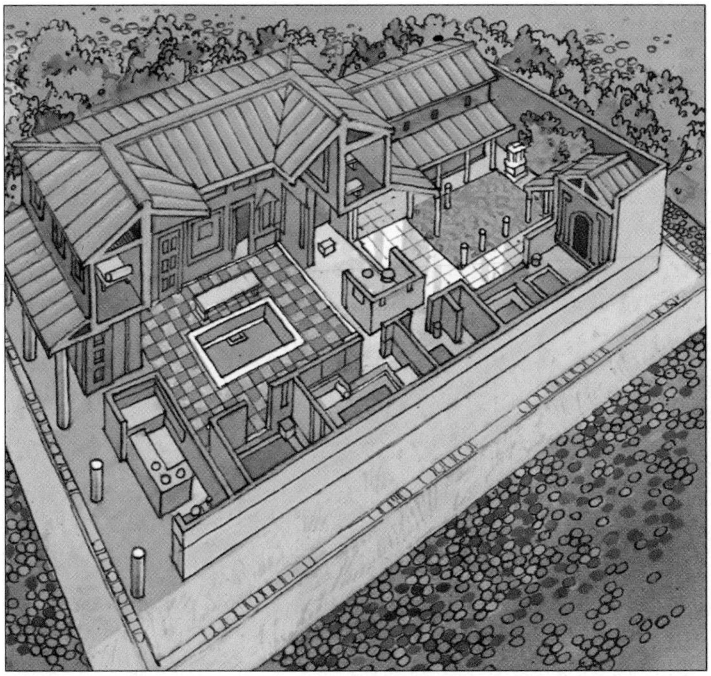

ROMAN FLOOR PLAN This is a typical floor plan of a *domus.* **What class of Romans would live in a house such as this?**

Then & Now

The Atrium Many shopping malls today have an atrium, a sky-lit central court. The idea for the atrium comes from ancient Rome. In a Roman house, the atrium was the central room. It was often open to the sky and had a pool to collect rainwater.

blocks of islands for every private house in Rome. The ground floor of most islands was given over to shops. These opened onto the street from large arched doorways.

Rents were high in Rome. They varied according to the apartment floor—the higher up the apartment, the lower the rent.

The Family

In Rome, the family was all-important. The father was head of the household. His word was law. He arranged the children's marriages to improve social position or to increase wealth. Cousins were expected to help one another politically.

Until they were 12 years old, most Roman boys and girls went to school together. Then, the sons of poor families went to work, while the sons of rich families began their formal education. They studied reading, grammar, writing, music, geometry, commercial arithmetic, and shorthand. When they were 15 years old, they entered a school of *rhetoric* (ret' uhr ik), or speech and writing, to prepare for a political career. Some went to schools in Athens or Alexandria for philosophy or medicine.

Girls received a different kind of education. When they were 12 years old, their formal education stopped. Instead of going to school, the daughters of the rich were given private lessons at

Painting of Roman Couple

L2 **Daily Life** Have students assume the role of one ancient Roman and write a first-person narrative of a typical day. Students might choose to be a Roman legionary, a shopkeeper, a senator, a public official in the provinces, an enslaved person, or a gladiator. After researching, students should relate details of the person's occupational functions and responsibilities, together with details of his or her family and social life.

CAPTION ANSWER

wealthy people

LINKING PAST TO PRESENT

In 46 B.C. Julius Caesar ordered the calendar revised. His so-called Julian calendar fixed the length of the year at 365 days with 12 months of 30 or 31 days except for February (29 days). He named one of the months Julius (now July) after himself. Later, Augustus lengthened his month, August, to 31 days by taking one day from February (leaving it 28 days). In A.D. 1582 Pope Gregory XIII formalized the system of leap years we know today.

COOPERATIVE LEARNING

Divide the class into groups, and tell them to pretend they are tutors assigned to give lessons to the children of a well-to-do Roman family. Have students plan what they would teach in a day's lesson. Encourage them to devise mathematical problems (using Roman numerals), a reading assignment (perhaps from *Plutarch's Lives*), a music lesson (perhaps practicing the scale on a flute), and a rhetoric assignment (perhaps on the topic of Roman government). When students are done, call on them to present their lesson plans to the class. If time allows, you might test out the lessons by having groups teach each other.

Assign Chapter 15 ***Cooperative Learning Activity*** in the TCR.

MAKING CONNECTIONS

>> **Daily Life** The father of a Roman household conducted religious rituals in the home, controlled property, and had the power to sell family members into enslavement or kill them.

Linking Across Time

Under the republic, the games had generally been staged by politicians looking for votes. Under the empire, they were staged by the government.

DID YOU KNOW ??

In ancient Rome the handkerchief was a status symbol, since only wealthy Romans could afford the precious white linen. Originally the handkerchief was used to wipe away perspiration, but later it was used to wave as a way of voting life or death for a defeated gladiator.

Reading Check Answer Most **gladiators** were enslaved people, prisoners of war, criminals, or poor people.

Linking Across Time

Stadiums During Roman times, people filled stadiums such as the Colosseum (left) to watch gladiator fights and other public games. Stadiums remain popular today but are usually used for team sports such as baseball, football, or soccer (right). **Who staged the public games held at stadiums in Rome?**

home. As a result, many Roman women were as well as or better informed than Roman men. Some women worked in or owned small shops. Wealthy women had enslaved people to do their housework. This left them free to study the arts, literature, and fashions, or to ride chariots in the countryside for a day's *pig-sticking,* or a type of hunt.

At Leisure

At home, the Romans enjoyed gambling with dice. They met friends at public bathhouses where they could take warm, cold, or steam baths. The bathhouses of Rome, however, provided more than baths. Some had gymnasiums, sports stadiums, and libraries. There, the Romans could watch or play games. They also could listen to lectures, see musical shows, exercise, or just sit and talk.

The Romans had no team sports to watch. Instead, they flocked to see free public games, which often ran from dawn to dusk. Under the republic, the games had generally been staged by politicians who were looking for votes. Under the empire, the games were staged by the government. The games included circuses, chariot races, and gladiatorial games. The most exciting chariot races were held at the Circus Maximus, an oval arena that could seat more than 200,000 people.

The people who fought animals and one another in arenas were called **gladiators** (glad' ē ā tuhrz). Most were enslaved people, prisoners of war, criminals, or poor people. They were

Reading Check Which groups of people were trained as **gladiators?**

MULTICULTURAL PERSPECTIVES

Most men in Rome had three names. The middle name told from which clan a man was descended. The last name told to which branch of the clan he belonged. The first name identified the person. Thus, Caius Julius Caesar was a member of the Caesarian branch of the Julian clan. His personal name was Caius. Unmarried women had two names—the feminine form of their father's middle name, and a last name that indicated chronological rank among the girls of the family. For example, if Caesar had fathered two daughters, the older would have been called Julia Prima and the other Julia Secunda. When a woman married, a form of her husband's last name was added to her other two names.

trained by managers who hired them out. A few gladiators were upper-class Romans who wanted excitement and public attention.

The night before they were to fight, gladiators would appear at a feast. There, they could be looked over by fans and gamblers who wanted to bet on the outcome of a match. When the gladiators entered the arena on the day of the games, they would walk past the emperor's box and say, "Hail Emperor, those who are about to die salute you."

Many gladiators did die. Those whose fighting pleased the crowd became idols of the people. A few won their freedom. Those who gave a poor performance were killed, even if they survived the fight.

All kinds of animals were used in the public games. Some animals pulled chariots or performed tricks. Most, however, fought one another or gladiators. Sometimes, as many as 5,000 wild animals were killed in a single day. In some cases, such as that of the Mesopotamian lion and the North African elephant, whole species were eventually wiped out.

HISTORY Online

Student Web Activity

Visit the *Human Heritage* Web site at humanheritage.glencoe.com and click on ***Chapter 15—Student Web Activities*** to find out more about early Roman life.

A ROMAN BANQUET MENU
APPETIZERS AND SOUPS
Snails Fed on Milk
Fried Bulbs
Grilled Truffles in Sausage Skin
Minced Sea-Crayfish-Tail Balls
Barley Soup with Dried Vegetables Topped with Cabbage Leaves
Puree of Lettuce-Leaves with Onions
MAIN COURSES
Boiled Electric Ray with Hot Raisins
Boiled Crane with Turnips
Smoked Pig's Stomach Stuffed with Brains, Pine Kernels, and Peppercorns
Roast Hare in White Sauce
Leg of Boar
Roast Flamingo with Jericho Dates, Dried Onion, Honey, and Wine
Wood-Pigeon Baked in Oil-Flour Pastry
DESSERTS
Sweet Fricassee of Pumpkin
Egg Sponge with Milk in Honey
Stew of Apricots

HISTORY Online

Student Web Activity objectives and answers can be found at the ***Chapter 15 Web Activity Lesson Plan*** at humanheritage.glencoe.com

DID YOU KNOW ??

Gladiators who were killed during combat were dragged from the arena by men wearing the mask of an Etruscan demon of the underworld.

MAKING CONNECTIONS

➤➤ **Culture** All Roman households had a central place to honor the spirits of the hearth and household. The hearth of the home was watched over by the goddess Vesta (or Hestia), spirit of the home fire. Family meals began and ended with thanks to her. A newborn child was carried around the hearth to symbolize becoming part of the family. Lares and Penates were the Roman spirits of everyday things. They came from ancient times when the Romans were mostly farmers. Each family had its own Lar, perhaps the spirit of an ancestor, to guide it. A household had several Penates representing prosperity.

MEETING SPECIAL NEEDS

Have interested students research and present an oral report on Hadrian's Wall built by Romans in northern Britain in the 120s A.D. Ask students to indicate the location of the wall on a map of Britain.

Refer to ***Inclusion for the Middle School Social Studies Classroom: Strategies and Activities*** for additional resources.

L3 **Health** Have students work together in small groups to research Roman diets. Suggest they prepare a day's menu for a peasant family similar to the Patrician menu shown in the illustration on this page.

L3 **Critical Thinking** Before students read the information about Diocletian and Constantine I, have them brainstorm ways in which a Roman emperor might have strengthened the empire to save it from collapse. Write their ideas on the board and revisit the lists after students have read Section 4.

Use **Interactive Tutor Self-Assessment CD-ROM** to review Section 3.

DID YOU KNOW ??

Marcus Aurelius was so loved by the Romans that there was no mourning when he died. They were sure he had come from the gods and had now returned to heaven.

Reading Check Answer
Inflation is a period of ever-rising prices.

Economics at a Glance

Inflation Inflation is an increase in the amount of money compared to the availability of goods. This results in increased prices. Today, the Federal Reserve System, which is the central bank of the United States, tries to keep the amount of money in circulation from changing too quickly in order to prevent inflation. Organize the class into groups of four and have them use the Internet to research the responsibilities of the Federal Reserve System. Students should identify the role of the Fed in the economy and how it controls the money supply. Students should present the information in a graphic organizer on poster board.

Use the **Vocabulary PuzzleMaker CD-ROM** to create crossword and word search puzzles.

Section 3 Assessment

1. **Define:** *domus,* gladiators.
2. What kind of schooling did Roman children receive?
3. What did the Romans do for entertainment?

Critical Thinking

4. **Drawing Conclusions** What conclusions can you draw about Roman society based upon popular leisure activities?

Graphic Organizer Activity

5. Draw this diagram, and use it to compare family life in the United States with Roman family life during the *Pax Romana.*

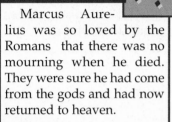

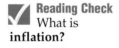

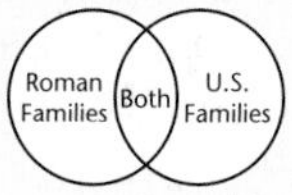

SECTION 4 Fall of the Empire

The *Pax Romana* ended after about 200 years. From then on, conditions in the Roman Empire grew worse. By 476 A.D., there was no empire left. Instead, much of western Europe was a patchwork of Germanic kingdoms. The eastern part of the empire, however, lasted about 1,000 years longer as part of the Byzantine (biz' n tēn) Empire.

There are many reasons the Roman Empire fell. The first was political. The emperors had no written rule about who was to inherit the throne upon an emperor's death. Sometimes, the title was inherited by a son. Sometimes, an emperor adopted an heir to the throne. Between 96 and 180 A.D., all the emperors were adopted. The system worked well until 180 A.D.

Marcus Aurelius (ah rē' lē uhs) became emperor in 161 A.D. He was kind, intelligent, and devoted to duty. His son Commodus (kahm' uh duhs), however, was the opposite. He became emperor when Marcus Aurelius died in 180 A.D. He was so cruel and hated that in 192 A.D. he was strangled by the Praetorian (prē tōr' ē uhn) Guard, or the emperor's bodyguards. The Praetorian Guard then sold the throne to the highest bidder. This set a terrible example. For nearly 100 years, legion fought legion to put its own emperor on the throne. By 284 A.D., Rome had 37 different emperors. Most were murdered by the army or the Praetorian Guard.

Then & Now

The Pantheon The "good emperor" Hadrian built the Pantheon in Rome as a temple to honor all the gods. Today the beautiful building is a national shrine, a church, and the burial place of two kings of Italy.

The second reason for Rome's downfall was economic. To stay in office, an emperor had to keep the soldiers who supported him happy. He did this by giving them high wages. This meant more and more money was needed for the army payroll. As a result, the Romans had to pay higher taxes.

Reading Check What is **inflation?**

In addition to higher taxes, the Romans began to suffer from **inflation,** or a period of ever-increasing prices. Since there were

Section 3 Assessment Answers

1. *domus,* house (p. 236); gladiators, people who fought in Roman arenas (p. 238)
2. Until age 12, boys and girls went to school. Wealthy males continued their studies while girls did not. Wealthy females may have been taught at home.
3. They gambled with dice, met at public bathhouses, and watched public games.
4. Answers will vary, but students should be prepared to present evidence that supports their conclusions.
5. Diagrams will vary. To get students started, you might provide these examples. *Roman families*—fathers arranged children's marriages. *U.S. families*—Children usually select their own partners. *Both*—Education of young children is important.

Assign Chapter 15 **Section 3 Quiz** in the TCR. Testmaker available.

no new conquests, gold was no longer coming into Rome. Yet, much gold was going out to pay for luxury items. This meant there was less gold to use in coins. As the amount of gold used in coins decreased, money began to lose its value. Prices went up. Many people stopped using money altogether. Instead, they began to **barter**, or exchange goods without using money.

The third major reason Rome fell centered on foreign enemies. While the Romans fought each other over politics and money, they left Rome's frontiers open to attack. Germanic hunters and herders from northern and central Europe began to raid Greece and Gaul.Trade and farming in those areas declined. Cities again began to surround themselves with protecting walls.

Reading Check Why did Romans begin to **barter?**

Diocletian and Constantine I Two emperors, Diocletian (dī ō klē′ shuhn) and Constantine I (kon stan tēn′), tried very hard to save the Roman Empire from collapse.

EMPERORS DURING THE *PAX ROMANA*

Emperor	Reign	Accomplishments
Augustus	27 B.C.–14 A.D.	first emperor of Roman Empire reorganized government of Rome; brought peace to Rome
Tiberius	14 A.D.–37 A.D.	reformed taxes and improved financial state of government
Caligula	37 A.D.–41 A.D.	repaired roads and began construction of two aqueducts
Claudius	41 A.D.–54 A.D.	conquered most of England extended citizenship to many people outside Rome set up ministries to handle government administration
Nero	54 A.D.–68 A.D.	rebuilt Rome after the fire of 64 A.D. and gave it a city plan
Flavian Emperors **Vespasian** **Titus** **Domitian**	69 A.D.–96 A.D.	brought people from the provinces into the Senate secured frontier regions brought Rome new prosperity built the Coliseum
Five Good Emperors **Nerva** **Trajan** **Hadrian** **Antoninus Pius** **Marcus Aurelius**	96 A.D.–180 A.D.	built aqueducts, bridges, and harbors extended citizenship to more provinces cut dishonesty in business and government

Reading Check Answer Romans began to **barter** because gold fell into short supply and money lost its value.

Independent Practice

L3 Art Ask students to research and present an oral report about the artifacts that have been found from the destruction of Pompeii, Italy, after the eruption of Mount Vesuvius in 79 A.D. Students' reports should include a variety of artifacts that have been found in excavations and what they explain about life in Pompeii.

L1 History Have students work in pairs to create five questions based on the chart of Roman emperors on this page. Collect the questions, ask for a volunteer moderator, and have students play a game of "Who Am I?" using their questions.

A&E HOME VIDEO.

The following videotape program is available from Glencoe to enrich Chapter 15:

- **The Incredible Monuments of Rome**

To find classroom resources to accompany this video, check the following home page:

A&E Television:
www.aande.com

SPOTLIGHT ON: ZENOBIA

One of the most celebrated women in the Roman Empire was Zenobia, queen of Palmyra—located in central Syria—from 267 to 272 A.D. As queen she helped her husband lead the army and rule the lands entrusted to him. She became known for her leadership and bravery. In 267 A.D. she succeeded her husband who had died, as ruler. Most of the people of Palmyra supported her because she was a just ruler, selected competent advisers, and was tolerant of other's beliefs. In 269 A.D. she seized Egypt, conquered most of Asia Minor, and declared her country independent from Rome. From 270 to 272 A.D., she was ruler of the Eastern Roman Empire.

CRITICAL THINKING SKILLS

TEACH

Identifying the Main Ideas

Write this phrase on the board: *What's the big idea?* Ask students what this phrase means to them. *(What is this all about? What are you trying to do?)* Explain that people usually ask this question when they want an explanation for someone's behavior. Call on students to suggest reasons they should also ask this question of historians, reporters, or any other person providing information. *(to find out why they are writing or saying something)*

Explain to students that they can discover the "big idea" even if the writer or speaker is not available to answer the question. To find out how, assign the skills lesson and the accompanying questions.

Answers to Skill Practice

1. to announce laws regulating the maximum price of goods
2. widespread high prices
3. possible details: prices stay high even in good years or time of ample supply, some greedy merchants have enough wealth to satisfy entire nations, a single purchase might rob a soldier of his bonus or salary
4. He says, "the penalty for violating this law shall be death."

CRITICAL THINKING SKILLS

Identifying the Main Idea

As you read about world history, you come across historical dates, events, and names. These details are easier to understand and remember when they are connected to one main idea.

Understanding the main idea allows you to grasp the whole picture or story. The details then become more easily understood.

Learning the Skill Follow these steps to identify a main idea:

- Before you read the material, find out the setting of the article or document: the time, the place, and who the writer is.
- Read the material and ask, "What is the purpose of this information?"
- Study any photographs or illustrations that accompany the material.
- Ask, "What are the most forceful statements in this material?"
- Identify supporting details.
- Identify the main idea, or central issue.

Skill Practice

The passage that follows comes from a document issued by Diocletian, the emperor of Rome from 284 to 305 A.D. In it, he describes a plan for ending Rome's economic problems. Read this passage and answer the questions that follow.

In the commerce carried on in the markets or involved in the daily life of cities, high prices are so widespread that they are not lowered even by abundant supplies or good years. . . . There are men who try . . . to profit in good as well as poor years even though they have enough wealth to satisfy entire nations. . . . Prices have been driven so high that sometimes in a single purchase a soldier is deprived of his bonus and salary. . . .

We have decreed that there be established . . . maximum prices. . . . It is our pleasure, therefore, that the prices . . . be observed in the whole of our empire and the penalty for violating this law shall be death. . . . We urge obedience to this law, since it provides . . . against those whose greed could not be satisfied.

1. **Why has Diocletian issued this document?**
2. **What main idea, or central issue, is discussed by the document?**
3. **What supporting details are used to support the main idea?**
4. **What forceful statement does Diocletian use to make sure people do not miss the seriousness of the central issue?**

GO TO Glencoe's **Skillbuilder Interactive Workbook CD-ROM, Level 1,** provides instruction and practice in key social studies skills.

TEAM TEACHING STRATEGIES

Art Work with an art teacher to present a lesson on identifying the main idea in a painting or other work of art. Tell students that artists (or photographers) can get across an idea through a number of techniques. They might emphasize certain details over others. They might draw a viewer's eyes to a key figure or event. They might also use familiar symbols to convey emotion or paint figures from an emotional standpoint.

Then refer students to the sculptures on page 232. Ask: What is the subject of the sculptures? *(Roman teacher and student)* How does the artist convey this? *(sample response: older man appears to be teaching/talking to young boy)* What techniques or details did the artist use to support this idea? *(Answers will vary, but might include details such as the scroll that the boy student is holding, and the way the older man appears to be instructing.)*

Diocletian, who was the son of a freedman, ruled from 284 to 305 A.D. He made many changes as emperor. He fortified the frontiers to stop invasions. He reorganized the state and provincial governments to make them work better. To keep prices from rising, he set maximum prices for wages and goods. To make sure goods were produced, he ordered workers to stay in the same jobs until they died. He also made city officials personally responsible for the taxes their communities had to pay.

One of the most important changes Diocletian made concerned the position of the emperor. Diocletian established the official policy of **rule by divine right.** This meant the emperor's powers and right to rule came not from the people but from the gods.

Diocletian realized the Roman Empire covered too much area for one person to rule well. So, he divided it into two parts. He allowed someone else to govern the western provinces, while he ruled the richer eastern provinces.

In 312 A.D., Constantine I became emperor. He ruled until 337 A.D. Constantine took even firmer control of the empire than Diocletian. To keep people from leaving their jobs when things got bad, he issued several orders. The sons of workers had to follow their fathers' trades. The sons of farmers had to stay and work the land their fathers worked. The sons of ex-soldiers had to serve in the army.

To escape government pressure and control, wealthy landowners moved to their *villas,* or country estates. Most villas were like small, independent cities or kingdoms. Each produced enough food and goods to meet the needs of everyone who lived on the estate.

Despite the changes made by Diocletian and Constantine, the Roman Empire continued to decline in the west. In 330 A.D., Constantine moved the capital from a dying Rome east to the newly built city of Constantinople (kon stan tuh nō′ puhl) in present-day Turkey.

End of the Empire Both Diocletian and Constantine I worked hard to save the Roman Empire. However, neither emperor succeeded in the end.

German attacks increased, especially in western Europe. There, the Germans crossed the Danube River in order to escape from the Huns, nomadic herders who had wandered west from Outer Mongolia in Asia. In 378 A.D., a Germanic group defeated Roman legions at the Battle of Adrianople (ā drē uh nō′ puhl). One reason the Germans were able to defeat the Romans was because of an invention they borrowed from the Huns. This invention was the iron stirrup. Using iron stirrups made cavalry stronger than infantry, even the powerful Roman legions. This was because the force of the charging horse was added to the force of the weapon.

Reading Check What does **rule by divine right** mean?

People in History

Diocletian
245 A.D.–313 A.D.

Roman Emperor

Diocletian was born of humble parents in what is now Croatia, an area in eastern Europe ruled by the Romans. He rose to power as an officer in the Roman army, and it was his troops who proclaimed him emperor in 284 A.D. Diocletian's division of the empire into parts earned him the loyalty of powerful supporters such as Constantine I. In 305 A.D., he retired to a castle in present-day Split, Croatia.

EXTENDING THE CONTENT

The German invaders did not intend to destroy the Roman Empire. Rather they sought safety from the Huns and a share of farmlands and prosperity within the empire. The Germans included many different groups. The Visigoths crossed the Danube into Romania and won at Adrianople (now Turkey). Thirty years later, the Visigoths asked the Romans for land in Austria. When this was refused, Alaric, their leader, sacked Rome. As the Roman Empire in the West declined, other Germanic groups and kingdoms gained control. They included the Ostrogoths (East Goths), Burgundians, Franks, and Vandals.

L1 **Geography: Environment and Society** Have students trace a map of Italy. Ask them to research the Appian Way and other Roman roads and draw these on their maps. Have students include the names of towns or cities connected by the Appian Way and the other Roman roads. ELL

Reading Check Answer
Rule by divine right means that a leader's right to rule comes not from the people but from the gods.

MAKING CONNECTIONS

>> **History** Diocletian hired Germanic soldiers to fill the ranks of the Roman army, which had been depleted by plagues and war. As a result, the army no longer was the loyal citizen's army it had been in earlier Roman days.

GEOGRAPHY AND HISTORY

One reason the Huns moved into Europe was that the Great Wall, completed by the Chinese emperor Shi Huangdi, prevented the Huns from entering China.

ASSESS

Check for Understanding

Ask students to summarize the main points of the chapter. Discuss the answers to Section and Chapter Assessment questions.

Evaluate

Assign Chapter 15 **Performance Assessment Activity** in the TCR.

Administer the **Chapter 15 Test** in the TCR. Testmaker available.

Reteach

Have students work in small groups to list the Roman emperors and their accomplishments.

Assign the Chapter 15 **Reteaching Activity** in the TCR.

Enrich

Have students imagine they are a friend of a Roman emperor and write a feature describing the most difficult problems that this emperor faced.

Assign Chapter 15 **Enrichment Activity** in the TCR.

CLOSE

Write these headings on the board: *Trade, Science, Literature, Government, Law, Religion, Entertainment, Military,* and *Architecture.* Have students describe the characteristics of each of these aspects of the *Pax Romana.*

Use **Interactive Tutor Self-Assessment CD-ROM** to review Section 4.

HISTORY Online

Self-Check Quiz gives students an interactive chapter tutorial. Have them access ***Chapter 15 Quiz*** at humanheritage.glencoe.com

By about 400 A.D., Rome had grown quite weak. In the winter of 406 A.D., the Rhine River froze. Groups of Germans crossed the frozen river and entered Gaul. The Romans were not able to force them back across the border.

In 410 A.D., the Germanic chief Alaric (al' uhr ik) and his soldiers invaded Rome. They burned records and looted the treasury. The Roman Senate told the people, "You can no longer rely on Rome for finance or direction. You are on your own."

Section 4 Assessment

1. **Define:** inflation, barter, rule by divine right.
2. How did wealthy landowners react to economic reforms by Diocletian and Constantine?
3. How did the Germans gain control of the Roman Empire?

Critical Thinking

4. **Identifying Alternatives** What do you think could have been done by either Diocletian or Constantine to save the Roman Empire?

Graphic Organizer Activity

5. Draw this diagram, and use it to summarize the causes for the fall of the Roman Empire.

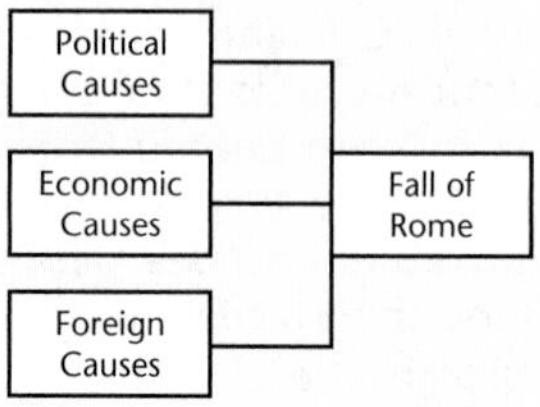

Chapter Summary & Study Guide

1. Octavian, better known as Augustus, became the first Roman emperor in 27 B.C.
2. Reorganization of the empire by Augustus introduced a 200-year period of peace, called the *Pax Romana.*
3. During the *Pax Romana,* trade increased, and Roman law became standardized.
4. During the *Pax Romana,* about one million people lived in Rome, where they suffered from such problems as overcrowding, pollution, crime, and unemployment.
5. Whether rich or poor, most Roman children went to school until age 12.
6. The Roman government staged free public games to entertain the people.
7. Reasons for the fall of Rome include the lack of a formal rule for inheriting the throne, inflation, and attacks by Germanic invaders.
8. Despite efforts by Diocletian and Constantine I to save the empire, Rome fell to Germanic invaders in 410 A.D.

HISTORY Online

Self-Check Quiz

Visit the *Human Heritage* Web site at humanheritage.glencoe.com and click on ***Chapter 15—Self-Check Quiz*** to assess your understanding of this chapter.

Section 4 Assessment Answers

1. inflation, increasing prices (p. 240); barter, exchange goods without using money (p. 241); rule by divine right, emperor's right to rule from the gods (p. 243)
2. They opposed the economic reforms or tried to escape them.
3. They defeated Roman legions at the Battle of Adrianople with the help of the iron stirrup, crossed the frozen Rhine River and entered Gaul, and invaded Rome.
4. Answers will vary. Students should explain their ideas.
5. Sample responses: *political*—no written rules on inheriting the throne, influence of the Praetorian Guard; *economic*—high taxes to buy loyalty of soldiers, inflation, gold shortages and declining value of money; *foreign*—frontiers left open to invaders, attacks by German hunters and herders, pressure from the Huns.

Assign Chapter 15 **Section 4 Quiz** in the TCR. Testmaker available.

CHAPTER 15 Assessment

Using Key Terms

Imagine you are living in Rome around 400 A.D. Use the following words to write a letter to a friend explaining some of the reasons for the decline of the Roman Empire.

emperor	freedmen	census
juris prudentes	tariffs	*domus*
gladiators	inflation	barter
rule by divine right		

Understanding Main Ideas

1. How did Augustus make life safer for people living in Rome?
2. How did increased trade during the *Pax Romana* affect the Romans?
3. Why did the Romans change the laws set down in the Twelve Tables?
4. Why was it important to make Roman law standardized across the empire?
5. What happened to some animal species as a result of the public games?
6. How did the Praetorian Guard contribute to the empire's decline?
7. Why did Diocletian divide the Roman Empire in two?
8. What were the main reasons for the fall of the Roman Empire?

Critical Thinking

1. What were Augustus's strengths and weaknesses as a ruler?
2. Why would the absence of tariffs increase trade?
3. Would you have enjoyed living in Rome during the *Pax Romana*? Explain.
4. What happens to a government if it does not have rules for passing on power from leader to leader?

Graphic Organizer Activity

Culture Create this diagram, and use it to compare the education of Roman children with the education of children in the United States.

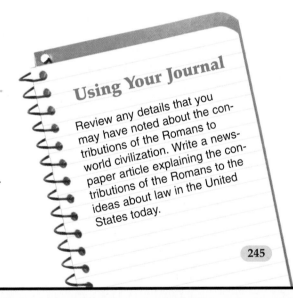

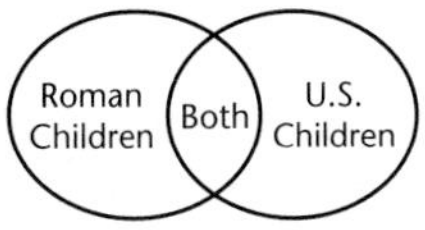

Geography in History

The World in Spatial Terms Refer to the map on page 235. Describe the general location of the Roman Empire according to its longitude and latitude. Also identify the location of the imaginary dividing line between the western and eastern empires.

Using Your Journal

Review any details that you may have noted about the contributions of the Romans to world civilization. Write a newspaper article explaining the contributions of the Romans to the ideas about law in the United States today.

245

CHAPTER 15 Assessment Answers

Using Key Terms

Letters will vary but should include all the words in explaining the end of the Roman Empire.

Understanding Main Ideas

1. by setting up a fire brigade and a police force
2. It brought more business and wealth, turning Italy into a manufacturing center.
3. because the times were different and the old laws did not apply to conquered territories
4. helped govern a large area
5. They were eventually wiped out.
6. They weakened Rome by murdering the emperor and selling the throne.
7. The Roman Empire was too big for one person to rule well.
8. the absence of a written rule for inheriting the throne, high taxes and inflation, and the Germanic invasions

Critical Thinking

1. Answers will vary but should be explained.
2. Answers will vary, but without tariffs, the prices of goods are lower.
3. Answers will vary, but students should provide reasons.
4. Answers will vary.

Graphic Organizer Activity

Review or repeat the discussion of the artifacts on page 232. Then have students complete this exercise, comparing things like subjects studied, length of education, place of schooling, and so on.

Bonus Test Question

For Chapter 15 Test

The Roman Empire's employment office has published a list of job openings, and all people are invited to apply. During the rule of which later Roman emperor, Marcus Aurelius or Diocletian, might this have occurred?

Using Your Journal

Articles will vary but might include making laws fair to everyone; considering a person innocent until proven guilty; requiring the accuser to have to prove a case; standardizing legal procedures.

Geography in History

The empire stretched from about 10° W to 45° E longitude, and north and south from 25° N to 40° N latitude. The division between empires approximately paralleled 20°E longitude.

Chapter 16 Planning Guide

Timesaving Tools

TeacherWorks™ All-In-One Planner and Resource Center

- **Interactive Teacher Edition** Access your Teacher Wraparound Edition and your classroom resources with a few easy clicks.
- **Interactive Lesson Planner** Planning has never been easier! Organize your week, month, semester, or year with all the lesson helps you need to make teaching creative, timely, and relevant.

PRESENTATION Plus!

Use Glencoe's **Presentation Plus!** multimedia teacher tool to easily present dynamic lessons that visually excite your students. Using Microsoft PowerPoint® you can customize the presentations to create your own personalized lessons.

Objectives	Reproducible Resources	Multimedia Resources
Section 1 **The Beginnings** Explain how Jesus' life and teachings formed the basis of Christianity.	Reproducible Lesson Plan Chapter 16 Vocabulary and Guided Reading Activity Reading Essentials and Study Guide 16-1 Chapter 16 Enrichment Activity Section 1 Quiz	Interactive Student Edition CD-ROM Graphic Organizer Transparency 8 Vocabulary PuzzleMaker CD-ROM Interactive Tutor Self-Assessment CD-ROM ExamView® Pro Testmaker CD-ROM Glencoe Skillbuilder Interactive Workbook CD-ROM, Level 1 Presentation Plus! CD-ROM
Section 2 **Christianity and Rome** Summarize how Christianity spread throughout the Roman Empire.	Reproducible Lesson Plan Reading Essentials and Study Guide 16-2 Chapter 16 Geography and Map Activity Chapter 16 Cooperative Learning Activity Section 2 Quiz	Vocabulary PuzzleMaker CD-ROM Interactive Tutor Self-Assessment CD-ROM ExamView® Pro Testmaker CD-ROM Glencoe Skillbuilder Interactive Workbook CD-ROM, Level 1
Section 3 **The Church** Explain how the early Christian church was organized and what relationship existed between Christianity and Roman society before and after the time of Constantine I.	Reproducible Lesson Plan Reading Essentials and Study Guide 16-3 Chapter 16 Chart and Graph Skill Activity Section 3 Quiz	Teaching Transparencies and Activities 16A & 16B Vocabulary PuzzleMaker CD-ROM Interactive Tutor Self-Assessment CD-ROM ExamView® Pro Testmaker CD-ROM Glencoe Skillbuilder Interactive Workbook CD-ROM, Level 1
Chapter 16 **Review and Evaluation**	Chapter 16 Reteaching Activity Chapter 16 Performance Assessment Activity Unit 5 Standardized Test Practice Spanish Chapter Summary and Glossary Chapter 16 Test	Vocabulary PuzzleMaker CD-ROM Interactive Tutor Self-Assessment CD-ROM Glencoe Skillbuilder Interactive Workbook CD-ROM, Level 1 Audiocassettes* ExamView® Pro Testmaker CD-ROM

*Also available in Spanish.

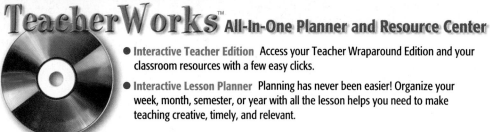

Performance Assessment Activities

Religion Have students imagine that they are Constantine I. Tell them to write a speech in which Constantine explains to his soldiers that he has converted to Christianity. Call on students to read their speeches to the class.

CHAPTER RESOURCES

LITERATURE ABOUT THE PERIOD

Comte, Fernand. *Sacred Writings of World Religions.* Chambers, 1992. Examines the history, beliefs, and major figures of more than 20 religions, among them Judaism, Islam, and Christianity.

READINGS FOR THE STUDENT

Rice, Edward. *The Early Christians: A Young People's Pictorial History of the Church.* Farrar Straus, 1963. An adaptation of a well-known Roman Catholic scholar's history of the early Church.

READINGS FOR THE TEACHER

Chadwick, Henry and G. R. Evans, eds. *Atlas of the Christian Church.* Facts on File, 1987. Offers an authoritative survey of the impact of the Christian Church on world civilization.

Gibbon, Edward. *The Early Growth of Christianity & the History of the First Christians.* American Classical College Press, 1986. Discusses the history of the first Christians.

KEY TO ABILITY LEVELS

Teaching strategies have been coded for varying learning styles and abilities.

L1 Level 1 activities are **basic** activities and should be within the ability range of all students.

L2 Level 2 activities are **average** activities and should be within the ability range of the average to above-average student.

L3 Level 3 activities are **challenging** activities designed for the ability range of above-average students.

ELL ELL activities should be within the ability range of English Language Learning students.

NATIONAL GEOGRAPHIC Teacher's Corner

INDEX TO NATIONAL GEOGRAPHIC MAGAZINE

The following articles relate to this chapter:

- "Abraham: Journey of Faith," by Tad Szulc, December 2001.
- "The Three Faces of Jerusalem," by Alan Mairson, April 1996.

NATIONAL GEOGRAPHIC SOCIETY PRODUCTS AVAILABLE FROM GLENCOE

To order the following, call Glencoe at 1-800-334-7344:

- *PicturePack: Ancient Rome (Transparencies)*
- *PictureShow: Ancient Civilizations: Greece and Rome (CD-ROM)*
- *PicturePack: Ancient Civilizations Library, Part I (Transparencies)*

ADDITIONAL NATIONAL GEOGRAPHIC SOCIETY PRODUCTS

To order the following, call National Geographic at 1-800-368-2728:

- *Jerusalem: Within These Walls (Video)*

Access *National Geographic's* new dynamic MapMachine Web site and other geography resources at:
www.nationalgeographic.com
www.nationalgeographic.com/maps

THE HISTORY CHANNEL. A&E HOME VIDEO. Biography

The following videotape programs are available from Glencoe:

- **Constantine: The Christian Emperor**
  0-7670-0577-5
- **Shroud of Turin**
  1-56501-557-6
- **Who Built the Catacombs?**
  1-56501-881-8

To order, call Glencoe at 1-800-334-7344. To find classroom resources to accompany many of these, check:
A&E Television: www.aande.com
The History Channel: www.historychannel.com

Introducing **CHAPTER 16**

OVERVIEW

Chapter 16 describes the rise of Christianity and its impact on the Roman Empire.

- ➤ **Section 1** discusses the origins of Christianity.
- ➤ **Section 2** describes the difficulties Christianity faced in a hostile Roman society.
- ➤ **Section 3** explains the organization of the Roman Catholic church.

CHAPTER OBJECTIVES

After reading Chapter 16, students will be able to:

1. explain how Jesus' life and teachings formed the basis of Christianity.

2. trace the spread of Christianity.

3. explain how the early Christian church was organized.

4. discuss the relationship between Christianity and Roman society before and after the time of Constantine I.

EXAMINING ARTIFACTS

Ask students why, based on the jeweled artifact, Roman officials might consider Jesus a threat. *(Students may note that he is seated on a throne, a symbol of royal power, and portrayed as a sacred figure, which challenged Roman gods.)* Tell students that in this chapter they will learn how Romans tried to stop Christianity and how it spread nonetheless.

PERFORMANCE ASSESSMENT

Use the Performance Assessment Activities on page 246B to help you evaluate students as they complete the chapter.

CHAPTER 16

Christianity

1 B.C.–1054 A.D.

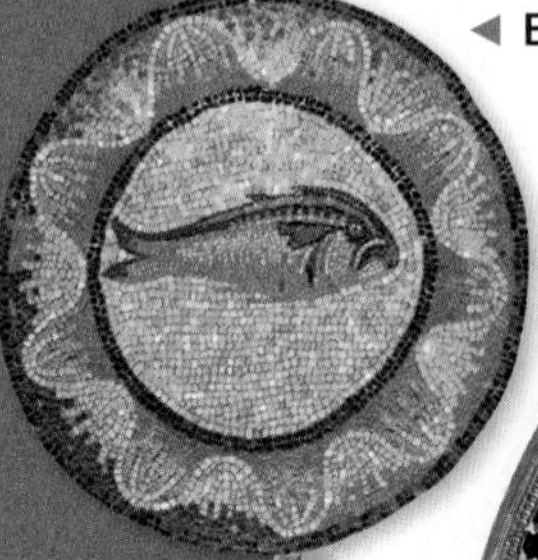

◄ Early Christian symbol

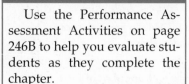

Jesus on his throne ►

30 A.D. Jesus is crucified by Romans

64 A.D. Romans ban Christianity

312 A.D. Constantine I accepts Christianity

392 A.D. Christianity becomes official religion of Roman Empire

1054 A.D. Latin and Greek churches separate

TEACHING RESOURCES

TEACHER PLANNING AND SUPPORT

- Reproducible Lesson Plan 16-1, 16-2, 16-3
- Teaching Strategies for the World History Classroom (Including Block Scheduling Pacing Guides)
- Presentation Plus! CD-ROM

REVIEW AND REINFORCEMENT

- Reading Essentials and Study Guide 16-1, 16-2, 16-3
- Chapter 16 Vocabulary and Guided Reading Activity
- Vocabulary PuzzleMaker CD-ROM
- Teaching Transparencies 16A & 16B
- Chapter 16 Reteaching Activity
- Chapter 16 Cooperative Learning Activity
- Chapter 16 Activity Book Activity
- Chapter 16 Chart and Graph Skill Activity
- Reading and Study Skills Foldables
- Interactive Tutor Self-Assessment CD-ROM
- Unit 5 MindJogger VideoQuiz

APPLICATION AND HANDS-ON ACTIVITIES

- Daily Questions in Social Studies
- Student Presentation Builder CD-ROM

GEOGRAPHY ACTIVITIES

- Chapter 16 Geography and Map Activity
- Outline Map Resource Book

Chapter Focus

Read to Discover

- How Jesus' life and teachings formed the basis of Christianity.
- How Christianity spread throughout the Roman Empire.
- How the early Christian church was organized.
- What relationship existed between Christianity and Roman society before and after the time of Constantine I.
- What life was like for the early monks and nuns.

HISTORY Online

Chapter Overview

Visit the *Human Heritage* Web site at **humanheritage.glencoe.com** and click on ***Chapter 16—Chapter Overviews*** to preview this chapter.

Terms to Learn

scriptures
messiah
gentiles
missionary
churches
apostles
priest
bishop
heresy
monks
nuns

People to Know

Jesus
Paul
Constantine I
Theodosius
Jerome
Augustine

Places to Locate

Bethlehem
Nazareth
Jerusalem

Why It's Important Christians brought new ideas and important changes to the Roman Empire. Their religion, Christianity, started in Palestine among the Jews and later spread throughout the empire and the world. Despite cruel treatment, the early Christians clung to their faith, and by 400 A.D. most Romans had come to accept the religion as their own.

SECTION 1 The Beginnings

Christianity is based on the life and teachings of Jesus (jē′ zuhs), who lived in Palestine during the reign of Augustus. After Jesus died, his teachings were spread by his followers. Christianity survived the fall of Rome and grew to be one of the major influences on western civilization.

The Life of Jesus Jesus, born a Jew in the town of Bethlehem (beth′ luh hem), grew up in Nazareth (naz′ uhr uhth). There, he received a Jewish education. He studied the **scriptures**

Reading Check What are the **scriptures?**

HISTORY Online

Chapter Overview introduces students to chapter content and key terms. Have them access ***Chapter 16 Overview*** at **humanheritage.glencoe.com**

FOCUS

Bellringer

Write the following unfinished statement on the chalkboard. *"When I hear the word Christianity, the first thing I think of is_______."* Ask students to fill in the blank.

Motivational Activity

Discuss student responses to the unfinished statement. Explain that in this chapter they will learn about the teachings of Jesus and the religion that eventually became Christianity.

GUIDE TO READING

Reading Strategy

Ask students to read "Why It's Important" and summarize the chapter's main theme. *(Despite early resistance, Romans came to accept Christianity—a religion that started in Palestine among the Jews.)*

Vocabulary Precheck

Ask students to define each of the "Terms to Learn." Have a volunteer consult the dictionary for any unfamiliar words. L1 ELL

Use the Vocabulary PuzzleMaker CD-ROM for Chapter 16 to create a crossword puzzle. L1

Assign Chapter 16 Vocabulary and Guided Reading Activity.

Assign Reading Essentials and Study Guide 16-1.

Reading Check Answer **Scriptures** are sacred writings.

INTERDISCIPLINARY CONNECTIONS

- World Art & Architecture Transparency 13, *Cover of the Lindau Gospels*
- World Music: A Cultural Legacy

ENRICHMENT AND EXTENSION

- World History Primary Source Document Library CD-ROM
- Chapter 16 Enrichment Activity
- Foods Around the World

ASSESSMENT AND EVALUATION

- Chapter 16 Performance Assessment Activity
- Chapter 16 Section Quizzes 16-1, 16-2, 16-3
- Chapter 16 Test
- Unit 5 Standardized Test Practice
- Chapter 16 ExamView® Pro Testmaker CD-ROM
- Chapter 16 Digests Audiocassettes Activities and Tests

SPANISH RESOURCES

- Chapter 16 Spanish Chapter Summary and Glossary
- Chapter 16 Spanish Digests Audiocassettes Activities and Tests

TEACH

Guided Practice

L1 **Writing** Ask the students to rewrite the parable of the man from Samaria (the Good Samaritan) as if the story took place in modern times. Have students read their parables to the class and explain any changes in the meaning from the original that occurred in modernizing it.

DID YOU KNOW ??

During the time that Jesus preached, there were about 2.5 million Jews in Palestine and another 4 million elsewhere in the Roman Empire.

Reading Check Answer

Jews waited for the arrival of a **messiah** who would save them.

Mosaic of Christian Symbol

(skrip' churz), or sacred writings, and learned prayers in the Hebrew language. Later, he went to work as a carpenter.

When he was about 30 years old, Jesus began to travel around Palestine preaching to people. Men and women came in large numbers from all over the country to see and hear him. Jesus taught that God created all people and loves them the way a father loves his children. Therefore, people should behave like God's children and love God and one another. Jesus said that God loves even people who have sinned. Jesus told people that if they were truly sorry and placed their trust in God, they would be forgiven.

Jesus spoke in the everyday language of the people. He presented his teachings in *parables* (par' uh buhlz), or stories, about persons and things that were familiar to his listeners. In this way, they could better understand the religious principles he was trying to teach. For example, in the parable of the Good Samaritan (suh mar' uh tuhn), Jesus told about a man from Jerusalem who was attacked by robbers. They beat the man severely and left him lying in the road. Two passers-by from Jerusalem saw him there but did nothing. Then came a man from the city of Samaria (suh mar' ē uh). He stopped, washed the man's wounds, and carried him to a nearby inn. The parable taught that people should not ignore wrong but should do something about it. The parable also taught that people should help everyone, not just those from their own community.

In 30 A.D., after about three years of preaching, Jesus and 12 of his disciples went to Jerusalem to celebrate Passover, the holiday that marks the exodus of the Jews from Egypt. At the time, there was much unrest in the city. Many Romans were angry because the Jews refused to worship statues of the Roman emperor. The Jews were tired of the high taxes they had to pay and of the pressure put on them by the Romans. They hoped and waited for a **messiah** (muh sī' uh), or someone who would save them.

Reading Check Why did Jews await the arrival of a **messiah?**

When Jesus arrived in Jerusalem, many Jews greeted him as the messiah. This worried other Jews and Romans alike. Jesus was convicted of treason under Roman law and was *crucified* (krū' suh fīd), or executed on a cross, outside Jerusalem. Usually, only lower-class criminals were killed in this way.

Painting of Some of Jesus' Disciples

The loss of their leader greatly saddened Jesus' disciples. Then, according to Christian tradition, Jesus rose from the dead. He remained on Earth for 40 days before going directly to heaven. His *resurrection* (rez uh rek' shuhn), or rising from the dead, convinced his disciples that Jesus was the Son of God who had become man. They believed that because Jesus had suffered death and had risen to life, he could forgive the sins of all people. They thought that anyone who believed in Jesus and lived by his teachings would know eternal life after death. From then on, the disciples called him Christ, after the Greek word *Christos* (khrēs tōs'), meaning "messiah."

MEETING SPECIAL NEEDS

Have auditory learners interview a Christian minister, a priest, or a Jewish rabbi about the Jewish roots of Christianity. Students should prepare a list of questions in advance of their interview, and then they should tape record their interviews. Have students report orally on their interviews.

Refer to ***Inclusion for the Middle School Social Studies Classroom: Strategies and Activities*** for additional resources.

THE LAST SUPPER The night before he was crucified, Jesus met with his closest disciples for the meal that marks the start of Passover. At this meal, known as the Last Supper, Jesus set the guidelines for later Christian ceremonies. **Why did Jesus and his disciples go to Jerusalem?**

Paul The disciples were among the first people to become Christians. After Jesus died, they tried to spread his *gospel,* or teachings, among the Jews in Palestine. They had little success, however. Most Palestinian Jews wanted a political messiah. They were not interested in a religious one. The disciples then began to spread their message to Jews who lived outside Palestine. Soon, small groups of people who believed in Christ were meeting in Antioch (ant' ē ahk), Corinth, Rome, and other trading cities of the Mediterranean area.

At about the same time, a Jew named Paul decided to teach Christianity to **gentiles** (jen' tīls), or non-Jews, as well as to Jews. Paul had once been a close follower of Judaism. Then, according to Christian tradition, while he was traveling on the road to Damascus (duh mas' kuhs), Paul was blinded by a bright light and heard Christ's voice. After he was able to see again, Paul became a Christian. He spent the rest of his life spreading the Christian message throughout the Roman world.

Reading Check Who were the **gentiles?**

CAPTION ANSWER

to celebrate the Jewish holiday of Passover

LINKING PAST TO PRESENT

About 1497, Italian Leonardo da Vinci painted the scene "The Last Supper" on a monastery wall. Soon after he finished the scene, the paint began to peel. Today the painting, although still greatly admired and considered a masterpiece, is in poor condition.

Reading Check Answer The **gentiles** were non-Jews.

A&E HOME VIDEO.

The following videotape program is available from Glencoe to enrich Chapter 16:

- **Shroud of Turin**

To find classroom resources to accompany this video, check the following home page:

A&E Television:
www.aande.com

MULTICULTURAL PERSPECTIVES

Messiah comes from a Hebrew word that means "the anointed one." The term derives from an ancient but widespread custom of using sacred oil in certain kinds of religious ceremonies. A priest might, for instance, place holy oil on the head of a new ruler to indicate God's approval. Anointing was also used in times of danger to give symbolic protection. Sometimes objects (even weapons) were anointed. The Greek word *Christos* also means "anointed one."

MAKING CONNECTIONS

>> **History** The last Roman emperor to persecute large numbers of Christians was Diocletian. In A.D. 311, Galerius, ruler of the Eastern Roman Empire, permitted freedom of worship.

Reading Check Answer

Paul is considered the first Christian **missionary** because he worked to spread religious beliefs to those who did not believe.

DID YOU KNOW ??

According to traditional legend, the emperor Nero sat in his palace and "fiddled" while Rome burned. In reality there were no fiddles at the time; Nero played a harp. One story hinted that Nero himself set fire to the city so he could admire the sight of Rome in flames.

Use **Interactive Tutor Self-Assessment CD-ROM** to review Section 1.

HISTORY Online

Student Web Activity objectives and answers can be found at the ***Chapter 16 Web Activity Lesson Plan*** at **humanheritage.glencoe.com**

Use the **Vocabulary PuzzleMaker CD-ROM** to create crossword and word search puzzles.

In each city where Paul preached, new Christian communities formed. Paul wrote letters to these groups to help guide the members. In his letters, he stated that gentiles who became Christians did not have to follow Jewish rituals and laws. All they needed was to have faith in Jesus. This appealed to many people.

Reading Check Why is Paul considered the first Christian **missionary**?

Paul was very important to the growth of Christianity. He was its first **missionary** (mish' uh ner ē), or person who spreads religious beliefs to those who do not believe. After Paul's death, other Christian missionaries continued his work.

Section 1 Assessment

1. **Define:** scriptures, messiah, gentiles, missionary.
2. Why did the Romans charge Jesus with treason?
3. What changes did Paul make in the Christian religion?

Critical Thinking

4. **Demonstrating Reasoned Judgment** Of the people you know about today, who could be called a Good Samaritan? Give examples.

Graphic Organizer Activity

5. Draw this diagram, and use it to show some of the Christian beliefs taught by Jesus.

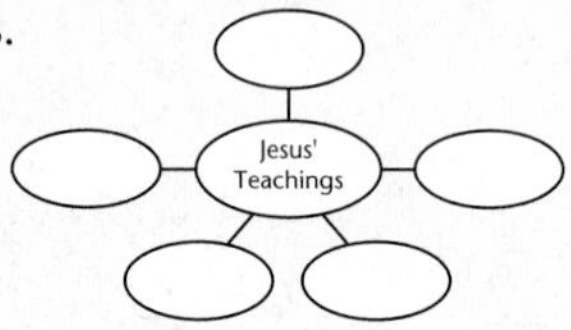

SECTION 2 Christianity and Rome

The Roman Empire helped Christianity spread. The *Pax Romana* allowed missionaries to move across Roman lands in safety. The Roman system of roads helped them go from one place to another quickly. Since most people spoke either Latin or Greek, the missionaries could talk with them directly.

Political Conditions Political conditions did not favor the spread of Christianity, however. Although all people in the Roman Empire were generally allowed to worship freely, the Romans expected everyone to honor the emperor as a god. The Christians, like the Jews, refused to do this. They claimed that only God could be worshiped. This made the Romans angry.

HISTORY Online

Student Web Activity
Visit the *Human Heritage* Web site at **humanheritage.glencoe.com** and click on ***Chapter 16—Student Web Activities*** to find out more about early Christianity.

The Romans also did not like other Christian ideas. For example, Christians did not want to serve in the army or hold public office. They often criticized Roman festivals and games. They taught that all people would be equal in heaven if they followed Jesus' teachings.

Because of these differences, the Romans blamed and punished Christians for all kinds of disasters, such as plagues and famines (fam' uhnz). In 64 A.D., the Romans accused the Chris-

Section 1 Assessment Answers

1. scriptures, sacred writings (p. 247); messiah, savior (p. 248); gentiles, non-Jews (p. 249); missionary, person who spreads religious beliefs to nonbelievers (p. 250)
2. because many Jews greeted him like the messiah, which threatened the power of the Roman emperor
3. that gentiles who became Christians did not have to follow Jewish rituals and laws but needed only to have faith in Jesus
4. Answers will vary but should be examples of situations in which a person came to the help of another person.
5. Sample beliefs: God created all people and loves them, people should behave like God's children and love one another, God loves even people who have sinned, anyone who puts trust in God will be forgiven, and people should help each other.

Assign Chapter 16 **Section 1 Quiz** in the TCR. Testmaker available.

tians of starting a fire that burned much of Rome. Christianity was then made illegal, and many Christians were killed.

Some officials paid no attention to the law that made Christianity illegal. However, Christians still had a hard time in most areas. In Rome, they were not allowed to use Roman burial places. They had to bury their dead in crowded catacombs.

The Spread of Christianity Even with all of the hardships, Christianity spread. It was of more interest to the poor workers and enslaved people in the cities. They led very hard lives. They liked a religion that promised a happier life after death.

Over time, however, Christianity began to draw people from all classes. After 250 A.D., many Romans grew tired of war and

MAP STUDY

HUMAN SYSTEMS
By 1100 Christianity had spread throughout most of Europe and parts of Asia and North Africa. **How did Paul's journeys help the spread of Christianity?**

The Spread of Christianity

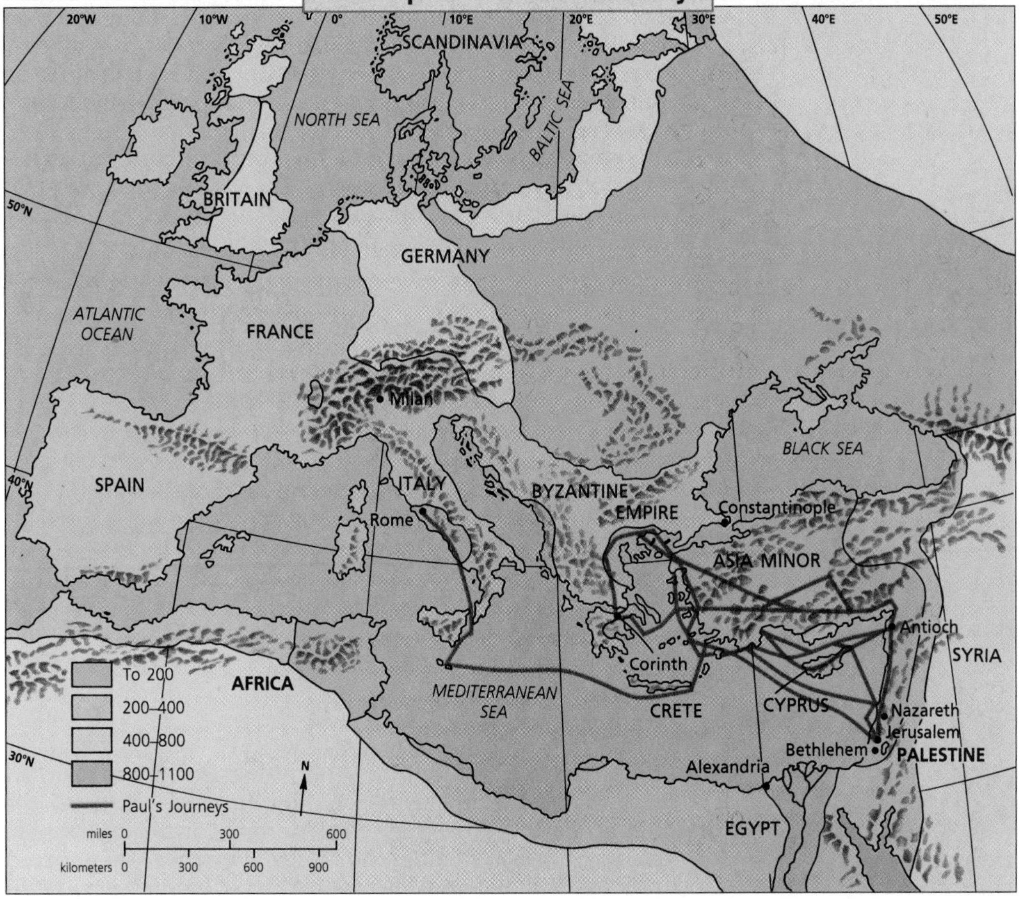

L3 Geography: Places and Regions Have students refer to the map of "The Spread of Christianity." Have them discuss the difference in size of the religion's area of influence from 200 to 1100, and the pattern, if any, that it followed. Then have students use the map scale to calculate the approximate length of the empire, from west to east, by the year 1100.

L2 Critical Thinking Have students discuss the major differences in attitudes that existed between some Roman non-Christians and Christians. Have students list these differences in two columns under the headings *Christian* and *non-Christian*. *(Students should mention differences over army service, and who should be honored as a god, hold public office, and be blamed for disasters.)* ELL

MAP STUDY

Answer

Paul traveled extensively throughout the Mediterranean region spreading the ideas of Christianity.

Assign Chapter 16 **Geography and Map Activity** in the TCR.

DID YOU KNOW ??

Early Christians tried to escape Roman persecution by worshiping in catacombs—underground passages dug by the Christians.

COOPERATIVE LEARNING

Divide students into several groups. Have each group research one of the various religions practiced in the Roman Empire. Make sure each group member is responsible for either research, compiling information, providing illustrations, preparing answers for possible questions, or presenting to the class. Religions to be researched include the official religion of Rome, Judaism, Christianity, and the Persian and Egyptian mystery religions, such as Mithraism and the cult of Isis. Have the groups act as a panel, answering questions from the class about the religion it studied.

Assign Chapter 16 ***Cooperative Learning Activity*** in the TCR.

feared the end of the empire. They began to admire the certainty and courage of the Christian missionaries. They wanted the love, kindness, and feeling of safety that Christianity offered. At the same time, many Christians started to accept the empire.

Constantine I and Theodosius In 312 A.D., Constantine I, who was a general at the time, accepted Christianity. Legend says that as he was about to go into battle, Constantine saw a flaming cross in the sky. Written beneath the cross were the Latin words *in hoc signo vinces* (in hok sig′ nō win′ kās). This means, "In this sign thou shalt conquer." Constantine won the battle and with it the throne of the Roman Empire. Constantine believed God had helped him gain his victory. Because of this, he ordered his soldiers to paint crosses on their shields.

The following year, the Edict (ē′ dikt) of Milan (mi lan′) was issued. It gave religious freedom to all people. It also made Christianity legal. Constantine I did many other things to help Christianity grow. He had churches built in Rome and Jerusalem. He used government money to pay for Christian schools. He let church leaders enter government service and excused them from paying taxes.

The emperor who followed Constantine I continued pro-Christian policies. In 392 A.D., Emperor Theodosius (thē uh dō′ shē uhs) made Christianity the official religion of the Roman Empire. At the same time, he outlawed all other religions.

Section 2 Assessment

1. What factors brought about a change in attitude between Romans and Christians?
2. What did Christians believe would happen to people in heaven?

Critical Thinking

3. **Making Inferences** Why do you think the hardships put on Christians by the Romans could not stop the spread of Christianity?

Graphic Organizer Activity

4. Draw this diagram, and use it to show what life was like for Christians before and after the rule of Constantine I.

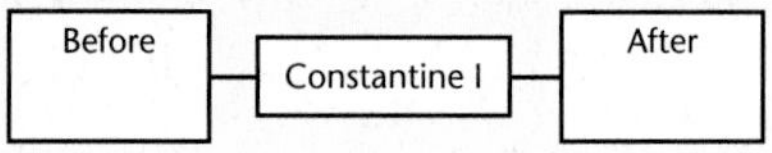

SECTION 3 The Church

Reading Check Why did early Christians form **churches**?

Early Christians thought the end of the world was near. At the time, they believed Jesus would return to set up God's kingdom on Earth. While they were waiting for this to happen, they lived together in small groups called **churches.** They shared their possessions and took turns leading worship services in

L3 **Culture** Write the following headings on the board: *Roman Soldiers, Wealthy Landowners, Farming Families.* Ask the class to discuss what each group might say about the spread of Christianity if interviewed. List students' responses under the appropriate headings. Then ask students to explain reasons for their answers. ELL

Economics at a Glance

Nonprofit Organizations Most businesses produce goods and services in the hopes of earning a profit for their owners. Nonprofit organizations operate on a "not-for-profit" basis. They operate like a business, but they provide services to their members while they seek other rewards. Nonprofit organizations include schools, hospitals, and churches. These organizations work to improve education and help the sick and those in need. These organizations do not pay income taxes. Have students write a list of nonprofit organizations in their community. Organize students into pairs and have them contact one of the organizations to find out what it does and how it spends its money. Students should report their findings to the class.

Reading Check Answer Christians formed **churches** where they could live and worship together until Jesus returned.

Use **Interactive Tutor Self-Assessment CD-ROM** to review Section 2.

Use the **Vocabulary PuzzleMaker CD-ROM** to create crossword and word search puzzles.

Section 2 Assessment Answers

1. The Romans grew tired of war and began to admire the courage of Christian missionaries and Christian values.
2. They would live happier lives.
3. Answers will vary but could note that people were tired of the Roman Empire and its decline.
4. Sample responses: *Before*—Romans blamed Christians for many wrongs, banned their religion, killed or persecuted them, and forbade them from burying their dead in Roman cemeteries. *After*—Christians could worship freely in their own churches, receive government money for schools, serve in government, and so on.

Assign Chapter 16 **Section 2 Quiz** in the TCR. Testmaker available.

homes and outdoors. Each group was in charge of its own affairs. **Apostles** (uh pos' uhls), or those people Jesus chose to teach his gospel, visited the different groups. The apostles taught and gave advice. They also provided a sense of unity.

Reading Check Who were the **apostles?**

Church Structure After the apostles died, Christians realized that Jesus was not going to return to Earth as quickly as they had expected. They looked for ways to hold their churches together. One way was by organizing the churches. They used the Roman Empire's structure of government as a model for this organization.

By 300 A.D., each church was called a **parish** (par' ish). Each had a leader known as a **priest.** Several parishes were put together into larger groups. Each group was called a **diocese** (dī' uh sis), a word that originally meant a Roman military district. A **bishop** headed each diocese. The most important bishops were called **archbishops.** They governed churches in larger cities. The five leading archbishops were called **patriarchs** (pā' trē arks).

Reading Check What is a **parish?** What was the role of an early **priest?** What was the original meaning of **diocese?**

Reading Check What was the role of the **bishop?** Who were the **archbishops** and **patriarchs?**

As time went on, the archbishop of Rome began to claim power over the other archbishops. By 600 A.D., he was called Pope. This comes from a Latin word meaning "father." Christians who spoke Latin saw him as the head of all the churches. Christians who spoke Greek, however, would not accept him as the leader of their churches. They turned instead to the archbishop of Constantinople. In 1054 A.D., the two church groups separated. The Latin churches as a group became known as the Roman Catholic Church. The Greek churches became known as the Eastern Orthodox Church.

The New Testament At the same time Christians were developing a church organization, they were deciding what writings to put into the New Testament, or Christian scriptures. Jesus had left no written records. However, after his death, others wrote about Jesus' life and teachings.

Toward the end of the 300s A.D., four accounts were accepted as part of the New Testament. The accounts were believed to have been written by Matthew, Mark, Luke, and John. These men were four of Jesus' early followers. A number of letters written by Paul and other disciples were also accepted as part of the New Testament.

At about the same time, bishops met to discuss questions about Christian thinking. Decisions they reached at these meetings came to be accepted as official *doctrine* (dok' truhn), or statements of faith. The points of view the bishops did not accept were declared to be **heresy** (her' uh sē), or false doctrines.

Reading Check What did bishops consider as **heresy?**

Fathers of the Church Between 100 and 500 A.D., different scholars wrote works that greatly influenced later Christians. These scholars became known as the "Fathers of the Church."

Reading Check Answer The **apostles** were the people Jesus chose to spread his teachings.

Reading Check Answer A **parish** is a local church. A **priest** was the leader of a parish. The word **diocese** originally meant a Roman military district.

MAKING CONNECTIONS

>> **Language** The word *church* means "belonging to the Lord."

Reading Check Answer A **bishop** headed each diocese. **Archbishops** were the most important bishops, and the five leading archbishops were called **patriarchs.**

Independent Practice

L3 **Critical Thinking** Ask students to write a brief description of everything they can remember that happened in class the day before. Have students read descriptions aloud to compare details. After students conclude that some differences are bound to appear, ask them why they think the same events are retold in different chapters of the New Testament.

Reading Check Answer Bishops considered views contrary to official church teachings as **heresy**.

MULTICULTURAL PERSPECTIVES

The Bible is the most sacred book to Christians. They consider the Bible to be the word of God. The word *Bible* comes from a Greek word that means "books." The Bible is not one book but actually a collection of books, or sections. The number of books in the Bible depends on the Christian group. The Roman Catholic Bible includes 73 books, while most Protestant groups include 66 books in their Bible. It is the most-read book in history.

Linking Across Time

Religious Orders The religious order that lived at the monastery at Monte Cassino (left) followed the teachings of Benedict and were known as Benedictines. In 1950, Mother Teresa, an eastern European nun, continued this tradition by founding the Missionaries of Charity, an order dedicated to helping the poor of India (right). **What rules did early members of the Benedictine order follow?**

People in History

Saint Augustine
354 A.D.–430 A.D.

Christian Scholar

Augustine was born in present-day Algeria. In 387 A.D., he embraced Christianity. As invaders poured into Rome, Augustine became one of the leading defenders of Christianity. After his death, church leaders declared him a saint.

One such scholar was Jerome (juh rōm'). He translated the Old and New Testaments into Latin. His translation was called the *Vulgate* (vul' gāt). It became the official Bible used by the Roman Catholic Church.

Augustine (o' guh stēn) was an important leader of Christian thought. His best-known work was *City of God.* In it, he defended Christianity against those who said that Rome would not have fallen if it had not accepted Christianity. Augustine said that Rome fell because it became rich and corrupt and persecuted Christians.

Monasteries

In the early years of Christianity, thousands of Christians left the cities to live and pray alone in isolated areas. Such people were known as *hermits.* In Egypt and Syria especially, thousands of hermits lived in the desert. They believed that this would help them grow closer to Christ.

A hermit was protected from the temptations of daily life. At the same time, however, such a person was not doing anything to improve the world. Near the end of the 300s A.D., a bishop named Basil (baz' uhl) suggested a different way of life. He said that Christians should form religious settlements near cities. In this way, they would be protected from the evils of the world. At the same time, they could help other people by doing good deeds and

Linking Across Time

Followers of Benedict promised to give up all their possessions, wear simple clothes, and eat only certain foods. They agreed not to marry, obeyed abbots without question, and attended religious services day and night. They also worked in the fields and church and spent their lives serving Christ.

DID YOU KNOW ??

St. Augustine was born a Christian but left Christianity at age 17. In 387 A.D., he met St. Ambrose, the bishop of Milan, who influenced him to return to Christianity.

L1 **The Arts** Many movies have been made about the life of Jesus or the impact of Christianity on the people of ancient Rome. Have students view a videotape of *The Robe, Ben Hur, The Silver Chalice,* or *The Greatest Story Ever Told* and then write a review of the film. Tell them to include descriptions of details they learned about life under *Pax Romana.* (For example, in *Ben Hur,* the chariot races; in *The Robe,* the Roman legionaries). ELL

A&E HOME VIDEO.

The following videotape program is available from Glencoe to enrich Chapter 16:

- **Constantine: The Christian Emperor**

To find classroom resources to accompany this video, check the following home page:

A&E Television:
www.aande.com

EXTENDING THE CONTENT

The first significant translation of the scriptures was by St. Jerome, which he began in about 383 at the request of the Pope. Jerome first translated the Gospels. They came from several sources, mainly Greek. The scholarly Jerome then decided the standard Greek translation of the Old Testament would not do. He went back to Hebrew sources and made a new translation. His work completed in about 405, was called *Vulgate,* from the Latin word meaning popular.

by setting an example of Christian living. Many Christians took Basil's advice.

Christian men who did as Basil suggested were called **monks.** Their settlements, or communities, were known as **monasteries** (mon' uh ster ēz). Christian women who did the same were called **nuns.** They lived in quarters of their own called **convents** (kon' vents). Basil drew up a list of rules for these religious communities. This list, which is known as the Basilian (buh zil' ē uhn) Rule, became the model for Eastern Orthodox religious life.

In the West, another set of rules called the Benedictine (ben uh dik' tuhn) Rule was followed. It was drawn up about 529 A.D. by an Italian named Benedict (ben' uh dikt). The monks who followed Benedict's rule promised to give up all their possessions before entering a monastery. They agreed to wear simple clothes and eat only certain foods. They could not marry. They had to obey without question the orders of the **abbot** (ab' uht), or leader of the monastery. They had to attend religious services seven times during the day and once at midnight. They also were expected to work six or seven hours a day in the fields around the monastery. When they grew older, they did clerical work or worked as carpenters and weavers. They spent their whole lives serving Christ.

Reading Check Why did **monks** build the first **monasteries?** Why did Christian women become **nuns** and live at **convents?**

Reading Check What was the role of an **abbot?**

EARLY CHRISTIANS Church leaders often dictated their thoughts as Pope Gregory is shown (left) doing. Those thoughts were studied by a church monk shown here (right) in order to improve his knowledge of Christianity. **Where did monks at this time live?**

EXTENDING THE CONTENT

Many monks copied ancient manuscripts. Without their efforts many literature classics would have been lost. Monks also served as missionaries, sent by the monasteries to spread the religious message to neighboring people. Nuns taught needlework and the medicinal use of herbs to the daughters of nobles.

Reading Check Answer **Monks** built the first **monasteries** to do good works and serve as an example of Christian living.
Christian women became **nuns** and lived at **convents** for much the same reason as monks.

Reading Check Answer An **abbot** was the leader of a monastery.

CAPTION ANSWER

monasteries

ASSESS

Check for Understanding

Ask students to summarize the main points of the chapter, orally or in writing. Discuss the answers to the Section and Chapter Assessment questions.

Evaluate

Assign Chapter 16 **Performance Assessment Activity** in the TCR.

Administer **Chapter 16 Test** in the TCR. Testmaker available.

Reteach

Help students create an outline of the chapter on the board. Have students work in pairs to ask one another questions using the outline.

Assign Chapter 16 **Reteaching Activity** in the TCR.

Enrich

Have students research the parables told by Jesus. Have students retell a parable to the class and explain its meaning.

Assign Chapter 16 **Enrichment Activity** in the TCR.

GLENCOE TECHNOLOGY

MindJogger Videoquiz

Use **MindJogger Videoquiz** to review students' knowledge of the unit.

Available in DVD and VHS

CLOSE

Ask students to discuss what Jesus meant when he said that he would make his disciples "fishers of men." *(He would teach them to convert others to Christianity.)* Ask students if they think Jesus succeeded in making his disciples "fishers of men."

Use **Interactive Tutor Self-Assessment CD-ROM** to review Section 3.

HISTORY Online

Self-Check Quiz gives students an interactive chapter tutorial. Have them access ***Chapter 16 Quiz*** at **humanheritage.glencoe.com**

By 800 A.D., monks were playing an important role in spreading Christianity throughout Europe. By preserving old Roman and Greek writings, they helped western civilization survive and progress.

Section 3 Assessment

1. **Define:** churches, apostles, parish, priest, diocese, bishop, archbishops, patriarchs, heresy, monks, monasteries, nuns, convents, abbot.
2. How was the early Christian church organized?
3. How did monks help western civilization survive?

Critical Thinking

4. **Making Generalizations** What general statement can you make about the main purpose of monastic life?

Graphic Organizer Activity

5. Draw this diagram, and use it to compare the lives of hermits with the lives of monks and nuns.

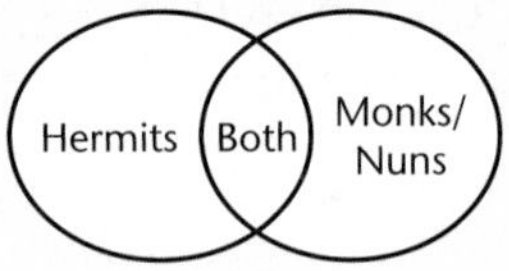

Chapter Summary & Study Guide

1. Jesus' teachings angered Roman officials, who arrested and executed him around 30 A.D.
2. Paul preached Christianity to Jews and non-Jews alike, helping to make Christianity a world religion.
3. Some Romans, particularly the emperors, tried unsuccessfully to stop the spread of Christianity.
4. In 313 A.D., Christianity became legal in Rome. In 392 A.D., it became the empire's official religion.
5. By the end of the 500s A.D., early Christians had organized a church and decided which writings should appear in the New Testament.
6. By 600 A.D., most Latin-speaking Christians looked on the Pope in Rome as the head of the Church.
7. In 1054 A.D., most Greek-speaking Christians split from the Latin Church to form the Eastern Orthodox Church.
8. Religious scholars and monks helped preserve Greek and Roman writings and wrote works that greatly influenced later Christian thinkers.

HISTORY Online

Self-Check Quiz

Visit the *Human Heritage* Web site at **humanheritage.glencoe.com** and click on ***Chapter 16—Self-Check Quiz*** to assess your understanding of this chapter.

Section 3 Assessment Answers

1. All terms are defined in the text Glossary.
2. It was modeled after the Roman government. Each church or parish was led by a priest. Several parishes formed a diocese headed by a bishop. The archbishops led city churches.
3. by preserving old Roman and Greek writings
4. Answers will vary, but most statements will focus on a desire to do good deeds and set an example for Christian living.
5. Comparisons will vary, but both hermits and monks and nuns followed lives of religious devotion, and both tried to escape worldly evils. Hermits, however, lived apart from society, while monks and nuns tried to help other people through example and teaching.

Assign Chapter 16 **Section 3 Quiz** in the TCR. Testmaker available.

CHAPTER 16 Assessment

Using Key Terms

Sort the following words into these categories: *people, places,* and *other*, as they apply to the beginning of Christianity. Then write one sentence explaining each term you classified as *other*.

scriptures	messiah	gentiles
missionary	churches	apostles
parish	priest	diocese
bishop	archbishops	patriarchs
heresy	monks	monasteries
nuns	convents	abbot

Understanding Main Ideas

1. Where did Christianity start?
2. Why did Jesus teach in parables?
3. Why did the Romans blame and punish the Christians for many disasters?
4. What groups of people were first attracted to Christianity?
5. What legend is told about Constantine I?
6. Why did Christians develop a church organization?
7. Why did the Latin and Greek churches split into two groups?
8. What kinds of work did the monks do?

Critical Thinking

1. Why do you think people seemed to remember Jesus' teachings more when he used parables?
2. Do you think citizens should have religious freedom or be required to follow one official religion? Explain.
3. What do you think could have been done to prevent the split between the Latin and Greek churches?

Graphic Organizer Activity

Culture Create a chart like the one shown, and use it to show the organization of the early Church. From the top, arrange these religious offices in order of authority: monks and nuns, patriarchs, bishops, pope, archbishops, priests.

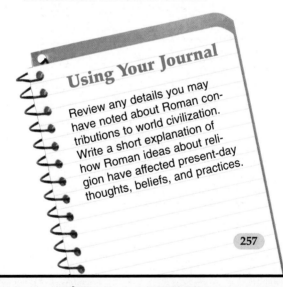

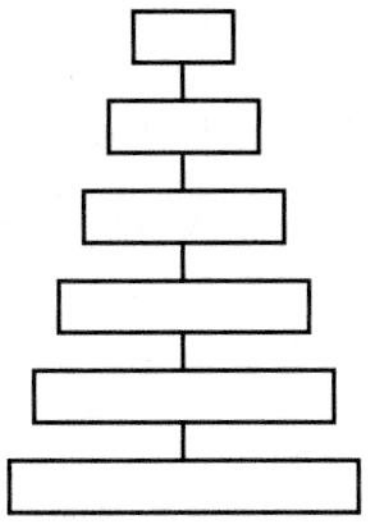

Geography in History

Places and Regions Refer to the map on page 251, noting Paul's journeys. Describe what geographic features and landscapes Paul would have seen as he traveled from Antioch to Corinth.

Using Your Journal

Review any details you may have noted about Roman contributions to world civilization. Write a short explanation of how Roman ideas about religion have affected present-day thoughts, beliefs, and practices.

CHAPTER 16 Assessment Answers

Building Vocabulary

People
messiah
gentiles
missionary
apostles
priest
bishop
archbishop
patriarchs

Places
parish
diocese
monasteries
convents

Other
scriptures
heresy

Check For Understanding

1. in Palestine among the Jews
2. so listeners could better understand his religious principles
3. because the Romans did not like Christian ideas
4. the poor and enslaved
5. he saw a flaming cross in the sky with the words *in hoc signo vinces* written beneath it
6. to hold their churches together while they waited for Jesus to return to Earth
7. because the Greek Christians would not accept the Pope
8. They attended religious services, worked in the fields, and did clerical work, carpentry, and weaving.

Critical Thinking

1. Answers will vary, but students could note that stories are easy to remember.
2. Answers will vary, but students should explain.
3. Answers will vary, but students should give reasons.

Graphic Organizer Activity

From top to bottom: pope, patriarchs, archbishops, bishops, priests, monks and nuns

Bonus Test Question

For Chapter 16 Test
Two Romans are talking. One states "If the winter of 406 had been milder, the empire would not have fallen." The other claims, "No. The winter had no effect. The empire was doomed." With whom do you agree? Why?

Using Your Journal

Essays will vary but should include the idea that Christianity is a strong religious force in Western civilization today.

Geography in History

As Paul traveled from Antioch to Corinth overland he would encounter arid land, seacoast, mountains, islands, and a peninsula. Traveling by sea, he would have viewed the same features.

UNIT 5 Around the World

FOCUS

Objectives

Your students will be able to:

1. state where and when the Moche built their civilization.

2. link geography to the population boom among the Moche.

3. explain the archaeological and cultural importance of the Pyramid of the Sun.

Bellringer

Remind students that they have now studied ancient civilizations all over the world. Ask: If you were to choose a location for a civilization, what would be some ideal features? *(fertile soil, water for farming, waterways for trade, natural barriers to discourage invasion, rich natural resources)*

Motivational Activity

Compile and discuss a list of student respones to the Bellringer question. Then tell students that a people called the Moche built their civilization in the coastal deserts of present-day Peru—one of the driest areas on earth. Refer them to the map. Ask: What geographic advantages did this location possess? *(rivers to provide water for farming, mountains and deserts to protect from invasion, fish from the ocean, and minerals from the desert)*

TEACH

Geography: Environment and Society Have students study the Around the World feature, looking for ways in which the Moche changed and adapted to their environment. (changes—*dug irrigation ditches, planted gardens, built huge pyramids;*

UNIT 5 Around

THE MOCHE

As the Roman Empire reached its height, a people named the Moche rose to power in the coastal deserts of present-day Peru. The Moche civilization lasted from roughly 100 A.D. to 800 A.D.

Although the Moche did not develop a written language, the story of their culture is told through the buildings and artwork that they left behind.

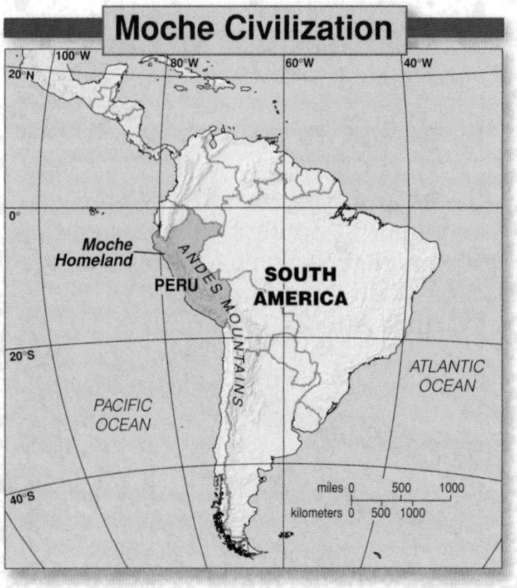

▲ A series of rivers runs out of the Andes Mountains and cuts through the dry deserts of Peru's northern coast. The Moche dug irrigation ditches and used water from these rivers to turn the deserts into farmland. They produced so much food that the population boomed. One river valley may have supported more than 10,000 people.

▲ One of the most powerful groups in Moche society was that of the warrior-priests—nobles who served as both military and religious leaders. A curved, gold headdress symbolized their power.

SPOTLIGHT ON: THE MOCHE

Nobody knows for sure why the Moche disappeared. Some experts suggest an earthquake, such as those that still occur along the Pacific Rim. Many others, however, trace the problem to El Niño—the name given to the periodic change in the temperatures of an ocean current off the coast of South America.

The Moche had mastered living in a nearly rainless area and knew how to survive droughts. However, they had little experience with the torrential downpours that an El Niño can bring. Scientists think that an El Niño of mammoth proportions hit the Moche somewhere around 750 A.D. The deluge washed out fields, overwhelmed irrigation systems, and melted clay-brick buildings. When the flood waters receded, so did the Moche civilization.

adaptations—*settled near rivers, used sand and stone as building materials, fashioned large jugs to hold water.)*

the World

◄ When a warrior-priest died, the Moche filled his grave with a wealth of treasures to accompany him to the next life. Talented metal workers, Moche artists produced complicated designs. This gold-and-turquoise ear ornament shows what a Moche warrior-priest looked like.

The Moche built hundreds of flat-topped ► pyramids. Temples and platforms on the top of the pyramids made them religious and administrative centers. The biggest Moche pyramid—the Pyramid of the Sun—covered over 12.5 acres. It was the largest structure built in the ancient Americas.

Pottery often took the form of animals important ► to the Moche, such as the llama. The llama served as a pack animal for long-distance trips. It also provided meat for food and wool for weaving.

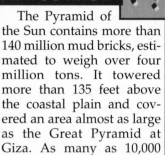

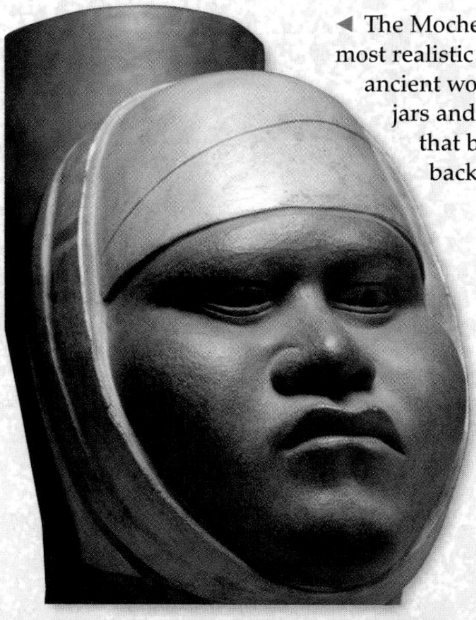

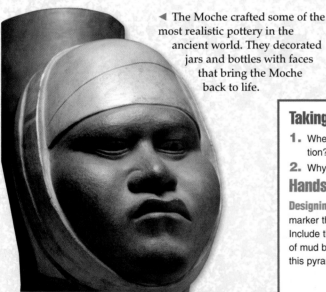

◄ The Moche crafted some of the most realistic pottery in the ancient world. They decorated jars and bottles with faces that bring the Moche back to life.

Taking Another Look

1. Where and when did the Moche build their civilization?
2. Why did the Moche experience a population boom?

Hands-On Activity

Designing a Historical Marker Design a historical marker that might be placed at the Pyramid of the Sun. Include this fact: The Spanish word for pyramids made of mud bricks is *huacas.* Thus the Spanish name for this pyramid is *Huaca del Sol.*

ANSWERS TO TAKING ANOTHER LOOK

1. The Moche built their civilization roughly around 100 A.D. in the coastal deserts of present-day Peru.

2. The Moche population boomed when irrigation allowed farmers to coax large crops of food from the desert.

Hands-On Activity
The markers will vary, but students should include an explanation of the pyramid's name and its importance to the history of the Americas, and identification of the Moche.

DID YOU KNOW ??

The Pyramid of the Sun contains more than 140 million mud bricks, estimated to weigh over four million tons. It towered more than 135 feet above the coastal plain and covered an area almost as large as the Great Pyramid at Giza. As many as 10,000 people may have lived there.

ASSESS

Check for Understanding

Have students answer the questions in **Taking Another Look** on page 259.

Enrich

Share the information at the bottom of page 258. Then assign interested students to research articles on how El Niño affects weather patterns in the Americas today. Ask students to present their findings to the class.

CLOSE

Have students compare the Moche with one other ancient desert civilization and record their findings in the form of a Venn diagram.

Answers and Analyses

1B History

According to page 219, the plebeians paid taxes and served in the army, but they could not serve in the government.

2F History

According to pages 179–180, a Greek oracle gave advice about *what might happen in the future.* Of the choices given, this is the closest match to a soothsayer.

THE PRINCETON REVIEW **TEST-TAKING TIP**

Remind students to scrutinize the language of the question. Very often there is a word or phrase that is key to finding the best answer. In this case the question asks specifically for something or someone who can predict the future. This information should allow students to eliminate G, H, and J.

3A Geography

According to the map, most of the Roman Empire was on the Mediterranean Sea.

4J Geography

According to the map, Spain is the only country that is both west of the Prime Meridian and part of the Roman Empire in 146 B.C.

THE PRINCETON REVIEW **TEST-TAKING TIP**

Review with students the terms *longitude, latitude,* and *Prime Meridian.*

THE PRINCETON REVIEW

Standardized Test Practice

Directions: Choose the *best* answer to each of the following multiple choice questions. If you have trouble answering a question, use the process of elimination to narrow your choices. Write your answers on a separate piece of paper.

1. Plebeians made up a majority of ancient Rome's total population. However, early Roman laws did not treat the plebeians fairly. Which of the following is an example of a law that was unfair to the plebeians?

A Senators in Rome held their positions for their whole lives.

B Plebeians had to pay taxes but could not serve in the government.

C There were only two consuls chosen to lead the Roman Republic each year.

D Tribunes were set up to represent plebeians in Roman government.

> ***Test-Taking Tip:*** The important phrase in this question is *unfair to the plebeians.* Answer A may seem unfair, but was it specifically *unfair to the plebeians?*

2. Early Romans believed that certain people, called *soothsayers,* could predict the future. Roman soothsayers were most similar to

F Greek oracles

G modern-day priests

H philosophers like Socrates

J Egyptian pharaohs

> ***Test-Taking Tip:*** This question asks you to make a *comparison.* Although oracles, priests, philosophers, and pharaohs may have all been consulted for *advice,* they did not all *predict the future.*

Use the map on the top of the next page to answer questions 3 and 4.

3. In 130 A.D., the Roman Empire surrounded which body of water?

A The Mediterranean Sea

B The Atlantic Ocean

C The North Sea

D The Red Sea

> ***Test-Taking Tip:*** Make sure that your answer is supported by information *on the map.* Use the *map key,* or *legend,* to help you understand how the map is organized. Remember that all the different patterns and shades of gray in the key refer to the Roman Empire. They just help to differentiate it at different points during its expansion.

4. In 146 B.C., which part of the Roman territory was west of the Prime Meridian?

F Great Britain

G Syria

H Italy

J Spain

> ***Test-Taking Tip:*** This question requires you to remember the term *Prime Meridian.* The Prime Meridian is the line of longitude that divides *east* and *west.* What degree represents it?

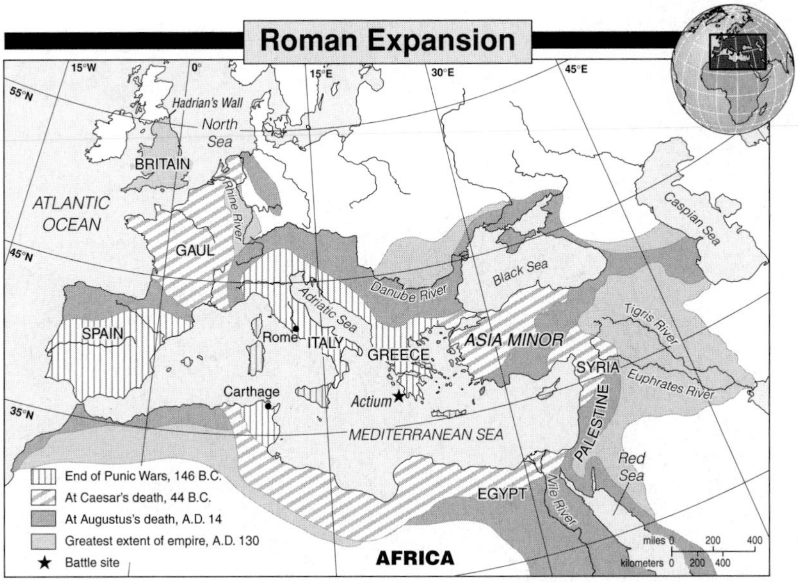

5. During the *Pax Romana*, when Rome was at peace for 200 years, Augustus

A established the principle that laws must be fair to everyone

B focused on conquering other lands to increase trade opportunities

C paid pirates to patrol the trade routes that Roman merchants used

D failed to maintain a strong army, leaving Rome open to foreign attacks

Test-Taking Tip: Eliminate answers that do not make sense. For example, if Rome was *at peace*, then Romans were probably not *conquering other lands* (answer B) or *open to foreign attacks* (answer D).

6. Which of the following was NOT a factor that facilitated the spread of Christianity through the Roman Empire?

F Missionaries spread the religion along the trade routes established by the Romans.

G Many people in the Empire understood the same languages, so Christians could spread their ideas.

H Christianity appealed to poor people by saying that there was a better life after death.

J People who became Christians were still allowed to worship Roman gods.

Test-Taking Tip: Be careful when a question says NOT or EXCEPT. Look for the answer choice that does NOT fit. For instance, answer G, that people spoke the same languages, would be very helpful in communicating any ideas. Therefore, it was probably helpful in spreading Christianity, and you can eliminate it as a possible correct answer.

STOP

Answers and Analyses

5A History

The *Pax Romana* is discussed on pages 234–236. There it states *that certain principles of law that were fair to everyone* were developed, and that Roman law was standardized. Therefore, A is the best choice.

6J History

The ways in which the Roman Empire helped Christianity to spread are discussed on pages 250–251. There it states that the Roman system of roads facilitated the movement of missionaries, and the common languages of Latin and Greek made it easy for people to communicate. Therefore, choices F and G can be eliminated. The top of page 251 states that Christianity appealed to poor people, so choice H can be eliminated. Since page 250 states that Christians refused to worship Roman gods, choice J is the best answer.

THE PRINCETON REVIEW TEST-TAKING TIP

Remind students to take enough time to understand the question thoroughly. Have students reword the question in their own words as another tactic to arriving at the answer.

Tested Objectives

Questions	Reading Objective
1	Evaluate information
2	Make comparisons
3, 4	Analyze information
5	Identify central issues
6	Make inferences and generalizations

Introducing **UNIT 6**

OVERVIEW

Unit 6 discusses the early Middle Ages, which began in western Europe after the fall of Rome and lasted until about 1000 A.D.

- **Chapter 17** describes how Germanic peoples replaced the Roman Empire with their own kingdoms.
- **Chapter 18** analyzes the rise of the Franks.
- **Chapter 19** describes the civilizations that emerged in the British Isles after the fall of the Roman Empire.
- **Chapter 20** summarizes the Viking expansion and how they influenced other people.

UNIT OBJECTIVES

After reading Unit 6, students will be able to:

1. explain why the early Middle Ages is an important period in European history.

2. describe changes in government, economy, and learning in the early Middle Ages.

3. analyze what role religion played in the lives of the people during the early Middle Ages.

UNIT PROJECT

Organize students into five groups. Assign each group one of the following peoples: the Germans (500s A.D.), the Franks (800s A.D.), the Irish (400s A.D.), the Anglo-Saxons (600s A.D.), or the Vikings (1000s A.D.). Have each group create a newspaper about their assigned people during the given period of time. The newspaper should include headlines, articles, ads, editorials, and an entertainment section.

UNIT 6

The Early Middle Ages

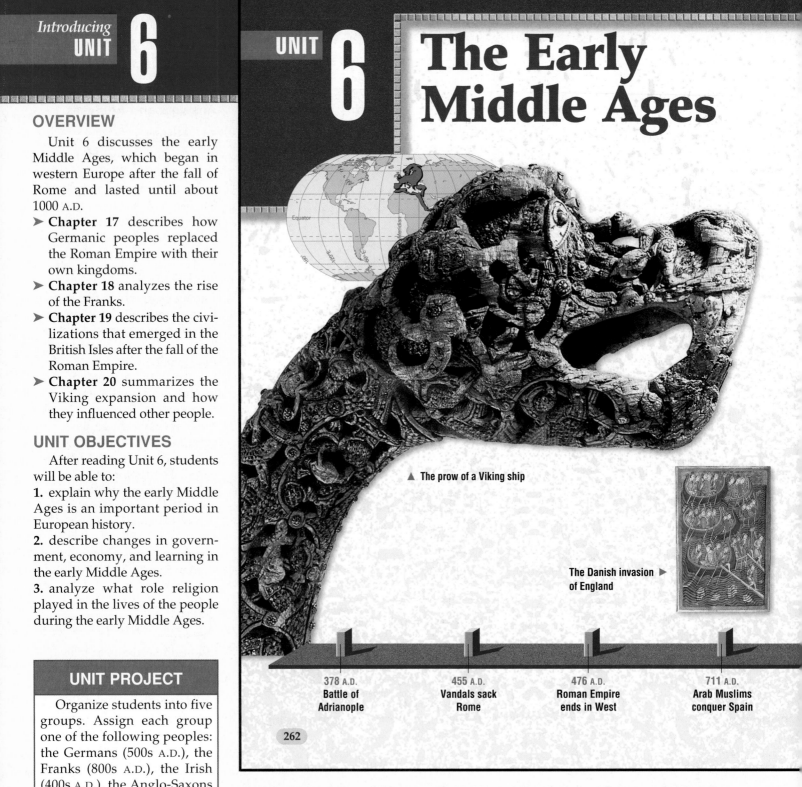

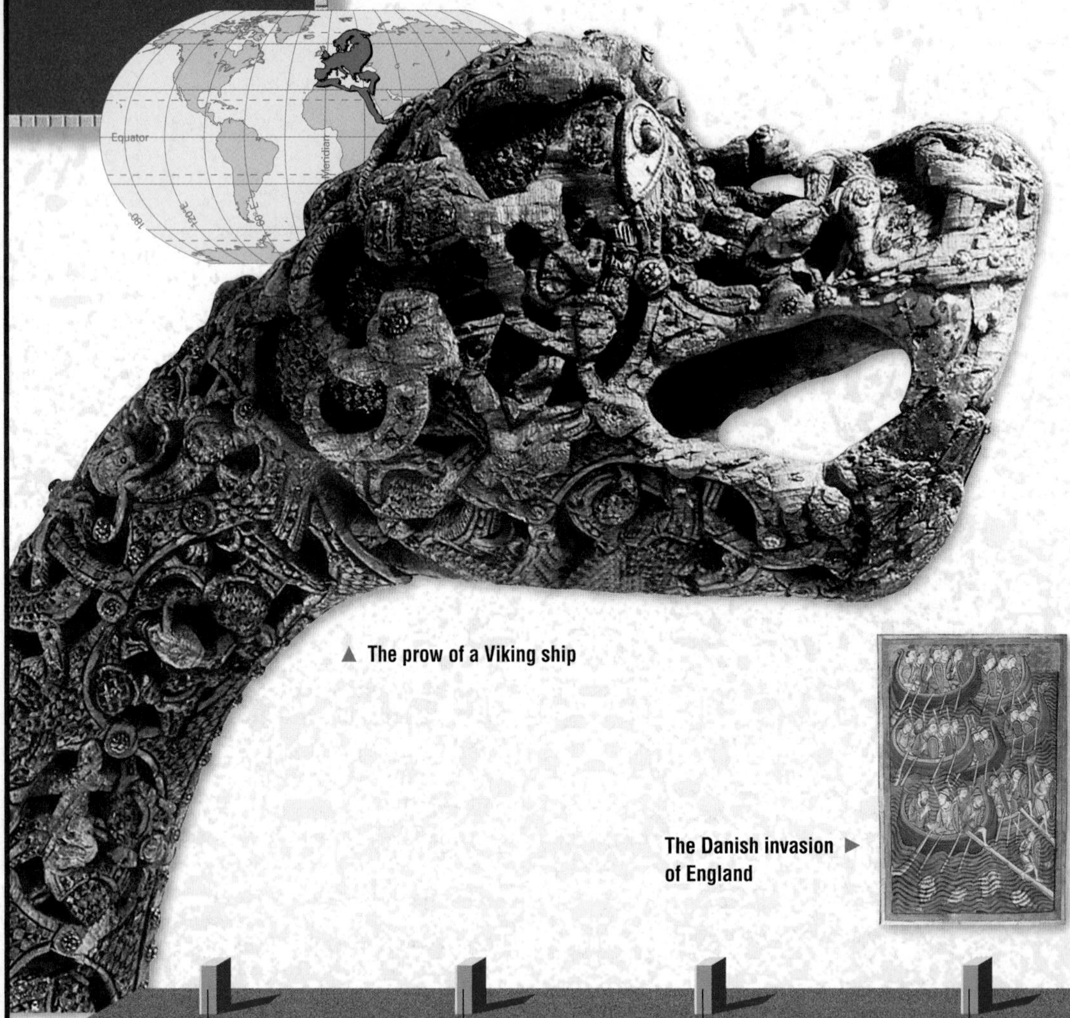

▲ The prow of a Viking ship

The Danish invasion of England ▶

378 A.D.	455 A.D.	476 A.D.	711 A.D.
Battle of Adrianople	Vandals sack Rome	Roman Empire ends in West	Arab Muslims conquer Spain

About the Unit Opening

Examining Artifacts

Ask students to study the artifacts on this page. What inferences can they make about life in the early Middle Ages? *(Lead students to understand that it was a period of fighting, invasion, and conquest.)* Have students determine what events in the time line support their inferences.

Global Chronology

Ask students what the time line covers. *(major events during the early Middle Ages in Europe)* Have students explain the connection between the end of the Roman Empire in the West and conquest of Spain by Arab Muslims. *(After Rome fell, there was no strong government to stop invaders from marching into Europe.)*

FOLDABLES™ Study Organizer

Summarizing Information Study Foldable *Make this foldable to help you organize and summarize information about the western European civilization that developed during the early Middle Ages.*

Step 1 *Mark the midpoint of a side edge of one sheet of paper. Then fold the outside edges in to touch the midpoint.*

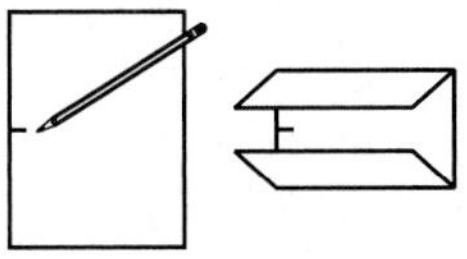

Step 2 *Fold the paper in half again from side to side.*

Step 3 *Open the paper and cut along the inside fold lines to form four tabs.*

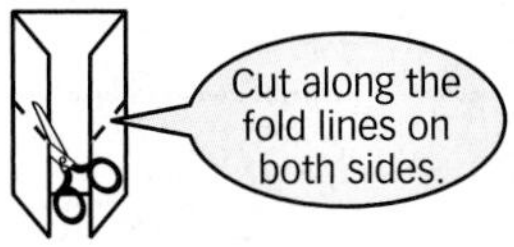

Step 4 *Label as shown.*

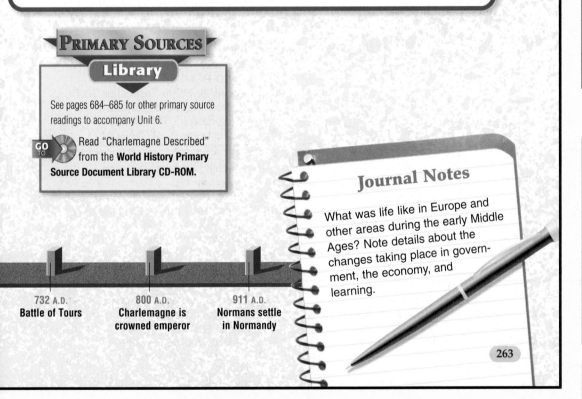

Reading and Writing *As you read the unit, write information under each appropriate tab. Be sure to summarize the information you find by writing only main ideas and supporting details.*

PRIMARY SOURCES Library

See pages 684–685 for other primary source readings to accompany Unit 6.

GO TO Read "Charlemagne Described" from the **World History Primary Source Document Library CD-ROM.**

Journal Notes

What was life like in Europe and other areas during the early Middle Ages? Note details about the changes taking place in government, the economy, and learning.

732 A.D.
Battle of Tours

800 A.D.
Charlemagne is crowned emperor

911 A.D.
Normans settle in Normandy

263

GLENCOE TECHNOLOGY

MindJogger Videoquiz

Use **MindJogger Videoquiz** to preview the unit content.

Available in DVD and VHS

FOLDABLES™ Study Organizer

Purpose Students will create and use a foldable to organize information about the early Middle Ages. As students read the chapters in this unit, they should summarize information about the Germans, Franks, Irish and Anglo-Saxons, and Vikings under the appropriate tabs of their foldables.

Have students complete **Reading and Study Skills Foldables** Activity 6.

RECORDING JOURNAL NOTES

Have students list major changes that have taken place in the world in their lifetimes. As they read the text, have students note details in their journal about the changes that took place in government, the economy, and learning in Europe and other areas during the early Middle Ages.

PRIMARY SOURCES Library

Additional primary sources from the **World History Primary Source Document Library CD-ROM** can be used during the study of Unit 6, including:

- "The Song of Roland"

Primary sources about Vikings can be found on pages 684–685.

Geographic Location

Have students use their text Atlas to locate the places in this unit that are in western Europe. *(England, Ireland, France, Spain, Italy, Germany, Denmark, Sweden, and Norway)* Ask them to locate Paris, Cluny, Canossa, Worms, and other cities in which important events in this unit take place.

Chapter 17 Planning Guide

Timesaving Tools

TeacherWorks™ All-In-One Planner and Resource Center

- **Interactive Teacher Edition** Access your Teacher Wraparound Edition and your classroom resources with a few easy clicks.
- **Interactive Lesson Planner** Planning has never been easier! Organize your week, month, semester, or year with all the lesson helps you need to make teaching creative, timely, and relevant.

PRESENTATION Plus!

Use Glencoe's **Presentation Plus!** multimedia teacher tool to easily present dynamic lessons that visually excite your students. Using Microsoft PowerPoint® you can customize the presentations to create your own personalized lessons.

Objectives	Reproducible Resources	Multimedia Resources
Section 1 **Village Life** Characterize family life in German villages, and analyze Germans' love of battle and how their laws influenced their lives.	Reproducible Lesson Plan Chapter 17 Vocabulary and Guided Reading Activity Reading Essentials and Study Guide 17-1 Chapter 17 Cooperative Learning Activity Section 1 Quiz Unit 6 Hands-On History Lab	Interactive Student Edition CD-ROM Graphic Organizer Transparency 14 Teaching Transparency and Activity 17A Vocabulary PuzzleMaker CD-ROM Interactive Tutor Self-Assessment CD-ROM ExamView® Pro Testmaker CD-ROM Glencoe Skillbuilder Interactive Workbook CD-ROM, Level 1 Presentation Plus! CD-ROM
Section 2 **The Conquerors** Discuss what role the Goths and the Vandals played in the decline of the Roman Empire, and describe what replaced the Roman Empire in the West.	Reproducible Lesson Plan Reading Essentials and Study Guide 17-2 Chapter 17 Chart and Graph Skill Activity Chapter 17 Geography and Map Activity Chapter 17 Enrichment Activity Section 2 Quiz	Teaching Transparency and Activity 17B Vocabulary PuzzleMaker CD-ROM Interactive Tutor Self-Assessment CD-ROM ExamView® Pro Testmaker CD-ROM Glencoe Skillbuilder Interactive Workbook CD-ROM, Level 1
Chapter 17 **Review and** **Evaluation**	Chapter 17 Reteaching Activity Chapter 17 Performance Assessment Activity Spanish Chapter Summary and Glossary Chapter 17 Test	Vocabulary PuzzleMaker CD-ROM Interactive Tutor Self-Assessment CD-ROM Glencoe Skillbuilder Interactive Workbook CD-ROM, Level 1 Audiocassettes* ExamView® Pro Testmaker CD-ROM

*Also available in Spanish.

✓ Performance Assessment Activities

Laws Remind students that German laws during the early Middle Ages were not written down, but instead were passed on by word of mouth. Have students imagine that they have been assigned the task of writing down the German laws. Have them write a German Law Book based on the information in the textbook and in other reference sources. Have students read their laws to the class.

Chapter Resources

Literature About the Period

Newark, Tim. *The Barbarians: Warriors and Wars of the Dark Ages.* Poole (Sterling), 1985. Account by a military historian of the medieval period.

Readings for the Student

Lyttle, Richard B. *Land Beyond the River: Europe in the Age of Migration.* Atheneum, 1986. Overview of the second through ninth centuries and the customs and characters of the various peoples on the move in Europe, including Germans, Huns, Mongols, and Gypsies.

Readings for the Teacher

Barbor, Richard. *The Penguin Guide to Medieval Europe.* Penguin Books, 1984. Describes the political and intellectual climate of Europe from 800 A.D. to 1400 A.D.

Burns, Thomas S. *A History of the Ostro-Goths.* Indiana University Press, 1984. Highlights the history of the Ostrogoths.

Simons, George E., gen. ed. *Barbarian Europe.* Time-Life Books, 1968. Surveys the history of Europe from 406 A.D. to 1200 A.D.

National Geographic Teacher's Corner

National Geographic Society Products Available from Glencoe

To order the following, call Glencoe at 1-800-334-7344:

- *Europe (Laminated Desk Maps)*
- *PicturePack: Physical Geography of the World (Transparencies)*
- *PicturePack: The Middle Ages (Transparencies)*
- *PictureShow: The Middle Ages (CD-ROM)*
- *Picture Atlas of the World (CD-ROM)*
- *PicturePack: Physical Geography of the World (Transparencies)*

Additional National Geographic Society Products

To order the following products for use with this chapter, call National Geographic Society at 1-800-368-2728:

- *Physical Geography of the Continents Series: Europe (Video)*
- *National Geographic Atlas of World History (Book))*
- *Wonders of the Ancient World: National Geographic Atlas of Archaeology (Book)*

Access *National Geographic*'s new dynamic MapMachine Web site and other geography resources at:
www.nationalgeographic.com
www.nationalgeographic.com/maps

Key to Ability Levels

Teaching strategies have been coded for varying learning styles and abilities.

L1 Level 1 activities are **basic** activities and should be within the ability range of all students.

L2 Level 2 activities are **average** activities and should be within the ability range of the average to above-average student.

L3 Level 3 activities are **challenging** activities designed for the ability range of above-average students.

ELL ELL activities should be within the ability range of English Language Learning students.

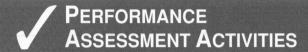

Introducing CHAPTER 17

OVERVIEW

Chapter 17 discusses the Germanic impact on western Europe.

- **Section 1** compares the cultures of the Romans and the Germans.
- **Section 2** describes the Germanic invasions and the end of the Roman Empire.

CHAPTER OBJECTIVES

After reading Chapter 17, students will be able to:

1. describe family life in German villages.
2. analyze how the love of battle and their laws influenced the Germans.
3. discuss what role the Goths and the Vandals played in the decline of the Roman Empire.
4. describe what replaced the Roman Empire in the West.

EXAMINING ARTIFACTS

Tell students that the Romans often used the word "barbarian" to describe the Germans who moved into their empire from the north. Call on students to define this word. *(a person whose culture is considered uncivilized)* Ask students how these artifacts disprove this description.

PERFORMANCE ASSESSMENT

Use the Performance Assessment Activities on page 264B to help you evaluate students as they complete the chapter.

CHAPTER 17 The Germans

300 A.D.–550 A.D.

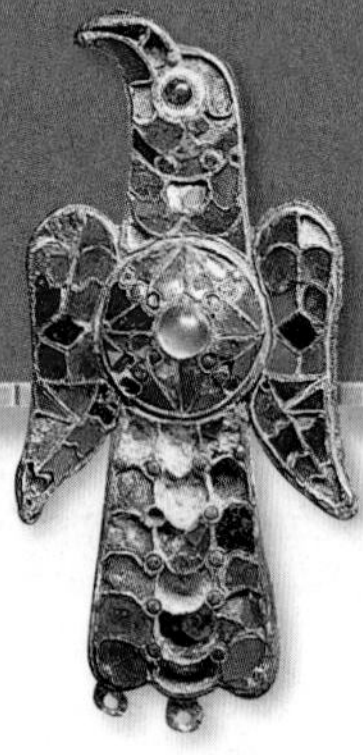

▲ A Germanic brooch in the shape of an eagle

The mausoleum ▶ of Theodoric the Great

300 A.D.	378 A.D.	410 A.D.	455 A.D.	550 A.D.
Romans allow groups of Germans to cross their borders	Battle of Adrianople	Alaric captures Rome	Vandals sack Rome	Roman Empire is replaced by Germanic kingdoms

TEACHING RESOURCES

TEACHER PLANNING AND SUPPORT

- Reproducible Lesson Plan 17-1, 17-2
- Teaching Strategies for the World History Classroom (Including Block Scheduling Pacing Guides)
- Presentation Plus! CD-ROM

REVIEW AND REINFORCEMENT

- Reading Essentials and Study Guide 17-1, 17-2
- Chapter 17 Vocabulary and Guided Reading Activity
- Vocabulary PuzzleMaker CD-ROM
- Teaching Transparencies 17A & 17B
- Chapter 17 Reteaching Activity
- Chapter 17 Cooperative Learning Activity
- Chapter 17 Activity Book Activity
- Chapter 17 Chart and Graph Skill Activity
- Reading and Study Skills Foldables
- Interactive Tutor Self-Assessment CD-ROM
- Unit 6 MindJogger VideoQuiz

APPLICATION AND HANDS-ON ACTIVITIES

- Daily Questions in Social Studies
- Unit 6 Hands-On History Lab Activity
- Student Presentation Builder CD-ROM

Chapter Focus

Read to Discover

- What life was like in German villages.
- How the Germans' laws and love of battle influenced them.
- What role the Goths and Vandals played in the decline of the Roman Empire.
- What replaced the Roman Empire in the West.

HISTORY Online

Chapter Overview

Visit the *Human Heritage* Web site at **humanheritage.glencoe.com** and click on ***Chapter 17—Chapter Overviews*** to preview this chapter.

Terms to Learn
clans
chieftain
blood feuds
oath-helpers
ordeal
wergeld

People to Know
Wodan
Thor
Atilla
Alaric
Odoacer
Theodoric

Places to Locate
Danube River valley
Valhalla

Why It's Important During the first 400 years after the birth of Christ, the Germans left the forests and marshes of northern Europe in search of warmer climates and better grazing land for their cattle. They slowly drifted south toward the Roman Empire.

Attracted by Rome's wealth and culture, the Germans hoped to live peacefully within the empire's borders. However, the Romans considered them enemies and for many years fought to keep the Germans out of Rome. By 300 A.D., however, the empire had begun its long decline and could no longer turn back the Germans. So the Romans allowed groups of Germans to move into the Danube River valley, where a blending of German and Roman ways took place.

SECTION 1 Village Life

Although the Germans took part in Roman life, they also kept much of their own culture. They lived in villages surrounded by farmlands and pastures. Most of the homes were long thatched-roof huts with an open space around them. The family lived in one end of the hut and divided the other end into animal stalls.

GEOGRAPHY ACTIVITIES

- Chapter 17 Geography and Map Activity
- Outline Map Resource Book

INTERDISCIPLINARY CONNECTIONS

- World Music: A Cultural Legacy

ENRICHMENT AND EXTENSION

- World History Primary Source Document Library CD-ROM
- Chapter 17 Enrichment Activity
- Foods Around the World

ASSESSMENT AND EVALUATION

- Chapter 17 Performance Assessment Activity
- Chapter 17 Section Quizzes 17-1, 17-2
- Chapter 17 Test
- Chapter 17 ExamView® Pro Testmaker CD-ROM
- Chapter 17 Digests Audiocassettes Activities and Tests

SPANISH RESOURCES

- Chapter 17 Spanish Chapter Summary and Glossary
- Chapter 17 Spanish Digests Audiocassettes Activities and Tests

HISTORY Online

Chapter Overview introduces students to chapter content and key terms. Have them access ***Chapter 17 Overview*** at **humanheritage.glencoe.com**

FOCUS

Bellringer

Have students answer the following: *What caused the fall of the Roman Empire?*

Motivational Activity

Discuss students' responses. Then read the following quote written by a Christian bishop of the 400s A.D. as his province was being overrun by the Germans: *We have planted our crops only for the enemy to burn. All our resources are gone—the flocks of sheep, the herds of camels and horses. I am writing this behind walls, under siege.* Tell students that they will learn more about Germanic groups who helped cause the end of the Roman Empire.

GUIDE TO READING

Reading Strategy

Ask students to read "Why It's Important" and summarize the chapter's main theme. *(As the Roman Empire declined, the Germans and Romans influenced each other's way of life.)*

Vocabulary Precheck

Ask students to define each of the "Terms to Learn." L1 ELL

Use the Vocabulary PuzzleMaker CD-ROM for Chapter 17 to create a crossword puzzle. L1

Assign Chapter 17 Vocabulary and Guided Reading Activity.

Assign Reading Essentials and Study Guide 17-1.

TEACH

Guided Practice

L1 **Daily Life** Ask the students to imagine they are teenagers living in a German village during the Roman Empire and have them write a diary entry describing a day in their lives. Ask students to share their entries with the class. ELL

CAPTION ANSWER

Most homes were long, thatched-roof huts with an open space around them. Families lived in one end of the hut and divided the other end into animal stalls. Wooden tables and benches were the only furniture.

DID YOU KNOW ??

The Germans were divided into groups that ranged in size from about 10,000 individuals to as many as 300,000.

HISTORY Online

Student Web Activity objectives and answers can be found at the ***Chapter 17 Web Activity Lesson Plan*** at humanheritage.glencoe.com

GERMAN VILLAGE The Germans built their villages just within the borders of the Roman Empire. There they became farmers. They lived in family groups that included parents, children, grandparents, aunts, uncles, and cousins. **What was a German home like?**

The body heat of the animals helped to warm the hut during the cold winters. Wooden tables and benches placed along the walls of the hut were the only furniture. A few wealthier villagers added wall hangings or carpets.

German villagers made their living herding cattle, which provided food and clothing. They also traded cattle for Roman glass vessels, table articles, and jewelry. The Germans farmed as well. They grew barley, rye, wheat, beans, and peas. Most farm work was done by women, children, and enslaved people. When the women were not working in the fields or cooking, they spun wool and wove cloth on upright looms.

German dress was simple. The women wore long skirts made of different yarns, or one-piece sack-like dresses that extended from the shoulders to the feet. Sometimes, they wore scarves or shawls fastened with a bone pin. The men wore short woolen *tunics*, or coat-like garments, and close-fitting trousers. They covered the tunics with cloaks fastened on the right shoulder with a brooch.

HISTORY Online

Student Web Activity

Visit the *Human Heritage* Web site at humanheritage.glencoe.com and click on ***Chapter 17—Student Web Activities*** to find out more about Germanic tribes.

SPOTLIGHT ON: TACTICUS

Most of what modern historians know about the customs, appearance, and beliefs of the Germanic tribes comes from a Roman—not a Germanic—historian. Cornelius Tacticus, a Roman lawyer, official, and historian, wrote about people in two distant parts of the Roman Empire in the 100s A.D. and early 200s A.D. His book *Germania,* written in 98 A.D., describes the Germans along the Rhine River frontier of the empire. He uses the Germanic tribes as moral examples of upright, if primitive, people who still hold on to the simple virtues that many Romans have forgotten. He also writes about the laws, customs, and fighting methods of the Germans that developed from nearly 100 years of Roman wars and other contacts.

The Germans believed in hospitality. So strong was this belief that it was against the law to turn away anyone who came to the door. Invited guests and strangers alike were welcomed, fed, and entertained. Feasting, drinking, and dancing were favorite German pastimes. Men also enjoyed gambling with dice. Sometimes, they took part in such organized sports as boxing and wrestling. In winter, they skated on frozen ponds and lakes using skates made of flat bone.

The Germans spoke a language that later became modern German. At first, they could not read or write because their language had no alphabet. However, some learned to speak and write Latin. Gradually, they began to use Roman letters to write their own language.

Warriors German men were warriors. They spent most of their time fighting, hunting, or making weapons. They began training for war when they were young boys. When a male reached manhood, he was brought before a special gathering held in a sacred grove under a full moon. There, he received a shield and a spear, which he had to carry with him at all times. The loss of the shield and spear meant loss of honor.

The Germans were divided into **clans,** or groups based on family ties. At first, the Germans gave their greatest loyalty to their clan. After a while, however, they developed a strong feeling of loyalty toward a military leader called a **chieftain** (chēf′ tuhn). A man had to fight well to become a chieftain. In the beginning, a chieftain was elected by a band of warriors. Later, this office became hereditary.

Chieftains gave their men leadership, weapons, and a chance for wealth and adventure. They also kept peace among their warriors. In some cases, they gave their warriors food and shelter. In return, warriors gave their chieftains complete loyalty. Some even gave their chieftains credit for the brave deeds they themselves did. In battle, chieftains fought for victory, and warriors fought for their chieftains.

German warrior bands did not have fixed plans of fighting. Each band was small and usually fought on its own, apart from other bands. The bands made surprise raids against their enemies. Warriors on foot and on horseback would charge wildly, yelling in loud voices to frighten their foes. They fought with daggers, short swords, and heavy axes made of metal and stone. They carried light wooden shields and wore suits of leather. A successful attack provided warriors with enslaved people, cattle, and other treasures.

The Germans' love of battle was closely linked to their religion. Germans had many gods who liked to fight and to hunt. The chief god, Wodan (wōd′ n), was the god of war, poetry, learning, and magic. Another god of war was Wodan's

People in History

Theodoric the Great
c. 454 A.D.–526 A.D.

Germanic King

Theodoric was king of the East Goths, a Germanic people from eastern Europe. When Rome fell in 476 A.D., he took part in the struggle. About 500 A.D., Theodoric declared himself king of Italy. As king, he encouraged the Roman and Germanic peoples to get along. He respected Roman customs, and during his reign peace and prosperity returned.

Reading Check
What are **clans?** How did a German leader become a **chieftain?**

L2 Critical Thinking Have students work in pairs to learn more about the German belief in hospitality. Have them create a presentation that compares and contrasts German hospitality in the 400s to that of today. Suggest they share their presentations with the class. ELL

MAKING CONNECTIONS

➤➤ **Religion** The warlike Wodan became the chief god of German warriors and chieftains. Earlier, these people held beliefs that centered on Mother Earth—Erce or Nerthus. Even after the Germans adopted Christianity, they kept some old beliefs in the spirits of the earth and forest. Customs such as the Yule log and the lighted Christmas tree, for instance, derive from rituals of the Germanic forest tribes.

Reading Check Answer
Clans are groups based on family ties.
A German leader became **chieftain** by fighting well. At first, he was elected by warriors, but later the office became hereditary.

COOPERATIVE LEARNING

Tell students that our seven-day week comes from the Babylonians, but the days of the week come mainly from the Germanic calendar. The Germans picked up Sun Day and Moon Day from the Greeks and Romans. They also kept Saturn's Day, in honor of the Roman god of agriculture. However, they gave the rest of the days to their own deities.

Divide the class into four groups, and assign students to research and design posters for each of the following days: **Tiu's Day** (in honor of the Germanic god of war)**; Wodan's Day** (in honor of the chief Germanic god)**; Thor's Day** (in honor of the Germanic god of thunder)**; Freya's Day** (in honor of the Germanic goddess of clouds, the sky, love and wife of Wodan).

Assign Chapter 17 *Cooperative Learning Activity* in the TCR.

L3 **Critical Thinking** Ask students how the Germans' belief in Valhalla typified their culture. Ask students to compare this German belief with Greek or Roman beliefs about the afterlife.

Linking Across Time

The Germans memorized their laws and passed them from parent to child.

LINKING PAST TO PRESENT

A remnant of German mythology on our calendar is Easter, a Christian festival that takes its name from the Germanic spring goddess, Eostre.

L2 **Civics** Write the following scenario on the board: *The son of a German chieftain is accused of displaying cowardice in battle. He is brought to trial in front of a panel of judges.* Ask volunteers to role-play the following in acting out the trial: the warrior, the accuser, two oath-helpers, and four judges. Once all testimony is given, have the judges reach a verdict. If a guilty verdict is reached, the judges should also decide on a sentence. Discuss the proceedings with the class.

Linking Across Time

Public Assemblies Germanic people picked leaders and decided laws in public assemblies. All freemen—except "cowards"—took part in these meetings (left). The Germanic conquest of the Roman Empire helped spread this practice. It became the basis of later democratic assemblies, including modern-day town meetings (right). **How did the Germans record their laws?**

son Thor (thōr), who was also the god of thunder. The Germans believed that the sound of thunder came from Thor's chariot wheels.

The Germans admired bravery. Like the Spartans, they expected their warriors to win in battle or to die fighting. The only German shields left on a battlefield were those of dead warriors. The Germans believed that goddesses carried the spirits of warriors who died in battle into the afterlife. There, in the hall of Wodan, called Valhalla (val hal' uh), the warriors would feast and fight forever.

German Shield

Law

The Romans believed that law came from the emperor. The Germans believed it came from the people. German rulers could not change a law unless the people approved.

The Germans based their laws on the customs of their ancestors. Instead of writing down the laws, the Germans memorized them and passed them from parent to child.

Reckless fighting, often caused by too much drinking, caused problems in German villages. The Germans wanted to keep such

MEETING SPECIAL NEEDS

Have tactile/kinesthetic learners make models or dioramas of German villages. Students can use the information in the textbook or from reference books. Display the models and dioramas in the classroom.

Refer to ***Inclusion for the Middle School Social Studies Classroom: Strategies and Activities*** for additional resources.

fights from becoming **blood feuds** (fyūds), or quarrels in which the families of the original fighters seek revenge. Blood feuds could go on for generations. To keep this from happening, the Germans set up courts. Judges listened to each side and tried to find a settlement that would bring peace to the village.

The Germans decided who was guilty or innocent in different ways. One way was by oath-taking. People accused of crimes would declare their innocence by oath. Then, they would be defended by **oath-helpers.** These were people who swore that the accused was telling the truth. The Germans believed that anyone who lied when taking an oath would be punished by the gods.

People accused of crimes could not always find oath-helpers to come to their aid. In such cases, guilt or innocence was decided by **ordeal** (ō r dēl′), or a severe trial. Accused persons had to walk barefoot over red-hot coals or put an arm into boiling water. The burns of the innocent were supposed to heal within three days. There was also ordeal by water. A person was tied hand and foot and thrown into a lake or river. The Germans viewed water as a symbol of purity. If a person sank to the bottom, he or she was innocent. If a person floated, he or she was guilty.

A person who was judged guilty was not always punished physically. Courts could impose fines called ***wergeld*** (wuhr′ geld). The exact amount of the payment varied. For example, the wergeld for harming a chieftain was higher than the one for harming a warrior. In the same way, a fine for killing a young girl was greater than one for killing a woman too old to have children. Although courts could set these fines, they did not have the power to collect them. They had to depend on public opinion to make a guilty person pay the fine.

The German legal system did not treat all people fairly. A person's wealth and importance, rather than the seriousness of the crime, determined the penalty. German laws did, however, keep the peace.

Reading Check How did Germans try to prevent **blood feuds?**

Reading Check How did **oath-helpers** take part in German trials?

Reading Check Why would an accused person be required to go through an **ordeal?**

Reading Check What was a *wergeld?*

Section 1 Assessment

1. **Define:** clans, chieftain, blood feuds, oath-helpers, ordeal, *wergeld.*
2. What were some of the duties of a German chieftain?
3. What were some features of German religion?

Critical Thinking

4. **Making Inferences** Why do you think hospitality was so important to the Germans?

Graphic Organizer Activity

5. Draw this diagram, and use it to compare strengths and weaknesses of German law.

Strengths	Weaknesses

Reading Check Answer The Germans tried to prevent **blood feuds** by setting up courts to settle the quarrels.

Reading Check Answer The **oath-helpers** swore the accused was telling the truth.

Reading Check Answer If oath-helpers did not come forward, an accused person went through an **ordeal,** or severe trial, to decide guilt or innocence.

Reading Check Answer A *wergeld* was a fine imposed as punishment for a crime.

Use **Interactive Tutor Self-Assessment CD-ROM** to review Section 1.

Section 1 Assessment Answers

1. clans, family groups (p. 267); chieftain, military leader (p. 267); blood feuds, quarrels between families (p. 269); oath-helpers, swore the accused was truthful (p. 269); ordeal, severe trial (p. 269); *wergeld,* fines (p. 269)
2. gave their men leadership, weapons, and a chance for wealth and adventure; also kept peace among warriors and sometimes provided them with food and shelter
3. It had many gods who fought and hunted; the chief gods were Wodan and Thor; and goddesses carried the spirits of warriors to Valhalla.
4. Answers will vary but should refer to German beliefs.
5. Sample responses: *strengths*—helped settle quarrels; *weaknesses*—did not treat people fairly since penalties were determined by a person's wealth and importance.

Assign the Chapter 17 **Section 1 Quiz** in the TCR. Testmaker available.

MAKING CONNECTIONS

>> **History** Most Germanic groups had an assembly made up of free men from the village that met once a year to discuss war, laws, and punishment for crimes. Before a chieftain could go to war, he had to get the assembly's approval. To show approval, assembly members banged their weapons against their shields.

DID YOU KNOW ??

The value of a person—and therefore the amount of his or her *wergeld*—was tied directly to that person's importance in warfare.

Evaluate

Assign Chapter 17 **Performance Assessment Activity** in the TCR.

Administer **Chapter 17 Test** in the TCR. Testmaker available.

Reteach

Have students summarize factors that led to the fall of Rome and their importance.

Assign Chapter 17 **Reteaching Activity** in the TCR.

Enrich

Have students research Germanic mythology and report on the gods and goddesses that were worshiped in the early Middle Ages.

Assign the Chapter 17 **Enrichment Activity** in the TCR.

CLOSE

Ask students to discuss whether they think the Western Roman Empire would have fallen even if the Germanic tribes had not invaded the empire.

Use **Interactive Tutor Self-Assessment CD-ROM** to review Section 2.

HISTORY Online

Self-Check Quiz gives students an interactive chapter tutorial. Have them access ***Chapter 17 Quiz*** at humanheritage.glencoe.com

The Germanic invasions were one of the three main reasons the Roman Empire in the West began to fall. While the Roman Empire in the East prospered, generals in the West fought for control of Rome and Italy.

In 476, a German general named Odoacer (ŏd' uh wā suhr) took control. He did not appoint an emperor. Instead, he ruled the western empire in his own name for almost 15 years. Then, a group of East Goths invaded Italy, killed Odoacer, and set up a kingdom under their leader Theodoric (thē ahd' uh rik).

By 550, the Roman Empire in the West had faded away. In its place were six major and a great many minor Germanic kingdoms. Many Roman beliefs and practices remained in use, and would shape later civilizations.

Section 2 Assessment

1. What happened to the East Goths in the late 300s? What effect did this have on the West Goths?
2. What did the Vandals do after leaving Spain?
3. What replaced the Roman Empire in the West?

Critical Thinking

4. **Predicting Consequences** What do you think might have happened if Roman officials had treated the West Goths fairly? Explain.

Graphic Organizer Activity

5. Draw this diagram, and use it to describe important events in the fall of Rome. (Key dates are given.)

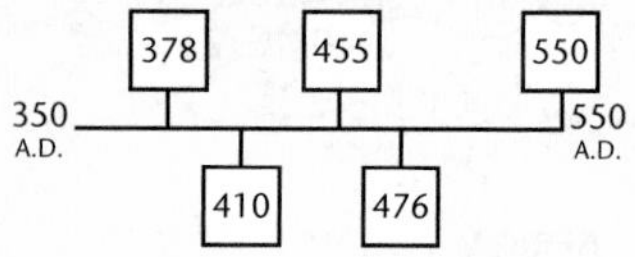

Chapter Summary & Study Guide

1. About 300 A.D., groups of Germans began settling in the Roman Empire.
2. German warriors were organized into bands headed by military chieftains.
3. The Germans' love of battle was closely linked to their religion.
4. The Germans determined a person's guilt or innocence through use of oath-helpers and by ordeal.
5. The Germans believed that law came from the people.
6. The Huns conquered the East Goths and forced the West Goths to turn to Rome for protection.
7. Harsh treatment of the West Goths by the Romans set off a chain of events leading to the capture of Rome in 410 A.D.
8. A Germanic chieftain took control of Rome in 476 A.D., and by 550 A.D., the Roman Empire had been replaced by a number of Germanic kingdoms.

HISTORY Online

Self-Check Quiz

Visit the *Human Heritage* Web site at humanheritage.glencoe.com and click on ***Chapter 17—Self-Check Quiz*** to assess your understanding of this chapter.

Section 2 Assessment Answers

1. They were conquered by the Huns. It led them to ask the Roman emperor for protection.
2. They crossed the Mediterranean to North Africa, became pirates, and attacked and burned Rome.
3. six major and a great many minor Germanic kingdoms
4. Answers will vary but will probably mention that the West Goths might not have rebelled.
5. 378—Romans defeated at Battle of Adrianople; 410—West Goths capture Rome; 455—Vandals attack and burn Rome; 476—Odoacer takes control of the western empire; 550—six major and many minor Germanic kingdoms replace the Western Roman Empire

Assign Chapter 17 **Section 2 Quiz** in the TCR. Testmaker available.

CHAPTER 17 Assessment

Using Key Terms

Write a short story describing the daily life of a person in one of the early Germanic groups. Use the following words in your story.

clans	chieftain	blood feuds
oath-helpers	ordeal	*wergeld*

Understanding Main Ideas

1. Why did the Germans begin to move south toward the Roman Empire?
2. Why were the Germans allowed to cross the borders of the Roman Empire?
3. How did German warriors show their loyalty to their chieftain?
4. What did the Germans believe the afterlife would be like for warriors?
5. According to German beliefs, from what source did law come?
6. What was the reason for the German ordeal by water?
7. Why did the West Goths want to enter the Roman Empire?
8. What happened to Rome after its capture by Odoacer in 476 A.D.?

Critical Thinking

1. What parts of Roman culture did the Germans adopt? What parts of their own culture did they keep?
2. Imagine you will soon become a Germanic chieftain. Explain what you would provide for your warriors.
3. What would you have liked and disliked about living in a German village?
4. Do you believe the penalty for a crime should depend on a person's wealth or importance? If not, on what should it depend? Explain.

Graphic Organizer Activity

Citizenship Create a diagram like the one shown, and use it to show German contributions to Western ideas about law and government.

German Contributions	
	1.
	2.
	3.

Geography in History

Places and Regions Refer to the map on page 271. Access to the sea played an important role in the economy of each Germanic kingdom. Which kingdom had the longest seacoast? About how many miles (km) long was it?

Using Your Journal

Review any details you may have noted about the changes that took place during the early Middle Ages. Imagine you are in a German village at that time. Write a letter to a friend describing the important traits of a German leader. Compare these traits to the ones that you would look for in a leader today.

273

Bonus Test Question

For Chapter 17 Test

"If I may join your army I swear on our god of war, Mars, I will fight hard. I have a letter from my chieftain saying I am a good warrior." Why would this warrior speaking to a Roman not be considered a true German?

Using Your Journal

Letters will vary but should compare and contrast the ideas of German law with ideas of law today.

Geography in History

Ostrogoth; about 2,000 miles (or 3,226 km)

CHAPTER 17 Assessment Answers

Using Key Terms

Short stories should include a description of daily activities and use all the words.

Understanding Main Ideas

1. looking for a warmer climate, grazing land, wealth, culture
2. because the Romans realized they were not strong enough to keep them out
3. They obeyed in battle and some gave their chieftains credit for their own brave deeds
4. spent in Valhalla, where they would feast and fight forever
5. from the people
6. They believed water would accept anyone who was pure and reject anyone who was not pure.
7. because they were afraid the Huns would conquer them.
8. Odoacer did not pick an emperor. Instead, he ruled the empire in his own name for 15 years, until the East Goths invaded and killed him.

Critical Thinking

1. They became farmers, traded with Romans, and joined the Roman army. Some became Christians. They lived in villages and spoke what later became modern German.
2. Answers will vary but should include some responsibilities of chieftains.
3. Answers will vary but should include specific details.
4. Answers will vary.

Graphic Organizer Activity

Contributions will vary but might include: the use of public assemblies to pick leaders; the belief that law came from the people instead of the gods; the use of courts to settle quarrels.

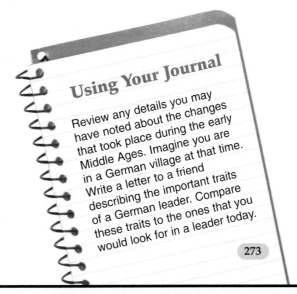

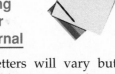

Chapter 18 Planning Guide

Timesaving Tools

TeacherWorks™ All-In-One Planner and Resource Center

- **Interactive Teacher Edition** Access your Teacher Wraparound Edition and your classroom resources with a few easy clicks.
- **Interactive Lesson Planner** Planning has never been easier! Organize your week, month, semester, or year with all the lesson helps you need to make teaching creative, timely, and relevant.

Use Glencoe's **Presentation Plus!** multimedia teacher tool to easily present dynamic lessons that visually excite your students. Using Microsoft PowerPoint® you can customize the presentations to create your own personalized lessons.

Objectives	Reproducible Resources	Multimedia Resources
Section 1 **Clovis** Explain how Clovis united the Franks and brought them Christianity.	Reproducible Lesson Plan Chapter 18 Vocabulary and Guided Reading Activity Reading Essentials and Study Guide 18-1 Section 1 Quiz	Interactive Student Edition CD-ROM Graphic Organizer Transparency 6 Teaching Transparency and Activity 18A Vocabulary PuzzleMaker CD-ROM Interactive Tutor Self-Assessment CD-ROM ExamView® Pro Testmaker CD-ROM Glencoe Skillbuilder Interactive Workbook CD-ROM, Level 1 Presentation Plus! CD-ROM
Section 2 **Charles the Hammer** Describe how Charles Martel's defeat of the Arabs kept western Europe Christian.	Reproducible Lesson Plan Reading Essentials and Study Guide 18-2 Chapter 18 Chart and Graph Skill Activity Section 2 Quiz	Vocabulary PuzzleMaker CD-ROM Interactive Tutor Self-Assessment CD-ROM ExamView® Pro Testmaker CD-ROM Glencoe Skillbuilder Interactive Workbook CD-ROM, Level 1
Section 3 **Charlemagne** Discuss how Charlemagne brought all of western Europe under his rule, what daily life was like in Charlemagne's empire, and why Charlemagne's empire collapsed.	Reproducible Lesson Plan Reading Essentials and Study Guide 18-3 Chapter 18 Cooperative Learning Activity Chapter 18 Geography and Map Activity Chapter 18 Enrichment Activity Section 3 Quiz	Teaching Transparency and Activity 18B Vocabulary PuzzleMaker CD-ROM Interactive Tutor Self-Assessment CD-ROM ExamView® Pro Testmaker CD-ROM Glencoe Skillbuilder Interactive Workbook CD-ROM, Level 1
Chapter 18 **Review and Evaluation**	Chapter 18 Reteaching Activity Chapter 18 Performance Assessment Activity Spanish Chapter Summary and Glossary Chapter 18 Test	Vocabulary PuzzleMaker CD-ROM Interactive Tutor Self-Assessment CD-ROM Glencoe Skillbuilder Interactive Workbook CD-ROM, Level 1 Audiocassettes* ExamView® Pro Testmaker CD-ROM

*Also available in Spanish.

Chapter 18 Planning Guide

✓ Performance Assessment Activities

Writing Have students research the many inventions from the Middle Ages. Then have them create advertisements for some of these inventions, using both text and drawings. Some possibilities are portable clocks (the first watches), pies, fireplaces for warming drafty castles, improved farming equipment such as wheelbarrows and plows, and buttons and buttonholes. Display the advertisements in the classroom.

CHAPTER RESOURCES

LITERATURE ABOUT THE PERIOD

Sayers, Dorothy, trans. *The Song of Roland.* Penguin, 1957. Chronicles the events and legends in Charlemagne's career and the career of his young nephew Roland.

READINGS FOR THE STUDENT

Heer, Friedrich. *Charlemagne and His World.* Macmillan, 1975. Large, lavishly illustrated description of the period.

READINGS FOR THE TEACHER

Editors of Time-Life. "The Changing Face of Europe," in *TimeFrame AD 600–800: The March of Islam.* Time-Life Books, 1988. Shows how Frankish kings helped preserve Christianity and usher in important cultural changes.

KEY TO ABILITY LEVELS

Teaching strategies have been coded for varying learning styles and abilities.

L1 Level 1 activities are **basic** activities and should be within the ability range of all students.

L2 Level 2 activities are **average** activities and should be within the ability range of the average to above-average student.

L3 Level 3 activities are **challenging** activities designed for the ability range of above-average students.

ELL ELL activities should be within the ability range of English Language Learning students.

NATIONAL GEOGRAPHIC Teacher's Corner

NATIONAL GEOGRAPHIC SOCIETY PRODUCTS AVAILABLE FROM GLENCOE

To order the following, call Glencoe at 1-800-334-7344:

- *Europe (Laminated Desk Maps)*
- *PicturePack: Physical Geography of the World (Transparencies)*
- *PicturePack: The Middle Ages (Transparencies)*
- *PictureShow: The Middle Ages (CD-ROM)*
- *Picture Atlas of the World (CD-ROM)*

ADDITIONAL NATIONAL GEOGRAPHIC SOCIETY PRODUCTS

To order the following, call National Geographic at 1-800-368-2728:

- *PicturePack: Physical Geography of the World (Transparencies)*
- *Physical Geography of the Continents Series: Europe (Video)*
- *National Geographic Atlas of World History (Book)*
- *Wonders of the Ancient World: National Geographic Atlas of Archaeology (Book)*

Access *National Geographic's* new dynamic MapMachine Web site and other geography resources at:
www.nationalgeographic.com
www.nationalgeographic.com/maps

Introducing **CHAPTER 18**

OVERVIEW

Chapter 18 discusses the Franks and the first strong kingdom in medieval Europe.

- **Section 1** discusses the goals of Clovis and the role of the Catholic Church in the political affairs of the Franks.
- **Section 2** describes the rule of Charles Martel and the Battle of Tours.
- **Section 3** explains important developments during the reign of Charlemagne.

CHAPTER OBJECTIVES

After reading Chapter 18, students will be able to:

1. explain how Clovis united the Franks under Christianity.
2. describe how Charles Martel's defeat of the Arabs kept western Europe Christian.
3. discuss how Charlemagne brought all of western Europe under his rule.
4. characterize what life was like in Charlemagne's empire.
5. summarize why Charlemagne's empire collapsed.

EXAMINING ARTIFACTS

Focus student attention on the artifacts, and ask them to describe how the artist who created the bronze statue wanted people to view Charlemagne. *(as a noble and perhaps holy warrior-king)* Tell students that in this chapter they will decide whether Charlemagne lived up to the artist's vision of him.

PERFORMANCE ASSESSMENT

Use the Performance Assessment Activities on page 274B to help you evaluate students as they complete the chapter.

CHAPTER 18

The Franks

400 A.D.–843 A.D.

▲ Frankish jewelry

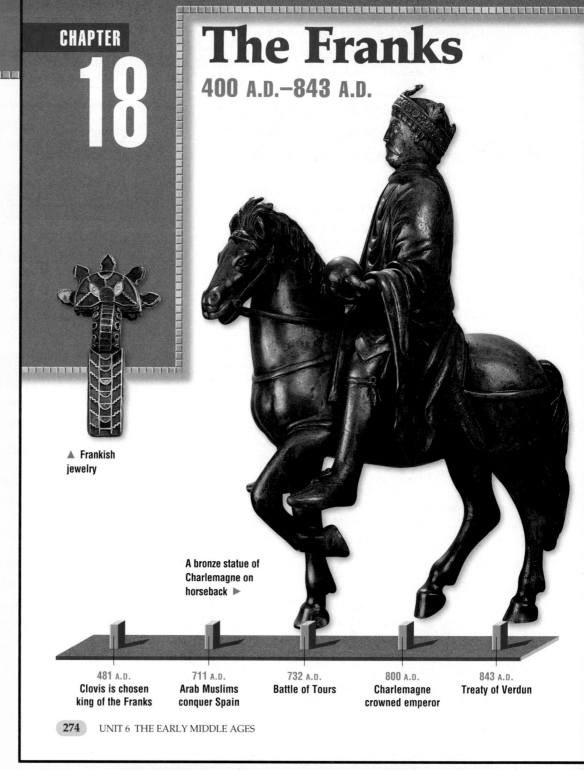

A bronze statue of Charlemagne on horseback ▶

481 A.D.	711 A.D.	732 A.D.	800 A.D.	843 A.D.
Clovis is chosen king of the Franks	Arab Muslims conquer Spain	Battle of Tours	Charlemagne crowned emperor	Treaty of Verdun

TEACHING RESOURCES

TEACHER PLANNING AND SUPPORT

- Reproducible Lesson Plan 18-1, 18-2, 18-3
- Teaching Strategies for the World History Classroom (Including Block Scheduling Pacing Guides)
- Presentation Plus! CD-ROM

REVIEW AND REINFORCEMENT

- Reading Essentials and Study Guide 18-1, 18-2, 18-3
- Chapter 18 Vocabulary and Guided Reading Activity
- Vocabulary PuzzleMaker CD-ROM
- Teaching Transparencies 18A & 18B
- Chapter 18 Reteaching Activity
- Chapter 18 Cooperative Learning Activity
- Chapter 18 Activity Book Activity
- Chapter 18 Chart and Graph Skill Activity
- Reading and Study Skills Foldables
- Interactive Tutor Self-Assessment CD-ROM

APPLICATION AND HANDS-ON ACTIVITIES

- Daily Questions in Social Studies
- Student Presentation Builder CD-ROM

Chapter Focus

Read to Discover

- How Clovis united the Franks and brought them Christianity.
- How Charles Martel's defeat of the Arabs kept western Europe Christian.
- How Charlemagne brought all of western Europe under his rule.
- What life was like in Charlemagne's empire.
- Why Charlemagne's empire collapsed.

HISTORY Online

Chapter Overview

Visit the *Human Heritage* Web site at **humanheritage.glencoe.com** and click on ***Chapter 18—Chapter Overviews*** to preview this chapter.

Terms to Learn	People to Know	Places to Locate
converted	Clovis	Paris
anointed	Charles Martel	Tours
counts	Pepin	Aachen
lords	Charlemagne	
serfs	Roland	
minstrels	Louis the Pious	

Why It's Important The decline of the Roman Empire led to disorder everywhere in western Europe. Many of the Germanic invaders were too weak to govern well. As a result, towns and villages fell into ruin. Roads and bridges were not repaired. Robbers roamed the countryside, making it unsafe for travelers. Trading and business slowed down, and there were shortages of food and other goods. People were no longer interested in learning, and many books and works of art were damaged or lost.

SECTION 1 Clovis

During this period, a Germanic people called the Franks became very important. They began to build a new civilization, one that later developed into modern France and Germany. The Franks lived along the Rhine River in what is now Germany. They were more successful in governing than other Germans. One reason for this was that the area in which they lived was close to their homeland, and they felt fairly secure. Also, unlike the Goths and Vandals, the Franks did more than just fight and rule. They became farmers.

At first, the Franks were divided into separate groups without a common ruler. In 481, one Frankish group chose a man named

HISTORY Online

Chapter Overview introduces students to chapter content and key terms. Have them access ***Chapter 18 Overview*** at **humanheritage.glencoe.com**

FOCUS

Bellringer

Ask students to respond in writing to the term *Dark Ages.*

Motivational Activity

Discuss students' responses to the term *Dark Ages*. Tell students that by 500 A.D. western Europe was so backward compared to other contemporary societies that scholars once called the early part of the Middle Ages the Dark Ages. Tell students that in this chapter they will learn about events that helped move western Europe out of the Dark Ages and into an age of enlightenment.

GUIDE TO READING

Reading Strategy

Ask students to read "Why It's Important" and summarize the chapter's main theme. *(The decline of the Roman Empire led to a decline of order and a loss of interest in learning.)*

Vocabulary Precheck

Ask students to define each of the "Terms to Learn." Have a volunteer consult the dictionary for any unfamiliar words. L1 ELL

Use the Vocabulary PuzzleMaker CD-ROM for Chapter 18 to create a crossword puzzle. L1

Assign Chapter 18 Vocabulary and Guided Reading Activity.

Assign Reading Essentials and Study Guide 18-1.

GEOGRAPHY ACTIVITIES

- Chapter 18 Geography and Map Activity
- Outline Map Resource Book

INTERDISCIPLINARY CONNECTIONS

- World Music: A Cultural Legacy

ENRICHMENT AND EXTENSION

- World History Primary Source Document Library CD-ROM
- Chapter 18 Enrichment Activity
- Foods Around the World

ASSESSMENT AND EVALUATION

- Chapter 18 Performance Assessment Activity
- Chapter 18 Section Quizzes 18-1, 18-2, 18-3
- Chapter 18 Test
- Chapter 18 ExamView® Pro Testmaker CD-ROM
- Chapter 18 Digests Audiocassettes Activities and Tests

SPANISH RESOURCES

- Chapter 18 Spanish Chapter Summary and Glossary
- Chapter 18 Spanish Digests Audiocassettes Activities and Tests

TECHNOLOGY SKILLS

TEACH

Developing Multimedia Presentations

You might introduce the lesson by writing this statement on the board: "Computers—More Than Just Typewriters." Ask students to brainstorm some of the things computers can do besides word processing. *(draw pictures, design tables and graphs, download/scan photos, create animation, record sound, and so on)*

Next, identify the "computer experts" in your class—those students who are comfortable with multimedia programs. Divide the class into groups, making sure each group has at least one technology advisor. Assign the skills lesson, which helps students plan a multimedia presentation on the Frankish empire.

Performance Assessment

To encourage self-assessment of the multimedia presentation, have each student complete this individual task management plan.

Self-Management Plan

Name: ____________________

Task: ____________________

Audience: ____________________

Steps to accomplish the task:

Problems to completing the task:

Solutions or attempted solutions:

Signed: ____________________

TECHNOLOGY SKILLS

Developing Multimedia Presentations

You want to present a research report to your class, and you want to really hold their attention. How do you do it? Your presentation can be exciting if you use various forms of media.

Learning the Skill At its most basic, a multimedia presentation involves using several types of media. To discuss life under the Frankish kings, for example, you might show photographs of historic paintings. You could also record selections from *The Song of Roland* or ballads sung by minstrels. Or you might present a video of Charlemagne's life.

You can also develop a multimedia presentation on a computer. Multimedia as it relates to computer technology is the combination of text, video, audio, and animation in an interactive computer program.

In order to create multimedia productions or presentations on a computer, you need to have certain tools. These may include traditional computer graphic tools and art programs, animation programs that make still images move, and authoring systems that tie everything together. Your computer manual will tell you what tools your computer can support.

This chapter focuses on the growth of the Frankish empire in the early Middle Ages. Ask yourself questions like the following to create a multimedia presentation on the cultural and political developments of that era:

- Which forms of media do I want to include? Video? Sound? Animation? Photographs? Graphics? Other?
- Which of these media forms does my computer support?
- What kind of software programs or systems do I need? An art program? A program to create interactive, or two-way, communication? An authoring system that will allow me to change images, sound, and motion?
- Is there a "do-it-all" program I can use to develop the kind of presentation I want?

Skill Practice

Developing Multimedia Presentations

Keeping in mind the four guidelines given above, write a plan describing a multimedia presentation you would like to develop. Indicate what tools you will need and what steps you must take to make the presentation a reality.

TEAM TEACHING STRATEGIES

Art Work together with the art teacher in your school to develop visual materials and/or original drawings that students might scan into their computers. The visuals/drawings should focus on the political and cultural accomplishments of the Frankish empire. Students might also consult with the art teacher on the selection of computer fonts and styles to use with their presentations.

Clovis (klō′ vis) as king. Although he was cruel and greedy, Clovis was a good general and an able king. He eventually brought all the Franks under one rule. Part of Clovis's kingdom later became France, which took its name from the Franks.

Clovis was the first Germanic king to accept the Catholic religion. Clovis was not happy with the Frankish gods. Although he prayed to them faithfully, they failed to help him win battles. Clovis decided that if he defeated the enemy, he would become a Christian. Clovis's army won its next battle. Clovis and some 3,000 Frankish soldiers, still in full battle dress, immediately **converted** (kuhn ver′ tuhd), or changed religion, to Christianity. It was not long before all the Franks followed his example.

When Clovis became a Christian, he gained the support of the Romans in his kingdom. Before long, the Franks began speaking a form of Latin that later became the modern French language. Now, all the people in Clovis's kingdom practiced the same religion, spoke the same language, and felt united.

The Pope and other church officials gave Clovis their support. Priests served in his government. In return for the Church's help, Clovis was expected to protect the Church against all non-believers.

Clovis extended his rule over what is now France and western Germany and set up his capital in Paris. He admired the Roman Empire. He wore purple robes similar to those of the Roman emperors and made Latin the official language of the court.

Reading Check What happened after Clovis **converted** to Christianity?

Section 1 Assessment

1. **Define:** converted.
2. What modern nations developed out of the civilization built by the Franks?
3. Why were the Franks more successful at governing than other Germanic peoples?

Critical Thinking

4. **Drawing a Conclusion** Why was it important for Clovis to have the Pope's blessing and the support of the Church?

Graphic Organizer Activity

5. Draw this diagram, and use it to show the cause and effects of Clovis's conversion to Christianity.

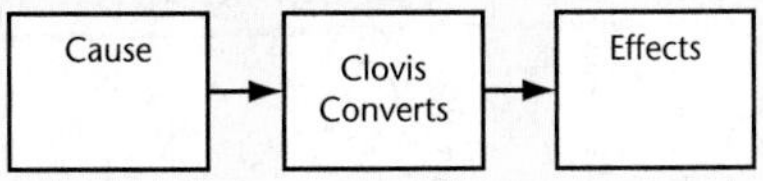

SECTION 2 Charles the Hammer

The Frankish kings who followed Clovis were weak rulers. Instead of keeping the kingdom united, they divided it among their sons. The sons often fought over their shares of land. They

TEACH

GUIDED PRACTICE

L1 **Government** Write the following question on the chalkboard: *How was Clovis able to unify the Franks?* Lead a discussion in which students answer this question. Direct the discussion with the following questions: Why did Clovis's conversion to Christianity gain the support of the Romans in his kingdom? Do you think Clovis would have had a united kingdom if he had not become a Christian and adopted the Latin language? Why or why not?

Reading Check Answer After Clovis **converted** to Christianity, other Franks followed his example and the Frankish empire underwent many changes.

Use **Interactive Tutor Self-Assessment CD-ROM** to review Section 1.

Use the **Vocabulary PuzzleMaker CD-ROM** to create crossword and word search puzzles.

Section 1 Assessment Answers

1. converted, changed religion (p. 277)
2. France and western Germany
3. because the area in which they lived was close to their homeland, and they felt fairly secure; also, they became farmers instead of just fighting and ruling
4. Answers will vary but might include that through this, Clovis gained the support of the Romans in his kingdom.
5. sample responses: *causes*—unhappy with Frankish gods, decided to convert if defeated enemy in next battle, won battle and converted; *effects*—gained support of Romans within kingdom, began speaking a form of Latin, promoted unity through use of same language and religion, won support of Pope and church officials, extended rule

Assign Chapter 18 **Section 1 Quiz** in the TCR. Testmaker available.

L2 **History** Ask the students to imagine that they are Charles Martel after his defeat of the Arabs and Berbers at the Battle of Tours in 732. Tell them that they are to write a letter to the Pope presenting an eyewitness account of what has taken place and giving reasons why the event is certain to be of great significance for Christianity and western Europe. Then have students imagine that they are the Pope and have them write a response to Charles Martel's letter. Have students read their letters to the class.

L2 **Critical Thinking** Remind students that they have read about several rulers who were given nicknames in addition to their given names. Ask students to name a few. ***(Charles the Hammer, Alexander the Great)*** Ask students to explain why they think many rulers were given nicknames. ELL

CAPTION ANSWER

They hoped to spread their religion of Islam throughout Europe.

Fun Facts...

Mounted Knights
Charles Martel could not follow up his victory at Tours because he had too few mounted soldiers. From then on, he required every landowner to provide him with at least one fully outfitted knight. Over time, mounted knights became the core of the Frankish army.

spent so much time and energy fighting that they lost much of their power to local nobles.

It was not long before the Franks began to accept the leadership of a government official known as the "Mayor of the Palace." The Mayor was a noble and the most important official in the king's household. As the Frankish kings grew weaker, the Mayors took over many of their duties. In time, the Mayors were conducting wars, giving out land, and settling disputes. Of all the Mayors, the most powerful was Charles Martel (mahr tel'). He wanted to reunite all the Frankish nobles under his rule. Before long, Charles Martel had gained the support of the Church.

Charles Martel became known as "The Hammer" because of his strength in battle. In 732, he led the Franks in the Battle of

BATTLE OF TOURS Charles Martel (shown center in this painting) leads his army against the Muslims at the Battle of Tours. The Frankish victory halted the Muslim advance into western Europe. It also helped the Frankish rulers to build a strong kingdom. **Why were the Muslims invading western Europe?**

EXTENDING THE CONTENT

Charles Martel, who held power effectively from about 720 until his death in 741, depended in part on having the backing of the Church. In return, and to help unify the empire, he encouraged Christianity and protected missionaries from the pagan Germans across the Rhine River. The most famous missionary was St. Boniface, an Anglo-Saxon priest from England.

Tours (tūrz), one of the most important battles in European history. The Franks defeated an army of Arabs and Berbers who had conquered Spain in 711. The Arabs and Berbers were Muslims, who hoped to spread their religion of Islam everywhere. The Franks' victory at the Battle of Tours enabled Christianity to survive in western Europe.

When Charles Martel died, his son Pepin (pep′ in) became Mayor of the Palace. With the help of the Pope and most Frankish nobles, Pepin removed the king and started a new dynasty. Pepin was the first Frankish king to be **anointed** (uh noin′ tuhd), or blessed with holy oil, by the Pope. In return for the Church's support, Pepin helped the Pope when he was threatened by a group of Germans known as Lombards (lahm′ bahrdz). Pepin led an army into Italy, defeated the Lombards, and gave the land they held in central Italy to the Pope. This gift made the Pope the political ruler of much of the Italian Peninsula.

Reading Check Who **anointed** Pepin, and why was this an important event?

Section 2 Assessment

1. **Define:** anointed.
2. Why was the Battle of Tours a turning point in history?
3. How did Pepin help the Pope?

Critical Thinking

4. **Predicting Consequences** What might western Europe have been like if the Arabs and Berbers had won the Battle of Tours?

Graphic Organizer Activity

5. Draw this diagram, and use it to compare the accomplishments of Charles Martel and his son Pepin.

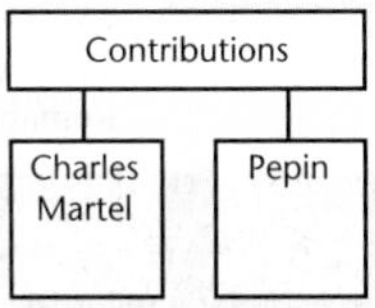

SECTION 3 Charlemagne

When Pepin died in 768, his kingdom was divided between his two sons. His son Carloman died within a few years. Pepin's other son Charles then became king of the Franks. He is best known by his French name Charlemagne (shar′ luh mān), which means "Charles the Great."

A powerful leader, Charlemagne wanted to bring all of western Europe under his rule. He also wanted all the Germanic people to become Christian. To achieve these goals, he waged a series of wars.

First, Charlemagne went to Italy and defeated the Lombards. Next, Charlemagne attacked Saxons (sak′ suhnz), who lived in what is now northern Germany. For years, the Saxons had been raiding towns and monasteries inside the Frankish border. He

HISTORY Online

Student Web Activity
Visit the *Human Heritage* Web site at **humanheritage.glencoe.com** and click on ***Chapter 18—Student Web Activities*** to find out more about Charlemagne.

Section 2 Assessment Answers

1. anointed, blessed with holy oil (p. 279)
2. It enabled Christianity to survive in western Europe.
3. He led an army into Italy, defeated the Lombards, and gave the land they held in central Italy to the Pope.
4. Answers will vary but could include the idea that it might have meant the end of Christianity as the major religion of western Europe.
5. sample responses: *Martel*—stopped the spread of Islam to Europe, united Frankish nobles; *Pepin*—removed the king and started a new dynasty; helped make the Pope the political ruler of much of Italy by defeating the Lombards and giving the Pope a gift of land

Assign the Chapter 18 **Section 2 Quiz** in the TCR. Testmaker available.

MAKING CONNECTIONS

>> **History** Pepin, known as "Pepin the Short," began the Carolingian line of kings in 751.

Reading Check Answer
The Pope **anointed** Pepin, showing his approval of the new dynasty and strengthening ties between Pepin and the Roman Catholic Church.

Use **Interactive Tutor Self-Assessment CD-ROM** to review Section 2.

HISTORY Online

Student Web Activity objectives and answers can be found at the ***Chapter 18 Web Activity Lesson Plan*** at **humanheritage.glencoe.com**

Use the **Vocabulary PuzzleMaker CD-ROM** to create crossword and word search puzzles.

L2 Critical Thinking Ask students why the Middle Ages might be considered a bridge to the modern world. Have them explain how western European society was clinging to the past but also moving slowly toward an age of great learning and enlightenment.

CAPTION ANSWER

He wanted to push back the darkness that followed the fall of the Roman Empire by educating his people.

Independent Practice

L2 History Have students research and write a biographical sketch of the life and work of Alcuin. Encourage students to illustrate their writing.

DID YOU KNOW ??

The emperor Charlemagne admired and encouraged learning, although he could not even write his own name. He reportedly slept with a slate beneath his pillow every night so that if he awoke he might practice his writing. Unfortunately, he never mastered the art of writing that he so admired.

CHARLEMAGNE'S SCHOOL Charlemagne often visited his palace school, which was attended by children of the court. Directed by the monk Alcuin, the school also provided a place where scholars could gather to share their knowledge and to inspire one another. **Why was Charlemagne interested in learning?**

to found schools. He had a scholar named Alcuin (al' kwin) start a school in one of the palaces to train the children of government officials to serve in the Church or in the royal household. The children studied such subjects as religion, Latin, music, literature, and arithmetic.

Scholars came from all over Europe to teach in Charlemagne's school. One of their many tasks was to copy manuscripts. This led to the development of a new form of writing. The Roman writing the scholars used contained only capital letters. These letters took up a lot of space on a page. So, the scholars began to write with small letters instead of capital ones. The new letters not only took up less space, but they were also easier to read. The new letters became the model for the lower-case letters used today.

Under Charlemagne, the arts began to flower again. Painters, sculptors, and metalworkers developed their talents. They built palaces and churches around a large courtyard as the Romans did. Artists covered palace and church walls with pictures showing stories from the Bible. They made book covers and ornamental weapons, and they decorated the manuscripts copied by scholars.

Fun Facts...

Deep Sleep Many legends spread about Charlemagne. According to one legend, he did not die but was only sleeping, and would awaken at the hour of his country's need.

MEETING SPECIAL NEEDS

Ask students with strong organizational skills to work in small groups with students who are having difficulty accessing the material in the chapter. Ask the groups to create descriptive outlines that show the movement of power from Clovis to the heirs of Charlemagne. Have students include biographical details and important events for each ruler. Students might also add relationships to other rulers, and major accomplishments. Have the groups compare their information in a class discussion. Create a master descriptive outline on the chalkboard. Let students decide what information is most important and should be included in the master outline.

Refer to **Inclusion for the Middle School Social Studies Classroom: Strategies and Activities** for additional resources.

Estate Life **Lords,** or nobles, were the most powerful people in Charlemagne's empire. They were the descendants of Frankish warriors and Roman landowners. Most of the lords' wealth came from goods grown or made on their estates. As there was little trade in Charlemagne's empire, each estate took care of its own needs. There were shoemakers, carpenters, and blacksmiths on each estate. There were also artisans who made weapons, cooking vessels, and jewelry.

Lords lived in stone farmhouses. Wooden *stockades* (stah kādz'), or fences, often were built around the houses. Each farmhouse had a banquet hall, sleeping quarters, cellars, stables, storage places, and a small chapel.

Farmers lived in simple wooden houses in small villages on the estates. They worked in the fields, vineyards, orchards, and forests around their villages. The fields were owned by the lords, but the farmers worked them three days a week. The rest of the time they worked small pieces of land the lords had given them.

Reading Check Who were the **lords,** and from where did they get their wealth?

Linking Across Time

Writing in Minuscule Today the word *minuscule* means "extremely small." However, during the rule of Charlemagne, it referred to small letters used in writing (below). The use of small letters replaced the all-capital letters used by the Romans. This writing style later developed into the capital and lowercase letters used in all Western languages (right). **What subjects did the children of government officials study?**

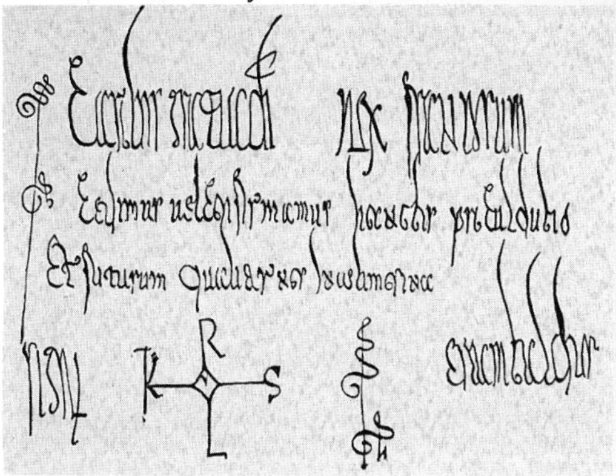

Reading Check Answer The **lords** were nobles who got most of their wealth from goods grown or made on their estates.

Linking Across Time

Children studied religion, Latin, music, literature, and arithmetic.

GEOGRAPHY AND HISTORY

Long-distance trade with the near East improved during the reign of Charlemagne. Items traded consisted mostly of spices and silks. The trade was carried on by Jewish merchants, who were acceptable to both Christians and Muslims. Charlemagne's protection of the Jewish merchants led to the rise of the new middle class in the later Middle Ages.

COOPERATIVE LEARNING

Have students work in small groups to create diagrams, dioramas, or models of estates in Charlemagne's empire. Students can use the information in the textbook and in reference books to create their estates. Each member of the group should be assigned a particular task in order to complete the assignment. Display students' work in the classroom.

Assign the Chapter 18 *Cooperative Learning Activity* in the TCR.

MAP SKILLS

TEACH

Understanding Inset Maps

Have students read the instructional part of the feature to answer the following questions: What are inset maps? *(small maps that are set within larger ones)* What are two reasons that inset maps are used? *(to show parts of the main map enlarged and in greater detail; to show in a different way an area on the main map)* Direct students to study the map to answer the following questions: What kingdom did the Saxons become part of after the Treaty of Verdun? *(Kingdom of Louis)* What kingdom did most Lombards become part of after the Treaty of Verdun? *(Kingdom of Lothair)*

Assign the Chapter 18 **Geography and Map Activity** in the TCR.

Answers to Skill Practice

1. Paris and Tours
2. Lothair
3. Kingdom of Louis

Use the **Glencoe Skillbuilder Interactive Workbook CD-ROM, Level 1,** to provide instruction and practice in key social studies skills.

MAP SKILLS

Understanding Inset Maps

Sometimes, there is not enough space on a map for information to be shown clearly. Mapmakers have solved this problem by using **inset maps,** or small maps that are set within larger ones. Often placed in a corner of the main map, inset maps may have their own scales and legends.

Inset maps are used for two reasons. One is to show parts of the main map enlarged and in greater detail. Maps of countries or states often include inset maps showing individual cities.

Another reason inset maps are used is to show in a different way an area on the main map. For example, on the map below, the main map shows the Frankish Empire from Clovis through Charlemagne. The inset map in the upper right shows what happened to the same territory after the death of Charlemagne.

Map Practice

1. **What two cities were in the kingdom of Charles?**
2. **Who controlled Rome after the Treaty of Verdun?**
3. **Through which kingdom did the Danube River flow?**

The Frankish Empire

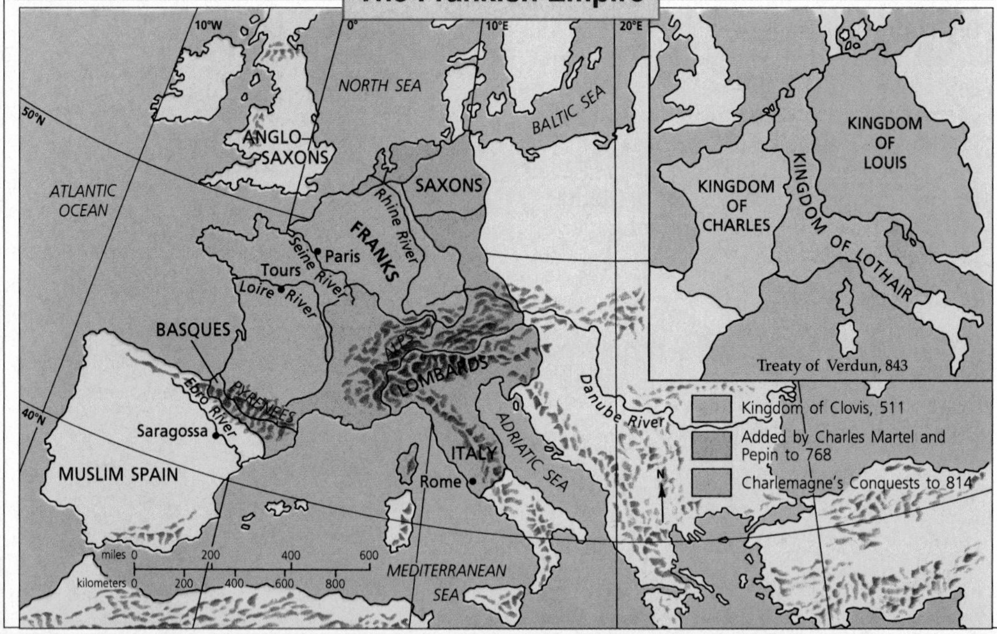

SPOTLIGHT ON: THE FRANKISH EMPIRE

A large part of the central Frankish Empire was made up by the extremely fertile North European Plain which has fed many nations for centuries. This area of western Europe, also known as the heartland, is today occupied by seven countries: France, Luxembourg, Switzerland, Germany, Belgium, Austria, and the Netherlands.

The farmers divided the land into three sections. They let one section lie *fallow* (fal' ō), or not planted. On the other two sections, they used heavy metal plows to prepare the hard but fertile soil. In autumn, they planted wheat or rye in one section. In spring, they planted oats or barley in the other section. Each year, the farmers *rotated* (rō' tā tuhd), or changed by turns, the kind of crops they grew in each section. They also let a different section lie fallow. These changes helped them grow larger crops.

Besides working the land, the farmers had to give the nobles food and animals. The farmers had to perform many services for the nobles, too. Men repaired buildings on the estates, cut down trees, carried loads, gathered fruits, and served in the army. Women worked as hard as men. They looked after the children and small animals, wove cloth, and sewed clothing copied from earlier Roman styles. The farmers gradually did more for the nobles and less for themselves. They were becoming **serfs,** or people bound to the land.

Neither the nobles nor the farmers had much time to learn to read or write or to think about religion. Both groups accepted Christianity, but the new religion had little to do with their daily lives. However, on religious holidays, both rich and poor sang, danced, and feasted. They listened to traveling musicians called **minstrels** (min' struhlz). The minstrels journeyed from place to place singing the praises of Charlemagne and his empire.

Painting of Minstrel

Reading Check How did farmers gradually become **serfs?**

Reading Check How did **minstrels** increase Charlemagne's popularity?

The Collapse of the Empire

The glory of the empire did not last long after Charlemagne's death in 814. The empire needed a strong and able ruler. Charlemagne's heirs were neither. Many counts and lords became increasingly independent. They cared more about their own estates than about the good of the empire. They refused to obey Louis the Pious (pī' uhs), Charlemagne's son.

Louis the Pious unknowingly weakened the empire further when he divided it among his three sons. After he died, they began fighting among themselves over their shares. Lothair (lō thahr'), Louis's oldest son, received the title of emperor. His younger brothers, Charles and Louis, were jealous of Lothair.

In 843, the brothers agreed to a new and different division of the empire. Under the Treaty of Verdun (ver duhn'), Lothair kept the title of emperor, but he ruled only a narrow strip of land that stretched from the North Sea to the Italian Peninsula. Louis received the area to the east. Called the East Frankish Kingdom, it later became the nation of Germany. Charles received the area to the west. Called the West Frankish Kingdom, it later became France.

The brothers were weak rulers who allowed the counts and nobles to have most of the power. Once again, a united western Europe was divided into smaller territories.

L3 **Literature** Have students read *The Song of Roland* and write a report on the characters and personalities of Charlemagne and Roland as presented in the poem. Ask students to comment on their reports on the mythical and legendary quality given to historical figures in poems.

Reading Check Answer In exchange for a noble's protection, farmers became bound to the land as **serfs.**

Reading Check Answer The **minstrels** journeyed from place to place singing the praises of Charlemagne and his empire.

ASSESS

Check for Understanding

Ask students to summarize orally or in writing the main points of the chapter. Discuss the answers to the Section and Chapter Assessment questions.

Evaluate

Assign the Chapter 18 **Performance Assessment Activity** in the TCR.

Administer the **Chapter 18 Test**. Testmaker available.

MEETING SPECIAL NEEDS

Have auditory learners or gifted learners debate the following topic: *The collapse of Charlemagne's empire was inevitable.* Form two teams, one to defend the idea that the collapse of the empire was inevitable and one to defend the idea that the collapse of the empire could have been prevented. Allow each team enough time to research and develop its arguments before beginning the debate.

Refer to **Inclusion for the Middle School Social Studies Classroom: Strategies and Activities** for additional resources.

Reteach

Ask students to explain how each of the following influenced the early Middle Ages: Germanic invasions, the donation of the land held by the Lombards to the Pope, and Charlemagne's dedication to education.

Assign the Chapter 18 **Reteaching Activity** in the TCR.

Enrich

Have students research and share with the class illustrations of Charlemagne's tomb and/or manuscripts of the period.

Assign the Chapter 18 **Enrichment Activity** in the TCR.

CLOSE

Ask students to explain how during the early Middle Ages, western Europe was in a dark age, and how it was moving toward an age of enlightenment—creating a bridge between an old world and a new one.

Use **Interactive Tutor Self-Assessment CD-ROM** to review Section 3.

HISTORY Online

Self-Check Quiz gives students an interactive chapter tutorial. Have them access ***Chapter 18 Quiz*** at **humanheritage.glencoe.com**

Section 3 Assessment

1. **Define:** counts, lords, serfs, minstrels.
2. Why did Charlemagne object to the Pope crowning him emperor?
3. What did Charlemagne do to encourage learning?

Critical Thinking

4. **Identifying Alternatives** What might have prevented the collapse of Charlemagne's government?

Graphic Organizer Activity

5. Draw this diagram, and use it to summarize Charlemagne's political, educational, and cultural accomplishments.

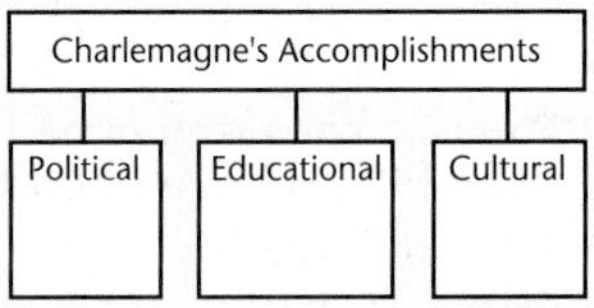

Chapter Summary & Study Guide

1. During the late 400s, the Franks began to build a civilization that would later develop into the modern nations of France and Germany.
2. Clovis united the Franks and was the first Germanic king to accept the Catholic religion.
3. Clovis gained the support of the Romans in his kingdom and made Latin the official language of the royal court.
4. A series of weak kings followed Clovis, and leadership gradually came into the hands of a government official known as the "Mayor of the Palace."
5. In 732, a Mayor of the Palace named Charles Martel defeated the Muslim army at the Battle of Tours. This kept western Europe Christian.
6. Charles Martel's son Pepin started a new dynasty and became the first Germanic king to be anointed by the Pope.
7. Pepin's son Charlemagne brought all of western Europe under his control.
8. In 800, the Pope crowned him the new Roman emperor.
9. Charlemagne was a wise and just ruler who wrote new laws.
10. Charlemagne was very interested in learning and encouraged the founding of schools in his empire.
11. During the rule of Charlemagne, powerful lords grew wealthy from goods grown or made on their estates.
12. Louis the Pious divided the Frankish Empire among his three sons, which led to its final collapse.

HISTORY Online

Self-Check Quiz

Visit the *Human Heritage* Web site at **humanheritage.glencoe.com** and click on ***Chapter 18— Self-Check Quiz*** to assess your understanding of this chapter.

Section 3 Assessment Answers

1. counts, court officials (p. 281); lords, nobles (p. 283); serfs, people bound to the land (p. 285); minstrels, traveling musicians (p. 285)
2. It seemed the emperor's right to rule came from the Pope rather than from God.
3. He encouraged churches and monasteries to found schools, and had Alcuin teach the children of government officials.
4. Answers will vary but could include that Charlemagne might have chosen a strong and able successor.
5. Answers will vary but may include the creation of courts and closely supervised counts to manage local affairs (political), spread of literacy through the establishment of schools (education), and flourishing of religious art and popular art such as minstrels (culture).

Assign the Chapter 18 **Section 3 Quiz** in the TCR. Testmaker available.

CHAPTER 18 Assessment

Using Key Terms

Write a paragraph about the Franks and their rule in western Europe. Highlight one of the people mentioned in the chapter in your paragraph. Use the following words.

converted	anointed	counts
lords	serfs	minstrels

Understanding Main Ideas

1. What happened to western Europe after the decline of the Roman Empire?
2. How did Clovis help people within his empire feel united?
3. What was the relationship between the Church and Clovis?
4. Why did the Mayor of the Palace become important?
5. What were Charlemagne's main goals when he became king of the Franks?
6. How did Frankish farmers become serfs?
7. What happened to western Europe after Charlemagne's heirs came to power?

Critical Thinking

1. Do you think that Charlemagne's traveling all over the empire was a wise idea? Why or why not?
2. Why was the title "the Great" good for Charlemagne? What other title might have been better? Why?
3. What parts of life in Charlemagne's empire would you have liked? What parts would you have disliked?
4. What do you think Louis the Pious could have done with the Frankish Empire instead of dividing it among his three sons?

Graphic Organizer Activity

Economics Create a diagram like the one shown, and use it to show details that support this main idea: "Life in the Frankish Empire centered around the estates of lords."

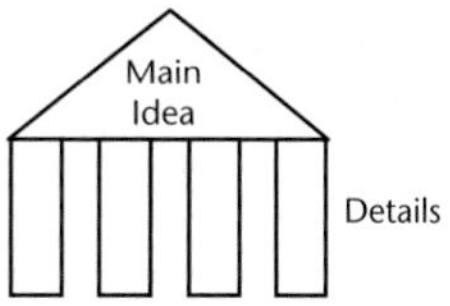

Geography in History

Places and Regions Refer to the map on page 284 and compare the locations of Saragossa, Paris, and Rome. Each of these was an important city in the Frankish Empire. What geographic similarities and differences can you see in these places?

Using Your Journal

Review any details you may have noted about the changes that took place during Charlemagne's empire. Write a diary entry describing how some of these changes can still be seen today.

CHAPTER 18 Assessment Answers

Building Vocabulary

Paragraphs will vary but should include specific details and use all the words.

Understanding Main Ideas

1. There was disorder, towns and roads fell into ruin, the countryside was unsafe, trading slowed, and there were shortages of food.
2. They all had the same religion and language.
3. The Pope and other Church officials supported Clovis's government. In return, Clovis was expected to protect the Church.
4. because he took over many of the king's duties
5. to rule all of western Europe and to have all Germanic peoples become Christian
6. They began to work more for the nobles on estates.
7. It was divided into smaller territories.

Critical Thinking

1. Answers will vary but might include that it was wise because it made him appear strong and in control.
2. Answers will vary but might include that Charlemagne unified his empire.
3. Answers will vary but should include examples.
4. Answers will vary.

Graphic Organizer Activity

Details will vary but might include: most goods were grown or made on estates, little trade existed so each estate had to take care of its own needs, farmers and artisans worked on estates in exchange for protection.

Bonus Test Question

For Chapter 18 Test

A historian has incorrectly reported several facts in the following statement. *Scholars from Europe and the Americas came to teach in Charlemagne's school. Most people could not read or write. Religion, however, was not taught.* Identify the errors.

Using Your Journal

Diary entries will vary. Changes may include heads of government keeping in touch with the people they govern, the use of lowercase letters, and the importance of art in public buildings.

Geography in History

Paris and Saragossa are both located on rivers; all three cities lie on flat lands somewhat near a seacoast; Paris is centrally located while Saragossa and Rome are not.

Chapter 19 Planning Guide

Timesaving Tools

TeacherWorks™ All-In-One Planner and Resource Center

- **Interactive Teacher Edition** Access your Teacher Wraparound Edition and your classroom resources with a few easy clicks.
- **Interactive Lesson Planner** Planning has never been easier! Organize your week, month, semester, or year with all the lesson helps you need to make teaching creative, timely, and relevant.

Use Glencoe's **Presentation Plus!** multimedia teacher tool to easily present dynamic lessons that visually excite your students. Using Microsoft PowerPoint® you can customize the presentations to create your own personalized lessons.

Objectives	Reproducible Resources	Multimedia Resources
Section 1 **Celtic Ireland** Discuss Rome's influence on the area known today as the British Isles and what life was like in Celtic Ireland.	Reproducible Lesson Plan Chapter 19 Vocabulary and Guided Reading Activity Reading Essentials and Study Guide 19-1 Chapter 19 Geography and Map Activity Section 1 Quiz	Interactive Student Edition CD-ROM Graphic Organizer Transparency 15 Teaching Transparencies and Activities 19A & 19B Vocabulary PuzzleMaker CD-ROM Interactive Tutor Self-Assessment CD-ROM ExamView® Pro Testmaker CD-ROM Glencoe Skillbuilder Interactive Workbook CD-ROM, Level 1 Presentation Plus! CD-ROM
Section 2 **Christianity** Explain how Christianity developed in Ireland and England and why the Anglo-Saxons united under Alfred the Great.	Reproducible Lesson Plan Reading Essentials and Study Guide 19-2 Chapter 19 Cooperative Learning Activity Chapter 19 Chart and Graph Skill Activity Chapter 19 Enrichment Activity Unit 6 World Literature Reading 2 Section 2 Quiz	Vocabulary PuzzleMaker CD-ROM Interactive Tutor Self-Assessment CD-ROM ExamView® Pro Testmaker CD-ROM Glencoe Skillbuilder Interactive Workbook CD-ROM, Level 1
Chapter 19 **Review and Evaluation**	Chapter 19 Reteaching Activity Chapter 19 Performance Assessment Activity Spanish Chapter Summary and Glossary Chapter 19 Test	Vocabulary PuzzleMaker CD-ROM Interactive Tutor Self-Assessment CD-ROM Glencoe Skillbuilder Interactive Workbook CD-ROM, Level 1 Audiocassettes* ExamView® Pro Testmaker CD-ROM

*Also available in Spanish.

Chapter 19 Planning Guide

✓ Performance Assessment Activities

Travel Journals Have students imagine they are Romans traveling through the British Isles in the year 250 A.D. On their trip, they see many sights and talk with many people. Tell students to write a travel journal describing the Roman influences they have noticed in the region and the different people they have encountered. Encourage volunteers to read their journal entries for the class.

Chapter Resources

Literature About the Period

Guerber, H.A., ed. *Middle Ages.* Avenel Books, 1985. From the *Myths and Legends Series,* covers Beowulf, Charlemagne, Arthur and his knights, and other tales of the Middle Ages.

Readings for the Student

Corfe, Tom. *St. Patrick and Irish Christianity* (A Cambridge Topic Book). Lerner Publications, 1979. Brief overview with illustrations.

Crossley-Holland, Kevin. *Green Blades Rising: The Anglo-Saxons.* Seabury Press, 1976 (A Clarion Book). An introduction to Anglo-Saxon culture through artifacts and literature.

Readings for the Teacher

Cunliffe, Barry. *The Celtic World.* McGraw-Hill, 1979. Portrays the civilization of the Celts from prehistoric Europe to present-day Ireland.

Thompson, E.A. *Who Was St. Patrick?* St. Martin's Press, 1985. Focuses on the writings of St. Patrick.

THE HISTORY CHANNEL. A&E HOME VIDEO. Biography

The following videotape program is available from Glencoe:

- **A Celtic Journey Through Time**
  0-7670-0864-2

To order, call Glencoe at 1-800-334-7344. To find classroom resources to accompany this video, check:

A&E Television: www.aande.com
The History Channel: www.historychannel.com

NATIONAL GEOGRAPHIC Teacher's Corner

INDEX TO NATIONAL GEOGRAPHIC MAGAZINE

The following articles relate to this chapter:

- "The Celts," by Merle Severy, May 1977

NATIONAL GEOGRAPHIC SOCIETY PRODUCTS AVAILABLE FROM GLENCOE

To order the following, call Glencoe at 1-800-334-7344:

- *Europe (Laminated Desk Maps)*
- *PicturePack: Physical Geography of the World (Transparencies)*
- *Picture Atlas of the World (CD-ROM)*
- *PicturePack: Physical Geography of the World (Transparencies)*

ADDITIONAL NATIONAL GEOGRAPHIC SOCIETY PRODUCTS

To order the following, call National Geographic at 1-800-368-2728:

- *Physical Geography of the Continents Series: Europe (Video)*
- *National Geographic Atlas of World History (Book)*
- *Wonders of the Ancient World: National Geographic Atlas of Archaeology (Book)*

Access *National Geographic's* new dynamic MapMachine Web site and other geography resources at:
www.nationalgeographic.com
www.nationalgeographic.com/maps

Key to Ability Levels

Teaching strategies have been coded for varying learning styles and abilities.

L1 Level 1 activities are **basic** activities and should be within the ability range of all students.

L2 Level 2 activities are **average** activities and should be within the ability range of the average to above-average student.

L3 Level 3 activities are **challenging** activities designed for the ability range of above-average students.

ELL ELL activities should be within the ability range of English Language Learning students.

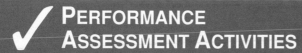

Introducing **CHAPTER 19**

OVERVIEW

Chapter 19 discusses the development of civilization in the British Isles.

- **Section 1** describes the development of an independent Celtic culture in Ireland.
- **Section 2** explains the development of English government and society under the Anglo-Saxon kings.

CHAPTER OBJECTIVES

After reading Chapter 19, students will be able to:

1. summarize what life was like in Celtic Ireland.
2. describe how Christianity developed in both Ireland and England.
3. explain why the Anglo-Saxons united under Alfred the Great.
4. describe what life was like in Anglo-Saxon England.

EXAMINING ARTIFACTS

Ask students who they think might wear a helmet such as the one pictured. *(soldier or warrior-leader)* Explain that this particular helmet belonged to the king that inspired the jewel on this page. Explain that in this chapter, students will learn how leaders such as King Alfred helped shape the history of the British Isles.

PERFORMANCE ASSESSMENT ✓

Use the Performance Assessment Activities on page 288B to help you evaluate students as they complete the chapter.

CHAPTER 19

The Irish and the Anglo-Saxons

55 B.C.–911 A.D.

▲ The Alfred jewel

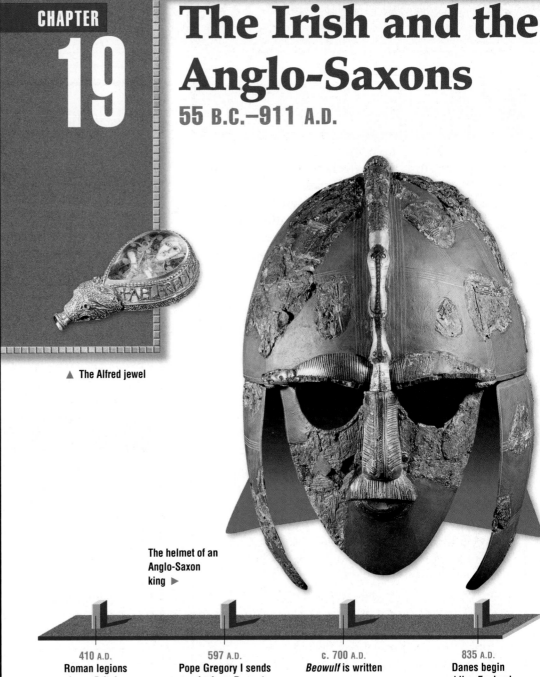

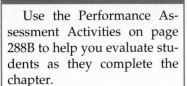

The helmet of an Anglo-Saxon king ▶

410 A.D.	597 A.D.	c. 700 A.D.	835 A.D.
Roman legions leave Britain	Pope Gregory I sends monks from Rome to England	*Beowulf* is written	Danes begin raiding England

TEACHING RESOURCES

TEACHER PLANNING AND SUPPORT

- Reproducible Lesson Plan 19-1, 19-2
- Teaching Strategies for the World History Classroom (Including Block Scheduling Pacing Guides)
- Presentation Plus! CD-ROM

REVIEW AND REINFORCEMENT

- Reading Essentials and Study Guide 19-1, 19-2
- Chapter 19 Vocabulary and Guided Reading Activity
- Vocabulary PuzzleMaker CD-ROM
- Teaching Transparencies 19A & 19B
- Chapter 19 Reteaching Activity
- Chapter 19 Cooperative Learning Activity
- Chapter 19 Activity Book Activity
- Chapter 19 Chart and Graph Skill Activity
- Reading and Study Skills Foldables
- Interactive Tutor Self-Assessment CD-ROM

APPLICATION AND HANDS-ON ACTIVITIES

- Daily Questions in Social Studies
- Student Presentation Builder CD-ROM

Europe, religion would also provide the subjects for much early literature. This literature reflected the lives of the people of the time and their culture.

Alfred the Great About 835 A.D., bands of Danes began attacking the coast of England. Before long, they were making permanent settlements in conquered areas. The English kingdoms decided to resist the invaders. They chose as their leader Alfred, King of Wessex (wes' iks). Alfred later became known as Alfred the Great, one of England's best-loved rulers.

Alfred knew the Anglo-Saxons were not yet strong enough to drive out the Danes. To gain time to build a stronger army, he paid the Danes a sum of money each year to leave England alone. When he felt his army was strong enough, he refused to make any more payments. The Danes invaded England and defeated the

Fun Facts . . .

Early History The *Anglo-Saxon Chronicle,* begun in the reign of Alfred the Great, records events in England from the beginning of the Christian era to the middle of the 12th century. It is the earliest known history of a European people written in the vernacular, or everyday spoken language.

Linking Across Time

Keeping the Peace In Anglo-Saxon times, the job of peacekeeping fell to local nobles known as sheriffs (below). In the United States, the job of sheriff now belongs to a paid public official (right). **What conditions in England made it necessary for nobles to enforce the law?**

L3 **Writing** Remind students that a common element in Anglo-Saxon folklore is the slaying of a monster or dragon, such as in *Beowulf.* Ask students to write their own folktale that involves a similar situation of a hero or heroine destroying a monster or evil force. Encourage students to share their folktales.

Linking Across Time

The central government was too weak to govern the whole country. Some students may also mention the inability of the king to drive out invaders, especially the Danes.

DID YOU KNOW ??

Alfred the Great's united kingdom became known as "Angleland" or England.

SPOTLIGHT ON: ALFRED THE GREAT

Alfred the Great encouraged a revival of English culture and learning. He wrote, "So completely had learning decayed in the English nation that there were very few from here to the Humber [River] who could understand their mass-books in English . . . and I think there were not many beyond the Humber." Alfred learned Latin so he could make his own Old English translations, including comments, of classic works that he thought people ought to be able to read in their own language.

INDEPENDENT PRACTICE

L3 **Religion** Have students research one of the following saints: Saint Patrick, Saint Augustine, or Saint Columba. Students should investigate why the saint was important and how he contributed to the spread of Christianity in Ireland or England.

MAKING CONNECTIONS

➤➤ **History** Alfred risked his life many times for his country. Legend states that he once disguised himself as a minstrel to go into the Danes' camp to find out their plan of attack. The next day, he and his army ambushed and defeated them.

MAP STUDY Answers

the North Sea and the Irish Sea; London, Canterbury

Assign the Chapter 19 **Geography and Map Activity** in the TCR.

Anglo-Saxons. The next year, Alfred again gathered his army and met the Danes in battle. This time, the Danes were defeated.

Alfred continued to strengthen his army. He built the first English fighting ships and constructed fortresses throughout England. The entire country rallied behind him. He was no longer just King of Wessex but King of England.

Alfred never became strong enough to drive the Danes completely out of England. So, he signed a treaty with them. The treaty recognized the right of the Danes to rule the northeast part of England, an area that became known as the Danelaw (dān' lah). In return, the Danes promised to remain inside the Danelaw and not try to conquer more English land. In later years, the English took control of the Danelaw and made it part of their kingdom.

The Danes had destroyed part of the English city of London. Alfred had it rebuilt. Before long, it became the country's leading city. To gain the continued loyalty and obedience of the people, Alfred set forth new laws based on old Anglo-Saxon customs. These customs protected the weak against the strong and stressed honesty in making agreements.

England and the Danelaw

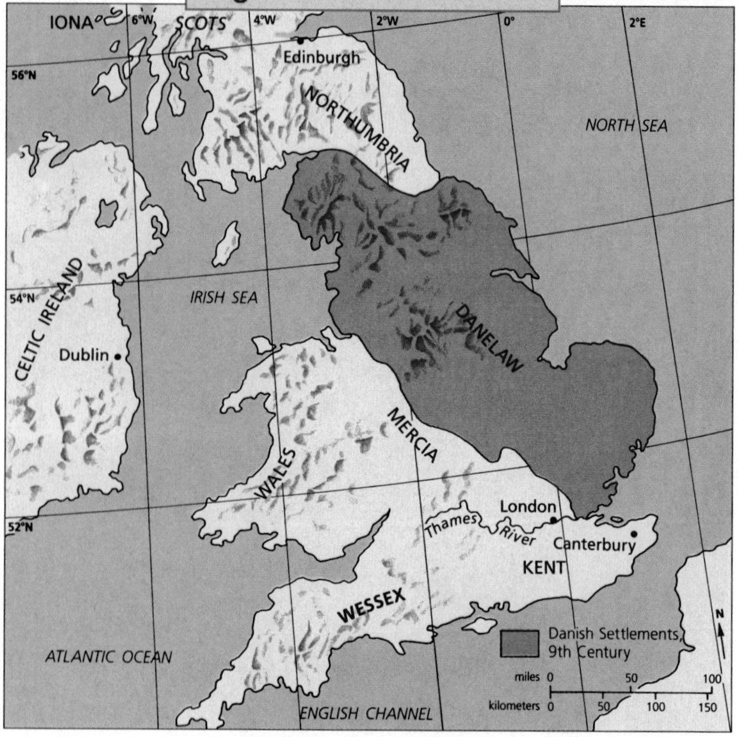

MAP STUDY

THE WORLD IN SPATIAL TERMS
The Danes had conquered an area north of the Thames River and established permanent settlements there. **What bodies of water bordered Danelaw? What two cities were located south of Danelaw?**

MEETING SPECIAL NEEDS

Have visual learners create murals or wall hangings to illustrate what life was like in Anglo-Saxon England. Organize the class into two groups. Have one group illustrate what life was like for nobles, and the other group illustrate what life was like for peasants. The murals should feature the dress, housing, and activities of the nobles or peasants.

Refer to ***Inclusion for the Middle School Social Studies Classroom: Strategies and Activities*** for additional resources.

Alfred was well-educated and interested in learning. He did much to educate the English. Like Charlemagne, Alfred started a palace school to train nobles' sons for government posts. At that time, books were generally written in Latin, a language most English church and government officials did not know. Alfred's scholars translated the books into English. So that the people would become familiar with their history, Alfred had monks begin a record of English history starting with Roman times.

The Government The government of Anglo-Saxon England centered on the king. A council of lords generally elected kings from among members of the royal family. After 700 A.D., the Church usually crowned the new rulers. The king directed the central government, which was made up of royal servants and advisers. They handled the king's needs and wishes.

The central government, however, was too weak to govern the whole country. So, the king set up local governments. England was divided into districts called **shires** (shīrz). Each was run by a **sheriff,** who was a local noble chosen by the king. The sheriff collected money, enforced the law, called out soldiers when needed, and told the king what was happening in the shire.

The king and his household moved around instead of remaining in a capital city. Whatever area the royal household was in was under the **king's peace,** or royal protection. Lawless acts were not allowed. Anyone who committed a crime was punished under the king's laws rather than local laws. In time, the king's peace spread to all areas of the kingdom, whether the king was there or not. This helped unite Anglo-Saxon England.

Nobles and church officials gave the king advice on how to run the country. They could not, however, order a king to act against his will. A group of nobles and church leaders, known as the **witenagemot** (wit uhn uh' guh mōt), met with the king to talk over problems. Each member of the group was known as a **witan** (wi' tuhn), or wiseman. The group approved laws drawn up by the king and his household. It also acted as a court.

The People The people in Anglo-Saxon England were generally divided into two classes. One was the nobles. An Anglo-Saxon became a noble by birth or as a reward for special service to the king. Nobles had to attend the witenagemot, keep peace in local areas, and serve the king in war. Noblemen wore pants and tunics covered by silk or fur cloaks. Noblewomen wore tunics and long cloaks held in place on each shoulder by a brooch.

The king rewarded many nobles with gifts of gold, silver, horses, and weapons. He also gave them estates throughout the kingdom. As a result, nobles spent a great deal of time moving from place to place with their families and servants. A noble's house had a large hall where meals were served and guests

Reading Check Why did early English kings divide the country into **shires?** What were some of the jobs of the **sheriff?**

Reading Check How did the **king's peace** help unite England?

Reading Check What was the purpose of the **witenagemot?** Who might become a **witan?**

L1 **Writing** Have students imagine that they are monks assigned the task of recording English history. Have them choose an event from early English history and write an account for the *Anglo-Saxon Chronicle.*

Reading Check Answer Early English kings divided the country into **shires** because the government was too weak to govern the entire country.
The **sheriff** collected money, enforced the law, called out soldiers when needed, and told the king what was happening in the shire.

Reading Check Answer The **king's peace** spread to all areas of the kingdom, and people followed it whether the king was there or not.

Reading Check Answer The **witenagemot** advised the king on how to handle problems.
A **witan** was one of the nobles or church leaders who served on the witenagemot.

ASSESS

Check for Understanding

Ask students to summarize orally or in writing the main points of the chapter. Discuss the answers to the Section and Chapter Assessment questions.

Evaluate

Assign Chapter 19 **Performance Assessment Activity** in the TCR.

Administer **Chapter 19 Test** in the TCR. Testmaker available.

COOPERATIVE LEARNING

Have students choose a historical event presented in this chapter and plan the presentation of a pictorial record. Organize the class into three groups. One group will determine the style and nature of the record and how it will be produced, choose particular scenes to present, and make recommendations during its execution. Another group will be responsible for the actual production. The third group will be responsible for creating a narrative to accompany the record. Groups should come together to present the finished record.

Assign Chapter 19 *Cooperative Learning Activity* in the TCR.

Reteach

Have students work in small groups to write a sentence that summarizes each section in the chapter.

Assign the Chapter 19 **Reteaching Activity** in the TCR.

Enrich

Have students role-play a scene from one of the many legends of King Arthur and the Knights of the Round Table.

Assign the Chapter 19 **Enrichment Activity** in the TCR.

CLOSE

Have students discuss how the settlements in the British Isles during the early Middle Ages might have been different if Christianity had not been an important part of everyday life.

Use **Interactive Tutor Self-Assessment CD-ROM** to review Section 2.

HISTORY Online

Self-Check Quiz gives students an interactive chapter tutorial. Have them access ***Chapter 19 Quiz*** at **humanheritage.glencoe.com**

entertained. Its walls were covered with *tapestries* (tap' uh strēz), or woven hangings with pictures on them. Tables and benches were the hall's only furniture. The bedrooms of nobles and their families were next to the hall or in a separate building.

The other class of people in Anglo-Saxon England was the peasants. They lived in small villages on or near a noble's estate and led a hard life. Most did not own their own land but worked fields belonging to the noble. Every year, the noble redivided the land, and each peasant received different strips. This was done to make sure that peasants would be treated equally. They helped each other farm the land by sharing tools and oxen. The peasants kept part of the crop for food and gave part to the noble. In return, the noble protected his peasants from enemy attacks.

Peasants lived in one-room wood and plaster huts. Both the family and the animals shared the same room. An open fireplace, which provided heat during winter, stood in the center. Smoke from the fire escaped through a hole in the straw roof.

Section 2 Assessment

1. **Define:** shires, sheriff, king's peace, witenagemot, witan.
2. How did Christianity come to the Anglo-Saxon kingdoms of England?
3. What did Alfred do to unite Anglo-Saxon England?

Critical Thinking

4. **Drawing Conclusions** Why do you think Alfred was given the title of "the Great"?

Graphic Organizer Activity

5. Draw this diagram, and use it to record the things that nobles and peasants gave to each other.

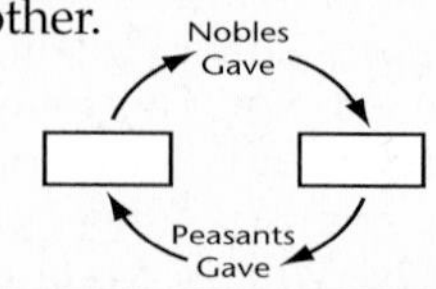

Chapter Summary & Study Guide

1. After Roman legions left Britain in 410 A.D., it was overrun by the Angles, Saxons, and Jutes, who united to become the Anglo-Saxons.
2. After the Anglo-Saxons drove most of the Celts from Britain, Ireland became a center of Celtic culture.
3. Monasteries became centers of Irish life.
4. In 597 A.D., Pope Gregory I sent monks to England, and by 700 A.D. England had become Christian.
5. When bands of Danes began raiding England in the 800s, the Anglo-Saxons united behind Alfred the Great.
6. English kings directed the central government, but they relied on help from local governments, nobles, and church leaders.

HISTORY Online

Self-Check Quiz

Visit the *Human Heritage* Web site at **humanheritage.glencoe.com** and click on ***Chapter 19—Self-Check Quiz*** to assess your understanding of this chapter.

Section 2 Assessment Answers

1. shires, districts (p. 295); sheriff, noble who ran a district (p. 295); king's peace, royal protection (p. 295); witenagemot, group of nobles and Church leaders (p. 295); witan, wise man (p. 295)
2. Pope Gregory I sent Augustine and other monks to England to convert the Anglo-Saxons. After King Ethelbert converted, other people quickly accepted the religion.
3. He defeated the Danes, built ships, constructed fortresses, and set forth new laws.
4. Answers will vary, but students will most likely point to his achievements.
5. Sample response: *nobles gave*—land and protection; *peasants gave*—their labor and part of their crops.

Assign the Chapter 19 **Section 2 Quiz** in the TCR. Testmaker available.

CHAPTER 19 Assessment

Using Key Terms

Write a paragraph to be used in a book on the Celts and Anglo-Saxons describing one part of their lives. Use the following words in your paragraph.

coracles	shires	sheriff
king's peace	witenagemot	witan

Understanding Main Ideas

1. Why did the Romans have trouble ruling Britain?
2. Why did Roman rule in Britain crumble during the 300s A.D.?
3. What happened to Britain when the Roman legions left?
4. What country became the major center of Celtic culture?
5. Why did the Irish church turn to its abbots for leadership?
6. Why did Alfred the Great pay the Danes to leave England alone?
7. Why did the king set up local governments in England?
8. What were the duties of nobles?

Critical Thinking

1. What effect did the Germanic invasions of the Roman Empire have on the history of England?
2. How did Ireland's location affect the development of Celtic culture? Explain your answer.
3. Would you agree or disagree that the king had too much power in Anglo-Saxon England? Explain.
4. What parts of an Anglo-Saxon noble's life would you have liked? What parts would you not have liked?

Graphic Organizer Activity

Culture Create a diagram like this one, and use it to compare the development of Christianity in Ireland and in the Frankish Empire.

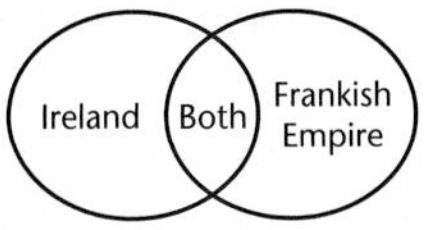

Geography in History

The World in Spatial Terms Refer to the map on page 294, and determine the most direct route from Edinburgh to London. How far would a person using this route have to travel? How much farther would that person have to travel to meet with priests of the church in Canterbury?

Using Your Journal

Review the role of a witan in the Anglo-Saxon government. Imagine you are a witan today working with the President of the United States. Write a letter to the President explaining the problems you think should be solved.

Bonus Test Question

For Chapter 19 Test

Two Anglo-Saxon people were arguing. One said, "My family has been here since the Romans left the British Isles so my family is older." The other said, "My family has been here since the Celts fled to Ireland." Whose family history is the oldest? *(neither—both began at about the same time)*

Using Your Journal

Letters will vary but should include specific problems. You might call on volunteers to read their letters to the class.

Geography in History

About 310 miles (or 500 km); about 55 miles (or 85 km)

CHAPTER 19 Assessment Answers

Using Key Terms

Paragraphs describing the lives of the Celts and Saxons will vary but should include all the vocabulary words.

Understanding Main Ideas

1. They could not win over the Celts.
2. because Roman soldiers were called home to defend the empire's borders against the Germanic invasions
3. It was gradually overrun by Angles, Saxons, and Jutes.
4. Ireland
5. because Ireland lost contact with Rome and the Pope during the Germanic invasions
6. to gain time to build a stronger army
7. because the central government was too weak to govern the whole country
8. They had to attend the witenagemot, keep peace, and serve the king in war.

Critical Thinking

1. They forced Roman soldiers to be called home, which allowed Angles, Saxons, and Jutes to overrun the island.
2. Its isolation allowed it to remain free of Germanic attacks. This allowed Celtic culture to develop.
3. Answers will vary, but students should support their conclusions with examples.
4. Answers will vary but should include specific examples.

Graphic Organizer Activity

Diagrams will vary, but should show that the Frankish Empire had close ties with Rome while Ireland did not. Similarities might include practices such as the use of monasteries, activities of monks, and so on.

Chapter 20 Planning Guide

Timesaving Tools

TeacherWorks™ All-In-One Planner and Resource Center

- **Interactive Teacher Edition** Access your Teacher Wraparound Edition and your classroom resources with a few easy clicks.
- **Interactive Lesson Planner** Planning has never been easier! Organize your week, month, semester, or year with all the lesson helps you need to make teaching creative, timely, and relevant.

Presentation Plus! Use Glencoe's **Presentation Plus!** multimedia teacher tool to easily present dynamic lessons that visually excite your students. Using Microsoft PowerPoint® you can customize the presentations to create your own personalized lessons.

Objectives	Reproducible Resources	Multimedia Resources
Section 1 **The Land** Describe the effects of climate and environment in the development of the Vikings as seafaring people.	Reproducible Lesson Plan Chapter 20 Vocabulary and Guided Reading Activity Reading Essentials and Study Guide 20-1 Chapter 20 Cooperative Learning Activity Section 1 Quiz	Interactive Student Edition CD-ROM Graphic Organizer Transparency 2 Teaching Transparencies and Activities 20A & 20B Vocabulary PuzzleMaker CD-ROM Interactive Tutor Self-Assessment CD-ROM ExamView® Pro Testmaker CD-ROM Glencoe Skillbuilder Interactive Workbook CD-ROM, Level 1 Presentation Plus! CD-ROM
Section 2 **Daily Life** Summarize the daily life and culture of the Vikings in their towns and villages.	Reproducible Lesson Plan Reading Essentials and Study Guide 20-2 Section 2 Quiz	Vocabulary PuzzleMaker CD-ROM Interactive Tutor Self-Assessment CD-ROM ExamView® Pro Testmaker CD-ROM Glencoe Skillbuilder Interactive Workbook CD-ROM, Level 1
Section 3 **Raiders and Adventurers** Explain the extent of Viking influence in shaping the cultures of England, France, Russia, and islands in the North Atlantic.	Reproducible Lesson Plan Reading Essentials and Study Guide 20-3 Chapter 20 Chart and Graph Skill Activity Chapter 20 Geography and Map Activity Chapter 20 Enrichment Activity Unit 6 Primary Source Readings Section 3 Quiz	Vocabulary PuzzleMaker CD-ROM Interactive Tutor Self-Assessment CD-ROM ExamView® Pro Testmaker CD-ROM Glencoe Skillbuilder Interactive Workbook CD-ROM, Level 1
Chapter 20 **Review and Evaluation**	Chapter 20 Reteaching Activity Chapter 20 Performance Assessment Activity Unit 6 Standardized Test Practice Spanish Chapter Summary and Glossary Chapter 20 Test	Vocabulary PuzzleMaker CD-ROM Interactive Tutor Self-Assessment CD-ROM Glencoe Skillbuilder Interactive Workbook CD-ROM, Level 1 Audiocassettes* ExamView® Pro Testmaker CD-ROM

*Also available in Spanish.

Chapter 20 Planning Guide

Performance Assessment Activities

Re-creations Have students research and draw illustrations of Viking ships or make models of them. These creations should be accompanied by explanations of ship construction and parts.

Chapter Resources

Literature About the Period

Treece, Henry. *The Invaders*. Crowell, 1972. Three stories about the Vikings.

Readings for the Student

Wernick, Robert. *The Vikings: The Seafarers*. Time-Life Books, 1979. An in-depth look at the Viking traders, raiders, and conquerors.

Readings for the Teacher

Jones, Gwyn. *A History of the Vikings*. Oxford University Press, 1984. Surveys the Viking world, including archaeological findings.

Key to Ability Levels

Teaching strategies have been coded for varying learning styles and abilities.

L1 Level 1 activities are **basic** activities and should be within the ability range of all students.

L2 Level 2 activities are **average** activities and should be within the ability range of the average to above-average student.

L3 Level 3 activities are **challenging** designed for the ability range of above-average students.

ELL ELL activities should be within the ability range of English Language Learning students.

National Geographic Teacher's Corner

Index to National Geographic Magazine

The following articles relate to this chapter:

- "In Search of Vikings," by Priit Vesilind, May 2000.

National Geographic Society Products Available from Glencoe

To order the following, call Glencoe at 1-800-334-7344:

- Europe (Laminated Desk Maps)
- *PicturePack: Physical Geography of the World (Transparencies)*

Additional National Geographic Society Products

To order the following, call National Geographic at 1-800-368-2728:

- *Physical Geography of the Continents Series: Europe (Video)*
- *National Geographic Atlas of World History (Book)*

Access *National Geographic's* new dynamic MapMachine Web site and other geography resources at:
www.nationalgeographic.com
www.nationalgeographic.com/maps

The History Channel / A&E Home Video / Biography

The following videotape programs are available from Glencoe:

- **The Vikings in North America**
  1-56501-663-7
- **Leif Ericson: Voyages of a Viking**
  1-56501-673-4

To order, call Glencoe at 1-800-334-7344. To find classroom resources to accompany many of these videos, check:

A&E Television: www.aande.com
The History Channel: www.historychannel.com

Introduce **CHAPTER 20**

OVERVIEW

Chapter 20 discusses the development of Scandinavia and the Vikings' impact upon world civilization.

- ➤ **Section 1** describes the effects of geography on the development of the Vikings as seafaring people.
- ➤ **Section 2** describes the culture of the Viking people.
- ➤ **Section 3** discusses Viking influence in England, France, Russia, and the North Atlantic.

CHAPTER OBJECTIVES

After reading Chapter 20, students will be able to:

1. explain how the Vikings earned their living.

2. summarize what daily life was like for the Vikings.

3. describe how Viking warriors traded and raided.

4. explain what role the Danish Vikings played in the histories of England and France.

EXAMINING ARTIFACTS

Refer students to the artifacts. Ask: What does the ice skate tell you about the Viking homeland? *(that it was cold enough for ice at least part of the year)* What does the picture of the dragon slayer reveal? *(that the Vikings were warriors and/or valued stories about warriors)* Direct students to find events in the time line that confirm their answers.

PERFORMANCE ASSESSMENT ✓

Use the Performance Assessment activities on page 298B to help you evaluate students as they complete the chapter.

CHAPTER 20

The Vikings

900 A.D.–1035 A.D.

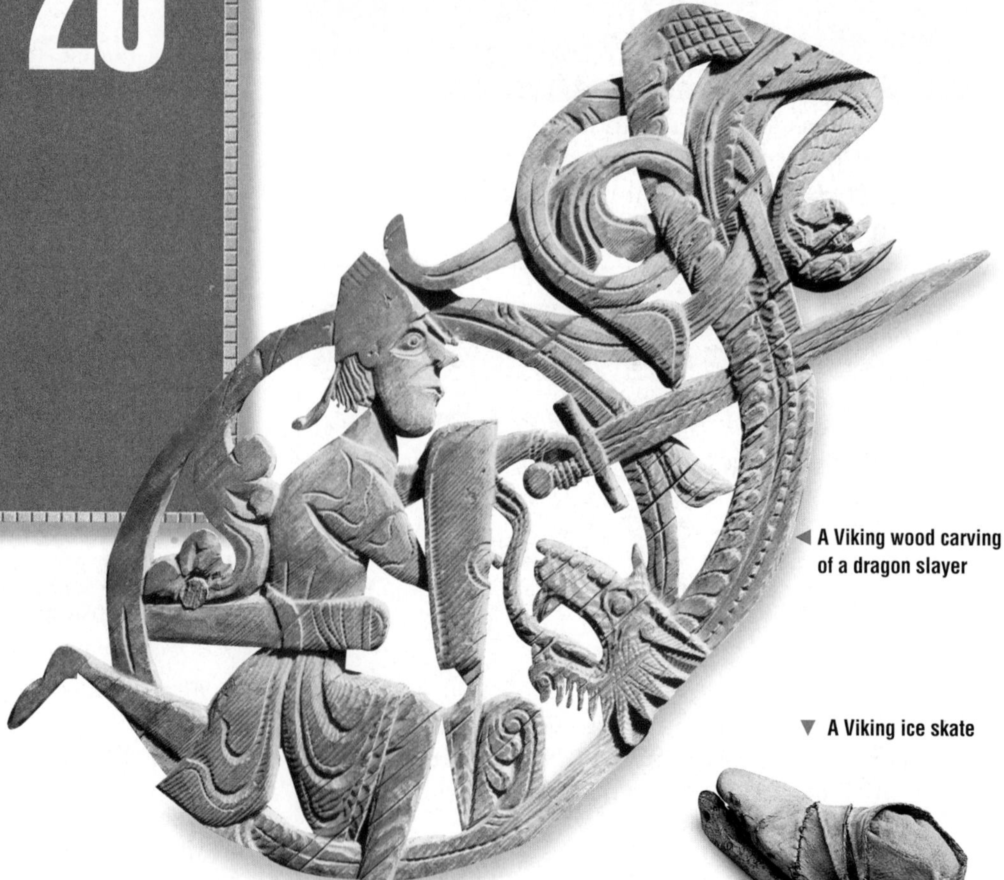

◄ A Viking wood carving of a dragon slayer

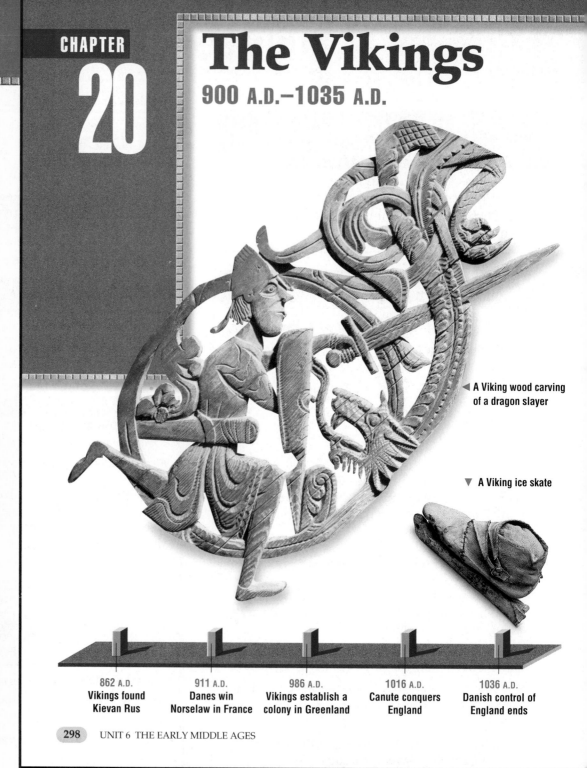

▼ A Viking ice skate

862 A.D.	911 A.D.	986 A.D.	1016 A.D.	1036 A.D.
Vikings found Kievan Rus	Danes win Norselaw in France	Vikings establish a colony in Greenland	Canute conquers England	Danish control of England ends

TEACHING RESOURCES

TEACHER PLANNING AND SUPPORT

- Reproducible Lesson Plan 20-1, 20-2, 20-3
- Teaching Strategies for the World History Classroom (Including Block Scheduling Pacing Guides)
- Presentation Plus! CD-ROM

REVIEW AND REINFORCEMENT

- Reading Essentials and Study Guide 20–1, 20–2, 20–3
- Chapter 20 Vocabulary and Guided Reading Activity
- Vocabulary PuzzleMaker CD-ROM
- Teaching Transparencies 20A & 20B
- Chapter 20 Reteaching Activity
- Chapter 20 Cooperative Learning Activity
- Chapter 20 Activity Book Activity
- Chapter 20 Chart and Graph Skill Activity
- Reading and Study Skills Foldables
- Interactive Tutor Self-Assessment CD-ROM
- Unit 6 MindJogger VideoQuiz

APPLICATION AND HANDS-ON ACTIVITIES

- Daily Questions in Social Studies
- World Games Card 5
- Student Presentation Builder CD-ROM

Chapter Focus

Read to Discover

- How the Vikings earned a living.
- What daily life was like for the Vikings.
- How Viking warriors and adventurers traded and raided.
- What role the Danish Vikings played in the histories of England and France.

HISTORY Online

Chapter Overview

Visit the *Human Heritage* Web site at **humanheritage.glencoe.com** and click on ***Chapter 20—Chapter Overviews*** to preview this chapter.

Terms to Learn	People to Know	Places to Locate
jarls	Rurik	Scandinavia
berserkers	Erik the Red	Jutland
Eddas	Leif Eriksson	Vinland
runes	Canute	Norselaw
	Rollo	

Why It's Important During the 900s, Charlemagne's empire and Anglo-Saxon England were attacked by new invaders known as Norseman, or Vikings (vī' kēngs). They came from the far northern part of Europe now called Scandinavia (skan duh nā'vē uh). They spread fear and destruction throughout western Europe. However, they opened up new trade routes and taught seafaring skills to other Europeans.

The Vikings captured parts of Britain and France. They ruled cities in Russia and set up colonies on islands in the North Atlantic. They even traveled to North America. Those who went abroad married the people they conquered and accepted a new religion and new customs. Others stayed in Scandinavia and set up the kingdoms of Norway, Sweden, and Denmark.

SECTION 1 The Land

The Viking homeland of Scandinavia was an area made up mostly of forests and long, rugged coastlines. The southern part, known as Jutland (juht' luhnd), or Denmark, had many natural harbors and was well suited for farming. It had large plains where the Vikings grew grains and pastured their cattle, sheep, and pigs.

The rest of Scandinavia was not as well suited to farming. The soil was rocky, and the growing season was short. The coastline, however, had many *fjords* (fē yōrdz'), or narrow bays. Because of this, the people turned to the sea to make a living.

GEOGRAPHY ACTIVITIES

- Chapter 20 Geography and Map Activity
- Outline Map Resource Book

INTERDISCIPLINARY CONNECTIONS

- World Music: A Cultural Legacy

EXTENSION AND ENRICHMENT

- Unit 6 Primary Source Readings
- World History Primary Source Document Library CD-ROM
- Chapter 20 Enrichment Activity
- Foods Around the World

ASSESSMENT AND EVALUATION

- Chapter 20 Performance Assessment Activity
- Chapter 20 Section Quizzes 20–1, 20–2, 20–3
- Chapter 20 Test
- Unit 6 Standardized Test Practice
- Chapter 20 ExamView® Pro Testmaker CD-ROM
- Chapter 20 Digests Audiocassettes Activities and Tests

SPANISH RESOURCES

- Chapter 20 Spanish Chapter Summary and Glossary
- Chapter 20 Spanish Digests Audiocassettes Activities and Tests

HISTORY Online

Chapter Overview introduces students to chapter content and key terms. Have them access ***Chapter 20 Overview*** at **humanheritage.glencoe.com**

FOCUS

Bellringer

Ask students to write down three ideas that occur to them when they think of the word *Viking*.

Motivational Activity

Have students read their responses to the word *Viking*. Explain that much of what we know about the Vikings comes from church records. Clerics and monks, who were often victims of Viking raids, portray a predominantly negative picture of the Vikings. Tell students that they will read more about the Vikings in this chapter.

GUIDE TO READING

Reading Strategy

Ask students to read "Why It's Important" and summarize the chapter's main theme. *(The Vikings were fearless conquerors and explorers who influenced European cultures and were in turn influenced by those they conquered.)*

Vocabulary Precheck

Ask students to define each of the "Terms to Learn." Have a volunteer consult the dictionary for any unfamiliar words. L1 ELL

Use the Vocabulary PuzzleMaker CD-ROM for Chapter 20 to create a crossword puzzle. L1

Assign Chapter 20 Vocabulary and Guided Reading Activity.

Assign Reading Essentials and Study Guide 20-1.

HISTORY Online

Student Web Activity objectives and answers can be found at the ***Chapter 20 Web Activity Lesson Plan*** at humanheritage.glencoe.com

TEACH

Guided Practice

L1 **Daily Life** Have students help complete an informational bulletin board about the daily life of the Vikings. Ask them to make illustrations about one of the following areas of Viking life: family life, occupations, or religion. Have them write captions to explain their illustrations. Display the illustrations and captions on the bulletin board. ELL

MAKING CONNECTIONS

➤➤ **Language** The word *Viking* comes from the word *vik* which means "creek" in all the Scandinavian languages. *Vik* was also the name of a pirate lair in southern Norway. The phrase *to go a Viking* meant "to fight as a pirate."

CAPTION ANSWER

silk, wine, and wheat

HISTORY Online

Student Web Activity

Visit the *Human Heritage* Web site at humanheritage.glencoe.com and click on ***Chapter 20—Student Web Activities*** to find out more about the Vikings.

Ships and Trade The Vikings built ships with timber from the dense forests. These ships were large and well suited for long voyages. The bodies were long and narrow. The sides, where a single row of 16 oars was placed, were usually decorated with black or yellow shields. The tall bows were carved in the shape of a dragon's head. This was supposed to frighten both enemies and the evil spirits of the ocean. The strongly sewn sails were square and often striped red and yellow. The ships bore names like "Snake of the Sea," "Raven of the Wind," and "Lion of the Waves."

An awning in the forepart of the ship protected sailors from bad weather. They slept in leather sleeping bags and carried bronze pots in which to cook meals. Whenever possible, they cooked meals ashore to avoid the danger of a fire onboard ship.

The Vikings plotted their courses by the positions of the sun and the stars. They sailed far out into the North Sea and the Atlantic Ocean in search of good fishing areas and trade. They did most of their traveling and trading in spring after their fields were sown or in fall after their crops were harvested. They spent the long winters repairing their boats and weapons.

The Vikings were as successful in trade as the Phoenicians. Viking traders carried furs, hides, fish, and enslaved people to western Europe and the Mediterranean. They returned from these areas with silk, wine, wheat, and silver.

VIKING TRADE The Vikings traveled very far in order to trade. They sailed to the Mediterranean and traded for Arabic silver coins. The Vikings then melted down the coins and used the silver to make jewelry. **What other items did the Vikings trade for?**

Then & Now

Berserk Of the many words that entered English from Old Norse, one of the most threatening is *berserk.* It comes from the Viking warriors known as *berserkers,* who rushed headlong into battle shrieking, leaping, and seemingly unaware of pain.

MULTICULTURAL PERSPECTIVES

Perhaps one of the best indications of how important the ship was in Viking life is the custom of ship burials. Sometimes the body of a dead chief or hero was set adrift on his boat. Sometimes the entire ship was buried on land, richly equipped for the afterlife much as an Egyptian pyramid was. Archaeologists have discovered many interesting and beautiful Viking artifacts in ship burials, including solid gold jewelry and ornaments. Two of the most famous ship burials are at Sutton Hoo in England and Gokstad in Norway.

Towns, Villages, and Jarls Trade led to the growth of market towns in Scandinavia. These towns generally had two main streets that ran along the water's edge. Buyers and sellers set up booths along these streets where they showed their wares. The towns were protected on their land side by mounds of earth surrounded by wooden walls with towers.

Most Vikings lived in villages scattered all through the country. Their houses were made of logs or boards. The roofs, which were made of sod-covered wood, slanted deeply to shed the heavy winter snows. Carved dragons decorated the roofs at either end. Each house had a small porch at its front that was held up by carved pillars.

Distance and the cold winters isolated the people of one village from those of another. Because of this, there was no central government. The people were divided into groups ruled by military chiefs called ***jarls*** (yahrlz). Some jarls were elected, while others inherited their position. Sometimes, a jarl became strong enough to take over neighboring lands. When a jarl had enough land under his rule, he was looked upon as a king.

Reading Check Who were the *jarls,* and how were they selected?

Section 1 Assessment

1. **Define:** *jarls.*
2. How did people in Scandinavia make a living?
3. What were some of the features of Viking towns?

Critical Thinking

4. **Making Generalizations** How did the Vikings use their natural resources?

Graphic Organizer Activity

5. Draw this diagram, and use it to describe geographic features of the Viking homeland.

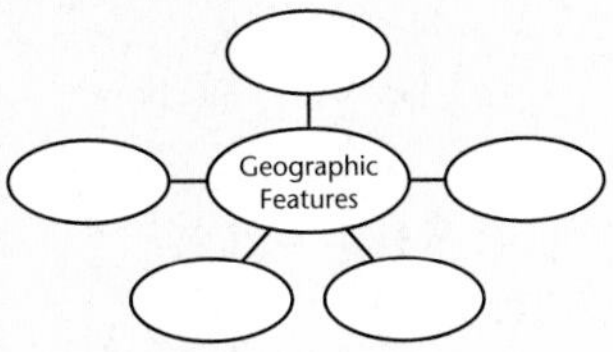

SECTION 2 Daily Life

Family life was important to the Vikings. Most households had 20 to 30 members, including parents, grandparents, married children, and grandchildren. Families often fought bloody feuds to defend their honor. The payment of fines later ended such feuds.

The People Viking warriors were called ***berserkers*** (ber zerk' erz). They believed in a life of action and valued deeds that called for strength and courage. They fought to gain wealth, honor, and fame. They believed that a liking for war brought special honors from the gods.

To call their warriors to battle, the Vikings lit bonfires on the tops of mountains. Those who saw a fire would light a new one to

Reading Check Who were the Viking *berserkers,* and why did they fight?

GEOGRAPHY AND HISTORY

Viking boats were sturdy enough to cross the Atlantic Ocean, shallow enough to navigate Europe's rivers, and light enough to be carried past fortified bridges. The Vikings became known for surprise attacks and speedy retreats. What they could not steal, they burned.

Reading Check Answer Viking *jarls* were military chiefs. Some were elected; others inherited their position.

Use **Interactive Tutor Self-Assessment CD-ROM** to review Section 1.

Reading Check Answer Viking *berserkers* were warriors who fought to gain wealth, honor, and fame.

Use the **Vocabulary PuzzleMaker CD-ROM** to create crossword and word search puzzles.

Section 1 Assessment Answers

1. *jarls,* Viking military chiefs (p. 301)
2. by farming, fishing, and trading
3. They generally had two main streets that ran along the water's edge and were lined with booths. They were protected on their land side by mounds of earth surrounded by wooden walls with towers.
4. The Vikings built ships and houses with timber from the dense forests, turned to the sea to make a living, and grew herbs that were used as medicines.
5. sample responses: mostly forests; long, rugged coastlines; many natural harbors in southern part (Jutland); large plains suitable for farming in south; region north of harbor area not well suited to farming; rocky soil and short growing season

Assign the Chapter 20 **Section 1 Quiz** in the TCR. Testmaker available.

L3 **Critical Thinking** Ask students to examine the role women played in Viking society. Ask why they think the position of Viking women was quite high.

DID YOU KNOW ??

Some Viking swords were handed down from father to son. The weapons bore fanciful names, such as Thorn of the Shields, Fire of the Sea Kings, and Serpent of the Wound.

CAPTION ANSWER

so the evil spirits would be scared away and the Vikings would appear fierce

Viking Sword Hilt

spread the message. Warriors fought with battle axes, swords, and spears. Metal helmets decorated with animal figures protected their heads. Shirts made of iron rings and covered by a large cloth protected their bodies. Warriors preferred to die by their own hand rather than give their enemies the satisfaction of capturing or killing them.

The women encouraged their men to fight. A Viking groom bought his wife from her family on their wedding day. If he was not pleased with her, he could sell her. Yet, the position of Viking women was quite high. They took complete charge of the home. They could attend public meetings and talk with men other than their husbands. They could own property and get a divorce. Many Viking women grew herbs that were used as medicine.

Both men and women liked fine clothes. Men usually dressed in trousers and woolen shirts covered by knee-length tunics. Broad leather belts held the clothing in place. Sheepskin hoods and caps kept their heads warm. For special events, men wore red cloaks with brooches and carried decorated swords and daggers. Women also wore tunics held in place by a belt. They covered their heads with woolen or linen caps and wore large brooches, pins, and bracelets. Both men and women wore their hair long. The men took great pride in their mustaches and beards. Calling a

VIKING ADVENTURES This painting of Vikings at sea shows the detail and decoration these north people put into their ships. The bows of their ships were usually elaborately carved. **Why did many Viking ships display the head of a dragon on the bow?**

COOPERATIVE LEARNING

Have students create a historical account of a medieval village under Viking attack. Some students will take on the roles of Vikings, who keep a record of their voyage, their intentions, and their strategies for attack. Other students can assume the roles of clergy members, who keep the official records of the village. Still others can represent the villagers who record the raid with drawings of the long ships as they approach. Some of the few villagers who could read and write might keep journal accounts of their fate. Encourage students to do outside research and to include vivid details in their drawings and writing projects.

Assign the Chapter 20 ***Cooperative Learning Activity*** in the TCR.

Viking man "beardless" was an insult that could be wiped out only by death.

The Vikings had no schools. Girls were taught household skills, such as spinning, weaving, and sewing, by their mothers. Boys were taught to use the bow and arrow and to be good fighters by their fathers. Boys also memorized tales of heroes and gods and competed in games that tested their strength and endurance.

Viking Rune Stone

Religion The Vikings worshiped many gods that at first were similar to the Germanic gods. Over time, they changed their gods to suit the hard life of Scandinavia. The Vikings believed that the gods were responsible for the weather and for the growth of crops. Since the gods liked to hunt, fish, and play tricks on one another, the Vikings viewed them as extra-powerful humans.

The Vikings bargained with their gods to get what they wanted. Priests offered sacrifices of crops and animals for the whole village. Most Vikings also had small shrines in their homes where they could pray or offer sacrifices.

The Vikings were proud of their gods and told stories of the gods' great deeds. These stories later became written poems called ***Eddas*** (ed' uhz). The Vikings also made up *sagas* (sah' guhz), or long tales. At first, storytellers used to recite them at special feasts. One such tale took 12 days to recite. After 1100, the Vikings wrote down their sagas. With the coming of Christianity, however, the people lost interest in them. Many were forgotten or were forbidden by the Church. Only the people on the isolated island of Iceland passed on the old tales.

Reading Check What were the *Eddas?*

Early on, the Vikings spoke a language similar to that of the Germans. In time, the one language developed into four—Danish, Norwegian (nor wē' juhn), Swedish, and Icelandic. These languages were written with letters called ***runes*** (rūnz), which few people except priests could understand or use. The Vikings used the runes as magic charms. They wrote the runes in metal and carved them in bone in the hope that they would bring good luck. When the Vikings accepted Christianity, they began to write their languages with Roman letters.

Reading Check What were some of the ways that the Vikings used *runes?*

Section 2 Assessment

1. **Define:** *berserkers, Eddas, runes.*
2. What kind of education did Viking children receive?
3. How did the Vikings view their gods?

Critical Thinking

4. **Demonstrating Reasoned Judgment** What might have been some of the advantages and disadvantages of living in the large Viking households?

Graphic Organizer Activity

5. Draw this diagram, and use it to compare the role of Viking women with the role of women in the United States today.

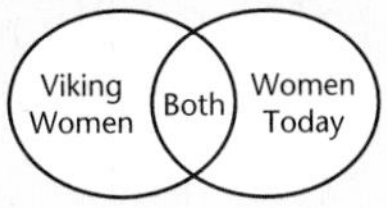

MAKING CONNECTIONS

>> **History** The Vikings believed in a heaven called Asgard, which contained 12 great halls. Warriors wanted to go to the Hall of the slain, called Valhalla. There, the chief Viking god, Odin, held court.

Reading Check Answer The *Eddas* were written poems about the deeds of Viking gods.

Reading Check Answer The Vikings used ***runes*** as letters to write their language and as magic charms.

Use **Interactive Tutor Self Assessment CD-ROM** to review Section 2.

Section 2 Assessment Answers

1. berserkers, Viking warriors (p. 301); *Eddas*, Viking poems (p. 303); *runes*, Viking letters and magic charms (p. 303)
2. Girls were taught household skills. Boys were taught to use the bow and arrow and to be good fighters, and they memorized tales of heroes and gods and competed in games.
3. as extra-powerful humans
4. sample responses: *advantages*—a lot of people to help with the work, protection and care for the sick; *disadvantages*—blood feuds between large families, lack of privacy, payment of the fines charged to the family
5. Answers will vary, but might point out that women today have equal rights and cannot be sold by their husbands. Both Viking and modern women can take charge of the home, attend public meetings, talk to men, own property, and get a divorce.

Assign the Chapter 20 **Section 2 Quiz** in the TCR. Testmaker available.

L2 **Myths and Legends** Have students write a list of the Norse gods and goddesses and their realms. Then have them brainstorm a list of where these names are used in modern times. For example, names are used as calendar items, in advertising, in city names, and so on. ELL

LINKING PAST TO PRESENT

In 1991, 3 authentically built Viking ships retraced early Norse exploration routes, sailing from Norway to L'Anse aux Meadows, Newfoundland, Canada. The trip, lasting 3 months, was made to honor the Vikings who sailed to America 1,000 years before.

Economics at a Glance

Scarcity
One of the basic economic problems facing all societies is *scarcity*. Scarcity occurs because society does not have enough resources to produce all the things people need or would like to have. Scarcity is always present because there is no limit to what people want. The ability to produce all the goods and services that people want and need, however, is limited. Lead the class in a discussion of what life would be like if no economic scarcity existed. Note ideas on the board as students offer them. Then ask students to use the information on the board to write a paragraph that begins: "If there were no economic scarcity then . . ."

Use the **Vocabulary PuzzleMaker CD-ROM** to create crossword and word search puzzles.

NORSE GODS

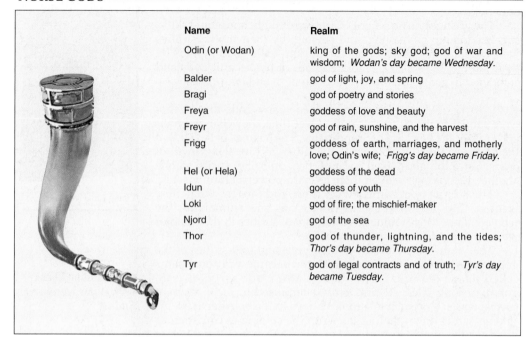

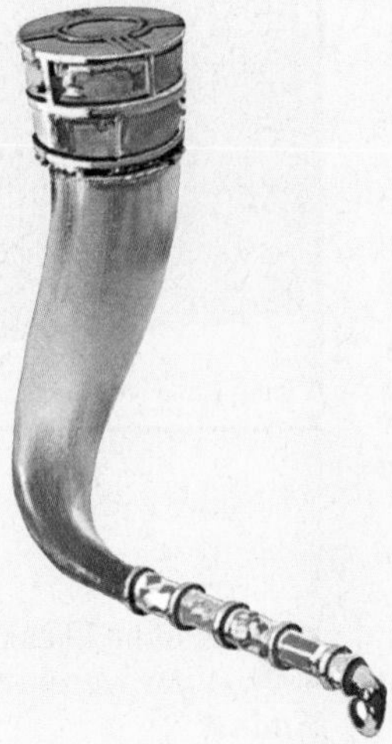

Name	Realm
Odin (or Wodan)	king of the gods; sky god; god of war and wisdom; *Wodan's day became Wednesday.*
Balder	god of light, joy, and spring
Bragi	god of poetry and stories
Freya	goddess of love and beauty
Freyr	god of rain, sunshine, and the harvest
Frigg	goddess of earth, marriages, and motherly love; Odin's wife; *Frigg's day became Friday.*
Hel (or Hela)	goddess of the dead
Idun	goddess of youth
Loki	god of fire; the mischief-maker
Njord	god of the sea
Thor	god of thunder, lightning, and the tides; *Thor's day became Thursday.*
Tyr	god of legal contracts and of truth; *Tyr's day became Tuesday.*

SECTION 3 Raiders and Adventurers

Scandinavia's population kept increasing. By the end of the 800s, many Viking villages were overcrowded, and there was not enough food for everyone. Since there was no central government, the kings constantly fought one another and made life difficult for their enemies. Before long, many Viking warriors began to seek their fortunes in other lands. They set sail on their long, deckless ships that were propelled through the water with oars. On them, the Vikings could safely sail the deep water of the Atlantic Ocean or the shallow rivers of Europe.

From East Europe to North America Viking adventurers traveled to and raided areas from east Europe to North America. Swedish Vikings crossed the Baltic Sea and traveled down the rivers toward what is now Belarus, Ukraine, and Russia. They established a trade water route from the Baltic to the

MEETING SPECIAL NEEDS

Help students who are having difficulty accessing the information in the chapter by creating cause-and-effect graphic organizers of the major events in the chapter on the chalkboard.

Refer to ***Inclusion for the Middle School Social Studies Classroom: Strategies and Activities*** for additional resources.

Black Sea and on to the wealthy city of Byzantium (bi zan' tē uhm). This water route became known as the Varangian (vah rahng ē'uhn) Route. In 862, a Swedish chief named Rurik (rū' rik) founded a Viking settlement that became the Kievan Rus state.

Norwegian Vikings set up trading towns in Ireland, explored the North Atlantic, and founded a colony on Iceland. Led by an adventurer named Erik the Red, they founded a colony on the island of Greenland in 986. Then, Erik's son, Leif Eriksson (lēf er' ik suhn), landed on the northeast coast of North America. He and his followers named the spot where they landed Vinland because of the wild grapes they found growing there. Today, the area is called Newfoundland (nū' fuhn luhnd). The Vikings did not set up a colony in Vinland because it was so far away from home and because they were repeatedly attacked by Native Americans.

Most Viking adventurers, however, went to western and southern Europe in search of food and valuables. They disguised their ships to look like wooded islands by covering them with tree branches. Then they traveled far up the rivers to make surprise

Linking Across Time

Iceland Around 930, the Vikings drew up a constitution that provided for a legislative assembly called the Althing (left). The Althing still meets today (right), making it the oldest practicing legislative assembly in the world. **What conditions in Scandinavia led the Vikings to settle in Iceland?**

GEOGRAPHY AND HISTORY

Some historians believe that Viking sailors first spotted the North American continent in 986 when Bjarni Herjulfsson was blown off course on a trip to the Greenland settlement. Leif Eriksson's voyage included stops at what he called "Helluland" (perhaps Baffin Island), "Markland" (Labrador), and "Vinland" (Newfoundland), so called because of the grapes that grew there.

Linking Across Time

Overcrowding in Scandinavia and a lack of food led the Vikings to settle in Iceland.

PRIMARY SOURCES Library

You might assign "The Age of Viking Conquest" on pages 684–685 of the Primary Sources Library.

THE HISTORY CHANNEL.

The following videotape program is available from Glencoe to enrich Chapter 20:

- **The Vikings in North America**

To find classroom resources to accompany this video, check the following home page:

A&E Television:
www.aande.com

SPOTLIGHT ON: VIKINGS

Viking adventurers made many voyages across the Northern Atlantic. One such Viking believed the first to set eyes on North America was Bjarni Herjulfsson. Bjarni, living in Iceland, set sail for Greenland in search of his father. Following the North Star, he reached the coast of Labrador, Canada, instead. According to Norse sagas, it was his course that Leif Eriksson and his men followed years later to reach Vinland.

MAP SKILLS

TEACH

Tracing Historical Routes

Have students read the introductory section of the skill on page 306. Ask: Why are historical routes often colored? *(to show information more clearly and to make the map easier to read)* Why do historical routes on maps often have arrows at their beginning or several arrows along its length? *(to point out the directions taken by people or goods)* Where should you look to find out the meaning of the different lines and colors on a map? *(in the legend or key)* Direct students' attention to the map on the skills page. Ask: What rivers did the Viking invasion routes follow? *(Volga River, Dnieper River)* What bodies of water did the Vikings cross on their trade routes? *(North Sea, Baltic Sea, Atlantic Ocean)*

Assign the Chapter 20 **Geography and Map Activity** in the TCR.

Answers to Map Practice

1. England, Ireland, Iceland, Greenland, Vinland, France, Spain, Italy, Norway, Sweden, and Denmark

2. invasion routes and the Varangian Route

3. Kiev and Baghdad

Use the **Glencoe Skillbuilder Interactive Workbook CD-ROM, Level 1,** to provide instruction and practice in key social studies skills.

MAP SKILLS

Tracing Historical Routes

Lines on maps generally show boundaries or rivers. On some maps, however, lines may show other things, such as **historical routes.** These are roads or courses over which people or goods have traveled all through history.

Such routes are often colored to make the map easier to read. A colored line may have arrows to point out the direction taken by people or goods. If there is a legend on the map, it may provide clues to the meaning of the different lines and colors.

For example, on the map of "Viking Trade and Expansion" below, the legend shows that the brown line is the Varangian Route. The two arrows along the line point out that the route began in Sweden and ended in Byzantium.

Map Practice

1. **What were some places visited by Vikings along their trade routes?**
2. **Which routes ran through the largest area of Viking settlement?**
3. **What two cities lay along Viking invasion routes?**

Viking Trade and Expansion

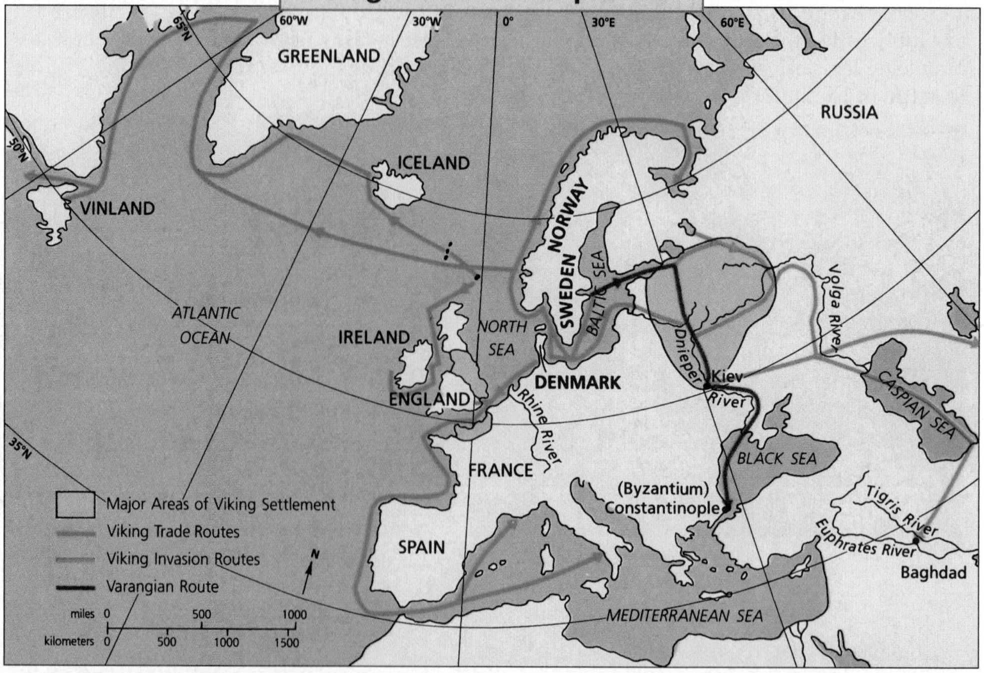

306

COOPERATIVE LEARNING

Organize the class into five groups. Have each group do research and prepare a report on one of the following Viking leaders: Eric the Red, Leif Eriksson, Rurik, Canute, or Rollo. Each report should describe the Viking leader's life and achievements. Have students illustrate their reports. Each member of the group should be assigned a specific task in preparing the report. Have a spokesperson from each group read its report to the class.

VIKING SHIPS The Vikings were among the best shipbuilders of their time. At sea, the Vikings depended on the wind and sails for power. On a river, rowers powered the ship. The Viking ships in this painting pursue enemy trading ships. **How did Vikings disguise their ships on rivers?**

attacks. They stole goods, destroyed homes, burned churches, and killed or enslaved people they captured. All Europe feared the Vikings. In their churches, the people prayed, "From the fury of the Norsemen, Good Lord, deliver us!"

The Danes The Danes were among those Vikings who raided western and southern Europe. One group invaded England and set up settlements there in the Danelaw. Their right to rule this area had been recognized by Alfred the Great. In 954, an heir of Alfred the Great forced the Danes to leave. In 978, Ethelred (eth' uhl red), nicknamed the Unready, became king of England. The Danes saw their chance and began raiding England again. At first, Ethelred was able to buy them off with silver. In 1016, however, a Danish king called Knut, or Canute (kuh nūt'), conquered England and made it part of his North Sea Empire. Canute was a powerful and just ruler. He converted to Christianity and brought peace and prosperity to England. Soon after his death in 1035, however, Danish control of the country came to an end. Some Danes left England. Those who remained became a part of the English people and culture.

Another group of Danes tried to take the city of Paris in France, but the French managed to fight them off. In 885, the

People in History

Canute
c. 995–1035

Danish King

Canute followed in the footsteps of his father, who conquered England in 1013. When his father died, the Anglo-Saxons refused to make Canute king, so he led the Danes in a second war of conquest. In 1016, he became the sole king of England. In 1018 he inherited the Danish throne, and in 1028 he seized the throne of Norway. Although Canute's sons lost England, a distant kinsman from Normandy—William the Conqueror—would reclaim it in 1066.

Independent Practice

L2 **Time Line** Have students make a time line of events in the chapter. Have students draw conclusions about the possible similarities among events on their time lines; explain the causes and effects of the events; and describe the Vikings with two adjectives. ELL

L3 **Critical Thinking** Ask students to write a paragraph comparing the importance of Christianity in the everyday lives of the Celts and the Anglo-Saxons during the Middle Ages with the importance of Christianity in the everyday life of the Vikings.

CAPTION ANSWER

covered the ships with tree branches to look like wooded islands

LINKING PAST TO PRESENT

A Viking settlement called *L'Anse aux Meadows* on the northern tip of Newfoundland has been carefully studied and is believed to be the site of Vinland. Archaeologists have excavated the remains of several houses with turf walls. One was a Norse "longhouse" with a great hall and other rooms. This and other houses resembled those in Greenland.

SPOTLIGHT ON: CANUTE

To extend People in History, *provide these additional details on Canute.*

Canute was the first Danish king of England. Legend states that he wanted to end the flattery of his nobles, who declared that he was all-powerful. To teach the nobles a lesson, he took them to the edge of the sea, where he commanded the incoming tide to come no further. His failure to stop the water proved to his nobles that a king's power was limited.

ASSESS

Check for Understanding

Ask students to summarize the main points of the chapter. Discuss answers to the Section and Chapter Assessment questions.

GLENCOE TECHNOLOGY

MindJogger Videoquiz

Use **MindJogger Videoquiz** to review students' knowledge of the unit.

Available in DVD and VHS

Evaluate

Assign the Chapter 20 **Performance Assessment Activity** in the TCR.

Administer the **Chapter 20 Test** in the TCR. Testmaker available.

Reteach

Assign Chapter 20 **Reteaching Activity** in the TCR.

Enrich

Assign the Chapter 20 **Enrichment Activity** in the TCR.

CLOSE

Have students discuss the importance of poems, myths, legends, and sagas in the everyday life of the Vikings.

Use **Interactive Tutor Self Assessment CD-ROM** to review Section 3.

HISTORY Online

Self-Check Quiz gives students an interactive chapter tutorial. Have them access ***Chapter 20 Quiz*** at humanheritage.glencoe.com

---

Danes tried again. The people of Paris held them off for ten months. Finally, the French king paid the Danes gold to abandon their attack.

Led by a warrior named Rollo (rahl' ō), the Danes began settling along the French coast opposite England. In 911, the French king signed a treaty with Rollo. He gave the Danes this land. In return, the Danes became Christians and promised to be loyal to the French king. The region in which the Danes settled became known first as the Norselaw and then as Normandy (nōr' muhn dē). The people became known as Normans.

Section 3 Assessment

1. Why did many Vikings leave Scandinavia?
2. Why did Europeans fear the Vikings?
3. What happened to the Danes who settled in England?

Critical Thinking

4. **Predicting Consequences** How might life have been different for the Vikings if there had been a central government in Scandinavia?

Graphic Organizer Activity

5. Draw the following diagram, and use it to summarize key dates in Viking history.

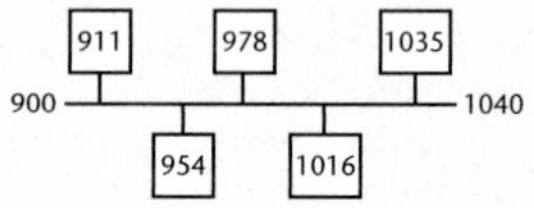

Chapter Summary & Study Guide

1. The Vikings lived in northern Europe in an area called Scandinavia.
2. The geography of the Viking homeland led people to become excellent sailors who earned their living through fishing, trading, and raiding.
3. The Vikings worshiped many gods and often told stories about them.
4. When the Vikings accepted Christianity, they stopped writing their languages in runes and began using Roman letters.
5. Overpopulation in Scandinavia in the 800s led many Vikings to establish settlements elsewhere, including Kievan Rus and Greenland.
6. In 1016, a Danish king called Canute conquered England, but after his death, Danish control of the country came to an end.
7. After besieging Paris, Danish Vikings settled along the French coast in an area known as Norselaw.

HISTORY Online

Self-Check Quiz

Visit the *Human Heritage* Web site at humanheritage.glencoe.com and click on ***Chapter 20—Self-Check Quiz*** to assess your understanding of this chapter.

Section 3 Assessment Answers

1. Viking villages were overcrowded and had food shortages, and the kings constantly fought one another.
2. because they stole, destroyed homes, and killed or enslaved people
3. Danes in England lost control of England after Canute died. Danes in France settled in Normandy and became Christians.
4. Answers will vary but could include that life might have been more stable.
5. 911—Danes win Norselaw in France; 954—heir to Alfred the Great forces the Danes to leave England; 978—Ethelred the Unready becomes king of England and Danes resume raids; 1016—Canute conquers England; 1035—Danish control of England ends.

Assign the Chapter 20 **Section 3 Quiz** in the TCR. Testmaker available.

CHAPTER 20 Assessment

Using Key Terms

Imagine you are a journalist writing a magazine article about Scandinavia. Use the following words to write a paragraph describing the Viking way of life.

jarls *Eddas*
runes *berserkers*

Understanding Main Ideas

1. Why did many Vikings turn to the sea to make a living?
2. How did the Vikings plot the courses of their voyages?
3. How were Viking houses protected from the winter?
4. Why was there no central government in Scandinavia?
5. How did a *jarl* bacome a king?
6. What role did women play in Viking society?
7. What were Viking stories about?
8. How did the Vikings use *runes*?
9. What effect did the Vikings have on Kievan Rus?
10. Why did the Vikings decide not to set up a colony in North America?

Critical Thinking

1. What effect did Christianity have on Viking life?
2. What would you have liked about being a Viking? What would you have disliked?
3. What do you think might have happened in Scandinavia if many Viking warriors had not left the area during the 800s?
4. What effect did Vikings have on the development of Europe during the Middle Ages?

Graphic Organizer Activity

Culture Create a diagram like the one shown, and use it to compare Viking culture before and after the arrival of Christianity in Scandinavia.

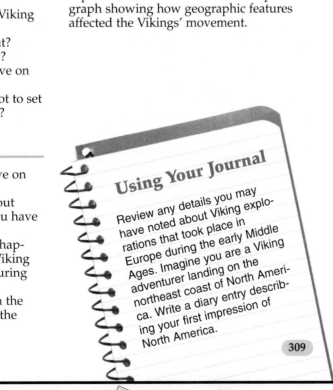

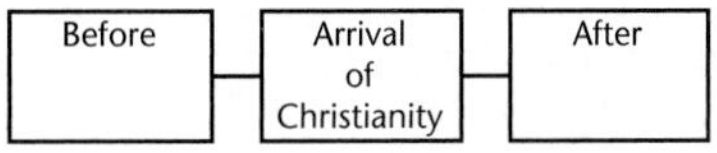

Geography in History

Places and Regions Look at the map on page 306. The Vikings settled in areas beyond the Scandinavian region. What geographic features of Scandinavia may have contributed to the Vikings' expansion and movement? Write a paragraph showing how geographic features affected the Vikings' movement.

Using Your Journal

Review any details you may have noted about Viking explorations that took place in Europe during the early Middle Ages. Imagine you are a Viking adventurer landing on the northeast coast of North America. Write a diary entry describing your first impression of North America.

CHAPTER 20 Assessment Answers

Understanding Key Terms

Paragraphs will vary but should use all the key terms.

Understanding Main Ideas

1. because the land was not suited to farming
2. by the positions of the sun and the stars
3. Their roofs slanted deeply to shed the heavy winter snows.
4. because distance and the cold winters isolated the people
5. seizing neighboring lands
6. They took charge of the home and could attend public meetings, talk with all men, own property, and get a divorce.
7. the gods' great deeds
8. as letters and magic charms
9. They founded a settlement that became the Russian nation.
10. It was too far from home, and Native Americans attacked them.

Critical Thinking

1. It caused the people to lose interest in their sagas and to write with Roman letters.
2. Answers will vary but should include examples.
3. Answers will vary but could include that there might not have been any explorations to North America.
4. They spread fear but also opened up new trade routes and taught seafaring skills.

Graphic Organizer Activity

sample responses: *before*—worshiped many gods, viewed gods as extra-powerful humans who could influence weather and other phenomena, bargained with gods and built shrines, told stories and wrote poems about the feats of gods; *after*—lost interest in the sagas and *Eddas,* adopted use of Roman letters to write their languages, abandoned most old religious practices

Bonus Test Question

For Chapter 20 Test

If the Vikings had sailed directly from Norway to Newfoundland, they could have covered the approximate 2,500-mile distance in under 20 days. About how many miles per hour would their speed have to be to make the trip? *(slightly over 5 miles per hour)*

Using Your Journal

Diary entries will vary but could include a description of their emotional reactions. You might ask volunteers to read their entries to the class.

Geography in History

Viking expansion was caused by limited space and mountains on their peninsula, and their access to the Baltic Sea and the Atlantic Ocean.

FOCUS

OBJECTIVES

After reading the Around the World for Unit 6, your students will be able to:

1. identify the years that the Gupta culture reached its peak and flourished.

2. cite features of the Gupta empire.

3. appreciate the importance of Gupta achievements in mathematics and other areas.

Bellringer

Instruct students to write the following information on a sheet of paper: their age in years, the age of their best friend, and the number of years they expect to be in school.

Motivational Activity

Call on volunteers to write their answers on the board. Then tell students they have just used symbols invented more than 1,500 years ago by a people from India. Have students quickly scan the photos in the Around the World feature. Ask: What are some of the other things accomplished by the people known as the Guptas? *(Students will probably note the architectural and artistic achievements, such as painting and sculpture. Use this as a springboard to examine the Gupta more closely.)*

TEACH

Geography: Places and Regions Remind students that a geographic region shares certain common characteristics. Based on the map on this page, ask: What were some of the landforms that defined northern India as a region? *(the Himalayan and Hindu Kush mountains that formed a natural border and barrier, the rivers that flowed out of*

UNIT 6 Around

THE GUPTAS

As the Roman Empire crumbled, the Gupta (gup′ tuh) Empire in what is now northern India entered a Golden Age. Beginning around 310 A.D., the Guptas began a period of great achievement and expansion.

Among the Gupta's contributions are many folktales and stories. In mathematics, the Gupta invented the concept of zero and developed symbols for the numbers 1 through 9. These symbols were carried to the West by traders and came to be called "Arabic numerals."

The empire lasted until about 600 A.D., when it dissolved into a collection of small states much like Europe.

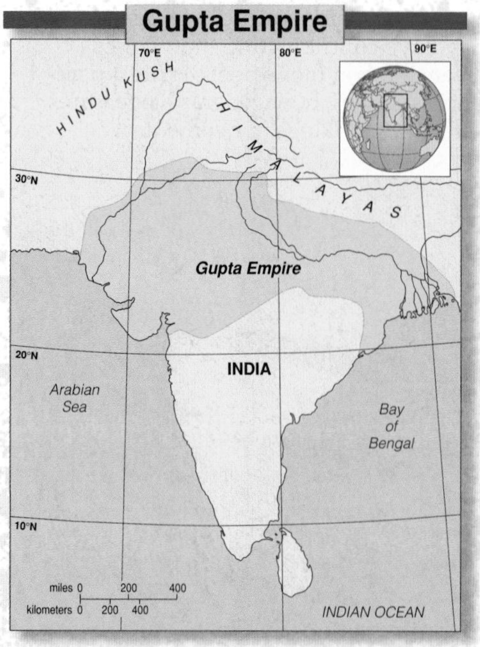

▲ The Gupta Empire covered much of India and reached into parts of southwest Asia.

► The Guptas practiced Hinduism, but they tolerated other religions, especially Buddhism. Buddhism was founded about 563 B.C. by Siddartha Gautama (si dahr′ tuh gow′ tuh muh), who later became known as the Buddha. The Buddha, meaning the "Enlightened One," became the subject of many huge Gupta sculptures.

SPOTLIGHT ON: THE GUPTAS

Share these extra facts about the Guptas:

- The Gupta period is known as the "Golden Age" of ancient India.
- Rulers gave money to artists, writers, and scholars to encourage their work.
- People in the Gupta empire received free medical care, including simple surgery.
- Villages were protected by local military squads made up of one elephant, one chariot, three cavalrymen, and five foot soldiers.
- In times of war, all the squads were brought together to form the royal army.
- The Guptas did not believe in capital punishment. They issued fines instead.
- With the coming of Buddhism and the reform of Hinduism, most Guptas lived as vegetarians.
- In a popular marriage practice called the Swayamvara, suitors met at a bride's house and the bride picked her own groom.

the World

◄ Despite the continued influence of Buddhism, Hinduism became the dominant religion of the Gupta Empire. During this period, rulers ordered the construction of stone or brick temples to honor Hindu gods and goddesses.

The great Gupta conqueror Samudra Gupta (suh mu' druh gup' tuh) minted his own coins. Ruling from about 335 A.D. to 375 A.D., he took over much of northern India and expanded trade as far south as islands in the Indian Ocean. The Sanskrit inscription on this coin describes Samudra Gupta as "the unconquered one, whose victory was spread in hundreds of battles, having conquered his enemies, conquers heaven." ►

◄ Under the Guptas, Buddhist monks decorated the inside of caves, which were used as temples and monasteries, with paintings, statues, and carved pillars. Most paintings illustrated stories from the life of Buddha. Some paintings, however, show Gupta rulers and scenes from daily life, such as this woman.

Taking Another Look

1. During what years did the Gupta Empire flourish?
2. How did Gupta rulers try to unify their empire?

Hands-On Activity

Writing a Speech Write a one-minute speech in which you recommend that the phrase "Arabic numerals" be changed to "Gupta numerals."

311

ANSWERS TO TAKING ANOTHER LOOK

1. The Gupta empire flourished from roughly 310 A.D. to 600 A.D.
2. Sample response: The Guptas promoted unity in their empire through religious tolerance, trade, and spread of the Hindu religion.

Hands-On Activity
Speeches will vary, but most students will credit the Guptas with inventing the concept of zero and symbols for the numbers 1 through 9. Some students may suggest the need to "set the record straight" or the relevance of historical inaccuracies.

the mountains, the location on the Indian subcontinent, and so on)

Next, direct students, working individually or in small groups, to use information in the Around the World feature to find other features that distinguished the Gupta empire as a region. *(Encourage students to identify such things as religion, shared history, common government, and so on.)*

DID YOU KNOW ??

Hindu legend holds that a curse lays over the Buddhist caves at Ajanta. The story claims that some deities angered Indra, the king of gods, by overstaying a visit on earth. As punishment, Indra turned them into pictures on the Buddhist walls of Ajanta, frozen there for all time. The gods, say the legend, retaliate against any mortal who tries to copy or destroy their beauty.

ASSESS

Check for Understanding

Have students answer the questions in Taking Another Look on page 311.

Enrich

Build on the Technology Skill lesson on page 276 of this unit, and assign interested students to prepare a multimedia presentation on the artwork at the Ajanta and Ellora caves. Encourage students to include maps, photos, sound clips, and more.

CLOSE

Review the attitude of the Gupta toward other religions. *(They practiced tolerance.)* Ask: How did religious tolerance help explain the success of Gupta rule? *(reduced religious dissension, promoting peace and unity)*

Answers and Analyses

1A Geography

Since this map shows the boundaries of kingdoms, it is a political map.

THE PRINCETON REVIEW **TEST-TAKING TIP**

Review with students the characteristics of various kinds of maps and the different purposes they serve.

2G Culture/Environment

A table of Norse gods, including Thor, "the god of thunder, lightning, and the tides," is on page 304. According to page 268, the Germans also believed *that the sound of thunder came from Thor's chariot wheels.*

THE PRINCETON REVIEW **TEST-TAKING TIP**

Encourage students to use the process of elimination and to guess aggressively, even if their knowledge is incomplete. Even if all they recall is that Thor was a powerful god, they can probably eliminate H and J.

THE PRINCETON REVIEW

Standardized Test Practice

Directions: Choose the *best* answer to each of the following multiple choice questions. If you have trouble answering a question, use the process of elimination to narrow your choices. Write your answers on a separate piece of paper.

Use the map below to answer question 1.

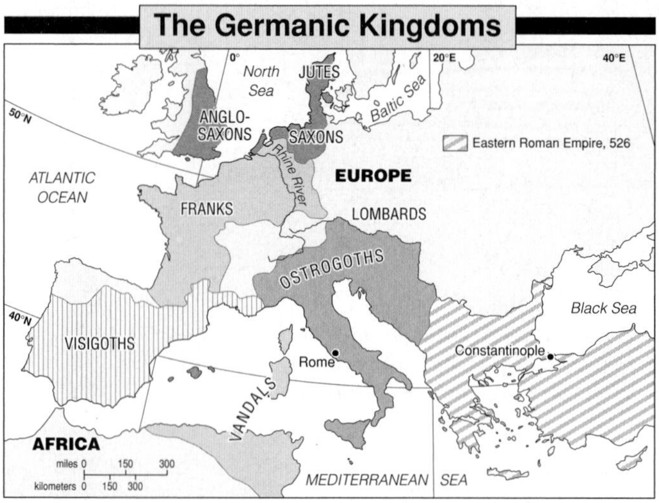

1. This type of map is called a

- **A** political map
- **B** physical map
- **C** military map
- **D** demographic map

Test-Taking Tip: Even though this map does show some landforms, such as rivers, it is *not* primarily a physical map (answer B). What is the map's *main purpose?* A map's title—or legend (if there is one)—can give you clues.

2. The legend of the Norse god Thor was used to explain

- **F** why the Vikings were such good warriors
- **G** the sound of thunder
- **H** the story of Adam and Eve
- **J** the origins of language

Test-Taking Tip: Eliminate answers that you know are incorrect. For example, the story of Adam and Eve (answer H) is a Bible story, and it is not related to the Vikings' religion.

3. The early Dark Ages were characterized by

A the development of strong trade routes in eastern Europe

B the failure of Christianity to spread to most parts of Europe

C a darkening of the sky due to air pollution around Europe

D an emphasis on war and conquest over education and trade

Test-Taking Tip: This question asks you to make a *generalization* about the Dark Ages. A generalization is a type of conclusion based on facts. Which of the answer choices *best* summarizes the Dark Ages? If you cannot remember any specific facts about the Dark Ages, ask yourself if it sounds like it was a positive or a negative time. In other words, what does the word *dark* suggest? Are there any answer choices you can eliminate as a result?

4. The battles waged by Charlemagne were different from earlier battles because

F for the first time, the purpose of war was to convert people to Christianity

G for the first time, wars were fought primarily on the water

H legends were written about the battles and Charlemagne's military leaders

J Charlemagne was the first to fight a war against the Pope

Test-Taking Tip: Always read the question and *all* the answer choices carefully. For example, Charlemagne fought *for* the Pope, not *against* the Pope, so you can eliminate answer J.

5. The Roman Catholic Church lost control of the Irish Church during the Germanic wars. What do you think was the reason for this?

A Ireland was far away, isolated, and relatively unimportant to Rome.

B Irish monks refused to follow the laws set by the Pope.

C Irish nobles refused to pay the taxes demanded by the Pope.

D The Irish refused to accept Christianity and kept worshiping their Celtic gods.

Test-Taking Tip: Make sure that you know where the major European countries are located on a map. How far was Ireland from Rome? Eliminate answer choices that do not make sense. If the Irish were already part of the Church, they must have accepted Christianity. Therefore, you can eliminate answer D.

6. After their encounters with the Germanic people in Europe, the Vikings stopped writing down their *sagas*, or long stories, about their gods. Why?

F They decided that they no longer had time to recite the long sagas.

G The Germanic people convinced the Vikings that stories were only for children.

H The Vikings were no longer interested in tales of warriors and exciting battles.

J The Vikings accepted Christianity, which outlawed stories about other gods.

Test-Taking Tip: For this question, you will have to think about the *influence* of the Germans on the Vikings. Since it is unlikely that the Vikings simply lost interest in these stories, you can get rid of answer H.

STOP

313

Tested Objectives

Questions	Reading Objective
1	Analyze information
2	Identify supporting ideas
3	Identify central issues
4	Make comparisons
5, 6	Draw conclusions

3D History

Pages 270–272 discuss the invasions that marked the end of the Roman Empire and the beginning of the Dark Ages. According to the introduction to Chapter 18 (page 275), *The decline of the Roman Empire led to disorder everywhere in western Europe. . . . People were no longer interested in learning, and many books and works of art were damaged or lost.*

4F History

No mention is made of battles on water, so choice G can be eliminated. Charlemagne fought *for* the Pope, so choice J can be eliminated. There were earlier war legends, such as the *Iliad,* so choice H can be eliminated. According to page 279, Charlemagne waged wars because he wanted *all the Germanic people to become Christian.*

5A History

No mention is made of taxes or laws demanded by the Pope in the discussion of Ireland on pages 289–291, so choices B and C can be eliminated. According to page 290, Ireland was not a target for Germanic attacks because it was farther out than Britain. Likewise, it might have been too far away for the Roman Catholic Church to remain in contact.

6J History

The Viking sagas are discussed on page 303. There it states that after meeting Christians, the sagas were forgotten or were forbidden by the Church.

Introducing UNIT 7

OVERVIEW

Unit 7 discusses the emergence of new empires in the Middle East and eastern Europe from the fall of Rome to A.D. 1600, focusing on the Byzantines, the Arabs, and the Eastern Slavs and the emergence of Russia.

- **Chapter 21** describes how the Byzantines forged an empire based on Greco-Roman culture and the Eastern Orthodox Church.
- **Chapter 22** analyzes the role of Muhammad in the emergence and spread of Islam and the creation of the Arab Empire.
- **Chapter 23** discusses the Eastern Slavic civilization from the founding of their early settlements to the establishment of a powerful Rus state centered around Moscow that later developed as modern Russia.

UNIT OBJECTIVES

After reading Unit 7, students will be able to:

1. discuss how religion influenced the growth and development of the Middle East and eastern Europe from 500 to the 1500s.
2. analyze how the Arabs influenced the civilization of western Europe.
3. explain how the Byzantines influenced Russia.

UNIT PROJECT

Organize the class into three groups. Assign each group one of the following leaders: Justinian, Muhammad, or Ivan the Great. Tell each group that it will be responsible for writing and performing a short play based on the life of their assigned leader.

UNIT 7

Emergence of New Empires

▲ A mosaic of a Byzantine woman

A gold Byzantine incense burner in the shape of a church ▶

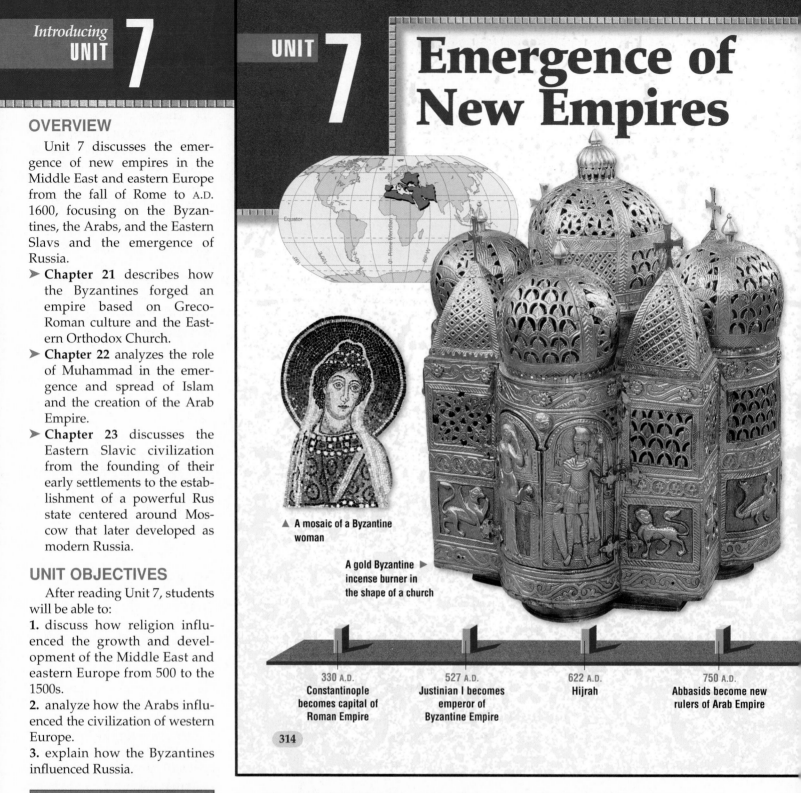

330 A.D.	527 A.D.	622 A.D.	750 A.D.
Constantinople becomes capital of Roman Empire	Justinian I becomes emperor of Byzantine Empire	Hijrah	Abbasids become new rulers of Arab Empire

314

ABOUT THE UNIT OPENING

Examining Artifacts

Based on the artifacts, what can students infer about the role of religion in the Byzantine Empire? *(It was important.)* Ask: How do you know this? *(the use of a church as the subject of art, the intricate detail of the church, the use of gold to depict the church, and so on)* What other inferences can students make about the Byzantine Empire?

Global Chronology

Ask students to explain what time period the time line covers. *(330 to 1500)* According to the time line, what empires existed during this time period? *(Roman, Byzantine, Arab empires)*

FOLDABLES™ Study Organizer

Organizing Information Study Foldable *Make the following foldable to help you organize information about how empires in the Middle East and eastern Europe influenced other civilizations.*

Step 1 *Fold a sheet of paper in half from side to side.*

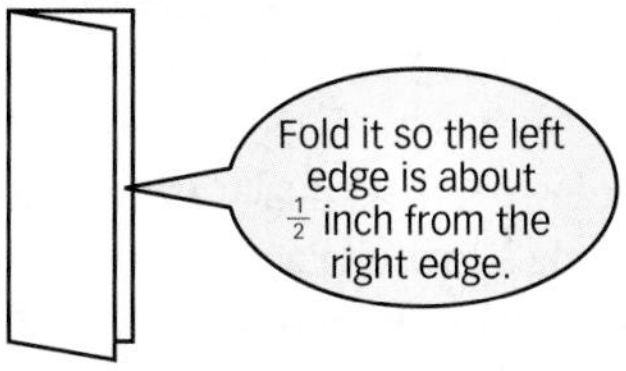

Fold it so the left edge is about ½ inch from the right edge.

Step 2 *Turn the paper and fold it into thirds.*

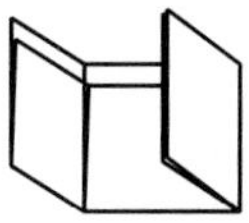

Step 3 *Unfold and cut the top layer only along both folds.*

This will make three tabs.

Step 4 *Label as shown.*

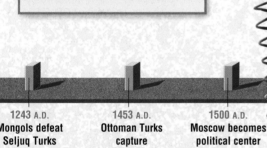

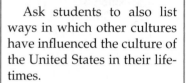

Reading and Writing *As you read the unit, use your foldable to help you organize information about how empires affected other civilizations. Write the main ideas about each empire under the appropriate tab of your foldable.*

PRIMARY SOURCES Library

See pages 686–687 for another primary source reading to accompany Unit 7.

GO TO Read "The Fall of Constantinople" from the **World History Primary Source Document Library CD-ROM.**

1243 A.D. **Mongols defeat Seljuq Turks**

1453 A.D. **Ottoman Turks capture Constantinople**

1500 A.D. **Moscow becomes political center of Rus**

Journal Notes

In what ways did the new empires that developed in the Middle East and in the eastern part of Europe influence other civilizations? Note details about these empires as you read.

GLENCOE TECHNOLOGY

MindJogger Videoquiz

Use **MindJogger Videoquiz** to preview the unit content.

Available in DVD and VHS

FOLDABLES™ Study Organizer

Purpose The purpose of this foldable is to help students group facts into categories. As students read the chapters in this unit, they will use their foldables to record and organize main ideas and facts about the Byzantine Empire, the spread of Islam, and the Eastern Slavs. Point out to students that each civilization changed throughout history. Ask them to think about what impact these changes had.

Have students complete **Reading and Study Skills Foldables** Activity 7.

RECORDING JOURNAL NOTES

Ask students to also list ways in which other cultures have influenced the culture of the United States in their lifetimes.

Geographic Location

Have students use their text Atlas to locate the places in this unit that are in the Mediterranean area, identifying the Balkan Peninsula and the waterways from the Mediterranean Sea to the Black Sea and up to Russia. Then have students locate the Arabian Peninsula and identify the areas where Islam spread.

ABCNEWS INTERACTIVE™

VIDEOCASSETTE
Turning Points in World History

Have students view **Tape 1 Chapter 6** to learn about Jerusalem and how it is now the center of three of the world's major religions.

PRIMARY SOURCES Library

Additional primary sources from the **World History Primary Source Document Library CD-ROM** include:

- "Belisarius, Justinian's Virtuous General," by Procopius

Primary sources about Byzantine women can be found on pages 686–687.

Chapter 21 Planning Guide

Timesaving Tools

TeacherWorks™ All-In-One Planner and Resource Center

- **Interactive Teacher Edition** Access your Teacher Wraparound Edition and your classroom resources with a few easy clicks.
- **Interactive Lesson Planner** Planning has never been easier! Organize your week, month, semester, or year with all the lesson helps you need to make teaching creative, timely, and relevant.

Use Glencoe's **Presentation Plus!** multimedia teacher tool to easily present dynamic lessons that visually excite your students. Using Microsoft PowerPoint® you can customize the presentations to create your own personalized lessons.

Objectives	Reproducible Resources	Multimedia Resources
Section 1 **Constantinople** Explain why the Byzantine Empire survived and prospered for 1,000 years.	Reproducible Lesson Plan Chapter 21 Vocabulary and Guided Reading Activity Reading Essentials and Study Guide 21-1 Section 1 Quiz Unit 7 Hands-On History Lab	Interactive Student Edition CD-ROM Graphic Organizer Transparency 14 Vocabulary PuzzleMaker CD-ROM Interactive Tutor Self-Assessment CD-ROM ExamView® Pro Testmaker CD-ROM Glencoe Skillbuilder Interactive Workbook CD-ROM, Level 1 Presentation Plus! CD-ROM
Section 2 **Justinian I** Discuss why Constantinople was important to the empire.	Reproducible Lesson Plan Reading Essentials and Study Guide 21-2 Chapter 21 Cooperative Learning Activity Chapter 21 Chart and Graph Skill Activity Chapter 21 Geography and Map Activity Unit 7 Primary Source Readings Section 2 Quiz	Teaching Transparencies and Activities 21A & 21B Vocabulary PuzzleMaker CD-ROM Interactive Tutor Self-Assessment CD-ROM ExamView® Pro Testmaker CD-ROM Glencoe Skillbuilder Interactive Workbook CD-ROM, Level 1
Section 3 **The Church** Analyze practices of the Eastern Orthodox Church and the role these practices played in the Byzantine Empire.	Reproducible Lesson Plan Reading Essentials and Study Guide 21-3 Chapter 21 Enrichment Activity Section 3 Quiz	Vocabulary PuzzleMaker CD-ROM Interactive Tutor Self-Assessment CD-ROM ExamView® Pro Testmaker CD-ROM Glencoe Skillbuilder Interactive Workbook CD-ROM, Level 1
Section 4 **Decline of the Empire** Summarize reasons the Byzantine Empire declined.	Reproducible Lesson Plan Reading Essentials and Study Guide 21-4 Section 4 Quiz	Vocabulary PuzzleMaker CD-ROM Interactive Tutor Self-Assessment CD-ROM ExamView® Pro Testmaker CD-ROM Glencoe Skillbuilder Interactive Workbook CD-ROM, Level 1
Chapter 21 **Review and Evaluation**	Chapter 21 Reteaching Activity Chapter 21 Performance Assessment Activity Spanish Chapter Summary and Glossary Chapter 21 Test	Vocabulary PuzzleMaker CD-ROM Interactive Tutor Self-Assessment CD-ROM Glencoe Skillbuilder Interactive Workbook CD-ROM, Level 1 Audiocassettes* ExamView® Pro Testmaker CD-ROM

*Also available in Spanish.

Chapter 21 Planning Guide

✓ Performance Assessment Activities

Word Puzzles Have students create a list of important people, places, buildings, or religious terms mentioned in this chapter. Tell them to use these lists to create crossword puzzles.

CHAPTER RESOURCES

LITERATURE ABOUT THE PERIOD

Dickinson, Peter. *The Dancing Bear*. Dell, 1972. Tells an adventure story that takes place during the time of the Byzantine Empire.

READINGS FOR THE STUDENT

Browning, Robert. *The Byzantine Empire*. Charles Scribner's Sons, 1980. Byzantine world from 500 A.D. to fall of Constantinople in 1453.

READINGS FOR THE TEACHER

Browning, Robert. *Justinian and Theodora: The Byzantine Recovery*. Thames & Hudson, 1987. Explores the relationship between Justinian and Theodora and their attempt to re-create the Christian Roman Empire of Constantine.

Mango, Cyril. *Byzantium: The Empire of New Rome*. Charles Scribner's Sons, 1980. Considers Byzantine life from a thematic perspective.

KEY TO ABILITY LEVELS

Teaching strategies have been coded for varying learning styles and abilities.

L1 Level 1 activities are **basic** activities and should be within the ability range of all students.

L2 Level 2 activities are **average** activities and should be within the ability range of the average to above-average student.

L3 Level 3 activities are **challenging** activities designed for the ability range of above-average students.

ELL ELL activities should be within the ability range of English Language Learning students.

NATIONAL GEOGRAPHIC Teacher's Corner

INDEX TO NATIONAL GEOGRAPHIC MAGAZINE

The following article relates to this chapter:

- "Albanians: A People Undone," by Priit Vesilind, February 2000.

NATIONAL GEOGRAPHIC SOCIETY PRODUCTS AVAILABLE FROM GLENCOE

To order the following, call Glencoe at 1-800-334-7344:

- *PicturePack: Physical Geography of the World (Transparencies)*
- *PicturePack: The Middle Ages (Transparencies)*
- *Picture Show: The Middle Ages (CD-ROM)*
- *Picture Atlas of the World (CD-ROM)*
- *Picture Pack: World Geography Library (Transparencies)*

ADDITIONAL NATIONAL GEOGRAPHIC SOCIETY PRODUCTS

To order the following, call National Geographic at 1-800-368-2728:

- *National Geographic Atlas of World History (Book)*
- *Wonders of the Ancient World: National Geographic Atlas of Archaeology (Book)*

Access *National Geographic's* new dynamic MapMachine Web site and other geography resources at:
www.nationalgeographic.com
www.nationalgeographic.com/maps

Introduce
CHAPTER 21

OVERVIEW

Chapter 21 describes the Byzantine Empire from the founding of Constantinople to the Turkish conquest.

- **Section 1** describes Constantinople as the "New Rome."
- **Section 2** discusses the Byzantine contributions to government and law.
- **Section 3** discusses the effects of Orthodox Christianity on Byzantine and eastern European culture.
- **Section 4** traces the decline of the Byzantine Empire.

CHAPTER OBJECTIVES

After reading Chapter 21, students will be able to:

1. explain why the Byzantine Empire survived and prospered for 1,000 years.
2. discuss why Constantinople was important to the empire.
3. describe the Eastern Orthodox Church and the role it played in the Byzantine Empire.
4. summarize causes of the decline of the Byzantine Empire.

EXAMINING ARTIFACTS

Have students examine the Byzantine crown, and ask: What does this artifact tell you about the relationship between church and government in the Byzantine Empire? *(They were closely tied.)* Call on students to explain how they reached their answer. *(the cross and icons on the crown)* Tell students to use the time line to figure out how long the empire prospered.

PERFORMANCE ASSESSMENT

Use the Performance Assessment Activities on page 316B to help you evaluate students as they complete the chapter.

CHAPTER 21

The Byzantine Empire

330 A.D.–1455 A.D.

◄ A gold Byzantine crown

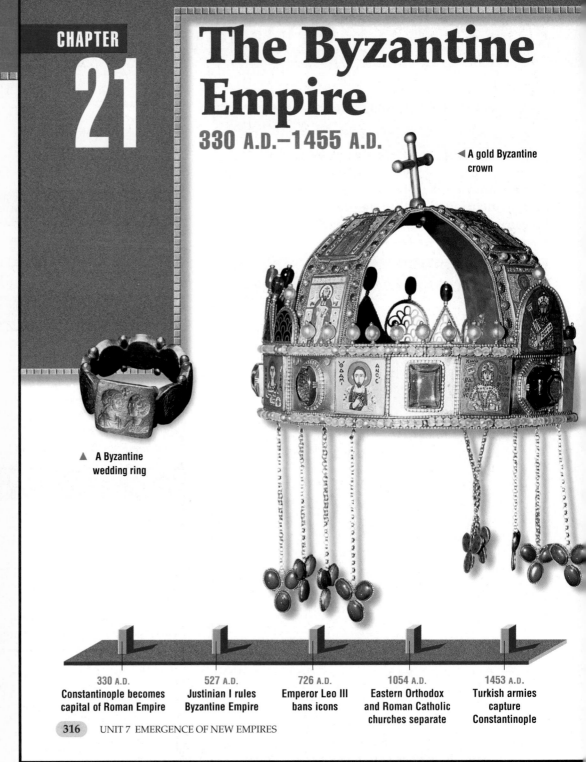

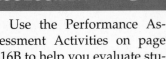

▲ A Byzantine wedding ring

330 A.D.	527 A.D.	726 A.D.	1054 A.D.	1453 A.D.
Constantinople becomes capital of Roman Empire	Justinian I rules Byzantine Empire	Emperor Leo III bans icons	Eastern Orthodox and Roman Catholic churches separate	Turkish armies capture Constantinople

TEACHING RESOURCES

TEACHER PLANNING AND SUPPORT

- Reproducible Lesson Plan 21-1, 21-2, 21-3, 21-4
- Teaching Strategies for the World History Classroom (Including Block Scheduling Pacing Guides)
- Presentation Plus! CD-ROM

REVIEW AND REINFORCEMENT

- Reading Essentials and Study Guide 21-1, 21-2, 21-3, 21-4
- Chapter 21 Vocabulary and Guided Reading Activity
- Vocabulary PuzzleMaker CD-ROM
- Teaching Transparencies 21A & 21B
- Chapter 21 Reteaching Activity
- Chapter 21 Cooperative Learning Activity
- Chapter 21 Activity Book Activity
- Chapter 21 Chart and Graph Skill Activity
- Reading and Study Skills Foldables
- Interactive Tutor Self-Assessment CD-ROM
- Unit 7 MindJogger VideoQuiz

APPLICATION AND HANDS-ON ACTIVITIES

- Daily Questions in Social Studies
- Unit 7 Hands-On History Lab Activity
- Student Presentation Builder CD-ROM

Chapter Focus

Read to Discover

- Why the Byzantine Empire survived and prospered for 1,000 years.
- Why Constantinople was important to the empire.
- What role the Eastern Orthodox Church played in the Byzantine Empire.
- What forces helped bring about the decline of the Byzantine Empire.

HISTORY Online

Chapter Overview

Visit the *Human Heritage* Web site at **humanheritage.glencoe.com** and click on ***Chapter 21—Chapter Overviews*** to preview this chapter.

Terms to Learn	People to Know	Places to Locate
relics	Constantine I	Constantinople
theology	Justinian	Byzantium
Greek fire	Theodora	Hagia Sophia
icons	Leo III	

Why It's Important Emperor Constantine I moved the capital of the Roman Empire from Rome to Constantinople in about 330. About 100 years later, the Roman Empire in the West fell. The Roman Empire in the East, however, survived and prospered. It became known as the Byzantine Empire. Its people were called Byzantines. The Byzantines built a civilization based on a blend of Greek, Roman, and Christian ideas.

The empire in the East survived for several reasons. Constantinople was a mighty fortress that needed few soldiers to defend it. This freed soldiers to protect other areas of the empire. The empire's wealth supported a large army and was used to pay invaders to move farther and farther west.

SECTION 1 Constantinople

When Constantine first chose the old Greek city of Byzantium as the place for his new capital, he was aware of its advantages. The Roman Empire depended on trade, and the great centers of trade lay to the east. Byzantium was on the waterway between the Black and Aegean seas. Its harbor offered a safe haven for fishing boats, merchant ships, and warships. The city sat at the crossroads of the trading routes between Europe and Asia. Its location gave it control of the sea trade between Kievan Rus and the Mediterranean area. One of the most important east-west land routes passed through the city, too.

HISTORY Online

Chapter Overview introduces students to chapter content and key terms. Have them access ***Chapter 21 Overview*** at **humanheritage.glencoe.com**

FOCUS

Bellringer

Write the following on the board: *Make a list of some things you know about the country of Turkey.*

Motivational Activity

Discuss students' lists of what they know about Turkey. Ask them if they realize that Istanbul is the ancient city of Constantinople. Explain that they will learn about the importance of this city in history.

GUIDE TO READING

Reading Strategy

Ask students to read "Why It's Important" and summarize the chapter's main theme. *(The Byzantine Empire survived and prospered, creating a civilization that blended Greek, Roman, and Christian ideas.)*

Vocabulary Precheck

Ask students to define each of the "Terms to Learn." Have a volunteer consult the dictionary for any unfamiliar words. L1 ELL

Use the Vocabulary PuzzleMaker CD-ROM for Chapter 21 to create a crossword puzzle. L1

Assign Chapter 21 Vocabulary and Guided Reading Activity.

Assign Reading Essentials and Study Guide 21-1.

GEOGRAPHY ACTIVITIES

- Chapter 21 Geography and Map Activity
- Outline Map Resource Book

INTERDISCIPLINARY CONNECTIONS

- World Art & Architecture Transparency 12, *Theodora and Attendants*
- World Music: A Cultural Legacy

ENRICHMENT AND EXTENSION

- Unit 7 Primary Source Readings
- World History Primary Source Document Library CD-ROM
- Chapter 21 Enrichment Activity
- Foods Around the World

ASSESSMENT AND EVALUATION

- Chapter 21 Performance Assessment Activity
- Chapter 21 Section Quizzes 21-1, 21-2, 21-3, 21-4
- Chapter 21 Test
- Chapter 21 ExamView® Pro Testmaker CD-ROM
- Chapter 21 Digests Audiocassettes Activities and Tests

SPANISH RESOURCES

- Chapter 21 Spanish Chapter Summary and Glossary
- Chapter 21 Spanish Digests Audiocassettes Activities and Tests

TEACH

Guided Practice

L1 **Geography: The World in Spatial Terms** Ask students to make an outline map of Europe, the Middle East, and North Africa similar to the one on page 323. Have them locate and label Rome, Constantinople, Athens, the Mediterranean and Black seas, the Bosphorus, Asia Minor, Syria, Egypt, Italy, Greece, and the Balkan Peninsula. Explain that the boundaries of the Byzantine Empire varied over time, but that it remained a geographic crossroads of sea and land travel. ELL

DID YOU KNOW ??

Constantinople's oval arena was called the Hippodrome.

CAPTION ANSWER

because it was modeled after Rome

NATIONAL GEOGRAPHIC

NGS PICTURESHOW CD-ROM

Picture Atlas of the World

You and your students can see the present-day skyline of Istanbul and the beautiful Hagia Sophia by clicking the "Photos" button of Istanbul, Turkey.

People in History

Constantine I
c. 288 A.D.–337 A.D.

Roman Emperor

Born in what is now Serbia, Constantine grew up the son of a Roman army officer. In 305 A.D., he became the co-emperor of Rome, but he continued to fight alongside the troops. During one battle, he saw a vision that convinced him to become the first Roman Emperor to accept Christianity. In 324 A.D., he triumphed as sole ruler of Rome and ordered a new capital city built at Byzantium. His rule helped ensure the eastward spread of Christianity.

The location also favored the city's defense. The sea protected it on three sides, and a huge wall protected it on the fourth side. Later, a huge chain was even strung across the city's north harbor for greater protection. Invaders would not easily take the new capital, which was renamed Constantinople.

It took more than four years to build Constantinople. Constantine modeled it after Rome. The city stood on seven hills. Government buildings and palaces were designed in the Roman style. Streets were narrow and apartment houses crowded. Constantinople even had an oval arena like the Circus Maximus where races and other events were held.

The city's political and social life was patterned on that of Rome, too. The emperor operated under Roman laws and ruled with the help of highly trained officials, who took charge of building roads, bridges, wells, and caravan shelters. The army followed Roman military customs. The poor people of Constantinople received free bread and enjoyed circuses and chariot races put on by the government. The wealthy people lived in town or on large farming estates. In fact, Constantine convinced many of the wealthy Romans to move to Constantinople by offering to build them palaces.

CONSTANTINOPLE Constantinople's location made it an important center for trade. The wealth from this trade was used to make Constantinople an ornate and beautiful city. Citizens shown in this painting gather to watch a royal procession. **Why was Constantinople called the "new Rome"?**

MULTICULTURAL PERSPECTIVES

A contemporary historian points out that a modern-day time traveler would feel more at home in the Byzantine world of Constantinople than in any of the depressed, dangerous countries of early medieval western Europe. The city had shops, factories, and banking houses. It had a well-educated population who was curious and informed about current events, politics, and literature. The Byzantines were enthusiastic sports fans at games and chariot races. They loved ornamentation and rich colors especially in their illuminated manuscripts and stained-glass windows.

The family was the center of social life for most Byzantines. The majority of them made their living through farming, herding, or working as laborers. There was, however, one important difference between Constantinople and Rome. From the beginning, Constantinople was a Christian city. It had been dedicated to God by Constantine, who viewed it as the center of a great Christian empire. Church leaders were consulted about all important events of everyday life and had great influence over the people. For a young man of Constantinople, a career in the church was considered a very high goal.

Constantinople had many Christian churches. Constantine saw to it that they were the most magnificent buildings in the city. Government and church leaders gathered **relics** (rel' iks), or valued holy objects from the past, from throughout the Christian world. These were placed in public monuments, palaces, and churches. The bodies of saints rested in beautiful shrines. Thousands of people came to these shrines to pray to God for cures for their ills.

The city's Christian values could be seen in the way needy people were treated. The Byzantines believed that each Christian was responsible for the well-being of other Christians. Wealthy Byzantines formed organizations to care for the poor, the aged, and the blind. Even members of the emperor's household took great pride in founding and supporting good causes.

About 600,000 people lived in Constantinople during Constantine's rule. There were Greeks, Turks, Italians, Slavs, Persians, Armenians, and Jews. They spoke Greek among themselves but used Latin, the official language, for government business. Most people became Christians, and all called themselves Romans. Byzantine nobles and rulers continued to boast of their ties to Rome for the next 1,100 years.

Byzantine Coins

Reading Check What are **relics,** and why did they attract thousands of people to Constantinople?

HISTORY Online

Student Web Activity Visit the *Human Heritage* Web site at humanheritage.glencoe.com and click on ***Chapter 21—Student Web Activities*** to find out more about the city of Constantinople.

Section 1 Assessment

1. **Define:** relics.
2. Why did Constantine choose Byzantium as the site for the empire's new capital?
3. How could the influence of Christianity be seen in the city?

Critical Thinking

4. **Demonstrating Reasoned Judgment** In your opinion, what were some of the good things about living in Constantinople?

Graphic Organizer Activity

5. Draw this diagram, and use it to compare the cities of Rome and Constantinople.

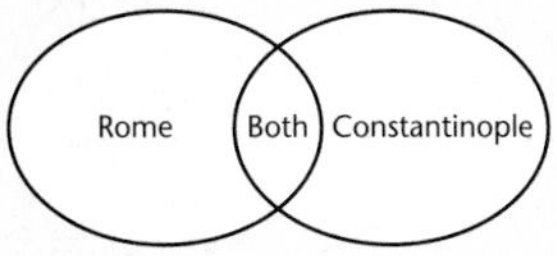

L3 Critical Thinking Have students create a chart comparing features of the Old Rome to the New Rome. They might compare elements such as language, people, and architecture.

Reading Check Answer Thousands of people came to Constantinople to pray for cures for their illnesses at shrines that contained **relics,** valued holy objects from the past.

HISTORY Online

Student Web Activity objectives and answers can be found at the ***Chapter 21 Web Activity Lesson Plan*** at humanheritage.glencoe.com

LINKING PAST TO PRESENT

Trade and industry in Constantinople were strictly controlled by the government. The main industry was textiles. About 550, silkworms smuggled out of China were brought to Constantinople, where beautiful fabrics and clothes were made from raw silk. Silkworms are still raised today to commercially produce this fine fabric.

Section 1 Assessment Answers

1. relics, holy objects from the past (p. 319)
2. because it lay at the crossroads of the trading routes between Europe and Asia
3. sample responses: dedicated to God by Constantine, influence of Church leaders on Constantine and everyday life, presence of many churches and relics, efforts by individuals and organizations to help the needy
4. Answers will vary, but students should include examples.
5. Answers will vary, but similarities should reflect information on pages 318–319. An important difference was that Constantine dedicated his capital to God. Students might go beyond the text and note other differences such as absolute location, population makeup (more Turks in Constantinople), histories (influence of Etruscans on Rome), and so on.

Assign Chapter 21 **Section 1 Quiz** in the TCR. Testmaker available.

Use **Interactive Tutor Self Assessment CD-ROM** to review Section 1.

L3 **Critical Thinking** Ask students to pretend that they are public relations advisers to Justinian I and have been asked to write a speech for the emperor to deliver to the people of the Byzantine Empire. The purpose of the speech is to improve the people's level of satisfaction with their lives under Justinian rule. Speeches should include references to Justinian's life and work, accomplishments, and influence on the daily life of the people. The speech should be based on factual information.

Reading Check Answer **Theology** is the study of religion.

CAPTION ANSWER

Theodora was an actress, and there was a law forbidding marriages between actresses and high government officials. After Justinian became emperor, he abolished the law.

Use the **Vocabulary PuzzleMaker CD-ROM** to create crossword and word search puzzles.

SECTION 2 Justinian I

After Constantine died, his sons ruled the empire. They were followed first by a general named Julian and then by a series of other emperors. Finally, in 527, a Macedonian named Justinian (juh stin′ ē uhn) came to the throne. He was a strong ruler who came to be considered the greatest Byzantine emperor.

Justinian had served in the army and was a good general. He was well trained in law, music, architecture, and **theology** (thē ol′ uh jē), or the study of religion. The people who served him were chosen for their abilities rather than for their wealth or social positions.

Reading Check What is **theology?**

As emperor, Justinian controlled the army and navy, made the laws, headed the Church and the government, and was supreme judge. He could declare war or make peace. The Church taught that the emperor's acts were inspired by God. Therefore, what Justinian did could not be questioned. Those who came into contact with him were expected to bow down before him and kiss his feet and hands.

Theodora

Justinian's wife, the empress Theodora (thē uh dor′ uh), was a great help to him. Theodora's family had been poor, and she had worked as an actress before meeting Justinian.

Fun Facts. . . .

Theodora Although Theodora was the daughter of a bear-keeper with a traveling circus, her strong will took her as far as the royal court. Justinian's court historian commented: "She never did anything at any time as the result of persuasion. . . . She claimed the right to govern the whole Roman Empire."

JUSTINIAN AND THEODORA Theodora had a much greater influence on Byzantine government than other empresses. In this painting she urges Justinian to take action against a revolt. **What problems did Justinian face in marrying Theodora?**

COOPERATIVE LEARNING

Organize a travel agency in which student teams will assume responsibility for providing information to people traveling to Constantinople during Justinian's rule. One team will plan the important stops, another will give information on climate and food, and another group will prepare one or two travel posters. The team that plans the stops will provide a map showing the route. Each team should research the various points of interest and be able to contribute to the packet of information.

Assign Chapter 21 *Cooperative Learning Activity* in the TCR.

Making Generalizations

If you say, "We have a good soccer team," you are making a generalization, or general statement, about your team. If you go on to say that the team has not lost a game this season and is the top-rated team, you are providing evidence to support your generalization. When studying history, it is often necessary to put together pieces of information—supporting statements—to arrive at a full picture.

Learning the Skill In some cases, authors provide only supporting statements, and you will need to make generalizations on your own. To make generalizations, follow these steps:

- Identify the subject matter and gather facts and examples related to it.
- Identify similarities or patterns among these facts.
- Use these similarities or patterns to form general ideas about the subject.

Read the passage about Hagia Sophia, a cathedral built by Justinian, and study the picture on this page. Then answer the questions that follow.

Hagia Sophia is the fourth largest cathedral in the world. Only St. Paul's Cathedral in England and St. Peter's Cathedral and Milan Cathedral in Italy are larger.

The building's huge round dome can be seen from everywhere in the church. The dome rests on four arches and four gigantic piers. It measures 102 feet (31 m) in diameter and stands 184 feet (56 m) high. A series of 40 arching windows flood the interior with light and draw the visitor's eyes upward.

GENERALIZATIONS:

a. It took great engineering skills to build Hagia Sophia.
b. Hagia Sophia made Constantinople the center of the Christian world.
c. Hagia Sophia is one of the world's greatest churches.
d. The arching windows are Hagia Sophia's most impressive feature.

Skill Practice

1. **Which of the generalizations above are supported by details in the passage?**
2. **Which of the generalizations are not supported by the passage?**
3. **Read Section 2 on pages 320–324. Write two generalizations about Justinian's wife, Theodora.**

GO TO Glencoe's **Skillbuilder Interactive Workbook CD-ROM, Level 1,** provides instruction and practice in key social studies skills.

CRITICAL THINKING SKILLS

TEACH

Making Generalizations

You might introduce this lesson by writing this information from a survey conducted in the late 1990s on the board.

- Some 89 percent of all teenagers report using the Internet at least once.
- On average, teens surf the Internet 5.1 hours per week.
- More than 75 percent of teenagers say they would rather look something up on the Internet than in a book.

Ask students to form a statement that summarizes these facts in some way. *(An example might be: Teenagers feel comfortable using the Internet.)* Have students share their responses. Then introduce the definition of a generalization—a statement that ties together facts in a general but accurate way.

Next, assign the skills lesson and accompanying questions on this page.

Answers to Skill Practice

1. a, c
2. b, because there are no facts to support this statement; d, because it is an opinion (Someone else may think other features are more impressive.)
3. Generalizations will vary, but should take into account all facts.

TEAM-TEACHING STRATEGY

Art Work with an art teacher to help students design a brochure on Hagia Sophia that might be given to tourists visiting the famous structure. Encourage students to use the Internet to locate such things as street maps, photographs, and other items that might be included in the brochure.

After collecting information, assign students to plan the brochure's design by drawing storyboards. Have them review their storyboards with the art teacher, making any necessary improvements. When students have written their rough drafts, direct them to exchange the copy with each other for editing. Urge students to watch for any faulty or unsupported generalizations. When students have edited each other's work, have them produce their final version for display on a bulletin board and/or inclusion in their portfolios.

DID YOU KNOW ??

Theodora built many hospitals for the poor and established a home for destitute actresses.

Reading Check Answer

A **dowry** is the wealth a bride brings with her when she marries. Theodora said that the dowry should be used to measure the amount of land a woman could own.

PRIMARY SOURCES Library

You might assign "Byzantine Women" on pages 686–687 of the Primary Sources Library.

The people of the empire had a low opinion of actresses. There was even a law forbidding marriages between them and high government officials. Justinian, however, wanted to marry Theodora. After he became emperor, he abolished the law and made Theodora his empress.

At first, Theodora only entertained guests and attended palace ceremonies. Gradually, however, she began to take an interest in politics. Soon she was helping Justinian fill government and church offices. She also convinced Justinian to allow women more rights. For the first time, a Byzantine wife could own land equal in value to her **dowry** (dow′ rē), or the wealth she brought with her when she married. A widow could raise and support her young children without government interference.

Reading Check What is a **dowry,** and what did Theodora say it should be used to measure?

In 532, Theodora made her most important contribution. A group of senators had organized a revolt to protest high taxes. They were able to gain much support from both the poor and the rich. The poor were angry because they were receiving less free food and entertainment. The rich were angry because, for the first time, they had to pay taxes. The leaders of the revolt were prepared to crown a new emperor. Justinian's advisers urged him to leave the city. Theodora, however, urged him to stay and fight. Justinian and his supporters took Theodora's advice. They stayed in Constantinople, trapped the rebels, killed 300,000 of them, and crushed the uprising. As a result, Justinian kept control of the government and became an even stronger ruler.

Law and Public Works

Justinian was very interested in law and spent much time reading the laws made by other emperors. He decided that the old legal system was too complicated and disorganized. He chose ten men to work out a simpler and better system. This group was headed by a legal scholar named Tribonian (tri bō′ nē ahn).

Tribonian and the others studied the existing laws. They did away with those that were no longer needed. They organized and rewrote those laws that remained. In six years, they had developed a legal code that became the law of the land.

This code came to be known as the Justinian Code. It is considered one of Justinian's greatest achievements. It provided a summary of Roman legal thinking. It also gave later generations insight into the basic ideas of Roman law. It has had a great influence on the legal systems of almost every western country.

Then & Now

Hagia Sophia Hagia Sophia, first built in the reign of Constantine, was twice destroyed by fire. When Justinian rebuilt the church, he ordered it be made fireproof. Earthquakes caused the dome to collapse in 559, but it too was rebuilt. The building became a mosque in 1453, and today it is a museum.

Justinian was as interested in public works as he was in law. He was almost always busy with some building program. He built churches, bridges, monasteries, and forums. He also built a system of forts connected by a large network of roads. When an earthquake destroyed Antioch, he had the whole city rebuilt.

One of Justinian's greatest accomplishments was the church called Hagia Sophia (hag′ē ī sō fē′ uh), or "Holy Wisdom."

EXTENDING THE CONTENT

In May 542, a plague struck Constantinople and raged for four months. The Greek historian Procopius witnessed the epidemic and wrote detailed accounts. At its height, the disease killed 10,000 people a day. By the end of that summer, 300,000 people had died. Justinian contracted the plague, which caused serious political concern because he and Theodora had no children and a successor had yet to be named. Theodora called a secret meeting with her ministers to plan for her husband's nephew to succeed him. Justinian survived the plague. During the months when he was sick, Theodora was in charge and dealt with the plague's devastation.

CHAPTER 21 Assessment

Using Key Terms

You live in ancient Byzantium and are asked to write a paragraph describing your culture. Your paragraph is to be put in a time capsule to be opened by a future generation. Write your paragraph, including the following words.

relics	theology	dowry
mosaics	Greek fire	metropolitans
icons		

Understanding Main Ideas

1. Why did the Roman Empire in the East survive the fall of Rome?
2. How did Constantinople's location help it become a great trading center?
3. How did Christianity affect Byzantine attitudes toward the care of needy people?
4. How did Theodora help women within the Byzantine Empire?
5. What led to the separation of the Eastern Orthodox Church and the Roman Catholic Church in 1054?
6. Why did Byzantine farmers gradually lose their loyalty to the empire?

Critical Thinking

1. What is your opinion of the following statement: "Constantine was wise to model Constantinople after Rome"?
2. What are the advantages for a government to have an offical religion? What are the disadvantages?
3. What do you think had the most to do with the decline of the Byzantine Empire? Explain.
4. What contribution made by the Byzantines do you think was the most important? Explain.

Graphic Organizer Activity

Citizenship Create a chart like the one shown, and use it to show the causes and effects of Justinian's decision to draw up a new code of laws.

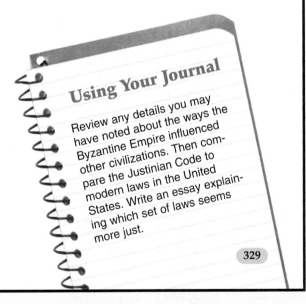

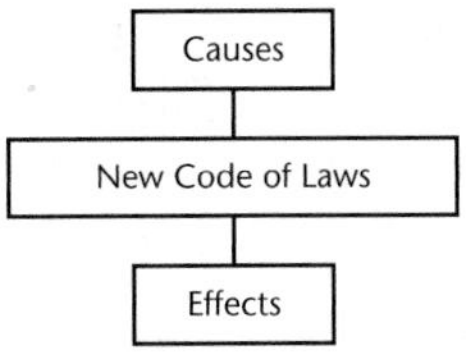

Geography in History

Human Systems Justinian expanded his empire greatly. Refer to the map on page 323. If you had been Justinian, in which direction would you have sent troops next to gain new territory? Why?

Using Your Journal

Review any details you may have noted about the ways the Byzantine Empire influenced other civilizations. Then compare the Justinian Code to modern laws in the United States. Write an essay explaining which set of laws seems more just.

CHAPTER 21 Assessment Answers

Using Key Terms

Paragraphs will vary, but should use descriptive phrases and all the Key Terms.

Understanding Main Ideas

1. Most Christians were united; Constantinople was strong and supported a large army and paid invaders.
2. gave Constantinople control of the sea trade to the Mediterranean and a key land route
3. The Byzantines formed organizations to care for the poor.
4. She convinced Justinian to allow a wife to own land and widows to raise children.
5. disputes over icons and the power of the Pope
6. because the emperor no longer helped protect them

Critical Thinking

1. Answers will vary but students should support opinions.
2. Answers will vary. An advantage might be that it would end conflict. A disadvantage is that it would end freedom of religion.
3. Answers will vary but could include loss of trade and invasions.
4. Answers will vary.

Graphic Organizer Activity

sample responses: *causes*—Justinian's interest in law, disorganization and complication of old laws; *effects*—summarized Roman legal thinking, provided later generations with an insight into the basic ideas of Roman law, had an impact on the legal systems of almost every western country

Bonus Test Question

For Chapter 21 Test

Imagine you were a citizen of Constantinople during the Byzantine Empire and you met a man named Cyril, about whom everyone was talking. What were people saying about this man?

Using Your Journal

Essays will vary. You might call on volunteers to read their essays to the class and have the class weigh the comparison.

Geography in History

Answers will vary but should reflect a logical plan for avoiding geographical features that might make an invasion difficult.

Chapter 22 Planning Guide

Timesaving Tools

TeacherWorks™ All-In-One Planner and Resource Center

- **Interactive Teacher Edition** Access your Teacher Wraparound Edition and your classroom resources with a few easy clicks.
- **Interactive Lesson Planner** Planning has never been easier! Organize your week, month, semester, or year with all the lesson helps you need to make teaching creative, timely, and relevant.

Use Glencoe's **Presentation Plus!** multimedia teacher tool to easily present dynamic lessons that visually excite your students. Using Microsoft PowerPoint® you can customize the presentations to create your own personalized lessons.

Objectives	Reproducible Resources	Multimedia Resources
Section 1 **Islam** Explain how Islam developed around the teachings of Muhammad and the religious beliefs held by Muslims.	Reproducible Lesson Plan Chapter 22 Vocabulary and Guided Reading Activity Reading Essentials and Study Guide 22-1 Chapter 22 Enrichment Activity Section 1 Quiz	Interactive Student Edition CD-ROM Graphic Organizer Transparency 10 Teaching Transparency and Activity 22A Vocabulary PuzzleMaker CD-ROM Interactive Tutor Self-Assessment CD-ROM ExamView® Pro Testmaker CD-ROM Glencoe Skillbuilder Interactive Workbook CD-ROM, Level 1 Presentation Plus! CD-ROM
Section 2 **The Arab Empire** Describe how Islam spread beyond the Arabian Peninsula and what Islamic life was like.	Reproducible Lesson Plan Reading Essentials and Study Guide 22-2 Chapter 22 Chart and Graph Skill Activity Chapter 22 Geography and Map Activity Section 2 Quiz	Teaching Transparency and Activity 22B Vocabulary PuzzleMaker CD-ROM Interactive Tutor Self-Assessment CD-ROM ExamView® Pro Testmaker CD-ROM Glencoe Skillbuilder Interactive Workbook CD-ROM, Level 1
Section 3 **Arab Contributions** Discuss what ideas and inventions the Arab Empire contributed to science, mathematics, medicine, and the arts.	Reproducible Lesson Plan Reading Essentials and Study Guide 22-3 Unit 7 World Literature Reading 1 Section 3 Quiz	Vocabulary PuzzleMaker CD-ROM Interactive Tutor Self-Assessment CD-ROM ExamView® Pro Testmaker CD-ROM Glencoe Skillbuilder Interactive Workbook CD-ROM, Level 1
Chapter 22 **Review and Evaluation**	Chapter 22 Reteaching Activity Chapter 22 Performance Assessment Activity Spanish Chapter Summary and Glossary Chapter 22 Test	Vocabulary PuzzleMaker CD-ROM Interactive Tutor Self-Assessment CD-ROM Glencoe Skillbuilder Interactive Workbook CD-ROM, Level 1 Audiocassettes* ExamView® Pro Testmaker CD-ROM

*Also available in Spanish.

Chapter 22 Planning Guide

✓ Performance Assessment Activities

Sharing Religion Have students research Muslim celebrations other than Ramadan. Suggest they choose either a religious or national holiday to describe in an oral presentation. Encourage students to include visuals displays.

CHAPTER RESOURCES

LITERATURE ABOUT THE PERIOD

Arnold, T.W. and A. Guillame. *The Legacy of Islam.* Gordon Press, 1976.

READINGS FOR THE STUDENT

Powell, Anton. *The Rise of Islam.* Warwick Press, 1980. An overview of Islamic culture.

READINGS FOR THE TEACHER

Editors of Time-Life Books. *What Life Was Like in the Land of the Prophet: Islamic World A.D. 570–1405.* Time-Life Books, 1999. Richly illustrated story of life in the medieval Islamic world.

Mahmud, S.F. *A Short History of Islam.* Oxford University Press, 1989. A study of Islamic civilization and a history of the Islamic Empire.

KEY TO ABILITY LEVELS

Teaching strategies have been coded for varying learning styles and abilities.

L1 Level 1 activities are **basic** activities and should be within the ability range of all students.

L2 Level 2 activities are **average** activities and should be within the ability range of the average to above-average student.

L3 Level 3 activities are **challenging** activities designed for the ability range of above-average students.

ELL ELL activities should be within the ability range of English Language Learning students.

NATIONAL GEOGRAPHIC Teacher's Corner

INDEX TO NATIONAL GEOGRAPHIC MAGAZINE

The following articles relate to this chapter:

- "Long Road Home: A Story of War and Revelation in Afghanistan," by Lois Raimondo, June 2002.
- "In Focus: World of Islam," by Don Belt, January 2002.
- "Eyewitness Afghanistan," by Edward Girardet, December 2001.
- "Petra, Ancient City of Stone," by Don Belt, December 1998.
- "The Promise of Pakistan," by John McCarry, October 1997.
- "India," by Geoffrey C. Ward, May 1997.

NATIONAL GEOGRAPHIC SOCIETY PRODUCTS AVAILABLE FROM GLENCOE

To order the following, call Glencoe at 1-800-334-7344:

- *PicturePack: Physical Geography of the World (Transparencies)*

ADDITIONAL NATIONAL GEOGRAPHIC SOCIETY PRODUCTS

To order the following, call National Geographic at 1-800-368-2728:

- *Arabia: Sand, Sea, and Sky (Video)*
- *Asia (Laminated Desk Maps)*
- *The Soul of Spain (Video)*
- *National Geographic Atlas of World History (Book)*
- *Wonders of the Ancient World: National Geographic Atlas of Archaeology (Book)*

Access *National Geographic's* new dynamic MapMachine Web site and other geography resources at:
www.nationalgeographic.com
www.nationalgeographic.com/maps

THE HISTORY CHANNEL. A&E HOME VIDEO. Biography

The following videotape program is available from Glencoe:

- **Legends of the Arabian Knights**
  0-7670-0232-6

To order, call Glencoe at 1-800-334-7344. To find classroom resources to accompany this video, check the following home pages:

A&E Television: www.aande.com
The History Channel: www.historychannel.com

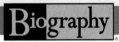

OVERVIEW

Chapter 22 discusses the rise of Islam and its central role in the creation of the Arab Empire.

- **Section 1** describes the rise of Islam.
- **Section 2** discusses the formation of the Arab Empire and the spread of Islam.
- **Section 3** describes the Arab contributions to world civilizations.

CHAPTER OBJECTIVES

After reading Chapter 22, students will be able to:

1. explain the teachings of Muhammad.
2. discuss the religious beliefs held by Muslims.
3. describe how Islam spread beyond the Arabian Peninsula.
4. describe Arab contributions to science, mathematics, medicine, and the arts.

EXAMINING ARTIFACTS

Point out that Islamic beliefs forbade artists from trying to capture living creatures in their work. Nobody, said Muslim Arabs, could re-create the work of God. Call on students to describe the artistic techniques developed to replace representational art. *(Students should note the use of geometric patterns, bright color, beautiful calligraphy, and so on.)* Tell students that they will learn more about the beliefs and accomplishments of Muslim Arabs in this chapter.

PERFORMANCE ASSESSMENT ✓

Use the Performance Assessment activities on page 330B to help you evaluate students as they complete the chapter.

CHAPTER 22

The Spread of Islam

500 A.D.–1300 A.D.

▲ A page from the Quran

A highly decorated ▶ Islamic ceramic lamp

570 A.D.	622 A.D.	710 A.D.	750 A.D.	C. 1290 A.D.
Muhammad born	Muhammad flees from Makkah to Yathrib	Moors invade Spain	Abbasids become rulers of Arab Empire	Ottoman dynasty founded in Asia Minor

TEACHING RESOURCES

TEACHER PLANNING AND SUPPORT

- Reproducible Lesson Plan 22-1, 22-2, 22-3
- Teaching Strategies for the World History Classroom (Including Block Scheduling Pacing Guides)
- Presentation Plus! CD-ROM

REVIEW AND REINFORCEMENT

- Reading Essentials and Study Guide 22-1, 22-2, 22-3
- Chapter 22 Vocabulary and Guided Reading Activity
- Vocabulary PuzzleMaker CD-ROM
- Teaching Transparencies 22A & 22B
- Chapter 22 Reteaching Activity
- Chapter 22 Cooperative Learning Activity
- Chapter 22 Activity Book Activity
- Chapter 22 Chart and Graph Skill Activity
- Reading and Study Skills Foldables
- Interactive Tutor Self-Assessment CD-ROM

APPLICATION AND HANDS-ON ACTIVITIES

- Daily Questions in Social Studies
- World Games Activity Card 9
- Student Presentation Builder CD-ROM

GEOGRAPHY ACTIVITIES

- Chapter 22 Geography and Map Activity
- Outline Map Resource Book

The Quran describes the **pillars of faith,** or the five duties all Muslims must fulfill. The first duty is the confession of faith. All Muslims must recite the Islamic creed that states, "There is no God but Allah, and Muhammad is his prophet."

The second duty deals with prayer. Muslims must pray five times a day, facing Makkah each time. The prayers are said at dawn, noon, late afternoon, sunset, and evening. The prayers can be said anywhere. The only exception is the Friday noon prayer. It is usually recited at a **mosque** (mosk), or Muslim house of worship. There, believers are led by an **imam** (i mam'), or prayer leader.

The third duty has to do with the giving of ***zakah,*** or charity. This is a donation that every Muslim has to give at the rate of 2.5 percent of his or her annual savings. It can be given to needy people or to institutions that are involved in education and social services.

Reading Check What are the **pillars of faith?**

Reading Check What is a **mosque,** and what does an **imam** do there? What action is called for in the giving of ***zakah?***

ISLAMIC FAITH Muslims learn the teachings of the Quran at an early age. A child in the photograph (left) studies passages from the Quran. From the prayer tower (right) of each mosque, announcers call the people to prayer. **What are the five duties that all Muslims must fulfill called?**

Reading Check Answer The **pillars of faith** are five duties that all Muslims must fulfill.

Reading Check Answer A **mosque** is a Muslim house of worship, and an **imam** is the prayer leader at a mosque.
The ***zakah*** calls upon Muslims to give donations at a rate of 2.5 percent of his or her annual savings.

MAKING CONNECTIONS

➤➤ **Religion** Until the Muslims took Makkah and made it their holy city, Muslims would pray facing Jerusalem. To offer a prayer, a Muslim kneels, bows, and touches the forehead to the ground as a symbol of submitting to God.

CAPTION ANSWER

the pillars of faith

DID YOU KNOW ??

Arabic, the language of the Quran, belongs to the Semitic language group. Although no one knows for sure when the language developed, it is known from poets writing before the time of Muhammad that it had reached its present stage 100 years before the prophet was born.

MULTICULTURAL PERSPECTIVES

Up until the 1800s, there were three main caravans to Makkah. One caravan formed in Damascus, Syria, and moved south by way of Madina, and reached Makkah in about 30 days. When Constantinople was captured by the Ottoman Turks in 1453, this caravan started in Constantinople and then went through Damascus to Makkah. Along the way, pilgrims throughout Asia Minor joined the caravan. A second caravan assembled in Cairo and crossed the Sinai Peninsula following the coastal plain of western Arabia to Makkah. This journey took from 30 to 45 days and included pilgrims from North Africa. A third much more sizable caravan crossed the peninsula from Baghdad.

Reading Check Answer
In a ***hajj,*** a Muslim must travel to Makkah, where Muslims from all over the world go to gather two months after Ramadan.

MAKING CONNECTIONS

➤➤ **Religion** The purpose of fasting is to remind Muslims about spiritual values. Ramadan is the ninth month in the Islamic calendar, the month in which the Quran was first revealed to Muhammad.

Use the **Interactive Tutor Self-Assessment CD-ROM** to review Section 1.

L2 **Geography: Human Systems** Discuss the spread of Islamic influence beyond the Arabian Peninsula. Have students use the map on page 337 and a map of the world to identify the modern countries that were partially or totally included in the Arab Empire. ELL

Reading Check Answer
A **caliph** is one of the successors of Muhammad who leads Muslims in the practice of their faith. The first caliph was Abu Bakr, Muhammad's father-in-law.

Use the **Vocabulary Puzzle-Maker CD-ROM** to create crossword and word search puzzles.

The fourth duty deals with fasting. The young, sick people, pregnant women, and travelers do not have to fast. Everyone else, however, must fast each year during the daylight hours of the holy month of Ramadan (ram′ uh dahn).

The fifth duty involves a pilgrimage. Each able Muslim, at least once in his or her lifetime, must travel to Makkah two months after Ramadan. The journey is called the ***hajj*** (haj). For three days, Muslims from all over the world come together for ceremonies and sacrifice.

Reading Check What religious duty is performed in the ***hajj?***

The Quran promises that all believers who fulfill their duties will go to Paradise, which has shade, fruit trees, beautiful flower gardens, cold springs, and singing birds. Hell is a flame-filled pit where drinking water comes from a salty well and where food is a strong-smelling plant that causes hunger.

Section 1 Assessment

1. **Define:** pilgrims, pillars of faith, mosque, imam, *zakah, hajj.*
2. According to Muslim tradition, what caused Muhammad to begin his preachings?
3. What does the Quran say will happen after death?

Critical Thinking

4. **Identifying Cause and Effect** What effect did the rise of Islam have on Byzantium and Persia?

Graphic Organizer Activity

5. Draw this diagram, and use it to summarize the five pillars of faith.

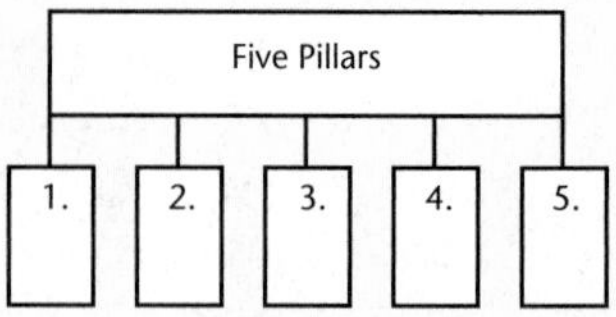

SECTION 2 The Arab Empire

When Muhammad died in 632, his followers needed a new leader. Without someone to guide them, the community could have broken up, and the faith could have been lost. A group of Muslims chose a new leader whom they called *khalifa,* or **caliph** (kā′lif), which means "successor."

Reading Check What is a **caliph,** and who was the first caliph chosen?

The Rightly Guided Caliphs

The first caliph was Abu Bakr (uh bū′ bak′ uhr), Muhammad's father-in-law and close friend. Bakr and the next three caliphs were elected for life. These caliphs ruled from Madina. They kept in close touch with the people and asked advice of their most trusted friends. For this reason, they were called the Rightly Guided Caliphs.

Section 1 Assessment Answers

1. pilgrims, travelers to a shrine (p. 332); pillars of faith, five Muslim duties (p. 335); mosque, house of worship (p. 335); imam, prayer leader (p. 335); *zakah*, charity (p. 335); *hajj*, journey to Makkah (p. 336)
2. The angel Gabriel told him to.
3. All who fulfill their duties will go to Paradise.
4. It shook their foundations.
5. Diagrams should accurately reflect these duties: confession of faith, prayer five times a day, giving of *zakah*, fasting during daylight hours of Ramadan, and pilgrimage to Makkah.

Assign Chapter 22 **Section 1 Quiz** in the TCR. Testmaker available.

Many Arab scientists tried to turn base metals, such as tin, iron, and lead, into gold and silver. These scientists, called **alchemists** (al′ kuh mists), used both chemistry and magic in their work. The word "chemistry" comes from the Arabic word "Al-Chemist." Alchemists were never able to turn base metals into gold and silver. However, their work led to the practice of making experiments and keeping records of the results. The Arabs are considered the founders of modern chemistry.

Arab astronomers studied the heavens. They gave many stars the names they still carry today. They correctly described the eclipses of the sun. They also proved that the moon affects the *tides,* or the rise and fall of the oceans. The astronomers worked with Arab geographers to determine the size of Earth and the distance around it. From their studies, they decided that Earth might be round. The astronomer-geographer al-Idrisi (al i drē′ si) drew the first accurate map of the world.

Arab mathematicians invented algebra and taught it to Europeans. Arab mathematicians also borrowed the numerals 0-9 from Gupta mathematicians and passed them to Europeans.

The Arabs gave much to the field of medicine. Unlike doctors in most other countries, Arab doctors had to pass a test before they could practice medicine. The Arabs set up the world's first school of pharmacy. They also opened the world's first drugstores. They organized medical clinics that traveled all through the empire giving care and medicines to the sick.

Arab doctors were the first to discover that blood *circulates,* or moves, to and from the heart. They were the first to diagnose certain diseases. The Persian doctor ar-Razi (al rā sē′) discovered differences between measles and smallpox. Another Persian, Avicenna (ä vä sēn ä), was the first to understand that tuberculosis is *contagious,* or can be passed from person to person.

Arab doctors informed the scientific community about their discoveries by publishing their findings. Avicenna's *Canon of Medicine,* an encyclopedia of medicine, was used in European medical schools for 500 years.

The Arabs also made many contributions to the arts. One of their best known writings is *The Arabian Nights,* a collection of tales put together from Persian stories. The tales paint an exciting picture of Islamic life at the height of the empire. The Persian poet Omar Khayyám's (ō′ mahr kī yahm′) *Rubáiyát* (rū′ bē aht) has been translated into many languages. It is considered one of the finest poems ever written.

Islamic art is distinct and full of color. It is used on walls, books, rugs, and buildings. It differs from most other art because of the Muslim belief that Allah created all living creatures. Islamic artists think it is a sin to make pictures of Allah's creations. As a result, most of their art is made up of geometric designs entwined with flowers, leaves, and stars.

Reading Check
Why are Arab **alchemists** considered the founders of modern chemistry?

Fun Facts . . .

Arabic Numerals
Europeans resisted the use of Arabic numerals well into the 1400s. An Italian bookkeeping manual insisted that Roman numerals "cannot be falsified as easily as those of the new art of computation, of which one can, with ease, make one out of another, such as turning the zero into a 6 or a 9."

Islamic Medical Diagram

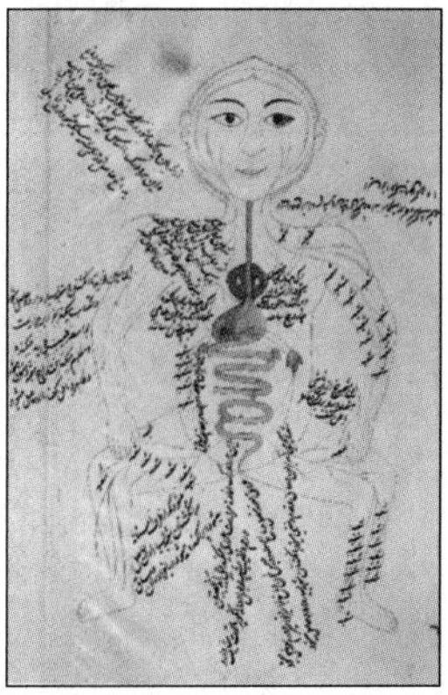

EXTENDING THE CONTENT

Carpets made by craftspeople in the Islamic world are famous for their glowing colors and intricate designs of interwoven leaves and flowers, and geometric figures. From the silk rugs that adorned the caliph's palaces to the carpets of sheep's wool that served as walls between different sections of a tent, carpets have always been far more than floor coverings in this culture. Most Muslims owned small rugs that they used in daily prayer. Today, carpets from Iran, Afghanistan, and other parts of the Islamic world are prized.

Reading Check Answer
Arab **alchemists** made experiments and kept records of their results, laying the foundation for modern chemistry.

DID YOU KNOW ??
The symbol of Islam, the crescent and star, appears on the flags of several nations whose population has a Muslim majority.

A&E HOME VIDEO.

The following videotape program is available from Glencoe to enrich Chapter 22:

- **Legends of the Arabian Knights**

To find classroom resources to accompany this video, check the following home page:

A&E Television:
http://www.aande.com

ASSESS

Check for Understanding

Ask students to summarize orally or in writing the main points of the chapter. Discuss the answers to the Section and Chapter Assessment questions.

Evaluate

Assign Chapter 22 **Performance Assessment Activity** in the TCR.

Administer the **Chapter 22 Test** in the TCR. Testmaker available.

Reteach

Have students review the chapter sections and list the main ideas. Discuss the lists in class.

Assign Chapter 22 **Reteaching Activity** in the TCR.

Enrich

Have students research caravans in the Middle East during this time period. Have them write a description of a typical caravan and the importance of oases to the caravans.

Assign the Chapter 22 **Enrichment Activity** in the TCR.

CLOSE

Write these names on the board: *Abu Bakr, Ali, Umayyads,* and *Abbasids.* Have students identify the names and explain the importance of each in the history of Islam and the expansion of the Arab Empire.

Use the **Interactive Tutor Self-Assessment CD-ROM** to review Section 3.

HISTORY Online

Self-Check Quiz gives students an interactive chapter tutorial. Have them access ***Chapter 22 Quiz*** at humanheritage.glencoe.com

Much of what is known about this time comes from Arabs who wrote down the history of Islam. They began to write about events centered around rulers and peoples. This is how most historians present history today. The Muslim historian Ibn Khaldun (ib' uhn kal dun') wrote about the Arabs, the Berbers, and the Persians. His writings were the first to take into account the influence of geography and climate on people.

Section 3 Assessment

1. **Define:** alchemists.
2. How did the use of the Arabic language promote learning?
3. What are two of the best-known Arab writings?

Critical Thinking

4. **Drawing Conclusions** Do you think the numerals 0 through 9 should be called Arabic or Gupta numerals? Explain.

Graphic Organizer Activity

5. Draw this diagram, and use it to show Arab contributions to science, math, and the arts.

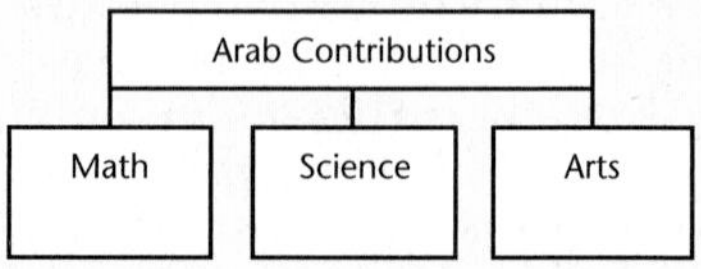

Chapter Summary & Study Guide

1. Muhammad was born in Makkah in 570.
2. In 613, Muhammad began to preach that the only god is Allah. This was the start of the Islamic religion.
3. In 622, Muhammad and his followers went from Makkah to Yathrib, where they organized a new government and army.
4. In 630, Muhammad led his followers into Makkah and dedicated the Ka'bah to Allah.
5. In 631, delegates throughout Arabia declared their loyalty to Muhammad and their belief in teachings such as the five pillars.
6. After Muhammad's death in 632, his followers chose a new leader, known as a caliph, and began building a huge empire.
7. In 661, the capital of the Arab Empire was moved to Damascus and the Umayyad Dynasty began.
8. In 750, the Abbasids took control of the Arab Empire and concentrated on trade rather than war.
9. The Moors in Spain combined Arab and Jewish cultures and allowed religious freedom.
10. The Arabs made many contributions to modern civilization, especially in science, math, and the arts.

HISTORY Online

Self-Check Quiz

Visit the *Human Heritage* Web site at humanheritage.glencoe.com and click on ***Chapter 22—Self-Check Quiz*** to assess your understanding of this chapter.

Section 3 Assessment Answers

1. alchemists, Arab scientists (p. 343)
2. It helped unite scholars throughout the Arab Empire.
3 *The Arabian Nights* and *Rubáiyát*
4. Answers will vary, but students should support their opinions about the development of numbering systems with reasons.
5. Completed charts should include the many accomplishments cited on pages 343–344. In a follow-up activity, you might challenge students to vote on the top five Arab ideas or inventions.

Assign Chapter 22 **Section 3 Quiz** in the TCR. Testmaker available.

CHAPTER 22 Assessment

Using Key Terms

Imagine you are a traveler in the Arab Empire. Use the following words to write a journal entry describing your impressions of the empire.

pilgrims	pillars of faith	mosque
imam	*zakah*	*hajj*
caliph	vizier	alchemists

Understanding Main Ideas

1. How did Bedouins earn a living?
2. Why did Muhammad begin to spend time alone in a cave outside Makkah?
3. Why did Makkah's leaders persecute Muhammad and his followers?
4. What is the Islamic creed?
5. In what direction do Muslims face when they pray?
6. What does the Quran promise all believers who fulfill their duties?
7. What brought about the downfall of the Umayyad Dynasty?
8. What did the name "Arab" mean under the Abbasids?
9. What discoveries did Arab doctors make?

Critical Thinking

1. What role did religion play in Arab life?
2. How did the Moorish kingdom in Spain show it had been influenced by different cultures?
3. Which Arab contribution do you think has most affected other civilizations? Explain your choice.
4. What parts of life in the Arab Empire would you have liked? What parts would you have disliked?

Graphic Organizer Activity

History Create a time line like the one shown, and use it to summarize the main events in Muhammad's life. (Dates have been provided to help you get started.)

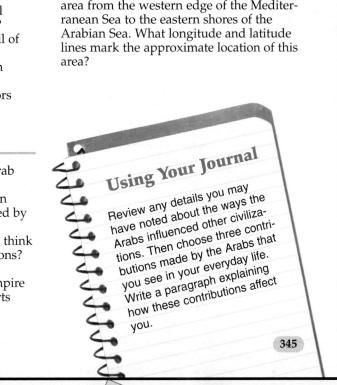

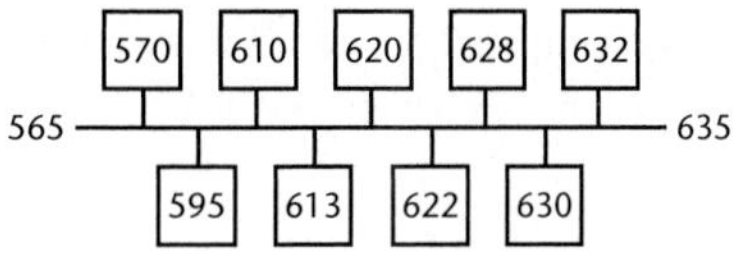

Geography in History

The World in Spatial Terms Islam spread across a wide area, as seen on the map on page 337. It included most of the area from the western edge of the Mediterranean Sea to the eastern shores of the Arabian Sea. What longitude and latitude lines mark the approximate location of this area?

Using Your Journal

Review any details you may have noted about the ways the Arabs influenced other civilizations. Then choose three contributions made by the Arabs that you see in your everyday life. Write a paragraph explaining how these contributions affect you.

CHAPTER 22 Assessment Answers

Using Key Terms

Journal entries will vary.

Understanding Main Ideas

1. as herders and traders
2. because he was troubled by the corruption in Makkah
3. They were afraid of losing money because fewer pilgrims would come to Makkah.
4. a confession of faith stating "There is no God but Allah, and Muhammad is His prophet."
5. toward Makkah
6. They will go to Paradise.
7. conquered people who became Muslim felt unfairly treated; the division of Muslims into the Shi'ah and the Sunni
8. any subject who spoke Arabic
9. the circulation of the blood, the differences between measles and smallpox, and that tuberculosis is contagious

Critical Thinking

1. brought pilgrims to Makkah, which helped its economy; united Muslims; set guidelines for the way Muslims lived
2. Many groups lived there; and Muslims, Jews, and Christians studied medicine and philosophy together.
3. Answers will vary.
4. Answers will vary, but students should cite specific examples.

Graphic Organizer Activity

570—birth; 595—marriage; 610—vision of Gabriel; 613—starting of preaching in Makkah; 620—invitation to come to Yathrib; 622—flight from Makkah to Yathrib; 628—peace treaty with people of Makkah; 630—violation of treaty and conquest of Makkah by Muhammad and his followers; 632—death

Bonus Test Question

For Chapter 22 Test

What is false about the following: A man and woman move to Madina in 613, the year Muhammad began preaching. That year, called the *Anno Hijrah,* they joined the thousands who supported Muhammad.

Using Your Journal

Paragraphs will vary but should include three specific examples. You might ask volunteers to read their paragraphs to the class.

Geography in History

The area spanned from about 45° N to 25° N and 5° W to 65° E.

Chapter 23 Planning Guide

Timesaving Tools

TeacherWorks™ All-In-One Planner and Resource Center

- **Interactive Teacher Edition** Access your Teacher Wraparound Edition and your classroom resources with a few easy clicks.
- **Interactive Lesson Planner** Planning has never been easier! Organize your week, month, semester, or year with all the lesson helps you need to make teaching creative, timely, and relevant.

PRESENTATION Plus!

Use Glencoe's **Presentation Plus!** multimedia teacher tool to easily present dynamic lessons that visually excite your students. Using Microsoft PowerPoint® you can customize the presentations to create your own personalized lessons.

Objectives	Reproducible Resources	Multimedia Resources
Section 1 **Early Eastern Slavs** Describe what life and economic development was like for the earliest Eastern Slavs.	Reproducible Lesson Plan Chapter 23 Vocabulary and Guided Reading Activity Reading Essentials and Study Guide 23-1 Chapter 23 Chart and Graph Skill Activity Section 1 Quiz	Interactive Student Edition CD-ROM Graphic Organizer Transparency 11 Vocabulary PuzzleMaker CD-ROM Interactive Tutor Self-Assessment CD-ROM ExamView® Pro Testmaker CD-ROM Glencoe Skillbuilder Interactive Workbook CD-ROM, Level 1 Presentation Plus! CD-ROM
Section 2 **Kievan Rus** Summarize how early Rus states developed around Kiev.	Reproducible Lesson Plan Reading Essentials and Study Guide 23-2 Chapter 23 Cooperative Learning Activity Chapter 23 Enrichment Activity Section 2 Quiz	Teaching Transparencies and Activities 23A & 23B Vocabulary PuzzleMaker CD-ROM Interactive Tutor Self-Assessment CD-ROM ExamView® Pro Testmaker CD-ROM Glencoe Skillbuilder Interactive Workbook CD-ROM, Level 1
Section 3 **The Mongol Conquest** Analyze how the Mongol invasion influenced internal development and foreign relations of Rus states.	Reproducible Lesson Plan Reading Essentials and Study Guide 23-3 Section 3 Quiz	Vocabulary PuzzleMaker CD-ROM Interactive Tutor Self-Assessment CD-ROM ExamView® Pro Testmaker CD-ROM Glencoe Skillbuilder Interactive Workbook CD-ROM, Level 1
Section 4 **The Rise of Moscow** Discuss how Moscow became powerful and how the czars affected life in Rus states.	Reproducible Lesson Plan Reading Essentials and Study Guide 23-4 Chapter 23 Geography and Map Activity Unit 7 World Literature Reading 2 Section 4 Quiz	Vocabulary PuzzleMaker CD-ROM Interactive Tutor Self-Assessment CD-ROM ExamView® Pro Testmaker CD-ROM Glencoe Skillbuilder Interactive Workbook CD-ROM, Level 1
Chapter 23 **Review and Evaluation**	Chapter 23 Reteaching Activity Chapter 23 Performance Assessment Activity Unit 7 Standardized Test Practice Spanish Chapter Summary and Glossary Chapter 23 Test	Vocabulary PuzzleMaker CD-ROM Interactive Tutor Self-Assessment CD-ROM Glencoe Skillbuilder Interactive Workbook CD-ROM, Level 1 Audiocassettes* ExamView® Pro Testmaker CD-ROM

*Also available in Spanish.

Chapter 23 Planning Guide

✓ Performance Assessment Activities

Newspaper Articles Have students write five newspaper headlines about major events in the life of Ivan the Great or one of the other czars of the early Rus states. Then have the students choose one of the headlines and write a newspaper article explaining the details of the headline.

CHAPTER RESOURCES

LITERATURE ABOUT THE PERIOD

Kimmel, Eric A. *Mishka, Pishka, and Fishka.* Coward, McCann & Geoghan, 1976. English translations of folktales from Ukraine.

READINGS FOR THE STUDENT

Sutcliff, Rosemary. *Blood Feud.* E.P. Dutton, 1977. Young adult novel about an English boy sold as an enslaved person to Varangian traders.

READINGS FOR THE TEACHER

Chambers, John. *The Devil's Horsemen: The Mongol Invasion of Europe.* Atheneum, 1985. Traces the westward push of the Mongols, beginning with the invasion of Russia.

Klein, Mina C. *The Kremlin: Citadel of History.* Macmillan, 1973. Describes the origin and growth of the Kremlin from the ninth century to modern times.

KEY TO ABILITY LEVELS

Teaching strategies have been coded for varying learning styles and abilities.

L1 Level 1 activities are **basic** activities and should be within the ability range of all students.

L2 Level 2 activities are **average** activities and should be within the ability range of the average to above-average student.

L3 Level 3 activities are **challenging** activities designed for the ability range of above-average students.

ELL ELL activities should be within the ability range of English Language Learning students.

NATIONAL GEOGRAPHIC Teacher's Corner

INDEX TO NATIONAL GEOGRAPHIC MAGAZINE

The following articles relate to this chapter:

- "Russia's Frozen Inferno," by Jeremy Schmidt, August 2001.
- "Hunting with Eagles" by Candice S. Millard, September 1999.
- "A Comeback for the Cossacks," by Mike Edwards, November 1998.

NATIONAL GEOGRAPHIC SOCIETY PRODUCTS AVAILABLE FROM GLENCOE

To order the following, call Glencoe at 1-800-334-7344:

- *PicturePack: Physical Geography of the World (Transparencies)*
- *PicturePack: World Geography Library (Transparencies)*

ADDITIONAL NATIONAL GEOGRAPHIC SOCIETY PRODUCTS

To order the following, call National Geographic at 1-800-368-2728:

- *The Mongols (Maps)*
- *Physical Geography of the Continents Series: Asia (Video)*

Access *National Geographic*'s MapMachine Web site and other geography resources at:

www.nationalgeographic.com
www.nationalgeographic.com/maps

THE HISTORY CHANNEL. A&E HOME VIDEO. Biography

The following videotape programs are available from Glencoe:

- **Genghis Khan: Terror and Conquest**
  1-56501-578-9
- **Faberge: Imperial Jeweler**
  1-56501-878-8

To order, call Glencoe at 1-800-334-7344. To find classroom resources to accompany these videos, check:

A&E Television: www.aande.com
The History Channel: www.historychannel.com

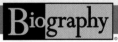

Introducing CHAPTER 23

OVERVIEW

Chapter 23 discusses the Eastern Slav civilization.

➤ **Section 1** describes the influences that transformed the early Slav agricultural settlements into trading centers.

➤ **Section 2** discusses the emergence of a Rus state.

➤ **Section 3** describes the effects of the Mongol invasions on the Rus states.

➤ **Section 4** discusses the reigns of Ivan the Great and Ivan the Terrible.

CHAPTER OBJECTIVES

After reading Chapter 23, students will be able to:

1. describe what life was like for the earliest Eastern Slavs.

2. summarize how early Rus states developed around Kiev.

3. analyze how Eastern Christianity influenced the Rus.

4. explain changes the Mongols brought about in Rus life.

5. examine how the czars affected life in Rus states.

EXAMINING ARTIFACTS

Direct students to study the artifacts for evidence of contact between the Eastern Slavs and the Byzantines. *(Students may note the influence of Christianity, the use of icons, and so on.)* Tell students to study the time line on this page. Ask: What other people influenced the civilization developed by the Eastern Slavs? *(Mongols)*

PERFORMANCE ASSESSMENT ✓

Use the Performance Assessment activities on page 346B to help you evaluate students as they complete the chapter.

CHAPTER 23

The Eastern Slavs

500 A.D.–1035 A.D.

▲ A Russian icon, the archangel Michael

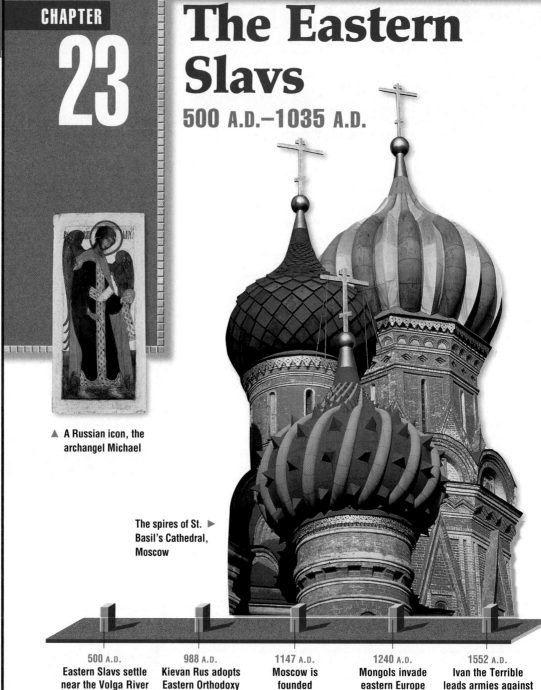

The spires of St. Basil's Cathedral, Moscow ►

500 A.D.	988 A.D.	1147 A.D.	1240 A.D.	1552 A.D.
Eastern Slavs settle near the Volga River	Kievan Rus adopts Eastern Orthodoxy	Moscow is founded	Mongols invade eastern Europe	Ivan the Terrible leads armies against the Mongols

TEACHING RESOURCES

TEACHER PLANNING AND SUPPORT

- Reproducible Lesson Plan 23-1, 23-2, 23-3, 23-4
- Teaching Strategies for the World History Classroom (Including Block Scheduling Pacing Guides)
- Presentation Plus! CD-ROM

REVIEW AND REINFORCEMENT

- Reading Essentials and Study Guide 23-1, 23-2, 23-3, 23-4
- Chapter 23 Vocabulary and Guided Reading Activity
- Vocabulary PuzzleMaker CD-ROM
- Teaching Transparencies 23A & 23B
- Chapter 23 Reteaching Activity
- Chapter 23 Cooperative Learning Activity
- Chapter 23 Activity Book Activity
- Chapter 23 Chart and Graph Skill Activity
- Reading and Study Skills Foldables
- Interactive Tutor Self-Assessment CD-ROM
- Unit 7 MindJogger VideoQuiz

APPLICATION AND HANDS-ON ACTIVITIES

- Daily Questions in Social Studies
- World Games Activity Card 7
- World Crafts Activity Card 8
- Student Presentation Builder CD-ROM

Chapter Focus

Read to Discover

- What life was like for the earliest Eastern Slavs.
- How early Rus states developed around Kiev.
- How Eastern Christianity influenced the people of Rus.
- What changes the Mongols brought about in Rus life.
- How Moscow became powerful.
- How the czars affected life in Muscovy.

HISTORY Online

Chapter Overview

Visit the *Human Heritage* Web site at **humanheritage.glencoe.com** and click on ***Chapter 23—Chapter Overviews*** to preview this chapter.

Terms to Learn

izbas
boyars
veche
khan
kremlin
czar

People to Know

Rurik
Vladimir I
Ivan the Great
Ivan the Terrible

Places to Locate

Volga River
Kiev
Dnieper River
Moscow

Why It's Important North of the Byzantine Empire lived a people that historians today call Slavs. All that is known about their origins is that they were Indo-Europeans, like the Aryans who entered the Indus Valley and the Dorians who conquered the Mycenaeans. About 500 A.D., the Slavs began to develop well-organized settlements in eastern Europe in the areas now known as eastern Poland and western Ukraine.

SECTION 1 Early Eastern Slavs

About 500 A.D., a group of Eastern Slavs began to move eastward toward the Volga (vol' guh) River. They were hunters and farmers who were the ancestors of Ukrainians, Belarussians, and Russians. They settled in villages made up of about 25 related families. Each family owned a house that was built partly underground to provide warmth during the cold winter months. The land, animals, tools, and seed belonged to the village.

The oldest male governed the village with the help of a council. He assigned villagers different farming tasks and judged quarrels. During attacks, he acted as military leader.

By the 600s, the Eastern Slavs controlled all the land as far east as the Volga River. To clear this heavily forested land for farming, farmers used a method called *slash-and-burn*. They cut

HISTORY Online

Chapter Overview introduces students to chapter content and key terms. Have them access ***Chapter 23 Overview*** at **humanheritage.glencoe.com**

FOCUS

Bellringer

Write this direction on the board: *List as many cities in Russia as you can.*

Motivational Activity

Have students share their lists of Russian cities. One city likely to be on their lists is Moscow. Tell students that they will learn about the early history of Moscow and other Russian cities in this chapter.

GUIDE TO READING

Reading Strategy

Ask students to read "Why It's Important" and summarize the chapter's main theme. *(The Slavs developed well-organized settlements and spread their influence through part of what is now eastern Europe.)*

Vocabulary Precheck

Ask students to define each of the "Terms to Learn." Have a volunteer consult the dictionary for any unfamiliar words. L1 ELL

Use the Vocabulary PuzzleMaker CD-ROM for Chapter 23 to create a crossword puzzle. L1

Assign Chapter 23 Vocabulary and Guided Reading Activity.

Assign Reading Essentials and Study Guide 23-1.

GEOGRAPHY ACTIVITIES

- Chapter 23 Geography and Map Activity
- Building Geography Skills for Life
- Outline Map Resource Book

INTERDISCIPLINARY CONNECTIONS

- Unit 7 World Literature Reading 2
- World Art & Architecture Transparency 14, *Ukrainian Easter Eggs*
- World Music: A Cultural Legacy

ENRICHMENT AND EXTENSION

- World History Primary Source Document Library CD-ROM
- Chapter 23 Enrichment Activity

ASSESSMENT AND EVALUATION

- Chapter 23 Performance Assessment Activity
- Chapter 23 Section Quizzes 23-1, 23-2, 23-3, 23-4
- Chapter 23 Test
- Chapter 23 ExamView® Pro Testmaker CD-ROM
- Chapter 23 Digests Audiocassettes Activities and Tests

SPANISH RESOURCES

- Chapter 23 Spanish Chapter Summary and Glossary
- Chapter 23 Spanish Digests Audiocassettes Activities and Tests

TEACH

Guided Practice

L1 **Daily Life** Have students imagine they are members of the early Eastern Slavs and write an entry in their diaries describing a day in their lives. Have students share their entries with the class. ELL

Reading Check Answer *Izbas* were one-room cabins with gabled roofs and wooden window frames.

GEOGRAPHY AND HISTORY

Russia's rivers form a unique network of navigable waterways. Although all the major rivers run north-south, their lateral branches provide east-west access to land. This helped increase trade for the early Eastern Slavs.

CAPTION ANSWER

It was only one room. Although each *izba* had a fireplace, some did not have chimneys, and smoke had to escape through the shutters that covered the windows.

down trees, which they burned for fertilizer. On the cleared land, they planted crops such as barley, rye, and flax. After a few years, when the wood fertilizer in the soil had been used up, the farmers moved to a new place. There, they repeated the process.

The forests provided the East Slavs with all the timber they needed. The East Slavs soon became skilled in building with wood. They made musical instruments out of wood and used logs to make boats and ***izbas*** (uhz bahs'). An izba was a one-room log cabin with a gabled roof and wooden window frames. The whole family lived, worked, ate, and slept in the single room. Although each izba had a fireplace, some did not have a chimney. Smoke from fires had to escape through shutters that covered the windows.

Reading Check What did Eastern Slavic ***izbas*** look like?

The villagers worshiped many gods and honored nature, spirits, and ancestors. The most popular gods were Volos (vō' lōs), who protected cattle and sheep; Perun (pār' uhn), the god of thunder and lightning; and the Great Mother, the goddess of the land and harvest. The people built wooden images of their favorite gods on the highest ground outside the villages.

There were many slow-moving rivers in the area west of the Volga. At first, the East Slavs used them as roads between their villages. Before long, they began using them for trade as well. They set up a trade route that ran from the Baltic Sea in the north to the Caspian Sea in the south.

RUS CABIN Houses in early Rus towns and villages were made of wood from the surrounding thick forests. Here, a modern Russian cabin is shown that is a good example of decorative styles passed on from early Rus artisans. **What was the inside of an izba, or Rus log cabin, like?**

Then & Now

Slavic Peoples Descendants of the West Slavs include the people of Poland, the Czech Republic, and Slovakia. Descendants of the South Slavs include Serbs, Croats, Slovenes, and Bosnians. Most West Slavs follow the Roman Catholic Church. South Slavs generally follow Eastern Orthodox Christianity, except for those Bosnians who follow Islam.

MEETING SPECIAL NEEDS

Have students who are tactile/kinesthetic learners make models or dioramas of early Russian towns or villages. Students can use the information in the textbook and in other resources. Display the models or dioramas in the classroom.

Refer to ***Inclusion for the Middle School Social Studies Classroom: Strategies and Activities*** for additional resources.

By the end of the 800s, the East Slavs had built many trading towns along the riverbanks. During the five months of winter, merchants who lived in the towns gathered furs, honey, and other forest products from the people in neighboring villages. In spring, when the ice on the rivers had melted, the merchants loaded their goods on boats and floated south to Byzantium. There, they traded their goods for cloth, wine, weapons, and jewelry. Trade helped the East Slavs to live more comfortably and to develop their civilization.

Drawing of Rus Sled

The Eastern Slavs, to protect their trade route, relied on Viking warriors from Scandinavia. These men were known as Varangians, and the route was called the Varangian Route or the route from the Varangians to the Greeks. Eventually, the Varangians became part of the larger Slav population.

Section 1 Assessment

1. **Define:** *izbas.*
2. How were early Eastern Slavic villages governed?
3. Why were rivers important to the Eastern Slavs?

Critical Thinking

4. **Making Inferences** Why do you think the Eastern Slavs chose the Vikings to protect their trade routes?

Graphic Organizer Activity

5. Draw this diagram, and use it to show details about early Eastern Slavic life.

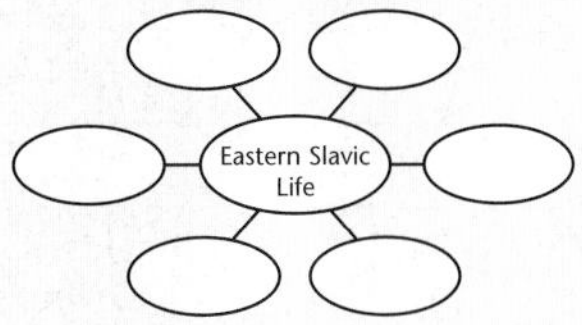

SECTION 2 Kievan Rus

In 862, a Varangian named Rurik became the prince of Novgorod (nahv′ guh rahd), a northern town on the East Slav trading route. About 20 years later, Rurik's Varangian friend Oleg (ō′ leg) established the state of Kievan Rus. The term "Rus" meant "warrior band." He set up his capital at Kiev (kē ev′).

Kiev stood on a group of hills overlooking the main bend in the Dnieper (nē′ puhr) River. It was the southernmost town on the Varangian trading route. Whoever ruled Kiev controlled trade with Byzantium. Kiev also lay close to where the Ukraine forest turned into a *steppe* (step), or grassland. For hundreds of years, this steppe had served central Asian warriors as a highway into Europe. Because of this, Kiev was in a good location to protect merchant ships from attack.

Painting of Eastern Slav Warriors

The Kievan Rus state that Oleg established was really a group of small territories. The main ruler was the Grand Prince of Kiev. He was helped by local princes, rich merchants, and

L2 **Culture** Discuss the influences from the Byzantines on early Slav people *(trade items such as silk, jewels, food; the Cyrillic alphabet; and Christianity).* Ask students to consider how they think the early Eastern Slavs might have felt about these influences on their traditional culture and practices. Suggest they write a dialogue that expresses the feelings of two Eastern Slavs.

MAKING CONNECTIONS

➤➤ **History** Around 1100 A.D. Slavic traditions were written down in the *Primary Chronicle,* a record that combines legends and facts. According to the *Primary Chronicle,* in about 860 A.D. the Slavic people from the northern forest village of Novgorod asked Vikings from Scandinavia for aid: "Our land is great and rich, but there is no order in it. Come to rule and reign over us." The Viking leader Rurik accepted the invitation.

Use **Interactive Tutor Self-Assessment CD-ROM** to review Section 1.

Use the **Vocabulary PuzzleMaker CD-ROM** to create crossword and word search puzzles.

Section 1 Assessment Answers

1. *izbas,* one-room log cabins (p. 348)
2. by the oldest male with the help of a council
3. because they were used like roads between the Rus villages and for trade
4. Answers will vary but might include that they needed people to protect their trade route.
5. sample details: lived in villages made up of about 25 related families; built houses partly underground; land, tools, animals, and seed belonged to village; oldest male, with help of a council, governed village; used slash-and-burn farming; skilled at building and making things out of wood; worshiped many gods, nature spirits, and ancestors

Assign Chapter 23 **Section 1 Quiz** in the TCR. Testmaker available.

L1 Geography: Places and Regions Have students trace an outline map of eastern Europe and draw and label the following on the map: Dnieper, Don, and Volga rivers; Novgorod, Smolensk, Moscow, Kiev, and Constantinople; the Black and Baltic seas. Then have students draw and label the Varangian Route. Point out the openness of the land to attackers. ELL

L2 Geography: Places and Regions Refer students to the map, "Kievan Rus" on page 350, and have them trace the Varangian Route. Ask students to identify the part of the route that did not follow a river or body of water. ***(the north central part of Kievan Rus)***

MAP STUDY

Answer

Baltic Sea, Dnieper River, Black Sea (to Mediterranean Sea)

Assign the Chapter 23 **Geography and Map Activity** in the TCR.

Reading Check Answer

The **boyars** were landowning nobles.

The *veche* did everything from settling business disputes to accepting or removing a prince.

DID YOU KNOW ??

Tribute usually consisted of one animal skin—black marten, fox, or squirrel—per year from each household.

Kievan Rus

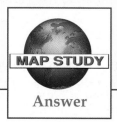

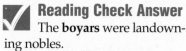

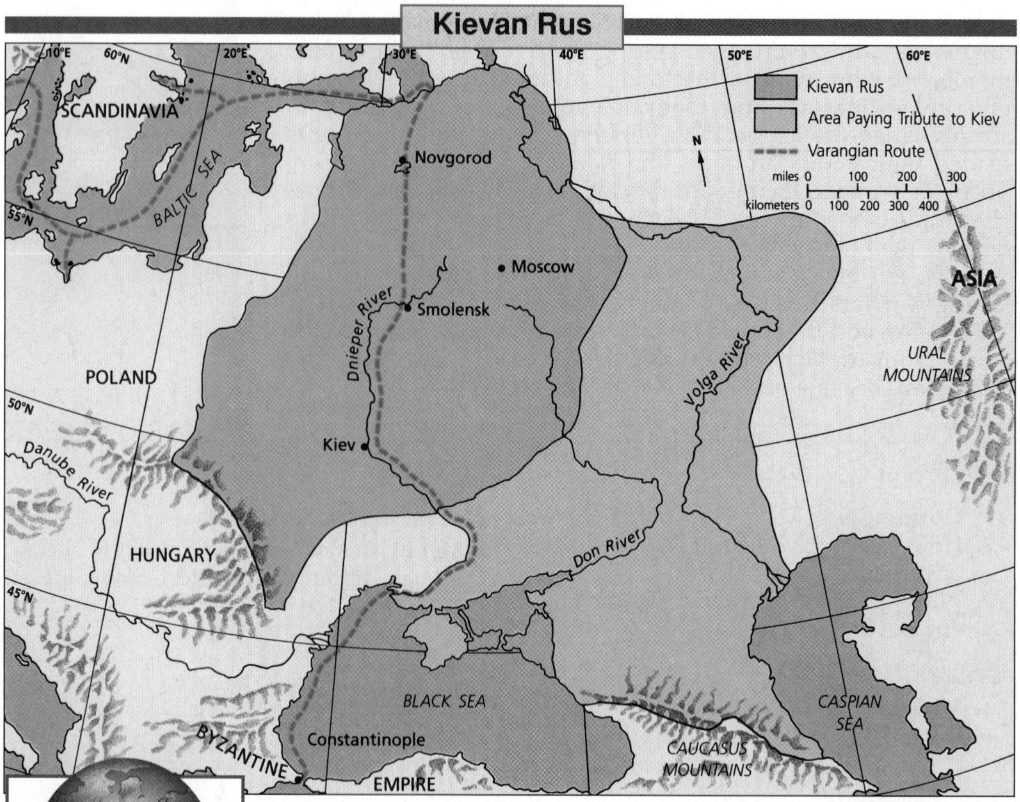

MAP STUDY

PLACES AND REGIONS **Along what bodies of water did the Varangian Route extend?**

boyars (bō yahrs'), or landowning nobles. The Grand Prince collected tribute from the local princes who in turn collected it from the people in their territories.

A ***veche*** (ve' chuh), or assembly, handled the daily matters of the towns. It did everything from settling business differences to accepting or removing a prince. Any free man could call a meeting of the veche by ringing the town bell.

Reading Check Who were the **boyars?** What daily matters were handled by the ***veche?***

Vladimir I and the Eastern Orthodox Church

One of the most important princes of Kiev was Vladimir I (vlad' uh mēr), a good soldier and a strong ruler. He spent the early years of his reign expanding Kievan Rus territory. His armies pushed the country's borders west into Poland and north along the stormy Baltic coast.

In 988, Vladimir chose Eastern, or Byzantine, Christianity as the country's official religion. The story is told about Vladimir's long search for a new faith that would unite the people. Vladimir sent a number of people to other countries to observe different

MEETING SPECIAL NEEDS

Students with a hearing impairment may need extra visual help when learning the material in this chapter. Select an advanced student to prepare a graphic organizer of key events in the chapter. Have students list Key Terms under appropriate events once organizers are complete. Have students share their organizers in small groups.

Refer to ***Inclusion for the Middle School Social Studies Classroom: Strategies and Activities*** for additional resources.

religions. Those sent were not impressed with what they saw in Islamic, Jewish, or Roman Catholic worship. Then, in Byzantium's Hagia Sophia, they saw Eastern Orthodox worship. They were stunned by its beauty. When they returned to Kievan Rus, Vladimir accepted Eastern Orthodoxy as the official religion.

The Eastern Orthodox Church brought Byzantine culture to Kievan Rus. Priests from Byzantium taught the people religious rituals and the art of painting icons. They learned to write their language in the Cyrillic alphabet. Sons of boyars and priests were sent to newly built schools. The look of Kievan Rus towns changed as stone churches with domes and arches rose among the wooden buildings. Monasteries appeared.

Eastern Orthodoxy gave the Kievan Rus people a sense of belonging to the civilized world. However, it separated them

RELIGIOUS LIFE Eastern Orthodoxy inspired art and architecture in Kievan Rus. These later Russian icons (left) closely resembled Byzantine examples. Stone churches with ornate, tiled domes (right) were built in Rus towns. **How did Eastern Orthodoxy separate Kievan Rus from the culture of western Europe?**

L2 **Daily Life** Ask students to imagine they are going to be exchange students from Kiev to another country. Have them write letters to their host families describing their own city, home, and family.

MAKING CONNECTIONS

>> **Language** The Kievan Rus people told stories about Vladimir and the *bogatyrs,* or knights, that are similar to western European tales about King Arthur and his Knights of the Round Table.

CAPTION ANSWER

Since Russian scholars had books in their own language, they developed their own body of learning separate from that of the West.

COOPERATIVE LEARNING

Tell students that Russian artists excelled at painted lacquer boxes. One of their favorite themes was scenes from traditional Russian fairy tales. Request several students to locate some of these tales for reading or retelling to the class. Many of these tales can be located on the Internet or in children's collections at the library. Possible stories include: "Prince Ivan and the Firebird," "The Little Humpbacked Pony," "The Magic Golden Fish," "The Tale of the Dead Princess," "Old Man Winter," and "The Snow Maiden."

After students have heard the stories, show some samples or pictures of lacquered boxes to the class. Then organize the class into groups, and have them design sketches for lacquered boxes based on the fairy tales told in class.

Assign Chapter 23 *Cooperative Learning Activity* in the TCR.

L1 **History** Have students write a short personality sketch from what they learn about the life and achievements of one of the following: Oleg, Vladimir I, Yaroslav the Wise. Have students share their personality sketches with the class.

L3 **The Arts** Have students find examples of Eastern Slavic folktales or legends, music, or art. Traditional musical instruments, art tools, or popular art media could also be included. They should give a brief presentation to the class on the subject of the research including any examples they found.

MAKING CONNECTIONS

>> **History** The marriages of Yaroslav's sister to the king of Poland and his daughters to the kings of France, Hungary, and Norway indicated Yaroslav's prestige among European rulers.

Use **Interactive Tutor Self-Assessment CD-ROM** to review Section 2.

Fur-lined Crown

from western Europe. Since Kievan scholars had books in their own language, they had developed their own body of learning separate from that of the West.

Yaroslav the Wise Another important ruler of early Rus was Yaroslav (yuh ruh slahf'), son of Vladimir I. Yaroslav became the Grand Prince of Kiev in 1019, after a long struggle with his brothers. Yaroslav was very interested in learning. He invited scholars from Byzantium to live in Kiev, and he was called Yaroslav the Wise.

Yaroslav encouraged artisans to practice their skills. The artisans built magnificent brick churches covered with white plaster and decorated with gold. Artists covered the walls of Yaroslav's palace in Kiev with scenes of music and hunting.

Under Yaroslav's rule, Kievan Rus enjoyed a golden age of peace and prosperity. Kiev grew until the city was larger than either Paris or London. Yaroslav developed closer ties with western Europe by family marriages.

Yaroslav also organized Kievan Rus laws based on old Slavic customs and Byzantine law. Under Yaroslav's code, crimes against property were thought to be more serious than those against people. There was no death penalty. In fact, criminals usually were not punished physically but had to pay a fine.

Then . . . & Now

Pravda The Russian word *pravda* means "truth," but during Yaroslav's reign it also meant "justice." The Kievan legal system that Yaroslav organized was called *Russkaya Pravda.* In modern times, the word became familiar to the West as the name of a Moscow newspaper.

Decline of Kievan Rus Kievan Rus began to decline around 1054. After Yaroslav's death, the princes of Kiev began to fight over the throne. People from the steppe took advantage of this fighting and attacked Kievan Rus's frontiers. This upset the trade flow which meant the loss of Kiev's major source of wealth. Kievan Rus became more isolated. In 1169 Kiev was attacked and plundered by Andrei Bogoliubsky, who wanted Kiev destroyed. The area never recovered.

Gradually, Kievan Rus changed from a trading land of towns into a farming land of peasants. To escape the invaders from the steppe, many of its people fled to the north and settled in the dense forests along the upper Volga.

Section 2 Assessment

1. **Define:** boyars, *veche.*
2. Why was Kiev a good location to build a city?
3. How did the decline of Kiev affect the area and people?

Critical Thinking

4. **Demonstrating Reasoned Judgment** How would you have felt about Yaroslav's code of laws and his ways to punish criminals? Explain.

Graphic Organizer Activity

5. Draw this diagram, and use it to show the causes and effects of Vladimir I's acceptance of Eastern Orthodoxy as the official religion of Kievan Rus.

Causes	Acceptance of Eastern Orthodoxy	Effects

Section 2 Assessment Answers

1. boyars, landowning nobles (p. 350); *veche*, Rus assembly (p. 350)
2. stood on a group of hills overlooking the main bend of the Dnieper River; at the southernmost end of the Varangian trading route; controlled trade with Byzantium; close to steppe; able to protect merchant ships from attack
3. It changed Rus states into a farming land of peasants, and more people fled north.
4. Answers will vary, but students should include reasons for their feelings about the punishments.
5. *causes*—sent people to observe different religions; stunned by the beauty of Hagia Sophia; *effects*—learned rituals, the art of icon painting, and the Cyrillic alphabet from Byzantine priests; domes appeared on churches; monasteries built; gained a sense of belonging to a broader world

Assign Chapter 23 **Section 2 Quiz** in the TCR. Testmaker available.

SECTION 3 The Mongol Conquest

About 1240, a group of different but united tribes known as Mongols (mon′ guhls) swept out of central Asia and took control of Rus principalities, or states. They destroyed villages and towns and killed many people. They made the Rus people pay tribute to the **khan** (kahn), or Mongol leader. They also made the Rus citizens serve in the Mongol armies.

Reading Check What duties did the Rus people have to perform for the **khan?**

The Church The Eastern Orthodox Church remained strong during the Mongol invasion. Priests continued to preach and to write. They encouraged the people to love their land and their religion.

During this time, monks began to found monasteries deep in the northern forests. They were followed by Rus farmers searching for new land. Soon, towns and villages began to grow up around the monasteries. Although the Mongol rule caused Rus people to cling more to their religion, it also made them distrustful of ideas and practices from other countries.

Fun Facts . . . .

A Lone Cathedral Mongol invaders completely destroyed Kiev. The only building left standing was the cathedral of Saint Sophia, which contains the tomb of Yaroslav.

Linking Across Time

Easter Eggs The Eastern Orthodoxy practiced by the Rus people included elements of early Eastern Slavic religions. Painted clay eggs (below) associated with springtime became the models for the eggs associated with the Christian festival of Easter. In the late 1800s and early 1900s, Russian goldsmith Carl Faberge elevated these eggs into what are now priceless works of art (right) housed in museums around the world. **How did the Mongol conquest strengthen the Rus Church?**

Reading Check Answer Under the **khan,** the Rus people paid tribute and served in Mongol armies.

Linking Across Time

Mongol conquest led monks to establish monasteries deep in the northern forests. The Rus farmers who followed them built villages and clung more deeply to their religious beliefs.

Biography®

The following videotape programs are available from Glencoe to enrich Chapter 23:

- **Genghis Khan: Terror and Conquest**
- **Faberge: Imperial Jeweler**

To find classroom resources to accompany this video, check the following home page:

A&E Television:
www.aande.com

Use the **Vocabulary PuzzleMaker CD-ROM** to create crossword and word search puzzles.

EXTENDING THE CONTENT

Mongols were not the only invaders of the Rus states in the thirteenth century. Although the northerly town of Novgorod was out of the direct wave of Mongol destruction, it still had to contend with invaders from the west. Its leader, Prince Alexander, was an outstanding military leader who became one of the great heroes of Rus history.

Independent Practice

L2 **Daily Life** Have students prepare a report with illustrations on some traditional Russian dress for both the wealthy and the peasants. Encourage students to include what influence this dress has had on modern fashion styles. ELL

LINKING PAST TO PRESENT

From a small unimportant town on the Moskva River, Muscovy grew to be a center of an empire. Troikas, or sleighs, guided by horses, still glide over snowy trails on the city's outskirts. Today the golden-domed Kremlin has walls of brick and stone instead of the wooden ones of the thirteenth century.

Use **Interactive Tutor Self-Assessment CD-ROM** to review Section 3.

Use the **Vocabulary PuzzleMaker CD-ROM** to create crossword and word search puzzles.

Reading Check Answer The **kremlin** was a fortress located at Moscow.

Church Vestment

The Mongol conquest somewhat isolated the Rus Church from other Christian churches. Because of this, the Church developed local rituals and practices. This united the people and made them proud of their own culture.

Daily Life Even under Mongol rule, differences between the lives of the rich in Rus and the lives of peasants remained. The wealthy sometimes entertained guests with feasts of deer and wild pig. Peasants, on the other hand, rarely ate meat. Instead, they ate dark rye bread, cabbage, salted fish, and mushrooms.

The few pleasures the peasants had came from visiting one another. They told stories that praised the brave deeds of their warriors and other heroes. The stories were passed from old to young and became part of the Rus heritage.

Common dress for peasant men was white tunics, wide linen trousers, and heavy shoes woven from long strips of tree bark. They tied rags around their legs and feet instead of stockings to keep out the cold. Rich merchants and boyars wore tall fur hats and *caftans* (kaf′ tanz), or long robes tied at the waist with a sash.

Rus women of all classes wore blouses or smocks, skirts, and long shawls. On holidays, they added headdresses with decorations that indicated the region from which a woman came and if she was married.

Section 3 Assessment

1. **Define:** khan.
2. Where did the Mongols come from?
3. What did the Mongols do to the Rus people when they invaded Rus lands?

Critical Thinking

4. **Predicting Consequences** How might life have been different in the Rus states if the Mongols had not conquered these lands?

Graphic Organizer Activity

5. Draw this diagram, and use it to compare the lives of the rich and the lives of the peasants in Rus during Mongol rule.

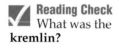

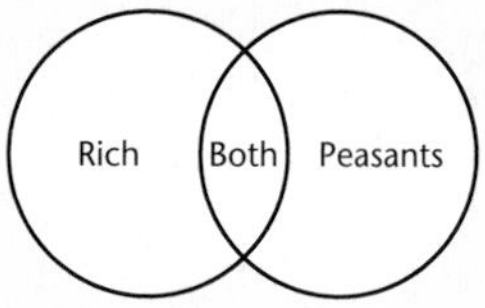

SECTION 4 The Rise of Moscow

Reading Check What was the **kremlin?**

At the time of the Mongol conquest, Moscow (mos′ kō), or Muscovy, founded in 1147, was a small trading post on the road from Kiev to the forests in the north. As more Rus people moved north to escape the Mongols, many artisans settled in or near Moscow's **kremlin** (krem′ luhn), or fortress.

Section 3 Assessment Answers

1. khan, Mongol leader (p. 353)
2. central Asia
3. They murdered people, destroyed villages, and made Rus people pay tribute and serve in the Mongol armies.
4. Answers will vary but could include that if the Mongols had not conquered Rus, these states might have been less isolated.
5. sample responses: *rich*—sometimes entertained guests with large feasts of deer and other meat, wore tall fur hats and caftans; *poor*—rarely ate meat, entertainment consisted of visits to friends and storytelling, wore linen clothes, wrapped rags around their legs for warmth, wore shoes made of woven tree bark

Assign Chapter 23 **Section 3 Quiz** in the TCR. Testmaker available.

The princes of Moscow were bold and ambitious. They learned to cooperate with the Mongols and even recruited Muscovy soldiers for the Mongol army. In return, the Mongols gave the princes of Moscow the power to collect taxes throughout the country. If a Rus territory could not provide soldiers or tax money for the Mongols, Moscow's princes took it over. In this way, Moscow, the principality of Muscovy, began to expand.

As Moscow grew in size, it became stronger. The princes passed their thrones from father to son. Thus, there was no fighting over who the next ruler would be, and the people remained united.

The Muscovite metropolitan lived in Moscow. This created a second center for the Eastern Orthodox Church outside of Kiev. The metropolitan blessed the princes for their efforts to make Moscow a great city. The people obeyed the prince as a ruler chosen and protected by God.

Meanwhile, Mongol chiefs started fighting among themselves. As a result, they grew weaker, while Moscow grew stronger. In 1380, an army formed by Dmitry (duh mē′ trē), the prince of Moscow, attacked and defeated the Mongols. The Mongols still remained powerful but no longer were feared or obeyed as they had been in the past.

Painting of Ivan the Great

HISTORY Online

Student Web Activity

Visit the *Human Heritage* Web site at humanheritage.glencoe.com and click on ***Chapter 23—Student Web Activities*** to find out more about the history of Moscow.

Ivan the Great

In 1462, Ivan III (ī′ vuhn), known as Ivan the Great, became prince of Moscow. In 1480, he ended Mongol control of Muscovy. He also expanded its boundaries to the north and west.

A few years before Mongol rule ended, Ivan married Sophia, a niece of the last Byzantine emperor. The Muscovite people felt this marriage gave Ivan all the glory of past Byzantine emperors. The Church believed it meant that Moscow had taken Byzantium's place as the center of Christianity.

Ivan began living in the style of the Byzantine emperors. He used the two-headed eagle of Byzantium on his royal seal. He brought Italian architects to Moscow to build fine palaces and large cathedrals in the kremlin. He raised the huge walls that still guard the kremlin. He called himself **czar** (zahr), or emperor. This later became the official title of the emperor.

Ivan died in 1505. By then, the people were convinced that their ruler should have full and unquestioned power over both Church and state.

Reading Check What did the official title of **czar** mean?

Ivan the Terrible

In 1533, Ivan IV, the three-year-old grandson of Ivan III, became czar of Muscovy. He was not crowned until 1547, however. While he was growing up, a council of boyars governed the country for him. The boyars, however, wanted more power. To frighten Ivan into obeying

L3 Political Cartoons Have the students write a political cartoon concerning one of the following events: Ivan the Great's marriage to Sophia, Ivan the Great's end of Mongol control of Rus, Ivan the Terrible's order to peasants not to leave their land, Ivan the Terrible's move to a monastery, or Ivan the Terrible's takeover of boyar lands. Display cartoons on a bulletin board.

HISTORY Online

Student Web Activity objectives and answers can be found at the ***Chapter 23 Web Activity Lesson Plan*** at humanheritage.glencoe.com

Reading Check Answer The title of **czar** meant emperor.

EXTENDING THE CONTENT

Moscow was first settled on a trail by a river where people built a blockhouse as a place to stop on the way to Kiev. The site—a hill of pines—was chosen because it offered protection and provided a good observation point. Around 1155 A.D., a log stockade was built to protect against raiders. Huts and storehouses were later added, and eventually the area became known as the *kremlin,* or fortress. The heart of today's Moscow is still the Kremlin, although Moscow has spread and grown since then. The "new" Kremlin has a massive red brick wall surrounding a medieval fortress that was built in the fifteenth century.

MAP SKILLS

TEACH

Analyzing Historical Maps

Have students read the introductory section of the skill on page 356. Ask: What do historical maps show? *(boundary changes over time)* Direct students' attention to the map on the skill page. Ask: In what year was Muscovy smallest? *(1300)* In what year did Moscow first acquire part of the Volga River? *(1462)* Under which czar did Moscow gain control of Novgorod? *(Ivan III)*

Next, have students refer to a current map of the area shown on the map "The Growth of Moscow" and name the countries that were once controlled by Moscow.

Answers to Map Practice

1. 1462
2. 1505
3. Ivan IV

Use the **Glencoe Skillbuilder Interactive Workbook CD-ROM, Level 1,** to provide instruction and practice in key social studies skills.

Analyzing Historical Maps

Some maps show how a certain country expanded and changed its boundaries over time. Maps that show boundary changes are called **historical maps.**

The map of "The Growth of Moscow" below shows the changes in Moscow's borders from 1300 to 1584. The color used to shade a certain area shows when that land became part of Moscow. It also shows the exact location of the land that was added. For example, green is the color used to show the land acquired by the time of Ivan IV's death. The shading on the map indicates that this land extended to the Caspian Sea in the southeast and to the Black Sea in the southwest.

Map Practice

1. **By what year did Moscow include part of the Don River?**
2. **By what year had Moscow acquired territory bordering on the Arctic Ocean?**
3. **Under which czar did Moscow control the largest amount of territory?**

The Growth of Moscow

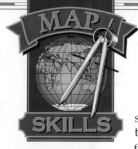

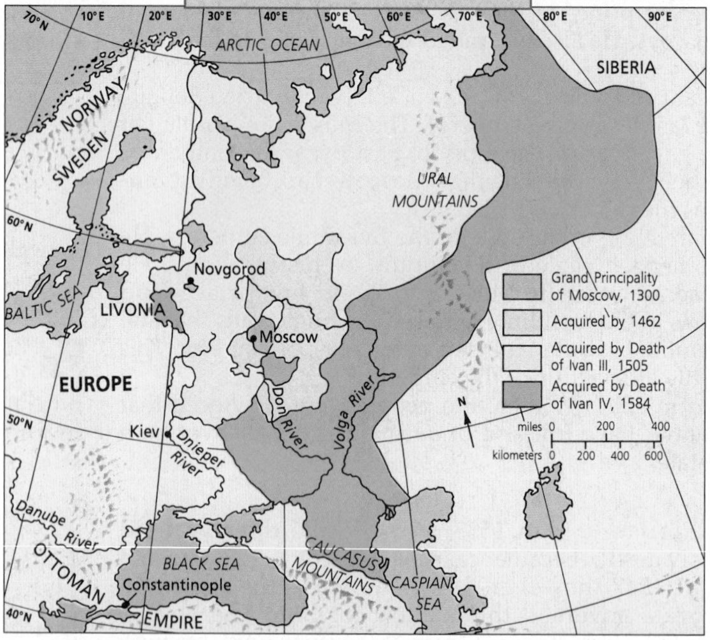

356

SPOTLIGHT ON: MOSCOW

The area around Moscow was dependent on both the Don and Volga rivers. The Volga is Europe's largest river, being comprised of 151,000 rivers, streams, and temporary streams, and having a length of 357,000 miles (or 574,000 km). The Volga River basin occupies a huge area stretching from the Valdi and Central Russian hills on the west to the Ural Mountains in the east, to the Caspian Sea in the south. Snow accounts for 60 percent of the river's annual drainage.

the World

▼ The Anasazi used turquoise as a trade item. At Chaco (cha' kō) Canyon, New Mexico, over 500,000 pieces of turquoise have been found. The Anasazi fashioned turquoise into beads for necklaces or used it to decorate everyday objects.

The Anasazi moved into the cliffs and canyons of the Southwest and built houses made of mud bricks. Perhaps 1,000 people lived in what is known as the Cliff Palace. Located in Mesa Verde, Colorado, the Cliff Palace had about 200 rooms and looked something like a modern apartment complex. When Spanish explorers first saw these houses, they called them *pueblos*—the Spanish word for "villages." ▼

Nearly all Anasazi villages included large circular underground chambers known as *kivas* (kē' vas). Scholars believe that the Anasazi used the kivas as religious centers and as clubhouses. They also believe that the kivas were restricted to men, with women entering the kivas only on special occasions. ▼

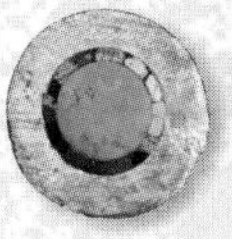

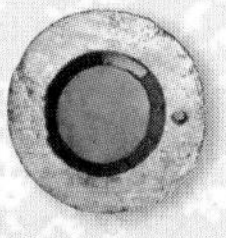

Taking Another Look

1. What was the purpose of the kivas?
2. What were the main economic activities of the Anasazi?

Hands-on Activity

Designing a Postcard Design a postcard that you might send from the Four Corners area that shows a picture of an Anasazi artifact. On the back, include a description of your experiences.

ANSWERS TO TAKING ANOTHER LOOK

1. Scholars believe the kivas were used for religious purposes and as clubhouses.
2. The Anasazi farmed and traded with people as far away as Central America.

Hands-On Activity
Postcards will vary but should accurately reflect the geographic conditions in the Anasazi homeland as well as the significance of the artifact. You might give extra credit to those students who do additional research on a site not shown in the feature, such as Chaco Canyon or Canyon de Chelly.

Features of the Anasazi Homeland	
Physical Features	Human Features

DID YOU KNOW ??

Charles Lindbergh and his wife Lynn took some of the first aerial photographs of Chaco Canyon and other Anasazi sites in the Southwest. The photos taken by Lindbergh revealed new sites and some of the more than 400 miles of roads that radiate from the Chaco area.

ASSESS

Check for Understanding

Have students answer the questions in Taking Another Look on page 361.

Enrich

Request interested students to research important Anasazi landmarks in the Four Corners area. Have them display their findings in an illustrated map of the region. A possible source of information is *North American Indian Landmarks: A Traveler's Guide,* by George Cantor, Gale Research Inc., 1993.

CLOSE

Have students compare economic activities in medieval Europe with those conducted by the Anasazi. Ask: What is one of the biggest differences that you notice? *(Help students to understand that while trade collapsed in most of western Europe, the Anasazi built a trading network that reached far and wide.)*

STANDARDIZED TEST PRACTICE

Answers and Analyses

1D History

Theodora is discussed on page 322. She never served as emperor, nor in the army, so choices B and C can be eliminated. Page 322 states, however, that she helped Justinian *fill government and church offices,* and that she was an important adviser to him.

THE PRINCETON REVIEW **TEST-TAKING TIP**

As with any specific question, students should begin by eliminating the improbable. Choices A and C are unlikely.

2H History

Page 326 discussed the split between the Orthodox and Catholic churches. There it states that *An argument also developed between the Pope and the Patriarch. The Patriarch would not recognize the Pope as head of the Church.*

3B History

Muhammad was born in Makkah, not Palestine, and had nothing to do with the Pope. Therefore, choices A and D can be eliminated. According to page 333, the leaders of Makkah began to fear Muhammad and began to persecute him and his followers. According to page 248, the same was true of Jesus.

4F History

The split between the Sunni and the Shi'ites is discussed on page 338. There it states that the Shi'ites believed that *the office of caliph should be held only by descendants of Ali.* This information makes F the best choice.

THE PRINCETON REVIEW

Standardized Test Practice

Directions: Choose the *best* answer to each of the following multiple choice questions. If you have trouble answering a question, use the process of elimination to narrow your choices. Write your answers on a separate piece of paper.

1. How was Justinian's wife, Theodora, different from the wives of previous emperors?

- **A** She bore a male heir to the emperor's throne.
- **B** She was the first female to serve as emperor.
- **C** She fought as a member of the army to defend her husband.
- **D** She played a large role in shaping law and public policy.

Test-Taking Tip: Eliminate answers that do not make sense. Since it is unlikely that Theodora was the first emperor's wife to give birth to a son (answer A), you can easily eliminate this answer choice.

2. The Eastern Orthodox Church split from the Roman Catholic Church because of a disagreement over

- **F** the content of the Old and New Testaments
- **G** what kinds of work missionaries should perform
- **H** who the leader of the Christian church should be
- **J** the role of women in the church

Test-Taking Tip: This question requires you to remember a *fact* about the Eastern Orthodox Church. Make sure that you read the question and *all* of the answer choices carefully before selecting the *best* answer.

3. In which of the following ways were Muhammad and Jesus similar?

- **A** Both were born in Palestine.
- **B** Both were seen as threats to the existing governments.
- **C** Both stopped gaining followers after their deaths.
- **D** Both required their followers to accept the power of the Pope.

Test-Taking Tip: This question asks you to make a *comparison* between these two leaders. Since Islam and Christianity are still gaining followers today, answer C is an unlikely choice.

4. Like the Catholic Church, the Muslims split into two groups. How were the Sunni different from the Shiites?

- **F** They believed that Islamic rulers did not have to be descendents of Ali.
- **G** They wanted the religious center of Islam to be Constantinople.
- **H** They were opposed to the use of religious icons as a part of ceremonies.
- **J** They wanted to recognize the Pope as their religious leader.

Test-Taking Tip: This question also asks you to make a comparison, but this time it asks for a *difference* rather than a *similarity*. Be careful: even though the question mentions the split in the Catholic Church, it is *not* asking for a comparison between Catholicism and Islam. Therefore, you can eliminate any answers that have to do with the Catholic Church, like answer J.

362

The Growth of Moscow

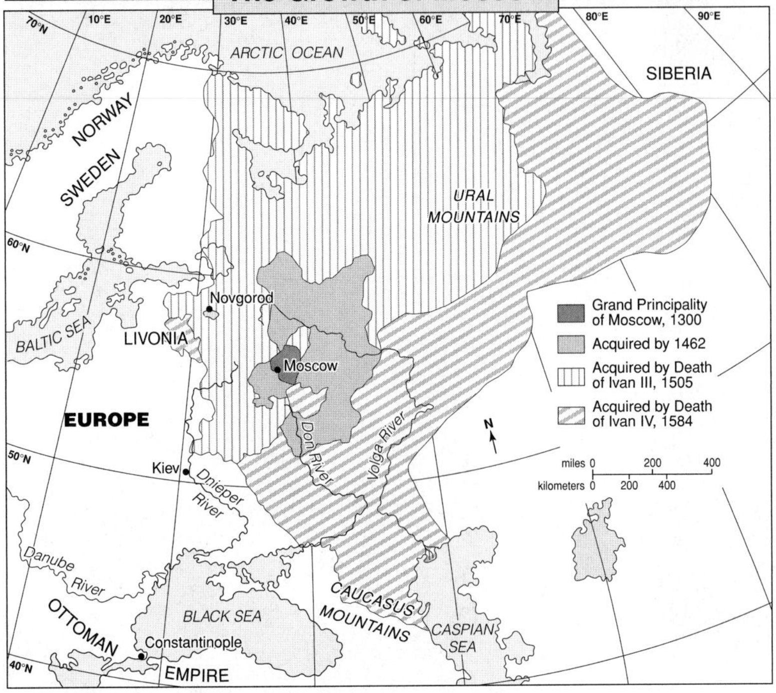

5. Based on the map above, what important contribution to Moscow's potential for trade was made by the time of Ivan IV's death?

A Moscow gained access to the Ottoman Empire through the Volga and Don rivers.

B Moscow gained access to trade routes to Norway and Sweden through the Baltic Sea.

C Moscow gained access to western Europe through the Danube River.

D Moscow gained control of land reaching to the Arctic Ocean.

Test-Taking Tip: Use the *map key*, or *legend*, to help you understand how the map is organized. Make sure that your answer is supported by information on the map.

6. The distance between Moscow and Novgorod is approximately

F 200 kilometers

G 400 kilometers

H 600 kilometers

J 700 kilometers

Test-Taking Tip: The map's *scale* will help you answer this question. If you do not have a ruler, you can copy the scale onto a small piece of paper to measure the distance. Notice that the answer choices are given in *kilometers*, not miles. The scale shows both: miles on the top, and kilometers below.

STOP

5A Geography

According to the map, only the Volga and Don rivers, as well as the Arctic Ocean, fell within the area acquired by the time of Ivan IV's death. The Arctic Ocean, however, did not have great potential for trade.

THE PRINCETON REVIEW **TEST-TAKING TIP**

Students need to understand how to read the legend and to determine what areas were under Moscow's control at this time. The Volga and Don rivers are the only choices listed that were both under Moscow's control *and* valuable for trade.

6H Geography

The scale on the map indicates that the distance between Moscow and Novgorod is about 600 kilometers.

THE PRINCETON REVIEW **TEST-TAKING TIP**

All of the information needed to answer the question is on the map, but students need to read very carefully to avoid mistakes. In this case, students need to make sure that they do not confuse miles and kilometers on the scale.

Tested Objectives

Questions	Reading Objective
1	Make generalizations
2	Determine cause and effect
3, 4	Make comparisons
5, 6	Analyze information

Introducing
UNIT 8

OVERVIEW

Unit 8 discusses the changes that took place in western Europe during the late Middle Ages.

- **Chapter 24** describes feudalism.
- **Chapter 25** discusses the role of the Roman Catholic Church in medieval life.
- **Chapter 26** describes how the growth of trade during the Middle Ages led to the rise of towns in western Europe.
- **Chapter 27** examines the development of strong national governments under monarchs in France, England, Germany, and Spain.

UNIT OBJECTIVES

After reading Unit 8, students will be able to:

1. discuss what roles the clergy, nobles, and peasants played during the late Middle Ages.
2. explain what led to the growth of trade and towns in western Europe.
3. describe how kings in western Europe built strong nations during the late Middle Ages.

UNIT PROJECT

Organize the class into four teams to play "The Late Middle Ages Quiz Bowl." Assign each team one chapter from this unit. Have the teams each prepare strips of paper with the names of important people, places, events, and themes discussed in their chapter, and place them in a large container. Have a moderator select a paper and read it aloud. The first team member must explain, define, or give information about the topic. If the team member is unable to do so, the question passes to the next team.

UNIT 8

The Late Middle Ages

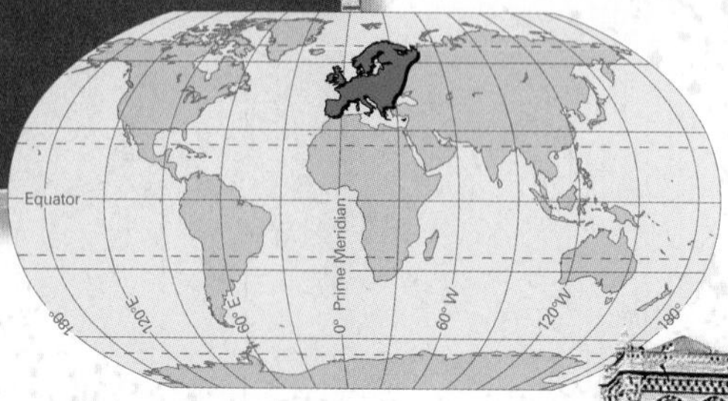

▲ Stained-glass image of a knight

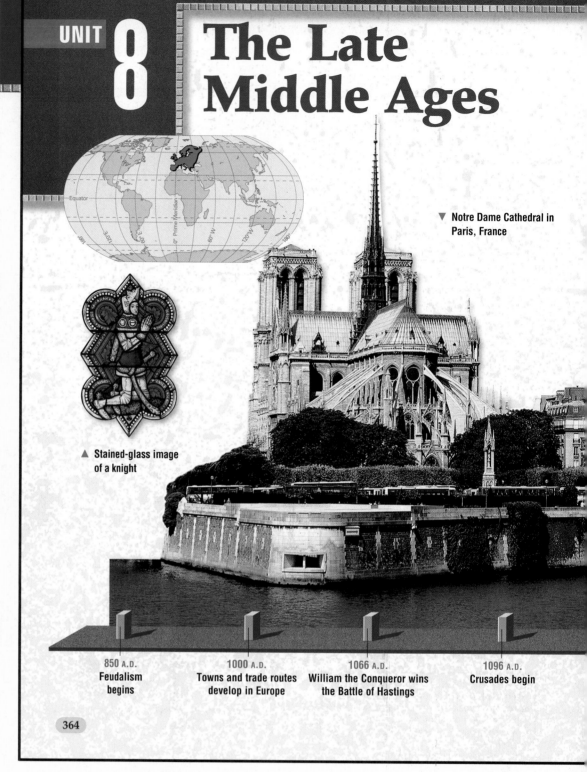

▼ Notre Dame Cathedral in Paris, France

850 A.D. Feudalism begins

1000 A.D. Towns and trade routes develop in Europe

1066 A.D. William the Conqueror wins the Battle of Hastings

1096 A.D. Crusades begin

364

ABOUT THE UNIT OPENING

Examining Artifacts

Based on these two artifacts, what can students infer about the role of religion in the late Middle Ages. *(It was very important.)* Ask students how they reached this answer. *(sample responses: complexity and grandeur of the cathedral, the knight kneeling in prayer, and so on)* Tell students that this unit examines the influence of the Roman Catholic Church and its relationship with emerging national governments.

Global Chronology

Ask students to explain what time period the time line covers. *(850 to 1337)* How many years passed between the beginning of feudalism and the development of towns and trade routes? *(150 years)* When did the Hundred Years' War begin? *(1337)* Who were some important people during this time? *(William the Conqueror, Frederick I)*

FOLDABLES™ Study Organizer

Organizing Information Study Foldable *Make the following foldable to help you organize information about the changes that occurred during the late Middle Ages.*

Step 1 *Fold two sheets of paper in half from top to bottom.*

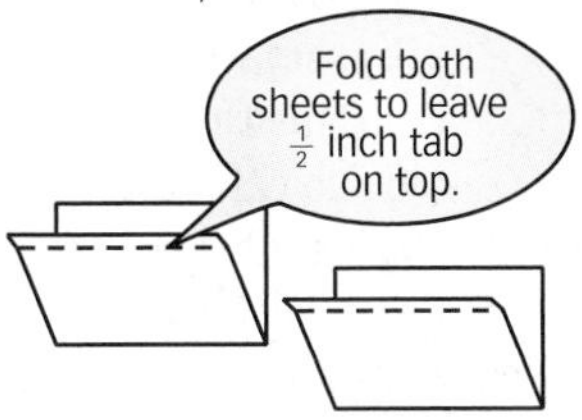

Step 2 *Place glue or tape along both ½ inch tabs.*

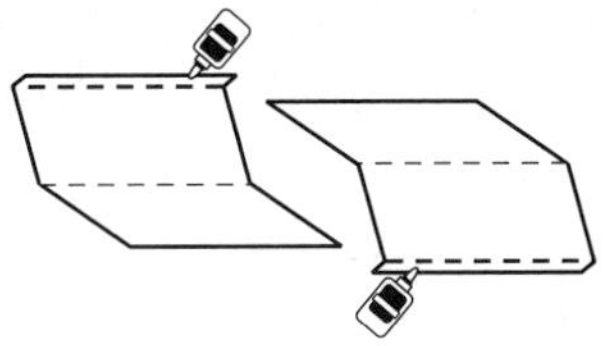

Step 3 *Fit both sheets of paper together to make a cube as shown.*

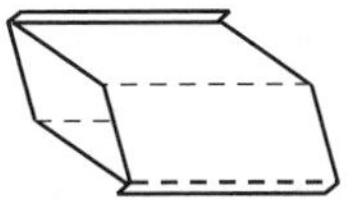

Step 4 *Turn the cube and label the foldable as shown.*

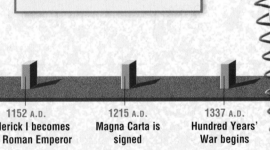

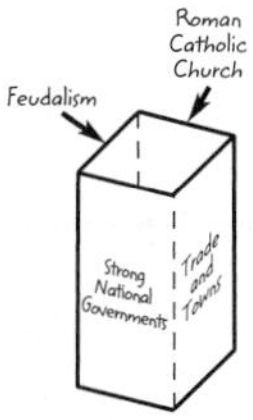

Reading and Writing *As you read the unit, list the developments that occurred in western Europe during the late Middle Ages. Write the developments under the correct foldable category.*

PRIMARY SOURCES Library

See pages 688–689 for other primary source readings to accompany Unit 8.

GO TO Read "Plan for a Crusade" from the **World History Primary Source Document Library CD-ROM.**

Journal Notes

What was life like during the late Middle Ages? Note details about it as you read.

1152 A.D. Frederick I becomes Holy Roman Emperor

1215 A.D. Magna Carta is signed

1337 A.D. Hundred Years' War begins

365

GLENCOE TECHNOLOGY

MindJogger Videoquiz

Use **MindJogger Videoquiz** to preview the unit content.

Available in DVD and VHS

FOLDABLES Study Organizer

Purpose Students will recognize and identify changes or developments that occurred in western Europe during the late Middle Ages and write these on their foldables. Explain to students that this was a time of turbulent change and many of the institutions in existence today had their origins in the late Middle Ages.

Have students complete **Reading and Study Skills Foldables** Activity 8.

RECORDING JOURNAL NOTES

Set aside time for the students to record details about life in the late Middle Ages after reading each chapter in the unit.

PRIMARY SOURCES Library

Additional primary sources from the **World History Primary Source Document Library CD-ROM** can be used during the study of Unit 8, including:

- "Battle of Hastings, 1066," by William of Malmesbury
- "The Magna Carta," by English nobles

Primary sources about the medieval manor can be found on pages 688–689.

Geographic Location

Have students look at their text Atlas to find the city of Jerusalem. *(located in the present state of Israel)* Discuss some of the difficulties an army in the Middle Ages might encounter traveling from Europe to Jerusalem. *(crossing mountains, crossing or going around the Black Sea, or crossing the Mediterranean Sea)*

ABC NEWS INTERACTIVE™

VIDEOCASSETTE
Turning Points in World History

Have students view **Tape 1 Chapter 7** to learn about the Crusades.

Chapter 24 Planning Guide

Timesaving Tools

TeacherWorks™ All-In-One Planner and Resource Center

- **Interactive Teacher Edition** Access your Teacher Wraparound Edition and your classroom resources with a few easy clicks.
- **Interactive Lesson Planner** Planning has never been easier! Organize your week, month, semester, or year with all the lesson helps you need to make teaching creative, timely, and relevant.

Presentation Plus!

Use Glencoe's **Presentation Plus!** multimedia teacher tool to easily present dynamic lessons that visually excite your students. Using Microsoft PowerPoint® you can customize the presentations to create your own personalized lessons.

Objectives	Reproducible Resources	Multimedia Resources
Section 1 **Land and Government** Explain why feudalism developed in western Europe.	Reproducible Lesson Plan Chapter 24 Vocabulary and Guided Reading Activity Reading Essentials and Study Guide 24-1 Chapter 24 Chart and Graph Skill Activity Unit 8 World Literature Reading 2 Section 1 Quiz Unit 8 Hands-On History Lab	Interactive Student Edition CD-ROM Teaching Transparencies and Activities 24A & 24B Graphic Organizer Transparency 2 Vocabulary PuzzleMaker CD-ROM Interactive Tutor Self-Assessment CD-ROM ExamView® Pro Testmaker CD-ROM Glencoe Skillbuilder Interactive Workbook CD-ROM, Level 1 Presentation Plus! CD-ROM
Section 2 **The Nobility** Describe the roles played by lords and vassals.	Reproducible Lesson Plan Reading Essentials and Study Guide 24-2 Chapter 24 Cooperative Learning Activity Section 2 Quiz	Vocabulary PuzzleMaker CD-ROM Interactive Tutor Self-Assessment CD-ROM ExamView® Pro Testmaker CD-ROM Glencoe Skillbuilder Interactive Workbook CD-ROM, Level 1
Section 3 **Knighthood** Discuss the training and duties of a knight.	Reproducible Lesson Plan Reading Essentials and Study Guide 24-3 Chapter 24 Enrichment Activity Section 3 Quiz	Vocabulary PuzzleMaker CD-ROM Interactive Tutor Self-Assessment CD-ROM ExamView® Pro Testmaker CD-ROM Glencoe Skillbuilder Interactive Workbook CD-ROM, Level 1
Section 4 **The Manor** Characterize manor life, identifying the relationship between nobles and serfs.	Reproducible Lesson Plan Reading Essentials and Study Guide 24-4 Chapter 24 Geography and Map Activity Unit 8 Primary Source Readings Section 4 Quiz	Vocabulary PuzzleMaker CD-ROM Interactive Tutor Self-Assessment CD-ROM ExamView® Pro Testmaker CD-ROM Glencoe Skillbuilder Interactive Workbook CD-ROM, Level 1
Chapter 24 **Review and Evaluation**	Chapter 24 Reteaching Activity Chapter 24 Performance Assessment Activity Spanish Chapter Summary and Glossary Chapter 24 Test	Vocabulary PuzzleMaker CD-ROM Interactive Tutor Self-Assessment CD-ROM Glencoe Skillbuilder Interactive Workbook CD-ROM, Level 1 Audiocassettes* ExamView® Pro Testmaker CD-ROM

*Also available in Spanish.

Performance Assessment Activities

Tapestry Mural Have students create murals modeled after tapestry made during the Middle Ages such as the Bayeux Tapestry. (This tapestry has 72 scenes depicting the Norman invasion of England.) Have them include portraits of people from the chapter, showing details of their dress and objects that symbolize their station in life. For instance, students might depict a knight in full armor with a shield displaying his coat of arms.

CHAPTER RESOURCES

LITERATURE ABOUT THE PERIOD

Scott, Sir Walter. *Ivanhoe.* Longmans, Green, and Co., 1897. Twelfth-century story of hidden identity, intrigue, and romance among the English nobility.

READINGS FOR THE STUDENT

McEvedy, Colin. *The New Penguin Atlas of Medieval History.* Penguin, 1992. Details the medieval history of the Mediterranean, Europe, and the nomad steppelands. Details enhanced with 45 maps.

READINGS FOR THE TEACHER

Gies, Frances, and Joseph Gies. *Marriage and the Family in the Middle Ages.* Harper and Row, 1987. Summarizes family history during the medieval period.

THE HISTORY CHANNEL. A&E HOME VIDEO. Biography

The following videotape programs are available from Glencoe:

- **Knights and Armor**
  1-56501-443-X
- **King Arthur: His Life and Legends**
  1-56501-644-0

To order, call Glencoe at 1-800-334-7344. To find classroom resources to accompany many of these videos, check:

A&E Television: www.aande.com
The History Channel: www.historychannel.com

NATIONAL GEOGRAPHIC Teacher's Corner

INDEX TO NATIONAL GEOGRAPHIC MAGAZINE

The following articles relate to this chapter:

- "The Basques," by Thomas J. Abercrombie, November 1995.
- "Oxford," by Bill Bryson, November 1995.

NATIONAL GEOGRAPHIC SOCIETY PRODUCTS AVAILABLE FROM GLENCOE

To order the following, call Glencoe at 1-800-334-7344:

- *PicturePack: Europe (Transparencies)*
- *PicturePack: Middle Ages (Transparencies)*
- *PictureShow: Middle Ages (CD-ROM)*

Access *National Geographic*'s new dynamic MapMachine Web site and other geography resources at:
www.nationalgeographic.com
www.nationalgeographic.com/maps

KEY TO ABILITY LEVELS

Teaching strategies have been coded for varying learning styles and abilities.

L1 Level 1 activities are **basic** activities and should be within the ability range of all students.

L2 Level 2 activities are **average** activities and should be within the ability range of the average to above-average student.

L3 Level 3 activities are **challenging** activities designed for the ability range of above-average students.

ELL ELL activities should be within the ability range of English Language Learning students.

OVERVIEW

Chapter 24 discusses the development of feudal society in western Europe after the collapse of Charlemagne's empire.

- **Section 1** describes the origins of feudalism.
- **Section 2** discusses the feudal social hierarchy.
- **Section 3** describes the duties of feudal knights.
- **Section 4** explains the lifestyles of the people in feudal society and the organization of the manors.

CHAPTER OBJECTIVES

After reading Chapter 24, students will be able to:

1. explain why feudalism developed in western Europe.
2. describe what roles were played by lords and vassals.
3. discuss a knight's duties.
4. describe manor life.

EXAMINING ARTIFACTS

Ask students what these artifacts tell them about the daily life of peasants. *(milled their own grain, used simple tools, worked as farmers, and so on)* Next, have students examine the time line for other clues about life during this time period. Tell them that in this chapter they will learn about the relationship that developed between peasants and nobles as they struggled to survive.

PERFORMANCE ASSESSMENT ✓

Use the Performance Assessment Activities on page 366B to help you evaluate your students as they complete the chapter.

CHAPTER 24

Feudal Society

700 A.D.–1200 A.D.

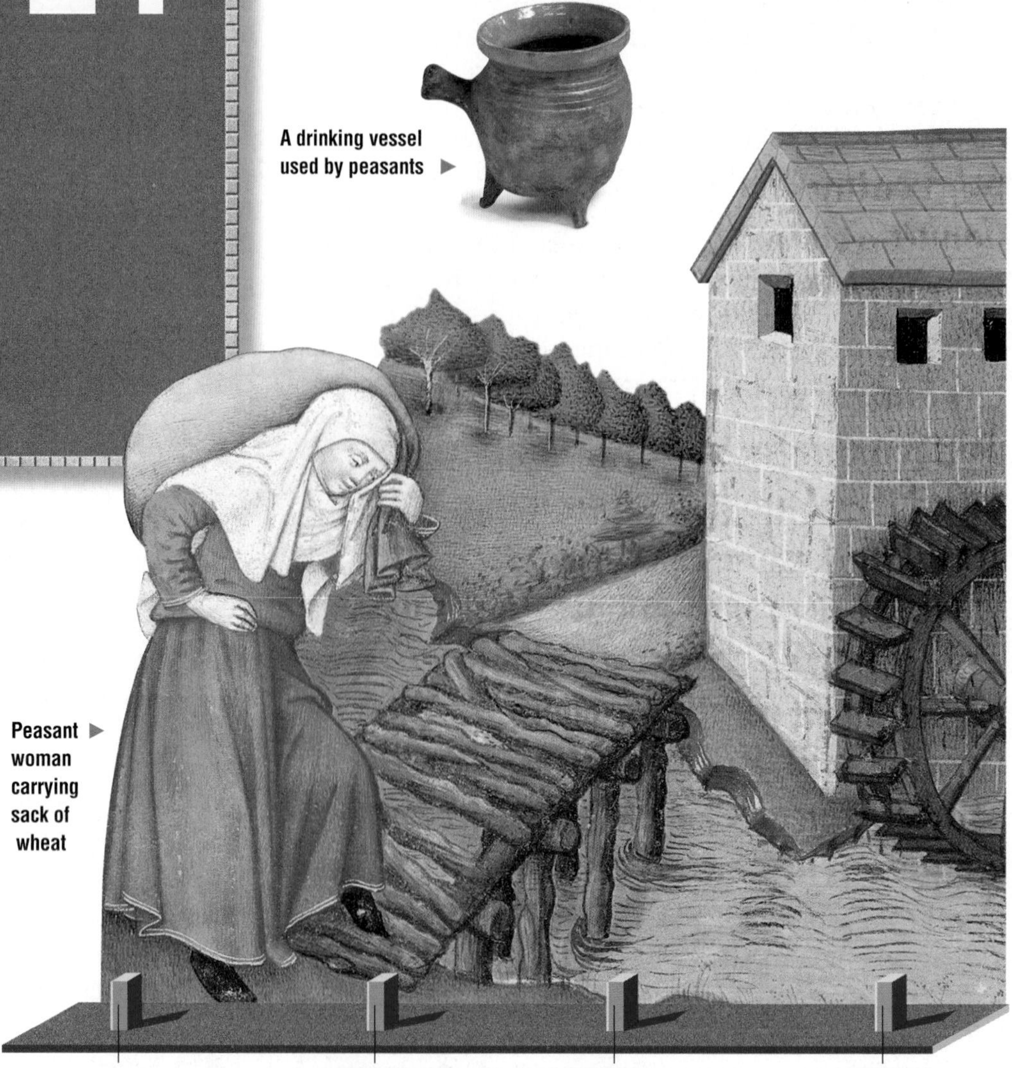

A drinking vessel used by peasants ►
Peasant ► woman carrying sack of wheat

814 A.D. Charlemagne dies

900 A.D. Nobles defend themselves against the Vikings

1000 A.D. Western Europe is divided into feudal territories

1100s A.D. Most nobles live in stone castles

TEACHING RESOURCES

TEACHER PLANNING AND SUPPORT

- Reproducible Lesson Plan 24-1, 24-2, 24-3, 24-4
- Teaching Strategies for the World History Classroom (Including Block Scheduling Pacing Guides)
- Presentation Plus! CD-ROM

REVIEW AND REINFORCEMENT

- Reading Essentials and Study Guide Guide 24-1, 24-2, 24-3, 24-4
- Chapter 24 Vocabulary and Guided Reading Activity
- Vocabulary PuzzleMaker CD-ROM
- Teaching Transparencies 24A & 24B
- Chapter 24 Reteaching Activity
- Chapter 24 Cooperative Learning Activity
- Chapter 24 Activity Book Activity
- Chapter 24 Chart and Graph Skill Activity
- Reading and Study Skills Foldables
- Interactive Tutor Self-Assessment CD-ROM
- Unit 8 MindJogger VideoQuiz

APPLICATION AND HANDS-ON ACTIVITIES

- Daily Questions in Social Studies
- Unit 8 Hands-On History Lab Activity
- Student Presentation Builder CD-ROM

Chapter Focus

Read to Discover

- Why feudalism developed in western Europe.
- What roles were played by lords and vassals.
- What the duties of a knight were.
- What life was like on a manor.

HISTORY Online

Chapter Overview

Visit the *Human Heritage* Web site at **humanheritage.glencoe.com** and click on ***Chapter 24—Chapter Overviews*** to preview this chapter.

Terms to Learn

feudalism	castles	tournaments
clergy	keep	joust
fiefs	ladies	manors
vassal	code of chivalry	seneschal
act of homage	page	bailiff
knight	squire	freemen
	dubbing	

Why It's Important Central government collapsed after the death of King Charlemagne. As the Vikings invaded western European kingdoms, local nobles took over the duty of raising armies and protecting their property. Power passed from kings to local lords, giving rise to a system known as **feudalism** (fyoo' dul ih zum). Under feudalism, landowning nobles governed and protected the people in exchange for services, such as fighting in a noble's army or farming the land.

The **clergy,** or religious leaders, also owned land and held power. Members of the clergy taught Christianity, helped the poor and sick, and advised the nobles who belonged to the Church. With western Europe divided into thousands of feudal territories, the Church served as a unifying force and exerted a strong influence over the culture of the Middle Ages.

Reading Check What was **feudalism?**

Reading Check Who were the **clergy?**

SECTION 1 Land and Government

During feudal times, power was based on the ownership of land. Before feudalism, kings owned all the land within their territories. Then Charles Martel, the Frankish leader, began giving his soldiers **fiefs** (fēfs), or estates, as a reward for their service and loyalty. From their fiefs, the soldiers got the income they needed to buy horses and battle equipment. After 800, the kings of Europe followed Martel's example. From that time on, land ownership was tied to military service. With land ownership went power and wealth, giving soldiers a base from which to rule Europe.

Reading Check Why did soldiers receive **fiefs** during the Middle Ages?

GEOGRAPHY ACTIVITIES

- Chapter 24 Geography and Map Activity
- Building Geography Skills for Life
- Outline Map Resource Book

INTERDISCIPLINARY CONNECTIONS

- Unit 8 World Literature Reading 2
- World Music: A Cultural Legacy

ENRICHMENT AND EXTENSION

- Unit 8 Primary Source Readings
- World History Primary Source Document Library CD-ROM
- Chapter 24 Enrichment Activity
- Foods Around the World

ASSESSMENT AND EVALUATION

- Chapter 24 Performance Assessment Activity
- Chapter 24 Section Quizzes 24-1, 24-2, 24-3, 24-4
- Chapter 24 Test
- Chapter 24 ExamView® Pro Testmaker CD-ROM
- Chapter 24 Digests Audiocassettes Activities and Tests

SPANISH RESOURCES

- Chapter 24 Spanish Chapter Summary and Glossary
- Chapter 24 Spanish Digests Audiocassettes Activities and Tests

HISTORY Online

Chapter Overview introduces students to chapter content and key terms. Have them access ***Chapter 24 Overview*** at **humanheritage.glencoe.com**

FOCUS

Bellringer

Ask students to write a one-sentence description of the following: a knight, a squire, a page, a noblewoman, and a serf.

Motivational Activity

Have students read their sentences, and discuss their ideas about people in the Middle Ages.

Reading Check Answer Under **feudalism,** landowning nobles governed and protected the people in exchange for services.
The **clergy** were religious leaders.
Soldiers received **fiefs** as a reward for service and loyalty.

GUIDE TO READING

Reading Strategy

Ask students to read "Why It's Important" and summarize the chapter's main theme. *(Collapse of central government and Viking invasions gave rise to feudalism—a time when the Church served as the main unifying force in Europe.)*

Vocabulary Precheck

Ask students to define each of the "Terms to Learn." L1 ELL

Use the Vocabulary PuzzleMaker CD-ROM for Chapter 24 to create a crossword puzzle. L1

Assign Chapter 24 Vocabulary and Guided Reading Activity.

Assign Reading Essentials and Study Guide 24-1.

TEACH

Guided Practice

L1 **Daily Life** Draw a simple figure to represent the human body on the chalkboard and label its parts as you explain the following comparison made by one medieval scholar who compared feudal society to the human body. He identified priests and clerks as spiritual guides, or the head and eyes; nobles as protectors and defenders, or the arms and hands; and peasants, the workers on whose labor all society was based, as the legs and feet. ELL

L2 **Critical Thinking** Ask: Was feudalism an effective system of government? Why or why not? Have students write a list of recommendations of changes they would submit to improve government.

Reading Check Answer

A **vassal** served a lord of a higher rank and gave him loyalty.

During an **act of homage,** the vassal and lord took part in a ceremony in which their tie became official.

NATIONAL GEOGRAPHIC

Use these materials to enrich student understanding of the Middle Ages.

NGS PICTUREPACK TRANSPARENCIES
Middle Ages

NGS PICTURESHOW CD-ROM
Middle Ages

The Rise of Feudal Territories

After Charlemagne's death in 814, Europe had no central government. The kings who followed Charlemagne were so weak they could not even rule their own kingdoms well. They ignored their responsibilities and spent most of their time traveling from one royal estate to another. Before long, they began to depend on the nobles for food, horses, and soldiers. Some nobles grew more powerful than the king and became independent rulers. They gained the right to collect taxes and to enforce the law in their areas. Many nobles raised armies and coined their own money.

Around 900, the nobles took on the duty of protecting their lands and people from the Vikings. They built fortresses on hilltops and fenced their lands. The peasants asked these powerful nobles to protect them. In return, the peasants gave their lands to nobles and promised to work for them in the fields. However, most peasants ended up giving the nobles not only their land but also their freedom.

By 1000, the kingdoms of western Europe were divided into thousands of feudal territories. Each was about the size of an ancient Greek city-state. Unlike the polis, however, a feudal territory had no central city. The noble who owned the land also had the political power. He made the laws for his fief, and the people obeyed them. Peasants, unlike Greek citizens, had no say in the government.

Although the peasants and townspeople made up the largest group, they had fewer rights than the clergy and nobles. Almost everyone believed that God wanted it that way. As a result, few people tried to improve society or change their own way of life. Most people remained in the group into which they were born.

Lord and Vassal

Feudalism was based on ties of loyalty and duty among nobles. Nobles were both lords and vassals. A **vassal** (vas' uhl) was a noble who served a lord of higher rank and gave him loyalty. In return, the lord protected the vassal. All nobles were ultimately vassals of the king, who might even be the vassal of another king.

Reading Check What were the duties of a **vassal?** What took place during an **act of homage?**

The tie between lord and vassal was made official in a special ceremony known as the **act of homage** (om' ij). The vassal, his head bare to show respect, knelt on one knee and placed his hands between those of the lord. He promised to serve the lord and to help him in battle. The lord accepted the promise, helped the vassal to his feet, and kissed him.

In return for the promise of loyalty and service, the lord gave his vassal a fief. Since there were few written agreements in the Middle Ages, the lord gave his vassal a glove, a stick, or a stone. This was to show that the lord's word could be trusted. He also gave the vassal the right to govern the people who lived on the

EXTENDING THE CONTENT

The basic structure of feudalism can take the shape of a pyramid but was sometimes complicated. Many lords simply had peasants or very minor knights as their vassals. On the other hand, in the higher ranks of feudalism, lords and vassals often were social equals. Even a poor knight with a run-down manor might come from a family as proud as that of his overlord. At several times in history, the kings of England were vassals of the kings of France for territories such as Anjou and Aquitaine.

fief. The lord promised to protect his vassal from enemy attacks. If the lord failed in this, the vassal no longer owed him loyalty.

Vassals had certain duties to perform. Their most important duty was to help the lord in battle. Vassals had to bring their own knights with them. They themselves were expected to take part in military service 40 to 60 days a year.

Vassals had to make payments to their lord. When a lord's daughter married, or his son became a **knight,** or a warrior on horseback, his vassals had to give the lord money. If a lord were captured in battle, his vassals either became prisoners in his place or paid his *ransom.* This is a sum of money given in exchange for a person's release.

Reading Check What was a **knight?**

Another duty of vassals was to attend the lord's court. Vassals were also expected to provide food and entertainment when their lord visited them. If a vassal failed in his duties to his lord, the lord had the right to take away the vassal's fief. When a vassal died, his fief usually passed on to his oldest son. The son then performed the act of homage.

Section 1 Assessment

1. **Define:** feudalism, clergy, fiefs, vassal, act of homage, knight.
2. How did land ownership become tied to military service?
3. How did nobles become so powerful?
4. What were some duties of a vassal?

Critical Thinking

5. **Demonstrating Reasoned Judgment** What were the advantages of being a vassal? What were the disadvantages?

Graphic Organizer Activity

6. Draw this diagram, and use it to show some of the causes of feudalism.

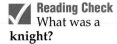

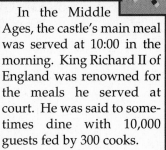

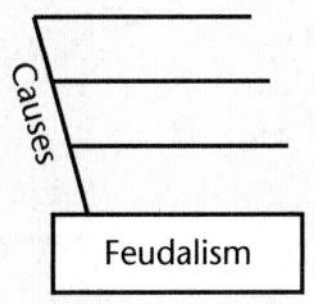

SECTION 2 The Nobility

Life was not always easy or pleasant for nobles during feudal times. They did, however, enjoy more benefits than the common people.

From the 800s to the 1000s, nobles and their families lived in wooden houses surrounded by *palisades* (pal uh sāds'), or high wooden fences built for protection. In case of attack, people from nearby villages sought shelter inside the palisade.

The house consisted of one room with a high ceiling and a straw-covered floor. All activity took place in that one room. There, nobles met with vassals, carried out the laws, and said their prayers. The nobles, their families, servants, and warriors

Reading Check Answer A **knight** was a warrior on horseback.

L1 **Critical Thinking** Ask students to create lists of the responsibilities of lords and vassals. Then create two columns on the chalkboard titled, "Lords" and "Vassals." Have students write their ideas in the appropriate column. Then ask students to explain why the relationship between the lords and vassals developed and whether they think it was a fair one. ELL

Use the **Interactive Tutor Self-Assessment CD-ROM** to review Section 1.

MAKING CONNECTIONS

➤➤ **History** The ties between lord and vassal could be confusing because a vassal could owe loyalty to several lords at once in times of war. In such cases, the vassal chose one lord to whom he was the most loyal. Some vassals simply supported the side most likely to win.

DID YOU KNOW

In the Middle Ages, the castle's main meal was served at 10:00 in the morning. King Richard II of England was renowned for the meals he served at court. He was said to sometimes dine with 10,000 guests fed by 300 cooks.

Use the **Vocabulary PuzzleMaker CD-ROM** to create crossword and word search puzzles.

Section 1 Assessment Answers

1. feudalism, government by landowning nobles (p. 367); clergy, religious leaders (p. 367); fiefs, estates (p. 367); vassal, a noble who served a lord (p. 368); act of homage, ceremony tying a lord and his vassal (p. 368); knight, warrior on horseback (p. 369)
2. Fiefs were given to soldiers as a reward.
3. Kings depended on nobles for food, horses, soldiers, and taxes.
4. to serve the lord in battle, make payments to the lord, become a prisoner in his place or pay his ransom, and entertain him
5. Answers will vary but should show an understanding of feudal relationships.
6. sample causes: lack of a central government, the weak kings who followed Charlemagne, the increasing power of nobles, the willingness of peasants to give their land to nobles for protection against the Vikings

Assign the Chapter 24 **Section 1 Quiz** in the TCR. Testmaker available.

L2 **Daily Life** Ask students to imagine they are cooks during the Middle Ages. Tell them that they are to prepare a banquet for the king and his court. What foods would they serve? How would they be cooked? Encourage students to research the menu of such a meal and share their research with the class.

CAPTION ANSWER

Wooden tables were set up in the castle's main room where all people gathered.

Reading Check Answer

Castles looked like thick-walled fortresses with lookout towers on each corner. Some had moats and bridges.

Fun Facts . . .

Too Much! Guests at a noble's banquet consumed huge amounts of food. In the 1340s, Pope Clement VI gave a feast that included 13,000 birds, 1,000 sheep, 50,000 fruit pies, and 200 casks of wine. At the 1403 wedding of Henry IV of England and Joan of Navarre, the royal couple tasted about 100 separate dishes.

NOBLE'S FEAST Nobles celebrated special occasions with elaborate feasts. Such meals often included many courses of meats, fruits, and vegetables. In this painting a noble sits down to dinner while his many servants bring out more food. **Where were meals for nobles held?**

also ate and slept in that room. At mealtime, wooden tables were set up and piled high with meat, fish, vegetables, fruits, and honey. People ate with their fingers and threw scraps of food on the floor for the dogs. The straw got so dirty with mud, bones, and food that every few months it had to be swept outdoors and burned.

The fires that cooked the meals were also used to heat the house. Actually, the fires did little to keep out the cold. Smoke from them often stung the eyes and darkened the walls and ceiling.

Reading Check What did **castles** look like?

The Castle By the 1100s, nobles were living in stone houses called **castles.** Because they were designed as fortresses, the castles made nobles secure and independent. Castles had thick stone walls, one within another. Each corner had its own lookout tower with archers in it. Some castles were further protected by a moat with a soft and muddy bottom that stopped attackers from using ladders to climb over the outer walls. To cross the moat, a

MULTICULTURAL PERSPECTIVES

During the Middle Ages, several books on courtesy were written to teach the nobility table manners. Since fingers were used to transport food from large platters to individual trenchers, and from there to one's mouth, the cleanliness of one's fingers was a matter of concern for all the diners. One author wrote, "Thou must not put thy fingers into thine ears." Other writers asked their readers not to blow their noses with their fingers or scratch their heads, especially since fleas and lice were common.

person had to use the castle's drawbridge, which could be raised to prevent entry. The drawbridge led to the *portcullis* (pōrt kul' is), an iron gate that often served as the entrance to the castle.

Within the castle walls was a large open area. In the middle of this area was a **keep,** or tall tower with thick walls. It contained a great hall, many rooms, and a dungeon. The people of the household lived in the keep, which could be defended even if the rest of the castle fell to attackers. Shops, kitchens, stables, and rooms for troops and guests were also built inside the castle walls.

Many people, including the noble's servants and officials, lived in the castle. Since the noble was away fighting most of the time, the servants and officials were responsible for the castle's care and defense. Most castles had enough space to store a large supply of food and drink. As a result, people inside a castle could hold out against attackers for as long as six months.

Reading Check Why did the people of a household live inside the **keep?**

HISTORY Online

Student Web Activity Visit the *Human Heritage* Web site at **humanheritage.glencoe.com** and click on ***Chapter 24—Student Web Activities*** to find out more about castles.

CASTLE A castle was both a noble's home and a military fortress. During enemy attack, people from the surrounding area sought protection within the castle walls. Here, the moat and entrance of an English castle are shown. **Who was responsible for a castle's care and defense?**

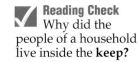

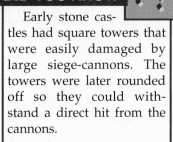

Reading Check Answer People of a household lived inside the **keep** because they could defend it even if the rest of the castle fell.

HISTORY Online

Student Web Activity objectives and answers can be found at the ***Chapter 24 Web Activity Lesson Plan*** at **humanheritage.glencoe.com**

CAPTION ANSWER

servants and officials

GEOGRAPHY AND HISTORY

Castles were often built on top of hills or mounds so sentries could easily spot attackers. Castles had their own wells so that defenders would have water if the castle came under attack.

DID YOU KNOW

Early stone castles had square towers that were easily damaged by large siege-cannons. The towers were later rounded off so they could withstand a direct hit from the cannons.

COOPERATIVE LEARNING

Have the class work in small groups to create plans for a medieval castle like the one described in this section. Tasks may be divided in several ways: researching medieval architecture, organizing data, writing plans, and illustrating the finished design by blueprint and sketch on poster board. Another group can present the finished project, describing various aspects of the castle and explaining the rationale.

Assign Chapter 24 ***Cooperative Learning Activity*** in the TCR.

L3 Critical Thinking Ask students why they think chess was a favorite game in the Middle Ages. Then ask them how the game pieces relate to feudal society. Students may wish to research the history of chess and present an oral report to the class.

Reading Check Answer
The marriages of most **ladies** were planned to unite families.

Linking Across Time

Other popular activities included hunting and fishing, and listening to wandering minstrels.

DID YOU KNOW ??

Some knights attacked and robbed passersby, especially traveling merchants, and raided their neighbors' lands for sheep and cattle.

MAKING CONNECTIONS

➤➤ **The Arts** Many ladies of the Middle Ages could read and were interested in music and poetry. They also spent time riding, hunting, and exercising.

Reading Check What was the main purpose of marriage for most **ladies** in the Middle Ages?

Castle Life When nobles were at home, they looked after their estates, went hunting and fishing, and held court. During long winter evenings, they often played chess with family members. Wandering minstrels sometimes came to entertain the nobles and their guests by singing songs and playing stringed instruments.

Noblewomen were called **ladies.** Once they married, their husbands had complete authority over them. Most marriages were planned to unite important families, and a woman had little say about who was chosen for her. The bride's family gave the groom a dowry. Most nobles looked for wives with large dowries. Women were often married by the time they were 12 years old. Those who were not married by the time they were 21 could expect to stay single for the rest of their lives.

Wives helped their husbands run their estates. When the men were away, the women had to defend the castle. The main duties of a wife, however, were to have and raise children and to

Linking Across Time

Chess After the game arrived in Europe from India about 1000 A.D., noble lords and ladies played chess (above) to pass the hours. In recent years, chess masters such as Russian expert Gary Kasparov (right) have matched their wits with chess-playing computers. **What other activities were popular in the Middle Ages?**

SPOTLIGHT ON: NOBLEWOMEN

The noblewoman was technically under her husband's control, although she could exert power both inside and outside of the castle. If her dowry included lands and manors or abbeys, they remained under her control. When the lord was away or at war—sometimes a matter of many years—the lady was in charge of the castle. If necessary, she organized its defenses. Some women actually led the castle troops into battle.

take care of the household. She was also expected to train young girls from other castles in household duties and to supervise the making of cloth and fine embroidery. Another duty was to use her knowledge of plants and herbs to care for the poor and sick on her husband's fief.

Section 2 Assessment

1. **Define:** castles, keep, ladies.
2. What activities took place in the noble's house?
3. How did the design of a castle protect people?
4. What were the duties of a feudal noblewoman?

Critical Thinking

5. **Drawing Conclusions** What parts of castle life would you have liked? What parts would you have disliked?

Graphic Organizer Activity

6. Draw this diagram, and use it to compare the living conditions of nobles before and after the rise of castles.

Before	Rise of Castles	After

SECTION 3 Knighthood

Almost all nobles were knights. However, knighthood had to be earned. Knights were expected to follow certain rules known as the **code of chivalry** (kōd of shiv' uhl rē). These rules stated that a knight was to obey his lord, show bravery, respect women of noble birth, honor the Church, and help people. A knight was also expected to be honest and to fight fairly against his enemies. The code of chivalry became the guide to behavior from which the western idea of good manners developed.

Reading Check What was the **code of chivalry?**

Training A noble began training to be a knight when he was seven years old. He was sent away from his family to the castle of another lord. There, he learned to be a **page,** or a person who helped the knights of the castle care for their *destriers* (dā trē' uhrs), or war-horses. Pages also polished the knights' armor, some of which weighed up to 80 pounds, or 36 kilograms.

Reading Check What did a **page** hope to become?

A page learned good manners and ran errands for the ladies. He was taught to ride and fight. By the age of 14, he could handle a lance and sword while on horseback.

When he was 15 years old, a page became a **squire.** Each squire was put under the care and training of one knight. The squire's duty was to go into battle with his knight. He was expected to rescue the knight if he was wounded or fell off his horse.

Reading Check What were the duties of a **squire?**

If the squire proved to be a good fighter, he was rewarded by being made a knight. This was done in a special ceremony

A&E HOME VIDEO.

The following videotape programs are available from Glencoe to enrich Chapter 24:

- **King Arthur: His Life and Legends**
- **Knights and Armor**

To find classroom resources to accompany these videos, check the following home page:

A&E Television:
www.aande.com

Use the **Interactive Tutor Self-Assessment CD-ROM** to review Section 2.

Reading Check Answer
The **code of chivalry** was a set of rules that a knight was expected to follow.

Reading Check Answer
A **page** hoped to become a knight.

Use the **Vocabulary PuzzleMaker CD-ROM** to create crossword and word search puzzles.

Reading Check Answer
The duties of a **squire** including going into battle with a knight and rescuing him if he was wounded or fell off his horse.

Section 2 Assessment Answers

1. castles, stone houses of nobles (p. 370); keep, tall tower (p. 371); ladies, noblewomen (p. 372)
2. Nobles met with vassals, carried out laws, and said their prayers; people slept there; meals were cooked and eaten there.
3. Student answers should reflect the description of a castle on pages 370–371.
4. She helped her husband run their estates, defended the castle when the men were away, raised children, took care of the household, and cared for the poor and sick.
5. Answers will vary, but students should provide specific examples of castle life.
6. Sample response: *Before*—lived in one-room wooden houses surrounded by palisades; *After*—lived in stone fortresses.

Assign the Chapter 24 **Section 2 Quiz** in the TCR. Testmaker available.

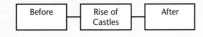

L1 **Language Arts** Organize students into two teams. Have each team write an interview between a squire and a knight on how nobles achieved knighthood and what a knight's duties were. Then have each team read the dialogue to the rest of the class, with one student playing the role of the knight and the other, the role of the squire.

CAPTION ANSWER

because men and horses might be killed, equipment damaged, and hundreds of people who attended were fed

Reading Check Answer At a **dubbing** ceremony, a squire officially became a knight.

Reading Check Answer At medieval **tournaments,** knights trained for war.

Reading Check Answer In a **joust,** two armored knights with dull lances galloped toward each other from opposite ends of a field in an effort to knock one or the other to the ground.

DID YOU KNOW ??

There were two types of medieval jousts. One was held for pleasure or exercise, and the knights used lances with blunt tips and swords that were not pointed. The other was a fight to the death in which sharp weapons were used. The arms of a defeated man belonged to the victor and could be ransomed for money. Because of this, tournaments were a way for poor but powerful fighters to earn a living.

Fun Facts...

Coats of Arms To identify themselves in battle, knights had individual designs, or "coats of arms," painted on their shields and tunics. In noble families, the coat of arms passed down through the generations. The flags of some modern European nations are based on medieval coats of arms.

MEDIEVAL TOURNAMENT In this painting knights on horseback joust during a tournament while other knights fight hand to hand. **Why were medieval tournaments costly events?**

Reading Check What took place during the ceremony known as **dubbing?**

known as **dubbing.** The squire knelt before his lord with his sword suspended from his neck. He then promised to defend the Church and his lord, and to protect the weak. Then, the lord tapped the squire on his shoulder with the blade of a sword and pronounced him a knight. The knight's sword was placed in a *scabbard,* or sword holder, at the knight's side. This showed that the knight would fight by the side of his lord.

Reading Check What was the purpose of medieval **tournaments?**

Reading Check What was the event known as the **joust?**

Tournaments

Knights trained for war by fighting each other in **tournaments,** or special contests that tested strength, skill, and endurance. Tournaments were held in large fields. They were exciting gatherings that brought in lords, ladies, and knights who watched the events from stands. The most popular event was the **joust** (jowst). Two armored knights on horseback carrying dull lances galloped towards each other from opposite ends of the field. Each tried with all his strength and skill to knock the other to the ground with his lance.

The cost of tournaments was high. Men and horses were killed and wounded. Lances, swords, and suits of armor were damaged. The noble who gave the tournament had to feed hundreds of people. In spite of the cost, however, tournaments remained popular. In fact, it was believed that a knight who had not learned to fight in one could not fight well in battle.

MEETING SPECIAL NEEDS

Have tactile/kinesthetic or gifted learners research the styles of armor worn by knights in the various regions of western Europe. Then have students make armor and model it or draw pictures of its various styles and designs. Students may wish to write a report explaining their findings.

Refer to ***Inclusion for the Middle School Social Studies Classroom: Strategies and Activities*** for additional resources.

Section 3 Assessment

1. **Define:** code of chivalry, page, squire, dubbing, tournaments, joust.
2. Why did noble families send their sons to other castles to work as pages?
3. How did knights train for war?

Critical Thinking

4. **Making Comparisons** How were tournaments similar to the Olympic games in ancient Greece? How were they different?

Graphic Organizer Activity

5. Draw this diagram, and use it to show the steps leading to knighthood.

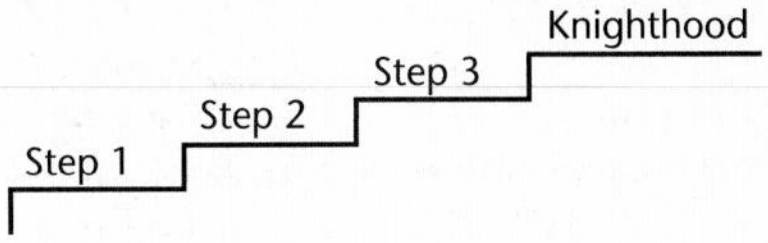

SECTION 4 The Manor

Nobles, knights, and peasants all depended on the land for everything they needed. The land was divided into **manors,** or farming communities. Manors were found on fiefs and were owned by nobles.

Reading Check What were **manors?**

Daily Life The noble chose a number of officials to run his manor. They were loyal to the noble and made sure his orders were carried out. One official was the **seneschal** (sen' uh shuhl).

Reading Check Who was the **seneschal?**

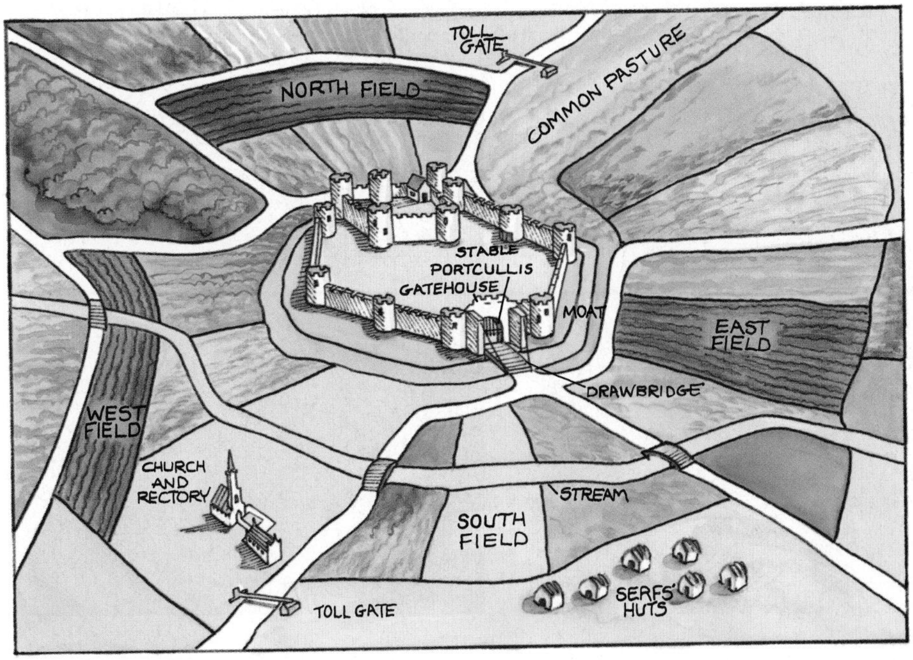

Independent Practice

L3 **Science** There were many diseases and medical problems during the Middle Ages. Ask students to research and present information about the following to the class: Who would treat peasants' diseases? Who did a king go to for medical problems? What kinds of treatments were commonly used?

Reading Check Answer
Manors were the farming communities found on all fiefs.

Reading Check Answer
The **seneschal** looked after the noble's fiefs, visiting them regularly.

Use the **Interactive Tutor Self-Assessment CD-ROM** to review Section 3.

Use the **Vocabulary PuzzleMaker CD-ROM** to create crossword and word search puzzles.

MAKING CONNECTIONS

>> **History** Manors formed the basis of the medieval agricultural system known as manorialism. While feudalism involved ties among nobles, manorialism concerned agreements between the nobles and peasants.

PRIMARY SOURCES Library

You might assign "The Medieval Manor" on pages 688–689 of the Primary Sources Library.

Section 3 Assessment Answers

1. code of chivalry, rules for knights (p. 373); page, person who helped the knights (p. 373); squire, second step in becoming a knight (p. 373); dubbing, ceremony in which a squire became a knight (p. 374); tournament, contests for knights (p. 374); joust, an event in a tournament (p. 374)
2. so they could become a knight
3. by taking part in tournaments with events such as the joust
4. Similar: many events watched by many people outside. Different: tournaments prepared knights for war while the Olympic games were held to honor the gods. Unlike the Olympics, women were allowed to view the tournaments.
5. Step 1—receive training as a page; Step 2—serve as squire to a knight; Step 3—take part in the dubbing ceremony

Assign the Chapter 24 **Section 3 Quiz** in the TCR. Testmaker available.

Reading Check Answer The **bailiff** made sure the peasants worked hard in the fields.

L3 Daily Life Have students research the roles of women from different classes (nobility, clergy, common people, merchants). Have them report on what they discover and include a comparison of the roles, goals, and beliefs of medieval women with those of women today.

DID YOU KNOW ??

The roofs of the cottages were thatched with bundles of straw fastened on a wood frame. The thick thatch kept the cottage warm in winter and cool in summer.

CAPTION ANSWER

anything the noble asked of them in maintaining the manor

Economics at a Glance

Subsistence Life on the manor was reduced to *subsistence*. Subsistence is when the population produces only enough of the necessary goods to support itself. Few crops are available for trade or to feed industrial workers. Have students research and write a one-page summary about agriculture in the U.S. Students should identify what crops are produced and how farming in the U.S. is different from feudal farming. *(The U.S. produces about one-half of the world's corn and about one-tenth of its wheat. American farmers raise about 20 percent of the world's beef, pork, and lamb. Commercial farms in the U.S. provide large amounts of products that are used by Americans and traded to other countries.)*

Reading Check What was the main job of a **bailiff?**

Fun Facts . . .

Peasant Life A typical peasant's cottage had one door that opened into a central room with a pressed dirt floor. Often a number of animals—piglets, ducklings, cats, and hens—shared the space with a married couple and their children. In cold weather, a cow might be brought inside to be near the warmth of the fire.

He looked after the noble's fiefs by visiting each fief regularly. Another official was the **bailiff** (bā′ lif). He made sure the peasants worked hard in the fields. Every manor had its own court of law. The court settled differences, gave out fines and punishments, and discussed manor business.

Poor transportation and frequent fighting isolated manors from one another. The men and women of each manor produced food, clothing, and shelter for themselves and the noble. They raised sheep for wool and cattle for meat and milk. They also grew grain and vegetables, made cloth, built homes, and fashioned tools.

The noble of each manor lived in a wooden house or a castle. Nearby stood a small village of cottages in which the peasants lived. Most villages also had a church, a mill, a bread oven, and a wine press. Around the village were forests, meadows, pastures, and fields.

The cottages were crowded around an open area called the village green. They were made of wood and earth and had thatched roofs. Most had only one room. At night, family members slept there on piles of straw or on the dirt floor. Three-legged stools and a table were the only furniture. Diseases and fleas from the animals that also slept in the cottage often sickened the people.

PEASANTS AT WORK Peasants spent long hours working in the fields of a manor. In these paintings, peasants are shown plowing the fields and doing other tasks on the manor. **What other work did the peasants do?**

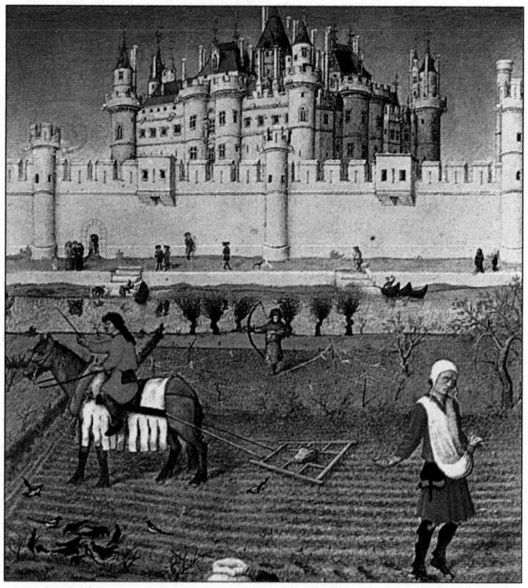

MULTICULTURAL PERSPECTIVES

Commercial fairs served as centers of trade for medieval Europe. These fairs were great annual events that attracted merchants from all over Europe, and brought many people from different cultures together.

PEASANT CELEBRATION Although peasants' lives were mostly long hours of hard work, there were times for celebration. Peasants celebrated special occasions with music, dancing, and feasting. Here, the festivities at a peasant wedding are shown. **What sports did peasants enjoy?**

Freemen and Serfs Two groups of peasants worked on a manor. One was the **freemen,** or peasants who paid the noble for the right to farm land. They worked only on their own strips of land and had rights under the law. They moved wherever and whenever they wished. The noble, however, had the right to throw them off the manor without warning.

The other group was the serfs. Serfs and their descendants were a noble's property. They could not move to another area, own their own property, or marry without the noble's permission. Serfs, however, could not be driven off the land and did not have to serve in the army.

It was not easy for serfs to gain their freedom. One way was to escape to the towns. If a serf was not caught and remained in town for more than a year, he or she was considered free. By the end of the Middle Ages, serfs were allowed to buy their freedom.

As in Charlemagne's time, the serfs worked long hours in the fields and performed many services for the nobles. Serfs spent three days of the week working the lord's strips of land and the rest of the week caring for their own strips. However, they had to give part of their own crops to the noble. They also paid him for the use of the village's mill, bread oven, and wine press.

In spite of the difficulties, a serf's life had some bright moments. Sunday was a day of rest from work. At Christmas, the

People in History

Trotula of Salerno
c.1097 A.D.

Doctor

Both noble and peasant women took care of the sick, but Trotula broke with tradition by becoming a trained doctor. She studied and taught at the medical school at Salerno, Italy. Trotula specialized in the health of women and wrote a book called *The Diseases of Women*. Her book influenced doctors for centuries. Today she is considered one of Europe's early women of science.

Reading Check How did **freemen** differ from serfs?

Fun Facts . . .

Serf Work A monk at Canterbury recorded an English serf's account of his day: "I work very hard. I go out at dawn, driving the oxen to the field, and I yoke them to the plough. However hard the winter, I dare not stay home for fear of my master."

CAPTION ANSWER

wrestling, archery, soccer

Reading Check Answer Unlike serfs, **freemen** paid a noble for the right to farm the land and could move about freely.

GEOGRAPHY AND HISTORY

In the three-field system of planting, one field might be planted with winter wheat, a second with spring wheat and vegetables, and a third left fallow. The next year, different crops were planted in the fallow field. One of the two remaining fields was planted and the other one was left fallow until the next year.

ASSESS

Check for Understanding

Ask students to summarize the main points of the chapter, orally or in writing. Discuss the answers to the Section and Chapter Assessment questions.

EXTENDING THE CONTENT

Peasant meals varied from country to country, just as basic cuisines do today. Bread—whole wheat, rye, or barley—was basic, along with several kinds of pasta in Italy. Porridges and oatmeal made of grain with peas or beans were common everywhere. In France, peasants ate hearty soups, stews, and vegetables and drank wine or cider. They grew apples and grapes and stored them over the winter by drying or cooking them in honey. The English had several kinds of cheese and curds. They made ale, cider, and mead—a fermented honey drink. Germans made lentils, sauerkraut, cabbage, peas, and turnips.

Evaluate

Assign the Chapter 24 **Performance Assessment Activity** in the TCR. Administer the **Chapter 24 Test.** Testmaker available.

Reteach

Organize the class into small groups. Have each group summarize a particular part of the chapter.

Assign the Chapter 24 **Reteaching Activity** in the TCR.

Enrich

Have students research the kinds of "mystery plays" that serfs attended for amusement. Students may perform a skit similar to one of the plays.

Assign the Chapter 24 **Enrichment Activity** in the TCR.

CLOSE

Ask students to share their opinions of people in the Middle Ages. If students had to travel back in time to medieval England, what kind of life would they choose? Why?

Use the **Interactive Tutor Self Assessment CD-ROM** to review Section 4.

HISTORY Online

Self-Check Quiz gives students an interactive chapter tutorial. Have them access ***Chapter 24 Quiz*** at humanheritage.glencoe.com

lord paid for a great feast and entertainment. Certain holidays were celebrated with singing and dancing on the village green. When they could, serfs took part in such sports as wrestling, archery, and soccer.

By the 1200s, peasants began to learn better farming methods. They used the three-field system of farming and started to use a heavy iron plow. The horse collar was invented, allowing horses instead of slow-moving oxen to plow fields. All of this enabled the peasants to grow more food.

Section 4 Assessment

1. **Define:** manors, seneschal, bailiff, freemen.
2. What were some features of a manor village?
3. What rights did freemen have?
4. What did serfs contribute to a manor?

Critical Thinking

5. **Making Comparisons** What interests did nobles and serfs have in common?

Graphic Organizer Activity

6. Draw this diagram, and use it to show technological improvements in farming in the 1200s.

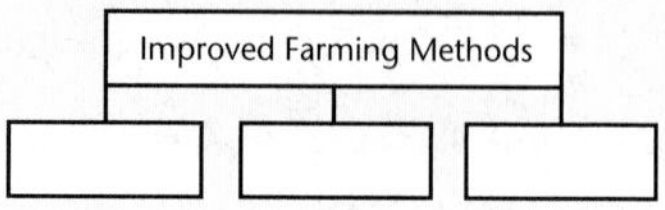

Chapter Summary & Study Guide

1. Following Charlemagne's death, kings began to depend on nobles for food, horses, and soldiers.
2. Some nobles began to collect their own taxes, run their own courts, coin their own money, and raise their own armies.
3. As the power of kings declined, the nobles took on the duty of defending their land and people from Viking attacks.
4. By 1000, the kingdoms of western Europe were divided into thousands of feudal territories.
5. Under feudalism, landowning nobles gave vassals land in exchange for loyalty and military service.
6. Knights followed the code of chivalry and trained for war by fighting in tournaments.
7. Fiefs were owned by nobles and worked by peasants.
8. Peasants included freemen and serfs. While freemen could leave the land if they wished, serfs were considered a noble's property.
9. By the 1200s, improvements in farming methods helped the peasants to grow more food.

HISTORY Online

Self-Check Quiz

Visit the *Human Heritage* Web site at humanheritage.glencoe.com and click on ***Chapter 24—Self-Check Quiz*** to assess your understanding of this chapter.

Section 4 Assessment Answers

1. manors, farming communities (p. 375); seneschal, overseer of a noble's fief (p. 375); bailiff, official who supervised peasants (p. 376); freemen, peasants who paid for the right to farm land (p. 377)
2. peasant cottages surrounded by forests, meadows, pastures, and fields; usually with a church, mill, bread oven, and wine press
3. to move about freely
4. They worked long hours in the fields, obeyed nobles' wishes, and had to give the noble part of their crops.
5. Answers will vary but might indicate that nobles and serfs depended upon each other to survive.
6. sample improvements: three-field system, use of iron plow, invention of horse collar

Assign the Chapter 24 **Section 4 Quiz** in the TCR. Testmaker available.

CHAPTER 24 Assessment

Using Key Terms

Imagine you are living in the late Middle Ages. Write an interview with a noble and a serf in which they describe their lives. Use the following words in your interview.

feudalism	clergy	fiefs
vassal	act of homage	knight
castles	keep	ladies
code of chivalry	page	squire
dubbing	tournaments	joust
manors	seneschal	bailiff
freemen		

Understanding Main Ideas

1. Into what three groups were people divided under feudalism?
2. Who held the political power within a feudal territory?
3. Who usually received a vassal's fief when the vassal died?
4. What was expected of a knight?
5. Why did people on a manor produce everything they needed?
6. How could serfs obtain their freedom?
7. What changes had taken place in farming by the 1200s?

Critical Thinking

1. What advantages would there be to being a vassal rather than a lord?
2. Why do you think women provided the medical care in a fief?
3. What would you have enjoyed about being a knight? What would you have disliked?
4. How do you think a serf's life would be affected by the improved farming methods of the thirteenth century?

Graphic Organizer Activity

Citizenship Create a diagram like this one, and use it to show the organization of government under feudalism. Each of these groups should appear on the chart: serfs, landowning nobles, freemen, knights.

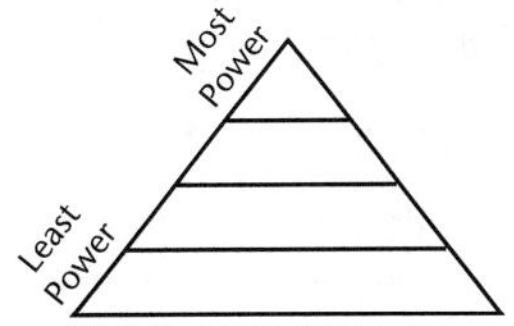

Geography in History

Environment and Society The people of the manor made good use of their natural resources to support themselves. Predict and describe how you think manor life would have changed if a plant disease had killed all the trees in an area.

Using Your Journal

Compare any details you may have noted about the lives of women in the late Middle Ages with the lives of women today. Write a paragraph explaining the similarities and differences as if you were explaining them to someone who lived on a European manor.

Bonus Test Question

For Chapter 24 Test

Who is not telling the truth here? *Noble 1*: "The king gave this manor to my mother. Here is the paper to prove it." *Noble 2*: "This is my land. I served the king in battle, was held hostage in his place, and he awarded it to me."

Using Your Journal

Paragraphs will vary but may include issues of basic human freedoms. You might ask volunteers to read their paragraphs to the class.

Geography in History

Answers will vary but should reflect the uses of wood in the lives of serfs and the impact of the loss of trees. Students may also suggest other plants may have been affected by the same disease.

CHAPTER 24 Assessment Answers

Using Key Terms

Interviews will vary, but students should use all the terms.

Understanding Main Ideas

1. the clergy, the nobles, and the peasants and townspeople
2. the noble who owned the land
3. his oldest son
4. to follow the code of chivalry
5. because the manors were isolated from one another
6. by escaping to the towns for more than a year or by buying their freedom
7. Peasants began to learn better farming methods, used the heavy iron plow, and used horses instead of slow-moving oxen to plow their fields.

Critical Thinking

1. Answers will vary but should include the ideas that vassals had fewer responsibilities, received a fief, and had the protection of a noble.
2. Answers will vary but might include that she was usually there, and medical care was considered a domestic concern.
3. Answers will vary, but students should give some specific examples.
4. Answers will vary but might include that serfs would have more time for themselves. With more food grown, they would be healthier.

Graphic Organizer Activity

From top to bottom, groups should appear in this order: landowning nobles, knights, freemen, serfs.

Chapter 25 Planning Guide

Timesaving Tools

TeacherWorks™ All-In-One Planner and Resource Center

- **Interactive Teacher Edition** Access your Teacher Wraparound Edition and your classroom resources with a few easy clicks.
- **Interactive Lesson Planner** Planning has never been easier! Organize your week, month, semester, or year with all the lesson helps you need to make teaching creative, timely, and relevant.

Use Glencoe's **Presentation Plus!** multimedia teacher tool to easily present dynamic lessons that visually excite your students. Using Microsoft PowerPoint® you can customize the presentations to create your own personalized lessons.

Objectives	Reproducible Resources	Multimedia Resources
Section 1 **Catholic Influence** Discuss how the Roman Catholic Church influenced life during the Middle Ages.	Reproducible Lesson Plan Chapter 25 Vocabulary and Guided Reading Activity Reading Essentials and Study Guide 25-1 Section 1 Quiz	Interactive Student Edition CD-ROM Teaching Transparency and Activity 25A Graphic Organizer Transparency 13 Vocabulary PuzzleMaker CD-ROM Interactive Tutor Self-Assessment CD-ROM ExamView® Pro Testmaker CD-ROM Glencoe Skillbuilder Interactive Workbook CD-ROM, Level 1 Presentation Plus! CD-ROM
Section 2 **Attempts to Reform** Summarize attempts made to reform the Church and Church practices during the Middle Ages.	Reproducible Lesson Plan Reading Essentials and Study Guide 25-2 Chapter 25 Enrichment Activity Section 2 Quiz	Vocabulary PuzzleMaker CD-ROM Interactive Tutor Self-Assessment CD-ROM ExamView® Pro Testmaker CD-ROM Glencoe Skillbuilder Interactive Workbook CD-ROM, Level 1
Section 3 **Learning** Describe what learning was like during the Middle Ages.	Reproducible Lesson Plan Reading Essentials and Study Guide 25-3 Section 3 Quiz	Teaching Transparency and Activity 25B Vocabulary PuzzleMaker CD-ROM Interactive Tutor Self-Assessment CD-ROM ExamView® Pro Testmaker CD-ROM Glencoe Skillbuilder Interactive Workbook CD-ROM, Level 1
Section 4 **The Crusades** Explain why the Crusades took place, and analyze the effect of the Crusades upon the Middle Ages.	Reproducible Lesson Plan Reading Essentials and Study Guide 25-4 Chapter 25 Cooperative Learning Activity Chapter 25 Geography and Map Activity Chapter 25 Chart and Graph Skill Activity Section 4 Quiz	Vocabulary PuzzleMaker CD-ROM Interactive Tutor Self-Assessment CD-ROM ExamView® Pro Testmaker CD-ROM Glencoe Skillbuilder Interactive Workbook CD-ROM, Level 1
Chapter 25 **Review and Evaluation**	Chapter 25 Reteaching Activity Chapter 25 Performance Assessment Activity Spanish Chapter Summary and Glossary Chapter 25 Test	Vocabulary PuzzleMaker CD-ROM Interactive Tutor Self-Assessment CD-ROM Glencoe Skillbuilder Interactive Workbook CD-ROM, Level 1 Audiocassettes* ExamView® Pro Testmaker CD-ROM

*Also available in Spanish.

Chapter 25 Planning Guide

✓ Performance Assessment Activities

Historic Imagination Have students imagine they are a member of the Children's Crusade. Tell students to each prepare a list of supplies and a map showing their planned route. Have students share their plans with the rest of the class.

CHAPTER RESOURCES

LITERATURE ABOUT THE PERIOD

Konisburg, E. L. *A Proud Taste for Scarlet and Miniver.* Atheneum, 1973. A biography of Eleanor of Aquitaine.

READINGS FOR THE STUDENT

Boyd, Anne. *Life in a 15th-Century Monastery* (A Cambridge Topic Book). Lerner Publications, 1979. An account of the daily life of monks in the monastery at Durham, England.

READINGS FOR THE TEACHER

Gies, Frances, and Joseph Gies. *Women in the Middle Ages: The Lives of Real Women in a Vibrant Age of Transition.* Barnes and Noble, 1978. Highlights women's lives in the Middle Ages.

KEY TO ABILITY LEVELS

Teaching strategies have been coded for varying learning styles and abilities.

L1 Level 1 activities are **basic** activities and should be within the ability range of all students.

L2 Level 2 activities are **average** activities and should be within the ability range of the average to above-average student.

L3 Level 3 activities are **challenging** activities designed for the ability range of above-average students.

ELL ELL activities should be within the ability range of English Language Learning students.

NATIONAL GEOGRAPHIC Teacher's Corner

INDEX TO NATIONAL GEOGRAPHIC MAGAZINE

The following articles relate to this chapter:

- "The Gothic Revolution," by James L. Stanfield and Victor R. Boswell, Jr., July 1989.
- "A Renaissance for Michelangelo," by David Jeffery, December 1989.

NATIONAL GEOGRAPHIC SOCIETY PRODUCTS AVAILABLE FROM GLENCOE

To order the following, call Glencoe at 1-800-334-7344:

- *PicturePack: Middle Ages (Transparencies)*
- *PictureShow: Middle Ages (CD-ROM)*

Access *National Geographic*'s new dynamic MapMachine Web site and other geography resources at:
www.nationalgeographic.com
www.nationalgeographic.com/maps

THE HISTORY CHANNEL. A&E HOME VIDEO. Biography

The following videotape programs are available from Glencoe:

- **The Crusades**
  1-56501-505-3
- **Richard the Lionheart**
  1-56501-916-4

To order, call Glencoe at 1-800-334-7344. To find classroom resources to accompany many of these, check:
A&E Television: www.aande.com
The History Channel: www.historychannel.com

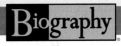

Introducing CHAPTER 25

OVERVIEW

Chapter 25 discusses the role of the Roman Catholic Church during the Middle Ages.

- **Section 1** describes the influence of the Church in daily life in western Europe.
- **Section 2** discusses Church reforms.
- **Section 3** explains the spread of Christian teachings in western Europe.
- **Section 4** describes reasons for the Crusades.

CHAPTER OBJECTIVES

After reading Chapter 25, students will be able to:

1. discuss how the Roman Catholic Church influenced life during the Middle Ages.
2. summarize attempts to reform the Church.
3. describe education during the Middle Ages.
4. explain why the Crusades took place.
5. list effects of the Crusades.

EXAMINING ARTIFACTS

Connect these two works of art by pointing out the cross worn by the crusader. Ask: What do you think the crusader would be willing to do for the Church? *(to fight for it)* Bridge chapters 24 and 25 by having students name groups in medieval society who they think might go on a crusade. Save their responses to review as students read this chapter.

PERFORMANCE ASSESSMENT

Use the Performance Assessment Activities on page 380B to help you evaluate students as they complete the chapter.

CHAPTER 25

The Church

1000 A.D.–1300 A.D.

◄ Christian crusader and his wife

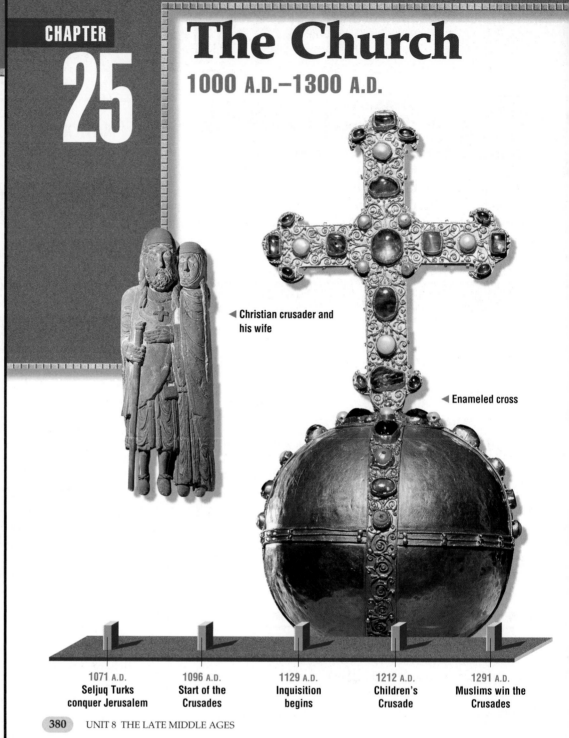

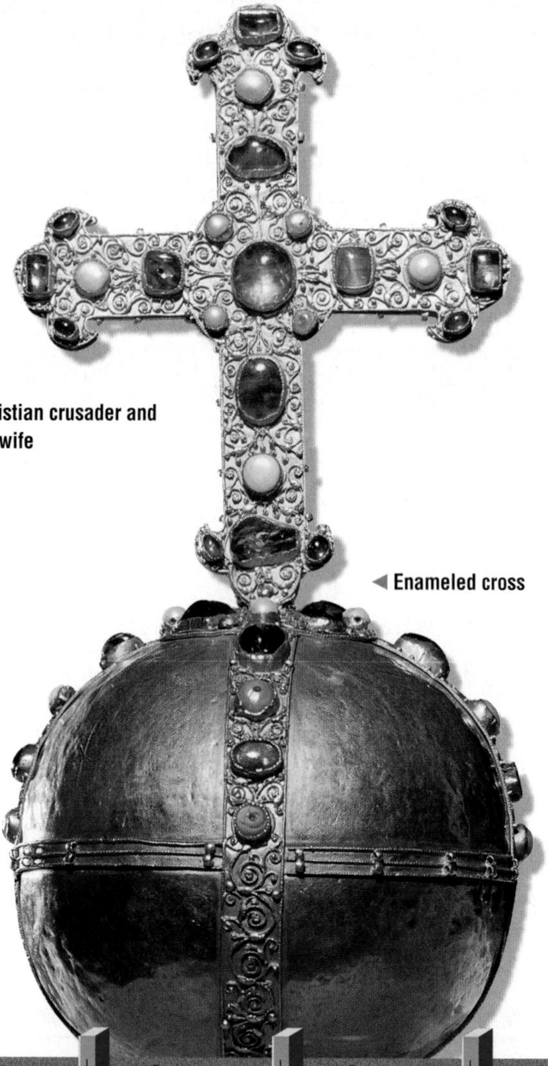

◄ Enameled cross

1071 A.D.	1096 A.D.	1129 A.D.	1212 A.D.	1291 A.D.
Seljuq Turks conquer Jerusalem	Start of the Crusades	Inquisition begins	Children's Crusade	Muslims win the Crusades

TEACHING RESOURCES

TEACHER PLANNING AND SUPPORT

- Reproducible Lesson Plan 25-1, 25-2, 25-3, 25-4
- Teaching Strategies for the World History Classroom (Including Block Scheduling Pacing Guides)
- Presentation Plus! CD-ROM

REVIEW AND REINFORCEMENT

- Reading Essentials and Study Guide 25-1, 25-2, 25-3, 25-4
- Chapter 25 Vocabulary and Guided Reading Activity
- Vocabulary PuzzleMaker CD-ROM
- Teaching Transparencies 25A & 25B
- Chapter 25 Reteaching Activity
- Chapter 25 Cooperative Learning Activity
- Chapter 25 Activity Book Activity
- Chapter 25 Chart and Graph Skill Activity
- Reading and Study Skills Foldables
- Interactive Tutor Self-Assessment CD-ROM

APPLICATION AND HANDS-ON ACTIVITIES

- Daily Questions in Social Studies
- World Crafts Activity Card 5
- Student Presentation Builder CD-ROM

GEOGRAPHY ACTIVITIES

- Chapter 25 Geography and Map Activity

Chapter Focus

Read to Discover

- How the Roman Catholic Church influenced life during the Middle Ages.
- What attempts were made to reform the Church during the Middle Ages.
- What learning was like during the Middle Ages.
- Why the Crusades took place during the Middle Ages.
- What the effects of the Crusades were.

HISTORY Online

Chapter Overview

Visit the *Human Heritage* Web site at **humanheritage.glencoe.com** and click on ***Chapter 25—Chapter Overviews*** to preview this chapter.

Terms to Learn	People to Know	Places to Locate
mass	Gregory VII	Cluny
tithes	Francis of Assisi	Palestine
cathedrals	Thomas Aquinas	Outremer
unions	Urban II	Venice
chancellor	Saladin	Acre
crusades	Richard the Lionheart	
emirs		

Why It's Important Leaders in the Roman Catholic Church wanted to develop a civilization in western Europe that was based on Christian ideals. By 1000, missionary monks had brought the Church's teachings to most of Europe. They converted people and built new churches and monasteries. The Roman Catholic Church united western Europeans and took the lead in government, law, art, and learning for hundreds of years. The Church helped pass on the heritage of the Roman Empire. Latin became the official language of the Church.

SECTION 1 Catholic Influence

The Roman Catholic Church had great influence during the Middle Ages. It was the center of every village and town. It played an important part in the political life of the period. At times, it even had the power of life or death over people.

Daily Life In every village and town, daily life revolved around the Church. To become a king, vassal, or knight, a man had to take part in a religious ceremony. Most holidays were in honor of saints or religious events. On Fridays, the people obeyed the Church's rule not to eat meat. On Sundays, they went to

HISTORY Online

Chapter Overview introduces students to chapter content and key terms. Have them access ***Chapter 25 Overview*** at **humanheritage.glencoe.com**

FOCUS

Bellringer

Write this question on the chalkboard: *What would cause you to voluntarily join an army and go to war in a foreign land?*

Motivational Activity

Have students read their responses. They may mention patriotism, a desire to help others, and so on. Point out that religion motivated many of the crusaders who went to war. Discuss whether religious motivation is a force anywhere in the world today.

GUIDE TO READING

Reading Strategy

Ask students to read "Why It's Important" and summarize the chapter's main theme. *(The Roman Catholic Church united western Europeans and took a leading role in most aspects of life.)*

Vocabulary Precheck

Ask students to define each of the "Terms to Learn." Have a volunteer consult the dictionary for any unfamiliar words. L1 ELL

Use the Vocabulary PuzzleMaker CD-ROM for Chapter 25 to create a crossword puzzle. L1

Assign Chapter 25 Vocabulary and Guided Reading Activity. L1

Assign Reading Essentials and Study Guide 25-1.

- Building Geography Skills for Life
- Outline Map Resource Book

INTERDISCIPLINARY CONNECTIONS

- World Art Print 6, *Shrine of the Three Magi*
- World Music: A Cultural Legacy

ENRICHMENT AND EXTENSION

- World History Primary Source Document Library CD-ROM
- Chapter 25 Enrichment Activity
- Foods Around the World

ASSESSMENT AND EVALUATION

- Chapter 25 Performance Assessment Activity
- Chapter 25 Section Quizzes 25-1, 25-2, 25-3, 25-4
- Chapter 25 Test
- Chapter 25 ExamView® Pro Testmaker CD-ROM
- Chapter 25 Digests Audiocassettes Activities and Tests

SPANISH RESOURCES

- Chapter 25 Spanish Chapter Summary and Glossary
- Chapter 25 Spanish Digests Audiocassettes Activities and Tests

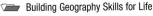

TEACH

Guided Practice

L1 **Discussion** Lead students in a discussion about the influence of the Catholic Church on all aspects of life in western Europe during the Middle Ages. Ask: How was the Church a force that brought people together in western Europe during the Middle Ages? How did the Church influence daily life?

Reading Check Answer
The parish priest usually held **mass** in medieval villages and towns.

CAPTION ANSWER

Priests recorded births, performed marriages, and conducted burials.

Reading Check Answer
Canon laws are laws set up by the Church.
People who were **excommunicated** lost their membership in the Church as well as their political rights.

MAKING CONNECTIONS

>> **Religion** The religion of most people in the Middle Ages was a mixture of Christian and pagan beliefs. Prayer was viewed as a way of working magic, and the saints were believed to have the same miracle-working powers as the gods and goddesses.

VILLAGE CHURCH During the Middle Ages, the church was the religious and social center of the village. Both the local noble and the peasants contributed to the building of the church and its upkeep. **What were some daily tasks performed by the parish priest?**

Reading Check Who usually held **mass** in medieval villages and towns?

mass, or a worship service, held by the parish priest. Church leaders ran schools and hospitals. Monks and nuns provided food and shelter for travelers. Priests recorded births, performed marriages, and conducted burials.

Political Life The Church played an important role in the political life of the Middle Ages. Together with kings and nobles, Church officials helped govern western Europe. As large landowners, high Church leaders were both lords and vassals of other lords. They served as advisers to kings and other nobles, keeping records for the kings who could not read or write. Parish priests also played a part in government. They were chosen by local nobles and were expected to tell the people to respect the king, the nobles, and other government officials.

The Church told people to obey the king's laws unless they went against **canon laws,** or laws set up by the Church. People who disobeyed the Pope or canon laws were **excommunicated** (ek skuh myū' nuh kā ted), or lost their membership in the Church. They also lost their political rights.

Reading Check What are **canon laws?** What happened to people who were **excommunicated?**

The Inquisition Despite its power, the Church faced the problem of heresy. At first, it tried to stop the spread of heresy by preaching. Then, in 1129, a council of bishops set up the Inquisition (in kwuh zish' uhn), or Church court, to end heresy by force.

The Church gave people it suspected of heresy one month to confess. Those who appeared in front of the Inquisition before the month ended were whipped or sent to prison for a short time. Those who did not appear were seized and brought to trial.

EXTENDING THE CONTENT

Nobles thought little of hurting or killing peasants, serfs, and villagers, burning their crops and barns, or killing their livestock. Within the Church there were those who tried to stop the bloodshed. Late in the 900s, a movement within the Church called the Peace of God tried to protect certain persons or places from violence. For instance, there was to be no fighting in church. Knights were not to attack people on their way to church. In 1017, the Church tried putting a further ban on casual fighting called the Truce of God. This forbade fighting from early Saturday until Monday.

The reason for the trial was to get a confession. The court called only two witnesses. Based on what they said, the court decided whether or not a person was a heretic. Heretics who confessed were punished. Then, they were allowed to become Church members again. Heretics who refused to confess were often tortured. A number of people were burned at the stake.

Section 1 Assessment

1. **Define:** mass, canon laws, excommunicated.
2. What part did parish priests play in government?

Critical Thinking

3. **Making Inferences** How do you think a king might have felt about being excommunicated from the Church?

Graphic Organizer Activity

4. Draw this diagram, and use it to show examples of Church powers during the Middle Ages.

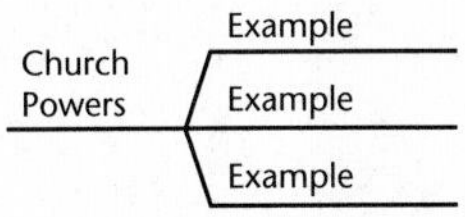

THE INQUISITION The Inquisition was established to strengthen the beliefs of the Church in France, Germany, Italy, and Spain. In this painting, a heretic under trial confesses. **What punishment came to those who confessed to heresy?**

LINKING PAST TO PRESENT

Unlike American courts, which hold that a defendant is innocent until proven guilty, the Inquisition assumed that a defendant was guilty. Also, during the Middle Ages, Church leaders sought to maintain their authority and to limit state influence. Today in the United States, the state usually favors separation of church and state so that neither religious beliefs nor government infringe on one another.

DID YOU KNOW ??

Monks and nuns worked hard to make monastery lands productive. They became known as the best farmers of western Europe.

CAPTION ANSWER

They were whipped or sent to prison for a short time.

Section 1 Assessment Answers

1. mass, a worship service (p. 382); canon laws, laws set up by the Church (p. 382); excommunicated, lost membership in the Church (p. 382)
2. They were expected to tell the people to respect the kings, the nobles, and other government officials.
3. Answers will vary but might include that it would not be desirable for a king to be excommunicated because then the king would lose his political rights.
4. Student answers should reflect the many Church powers identified on pages 381–382. You might adapt the graphic organizer to display examples by category, such as political powers, legal powers, social powers, and so on.

Assign the Chapter 25 **Section 1 Quiz** in the TCR. Testmaker available.

L3 Critical Thinking Explain to students that as institutions of religious faith and devotion, monasteries fulfilled an important function in medieval society. By providing schools for the young, medical care for the sick, food for the hungry, and rest for the weary, monasteries were forerunners of modern charitable organizations. Ask students to list examples of contemporary organizations who answer social needs. Then have students compare these modern organizations with monasteries of the Middle Ages.

Reading Check Answer
Tithes were offerings equal to 10 percent of the incomes of Church members.

Linking Across Time

Church leaders raised money to pay for works of art through tithes and donations by wealthy nobles. (You might point out that merchants and guilds later gave donations, too.)

Use the **Vocabulary PuzzleMaker CD-ROM** to create crossword and word search puzzles.

SECTION 2 Attempts at Reform

Reading Check What were **tithes?**

The Church became rich during the Middle Ages. Church members supported it by giving **tithes** (tīthz), or offerings equal to 10 percent of their income. Rich nobles donated money to build large churches and gave land to monasteries. The wealthier the monasteries became, however, the more careless many monks grew about carrying out their religious duties.

Monks were not the only ones to grow careless about religious duties. When a bishop died, his office and lands were taken over by the local noble. The noble often chose a close relative as the new bishop or sold the office for money or favors.

Linking Across Time

Stained-Glass Windows During the time of Charlemagne, Europeans started designing windows made from individual pieces of colored glass and held together by lead. The art form reached its peak in the church windows of the late Middle Ages (below). In the late 1800s and early 1900s, artists such as Louis Comfort Tiffany revived this art form in stained-glass windows and lamps (right). **How did church leaders raise money to pay for works of art like stained-glass windows?**

MULTICULTURAL PERSPECTIVES

Inquisition officials often accused people of heresy without sufficient proof; sometimes they even used torture to obtain confessions. The Church welcomed back those who repented, but those who did not were punished with imprisonment, loss of property, or execution. According to Church teachings, these punishments were necessary to save the souls of the heretics.

The crusaders changed their eating habits, too. It was too hot to eat the heavy, solid foods they were used to. They learned to have light meals with less meat and more fruits and vegetables. They also ate new foods such as rice, oranges, figs, and melons.

The crusaders led an easier life in Palestine than they had at home. Still, they had trouble adjusting. Many died in battle against the Turks or in fights among themselves over rights and lands. Others could not survive the hot climate.

Painting of Arab Scholars

Saladin and the Crusade of Kings

In 1174, a Muslim military leader named Saladin (sal′ uhd uhn) became the ruler of Egypt. He united the Muslims throughout the Near East and started a war against the Christian occupation of Palestine by western Crusaders. Saladin's armies were well organized and devoted to Islam. Groups of soldiers headed by leaders called **emirs** (i miuhrs′) made up the armies. Many emirs were known for their honesty and for the consideration they showed their captives. The emirs often were shocked by the cruelty and greed of the Christian soldiers.

Reading Check What were **emirs** known for?

Saladin's soldiers rode into battle on swift ponies. Their weapons were short bows. The crusaders found it hard to fight them. The crusaders' armor was heavy, their swords were too long to handle easily, and their horses were not protected. They had to learn to depend on a new weapon called the *crossbow,* which fired an arrow with great force and speed. In 1187, Saladin's armies took Jerusalem. When he refused to massacre the city's Christians, he won the respect of many of the crusaders.

After Saladin's victory, the Church urged another crusade. This time the western armies were led by King Richard I of England, Emperor Frederick Barbarossa (bahr buh ros′ uh) of Germany, and King Philip II Augustus of France. They were the three most powerful rulers in Europe.

This Crusade of Kings, as it was called, was a failure. Frederick died in Asia Minor, and many of his troops returned home without ever having fought a battle. Richard and Philip were enemies and were always quarreling. They did take a few coastal cities in Palestine together. Then, Philip returned home. Richard and his armies had to continue the crusade alone.

Richard was a brave warrior. Because of this, he was called "the Lionheart." Nevertheless, he could not defeat Saladin. After three years, he gave up and signed a truce with the Muslim leader. Although the crusaders still controlled large areas of Palestine, Jerusalem remained in Muslim hands.

Painting of Saladin

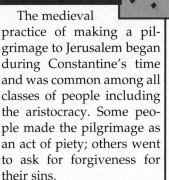

The Loss of an Ideal

In 1202, Pope Innocent III called for yet another crusade. Knights from all over Europe answered the call. They decided not to take a land route to Palestine but to go by ship from the Italian port of Venice. Rich merchants there wanted

MAKING CONNECTIONS

>> **Religion** The truce signed by King Richard and Saladin allowed both Muslims and Christians to visit the Holy Land in peace and safety.

Reading Check Answer

Emirs were known for their honesty and for the consideration they showed their captives.

DID YOU KNOW ??

The medieval practice of making a pilgrimage to Jerusalem began during Constantine's time and was common among all classes of people including the aristocracy. Some people made the pilgrimage as an act of piety; others went to ask for forgiveness for their sins.

Biography

The following videotape program is available from Glencoe to enrich Chapter 25:

- **Richard the Lionheart**

To find classroom resources to accompany this video, check the following home page:

A&E Television:
www.aande.com

SPOTLIGHT ON: SALADIN

Saladin made the following reply to King Richard I of England after Richard wrote Saladin that he and his men would continue to fight for Jerusalem:

"To us Jerusalem is as precious, aye and more precious than it is to you, in that it was the place whence our Prophet made his journey by night and is destined to be the gathering place of our nation at the last day. Do not dream that we shall give it up to you. . . It belonged to us originally, and it is you who are the aggressors."

MAP SKILLS

TEACH

Determining Exact Location

Have students read the introductory section of the skill on page 394. Ask: Why do most maps have grids? *(to help find different points on a map)* What do you need to find in order to know the exact location of a place? *(the line of latitude and the line of longitude that cross at that exact location)* Direct students to the map on this page. Ask: What are the coordinates of Constantinople? *(41 °N, 29 °E)*

Next, have students write five questions about the Crusades based on the information on the map. Then collect the questions and quiz the class on the map using the questions written by the students.

Assign the Chapter 25 **Geography and Map Activity** in the TCR.

Answers to Map Practice

1. Jerusalem
2. 45° N, 12° E

Use the **Glencoe Skillbuilder Interactive Workbook CD-ROM, Level 1,** to provide instruction and practice in key social studies skills.

MAP SKILLS

Determining Exact Location

Most maps have **grids,** or patterns of horizontal and vertical lines that cross each other. Generally, the horizontal lines are lines of latitude, and the vertical ones are lines of longitude. Grids make it easier to determine the exact location of a place on Earth.

To find a place exactly, it is necessary to find what lines of latitude and longitude cross at that place. The point at which they cross is the exact location.

Exact location may be shown by a set of numbers that lists latitude first and then longitude (30°N, 60°E). Such sets are called **coordinates** (kō ōr′ din uhts).

Look at the map of "The Crusades" below. Locate the city of Marseilles on the southern coast of France. The line of latitude that passes through the city is 43°N. The line of longitude that passes through it is 5°E. This means that the exact location of Marseilles is 43°N, 5°E.

Map Practice

1. **What city is located at 32°N, 35°E?**
2. **What are the coordinates of Venice's location?**

The Crusades

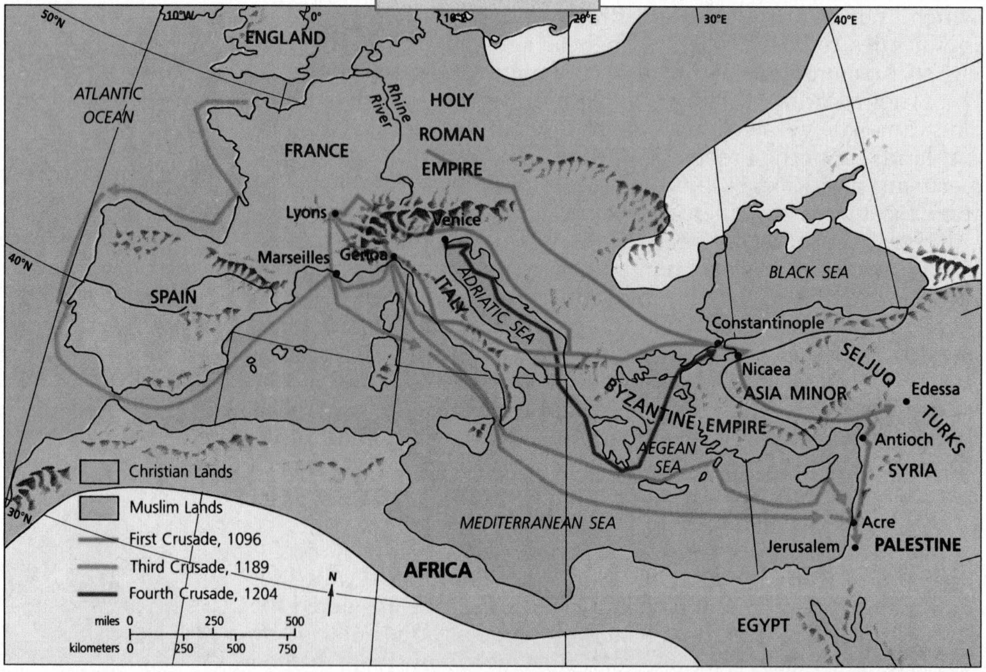

SPOTLIGHT ON: THE CRUSADES

The general climate of the area through which the crusaders traveled was not unlike that of the western United States and Mexico—a combination of desert and mediterranean climates. The average annual temperature fell in the range of 60°–70° F (16°–21° C), which is similar to the temperatures in the southern half of the United States.

Venice to replace Constantinople as the trading center of the eastern Mediterranean. The crusaders agreed to pay these merchants a large sum of money and to share one half of all their conquests with the Venetians. In return, the Venetians agreed to supply the crusaders with ships and equipment.

When the soldiers found they could not pay all they owed, they agreed to conquer the city of Zara for the Venetians. Then, the Venetians convinced them to capture Constantinople. For three days, the crusaders and the Venetians burned and looted Constantinople. Many priceless manuscripts and works of art were either taken to Venice, lost, or destroyed.

Jeweled Box

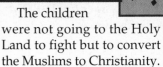

The crusaders finally decided not to go to Palestine. Instead, they stayed in Constantinople and divided the city with the Venetians. Their conduct shocked many western Europeans, who lost respect for the crusader ideal.

Several other crusades were fought during the 1200s, but the Europeans did not win any of them. The saddest of all was the Children's Crusade. A group of French children, led by a peasant boy named Stephen of Cloyes, set sail from Marseilles (mahr sā'), France, in 1212. Most of the children never reached Palestine. Along the way they were sold into slavery by captains of the ships on which they sailed. At the same time, another group of children set forth on foot from Germany, intending to march toward Italy. Most of them, however, starved to death or died from disease.

In 1291, the Muslims took over the city of Acre (ah' kuhr), the last Christian stronghold. The Muslims had won the Crusades. They also gained back all the land in Palestine that the crusaders had taken earlier.

Effects of the Crusades The Crusades affected both the Near East and western Europe. The Byzantines were so angry at the actions of western Europeans that the split between eastern and western Christianity became permanent. At the same time, the Byzantine Empire was so weakened by the Crusades that it could no longer defend itself. This left Europe open to Turkish attack.

The Crusades helped to break down feudalism in western Europe. While feudal lords were fighting in Palestine, kings at home increased their authority. The desire for wealth, power, and land grew and began to cloud the religious ideals of many western Europeans.

The crusaders' contact with the cultured Byzantines and Muslims led western Europeans to again become interested in learning. At the same time, Europeans began to demand such luxuries as spices, sugar, lemons, rugs, tapestries, and richly woven cloth. To meet these demands, European merchants opened up new trade routes. As trade grew, so did the towns of western Europe.

MULTICULTURAL PERSPECTIVES

Have students debate the following: *The Crusades took place only for religious reasons and purposes.* Organize students into two groups, one group to defend the idea that the motivations of the crusaders were solely religious and the other to defend the idea that the crusaders had other reasons for going to the Holy Land. Allow each group time to research and develop their arguments. Then have each group present its views.

Economics at a Glance

Demand Demand is the desire, ability, and willingness to buy a product. The terms *demand* and *want* have two different meanings in economics. Have students use a dictionary to find the definition for *want*. Ask students to compare this definition with the definition for demand. Ask: What is the difference between *demand* and *want*? *(Demand is the desire, ability, and willingness to buy a product. Want expresses the desire for a product but does not mean that a person has the ability or willingness to pay for it.)*

DID YOU KNOW ??

The children were not going to the Holy Land to fight but to convert the Muslims to Christianity.

ASSESS

Check for Understanding

Ask students to summarize the main points of the chapter, orally or in writing. Discuss the answers to the Section and Chapter Assessment questions.

Evaluate

Assign the Chapter 25 **Performance Assessment Activity** in the TCR.

Administer the **Chapter 25 Test.** Testmaker available.

Reteach

Have students work in small groups to list the important features of each crusade. Have the groups compare and discuss their lists.

Assign the Chapter 25 **Reteaching Activity** in the TCR.

Enrich

Have students investigate accounts of Saladin and King Richard I of England during the Crusade of Kings. Ask students to give a brief oral report on the character of these two men, their motives for fighting, and how they regarded each other.

Assign the Chapter 25 **Enrichment Activity** in the TCR.

CLOSE

Discuss how the Crusades changed western civilization. Ask: Did the crusaders help or hurt western civilization? Have students debate their conclusions.

Use the **Interactive Tutor Self-Assessment CD-ROM** to review Section 4.

HISTORY Online

Self-Check Quiz gives students an interactive chapter tutorial. Have them access ***Chapter 25 Quiz*** at humanheritage.glencoe.com

Section 4 Assessment

1. **Define:** crusades, crusaders, emirs.
2. Why were western Europeans of all classes of society eager to go on a crusade?
3. What effect did the Crusades have on trade?

Critical Thinking

4. **Understanding Cause and Effect** What do you think was the most important effect of the Crusades on the entire civilized world (not just on western Europe)? Explain.

Graphic Organizer Activity

5. Draw this diagram, and use it to support a generalization about the effect of the Crusades on feudalism.

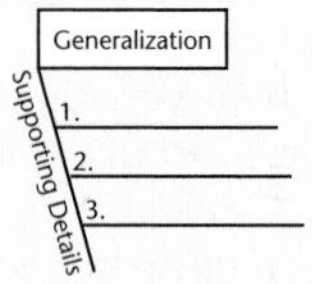

Chapter Summary & Study Guide

1. The Roman Catholic Church was the center of life in Europe during the Middle Ages.
2. Increased wealth led many members of the clergy to grow careless about their religious duties, sparking a spirit of reform.
3. During the Middle Ages, monks and friars worked to win the respect of the people.
4. In 1075, Pope Gregory VII issued a document placing the power of the Pope above all kings and feudal lords.
5. By the 1200s, students and teachers at cathedral schools had helped form universities, which soon spread throughout Europe.
6. Scholars such as Thomas Aquinas tried to bring faith and reason together.
7. In 1071, the Seljuq Turks conquered the Holy Land and took control of the Christian shrines there.
8. In 1095, Pope Urban II agreed to help the Byzantines against the Turks and called on the people of western Europe to join in a crusade.
9. The Nobles' Crusade of 1097 succeeded in capturing Jerusalem, but the Christians could not hold on to the city.
10. Richard the Lionheart, who set out on a crusade with two other kings, could not defeat Saladin and signed a truce with him.
11. In 1202, crusaders, with the help of the Venetians, burned and looted Constantinople. This event badly damaged the crusading ideal.
12. Even though the Muslims regained all of Palestine in 1291, the Crusades brought lasting changes to Europe, including the end of feudalism.

HISTORY Online

Self-Check Quiz

Visit the *Human Heritage* Web site at humanheritage.glencoe.com and click on ***Chapter 25—Self-Check Quiz*** to assess your understanding of this chapter.

Section 4 Assessment Answers

1. crusades, a series of holy wars (p. 388); crusaders, people on crusades (p. 391); emirs, Muslim military leaders (p. 393)
2. They felt it was their duty as Christians to win back the Holy Land; nobles hoped to acquire more land and gain glory; and peasants wanted to escape hard work.
3. They led to the opening up of new trade routes and an increase in trade.
4. Answers will vary, but students should provide reasons for their choices.
5. Supporting details will vary with the generalization written by students. If you need to provide an example of a generalization, offer this statement from page 395: "The Crusades helped to break down feudalism in western Europe."

Assign the Chapter 25 **Section 4 Quiz** in the TCR. Testmaker available.

CHAPTER 25 Assessment

Using Key Terms

Imagine that you are a traveler in Europe during the Middle Ages. Write an article for a travel magazine describing the influence of the Roman Catholic Church. Use the following words.

mass	canon laws	excommunicated
tithes	friars	orders
cathedrals	unions	universities
chancellor	crusades	crusaders
emirs		

Understanding Main Ideas

1. What role did Church officials play in the political life of the Middle Ages?
2. Why did many monks grow careless about carrying out their religious duties?
3. Why were universities started?
4. Why did Urban II encourage people to go on a crusade?
5. What effect did the climate in Palestine have on the crusaders?
6. What happened during the Children's Crusade?
7. Why did the split in the Roman Catholic Church become permanent?
8. How did the Crusades affect the power of western Europe's kings?

Critical Thinking

1. What were the advantages and disadvantages of having Church leaders run the government during the Middle Ages?
2. What would have been enjoyable about being a student in a medieval university?
3. How would you have responded to Urban II's call for a crusade?
4. How do you think crusaders felt about settling in Palestine?

Graphic Organizer Activity

Economics Create a diagram like the one below, and use it to show how the Crusades affected western Europe's economy.

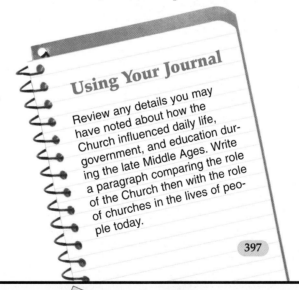

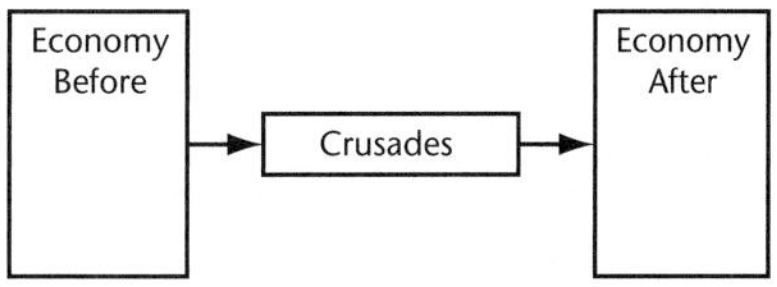

Geography in History

The World in Spatial Terms Refer to the map on page 394. Soldiers in the Fourth Crusade sailed from Venice to Constantinople. About how many miles long was their voyage? Was their voyage longer or shorter than it would have been if they had sailed to Jerusalem as planned?

Using Your Journal

Review any details you may have noted about how the Church influenced daily life, government, and education during the late Middle Ages. Write a paragraph comparing the role of the Church then with the role of churches in the lives of people today.

397

CHAPTER 25 Assessment Answers

Using Key Terms

Articles will vary but should describe highlights of the area and dominance of the Church.

Understanding Main Ideas

1. They served as advisers and kept records for illiterate kings.
2. because they became wealthy
3. because students complained that teachers were poor and held few classes, and untrained people were teaching
4. to free Jerusalem from the Seljuq Turks; to win a chance to regain control of the Eastern Orthodox Church
5. They were not accustomed to the heat and lack of water. Many died of thirst or starvation.
6. Many of the children were sold into enslavement, starved to death, or died from disease.
7. because the Byzantines were so angry at the actions of western Europeans in burning and looting Constantinople
8. They increased the kings' authority.

Critical Thinking

1. Answers will vary, but one advantage was that the Church was a unifying force. A disadvantage was that Church officials became wealthy and corrupt.
2. Answers will vary but should include examples.
3. Answers will vary.
4. Answers will vary, but students should indicate why they would or would not have liked to settle there.

Graphic Organizer Activity

Graphic organizers will vary but should contrast the largely self-sufficient manors prior to the Crusades with the revival of trade and cities after the Crusades.

Bonus Test Question

For Chapter 25 Test

You are a Monk of Cluny faced by an angry bishop who resents your activities. Explain your beliefs and convince the bishop to work with you. *(Answers may vary, but students should indicate that the Cluny monks were trying to reform the Church.)*

Using Your Journal

Paragraphs will vary but might indicate that churches have a more personal effect on people today rather than the all-encompassing effect the Church had in the Middle Ages.

Geography in History

about 1,400 miles (or 2,250 km); shorter

Chapter 26 Planning Guide

Timesaving Tools

TeacherWorks™ All-In-One Planner and Resource Center

- **Interactive Teacher Edition** Access your Teacher Wraparound Edition and your classroom resources with a few easy clicks.
- **Interactive Lesson Planner** Planning has never been easier! Organize your week, month, semester, or year with all the lesson helps you need to make teaching creative, timely, and relevant.

Use Glencoe's **Presentation Plus!** multimedia teacher tool to easily present dynamic lessons that visually excite your students. Using Microsoft PowerPoint® you can customize the presentations to create your own personalized lessons.

Objectives	Reproducible Resources	Multimedia Resources
Section 1 **Trading Centers** Analyze how the growth of trade led to the rise of towns in the Middle Ages.	Reproducible Lesson Plan Chapter 26 Vocabulary and Guided Reading Activity Reading Essentials and Study Guide 26-1 Chapter 26 Geography and Map Activity Section 1 Quiz	Interactive Student Edition CD-ROM Graphic Organizer Transparency 4 Vocabulary PuzzleMaker CD-ROM ExamView® Pro Testmaker CD-ROM Glencoe Skillbuilder Interactive Workbook CD-ROM, Level 1 Presentation Plus! CD-ROM
Section 2 **Merchants** Summarize how merchants became an important part of European life.	Reproducible Lesson Plan Reading Essentials and Study Guide 26-2 Section 2 Quiz	Vocabulary PuzzleMaker CD-ROM Interactive Tutor Self-Assessment CD-ROM ExamView® Pro Testmaker CD-ROM Glencoe Skillbuilder Interactive Workbook CD-ROM, Level 1
Section 3 **Living Conditions** Describe what living conditions were like in medieval towns.	Reproducible Lesson Plan Reading Essentials and Study Guide 26-3 Section 3 Quiz	Teaching Transparencies and Activities 26A & 26B Vocabulary PuzzleMaker CD-ROM Interactive Tutor Self-Assessment CD-ROM ExamView® Pro Testmaker CD-ROM
Section 4 **The Rise of Guilds** Explain why guilds were formed and why they were later opposed.	Reproducible Lesson Plan Reading Essentials and Study Guide 26-4 Chapter 26 Cooperative Learning Activity Chapter 26 Enrichment Activity Section 4 Quiz	Vocabulary PuzzleMaker CD-ROM Interactive Tutor Self-Assessment CD-ROM ExamView® Pro Testmaker CD-ROM Glencoe Skillbuilder Interactive Workbook CD-ROM, Level 1
Section 5 **Cultural Changes** Summarize the cultural changes that took place in Europe during the 1400s.	Reproducible Lesson Plan Reading Essentials and Study Guide 26-5 Chapter 26 Chart and Graph Skill Activity Unit 8 World Literature Reading 1 Section 5 Quiz	Vocabulary PuzzleMaker CD-ROM Interactive Tutor Self-Assessment CD-ROM ExamView® Pro Testmaker CD-ROM Glencoe Skillbuilder Interactive Workbook CD-ROM, Level 1
Chapter 26 **Review and Evaluation**	Chapter 26 Reteaching Activity Chapter 26 Performance Assessment Activity Spanish Chapter Summary and Glossary Chapter 26 Test	Vocabulary PuzzleMaker CD-ROM Interactive Tutor Self-Assessment CD-ROM Glencoe Skillbuilder Interactive Workbook CD-ROM, Level 1 Audiocassettes* ExamView® Pro Testmaker CD-ROM

*Also available in Spanish.

Chapter 26 Planning Guide

✓ Performance Assessment Activities

Literature Collages As students learn about people in the Middle Ages , read the following portraits from Chaucer's Prologue to *The Canterbury Tales* aloud to them: the Knight, the Wife of Bath, the Squire, the Monk, the Friar, the Parson, the Prioress. Have students create collages to represent the people as described by Chaucer.

CHAPTER RESOURCES

LITERATURE ABOUT THE PERIOD

Chaucer, Geoffrey. *The Canterbury Tales.* In *The Complete Poetry and Prose of Geoffrey Chaucer*. Holt, Rinehart and Winston, 1977. This English classic gives insight into the characters of the Middle Ages.

READINGS FOR THE STUDENT

Clarke, Charles Cowden. *Tales from Chaucer.* The Heritage Press, 1947. A selection of nine tales (and the Prologue) re-told in prose for young readers.

READINGS FOR THE TEACHER

Editors of Time-Life Books. *What Life was Like in the Age of Chivalry.* Time-Life Books, 1997. Illustrated look at daily life in the period 800–1500.

Tuchman, Barbara W. *A Distant Mirror.* Ballantine Books, 1978. Examines problems of the fourteenth century.

KEY TO ABILITY LEVELS

Teaching strategies have been coded for varying learning styles and abilities.

L1 Level 1 activities are **basic** activities and should be within the ability range of all students.

L2 Level 2 activities are **average** activities and should be within the ability range of the average to above-average student.

L3 Level 3 activities are **challenging** activities designed for the ability range of above-average students.

ELL ELL activities should be within the ability range of English Language Learning students.

NATIONAL GEOGRAPHIC Teacher's Corner

INDEX TO NATIONAL GEOGRAPHIC MAGAZINE

The following articles relate to this chapter:

- "A World Together," by Erla Zwingle, August 1999.
- "The Hanseatic League," by Edward Von der Porten, October 1994.
- "The Power of Money," by Peter T. White, January 1993.

NATIONAL GEOGRAPHIC SOCIETY PRODUCTS AVAILABLE FROM GLENCOE

To order the following, call Glencoe at 1-800-334-7344:

- *PicturePack: Middle Ages (Transparencies)*
- *PictureShow: Middle Ages (CD-ROM)*

ADDITIONAL NATIONAL GEOGRAPHIC SOCIETY PRODUCTS

To order the following, call National Geographic at 1-800-368-2728:

- *National Geographic Atlas of World History (Book)*
- *The Builders: Marvels of Engineering (Book)*

Access *National Geographic*'s new dynamic MapMaker Web site and other geography resources at:
www.nationalgeographic.com
www.nationalgeographic.com/maps

THE HISTORY CHANNEL. A&E HOME VIDEO. Biography

The following videotape programs are available from Glencoe:

- **Marco Polo: Journey to the East**
  1-56501-668-8
- **Scourge of the Black Death**
  0-7670-0534-1

To order, call Glencoe at 1-800-334-7344. To find classroom resources to accompany many of these, check:

A&E Television: www.aande.com
The History Channel: www.historychannel.com

Introducing CHAPTER 26

OVERVIEW

Chapter 26 examines the rise of towns in western Europe during the Middle Ages.

➤ **Section 1** explains the growth of trade and rise of towns.
➤ **Section 2** discusses the medieval merchant class.
➤ **Section 3** identifies living conditions in the towns.
➤ **Section 4** describes the guilds.
➤ **Section 5** summarizes the cultural developments in medieval towns.

CHAPTER OBJECTIVES

After reading Chapter 26, students will be able to:

1. link the growth of trade to the rise of medieval towns.
2. tell how merchants became a key part of European life.
3. describe medieval town life.
4. explain why guilds were formed and later opposed.
5. summarize the cultural changes that took place in Europe during the 1400s.

EXAMINING ARTIFACTS

Have students compare these artifacts to the ones on page 380. How do these artifacts differ? *(Craftsmen and guilds are the subjects rather than crusaders and the Church.)* Focus on the fact that medieval craftsmen now appear in stained-glass windows—a place once reserved for religious figures and nobles. Ask: What does this suggest to you? *(that craftsmen have become more influential)*

PERFORMANCE ASSESSMENT ✓

Use the Performance Assessment activities on page 398B to help you evaluate students as they complete the chapter.

CHAPTER 26

Rise of Trade and Towns

500 A.D.–1400 A.D.

The woolworkers' ▶ guild badge from Florence, Italy

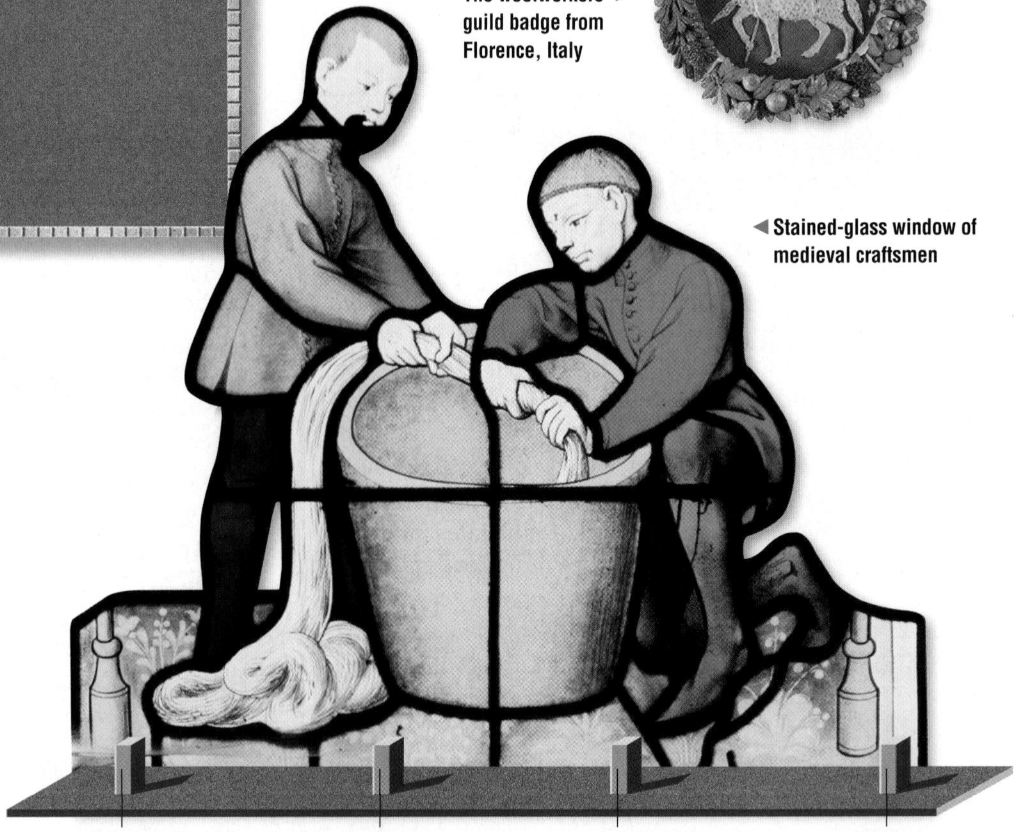

◀ Stained-glass window of medieval craftsmen

500s A.D. Venice founded

1000s A.D. Trade increases between Europe and the Near East

1100 A.D. Italian trading towns drive Muslims from the Mediterranean

1300 A.D. Flemish develop thriving trade with England

TEACHING RESOURCES

TEACHER PLANNING AND SUPPORT

- Reproducible Lesson Plan 26-1, 26-2, 26-3, 26-4, 26-5
- Teaching Strategies for the World History Classroom (Including Block Scheduling Pacing Guides)
- Presentation Plus! CD-ROM

REVIEW AND REINFORCEMENT

- Reading Essentials and Study Guide 26-1, 26-2, 26-3, 26-4, 26-5
- Chapter 26 Vocabulary and Guided Reading Activity
- Vocabulary PuzzleMaker CD-ROM
- Teaching Transparencies 26A & 26B
- Chapter 26 Reteaching Activity
- Chapter 26 Cooperative Learning Activity
- Chapter 26 Activity Book Activity
- Chapter 26 Chart and Graph Skill Activity
- Reading and Study Skills Foldables
- Interactive Tutor Self-Assessment CD-ROM

APPLICATION AND HANDS-ON ACTIVITIES

- Daily Questions in Social Studies
- Student Presentation Builder CD-ROM

GEOGRAPHY ACTIVITIES

- Chapter 26 Geography and Map Activity
- Building Geography Skills for Life
- Outline Map Resource Book

Chapter Focus

Read to Discover

- How the growth of trade led to the rise of towns in the Middle Ages.
- What living conditions were like in medieval towns.
- Why guilds were formed and why they were later opposed.
- What cultural changes to civilization took place in Europe during the 1400s.

HISTORY Online

Chapter Overview

Visit the *Human Heritage* Web site at **humanheritage.glencoe.com** and click on ***Chapter 26—Chapter Overviews*** to preview this chapter.

Terms to Learn
guilds
apprentice
masters
journeyman

People to Know
Dante
Geoffrey Chaucer

Places to Locate
Venice
Flanders

Why It's Important Beginning in the 1000s, the population of western Europe grew for the first time since the fall of Rome. Better ways of farming helped farmers grow more food. Many peasants left the fields to work in villages. They began to turn out cloth and metal products.

Western nobles, however, wanted such luxury items as sugar, spices, silks, and dyes. These goods came from the East. So, European merchants carried western products to the East to exchange for luxury goods.

SECTION 1 Trading Centers

The growth of trade led to the rise of the first large trading centers of the later Middle Ages. They were located on the important sea routes that connected western Europe with the Mediterranean Sea, Russia, and Scandinavia. Two of the earliest and most important trading centers were Venice and Flanders.

Venice Venice was an island port in the Adriatic (ā drē at' ik) Sea close to the coast of Italy. It was founded in the 500s by people fleeing from the Germans.

HISTORY Online

Chapter Overview introduces students to chapter content and key terms. Have them access ***Chapter 26 Overview*** at **humanheritage.glencoe.com**

FOCUS

Bellringer

Ask students this question: *What if there were no place to take the garbage?*

Motivational Activity

Review student responses. Then explain that during the Middle Ages, peasants began moving to towns from manorial estates. Although the towns were safer, they were also dirty, noisy, and crowded. Garbage as well as raw sewage was thrown into the streets, and wooden houses with thatched roofs were fire hazards. Tell students that in this chapter they will learn about living conditions in towns in the Middle Ages.

GUIDE TO READING

Reading Strategy

Ask students to read "Why It's Important" and summarize the chapter's main theme. *(Better farming methods and the Crusades helped give rise to a class of artisans and an interest in trade.)*

Vocabulary Precheck

Ask students to define each of the "Terms to Learn." Have a volunteer consult the dictionary for any unfamiliar words. L1 ELL

Use the Vocabulary PuzzleMaker CD-ROM for Chapter 26 to create a crossword puzzle. L1

Assign Chapter 26 Vocabulary and Guided Reading Activity.

Assign Reading Essentials and Study Guide 26-1.

INTERDISCIPLINARY CONNECTIONS
- Unit 8 World Literature Reading 1
- World Art & Architecture Transparency 22, *May*
- World Music: A Cultural Legacy

ENRICHMENT AND EXTENSION
- World History Primary Source Document Library CD-ROM
- Chapter 26 Enrichment Activity
- Foods Around the World

ASSESSMENT AND EVALUATION
- Chapter 26 Performance Assessment Activity
- Chapter 26 Section Quizzes 26-1, 26-2, 26-3, 26-4, 26-5
- Chapter 26 Test
- Chapter 26 ExamView® Pro Testmaker CD-ROM
- Chapter 26 Digests Audiocassettes Activities and Tests

SPANISH RESOURCES
- Chapter 26 Spanish Chapter Summary and Glossary
- Chapter 26 Spanish Digests Audiocassettes Activities and Tests

TEACH

Guided Practice

L1 **Discussion** Lead a discussion on how the growth of trade led to the rise of towns in western Europe during the Middle Ages. Ask: *What effect did increased trade have on western European life? Where were some of the most important trading centers located? What did these centers have in common?* ELL

MAP STUDY

Answer

a land route to Genoa and then a water route to Alexandria

Assign the Chapter 26 **Geography and Map** Activity in the TCR.

MAKING CONNECTIONS

➤➤ **Economics** Italian merchants loaned money to the kings of France and England. In return, the merchants were allowed to conduct trade and collect taxes there. As a result, French and English townspeople often disliked the merchants.

GEOGRAPHY AND HISTORY

Two reasons for the population growth during the 1000s and 1100s were the decline of foreign invasions and good weather, caused by a retreat of polar ice.

Since the land was not very fertile, the early Venetians had to depend on the sea for a living. They fished in the Adriatic and produced salt from the seawater. They exchanged their products for wheat from towns on the mainland of Italy. They also traded wheat, wine, and slaves to the Byzantines for fabrics and spices.

During the 1100s, Venice became a leading port and many of its citizens became fulltime merchants. Venetian merchants learned to read and write, use money, and keep records. In time, they developed an effective banking system.

Venice's prosperity soon spread to other parts of Italy. Towns on the Italian mainland began to make cloth, which was sent to Venice to be shipped to other areas. Before long, other Italian towns along the seacoast became shipping centers.

The navies of the Italian trading towns drove the Muslims from the Mediterranean, making it safe for Italian seafarers. As a result, the Italians opened the Near East to Europeans.

However, the Italian trading towns quarreled among themselves over profits and trade routes. While they were quarreling,

MAP STUDY

HUMAN SYSTEMS Trade routes tied all parts of western Europe together. **What was the most direct route merchants could take from Milan to Alexandria?**

Medieval Towns and Trade Routes

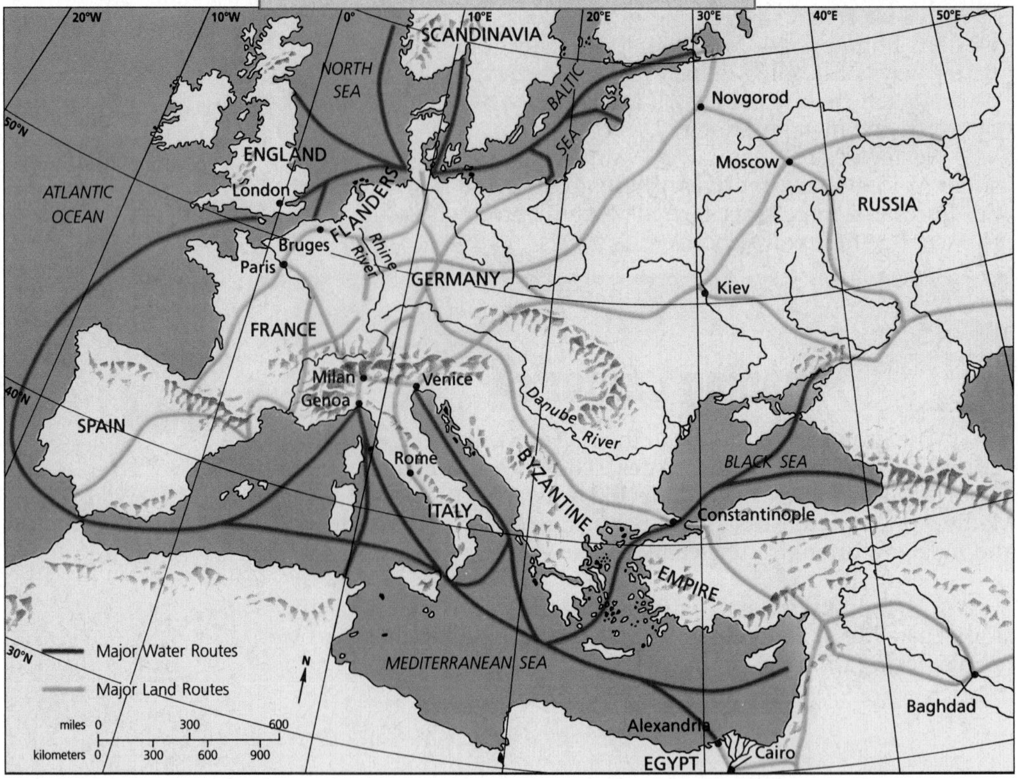

EXTENDING THE CONTENT

The most famous Venetian traveler is Marco Polo who wrote a colorful journal of his adventures in Mongol China. Marco's father and uncle were wealthy jewel merchants and the first Polos to trade in Asia. In about 1260, they traded in central Asia with the Khan of the Golden Horde and then went on to the court of Kublai Khan, emperor of China. On their second trip in 1271, the Polos took Marco, then about age 17. They traveled overland through Tibet on the Silk Road. Marco had a flair for languages and a gift for diplomacy, which allowed him to become a trusted official for the Khan.

towns along Europe's Atlantic coast developed trade routes. By 1500, these towns had become more powerful than those in Italy.

Flanders Flanders, which today is part of Belgium, was an area of small towns on the northwest coast of Europe. The Flemish (flem' ish) people raised sheep and used the wool to develop a weaving industry. The cloth they produced became famous for its quality and soon was in heavy demand.

Flanders became the earliest Atlantic trading center. Its rivers joined together before they emptied into the North Sea. Where the rivers met, the Flemish built harbors. From these harbors, they shipped their valuable woolen cloth to other lands.

Flanders became an important stopping place for ships traveling along the Atlantic coast from Scandinavia to the Mediterranean. It also became an important link in the trade route between Constantinople and the North Sea.

By 1300, the most important trading partner of Flanders was England. Flemish traders set up shop in the dockyards of London. They relied on English shepherds to supply them with wool to be made into cloth. The finished cloth was then shipped back to England. In this way, the Flemish developed an international industry.

Section 1 Assessment

1. What led to the growth and development of Venice's trade?
2. How did the location of Flanders help it become an important trading center?
3. How did the Flemish develop an international industry?

Critical Thinking

4. **Demonstrating Reasoned Judgment** How effective do you think the Flemish were in using geography to benefit their economy?

Graphic Organizer Activity

5. Draw this diagram, and use it to compare the trading towns of Italy and Flanders.

	Italy	Flanders
Location		
Trade Items		
Key Trade Routes		

SECTION 2 Merchants

As sea trade grew, so did overland trade. Italian towns began sending goods across the Alps to areas in the north. Soon, an overland trade route connected Italy and Flanders. From this route, other routes developed and spread across Europe.

Merchants became an important part of European life during the late Middle Ages. The first merchants were mostly adventurers who traveled from place to place. As protection

Section 1 Assessment Answers

1. Because the land was not very fertile, the early Venetians had to depend on the sea for a living. Venice became a leading port, and its merchants learned to read and write, use money, keep records, and develop a banking system.
2. It had many rivers, a seacoast, and water deep enough for harbors.
3. Flemish traders relied on English shepherds for wool, which they sent to Flanders to be made into cloth. The finished cloth was then shipped back to England.
4. Answers will vary but could say effective, because they built harbors on the seacoast to ship woolen cloth.
5. Charts comparing Venice and Flanders should accurately describe the bodies of water, trade routes, and natural resources that contributed to each city's success as a center of trade.

Assign the Chapter 26 **Section 1 Quiz** in the TCR. Testmaker available.

Use the **Interactive Tutor Self-Assessment CD-ROM** to review Section 1.

DID YOU KNOW

Medieval fairs were much more than a chance to buy goods from faraway places, though that was rare and exciting. They also broadened the world of the medieval townspeople. Though they might never have traveled more than a few miles from home, the fair drew travelers with exciting stories and visitors from distant places.

NATIONAL GEOGRAPHIC

Use these materials to enrich student understanding of the Middle Ages.

NGS PICTURESHOW CD-ROM
Middle Ages

NGS PICTUREPACK TRANSPARENCY SET
Middle Ages

Biography®

The following videotape program is available from Glencoe to enrich Chapter 26:

- **Marco Polo: Journey to the East**

To find classroom resources to accompany this video, check the following home page:

A&E Television:
www.aande.com

Use the **Vocabulary PuzzleMaker CD-ROM** to create crossword and word search puzzles.

Reading Check Answer Most medieval **fairs** were sponsored by nobles who collected taxes on sales.

CAPTION ANSWER

to help protect themselves from robbers and fights between nobles

DID YOU KNOW

Most of the important fairs were held on saints' days. Before a fair could be held, a charter had to be obtained from the lord or bishop who owned the land on which the fair was to be held. Usually, no two fairs could be set up within 7 miles (or 11 km) of each other.

Economics at a Glance

The Three Functions of Money Money has three functions. Money must serve as a *medium of exchange*. This means that people can trade money for goods and services. Money serves as a *measure of value*. Money is like a measuring stick that can be used to give value to a good or service. Finally, money serves as a *store of value*, which means that people can hold their wealth in the form of money until they are ready to use it. Organize the class into small groups. Direct groups to use library resources and the Internet to discover the various items that have been used for money throughout history. Have groups use their findings to create an illustrated chart titled "Money— Not Just Bills and Coins."

against robbers, they traveled in armed groups. They carried their goods in open wagons pulled by horses.

Fairs Merchants traveling along the chief route through eastern France stopped to trade with each other at special gatherings called **fairs.** The fairs were sponsored by nobles who collected taxes on sales. Fairs were held once a year for a few weeks at selected places. Over time, they attracted merchants from as far away as England and Egypt.

At the fairs, merchants could buy and sell goods or settle debts. They set up booths to show *wares,* or things for sale, such as pots, swords, armor, and clothing. Before long, merchants began to pay for goods with precious metals instead of bartering. Italian money changers tested and weighed coins from many different lands to determine their value. From the *banc,* or bench, at which the money changers sat comes the English word "bank."

Reading Check Who sponsored most medieval **fairs?**

Fun Facts . . .

Wandering Musicians
In southern France, wandering poet-musicians called troubadours visited towns and nobles' courts, composing songs about love and the brave deeds of heroes. Some troubadours also traveled to parts of southern Spain, singing lyrics in Arabic, Hebrew, and Spanish.

The Growth of Towns After awhile, merchants grew tired of moving around. They began to look for places where they could settle permanently and store their goods. They generally chose places along trade routes near waterways or road crossings. They also tried to settle close to a castle or monastery. This helped protect them from robbers and fights between nobles. The merchants surrounded their settlements with high stake

MEDIEVAL MARKETPLACE During the Middle Ages merchants set up permanent shops that eventually developed into towns. Medieval merchants in this painting sell shoes, cloth, and tableware. **Why did merchants try to settle near castles or monasteries?**

MEETING SPECIAL NEEDS

Have gifted students research and create a medieval fair or marketplace. Have students set up several booths with wares that would have been sold at the time. Include money changers. Invite other classes to the fair or marketplace.

Refer to ***Inclusion for the Middle School Social Studies Classroom: Strategies and Activities*** for additional resources.

fences and moats. Most towns of the Middle Ages developed from these merchant settlements.

The Germans called castles *burgs* (bergs). Towns came to be called **burgs** because they were often near castles. The new towns grew steadily and attracted people from the surrounding countryside. Markets became centers of business and social life. Once a week, nobles and peasants sold food for goods they could not make on the manor. Artisans came from the villages to find work. Often they brought their families with them. Over time, the towns became more than just centers of trade. They became communities in which people lived.

Reading Check How did **burgs** get their name?

Section 2 Assessment

1. **Define:** fairs, burgs.
2. Why did nobles sponsor fairs?
3. Where did merchants set up their marketplaces?

Critical Thinking

4. **Making Generalizations** How did merchants contribute to the growth of towns?

Graphic Organizer Activity

5. Draw the diagram below, and use it to compare the activities at medieval fairs with the activities at fairs today.

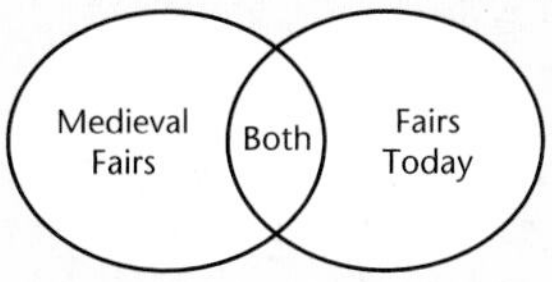

SECTION 3 Living Conditions

By the 1200s, many towns were wealthy and large enough to have their fences replaced by walls and towers. Inside the walls, public buildings of stone and houses of wood were jammed close together. To save even more space, the houses had extra stories that extended over crooked narrow alleys.

The crowded conditions often made towns unhealthy places in which to live. Sewers were open, and there was little concern for cleanliness. People threw garbage out of windows onto the streets below. Rats were everywhere.

During the 1300s, diseased rats came to Europe on trading ships from the Middle East. They carried with them a plague called the "Black Death." This disease swept through Europe, killing millions of people. Experts think that one out of three Europeans died in the plague. To escape it, people fled from the towns and settled in the countryside. Trading, farming, and war came to a temporary halt.

Then... & Now

Between 1348 and 1350, the Black Death claimed nearly 25 million lives. The epidemic stopped wars and slowed trade. Officials sealed off infected homes, suspended religious services, and made it illegal to meet in groups. It took almost 200 years for Europe to regain its pre-1348 level of population.

Burgher Life Merchants and artisans controlled a town's business and trade. They hired workers from the countryside to

Reading Check Answer Towns came to be called **burgs** because they often lay near castles, which the Germans called *burgs*.

L2 Environment Have students discuss the garbage problem that faced medieval towns. Encourage them to brainstorm solutions to the problem. Then have them devise the best way to inform the people of what they must do to clean up the town. ELL

Use the **Interactive Tutor Self-Assessment CD-ROM** to review Section 2.

THE HISTORY CHANNEL®

The following videotape program is available from Glencoe to enrich Chapter 26:

- **Scourge of the Black Death**

To find classroom resources to accompany this video, check the following home page:

A&E Television
www.aande.com

GEOGRAPHY AND HISTORY

In Switzerland and western Germany, the Jews were blamed for the Black Death, and thousands were burned to death or hanged. As a result, there was a movement of Jews into eastern Germany and Poland.

Use the **Vocabulary PuzzleMaker CD-ROM** to create crossword and word search puzzles.

Section 2 Assessment Answers

1. fairs, special gatherings for trade (p. 402); burgs, medieval towns (p. 403)
2. because they collected taxes on sales
3. along a trade route near waterways or road crossings, and close to a castle or monastery
4. Sample generalization: Most of the towns developed from merchant settlements.
5. Diagrams will vary but should show an accurate understanding of medieval fairs, especially in promoting trade and the use of money. Shared features of both fairs might be such things as: largely an annual event, draw people from all over, and so on. Differences might include the kinds of technological entertainment at modern fairs or the use of credit to purchase goods.

Assign the Chapter 26 **Section 2 Quiz** in the TCR. Testmaker available.

Reading Check Answer At first, the merchants, artisans, and workers who lived in towns were all called **burghers.**

LINKING PAST TO PRESENT

The term *burg* originally meant a fortified town or castle. As part of town names, it appeared in the Germanic *-burg*, the French *-bourg*, and the English *-borough* and *-bury*. Today, in Europe, we find Hamburg, Strasbourg, Edinburgh, and Canterbury; in the United States, Pittsburgh, Harrisburg, and Salisbury.

Linking Across Time

Diseased rats that came to Europe on trading ships from the Middle East carried the Black Death through Europe.

DID YOU KNOW ??

Peasants ate dark bread, broth, cheese, and curds. Other dishes of the burghers and manor nobility included miniature cod liver pastries, beef marrow fritters, a sauce of pounded crayfish tails, and other types of fish. Aristocrats ate many of the foods that the burghers ate, but in larger quantities.

make goods for them. At first, the merchants, artisans, and workers who lived in towns were all called **burghers** (ber′ guhrz). Later the title was used to refer to rich merchants.

The daily life of burghers and their families started with prayers at dawn. The burgher hurried off to the docks and market to see how his products were selling. Then, he met with his business partners.

The burgher's wife kept house, managed servants, and cared for children. The family ate two large meals a day—one at ten o'clock in the morning and another at six o'clock in the evening. A typical meal consisted of eel, roast beef, lark pastry, and curded milk. About nine o'clock in the evening, the family went to bed.

Changing Ways Under the feudal system, the land on which towns were built was owned by kings, nobles, and bishops. They taxed the people in the towns and charged them

Reading Check At first, what groups were called **burghers?**

Fun Facts . . .

Manners Robert of Blois, a French poet, listed rules of correct conduct for daughters of burghers. They included:
- A lady must walk straight and not trot or run.
- Take care: glances are messengers of love; men are prompt to deceive themselves by them.

Linking Across Time

Health Care The unhealthy, overcrowded conditions of medieval cities encouraged the rapid spread of diseases such as measles, smallpox, polio, flu, and the "Black Death" (below). Today doctors know that most diseases are caused by bacteria and viruses. Many diseases common in medieval times have been wiped out or curbed through good health practices such as washing hands or receiving vaccinations like the polio shot (right). **What carried the "Black Death" through Europe in the 1300s?**

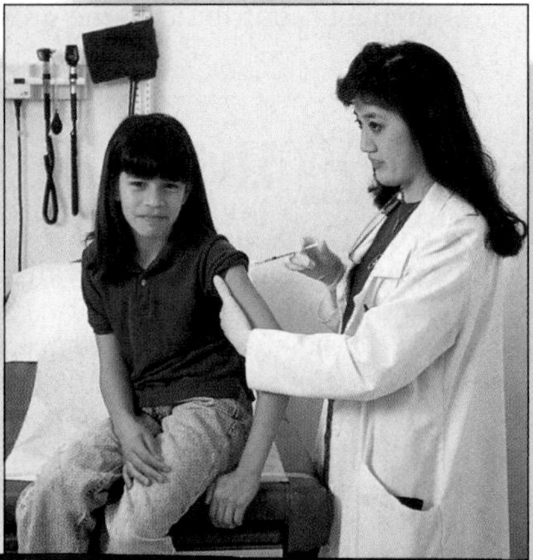

MULTICULTURAL PERSPECTIVES

Town life in the Middle Ages gave middle-class women many new opportunities. They not only worked with their husbands or sons in family shops and businesses, but they also had the freedom to operate their own enterprises in what became known as *femme sole*. It is true that women were kept out of certain crafts and guilds unless they were a master's wife, widow, or daughter. In other guilds, however, women had equal status with men, and in some trades and businesses they had a near monopoly. Women dominated the silk-making industry in Paris and London and were important in the cloth trades such as spinning, weaving, dyeing, tailoring, and glove making. Women also worked in the medieval food industry as bakers, fishmongers, and poultry sellers.

fees to use the marketplace. The burghers did not like this or the other restrictions placed on them. They resented having to get a noble's permission to marry, move around, or own land. They also did not like serving in the noble's army.

Many nobles viewed the rise of towns as a threat to their power. They resented the wealth of the burghers and began to use feudal laws to keep them in their place. The Church was also against the rise of towns. Its leaders feared that the making of profit would interfere with religion.

The burghers, however, resented feudal laws. They thought these laws were not suited to business. The burghers now had wealth and power. Thus, they began to depend less on nobles and bishops. Instead, they developed a sense of loyalty toward their town. They worked together to build schools, hospitals, and churches. They began to demand changes.

HISTORY Online

Student Web Activity
Visit the *Human Heritage* Web site at humanheritage.glencoe.com and click on ***Chapter 26—Student Web Activities*** to find out more about the towns of the Middle Ages.

Communes and Charters

In the 1100s, townspeople in northern Italy formed political groups called **communes** (kom' yūnz). Their purpose was to work against the nobles and bishops and for the people by establishing local self-government. The Italian communes were successful. Soon, the idea of communes spread to the towns of northern Europe. Some kings and nobles gave the townspeople **charters,** or documents allowing towns to run their own affairs.

The charters gave the townspeople the right to elect officials to run their towns. A council collected taxes and set charges for merchants who bought and sold goods in the town market. It also repaired streets, formed citizen armies, and ran hospitals, orphanages, and special homes for the poor.

The towns enforced their own laws and set up special courts. To reduce crime, the towns severely punished those who broke the law. Murderers were hanged. Robbers lost a hand or an arm. Those who committed minor crimes, such as disturbing the peace, were whipped or put in the *stocks,* or a wooden frame with holes in which a person's feet and hands were locked.

Reading Check What was the purpose of **communes?**

Reading Check What did **charters** allow townspeople to do?

Section 3 Assessment

1. **Define:** burghers, communes, charters.
2. What were some of the problems faced by medieval towns?
3. What changes did burghers want to make in feudal laws?

Critical Thinking

4. **Demonstrating Reasoned Judgment** What laws or regulations would you have written to further improve conditions in medieval towns?

Graphic Organizer Activity

5. Draw this diagram, and use it to show characteristics of towns in the late Middle Ages.

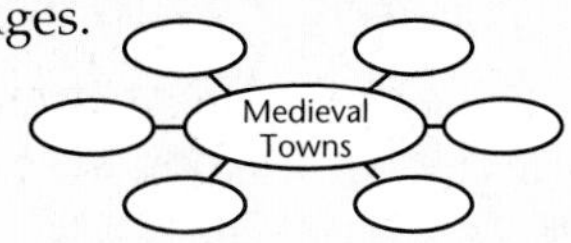

HISTORY Online

Student Web Activity objectives and answers can be found at the ***Chapter 26 Web Activity Lesson Plan*** at humanheritage.glencoe.com

L2 **Critical Thinking** Ask students to compare the forms of punishment for crimes committed during the Middle Ages with the forms of punishment for crimes committed today. Ask them to create a chart showing each. Then ask students to vote on which society seems more humane.

Reading Check Answer
Communes worked against nobles and bishops and helped the people set up local self-government.

Reading Check Answer
Medieval **charters** allowed townspeople to run their own affairs.

MAKING CONNECTIONS

>> **Economics** Burghers got around the Church's opposition to interest in two ways. First, they used Jews as moneylenders. Second, they lent money at no interest but charged "damages" if the loan was not repaid at once. By the 1200s, the Church changed its position, and interest became acceptable.

Section 3 Assessment Answers

1. burghers, rich merchants (p. 404); communes, political groups (p. 405); charters, documents allowing towns to run their own affairs (p. 405)
2. They were overcrowded, unhealthy, and dirty.
3. They wanted to run their own affairs and to have their own courts and laws.
4. Answers will vary, but students might suggest regulations to relieve overcrowding, to plan for growth, and to determine disposal of sewage.
5. sample characteristics: crowded conditions, open sewers, lack of sanitation, crooked narrow streets, large population of merchants and artisans, enforced own laws, and so on

Assign the Chapter 26 **Section 3 Quiz** in the TCR. Testmaker available.

Use the **Interactive Tutor Self-Assessment CD-ROM** to review Section 3.

Use the **Vocabulary Puzzle-Maker CD-ROM** to create crossword and word search puzzles.

Reading Check Answer Merchants, artisans, and workers formed **guilds** to ensure that members were treated equally.

L3 **Critical Thinking** Ask students to discuss how well the guild system would work in present-day society. Suggest they write a case study of its application in modern times.

LINKING PAST TO PRESENT

Medieval guilds controlled all the business in a town, establishing rules on prices, wages, and unemployment. In the United States today, laws prohibit price fixing and monopolies. In addition, the Taft-Hartley Act outlaws both hiring only union members and forcing employees to join unions.

Reading Check Answer An **apprentice** was a trainee in a trade, usually for two to seven years.
The **masters** were the experts in a guild.

Reading Check Answer Unlike an apprentice, a **journeyman** worked under a master for a daily wage until ready to take a test for guild membership.

MAKING CONNECTIONS

➤➤ **History** Often, masters were required to teach their apprentices to read and write and to provide them with clothing and a salary. Masters were also responsible for their behavior.

SECTION 4 The Rise of Guilds

Reading Check Why did merchants, artisans, and workers form **guilds?**

Around the 1100s, merchants, artisans, and workers formed **guilds** (gildz). These were business groups that made sure that their members were treated equally. Each craft had its own guild, whose members lived and worked in the same area of town.

Craft guilds controlled the work of artisans such as carpenters, shoemakers, blacksmiths, masons, tailors, and weavers. Women working as laundresses, seamstresses, embroiderers, and maidservants had their own trade associations. Guild members were not allowed to compete with one another or to advertise. Each member had to work the same number of hours, hire the same number of workers, and pay the same wages.

Guilds controlled all business and trade in a town. Only members could buy, sell, or make goods there. Outsiders who wanted to sell their goods in the town market had to get permission from the guilds. The guild decided the fair price for a product or service, and all members had to charge that price. Guild members who sold poorly made goods or cheated in business dealings had to pay large fines. They could also be expelled from the guild.

Guilds were more than business or trade groups. If members became ill, other members took care of them. If members were out of work, the guild gave them food. When members died, the other members prayed for their souls, paid for funerals, and supported the families. Guilds were also centers of social life. Holy day celebrations, processions, and outdoor plays were sponsored by the guild. Close friendships often developed among guild members.

Reading Check What was an **apprentice?** Who were the **masters** in a guild?

Reading Check How did a **journeyman** differ from an apprentice?

Job Training

It was not easy to become a member of a guild. A person had to be an **apprentice** (uh pren′ tis), or trainee, in a trade for two to seven years. Apprentices were taught their trade by **masters,** or experts. They had to live with and obey their masters until their training was finished.

The next step was becoming a **journeyman** (jer′ nē muhn), or a person who worked under a master for a daily wage. After a certain amount of time, journeymen took a test to become masters. The test was given by guild officials. Journeymen had to make and present a "masterpiece" to prove they had learned their craft. Those who passed the test were considered masters and could make their own goods. Often, they worked in the back of their houses and sold their goods in a shop in the front of the house.

By 1400, many merchants and artisans had begun challenging the control of the guilds. They felt the guilds kept them from

COOPERATIVE LEARNING

Have students work in groups to write and present a brief skit showing daily life in a medieval town. Assign small groups to research the daily work, clothing, food, and homes of townspeople. Assign each student a specific task such as selecting an event and characters, outlining and writing parts of the script, and obtaining or making props. Students can choose to portray such characters as apprentices, journeymen, masters of various guilds, university students, clergy, money changers, or troubadours.

Assign Chapter 26 *Cooperative Learning Activity* in the TCR.

increasing their trade and profits. Then, too, apprentices disliked the strict rules set by guilds. It was getting harder and harder for apprentices to become masters. Many masters were grouping together and hiring unskilled workers instead of apprentices.

Section 4 Assessment

1. **Define:** guilds, apprentice, masters, journeyman.
2. What rules did guild members have to obey?
3. Why did people begin to challenge guilds in the 1400s?

Critical Thinking

4. **Analyzing Information** "The steps taken to become a master were too difficult." Do you agree or disagree with this statement? Give reasons for your opinion.

Graphic Organizer Activity

5. Draw this diagram, and use it to show the steps in joining a guild.

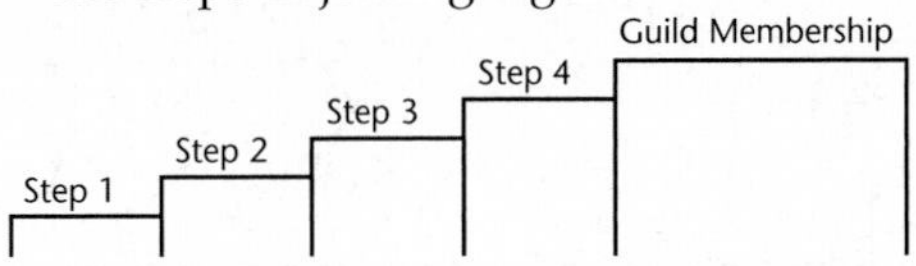

SECTION 5 Cultural Changes

During the 1400s, merchants, artisans, and bankers became more important than they had been in the past. Their growing power led to the decline of feudalism.

Many townspeople were as rich as, or richer than, the nobles. Bankers lent money to kings, nobles, and church officials for wars, building repairs, and entertainment. With their new wealth, merchants turned their homes into mansions. Some even bought castles from nobles who had lost their money. They began to set fashions. Women wore furs and gowns made of *brocade* (bro kād'), or a cloth woven with raised designs on it. Men dressed in colorful jackets, stockings, and feathered caps.

The townspeople had more leisure time and money to spend on their interests. Many hired private teachers to educate their sons. The sons later went to universities to study law, religion, and medicine. There was time to enjoy art and books, so townspeople began to support the work of painters and writers.

Most townspeople used such languages as German, French, and English. A scholar named Dante (dahn' tā) wrote the *Divine Comedy* in Italian. It is one of the most famous poems of the Middle Ages. Geoffrey Chaucer (jef' rē cho' suhr) wrote the *Canterbury Tales* in English. These tales are still popular today.

Townspeople began to think differently from nobles and peasants. The townspeople came to believe that they should be free to develop their talents and to improve their way of life. They wanted a strong central government. They began to look toward kings to provide leadership.

People in History

Geoffrey Chaucer
c. 1340–1400

English Poet

Chaucer's poems include the *Legend of Good Women,* an unfinished work about heroines from the past. His most famous poem is the *Canterbury Tales,* which tells the tales told by a group of travelers on their way to a shrine.

Independent Practice

L3 **Writing** Have students imagine that they are editors of a newspaper during the Middle Ages. Tell them to write two editorials, one written in 1220 titled, "Why We Need to Establish Guilds," the other one written in 1400, titled, "Why We Need to Abolish Guilds."

Use the **Interactive Tutor Self-Assessment CD-ROM** to review Section 4.

MAKING CONNECTIONS

>> **Literature** Dante's *Divine Comedy* is divided into three parts—*Inferno* (Hell), *Purgatorio* (Purgatory), and *Paradiso* (Paradise). The epic's main theme is life after death.

Use the **Vocabulary PuzzleMaker CD-ROM** to create crossword and word search puzzles.

DID YOU KNOW ??

Chaucer was a government official who wrote poetry as an avocation. His *Canterbury Tales* is a collection of stories told by a group of pilgrims on a journey to Thomas á Becket's shrine in Canterbury.

ASSESS

Check for Understanding

Ask students to summarize the main points of the chapter. Discuss the answers to the Section and Chapter Assessment questions.

Section 4 Assessment Answers

1. guilds, business groups organized to protect members (p. 406); apprentice, trainee (p. 406); masters, experts (p. 406); journeyman, person who worked under a master (p. 406)
2. were not allowed to compete with one another or to advertise; had to work the same number of hours, hire the same number of workers, and pay the same wages
3. because they felt the guilds kept them from increasing their trade and profits, and because apprentices found it hard to become masters
4. Answers will vary, but students should provide evidence to support their opinions.
5. Step 1—apprentice; Step 2—journeyman; Step 3—presentation of masterpiece; Step 4—approval of masterpiece by guild officials

Assign the Chapter 26 **Section 4 Quiz** in the TCR. Testmaker available.

Evaluate

Assign the Chapter 26 **Performance Assessment Activity** in the TCR.

Administer the **Chapter 26 Test**. Testmaker available.

Reteach

Have students in groups prepare charts of significant medieval innovations in economics, trade, literature, and art.

Assign the Chapter 26 **Reteaching Activity** in the TCR.

Enrich

Have students investigate the death rates of western European countries during the Black Death and graph their findings.

Assign the Chapter 26 **Enrichment Activity** in the TCR.

CLOSE

Have students summarize how medieval life shifted from the feudal manor to the towns.

Use the **Interactive Tutor Self-Assessment CD-ROM** to review Section 5.

HISTORY Online

Self-Check Quiz gives students an interactive chapter tutorial. Have them access ***Chapter 26 Quiz*** at **humanheritage.glencoe.com**

Section 5 Assessment

1. In what ways did the cultural life of townspeople change during the 1400s?
2. What did townspeople want government to do?

Critical Thinking

3. **Making Inferences** Why might nobles have disliked the success of merchants during the Middle Ages?

Graphic Organizer Activity

4. Draw this diagram, and use it to show details that support the following main idea: "The growing power of merchants, artisans, and bankers led to the decline of feudalism."

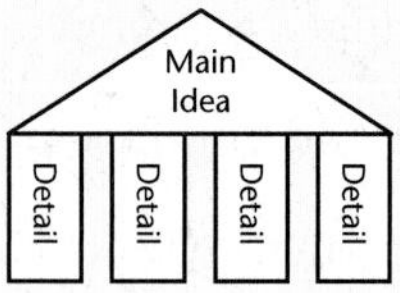

Chapter Summary & Study Guide

1. During the 1000s and 1100s, increased trade between Europe and the Near East led to the rise of trading centers, such as Venice and Flanders.
2. Venetian traders developed an effective banking system and, with the help of other Italian trading towns, drove the Muslims from the Mediterranean.
3. Flanders was the earliest Atlantic trading center, and, by 1300, it had developed a flourishing international trade with England.
4. The first medieval merchants traveled overland in armed groups and traded with each other at fairs.
5. After a while, merchants began to settle in towns known as burgs.
6. Most medieval towns were overcrowded, unhealthy places to live.
7. Artisans and rich merchants controlled the business and trade of towns.
8. Nobles and church officials viewed the rise of towns as a threat to their power and wealth.
9. Burghers resented feudal laws, and they resisted nobles and demanded charters for greater self-government.
10. Guilds set wages, prices, and working conditions, and helped members who were sick or out of work.
11. By the 1400s, many masters and artisans resented the control of guilds over profits, and they began to hire untrained workers instead of apprentices.
12. As townspeople grew richer and more powerful, they looked to kings for leadership, and feudalism declined.

HISTORY Online

Self-Check Quiz

Visit the *Human Heritage* Web site at **humanheritage.glencoe.com** and click on ***Chapter 26—Self-Check Quiz*** to assess your understanding of this chapter.

Section 5 Assessment Answers

1. Many became as rich as nobles and spent their new wealth on homes and clothes. They hired private teachers for their sons and supported painters and writers.
2. give them peace and security
3. Answers will vary, but students might indicate that nobles were envious and somewhat afraid of the wealth and power the merchants had acquired.
4. Sample details: bankers lent money to kings, nobles, and church officials; merchants turned homes into mansions and began to set fashions; townspeople began to think differently than nobles and peasants; townspeople looked toward kings instead of nobles for leadership.

Assign the Chapter 26 **Section 5 Quiz** in the TCR.

CHAPTER 26 Assessment

Using Key Terms

Imagine you are living in a town in western Europe during the late Middle Ages. Write a diary entry describing your life there. Use the following words in your diary.

fairs	burgs	burghers
communes	charters	guilds
apprentice	masters	journeyman

Understanding Main Ideas

1. What led to the development of trade between Europe and the Near East during the 1000s and 1100s?
2. What led to the decline of Italian trading centers?
3. How did fairs affect the development of banking?
4. What effects did the "Black Death" have on Europe?
5. How did a person become a master in a guild?
6. Why were nobles and church officials against the rise of towns?
7. How were the ideas of townspeople different from those of the nobles and peasants?

Critical Thinking

1. What would you have liked about being a merchant in the Middle Ages? Explain.
2. Would you have supported or opposed the position taken by Italian communes during the 1100s? Explain.
3. Would you have preferred to be a burgher or a noble during the Middle Ages? Explain.
4. Do you approve or disapprove of the rules established by the guilds? Explain.

Graphic Organizer Activity

Culture Create a diagram like the one below, and use it to compare life on a medieval manor with life in a medieval trading town.

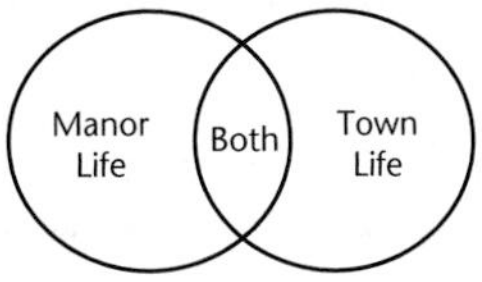

Geography in History

Places and Regions Refer to the map on page 400. At what places do you think European trading ships could have been attacked by pirates? How would geographic features increase the possibility of an attack? Explain.

Using Your Journal

Review any details you may have noted about life during the late Middle Ages. Write a paragraph explaining what developments started in the towns of Europe during the Middle Ages that are evident in life today.

409

Bonus Test Question

For Chapter 26 Test

How did the Flemish become one of the first to develop an international industry? *(They were able to create an economic bridge between the supply source, production source, and customer; became merchants of products people needed and wanted.)*

Using Your Journal

Paragraphs will vary but students might indicate commerce, fairs, banks, towns, town charters, business associations, fashion, and literature.

Geography in History

Likely spots for pirates were the passage between Spain and Africa, or near Constantinople. Narrow passages would make it difficult for ships to escape an attack.

CHAPTER 26 Assessment Answers

Using Key Terms

Entries will vary, but students should use all the terms.

Understanding Main Ideas

1. Nobles wanted luxury goods from the Near East.
2. They quarrelled among themselves over profits and routes.
3. Merchants began to pay for goods with precious metals and coins from many different lands.
4. It killed millions of people and halted trading, farming, and war.
5. by becoming an apprentice first, then a journeyman, then passing a master's test, and finally creating a masterpiece
6. They viewed towns and burghers as a threat to their power.
7. Townspeople believed they should be free to improve their way of life.

Critical Thinking

1. Answers will vary, but students should include specific examples.
2. Answers will vary, but students should support their opinion with reasons.
3. Answers will vary, but students should explain their preference of burgher or noble.
4. Answers will vary.

Graphic Organizer Activity

Diagrams will vary. Some sample responses might include: *manors*—largely self-sufficient, ruled by the noble or lord, little freedom for peasants; *both*—large class differences, poor health conditions; *towns*—enriched by trade, greater freedom, strongly influenced by merchants and artisans.

Chapter 27 Planning Guide

Timesaving Tools

TeacherWorks™ All-In-One Planner and Resource Center

- **Interactive Teacher Edition** Access your Teacher Wraparound Edition and your classroom resources with a few easy clicks.
- **Interactive Lesson Planner** Planning has never been easier! Organize your week, month, semester, or year with all the lesson helps you need to make teaching creative, timely, and relevant.

Use Glencoe's **Presentation Plus!** multimedia teacher tool to easily present dynamic lessons that visually excite your students. Using Microsoft PowerPoint® you can customize the presentations to create your own personalized lessons.

Objectives	Reproducible Resources	Multimedia Resources
Section 1 **France** Describe how the Capetian kings strengthened the French monarchy.	Reproducible Lesson Plan Chapter 27 Vocabulary and Guided Reading Activity Reading Essentials and Study Guide 27-1 Section 1 Quiz	Interactive Student Edition CD-ROM Graphic Organizer Transparency 3 Vocabulary PuzzleMaker CD-ROM ExamView® Pro Testmaker CD-ROM Glencoe Skillbuilder Interactive Workbook CD-ROM, Level 1 Presentation Plus! CD-ROM
Section 2 **England** Explain what changes took place in the English monarchy during the Middle Ages.	Reproducible Lesson Plan Reading Essentials and Study Guide 27-2 Section 2 Quiz	Vocabulary PuzzleMaker CD-ROM Interactive Tutor Self-Assessment CD-ROM ExamView® Pro Testmaker CD-ROM Glencoe Skillbuilder Interactive Workbook CD-ROM, Level 1
Section 3 **The Hundred Years' War** Analyze the causes and results of the Hundred Years' War.	Reproducible Lesson Plan Reading Essentials and Study Guide 27-3 Chapter 27 Cooperative Learning Activity Chapter 27 Chart and Graph Skill Activity Section 3 Quiz	Teaching Transparencies and Activities 27A & 27B Vocabulary PuzzleMaker CD-ROM Interactive Tutor Self-Assessment CD-ROM ExamView® Pro Testmaker CD-ROM
Section 4 **Germany** Trace the start of the Holy Roman Empire, and describe how it was ruled.	Reproducible Lesson Plan Reading Essentials and Study Guide 27-4 Section 4 Quiz	Vocabulary PuzzleMaker CD-ROM ExamView® Pro Testmaker CD-ROM Glencoe Skillbuilder Interactive Workbook CD-ROM, Level 1
Section 5 **Spain** Summarize how the Catholic monarchs governed Spain.	Reproducible Lesson Plan Reading Essentials and Study Guide 27-5 Chapter 27 Geography and Map Activity Section 5 Quiz	Vocabulary PuzzleMaker CD-ROM Interactive Tutor Self-Assessment CD-ROM ExamView® Pro Testmaker CD-ROM Glencoe Skillbuilder Interactive Workbook CD-ROM, Level 1
Chapter 27 **Review and Evaluation**	Chapter 27 Reteaching Activity Chapter 27 Performance Assessment Activity Unit 8 Standardized Test Practice Spanish Summary and Glossary Chapter 27 Test	Interactive Tutor Self-Assessment CD-ROM Glencoe Skillbuilder Interactive Workbook CD-ROM, Level 1 Audiocassettes* ExamView® Pro Testmaker CD-ROM

*Also available in Spanish.

Chapter 27 Planning Guide

✓ Performance Assessment Activities

News Account Have students imagine that they are English newspaper reporters who have just witnessed the 1066 Battle of Hastings. Assign them to create headlines and accounts of the battle. Some students may also choose to illustrate their stories.

CHAPTER RESOURCES

LITERATURE ABOUT THE PERIOD

Warner, Marina. *Joan of Arc: The Image of Female Heroism.* Random House, 1982. Account of Joan of Arc.

READINGS FOR THE STUDENT

McKendrick, Melveena. *Ferdinand and Isabella.* American Heritage, 1968. Photographs and contemporary paintings help re-create the period.

READINGS FOR THE TEACHER

Brown, R. Allen. *The Normans.* St. Martin's Press, 1984. Concentrates on Norman influence on the western world.

Hallam, Elizabeth, ed. *The Plantagenet Chronicles.* Weidenfeld and Nicholson, 1986. Examines the reigns of Henry II, Richard I, and King John and discusses the Magna Carta, the Crusades, and life in England during the 1100s.

KEY TO ABILITY LEVELS

Teaching strategies have been coded for varying learning styles and abilities.

L1 Level 1 activities are **basic** activities and should be within the ability range of all students.

L2 Level 2 activities are **average** activities and should be within the ability range of the average to above-average student.

L3 Level 3 activities are **challenging** activities designed for the ability range of above-average students.

ELL ELL activities should be within the ability range of English Language Learning students.

NATIONAL GEOGRAPHIC Teacher's Corner

INDEX TO NATIONAL GEOGRAPHIC MAGAZINE

The following articles relate to this chapter:

- "Japan's Imperial Palace: Beyond the Moat," by Robert M. Poole, January 2001.
- "New Caledonia: France's Untamed Pacific Outpost," by Thomas O'Neill, May 2000.

NATIONAL GEOGRAPHIC SOCIETY PRODUCTS AVAILABLE FROM GLENCOE

To order the following, call Glencoe at 1-800-334-7344:

- *PicturePack: Physical Geography of the World (Transparencies)*

ADDITIONAL NATIONAL GEOGRAPHIC SOCIETY PRODUCTS

To order the following, call National Geographic at 1-800-368-2728:

- *Atocha: Quest for Treasure (Video)*
- *National Geographic Atlas of World History (Book)*

Access *National Geographic*'s new dynamic MapMachine Web site and other geography resources at:
www.nationalgeographic.com
www.nationalgeographic.com/maps

Introducing CHAPTER 27

OVERVIEW

Chapter 27 describes the growth of central governments in France, Germany, and Spain.

- **Section 1** discusses the powers of the French monarchy.
- **Section 2** describes the English monarchy, the Magna Carta, and the Parliament.
- **Section 3** analyzes the Hundred Years' War.
- **Section 4** explains the role of the Holy Roman Empire.
- **Section 5** summarizes the unification of Spain.

CHAPTER OBJECTIVES

After reading Chapter 27, students will be able to:

1. describe how the Capetian kings strengthened the French monarchy.
2. discuss limits placed on the English monarchy.
3. analyze the causes and results of the Hundred Years' War.
4. explain how the Holy Roman Empire was created and ruled.
5. summarize how the Catholic monarchs united Spain.

EXAMINING ARTIFACTS

Direct students to study both the artifacts and the time line. Ask: What groups of people seem to be shaping history? *(kings, soldiers, and conquerors)* What effect do students think this trend might have on western Europe? Save student responses for review as they read the chapter.

PERFORMANCE ASSESSMENT ✓

Use the Performance Assessment activities on page 410B to help you evaluate students as they complete the chapter.

CHAPTER 27

Rise of Monarchies

900 A.D.–1500 A.D.

▲ Coronation robe worn by King Roger II of Sicily

Joan of Arc ▶

1066 A.D. William the Conqueror invades England
1215 A.D. Magna Carta is signed
1272 A.D. Edward I sets up Parliament
1273 A.D. Hapsburg dynasty is founded
1337 A.D. Hundred Years' War begins
1492 A.D. Ferdinand and Isabella unite Spain

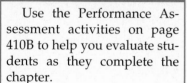

TEACHING RESOURCES

TEACHER PLANNING AND SUPPORT

- Reproducible Lesson Plan 27-1, 27-2, 27-3, 27-4, 27-5
- Teaching Strategies for the World History Classroom (Including Block Scheduling Pacing Guides)
- Presentation Plus! CD-ROM

REVIEW AND REINFORCEMENT

- Reading Essentials and Study Guide 27-1, 27-2, 27-3, 27-4, 27-5
- Chapter 27 Vocabulary and Guided Reading Activity
- Vocabulary PuzzleMaker CD-ROM
- Teaching Transparencies 27A & 27B
- Chapter 27 Reteaching Activity
- Chapter 27 Cooperative Learning Activity
- Chapter 27 Activity Book Activity
- Chapter 27 Chart and Graph Skill Activity
- Reading and Study Skills Foldables
- Interactive Tutor Self-Assessment CD-ROM
- Unit 8 MindJogger VideoQuiz

APPLICATION AND HANDS-ON ACTIVITIES

- Daily Questions in Social Studies
- Student Presentation Builder CD-ROM

Chapter Focus

Read to Discover

- How the Capetian kings strengthened the French monarchy.
- What changes took place in the English monarchy during the Middle Ages.
- What the main causes and results were of the Hundred Years' War.
- How the Holy Roman Empire was created and ruled.
- How the Catholic monarchs united Spain.

HISTORY Online

Chapter Overview
Visit the *Human Heritage* Web site at **humanheritage.glencoe.com** and click on ***Chapter 27—Chapter Overviews*** to preview this chapter.

Terms to Learn
monarchies
circuit judges
grand jury
trial jury
dauphin
diet
corregidores

People to Know
Hugh Capet
William the Conqueror
Joan of Arc
Frederick II
Ferdinand and Isabella

Places to Locate
Hastings
Orleans
Sicily
Holy Roman Empire
Granada

Why It's Important The growth of trade and towns during the late Middle Ages led to many changes in western Europe. Some of these changes were political. The rise of **monarchies** (mon' uhr kēz), or countries governed by one ruler, led to the decline of feudalism.

Reading Check What are **monarchies?**

SECTION 1 France

In 987, Hugh Capet (ka pā'), a French noble, was chosen as the new king of France. At the time, France consisted of many feudal territories. As king, Capet ruled only a small area between the Seine (sān) and Loire (lwahr) rivers. Capet, who died in 996, was the first of a line of Capetian (kuh pē' shuhn) kings who ruled France for some 300 years. For 100 years after his death, however, these kings were weak and did little to increase royal power.

In 1108, Louis VI, known as "Louis the Fat," became king and increased the power of the monarchy. He got rid of disloyal nobles and put loyal persons of lower birth in their place. He stopped the raids of lawless vassals and granted charters to many towns, thus winning the loyalty of the townspeople.

The king's power was further increased under Philip II, also known as Philip Augustus. Philip, who ruled from 1179 to 1223,

HISTORY Online

Chapter Overview introduces students to chapter content and key terms. Have them access ***Chapter 27 Overview*** at **humanheritage.glencoe.com**

FOCUS

Bellringer

Have students reply to this question: *What do you think it means to be a king?*

Motivational Activity

Discuss student responses. Then explain that over time the power of kings has varied dramatically. Sometimes they were absolute rulers, and sometimes they were nothing more than figureheads. Ask students to discuss what problems might arise for our federal government if our leaders collected their own taxes and raised their own armies.

Reading Check Answer
Monarchies are countries governed by one ruler.

GUIDE TO READING

Reading Strategy

Ask students to read "Why It's Important" and summarize the chapter's main theme. *(As the power of monarchs increased, feudalism declined.)*

Vocabulary Precheck

Ask students to define each of the "Terms to Learn." Have a volunteer consult the dictionary for any unfamiliar words. L1 ELL

Use the Vocabulary PuzzleMaker CD-ROM for Chapter 27 to create a crossword puzzle. L1

Assign Chapter 27 Vocabulary and Guided Reading Activity.

Assign Reading Essentials and Study Guide 27-1.

GEOGRAPHY ACTIVITIES
- Chapter 27 Geography and Map Activity
- Building Geography Skills for Life
- Outline Map Resource Book

INTERDISCIPLINARY CONNECTIONS
- World Music: A Cultural Legacy

ENRICHMENT AND EXTENSION
- World History Primary Source Document Library CD-ROM
- Chapter 27 Enrichment Activity
- Foods Around the World

ASSESSMENT AND EVALUATION
- Chapter 27 Performance Assessment Activity
- Chapter 27 Section Quizzes 27-1, 27-2, 27-3, 27-4, 27-5
- Chapter 27 Test
- Chapter 27 ExamView® Pro Testmaker CD-ROM
- Chapter 27 Digests Audiocassettes Activities and Tests

SPANISH RESOURCES
- Chapter 27 Spanish Chapter Summary and Glossary
- Chapter 27 Spanish Digests Audiocassettes Activities and Tests

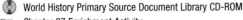

TEACH

Guided Practice

L2 **Panel Discussion** Organize the class into five groups. Assign each group one of the following Capetian monarchs: Hugh Capet, Louis VI, Philip Augustus, Louis IX, and "Philip the Fair." Tell the students to decide how their monarch strengthened the French monarchy and prepare an index card containing at least three points to share in a panel discussion of the Capetian kings.

MAKING CONNECTIONS

➤➤ **Architecture** Philip Augustus built a fortress called the Louvre, which is now France's national art museum. He was also responsible for the construction of the great Cathedral of Notre Dame.

CAPTION ANSWER

the Capetians

DID YOU KNOW ??

Hugh Capet always wore beautiful capes. At first, he had no last name. He was given the name *Capet* from the French word meaning "cape."

Fun Facts. . . .

Royal Advice Louis IX gave his son this advice on governing: "Hold yourself steadfast to your subjects and vassals. . . . And if a poor man have a quarrel with a rich man, sustain the poor rather the rich, until this truth is made clear."

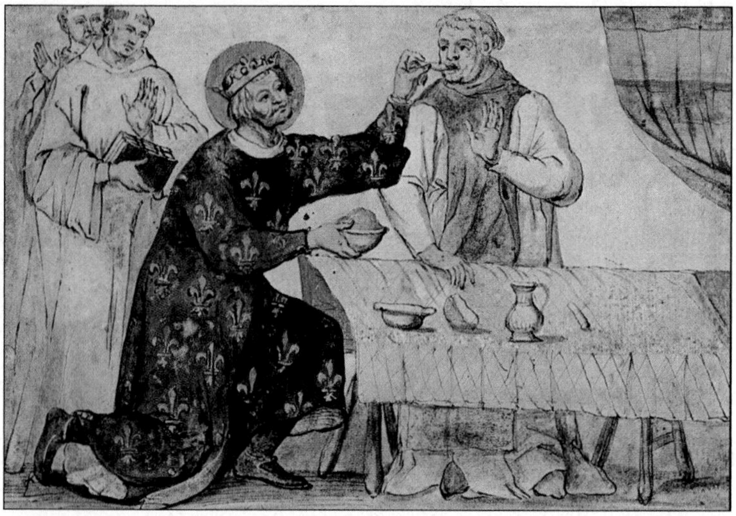

LOUIS IX King Louis IX of France was known for his honesty and just dealings. After his death, he was made a saint of the Roman Catholic Church. Louis's support of the Church is expressed in this painting of the king feeding a church official. **To what line of French kings did Louis IX belong?**

made Paris the center of government. He increased the size of his kingdom through marriage and by winning back French lands held by the English. To make sure the nobles did not become too powerful while he was fighting in the Crusades, Philip II appointed royal agents to keep a close watch on them.

In 1226, Philip's grandson became King Louis IX. He brought peace to France and helped unite the French people. He ordered the nobles to stop feuding and forbade them to settle disputes by fighting duels. Most nobles minted their own money. Louis IX made it illegal to use coins made anywhere else but the royal mint. He set up a royal court to which anyone could bring disputes.

Painting of Philip the Fair

Philip IV, Louis's grandson, ruled from 1285 to 1314. Known as "Philip the Fair," Philip IV believed the interests of the state came first. So, he seized the English fortresses in France that he felt were necessary for his kingdom's security. He also went to war with the Flemish when they refused to let France control their cloth trade. Philip believed a kingdom could not exist without taxes. So, he made sure that taxes were collected regularly. He also taxed the clergy, who had not been taxed before. To help him run the country, Philip IV formed the Estates-General, an assembly of nobles, clergy, and townspeople. This marked the beginning of a national government in France. By the time Philip IV died in 1314, France was united under one ruler.

MULTICULTURAL PERSPECTIVES

The structure of the Estates-General reflected medieval French society (and did so until the French Revolution). The First Estate was the clergy. The Second Estate was the nobility. The Third Estate was the townspeople, or the *bourgeoisie*. Philip IV had the support of all three estates, including the French clergy, in his struggle for power with the Pope. Philip IV had a French Pope elected in 1305 and installed at Avignon, France, not Rome. This papacy lasted until 1378. There was a period of time in which there were two popes—one in Rome and one in Avignon.

Section 1 Assessment

1. **Define:** monarchies.
2. How did Louis VI increase the power of the monarchy?
3. What did Louis IX and Philip the Fair do to help unite France?

Critical Thinking

4. **Drawing Conclusions** Why do you think Louis IX made it illegal for nobles to coin their own money?

Graphic Organizer Activity

5. Draw this diagram, and use it to summarize the accomplishments of these French kings: Hugh Capet, Louis VI, Philip II, Louis IX, and Philip IV.

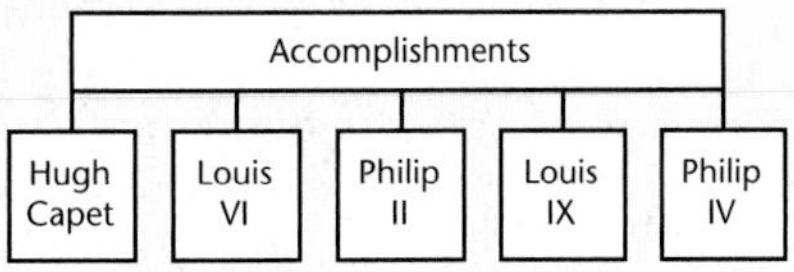

SECTION 2 England

In 1042, the witenagemot made Edward the Confessor, an Anglo-Saxon prince, king of England. Edward gave money to the poor and sponsored the building in London of Westminster Abbey, the church in which later English kings and queens were crowned. He spent so much time in religious work, however, that he failed to carry out his royal duties. As a result, the nobles increased their hold on the country. The most powerful noble was Harold Godwinson. When Edward died in 1066 without an heir, Harold became the new king.

William the Conqueror Harold Godwinson did not remain king for long. William, Duke of Normandy, a cousin of Edward the Confessor, claimed that before Edward died, he had promised him the English throne.

In 1066, William led an army of between 4,000 and 7,000 Norman knights across the channel to England. They met Harold's army in battle near Hastings, a town just south of London. To stop the Norman charge, English foot soldiers armed with axes formed a wall of shields on the edge of a low hill. William knew he could not break through the wall. So, he had his soldiers pretend to retreat. When the English broke formation to follow them, the Normans turned on the English. By nightfall, King Harold was dead, and the English were defeated. William the Conqueror was crowned King William I of England.

At first, the English resisted William's rule. To crush English revolts—and to keep the Normans in line—William introduced feudalism. He seized the lands of English nobles and divided them among Norman nobles. In return, they became his vassals. They promised to be loyal and to provide him with soldiers.

Then & Now

Language For years after the Norman conquest, the upper classes in England spoke Norman French, the lower classes Anglo-Saxon English. Modern English preserves this double heritage. Words for farm animals are mainly Anglo-Saxon: *ox, cow, pig, sheep*. Words for cooked meat, once served mainly to the upper classes, come from French: *beef, pork, mutton* (from *boeuf, porc, mouton*).

L1 **Government** Each of the French kings detailed in Section 1 made reforms that made life easier for peasants. Help students make a chart that lists the kings and at least one beneficial reform they instigated. Have students decide what information should be included in the chart, and have several students put the information on a large poster board. ELL

Use the **Interactive Tutor Self-Assessment CD-ROM** to review Section 1.

DID YOU KNOW ??

The witenagemot was a group of church officials and nobles that advised the king.

MAKING CONNECTIONS

>> **History** William's and Harold's armies were very different. William's soldiers were knights and full-time fighters. Harold's were farmers who left their fields when called to battle.

Use the **Vocabulary PuzzleMaker CD-ROM** to create crossword and word search puzzles.

Section 1 Assessment Answers

1. monarchies, countries governed by one ruler (p. 411)
2. He got rid of nobles who did not fulfill their feudal duties and put loyal persons of lower birth in their place; stopped raids of lawless vassals; and granted charters of freedom to many towns.
3. Louis IX ordered the nobles to stop feuding and fighting duels, required use of royal coins, and set up a royal court. Philip the Fair seized the English fortresses in France, went to war with the Flemish, set up a tax system, and formed the Estates-General.
4. sample conclusions: to increase his power; to promote unity
5. Accomplishments should reflect information in the text and show efforts of each to increase royal power. As an extension, you might ask students to vote on which of these kings they think did the most to strengthen France.

Assign the Chapter 27 **Section 1 Quiz** in the TCR. Testmaker available.

MAKING CONNECTIONS

➤➤ **Language** The Old Saxon language continued to be spoken only by farmers and tradespeople. In time, many French words were used in common speech and greatly altered what became the English language.

LINKING PAST TO PRESENT

The Domesday Book, completed in the 1060s, was the first official record of English property owners and the amount of land they owned. The first modern census in the United States occurred in 1790. The U.S. Constitution required an official account not only for taxation but also to determine representation for each state.

CAPTION ANSWER

He became King William I of England.

Fun Facts . . .

The Final Say The *Domesday Book* got this popular name because people said there was no chance of arguing with its records. That is, its determinations were as final as those of God on doomsday—the Day of Judgment.

William kept many English laws and government practices. He received advice from the witenagemot, now called the Great Council. He depended on such local officials as the sheriff. William also made many changes. In 1086, he took a census and a survey of the land in order to tax the people properly. This information was recorded in two huge volumes called the *Domesday Book.* The title comes from the Anglo-Saxon word *doom,* meaning "judgment."

William brought *continental,* or European mainland, ways to England. Under his rule, the English learned Norman customs and the French language. The wealthy built castles, cathedrals, and monasteries in the French style. The people learned new skills from Norman weavers and other artisans.

Henry II After William died in 1087, there was confusion in England until 1154 when William's great-grandson became King Henry II. Henry ruled England, most of Ireland, Scotland, and Wales. He was also a feudal lord in France, where he owned more land than he did in England. Some of the French lands belonged to his wife, Eleanor of Aquitaine.

BATTLE OF HASTINGS William the Conqueror took the throne of England after his army defeated the English army at the Battle of Hastings in 1066. This painting shows Norman knights on horseback attacking the English soldiers. **What title did William the Conqueror take after his victory at Hastings?**

COOPERATIVE LEARNING

Organize the class into four groups. Assign each group one of the following topics: William the Conqueror, Henry II, Magna Carta, and Parliament. Each group is responsible for researching and preparing a report explaining how these rulers and institutions brought about changes in the English monarchy during the Middle Ages. Have a spokesperson from each group present their group's report to the class.

Henry II restored order and forced the nobles to give him their loyalty. He also used the law to gain more power, and he worked to reform English courts. A central royal court was set up in London with trained lawyers as judges. **Circuit judges,** or judges who traveled throughout the country, brought the king's law to all parts of England. They made it the common law of the land, thus helping to unite the country.

Henry also set up juries to settle quarrels about land. After a while, two kinds of juries came into being. One was the **grand jury,** or a group of people who present to judges the names of people suspected of crimes. The other was the **trial jury,** or a group of people who decide whether a person accused of a crime is innocent or guilty. The trial jury took the place of the medieval trial by ordeal.

Henry II believed that everyone, even church officials, should be tried in the king's courts. Thomas à Becket, Henry's close friend and the Archbishop of Canterbury, did not agree. Becket wanted Church officials to be free of royal control. The quarrel between the king and the archbishop ultimately led to the murder of Becket by four of Henry's knights. After the murder, Henry II made peace with the Church by allowing some of the clergy to be tried in Church courts.

Reading Check How did **circuit judges** spread English law?

Reading Check What was the difference between a **grand jury** and a **trial jury?**

Magna Carta and Parliament

When Henry II died in 1189, his oldest son Richard became king. Richard, however, was more interested in his French lands than in ruling England. He spent most of his time fighting in the Near East on the Crusades.

When Richard died in 1199, his brother John became king of England. John lost most of his lands in France to the French king. When he increased England's taxes and began to ignore the law, the country's nobles became angry. They refused to obey him unless he agreed to give them certain rights. In 1215, John met the nobles in the meadow of Runnymede (ruhn' ē mēd), where they forced him to sign the *Magna Carta* (mag' nuh kar' tuh), or Great Charter.

The Magna Carta took away some of the king's power and increased that of the nobles. A king could no longer collect taxes unless the Great Council agreed. Freemen accused of crimes had the right to a trial by their *peers,* or equals. The Magna Carta was viewed as an important step toward democracy. It brought to government the new idea that even a king is not above the law.

John died in 1216, and his son became King Henry III. Henry, however, was a weak ruler who allowed the feudal lords in the Great Council to rule England. In 1264, Simon de Montfort (mahnt' fuhrt), Henry's brother-in-law, came to power. He gave the people a voice in government by letting them have representatives in the Great Council.

MEETING SPECIAL NEEDS

Have auditory learners hold a debate between representatives of the English monarchy and the Church of Rome. Organize the class into three groups. One group should gather information from the text and from other references. The second group should prepare arguments, questions and possible answers to be used during the debate. The third group should form a committee to hear the arguments from each side, weigh the merits of each argument, and determine the winning position.

Refer to ***Inclusion for the Middle School Social Studies Classroom: Strategies and Activities*** for additional resources.

Reading Check Answer **Circuit judges** traveled throughout the country, making the king's law the common law of the land.

Reading Check Answer A **grand jury** presented judges with the names of people suspected of crimes, while the **trial jury** decided a person's guilt or innocence.

L2 **Language Arts** Discuss the word *conflict* as it applies to the conflicts between the English monarch and the Church. Ask students for other words that could be used in place of *conflict.* List these on the board and have volunteers research their origins and meanings for comparison. ELL

DID YOU KNOW ??

Thomas à Becket was murdered in his own cathedral during Christmastime. He became an instant medieval celebrity. Within months, miracles were reported at Becket's tomb and pilgrims flocked to the site.

MAKING CONNECTIONS

>> **History** During the 10 years of his rule, Richard spent less than a year in England. Most of his time was spent on the Crusades. On his way home from the Third Crusade, he was shipwrecked in the Adriatic Sea. While trying to make his way home by land, the Duke of Austria took him prisoner. He was released after the English people collected and paid a large ransom.

CAPTION ANSWER

the idea that even the king is not above the law

L3 Debate Have students learn more about the importance of the Magna Carta. Form two groups of students, one to represent King John and the other to represent the nobles. Have students prepare their arguments to debate the need for the Magna Carta. Students should hold their debate, and the other students, as an audience, can judge who presents the most convincing arguments.

MAKING CONNECTIONS

➤➤ **Language** The word *parliament* introduced by Simon de Montfort, comes from *parler,* the French word meaning "to talk or discuss." Because it set the precedent for the holding of future parliaments, Edward I's gathering was later called the Model Parliament.

L2 History Ask students to imagine that they were newspaper reporters living during the Middle Ages. They have been asked to write two articles on the Hundred Years' War. One article should discuss the causes of the war between France and England in 1339. The other should deal with the end of the war in 1453 and emphasize the results of the war. Students should write appropriate headlines for the two articles. Have students read their articles to the class.

Use the **Interactive Tutor Self-Assessment CD-ROM** to review Section 2.

Then... & Now

Constitutions Unlike the United States, the United Kingdom does not have a single written document called a "constitution." Instead, British leaders govern according to a series of laws and charters. The oldest of those is the Magna Carta.

MAGNA CARTA The Archbishop of Canterbury and merchants joined the nobles at Runnymede to force King John to sign the Magna Carta. In this painting, as the Archbishop looks on, a noble shows King John where to sign the document. **What new idea did the Magna Carta bring to government?**

Eight years later, the new king, Edward I, went even further. He called for a meeting of representatives to advise him and to help him make laws. This gathering, known as Parliament (par' luh muhnt), gave the people a greater share in the ruling of England. Parliament later broke into two separate groups. Nobles and clergy met as the House of Lords, while knights and townspeople met as the House of Commons.

Section 2 Assessment

1. **Define:** circuit judges, grand jury, trial jury.
2. How did the Normans win the Battle of Hastings?
3. Why was King John forced to sign the Magna Carta?

Critical Thinking

4. **Predicting Consequences** How might the history of English government have been different if nobles had not forced King John to sign the Magna Carta?

Graphic Organizer Activity

5. Draw this diagram, and use it to show some of the milestones in democracy that took place in medieval England.

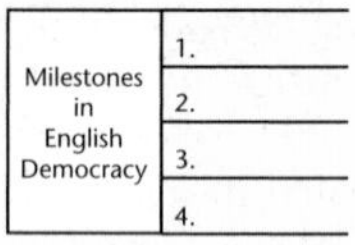

Section 2 Assessment Answers

1. circuit judges, judges who travel (p. 415); grand jury, people who name others suspected of crimes (p. 415); trial jury, group who decides innocence or guilt (p. 415)
2. William's soldiers pretended to retreat and attacked when the English broke formation to follow after them.
3. because he had increased taxes and had begun to ignore the law
4. Most students will probably indicate that England would not have developed a system of government in which the people have a share in ruling.
5. Sample milestones: invasion of William the Conqueror and his efforts to end feudalism; 1086 census to determine fair taxation; use of circuit judges, grand jury, and trial by jury under Henry II, signing of Magna Carta, creation of Parliament.

Assign the Chapter 27 **Section 2 Quiz** in the TCR. Testmaker available.

SECTION 3 The Hundred Years' War

In the early 1300s, the English still held a small part of southwest France. The kings of France, who were growing more powerful, wanted to drive the English out. In 1337, the English king, Edward III, declared himself king of France. This angered the French even more. In 1337, England and France fought the first in a long series of battles known as the Hundred Years' War.

The Hundred Years' War began when the English defeated the French fleet and won control of the sea. The English then invaded France. They defeated the French at the Battle of Crécy (krā sē') in 1346 and again at the Battle of Agincourt (aj' uhn kōrt) in 1415.

The English owed their success on land mostly to a new weapon called the *longbow,* which shot steel-tipped arrows. The French still used the shorter crossbow. The crossbow could not send arrows as far as the longbow, and the French arrows were not as sharp as the steel-tipped English arrows.

At Crécy the English forces also used the first portable firearm in European warfare—a very crude cannon. This early weapon was made of a long iron tube mounted on a pole. The weapon was difficult to carry and use, but led to the development of a more refined cannon that was a major weapon in many later wars.

Joan of Arc

By 1429, much of France was in English hands. Charles, the French ***dauphin*** (do' fuhn), or eldest son of the king, was fighting the English for the French throne. Then, a 17-year-old French peasant named Jeanne d'Arc (zhahn dark'), or Joan of Arc, appeared. She said that while praying, she had heard heavenly voices telling her she must save France. She went to see Charles and told him that God had sent her to help him. She said that if she had an army she would free Orleans (or lā ahn'), a city the English had been besieging for seven months. Charles gave Joan an army, a suit of armor, and a white linen banner.

Joan led an attack against the English army at Orleans. Within ten days, the city was free, and Joan became known as the "Maid of Orleans." Shortly after, with Joan at his side, the dauphin was crowned King Charles VII of France. Joan wanted to return home, but Charles convinced her to stay with the army. A few months later, a French traitor captured her and sold her to the English. After spending a year in prison, she was tried as a witch and burned at the stake. Joan died at the age of 18, a girl who could neither read nor write but who had led an army. A trial twenty-four years later proclaimed her innocence.

People in History

Joan of Arc
c. 1412–1431

French Heroine

Born a peasant, Joan began to hear heavenly voices as a child. They urged her to drive the English from France. At age 17, Joan convinced the king's son to give her an army. She battled the English for seven months before she was captured. The English turned her over to Church officials sympathetic to their cause. They demanded that Joan deny that she was guided by heaven. When she refused, they burned her at the stake. A later court found Joan innocent, and in 1920 the Catholic Church declared her a saint.

Reading Check Who was the French ***dauphin?***

L2 **Religion** Ask students why Joan of Arc was successful and why French soldiers accepted her reports of hearing heavenly voices. List the reasons on the board. Remind students that religion played an important role during the Middle Ages. ELL

L3 **Research** Ask students to research and report on the life of Joan of Arc. With their report, have students prepare a scenario of what might happen if she appeared in modern times in the same kind of situation. How do students think people today would react to her and her "messages?"

MAKING CONNECTIONS

>> **History** It is believed that gunpowder, invented in China, was used for the first time in European warfare at the Battle of Crécy. Its use helped bring the Middle Ages to an end by destroying the ability of castles to withstand an attack.

Reading Check Answer
The French ***dauphin*** was the eldest son of the king.

Use the **Vocabulary PuzzleMaker CD-ROM** to create crossword and word search puzzles.

COOPERATIVE LEARNING

Have groups of students prepare and present readings from the play *Saint Joan* by George Bernard Shaw, choosing suitable passages for presentation, assigning and reading the roles, preparing and presenting a summary of the play, and explaining scenes being presented.

Assign Chapter 27 ***Cooperative Learning Activity*** in the TCR.

HISTORY Online

Student Web Activity objectives and answers can be found at the ***Chapter 27 Web Activity Lesson Plan*** at humanheritage.glencoe.com

LINKING PAST TO PRESENT

Today, Joan of Arc is the second patron saint of France.

CAPTION ANSWER

She led an attack against the English army at Orleans and freed the city.

MAKING CONNECTIONS

➤➤ **Government** During the Hundred Years' War, English kings depended increasingly on Parliament to raise funds in order to support the war. This reliance on Parliament by England's monarchy strengthened Parliament's power. The arrangement strengthened the king as well, giving him power to work with Parliament to raise funds and change laws. In France, the Estates-General was the king's council. Because the king retained the right to raise money and make laws, the Estates-General never assumed the same powers as the English Parliament and eventually was disbanded. Without the Estates-General, the French king was an absolute monarch.

HISTORY Online

Student Web Activity

Visit the *Human Heritage* Web site at humanheritage.glencoe.com and click on ***Chapter 27—Student Web Activities*** to find out more about Joan of Arc.

The French continued to fight after Joan's death. By 1453, they had driven the English from all of France except the seaport of Calais (ka lā′), and the war came to an end.

Results of the War Both France and England were changed by the Hundred Years' War. By 1500, the last French feudal territories were under the king's rule, and France was unified. England, too, was unified by the war, but its monarchy was weakened. Not until 1485, when a Welshman named Henry Tudor (tū′ duhr) became king, did it become strong again.

Because of the Hundred Years' War, the common people in both England and France became more important. Many peasants had died during the war from disease or fighting. Those who remained were greatly needed as workers. The peasants knew this and began to make demands. They forced the nobles to pay them wages and allow them to move outside the manors. When the nobles tried to force them back to the old ways, they revolted. Most became farmers who rented land from the nobles.

JOAN OF ARC Claiming that heavenly voices had instructed her to do so, Joan of Arc led a French army against the invading English and helped return the French king to the throne. She became a national heroine and a saint of the Roman Catholic Church. **How did Joan earn her nickname "Maid of Orleans"?**

EXTENDING THE CONTENT

One of the most famous uprisings was the 1381 Peasant's Revolt in England, led by Wat Tyler and a priest, John Ball. Three ragged peasant armies marched on London in the summer of 1381. They kidnapped several high royal officials, including the Archbishop of Canterbury, and beheaded them. They demanded freedom and an end to all class distinctions or feudal duties. King Richard II began to bargain with the rioters. His army seized and punished the leaders, and the rebellion came to an end.

Section 3 Assessment

1. **Define:** *dauphin.*
2. Why did France and England go to war?
3. How did the Hundred Years' War affect French and English peasants?

Critical Thinking

4. **Understanding Cause and Effect** What was the connection between the Hundred Years' War and the end of feudalism?

Graphic Organizer Activity

5. Draw this diagram, and use it to show facts about Joan of Arc's life. (Add more answer circles as necessary.)

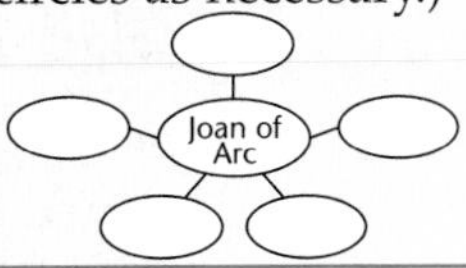

SECTION 4 Germany

During the 900s, Germany was the most important country in western Europe. Over time, though, German kings lost much of their authority to powerful nobles who wanted to rule their own territories. The king, however, still had the right to remove lords who would not obey him.

Otto I In 936, Otto I became king of Germany. He wanted to unite the country and rule without nobles. He removed lords who would not obey him and gave their estates to his family. Then, he turned to the Roman Catholic Church for help. Its leaders wanted him to set up a Christian Roman Empire in western Europe. So, Otto made many of his loyal followers bishops and abbots and gave them government posts. In return, they supplied him with money and soldiers.

Otto began expanding Germany. In 951, he marched south into Italy, where he took over the northern Italian trading cities. In 962, he led an army to Rome to free the Pope from the control of Roman nobles. In return, the Pope crowned Otto I emperor of the Holy Roman Empire, a large new state made up of Germany and northern Italy. Otto saw himself as the heir of the Roman emperors. For the next 90 years, Otto and the emperors who followed him controlled the office of Pope.

German Crown

Frederick I In 1152, Frederick I became emperor. Because of his full red beard, he was called Barbarossa, or "red beard." Frederick forced the powerful lords to promise him loyalty and to work for his government.

Frederick's attempts to control the nobles and unify the empire worked against him. The nobles grew rich from their government posts. At the same time, the Italian city-states, aided

Use the **Interactive Tutor Self-Assessment CD-ROM** to review Section 3.

L1 **Discussion** Lead a discussion of the following questions as students build a cause-and-effect graphic organizer on the chalkboard. Encourage volunteers to add to the graphics as the questions are answered. Ask: *How was the Holy Roman Empire created and ruled? What was the relationship between Otto I and the Roman Catholic Church? How did Otto I become emperor of the Holy Roman Empire? What caused the Holy Roman Empire to become weaker during the rule of Frederick I? Why did the Pope call for a crusade against Frederick II? What happened as a result of Hapsburg rule?* ELL

MAKING CONNECTIONS

>> **History** Otto was the son of Henry I, or Henry the Fowler, powerful German Duke of Saxony who was elected king of Germany in 919. Henry's bravery and ability won the respect of the nobles and paved the way for the rule of his son.

Use the **Vocabulary PuzzleMaker CD-ROM** to create crossword and word search puzzles.

Section 3 Assessment Answers

1. *dauphin,* eldest son of the French king (p. 417)
2. The kings of France wanted to drive the English out, and Edward III of England declared himself king of France.
3. They became more important.
4. Answers will vary but could include that kings took control of feudal territories, England and France were unified, and peasants became more important.
5. In selecting their sample facts, remind students to use the People in History on page 417, and include the declaration of Joan's innocence in 1920.

Assign the Chapter 27 **Section 3 Quiz** in the TCR. Testmaker available.

MAKING CONNECTIONS

>> **Legends** According to legend, when Frederick Barbarossa's red beard grows long enough to wrap completely around the large table next to which he "sleeps," Barbarossa will rise and destroy Germany's enemies.

CAPTION ANSWER

He founded a university at Palermo.

by the Pope, banded together and defeated Frederick's armies. Frederick had to accept a peace that recognized the independence of the city-states.

While leading the Third Crusade in 1190, Frederick drowned in a river in Asia Minor. Later, a legend about him spread among the Germans. It stated that he was not dead but under a magic spell that had put him to sleep somewhere high in the mountains. The people believed that one day he would awake and restore the glory of Germany.

Frederick II In 1220, Frederick II, Frederick I's grandson, became emperor. Frederick II was raised in Palermo (puh luhr' mō), Sicily, which his father had made part of the Holy Roman Empire. He ignored Germany and concentrated on ruling the people of Sicily.

Frederick was known as the best-educated monarch of his time. He spoke several languages and enjoyed doing scientific experiments. He supported many artists and scholars. He

FREDERICK II Frederick II was greatly interested in the sciences and medicine and encouraged their study during his reign. He had a special interest in the study of birds and wrote a book on the subject. This painting of Frederick shows him with his falcon handler. **How did Frederick II aid medieval learning?**

EXTENDING THE CONTENT

Today the Catholic Pope is elected by the College of Cardinals without interference from any political groups. The Popes have been traditionally Italian, but in 1978, the college elected the Polish Pope John Paul II.

Linking Across Time

Universities Scholarship was important to the Hapsburg family, which included Maximilian I. The Hapsburgs encouraged the growth of universities throughout the Holy Roman Empire (left). Universities spread throughout Europe and the rest of the world (below). **Why are universities important today?**

founded a university in Palermo so young men could study at home rather than in other countries. Although the Church was against it, Frederick even adopted many Muslim customs.

When Frederick began conquering land in Italy, the Pope became afraid that he would take over Church lands around Rome. To stop Frederick, the Pope excommunicated him in 1227. He also called for a crusade against Frederick. This gave the German princes the chance for which they had been waiting. They broke away from Frederick's rule and made Germany a loose grouping of states under their control.

The Hapsburgs Whenever an emperor of the Holy Roman Empire died, the German princes met in a **diet,** or assembly. There, they elected a new emperor. In 1273, the princes elected as emperor a member of the Hapsburg (haps' berg) family named Rudolf. He and members of his family served as Holy Roman emperors for about the next 650 years.

Reading Check What was the purpose of the German **diet?**

One important Hapsburg was Maximilian I (mak suh mil' yuhn), who became emperor in 1493. He worked to extend the empire's power all through Europe. When he married Mary of Burgundy, he gained control of Flanders and other areas of what are now the Low Countries, or Belgium, the Netherlands, and Luxembourg. By marrying his children into other European

Linking Across Time

Answers will vary, but students should mention the importance of universities as centers of learning.

L2 **Culture** One of the favorite pastimes of nobles was falconry. Suggest students research this sport, and report their findings to the rest of the class.

GEOGRAPHY AND HISTORY

Maximilian's older son Philip I, married Joanna, the daughter of Ferdinand and Isabella of Spain. His second son, Ferdinand, married Anna of Bohemia and Hungary. By 1520, the Hapsburgs ruled half of Europe and most of the settled areas in the Americas.

Reading Check Answer The German **diet** elected a new emperor whenever an emperor of the Holy Roman Empire died.

SPOTLIGHT ON: THE HAPSBURGS

Emperor Charles V retired to a monastery in 1556 after ruling much of Europe for 37 years. The resulting division of Hapsburg lands gave the family power in parts of Europe for hundreds of years, outlasting the Holy Roman Empire. Charles' son became king of Spain as Philip II, who ruled a vast empire in the Americas. The Spanish line continued until 1700. A lack of an heir caused the War of the Spanish Succession. The Austrian Hapsburg dynasty continued under Charles' brother Ferdinand. Hapsburg emperors and an empress ruled the Holy Roman Empire until the empire was ended in the early 1800s. They then ruled Austria-Hungary. The last Hapsburg emperor of Austria had to abdicate after World War I.

Independent Practice

L1 History Have students work in pairs to prepare a list of questions that a news reporter might ask one of the people mentioned in this chapter. Have them role-play the interview for the class.

L2 Geography: Places and Regions Have students create five geography-based questions based on the map "Europe in the Late Middle Ages." Collect the questions and use them to quiz the students. ELL

MAP STUDY

Answer

The Holy Roman Empire was larger than the other regions.

Assign the Chapter 27 **Geography and Map Activity** in the TCR.

Use the **Interactive Tutor Self-Assessment CD-ROM** to review Section 4.

royal families, he brought still more countries under Hapsburg control. He could not gain complete control, however, in Germany where the princes continued to have authority over their own lands.

Section 4 Assessment

1. **Define:** diet.
2. How were the German emperors able to control the office of Pope in the late 900s and early 1000s?
3. How did the Hapsburgs come to power?

Critical Thinking

4. **Drawing Conclusions** Why do you think a strong rule by a king or queen did not develop in Germany?

Graphic Organizer Activity

5. Draw this diagram, and use it to show the achievements of German rulers in the Middle Ages.

Ruler	Achievements

Europe in the Late Middle Ages

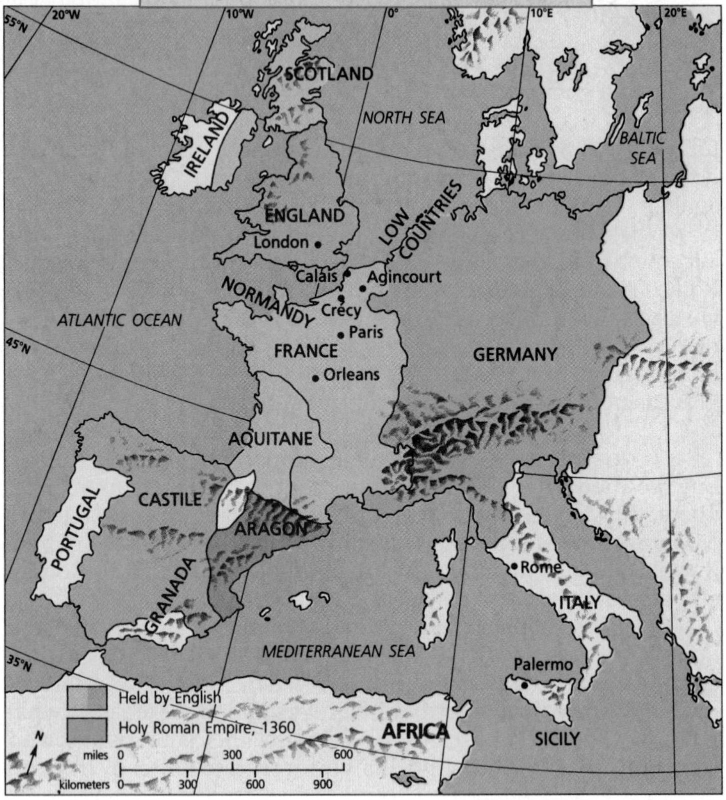

MAP STUDY

PLACES AND REGIONS Strong kings and queens appeared in England, France, Spain, and Portugal in the late Middle Ages. **How did the size of the Holy Roman Empire compare to other regions of western Europe during the late Middle Ages?**

Section 4 Assessment Answers

1. diet, assembly (p. 421)
2. Otto had freed the Pope from the control of Roman nobles. In return, the Pope crowned him Emperor of the Holy Roman Empire.
3. through election in a diet, or assembly, of German princes
4. Answers will vary but might include the idea that Germany was a loose grouping of states under the control of German princes. Also, emperors were elected by German princes versus inheriting the position.
5. Charts should show the accomplishments of Otto I, Frederick I, Frederick II, Rudolf, and Maximilian I. Completed charts should include each ruler's efforts to promote unity and expand German power.

Assign the Chapter 27 **Section 4 Quiz** in the TCR. Testmaker available.

SECTION 5 Spain

Painting of Spanish Hero El Cid and his father

While the western European monarchies were increasing their power, Spain was under the control of the Moors. When the Moors conquered Spain in 711, they brought with them learning and luxury. Most Spaniards, however, were Christians and opposed Muslim rule. They banded together to drive the Moors out of the country. By the 1200s, the Moors controlled only the small southern kingdom of Granada (gruh nahd' uh).

The rest of Spain was made up of several kingdoms, the most powerful of which were Castile (kas tēl') and Aragon (ar' uh gahn). In 1469, Prince Ferdinand of Aragon married Princess Isabella of Castile. Within ten years, they became king and queen and united their kingdoms into one country.

Ferdinand and Isabella accomplished this in different ways. To control the nobles, the king and queen took away some of their privileges. To keep order in the land, they sent royal officials called ***corregidores*** (kō rā hē dō' rās) to govern the towns. They also set up special courts in the countryside.

Reading Check What was the role of the *corregidores?*

The most important way in which they unified Spain, however, was through religion. Ferdinand and Isabella were known as the "Catholic Monarchs." They believed that to be truly united, all Spaniards should be Catholic. They turned their attention first to the Jews. The Jews had lived freely under the Moors. However, as Christians took over more of Spain, they killed thousands of Jews. To save themselves, many Jews converted.

Ferdinand and Isabella believed these new Christians were practicing their old religion in secret. So, they set up the Spanish Inquisition. The Spanish Inquisition tried and tortured thousands of people charged with heresy. More than 2,000 people were burned to death. Still, most Jews refused to change their faith. So, in 1492, Ferdinand and Isabella told the remaining Jews to convert or leave the country. Most left the country.

Next, the king and queen turned their attention to the Moors. In 1492, the last of the Moors had surrendered Granada to armies of Ferdinand and Isabella. The treaty signed at the time promised the Moors freedom of religion. Nevertheless, in 1502 the Catholic Monarchs ordered the remaining Moors to convert or leave. Most left Spain for northern Africa.

Although now a united Catholic monarchy, Spain was weaker than it had been before. This was because most of its artisans, merchants, bankers, doctors, and educators had been either Jews or Moors. After these people left, there were few trained Spaniards to take their place.

Then ... & Now

Equal Footing In 1990 Spain finally overturned the 1492 order calling for the expulsion or conversion of the Jews. Now both Judaism and Protestantism are on an equal basis with Roman Catholicism, giving all three religions the same tax breaks and privileges.

SPOTLIGHT ON: EL CID

Spain's national epic, which created a hero like England's King Arthur or France's Roland, comes out of the long period of wars between Moors and Christians known as the *Reconquista.* The Christians of the old Visigothic kingdoms had been pushed back into the Pyrenees. From there they moved southward city by city. Spanish rulers also warred against each other. In addition, Muslim kingdoms were resisting takeover by fanatic Almoravids from North Africa. The hero of the battle of Valencia in 1094 was El Cid. This was the name given to the military leader Rodrigo Díaz de Vivar who later became ruler of Valencia. More legends than facts are known about El Cid.

Use the **Vocabulary PuzzleMaker CD-ROM** to create crossword and word search puzzles.

L2 **The Arts** When Ferdinand and Isabella captured the Moorish province of Granada, they gained some remarkable examples of Moorish art and architecture, such as the Alhambra. Have students research and report on the art and architecture of the Spanish Moors. Have them give oral summaries of their reports including pictures of the art and architecture.

Reading Check Answer The *corregidores* governed towns and also set up special courts in the countryside.

ASSESS

Check for Understanding

Ask students to summarize the main points of the chapter, orally or in writing. Discuss the answers to the Section and Chapter Assessment questions.

Evaluate

Assign the Chapter 27 **Performance Assessment Activity** in the TCR.

Administer the **Chapter 27 Test.** Testmaker available.

Reteach

Have the students create a time line of events covered in this chapter.

Assign the Chapter 27 **Reteaching Activity** in the TCR.

GLENCOE TECHNOLOGY

MindJogger Videoquiz

Use **MindJogger Videoquiz** to review students' knowledge of the unit.

Available in DVD and VHS

Enrich

The son of the English King Edward III was known as the Black Prince because he wore black armor. Have students research the Black Prince and his role in the Hundred Years' War and write a first-person account of his career.

Assign the Chapter 27 **Enrichment Activity** in the TCR.

CLOSE

Have students debate the advantages and disadvantages of a strong monarchy during the Middle Ages.

Use the **Interactive Tutor Self-Assessment CD-ROM** to review Section 5.

HISTORY Online

Self-Check Quiz gives students an interactive chapter tutorial. Have them access ***Chapter 27 Quiz*** at humanheritage.glencoe.com

Section 5 Assessment

1. **Define:** *corregidores*.
2. How did Ferdinand and Isabella control the nobles and keep order in Spain?
3. How did Ferdinand and Isabella use religion to unite Spain?

Critical Thinking

4. **Predicting Consequences** How might Spain have been different if the Spanish king and queen had allowed freedom of religion?

Graphic Organizer Activity

5. Draw this diagram, and use it to show the causes and effects of Ferdinand and Isabella's united Catholic monarchy.

Chapter Summary & Study Guide

1. The rise of trade and towns in western Europe led to the rise of strong monarchies.
2. The Capetian dynasty strengthened the French monarchy by granting town charters and by setting up a national court, a national currency, a tax system, and the Estates-General.
3. William the Conqueror defeated the English at the Battle of Hastings in 1066 and brought the system of feudalism to England.
4. Henry II strengthened England by imposing his law on the land and by reforming courts.
5. In 1215, English nobles forced King John to sign the Magna Carta, which established the idea that a king was not above the law.
6. In 1272, Edward I set up Parliament to help him make laws.
7. During the Hundred Years' War, fought between 1337 and 1453, Joan of Arc led armies to force the English from France.
8. Because of the Hundred Years' War, both France and England were unified and the common people became more important.
9. The Pope crowned Otto I emperor of the Holy Roman Empire in 962. However, future German emperors had a hard time uniting unruly German princes.
10. The Hapsburg family ruled the Holy Roman Empire from 1273 until the early 1900s.
11. By 1492, Ferdinand and Isabella had conquered the Moors and made Spain a united Catholic country.

HISTORY Online

Self-Check Quiz

Visit the *Human Heritage* Web site at humanheritage.glencoe.com and click on ***Chapter 27—Self-Check Quiz*** to assess your understanding of this chapter.

Section 5 Assessment Answers

1. *corregidores,* Spanish royal officials (p. 423)
2. They took away some of their privileges, sent *corregidores* to govern the towns, and set up special courts in the countryside.
3. They forced the Jews and the Moors to convert to Christianity or leave the country.
4. Answers will vary but might include that the artisans, merchants, bankers, doctors, and educators who were needed to keep the nation strong would not have left Spain.
5. *sample causes*—opposition to Moorish control, marriage of Ferdinand and Isabella *sample effects*—decreased privileges for nobles; use of *corregidores;* persecution of non-Catholics and establishment of Inquisition; defeat of Moors at Granada; loss of most of Spain's artisans, merchants, bankers, doctors, and educators who had been Jews or Moors

Assign the Chapter 27 **Section 5 Quiz** in the TCR. Testmaker available.

CHAPTER 27 Assessment

Using Key Terms

Imagine that you are a news reporter who has a chance to interview one of the kings or queens you have read about in this chapter. Identify whom you will interview, and write five questions you would like to ask that person. Use the following words in your questions.

monarchies	circuit judges	grand jury
trial jury	*dauphin*	diet
corregidores		

Understanding Main Ideas

1. How did the Estates-General help strengthen the French monarchy?
2. What changes did the Magna Carta bring about in English government?
3. Why did the position of the common people in England and France improve as a result of the Hundred Years' War?
4. How did Otto I set up a Christian Roman Empire in western Europe?
5. What did the Moors bring to Spain?
6. What was the purpose of the Spanish Inquisition?

Critical Thinking

1. If you had been King John, how would you have reacted to the demand that you sign the Magna Carta? Explain your answer.
2. If you had been Joan of Arc, what decision would you have made about attacking the English at Orleans? Explain your answer.
3. How did the Hundred Years' War both help and hurt England and France?
4. Would you have agreed or disagreed with Ferdinand and Isabella that all people in a country should follow the same religion? Explain.

Graphic Organizer Activity

Citizenship Create a diagram like the one below, and use it to compare English government in 1275 with government in the United States today.

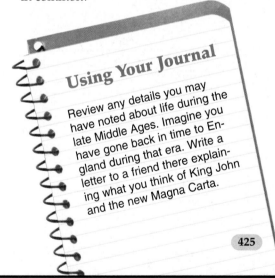

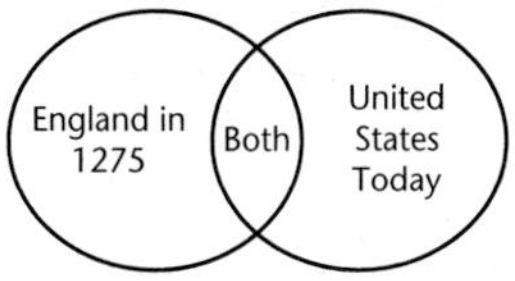

Geography in History

Places and Regions Refer to the map on page 422. There were several places outside the control of either the English or the Holy Roman Empire. What geographic features do these places have in common?

Using Your Journal

Review any details you may have noted about life during the late Middle Ages. Imagine you have gone back in time to England during that era. Write a letter to a friend there explaining what you think of King John and the new Magna Carta.

425

CHAPTER 27 Assessment Answers

Using Key Terms

Questions will vary according to the king or queen selected but should use all the terms.

Understanding Main Ideas

1. It united the nobles, clergy, and townspeople.
2. It increased the nobles' power, gave freemen the right to a trial, and said that the king had to obey laws.
3. because many had died, and those who remained were greatly needed as workers
4. He made his loyal followers bishops and abbots and gave them government posts.
5. learning and luxury
6. to deal with heresy

Critical Thinking

1. Answers will vary, but students might disagree with King John's acceptance.
2. Answers will vary.
3. Answers will vary, but might include that it helped by unifying them but hurt the countries by resulting in the deaths of many peasants.
4. Answers will vary, but students should explain why they agree or disagree.

Graphic Organizer Activity

Diagrams will vary but should show the roots of United States government in English law as well as the increased rights of United States citizens and additional curbs on executive power such as the system of checks and balances. Some features of both governments might include: a two-house assembly, trial by jury, written document setting limits on government, and so on.

Bonus Test Question

For Chapter 27 Test

If medieval monarchs had been able to access modern technology, they might have avoided some of their problems. Assume the role of one of these monarchs and name a modern invention you could have used and what problem it would have solved.

Using Your Journal

Letters will vary, but students might include thoughts about grand juries, trial juries, right to a trial by peers, and Parliament.

Geography in History

They are on the outer fringes of Europe and are widely spaced and most often surrounded by water.

FOCUS

Objectives

After reading the Around the World for Unit 8, your students will be able to:

1. explain how Japan's geography helped shape life during feudal times.

2. identify the Noh theater and other feudal Japanese accomplishments.

3. appreciate the meaning of a Zen garden to Japanese Buddhists.

Bellringer

Instruct students to write down the geographic features that can isolate a people or a culture.

Motivational Activity

Call on students to share their responses, compiling a list of geographic features that can promote cultural isolation. Then refer students to the map of Japan on page 426. Ask: Which of these features did Japan possess? *(Sample responses: its island location—i.e., surrounding oceans and seas.)*

TEACH

Geography: Places and Regions Tell students to look closely at the map. Is Japan one island or several islands? *(several)* What is the most common landform on these islands? *(mountains)* Challenge students to suggest how Japan's islands and mountains might encourage the rise of feudalism. *(It would divide people from one another, encouraging the growth of small independent kingdoms.)*

UNIT 8 Around

FEUDAL JAPAN

From about 1000 A.D.–1600 A.D., Japan went through its own feudal age. Like the feudal age in Europe, this was a time when power belonged to military leaders, known as *samurai*, and the soldiers who served them. The most powerful samurai became *daimyo*, or local lords. The samurai, like medieval knights, pledged their loyalty and military service to the daimyo. Individual states controlled by the daimyo battled for control of Japan and the right to claim the title of *shogun*—the head of Japan's military government. The principle of *bushido*, which means "the way of the warrior," shaped life in much of feudal Japan.

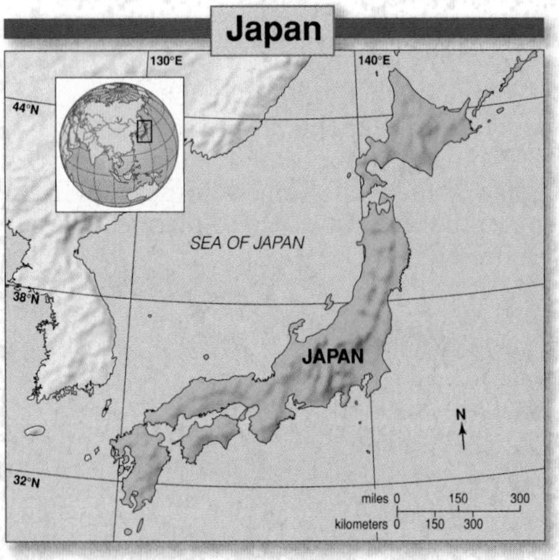

▲ Japan's island location helped isolate it from unwanted intruders. Its rugged terrain limited the amount of available land and increased the power of the land-owning daimyo and the samurai who served them.

► The Japanese considered a samurai's armor a work of art. The armor was made of horizontal rows of lacquered iron or leather held together by braided silk cords. The artisans who fashioned the armor—and the swords that went with it—were held in high regard.

SPOTLIGHT ON: FEUDAL JAPAN

Courtship and marriage in feudal Japan followed fixed rituals. Usually a bridegroom's family chose a suitable match from an equal or higher class. The royal family chose the husband for the daughters of emperors.

Courtship often began with a sentimental poem sent to the woman by the prospective bridegroom. Her reply was examined closely for its calligraphy and style. If the woman was willing and the man impressed, the two might then go through a series of meetings set by custom. A third meeting was considered a sign of commitment.

Marriages generally took place while the bride and groom were in their early teens. Since children this young could not manage their own affairs, they went to live with the wife's family. Houses and other property frequently passed from mothers to daughters, ensuring security for a woman in case she lost her husband to death or divorce.

the World

▲ Japanese nobles tried to include beauty and poetry in every aspect of their lives. Even everyday objects such as this tea pot were crafted with an artist's care.

The Japanese imported Zen Buddhism from China. Zen holds that enlightenment can be achieved by anyone who experiences a revelation, or vision, following meditation. To encourage meditation, the Japanese built Zen gardens where monks, samurai, and others came to meditate. ▼

▼ Swordsmiths produced beautiful—and sharp—swords.

The tales of ancient warriors and the bravery and suffering of women were told in the Noh theaters of medieval Japan. Noh theater combined music, dance, poetry, and elaborate customs. The Noh actors—all male—often wore wooden masks such as this one. ►

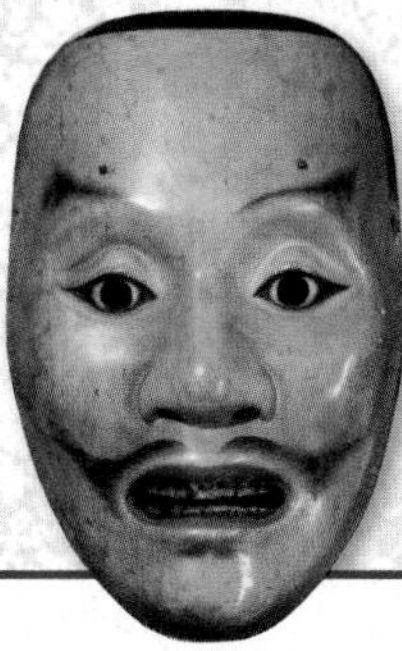

▼ The samurai received land for their loyal service. They built castles to protect themselves against attacks from rival states. This castle is called the White Heron for its white plaster walls and its location high on a hill that resembles a bird protecting its nest. The castle originally belonged to samurai Toyotomi Hideyoshi.

Taking Another Look

1. How did Japan's geography help shape life in feudal Japan?
2. What was Noh theater?

Hands-On Activity

Designing a Garden Design a plan for a Zen garden. It should be simple, with wandering paths and private spots for meditation.

427

ANSWERS TO TAKING ANOTHER LOOK

1. Japan's island location helped isolate it from other people and unwanted intruders. Its rugged, mountainous terrain limited the amount of available land and increased the power of the land-owning daimyo. The mountains also encouraged the rise of independent and warring feudal samurai.
2. The Noh theater combined several art forms—dance, music, poetry, and costume-making—to tell the stories of ancient warriors and the bravery and suffering of women.

Hands-On Activity

Plans should include paths and meditation sites. They should exhibit simplicity as well as use of natural features—i.e., rock benches instead of manufactured benches.

DID YOU KNOW ??

Women, like their brothers, inherited samurai status from their fathers. Although they rarely appeared on the battlefield, women samurai received martial-arts training and were expected to defend family estates. Women samurai also practiced *bushido,* which stressed loyalty, bravery, and self-discipline. One woman samurai named Oichi Nobunaga took her own life rather than surrender her castle to a rival samurai.

ASSESS

Check for Understanding

Have students answer the questions in Taking Another Look on page 427.

Enrich

Ask interested students to research information on the Japanese tea ceremony. Encourage them to share their findings by reenacting a tea ceremony for the rest of the class to observe.

CLOSE

Have students compare Japanese feudalism with European feudalism, noting similarities and differences. *(Sample responses:* similarities—*armored warriors, codes of loyalty [chivalry and* bushido*], construction of castles, lack of unity among kingdoms, and so on;* differences—*influence of Zen Buddhism [instead of Christianity], development of unique art forms such as Noh theater, historical connections with China [rather than Greece and Rome].*

Answers and Analyses

1B History

The rise of feudalism is discussed at the top of page 368. There it states that *The kings who followed Charlemagne were so weak they could not even rule their own kingdoms well . . . Before long they began to depend on the nobles.*

2J History

Page 385 describes the reforms begun by the monks of Cluny and continued by Pope Gregory VII. There it states that Gregory wanted to *rid the Church of control by kings and nobles.*

THE PRINCETON REVIEW **TEST-TAKING TIP**

Students probably recall the struggles for power between the monarchy and the Church, and this information is enough to make J a good guess. Choices F and H are unlikely, since these attempts have only been made in modern times.

3B History

The rise of universities is discussed on page 387. The text at the top of the page states that universities arose in part because *students began to complain that teachers held few classes and did not cover enough subjects.*

THE PRINCETON REVIEW

Standardized Test Practice

Directions: Choose the *best* answer to each of the following multiple choice questions. If you have trouble answering a question, use the process of elimination to narrow your choices. Write your answers on a separate piece of paper.

1. One reason for the growth of feudalism in western Europe was

A an increase in the population of lords and nobles
B the failure of kings to develop a centralized government
C the need for many more people to work farmland
D the desire of peasants to have a more secure future

> ***Test-Taking Tip:*** The key to being able to answer this question correctly is knowing what *feudalism* is. Always consult the **glossary** in the back of your book when you come across a word you are unsure of. In this case, *feudalism* was a medieval system of government by landowning nobles. Which answer choice *best* fits with this information?

2. During the Middle Ages, the Church attempted to institute reforms aimed at

F reuniting the Roman Catholic and the Eastern Orthodox churches
G obtaining more land and wealth for the Church
H expanding the role of women in the Church
J reducing the influence of kings, lords, and nobles in the Church

> ***Test-Taking Tip:*** Think about the meaning of the word *reform.* It means "change that leads to improvement." Usually, reforms are needed when an institution strays from its original purpose. In the Middle Ages, Church officials were often wealthy nobles who were more concerned with money than with religious ideals. Which answer choice do you think would *best* help the Church *improve,* so that it could fulfill its original *religious purposes?*

3. During the Middle Ages, universities arose

A because there was no more classroom space in the cathedrals
B to teach subjects not covered in cathedral schools
C to prepare future rulers and noblemen
D to provide the underprivileged with educational opportunity

> ***Test-Taking Tip:*** This question is looking for a *cause and effect* relationship. During the Middle Ages, governments were more secure, and the economy was stronger. Therefore, people had more time for—and more interest in—learning new things. Therefore, which of the answer choices would most likely have been the cause of the rise of universities?

4. What was one important result of the Crusades?

F Muslim and Byzantine culture was introduced to western Europe.

G The Eastern Orthodox Church accepted the Pope as its leader.

H Jerusalem came under control of the Roman Catholic Church.

J The Byzantine Empire was at last safe from the Turks.

> ***Test-Taking Tip:*** Always read *carefully.* Although the Crusades began as an attempt to help the Byzantine Empire, they were ultimately unsuccessful. Therefore, answer J is incorrect.

5. Why were craft guilds created?

A To help royalty regain control over the price of goods

B To protect the rights of people who bought goods and services

C To protect the rights of people working in these trades

D To make it easier for apprentices to become masters

> ***Test-Taking Tip:*** This question requires you to remember the meaning of the word *guild.* Craft guilds, like present-day unions, were business associations of artisans, such as carpenters, shoemakers, and weavers. What is the purpose of unions today?

Read the passage below, which is an excerpt from the Magna Carta, and answer the question that follows.

> We . . . have granted to all the freemen of our kingdom, for us and for our heirs forever, all the underwritten liberties, to be had and holden by them and their heirs . . .
>
> No freeman shall be taken or imprisoned, or diseased, or outlawed, or banished, or in any way destroyed, nor will we pass upon him, nor will we send upon him, unless by the lawful judgement of his peers, or by the law of the land.
>
> All merchants shall have safe and secure conduct to go out of, and to come into, England . . . without any unjust tolls. . . .

6. The main idea of the Magna Carta was

F to help the king further centralize his power

G to secure certain rights and liberties for noblemen

H to entitle people accused of crimes to a trial by jury

J for the Church to take on a greater role in England's government

> ***Test-Taking Tip:*** This question asks for the *main idea.* Remember, the main idea is a generalization about the *entire passage,* not just one detail. For example, the second paragraph does mention *the lawful judgement of peers* (a reference to trial by jury), but this is not the main idea of the *entire passage.*

STOP

Tested Objectives

Questions	Reading Objective
1, 4	Determine cause and effect
2, 6	Identify central issues
3	Identify supporting ideas
5	Perceive relationships and recognize outcomes

4F History

The Eastern Orthodox Church did not accept the Pope as its leader, so choice G can be eliminated. While Jerusalem was temporarily in the hands of Christians, it was retaken by the Muslims, so choice H can be eliminated. After the Crusades, the Byzantine Empire was weaker than ever, and so choice J can be eliminated. According to the bottom of page 395, the crusaders' contact with the Byzantine and Muslim cultures led to a taste for eastern luxuries and for the knowledge that the Muslims had.

5C History

The rise of guilds is discussed on pages 406–407. There it states that guilds *were business groups whose purpose was to make sure that their members were treated equally.* This information best supports choice C.

THE PRINCETON REVIEW **Test-Taking Tip**

Encourage students to use their common sense about political positions of individuals and groups. Since guilds were made up of artists, the guilds naturally protected the interests of the artists. Therefore, students can eliminate choices A and B.

6G History

According to page 415, *the Magna Carta took away some of the king's power and increased that of the nobles.*

Introducing **UNIT 9**

OVERVIEW

Unit 9 discusses the changes that took place in western Europe from the 1300s to the 1600s as the Middle Ages came to an end.

- **Chapter 28** describes the Renaissance when western Europeans experienced new attitudes about themselves and the world around them.
- **Chapter 29** discusses the Reformation and how differences in religions led to religious wars.
- **Chapter 30** summarizes the principal European voyages of discovery from the 1400s to the 1600s.

UNIT OBJECTIVES

After reading Unit 9, students will be able to:

1. describe what changes took place in learning in western Europe during the 1300s and 1400s.

2. summarize what changes took place in religion during the 1400s and 1500s.

3. discuss what western Europeans learned about the world during the Age of Discovery.

UNIT PROJECT

Tell students to imagine they are on an explorer's ship in the middle 1600s. Their ship has landed in an overseas port. The local ruler expresses interest in hearing about the Renaissance, the Reformation, and the Age of Discovery in western Europe. The captain asks for a historical sketch of important events and people during this time. Students should prepare their presentations for the captain.

UNIT 9

Beginning of Modern Times

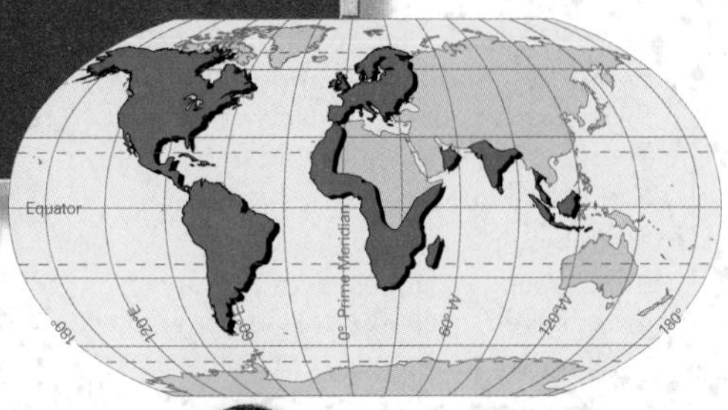

Compass and sundial ▶

◀ Master sh
wright, aided
his apprentic

1300
Scholars promote classical learning

1418
Prince Henry of Portugal starts school for navigators

1440
Johannes Gutenberg develops printing press

1478
Lorenzo de Medici rules Florence

430

About the Unit Opening

Examining Artifacts

Ask students what the two artifacts have in common. *(Both are related to ships or sailing.)* Explore reasons these artifacts might be used to illustrate this unit on the start of modern times. Explain to students the importance of exploration and trade in ushering in a new era.

Global Chronology

Ask students what time period the time line covers. *(1300 to 1519)* How do they know learning was important? *(scholars promoted learning, school for navigators started)* What entries indicate exploration? *(Prince Henry starts school for navigators; Columbus lands at San Salvador; Magellan begins voyage to Pacific)*

FOLDABLES™ Study Organizer

Sequencing Events Study Foldable *Make this foldable to help you sequence events that led to the Age of Discovery.*

Step 1 *Fold two sheets of paper in half from top to bottom.*

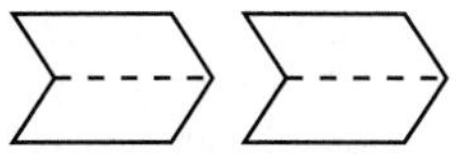

Step 2 *Turn the papers and cut each in half*

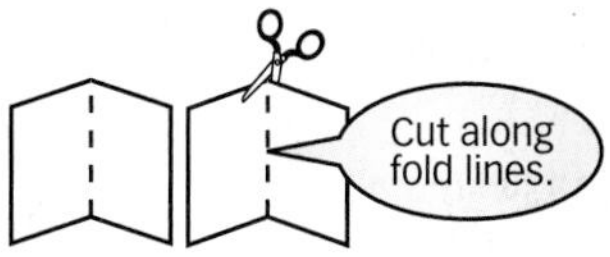

Cut along fold lines.

Step 3 *Fold the four pieces in half from top to bottom.*

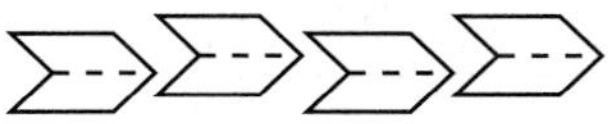

Step 4 *Tape the ends of the pieces together (overlapping the edges very slightly) to make an accordion time line.*

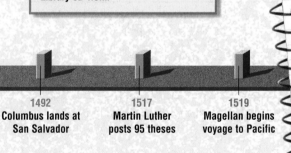

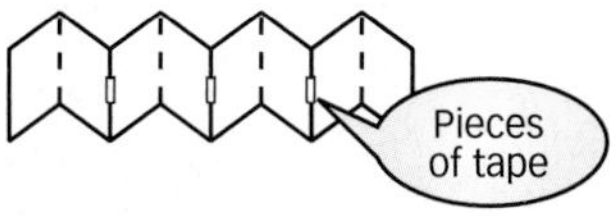

Pieces of tape

Reading and Writing *As you read the unit, sequence the events that led to European voyages of exploration by writing a date and an event on each part of the time line.*

PRIMARY SOURCES Library

See pages 690–691 for other primary source readings to accompany Unit 9.

GO TO Read "Columbus Reaches the Americas" from the **World History Primary Source Document Library CD-ROM.**

1492 Columbus lands at San Salvador

1517 Martin Luther posts 95 theses

1519 Magellan begins voyage to Pacific

Journal Notes

What changes took place in western Europe between 1300 and 1600? Note details about these changes as you read.

431

Geographic Location

Using a world map or globe, have students locate the countries of western Europe and North and South America, the islands of the Caribbean, Africa, and the East Indies. Discuss the dangers involved in sailing from western Europe to unknown lands during the 1400s–1600.

ABCNEWS INTERACTIVE™

VIDEOCASSETTE
Turning Points in World History

Have students view **Tape 1 Chapter 9** to learn about the Age of Exploration, which increased contact among the world's civilizations.

GLENCOE TECHNOLOGY

MindJogger Videoquiz

Use **MindJogger Videoquiz** to preview the unit content.

Available in DVD and VHS

FOLDABLES™ Study Organizer

Purpose Students will create this foldable to organize events leading up to the Age of Discovery. As students are reading this unit, they are required to sequence and describe important events. When students have completed the activity, they should have a time line of changes and innovations in western Europe in the 1300s and 1400s.

Have students complete **Reading and Study Skills Foldables** Activity 9.

RECORDING JOURNAL NOTES

Help students begin writing by asking them to name the changes that are on the time line. Explain that these are the kinds of changes they should detail in their journals.

PRIMARY SOURCES Library

Additional primary sources from the **World History Primary Source Document Library CD-ROM** include:

- "Da Vinci on Painting," by Leonardo da Vinci
- "Martin Luther's 95 Theses," by Martin Luther

Primary sources about the fall of the Aztec Empire are on pages 690–691.

Chapter 28 Planning Guide

Timesaving Tools

TeacherWorks™ All-In-One Planner and Resource Center

- **Interactive Teacher Edition** Access your Teacher Wraparound Edition and your classroom resources with a few easy clicks.
- **Interactive Lesson Planner** Planning has never been easier! Organize your week, month, semester, or year with all the lesson helps you need to make teaching creative, timely, and relevant.

Use Glencoe's **Presentation Plus!** multimedia teacher tool to easily present dynamic lessons that visually excite your students. Using Microsoft PowerPoint® you can customize the presentations to create your own personalized lessons.

Objectives	Reproducible Resources	Multimedia Resources
Section 1 **The Italian City-States** Explain how the Renaissance began and flourished in the Italian city-states.	Reproducible Lesson Plan Chapter 28 Vocabulary and Guided Reading Activity Reading Essentials and Study Guide 28-1 Chapter 28 Cooperative Learning Activity Chapter 28 Chart and Graph Skill Activity Unit 9 Primary Source Readings Chapter 28 Enrichment Activity Section 1 Quiz Unit 9 Hands-On History Lab	Interactive Student Edition CD-ROM Graphic Organizer Transparency 1 Teaching Transparencies and Activities 28A & 28B Vocabulary PuzzleMaker CD-ROM ExamView® Pro Testmaker CD-ROM Glencoe Skillbuilder Interactive Workbook CD-ROM, Level 1 Presentation Plus! CD-ROM
Section 2 **France** Identify ways in which France was influenced by the Italian Renaissance.	Reproducible Lesson Plan Reading Essentials and Study Guide 28-2 Section 2 Quiz	Vocabulary PuzzleMaker CD-ROM Interactive Tutor Self-Assessment CD-ROM ExamView® Pro Testmaker CD-ROM Glencoe Skillbuilder Interactive Workbook CD-ROM, Level 1
Section 3 **Germany and Flanders** Describe how the Renaissance spread to Germany and Flanders.	Reproducible Lesson Plan Reading Essentials and Study Guide 28-3 Chapter 28 Geography and Map Activity Section 3 Quiz	Vocabulary PuzzleMaker CD-ROM Interactive Tutor Self-Assessment CD-ROM ExamView® Pro Testmaker CD-ROM Glencoe Skillbuilder Interactive Workbook CD-ROM, Level 1
Section 4 **Spain** Discuss the influence of the Roman Catholic Church and government on the Renaissance in Spain.	Reproducible Lesson Plan Reading Essentials and Study Guide 28-4 Unit 9 World Literature Reading 2 Section 4 Quiz	Vocabulary PuzzleMaker CD-ROM Interactive Tutor Self-Assessment CD-ROM ExamView® Pro Testmaker CD-ROM Glencoe Skillbuilder Interactive Workbook CD-ROM, Level 1
Section 5 **England** Summarize how the English monarchy promoted the Renaissance in England.	Reproducible Lesson Plan Reading Essentials and Study Guide 28-5 Unit 9 World Literature Reading 1 Section 5 Quiz	Vocabulary PuzzleMaker CD-ROM Interactive Tutor Self-Assessment CD-ROM ExamView® Pro Testmaker CD-ROM Glencoe Skillbuilder Interactive Workbook CD-ROM, Level 1
Chapter 28 Review and Evaluation	Chapter 28 Reteaching Activity Chapter 28 Performance Assessment Activity Spanish Chapter Summary and Glossary Chapter 28 Test	Vocabulary PuzzleMaker CD-ROM Interactive Tutor Self-Assessment CD-ROM Glencoe Skillbuilder Interactive Workbook CD-ROM, Level 1 Audiocassettes* ExamView® Pro Testmaker CD-ROM

*Also available in Spanish.

Chapter 28 Planning Guide

Performance Assessment Activities

Art Museum Have students find books at the library with examples of Renaissance art and architecture. Students should use these books to set up their own Renaissance museum. Encourage students to tape an audio description for each art piece as many museums do.

CHAPTER RESOURCES

LITERATURE ABOUT THE PERIOD

Castiglione, Baldassare. *The Book of the Courtier.* Translated by George Bull. Penguin, 1976. Contemporary handbook of courtly etiquette.

READINGS FOR THE STUDENT

Mee, Charles L. *Daily Life in the Renaissance.* American Heritage, 1975. Illustrated with works of art showing people in their daily lives.

READINGS FOR THE TEACHER

Editors of Time-Life. *What Life Was Like In Europe's Golden Age.* Time-Life, Inc., 1999. A vividly illustrated study of northern Europe during the years 1500 to 1675.

Editors of Time-Life. *What Life Was Like at the Rebirth of Genius.* Time-Life, Inc., 1999. A look at the outburst of creativity that characterized Renaissance Italy.

KEY TO ABILITY LEVELS

Teaching strategies have been coded for varying learning styles and abilities.

L1 Level 1 activities are **basic** activities and should be within the ability range of all students.

L2 Level 2 activities are **average** activities and should be within the ability range of the average to above-average student.

L3 Level 3 activities are **challenging** activities designed for the ability range of above-average students.

ELL ELL activities should be within the ability range of English Language Learning students.

NATIONAL GEOGRAPHIC Teacher's Corner

INDEX TO NATIONAL GEOGRAPHIC MAGAZINE

The following article relates to this chapter:

- "Italy's Endangered Art: A Nation of Art Lovers Finds New Ways and Will to Save its Priceless Legacy," by Erla Zwingle, August 1999.

NATIONAL GEOGRAPHIC SOCIETY PRODUCTS AVAILABLE FROM GLENCOE

To order the following, call Glencoe at 1-800-334-7344:

- *PicturePack: Renaissance (Transparencies)*
- *PictureShow: Renaissance (CD-ROM)*

Access *National Geographic*'s new dynamic MapMaker Web site and other geography resources at:
www.nationalgeographic.com
www.nationalgeographic.com/maps

THE HISTORY CHANNEL. A&E HOME VIDEO. Biography

The following videotape programs are available from Glencoe:

- **Henry VIII**
  1-56501-917-2
- **Michelangelo**
  1-56501-425-1
- **The Miraculous Canals of Venice**
  1-56501-840-0

To order, call Glencoe at 1-800-334-7344. To find classroom resources to accompany many of these, check:

A&E Television: www.aande.com
The History Channel: www.historychannel.com

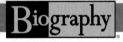

Introducing **CHAPTER 28**

OVERVIEW

Chapter 28 describes the Renaissance and the changes it brought to western Europe.

- **Section 1** discusses the start of the Renaissance in Italy.
- **Section 2** describes the Renaissance in France.
- **Section 3** analyzes the Renaissance in Germany and Flanders.
- **Section 4** explains the Renaissance in Spain.
- **Section 5** summarizes the Renaissance in England.

CHAPTER OBJECTIVES

After reading Chapter 28, students will be able to:

1. explain how the Renaissance flourished in Italy.
2. identify how France was influenced by the Renaissance.
3. describe how the Renaissance spread to Germany and Flanders.
4. discuss how the Church and the government influenced the Renaissance in Spain.
5. cite features of the Renaissance in England.

EXAMINING ARTIFACTS

Ask students what these artifacts reveal about Renaissance interests. *(People took an interest in music and invention.)* Based on the time line, have students identify other pursuits or pastimes. *(printing/reading; theater)* Encourage students to add to their lists of Renaissance activities as they read the chapter.

PERFORMANCE ASSESSMENT

Use the Performance Assessment activities on page 432B to help you evaluate students as they complete the chapter.

CHAPTER 28

The Renaissance

1300 A.D.–1600 A.D.

◄ Renaissance musicians

A replica of a bicycle designed by Leonardo da Vinci ▼

- c. 1440 Johannes Gutenberg develops printing press
- 1478 Lorenzo de Medici becomes ruler of Florence
- 1485 Tudors take over the English throne
- 1494 The Renaissance spreads to France
- 1580 First English theaters built

TEACHING RESOURCES

TEACHER PLANNING AND SUPPORT

- Reproducible Lesson Plan 28-1, 28-2, 28-3, 28-4, 28-5
- Teaching Strategies for the World History Classroom (Including Block Scheduling Pacing Guides)
- Presentation Plus! CD-ROM

REVIEW AND REINFORCEMENT

- Reading Essentials and Study Guide 28-1, 28-2, 28-3, 28-4, 28-5
- Chapter 28 Vocabulary and Guided Reading Activity
- Vocabulary PuzzleMaker CD-ROM
- Teaching Transparencies 28A & 28B
- Chapter 28 Reteaching Activity
- Chapter 28 Cooperative Learning Activity
- Chapter 28 Activity Book Activity
- Chapter 28 Chart and Graph Skill Activity
- Reading and Study Skills Foldables
- Interactive Tutor Self-Assessment CD-ROM
- Unit 9 MindJogger VideoQuiz

APPLICATION AND HANDS-ON ACTIVITIES

- Daily Questions in Social Studies
- World Crafts Activity Card 5
- Student Presentation Builder CD-ROM

Chapter Focus

Read to Discover

- How the Renaissance flourished in the Italian city-states.
- How France was influenced by the Italian Renaissance.
- How the Renaissance spread to Germany and Flanders.
- How the Roman Catholic Church and the government influenced the Renaissance in Spain.
- How the English monarchy promoted the Renaissance in England.

HISTORY Online

Chapter Overview

Visit the *Human Heritage* Web site at **humanheritage.glencoe.com** and click on ***Chapter 28—Chapter Overviews*** to preview this chapter.

Terms to Learn	People to Know	Places to Locate
classical writings	Leonardo da Vinci	Florence
humanists	Michelangelo	Venice
piazza	Johannes Gutenberg	Papal States
doge	El Greco	Toledo
chateaux	Henry VIII	
printing press	Elizabeth I	
	William Shakespeare	

Why It's Important Around 1300, scholars in western Europe developed a new interest in **classical writings**, or the writings of the ancient Greeks and Romans. The scholars improved their knowledge of Greek and Latin. They also began to accept some Greek and Roman ideas.

One idea that the scholars accepted was a belief in the importance of people. Because of this, the scholars were called **humanists** (hyū́ muh nists). Their work caused a break with the thinking of the Middle Ages and led to a new age called the Renaissance (ren' uh sahns), a French word meaning "rebirth." During this age, people became less concerned with the mysteries of heaven and more interested in the world around them.

Reading Check Where did **classical writings** come from?

Reading Check What was the main belief of the **humanists?**

SECTION 1 The Italian City-States

The first and leading center of the Renaissance was Italy, which consisted of small, independent city-states. The most important were Florence, Venice, and the Papal (pā' puhl) States. The Papal States in central Italy included Rome and were ruled by the Pope. All these city-states had grown wealthy from trade.

HISTORY Online

Chapter Overview introduces students to chapter content and key terms. Have them access ***Chapter 28 Overview*** at **humanheritage.glencoe.com**

FOCUS

Bellringer

Have students write down what they think of when they hear the name *Leonardo da Vinci.*

Motivational Activity

Discuss student responses. *(They may know that da Vinci painted the* Mona Lisa *or that he designed an early flying machine.)* Ask: What do da Vinci's accomplishments tell you about the time in which he lived? *(a renewed interest in science and technology)* Tell students that in this chapter they will learn about the ideas that inspired a Renaissance in western Europe.

Reading Check Answer **Classical writings** came from the works of the Greeks and Romans.

Reading Check Answer The **humanists** believed in the importance of people.

GUIDE TO READING

Reading Strategy

Ask students to read "Why It's Important" and summarize the chapter's main theme. *(The beliefs of the humanists caused a break with the Middle Ages and paved the way for a renewed interest in people and their accomplishments.)*

Vocabulary Precheck

Ask students to define each of the "Terms to Learn." L1 ELL

Use the Vocabulary PuzzleMaker CD-ROM for Chapter 28 to create a crossword puzzle. L1

Assign Chapter 28 Vocabulary and Guided Reading Activity.

Assign Reading Essentials and Study Guide 28-1.

GEOGRAPHY ACTIVITIES

- Chapter 28 Geography and Map Activity
- Building Geography Skills for Life
- Outline Map Resource Book

INTERDISCIPLINARY CONNECTIONS

- Unit 9 World Literature Readings 1 & 2
- World Art & Architecture Transparency 23, *Mona Lisa*
- World Music: A Cultural Legacy

ENRICHMENT AND EXTENSION

- World History Primary Source Document Library CD-ROM
- Chapter 28 Enrichment Activity
- Unit 9 Primary Source Readings
- Foods Around the World

ASSESSMENT AND EVALUATION

- Chapter 28 Performance Assessment Activity
- Chapter 28 Section Quizzes 28-1, 28-2, 28-3, 28-4, 28-5
- Chapter 28 Test
- Chapter 28 ExamView® Pro Testmaker CD-ROM
- Chapter 28 Digests Audiocassettes Activities and Tests

SPANISH RESOURCES

- Chapter 28 Spanish Chapter Summary and Glossary
- Chapter 28 Spanish Digests Audiocassettes Activities and Tests

TEACH

Guided Practice

L1 **The Arts** Organize students into small groups. Have each group write brief descriptions of the visuals in this chapter. How does this art look different from the medieval art shown in Chapters 24–27? Discuss the groups' descriptions as a class. *(Students' responses might include: three dimensional, less likely to have religious themes, and more emotional expression.)* ELL

MAKING CONNECTIONS

➤➤ **Daily Life** In their workshops, artists worked on dozens of projects at a time. In addition to painting and sculpting, Renaissance artists designed and carved furniture, made jewelry, painted festival cloaks and carnival masks, planned scenery for plays, molded candlesticks and chandeliers, and decorated cakes.

HISTORY Online

Student Web Activity objectives and answers can be found at the ***Chapter 28 Web Activity Lesson Plan*** at humanheritage.glencoe.com

NATIONAL GEOGRAPHIC

Use these materials to enrich student understanding of the Renaissance.

NGS PICTURESHOW CD-ROM
Renaissance

NGS PICTUREPACK TRANSPARENCY SET
Renaissance

Painting of Leonardo da Vinci

At first, each city-state was ruled by guilds. Later, powerful individuals or families took control. They often fought each other for land and wealth. At times, they had difficulty gaining the people's loyalty and had to govern by force.

The leaders of the Italian city-states, however, were interested in more than power. They wanted to be remembered as wise, generous rulers. To be sure this would happen, they spent money on ceremonies and parades to impress and entertain the people. They ordered the building of churches and palaces. They also encouraged scholars, poets, and philosophers to set up palace schools to educate the sons of the rich. In these schools, pupils learned to develop their minds and make their bodies stronger. They spent part of the day studying classical writings and learning good manners. They spent the rest of the day wrestling, fencing, and swimming.

Art Art was an important part of life in Renaissance Italy. City-states were proud of their artists. In fact, the city-states often competed for the services of certain painters and sculptors. The artists knew they were important and began to seek individual honor and attention. They worked hard to develop their own distinctive style.

Renaissance artists carefully studied ancient Greek and Roman art, science, and mathematics. They began to pay close attention to the details of nature. They became interested in *perspective* (puhr spek' tiv), or a way of showing objects as they appear at different distances. Above all, the artists studied the structure of the human body to learn how to draw it accurately. They began to experiment with light, color, and shade. As a result, they painted and sculpted works that were true to life and full of color and action.

HISTORY Online

Student Web Activity
Visit the *Human Heritage* Web site at humanheritage.glencoe.com and click on ***Chapter 28—Student Web Activities*** to find out more about Leonardo da Vinci.

Good artists were given money by the rulers of the city-states. In return, they were expected to make paintings and sculptures for the rulers' palaces and gardens. Artists often had workshops where they trained apprentices. The apprentices added backgrounds, costumes, or hands to the artists' paintings.

Many artists painted portraits for the rich. The artists tried to paint people's facial features so they showed what the people really looked like. At first, portraits were painted only to honor dead or famous people. Later, any merchant with money could have a portrait painted.

One of the greatest Renaissance artists was Leonardo da Vinci (lē uh nahr' dō dah vin' chē). He is known for the *Mona Lisa,* a portrait of an Italian noblewoman. He also painted a fresco called *The Last Supper* on the wall of an Italian monastery's dining room. It shows Christ and his disciples at their last meal before Christ's death. In these works, da Vinci tried to reveal people's feelings as well as their outward appearance.

COOPERATIVE LEARNING

Organize students into groups and have each group take on the role of da Vinci, the inventor. Tell each group they are to look around them and come up with an invention that would be helpful to them like da Vinci did. Within the group, have them choose an illustrator, planner, supply manager, builder, and whatever else they need to plan and create their invention. Have groups present their inventions, with explanations, to the class.

Assign Chapter 28 ***Cooperative Learning Activity*** in the TCR.

Da Vinci was a scientist as well as an artist. He filled notebooks with drawings of inventions that were far ahead of the times. Da Vinci designed the first parachute and made drawings of flying machines and mechanical diggers.

Another outstanding artist was Michelangelo Buonarroti (mī kuh lan′ juh lō bwah nah rō′ tē). He is known for his paintings on the ceiling and altar wall of Rome's Sistine (sis′ tēn) Chapel. He also sculpted the *Pietà* (pē ā′ tah), which shows the dead Christ in his mother's arms. Michelangelo went farther than the ancient Greeks and Romans in presenting the human body. His figures are large and muscular and show a sense of motion.

City Life Most Italian Renaissance cities had narrow paved streets with open sewers in the middle. Merchants and shopkeepers lived on the top floors of the buildings that housed their

Then & Now

Mona Lisa Near the end of his life, while living in France, Leonardo da Vinci sold the *Mona Lisa* to his patron Francis I, king of France. The painting is one of the major attractions of the Louvre in Paris, where it can be seen today.

RENAISSANCE ARTISTS Michelangelo Buonarroti and Leonardo da Vinci were two leading artists of the Italian Renaissance. Michelangelo carved a very large statue of Christ and his mother known as the *Pietà* (left). Da Vinci tried to capture the personality of an Italian noblewoman in the painting known as the *Mona Lisa* (right). **What did da Vinci try to reveal in his works of art?**

L3 **Language Arts** Have students research the life and works of an Italian artist mentioned in this chapter. Have them develop a dramatic monologue to present to the class portraying this artist. Encourage students to dress appropriately for their presentations.

MAKING CONNECTIONS

>> **The Arts** Another influential Italian artist was Raphael, who painted historical and religious frescoes. He became known for his portraits of the Madonna, or Virgin Mary. As an architect, he helped in the construction of St. Peter's Basilica in Rome.

CAPTION ANSWER

people's thoughts and feelings as well as their outward appearances

Biography®

The following videotape program is available from Glencoe to enrich Chapter 28:

- **Michelangelo**

To find classroom resources to accompany this video, check the following home page:

A&E Television:
www.aande.com

SPOTLIGHT ON: MICHELANGELO

Michelangelo was working on the sculpture of Moses for Pope Julius's tomb when the Pope asked him to paint the ceiling of the Sistine Chapel instead. Michelangelo painted scenes from the Bible on the ceiling while lying on his back on scaffolding 70 feet (or 21 m) above the floor. The Renaissance biographer Giorgio Vasari described the completion of Michelangelo's ceiling of the Sistine Chapel in the following way: "When the work was thrown open, the whole world came running to see what Michelangelo had done; and certainly it was such as to make everyone speechless with astonishment."

Reading Check Answer People gathered in the **piazza** to talk to friends, carry out business dealings, and watch or take part in parades and celebrations on holidays.

L1 **Geography: Places and Regions** Have students locate the various Italian city-states on the map on page 438 as they are mentioned in the chapter narrative. Have volunteers keep a running list of city-states on the chalkboard. Have students add one adjective to the list that describes each city. ELL

L2 **Daily Life** Ask students to create a list of manners that might appear in a modern book on etiquette. Have them compare their lists with the list on page 436. What conclusions about Renaissance manners can students draw? ELL

LINKING PAST TO PRESENT

The Renaissance revived the Greek ideal of the balanced individual who participated in a variety of activities, such as politics, arts, sports, and music. Today we still admire this ideal, and we apply the term "Renaissance man" or "Renaissance woman" to someone who has wide interests and many different talents. Ask students to think of someone today whom they would describe this way.

shops. The rich built homes in the classical style, with rooms that were large and had high ceilings. In the center of the homes stood courtyards filled with statues, fountains, and gardens. Most people in the cities, however, were poor. They worked for low wages and lived in run-down areas.

Reading Check What activities went on in the **piazza?**

The center of city life was the **piazza** (pē aht′ suh), or central square. There, markets were set up, and merchants traded goods. People gathered to talk to friends and to carry out business dealings. On holidays, the people often watched or took part in parades and ceremonies there.

Families were close-knit. Most family members lived and worked together in the same neighborhood. Marriages were arranged as if they were business deals. Women stayed at home, ran the household, and raised children. Men spent their days at work and talking with friends on the streets and in taverns.

Most men dressed in tights and tunics. Some also wore cloaks and caps. Women dressed in simply cut, flowing dresses with tight bodices. The rich often wore brightly colored clothing made from expensive silks and velvets trimmed with fur.

Florence The Italian Renaissance began in Florence, which was ruled by the Medici (med′ uh chē) family. One of its most

RENAISSANCE MANNERS

Do not blow your nose and then open and look inside your handkerchief as if pearls or rubies had dropped out of your head.

Do not offer anyone a fruit from which you have already taken a bite.

Do not tell sad stories at parties or mealtimes. If someone starts talking this way, gently and politely change the subject and talk about something more cheerful.

Do not brag about honors, wealth, or intelligence.

Do not speak while yawning.

Do not clean your teeth with your napkin or your finger.

Do not lie all over the dinner table or fill both sides of your mouth with so much food that your cheeks stick out widely.

Do not undress, comb, or wash your hair in front of others.

Do not stick out your tongue, rub hands together, or groan out loud.

Do not talk too much, especially if your knowledge is small.

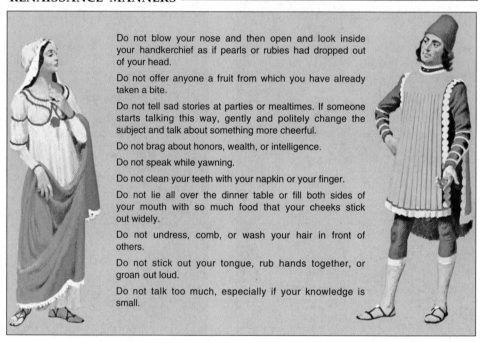

MULTICULTURAL PERSPECTIVES

The Renaissance revived the Greek notion that an ideal person participated in a variety of activities, including sports. Games and sports that were popular at this time included javelin hurling, chess, archery, fencing, boxing, snowfights, and gambling. Women as well as men participated in many sports, including *giuco della palla*—a game that led to the modern game of tennis.

Philip had a new granite palace built just outside Madrid. Called El Escorial (el es kō rē ahl'), it served as a royal court, art gallery, monastery, church, and tomb for Spanish royalty. El Escorial soon became a symbol of the power and religious devotion of Spanish rulers.

Despite strong Church and government controls, the arts flowered. The city of Toledo (tō lā' dō) became a center for painters and poets. One artist who settled there was a Greek whom the Spanish called El Greco (el grek' ō). He painted figures with very long bodies, parts of which stretched beyond normal size. Some art experts believe that El Greco copied his style from Byzantine artists. Others insist he painted as he did because of an eye problem that distorted his vision.

Painting of Don Quixote

The theater was also popular in Renaissance Spain. Miguel de Cervantes Saavedra (mē gel' dā suhr van' tēs suh vē druh) was one of the most noted authors of the time. He wrote many plays, short stories, and other works. His novel, *Don Quixote* (don ki hō' tā), which describes the adventures of a comical knight and his peasant squire, is still read today.

Section 4 Assessment

1. What factors influenced the Renaissance in Spain?
2. Why did Philip II mistreat Spanish scholars?

Critical Thinking

3. **Making Comparisons** How did Cardinal Jiménez and Philip II differ in their attitudes toward learning?

Graphic Organizer Activity

4. Draw this diagram, and use it to summarize the contributions of Jiménez, El Greco, and Cervantes to the Spanish Renaissance.

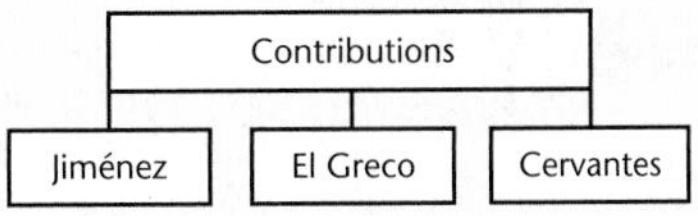

SECTION 5 England

Peace did not come to England after the Hundred Years' War. In 1455, two noble families, York and Lancaster, began a fight for the throne. The Yorkist symbol was a white rose, and the Lancastrian symbol was a red rose. For this reason, the struggles between the House of York and the House of Lancaster were called the Wars of the Roses.

When the wars ended in 1485, a family called the Tudors, who fought on the Lancastrian side, took over the English throne. The first Tudor king, Henry VII, prepared the way for the Renaissance. He made the monarchy stronger and built up trade, which made England both peaceful and rich.

Painting of English Singers

L2 **The Arts** Have students choose a Northern Renaissance painting (one by Brueghel or Van Eyck, for example) and compare it to one by an Italian Renaissance artist (such as Masaccio or Michelangelo). Ask students to compare how "real" the people look and tell what effect the paintings have on them. ELL

Use the **Interactive Tutor Self-Assessment CD-ROM** to review Section 4.

MAKING CONNECTIONS

>> **Architecture** It took 21 years to build El Escorial, which was finished in 1586. Philip often sat on a rock throne set on a nearby hilltop and supervised the workers. Lit by 200,000 oil lamps, the building was dedicated on the eve of the Feast of Saint Lorenzo, the saint for whom El Escorial was named.

LINKING PAST TO PRESENT

El Greco's real name was Doménikos Theotokópoulos. One of his most famous paintings, "View of Toledo," hangs in New York's Metropolitan Museum of Art.

Section 4 Assessment Answers

1. the close ties between the Roman Catholic Church and the government
2. He did not trust their work and considered much of it to be heretical.
3. Cardinal Jiménez believed in the value of learning and helped spread education. Philip II distrusted the work of scholars and charged many of them with heresy.
4. Sample contributions: Jiménez—founded universities, welcomed scholars from other countries, helped scholars produce a new version of the Bible in three languages; El Greco—spread new painting styles; Cervantes—wrote many plays, short stories, and other works, including the novel *Don Quixote*.

Assign the Chapter 28 **Section 4 Quiz** in the TCR. Testmaker available.

Use the **Vocabulary PuzzleMaker CD-ROM** to create crossword and word search puzzles.

L2 **History** Have students read more about the Wars of Roses and develop a graphic organizer showing the series of events that caused, continued, and concluded these wars.

CAPTION ANSWER

He made the monarchy stronger and built up trade, which made England both peaceful and rich.

Biography®

The following videotape program is available from Glencoe to enrich Chapter 28:

- **Henry VIII**

To find classroom resources to accompany this video, check the following home page:

A&E Television:
www.aande.com

DID YOU KNOW ??

Elizabeth I had been educated in the tradition of the Renaissance. She spoke English, French, and Italian as well as being skilled at translating Latin and Greek.

THE TUDORS These paintings of King Henry VIII of England (left) and his daughter Queen Elizabeth I (right) show members of the Tudor family, who ruled England from 1485 to 1603. Henry and Elizabeth both were strong and forceful rulers, and they were able to gain the respect and love of the English people. **How did the first Tudor king, Henry VII, pave the way for the English Renaissance?**

People in History

Henry VIII
1491–1547

English King

Henry VIII was a typical Renaissance ruler. He played tennis, liked to joust, and wrote music. He also built up the English navy and changed the course of history by convincing Parliament to declare him the head of the Church of England, splitting with the Roman Catholic Church (see Chapter 29).

Henry VII's work was continued by his son, Henry VIII, who became king in 1509. He enjoyed and encouraged art, literature, hunting, and parties. He played several musical instruments and even composed his own music. Under his rule, English nobles and merchants began to look to Renaissance Italy for guidance in politics, diplomacy, and behavior.

The English Renaissance reached its height, however, during the reign of Henry VIII's daughter, Elizabeth I. She became queen in 1558 when she was 25 years old. She was shrewd and well-educated. Although she had a sharp tongue and an iron will, she won the loyalty and confidence of her people.

Elizabeth often made journeys through the kingdom so that the people could see her. During her travels, she stayed at the homes of nobles who entertained her with banquets, parades, and dances. Poets and writers praised her in their writings. The sons of merchants, lawyers, and landowners copied Italian clothes and manners and came to court to capture her attention and favor.

Poetry, music, and the theater became a part of daily life. Most nobles wrote poetry. People of all classes enjoyed singing ballads and folk songs. Many played violins, guitars, and lutes.

EXTENDING THE CONTENT

Henry V died in France in 1422 leaving an infant son, Henry VI. Nobles from rival branches of the Plantagenet family (Henry II's line) began maneuvering for power, and Henry VI never gained control. When rivalry erupted into war in 1455, two parties formed around Richard, Duke of York, and Cardinal Beaufort, who backed King Henry VI. Shifting loyalties, intermittent fighting, and treachery marked the war. Over the next 30 years, four men became king of England and were deposed, murdered, or killed in battle. The young sons of Edward IV (York) were sent to the Tower of London and never seen again. The deaths of hundreds of nobles seriously weakened the English nobility.

The people of Renaissance England were especially fond of plays. Not since the days of ancient Greece had so many plays been written and performed. About 1580, the first theaters in England were built. Their stages stood in the open air. Most of the audience, however, sat under a roof or some sort of covering. Those who could not afford to pay for seats stood in the *pit,* or an open area in the front of the theater, and on the sides of the stage. Since there were no lights, plays were performed in the afternoon. They attracted large crowds.

One of the best known English *playwrights,* or authors of plays, was William Shakespeare (shāk′ spir). He drew ideas for his tragedies and comedies from the histories of England and ancient Rome. He often used Italian scenes, characters, and tales in his plays. Some of his most famous works are *Romeo and Juliet, Macbeth, Hamlet, Julius Caesar,* and *A Midsummer Night's Dream.* Many experts consider Shakespeare the greatest playwright in the English language.

ENGLISH THEATER The Globe Theater (left) stood near the south bank of the Thames River in the London suburb of Southwark. The Globe Theater became the home of William Shakespeare's (right) acting company in 1599. **What kind of reputation have the plays of William Shakespeare earned for him?**

DID YOU KNOW ??

Audiences that disliked a play would hurl insults and toss ripe fruit at the actors to drive them from the stage. Since women were not permitted on the stage, boys whose voices had not yet changed played the female roles, which were usually smaller and less important than the male roles.

CAPTION ANSWER

He is considered the greatest playwright in the English language.

ASSESS

Check for Understanding

Ask students to summarize the main points of the chapter, orally or in writing. Discuss the answers to the Section and Chapter Assessment questions.

Evaluate

Assign the Chapter 28 **Performance Assessment Activity** in the TCR.

Administer the **Chapter 28 Test** in the TCR. Testmaker available.

COOPERATIVE LEARNING

Assign students to small groups to develop a set of TV quiz-show-style questions about a Renaissance artist of their choice. Students should consult art history books and, as a group, analyze the artist's style, subjects of art, and also the facts of their lives. Each panel can present their questions in a class competition. Each member of the group should be responsible for a task: research, recording group discussion, developing questions, or acting as panel moderator in presenting the questions.

Reteach

Ask students to suggest the ways in which Italian Renaissance ideas spread to other areas of western Europe. Have volunteers write responses on the chalkboard.

Assign the Chapter 28 **Reteaching Activity** in the TCR.

Enrich

Have students choose an influential social critic who lived during the Renaissance, such as Erasmus or Rabelais, and report on the person's criticisms of the Catholic Church or Renaissance society.

Assign the Chapter 28 **Enrichment Activity** in the TCR.

CLOSE

Have students write an essay that summarizes major characteristics of the arts of the Renaissance—painting, literature, drama, and architecture.

Use the **Interactive Tutor Self-Assessment CD-ROM** to review Section 5.

HISTORY Online

Self-Check Quiz gives students an interactive chapter tutorial. Have them access ***Chapter 28 Quiz*** at humanheritage.glencoe.com

Section 5 Assessment

1. What did the Tudors do to encourage the Renaissance in England?
2. What were English theaters like?
3. From what did Shakespeare draw the ideas for his plays?

Critical Thinking

4. **Understanding Cause and Effect** What was the cause of the Wars of the Roses? How did these struggles affect English history?

Graphic Organizer Activity

5. Draw this diagram, and use it to write four facts about the English Renaissance.

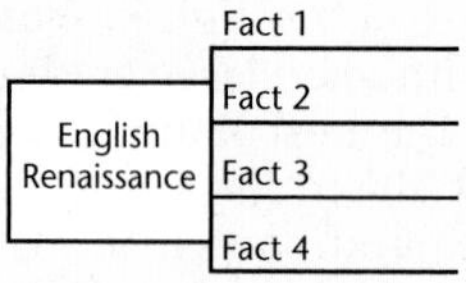

Chapter Summary & Study Guide

1. Around 1300, western European scholars showed a growing interest in classical writings, which in turn led to the Renaissance.
2. The Renaissance began in the Italian city-states, where the wealth from trade help fuel a burst of artistic achievement.
3. Leading figures in the Italian Renaissance included rulers such as the Medicis of Florence and artists like Michelangelo Buonarroti and Leonardo da Vinci.
4. The Renaissance moved from Florence to Rome when the Popes rebuilt the city to prove their power to the rulers of Europe.
5. In the late 1500s, the Renaissance spread from Rome to Venice.
6. After 1494, King Francis I helped bring the Renaissance to France.
7. An interest in religious reform and trading contacts with Italy helped bring the Renaissance to Germany and Flanders.
8. Development of a printing press by Johannes Gutenberg helped new Renaissance ideas to reach more people.
9. In the late 1400s and early 1500s the Renaissance spread to Spain, where it was influenced by strong ties with the Roman Catholic Church and strict government policies.
10. The Tudors paved the way for the arrival of the Renaissance in England, where it reached its peak under Elizabeth I.
11. The people of Renaissance England were very fond of plays, especially those by William Shakespeare.

HISTORY Online

Self-Check Quiz

Visit the *Human Heritage* Web site at humanheritage.glencoe.com and click on ***Chapter 28—Self-Check Quiz*** to assess your understanding of this chapter.

Section 5 Assessment Answers

1. They made the monarchy stronger, built up trade, and encouraged the arts.
2. open-air stages where the audience sat under a roof or stood in the pit to see afternoon plays
3. from the histories of England and ancient Rome and also from Italian tales
4. sample responses: *cause*—struggle for the throne waged by the York and Lancaster families; *effects*—the Tudors, who fought for the Lancasters, took the throne and paved the way for the English Renaissance
5. Facts will vary but should reflect the achievements of the Elizabethan era.

Assign the Chapter 28 **Section 5 Quiz** in the TCR. Testmaker available.

CHAPTER 28 Assessment

Using Key Terms

Imagine you are a drama critic writing about the literature of the Renaissance. Write a short magazine article explaining the kinds of plays being written and how they reflect the life of the times. Use the following words in your article.

classical writings	humanists	*piazza*
printing press	*chateaux*	*doge*

Understanding Main Ideas

1. Whose writings did the scholars of western Europe study during the Renaissance?
2. Why were the Renaissance scholars called humanists?
3. What did the rulers of the Italian city-states do to encourage learning and development of art?
4. Why did the people of Florence turn to Savonarola in 1494?
5. How was France introduced to the Renaissance?
6. What did Germany, Flanders, Spain, and England contribute to the Renaissance?
7. Of what did El Escorial become a well-known symbol?
8. How did the Wars of the Roses get their name?

Critical Thinking

1. How did the Renaissance differ from the Middle Ages?
2. What was the connection between trade and the start of the Renaissance?
3. Why was Lorenzo de Medici called "the Magnificent"?
4. If you could go back in time and talk with a Renaissance artist or ruler, whom would you choose? What questions would you ask? Explain your answer.

Graphic Organizer Activity

Culture Create a diagram like the one below, and use it to compare the Renaissance to the Middle Ages.

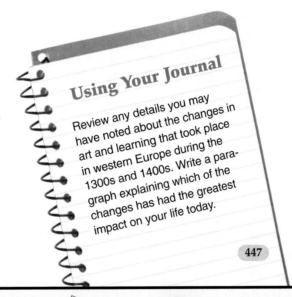

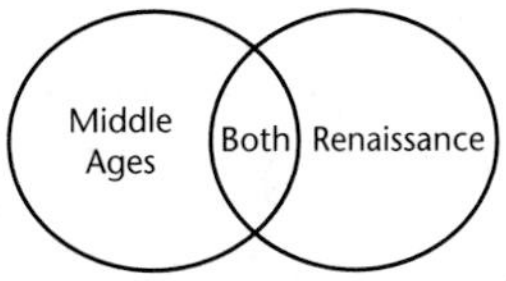

Geography in History

The World in Spatial Terms Refer to the map of Renaissance Italy on page 438. This country is often compared to the shape of a boot. Describe the location of Italy by giving its latitude and longitude. Then describe its relative location.

Using Your Journal

Review any details you may have noted about the changes in art and learning that took place in western Europe during the 1300s and 1400s. Write a paragraph explaining which of the changes has had the greatest impact on your life today.

CHAPTER 28 Assessment Answers

Using Key Terms

Magazine articles will vary, but students should use all the key terms.

Understanding Main Ideas

1. those of the ancient Greeks and Romans
2. because they believed in the importance of people
3. They spent money and encouraged scholars, poets, and philosophers and set up palace schools.
4. They thought he would stop government spending and solve the food and housing shortages.
5. through French invasions of Italy
6. Answers will vary but should reflect the achievements of each nation.
7. the power and religious devotion of Spanish rulers
8. from the symbols of the two noble families who fought

Critical Thinking

1. During the Renaissance, people became more interested in art, learning, and the world around them.
2. The Italian city-states had grown wealthy from trade and spent their wealth on the arts.
3. Answers will vary but might include that he made Florence prosper.
4. Answers will vary but students should write specific questions.

Graphic Organizer Activity

Diagrams will vary, but entries on the Middle Ages should reflect the influence of feudalism and the Church, while entries on the Renaissance should show the effects of trade and an increased interest in human potential. Entries for both periods might include: concern with religious topics, education at universities, creation of beautiful cathedrals, and so on.

Bonus Test Question

For Chapter 28 Test

Is the man charged with theft innocent or guilty? His alibi: "During the theft, at 3:00 P.M., I was at the Globe Theater watching Shakespeare's *Romeo and Juliet.* Afterward, it was so crowded along the Thames River that I didn't leave the area until after dark." *(innocent—facts are accurate)*

Using Your Journal

Paragraphs will vary, but students should explain that learning and art do have an impact on their lives. You might call on volunteers to read their paragraphs to the class.

Geography in History

Italy stretched from about 48°–38°N latitude, and from about 5°–18°E longitude. The relative location of Italy is in southern Europe northeast of Sardinia on a peninsula that extends into the Mediterranean Sea.

Chapter 29 Planning Guide

Timesaving Tools

TeacherWorks™ All-In-One Planner and Resource Center

- **Interactive Teacher Edition** Access your Teacher Wraparound Edition and your classroom resources with a few easy clicks.
- **Interactive Lesson Planner** Planning has never been easier! Organize your week, month, semester, or year with all the lesson helps you need to make teaching creative, timely, and relevant.

Use Glencoe's **Presentation Plus!** multimedia teacher tool to easily present dynamic lessons that visually excite your students. Using Microsoft PowerPoint® you can customize the presentations to create your own personalized lessons.

Objectives	Reproducible Resources	Multimedia Resources
Section 1 **Martin Luther** Explain why Martin Luther's beliefs brought him into conflict with the Roman Catholic Church.	Reproducible Lesson Plan Chapter 29 Vocabulary and Guided Reading Activity Reading Essentials and Study Guide 29-1 Chapter 29 Cooperative Learning Activity Section 1 Quiz	Interactive Student Edition CD-ROM Graphic Organizer Transparency 10 Teaching Transparencies and Activities 29A & 29B ExamView® Pro Testmaker CD-ROM Presentation Plus! CD-ROM
Section 2 **A New Religion** Describe how Protestantism developed.	Reproducible Lesson Plan Reading Essentials and Study Guide 29-2 Section 2 Quiz	Vocabulary PuzzleMaker CD-ROM Interactive Tutor Self-Assessment CD-ROM ExamView® Pro Testmaker CD-ROM
Section 3 **Catholic Reform** Identify how Catholic reformers worked to improve their Church.	Reproducible Lesson Plan Reading Essentials and Study Guide 29-3 Chapter 29 Chart and Graph Skill Activity Chapter 29 Enrichment Activity Section 3 Quiz	Vocabulary PuzzleMaker CD-ROM Interactive Tutor Self-Assessment CD-ROM ExamView® Pro Testmaker CD-ROM Glencoe Skillbuilder Interactive Workbook CD-ROM, Level 1
Section 4 **A Middle Way** Discuss how the reformation of the Church of England came about.	Reproducible Lesson Plan Reading Essentials and Study Guide 29-4 Section 4 Quiz	Vocabulary PuzzleMaker CD-ROM ExamView® Pro Testmaker CD-ROM Glencoe Skillbuilder Interactive Workbook CD-ROM, Level 1
Section 5 **Wars of Religion** Explain why Europeans became involved in religious wars.	Reproducible Lesson Plan Reading Essentials and Study Guide 29-5 Chapter 29 Geography and Map Activity Section 5 Quiz	Vocabulary PuzzleMaker CD-ROM Interactive Tutor Self-Assessment CD-ROM ExamView® Pro Testmaker CD-ROM
Section 6 **The Thirty Years' War** Discuss how the Thirty Years' War affected Europe.	Reproducible Lesson Plan Reading Essentials and Study Guide 29-6 Section 6 Quiz	Vocabulary PuzzleMaker CD-ROM Interactive Tutor Self-Assessment CD-ROM ExamView® Pro Testmaker CD-ROM Glencoe Skillbuilder Interactive Workbook CD-ROM, Level 1
Chapter 29 **Review and Evaluation**	Chapter 29 Reteaching Activity Chapter 29 Performance Assessment Activity Spanish Chapter Summary and Glossary Chapter 29 Test	Interactive Tutor Self-Assessment CD-ROM Glencoe Skillbuilder Interactive Workbook CD-ROM, Level 1 Audiocassettes* ExamView® Pro Testmaker CD-ROM

*Also available in Spanish.

Chapter 29 Planning Guide

✓ Performance Assessment Activities

Comparing Reformers Have students choose one of the following reformers to compare to a modern reformer of their choice: Teresa of Avila, William Tyndale, Charles Borromeo, John Knox, Jan Hus, or John Wycliffe. Tell students to create a poster that parallels the achievements of both reformers.

CHAPTER RESOURCES

LITERATURE ABOUT THE PERIOD

Dumas, Alexandre. *The Three Musketeers.* Translated by Henry L. Williams. Street and Smith, 1919. Exaggerated tale of four swashbucklers in France during the reign of Louis XIII.

READINGS FOR THE STUDENT

Cowie, Leonard W. *Martin Luther: Leader of the Reformation* (A Pathfinder Biography). Frederick Praeger, 1969. Detailed biography of Luther.

O'Dell, Scott. *The Hawk that Dare Not Hunt by Day.* Houghton Mifflin, 1975. Novel about a boy who helps the reformer Tyndale smuggle his translation of the Bible into England.

READINGS FOR THE TEACHER

Bainton, Roland H. *The Age of Reformation.* Van Nostrand Reinhold Company, 1956. Shows how the Christian faith shaped history during the Reformation.

KEY TO ABILITY LEVELS

Teaching strategies have been coded for varying learning styles and abilities.

L1 Level 1 activities are **basic** activities and should be within the ability range of all students.

L2 Level 2 activities are **average** activities and should be within the ability range of the average to above-average student.

L3 Level 3 activities are **challenging** activities designed for the ability range of above-average students.

ELL ELL activities should be within the ability range of English Language Learning students.

NATIONAL GEOGRAPHIC Teacher's Corner

INDEX TO NATIONAL GEOGRAPHIC MAGAZINE

The following article relates to this chapter:

- "The World of Martin Luther," by Merle Severy, October 1983.

NATIONAL GEOGRAPHIC SOCIETY PRODUCTS AVAILABLE FROM GLENCOE

To order the following, call Glencoe at 1-800-334-7344:

- *PicturePack: Europe (Transparencies)*
- *Picture Atlas of the World (CD-ROM)*

ADDITIONAL NATIONAL GEOGRAPHIC SOCIETY PRODUCTS

To order the following, call National Geographic at 1-800-368-2728:

- *National Geographic Atlas of World History (Book)*

Access *National Geographic's* new dynamic MapMachine Web site and other geography resources at:
www.nationalgeographic.com
www.nationalgeographic.com/maps

THE HISTORY CHANNEL. A&E HOME VIDEO. Biography

The following videotape program is available from Glencoe:

- **Elizabeth I: The Virgin Queen**
  0-7670-0209-1

To order, call Glencoe at 1-800-334-7344. To find classroom resources to accompany this video, check:

A&E Television: www.aande.com
The History Channel: www.historychannel.com

OVERVIEW

Chapter 29 examines the Protestant and Catholic reformations.

- **Section 1** discusses Martin Luther's excommunication.
- **Section 2** describes the founding of Protestantism.
- **Section 3** explains the work of Catholic reformers.
- **Section 4** examines the Reformation in England.
- **Section 5** summarizes the religious wars in Europe in the late 1500s and the 1600s.
- **Section 6** discusses the Thirty Years' War.

CHAPTER OBJECTIVES

After reading Chapter 29, students will be able to:

1. explain why Luther's beliefs brought him into conflict with the Roman Catholic Church.
2. describe how Protestantism developed.
3. identify how Catholic reformers changed their Church.
4. discuss the English Reformation.
5. explain why Europeans became involved in religious wars.
6. trace the Thirty Years' War.

EXAMINING ARTIFACTS

Have students state the connection between the two artifacts. *(Luther opposed the selling of indulgences.)* Explain that the boxes were used for documents (indulgences) sold to free people from their sins. Ask: Why might Luther object to this practice? Record student responses for review.

PERFORMANCE ASSESSMENT ✓

Use the Performance Assessment activities on page 448B to help you evaluate students as they complete the chapter.

CHAPTER 29

The Reformation

1475 A.D.–1650 A.D.

▲ Indulgence box

Martin Luther, Church reformer ►

1517	1534	1545	1588	1598	1618
Luther posts 95 theses	Henry VIII heads Church of England	Council of Trent meets	England defeats the Armada	Edict of Nantes is signed	Thirty Years' War begins

TEACHING RESOURCES

TEACHER PLANNING AND SUPPORT

- Reproducible Lesson Plan 29-1, 29-2, 29-3, 29-4, 29-5, 29-6
- Teaching Strategies for the World History Classroom
- Presentation Plus! CD-ROM

REVIEW AND REINFORCEMENT

- Reading Essentials and Study Guide 29-1, 29-2, 29-3, 29-4, 29-5, 29-6
- Chapter 29 Vocabulary and Guided Reading Activity
- Vocabulary PuzzleMaker CD-ROM
- Teaching Transparencies 29A & 29B
- Chapter 29 Reteaching Activity
- Chapter 29 Cooperative Learning Activity
- Chapter 29 Activity Book Activity
- Chapter 29 Chart and Graph Skill Activity
- Reading and Study Skills Foldables
- Interactive Tutor Self-Assessment CD-ROM

APPLICATION AND HANDS-ON ACTIVITIES

- Daily Questions in Social Studies
- Student Presentation Builder CD-ROM

GEOGRAPHY ACTIVITIES

- Chapter 29 Geography and Map Activity
- Building Geography Skills for Life
- Outline Map Resource Book

Chapter Focus

Read to Discover

- Why Martin Luther's beliefs brought him into conflict with the Roman Catholic Church.
- How Protestantism developed.
- How Catholic reformers worked to improve their Church.
- How and why the reformation of the Church of England came about.
- How the Thirty Years' War affected Europe.

HISTORY Online

Chapter Overview

Visit the *Human Heritage* Web site at **humanheritage.glencoe.com** and click on ***Chapter 29—Chapter Overviews*** to preview this chapter.

Terms to Learn	People to Know	Places to Locate
reformation	Martin Luther	Wittenberg
indulgences	Pope Leo X	Geneva
theses	John Calvin	
heretic	Henry VIII	
armada	Mary Tudor	
galleons	Elizabeth I	

Why It's Important The Roman Catholic Church did not adjust to the many changes taking place in western Europe during the 1400s and 1500s. Many Europeans began to call for a **reformation** (ref uhr mā' shuhn), or a change, in the way the Church taught and practiced Christianity.

Church leaders, however, were too busy with their own and government affairs to make changes. They did not like the reformers' ideas, especially those that could affect their power. Because of this, the unity of the Church was threatened.

Reading Check Why did many Europeans call for a **reformation?**

SECTION 1 Martin Luther

One reformer who challenged the Church was a German monk named Martin Luther. Luther, born in 1483, was the son of peasants. His family wanted him to be a lawyer, but he decided to become a monk. As a monk, Luther faithfully followed Church teachings and practices. However, he could find no peace of mind. He wondered how God would judge his actions.

While studying the New Testament, Luther found the answer to the questions that had been troubling him. He decided that trusting in Jesus, rather than doing good works, would save people from their sins. Luther's ideas soon brought him into conflict with the Church. In 1517, Pope Leo X wanted money to

INTERDISCIPLINARY CONNECTIONS

- Unit 9 World Literature Readings 1 & 2
- World Art & Architecture Transparency 25, *Herzogenburg Monastery*
- World Music: A Cultural Legacy

ENRICHMENT AND EXTENSION

- World History Primary Source Document Library CD-ROM
- Chapter 29 Enrichment Activity
- Foods Around the World

ASSESSMENT AND EVALUATION

- Chapter 29 Performance Assessment Activity
- Chapter 29 Section Quizzes 29-1, 29-2, 29-3, 29-4, 29-5, 29-6
- Chapter 29 Test
- Chapter 29 ExamView® Pro Testmaker CD-ROM
- Chapter 29 Digests Audiocassettes Activities and Tests

SPANISH RESOURCES

- Chapter 29 Spanish Chapter Summary and Glossary
- Chapter 29 Spanish Digests Audiocassettes Activities and Tests

HISTORY Online

Chapter Overview introduces students to chapter content and key terms. Have them access ***Chapter 29 Overview*** at humanheritage.glencoe.com

FOCUS

Bellringer

Write the following quote on the board: "It is neither safe nor prudent to do aught against conscience. Here I stand—I cannot do otherwise. God help me." Ask students to write down their first impressions of the quote.

Motivational Activity

Have students share their impressions of the quote above. Explain that the person quoted was Martin Luther, the reformer who shattered Christian unity in western Europe.

Reading Check Answer

They called for a **reformation** so that the Church would adjust its teachings and practices to the changing times.

GUIDE TO READING

Reading Strategy

Ask students to read "Why It's Important" and summarize the chapter's main theme. *(The unity of the Church was threatened by the unwillingness of Church officials to make changes or listen to the ideas of reformers).*

Vocabulary Precheck

Ask students to define each of the "Terms to Learn." L1 ELL

Use the Vocabulary PuzzleMaker CD-ROM for Chapter 29 to create a crossword puzzle. L1

Assign Chapter 29 Vocabulary and Guided Reading Activity.

Assign Reading Essentials and Study Guide 29-1.

TEACH

Guided Practice

L1 **History** Have students create a time line of major events during the Reformation of western Europe as they read this chapter. ELL

Reading Check Answer **Indulgences** were documents that freed their owners from the punishment they were due to receive for their sins.

Reading Check Answer In his list of 95 **theses**, Luther stated that only God could forgive sins and challenged anyone who disagreed to debate with him.

CAPTION ANSWER

Pope Leo X wanted money to rebuild Peter's Church in Rome.

Reading Check What were **indulgences?**

Reading Check What did Luther state in his list of 95 **theses?**

rebuild St. Peter's Church in Rome. He sent out monks to sell **indulgences** (in dul' juhnt sez), or documents that freed their owners from the punishment they were due to receive for their sins. Luther believed the sale of indulgences led people to think they could buy God's forgiveness for their sins.

One night Luther posted a list of 95 **theses** (thē' sēz), or statements of beliefs, on the door of the castle church in Wittenberg (wit' uhn buhrg), Germany. In the list, Luther stated that only God could forgive sins. He challenged anyone who disagreed to debate with him.

Luther began to attack other Catholic beliefs openly. He said that Popes could make mistakes; that the only true guide to religious truth was the Bible, which every Christian had the right to read; and that every Christian had the right to pray to God without the aid of a priest.

In 1520, Pope Leo condemned Luther's teachings and excommunicated him. Leo insisted that the German emperor,

SALE OF INDULGENCES Hoping to lessen God's punishment upon them, many Christians bought the indulgences offered by the Church. Here, indulgences are sold at the village marketplace. **Why was the Church selling indulgences?**

COOPERATIVE LEARNING

Organize students into two teams: one representing John Tetzel, the Church's agent for selling indulgences in northern Germany, and the other representing Martin Luther. Have students research the practice of selling indulgences and prepare arguments from the point of view of the person they represent. Have each team choose its representative to debate this proposition: The beauty of St. Peter's Church justifies the sale of indulgences to finance its reconstruction. One student should serve as moderator. Conclude by having the entire class analyze the arguments.

Assign the Chapter 29 *Cooperative Learning Activity* in the TCR.

Charles V, try Luther as a **heretic** (her′ uh tik), or person who holds a belief that is different from the accepted belief of the Church. Charles was loyal to the Church, but he relied on German princes who supported Luther. To keep their loyalty, Charles agreed to give Luther a fair trial. At the same time, he secretly promised the Pope that Luther would be condemned. In 1521, Luther was tried by the German Diet of Worms. When he refused to give up his ideas, he was condemned for heresy.

Reading Check Why did the Pope want to try Luther as a **heretic?**

Section 1 Assessment

1. **Define:** reformation, indulgences, theses, heretic.
2. Why did Luther come into conflict with the Church?
3. What happened to Luther at Worms?

Critical Thinking

4. **Identifying Central Issues** What was the central or underlying issue in the debate between Luther and Pope Leo X?

Graphic Organizer Activity

5. Draw this diagram, and use it to summarize Luther's beliefs about indulgences, the Bible, the Pope, and prayer.

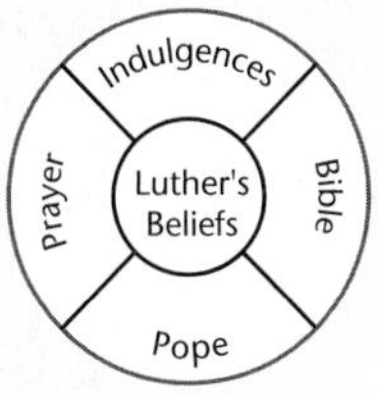

SECTION 2 A New Religion

By 1524, most people in northern Germany supported Luther. They left the Roman Catholic Church and formed the Lutheran (lū′ thuhr uhn) Church.

The Lutheran princes of Germany had strong armies, which Charles V could not defeat. In 1555, Charles realized he could not force the people to return to the Roman Catholic Church. He then agreed to sign a treaty known as the Peace of Augsburg (ogz′ buhrg). There could be both Catholic and Lutheran churches in Germany. The Peace of Augsburg kept German Lutherans and Catholics from fighting each other for nearly 50 years.

Protestant Groups Luther's ideas soon spread to other areas of Europe. People in Scandinavia founded Lutheran churches. Preachers and merchants in Switzerland (swit′ suhr luhnd) also left the Roman Catholic Church. They set up Reformed churches. Because they protested against Catholic ideas, Lutheran and Reformed churches were called Protestant (prot′ uh stuhnt). Protestant church leaders were called **ministers.** They spent more time teaching from the Bible. They conducted services in the language of the area instead of in Latin. This made services easier for people to understand.

Reading Check How did Protestant **ministers** differ from Catholic priests?

Section 1 Assessment Answers

1. reformation, a change (p. 449); indulgences, documents that freed owners from punishment for their sins (p. 450); theses, statements of beliefs (p. 450); heretic, person who holds a belief different from accepted Church beliefs (p. 451)
2. believed that trusting in Jesus, rather than doing good works, would save people from their sins
3. He was condemned for heresy.
4. that the purchase of indulgences would free people from punishment for their sins
5. sample responses: *indulgences*—that people could not buy forgiveness for their sins; *Bible*—that it was the only guide to religious truth; *Pope*—that the Pope could make mistakes; *prayer*—that every Christian had the right to pray to God without the aid of a priest

Assign the Chapter 29 **Section 1 Quiz** in the TCR. Testmaker available.

Reading Check Answer The Pope wanted to try Luther as a **heretic** because he disagreed with accepted Church beliefs.

L2 **Critical Thinking** Have students imagine they are the editor of the Worms newspaper. Tell them to write an editorial—from the Church's point of view—about Luther's appearance before the Diet.

Use the **Interactive Tutor Self-Assessment CD-ROM** to review Section 1.

MAKING CONNECTIONS

>> **History** After the Diet of Worms, Luther was "kidnapped" by his protector, Prince Frederick of Saxony, and hidden in his castle for a year. In 1525, Luther married Katherina con Bora, a former nun, thus emphasizing his rejection of monastic rules. He died in 1546 and was buried in the castle church in Wittenberg.

Reading Check Answer **Ministers** spent more time teaching from the Bible and conducted services in the language of the area instead of in Latin, which made services easier for people to understand.

Use the **Vocabulary PuzzleMaker CD-ROM** to create crossword and word search puzzles.

LINKING PAST TO PRESENT

Luther translated the New Testament from Greek to German. Later, he translated the Old Testament. Luther's German Bible greatly influenced the development of the modern German language.

MAKING CONNECTIONS

➤➤ **History** Geneva was newly independent (from Savoy) and self-governing. Its council at first rejected Calvin and his strict ideas but later asked him back. Calvin wrote books and pamphlets on every detail of church organization, personal conduct, and doctrine. His rules for the city inns, for example, not only forbade dancing and card playing but even set bedtime at 9:00 P.M. The city government carried out church laws. Church elders inspected people's homes and monitored their behavior.

L3 **Language Arts** Ask students to choose to be a publisher of Calvin's time that either supports Calvin's rules and ideas, or disagrees with the rules Calvin has forced on the people of Geneva. Have them write a pamphlet that supports their opinions to be distributed to the people. Encourage them to be thorough and convincing in presenting their ideas.

Use the **Interactive Tutor Self-Assessment CD-ROM** to review Section 2.

John Calvin

Ulrich Zwingli was important in leading the Protestant movement in Switzerland. Zwingli lived from 1484 to 1531. Unlike Luther, however, he wanted to break completely from Catholic rituals. He ordered the removal of images from churches, and he wanted to close monasteries. Zwingli led a group of Protestants from Zurich, Switzerland, in a battle against Catholic forces in 1531 and was killed. After Zwingli's death, the Protestant church was firmly established in Switzerland.

John Calvin The most powerful Reformed group was in the Swiss city of Geneva (juh nē' vuh). There, John Calvin set up the first Protestant church governed by a council of ministers and elected church members. Calvin also wrote books that became a guide for Protestants throughout Europe.

Calvin believed that there was nothing in the past, present, or future that God did not know about or control. He also held that from the beginning of time, God decided who would be saved and who would not. Calvin used the scriptures to support his ideas. He believed that God's will was written in the Bible, which ministers had the right to interpret. The ministers also had the right to make sure everyone obeyed God's will. Calvin had the Geneva town council pass laws to force people to follow strict rules of behavior. They could not dance, play cards, go to the theater, or take part in drinking parties. Those who refused to obey these laws were put in prison, executed, or banished.

Calvinism taught people to work hard and to save money. For this reason, many rich merchants supported Calvin. With their help, Calvin worked to improve Geneva. Streets and buildings were kept clean. New workshops opened, providing more jobs for people. Persecuted Protestants from all over Europe found safety in Geneva. Young men came to study at the school Calvin founded to train Reformed ministers. Many of them later returned to their own countries to set up Reformed churches.

Section 2 Assessment

1. **Define:** ministers.
2. What was the Peace of Augsburg?
3. Why were Lutheran and Reformed churches called Protestant?

Critical Thinking

4. **Analyzing Information** What ideas of Calvinism do you agree with? What ideas do you disagree with?

Graphic Organizer Activity

5. Draw this diagram, and use it to compare Protestant and Catholic practices.

Protestant Practices	Catholic Practices

Section 2 Assessment Answers

1. ministers, Protestant church leaders (p. 451)
2. treaty allowing both Catholic and Lutheran churches in Germany
3. because they protested against Catholic ideas
4. Answers will vary, but students should explain their choices.
5. sample responses: *Protestant practices*—conducted services in local languages, church leaders called ministers, simplified services and taught from the Bible, preached that everyone had a right to read the Bible and pray directly to God; *Catholic practices*—conducted services in Latin, church leaders called priests, used Church-approved services, priests interpreted the Bible and guided worshipers in prayer, accepted the idea of salvation through good works

Assign the Chapter 29 **Section 2 Quiz** in the TCR. Testmaker available.

SECTION 3 Catholic Reform

While Protestants formed new churches, Catholic reformers worked to improve their church. Many came from Spain and Italy, the leading countries of the Catholic reform movement.

One of the best known Catholic reformers was Ignatius (ig nā' shē uhs) of Loyola (loi ō' luh). In 1521, he gave up his life as a Spanish noble to serve God and the Roman Catholic Church. In 1540, he founded the Society of Jesus. Its members were called Jesuits (jezh' ū its). This group was formed to spread Roman Catholic ideas to all parts of the world. Jesuits also worked to help the people strengthen their faith. They wore black robes and lived simple lives. They set up schools, helped the poor, and preached to the people. They also taught in universities and served as advisers in royal courts. Jesuit missionaries were the first to carry Catholic ideas to India, China, and Japan.

Then & Now

Church Membership Worldwide, the Roman Catholic Church is still the largest Christian church, with about 968 million people. About 466 million follow some of the many varieties of Protestantism. The next largest Christian community, with nearly 218 million, includes the different congregations of the Eastern Orthodox Church, which was once centered in Constantinople.

Linking Across Time

St. Peter's Basilica In 1506, Donato Bramante proposed a bold design for the rebuilding of St. Peter's Basilica. Instead of medieval spires, he revived the Roman dome, as captured in a medal issued by Pope Julius II (left). Work progressed slowly, and in 1546, 71-year-old Michelangelo took over the project. Today the inner dome, built to Michelangelo's specifications, is considered one of the world's great architectural feats (right). **What other steps did Catholic reformers take to revive the Church's influences?**

EXTENDING THE CONTENT

In addition to Loyola, the movement for Catholic reform (or the Counter-Reformation) produced other outstanding and unforgettable figures. Francis Xavier, an early follower of Loyola, was perhaps the most untiring missionary since Paul. Following closely behind Portuguese explorers who reached India, Francis Xavier brought Catholic Christianity to Asia, establishing Jesuit communities in India, Goa, Ceylon (Sri Lanka), and Hong Kong. He was one of the first Europeans in Japan (1549).

Use the **Vocabulary PuzzleMaker CD-ROM** to create crossword and word search puzzles.

MAKING CONNECTIONS

>> Geography: Places and Regions In 1549, Jesuit missionaries began preaching in Japan. They were expelled in 1638. In 1600, Jesuit missionaries established themselves in Peking (Beijing), China, where they served for 200 years as advisers to the emperor in astronomy, mathematics, translation, and other areas. Encourage students to locate Beijing on a map.

Linking Across Time

Catholic reformers worked to improve their church by forming societies such as the Jesuits, acting as missionaries, living simple lives, helping people to strengthen their faith, setting up schools, helping the poor, and using reason and good deeds to defend the Church.

LINKING PAST TO PRESENT

The Catholic Reformation renewed religious enthusiasm in the arts, sparking a new style of art and music called *baroque*. Renaissance art had demonstrated symmetry, order, and restraint, but baroque art employed asymmetry and exaggeration for dramatic effect. This art style had great influence on later generations of artists.

L3 Critical Thinking Ask: Why do you think another name for the Catholic Reformation is the Counter-Reformation? *(The Catholic Church was reacting to the Protestant Reformation.)*

GEOGRAPHY AND HISTORY

The reason masses were spoken in only Latin was to insure religious uniformity regardless of what country or area in which the service was to be held.

CAPTION ANSWER

to discuss changes in the Church and to defend Catholic teachings

LINKING PAST TO PRESENT

The Catholic Church published the *Index Librorum Prohibitorum*—Index of Prohibited Books—until 1966.

Reading Check Answer The purpose of a **seminary** was to train priests.

COUNCIL OF TRENT Meeting three times between 1545 and 1563, the Council of Trent helped to renew Catholic life and worship. In this painting bishops and other church leaders from throughout Europe debate an issue at a session of the Council. **Why did the Pope call for the Council of Trent?**

The Jesuits used reason and good deeds to defend the Roman Catholic Church against criticisms. They also tried to bring Protestants back to the Church. Because of their work, people in eastern European countries such as Poland, Bohemia (bō hē mē uh), and Hungary once again became loyal to the Roman Catholic Church.

During this time, the Pope also took steps to strengthen the Roman Catholic Church. He called a council of bishops to discuss reforms and to defend Catholic teachings. The council met at different times between 1545 and 1563 at Trent, Italy. The Council of Trent ended many Church practices that had been criticized for hundreds of years such as the sale of indulgences. Church leaders were ordered to follow strict rules. Each diocese was told to build a **seminary** (sem′ uh ner ē), or a school to train priests.

Reading Check What was the purpose of a **seminary?**

The Council of Trent also explained Catholic doctrine. It said that good works, as well as faith, helped people get to heaven. It also held that the Church alone decided how the Bible was to be interpreted and that mass would be said in Latin only. Together, the Council of Trent and the Jesuit missionaries helped the Pope reclaim Protestant areas.

SPOTLIGHT ON: HENRY VIII

Henry VIII was typical of Renaissance rulers—a king who tried to excel in many areas. As a youth he had an athletic physique and a keen mind. He enjoyed tennis, jousting, music, and discussions about astronomy and geometry. He composed several pieces of music and has been credited with writing the song "Greensleeves." He also wrote the book called *Assertions of the Seven Sacraments,* in which, as a devout Catholic he attacked the views of Martin Luther.

Section 3 Assessment

1. **Define:** seminary.
2. What were the leading countries involved in the Catholic reform movement?
3. What did the Council of Trent do?

Critical Thinking

4. **Evaluating Information** "The Council of Trent was important in strengthening the Roman Catholic Church." What is your opinion of this statement? Explain.

Graphic Organizer Activity

5. Draw this diagram, and use it to describe the order of the Jesuits founded by Ignatius of Loyola.

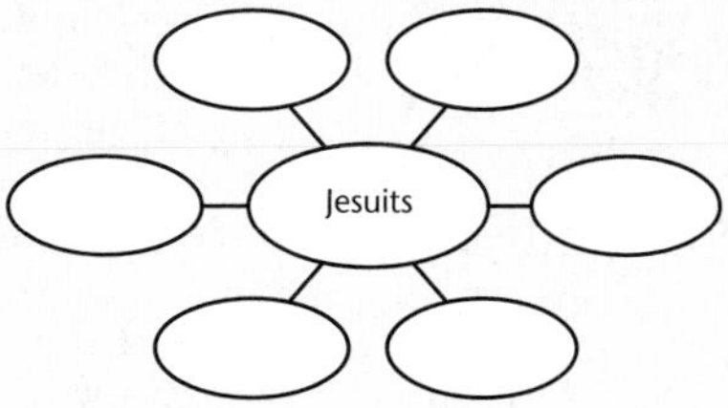

SECTION 4 A Middle Way

Reformation of the Church in England was led by a monarch, not by church leaders. It started as a political quarrel between the Tudor king Henry VIII and Pope Clement VII. Religious beliefs did not play a part in the struggle until later.

HENRY VIII AND ANNE BOLEYN Henry's hopes for a son made him determined to marry Anne Boleyn and led to a political break with the Pope. In this painting Henry and Anne are shown at the home of Thomas Wolsey, the king's chief adviser. **How was Henry eventually able to marry Anne Boleyn?**

Use the **Interactive Tutor Self-Assessment CD-ROM** to review Section 3.

Independent Practice

L2 **Critical Thinking** Have students watch a film portraying people from the time period discussed in this chapter, such as *Anne of a Thousand Days* (Anne Boleyn) or *A Man for All Seasons* (Thomas More). Have them write notes about the presentation and decide from what point of view these people are represented. ELL

CAPTION ANSWER

Henry set up the Anglican Church and received permission from the Archbishop of Canterbury to end his marriage to Catherine of Aragon.

DID YOU KNOW

Henry's desire for an heir and a happy marriage led him to marry six times.

Use the **Vocabulary PuzzleMaker CD-ROM** to create crossword and word search puzzles.

Section 3 Assessment Answers

1. seminary, school to train priests (p. 454)
2. Spain and Italy
3. It stopped the sale of indulgences, ordered Church leaders to follow strict rules of behavior, told each diocese to build a seminary, and explained Catholic doctrine more fully.
4. Answers will vary but might include that the council corrected many things in the Roman Catholic Church, although it may have been too late to strengthen the Church.
5. sample descriptions: formed to spread Roman Catholic ideas to all parts of the world; wore black robes; lived simple lives; set up schools; helped the poor; preached to the people; taught at universities; first to carry Catholic ideas to India, China, and Japan; used reason and good deeds to defend Catholic beliefs; tried to bring Protestants back into the Church

Assign the Chapter 29 **Section 3 Quiz** in the TCR. Testmaker available.

DID YOU KNOW

Thomas More, who served as the highest judicial official in England from 1529 to 1532, was beheaded for refusing to accept the king as the head of the English Church. The Roman Catholic Church declared Thomas More a saint in 1935.

MAKING CONNECTIONS

➤➤ **History** Lady Jane Grey was the Protestant noblewoman the council tried to put on the throne. Earlier, her guardian had tried unsuccessfully to convince Edward VI to marry her. After Edward's death, she ruled as queen for nine days before she was imprisoned in 1554. At the age of 17, she was beheaded.

Painting of Thomas Cranmer

The Break With Rome

The trouble between Henry VIII and the Pope began in 1527. At that time, Henry was married to Catherine of Aragon, the daughter of Ferdinand and Isabella of Spain and the aunt of German emperor Charles V. Henry and Catherine had only one living child, Mary. As Catherine grew older, Henry feared she could not have any more children. This was very important to Henry because he wanted a son to succeed to the throne.

At the same time, Henry had fallen in love with Anne Boleyn (bu lin′), a young woman of the court. He wanted Pope Clement to end his marriage to Catherine so that he could marry Anne, by whom he hoped to have a son. When the Pope refused, Henry declared that the Pope no longer had power over the Church in England. Henry was then excommunicated.

In 1534, the English Parliament passed a law stating that the king was head of the Church of England. Any English church leader who did not accept the law would stand trial as a heretic. Thomas Cranmer (kran′ muhr), the Archbishop of Canterbury and the most important church leader in England, supported Henry. Cranmer helped Henry end his marriage to Catherine. Henry then married Anne Boleyn, who gave him one child, a daughter named Elizabeth. A few years later, Henry had Anne executed for treason. He then married Jane Seymour (sē′ mōuhr), who died shortly after giving Henry the son he wanted.

Edward and Mary

When Henry VIII died, his nine-year-old son became King Edward VI. Since Edward was too young and sick to rule, a council of nobles governed England for him. Most of the council members were Protestants, and they brought Protestant doctrines into the English Church. Thomas Cranmer supported the council. He wanted the people to have an orderly form of Protestant worship. To help achieve this, he wrote a worship service in English called the *Book of Common Prayer.* It was used in all the churches in England.

Painting of Edward VI

When Edward died in 1553, the council of nobles tried to bring a Protestant noblewoman to the throne. Their attempt failed, however, because the people of England refused to accept any ruler who was not a Tudor. They wanted Henry's daughter, Mary, as their monarch.

Mary was Catholic. As soon as she became queen, she accepted the Pope as head of the English Church. She then insisted that all English men and women return to the Roman Catholic Church. Many Protestants refused and were persecuted. More than 300 of them, including Cranmer, were burned at the stake for heresy. The people turned against their queen, calling her "Bloody Mary."

Mary was married to King Philip II of Spain. The English were unhappy about the marriage because Spain was England's

MULTICULTURAL PERSPECTIVES

Anabaptists, Protestant sects in western Europe who admitted only adult members, denied the authority of local governments to direct their lives. They refused to hold office, bear arms, or swear oaths, and many lived separate from a society they saw as sinful. As a result, they were often persecuted by government officials, forcing many Anabaptists to wander from country to country seeking refuge. Many Anabaptist groups left Europe for North America during the 1600s. There they promoted the ideas of religious liberty and separation of church and state.

PHILIP II AND MARY TUDOR Queen of England from 1553 to 1558, Mary I shown in this painting (right) longed to bring England back to the Roman Catholic Church. Mary married Philip II (left) of Spain, shown here, who considered himself the champion of the Roman Catholic faith. **Why did the English people object to the marriage of Mary and Philip?**

enemy and the leading Catholic power in Europe. They feared that Philip and the Pope would become the real rulers of England. The people decided that England would remain free only if it became a Protestant country. For this reason, they wanted a Protestant ruler.

Elizabeth's Church Mary died in 1558 without a child to succeed her. Thus, her half-sister, Elizabeth, became queen. Elizabeth I was Protestant. With the help of Parliament, she ended the Pope's authority in the English Church.

Elizabeth was very popular with her subjects. She worked to set up the Church in a form that would appeal to as many people as possible. Elizabeth and Parliament decided that the Church should be Protestant. However, the Church would keep some Catholic features. The monarch would be head of the Church, which would use Cranmer's prayer book and teach Protestant beliefs.

L3 **Critical Thinking** Ask: How did the religious turmoil in England influence the colonization of America? Encourage students to brainstorm ideas, and then research to find how valid their ideas were. Encourage them to make a graphic organizer of their ideas.

CAPTION ANSWER

Spain was England's enemy and the leading Catholic power in Europe. The English people feared that Philip and the Pope would become the real rulers of England.

MAKING CONNECTIONS

➤➤ **Religion** The combination of Protestant beliefs and Catholic rituals devised by Elizabeth and Parliament became known as the beliefs of Anglicanism.

Biography®

The following videotape program is available from Glencoe to enrich Chapter 29:

- **Elizabeth I: The Virgin Queen**

To find classroom resources to accompany this video, check the following home page:

A&E Television:
www.aande.com

MEETING SPECIAL NEEDS

Help visual learners create an outline of Section 4 on the chalkboard. Place the following brief outline on the chalkboard. Then have students give details to complete the outline.

How the Reformation of the Church of England Came About:

I. Henry VIII
II. Edward VI
III. Mary Tudor
IV. Elizabeth I

Refer to ***Inclusion for the Middle School Social Studies Classroom: Strategies and Activities*** for additional resources.

HISTORY Online

Student Web Activity objectives and answers can be found at the ***Chapter 29 Web Activity Lesson Plan*** at humanheritage.glencoe.com

LINKING PAST TO PRESENT

Several new Protestant sects in western Europe, called Anabaptists, initiated the practice of baptizing only adult members. They based this practice on the belief that only people who could make a free and informed choice to become Christians should be allowed to do so. The Mennonite church originated among Anabaptists in Europe in the 1500s under the leadership of Menno Simons. Many of the Mennonites who migrated to the United States settled in Lancaster County, Pennsylvania.

CAPTION ANSWER

Queen Mary I

Use the **Interactive Tutor Self-Assessment CD-ROM** to review Section 4.

HISTORY Online

Student Web Activity
Visit the *Human Heritage* Web site at humanheritage.glencoe.com and click on ***Chapter 29—Student Web Activities*** to find out more about English monarchs of the Reformation.

ST. TERESA OF AVILA Another Church reformer, St. Teresa of Avila, Spain, lived from 1515–1582. As a nun she reformed convent life and wrote about religious life. **Which British monarch tried to restore the Pope as the head of the English Church?**

Most of the English people were pleased with the mix of Protestant belief and Catholic practice since many Catholic rituals remained. Those who were not pleased stayed outside the Church. Some Protestants also did not like Elizabeth's Church, but they did not leave it. Because these people wanted to purify the English Church of Catholic ways, they became known as Puritans (pyur' uh tuhnz).

Section 4 Assessment

1. What happened when Pope Clement refused to end Henry VIII's marriage?
2. What did Mary Tudor expect the people to do as soon as she became queen? How did the people feel about this?
3. What was the Church of England like under Elizabeth I?

Critical Thinking

4. **Demonstrating Reasoned Judgment** How effective do you think Elizabeth I was in establishing a new national church?

Graphic Organizer Activity

5. Draw this diagram, and use it to compare the reigns of Mary Tudor and Elizabeth I.

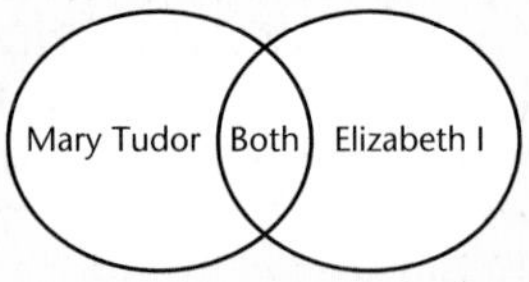

Section 4 Assessment Answers

1. Henry said he controlled the Church in England and was excommunicated.
2. return to the Roman Catholic Church; many refused and were persecuted
3. led by the monarch, used Cranmer's prayer book, and taught Protestant beliefs
4. Answers will vary, but students will conclude that Elizabeth successfully established the new Church. She set it up to appeal to as many people as possible.
5. Diagrams will vary, but should contrast Mary Tudor's efforts to restore Catholicism with Elizabeth's efforts to protect the Church of England. Both were Tudors, strong-willed daughters of Henry VIII and inherited a religious conflict started in part by their father.

Assign the Chapter 29 **Section 4 Quiz** in the TCR. Testmaker available.

SECTION 5 Wars of Religion

By the middle 1500s, most northern Europeans were Protestants, while most southern Europeans were Catholics. European monarchs had used religion to help unite their people and to build powerful nations. The ruler and people of each country were expected to belong to the same church. Those who refused were persecuted. This led to much bitterness between people of different faiths. Differences in religion also led to wars between countries. Toward the end of the 1500s, Europe entered a period of religious wars that lasted until 1648.

The Armada Under Elizabeth I, England became the leading Protestant power in Europe. Spain, under Philip II, remained the leading Catholic power. Philip knew that if he could defeat England, Protestant Europe would be open to Catholic control. Therefore, he ordered the building of an **armada** (ar mah′ duh), or a large group of warships.

After two years, the Spanish Armada, with its 130 ships, was ready. Its strength lay in its **galleons** (gal′ ēuhns), or heavy ships with square-rigged sails and long, raised decks. In 1588, the Armada sailed toward England. Its main purpose was to help the Spanish armies on the continent cross over to the English shore.

Reading Check Why did Philip II order the building of an **armada?**

Reading Check What did Spanish **galleons** look like?

SPANISH ARMADA In 1588, the English fleet faced the Spanish Armada in the English Channel. Here, English fire ships move toward the Armada. This action broke the curved formation of the Spanish ships and made possible a successful English attack. **What was the main strength of the Spanish Armada?**

Use the **Vocabulary PuzzleMaker CD-ROM** to create crossword and word search puzzles.

DID YOU KNOW ??

When the Spanish Armada faced the English ships, the Spanish ships carried 1,100 cannons and about 27,000 men, half of whom were soldiers. The English ships carried about 2,000 cannons and 16,000 sailors.

Reading Check Answer Philip II ordered the building of the **armada** so that he could launch an invasion of Protestant England.

Reading Check Answer Spanish **galleons** were heavy ships with square-rigged sails and long, raised decks.

CAPTION ANSWER

its galleons, or heavy ships with square-rigged sails and long, raised decks

MAKING CONNECTIONS

➤➤ **History** People expected that Elizabeth would marry and that her husband would rule. The common attitude of the time was that only men were fit to rule and that government matters were beyond a woman's ability. Elizabeth, however, feared that marrying a foreign prince would endanger England and that marrying an Englishman would cause jealousy among the English nobility.

COOPERATIVE LEARNING

Organize students into three research groups. Ask them to do research and write a report about one of the Spanish minorities during Philip's reign—Protestants, Marranos, and Moriscos. Reports should include information about daily life, professions, reasons for conversion or defiance in the face of danger, persecution during the Spanish Inquisition, and decisions people made to flee Spain or stay in spite of persecutions. Students should delegate tasks of finding information, organizing ideas, making outlines and note cards, and writing the drafts.

L2 Geography: Places and Regions Ask students to research and write about the Low Countries. Why were they called this? What geographical features do they have and how does this environment affect peoples' lives? Students should include basic facts about the area and its people.

GEOGRAPHY AND HISTORY

Spain and France posed the greatest naval threats to England. The attack of the Spanish Armada made England realize the dangers of an alliance between Spain and France. As a result, England relied on diplomacy as well as sea power to protect its interests. During Elizabeth's reign, England worked to balance the power of European nations.

MAKING CONNECTIONS

>> **History** Henry IV founded the Bourbon dynasty, which ruled France until the early 1800s.

People in History

Elizabeth I
1533–1603

English Queen

Elizabeth came to the throne at age 25. She faced a nation deeply in debt, caught up in European wars, and torn apart by religious conflicts at home. King Philip II offered to marry her, but Elizabeth rejected him—and all other suitors as well. Instead, she led England through one of its greatest eras, producing a united country, a strong navy, and a powerful European nation.

Elizabeth knew the Spanish forces were coming and prepared England for war. She had a naval commander, John Hawkins, reorganize the English fleet. He remodeled old ships and built new ones. He formed a new navy of 134 fighting ships and merchant vessels. Most of the ships were smaller than the Spanish ships, but they had larger guns and more ammunition. Expert sailors handled the English ships with much skill. One naval captain, Sir Francis Drake, was known for his overseas voyages and his capture of Spanish merchant ships.

The English knew they had to make the Spanish ships break their curved formation. Their chance came when the Spanish fleet anchored off the coast of Europe to wait for the Spanish armies to meet it. That night, the English set fire to eight small ships and sent them into the Spanish fleet. As the burning ships reached the Armada, the Spanish ships broke formation and began to drift. The English were then able to fight the Spanish ships one by one.

The Spanish naval command soon realized that the Armada was defeated. Short of food and water, it decided to return to Spain. A great storm came up, however, causing the voyage to be long and difficult. Only half the Armada reached home.

The English celebrated their victory with bonfires and parades. Although Spain was still a powerful enemy, England had shown it could defend itself. The English gained respect throughout Europe as champions of the Protestant cause. The defeat of the Armada allowed northern Europe to remain a Protestant stronghold.

The Huguenots

Most people in France during the 1500s were Catholics. Many nobles, lawyers, doctors, and merchants, however, were Protestants. These French Protestants, who were called Huguenots (hyū' guh nots), followed Calvin's teachings.

In 1534, King Francis I, who was Catholic, forbade the Huguenots to worship freely. He wanted all French people to support the Roman Catholic Church. Catholics began to persecute Huguenots, and by 1562 a civil war broke out. By then, Charles IX had become king. Since he was too young to rule, his mother, Catherine de Medici, ruled for him.

Catherine tried to keep peace by showing favor first to one group and then to the other. She finally decided to support the Roman Catholic Church. In 1572, she allowed Catholic nobles to kill the leading Huguenots in Paris. Catholic mobs in other parts of France began to kill Protestants and burn their homes. Many Protestants left the country. The few who remained to carry on the fight were led by Henry of Navarre (nuh var'), a Huguenot prince.

In 1589, the king of France was killed. Henry of Navarre, who was next in line for the throne, became Henry IV. He wanted to gain the loyalty of the people. Since most French people were still

EXTENDING THE CONTENT

Ruling France as regent for her sons, Catherine de Medici balanced Catholic and Huguenot rivalries for many years. The leader of the Huguenots was Henry of Navarre, who was in line for the throne after Catherine's sons. On August 24, 1572—St. Bartholomew's Day—the queen's daughter Margaret of Valois was to marry Henry of Navarre in Paris. Most Protestant nobles came to the wedding, where hired assassins attacked and murdered them all except Henry and another heir to the throne. At the same time, mobs of Catholic Parisians turned on their Protestant neighbors and slaughtered thousands of them. As the killing spread to the countryside, more than 10,000 Huguenots were killed in the next six weeks.

Drawing Conclusions

CRITICAL THINKING SKILLS

"Elementary, my dear Watson." Detective Sherlock Holmes often said these words to his assistant when he solved yet another mystery. Holmes would examine all the available evidence, or facts, and draw conclusions to solve the case.

Learning the Skill Drawing conclusions allows you to understand ideas that are not stated directly. Follow these steps in learning to draw conclusions:

- Review the facts that are stated directly.
- Use your knowledge and insight to develop some new conclusions about these facts.
- Look for information to check the accuracy of your conclusions.

GO TO Glencoe's **Skillbuilder Interactive Workbook CD-ROM, Level 1,** provides instruction and practice in key social studies skills.

Skill Practice

The excerpt on this page comes from a speech delivered to Parliament by Queen Elizabeth in 1601, just two years before her death. In it, she reviews her reign as queen. Read this excerpt, and then answer the questions that follow.

To be a king and wear a crown is a thing more glorious to them that see it than it is pleasing to them that bear it. For myself, I was never so much enticed with the glorious name of a king, or royal authority of a queen, as delighted . . . to defend this kingdom (as I said) from peril, dishonour, tyranny, and oppression.

There will never [be a] queen sit in my seat with more zeal to my country . . . and that sooner . . . will venture her life for your good and safety than myself. . . . And though you have had, and may have many princes, more mighty and wise sitting in this state; yet you never had, or shall have, any more careful and loving.

1. How does Elizabeth say she views the title of queen?
2. What aspect of being England's ruler has "delighted" her the most?
3. What conclusion can you draw from this speech about how Elizabeth would like to be remembered?
4. What evidence from the speech supports your conclusion?

461

CRITICAL THINKING SKILLS

TEACH

Drawing Conclusions

You might introduce this lesson by playing a quick game of "Who Am I?" Ask students to listen carefully as you or a volunteer read this statement:

I came to the throne at age nine. My father hoped that I would keep the monarchy safe for the Tudors, but I died too soon. The fate of England rested in the hands of my two half-sisters—one Catholic and one Protestant. Who Am I?

Call on students to guess the identity of the speaker. *(Edward VI)* Ask students to explain how they did their "detective work." Then assign the skills lesson and the accompanying questions.

Answers to Skill Practice

1. She feels the title of queen is more glorious to others than to the person who must fulfill the duties that go with it.
2. the chance to defend England
3. as a ruler who put her country and its people above her own well-being
4. claims that the power and glory of a royal title never delighted her as much as the chance to serve her people; that the English will never see a ruler more loving of the people than her

TEAM-TEACHING STRATEGY

Language Arts Work with a language arts teacher to describe some of the features of a mystery—a novel, play, or story centering on efforts to solve a crime. Explain to students that a mystery, a form of popular fiction, is sometimes called a "whodunit." Ask students how they think mysteries got this nickname. *(because stories center on efforts to figure out who committed a crime)*

Next, organize students into groups, and assign each group to create a mystery set in Elizabethan England. Somebody has kidnapped the queen, and the main character has the job of figuring out "whodunit." Tell students to fill their stories with clues and possible suspects. Each group should end their story with the question: Whodunit?

Call on students to read their mysteries aloud. Challenge the rest of the class to draw conclusions based on clues, about who kidnapped the queen.

DID YOU KNOW ??

Henry IV is credited with two famous statements. One, that "Paris is worth a Mass," was made when he converted to Catholicism. The other, "A chicken every Sunday in every peasant's pot," summed up his concern for the welfare of his people.

L1 Religion Before beginning the section on the Thirty Years' War, refer students to the map "The Religions of Europe" on page 463 and have them familiarize themselves with the religions of the areas involved in the war. ELL

L2 History Organize the class into two groups. Have students in one group imagine they are living in France in 1648 and students in the other group imagine they are living in Germany during the same year. Tell students that the Thirty Years' War has just ended. Ask students to write an eyewitness account of how life in their country has changed since the war ended. The account should include any changes that have occurred in religion. Have volunteers read their accounts to the class.

Use the **Interactive Tutor Self-Assessment CD-ROM** to review Section 5.

Use the **Vocabulary Puzzle-Maker CD-ROM** to create crossword and word search puzzles.

Catholic, he decided to convert. Nevertheless, Henry ended the fighting between Protestants and Catholics. Although he made Catholicism the national religion, he also made life easier for Protestants. In 1598, he signed the Edict of Nantes (nahnts), which gave Huguenots freedom of worship. France thus became the first European country to allow two Christian religions.

The Low Countries The Low Countries were part of the Spanish Empire. The people of the Low Countries were divided into Protestants and Catholics. Neither group liked Philip II's harsh rule. They did not like the heavy taxes imposed by Spain or the Spanish laws. Philip, however, made money from the wealth and trade of the Low Countries. He wanted to keep them under Spanish control.

Philip also wanted all his subjects to be Catholic. To achieve this, he set up an Inquisition in the Low Countries to stamp out Protestantism. In 1567, Protestants in the northern provinces revolted. Philip sent soldiers to restore order. They were joined by French Catholics from the southern provinces.

The fighting did not end until 1648. At that time, it was decided that the southern provinces, known today as Belgium, were to remain Catholic and continue under the rule of Spain. The northern provinces, known today as the Netherlands, were to be an independent Protestant country.

Section 5 Assessment

1. **Define:** armada, galleons.
2. How did the English defeat the Spanish Armada?
3. What led to civil war in France in 1562?

Critical Thinking

4. **Identifying Alternatives** How do you think the religious wars in Europe in the 1500s and 1600s might have been avoided?

Graphic Organizer Activity

5. Draw this diagram, and use it to show the causes and effects of the Edict of Nantes.

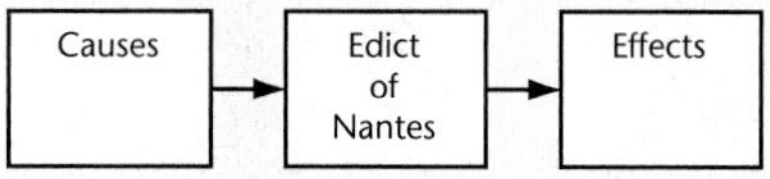

SECTION 6 The Thirty Years' War

During the 1590s and early 1600s, the German states began to quarrel over the terms of the Peace of Augsburg. They formed alliances based on religion. The Catholic alliance was led by the German emperor Ferdinand II.

Section 5 Assessment Answers

1. armada, group of warships (p. 459); galleons, ships with square-rigged sails (p. 459)
2. by causing the Spanish ships to break formation and fighting the Spanish ships one by one
3. King Francis I forbade Huguenots to worship freely, and Catholics began to persecute Huguenots.
4. Answers will vary, but could say by allowing different religions to exist in their countries.
5. sample responses: *causes*—conflicts between Catholics and Protestants in France, desire of Henry IV to win people's loyalty; *effects*—gave Huguenots freedom of worship; made France first European country to allow two Christian religions

Assign the Chapter 29 **Section 5 Quiz** in the TCR. Testmaker available.

One Protestant state that resisted Ferdinand was Bohemia. In 1618, the Protestant nobles of Bohemia revolted. They chose a German Protestant prince as their new king. Ferdinand's armies crushed the Bohemians in a fierce battle, and Ferdinand proclaimed himself king of Bohemia. He did not allow Protestant worship. He sent Jesuits throughout the country to win the people back to the Roman Catholic Church.

The revolt in Bohemia soon grew into the Thirty Years' War. During the war, half the armies of Europe fought in Germany. First Denmark and then Sweden invaded Germany. Their kings were Protestants who wanted to stop the spread of Catholicism. They also hoped to conquer German territory. When the Swedes were finally defeated in 1634, the French became involved. Although France was a Catholic country, it entered the war on the Protestant side. This changed the nature of the war. It became

MAP STUDY

PLACES AND REGIONS By 1560 many Europeans were either Protestants or Catholic. **In which European countries did Calvinism take hold?**

The Religions of Europe

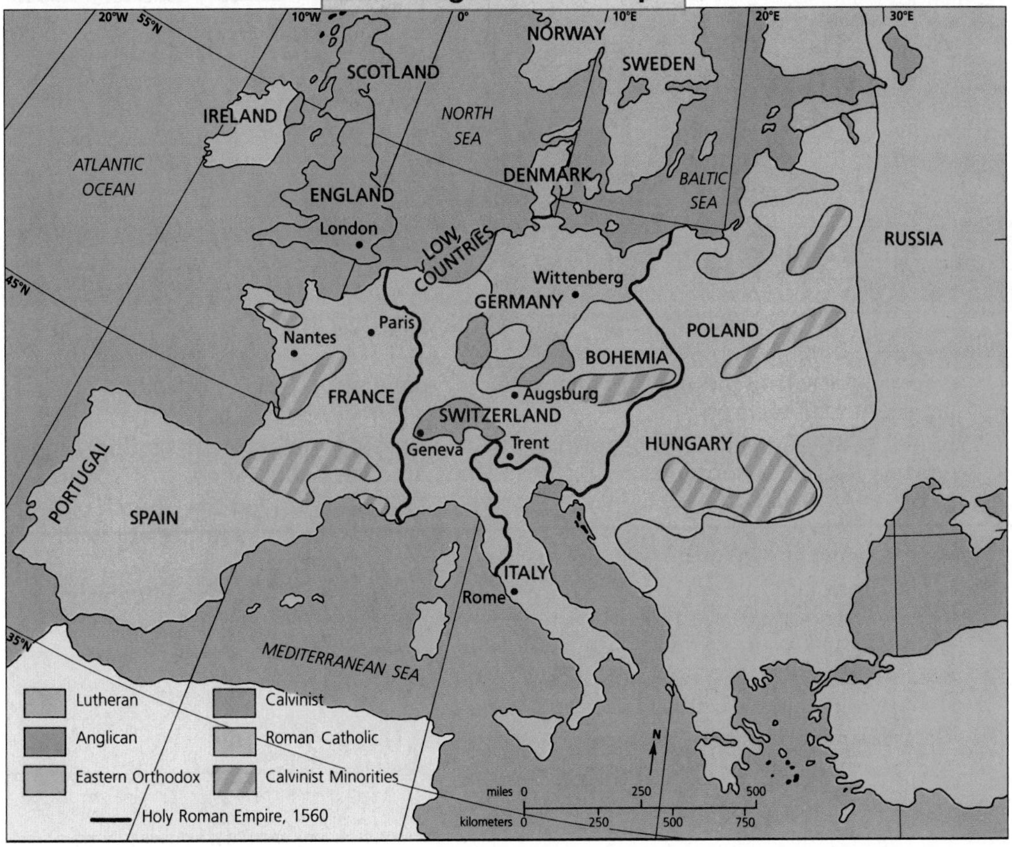

L1 Geography: The World in Spatial Terms Most of the Thirty Years' War took place in Germany, but soon other powers became involved. Have students list all the powers involved in the Thirty Years' War and locate them on the map on page 463.

DID YOU KNOW ??

In the midst of the brutal Thirty Years' War, traders brought tulip bulbs into Europe from Turkey. Public demand for tulips reached a peak in the 1630s. Frenzied buyers bid increasingly large sums for the flowers. Investing in tulips became big business.

MAP STUDY

Answer

Scotland, Low Countries, Germany, Switzerland

Assign the Chapter 29 **Geography and Map Activity** in the TCR.

GEOGRAPHY AND HISTORY

The splitting of the northern and southern provinces, as discussed in the section on Low Countries, was also part of the Peace of Westphalia.

EXTENDING THE CONTENT

The Thirty Years' War changed the balance of power in Europe. Before the war, huge landholdings and family ties between the Spanish and Austrian Hapsburgs combined to make the German Hapsburg emperors dominant. France under the Bourbon kings was the only serious political rival. Sweden, Denmark, and the Netherlands entered the war for religious and political reasons. Cardinal Richelieu, Louis XIII's adviser, then brought Catholic France into the war to resist the alarming growth in Hapsburg power. After the war, German princes were autonomous; Bourbon France dominated western Europe; and Sweden was locally powerful in the north.

ASSESS

Check for Understanding

Ask students to summarize the main points of the chapter. Discuss answers to the Section and Chapter Assessment questions.

Evaluate

Assign the **Chapter 29 Performance Assessment Activity** in the TCR.

Administer the **Chapter 29 Test** in the TCR. Testmaker available.

Reteach

Organize students into six groups. Assign each group a section from this chapter. Have the students write questions about the main ideas of their assigned section and quiz other groups.

Assign the Chapter 29 **Reteaching Activity** in the TCR.

Enrich

Ask students to summarize the main reasons Luther felt he must break away from the Roman Catholic Church.

Assign the Chapter 29 **Enrichment Activity** in the TCR.

CLOSE

Have students discuss how religious wars during this time seemed to have been started by one or two people, but ended up involving whole nations.

Use the **Interactive Tutor Self-Assessment CD-ROM** to review Section 6.

HISTORY Online

Self-Check Quiz gives students an interactive chapter tutorial. Have them access ***Chapter 29 Quiz*** at humanheritage.glencoe.com

less a war over religion and more a struggle for territory and wealth.

The German people suffered great hardships during the war. Finally, in 1643, after a serious defeat, the German emperor asked for peace. In 1648, representatives of European nations signed the Peace of Westphalia (west fāl′ yuh), which ended the war. The German emperor lost much of his power and France emerged as a strong nation. After this war, Europeans no longer fought over religion. Instead, nations tried to gain power through trade and expansion overseas.

Section 6 Assessment

1. What led to the Thirty Years' War?
2. What effect did the Thirty Years' War have on Europe?

Critical Thinking

3. **Drawing Conclusions** Based on the Thirty Years' War, what conclusions can you draw about the reasons nations go to war?

Graphic Organizer Activity

4. Draw this diagram, and use it to show the main events in the Thirty Years' War. (Add answer boxes as needed.)

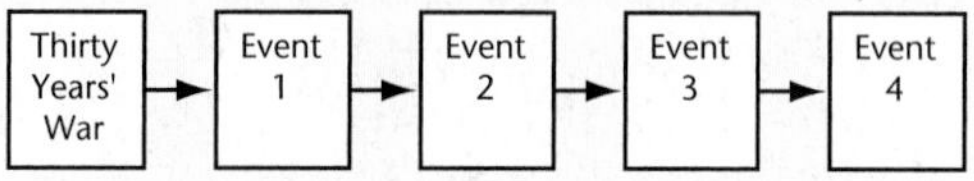

Chapter Summary & Study Guide

1. Luther posted his list of 95 theses to object to the sale of indulgences and other Church practices.
2. Luther's ideas spread, with people in northern Germany forming the Lutheran Church and people in Switzerland and elsewhere adopting what became known as Protestantism.
3. While Protestant reformers established new churches, Catholic reformers worked to improve their Church.
4. Between 1545 and 1563, the Council of Trent reformed many Catholic practices.
5. The reformation came to England when Parliament declared Henry VIII the head of the Church of England.
6. After Henry's death, advisers to his young son Edward introduced Protestant practices to the English Church.
7. Mary Tudor tried to return England to Catholicism, but failed.
8. Elizabeth I decided the Church of England should be Protestant with some Catholic features.
9. The English defeat of the Spanish Armada in 1588 kept northern Europe Protestant, but it did not prevent other religious wars.

HISTORY Online

Self-Check Quiz

Visit the *Human Heritage* Web site at humanheritage.glencoe.com and click on ***Chapter 29—Self-Check Quiz*** to assess your understanding of this chapter.

Section 6 Assessment Answers

1. the revolt in Bohemia against the German emperor Ferdinand II

2. The German emperor lost much of his power, France emerged as a strong nation, and nations tried to gain power through trade and expansion.

3. Sample conclusion: for religion, land, wealth, and political power. Students should be prepared to support their conclusions.

4. Events may vary, but should be in chronological order. For example: Denmark and Sweden invade Germany, Swedes defeated, France enters the war on Protestant side, Germans suffer serious defeat, German emperor asks for peace, warring nations sign Peace of Westphalia.

Assign the Chapter 29 **Section 6 Quiz** in the TCR. Testmaker available.

CHAPTER 29 Assessment

Using Key Terms

Use the following words to write a paragraph explaining the conflicts over religion among European countries during the 1500s and 1600s.

reformation	indulgences	theses
heretic	ministers	seminary
armada	galleons	

Understanding Main Ideas

1. How did Protestantism get its name, and what were some of the churches that belonged to this faith?
2. What rules of behavior did John Calvin propose for his followers?
3. What organization did Ignatius of Loyola form?
4. Why did Mary Tudor become known as "Bloody Mary"?
5. How did the defeat of the Spanish Armada help the Protestant cause?
6. What was the basis of alliances formed by German states in the 1590s and early 1600s?

Critical Thinking

1. What would you have liked about living in Geneva at the time of John Calvin? What would you have disliked? Explain your answer.
2. Do you approve or disapprove of the way Elizabeth I organized the Church of England? Explain your answer.
3. Explain whether you would or would not have converted to Catholicism if you had been Henry IV.
4. If you had been a Catholic in the mid-1500s, in which European country would you have preferred to live? Why?

Graphic Organizer Activity

History Create a diagram like the one below, and use it to summarize the causes and effects of the reformation on the history of western Europe.

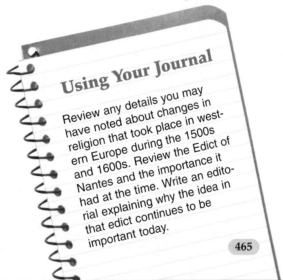

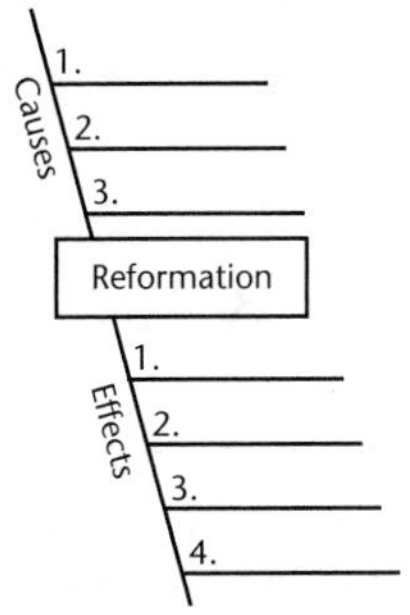

Geography in History

Places and Regions Refer to the location of Calvinist minorities on the map of western European religions on page 463. What connection might there be between their locations and the fact that they are minority groups (groups with fewer members than other religions)?

Using Your Journal

Review any details you may have noted about changes in religion that took place in western Europe during the 1500s and 1600s. Review the Edict of Nantes and the importance it had at the time. Write an editorial explaining why the idea in that edict continues to be important today.

465

CHAPTER 29 Assessment Answers

Using Key Terms

Paragraphs will vary but students should use all the terms.

Understanding Main Ideas

1. Protestants got their name because they protested teaching of the Roman Catholic Church. Some of their churches included the Lutheran and Reformed churches.
2. They could not dance, play cards, go to the theater, or take part in drinking parties.
3. the Society of Jesus
4. because under her rule, many Protestants were persecuted or burned at the stake for heresy
5. It allowed northern Europe to remain a Protestant stronghold.
6. religion

Critical Thinking

1. Answers will vary but should make reference to the agreement or disagreement with Calvinism.
2. Answers will vary, but students should explain why they approve or disapprove.
3. Answers will vary, but students should provide reasons for their choices.
4. Answers will vary, but students should choose a specific location and explain the reasons for their choices.

Graphic Organizer Activity

Sample responses: *causes*—sale of indulgences by the Church, posting of the 95 theses, excommunication of Luther; *effects*—formation of Lutheran and Reformed churches, start of a new form of Christianity known as Protestantism, reforms by the Roman Catholic Church to stop the spread of Protestantism, religious wars, and so on.

Bonus Test Question

For Chapter 29 Test

What work, written by Ignatius of Loyola, describes ways that people can develop a closer relationship with God? *(Spiritual Exercises)*

Using Your Journal

Editorials will vary but might include the idea that the Edict of Nantes had the beginnings of religious freedom, which is guaranteed in the U.S. today.

Geography in History

The minorities were spread all over Europe in small pockets, while other religious groups lived in larger areas. Smaller groups are more apt to remain minorities if cut off from others with the same beliefs.

Chapter 30 Planning Guide

Timesaving Tools

TeacherWorks™ All-In-One Planner and Resource Center

- **Interactive Teacher Edition** Access your Teacher Wraparound Edition and your classroom resources with a few easy clicks.
- **Interactive Lesson Planner** Planning has never been easier! Organize your week, month, semester, or year with all the lesson helps you need to make teaching creative, timely, and relevant.

Presentation Plus!

Use Glencoe's **Presentation Plus!** multimedia teacher tool to easily present dynamic lessons that visually excite your students. Using Microsoft PowerPoint® you can customize the presentations to create your own personalized lessons.

Objectives	Reproducible Resources	Multimedia Resources
Section 1 **The Portuguese** Identify reasons Europeans searched for a direct sea route to India, and cite achievements of Portuguese explorers.	Reproducible Lesson Plan Chapter 30 Vocabulary and Guided Reading Activity Reading Essentials and Study Guide 30-1 Chapter 30 Enrichment Activity Section 1 Quiz	Interactive Student Edition CD-ROM Graphic Organizer Transparency 3 Teaching Transparency and Activity 30A Vocabulary PuzzleMaker CD-ROM Interactive Tutor Self-Assessment CD-ROM ExamView® Pro Testmaker CD-ROM Glencoe Skillbuilder Interactive Workbook CD-ROM, Level 1 Presentation Plus! CD-ROM
Section 2 **The Spanish** List expeditions and voyages financed by Spain and name some of the explorers who led these voyages.	Reproducible Lesson Plan Reading Essentials and Study Guide 30-2 Chapter 30 Cooperative Learning Activity Chapter 30 Geography and Map Activity Section 2 Quiz	Teaching Transparency and Activity 30B Vocabulary PuzzleMaker CD-ROM Interactive Tutor Self-Assessment CD-ROM ExamView® Pro Testmaker CD-ROM Glencoe Skillbuilder Interactive Workbook CD-ROM, Level 1
Section 3 **Northwest Passage** Analyze how the search for a northwest passage changed the history of the Americas.	Reproducible Lesson Plan Reading Essentials and Study Guide 30-3 Chapter 30 Chart and Graph Skill Activity Unit 9 Primary Source Readings Section 3 Quiz	Vocabulary PuzzleMaker CD-ROM Interactive Tutor Self-Assessment CD-ROM ExamView® Pro Testmaker CD-ROM Glencoe Skillbuilder Interactive Workbook CD-ROM, Level 1
Chapter 30 **Review and** **Evaluation**	Chapter 30 Reteaching Activity Chapter 30 Performance Assessment Activity Unit 9 Standardized Test Practice Spanish Chapter Summary and Glossary Chapter 30 Test	Vocabulary PuzzleMaker CD-ROM Interactive Tutor Self-Assessment CD-ROM Glencoe Skillbuilder Interactive Workbook CD-ROM, Level 1 Audiocassettes* ExamView® Pro Testmaker CD-ROM

*Also available in Spanish.

Reviewing Map Legends

Legends, as explained in the map skill on page 75, are used to identify information shown on maps. Legends provide the key to the meaning of an unlimited number of symbols and colors that can be used on maps.

Sometimes, however, one legend may be used in several ways. For example, on the "European Voyages of Discovery" map below, five colors are used in the legend. On this particular map, these colors are used to show two different things. First, they point out the five European countries that took part in the voyages of discovery. Second, the colors show the different routes taken by explorers from these countries. For example, Portugal is shown in yellow. The routes that the Portuguese explorers took are also shown in yellow.

Map Practice

1. **What two countries had explorers sail around the world?**
2. **What country did not send any explorers south of 25°N latitude?**

European Voyages of Discovery

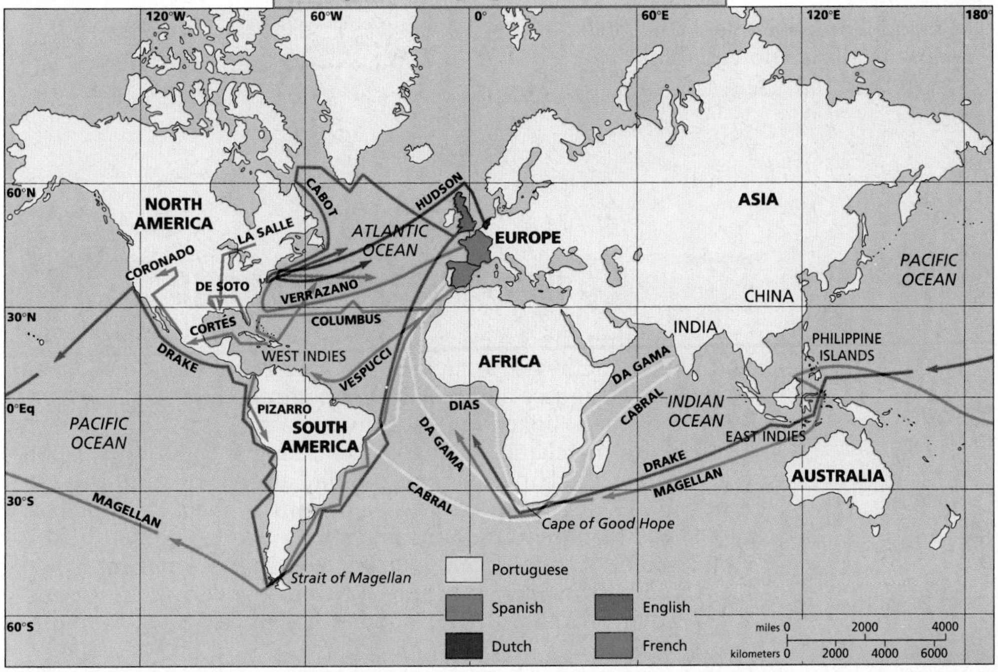

SPOTLIGHT ON: WORLD VOYAGES

After Spanish soldiers and explorers followed Columbus to the Americas, they returned to Europe with fantastic stories of the Seven Cities of Gold. One Spaniard, Estevanico, a black sailor shipwrecked in the Gulf of Mexico, spent many years wandering the deserts of southwest North America in search of these cities. He eventually died, unsuccessful in his quest, and the rumors of the existence of these golden cities persisted.

MAP SKILLS

TEACH

Reviewing Map Legends

Have students read the instructional part of the feature and answer the following questions: What are used to identify information shown on maps? *(legends)* In what two ways are colors used on the map on this page? *(to point out the five European countries that took part in the voyages of discovery and to show the routes taken by explorers from these countries)* Next, direct students to study the map to answer the following questions: What countries explored the coastline of South America? *(Portugal, Spain, England)* What countries explored North America? *(Spain, England, France, the Netherlands)* What countries explored the Philippine Islands and the East Indies? *(England, Spain)*

Assign the Chapter 30 **Geography and Map Activity** in the TCR.

Answers to Map Practice

1. Spain and England
2. France and the Netherlands

Use the **Glencoe Skillbuilder Interactive Workbook CD-ROM, Level 1,** to provide instruction and practice in key social studies skills.

L2 **Charts** Have students create charts of the following explorers who searched for the northwest passage to the Far East: John Cabot, Giovanni da Verrazano, Jacques Cartier, Martin Frobisher, and Henry Hudson. The charts should include the explorers' names, countries of origin, countries for which he explored, the date/dates of his explorations, the area explored/land claims made, and interesting facts about his explorations.

Use the **Interactive Tutor Self Assessment CD-ROM** to review Section 2.

NATIONAL GEOGRAPHIC

Use these materials to enrich student understanding of the age of exploration.

NGS PICTURESHOW CD-ROM
Age of Exploration, Parts 1 and 2

NGS PICTUREPACK TRANSPARENCY SET
Age of Exploration

GEOGRAPHY AND HISTORY

The English also made several attempts to reach the Far East by sailing northeast. Two of their ships reached Lapland, while a third got as far as the White Sea before being stopped by ice. Its crew then traveled to Moscow by horse-drawn sleds and started a trade with the Russians for furs and tallow.

Use the **Vocabulary PuzzleMaker CD-ROM** to create crossword and word search puzzles.

Painting of Ferdinand Magellan

later, it was almost helpless. The crew was suffering from scurvy and had no food of any kind.

After they had eaten and rested, Magellan and his crew set a southwest course for the Philippine (fil uh pēn') Islands. There, Magellan became involved in a local war and was killed. Shortly after, more crew members were killed, and two more ships were lost. The one remaining ship continued on into the Indian Ocean and around Africa. It finally arrived in Seville (suh vil'), Spain, in 1522 with 18 men and a load of spices.

The voyage was a great accomplishment. By *circumnavigating*, or sailing completely around the world, it proved that Earth is indeed round. The voyage opened the Pacific Ocean to European ships. It also proved that Columbus did not land in Asia but in the Americas.

Section 2 Assessment

1. **Define:** mutiny, papal line of demarcation, *conquistadores.*
2. What were some discoveries made by the Spanish between 1513 and 1540?
3. What did Magellan's voyage prove?

Critical Thinking

4. **Making Comparisons** Which of Spain's explorers do you think advanced knowledge of the world the most? Explain.

Graphic Organizer Activity

5. Draw this diagram, and use it to show some of the effects of Columbus's voyages.

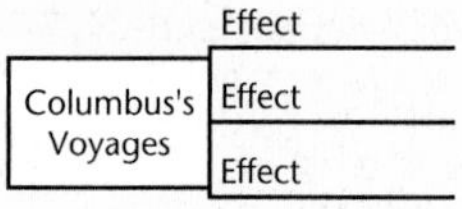

SECTION 3 Northwest Passage

Even after the Americas were reached, the English, French, and Dutch continued to look for another route to the Far East. Since the Portuguese and the Spanish controlled the southern sea lanes, the others looked for a northwest passage.

English merchants persuaded their king to send John Cabot (kab' uht), an Italian navigator, to the Far East by a northwest route. In 1497, Cabot set sail with a handful of men. He explored the coasts of Newfoundland and Nova Scotia (nō' vuh skō' shuh) and established claims for England in the Americas.

In 1523, the French hired Giovanni da Verrazano (jē uh vahn' ē dah ver rah tsah' nō), another Italian navigator, to find a

Section 2 Assessment Answers

1. mutiny, an overthrow of officers (p. 472); papal line of demarcation, an imaginary line of separation (p. 473); *conquistadores,* conquerors (p. 473)
2. Florida, Mexico, Peru, Mississippi River, Grand Canyon, and Pacific Ocean
3. that the earth is round
4. Answers will vary, but students should support their choice with evidence demonstrating the importance of the explorer's voyage or expedition.
5. sample effects: opened contact between Europe and the Americas, led to exploration and conquest by the *conquistadores,* changed the course of Native American history, paved the way for a Spanish empire in the Americas

Assign the Chapter 30 **Section 2 Quiz** in the TCR. Testmaker available.

northwest passage. He sailed along the Atlantic coast from North Carolina to New York. Eleven years later, Jacques Cartier (zhahk kahr tyā'), a French navigator, sailed up the St. Lawrence River as far as present-day Montreal (mahn trē ahl'). This gave the French a claim to eastern Canada.

In 1576, Sir Martin Frobisher (frō' bi shuhr), an English **sea dog,** or sea captain, sailed the coast of Greenland and fought a storm that almost wrecked one of his three ships. Frobisher finally discovered the bay that today bears his name.

Reading Check What was an English **sea dog?**

In 1609, the Dutch sent Henry Hudson, an English navigator, to locate the passage. He explored the Hudson River and sailed to what is today Albany, New York. In 1610 he set out on a second voyage. He became lost in a storm and was never seen again. Nevertheless, his first voyage gave the Dutch their claim in the Americas.

EXPLORERS

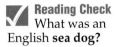

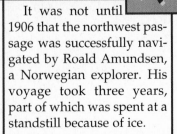

Name	Country	Achievements
Amerigo Vespucci	*Spain Portugal*	explored Atlantic coast of South America, 1497–1504; one of first to believe he had reached a new world
Pedro Alváres Cabral	*Portugal*	discovered Brazil and sailed east to India, 1500–1501
Vasco Núñez de Balboa	*Spain*	first European to sight eastern shore of Pacific Ocean, 1513
Alvar Núñez Cabeza de Vaca	*Spain*	explored Florida and Gulf region from Texas to Mexico, 1528–36
Juan Rodríguez Cabrillo	*Spain*	explored Pacific coast to Drake's Bay near San Francisco, 1542
Richard Chancellor	*England*	reached Moscow in search of northeast passage to Asia; opened trade with Russia, 1553–54
John Davis	*England*	explored west coast of Greenland in search of northwest passage to Asia, 1585
Sir Francis Drake	*England*	first Englishman to sail around the world, 1577–80
Father Jacques Marquette Louis Jolliet	*France*	explored Mississippi Valley to mouth of Arkansas River, 1673
Vitus Bering	*Russia*	explored coasts of Alaska and northeast Asia; discovered Bering Strait and Bering Sea, 1728, 1741

Reading Check Answer
An English **sea dog** was the name given to the sea captains who sailed for England.

LINKING PAST TO PRESENT

Vasco Núñez de Balboa led an expedition of soldiers and guides across the Isthmus of Panama in 1513 to search for a region rumored to be "flowing with golde [gold]," and to find "another sea, where they sayle [sail] with shippes [ships] as bigge [big] as yours." Balboa's company fought rain forest undergrowth, poisonous snakes, and angry inhabitants for about 25 days as they crossed the isthmus. Today, people travel by ship through the Panama Canal completed in 1914.

ASSESS

Check for Understanding

Ask students to summarize the main points of the chapter, orally or in writing. Discuss the answers to the Section and Chapter Assessment questions.

Evaluate

Assign the Chapter 30 **Performance Assessment Activity** in the TCR.

Administer the **Chapter 30 Test** in the TCR. Testmaker available.

EXTENDING THE CONTENT

In 1522, French pirates captured a Spanish treasure ship filled with gold, silver, and jade mosaics sent home from Mexico by Cortés. Amazed and covetous, King Francis I decided to send his own expedition to bring home wealth from the Americas. Francis chose the Italian navigator Giovanni da Verrazano to head the expedition in 1524. It was paid for by silk merchants of France who also had an interest in finding a route to China. Verrazano worked his way gradually up the coast from North Carolina to Nova Scotia. His ships sailed in and around Chesapeake Bay, the Hudson River, Cape Cod, and the Maine coast.

DID YOU KNOW

It was not until 1906 that the northwest passage was successfully navigated by Roald Amundsen, a Norwegian explorer. His voyage took three years, part of which was spent at a standstill because of ice.

GLENCOE TECHNOLOGY

MindJogger Videoquiz

Use **MindJogger Videoquiz** to review students' knowledge of the unit.

Available in DVD and VHS

Reteach

Assign the Chapter 30 **Reteaching Activity** in the TCR.

Enrich

Assign the Chapter 30 **Enrichment Activity** in the TCR.

CLOSE

Ask students to discuss the discoveries made by the explorers discussed in this chapter. Ask them to rank the discoveries in the order of importance. Then ask students to explain their rankings.

Use the **Interactive Tutor Self-Assessment CD-ROM** to review Section 3.

HISTORY Online

Self-Check Quiz gives students an interactive chapter tutorial. Have them access ***Chapter 30 Quiz*** at **humanheritage.glencoe.com**

All of these voyages failed in their search to find a northwest passage to the Far East. They did, however, establish claims in the Americas for England, France, and the Netherlands.

Section 3 Assessment

1. **Define:** sea dog.
2. How did English, French, and Dutch explorers plan to reach Asia?
3. What lands in the Americas were claimed by England? By France? By the Netherlands?

Critical Thinking

4. **Demonstrating Reasoned Judgment** What characteristics or kinds of personalities do you think the English, French, and Dutch explorers had to have to achieve what they did?

Graphic Organizer Activity

5. Draw this diagram, and use it to show the causes and effects of the search for a northwest passage.

Chapter Summary & Study Guide

1. During the 1500s, Europeans tried to break the Italian hold on trade by searching for an all-water route to India and beyond.
2. The development of better maps, ships, and navigational instruments helped Europeans in their search.
3. In the early 1400s, Prince Henry of Portugal opened the first school in Europe for navigators.
4. By 1473, Portuguese ships had crossed the equator. By 1498, they had reached India.
5. Between 1492 and 1504, Columbus made four voyages to what he thought was Asia but was really the Americas.
6. In 1494, the Treaty of Tordesillas divided non-Christian lands between Spain and Portugal, but other nations ignored the agreement.
7. In the first half of the 1500s, Cortés and Pizarro conquered the Aztec and Inca empires, encouraging other explorers to search for other empires in the Americas.
8. Between 1519 and 1522, Magellan's expedition sailed around the world, proving that Columbus did not land in Asia.
9. Between 1497 and 1609, England, France, and the Netherlands sent explorers to find a northwest passage through the Americas.
10. Early English, French, and Dutch voyages paved the way for future claims in North America.

HISTORY Online

Self-Check Quiz

Visit the *Human Heritage* Web site at **humanheritage.glencoe.com** and click on ***Chapter 30—Self-Check Quiz*** to assess your understanding of this chapter.

Section 3 Assessment Answers

1. sea dog, sea captain (p. 477)
2. by a northwest passage
3. Newfoundland, Nova Scotia; lands along the St. Lawrence River; lands along the Hudson River
4. Answers will vary but might include that these explorers were brave, adventurous, competitive, and persistent.
5. sample responses: *causes*—Spanish and Portuguese control of southern sea lanes, desire of other European nations for sea routes to the Far East; *effects*—exploration of North America's Atlantic coast; land claims by England, France, and the Netherlands

Assign the Chapter 30 **Section 3 Quiz** in the TCR. Testmaker available.

CHAPTER 30 Assessment

Using Key Terms

Imagine you are writing a newspaper column entitled "Great Explorer Achievements." Use each of the following words in a description of what you think some of these achievements were.

compass	astrolabe	caravel
mutiny	papal line of demarcation	*conquistadores*
sea dog		

Understanding Main Ideas

1. What were some of the problems that European explorers faced on their voyages of discovery?
2. What was the first European settlement in the Americas?
3. What are three bodies of water named after European explorers?
4. How long did it take Magellan's ship to sail around the world?
5. What did voyages in search of a northwest passage to Asia accomplish?

Critical Thinking

1. Why do you think Queen Isabella of Spain agreed to support Columbus when others had turned him down?
2. How do you think Native Americans felt about the *conquistadores?*
3. How did competition between nations affect European voyages of exploration?

Graphic Organizer Activity

History Create a chart like the one on this page, and use it to write a headline for an important event that occurred in each of the years shown.

Year	Headline
1473	
1487	
1492	
1494	
1497	
1499	
1521	
1522	
1532	
1609	

Geography in History

The World in Spatial Terms Refer to the map on page 475. Whose voyage from Portugal to India was longer in miles (or kilometers)—da Gama's or Cabral's? How many miles (or kilometers) longer was it?

Using Your Journal

Review any details you may have noted about the changes that took place in western Europe between 1300 and 1600. Imagine you are a peasant living in London, England, in 1550. Write a diary entry describing what you have learned about the world in recent years.

479

Bonus Test Question

For Chapter 30 Test

How did discoveries by non-Europeans help Europeans begin their voyages of exploration? Make a cause-and-effect chart showing these relationships. Add a summary statement to explain your chart.

Using Your Journal

Diary entries will vary but should include major events that affected England. You might ask volunteers to read their entries to the class.

Geography in History

da Gama's; about 2,900 miles (or 4,666 km) longer

CHAPTER 30 Assessment Answers

Using Key Terms

Columns will vary, but students should include some achievements and use all the key terms.

Understanding Main Ideas

1. storms, scurvy, spoiled food and water, and starvation
2. a fort built with wood from the Santa Maria
3. Strait of Magellan, Frobisher Bay, and Hudson River
4. three years
5. claims in the Americas for England, France, and the Netherlands

Critical Thinking

1. Answers will vary but might include that she thought finding a new route to Asia would make Spain richer.
2. Answers will vary but might include fear, dread, and sadness.
3. Each nation wanted to extend its trade and power, and to be richer than other nations. They thought they could do this by finding a new route to the Far East. The search led to the discovery of the Americas.

Graphic Organizer Activity

Headlines will vary but should show the importance of the event chosen for each date. To get students started, you might use this example for 1522: "Ragged Crew Completes Magellan's Voyage—The World is Round!"

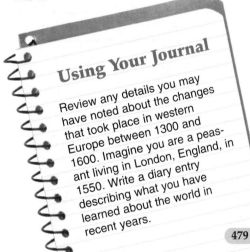

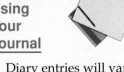

UNIT 9 Around the World

FOCUS

Objectives

After reading the Around the World for Unit 9, your students will be able to:

1. locate the region influenced by the Swahili culture, and name some of the nations or people that contributed to its development.

2. cite evidence proving that Swahili merchants traded throughout the Arab world and with China.

3. predict how Portuguese explorers might have reacted when they first arrived in one of the Swahili towns.

Bellringer

Ask students to write down what they think the word "simba" means.

Motivational Activity

Most students will probably correctly guess "lion." Tell them that they have just learned a Swahili word. If any of your students speak Swahili, have them share other words with the class. Then refer students to the Around the World feature, pointing out that today Swahili is the most widely spoken language on the African continent. Ask: From looking at the works of art on pages 480–481, what cultures do you think influenced the Swahili culture? *(sample answers: Chinese, Arabic, and African cultures)*

TEACH

Geography: Human Systems Focus student attention on the map on page 480. Ask: How does the location of the East African harbor towns explain the region's cultural diversity? To help students with their answer, trace the Swahili coast on a wall map of the world.

UNIT 9 Around

THE SWAHILI CULTURE

Between 1000 and 1700 A.D., the harbor towns of East Africa blossomed. Like other trading centers, they attracted a variety of influences. More than 1,200 years ago, Arab traders came to the area, bringing the Muslim religion with them. Other influences came from Persia, India, and China. Later, Portuguese explorers edging their way along the East African coast brought yet another influence to the area.

By far the strongest influence, however, was that of the African peoples who already lived in the region. The blending of their cultures with the cultures of other regions produced the Swahili culture, which is still alive and vibrant today.

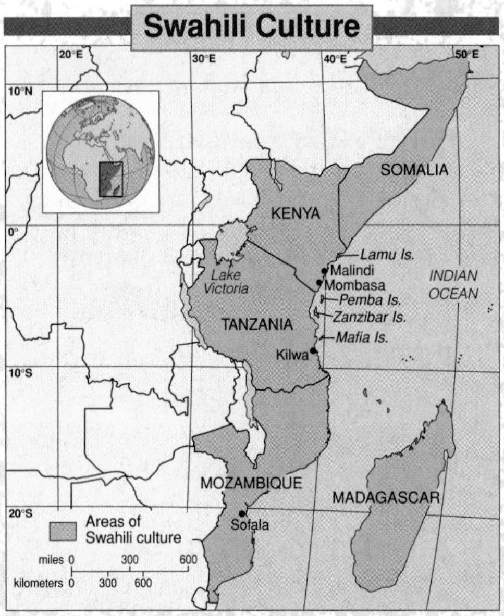

▲ The term *Swahili* comes from an Arab word meaning "coastal people." The Swahili culture includes African Muslims who live on African islands and lands bordering the Indian Ocean.

► In the early 1400s, Chinese explorer Zheng He made several voyages to East Africa. On his fourth voyage, the sultan of Malindi presented him with a giraffe—a gift to the Chinese emperor. The Chinese called the giraffe a "celestial unicorn" and saw it as a sign of good luck.

SPOTLIGHT ON: SWAHILI CULTURE

Swahili, the language spoken along the Swahili coast and in much of East Africa, reflects the region's far-flung contacts. Classified as a Bantu language, Swahili has borrowed words from many other languages, including Portuguese, Persian, Arabic, German, and English. Some Swahili words taken from English include: *basikeli* (bicycle), *pensili* (pencil), *mashine* (machine), and *komputya* (computer).

Millions of non-Africans learned Swahili when they watched the movie *The Lion King* and met the characters Simba (the Swahili word for "lion") and Rafiki (the Swahili word for "friend"). People who watched the original *Star Trek* learned yet another word when they met Lieutenant Uhura. In Swahili, *uhura* means "freedom," a rallying cry for East Africans during their struggle for independence.

the World

▲ Trade goods from China made their way to the Swahili coast as early as the 800s A.D. Pottery, such as this bowl made during the Ming dynasty, has been uncovered up and down the coast.

From the 100s to the early 1900s, Swahili merchants used a ship known as the *mtepe* to sail the coastal waters. Built without nails, the timbers of the boats were held together by rope woven from coconut husks and powered by sails made from the leaves of coconut trees. The Arabs introduced the *dhow* and its triangular cotton sail to the region around the 800s. Arab *dhows* can still be seen along the Swahili coast today. ▼

Gold coins found on Pemba, an island off the coast of Kenya, prove that Swahili merchants traded all over the Arab world in the 1000s. These coins come from Tunisia, Egypt, and Syria. The Swahili towns also minted their own coins. ►

▼ This present-day market shows the blend of people that make up the Swahili culture and the many goods, particularly spices, that have made the region famous.

Taking Another Look

1. Where are the Swahili peoples located?
2. What evidence proves that Swahili merchants traded with the Arab world? With China?

Hands-On Activity

Writing Diary Entries Imagine you are a Portuguese ship captain visiting a Swahili town for the first time. Write several diary entries describing the experience.

Use a pointer or ruler to point out nations along the northern rim of the Indian Ocean with which the Swahili harbor towns may have traded.

LINKING PAST TO PRESENT

European explorers hoped to reach the spice islands of Asia, but in Zanzibar they found spices that far exceeded their dreams. Although the island's main exports are cloves and coconuts, more than 50 different kinds of spices and fruits can still be found there: cinnamon, cardamom, nutmeg, pepper, pimentos, ginger, tamarind, vanilla, figs, lemons, litchi, bananas, pineapples, passion fruit, breadfruit, ten kinds of mangos, and more.

ASSESS

Check for Understanding

Have students answer the questions in Taking Another Look on page 481.

Enrich

Assign the Chapter 30 **Enrichment Activity** in the TCR. Have students compare the account from *The Kilwa Chronicle* with the journal entries that they wrote in the Hands-On Activity.

CLOSE

Ask students why the Swahili harbor towns might have been the envy of almost any European merchant during the period covered by this unit. *(sample responses: their location on an all-water route to the Far East, their direct contact with India and China, and so on)*

ANSWERS TO TAKING ANOTHER LOOK

1. Swahili peoples are located on the African islands and lands bordering the Indian Ocean. The culture reaches from present-day Somalia in the north to Mozambique in the south.

2. Coins found on Pemba come from all over the Arab world. Chinese prints record a picture of a giraffe that the Sultan of Malindi gave to the emperor of China. Pieces of Chinese pottery and other trade goods have been found up and down the Swahili coast.

Hands-On Activity

The entries will vary but will probably reflect surprise at the level of development or perhaps concern over the spread of Muslim influence. Some entries might express greed or an interest in claiming the coastal towns for Portugal.

STANDARDIZED TEST PRACTICE

Answers and Analyses

1C History

While each of these contributions occurred during the Renaissance, the most important element was the printing press. The Renaissance was essentially the rediscovery of Greek and Roman ideas. According to page 441, the printing press made books available to people, and therefore, *new ideas spread rapidly.*

2G History

Pages 434–435 state that da Vinci was an artist, scientist, and inventor. This information makes G the best choice.

THE PRINCETON REVIEW **TEST-TAKING TIP**

Students can probably answer this question by association: da Vinci was definitely an artist, so the word *artist* must figure into the correct answer. Only G then qualifies.

3D History

Luther is discussed on pages 449–451. There it states that he posted his theses, which brought him into conflict with Catholic doctrine, on the church in Wittenberg. For this action, he was condemned and excommunicated by the Pope.

4F History

According to page 451, Protestant church leaders *conducted services in the language of the area instead of in Latin.* This information makes F the best choice. No mention is made of improving the conditions of women or recognition by the Catholic Church.

THE PRINCETON REVIEW

Standardized Test Practice

Directions: Choose the *best* answer to each of the following multiple choice questions. If you have trouble answering a question, use the process of elimination to narrow your choices. Write your answers on a separate piece of paper.

1. Which of the following Renaissance contributions was most helpful in spreading new ideas?

A The creation of piazzas in the center of cities

B The use of perspective in artists' work

C The invention of the printing press

D The generosity of Lorenzo de Medici toward artists, poets, and philosphers

> ***Test-Taking Tip:*** Always read the question and *all* the answer choices carefully. Notice that all of the answer choices are examples of Renaissance contributions to European culture. Although Lorenzo de Medici's generosity (answer D) probably helped people *create* new ideas, there is another choice that was more helpful in *spreading* these ideas to many people.

2. Leonardo da Vinci was

F a scholar and a Church leader

G an artist, scientist, and inventor

H the founder of modern medicine

J a philosopher and historian

> ***Test-Taking Tip:*** Eliminate answers that are incorrect. Leonardo da Vinci was not a Church leader, so answer F can be eliminated.

3. Why was Martin Luther charged with heresy?

A He worshiped more than one god.

B He worked to secure rights for Spanish Jews.

C He declared himself the one true voice of God.

D His theses challenged the Pope and the Catholic Church.

> ***Test-Taking Tip:*** This question requires you to remember a *fact* about Martin Luther. Reading all the answer choices carefully may help you remember information about this important religious leader.

4. Which of the following was most responsible for the spread of the Protestant church through Europe?

F Services were not conducted in Latin, but rather in local languages.

G Women were given a greater role in the Protestant church.

H Church members could buy indulgences to free themselves from punishment.

J The Protestant church was recognized by the Roman Catholic Church.

> ***Test-Taking Tip:*** Again, read carefully. Lutheran and Reformed churches were known as *Protestant* because they *protested* against Catholic ideas, such as the sale of indulgences. Therefore, answer H can be eliminated.

European Voyages of Discovery

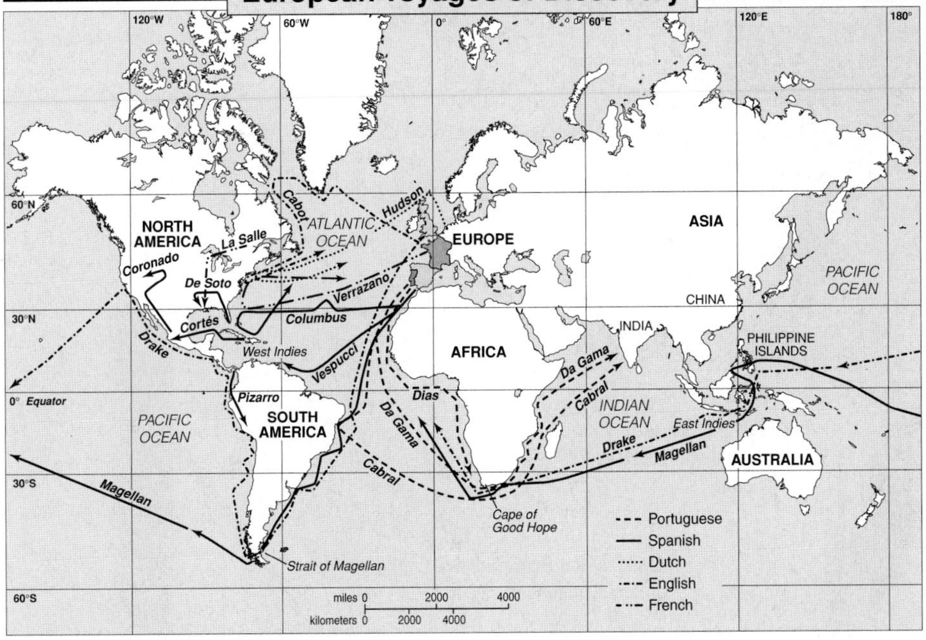

5. According to the map above, which nations' explorers sailed around the Cape of Good Hope?

A Portugal and Spain
B Portugal, France, and England
C Spain, England, and France
D Portugal, Spain, and England

> ***Test-Taking Tip:*** Use the *map legend*, or *key*, to help you understand how the map is organized. How does this map show the routes of different countries' explorers?

6. Which countries had explorers whose routes crossed the equator?

F England, Spain, and Portugal
G England, Spain, and France
H Spain, France, and Portugal
J Spain, Portugal, and Holland

> ***Test-Taking Tip:*** Make sure that you do not confuse the *equator* with the *Prime Meridian.* Although both are indicated by 0°, the equator is a line of latitude, and the Prime Meridian is a line of longitude. Do you remember which is which?

STOP

483

5D Geography

According to the map, Drake (English), Magellan (Spanish) and da Gama and Cabral (Portuguese) sailed around the Cape of Good Hope.

THE PRINCETON REVIEW **TEST-TAKING TIP**

All of the information needed to answer the question is on the map itself. Make sure that students understand how to read the legend, and remind them to work carefully to avoid making simple errors.

6F Geography

According to the map, Drake (English), Magellan (Spanish), and da Gama, Cabral, and Dias (Portuguese) crossed the equator.

THE PRINCETON REVIEW **TEST-TAKING TIP**

Be sure to help students understand lines of longitude and latitude, and how to identify the line that represents the equator.

Tested Objectives

Questions	Reading Objective
1	Evaluate information
2	Identify supporting ideas
3	Determine cause and effect
4	Identify central issues
5, 6	Analyze information

OVERVIEW

Unit 10 discusses the changes that took place in the world from the time the Europeans discovered the Americas to the 1800s.

- **Chapter 31** describes the colonizing efforts of Portugal, Spain, England, the Netherlands, and France from the early 1500s to 1763.
- **Chapter 32** outlines the revolutions in England, the American colonies, and France during the 1600s and the 1700s.
- **Chapter 33** summarizes the Industrial Revolution of the 1700s and 1800s, highlighting key developments in textiles, agriculture, mining, and transportation.

UNIT OBJECTIVES

After reading Unit 10, students will be able to:

1. describe how the Americas changed during the 1500s and 1600s.

2. discuss what changes in government took place in the West during the 1600s and 1700s.

3. analyze economic changes that took place in the West during the 1700s and early 1800s.

UNIT PROJECT

Tell students to create an advertising campaign that does one of the following: encourages Europeans in the 1500s to help colonize the Americas; supports a political uprising against a monarchy in the 1700s; or promotes the latest inventions and their uses and benefits. Encourage students to think of catchy slogans for their campaigns. Have them share their campaigns with the rest of the class.

UNIT 10 The Changing World

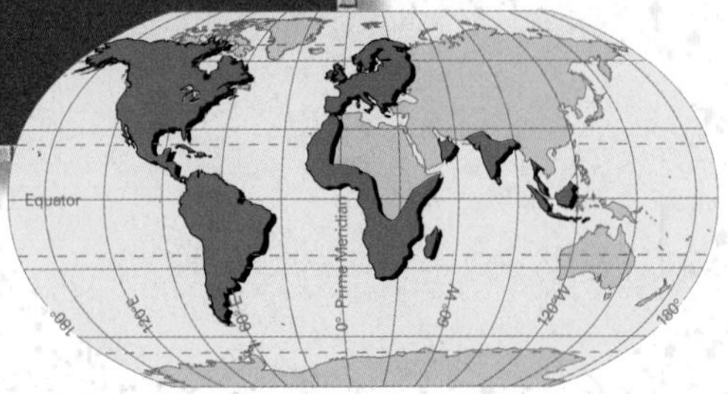

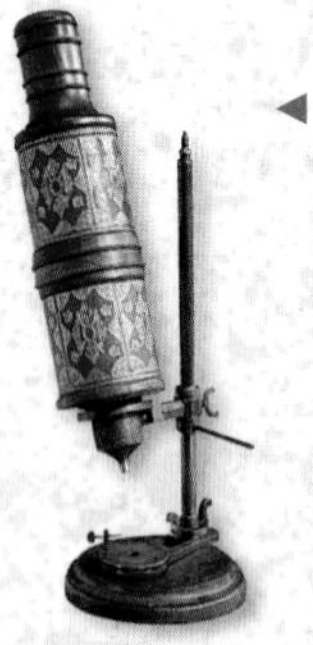

◀ Early microscope, which revolutionized science

Model of the *Rocket*, one of England's first steam locomotives ▼

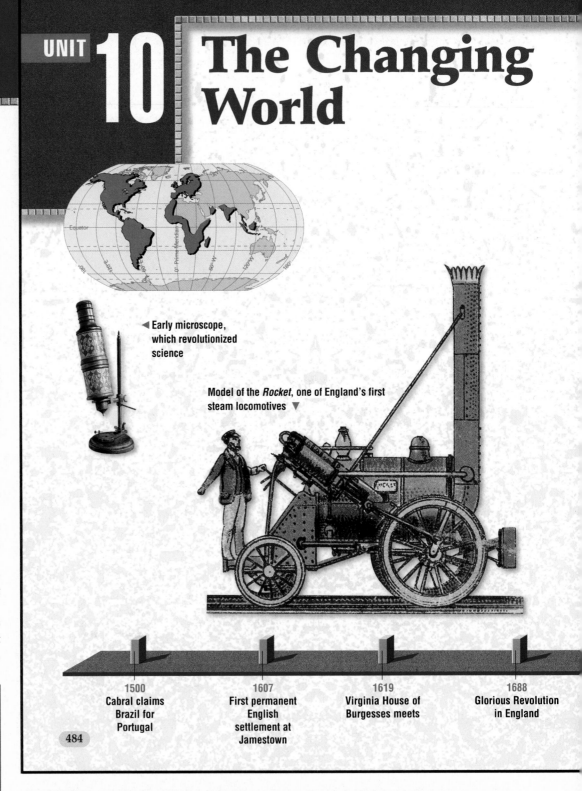

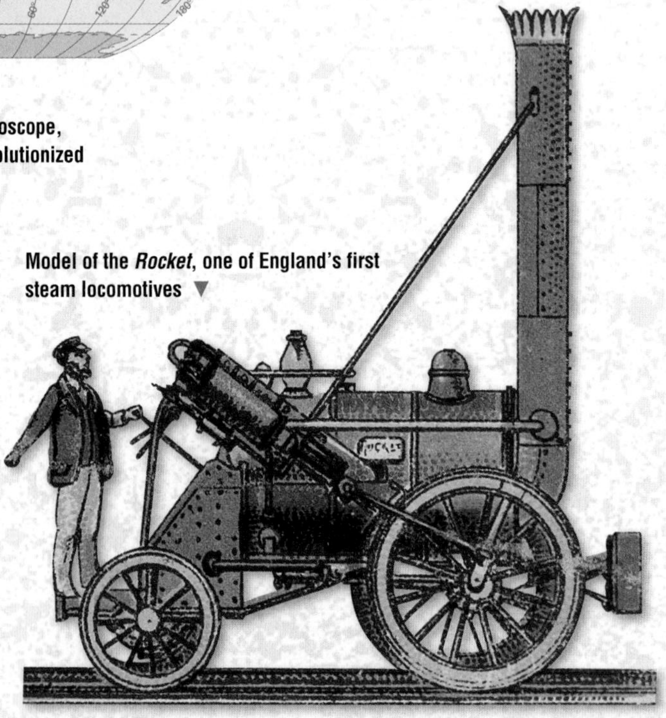

1500	1607	1619	1688
Cabral claims Brazil for Portugal	First permanent English settlement at Jamestown	Virginia House of Burgesses meets	Glorious Revolution in England

ABOUT THE UNIT OPENING

Examining Artifacts

Have students suggest the areas of life that these two artifacts may have changed. *(science, medical research, transportation, and so on)* Point out that the microscope opened a whole new world invisible to the naked eye and that the train carried people and goods faster than ever before. Tell students they will explore other far-reaching changes in this unit.

Global Chronology

Ask students to explain what time period the time line covers. *(1500 to 1847)* What entries indicate new ideas about government were taking place? *(Virginia House of Burgesses meets, Glorious Revolution in England, Declaration of Independence)*

FOLDABLES™ Study Organizer

Organizing Information Study Foldable *Make this foldable to help you organize what you learn about the changes that occurred in western Europe and the Americas during the 1800s.*

Step 1 *Fold a sheet of paper into fourths from top to bottom.*

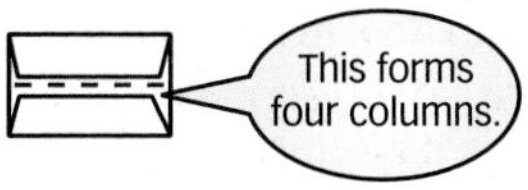
This forms four columns.

Step 2 *Open the paper and refold it into fourths from side to side.*

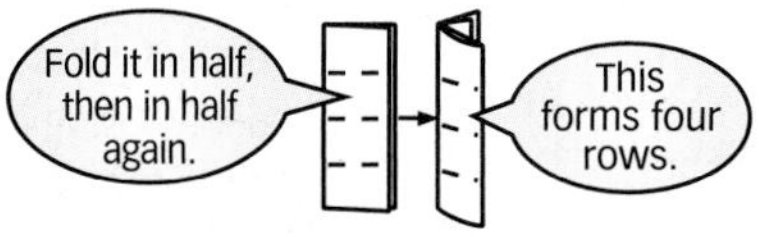
Fold it in half, then in half again.
This forms four rows.

Step 3 *Unfold, turn the paper, and draw lines along the folds.*

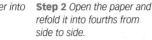

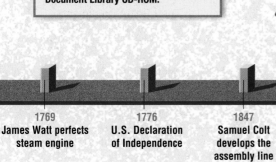

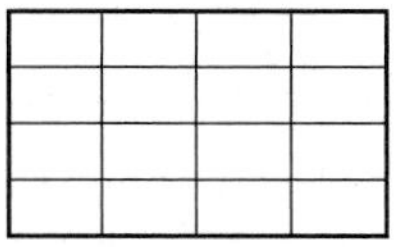

Step 4 *Label as shown.*

Unit 10	Terms	People	Places
Expansion			
Revolution			
Industry			

Reading and Writing *Complete your table foldable as you read the unit. Your foldable should contain main ideas about the political and economic developments of the 1800s.*

PRIMARY SOURCES Library

See pages 692–693 for other primary source readings to accompany Unit 10.

GO TO Read "Life at the Mill: Memoirs of a Child Laborer" from the **World History Primary Source Document Library CD-ROM.**

Journal Notes

What changes took place in the world between the 1500s and the 1800s? Note details about these changes as you read.

1769 **James Watt perfects steam engine**

1776 **U.S. Declaration of Independence**

1847 **Samuel Colt develops the assembly line**

485

GLENCOE TECHNOLOGY

MindJogger Videoquiz

Use **MindJogger Videoquiz** to preview the unit content.

Available in DVD and VHS

FOLDABLES™ Study Organizer

Purpose This foldable helps students organize information about the changing world from the time the Europeans discovered the Americas to the 1800s. Students should use this table foldable to write down facts—terms, people, and places—about European expansion, political revolutions, and the rise of industry.

Have students complete **Reading and Study Skills Foldables** Activity 10.

RECORDING JOURNAL NOTES

Help students begin writing by asking them to name time line entries that indicate the kinds of changes taking place in the world during this time. Tell students that these are the kinds of changes they should note in their journals as they read Unit 10.

PRIMARY SOURCES Library

Additional primary sources from the **World History Primary Source Document Library CD-ROM** can be used during the study of Unit 10, including:

- *Second Treatise of Government*, by John Locke

Primary sources about the "iron horse" can be found on pages 692–693.

Geographic Location

Have students locate the countries of western Europe and North and South America, the islands of the Caribbean, Africa, the Philippines, and the East Indies. Have students calculate the approximate distances between these places. Discuss the length of time that it might have taken colonists to get to these foreign lands in the 1500s–1700s.

ABC NEWS INTERACTIVE™

VIDEOCASSETTE
Turning Points in World History

Have students view **Tape 2 Chapter 3** to learn about the changes brought about by the Industrial Revolution.

Chapter 31 Planning Guide

Timesaving Tools

TeacherWorks™ All-In-One Planner and Resource Center

- **Interactive Teacher Edition** Access your Teacher Wraparound Edition and your classroom resources with a few easy clicks.
- **Interactive Lesson Planner** Planning has never been easier! Organize your week, month, semester, or year with all the lesson helps you need to make teaching creative, timely, and relevant.

Use Glencoe's **Presentation Plus!** multimedia teacher tool to easily present dynamic lessons that visually excite your students. Using Microsoft PowerPoint® you can customize the presentations to create your own personalized lessons.

Objectives	Reproducible Resources	Multimedia Resources
Section 1 **Portugal** Summarize the development and decline of Portugal's empire in the Americas.	Reproducible Lesson Plan Chapter 31 Vocabulary and Guided Reading Activity Reading Essentials and Study Guide 31-1 Section 1 Quiz Unit 10 Hands-On History Lab	Interactive Student Edition CD-ROM Graphic Organizer Transparency 12 Vocabulary PuzzleMaker CD-ROM ExamView® Pro Testmaker CD-ROM Presentation Plus! CD-ROM
Section 2 **Spain** Discuss the rise and decline of Spain's colonial empire in the Americas.	Reproducible Lesson Plan Reading Essentials and Study Guide 31-2 Chapter 31 Cooperative Learning Activity Section 2 Quiz	Vocabulary PuzzleMaker CD-ROM ExamView® Pro Testmaker CD-ROM Glencoe Skillbuilder Interactive Workbook CD-ROM, Level 1
Section 3 **England** Describe the colonies established by the English in the Americas.	Reproducible Lesson Plan Reading Essentials and Study Guide 31-3 Chapter 31 Chart and Graph Skill Activity Chapter 31 Geography and Map Activity Section 3 Quiz	Teaching Transparency and Activity 31B Vocabulary PuzzleMaker CD-ROM Interactive Tutor Self-Assessment CD-ROM
Section 4 **The Netherlands** Discuss how the Dutch established colonies in the Americas.	Reproducible Lesson Plan Reading Essentials and Study Guide 31-4 Section 4 Quiz	Vocabulary PuzzleMaker CD-ROM Interactive Tutor Self-Assessment CD-ROM Glencoe Skillbuilder Interactive Workbook CD-ROM, Level 1
Section 5 **France** Explain how and where the French established settlements in the Americas.	Reproducible Lesson Plan Reading Essentials and Study Guide 31-5 Section 5 Quiz	Interactive Tutor Self-Assessment CD-ROM ExamView® Pro Testmaker CD-ROM Glencoe Skillbuilder Interactive Workbook CD-ROM, Level 1
Section 6 **The Influence of Empires** Describe how empires in the Americas influenced Europe.	Reproducible Lesson Plan Reading Essentials and Study Guide 31-6 Section 6 Quiz	Vocabulary PuzzleMaker CD-ROM ExamView® Pro Testmaker CD-ROM Glencoe Skillbuilder Interactive Workbook CD-ROM, Level 1
Chapter 31 Review and Evaluation	Chapter 31 Reteaching Activity Chapter 31 Performance Assessment Activity Spanish Chapter Summary and Glossary Chapter 31 Test	Interactive Tutor Self-Assessment CD-ROM Glencoe Skillbuilder Interactive Workbook CD-ROM, Level 1 Audiocassettes* ExamView® Pro Testmaker CD-ROM

*Also available in Spanish.

Chapter 31 Planning Guide

Performance Assessment Activities

Mapmaking Have students research in historical atlases and create two maps of European claims in the Americas. One map should show the claims in 1650, and the other map should show the claims in 1753. Assign students to write five questions about the two maps and exchange them with each other.

CHAPTER RESOURCES

READINGS FOR THE STUDENT

Davis, James E. and Sharryl Davis Hawke. *Seeds of Change: The Story of Cultural Exchange After 1492.* Addison-Wesley, 1992. An account of the exchanges made between Europe and the Americas and their effects on each region.

Hooks, William H. *The Legend of White Doe.* Macmillan, 1988. A tale about Virginia Dare, the first child of English settlers born in the Americas.

READINGS FOR THE TEACHER

Scott, John Anthony. *Settlers on the Eastern Shore: The British Colonies in North America 1607-1750.* Facts on File, 1991. Eyewitness accounts and primary sources describe the first years of British settlement in the Americas.

KEY TO ABILITY LEVELS

Teaching strategies have been coded for varying learning styles and abilities.

L1 Level 1 activities are **basic** activities and should be within the ability range of all students.

L2 Level 2 activities are **average** activities and should be within the ability range of the average to above-average student.

L3 Level 3 activities are **challenging** activities designed for the ability range of above-average students.

ELL ELL activities should be within the ability range of English Language Learning students.

NATIONAL GEOGRAPHIC Teacher's Corner

INDEX TO NATIONAL GEOGRAPHIC MAGAZINE

The following articles relate to this chapter:

- "Unsettling Discoveries at Jamestown: Suffering and Surviving in 17th Century Virginia," by Karen E. Lange, June 2002.
- "Pilgrimage Through Sierra Madre," by Paul Salopek, June 2000.

NATIONAL GEOGRAPHIC SOCIETY PRODUCTS AVAILABLE FROM GLENCOE

To order the following, call Glencoe at 1-800-334-7344:

- *PicturePack: The Age of Exploration (Transparencies)*
- *PictureShow: The Age of Exploration, Parts 1 & 2 (CD-ROMs)*

ADDITIONAL NATIONAL GEOGRAPHIC SOCIETY PRODUCTS

To order the following, call National Geographic at 1-800-368-2728:

- *National Geographic Atlas of World History (Book)*

Access *National Geographic*'s new dynamic MapMachine Web site and other geography resources at:
www.nationalgeographic.com
www.nationalgeographic.com/maps

THE HISTORY CHANNEL. A&E HOME VIDEO. Biography

The following videotape program is available from Glencoe:

- **Pocahontas: Her True Story**
  1-56501-555-X

To order, call Glencoe at 1-800-334-7344. To find classroom resources to accompany many of these, check:

A&E Television: www.aande.com
The History Channel: www.historychannel.com

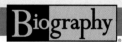

Introducing CHAPTER 31

OVERVIEW

Chapter 31 outlines European expansion into the Americas.

- **Section 1** discusses Portugal's empire in the Americas.
- **Section 2** describes Spanish expansion and the role of the Church.
- **Section 3** summarizes English settlement of the Americas.
- **Section 4** examines the Dutch colonies in the Americas.
- **Section 5** describes French settlements in the Americas.
- **Section 6** discusses the effects of colonization on Europe.

CHAPTER OBJECTIVES

After reading Chapter 31, students will be able to:

1. summarize why Europeans colonized the Americas.

2. discuss what European empires were established in the Americas.

3. explain why many colonial empires declined.

4. describe how the empires in the Americas influenced Europe.

EXAMINING ARTIFACTS

Explain that these artifacts are from Spanish settlements in North America. Ask: What aspects of European culture did Spanish settlers bring to the Americas? *(the idea of a university education, the practice of Christianity)* Tell students that in this chapter they will learn more about the changes that European expansion brought both to the Americas and to Europe.

PERFORMANCE ASSESSMENT ✓

Use the Performance Assessment activities on page 486B to help you evaluate students as they complete the chapter.

CHAPTER 31

Expansion Into the Americas

1500 A.D.–1700 A.D.

▼ Mural from the University of Mexico

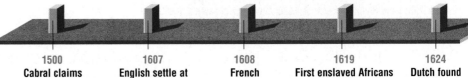

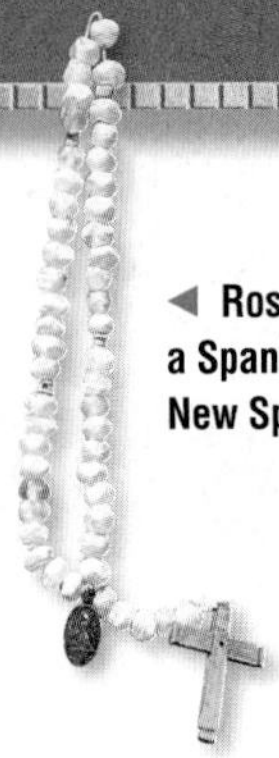

◀ Rosary beads from a Spanish mission in New Spain

1500	1607	1608	1619	1624
Cabral claims Brazil for Portugal	English settle at Jamestown	French found Quebec	First enslaved Africans brought to Jamestown	Dutch found New Amsterdam

TEACHING RESOURCES

TEACHER PLANNING AND SUPPORT

- Reproducible Lesson Plan 31-1, 31-2, 31-3, 31-4, 31-5, 31-6
- Teaching Strategies for the World History Classroom (Including Block Scheduling Pacing Guides)
- Presentation Plus! CD-ROM

REVIEW AND REINFORCEMENT

- Reading Essentials and Study Guide 31-1, 31-2, 31-3, 31-4, 31-5, 31-6
- Chapter 31 Vocabulary and Guided Reading Activity
- Vocabulary PuzzleMaker CD-ROM
- Teaching Transparency 31B
- Chapter 31 Reteaching Activity
- Chapter 31 Cooperative Learning Activity
- Chapter 31 Activity Book Activity
- Chapter 31 Chart and Graph Skill Activity
- Reading and Study Skills Foldables
- Interactive Tutor Self-Assessment CD-ROM
- Unit 10 MindJogger VideoQuiz

APPLICATION AND HANDS-ON ACTIVITIES

- Daily Questions in Social Studies
- World Crafts Activity Card 2
- Student Presentation Builder CD-ROM

Chapter Focus

Read to Discover

- Why Europeans colonized the Americas.
- What European empires were established in the Americas.
- Why many colonial empires declined.
- How empires in the Americas influenced Europe.

HISTORY Online

Chapter Overview

Visit the *Human Heritage* Web site at **humanheritage.glencoe.com** and click on ***Chapter 31—Chapter Overviews*** to preview this chapter.

Terms to Learn	People to Know	Places to Locate
colonize	Cabral	Brazil
viceroy	Sir Francis Drake	Peru
peninsulares	Sir Walter Raleigh	Roanoke Island
mestizos	John Smith	Jamestown
indentured servants	John Rolfe	Plymouth
	William Penn	New France

Why It's Important From the early 1500s to the 1700s, several western European countries set out to **colonize,** or build permanent settlements in, the Americas. Europeans wanted the riches of the Americas, which they thought would bring them power. They also wanted to spread Christianity.

Reading Check How did western Europeans **colonize** the Americas?

SECTION 1 Portugal

By 1512, the Portuguese had claimed all of Brazil. They had also established trading posts in Africa, India, Southeast Asia, and the Moluccas (muh luhk' uhz), or Spice Islands. They took most of the Asian coastal cities by force.

Portugal found it difficult to rule its new territories. One reason was that it did not have a large enough population to send settlers to all its territories. Also, most of Portugal's territories already had large populations. Then, too, the hot, wet climate of the trading posts was too uncomfortable for most Portuguese. As a result, Portugal had to depend on sea power and the cooperation of defeated leaders to protect its interests.

Brazil In 1500, the Portuguese explorer Pedro Alváres Cabral (pā' drō al vah' rez kah brahl') claimed Brazil for Portugal. Since no precious metals were found, Portugal paid little attention to the discovery. Then, other countries started to take *brazilwood,* or a red wood used to make dyes. When the Portuguese realized the value of the wood, they became more interested in Brazil.

GEOGRAPHY ACTIVITIES

- Chapter 31 Geography and Map Activity
- Building Geography Skills for Life
- Outline Map Resource Book

INTERDISCIPLINARY CONNECTIONS

- World Art & Architecture Transparency 33, *Quilled Buckskin Robe*
- World Music: A Cultural Legacy

ENRICHMENT AND EXTENSION

- World History Primary Source Document Library CD-ROM
- Chapter 31 Enrichment Activity
- Foods Around the World

ASSESSMENT AND EVALUATION

- Chapter 31 Performance Assessment Activity
- Chapter 31 Section Quizzes 31-1, 31-2, 31-3, 31-4, 31-5, 31-6
- Chapter 31 Test
- Chapter 31 ExamView® Pro Testmaker CD-ROM
- Chapter 31 Digests Audiocassettes Activities and Tests

SPANISH RESOURCES

- Chapter 31 Spanish Chapter Summary and Glossary
- Chapter 31 Spanish Digests Audiocassettes Activities and Tests

HISTORY Online

Chapter Overview introduces students to chapter content and key terms. Have them access ***Chapter 31 Overview*** at **humanheritage.glencoe.com**

FOCUS

Bellringer

Write the following quotation on the board. "Of gold is treasure made, and with it he who has it does as he wills in the world and it even sends souls to Paradise." Have students interpret this quote from Christopher Columbus.

Motivational Activity

Link students' interpretations with the establishment of empires in the Americas.

Reading Check Answer The Europeans set out to **colonize** the Americas by building permanent settlements.

GUIDE TO READING

Reading Strategy

Ask students to read "Why It's Important" and summarize the chapter's main theme. *(In colonizing the Americas, European nations hoped to increase their wealth and power and spread Christianity.)*

Vocabulary Precheck

Ask students to define each of the "Terms to Learn." L1 ELL

Use the Vocabulary PuzzleMaker CD-ROM for Chapter 31 to create a crossword puzzle. L1

Assign Chapter 31 Vocabulary and Guided Reading Activity.

Assign Reading Essentials and Study Guide 31-1.

TEACH

Guided Practice

L1 **History** Show students on a wall map of the world the city of Calicut, India, located in southwestern India. Tell them that Calicut was one of the world's five great harbors in the 1500s. The city reflected elements of Muslim and Asian culture because of its location at the junction of the Arabian-Indian sea trade. Ask students why they think Portugal wanted control of this seaport. *(The Portuguese wanted control of the spice trade.)*

Reading Check Answer
Captaincies were given to families who would establish towns, give out land, and raise armies.

Reading Check Answer
The ***bandeirantes*** were fortune hunters who expanded Portuguese land claims as they searched for precious stones and escaped enslaved people.

Glencoe Literature Library

The following novel from the **Glencoe Literature Library** may be used to enrich this chapter:

- *The Slave Dancer*, by Paula Fox. (Forced journey of Africans to the Americas.)

GEOGRAPHY AND HISTORY

Cabral wanted to sail around Africa but traveled too far west and accidentally landed in Brazil. The question of when Brazil was first discovered by Europeans is still argued by scholars.

In 1532, the Portuguese established their first permanent settlement in Brazil. The king of Portugal divided the area into 15 territorial strips called **captaincies** (kap' tuhn sēz). Each strip was given to a different Portuguese family who could establish towns, give out land, and raise armies. In return, they promised to colonize and protect their captaincies.

Reading Check How did the Portuguese use **captaincies** to colonize Brazil?

Portugal sent large numbers of settlers to Brazil. Portuguese sailors landed there and decided to stay. Criminals were sent to work off their sentences. Soldiers and officials came to protect royal interests. Ranchers arrived with herds of cattle. Missionaries came looking for converts to Christianity.

The Portuguese set up plantations in Brazil. Most plantations grew sugarcane, which was used to make sugar, molasses, and rum. About 2 million Native Americans were living in Brazil when Portugal claimed the land. The Portuguese settlers enslaved them to work the land. Most of the Native Americans, however, either ran away or died from diseases brought by the Europeans.

Before long, the Portuguese settlers began bringing over enslaved Africans. The number of Africans grew until, in some places, there were at least 20 enslaved Africans for each Portuguese settler. The Africans brought their religions with them. They also brought African music and dance to Brazil. They told folktales about their African history and carved wooden figures for churches. They also added many new words to the Portuguese language.

By the end of the 1600s, there was less demand for sugar. ***Bandeirantes*** (ban duh ran' tās), or fortune-hunters, looking for precious stones and escaped enslaved people began to appear. Bandeirantes were the frontiersmen of Brazil. Traveling in bands of fifty to several thousand men, they followed the rivers into the jungle. They established Portugal's claim to the far western and southern areas of Brazil.

Reading Check Who were the ***bandeirantes,*** and how did they increase Portuguese land claims?

Early Map of Brazil

Royal interest in Brazil grew when gold was discovered in the 1690s. The king sent government clerks to check the mineral resources and make sure the monarchy received one fifth of each miner's gold. Gold brought still more people to Brazil and more wealth to Portugal. The growing of coffee, which was introduced in the early 1700s, made Portugal richer.

In many ways, Brazil was a tolerant society. It welcomed people of different countries and religions. Many men of part-African ancestry rose to high positions in the Church and the government. Women, however, were allowed little freedom or power, and hardly anyone knew how to read and write.

The Loss of Empire By the middle of the 1500s, Portugal began losing its empire. The colonial government was not well

---

MULTICULTURAL PERSPECTIVES

Jesuit missionaries to Brazil set up mission villages in remote areas along the Amazon River. There, thousands of Native Americans were baptized, gathered into fortified settlements, and taught farming. These missions provided a place of safety for the Native Americans against raiders who enslaved people. They also became outposts of Portuguese political and economic influence. At the same time, however, they disrupted the hunting and gathering life of the Native Americans.

organized and the economy was in poor shape. Another reason was that the conquered peoples disliked the Portuguese for forcing Christianity on them. By the time the Portuguese king died in 1580, Portugal was very weak. The king left no heirs, and the throne was claimed by Philip II of Spain. Portugal was ruled by Spain until 1640. Then, Portugal regained its independence. During that time, the English and the Dutch took over most of the Portuguese trading centers, including those in Southeast Asia.

Section 1 Assessment

1. **Define:** colonize, captaincies, *bandeirantes.*
2. What kept Portugal from colonizing settlements?
3. What happened to the Native Americans who lived in Brazil when the Portuguese claimed the land?

Critical Thinking

4. **Making Inferences** How do you think the Native Americans felt about the Portuguese settlement of Brazil?

Graphic Organizer Activity

5. Draw this diagram, and use it to show the causes of the decline of the Portuguese empire.

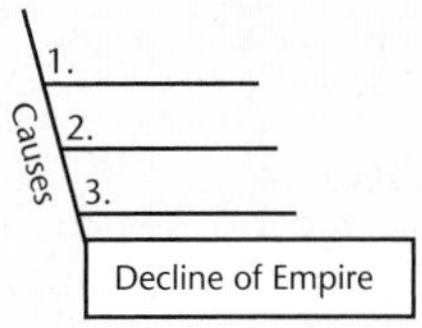

BRAZILIAN PLANTATION Early Portuguese settlers established plantations in Brazil. At first, Native American populations were enslaved to provide the needed labor. Most of the Native Americans, however, proved too rebellious or too sickly to perform the hard work required. Enslaved Africans were then brought to work on the plantations. **For what was the sugarcane grown on plantations used?**

Then & Now

Carnival The Brazilian capital of Rio de Janeiro is known for its annual Carnival. Celebrated just before the beginning of Lent, the Christian holy season that comes before Easter, Carnival runs for four days.

DID YOU KNOW

At this time, Brazil had only a few elementary schools. It lacked both a university and a printing press.

LINKING PAST TO PRESENT

The culture of modern Brazil, like its people, is a blend of Portuguese, African, and Native American influences. Although major elements—the Portuguese language, the Roman Catholic religion, and many customs—came from Portugal, a unique Brazilian blend has developed since colonial times. The Native American language Tupi is still spoken in the northern interior of Brazil. The words *cashew* and *tapioca* are Tupi words. African influences are strongest on the coast north of Rio de Janeiro. Foods and dances such as the samba and bossa nova have African influences.

CAPTION ANSWER

to make sugar, molasses, and rum

Section 1 Assessment Answers

1. colonize, to build permanent settlements (p. 487); captaincies, territorial strips into which the Portuguese divided Brazil (p. 488); *bandeirantes,* fortune-hunters (p. 488)
2. Portugal did not have a large enough population to send settlers to all its territories; most territories already had large populations; and the Portuguese were not accustomed to the hot, wet climate of the new colonies.
3. They were enslaved by the Portuguese.
4. Answers will vary but might include the idea that they were angry and overwhelmed.
5. sample causes: government not well organized, economy in poor shape, resentment of Portuguese among conquered peoples in Southeast Asia, no direct heirs to the throne

Assign the Chapter 31 **Section 1 Quiz** in the TCR. Testmaker available.

Use the **Interactive Tutor Self-Assessment CD-ROM** to review Section 1.

L1 Geography: The World in Spatial Terms Have students locate the Spanish colonies on the map "European Colonies in the Americas" on page 498. Ask them why they think the Spanish colonies were difficult to govern.

L2 Economics Discuss the use of enslaved people in the colonies by explaining how enslaved Africans contributed to colonial economic prosperity. Ask students why enslaved people were used on sugarcane and coffee plantations. *(Growing these crops required a great deal of manual labor.)* Ask why large numbers of Africans were not imported to Europe. *(Europe did not have large plantations that required a great deal of manual labor.)*

Reading Check Answer The **viceroyalties** were districts in New Spain. The **viceroy** ruled each viceroyalty as a representative of the king of Spain.

Glencoe Literature Library

The following novel from the **Glencoe Literature Library** may be used to enrich this chapter:

- *I, Juan de Pareja,* by Elizabeth Treviño. (Enslaved artist forced by Spanish law to hide his talent.)

Reading Check Answer The *peninsulares* were Spaniards born in Spain, while the *mestizos* were of mixed European and Native American ancestry.

Use the **Vocabulary PuzzleMaker CD-ROM** to create crossword and word search puzzles.

Colonial Vase

SECTION 2 Spain

By 1535, Spain had established the largest colonial empire in the Americas. Spain's colonies reached from southern North America through Central America and the West Indies to South America. Spain also had trade interests in the Philippines.

Unlike Portugal, Spain had a fairly large population. This allowed it to send thousands of people to its colonies in the Americas. Spain also had a strong, centralized colonial government.

Mexico and Peru

In the early 1500s, Spain conquered the Native American empires of Mexico and Peru. They set the example for other Spanish colonies. They were governed by the Council of the Indies, which met at the Spanish court. This council made laws, acted as a court of final appeal, and chose officials to send to the Americas. It even took charge of religious matters.

The colonies were divided into two **viceroyalties** (vīs' roi uhl tēz), or districts—New Spain, or Mexico, and New Castile, or Peru. Each viceroyalty was ruled by a **viceroy** (vīs' roi), or person who represented the king.

Reading Check What were the **viceroyalties?** What was the role of the **viceroy?**

The colonists in the viceroyalties sent large amounts of gold and silver back to Spain. They also ran plantations that produced cocoa, coffee, tobacco, tea, and sugar. They forced Native Americans to do all of the heavy work in mines and on plantations. Most of the Native Americans were badly treated. Many died of overwork, starvation, or such diseases as measles and smallpox.

After a time, the Spanish, like the Portuguese, brought enslaved Africans to the Americas. Most of these enslaved people worked on sugar plantations located on the islands of the Caribbean. There were still far more Portuguese-owned enslaved people in Brazil, however, than Spanish-owned enslaved people in the Caribbean.

By the middle 1500s, colonists in the Americas were divided into clear-cut social groups. At the top were ***peninsulares*** (puh nin sū la' rās), or Spaniards born in Spain. Then came Creoles (krē' ōlz), or those of Spanish descent born in the Americas. Next were ***mestizos*** (me stē' zōz), or people of mixed European and Native American ancestry. They were followed by Native Americans. At the lowest level were blacks. Each group held certain jobs. Peninsulares served as viceroys or important church leaders. Mestizos were mostly artisans and merchants.

Reading Check How did the *peninsulares* and *mestizos* differ from each other?

The way in which colonial cities developed also reflected this social structure. Most cities centered on a square. On one side of the square was the cathedral. On the other three sides stood the government headquarters and the houses of peninsulares. Farther out were the houses of Creoles and mestizos.

COOPERATIVE LEARNING

Organize the class into small groups and assign each group an oral report on the advantages and disadvantages of the introduction of the profit motive during the age of exploration. Each student is responsible for a specific task or area of research. Have students address these questions: What effect did the profit motive have on European countries? What effect did the profit motive have on the inhabitants of the Americas and Africa? One or more students in each group should compile the research and prepare the report, gather necessary supplies and visuals, and another student should present the report to the class.

Assign the Chapter 31 *Cooperative Learning Activity* in the TCR.

The Roman Catholic Church played a large role in Spanish colonization. It controlled most of the best land in the Spanish colonies. Although the Church itself did not pay taxes, it charged the people who rented or farmed its land a 10 percent income tax.

The Church worked to improve conditions in the colonies. Leaders, such as Bartholomé de Las Casas (bar tol uh mā' dā lahs kah' sahs), tried to improve life for the Native Americans. The Church built schools, hospitals, and *asylums* (uh sī' luhms), or places for the mentally ill, and staffed them mostly with nuns. It established the first two universities in the Americas. One was the University of Mexico. The other was San Marcos (mar' kuhs) University at Lima.

The Decline of an Empire Spain received a great deal of wealth from the colonies, but it did not hold on to that wealth. The Spanish Inquisition had driven out most of the Jews and Muslims who had been the backbone of Spanish industry. As a result, much of the gold and silver sent to Spain ended up going to northern Europe to pay for goods made there.

Fun Facts . . . .

Laziness In Inca times, anyone entering the city of Cuzco was greeted by the phrase *Ama Sua, Ama Quella, Ama Lulla*—Don't Lie, Don't Steal, Don't Be Lazy. To the Incas, laziness was such a serious offense that it was punishable by death.

Linking Across Time

Music The enslaved Africans brought to the Americas contributed to the development of the region's culture. They crafted drums (below) and other instruments similar to those in their homeland and shaped our musical heritage. Today the rhythms of Africa can be heard in the music of the steel drummers in the Caribbean (right) and in the sounds of reggae, calypso, salsa, rap, and other types of music. **What cultural contributions did Spanish settlers make?**

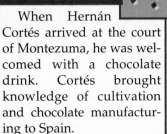

LINKING PAST TO PRESENT

Although Peru was appealing to the Spanish in the 1500s because of its gold reserves, its real wealth was hidden. Today Peru's most valuable export is oil.

DID YOU KNOW ??

When Hernán Cortés arrived at the court of Montezuma, he was welcomed with a chocolate drink. Cortés brought knowledge of cultivation and chocolate manufacturing to Spain.

Linking Across Time

sample contributions: built cities and cathedrals; established universities; started church-run schools, hospitals, and asylums

NATIONAL GEOGRAPHIC

Use these materials to enrich student understanding of the age of exploration.

NGS PICTURESHOW CD-ROM
Age of Exploration, Parts 1 and 2

NGS PICTUREPACK TRANSPARENCY SET
Age of Exploration

EXTENDING THE CONTENT

Even the huge amounts of silver and gold from Mexico and Peru paid only about a quarter of the war costs that Philip II and his successors accrued. Their leaders saw themselves as the defenders of the Roman Catholic Church and went to war against Muslims, Turks, Huguenots, Calvinists, and Protestants. Little revenue from trade or industry could be had in the country because of the lack of middle class and the expulsion of non-Catholics. The Spanish people were heavily taxed, and still the government ran out of money. The high taxes caused rebellions.

The Spanish also had trouble getting gold and silver from their colonies to Spain. Ships loaded with the precious metals were robbed at sea by English, French, and Dutch pirates. English sea dogs attacked Spanish treasure ships with the blessing of their queen, Elizabeth I. One of the most successful sea dogs was Sir Francis Drake. When the Spanish Armada was defeated by the English in 1588, Spain lost its power in the Atlantic. This opened the Americas to colonization by England, the Netherlands, and France.

Section 2 Assessment

1. **Define:** viceroyalties, viceroy, *peninsulares, mestizos.*
2. What role did the Roman Catholic Church play in the Spanish colonies?
3. Why did the Spanish have trouble transporting gold and silver from the Americas to Spain?

Critical Thinking

4. **Predicting Consequences** What do you think might have happened if Spain had used the gold and silver to develop industries in the Americas?

Graphic Organizer Activity

5. Draw this diagram, and use it to show the structure of Spanish society from the most powerful to the least powerful groups.

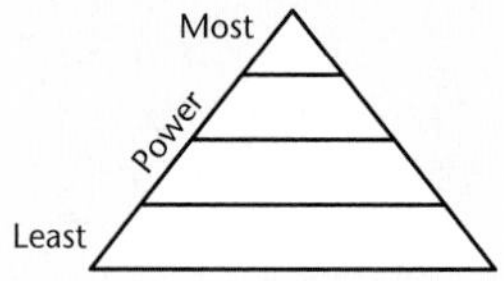

SECTION 3 England

Like Portugal and Spain, England looked to the Americas for wealth. English nobles and merchants saw it as a place to get raw materials as well as gold and silver. With enough gold, silver, and raw materials, the English could establish a favorable **balance of trade.** This meant England would be able to sell more products to other countries than it would have to buy from them. The English would no longer have to depend on other countries for their needs.

Reading Check How did the English try to establish a favorable **balance of trade?**

The English had other reasons for wanting colonies in the Americas. England had such a large population that jobs were becoming hard to find. New colonies meant more jobs. Then, too, the Anglican (ang′ gluh kuhn) Church had become England's official church and the English people were expected to follow Anglican beliefs. Because of this, Catholics and groups of Protestants called Separatists (sep′ uhr uh tists) were looking for a place where they could have religious freedom. They believed that in the Americas they would be able to worship freely.

MAKING CONNECTIONS

➤➤ **The Arts** Spaniards consider the 1500s and early 1600s a "Golden Century" in their culture. Spanish writers included Saavedra de Cervantes, Lope de Vega, and Calderón. In art and architecture, the early 1600s was the beginning of the baroque period, with artists such as El Greco and Diego Velázquez.

Use the **Interactive Tutor Self-Assessment CD-ROM** to review Section 2.

DID YOU KNOW ??

At the time England sent Sir Walter Raleigh to establish a colony in the Americas, well-established Native American civilizations existed across the continent. One of the oldest of these was the settlement of Anasazi, established in the Arizona-New Mexico area about four thousand years earlier.

Reading Check Answer The English hoped the raw materials and gold and silver supplied by colonies would allow them to establish a favorable **balance of trade** in which they sold more goods than they bought.

Use the **Vocabulary PuzzleMaker CD-ROM** to create crossword and word search puzzles.

Section 2 Assessment Answers

1. viceroyalties, districts (p. 490); viceroy, king's representative (p. 490); *peninsulares,* Spaniards born in Spain (p. 490); *mestizos,* people of mixed European and Native American ancestry (p. 490)
2. It controlled the best land, taxed the people who rented or farmed its land, and built schools, hospitals, and asylums.
3. Ships loaded with the precious metals were robbed at sea by English, French, and Dutch pirates.
4. Answers will vary but might include that Spain might have become more wealthy and powerful.
5. Groups from most powerful to least powerful include: *peninsulares,* Creoles, *mestizos,* Native Americans, blacks.

Assign the Chapter 31 **Section 2 Quiz** in the TCR. Testmaker available.

In 1585, a group of colonists financed by Sir Walter Raleigh (rahl′ ē) sailed for North America. There, they founded a colony on Roanoke (rō′ uh nōk) Island off the coast of North Carolina. After six years, however, the colonists disappeared. No one knows for certain what happened to them. For this reason, Roanoke Island became known as the "Lost Colony."

The English did not try again to found colonies in the Americas for more than 20 years. However, in 1600, English merchants formed the East India Company to trade with the East Indies. The company set up trading posts in India, Malaya (muh lā′ uh), and some islands in both the East and West Indies.

Jamestown In 1607, a group of English nobles and merchants formed the Virginia Company of London. The following year the company sent about 100 settlers to the Americas to search for gold and silver. They founded the first permanent English settlement in America. It was located near the mouth of Chesapeake (ches′ uh pēk) Bay. The settlers named it Jamestown after their king, James I.

The area in which the colony was founded had long been home to Native Americans. By the time Christopher Columbus arrived in the Americas, there were more than 1 million Native Americans scattered across the North American continent. They were divided into some 500 different groups.

Each group of Native Americans had its own language, religion, and way of life. Some, like the Pima (pē′ muh), Papago (pap′ uh gō), Creeks, and Cherokee (cher′ uh kē), were farmers. Others, like the Comanche (kuh man′ chē), Blackfoot, Sioux (sū), Apache (uh pach′ ē), and Navaho (nav′ uh hō), were hunters and warriors who traveled in bands.

The Native Americans who lived in the area near Jamestown were the Powhatan (pau uh tan′). Their chief, whom the settlers called Powhatan, controlled 128 Native American villages.

Life in Jamestown was hard. The land was swampy and filled with mosquitoes that carried disease. Winters were colder in Jamestown than in England. The colonists burned parts of their houses as fuel. Many became sick and died.

Captain John Smith kept the settlement from total failure. He made it clear that those who did not work would not eat. He also convinced the Powhatan to supply the colonists with corn and beans. When Smith returned to England in 1609, however, many of the colonists starved to death. Those still alive a year later were ready to go back to England. When an English fleet arrived with supplies, the colonists decided to stay.

The settlers worked the land, but they did not own it. It belonged to the Virginia Company. Then, in 1618, the company began granting land to individuals. All colonists who paid their own way to America were given 50 acres, or about 20 hectares, of

HISTORY Online

Student Web Activity

Visit the *Human Heritage* Web site at **humanheritage.glencoe.com** and click on ***Chapter 31—Student Web Activities*** to find out more about Jamestown.

John Smith

HISTORY Online

Student Web Activity objectives and answers can be found at the ***Chapter 31 Web Activity Lesson Plan*** at **humanheritage.glencoe.com**

L1 **Geography: The World in Spatial Terms** Ask students to locate Jamestown on the map of "European Colonies in the Americas" on page 498. Ask them to describe its location in reference to later British colonies. ELL

DID YOU KNOW

On August 18, 1587, Virginia Dare was born on Roanoke Island. She was the granddaughter of the governor of the island and the first child born in America of English parents.

Biography

The following videotape program is available from Glencoe to enrich Chapter 31:

- **Pocahontas: Her True Story**

To find classroom resources to accompany this video, check the following home page:

A&E Television:
www.aande.com

MEETING SPECIAL NEEDS

Help students that have difficulty accessing chapter information use a kind of rapid reading or scanning to locate specific information in the text. Show students how to scan by sliding a finger down the middle of the column rapidly. Demonstrate finding the date 1609 on page 493. Read the event that occurred on that date. Then have students use this method to find the following dates and the events in Section 3: 1585, 1600, 1606, 1612, 1618, 1619, 1630, 1634, 1681, 1691, 1733. Create a time line of events on the board as students respond.

Refer to ***Inclusion for the Middle School Social Studies Classroom: Strategies and Activities.***

L2 **Geography: Environment and Society** Provide students with an outline map of North America. Help them make a map of the regions where each of the Native American culture groups listed in the chart on page 494 lived in North America. Then have them compare their maps of the Native American culture groups with a climate map of North America. Discuss how the climate where each group lived affected their way of life. ELL

MAKING CONNECTIONS

➤➤ **Culture** In 1619, 20 enslaved African Americans were brought to Jamestown colony, the first of many such shipments. This important event changed the culture and social structure of the Americas from then on.

L3 **Science** John White, a Roanoke colonist and artist, painted pictures of the animals and vegetation that he encountered in the Americas. Ask students to research and write a report explaining how these paintings affected 16th-century science. Students might share examples of White's paintings with the class. ELL

NATIVE AMERICANS

REGION	WAY OF LIFE
Arctic	fished and hunted whales, seals, walruses, and caribou; lived in wood and stone houses or igloos in winter and animal skin tents in summer
Subarctic	hunted and gathered food; built wood-frame houses; traveled by snowshoes, canoe, and toboggan
Northwest Coast	fished and hunted; built cedar wood houses and sea-going canoes; carved totem poles to honor ancestors; held potlatches, or ceremonial feasts
Plateau	hunted bison, fished, and gathered food; lived in multifamily lodges; bred the Appaloosa horse
Great Basin	hunted and gathered food; traveled over territory; wove reed baskets decorated with beads, feathers, and shells
California	hunted, fished, and gathered food; settled in communities; used acorns to make bread
Southwest	farmed corn, beans, and squash; built pueblos of stone and adobe; wove straw and reed baskets and cotton cloth
Great Plains	farmed and hunted; lived in log houses or cone-shaped tepees; communicated with other tribes by hand signals
Eastern Woodlands	fished and hunted; lived in longhouses and birch lodges; women owned property, chose chief, and passed on family name
Southeast	farmed and hunted; built towns with open squares; women owned houses and land; counted descent through mothers

EXTENDING THE CONTENT

Many historians think that American settlers were influenced in their development of a new government by the confederations they observed among the Native Americans on the east coast. According to legend, a holy man in the 1500s tried to end the constant warfare among the related Iroquois-speaking peoples of the Five Nations. A Mohawk leader, Hiawatha, brought the tribes together in a political and military alliance that came to be known as the Iroquois League. In the confederation, each tribe continued to manage its internal affairs, but they cooperated against outside enemies. The Iroquois League served as a model for the Albany Plan of Union and the Articles of Confederation.

Chapter Focus

Read to Discover

- How revolution in England began during the 1600s.
- What British policies led to the American Revolution of the late 1700s.
- How the French Revolution came about in the late 1700s and what its results were.

HISTORY Online

Chapter Overview
Visit the *Human Heritage* Web site at **humanheritage.glencoe.com** and click on ***Chapter 32—Chapter Overviews*** to preview this chapter.

Terms to Learn	People to Know	Places to Locate
revolution	James I	Concord
mercantilism	Charles I	Lexington
monopoly	Oliver Cromwell	Yorktown
direct tax	Charles II	Bastille
boycott	John Locke	
estates	Voltaire	

Why It's Important By the 1700s, people in the western world had new ideas about government. They were less willing to be ruled without having a voice in politics. They also wanted equal justice under the law. They did not believe that monarchs or the Church had the right to tell them what to do. Thinkers and writers began spreading ideas about freedom and the right of people to change the government to meet their needs. The 1700s came to be known in Europe and the Americas as the Age of Enlightenment, or a time of increased knowledge.

SECTION 1 Revolution in England

In England, there was a struggle for power between the king and Parliament. After a civil war and a **revolution,** or an attempt to overthrow or change the government, Parliament won. From that point on, the monarch ruled in the name of the people.

Reading Check What is the goal of a political **revolution?**

Conflict with Parliament

In 1603, the last Tudor monarch, Queen Elizabeth I, died. Since she had never married, the Crown, or royal power, passed to a distant relative. This was James VI of Scotland, a member of the Stuart family. He became James I of England.

The Tudors had enjoyed great power. They had been careful, however, to get Parliament's opinion on their actions. James I, on the other hand, believed in rule by divine right. When Parliament

GEOGRAPHY ACTIVITIES
- Chapter 32 Geography and Map Activity
- Building Geography Skills for Life
- Outline Map Resource Book

INTERDISCIPLINARY CONNECTIONS
- Unit 10 World Literature Reading 1
- World Music: A Cultural Legacy

ENRICHMENT AND EXTENSION
- World History Primary Source Document Library CD-ROM
- Chapter 32 Enrichment Activity
- Foods Around the World

ASSESSMENT AND EVALUATION
- Chapter 32 Performance Assessment Activity
- Chapter 32 Section Quizzes 32-1, 32-2, 32-3
- Chapter 32 Test
- Chapter 32 ExamView® Pro Testmaker CD-ROM
- Chapter 32 Digests Audiocassettes Activities and Tests

SPANISH RESOURCES
- Chapter 32 Spanish Chapter Summary and Glossary
- Chapter 32 Spanish Digests Audiocassettes Activities and Tests

HISTORY Online

Chapter Overview introduces students to chapter content and key terms. Have them access ***Chapter 32 Overview*** at **humanheritage.glencoe.com**

FOCUS

Bellringer

Write this question on the board: Do you think that the destruction of another person's property can ever be justified? If yes, under what circumstances?

Motivational Activity

Tell students that in this chapter they will learn about incidents such as the Boston Tea Party in which people destroyed property to protest British policies. Ask students if they feel this justifies the protestors' actions.

Reading Check Answer
A political **revolution** seeks to overthrow or change a government.

GUIDE TO READING

Reading Strategy

Ask students to read "Why It's Important" and summarize the chapter's main theme. *(During the Age of Enlightenment, people were less willing to be ruled without a voice in politics and began to demand that governments change to meet their needs.)*

Vocabulary Precheck

Ask students to define each of the "Terms to Learn." L1 ELL

Use the Vocabulary PuzzleMaker CD-ROM for Chapter 32 to create a crossword puzzle. L1

Assign Chapter 32 Vocabulary and Guided Reading Activity.

Assign Reading Essentials and Study Guide 32-1.

TEACH

Guided Practice

L1 **Civics** Point out that the English civil war was the outcome of the deep conflict between the king and Parliament. Ask students to identify the source of that conflict. *(the king's belief in the divine rights of kings and Parliament's desire to have a voice in government)* ELL

L2 **Critical Thinking** Ask students to create a list of Parliament's grievances against the king. Putting themselves in the place of members of Parliament, have students rank the grievances from most to least important.

DID YOU KNOW ??

The mother of James I was Mary Queen of Scots, who had been put to death by Elizabeth I.

MAP STUDY Answer

from the southern and eastern part of England; from the northern and western part of England

objected to some of his actions, he dismissed it and ruled without a legislature for ten years.

Religious differences also caused trouble between the king and Parliament. James I wanted to force the Anglican Church on the people. Many members of Parliament, however, were Puritans. They wanted to be able to worship as they pleased. They believed in hard work and plain living and did not like the Crown's free-spending ways. They wanted a say in how the government raised and spent taxes. With the help of other groups, they worked against what they felt was the king's unjust power.

Although James I did not agree with many of his subjects about religion, it was his idea to have a new translation of the Bible. He appointed a committee of church officials who put together the King James version. Its style has greatly influenced English speech and literature. Many English-speaking Protestant churches today still use the King James version.

When James I died in 1625, his son became King Charles I. He held the same beliefs about the monarchy as his father.

The English Civil Wars

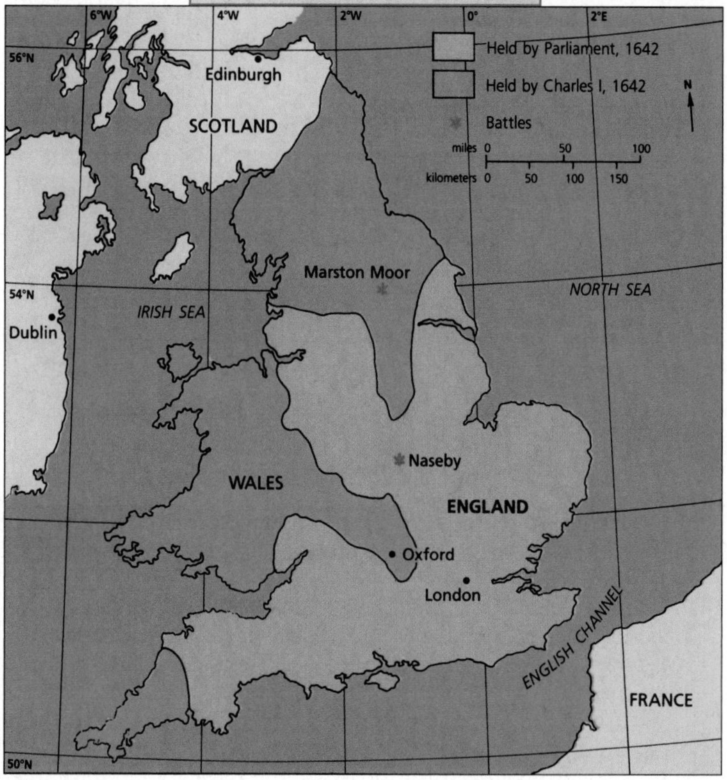

MAP STUDY

PLACES AND REGIONS The English civil war was both a religious and a political war. **From what part of England did Parliament draw its support? From what part did Charles I draw his support?**

MULTICULTURAL PERSPECTIVES

Many supporters of the Parliamentary cause were Puritans. Like other Protestants, Puritans believed that the Bible was the only source of religious authority. The Puritans were different from other Protestants, such as those belonging to the Church of England, in that Puritans were extremists in their religious discipline and the militancy of their beliefs. They wanted to "purify" the Church of England, which they felt retained too many vestiges of the Roman Catholic Church, and to purify the rest of society as well. Puritans considered themselves the spiritual elite, separate from the wickedness of the world.

In 1628, Charles I was forced to call a meeting of Parliament to approve new taxes to pay for wars with France and Spain. Parliament saw a chance to limit the Crown's power and gain more for itself. It drew up the Petition of Right. This said that the king could not declare **martial** (mar' shuhl) **law,** or rule by the army instead of by law. It also said that the Crown could not pass tax laws without Parliament's consent. In addition, people could not be put in prison just because the king wanted them out of the way. At first, Charles I agreed to the petition. Then, in 1629, he broke his word and dismissed Parliament.

In 1640, however, Charles I needed money to build a larger army to fight the Scots. He had tried to force the Anglican Church on the Presbyterian Scots, and they had revolted, taking over part of northern England. So, he called a meeting of Parliament.

Parliament again saw a chance to limit Charles's power. It passed a law abolishing taxes collected by the Crown without Parliament's consent. It also passed a law to set up regular meetings of Parliament and to do away with the Star Chamber. This was a royal court that tried people without a jury.

Reading Check What is **martial law?**

Civil War Once again, Charles I accepted the laws Parliament passed and then disregarded them. In 1642, civil war broke out between the Crown and Parliament.

Those who backed the Crown were called Cavaliers (kav uh lirz'). They wore their hair shoulder length, often in curls. They were mostly rich Roman Catholics and Anglicans. Those who backed Parliament were called Roundheads because they wore their hair short. They were mostly middle- and lower-class Puritans and other Calvinists.

Oliver Cromwell (krahm' wel), a Puritan leader who backed Parliament, formed a New Model Army. It drilled hard and followed strict rules against drinking, swearing, and robbing. It chose its officers because they were good fighters and leaders, not because they were of high birth. In 1646, the New Model Army defeated the king's forces and ended the war.

Most English leaders still believed that monarchy was the best form of government. They did not, however, trust Charles I and were afraid to allow him to return to the throne. Cromwell and his supporters put Charles I on trial for treason. The court found him guilty, and he was beheaded in 1649.

Oliver Cromwell After the king's death, Cromwell took over the rule of England, now called the Commonwealth. The Commonwealth was overwhelmed with troubles from the start. The Irish and the Scots both looked to Charles I's son as the true ruler of England. Cromwell had to put down their rebellion. He also had trouble balancing the English who felt enough changes had been made with those who wanted more. He finally did away

Then & Now

Religion Persecution of the Puritans under Charles I led to the Great Migration—the exodus of thousands of Puritans to America between 1630 to 1640. The Puritans founded the Massachusetts Bay Colony and later became known as the Congregationalist Church.

Reading Check Answer **Martial law** is rule by the army instead of by law.

L3 **History** Have students draw a political cartoon about the English civil war. For example, students might draw a cartoon that lampoons King Charles. They may also choose to draw a cartoon of Cromwell that expresses the ideas of the Parliamentarians. ELL

DID YOU KNOW

The region that became the state of Maryland was named for Queen Henrietta Maria, the Catholic French wife of Charles I.

MAKING CONNECTIONS

>> **History** Cromwell's New Model Army also became known for its religious devotion. Soldiers listened to sermons during their free time and often marched into battles singing psalms.

COOPERATIVE LEARNING

Organize students into three groups to stage the trial of King Charles. Explain that one group is to prosecute the king and one group is to defend the king. The third group is to act as witnesses for the prosecution and the defense. Make sure each student has a task to perform. Students should choose one student to role-play Charles and one to role-play Cromwell. Assign other students to research arguments for the prosecution and arguments used by the defense, and prepare dialogue for the role play. Then stage the trial.

CAPTION ANSWER

The Irish and the Scots were in rebellion, and groups of English did not agree on the charges that had been made.

LINKING PAST TO PRESENT

One of the radical revolutionary factions of English society was the Levellers, who believed that every citizen had the right to vote. Although Cromwell considered this a dangerous idea and destroyed a Leveller-inspired mutiny, the ideas of the Levellers have finally been fulfilled in today's American democracy.

MAKING CONNECTIONS

➤➤ **History** Richard Cromwell did not have the support of the army, and he resigned after ruling only nine months.

OLIVER CROMWELL AND KING CHARLES I Oliver Cromwell shown in this painting (left) organized the New Model Army that defeated the army of King Charles I shown in the painting (right) in 1646. This ended the four-year civil war between the Crown and Parliament. After Charles was beheaded, Cromwell took over the rule of England, which was then called the Commonwealth. **What problems did Cromwell face as he came to power?**

with Parliament and governed as a military dictator for the Puritan minority.

Many Puritans were very strict. They disapproved of dancing, theater-going, sports, and other popular amusements. They believed people should spend their free time praying and reading the Bible. Despite this, Puritan rule was not completely gloomy. Cromwell himself was fond of music and horses, and allowed women to act on stage for the first time. After Cromwell died, his son Richard took over. By 1660, however, Parliament decided that England again needed a monarch.

The Return of the Stuarts Parliament's choice was Charles I's son, who became Charles II. Charles II had spent most of the previous 15 years in France. He brought French dances, food, and clothing styles with him to London. Soon, the English court was a center of gaiety and fashion. Men copied the fashions of Paris and wore silks and velvets and huge wigs. The wealthy ate large meals. One meal might include rabbit and chicken stew, a leg of mutton, a side of lamb, roasted pigeons, lobsters, tarts, anchovies, and wine. The English nobility was ready for this kind of living, and Charles II became very popular.

SPOTLIGHT ON: CHARLES II

Under the rule of Charles II, the Restoration period (1660–1685) was a brilliant time for literature, drama, music, architecture, and science. In 1662, Charles chartered the Royal Society to encourage investigations in science. The king had his own laboratory where he performed experiments in chemistry. Charles also established the Royal Observatory at Greenwich. He hoped that discoveries in astronomy would produce better navigational instruments.

In September 1666, a great fire destroyed two-thirds of London's buildings. Charles II put Sir Christopher Wren, an architect, in charge of rebuilding the city. Wren designed St. Paul's Cathedral and 52 other churches. He also had most new houses and shops built of brick and stone instead of wood.

As king, Charles II tried to work with Parliament and not anger it. He refused, however, to consult with it about **foreign policy,** or relations with other countries. Parliament was worried by his friendship with the Roman Catholic king of France.

Reading Check Why did Parliament worry about the **foreign policy** of Charles II?

The Glorious Revolution

In 1685, Charles II died and his brother James became king. Openly Roman Catholic, James II named many Roman Catholics to high posts in the army and the government. This went against a law passed by Parliament under Charles II. James II also tried to have the Act of Habeas Corpus (hā' bē uhs kōr' puhs) **repealed,** or abolished. That act had also been passed under Charles II. It stated that a person could not be put in jail unless charged with a specific crime.

Reading Check What would have happened if James II had **repealed** the Act of Habeas Corpus?

The leaders of Parliament did not like James II. They did not move against him, however, until 1688 when his second wife, who was Roman Catholic, had a son. Fearing the ultimate establishment of Roman Catholic rule, they offered the throne to Mary, James's Protestant daughter by his first wife. Mary's husband William landed in England in 1688 with a large army, and James II fled to France. William and Mary were then named joint rulers. Because the change in monarchs took place without a shot being fired, it came to be called the "Glorious Revolution."

After becoming the new rulers of England in 1689, William and Mary accepted Parliament's Declaration of Rights. This made Parliament stronger and protected the rights of the English people. The declaration stated that the Crown could not tax people or keep an army in peacetime without Parliament's consent. Parliament had the right to debate openly, meet often, and be freely elected. People had the right to a fair and speedy trial by a jury of their peers. People could also petition the Crown without fear of being punished.

Painting of Queen Mary II

The Writings of John Locke

Many of the ideas behind the Glorious Revolution were explained in a book called *Two Treatises of Government.* It was written in 1690 by an English philosopher named John Locke. He believed that people are born with certain natural rights. Among them are the right to life, liberty, and property. Locke believed that the purpose of government is to protect these rights. If it fails to do so, then the people can revolt and set up a new government. Locke thought the best kind of government was a representative one. His writings were widely read, and his ideas became a basis for the American Revolution and, later, the French Revolution.

L2 **Architecture** Ask students to present a report on the life and works of Sir Christopher Wren, architect of Charles II. The report should include illustrations of some of the buildings Wren designed.

Reading Check Answer Parliament worried about the **foreign policy** of Charles II because of his friendship with the Roman Catholic king of France.

Reading Check Answer If James II had **repealed** the Act of Habeas Corpus, he could have put people in jail without charging them with a specific crime.

MAKING CONNECTIONS

>> **Daily Life** In 1665, London was hit by the plague. It was carried by rats, who flourished in the filthy streets and old buildings. As many as 7,000 persons died in one week. They had to be buried in great pits because the churchyards were full. Business came to a standstill, and the royal court fled to the countryside.

MEETING SPECIAL NEEDS

Have tactile/kinesthetic or gifted learners produce a "documentary" about the London fire of 1666. Make sure each student is assigned a specific task. Assign, or have students choose, a "producer" to coordinate the class effort. Some teams should be responsible for researching, writing, and presenting "news desk" reports about the fire. Other teams should prepare on-the-scene skits about the fire, such as interviews with local residents, fire fighters, or government officials. If possible, have students videotape their documentaries. Have students present their documentaries to the class.

Refer to ***Inclusion for the Middle School Social Studies Classroom: Strategies and Activities*** for additional resources.

L2 **Research** Have students research and report on the beliefs of one of the political thinkers, philosophers, or writers of the revolutionary time period, such as John Locke *(Two Treatises of Government)*, Montesquieu *(The Spirit of Laws)*, Thomas Paine *(Common Sense* and *The Rights of Man)*, or Jean-Jacques Rousseau *(Social Contract)*. Have students do a dramatic reading of the writings of their chosen philosopher.

Use the **Interactive Tutor Self-Assessment CD-ROM** to review Section 1.

Reading Check Answer

Under the system of **mercantilism,** colonies served as a source of raw materials and as a market for finished products.

Reading Check Answer

A **monopoly** is the sole right over the production and sale of an item.

MAKING CONNECTIONS

>> **Economics** Mercantilists believed that a nation's strength depended on how much gold and silver it had. They, therefore, emphasized foreign trade rather than the production of goods. Mercantilists also emphasized the role of the government in a nation's economy.

Use the **Vocabulary Puzzle-Maker CD-ROM** to create crossword and word search puzzles.

Section 1 Assessment

1. **Define:** revolution, martial law, foreign policy, repealed.
2. Why did civil war finally break out between the Crown and Parliament in 1642?
3. Why did Parliament remove James II from the throne?

Critical Thinking

4. **Identifying Central Issues** What was the central issue addressed by England's Declaration of Rights?

Graphic Organizer Activity

5. Draw this diagram, and use it to summarize the key ideas of John Locke's *Two Treatises of Government.*

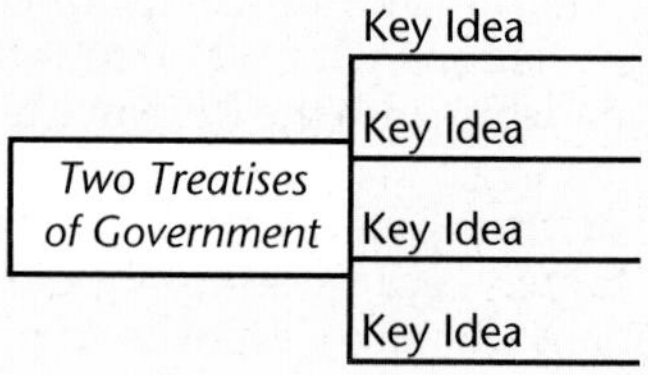

SECTION 2 The American Revolution

At first, England and its American colonies got along well. Over time, however, things changed. The colonists became angry over English controls. This led to revolution and the forming of a new country.

Reading Check How did the system of **mercantilism** work?

Reading Check What is a **monopoly?**

Mercantilism In 1660, when Charles II became king of England, most European leaders believed in an economic system called **mercantilism** (mer′ kuhn tēl iz uhm). Under it, colonies served as a source of raw materials and as a market for finished products. England's colonies in America were supposed to send goods to England that were scarce or could not be grown there, such as furs, lumber, tobacco, and cotton. The colonists were supposed to buy only goods made in England so that English merchants could make money. These goods could be carried only in ships built in England or in the colonies. The ships also had to be sailed by English crews. This was to make the shipbuilding industry and merchant marines stronger in case of war.

Mercantilism worked well until the 1700s. There were not enough skilled people in the American colonies to produce many goods. The colonists also enjoyed a **monopoly** (muh nop′ uh lē), or sole right, on the sale of several major crops. In addition, their ships were protected against pirates by the English navy.

Then, things changed. With the population in the colonies growing, the colonists wanted to make their own manufactured goods, such as iron products and beaver hats. Also, people in northern colonies were not able to sell as much to England as

Section 1 Assessment Answers

1. revolution, attempt to overthrow and change the government (p. 503); martial law, rule by the army instead of by the law (p. 505); foreign policy, relations with other countries (p. 507); repealed, abolished (p. 507)
2. because Charles accepted the laws Parliament passed and then disregarded them
3. because Parliament was afraid of control by the Roman Catholic Church
4. the power of the king versus the power of Parliament
5. Key ideas: people are born with certain rights; the purpose of government is to protect those rights; if a government fails to do so, people can revolt and set up a new government; the best kind of government is a representative one.

Assign the Chapter 32 **Section 1 Quiz** in the TCR. Testmaker available.

people in southern colonies did. Yet, they needed money to buy English goods. So, they began smuggling goods to and from the West Indies. Soon, a triangular, or three-way, trade grew up. The colonists shipped in sugar and molasses from the West Indies. They made rum and traded it for enslaved Africans. Then, they brought the enslaved Africans to the West Indies, where they traded them for sugar and molasses.

Stamp

Changes in British Policy Although England, now known as Great Britain, regulated colonial trade, the colonists handled local affairs. Their legislatures generally passed tax laws. Since colonial officials were paid out of taxes, they had to do as the colonial legislatures wished. This gave the legislatures a great deal of power.

In the middle of the 1700s, this changed. The French, who also had colonies in America, built a fort on the site of present-day Pittsburgh, Pennsylvania. The French and their Native American allies wanted to keep the British out of northern and western America. Great Britain, however, had already claimed the area for itself. The dispute led to the French and Indian War. By the time it ended in 1763, the British controlled nearly all of North America east of the Mississippi River.

The war left the British government deeply in debt. It wanted the colonies to pay a large share of the money owed. After all, the war had been fought partly to protect their western frontier. So, Great Britain moved to raise money by tightening its control over the colonies.

In 1765, Parliament passed the Stamp Act. It called for a tax on all newspapers, legal documents, calendars, and playing cards. All these items had to bear a stamp showing that the tax had been paid. This was the first **direct tax** Parliament placed on the colonies. That is, it was a tax paid directly to the government, not included in the price of the goods.

Reading Check Why was the Stamp Act considered a **direct tax?**

The Stamp Act hurt merchants, lawyers, and people in the newspaper business. These groups were among the most able to lead the colonists in a fight against British control. Angry mobs formed in many cities. Tax officials were threatened, and stamps were destroyed. People throughout the colonies decided to **boycott,** or refuse to buy, British goods.

Reading Check What action did the colonists take when they organized a **boycott?**

In October 1765, delegates from 9 of the 13 colonies met in New York to discuss the Stamp Act. They sent a letter to the British government. It stated that the colonies had not been taxed before by anyone except their own legislatures. It also said that Parliament had no right to tax them because they did not have representatives in Parliament.

In March 1766, Parliament finally voted to repeal the Stamp Act. At the same time, however, it passed the Declaratory Act, which stated that Parliament had the right to make laws on all

L2 **History** Have students write a report about the lasting impact of the French on North America, stating when the French first came. Have them note French influences that remain, such as in the names of cities, states, and other geographical features; French customs; French foods; and so on.

GEOGRAPHY AND HISTORY

In 1707, England and Scotland united to become Great Britain. Great Britain is still the name today.

Reading Check Answer
The Stamp Act was a **direct tax** because it was a tax paid directly to the government instead of a tax included in the price of goods.

Reading Check Answer
When the colonists organized a **boycott**, they refused to buy British goods.

THE HISTORY CHANNEL.

The following videotape program is available from Glencoe to enrich Chapter 32:

- **The American Revolution**

To find classroom resources to accompany this video, check the following home page:

A&E Television:
www.aande.com

MEETING SPECIAL NEEDS

Have each student choose an event discussed in the section, such as the Stamp Act, the Boston Tea Party, or the Boston Massacre. Ask them what it would have been like to live through the event. Then have students write a first-person narrative describing their experiences. Have students who are visual learners include drawings to help illustrate their main ideas. Encourage students to share their narratives in small groups or with the rest of the class.

Refer to ***Inclusion for the Middle School Social Studies Classroom: Strategies and Activities*** for additional resources.

HISTORY Online

Student Web Activity objectives and answers can be found at the ***Chapter 32 Web Activity Lesson Plan*** at humanheritage.glencoe.com

Glencoe Literature Library

The following novel from the **Glencoe Literature Library** may be used to enrich this chapter:

- *Johnny Tremain*, by Esther Forbes. (Events leading up to the American Revolution.)

MAKING CONNECTIONS

➤➤ **History** The song "Yankee Doodle" began as a song that mocked the colonists. *Macaroni* was a term used for British men who thought they were dressed in the latest styles but who actually looked ridiculous. British troops sang it as a song of ridicule. The colonists, however, loved the song and added their own verses to it. Ironically, it was to this tune that the British surrendered at Yorktown.

HISTORY Online

Student Web Activity

Visit the *Human Heritage* Web site at humanheritage.glencoe.com and click on ***Chapter 32—Student Web Activities*** to find out more about the American Revolution.

matters concerning the colonies. This showed that Parliament was not going to give in completely to the demands of the American colonists.

The Road to Revolution In 1767, Parliament passed a series of laws known as the Townshend Acts. These acts placed a tax on such goods as paper, paint, glass, lead, and tea that were shipped to the colonies. Part of the tax money was to be used to pay colonial officials. This took away the colonial legislatures' main source of power. The following year, the British sent soldiers to Boston to make sure the colonists obeyed the new laws. The colonists called the soldiers "redcoats" because of their bright red uniforms.

The Townshend Acts made the colonists angry. Soon, there were incidents of violence. One of the worst of these took place in Boston in 1770. A crowd of colonists began insulting British soldiers and throwing stones at them. The soldiers fired into the crowd. Five people were killed. This incident came to be called the Boston Massacre. Shortly after, all the Townshend taxes were repealed except the one on tea. The Boston Massacre itself would probably have been forgotten had not some colonists used it to stir up feelings against British rule.

Three years later, Parliament passed the Tea Act. It allowed the British East India Company to sell tea directly to the colonists rather than to colonial merchants, who took part of the profits. This hurt the merchants. The act also further angered those colonists already tired of British tax policies. In Massachusetts, a group of colonists dressed as Native Americans boarded a British ship in Boston harbor and dumped its cargo of tea into the water. This event is known as the Boston Tea Party.

To punish the colonists, Parliament, in 1774, passed the Coercive (kō er' siv) Acts. These acts closed Boston harbor and put the government of Massachusetts under military rule. These acts also said that British troops in the colonies should be *quartered,* or given a place to live, in private homes. Next, Parliament passed the Quebec Act, which extended the boundaries of Quebec west of the Appalachians and north of the Ohio River. This took in land that Massachusetts, Connecticut, and Virginia claimed as their own. The colonists called these laws the Intolerable Acts, or laws they could not bear.

Painting of Boston Tea Party

The Coercive Acts only made the colonists more determined than ever to fight for their liberties. In September 1774, delegates from 12 of the colonies met in Philadelphia. They called themselves the First Continental Congress. The Congress spoke out against the Coercive Acts and called for their repeal.

Colonial leaders, however, were divided about what to do. Some, like George Washington of Virginia, hoped to settle the differences with Great Britain. Others, like Samuel Adams of

MULTICULTURAL PERSPECTIVES

As the struggle for control of the colonies began, colonial leader John Adams wrote in his diary: "The people have become more attentive to their liberties, . . . and more determined to defend them. . . Our presses have groaned, our pulpits have thundered, our legislatures have resolved, our towns have voted; the crown officers have everywhere trembled, and all their little tools and creatures have been afraid to speak and ashamed to be seen."

Reading a Military Map

Maps that contain information about wars are called **military maps.** They show troop movements, battle sites and dates, and battle victories.

Look at the legend for the two maps below. Notice that different symbols and colors stand for American and British advances, retreats, and battle victories.

For example, the map has a solid red line to show that the British advanced to New York City, where they won a battle in August 1776. This victory is indicated by a red star. The Americans then retreated to Trenton, New Jersey, as shown by a dashed blue line.

Map Practice

1. **Which army won the battle at Saratoga, New York?**
2. **Which army advanced to Camden, South Carolina, after the Battle of Charleston?**
3. **Where did the British retreat to after the Battle of Guilford Courthouse?**

American Revolution: North **American Revolution: South**

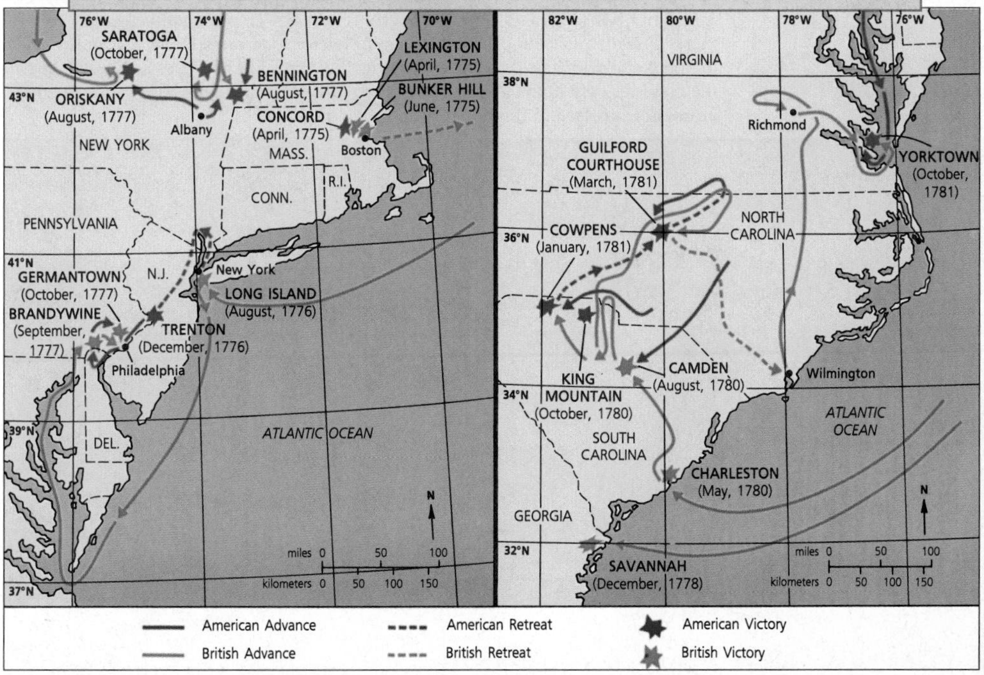

MAP SKILLS

TEACH

Reading a Military Map

Have the students read the instructional section of the feature. Ask: What kind of information is generally shown on a military map? *(information about wars such as troop movement, battle sites and dates, and battle victories)* Direct students to study the maps. Ask: Who won most of the battles along the Atlantic coast? *(the British)* According to the maps, where did most of the fighting during the American Revolution take place, North or South? *(North)*

Next, have students use the information on the maps to create charts about the battles of the American Revolution. The charts might include the following headings: "Battles," "Dates," and "Victories."

Assign the Chapter 32 **Geography and Map Activity** in the TCR.

Answers to Skill Practice

1. the American army
2. the British army
3. Wilmington

Use the Glencoe Skillbuilder Interactive Workbook, Level 1, to provide instruction and practice in key social studies skills.

SPOTLIGHT ON: AMERICAN REVOLUTION

African Americans played an important role in the military successes that the American army was able to achieve against the British during the Revolutionary War. In 1776, Congress recruited only free African Americans. By the winter of 1777, however, General George Washington welcomed all African Americans, free or enslaved. At the time the war ended, 5,000 African Americans from all 13 states except North Carolina had served in the Continental Army. Another 2,000 had served in the colonial navy.

L3 **Critical Thinking** Help students create a chart on the board showing the similarities and differences between the English civil war and the American Revolution. Begin by posing questions such as: What were the issues and goals of each uprising? Who were the opponents? What were the outcomes? **ELL**

MAKING CONNECTIONS

➤➤ **History** Thomas Paine had come to the American colonies from Great Britain shortly before he wrote the following thoughts in his pamphlet *Common Sense* in January 1776: "Everything that is right begs for separation from Britain. The Americans who have been killed seem to say, 'TIS TIME TO PART. England and America are located a great distance apart. That is itself strong and natural proof that God never expected one to rule over the other."

DID YOU KNOW ??

When the Second Continental Congress met, Georgia was the only colony without delegates.

CAPTION ANSWER

popular sovereignty and limited government

L1 **Government** Read the Preamble to the Declaration of Independence to the students. Discuss the certain basic rights that cannot be taken away by any government. **ELL**

Massachusetts and Patrick Henry of Virginia, wanted the colonies to become independent.

Fun Facts . . .

Peace Treaties Many peace treaties have been signed in Paris, France. In addition to the treaty ending the American Revolution, they include those that ended the French and Indian War (1763), the European allies' war with Napoleon (1814), and U.S. involvement in the Vietnam War (1973).

The Outcome

Before anything was decided, fighting broke out in Massachusetts between the colonists and British soldiers. The British set out to destroy a store of weapons at Concord. On the way there, they met the colonists at Lexington and fought the first battle of the American Revolution.

In May 1775, the Second Continental Congress met. George Washington was named head of the colonial army. The colonists then tried again to settle their differences with Great Britain. They appealed to King George III, who refused to listen.

On July 4, 1776, Congress issued the Declaration of Independence. Written mostly by Thomas Jefferson of Virginia, it stated that all men are created equal and have certain God-given rights. In the Declaration, the colonies broke away from Great Britain and declared themselves the United States of America.

War between the British and Americans dragged on. In 1778, the French, who were old enemies of Great Britain, agreed to help the Americans. In 1781, the Americans and French forced the British to surrender at Yorktown, Virginia. This ended the fighting. Two years later, the Treaty of Paris ended the war.

UNITED STATES CONSTITUTION In 1787, representatives from 12 states met in Philadelphia and drew up a constitution for the United States. George Washington is shown in this painting addressing the delegates. In 1789, Washington became the first President of the United States. **What are some principles of American government expressed in the Constitution?**

COOPERATIVE LEARNING

Tell students to imagine it is the eve of the American Revolution. Their village has just called a town meeting to decide the issue of independence. Next, organize the class into three teams. Tell one team to research arguments in support of independence, another team to research arguments against it, and the third team to research the events leading up to the current crisis.

Then have the pro and con teams state their cases. Instruct the third team to listen carefully to all of the arguments. After they have listened to the arguments, allow them to meet in a caucus for no more than 10 minutes. Call on each member of the group to vote "yea" or "nay," explaining why in two or three sentences.

Assign Chapter 32 *Cooperative Learning Activity* in the TCR.

In 1789, the United States adopted a constitution that set up a new form of government. The Constitution set forth certain principles of government. One of these is **popular sovereignty** (sov′ ruhn tē), or the idea that a government receives its powers from the people. Another is **limited government,** or the idea that a government may use only the powers given to it by the people.

Later, ten **amendments,** or formal changes, known as the Bill of Rights were added. The Bill of Rights guarantees all American citizens such rights as freedom of speech, press, and religion; the right to trial by jury; and freedom from unreasonable searches and seizures.

Reading Check What is the principle of **popular sovereignty?** What is the principle of **limited government?** What are the first ten **amendments** to the U.S. Constitution called?

Reading Check Answer **Popular sovereignty** is the idea that government gets its power from the people. The principle of **limited government** holds that a government may only use those powers given to it by the people. The first ten **amendments** are called the Bill of Rights.

Section 2 Assessment

1. **Define:** mercantilism, monopoly, direct tax, boycott, popular sovereignty, limited government, amendments.
2. Why were colonial legislatures powerful?
3. How did the Townshend Acts affect the power of the colonial legislatures?

Critical Thinking

4. **Evaluating Information** "The Bill of Rights is an important addition to the U.S. Constitution." What is your opinion of this statement? Explain.

Graphic Organizer Activity

5. Draw this diagram, and use it to show the causes and effects of the American Revolution.

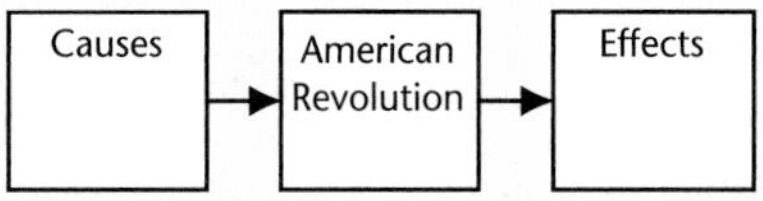

LINKING PAST TO PRESENT

The six fundamental principles on which the U.S. Constitution was based—popular sovereignty; separation of powers among legislative, executive, and judicial branches; checks and balances; federalism; supremacy of national law; and civilian control of government—were mostly derived from English political tradition. The U.S. Constitution became a model for other later democratic constitutions.

Use the **Interactive Tutor Self-Assessment CD-ROM** to review Section 2.

SECTION 3 The French Revolution

The events in America influenced people in France. The American example pointed to the need for political change and helped bring about a revolution.

Old Regime During the 1600s and early 1700s—the time of the Old Regime (ri zhēm′)—France was a divine-right monarchy. French society was divided into three **estates** (e stāts′), or classes. The First Estate was the clergy. Although they made up less than 1 percent of the people, they owned 10 percent of the land. They were not only *exempt,* or free, from taxes, but they also received income from church lands. Church income was not divided evenly, however. Most went to high church officials, who were generally nobles. They wore robes of purple and scarlet velvet

Reading Check Into how many **estates** was French society divided?

Reading Check Answer French society was divided into three **estates,** or classes.

Use the **Vocabulary PuzzleMaker CD-ROM** to create crossword and word search puzzles.

Section 2 Assessment Answers

1. mercantilism, system where colonies served as a source of raw materials and a market for finished goods (p. 508); monopoly, sole right (p. 508); direct tax, tax paid directly to the government (p. 509); boycott, refusal to buy (p. 509); popular sovereignty, idea that the government receives its power from the people (p. 513); limited government, idea that a government may only use the powers given to it by the people (p. 513); amendments, formal changes (p. 513)

2. because they passed tax laws and controlled officials

3. took away the legislatures' main power

4. Answers will vary.

5. *causes*—growing colonial population, conflict over colonial manufacturing, triangular trades, conflict over taxation and representation; *effects*—colonial independence, new constitution, Bill of Rights

Assign the Chapter 32 **Section 2 Quiz** in the TCR. Testmaker available.

L2 **Language Arts** Ask students to brainstorm definitions of the term *revolution.* Stimulate the discussion by asking, "When are people justified in choosing revolution as a solution to political problems?" Have students write a case study of a situation they feel would justify a revolution or people taking the government into their own hands.

Reading Check Answer
The **bourgeoisie** was made up of bankers, merchants, lawyers, doctors, manufacturers, and teachers.

Reading Check Answer
The *philosophes* were French writers and thinkers who wrote articles pointing out France's political problems.

MAKING CONNECTIONS

>> **History** From 1642 to 1715, France was ruled by Louis XIV. His was the longest rule in modern European history. Under Louis, France led Europe in the arts and had the most powerful army on the continent. After Louis, French power and influence began to decline.

trimmed with lace. Parish priests lived simply and served people's religious needs.

The Second Estate was the nobility. They made up about 2 percent of the people and also owned large areas of land. Nobles, too, were free from taxes. They lived off grants from the royal treasury and rents paid by the peasants. Some nobles spent their time at the royal court, dancing, hunting, and gambling. Others filled the highest posts in the government and the army.

Reading Check What groups made up the French **bourgeoisie?**

The Third Estate was everyone else in France. At the top of this class was the **bourgeoisie** (bur zhwah zē')—bankers, merchants, lawyers, doctors, manufacturers, and teachers. They controlled much of France's wealth and trade. Next were the city workers—artisans, day laborers, and servants. At the bottom were the peasants, who made up more than 80 percent of the French people.

Members of the Third Estate had no power in the government, but they paid the country's taxes. They paid taxes on income, personal property, land, and crops. They paid sales taxes on salt, tobacco, and wine. Parents even paid a tax when a child was born. In addition, the peasants still paid feudal dues.

Reading Check Who were the *philosophes?*

The Estates-General By the 1780s, the French government was in trouble. Educated French writers and thinkers called ***philosophes*** (fē luh zofs'), or philosophers, wrote articles pointing out the country's political problems. One of the most widely read philosophes was Francois Marie Arouet (fran' swah muh rē' ah rwe'), known as Voltaire (vōl tair'). Voltaire favored free speech, a free press, freedom of religion, and equal justice for everyone. One of his favorite sayings was: "I do not agree with a word you say, but I will defend to the death your right to say it."

Painting of Louis XVI and Family

The major problem facing the French government, however, was a lack of money. The French government had given so much help to the colonies during the American Revolution that it was almost bankrupt. King Louis XVI and his wife added to the problem by spending money on jewels, hunting parties, horse races, and balls. In fact, Queen Marie-Antoinette (muh rē an twuh net') spent so much that she was accused of increasing France's *deficit,* or shortage of money. For this reason, the French people called her Madame Deficit. The king wanted the clergy and nobles to give him money. They, however, had never paid taxes and saw no reason to start.

Finally, Louis XVI called a meeting of the French legislature to help decide how to raise money. It was the first time that this body, known as the Estates-General, had met since 1614. In the past, each of the estates had met separately, with each casting one vote. This meant the nobles and clergy together could outvote the Third Estate and protect themselves from change.

MULTICULTURAL PERSPECTIVES

Men and women were equally instrumental in spreading the Enlightenment ideas that helped to spark the French Revolution. Influential Parisian intellectuals such as Madame de Pompadour, Madame Geoffrin, and Madame du Deffand sponsored evenings of long political discussions in gatherings called salons. Here, writers, artists, and educated people of the middle class mingled with men and women of nobility.

posts. When it was released, the blade came crashing down and cut off the victim's head. The wave of killing came to be known as the "Reign of Terror." Because of it, the people began to turn against Robespierre. In 1794, government leaders had him executed.

The following year, a third constitution was written. It set up a government known as the Directory. Besides the legislature, there was an executive branch with five directors. Only people who owned land could vote.

Under the new government, most reforms of the Revolution came to an end. The people of France had grown more conservative. The Directory spent its time trying to handle food shortages, rising prices, government bankruptcy, and attacks by other countries.

One reform that did remain was the idea that all French people had the right to choose their government. Another was a standard system of weights and measures known as the metric

Linking Across Time

The Metric System After France adopted use of the metric system in 1791, the government attempted to educate people about its many uses (below). Today the metric system is followed in most technological nations in the world, except the United States. It is so widespread that the metric system is used for measurement at the Olympics. **What other lasting reform grew out of the French Revolution?**

MAKING CONNECTIONS

>> **History** Historians estimate that about 40,000 people were executed during the Reign of Terror.

DID YOU KNOW ??

The guillotine was considered a "humane" way of execution at the time. Beheading was quick and merciful. It was the official instrument of execution in 1792 and was used until capital punishment was officially abolished in France in 1981.

Linking Across Time

A lasting reform that came out of the French Revolution was the idea that all French people had the right to choose their own government.

Biography

The following videotape program is available from Glencoe to enrich Chapter 32:

- **Marie Antoinette: Tragic Queen**

To find classroom resources to accompany this video, check the following home page:

A&E Television:
www.aande.com

MULTICULTURAL PERSPECTIVES

The French Revolution destroyed an entire society and began a new era in France. Since France led European and colonial fashion, the styles of the revolutionary period influenced the rest of Europe and America. The revolutionary fashions were simplistic, at least in comparison to the brocade gowns, embroidered waistcoats, and large powdered wigs of the previous social system of France. During the Reign of Terror, wearing the old styles became dangerous. Anyone whose clothes suggested luxury was likely to be seized as an aristocrat and sent to the guillotine. Because England represented political freedom, the new fashions imitated English country styles, with muslin and broadcloth in place of silks and satins.

ASSESS

Check for Understanding

Ask students to summarize the main points of the chapter, orally or in writing. Discuss the answers to the Section and Chapter Assessment questions.

Evaluate

Assign the Chapter 32 **Performance Assessment Activity** in the TCR.

Administer the **Chapter 32 Test**. Testmaker available.

Reteach

Have students make time lines of the major events in the chapter.

Assign the Chapter 32 **Reteaching Activity** in the TCR.

Enrich

Have students read a book—fiction or nonfiction—related to events of this chapter, and deliver an oral report about the book to the class.

Assign the Chapter 32 **Enrichment Activity** in the TCR.

CLOSE

Have students discuss how the following slogan would have applied in each of the revolutions in this chapter: "No taxation without representation."

Use the **Interactive Tutor Self-Assessment CD-ROM** to review Section 3.

HISTORY Online

Self-Check Quiz gives students an interactive chapter tutorial. Have them access ***Chapter 32 Quiz*** at **humanheritage.glencoe.com**

system, which the National Assembly adopted in 1791. Metrics, a system of numbers that is based on powers of ten, helped scientists carry out experiments and made international trade easier. Today, metrics are used by all major countries in the world except the United States.

Section 3 Assessment

1. **Define:** estates, bourgeoisie, *philosophes*, tyranny, constitutional monarchy, *sans-culottes*, *émigrés*, guillotine.
2. What groups made up the three French estates?
3. What did the National Assembly do about the uprisings in 1789?
4. Why did most reforms of the French Revolution come to an end under the Directory?

Critical Thinking

5. **Understanding Cause and Effect** How did the storming of the Bastille help trigger the French Revolution?

Graphic Organizer Activity

6. Draw this diagram, and use it to compare the French Declaration of the Rights of Man and the Citizen to the U.S. Declaration of Independence.

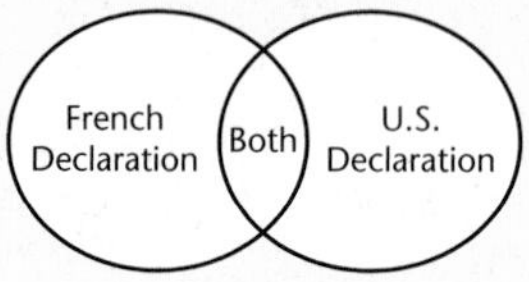

Chapter Summary & Study Guide

1. As a result of new ideas about freedom and government, the 1700s are known as the Age of Enlightenment.
2. England's political revolution began in the 1600s when the Crown and Parliament disagreed over issues of divine right and religion.
3. In 1689, Parliament passed the Declaration of Rights, which made Parliament stronger and protected the rights of the people.
4. In 1776, disagreements between the American colonies and Great Britain led to the Declaration of Independence, which defended the right to self-government.
5. In 1789, the United States adopted a new constitution based on the principles of popular sovereignty and limited government.
6. The French Revolution, which began in 1789, ended as a result of the Reign of Terror. However, two lasting reforms survived—use of the metric system and the idea that people had a right to choose their government.

HISTORY Online

Self-Check Quiz

Visit the *Human Heritage* Web site at **humanheritage.glencoe.com** and click on ***Chapter 32—Self-Check Quiz*** to assess your understanding of this chapter.

Section 3 Assessment Answers

1. All terms are defined in the text Glossary.
2. the clergy, the nobility, and the bourgeoisie, city workers, and peasants
3. It ended the privileges of the clergy and nobles.
4. because the people of France had grown more conservative
5. Sample response: News of the Bastille spurred peasant uprising throughout France and caused the National Assembly to take steps that would end the French monarchy.
6. Sample responses: Both documents stressed equality and the idea that power came from the people rather than the government. The French Declaration included specific individual freedoms, such as freedom of speech, that Americans later included in the Bill of Rights. The U.S. Declaration asserted independence from Great Britain.

Assign the Chapter 32 **Section 3 Quiz** in the TCR. Testmaker available.

CHAPTER 32 Assessment

Using Key Terms

Sort these words describing the revolutions in England, America, and France by the country to which each applies. (Words may be used more than once.) Use the words in each group to write a sentence or two about each country's revolution.

revolution	constitutional monarchy
mercantilism	monopoly
direct tax	popular sovereignty
boycott	estates
bourgeoisie	tyranny
martial law	
guillotine	

Understanding Main Ideas

1. What were some Puritan beliefs?
2. Why was the Glorious Revolution called "glorious"?
3. How did Great Britain tighten its control over the American colonies?
4. How did the British colonists respond to the Stamp Act?
5. Who had the most power in the French government before the French Revolution? After the Revolution?
6. Why were European rulers afraid of the ideas of the French Revolution?

Critical Thinking

1. What economic questions played a part in the American Revolution? In the French Revolution?
2. What were the most important political issues that played a part in England's Glorious Revolution? Explain your answer.
3. Do you agree with the idea that people have the right to rule themselves? Explain.
4. Why are the 1700s known as the Age of Enlightenment?

Graphic Organizer Activity

Citizenship Create a diagram like the one on this page, and use it to compare the reforms and rights sought by the leaders of the English, American, and French revolutions.

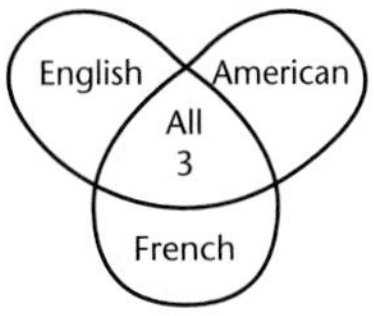

Geography in History

The World in Spatial Terms Look at the maps of the American Revolution on page 511. The advances and retreats of both armies are shown. About how many miles (or kilometers) did the British advance from the battle at Long Island, New York, to the battle at Brandywine, Pennsylvania?

Using Your Journal

Review any details you may have noted about the changes in government that took place during the 1700s. Imagine you are setting up your own country with its own government. Using ideas you have noted, write a description of how you think the government should be organized.

Bonus Test Question

For Chapter 32 Test

Choose one of the revolutions you have read about and identify one thing that could have been done to avoid that revolution. Explain. *(Answers will vary.)*

Using Your Journal

Descriptions will vary but should include some of the government principles discussed. You might call on volunteers to read their descriptions to the class.

Geography in History

about 575 miles (or 925 km)

CHAPTER 32 Assessment Answers

Using Key Terms

England: revolution, martial law, mercantilism, tyranny, direct tax; America: revolution, foreign policy, monopoly, boycott, popular sovereignty; France: revolution, *sans-culottes*, mercantilism, tyranny, estates, bourgeoisie, constitutional monarchy. Sentences will vary.

Understanding Main Ideas

1. freedom of worship, hard work, and having a say in government
2. because the change in monarchs took place without gunfire
3. by passing new tax laws and taking steps to enforce them
4. Angry mobs threatened tax officials, and British goods were boycotted.
5. the king; the Directory
6. because these ideas would weaken their own power

Critical Thinking

1. mercantilism, direct taxes, and a boycott of British goods; exemption of a few from taxes, the nation's deficit, and high food prices
2. the conflict between Parliament and the king
3. Answers will vary but students should provide reasons.
4. Answers will vary.

Graphic Organizer Activity

Answers will vary, but should show that leaders of all three revolutions sought to protect the basic rights of individuals and to give the people an increased voice in political affairs. The United States differed from the other two revolutions because it sought complete independence from another nation rather than a change in the balance of power.

Chapter 33 Planning Guide

Timesaving Tools

TeacherWorks™ All-In-One Planner and Resource Center

- **Interactive Teacher Edition** Access your Teacher Wraparound Edition and your classroom resources with a few easy clicks.
- **Interactive Lesson Planner** Planning has never been easier! Organize your week, month, semester, or year with all the lesson helps you need to make teaching creative, timely, and relevant.

Use Glencoe's **Presentation Plus!** multimedia teacher tool to easily present dynamic lessons that visually excite your students. Using Microsoft PowerPoint® you can customize the presentations to create your own personalized lessons.

Objectives	Reproducible Resources	Multimedia Resources
Section 1 **Scientific Revolution** Summarize the inventions and discoveries that marked the Scientific Revolution.	Reproducible Lesson Plan Chapter 33 Vocabulary and Guided Reading Activity Reading Essentials and Study Guide 33-1 Section 1 Quiz	Interactive Student Edition CD-ROM Graphic Organizer Transparency 13 Vocabulary PuzzleMaker CD-ROM ExamView® Pro Testmaker CD-ROM Glencoe Skillbuilder Interactive Workbook CD-ROM, Level 1 Presentation Plus! CD-ROM
Section 2 **Agricultural Revolution** Explain what the Agricultural Revolution was and how it contributed to the Industrial Revolution.	Reproducible Lesson Plan Reading Essentials and Study Guide 33-2 Section 2 Quiz	Vocabulary PuzzleMaker CD-ROM Interactive Tutor Self-Assessment CD-ROM ExamView® Pro Testmaker CD-ROM Glencoe Skillbuilder Interactive Workbook CD-ROM, Level 1
Section 3 **Industrial Revolution** Discuss the development of the Industrial Revolution.	Reproducible Lesson Plan Reading Essentials and Study Guide 33-3 Chapter 33 Cooperative Learning Activity Chapter 33 Chart and Graph Skill Activity Chapter 33 Geography and Map Activity Section 3 Quiz	Vocabulary PuzzleMaker CD-ROM Interactive Tutor Self-Assessment CD-ROM ExamView® Pro Testmaker CD-ROM Glencoe Skillbuilder Interactive Workbook CD-ROM, Level 1
Section 4 **Industrial Impact** Identify and describe the effects of industrialization.	Reproducible Lesson Plan Reading Essentials and Study Guide 33-4 Unit 10 Primary Source Readings Section 4 Quiz	Teaching Transparency and Activity 33A Vocabulary PuzzleMaker CD-ROM Interactive Tutor Self-Assessment CD-ROM ExamView® Pro Testmaker CD-ROM
Section 5 **Spread of Industry** Analyze how industrialization continued and spread.	Reproducible Lesson Plan Reading Essentials and Study Guide 33-5 Chapter 33 Enrichment Activity Unit 10 World Literature Reading 2 Section 5 Quiz	Teaching Transparency and Activity 33B Interactive Tutor Self-Assessment CD-ROM ExamView® Pro Testmaker CD-ROM
Chapter 33 **Review and Evaluation**	Chapter 33 Reteaching Activity Chapter 33 Performance Assessment Activity Unit 10 Standardized Test Practice Spanish Chapter Summary and Glossary Chapter 33 Test	Interactive Tutor Self-Assessment CD-ROM Glencoe Skillbuilder Interactive Workbook CD-ROM, Level 1 Audiocassettes* ExamView® Pro Testmaker CD-ROM

*Also available in Spanish.

Chapter 33 Planning Guide

✓ Performance Assessment Activities

Writing Commercials Ask each student to select an invention or discovery of the 1400s–1800s and write a promotional flyer or commercial promoting the product. Have students present their flyers or commercials to the class.

CHAPTER RESOURCES

LITERATURE ABOUT THE PERIOD

Dickens, Charles. *Oliver Twist.* Bantam Books, 1982. The saga of an orphan's adventures in industrial London.

READINGS FOR THE STUDENT

Macaulay, David. *Mill.* Houghton Mifflin, 1983. Detailed drawings and clear descriptions of the history and construction of a typical New England mill.

READINGS FOR THE TEACHER

Smith, Page. *The Rise of Industrial America.* Facts on File, 1980. Examines the industrialization of the United States between the years 1876 and 1901.

Thompson, Paul. *The Edwardians: The Remaking of British Society.* Indiana University Press, 1975. Focuses on social change and class differences in Great Britain in the late 1800s.

KEY TO ABILITY LEVELS

Teaching strategies have been coded for varying learning styles and abilities.

L1 Level 1 activities are **basic** activities and should be within the ability range of all students.

L2 Level 2 activities are **average** activities and should be within the ability range of the average to above-average student.

L3 Level 3 activities are **challenging** activities designed for the ability range of above-average students.

ELL ELL activities should be within the ability range of English Language Learning students.

NATIONAL GEOGRAPHIC Teacher's Corner

INDEX TO NATIONAL GEOGRAPHIC MAGAZINE

The following articles relate to this chapter:

- "Food: How Safe?" by Jennifer Ackerman, May 2002.
- "War on Disease," by Rick Weiss, February 2002.
- "The Future is Calling," by Thomas B. Allen, December 2001.

NATIONAL GEOGRAPHIC SOCIETY PRODUCTS AVAILABLE FROM GLENCOE

To order the following, call Glencoe at 1-800-334-7344:

- *Picture Atlas of the World (CD-ROM)*

ADDITIONAL NATIONAL GEOGRAPHIC SOCIETY PRODUCTS

To order the following, call National Geographic at 1-800-368-2728:

- *Physical Geography of the Continents Series: Europe (Video)*
- *Wired World (Video)*
- *Inventors and Inventions (Video)*
- *Technology's Price (Video)*

Access *National Geographic's* new dynamic MapMachine Web site and other geography resources at:

www.nationalgeographic.com
www.nationalgeographic.com/maps

THE HISTORY CHANNEL. A&E HOME VIDEO. Biography

The following videotape programs are available from Glencoe:

- **Alexander Graham Bell: Voice of Invention** 1-56501-946-6
- **The Electric Light** 1-56501-892-3
- **Marconi: Whisper in the Air** 1-56501-551-7
- **Sir Isaac Newton: The Gravity of Genius** 1-56501-982-2

To order, call Glencoe at 1-800-334-7344. To find classroom resources to accompany many of these videos, check:

A&E Television: www.aande.com
The History Channel: www.historychannel.com

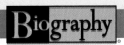

Introducing CHAPTER 33

OVERVIEW

Chapter 33 traces the rise of science and industry in Europe and North America during the 1700s and 1800s.

- **Section 1** traces the Scientific Revolution.
- **Section 2** describes developments in farming that led to the Agricultural Revolution.
- **Section 3** summarizes the major developments that led to the Industrial Revolution.
- **Section 4** examines the effects of industrialization.
- **Section 5** describes how industrialization spread.

CHAPTER OBJECTIVES

After reading Chapter 33, students will be able to:

1. summarize the inventions of the Scientific Revolution.
2. identify features of the Agricultural Revolution.
3. trace the rise of industry.
4. describe the social effects of industrialization .
5. analyze how industrialization spread.

EXAMINING ARTIFACTS

Ask students to speculate on the impact of the phonograph and steam engine. *(advanced communication; expanded the growth of industry and promoted mechanization)* Call on students to suggest effects of other ideas and inventions in the time line.

PERFORMANCE ASSESSMENT

Use the Performance Assessment activities on page 522B to help you evaluate students as they complete the chapter.

CHAPTER 33

Rise of Industry

1500 A.D.–1880 A.D.

▲ Parts of a steam engine

◄ Edison phonograph

1543	1733	1769	1847	1879
Copernicus proposes sun-centered solar system	John Kay invents the flying shuttle	James Watt perfects the steam engine	Samuel Colt develops assembly line	Thomas Edison develops electric light

TEACHING RESOURCES

TEACHER PLANNING AND SUPPORT

- Reproducible Lesson Plan 33-1, 33-2, 33-3, 33-4, 33-5
- Teaching Strategies for the World History Classroom (Including Block Scheduling Pacing Guides)
- Presentation Plus! CD-ROM

REVIEW AND REINFORCEMENT

- Reading Essentials and Study Guide 33-1, 33-2, 33-3, 33-4, 33-5
- Chapter 33 Vocabulary and Guided Reading Activity
- Vocabulary PuzzleMaker CD-ROM
- Teaching Transparencies 33A & 33B
- Chapter 33 Reteaching Activity
- Chapter 33 Cooperative Learning Activity
- Chapter 33 Activity Book Activity
- Chapter 33 Chart and Graph Skill Activity
- Reading and Study Skills Foldables
- Interactive Tutor Self-Assessment CD-ROM
- Unit 10 MindJogger VideoQuiz

APPLICATION AND HANDS-ON ACTIVITIES

- Daily Questions in Social Studies
- Student Presentation Builder CD-ROM

Chapter Focus

Read to Discover

- What inventions and discoveries marked the Scientific Revolution.
- How the Agricultural Revolution contributed to the Industrial Revolution.
- How the Industrial Revolution developed.
- What the effects of industrialization were.
- How industrialization continued and spread.

HISTORY Online

Chapter Overview

Visit the *Human Heritage* Web site at **humanheritage.glencoe.com** and click on ***Chapter 33—Chapter Overviews*** to preview this chapter.

Terms to Learn

enclosure
textile
factory system
cotton gin

People to Know

Galileo Galilei
Sir Isaac Newton
Robert Fulton
Samuel F.B. Morse

Why It's Important By the 1700s, people in the western world had new ideas about science. These led to new forms of power and ways of making goods. Industry and ways of living changed so much that historians call these changes the Industrial Revolution.

The Industrial Revolution involved the shift from animal and human power to machine power. This meant that society became less agricultural and more industrial. During the early years of the Industrial Revolution, Great Britain took the lead. Later, other countries rose to challenge Great Britain.

SECTION 1 Scientific Revolution

Many of the changes that occurred during the Industrial Revolution grew out of changes in scientific thinking. Beginning in the 1400s, scientists started to break away from old ideas. They used the scientific method to form and test their own hypotheses. This became known as the Scientific Revolution.

Nicolaus Copernicus (kuh per' nuh kuhs) was one of the first people to use the scientific method. Copernicus was a Polish astronomer who studied the motion of the planets. What he saw proved to him that Ptolemy was wrong and that Earth was not the center of the universe. In 1543, Copernicus published a book explaining his idea that planets revolve around the sun rather

HISTORY Online

Chapter Overview introduces students to chapter content and key terms. Have them access ***Chapter 33 Overview*** at **humanheritage.glencoe.com**

FOCUS

Bellringer

Hold a two-minute brainstorming session in which students name devices, equipment, or machines powered by steam, gas, oil, or electricity. Record the results on the board.

Motivational Activity

Note the many items on the board. Then quickly erase everything. Tell students that none of these things would be available without the Industrial Revolution—the subject of this chapter.

GUIDE TO READING

Reading Strategy

Ask students to read "Why It's Important" and summarize the chapter's main theme. *(New scientific ideas and new forms of energy produced such far-reaching changes in society and industry during the 1700s that historians call these changes the Industrial Revolution.)*

Vocabulary Precheck

Ask students to define each of the "Terms to Learn." Have a volunteer consult the dictionary for any unfamiliar words. L1 ELL

Use the Vocabulary PuzzleMaker CD-ROM for Chapter 33 to create a crossword puzzle. L1

Assign Chapter 33 Vocabulary and Guided Reading Activity.

Assign Reading Essentials and Study Guide 33-1.

GEOGRAPHY ACTIVITIES

- Chapter 33 Geography and Map Activity
- Outline Map Resource Book

INTERDISCIPLINARY CONNECTIONS

- Unit 10 World Literature Reading 2
- World Music: A Cultural Legacy

ENRICHMENT AND EXTENSION

- World History Primary Source Document Library CD-ROM
- Chapter 33 Enrichment Activity
- Unit 10 Primary Source Readings
- Foods Around the World

ASSESSMENT AND EVALUATION

- Chapter 33 Performance Assessment Activity
- Chapter 33 Section Quizzes 33-1, 33-2, 33-3, 33-4, 33-5
- Chapter 33 Test
- Unit 10 Standardized Test Practice
- Chapter 33 ExamView® Pro Testmaker CD-ROM
- Chapter 33 Digests Audiocassettes Activities and Tests

SPANISH RESOURCES

- Chapter 33 Spanish Chapter Summary and Glossary
- Chapter 33 Spanish Digests Audiocassettes Activities and Tests

TEACH

Guided Practice

L1 Critical Thinking New interest in science led to discoveries and philosophies based on reason. Lead students in defining reason. *(the logical and systematic way of proving a case by supporting it with facts)*

L2 Science Have students choose one of the scientists listed in the chart on this page. Have them research the inventions or discoveries of their chosen scientists, including lesser-known inventions. Then have students create a visual presentation of their inventor's achievements.

MAKING CONNECTIONS

➤➤ **History** Great Britain pioneered the Industrial Revolution because it possessed the factors of industrialization, including (1) capital, (2) a mobile labor force, (3) natural resources, (4) entrepreneurs, (5) a new technology, (6) markets, and (7) a supportive government.

SCIENTISTS

NAME	FIELD	ACCOMPLISHMENTS
Johannes Kepler *Germany*	*Astronomy*	announced laws of movement of planets, 1609
William Harvey *England*	*Medicine*	published theory on human blood circulation, 1628
Sir Isaac Newton *England*	*Physics*	stated laws of motion and theory of gravitation, 1687
Antoine-Laurent Lavoisier *France*	*Chemistry*	discovered nature of combustion, 1777
John Dalton *England*	*Chemistry*	announced atomic theory, 1803
Maria Mitchell *United States*	*Astronomy*	discovered new comet, 1847
Charles Darwin *England*	*Biology*	advanced theory on development of plants and animals, 1858
Gregor Mendel *Austria*	*Botany*	discovered principles of heredity, 1866
Louis Pasteur *France*	*Medicine*	advanced germ theory of disease, 1876; developed a rabies vaccine, 1885
Pierre Curie **Marie Curie** *France*	*Chemistry*	discovered radium and polonium, 1898

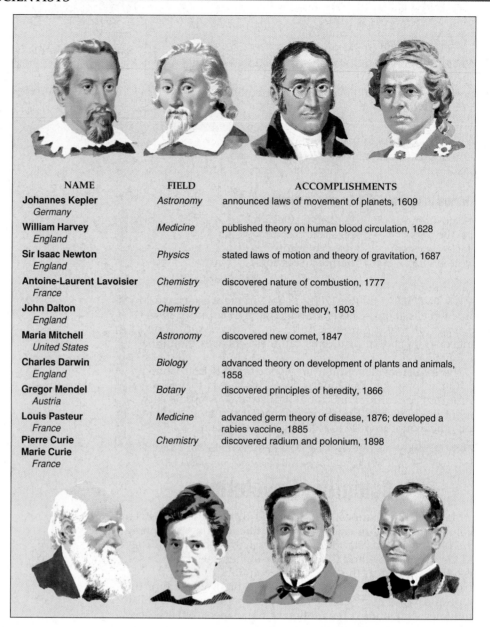

COOPERATIVE LEARNING

Organize the class into two groups to role-play a presentation on the solar system by Galileo before a group consisting of opposing academic and Church leaders. Have the first group plan Galileo's presentation in a manner that is convincing and tactful. The second group should prepare the academic and Church leaders' rebuttal. Within each group, have students assume tasks such as conducting research, listing arguments, anticipating responses, and taking part in the role play. After the presentation and rebuttal, have the class evaluate the statements and identify which group had the most convincing argument and why.

than around Earth. This book began a complete change in scientific thinking.

Another important scientist was the Italian astronomer Galileo Galilei (gal uh lē′ ō gal uh lā′ ē). He invented a telescope and began to study the stars and planets. He learned that the moon's surface is not smooth but has mountains and craters. He learned that the Milky Way holds a vast number of stars and that the sun rotates on its axis. Galileo was strongly criticized by the Roman Catholic Church for teaching that Earth revolves around the sun. Even so, Galileo's ideas spread throughout Europe.

In 1642, the same year Galileo died, another important scientist, Sir Isaac Newton (ī′ zuhk nūt′ n), was born in England. It was Newton who explained the theory of gravitation and how objects move through space. The technology for today's rockets and space satellites is based on his work.

It was at this time that scientists in Great Britain and France formed organizations in which they could discuss their ideas and research. In this way, scientific information began to spread more quickly. Soon, thousands of people were using the scientific method to add to their knowledge and improve their lives.

Copernicus

Section 1 Assessment

1. What scientific discoveries were made by Galileo Galilei?
2. Why were Sir Isaac Newton's theories important?

Critical Thinking

3. **Making Generalizations** Why were the early 1400s known as the Scientific Revolution?

Graphic Organizer Activity

4. Draw this diagram, and use it to show some of the new ideas developed during the Scientific Revolution. (Add circles as needed.)

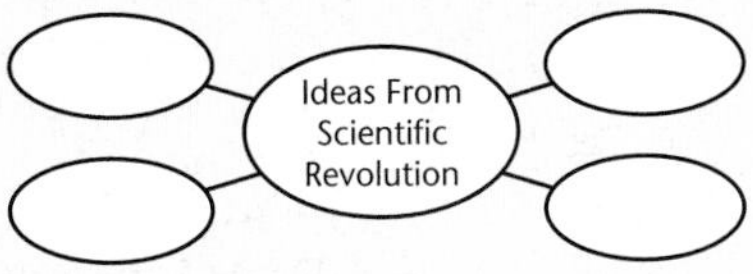

SECTION 2 Agricultural Revolution

As changes were taking place in science, there were new developments in farming. These changes were called the Agricultural Revolution. It set the stage for the Industrial Revolution.

By the 1700s, a system of land division called **enclosure** (en klō′ zhuhr) was in use in Great Britain. Landowners combined the many small strips of land worked by tenant farmers into large areas closed in by fences, hedges, or ditches. Enclosure allowed landowners to make more money. Whole areas could grow the same crop, which meant larger harvests and greater profits. Landowners also needed fewer workers.

Reading Check How did the system of **enclosure** work?

Section 1 Assessment Answers

1. that the planets revolve around the sun
2. because his work formed the basis for today's rockets
3. This was a time when scientists broke away from old theories and used the scientific method to form and test their own hypotheses.
4. sample ideas: idea of a sun-centered solar system, discovery of moon's topographic features, discovery of stars in the Milky Way, principle of gravity, any of the ideas or discoveries in the table on page 524

Assign the Chapter 33 **Section 1 Quiz** in the TCR. Testmaker available.

DID YOU KNOW

French law outlawed the dissection of any human bodies. English law allowed the dissection of executed criminals only. These laws prevailed in England until the English passed the Anatomy Act of 1832.

Use the **Interactive Tutor Self-Assessment CD-ROM** to review Section 1.

MAKING CONNECTIONS

>> **Science** Changes also took place in medicine. In 1628, Dr. William Harvey discovered that blood circulates in one direction through the body. In 1718, Lady Mary Wortley Montague brought the Chinese practice of inoculation against smallpox from Turkey to England.

Reading Check Answer
Under **enclosure,** landowners combined small strips of land worked by tenant farmers into large areas enclosed by fences, hedges, or ditches.

Biography

The following videotape program is available from Glencoe to enrich Chapter 33:

- **Sir Isaac Newton: The Gravity of Genius**

To find classroom resources to accompany this video, check the following home page:

A&E Television:
www.aande.com

Use the **Vocabulary PuzzleMaker CD-ROM** to create crossword and word search puzzles.

L1 **Critical Thinking** Ask students to analyze the term *revolution.* What revolutions have they studied besides the Industrial Revolution? *(English, American, and French political revolutions)* What changes occurred? *(changes in government and in society)* Ask if they think these changes were positive or negative. ELL

GEOGRAPHY AND HISTORY

In farming developments, Viscount Charles Townshend introduced the system of rotating crops. Instead of letting a field lie fallow for one year, Townshend planted such crops as alfalfa and clover, which restore nitrogen to the soil and make it more fertile. Townshend was nicknamed "Turnip" because he encouraged farmers to grow root crops.

Use the **Interactive Tutor Self-Assessment CD-ROM** to review Section 2.

Reading Check Answer
The **textile** industry produced wool and cotton cloth. Under the **domestic system,** work was done in workers' cottages.

Use the **Vocabulary PuzzleMaker CD-ROM** to create crossword and word search puzzles.

DID YOU KNOW ??

The 1800s saw many innovations in Great Britain's textile industry. In 1807, the die-stamped metal button was invented. In 1820, T. Hancock invented the first elastic fabric called webbing. It replaced the ribbons that secured women's shoes.

The tenant farmers had two choices. They could stay on as paid workers, or they could look elsewhere for jobs. Most left to find work in other places. They moved to cities and became industrial workers.

Enclosure was just part of the revolution in agriculture. New ways of growing crops and breeding animals were also developed. These changes led to greater production of food. More food meant better health and longer life spans. Population increased, and the demand for manufactured goods grew.

Section 2 Assessment

1. **Define:** enclosure.
2. How did landowners use the enclosure system?
3. How did the growth of population influence the Industrial Revolution?

Critical Thinking

4. **Making Comparisons** Do you think agriculture was more or less important in the 1700s than it is today in Great Britain?

Graphic Organizer Activity

5. Draw this diagram, and use it to show some of the effects of the enclosure system.

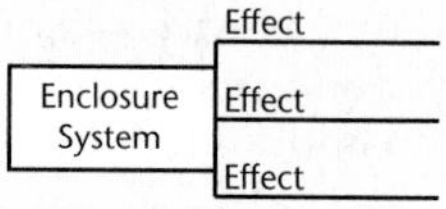

SECTION 3 Industrial Revolution

The Industrial Revolution began in the early 1700s. It was a long, slow process at first. However, as one development led to another, the revolution moved faster and faster. Much of the world changed. By the 1850s, the changes had become so widespread that people realized they were entering a new age.

Reading Check What did the **textile** industry produce? What was the **domestic system?**

The Textile Industry The Industrial Revolution began in Great Britain in the **textile** (tek' stuhl), or woven cloth, industry. In the 1600s and early 1700s, cloth was made by the **domestic system.** Under this system, most work was done in workers' cottages, where families worked together. Merchants went from cottage to cottage, bringing the workers raw wool and cotton. Using hand-powered spinning wheels and looms, the workers would spin the thread and weave it into wool and cotton cloth. The merchants then picked up the finished cloth to sell.

The domestic system could not meet the strong growing demand for cloth. Before long, people started looking for ways to make more cloth in less time. The first major breakthrough came in 1733 when a British inventor named John Kay invented the

Section 2 Assessment Answers

1. enclosure, land division (p. 525)
2. They could grow the same crop over a large area with fewer workers.
3. As the population increased, the demand for manufactured goods grew.
4. Answers will vary but might say less important because a lot of people moved to cities or just as important because there is a larger population to feed.
5. sample effects: allowed landowners to make more money; resulted in larger harvests at greater profits with fewer workers; forced many tenant farmers into cities; swelled the industrial labor force

Assign the Chapter 33 **Section 2 Quiz** in the TCR. Testmaker available.

flying shuttle. It was mounted on rollers, and one weaver could send it rapidly from one side of a loom to the other. It cut in half the time needed to weave cloth. Now, however, spinners could not keep up with the weavers. Then, in 1764, James Hargreaves (hahr′ grēvz), a British carpenter, invented the **spinning jenny.** It had a number of spindles fastened to a single wheel. The jenny made it possible for one person to spin many threads at the same time.

Reading Check Why was the **flying shuttle** important? Who invented the **spinning jenny?**

More progress was made when ways were found to use the power of falling water instead of hand power to run textile machines. This meant, however, that the machines had to be near a large water supply. Accordingly, factories were built next to rivers that could supply the necessary water power. This was the beginning of the **factory system,** which brought workers and machines together in one place to make goods. Workers still lived in their cottages, but they went to factories to work. In time, towns grew up around these factories.

Reading Check How did the **factory system** differ from the domestic system?

Water power did not work very well with heavy machinery. So, people began looking for still another source of power. In 1769, a Scottish mechanic named James Watt perfected the steam engine. Steam soon replaced water as the major source of power. Factories of all kinds could now be set up near raw materials and town markets.

Cotton farmers in America and in India could not supply enough raw cotton to meet the needs of British textile factories. Eli Whitney (ē′ lī hwit′ nē), an American inventor, found a way to solve this problem. While visiting a cotton plantation in Georgia, he learned that it took a great deal of time to clean the seeds out of cotton by hand. In 1793, with the help of Catherine Littlefield Greene, he invented the **cotton gin,** or cotton-cleaning machine. It could clean cotton 50 times faster than a person working by hand. If it were driven by water power, it could clean cotton 1,000 times faster.

Reading Check Who invented the **cotton gin,** and what did this machine do?

Organizing Production

About five years later, Whitney developed a new way of organizing production. This was the system of **interchangeable parts,** which means that a certain part of a product is the same size and shape as that same part in another product. Whitney first used interchangeable parts in the making of guns. Until that time, each gun was made individually, and no two guns were alike. Broken parts had to be specially made by a skilled worker in order to fit a specific gun. Whitney's use of parts of identical size and shape made it possible for less-skilled workers to make or fix guns much faster.

Reading Check What changes did the use of **interchangeable parts** bring to production?

Other Americans also developed new ways of organizing production. In the late 1700s, a shopkeeper-mechanic named Oliver Evans was the first to use **automation,** or the process in which machines instead of people do much of the labor. Evans's

Reading Check What is **automation?**

Reading Check Answer The **flying shuttle** cut in half the time needed to weave cloth. James Hargreaves invented the **spinning jenny.**

Reading Check Answer Under the **factory system,** workers left their cottages to work at machines located in buildings away from their cottages.

MAKING CONNECTIONS

➤➤ **History** The invention of the cotton gin brought about social changes as well as economic ones. Enslavement in the southern states of the United States increased partly because of it.

Reading Check Answer Eli Whitney invented the **cotton gin,** which cleaned seeds from cotton.

Reading Check Answer The use of **interchangeable parts** made it possible for less-skilled workers to make or fix products much faster.

Reading Check Answer **Automation** is the process in which machines, instead of people, do much of the labor.

MEETING SPECIAL NEEDS

To help students with Limited English Proficiency organize and remember information about the people in this chapter, have them make a graphic organizer of the names of these people and their achievements. Have the students work in pairs to classify and then quiz each other; for example, "Who was Galileo Galilei?" "He was an astronomer." After the students know these facts, have pairs add another fact about each person; then have them quiz each other again.

Refer to ***Inclusion for the Middle School Social Studies Classroom: Strategies and Activities*** for additional resources.

Reading Check Answer On an **assembly line,** each worker adds a part of the product and passes it on to the next worker, who also adds a part, until the entire product has been put together.

L3 **Research** Have students research one of the following inventors and their inventions: Samuel Crompton, Edmund Cartwright, Alessandro Volta, Richard Trevithnick, Cyrus McCormick, Charles Goodyear, Elias Howe, Zénobe T. Gramme, Christopher L. Stoles, Norbert Rillieux, Richard Arkwright. Have students re-create a model of the invention made by the inventor. Then hold an "Invention Convention" in which the students role-play the inventor and explain the invention.

CAPTION ANSWER

the cotton gin

LINKING PAST TO PRESENT

Henry Bessemer established his steel works at Sheffield, England, a city that is still noted for its fine steel products.

Reading Check How does an **assembly line** work?

People in History

Robert Fulton
1765–1815

American Inventor

Born near Lancaster, Pennsylvania, Robert Fulton had many talents. He was an expert gunsmith and an accomplished landscape painter. He also designed torpedoes and early submarines. Fulton is best known for launching the *Clermont,* the first commercially successful steamboat in America.

automated flour mill was water-powered and cut by four-fifths the number of workers needed to run it.

In 1847, Samuel Colt used Whitney's idea of interchangeable parts to develop the **assembly line.** On an assembly line, each worker adds a part of the product and passes it on to the next worker, who also adds a part, until the entire product has been put together. Colt used the assembly line to produce the Colt revolver. Before assembly lines, a skilled worker had to make one product at a time from start to finish. With the assembly line, work could be divided, and many products could be put together at one time by unskilled workers. All of these discoveries and new techniques greatly increased production.

Iron, Coal, and Steel To build machine parts, iron was needed. To fire steam engines, coal was needed. Without iron, coal, and steel, which replaced iron, the Industrial Revolution could not have continued.

By the early 1700s, ironmaking had become expensive. To smelt iron, the British used *charcoal,* a fuel that is made by burning wood. The British, however, were running out of

SEWING MACHINE Isaac Singer oversees a demonstration of his first sewing machine. **What invention benefited the textile industry during the early 1800s?**

SPOTLIGHT ON: JOSIAH WEDGWOOD

When china clay, used for pottery and chinaware, was found in nearby Cornwall, Josiah Wedgwood took the lead in establishing the famous potteries in 18th-century Great Britain. Wedgwood learned the craft of making pottery from his family and other famous potters and opened his own factory in Etruria. His first success was a cream-colored earthenware he called Queen's ware. Wedgwood's dishes became quite popular with the prosperous middle class. Wedgwood was the first pottery maker to use steam-powered engines.

forests, which made wood scarce and costly. In 1753, a way was found to use coal instead of charcoal for smelting. As a result, iron became cheaper, iron production grew, and coal mining became a major industry.

Iron, however, was too brittle for rails, bridge supports, and heavy equipment. In 1856, a British inventor named Henry Bessemer (bes' uh muhr) found a cheap way of removing the impurities from iron to make steel, which was harder and stronger than iron. The Bessemer Process lowered the cost of making steel from $200 a ton to $4 a ton. Seven years later, in 1863, Pierre-Emile Martin of France and William Siemens of England invented the **open-hearth process,** which used a special kind of furnace to make steel. It was even cheaper than the Bessemer Process and could turn out many different kinds of steel. Soon, mining towns and steel centers grew up in areas with supplies of iron ore and coal.

Reading Check What was the **open-hearth process?**

Transportation

Raw materials and finished products had to be moved quickly and cheaply. Before this could happen, transportation had to be improved. Until the 1700s, the chief means of transportation over land was by horse or horse-drawn wagon. Roads were no more than rough and narrow dirt paths. Travel was slow and uncomfortable. It was even worse when rain made the roads muddy.

Late in the 1700s, the British began to improve their roads. A Scottish engineer named Thomas Telford (tel' fuhrd) designed roadbeds so that water would drain off the roads. Another Scottish engineer, John L. McAdam, developed what became known as the **macadam** (muh kad' uhm) **road.** It had a surface made of layers of crushed stone. This surface allowed horse-drawn wagons to use the roads in all kinds of weather and to travel faster.

Reading Check How did the **macadam road** improve transportation?

The British also made their rivers wider and deeper and built canals to connect navigable rivers to factory and mining centers. Horses walked beside canals and pulled barges. The barges were slow but could carry 50 times the amount of goods that horse-drawn wagons could. By 1830, Great Britain had a complete system of inland waterways.

The biggest improvement in land transportation was the railroad. For years, donkeys had pulled carts over wooden rails inside coal mines. Then, the production of iron grew. The wooden rails were replaced by iron ones that could carry heavier loads. Inventors began to build locomotives to run on iron rails. In 1829, George Stephenson (stē' vuhn suhn), a British mining engineer, won a contest to see who could build the best locomotive. Stephenson's locomotive, the *Rocket,* could pull a train about 36 miles, or 58 kilometers, an hour. The *Rocket* started a railroad-building boom in Great Britain and around the world.

Then & Now

A High Railway In 1870, an American engineer named Henry Meiggs built what is still the world's highest railroad—the Central Railway—across the Andes Mountains in Peru. At its highest point, the Central Railway reaches an altitude of nearly 16,000 feet, or 4880 meters, higher than the tallest peak in the Alps.

Reading Check Answer The **open-hearth process** used a special kind of furnace to make steel cheaper than the Bessemer process.

PRIMARY SOURCES Library

You might assign "The Iron Horse," from pages 692–693 of the Primary Sources Library.

Reading Check Answer The **macadam road** allowed horse-drawn carriages to use the roads in all kinds of weather and to travel faster.

Economics at a Glance

The Economy of the Twenty-first Century

New terms are being used to describe the economic changes that we see today. The *knowledge economy* and the *weightless economy* describe an environment in which ideas and information are as valuable as material goods. There are many elements to this new economy: information and communications technology; intellectual property, such as patents and brand names; technical information, such as biotechnology and engineering; and information found in libraries, databases, and videos. Call on volunteers to describe the industrial economy and the knowledge, or weightless, economy. Note their responses on the board. Then organize students into several groups, and have groups create an illustration—a cartoon, poster, or graphic organizer—that shows the differences between the two economies. Ask groups to display their illustrations.

COOPERATIVE LEARNING

Organize students into groups. Have each group research innovations in one of these areas: farming, transportation, power sources, textiles, factories. Each team member should be assigned a specific topic. Students examining "power sources" could research the use of waterwheels or coal, for example. After researching, have groups share their findings. Have one member of each group present the group's findings in an oral report.

Assign Chapter 33 ***Cooperative Learning Activity*** in the TCR.

GEOGRAPHY AND HISTORY

It took sailing ships about two months to cross the Atlantic. Steamboats made the trip in ten days.

Independent Practice

L2 **Literature** Have students read parts of *Life on the Mississippi* by Mark Twain, an account of the author's years as a steamboat pilot. Have students consider what functions steamboats served and how they affected life and commerce in that area. Have students conclude by discussing what the book tells about society in the Mississippi River valley at that time.

Use the **Interactive Tutor Self-Assessment CD-ROM** to review Section 3.

HISTORY Online

Student Web Activity objectives and answers can be found at the ***Chapter 33 Web Activity Lesson Plan*** at humanheritage.glencoe.com

Use the **Vocabulary Puzzle-Maker CD-ROM** to create crossword and word search puzzles.

Railroads changed daily life as well as transportation. People started using such phrases as "keeping on track" and "tooting your own whistle." They also collected autographs of railway engineers. When American railroads adopted standard time zones in 1883, everyone else in the United States did too. The next year, time zones were established all over the world.

The biggest improvement in water transportation was the steamboat. The first practical one was developed by Robert Fulton (fūhl' tuhn), an American inventor. In 1807, Fulton's *Clermont,* powered by a British steam engine, set a record by making the trip from Albany to New York City in 32 hours. Soon, steamboats were carrying passengers and goods along the inland waterways of the United States and Europe. Steamboats, however, did not replace sailing ships in trans-oceanic travel until the late 1800s, when fuel-efficient engines were developed.

Section 3 Assessment

1. **Define:** textile, domestic system, flying shuttle, spinning jenny, factory system, cotton gin, interchangeable parts, automation, assembly line, open-hearth process, macadam road.
2. What effect did the assembly line have on the type of workers needed for production?
3. Why did transportation have to be improved during the Industrial Revolution?

Critical Thinking

4. **Predicting Consequences** Suppose the steam engine was never invented. Do you think the Industrial Revolution would have still occurred? Why or why not?

Graphic Organizer Activity

5. Draw this diagram, and use it to weigh the pros and cons of using an assembly line to produce goods.

Use of Assembly Line	
Pros	Cons

HISTORY Online

Student Web Activity

Visit the *Human Heritage* Web site at humanheritage.glencoe.com and click on ***Chapter 33—Student Web Activity*** to find out more about inventors who lived during the Industrial Revolution.

SECTION 4 Industrial Impact

The Industrial Revolution brought many changes in people's lives. These changes showed up first in Great Britain. They then spread to other countries.

Changes in Society In England, until the Middle Ages, there had been two major social classes—the nobles, who were the upper class, and the peasants, who were the lower class. Then, a middle class of rich merchants developed.

Section 3 Assessment Answers

1. All terms are defined in the text Glossary.
2. It made it possible for less-skilled workers to make or fix products much faster.
3. to move raw materials and finished products quickly and cheaply
4. Answers will vary, but students should mention the importance of the steam engine in the expansion of the factory system and growth of a market economy. Some students may suggest alternative inventions that could have had a similar impact as the steam engine.
5. Charts will vary but may indicate the advantage of increased productivity and the disadvantage of monotonous work.

Assign the Chapter 33 **Section 3 Quiz** in the TCR. Testmaker available.

During the Industrial Revolution, the middle class increased in numbers and grew richer. Many factory, railroad, and mine owners became as wealthy as the nobles. They began to keep servants and to dress like members of the upper class. Women wore lacy petticoats and hooped skirts with stiff linings. Men wore dark suits, with top hats in winter and *boaters*, or stiff straw hats, in summer. Members of the middle class had iron ranges for cooking and gave huge dinner parties. Middle-class families began spending their weekends at seaside resorts, which were easy to reach now that railroads were common. Middle-class children went to upper-class schools.

In time, the middle class gained political power. In Great Britain, its male members gained the right to vote and to be represented in Parliament.

The Industrial Revolution also created an industrial working class. Most members of this class were peasants who could no longer support themselves by farming. Since they had no property of their own to sell, they had to sell their labor in order to live.

Members of the working class did not benefit from the Industrial Revolution in its early years. They worked 12 to 16 hours a day, six days a week, for low wages. They had to work at the pace set by machines and factory owners and were fined or

Linking Across Time

Automation The development of automation reduced the number of workers needed to produce goods. One person, for example, could run a machine that spun rows and rows of spindles of thread (below). Today the use of robots has eliminated the use of humans entirely on some jobs (right). **How did the use of machines affect the lives of workers in the Industrial Revolution?**

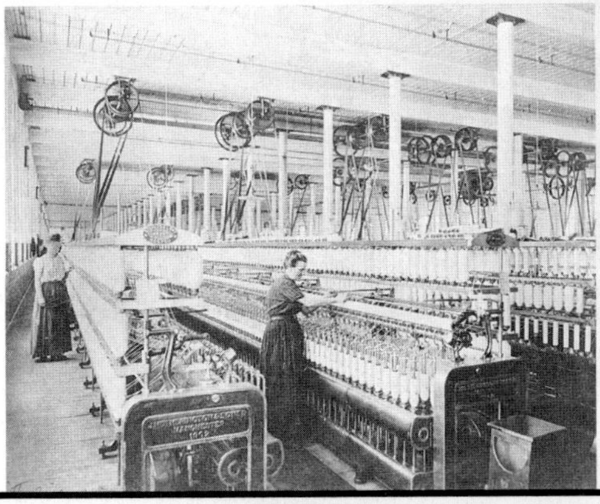

Glencoe Literature Library

The following novel from the **Glencoe Literature Library** may be used to enrich this chapter:

- *The Adventures of Tom Sawyer*, by Mark Twain.

Linking Across Time

Workers labored long hours for low wages, often under dangerous conditions. They had no job security and could be fined for falling behind.

SPOTLIGHT ON: ROBERT OWEN

Robert Owen tried to turn his mill town in New Lanark, Scotland, into an ideal community. He was a reformer who believed that better conditions would create better people and reduce crime and undesirable habits. Working hours were shortened and pay was increased at his mill. Owen built cottages for the workers. The town's stores offered affordable clothing and food. Children under age 10 did not work in the mill but attended free schools. Classes for older children were provided as well. By 1815, visitors from other parts of Great Britain and other countries came to observe the "ideal" town.

MAKING CONNECTIONS

>> **Daily Life** In 1841, an anonymous woman who worked in the textile mill in Lowell, Massachusetts, wrote about the poor working conditions in the workers' magazine *The Lowell Offering:* "I am going home, where I shall not be obliged to rise so early in the morning, . . . Up before day, at the clang of the bell—and out of the mill by the clang of the bell—into the mill, and at work in obedience to that ding-dong of a bell—just as though we were so many living machines."

L2 **Economics** Have students research and present an in-class report on the early railroad industry. Students should use the following questions to focus their reports. How did this new means of transportation affect the economies of countries such as Great Britain and the United States? How did railroads affect markets for goods, opportunities for travel, and communication?

L3 **Critical Thinking** Have students investigate reform movements to outlaw child labor in the United States. Who headed these movements? Were they successful?

CAPTION ANSWER

because workers had little economic power; it was against the law to form trade unions, and workers could not vote

beaten if they did not keep up. Working conditions were difficult, dirty, and dangerous. Many people were killed or injured by unsafe machinery. The working class did not have job security. Factory and mine owners hired and fired whenever they wanted.

Most children of the working class did not have time to go to school or to play. Instead, they worked in factories and mines along with men and women. Employers often preferred to hire children since they could be paid even less than adults. Another reason was that in mines, children could crawl through narrow tunnels into which adults could not fit. Children sometimes were crippled by this difficult work.

Then . . . & Now

A Growing Population
In 1800, less than 3 percent of the world's people lived in cities with 20,000 or more people. By the year 2000, however, as many as 50 percent lived in urban areas.

The Growth of Cities Another change brought by the Industrial Revolution was the growth of cities. Before the Industrial Revolution, less than 10 percent of the people in Great Britain lived in cities. By 1900, the number had reached 75 percent. Indeed, 10 percent of the people in the whole country lived in the city of London.

Some cities grew up around factories or mines that had been built in rural areas. Most factories, however, were built in existing cities, which grew rapidly as people moved there to find jobs. Soon, the cities became overcrowded. Houses could not be built fast enough. Sometimes, a dozen people had to live in one room. Many moved into damp basements or rooms with no windows. Garbage floated in the streets because sewers had not yet been built. Water supplies became polluted. Epidemics of cholera (kol' uhr uh), typhoid, and tuberculosis were common. The death rate

INDUSTRIAL CITIES The development of industry in England led to the growth of large cities. English industrial cities were located near coal or iron deposits. This painting shows a nineteenth-century steel factory in the city of Sheffield. **Why could workers in the city do nothing about their working or living conditions?**

EXTENDING THE CONTENT

The city of Manchester, England, had many geographic factors that an industrial city needed for growth, such as the availability of raw materials and accessible transportation routes. Manchester lies within 25 miles (or 40 km) of two coal fields, at the meeting point of three rivers, and has a canal that connects the city to the Irish Sea. During the 1800s, Manchester grew into one of the world's centers for the production of cotton textiles. Mills and warehouses replaced private homes in many areas.

among the working class was more than twice that of the middle and upper classes.

Workers had little economic or political power. It was against the law to form **trade unions,** or workers' associations. Workers did not have the right to vote. For these reasons, they could do nothing about their working or living conditions.

Reading Check What were **trade unions?**

Reform Most people in the middle and upper classes paid little attention to the suffering of the workers. Factory owners, for example, felt that raising wages and improving working conditions would raise the cost of goods and lower profits. Some, however, believed that higher wages and better working conditions could produce good profits. They began to work for reform.

The reformers started schools, orphanages, and hospitals for the poor. They also worked to change laws. In 1824, trade unions were made legal. During the 1830s and 1840s, children under ten years old and women were prohibited from working underground in mines. The workday was cut to ten hours.

The reformers also worked to improve living conditions. New laws required public sewer systems and the building of better houses. Every room had to have at least one window, and every house had to have piped-in water. Over time, life became better for the working class. There were fewer epidemics. Clothing, food, and other products became cheap enough for the workers to buy.

Section 4 Assessment

1. **Define:** trade unions.
2. What problems were caused by the rapid growth of cities?
3. Why were some people against reform?

Critical Thinking

4. **Demonstrating Reasoned Judgment** What reforms would you have worked for if you had lived during the Industrial Revolution?

Graphic Organizer Activity

5. Draw this diagram, and use it to support this generalization: The Industrial Revolution brought many changes to people's lives. (Add answer lines as needed.)

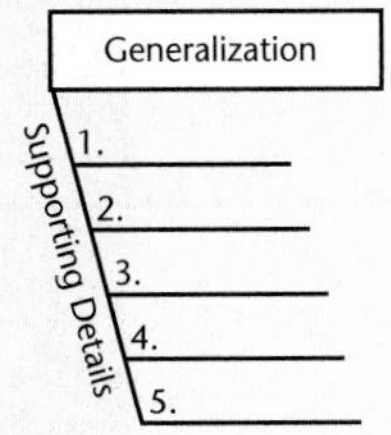

SECTION 5 Spread of Industry

Meanwhile, the Industrial Revolution spread from Great Britain to other countries. These countries, aided by technology, soon **industrialized,** or built up industry. The expansion of railroads and transportation were also important factors.

Reading Check What happened when countries **industrialized?**

Reading Check Answer **Trade unions** were workers' associations.

Economics at a Glance

Trade Unions A *trade union* is an association of skilled workers who perform the same kind of work. An industrial union is an association of all workers in the same industry, regardless of the job each worker performs. Have students use the Internet to find different trade and industrial unions. Students should then create a graphic organizer that shows which category each one belongs to and describe its responsibilities. Have volunteers present their graphic organizers to the class.

L1 **History** Have students investigate and present an oral report on child labor in the United States during the 1800s. Students should research the type of work young children performed, the length of their working day, and the amount they were paid. Suggest they create a list or daily schedule of what a day in the life of one of these children might have been like. What modern counterparts to these movements remain today? Have students report on their findings to the class.

Use the **Interactive Tutor Self-Assessment CD-ROM** to review Section 4.

Reading Check Answer When countries **industrialized,** they built up industry.

Use the **Vocabulary PuzzleMaker CD-ROM** to create crossword and word search puzzles.

Section 4 Assessment Answers

1. trade unions, workers' associations (p. 533)
2. overcrowding; disposing of garbage; obtaining fresh water supplies; and epidemics of cholera, typhoid, and tuberculosis
3. because they felt that raising wages and improving working conditions would raise the cost of goods and lower profits
4. Answers will vary, but students should give reasons for their answers.
5. Sample supporting details: middle class grew in size, wealth, and political power; an industrial working class appeared; industrial workers labored long hours for low wages; machines and factory owners set the pace of work; children went to work in factories and mines; cities expanded and the poor often lived in unhealthy conditions.

Assign Chapter 33 **Section 4 Quiz** in the TCR. Testmaker available.

L1 Geography: The World in Spatial Terms Have students use the world map in their text Atlas to locate the countries that were industrialized by the late 1800s.

Reading Check Answer Other countries welcomed skilled British **immigrants** because they brought British industrial secrets to their new homelands.

MAKING CONNECTIONS

>> **History** In 1789, a young British mechanic named Samuel Slater arrived in New York, bringing with him the secrets of new spinning and weaving machines built by British inventors. Slater was soon operating the first factory in the United States.

CAPTION ANSWER

British immigrants brought industrial secrets to their new homelands.

DID YOU KNOW ??

Crusader for workers' rights, especially those of African Americans, William Lloyd Garrison published his successful newspaper, *The Liberator*, in the early 1800s.

Reading Check Why did other nations welcome skilled British **immigrants?**

Then & Now

Weights and Measures As industrialization spread, people needed a common system of weights and measures. Most countries adopted the metric system, first developed in France in the 1790s. Its basic measurement, the meter, equals one ten-millionth of the distance along a meridian from the North Pole to the Equator.

Other Countries

At the beginning of the Industrial Revolution, Great Britain tried to keep its inventions secret. Machines or plans for machines were forbidden to be taken out of Great Britain. Skilled workers were forbidden to leave the country. By the 1800s, however, many workers had ignored the law and left. Other nations welcomed these **immigrants,** or people who settle permanently in a different country, because they brought British industrial secrets to their new homelands.

These countries used what they learned to build their own industries. Belgium, with its rich deposits of iron and coal, was the first country after Great Britain to industrialize. The next country was France. There, the process began in the 1700s but was slowed by war and revolution. The United States, with its many natural resources, soon followed France.

Then came Germany. Although Germany was well supplied with coal and iron, it was divided into more than 30 separate states. These states were not willing to cooperate in economic matters. Germany, therefore, did not make much industrial progress until after it was unified in 1871. It then matched the others as a leading industrial power.

WORLD'S FAIR In 1851, Great Britain held the first World's Fair in London to celebrate its industrial achievements. Other countries then began to hold similar fairs. This painting shows the royal family attending opening day. **How did the Industrial Revolution spread from Great Britain to other countries?**

SPOTLIGHT ON: SAMUEL SLATER

Samuel Slater was working as an engineer overseeing the machines in a British cotton mill when he heard about the rewards for textile-machine designs in the United States. Disguising himself as an apprentice, he sailed to New York. There, Moses Brown, a Quaker merchant from Rhode Island, hired him. Slater re-created from memory the Arkwright-designed spinning machines that he had worked with in England. His water-powered mill was built next to the falls of the Blackstone River. Slater later built other mills in New England. The Old Slater Mill in Pawtucket, Rhode Island, has been restored as a museum.

THOMAS EDISON Although best known for the electric light, Thomas Edison had numerous other important inventions. These include the first successful phonograph, an electric railroad, and an electric battery. This photograph shows Edison in his laboratory. **What advances in communications were powered by electricity?**

Technological Advances The development of new kinds of power helped continue the Industrial Revolution. One of these was electricity. In 1837, two Americans, Samuel F. B. Morse and Alfred Vail, built the first successful electric telegraph. It made quick communication possible. Some years later, Alexander Graham Bell, also an American, invented the telephone. Communications took another step forward. In 1895, an Italian physicist, Guglielmo Marconi (gū yel' mō mahr kō' nē), built the wireless telegraph, or radio. Six years later, he was able to send a message across the Atlantic Ocean.

Meanwhile, there were other advances in electricity. By 1879, Thomas Alva Edison, an American, developed the electric light. It would soon illuminate factories and homes all over the world.

Another new source of power was the **internal combustion engine,** or an engine that is fueled by gasoline. It was invented around 1885 by German engineer Gottlieb Daimler (gōt' lēb dīm' luhr). Daimler's engine was used to drive the first automobile as well as other machines. Another German engineer, Rudolf Diesel, developed an oil-burning internal combustion engine that could run large industrial plants, locomotives, and ocean liners. These developments helped open a whole new era in transportation.

Fun Facts . . .

Inspiration Guglielmo Marconi, inventor of the wireless telegraph, was inspired to experiment with science after reading a biography of Benjamin Franklin.

Reading Check What fueled the **internal combustion engine?**

Biography

The following video programs are available to enrich Chapter 33:

- **Alexander Graham Bell: Voice of Invention**
- **The Electric Light** (Edison)
- **Marconi: Whisper in the Air**

To find classroom resources to accompany these videos, check the following home page:

A&E Television:
www.aande.com

CAPTION ANSWER

the electric telegraph, the telephone, and the wireless telegraph (radio)

Reading Check Answer

The first **internal combustion engine** was fueled by gasoline.

ASSESS

Check for Understanding

Ask students to summarize the main points of the chapter, orally or in writing. Discuss the answers to the Section and Chapter Assessment questions.

Evaluate

Assign the Chapter 33 **Performance Assessment Activity** in the TCR.

Administer the **Chapter 33 Test.** Testmaker available.

Reteach

Have students create time lines that list important inventions that contributed to the Industrial Revolution.

Assign the **Chapter 33 Reteaching Activity** in the TCR.

EXTENDING THE CONTENT

The invention of the gasoline-powered engines carried aviation technology to new levels. In the 1890s, Ferdinand von Zeppelin streamlined the dirigible—a balloon-like craft that could carry passengers. Wilbur and Orville Wright achieved success in 1903 with the first flight of a motorized airplane. Airplanes and other vehicles needed a steady supply of fuel for power and rubber for tires and other parts. As a result, the worldwide petroleum and rubber industries skyrocketed.

GLENCOE TECHNOLOGY

MindJogger Videoquiz

Use **MindJogger Videoquiz** to review students' knowledge of the unit.

Available in DVD and VHS

Enrich

Have students write scripts and perform skits showing working-class life during the Industrial Revolution.

Assign the **Chapter 33 Enrichment Activity** in the TCR.

CLOSE

Tell students that people often use the phrase, "the good old days," out of nostalgia for the past. Have them discuss what people living in the United States during the Industrial Revolution might have meant when they used this phrase.

Use the **Interactive Tutor Self-Assessment CD-ROM** to review Section 5.

HISTORY Online

Self-Check Quiz gives students an interactive chapter tutorial. Have them access ***Chapter 33 Quiz*** at **humanheritage.glencoe.com**

Section 5 Assessment

1. **Define:** industrialized, immigrants, internal combustion engine.
2. How did the Industrial Revolution spread?
3. What were the first countries to industrialize after Great Britain?

Critical Thinking

4. **Drawing Conclusions** Which of the advances in technology made during the Industrial Revolution do you consider the most important? Explain.

Graphic Organizer Activity

5. Draw this diagram, and use it to show inventions that advanced communication and the use of new forms of energy or power.

New Inventions	
Communication	Energy/Power

Chapter Summary & Study Guide

1. In 1543, Copernicus triggered the Scientific Revolution with his idea of a sun-centered solar system.
2. The Scientific Revolution helped lead to the Agricultural Revolution—a new system of land division, animal breeding, and growing crops.
3. The invention of new machines helped workers produce more goods in less time.
4. Perfection of the steam engine replaced the use of water power and allowed factories to be built near sources of raw materials.
5. Eli Whitney and Catherine Littlefield Greene invented the cotton gin in 1793. Whitney also developed the principle of interchangeable parts.
6. Automation and the assembly line increased production and reduced the need for skilled workers.
7. The development of inexpensive ways to smelt iron and make steel provided cheaper building materials for industry.
8. Improvements in transportation—better roads, canal systems, railroads, and steam boats—helped speed industrialization.
9. The Industrial Revolution increased the size of the middle class and created a new industrial working class, many of whom suffered poor living conditions in industrial cities.
10. During the 1800s, the Industrial Revolution spread from Great Britain to other countries, where inventors developed even more new ideas such as electricity and the internal combustion engine.

HISTORY Online

Self-Check Quiz

Visit the *Human Heritage* Web site at **humanheritage.glencoe.com** and click on ***Chapter 33—Self-Check Quiz*** to assess your understanding of this chapter.

Section 5 Assessment Answers

1. industrialized, built up industry (p. 533); immigrants, people who settle in a different country (p. 534); internal combustion engine, engine fueled by gasoline (p. 535)
2. Workers who left England took British industrial secrets to their new homelands.
3. Belgium, France, Germany, and the United States
4. Answers will vary, but students should give reasons for their choices.
5. sample responses: *communication*—telegraph, telephone, wireless telegraph (radio); *energy/power*—electricity, internal combustion engines run by gasoline, internal combustion engine run by oil

Assign the Chapter 33 **Section 5 Quiz** in the TCR. Testmaker available.

CHAPTER 33 Assessment

Using Key Terms

Imagine that you are having a conversation with Thomas Jefferson about the most important ideas and innovations of the Industrial Revolution. Write out the dialogue using the following words.

enclosure	textile
domestic system	flying shuttle
spinning jenny	factory system
cotton gin	interchangeable parts
automation	assembly line
open-hearth process	macadam road
trade unions	industrialized
immigrants	internal combustion engine

Understanding Main Ideas

1. In what ways did ideas about science change in the 1400s, 1500s, and 1600s?
2. What effect did the Agricultural Revolution have on population growth?
3. How did the development of the macadam road affect transportation?
4. What benefits did people in the working class eventually receive from the Industrial Revolution?
5. What new sources of power helped spread the Industrial Revolution?

Critical Thinking

1. How did changes in agriculture influence the beginning of the Industrial Revolution?
2. Why did Great Britian want to keep its inventions secret from the rest of the world?
3. What things are necessary for a country to be able to industrialize?
4. Do you believe the Industrial Revolution was good or bad for most workers? Explain.

Graphic Organizer Activity

Economics Create a diagram such as the one shown, and use it to compare economic activities before and after the Industrial Revolution. (Tip: Think back to how people earned a living in the Renaissance and Middle Ages.)

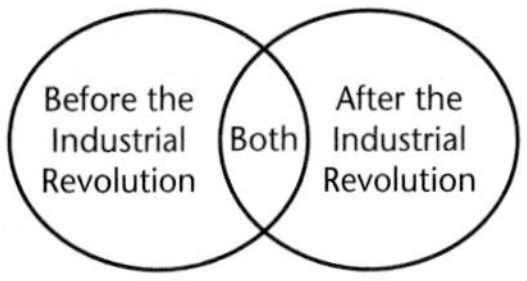

Geography in History

Environment and Society Progress that came about during the Industrial Revolution was caused by people interacting with their environment. What geographic features were involved in this progress? Explain.

Using Your Journal

Review any details you may have noted about the changes that took place in the world between the 1400s and the 1800s. Write a newspaper editorial in which you give your opinion about how developments during the Industrial Revolution might cause problems for people in the future.

537

Bonus Test Question

For Chapter 33 Test
How did the invention of the electric light change American society forever? Explain.

Using Your Journal

Editorials will vary. You might call on volunteers to read their editorials to the class and discuss them.

Geography in History

Factories were built next to rivers for water power and steam power, and near raw materials and markets. Transportation systems were improved so things could be moved quickly and cheaply.

CHAPTER 33 Assessment Answers

Using Key Terms

Dialogues will vary, but students should use all the terms.

Understanding Main Ideas

1. Scientists used the scientific method to test their hypotheses.
2. More food meant better health and longer life spans.
3. It allowed horse-drawn wagons to travel faster in all kinds of weather.
4. There were fewer epidemics, and products were cheaper.
5. electricity and the internal combustion engine

Critical Thinking

1. Farmers moved to cities; population grew and demand increased for manufactured goods.
2. because it wanted to monopolize profits
3. natural resources, technology, power sources, production, transportation, and workers
4. Answers will vary, but students should explain their reasons.

Graphic Organizer Activity

Diagrams will vary, but economic activities prior to the Industrial Revolution will probably focus on farming and skilled crafts while economic activities after the Industrial Revolution will include factory work, mining, and so on. Economic activities both before and after the Industrial Revolution might include trade, shipbuilding, and perhaps banking (starting in the Renaissance).

FOCUS

Objectives

After reading the Around the World for Unit 10, students will be able to:

1. identify the size and location of the Russian empire at its height.

2. link Russian expansion to the diversity of its population.

3. describe efforts to westernize Russia.

Bellringer

Ask students to write down what comes to mind when they hear the word "empire."

Motivational Activity

Discuss student responses. Then refer them to the Around the World feature on these pages. In what ways did Russia fulfill students' expectations of what an empire should look like? *(Students might note the empire's huge size, the grandeur of objects such as the crown, the existence of a noble class, and so on.)*

TEACH

Geography: The World in Spatial Terms Tell students to study the map on this page. Ask: On what continents was the Russian empire located at its height? *(parts of Europe, Asia, and North America)* Where were the two great Russian cities—St. Petersburg and Moscow—located? *(west of the Ural Mountains, in Europe)* Ask students why Russian rulers might have found it hard to modernize their empire. *(sheer size of the empire, great distance of the government from lands east of the Urals, existence of many traditional cultures, and so on)*

UNIT 10 Around

RUSSIA

While western European nations pushed into the Americas, Russian czars expanded their borders both in the east and in the west. By the 1800s, Russia covered one-sixth of the earth's surface. It extended from the Baltic Sea in the west to Alaska in the east and from the Arctic Ocean in the north to central Asia in the south. The greatest czars—rulers like Peter the Great and Catherine the Great—worked tirelessly to modernize Russia. No matter how hard they tried, however, Russia remained a mostly rural nation, with nearly all of its vast population working as serfs or living in remote villages.

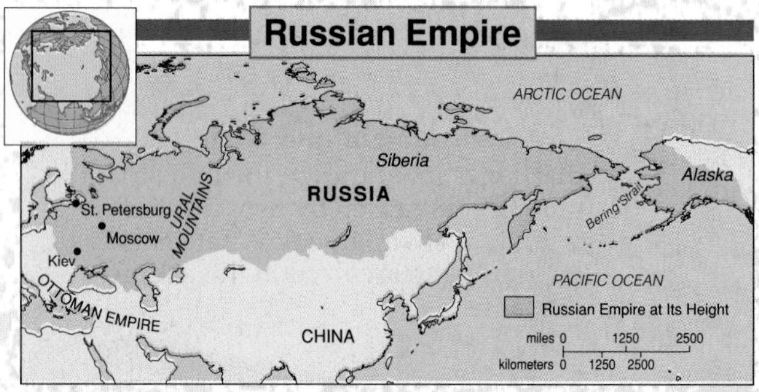

▲ Most of the Russian empire stretched east of the Ural Mountains—the traditional boundary between Europe and Asia. Even so, the heart of the empire always lay west of the Urals—the place where the states of Rus and Muscovy were born. It was here that Russian rulers built their greatest cities and set up governments to rule their sprawling lands.

▼ Both nobles and serfs loved the folktales that formed part of Russia's oral history. These tales drew an audience everywhere, whether it be in a peasant's cottage or a czar's palace. Russian artists captured scenes from these stories on beautiful lacquered boxes such as this one.

SPOTLIGHT ON: RUSSIA

The revolutions of the late 1700s did not escape Russian notice. Inspired by the American and French revolutions, some 3,000 army officers from the Russian aristocracy took part in the Decembrist uprising of 1825. On December 26, the so-called "Decembrists" gathered at a statue of Peter the Great located in St. Petersburg's Senate Square. There, leaders of the uprising demanded a constitution and an immediate end to serfdom, which they called "our national disgrace."

The Decembrists expected the peasants to join them in revolt. What they got instead was the wrath of Czar Nicolas I, who called out the imperial guard. The czar's troops crushed the uprising—and hopes for democratic reform. After a quick trial, the leaders were hanged and the remaining officers were sent into exile in Siberia.

▶ Peter the Great founded St. Petersburg on the Baltic Sea in the early 1700s. Peter tried to "westernize" Russia. He even worked to ban beards on Russian men.

▲ Russian serfs farmed the land, worked as servants, and generally served the nobles who owned the land on which they lived. In this painting, serfs escort a noble family through the winter countryside in a carriage.

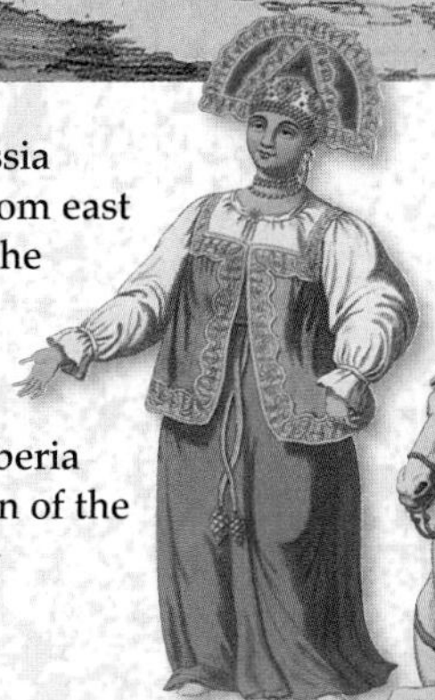

By the end of the 1700s, Russia reached some 6,000 miles from east to west. The larger it grew, the more diverse its population became. Peoples ranged from the hunters of the Tungus region in eastern Siberia (right) to the peasant women of the St. Petersburg area (left). ▶

◀ The skill of Russian artisans is shown in this fur-lined gold crown set with precious jewels. Crafted in the mid-sixteenth century, the crown is in a museum in the Kremlin today.

Taking Another Look

1. What was the size and location of the Russian empire at its height?
2. How did expansion affect the population makeup of Russia?

Hands-On Activity

Writing a Letter to the Editor Write a letter to the editor of a Russian newspaper commenting on the decision to ban all beards.

539

ANSWERS TO TAKING ANOTHER LOOK

1. At its height, the Russian empire covered one-sixth of the earth's surface. It extended from the Baltic Sea in the west to Alaska in the east and from the Arctic Ocean in the north to central Asia in the south.
2. The larger the empire grew, the more diverse its population became.

Hands-On Activity

Letters will vary but should reflect an understanding that the central issue is Peter's efforts to westernize Russia, rather than simply his ban on old-fashioned beards.

DID YOU KNOW ??

Russia acquired Siberia during the reign of Ivan the Terrible. Instead of sending criminals or troublemakers to prison, Ivan and the rulers who followed him often exiled them to Siberia, giving rise to the phrase "sent off to Siberia."

Biography®

The following videotape program is available from Glencoe to enrich the Around the World feature.

- **Faberge: Imperial Jeweler**

1-56501-878-8

To find classroom resources to accompany this video, check the following home page:

A&E Television:
www.aande.com

ASSESS

Check for Understanding

Have students answer the questions in Taking Another Look on page 539.

Enrich

Ask interested students to trace the Romanov dynasty that ruled imperial Russia. Have students present their findings in the form of an illustrated time line.

CLOSE

Have students compare Russia with western Europe in the late 1700s and early 1800s. Ask: What political and economic differences can you note between the two regions? *(the lack of democratic revolutions in Russia, the continued presence of a large population of serfs, lack of industry, and so on)*

Answers and Analyses

1C Geography

According to the map, St. Augustine is located next to the 30°N (30 degrees north) line and is just to the east of the 90° W (90 degrees west) line.

2F Geography

According to the graph, the largest population belonged to Virginia, with close to 60,000 people; the smallest belonged to Pennsylvania, with about 18,000 people.

3D Culture/Environment

Since Native Americans had established ways of life before the arrival of colonists, choice A can be eliminated. Choice B is unlikely, and since Native Americans did not believe in land ownership, choice C can also be eliminated.

THE PRINCETON REVIEW **TEST-TAKING TIP**

Students should always begin by eliminating the unreasonable, and then take their best guess from among the remaining choices. Choices A and C are limited to the encounter between the Native Americans and the American settlers. They are not likely the cause of the different lifestyles.

THE PRINCETON REVIEW

Standardized Test Practice

Directions: Choose the *best* answer to each of the following multiple choice questions. If you have trouble answering a question, use the process of elimination to narrow your choices. Write your answers on a separate piece of paper.

Spanish Colonies in the Americas

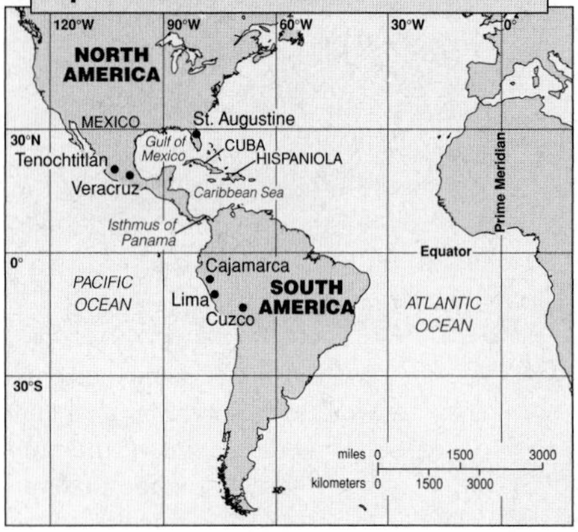

1. According to the map above, what colony was located at approximately 29°N and 82°W?

A Cuba

B Gulf of Mexico

C St. Augustine

D Cajamarca

Test-Taking Tip: Look at the map's labels carefully. How does it show which labels belong to *continents?* To *islands?* To *colonies?*

Population of Six English Colonies, 1700

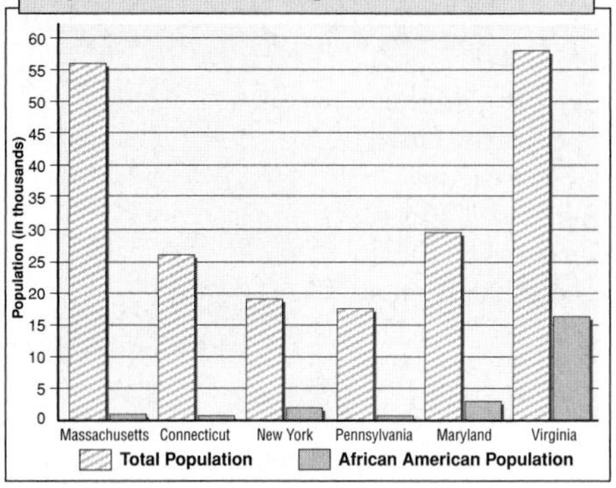

2. According to the graph above, which colonies had the largest and smallest total populations in 1700?

F Virginia and Pennsylvania

G Massachusetts and New York

H New York and Pennsylvania

J Connecticut and Maryland

Test-Taking Tip: Notice that the question asks for *total population.* This graph shows two different bars for each colony. Do you need to add the bars together to get the total population? Why or why not?

3. Native Americans in the Subarctic, Great Basin, and California areas relied on hunting, fishing, and gathering food. Native Americans in the Eastern Woodlands, Southwest, and Southeast became farmers. What might explain this difference?

A Native Americans in the Eastern Woodlands, Southwest, and Southeast learned how to farm from the colonists.

B Native Americans in the Subarctic, Great Basin, and California did not have farming tools.

C Native Americans in the Eastern Woodlands, Southwest, and Southeast were allowed to own land, so they could establish permanent farms.

D The climate and soil in the Subarctic, Great Basin, and California areas were not good for farming.

Test-Taking Tip: Since the "hunters" and the "farmers" came from different geographic regions, it is likely that the answer has something to do with geography. Which answer choice fits *best* with this information?

4. The civil war in England was fought between

F the government and serfs
G the monarchy and the feudal lords
H the king and Parliament
J England and France

Test-Taking Tip: Eliminate answers that do not make sense. A *civil war* is a type of war fought *within one country.* Therefore, answer J can be eliminated.

5. In *Two Treatises of Government,* John Locke wrote about certain natural rights with which all people are born. These rights did NOT include

A life
B liberty
C education
D property

Test-Taking Tip: It may be helpful to remember that Locke's ideas helped form the basis for the Declaration of Independence. What rights did the colonists *most* want to protect?

6. Like the English and American revolutions, the French Revolution was fought over

F the power of the monarchy
G the role of the Church
H the right to own property
J the rights of taxpaying citizens

Test-Taking Tip: This question asks you to make a *comparison.* What did *all three* revolutions have in common? For instance, did the American Revolution have anything to do with the role of the Church? No. Therefore, you can eliminate choice G.

7. The Agricultural Revolution led to

A a decrease in farm productivity
B more people moving to farms to work
C better farming technologies
D many bloody wars between farmers and the government

Test-Taking Tip: This question asks about a *different* type of revolution. Remember that the Agricultural Revolution set the stage for the Industrial Revolution a hundred years later. However, neither of these revolutions involved warfare. In this case, the word *revolution* refers to a change in the system of farming. Therefore, you can eliminate choice D.

STOP

541

Tested Objectives

Questions	Reading Objective
1, 2	Analyze information
3	Make inferences and generalizations
4, 5	Identify central issues
6	Make comparisons
7	Draw conclusions

4H History

The English civil war is discussed on page 505. There it states that *civil war broke out between the Crown and Parliament.*

5C Civics

Locke's *Two Treatises of Government* is discussed on the bottom of page 507. There it states that Locke believed in the rights of *life, liberty, and property.* Therefore, the answer is C.

6F History

While the American Revolution was fought, in part, over the rights of taxpayers, the English Revolution was not. Therefore, choice J can be eliminated. None of these revolutions was concerned with the role of the Church, so choice G can be eliminated. They were all concerned with the power of the monarchy, so choice F is the best answer.

THE PRINCETON REVIEW **TEST-TAKING TIP**

Since the question asks for something in common to all three revolutions, any choice that does not apply to even one revolution can be eliminated.

7C Culture/Environment

The top of page 526 states that the Agricultural Revolution led to *new ways of growing crops and breeding animals,* which resulted in *greater production of food.* This information makes C the best choice.

Introducing **UNIT 11**

OVERVIEW

Unit 11 discusses the changes in the world during the 1800s, focusing on the emergence of new nations and the building of empires in Africa and Asia.

- **Chapter 34** describes how the United States and Latin American countries developed different forms of governments and economies.
- **Chapter 35** discusses how the ideas of the French Revolution spread.
- **Chapter 36** summarizes the move toward imperialism by western European powers, the United States, and Japan.

UNIT OBJECTIVES

After reading Unit 11, students will be able to:

1. discuss how nationalism influenced the western world during the 1800s.

2. identify what economic ideas developed in Europe.

3. describe changes in Africa and Asia during the 1800s.

UNIT PROJECT

Have students choose one of the following topics: the Americas during the early 1800s; or the Americas, Europe, Africa, Asia and the Pacific, during the late 1800s. Have students write newspaper headlines and articles that characterize the assigned region's economic ideas, nationalism, and imperialism during that time. Ask volunteers to compile all the articles into a newspaper.

UNIT 11 Nations and Empires

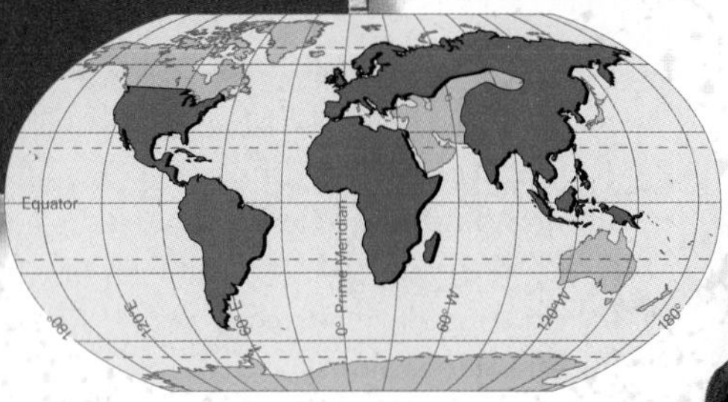

Yoruba carving of Catholic missionary arriving in West Africa, late 1800s ►

▲ Medicines to conquer the diseases that hindered colonization of Africa

1784	1804	1822	1839
Russian settlement of Kodiak Island	Haiti becomes independent	Mexico becomes independent	Opium War in China

542

ABOUT THE UNIT OPENING

Examining Artifacts

Based on these artifacts, ask students these questions: Where did European nations seek to build empires in the 1800s? *(Africa)* What was at least one of the motives behind expansion into Africa? *(to spread Christianity)* What was the link between European medicines and colonization? *(allowed Europeans to conquer African diseases)*

Global Chronology

Ask students what time period the time line covers. *(1784 to 1910)* What countries are mentioned? *(Russia, Haiti, Mexico, China, United States, South Africa)* What do the entries in 1804 and 1822 indicate? *(Latin American countries became independent.)* What dates indicate that this time period was turbulent? *(the wars and rebellions in 1839, 1846, and 1900)*

FOLDABLES™ Study Organizer

Organizing Information Study Foldable *Make the following foldable to help you organize what you learn about the nation and empire building during the 1800s.*

Step 1 *Collect 2 sheets of paper and place them about 1 inch apart.*

Keep the edges straight.

Step 2 *Fold up the bottom edges of the paper to form 4 tabs.*

This makes all tabs the same size.

Step 3 *When all the tabs are the same size, crease the paper to hold the tabs in place and staple the sheets together. Label each tab as shown.*

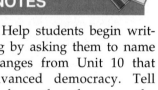

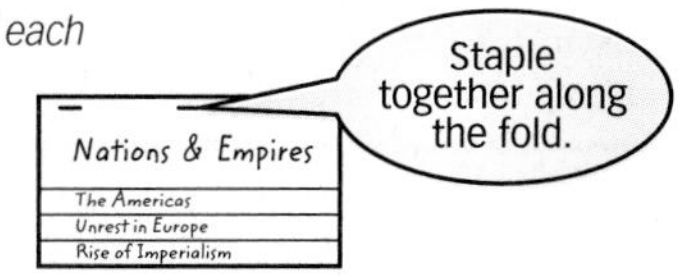
Staple together along the fold.
Nations & Empires
The Americas
Unrest in Europe
Rise of Imperialism

Reading and Writing *As you read the unit, write the main ideas presented in each of the three chapters under the tabs of your foldable. Note details that support the main ideas.*

PRIMARY SOURCES Library

See pages 694–695 for another primary source reading to accompany Unit 11.

Read "Victory at Waterloo" from the **World History Primary Source Document Library CD-ROM.**

1846 War between U.S. and Mexico begins

1900 Boxer Rebellion breaks out in China

1910 Union of South Africa formed

Journal Notes

How did world governments and ideas about democracy change during the 1800s? Note details about these changes as you read.

GLENCOE TECHNOLOGY

MindJogger Videoquiz

Use **MindJogger Videoquiz** to preview the unit content.

Available in DVD and VHS

FOLDABLES Study Organizer

Purpose The purpose of this foldable is to help students group facts about nation and empire building during the 1800s into categories. Students should also list details such as dates, terms, examples of cultural changes, and so on. This will help them better understand the main ideas of this unit.

Have students complete **Reading and Study Skills Foldables** Activity 11.

RECORDING JOURNAL NOTES

Help students begin writing by asking them to name changes from Unit 10 that advanced democracy. Tell students that these are the kinds of changes they should note as they read Unit 11.

PRIMARY SOURCES Library

Additional primary sources from the **World History Primary Source Document Library CD-ROM** include:

- *Napoleon at Moscow,* by Baron Claude François de Méneval

Primary sources about British India can be found on pages 694–695.

Geographic Location

Ask students to name the continents that will be discussed in this unit. *(all except Antarctica)* Tell students that in this unit they will learn how nationalism caused independence movements in countries and how industrialization increased the interest of some nations in building empires in non-industrialized countries.

Chapter 34 Planning Guide

Timesaving Tools

TeacherWorks™ All-In-One Planner and Resource Center

- **Interactive Teacher Edition** Access your Teacher Wraparound Edition and your classroom resources with a few easy clicks.
- **Interactive Lesson Planner** Planning has never been easier! Organize your week, month, semester, or year with all the lesson helps you need to make teaching creative, timely, and relevant.

Use Glencoe's **Presentation Plus!** multimedia teacher tool to easily present dynamic lessons that visually excite your students. Using Microsoft PowerPoint® you can customize the presentations to create your own personalized lessons.

Objectives	Reproducible Resources	Multimedia Resources
Section 1 **The United States** Describe the development of government in the United States, westward expansion in the 1800s, and the causes of the Civil War.	Reproducible Lesson Plan Chapter 34 Vocabulary and Guided Reading Activity Reading Essentials and Study Guide 34-1 Unit 11 World Literature Reading 1 Chapter 34 Enrichment Activity Section 1 Quiz Unit 11 Hands-On History Lab	Interactive Student Edition CD-ROM Graphic Organizer Transparency 3 Teaching Transparency and Activity 34A Vocabulary PuzzleMaker CD-ROM Interactive Tutor Self-Assessment CD-ROM ExamView® Pro Testmaker CD-ROM Glencoe Skillbuilder Interactive Workbook CD-ROM, Level 1 Presentation Plus! CD-ROM
Section 2 **Latin America** Describe the independence movements in Latin America and governments that were established in Latin America in the late 1800s.	Reproducible Lesson Plan Reading Essentials and Study Guide 34-2 Chapter 34 Cooperative Learning Activity Chapter 34 Chart and Graph Skill Activity Chapter 34 Geography and Map Activity Unit 11 Primary Source Readings Section 2 Quiz	Teaching Transparency and Activity 34B Vocabulary PuzzleMaker CD-ROM Interactive Tutor Self-Assessment CD-ROM ExamView® Pro Testmaker CD-ROM Glencoe Skillbuilder Interactive Workbook CD-ROM, Level 1
Chapter 34 **Review and Evaluation**	Chapter 34 Reteaching Activity Chapter 34 Performance Assessment Activity Spanish Chapter Summary and Glossary Chapter 34 Test	Vocabulary PuzzleMaker CD-ROM Interactive Tutor Self-Assessment CD-ROM Glencoe Skillbuilder Interactive Workbook CD-ROM, Level 1 Audiocassettes* ExamView® Pro Testmaker CD-ROM

*Also available in Spanish.

Chapter 34 Planning Guide

Performance Assessment Activities

Role Play Have students research the 19th-century leaders of voting-rights movements in some of the countries discussed in this chapter. After students complete their research, have them prepare scripts in which they role-play a leader of their choice, explaining their philosophies and methods.

CHAPTER RESOURCES

LITERATURE ABOUT THE PERIOD

Keith, Harold. *Rifles for Watie.* T.Y. Crowell, 1957. Story of a teenage soldier in the West during the American Civil War.

READINGS FOR THE STUDENT

Freedman, Russell. *Lincoln: A Photobiography.* Clarion Books, 1987. Newbery Award winner that offers a photo essay of the life of Abraham Lincoln.

Lester, Julius. *To Be A Slave.* Scholastic, 1968. A primary source of the feelings and experiences of African Americans from colonial times through the Civil War.

READINGS FOR THE TEACHER

Prago, Albert. *The Revolutions in Spanish America: The Independence Movements of 1808-1825.* Macmillan, 1970. Surveys the history of the independence movements in Latin America during the early 1800s.

KEY TO ABILITY LEVELS

Teaching strategies have been coded for varying learning styles and abilities.

L1 Level 1 activities are **basic** activities and should be within the ability range of all students.

L2 Level 2 activities are **average** activities and should be within the ability range of the average to above-average student.

L3 Level 3 activities are **challenging** activities designed for the ability range of above-average students.

ELL ELL activities should be within the ability range of English Language Learning students.

NATIONAL GEOGRAPHIC Teacher's Corner

INDEX TO NATIONAL GEOGRAPHIC MAGAZINE

The following articles relate to this chapter:

- "Lewis and Clark Get Lost," by Tim Cahill, April 2002.
- "Urban Sprawl," by John G. Mitchell, July 2001.
- "The Way West," by John G. Mitchell, September 2000.
- "The Missouri Breaks," by John Barsness, May 1999.

NATIONAL GEOGRAPHIC SOCIETY PRODUCTS AVAILABLE FROM GLENCOE

To order the following, call Glencoe at 1-800-334-7344

- *PictureShow: The Civil War (CD-ROM)*
- *PicturePack: Civil War (Transparencies)*
- *PictureShow: Story of America Library, 1 & 2 (CD-ROMs)*
- *PictureShow: The Westward Movement (CD-ROM)*
- *PicturePack: Westward Movement (Transparencies)*
- *Native Americans (Poster Set)*

ADDITIONAL NATIONAL GEOGRAPHIC SOCIETY PRODUCTS

To order the following, call National Geographic at 1-800-368-2728:

- *American Indians: A Brief History (Video)*
- *American West* (Classroom Library)
- *Steal Away: The Harriet Tubman Story (Video)*

Access *National Geographic*'s new dynamic MapMachine Web site and other geography resources at:

www.nationalgeographic.com
www.nationalgeographic.com/maps

THE HISTORY CHANNEL. A&E HOME VIDEO. Biography

The following videotape programs are available from Glencoe:

- **Civil War Journal (Set 1 and 2)**
  1-56501-200-3 (set 1) 1-56501-326-3 (set 2)
- **Lewis and Clark**
  1-56501-592-4
- **Mexico: A Story of Courage and Conquest**
  0-7670-1622-X

To order, call Glencoe at 1-800-334-7344. To find classroom resources to accompany many of these videos, check:

A&E Television: www.aande.com
The History Channel: www.historychannel.com

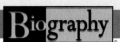

OVERVIEW

Chapter 34 examines the political, economic, and cultural developments in the Western Hemisphere during the 1800s.

- **Section 1** discusses changes in United States government, westward expansion, and the Civil War.
- **Section 2** describes the independence movements in Latin America.

CHAPTER OBJECTIVES

After reading Chapter 34, students will be able to:

1. describe the growth of democracy in the United States.
2. trace the expansion of the United States during the 1800s.
3. analyze causes of the Civil War.
4. identify cultural changes in the United States during the late 1800s and early 1900s.
5. discuss how colonies in Latin America won independence, and examine the types of governments they developed.

EXAMINING ARTIFACTS

Have students look at each of the artifacts. Then ask: How are these two items linked? *(Settlers pushed into Native American homelands. Items represent the groups that clashed in the West.)* Explain that this chapter traces the causes and effects of the expansion of the United States.

PERFORMANCE ASSESSMENT

Use the Performance Assessment Activities on page 544B to help you evaluate students as they complete the chapter.

CHAPTER 34

The Americas

1800 A.D.–1875 A.D.

◄ Native American dress

Covered wagons carrying U.S. settlers westward ▼

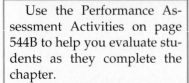

1803	1804	1822	1861
U.S. buys the Louisiana Territory	Haiti becomes first independent country in Latin America	Mexico wins independence	U.S. Civil War begins

TEACHING RESOURCES

TEACHER PLANNING AND SUPPORT

- Reproducible Lesson Plan 34-1, 34-2
- Teaching Strategies for the World History Classroom (Including Block Scheduling Pacing Guides)
- Presentation Plus! CD-ROM

REVIEW AND REINFORCEMENT

- Reading Essentials and Study Guide 34-1, 34-2
- Chapter 34 Vocabulary and Guided Reading Activity
- Vocabulary PuzzleMaker CD-ROM
- Teaching Transparencies 34A & 34B
- Chapter 34 Reteaching Activity
- Chapter 34 Cooperative Learning Activity
- Chapter 34 Activity Book Activity
- Chapter 34 Chart and Graph Skill Activity
- Reading and Study Skills Foldables
- Interactive Tutor Self-Assessment CD-ROM
- Unit 11 MindJogger VideoQuiz

APPLICATION AND HANDS-ON ACTIVITIES

- Daily Questions in Social Studies
- World Games Activity Cards 1 & 2
- Student Presentation Builder CD-ROM

Chapter Focus

Read to Discover

- What kind of government developed in the newly formed United States.
- How and why the United States expanded its boundaries during the 1800s.
- What led to the Civil War in the United States.
- What cultural changes took place in the United States during the late 1800s and early 1900s.
- How colonies in Latin America won their independence.
- Why democracy did not develop in Latin America.

HISTORY Online

Chapter Overview

Visit the *Human Heritage* Web site at **humanheritage.glencoe.com** and click on ***Chapter 34—Chapter Overviews*** to preview this chapter.

Terms to Learn	People to Know	Places to Locate
federal	Abraham Lincoln	Alamo
manifest destiny	Simón Bolívar	Rio Grande
		Haiti

Why It's Important Many changes took place in the Americas from 1800 to the early 1900s. The United States more than doubled in size, and its government was set on a firm base. This allowed the country to grow industrially and to become a world power. Latin America, which is made up of Mexico, Central America, the Caribbean islands, and South America, won independence from European rule. However, colonial traditions remained strong. So, despite many efforts, democracy did not develop in most of Latin America.

SECTION 1 The United States

In the years after winning independence, the Americans set up a democratic government and expanded the boundaries of their country. They fought each other in a civil war and then worked to reunite the nation after the war ended. Industry grew and brought about many changes in daily life. By 1900, the United States had become a powerful country.

Government One thing that helped the United States become powerful was its government. Americans developed a tradition of **stable government,** or a government that rules from year to year without great changes.

Reading Check Why was a **stable government** important to the future of the United States?

GEOGRAPHY ACTIVITIES

- Chapter 34 Geography and Map Activity
- Building Geography Skills for Life
- Outline Map Resource Book

INTERDISCIPLINARY CONNECTIONS

- Unit 11 World Literature Reading 1
- World Music: A Cultural Legacy

ENRICHMENT AND EXTENSION

- World History Primary Source Document Library CD-ROM
- Chapter 34 Enrichment Activity
- Foods Around the World

ASSESSMENT AND EVALUATION

- Chapter 34 Performance Assessment Activity
- Chapter 34 Section Quizzes 34-1, 34-2
- Chapter 34 Test
- Chapter 34 ExamView® Pro Testmaker CD-ROM
- Chapter 34 Digests Audiocassettes Activities and Tests

SPANISH RESOURCES

- Chapter 34 Spanish Chapter Summary and Glossary
- Chapter 34 Spanish Digests Audiocassettes Activities and Tests

HISTORY Online

Chapter Overview introduces students to chapter content and key terms. Have them access ***Chapter 34 Overview*** at **humanheritage.glencoe.com**

FOCUS

Bellringer

Tell students that in the 1800s many settlers wanted to expand the United States across the continent. Have students write three reasons Native Americans or Mexicans might be hostile to this attitude.

Motivational Activity

Tell students that in this chapter they will learn how U.S. expansion changed the lives of Native Americans and Mexicans.

GUIDE TO READING

Reading Strategy

Ask students to read "Why It's Important" and summarize the chapter's main theme. *(The 1800s saw the rise of the United States as a world power and the independence of Latin American nations from European rule.)*

Vocabulary Precheck

Ask students to define each of the "Terms to Learn." Have a volunteer consult the dictionary for any unfamiliar words. L1 ELL

Use the **Vocabulary PuzzleMaker CD-ROM** for Chapter 34 to create a crossword puzzle. L1

Assign Chapter 34 Vocabulary and Guided Reading Activity.

Assign Reading Essentials and Study Guide 34-1.

Reading Check Answer

A **stable government** prevented major upheavals and encouraged the country to grow.

TEACH

Guided Practice

L1 **History** To help students understand the swiftness of the expansion of the United States, guide them in developing a time line showing the acquisition of territory. ELL

Reading Check Answer The two **political parties** were the Federalist party and the Democratic-Republican party. The **federal** government is the national government.

Reading Check Answer In a **representative government,** officials are elected by the people.

Reading Check What two **political parties** had formed by 1800? What is the **federal** government?

By 1800, two **political parties,** or groups with different ideas about government, had come into being. One was the Federalist (fed' uhr uh list) party. It favored a strong **federal,** or national, government. Most Federalists believed that only people of wealth and education should hold office. They thought the economy should be based more on industry than on trade or agriculture. The other political party was the Democratic-Republican party. It favored more power for the states. Most Democratic-Republicans believed that average people should lead the country. They thought the economy should be based more on agriculture than on industry or trade.

Although in other countries wars were often fought when political power changed hands, in the United States the government changed hands through peaceful elections. For example, in 1800, Thomas Jefferson, who was a Democratic-Republican, was elected President. He took the place of John Adams, who was a Federalist. This was the first peaceful passing of power from one political group to another in the United States.

Reading Check How are officials chosen in a **representative government?**

The United States also had a tradition of **representative government.** This is a government in which officials are elected by the people. In 1800, however, only white males who owned property could vote. This changed over the next 30 years. New states in the West began to allow all adult white males to vote. Other states soon followed. By 1830, the number of voters had greatly increased. Although women, enslaved people, and Native Americans were not allowed to vote, the United States government was one of the most democratic in the world at the time.

With the growing number of voters, election campaigns changed. They became filled with entertainment and advertising. People sang songs and wore ribbons to show which candidates they supported. Political parties held parades, rallies, and dinners. Presidential races in particular were noted for slogans and symbols. For example, Andrew Jackson, who became President in 1829, was known as "Old Hickory." So, during his campaign, the newly formed Democratic party planted hickory trees in town squares and gave out hickory brooms and canes.

The Westward Movement

At the end of the American Revolution, the United States claimed most of the land east of the Mississippi River. Soon, thousands of Americans were putting their belongings into farm wagons and traveling across the Appalachian Mountains to find new homes. When they came to the Ohio River and other water routes, they loaded their goods and animals on flatboats and floated downstream.

The settlers were careful about choosing a spot for their new home. It had to be near a stream for water. It also had to be near a large settlement or fort for safety. After choosing a place, the settlers would clear the land of trees and build a log cabin. It

EXTENDING THE CONTENT

In the election of 1800, there was no distinction on the electoral ballot between president and vice president. Thomas Jefferson and Aaron Burr of the Democratic-Republican party ran against John Adams and Charles C. Pinckney of the Federalist party. During this election, the candidate who received the most electoral votes became president. The person who won the second-largest number of votes became vice president. Since both Jefferson and Burr received the same number of electoral votes, the House of Representatives had to vote to break the tie. They voted to make Jefferson president and Burr vice president. The Twelfth Amendment was passed in 1804 to ensure that an electoral tie could not happen again.

usually had one room, with a dirt-packed floor and a door made of wood planks. Each cabin had one or two tiny windows covered with deerskin. There was a fireplace that supplied heat for warmth and cooking.

The settlers' way of life was generally different from that of the Native Americans in the area. The settlers were farmers, while most Native Americans were hunters. The settlers claimed land for themselves. The Native Americans believed land belonged to everyone.

The Native Americans and the settlers did learn from one another, however. Many of the settlers wore Native American clothing, such as moccasins and deerskin leggings. They used Native American herbs as medicine and paddled Native American canoes. Many of the Native Americans used rifles, iron pots, and woolen blankets that were made in Great Britain.

The Native Americans tried to defend their lands against the settlers. However, there were many more settlers than Native Americans. Also, many Native Americans died from such diseases as measles and smallpox brought by the whites. Over time, the Native Americans were slowly pushed farther and farther west. In the 1830s, the United States government began forcing the Native Americans to live on reservations.

Territorial Expansion Many settlers chose land newly acquired by the United States. In 1803, the United States doubled its size by buying the Louisiana Territory from France for $15 million. The Louisiana Purchase, as it was called, provided an

NATIVE AMERICAN LIFE Many Native Americans west of the Mississippi were nomadic and hunted the great migrating herds of buffalo. The Native Americans depended on the buffalo's meat for food and its hide for clothing and shelter. **Why were the Native Americans unable to stop the movement of the settlers?**

L3 Geography: Human Systems Ask students to research and sketch maps about the changing center of population of the United States. (The Statistical Abstract of the United States *contains this data.)* Have students lead a class discussion that covers what the center of population is today, why it moves, and speculate what its next move, if any, will be. Display student maps.

CAPTION ANSWER

There were more settlers than Native Americans, and many Native Americans died from diseases.

Glencoe Literature Library

The following novels from the **Glencoe Literature Library** may be used to enrich this chapter:

- *Bearstone,* by Will Hobbs. (Troubled Native American youth rediscovers his heritage.)
- *Island of the Blue Dolphins,* by Scott O'Dell. (Native American woman on California island in the mid-19th century.)

Biography

The following videotape programs are available from Glencoe to enrich Chapter 34:

- **Tecumseh: The Dream of Confederacy**
- **Lewis and Clark**

To find classroom resources to accompany these videos, check the following home page:

A&E Television:
www.aande.com

MEETING SPECIAL NEEDS

Obtain a copy of David S. Lavender's book, *The Way to the Western Sea: Lewis and Clark Across the Continent.* Harper, 1988. Read excerpts from the book to auditory learners. Ask students to describe the journal entries of Lewis and Clark in their own words. Have students find the places described in the journal on a map of the United States.

Refer to ***Inclusion for the Middle School Social Studies Classroom: Strategies and Activities*** for additional resources.

CAPTION ANSWER

The Mexicans offered people from the United States large areas of free land if they would swear loyalty to Mexico and become Catholic.

MAKING CONNECTIONS

>> Geography: Human Systems The Spaniards had originally colonized California by establishing a series of 21 missions along the coast from San Diego to San Francisco. Each mission consisted of a central church, outlying buildings, and a fort. Father Junípero Serra was responsible for establishing the first of these missions.

Reading Check Answer
Manifest destiny held that it was the fate of the United States to stretch from the Atlantic Ocean to the Pacific Ocean.

THE HISTORY CHANNEL.

The following videotape programs are available from Glencoe to enrich Chapter 34:

- **The Alamo**
- **Mexico: A Story of Courage and Conquest**

To find classroom resources to accompany these videos, check the following home page:

A&E Television:
www.aande.com

THE ALAMO The Alamo was a Catholic mission in San Antonio, Texas. In 1836, during the war for Texan independence, 187 Texans used the Alamo as a fortress and held out for several days against nearly 4,000 Mexican soldiers before being defeated. **What conditions had the Mexicans placed on Americans settling in Texas?**

Fun Facts...

Manifest Destiny The spirit of manifest destiny was captured in this 1821 speech by Francis Baylies, a Massachusetts Congressman. "Our natural boundary is the Pacific Ocean. The swelling tide of our population must and will roll on until that mighty ocean . . . limits our territorial empire."

area rich in farmland, minerals, and forests. It also gave the United States control of the Mississippi River and the important seaport of New Orleans.

In 1819, the United States and Spain signed a treaty. This treaty, called the Adams-Onís Treaty, gave Florida to the United States and set the boundary between the Louisiana Purchase and the Spanish lands to the south and west.

One of the Spanish lands was Mexico. It became independent in 1821. The Mexicans wanted more people to settle in their territory, especially in Texas. So, they offered people from the United States large areas of free land if they would swear loyalty to Mexico and become Catholic. By the early 1830s, there were 30,000 Americans living in Texas. Most were from the South, and many owned enslaved people.

Enslavement and other issues soon led to quarrels between the Americans who moved to Texas and the Mexican government. Mexico had outlawed enslavement in 1824, and it objected to Texans enslaving people. It also began wondering whether American settlers were loyal to Mexico or to the United States. So, the Mexican government tried to stop more Americans from entering Texas. The Texans then asked for more control over their local affairs. Finally, in 1835, the Texans revolted. The following year, they declared their independence.

Reading Check What was the principle of **manifest destiny?**

Many Americans believed in the **manifest destiny** (man′ uh fest des′ tuh nē) of the United States, or the idea that it was the fate of the United States to stretch from the Atlantic Ocean to the Pacific Ocean. They wanted the federal government to allow the

EXTENDING THE CONTENT

Have students imagine the year is 1845, and many people want the United States to annex land from Mexico. Have students play the roles of Mexican peasants and landowners, Southern plantation owners, Northern industrialists, or Native Americans. Have students investigate the concerns of their group, and write speeches, articles, or posters promoting their view. Have students role-play their chosen group and share their information with the class.

annexation of Texas. **Annexation** (an ek sā′ shuhn) is the act of taking over a territory and combining it with an existing country or state. In 1845, the United States annexed Texas. This greatly angered Mexico. A dispute over the Texas-Mexico boundary caused more trouble. By the following year, the two countries were at war. American soldiers invaded California, which was part of Mexico. They also marched into Mexico City.

In 1848, Mexico signed the Treaty of Guadalupe Hidalgo (gwah dl ū′ pā huh duhl′ gō). It gave the United States almost one half of Mexico's land. It also set the Rio Grande (rē′ ō gran′ dā) as the boundary between Texas and Mexico.

Five years after the treaty, in 1853, the United States bought a piece of land from Mexico in order to build a railroad to the Pacific. This was called the Gadsden (gadz′ duhn) Purchase after James Gadsden, the American who arranged the purchase.

Meanwhile, the United States acquired the Oregon Territory. During the 1840s, thousands of American settlers made the long, hard trip over the Rocky Mountains to Oregon, which both the United States and Great Britain claimed. The presence of these settlers gave the United States control of much of the area. In 1846, the two countries agreed to divide the Oregon Territory at the 49th parallel.

Reading Check
How did the **annexation** of Texas affect U.S. relations with Mexico?

MAP STUDY

PLACES AND REGIONS The Louisiana Purchase eventually formed parts of 13 states. **What geographic features marked the western and eastern boundaries of the Louisiana Purchase?**

The Growth of the United States

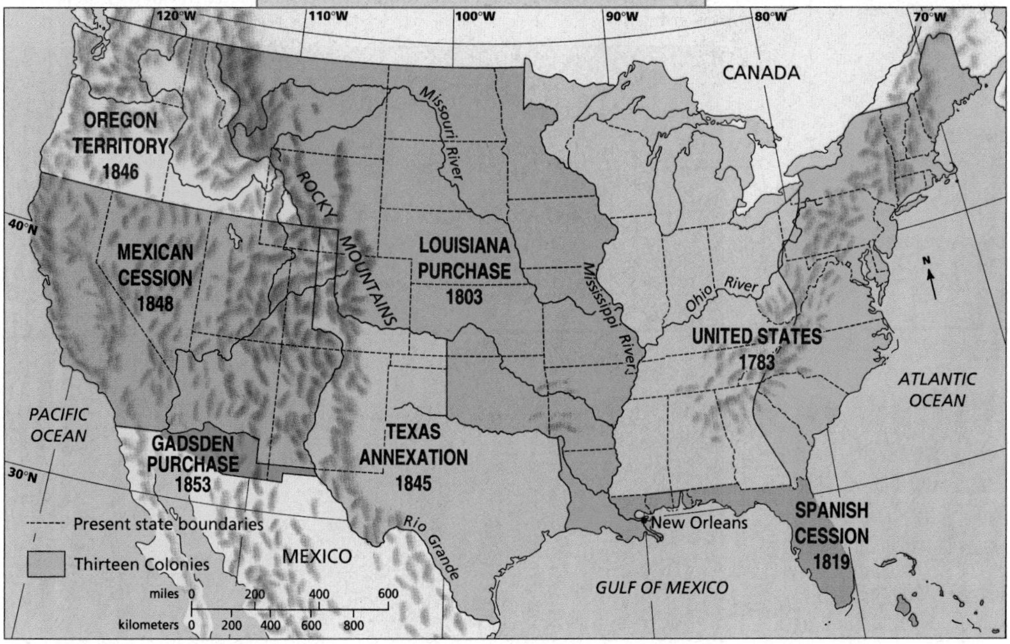

Reading Check Answer
The **annexation** of Texas by the United States greatly angered Mexico.

L1 **Geography: Places and Regions** Have students use the map "The Growth of the United States" to locate the areas of territorial expansion discussed in this section. Have them name present states that were part of each territory. In particular, have them locate their own state and determine where it fit into U.S. expansion. ELL

DID YOU KNOW ??

The locations of the first Spanish missions in California were decided according to how far and fast a priest could walk. Each mission was one week's travel time apart.

MAP STUDY

Answer

Rocky Mountains and Mississippi River

Glencoe Literature Library

The following novel from the **Glencoe Literature Library** may be used to enrich this chapter:

- *The Call of the Wild,* by Jack London. (Tale of the Yukon gold rush.)

EXTENDING THE CONTENT

Explain to students that the term "Manifest Destiny" was first used in a magazine in 1845 supporting the view that the United States was given the divine right to conquer and settle new land in North America and elsewhere. The phrase soon became popular. Ask students which acquisitions allowed the United States to reach its "Manifest Destiny" of spreading from sea to sea. *(Oregon Territory, 1846; Mexican Cession, 1848)*

L3 **Critical Thinking** Organize students into small groups to consider whether any state should have the right to withdraw from the United States if it feels it has just cause. Have each group draw from slips of paper on which you have written *yes* or *no* an equal number of times. Have each group gather information on their assigned side of the issue. Then have each group choose a member to participate in a panel debate on the issue.

DID YOU KNOW ??

Alaska became the 49th state of the Union in 1959.

CAPTION ANSWER

the Confederate States of America or the Confederacy

HISTORY Online

Student Web Activity objectives and answers can be found at the ***Chapter 34 Web Activity Lesson Plan*** at humanheritage.glencoe.com

THE HISTORY CHANNEL.

The following videotape programs are available from Glencoe to enrich Chapter 34:

- **Civil War Journal**
- **Underground Railroad**

To find resources to accompany these videos, check:

A&E Television: www.aande.com

Then & Now

Cotton Cotton remains a vital part of the Southern economy, providing $6.4 billion in annual revenue. Cotton is the largest cash crop in Alabama and is also important to the economies of Mississippi, Arkansas, Louisiana, Tennessee, and Georgia.

Later, another large area of land, Alaska, was added to the United States. In 1784, Russian fur hunters had established a permanent settlement at Kodiak (kōd′ ē ak) Island off the Alaskan coast. From there, they set up hunting and trading settlements as far south as California. After a time, however, Russia lost interest in Alaska and sold the territory to the United States in 1867.

Civil War and Reunion

As the United States expanded westward, different ways of life developed in the northern and southern states. The northern states were industrialized. They had most of the nation's factories, railroads, and canals. Labor in the North was done by hired workers. About 20 percent of the people lived in cities. Education was widespread, and immigration brought in all different kinds of people. Northern leaders wanted a strong national government. They also wanted the government to aid industry and improve transportation. They believed that enslavement should not be allowed in new areas of the country.

The southern states depended on agriculture. Tobacco, rice, sugar cane, and especially cotton were important. These crops

ABRAHAM LINCOLN As President during the Civil War, Abraham Lincoln led the United States through one of the most critical periods in the nation's history. Lincoln was assassinated by a southern sympathizer shortly after the North and South were reunited. **What did the southern states that seceded call their new government?**

HISTORY Online

Student Web Activity

Visit the *Human Heritage* Web site at **humanheritage.glencoe.com** and click on ***Chapter 34—Student Web Activities*** to find out more about the Civil War.

COOPERATIVE LEARNING

Organize the class into groups to discuss the ways American life might be different if the Civil War had not been fought and the country had remained divided into two separate nations. Have each group focus on a different topic, such as economy, international relations, labor, government, or culture. One person from each group should take notes on the discussion and report the group's ideas to the class. Encourage students from the other groups to ask questions after each group's presentation.

CHAPTER 34 Assessment

Using Key Terms

Write a newspaper article that gives an overview or summary of the major changes in government that took place in the United States and Latin America during the 1800s. Use the following words in your article.

stable government
political parties
federal
representative government
manifest destiny
annexation
seceding
urbanization
tenements
slums
junta
caudillo

Understanding Main Ideas

1. What was important about the American election of 1800?
2. What did the United States gain by the Louisiana Purchase?
3. What happened to Native Americans as the United States expanded its borders?
4. How did city life differ for lower-, middle-, and upper-class Americans?
5. How did Antonio Nariño help spread French democratic ideas throughout the Spanish colonies?
6. Why did Father Hidalgo revolt against Spanish rule?

Critical Thinking

1. What do you think are some ways the creation of public schools changed American life?
2. If you lived in Brazil in 1822, would you have supported the Portuguese government or the monarchy? Explain your answer.
3. How did the revolution in Brazil compare to the revolution in Mexico? Explain your answer.

Graphic Organizer Activity

Citizenship Create a diagram like the one shown, and use it to compare voting rights in the United States in 1830 with voting rights today. (Think of the groups who can vote today but could not vote in 1830.)

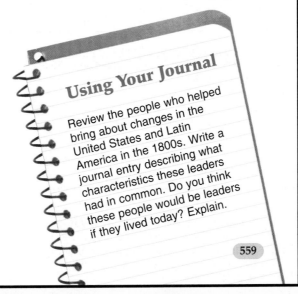

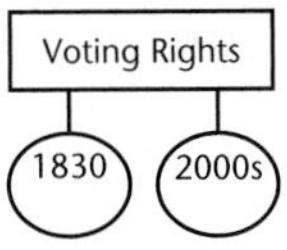

Geography in History

Places and Regions Refer to the map of Latin America on page 555. The three battle sites marked show that they were all fought near large cities. What other things do these battle sites have in common? Describe them in a paragraph.

Using Your Journal

Review the people who helped bring about changes in the United States and Latin America in the 1800s. Write a journal entry describing what characteristics these leaders had in common. Do you think these people would be leaders if they lived today? Explain.

CHAPTER 34 Assessment Answers

Using Key Terms

Newspaper articles will vary, but students should include major points and all the terms.

Understanding Main Ideas

1. It was the first peaceful passing of power from one political group to another.
2. It doubled its size; gained rich farmland, minerals, and forests; and gained control of the Mississippi River.
3. The government began forcing them to live on reservations west of the Mississippi.
4. in housing, in jobs, and in education
5. He translated into Spanish the Declaration of the Rights of Man and the Citizen.
6. because he was upset about the way the Native Americans were treated

Critical Thinking

1. Answers will vary but should indicate that it gave people a chance for a better life.
2. Answers will vary, but students should support their opinions.
3. Answers will vary, but revolution in Brazil came about more peacefully than in Mexico.

Graphic Organizer Activity

Diagrams will vary, but should show the expansion of voting rights to go beyond all adult white males and include all U.S. citizens age 18 and over.

Bonus Test Question

For Chapter 34 Test

Imagine that in Latin America around 1800, no one could translate French. How would this have changed the history of the region? Explain. *(Answers should refer to the* Declaration of the Rights of Man and the Citizen.*)*

Using Your Journal

Journal entries will vary but students should describe some characteristics of good and bad leaders. If negatives are not stated, discuss how corruption in leadership can develop.

Geography in History

Answers could include that the three sites are in mountainous regions and located centrally but are at opposite ends of the continent.

Chapter 35 Planning Guide

Timesaving Tools

TeacherWorks™ All-In-One Planner and Resource Center

- **Interactive Teacher Edition** Access your Teacher Wraparound Edition and your classroom resources with a few easy clicks.
- **Interactive Lesson Planner** Planning has never been easier! Organize your week, month, semester, or year with all the lesson helps you need to make teaching creative, timely, and relevant.

Presentation Plus!

Use Glencoe's **Presentation Plus!** multimedia teacher tool to easily present dynamic lessons that visually excite your students. Using Microsoft PowerPoint® you can customize the presentations to create your own personalized lessons.

Objectives	Reproducible Resources	Multimedia Resources
Section 1 **The Age of Napoleon** Discuss how Napoleon influenced France and formed the Grand Empire.	Reproducible Lesson Plan Chapter 35 Vocabulary and Guided Reading Activity Reading Essentials and Study Guide 35-1 Chapter 35 Cooperative Learning Activity Section 1 Quiz	Interactive Student Edition CD-ROM Graphic Organizer Transparency 6 Teaching Transparency and Activity 35A Vocabulary PuzzleMaker CD-ROM ExamView® Pro Testmaker CD-ROM Glencoe Skillbuilder Interactive Workbook CD-ROM, Level 1 Presentation Plus! CD-ROM
Section 2 **Revolution and Reform** Describe how the Congress of Vienna tried to bring peace to Europe through a balance of power and how liberals, nationalists, and socialists threatened the Congress System.	Reproducible Lesson Plan Reading Essentials and Study Guide 35-2 Section 2 Quiz	Vocabulary PuzzleMaker CD-ROM Interactive Tutor Self-Assessment CD-ROM ExamView® Pro Testmaker CD-ROM Glencoe Skillbuilder Interactive Workbook CD-ROM, Level 1
Section 3 **Growth of Nationalism** Examine the effects of nationalism on Italy, Germany, and Austria.	Reproducible Lesson Plan Reading Essentials and Study Guide 35-3 Chapter 35 Geography and Map Activity Chapter 35 Chart and Graph Skill Activity Unit 11 World Literature Reading 2 Section 3 Quiz	Teaching Transparency and Activity 35B Vocabulary PuzzleMaker CD-ROM Interactive Tutor Self-Assessment CD-ROM ExamView® Pro Testmaker CD-ROM Glencoe Skillbuilder Interactive Workbook CD-ROM, Level 1
Chapter 35 **Review and Evaluation**	Chapter 35 Reteaching Activity Chapter 35 Performance Assessment Activity Spanish Chapter Summary and Glossary Chapter 35 Test	Vocabulary PuzzleMaker CD-ROM Interactive Tutor Self-Assessment CD-ROM Glencoe Skillbuilder Interactive Workbook CD-ROM, Level 1 Audiocassettes* ExamView® Pro Testmaker CD-ROM

*Also available in Spanish.

Chapter 35 Planning Guide

Performance Assessment Activities

Flow Charts Have students create a flow chart or graphic organizer that shows the major events in Napoleon's career from beginning to end. Ask students to then imagine they could change history and intervene in Napoleon's career, having it end in a different way. Have them write an explanation that tells what the outcome would be.

Chapter Resources

LITERATURE ABOUT THE PERIOD

Hugo, Victor. *Les Misérables*. New American Library, 1987. Novel about the conflicts in France in the early 1800s.

READINGS FOR THE STUDENT

Lengyel, Emil. *The Congress of Vienna*. Franklin Watts, 1974. Account of the Congress and its participants.

Marrin, Albert. *Napoleon and the Napoleonic Wars*. Viking, 1991. Biography of Napoleon.

READINGS FOR THE TEACHER

Cate, Curtis. *The War of the Two Emperors: The Duel Between Napoleon and Alexander, Russia, 1812*. Random House, 1985. Discusses Napoleon's invasion of Russia.

Cloarec, Yann, Editor. *How to Make War*. Ediciones La Calavera, 1998. Napoleon's thoughts and sayings on war, as translated by Keith Sanborn.

KEY TO ABILITY LEVELS

Teaching strategies have been coded for varying learning styles and abilities.

L1 Level 1 activities are **basic** activities and should be within the ability range of all students.

L2 Level 2 activities are **average** activities and should be within the ability range of the average to above-average student.

L3 Level 3 activities are **challenging** activities designed for the ability range of above-average students.

ELL ELL activities should be within the ability range of English Language Learning students.

NATIONAL GEOGRAPHIC Teacher's Corner

INDEX TO NATIONAL GEOGRAPHIC MAGAZINE

The following articles relate to this chapter:

- "Reinventing Berlin," by Peter Ross Range, December 1996.
- "The Morning After: Germany Reunited," by William S. Ellis, September 1991.
- "Berlin's Ode to Joy," Priit J. Vesilind, April 1990.

NATIONAL GEOGRAPHIC SOCIETY PRODUCTS AVAILABLE FROM GLENCOE

To order the following, call Glencoe at 1-800-334-7344

- *PicturePack: Physical Geography of the World (Transparencies)*
- *Picture Atlas of the World (CD-ROM)*

ADDITIONAL NATIONAL GEOGRAPHIC SOCIETY PRODUCTS

To order the following, call National Geographic at 1-800-368-2728:

- *Europe (Laminated desk maps)*
- *Physical Geography of the Continents Series: Europe (Video)*
- *National Geographic Atlas of World History (Book)*

Access *National Geographic's* new dynamic MapMachine Web site and other geography resources at:
www.nationalgeographic.com
www.nationalgeographic.com/maps

THE HISTORY CHANNEL. A&E HOME VIDEO. Biography

The following videotape program is available from Glencoe:

- **Napoleon Bonaparte: The Glory of France**
  0-7670-1211-9

To order, call Glencoe at 1-800-334-7344. To find classroom resources to accompany this video, check:

A&E Television: www.aande.com
The History Channel: www.historychannel.com

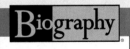

Introducing CHAPTER 35

OVERVIEW

Chapter 35 discusses the political conflicts that transformed Europe during the 1800s.

- **Section 1** analyzes how reforms and military conquests by Napoleon helped spread French revolutionary ideas.
- **Section 2** describes the political movements that challenged the traditional European political order.
- **Section 3** discusses how each European country accepted or resisted change.

CHAPTER OBJECTIVES

After reading Chapter 35, students will be able to:

1. discuss how Napoleon influenced France.

2. describe how the Congress of Vienna brought peace to Europe.

3. analyze how revolutions in the 1800s threatened the Congress System.

4. examine the effects of nationalism on Italy, Germany, and Austria.

EXAMINING ARTIFACTS

Based on the statue, what can students infer about Napoleon's greatest strength? *(his military leadership)* Explain that the urn is an example of the style of art favored by Napoleon. What does that tell students about how he saw himself? *(as emperor of France)* Ask students how Napoleon might have built his empire. *(by conquering European nations)*

PERFORMANCE ASSESSMENT ✓

Use the Performance Assessment activities on page 560B to help you evaluate students as they complete the chapter.

CHAPTER 35

Unrest in Europe

1755 A.D.–1875 A.D.

▲ An urn from Napoleon's time

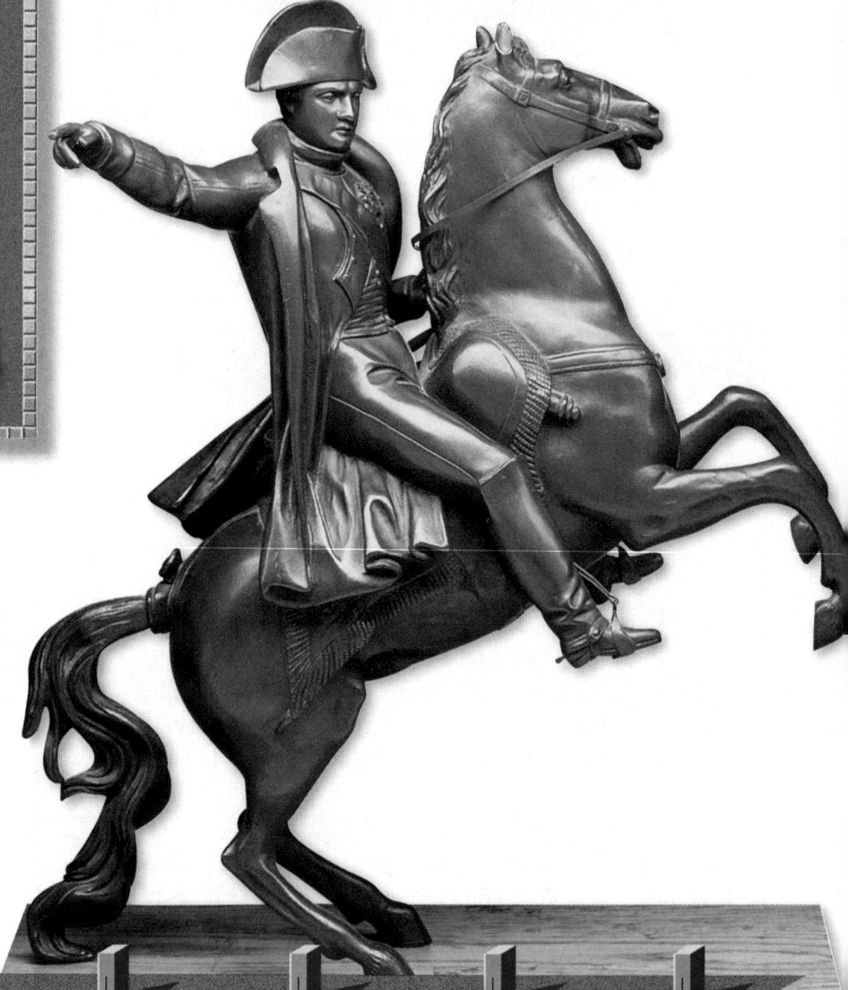

1804	1814	1815	1848	1867
Napoleon crowned	Congress of Vienna meets	Napoleon defeated	Universal male suffrage begins to spread	Dual monarchy of Austria-Hungary

TEACHING RESOURCES

TEACHER PLANNING AND SUPPORT

- Reproducible Lesson Plan 35-1, 35-2, 35-3
- Teaching Strategies for the World History Classroom (Including Block Scheduling Pacing Guides)
- Presentation Plus! CD-ROM

REVIEW AND REINFORCEMENT

- Reading Essentials and Study Guide 35-1, 35-2, 35-3
- Chapter 35 Vocabulary and Guided Reading Activity
- Vocabulary PuzzleMaker CD-ROM
- Teaching Transparencies 35A & 35B
- Chapter 35 Reteaching Activity
- Chapter 35 Cooperative Learning Activity
- Chapter 35 Activity Book Activity
- Chapter 35 Chart and Graph Skill Activity
- Reading and Study Skills Foldables
- Interactive Tutor Self-Assessment CD-ROM

APPLICATION AND HANDS-ON ACTIVITIES

- Daily Questions in Social Studies
- World Crafts Activity Card 6
- Student Presentation Builder CD-ROM

In September, Napoleon reached Moscow, which had been abandoned by the Russians. Shortly after the French arrived, the city caught fire and three fourths of it was destroyed. The French army now had neither food nor shelter. Napoleon sent several peace proposals to the Russians, which they ignored. He finally gave the order to withdraw. By then the bitter Russian winter had started. Hundreds of thousands of French soldiers froze to death as temperatures fell to 40 degrees below zero. Thousands more died from disease and lack of food. In the end, fewer than 100,000 soldiers made it back to France.

Reading Check How did the Russians use a **scorched-earth policy** to defeat the French?

Napoleon quickly raised another army, but the new soldiers were not well trained. They were defeated by the allied forces of Austria, Prussia, Russia, and Great Britain. This was the first time the four countries had joined together to fight Napoleon.

In 1814, the allies took Paris, and Napoleon was forced to **abdicate** (ab′ duh kāt), or give up the throne. He was sent into exile to the small island of Elba off the coast of Italy. He managed to escape, however, and gathered together enough troops to invade France. For 100 days, Napoleon again reigned as emperor. The allies, under the British leadership of the Duke of Wellington, finally defeated him in 1815 at the Battle of Waterloo. This time, Napoleon was sent to the island of St. Helena (huh lē′ nuh) off the west coast of Africa, where he died in 1821.

Reading Check Where did Napoleon go when he was forced to **abdicate** his throne?

Section 1 Assessment

1. **Define:** plebiscite, scorched-earth policy, abdicate.
2. What was the Grand Empire?
3. Why did Napoleon's invasion of Russia fail?

Critical Thinking

4. **Understanding Cause and Effect** How did weaknesses of government under the Directory help pave the way for the rise of Napoleon?

Graphic Organizer Activity

5. Draw this diagram, and use it to summarize Napoleon's accomplishments in the areas of government, education, law, transportation, and the arts.

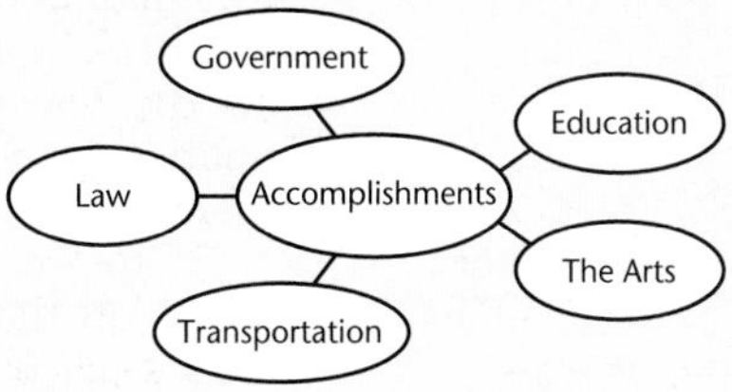

SECTION 2 Revolution and Reform

After Napoleon's defeat, representatives from Austria, Prussia, Russia, and Great Britain met in Vienna (vē en′ uh) to decide what to do about France and the rest of Europe. Although the settlement they agreed upon brought peace to Europe for a time, it also set the stage for revolution in many countries and reform in others.

Reading Check Answer The Russians used a **scorched-earth policy** to burn their villages and food supplies so the advancing French army would have nothing to help them survive.

L1 **History** Ask students to discuss some of the most important changes in Europe brought about by Napoleon's reign in France. Then ask them to predict how the European nations might react after Napoleon loses his power. ELL

Reading Check Answer When Napoleon was forced to **abdicate,** he went to Elba.

L3 **Music** Have interested students research composers such as Tchaikovsky or Beethoven, who were inspired to write music about the events in France under Napoleon. Encourage students to share samples of the music and analyze what comes across in phrases of the music.

Use the **Interactive Tutor Self-Assessment CD-ROM** to review Section 1.

Use the **Vocabulary PuzzleMaker CD-ROM** to create crossword and word search puzzles.

Section 1 Assessment Answers

1. plebiscite, popular vote (p. 563); scorched-earth policy, retreating army burns land (p. 564); abdicate, give up the throne (p. 565)
2. the empire created by Napoleon
3. because of the Russian scorched-earth policy and the bitter Russian winter
4. Answers will vary, but the disorder and debts of the Directory encouraged Napoleon to believe he could set up a new government without a lot of resistance, either from the Directory or the people.
5. Diagrams will vary, but the accomplishments should reflect information in the text. You might award extra credit to those students who list accomplishments through outside research.

Assign the Chapter 35 **Section 1 Quiz** in the TCR. Testmaker available.

L2 **Government** Help students make a chart on the board of the groups who were against the Congress System. The chart should explain the grievances of each group. Then suggest students put themselves in each group and choose the grievance they would *most* like to correct. ELL

Reading Check Answer
The Congress of Vienna hoped a **balance of power** would prevent any single country from starting another war.

DID YOU KNOW ??

The French representative, Prince Charles Maurice de Talleyrand, served under Louis XVI, the various revolutionary governments, Napoleon, and the restored French king, Louis XVIII.

Reading Check Answer
Liberals supported individual freedom, equal rights under the law, freedom of thought and religion, voting rights for landowners, and protection of private property.

Reading Check Answer
Nationalists opposed the Congress System because they wanted independence for areas where people shared the same language, customs, and history.

Painting of Metternich

Reading Check Why did the Congress of Vienna want to achieve a **balance of power?**

The Congress of Vienna

The Congress of Vienna was sometimes called the "Waltzing Congress." This was because the representatives spent much of their time at dinners, dances, and fox hunts. However, decisions were made by a few leaders. They included Prince Klemens von Metternich (met′ uhr nik), the Austrian foreign minister; Czar Alexander I of Russia; King Frederick William III of Prussia; and Viscount Castlereagh (vī′ kownt kas′ uhl rā), the British foreign secretary. Charles-Maurice de Talleyrand (tal′ ē ran) decided matters for France.

The leaders did not want to punish France too harshly. At the same time, they wanted to build a peaceful and stable Europe. They believed the best way to do this was by establishing a **balance of power,** or equal strength among countries. They hoped that a balance of power would prevent any single country from starting another war.

To accomplish this, the leaders divided Napoleon's Grand Empire. Russia got Finland and most of Poland. Sweden got Norway. Austria got part of northern Italy. Great Britain got the islands of Malta (mahl′ tuh) and Ceylon (sā lahn′), as well as the Dutch Cape Colony in South Africa. Belgium and Holland were made into a single nation. In addition, the 39 German states were combined into a loose confederation headed by Austria.

The leaders of the Congress of Vienna were against democracy. Hoping to crush revolutionary ideas, they brought back divine-right monarchy. They had already put Louis XVIII, younger brother of Louis XVI, on the French throne. Now, they brought back the monarchy in Spain and Portugal. The Pope was again made ruler of the Papal States.

Political Movements

The balance of power in Europe was maintained for a number of years. However, the revolutionary ideas that had been spread by Napoleon's Grand Empire did not die. Several groups were against the Congress System, or the political plan and division of Europe set up by the Congress of Vienna.

Reading Check What changes did the **liberals** support?

One group was the **liberals.** They wanted political reform based on the ideals of the French Revolution. These included individual freedom, equal rights under the law, and freedom of thought and religion. Most liberals were members of the middle class. They also wanted changes that would improve their own lives. Among these changes were voting rights for landowners and the protection of private property. Some liberals wanted a constitutional monarchy. Others wanted a republic. The liberals were strongest in Great Britain and France.

Reading Check Why did the **nationalists** oppose the Congress System?

Another group that was against the Congress System was the **nationalists** (nash′ uh nuh lists). They wanted political independence for areas where people shared the same language, customs, and history. The Congress of Vienna had paid no

EXTENDING THE CONTENT

Prince Klemmens von Metternich was the dominant figure at the Congress of Vienna. As an Austrian aristocrat, he disliked and feared nationalism, for the Austrian Empire included many minorities—Magyars, Czechs, Slavs, and others. Metternich believed that any upset in the established order might bring down the whole structure. To follow up the decisions made at the Congress of Vienna, Metternich put together a series of treaties aimed at involving all monarchs in preserving the status quo against liberalism and nationalism. The treaties called for periodic conferences and for settling international crises by diplomacy, if possible.

Comparing Historical Maps

A comparison of historical maps can reveal the changes that occur in the political features of an area over time.

Look at the map on page 564. Now, look at the map below. Note that both show about the same area, but at different times. The map on page 564 shows Europe's political divisions during Napoleon's rule. The map below shows Europe after the Congress of Vienna.

To compare historical maps, first look at both maps to make sure the same region is being illustrated. Then, study the boundaries and note any changes. Study also the names of the countries to see if they have changed.

For example, note that the Grand Duchy of Warsaw was subject to Napoleon. After the Congress of Vienna, however, both its boundaries and its name changed.

Compare both maps and answer the following questions.

Map Practice

1. **How was the French Empire divided after the Congress of Vienna?**
2. **What countries were not directly affected by either Napoleon's rule or the Congress of Vienna?**

Europe After the Congress of Vienna

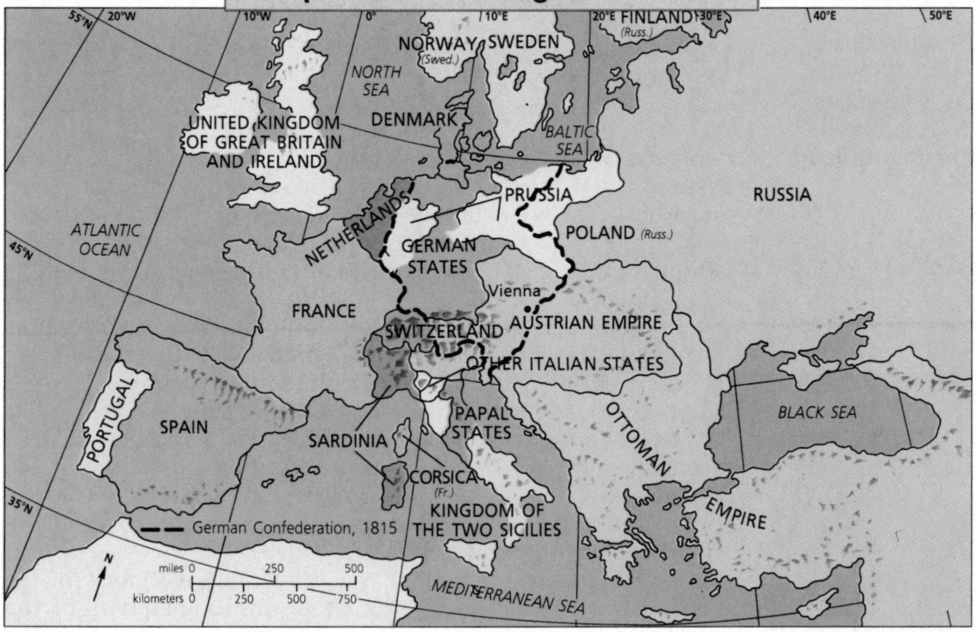

MAP SKILLS

TEACH

Comparing Historical Maps

Ask students the following: What can a comparison of historical maps of the same region show? *(the changes that occur in the political features of an area over time)* What are two things to study when comparing historical maps of the same region? *(boundaries, names of countries)*

Next, have students use the skills they have learned in this feature to compare the historical map "Europe After the Congress of Vienna" on this page with the map "Europe in the Late Middle Ages" on page 422. Ask them to write five questions that highlight similarities and differences between the maps. Then call on students to ask their questions of the class.

Answers to Map Practice

1. into France; the Netherlands; the Papal States; and parts of Italy, the Austrian Empire, and Prussia

2. Portugal, the United Kingdom of Great Britain and Ireland, Sweden, and the Ottoman Empire were not directly affected.

Use the **Glencoe Skillbuilder Interactive Workbook, Level 1,** to provide instruction and practice in key social studies skills.

SPOTLIGHT ON: EUROPE

Several European leaders met at the Congress of Vienna to reorganize the Napoleonic lands. One leader, Alexander I of Russia, called a Holy Alliance that would let God guide the Congress and their relations. Most countries agreed to join his alliance although they doubted it could be successful. Alexander later died mysteriously in a remote part of Russia with many doubting he was really dead. He was reportedly sighted alive all over Europe.

Independent Practice

L3 **Debate** Have students discuss the part of Marx's philosophy that states: "In a worker's revolution all people would be equal and government would not be needed." In a blind drawing, assign students to a team, either agreeing or disagreeing with Marx's philosophy. Have students conduct a debate with the rest of the class deciding who presents the best arguments.

Reading Check Answer The **socialists** wanted to end private ownership of land so the people as a whole could own it.

Reading Check Answer The **utopian socialists** wanted to set up ideal communities based on economic cooperation. Karl Marx expected the **proletariat** to rise up and take power.

Reading Check Answer Marx believed government would no longer be needed under **communism.**

GEOGRAPHY AND HISTORY

The delegates to the Congress of Vienna redrew national boundaries in Europe based on the desires of the rulers rather than those of the people they governed. The new boundaries ended the hopes of many groups. For example, the boundaries crushed the Polish people's hopes for a united nation. Instead their land was divided among Austria, Vienna, Prussia, and Russia.

Assign the Chapter 35 **Geography and Map Activity** in the TCR.

attention to nationalist feelings when it divided the Grand Empire. For example, the Belgians did not want to be part of Holland. The northern Italians did not want to be ruled by Austria.

A third group that was against the Congress System was the **socialists.** They wanted to end private ownership of land and factories. They believed the state, or the people as a whole, should own all means of production. In this way, the socialists believed, everyone would be treated fairly and the workers' lives would improve.

Reading Check How did the **socialists** feel about private property?

Some socialists tried to set up ideal communities based on economic cooperation. They thought these communities would show that theirs was a better way of life. Such socialists were known as **utopian socialists** (yū tō' pē uhn sō'shuh lists).

Other socialists believed the only way to bring about reform was by revolution. One such socialist was Karl Marx, a German. He believed the **proletariat** (prō luh tār' ē uht), or industrial working class, would rise up and take power. "The workers have nothing to lose . . . but their chains," he wrote in his book *The Communist Manifesto* (kahm' yū nist man uh fes' tō). "They have a world to gain. Workers of the world, unite!"

Reading Check Who were the **utopian socialists?** What did Karl Marx expect the **proletariat** to do?

Marx believed that after the workers' revolution, there would be no hunger or poverty. Everyone would become equal. Governments would not even be needed. People would work because they wanted to give something to society. In return, they would be able to develop their own interests and talents. Marx called his kind of socialism **communism** (kahm' yū niz uhm). He believed the workers' revolution would be led by his new Communist party.

Reading Check What did Marx believe would happen to government under **communism?**

Karl Marx

An Era of Revolution Beginning in 1820, liberals, nationalists, and socialists led revolutions against the Congress System. The earliest of these took place in Spain, Portugal, Italy, and Russia. They all failed. However, Greek nationalists were given hope by these attempts. In 1821, they rebelled against the Ottoman Empire. After eight years of fighting, Greece gained its independence.

In 1830, there was another revolution in France. After Louis XVIII died, his brother Charles X had taken the throne. He wanted to bring back the Old Regime. Just a few weeks after being crowned, Charles did away with the National Assembly. He took the right to vote away from the middle class and returned control of the schools to the Roman Catholic Church. In response to Charles's actions, middle-class liberals, helped by students and unemployed workers, overthrew the government. After three days of fighting, Charles X fled.

The July Revolution, as it was called, was a victory for the middle class. Members of this class, unlike members of the working class, wanted a constitutional monarchy rather than a

EXTENDING THE CONTENT

Karl Marx believed that capitalism was only a temporary phase. A crisis in one of the advanced industrial countries would cause the workers, or the proletariat, to seize control from the bourgeoisie, or middle class. The proletariat would build a society in which the people owned everything. Without private property, class distinctions would disappear, and the government would wither away. He felt that this last stage would be genuine communism. He wrote *The Communist Manifesto* along with Friedrich Engels. Marx expanded his views in *Das Kapital* written in 1867.

Linking Across Time

Universal Suffrage English author and teacher Mary Wollstonecraft (left) believed all people should vote, regardless of gender. In 1792, she published a widely read book defending the rights of women. Her book helped spark the start of the woman's suffrage movement, which eventually made it possible for Margaret Thatcher (right) to become Great Britain's first female Prime Minister. She held the office from 1979 to 1990. **What reforms helped increase suffrage in Great Britain in the 1830s?**

republic. So, they gave the throne to Charles X's cousin, Louis-Philippe (lū' ē fi lēp'). Under Louis-Philippe's rule, the number of people who could vote increased. However, of the middle class, only its richest members could vote. This angered other members of the middle class. Working-class people were also angry. They had wanted not only a republic but also **universal male suffrage** (suhf' rij), or the right of all adult males to vote.

News of the July Revolution touched off rebellions in other countries. In 1831, Belgian nationalists won independence from Holland. The Poles fought against Russia but were defeated. Uprisings in several German and Italian states also were put down and ended quickly.

In Great Britain, however, liberal reforms were made by gradual change instead of revolution. In 1832, the British government passed a law that lowered the amount of land a man had to own in order to vote. This increased by one half the number of voters. It also gave the new industrial towns more representation in Parliament. As a result, the British middle class had more say in the government.

Reforms also helped the working class. Labor unions gained the right to **strike,** or stop work, in order to obtain shorter hours,

Reading Check What group fought for **universal male suffrage** in France?

Reading Check Why did workers want the right to **strike?**

L2 **Government** Organize the class into three groups, and assign each one of the following political groups: the liberals, the nationalists, and the socialists. Have students write a speech, the purpose of which is to gain support for his or her assigned political group in response to the Congress System. The speeches should outline the basic goals of the group's philosophy and indicate how they plan to achieve them. Have students read their speeches.

Linking Across Time

In 1832, the British government passed a law that lowered the amount of land a man had to own in order to vote. It also gave new industrial towns more representation in Parliament.

Reading Check Answer The working class fought for **universal male suffrage** in France.

Reading Check Answer Workers wanted the right to **strike** in order to obtain shorter hours, higher wages, and better working conditions.

DID YOU KNOW ??

Only 3 percent of the French citizens could vote, even after the July Revolution.

MEETING SPECIAL NEEDS

Allow time for students with learning difficulties to make charts, diagrams, time lines, or other graphic organizers for each section. These organizers will help them retain a grasp of the relationships among people, dates, and events and will help them quickly review important data.

Refer to ***Inclusion for the Middle School Social Studies Classroom: Strategies and Activities*** for additional resources.

L2 **Critical Thinking** Ask students how the events described in this section can be called a continuation of the French Revolution of 1789. Encourage students to refer to pages 513–520 to refresh their memories. Then have them write a paragraph explaining the connections, if any, that they see.

MAKING CONNECTIONS

>> **History** Although workers had done most of the fighting in the 1830 revolution that put Louis-Philippe on the throne, he ignored their demands for economic reforms. Labor unions were declared illegal, and police were used to break up strikes. Napoleon III was aware of the problems of the industrial age. He favored aid for industries, banks, railroads, and the poor. He also favored nationalism and supported international conferences to settle disputes.

Reading Check Answer
National workshops provided jobs, but the number of people out of work grew faster than jobs could be created.

LINKING PAST TO PRESENT

In 1844, Antoine Joseph Sax performed in Paris on a new instrument he had invented—the saxophone—which is still played today.

higher wages, and better working conditions. By 1890, working-class males also obtained the right to vote.

The Revolutions of 1848

In 1848, another series of revolutions broke out. All over Europe, governments were overthrown. Once again, the rebellion started in France.

Louis-Philippe had tried to be a "citizen-king." He walked through the streets of Paris without any servants to show that he was a bourgeois rather than an aristocrat. He wore a frock coat and trousers like the men of the middle class. He was very rich himself, however, and his government served only the rich. Industrial workers and middle-class liberals became increasingly unhappy. At the same time, the economy was bad throughout Europe, including France. Many people did not have jobs. Then, in 1845 and 1846, the potato and wheat crops failed. There was not enough food to feed everyone.

In February of 1848, riots broke out in the streets of Paris. Louis-Philippe fled, and the revolutionary leaders declared the Second French Republic. They set up a temporary government to rule until a new National Assembly could be elected. Louis Blanc (lū ē blahnk), a socialist, was one of the leaders. He persuaded the other leaders to set up **national workshops**, or factories run by the workers but paid for by the government. The national workshops provided jobs for thousands of people. However, the number of people out of work grew faster than jobs could be created. Before long, the French government was supporting over 100,000 people.

Reading Check
What was the purpose of the **national workshops,** and why did they fail?

When the new National Assembly was finally elected in April, it did away with the workshops. The workers revolted, fighting violently for three days. They were defeated by the army, but not before over 10,000 people were killed.

The National Assembly then drew up a constitution. It called for a strong president to be elected by universal male suffrage. Napoleon's nephew, Louis-Napoleon Bonaparte, was elected president of the Second French Republic. He believed, however, that he had inherited his uncle's destiny. So, in 1851 he did away with the constitution. A year later, the people voted him Emperor Napoleon III. At the same time, the Second French Republic was renamed the Second French Empire. Louis-Napoleon remained on the throne until 1870.

Painting of Louis-Napoleon

The revolution in France was followed by revolutions in other parts of Europe. The Hungarians (hung ger' ē uhns), the Italians, and the Germans all rebelled. Their revolts failed. Even so, the revolutions of 1848 led to some important changes. In time, universal male suffrage spread to most northern and western European countries. Workers, who felt they had been cheated, began to form political parties. Soon, there was a socialist party in almost every European country.

COOPERATIVE LEARNING

Organize students into broadcast teams to provide coverage of the revolutions in France. Each team should divide up responsibility to research and prepare stories that provide a rounded picture of events in one of the revolutions. Each team member should have a role as a news anchor, on-the-scene reporter, or subject of an interview. Have teams report on events, reactions of royalists, republicans, leaders, and the commoner. Remind students to base their reports on actual events and actual people when possible. Have students write scripts and present their broadcasts to the class.

Predicting Consequences

CRITICAL THINKING SKILLS

Did you ever wish you could see into the future? Predicting future events is very difficult. You can, however, develop skills that will help you identify the logical consequences of decisions or actions.

Learning the Skill Follow these steps to help you accurately predict consequences.

- Review what you already know about a situation by listing facts, events, and people's responses. The list will help you recall events and how they affected people.
- Analyze patterns. Try to determine what the patterns show.
- Use your knowledge and observations of similar situations. In other words, ask yourself, "What were the consequences of a similar decision or action that occurred in the past?"
- Analyze each of the potential consequences by asking, "How likely is it that this will occur?"
- Make a prediction.

Louis-Philippe fled France in 1848

GO TO Glencoe's **Skillbuilder Interactive Workbook CD-ROM, Level 1,** provides instruction and practice in key social studies skills.

Skill Practice

Historians often make predictions about the future based on patterns from the past. Imagine you are a historian at the start of 1849. Use the information in the chart below to make predictions about what lies ahead for the 1850s and 1860s.

Events of the Early 1800s	Results and Reactions
Napoleon is defeated at the Battle of Waterloo.	The Congress of Vienna seeks to restore divine-right monarchy to Europe.
The July Revolution of 1830 returns constitutional monarchy to France.	Rebellions erupt in other European nations.
Worker riots in France lead to revolution and the Second French Republic.	The revolution in France is followed by revolutions in other parts of Europe.
The revolutions of 1848 fail to overturn the Congress System.	?

The following questions will serve as a guide.

1. **Review the information on the chart. What patterns do you notice? What do the facts tell you about political affairs in Europe during the early 1800s?**
2. **Suppose one of the leaders who took part in the Congress of Vienna asked you to predict what to expect in the mid-1800s. What would you say? Was the Congress System safe from future threats? Explain.**

CRITICAL THINKING SKILLS

TEACH

Predicting Consequences

You might open this lesson by asking students what would happen if they chose to watch a movie instead of handing in a homework assignment on time. Call on volunteers to explain how they are able to make these predictions. *(Students will probably cite past experiences.)*

Explore how the ability to predict consequences helps people to reach decisions—i.e., the importance of weighing alternative outcomes. Use this discussion to introduce the skills lesson and accompanying questions.

Answers to Skill Practice

1. Answers will vary, but most students will notice the pattern of revolution that spread across Europe. They will probably also indicate that the facts suggest a period of turbulent political affairs, filled with rebellions and efforts to restore order.

2. Answers will vary, but past patterns indicate a potential for future upheavals. As a result, the Congress System would probably face threats in the years ahead.

TEAM TEACHING STRATEGY

Math Along with the political turmoil of the 1800s came the turmoil of a population explosion. Invite a math teacher to develop word problems to help students interpret patterns on this table. Then ask these questions: (1) What population patterns do you notice? (2) What are some of the possible consequences of these patterns? (3) If you were a leader of one of these nations, what predictions or plans would you make for the future?

Population Growth (in millions)

Country	1800	1850	1880
British Isles	16.1	27.5	35.1
France	27.3	35.8	37.7
Russia	37.0	60.2	88.0
Germany	24.6	35.9	45.2
Italy	18.1	24.3	28.5

W. S. Woytinsky and E. S. Woytinsky, *World Population and Production: Trends and Outlooks*. New York. Twentieth Century Fund, 1953, 44, 46.

DID YOU KNOW ??

An 1816 French law prohibited the Bonapartes from living in France, so Napoleon III grew up in Italy, Germany, and Switzerland.

Use the **Interactive Tutor Self-Assessment CD-ROM** to review Section 2.

LINKING PAST TO PRESENT

Another result of the fighting between Austria and Sardinia and France was the founding of the International Red Cross by a Swiss stretcher-bearer who was named Henri Dunant. He was horrified by the death of thousands of wounded soldiers from typhus and poor care. The symbol of the new organization was the Swiss flag with its colors reversed.

Use the **Vocabulary PuzzleMaker CD-ROM** to create crossword and word search puzzles.

Section 2 Assessment

1. **Define:** balance of power, liberals, nationalists, socialists, utopian socialists, proletariat, communism, universal male suffrage, strike, national workshops.
2. What were two goals of the Congress of Vienna?
3. What were some of the results of the revolutions of 1848?

Critical Thinking

4. **Making Comparisons** Which one of the three groups—liberals, nationalists, or socialists—would you have supported in the 1800s? Why?

Graphic Organizer Activity

5. Draw this diagram, and use it to show predictions made by Karl Marx.

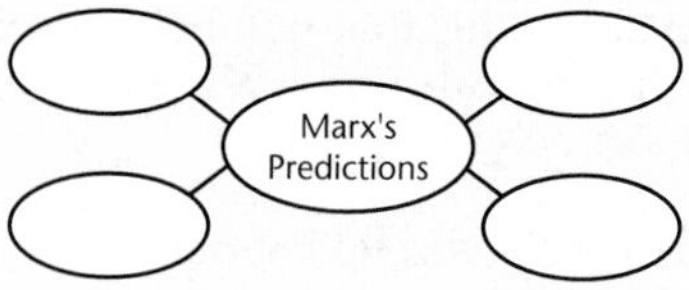

SECTION 3 Growth of Nationalism

After the revolutions of 1848 failed, the Congress System seemed stronger than ever. However, this was not the case. Before long, the growth of nationalism would destroy the balance of power that had been established at Vienna. Three countries that were affected by the growth of nationalism were Italy, Germany, and Austria.

Italy In 1848, eight of the nine Italian states were under Austrian control. Only Sardinia (sahr din′ ē uh) was independent. Ever since Napoleon's time, the Italians had been unhappy about this state of affairs. They remembered that Rome had once ruled the ancient world and that Italian city-states had led the Renaissance. They wanted to become a unified nation.

Many nationalists in Italy looked to Sardinia to take the lead. This was because of Sardinia's prime minister, Count Camillo di Cavour (kont kuh mē′ lō dē kuh vuhr′). Cavour believed in industrialization and favored a constitutional monarchy. He also realized that Sardinia needed help to drive the Austrians out of Italy. To this end, he made an agreement with Napoleon III. It stated that if the Austrians attacked Sardinia, the French would help the Sardinians. When Austria declared war on Sardinia in 1859, Napoleon III kept his word. Austria was defeated, and the Italian state of Lombardy (lahm′ bahr dē) was united with Sardinia. By 1860, the other northern Italian states also revolted against Austria and united with Sardinia.

That same year, an Italian nationalist named Giuseppe Garibaldi (jū zep′ ā gār uh bahl′ dē) led another revolution in

Fun Facts . . .

Charcoal and Freedom *Carbonari,* which means "charcoal burners" in Italian, was the name of one of the first secret societies formed to overthrow foreign rule in Italy. Charcoal is black, but it glows brightly when burning. Italian rebels associated the glow with the light of freedom and liberty.

Section 2 Assessment Answers

1. All terms are defined in the text Glossary.
2. to build a peaceful and stable Europe and to crush revolutionary ideas
3. In time, universal male suffrage spread to most northern and western European countries, and workers began to form political parties.
4. Answers will vary, but students should give reasons for their choices of one of the three groups.
5. Predictions include: the working class would rise up and take power; there would be no hunger or poverty; everybody would become equal; governments would not be needed; people would work because they wanted to give something to society; in return, they would be free to develop their talents and interests.

Assign the Chapter 35 **Section 2 Quiz** in the TCR. Testmaker available.

GIUSEPPE GARIBALDI Giuseppe Garibaldi led the fight for Italian unification in southern Italy. He was skilled in guerrilla warfare, having fought in other revolutionary wars. In this painting, Garibaldi leads his Red Shirts in an attack on troops from Naples. **Who became king of the united Italy?**

Fun Facts . . .

Garibaldi Between 1850 and 1860, Giuseppe Garibaldi lived on Staten Island in New York City. Here he made a meager living working in a friend's candle factory.

southern Italy. Garibaldi had spent much of his life in exile in Brazil and Uruguay (yūr′ uh gwī). There, he had learned how to lead small bands of soldiers behind enemy lines. The bands would hide in forests and on hillsides. They would make surprise attacks on the enemy and then go back into hiding. This kind of fighting is called **guerrilla warfare** (guh ril′ uh wōr fār). In guerrilla warfare, a small group of soldiers can often defeat a much larger army.

Garibaldi taught guerrilla warfare to his followers. They were called "Red Shirts" because they, like their leader, wore red shirts. They also wore loose grey trousers, silk handkerchiefs around their necks, grey cloaks, and black felt hats. In 1860, Garibaldi's Red Shirts conquered Sicily within three months. Then, they sailed to the Italian mainland and conquered the state of Naples.

In 1861, the northern and southern nationalist groups combined. The Kingdom of Italy was formed as a constitutional monarchy. Victor Emmanuel II (ē man′ yū el) of Sardinia became king. The Pope, who wanted to keep control over the Papal

Reading Check Why might rebels such as the "Red Shirts" engage in **guerrilla warfare?**

CAPTION ANSWER

Victor Emmanuel II

LINKING PAST TO PRESENT

Major wars are not generally won exclusively through guerrilla warfare, which has been used since the eighteenth century to wear down the enemy and keep opponents from winning. During the American Revolutionary War, Francis Marion, the "Swamp Fox," effectively led guerrilla groups in South Carolina against the British. Guerrilla warfare has proven effective in rough terrain, as in the rain forests of Latin America and Southeast Asia.

Reading Check Answer

Rebels like the "Red Shirts" might engage in **guerrilla warfare** because in this type of warfare, a small group can often defeat a much larger army.

MAKING CONNECTIONS

>> **Biography** Garibaldi's military skills were recognized worldwide. In 1861, the United States offered him command of a Union force at the outbreak of the American Civil War. Garibaldi refused the offer.

MEETING SPECIAL NEEDS

Organize students who are auditory learners into small groups. Ask the students in each group to discuss all the examples they can think of—both historical and current—where regional differences have been a source of tension within a nation. Have students also include any examples of such tensions that exist in their own state. Bring the students back together and make a list on the board of each group's examples. After discussing the kinds of factors that create regional differences, ask students if they can make any generalizations about the examples they have generated.

Refer to ***Inclusion for the Middle School Social Studies Classroom: Strategies and Activities*** for additional resources.

L2 **Critical Thinking** Ask students what they think Bismarck meant when he said he would unite Germany, not "by speeches and majority votes—but by blood and iron."

MAKING CONNECTIONS

>> **History** After Paris surrendered, a civil war broke out between the city's municipal government, called the Commune, and the national Assembly at Versailles. More people were killed in the civil war than during the entire French Revolution. After the Commune was defeated, some 20,000 persons were executed and another 7,000 were exiled to a penal colony on an island in the Pacific.

Reading Check Answer A **junker** was a rich landowner in Prussia.

Reading Check Answer William I of Prussia was the **kaiser** of the new German empire.

Then... & Now

Germany Bismarck fought three wars to unify Germany, but another war—World War II—left Germany divided for 45 years. In 1990, West Germany and East Germany were reunited as one country.

States, fought against Italian unity and lost. In 1870, the Papal States became part of Italy, and Italian unification was complete. The balance of power in Europe, however, was weakened.

Germany

Nationalist feelings were also strong in the 39 German states. German poets and writers, like Johann Wolfgang von Goethe (ger' tuh) and Friedrich von Schiller (shil' uhr), wrote about German nationalism. German composer Richard Wagner (vahg' nuhr) wrote operas based on German folk tales. In 1834, many of the German states signed a trade agreement. In it, they promised not to tax goods coming from other German states. Soon, the economy of these states improved. However, many of the rulers of the smaller states were not willing to give up their political power. Austria was also against any attempt to unify Germany.

These obstacles were overcome by the Kingdom of Prussia. In 1862, King William I named Count Otto von Bismarck (biz' mahrk) prime minister of Prussia. Bismarck was a **junker** (yung' kuhr), or rich landowner, who believed in divine-right monarchy. He said that he would unite Germany, not "by speeches and majority votes—but by blood and iron." He also believed that war against a common enemy would bring the German states closer together.

Reading Check What was a **junker?**

In 1864, Bismarck joined with Austria to defeat Denmark and to gain territory. Two years later, he used a dispute over this territory as an excuse to go to war against Austria. Prussia won the war in seven weeks. It had superior weapons, as well as an excellent railroad system that moved troops quickly from one battlefield to another. The resulting peace treaty ended the loose German Confederation. The North German Confederation, led by Prussia, was set up in its place.

In 1870, Bismarck found an excuse to go to war against France, Germany's oldest enemy. As Bismarck had hoped, the southern German states joined the northern German states in the struggle. Well-trained and well-equipped, the German army easily defeated the French army. Bismarck then laid siege to Paris. The city held out for four months. Food became so scarce that the people were forced to eat the animals in the zoo. The trees that Napoleon III had planted along the streets of Paris were cut down and used for fuel. At last, on January 28, 1871, the city surrendered.

Meanwhile, at Versailles (vuhr sī'), William I of Prussia was named **kaiser** (kī' zuhr), or emperor, of the new German Empire. This included both the northern and the southern German states, as well as the rich mining and manufacturing lands of Alsace (al' sas) and Lorraine (luh rān'), which had been won from France. A unified Germany, however, meant a further weakening of the balance of power.

Reading Check Who was the **kaiser** of the new German Empire?

EXTENDING THE CONTENT

Nationalism deeply influenced European literature during the 1800s. It inspired widespread interest in folktales, myths, and national history. In Germany, for instance, the Brothers Grimm (Jakob and Wilhelm) collected folktales in their famous collection, first printed in 1812–1815. Following the Grimm's example, Asbjornsen and Moe made a similar collection of Norwegian folktales, including stories like "East of the Sun and West of the Moon." Romantic novelists, playwrights, and poets found themes in national history. Sir Walter Scott collected Scottish ballads and wrote about medieval England in *Ivanhoe.* In Germany, Friedrich von Schiller wrote plays based on historical fighters for liberty, such as William Tell and Joan of Arc.

THE GERMAN EMPIRE The struggle for a united Germany was led by Count Otto von Bismarck, prime minister of Prussia. In this painting, Bismarck (center) proclaims King William I of Prussia (on platform) the emperor of a new German empire. **What effect did a unified Germany have on Europe?**

People in History

Otto von Bismarck
1815-1898

Prime Minister of Prussia

Otto von Bismarck grew up the son of a wealthy landowner, whose noble ancestry stretched back more than five centuries. He was only an average student and showed little promise until his 30s, when he married and entered politics. For the rest of his life, Bismarck demonstrated the discipline he had lacked as a youth. He was the architect of German unification and served as the first *chancellor*, or prime minister, of unified Germany. People called him the "Iron Chancellor."

Austria

Nationalists in Italy and Germany wanted to unify their nations. Nationalists in Austria, on the other hand, threatened the unity of the Austrian Empire.

The Austrian Empire was made up of many nationalities. Although its emperor, Francis Joseph, was German, four out of five people were not. Other nationalities included the Czechs, the Slovaks, the Poles, the Croats, the Slovenes, and the Magyars (mag' yahrs), the largest group in Hungary. Each had its own language and history and wanted self-rule.

By 1866, Austria had been defeated by both Sardinia and Prussia. Magyar nationalists saw their chance to become independent. They revolted. In 1867, a weakened Austria agreed to create a dual monarchy. Now, the emperor ruled over two separate kingdoms—Austria and Hungary. Each had its own official language, parliament, and laws. Although they were separate politically, the two countries needed each other economically. Austria supplied manufactured goods to Hungary. In return, Hungary supplied Austria with food products.

CAPTION ANSWER

The balance of power was weakened further.

DID YOU KNOW

In 1874 in Budapest, Hungary, Ehrich Weiss (later known as Harry Houdini, the world's greatest escape artist) was born.

LINKING PAST TO PRESENT

In addition to having a common ruler, Austria and Hungary had a single army and a common postal system. Systems today were modeled on these early examples.

ASSESS

Check for Understanding

Ask students to summarize the main points of the chapter, orally or in writing. Discuss the answers to the Section and Chapter Assessment questions.

MULTICULTURAL PERSPECTIVES

European composers in the 1800s were influenced by nationalism and drew on folk ballads or patriotic themes. Chopin, Liszt, and Smetana used traditional Polish, Hungarian, and Czech melodies. Folk melodies came from German and Austrian composers including Beethoven, Schubert, and Schumann. In Italy, a patriotic chorus from Giuseppe Verdi's opera *Nabucco* became virtually the national anthem of the movement for unification. In 1874, Verdi wrote his *Requiem Mass* to honor the poet and nationalist patriot Alessandro Manzoni.

Evaluate

Assign the Chapter 35 **Performance Assessment Activity**

Administer the **Chapter 35 Test.** Testmaker available.

Reteach

Have students work in small groups. Assign each group a section to outline. Ask a student from each group to write their outline on the board.

Assign the Chapter 35 **Reteaching Activity** in the TCR.

Enrich

Have students choose one of the people mentioned in this chapter and write a short biographical sketch of the person.

Assign the Chapter 35 **Enrichment Activity** in the TCR.

CLOSE

Have students compare the map "Europe After the Congress of Vienna" on page 567 with a present-day map of Europe in the text Atlas. Discuss boundary and country name changes.

Use the **Interactive Tutor Self-Assessment CD-ROM** to review Section 3.

Self-Check Quiz gives students an interactive chapter tutorial. Have them access ***Chapter 35 Quiz*** at humanheritage.glencoe.com

The Magyars were satisfied with the situation of having separate countries, but other nationalities in Austria-Hungary were not. Their unhappiness presented a continuing threat to the dual monarchy and the peace of Europe.

Section 3 Assessment

1. **Define:** guerrilla warfare, junker, kaiser.
2. What did Garibaldi do to further nationalism in Italy?
3. How was Austria-Hungary formed? How did most of its citizens feel about this?

Critical Thinking

4. **Drawing Conclusions** Why do you think the Italian city-states wanted to be a unified nation? Explain.

Graphic Organizer Activity

5. Draw this diagram, and use it to describe the importance of these dates in the drive for German unification: 1834, 1862, 1864, 1870.

1834 → 1862 → 1864 → 1870

Chapter Summary & Study Guide

1. In 1804, Napoleon became emperor of France. He then set out to conquer the rest of Europe—a plan that nearly succeeded.
2. Although Napoleon created a strong central government and a new code of laws, the people of France still lost certain rights.
3. After Napoleon's defeat, the Congress of Vienna tried to establish a balance of power in Europe and to restore divine-right monarchy.
4. Liberals, nationalists, and socialists opposed the Congress System.
5. A series of revolutions broke out in many European countries in 1820, 1830, and 1848.
6. Liberal reforms were made in Great Britain without a revolution.
7. The revolutions of 1848 failed to overthrow the Congress System, but they still had lasting results, including the spread of universal male suffrage and the rise of socialism among workers.
8. The rise of nationalism led to the unification of Italy between 1859 and 1870 and the unification of Germany between 1862 and 1871.
9. In the Austrian Empire, nationalism led to the Empire's division into two separate kingdoms—Austria and Hungary—each of which had many different national groups that wanted independence.

Self-Check Quiz

Visit the *Human Heritage* Web site at humanheritage.glencoe.com and click on ***Chapter 35—Self-Check Quiz*** to assess your understanding of this chapter.

Section 3 Assessment Answers

1. guerrilla warfare, a kind of fighting (p. 573); junker, rich landowner (p. 574); kaiser, German emperor (p. 574)

2. He led a revolution in southern Italy. Soon after, the northern and southern nationalist groups combined.

3. Magyar nationalists in Hungary revolted, and Austria agreed to create a dual monarchy with a common emperor but separate language, parliament, and laws.

4. They remembered ancient Rome's strength and that of Italian city-states. They wanted to be strong and dominant again.

5. 1834—many German states sign trade agreement; 1862—Otto von Bismarck becomes prime minister of Prussia; 1864—Bismarck joins Austria to defeat Denmark; 1870—Bismarck goes to war against France

Assign the Chapter 35 **Section 3 Quiz** in the TCR. Testmaker available.

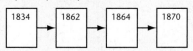

CHAPTER 35 Assessment

Using Key Terms

Imagine you are a writer in Europe in the 1800s. You have been asked to prepare a brief introduction to a revolutionary handbook—a book telling people how to bring about change or to resist unfair governments. Use the following words in your introduction.

plebiscite	scorched-earth policy
abdicate	balance of power
liberals	proletariat
communism	strike
guerrilla warfare	kaiser

Understanding Main Ideas

1. Why did the representatives at the Congress of Vienna try to bring back divine-right monarchy?
2. Why did the temporary French government of 1848 set up national workshops?
3. How did Napoleon III help Italian nationalists?
4. How did the German states become unified?
5. What were some of the results of the war between Prussia and France?
6. Why were national groups in Austria-Hungary unhappy in the 1860s?

Critical Thinking

1. What did Napolean reveal about himself at his crowning as emperor?
2. Do you think Napoleon's conquests were good or bad for Europe? Explain your answer.
3. How important was nationalism in Europe during the second half of the 1800s? Explain.
4. "Liberal reforms can only be made with a revolution." Do you agree or disagree with this statement? Explain.

Graphic Organizer Activity

History Create a diagram like the one shown, and use it to give details that support the following generalization: The Congress of Vienna failed in its goal to return Europe to the old order.

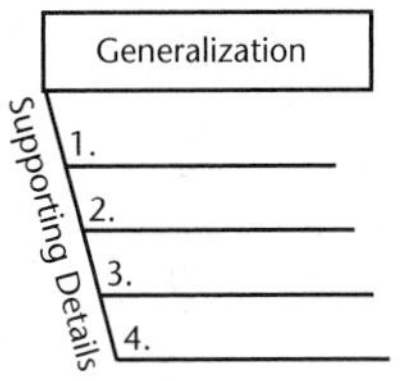

Geography in History

The World in Spatial Terms Refer to the map on page 564. During Napoleon's time, as during other historical eras, Paris was an important city. What is the latitude of Paris? What is the longitude? Describe its relative location.

Using Your Journal

Review the reasons why different revolutions took place in Europe during the 1800s. Write a brief editorial in which you give your opinion about one of these revolutions and whether the people had good reason to revolt. Use facts to support your opinions.

577

CHAPTER 35 Assessment Answers

Using Key Terms

Introductions will vary but should use all the terms.

Understanding Main Ideas

1. because they wanted to crush revolutionary ideas
2. to provide jobs for unemployed workers
3. He helped the Sardinians when Austria declared war on Sardinia.
4. by joining together to fight Denmark, Austria, and France
5. Prussia won from France the rich mining and manufacturing lands of Alsace and Lorraine.
6. because each had its own language and history and wanted to rule itself

Critical Thinking

1. He thought he was above the Church.
2. Answers will vary, but students should provide reasons for their answers.
3. very important because it led to important governmental changes in Italy, Austria, Germany, and France
4. Answers will vary but should include the idea that Great Britain adopted reforms without a revolution.

Graphic Organizer Activity

Sample responses: liberals, nationalists, and socialists led revolutions against the Congress System; Greece won its independence; July Revolution limited power of the French monarch; voters and labor unions increased their power in England; revolutions of 1848 helped spread universal male suffrage; worker parties formed; nationalism in Italy, Germany, and Austria upset the balance of power.

Bonus Test Question

For Chapter 35 Test

Think about the following group of words and list what they have in common with one another in the context of this chapter: *liberals, nationalists, socialists.* How are they different? *(Answers will vary.)*

Using Your Journal

Editorials will vary, but students should support their choices with reasons. They might point to the conflict in the former Yugoslavia and other modern revolutions as comparisons.

Geography in History

about 49° N, 2° E; relative location: in the French Empire during this time

Chapter 36 Planning Guide

Timesaving Tools

TeacherWorks™ All-In-One Planner and Resource Center

- **Interactive Teacher Edition** Access your Teacher Wraparound Edition and your classroom resources with a few easy clicks.
- **Interactive Lesson Planner** Planning has never been easier! Organize your week, month, semester, or year with all the lesson helps you need to make teaching creative, timely, and relevant.

Presentation Plus!

Use Glencoe's **Presentation Plus!** multimedia teacher tool to easily present dynamic lessons that visually excite your students. Using Microsoft PowerPoint® you can customize the presentations to create your own personalized lessons.

Objectives	Reproducible Resources	Multimedia Resources
Section 1 **Growth of Imperialism** Cite causes for the rise of imperialism.	Reproducible Lesson Plan Chapter 36 Vocabulary and Guided Reading Activity Reading Essentials and Study Guide 36-1 Section 1 Quiz	Interactive Student Edition CD-ROM Graphic Organizer Transparency 8 Vocabulary PuzzleMaker CD-ROM ExamView® Pro Testmaker CD-ROM Presentation Plus! CD-ROM
Section 2 **Africa** Discuss how Great Britain and other European powers established colonies in Africa.	Reproducible Lesson Plan Reading Essentials and Study Guide 36-2 Chapter 36 Geography and Map Activity Unit 11 Primary Source Readings Chapter 36 Enrichment Activity Section 2 Quiz	Vocabulary PuzzleMaker CD-ROM Interactive Tutor Self-Assessment CD-ROM ExamView® Pro Testmaker CD-ROM Glencoe Skillbuilder Interactive Workbook CD-ROM, Level 1
Section 3 **Asia** Describe how Asian countries were affected by imperialism.	Reproducible Lesson Plan Reading Essentials and Study Guide 36-3 Chapter 36 Chart and Graph Skill Activity Section 3 Quiz	Teaching Transparencies and Activities 36A & 36B Vocabulary PuzzleMaker CD-ROM Interactive Tutor Self-Assessment CD-ROM
Section 4 **Latin America** Explain why the United States became involved in the affairs of Latin America.	Reproducible Lesson Plan Reading Essentials and Study Guide 36-4 Chapter 36 Cooperative Learning Activity Section 4 Quiz	Vocabulary PuzzleMaker CD-ROM Interactive Tutor Self-Assessment CD-ROM ExamView® Pro Testmaker CD-ROM Glencoe Skillbuilder Interactive Workbook CD-ROM, Level 1
Section 5 **Effects of Imperialism** Analyze the effects of imperialism on global politics.	Reproducible Lesson Plan Reading Essentials and Study Guide 36-5 Section 5 Quiz	Vocabulary PuzzleMaker CD-ROM ExamView® Pro Testmaker CD-ROM Glencoe Skillbuilder Interactive Workbook CD-ROM, Level 1
Chapter 36 **Review and Evaluation**	Chapter 36 Reteaching Activity Chapter 36 Performance Assessment Activity Unit 11 Standardized Test Practice Spanish Chapter Summary and Glossary Chapter 36 Test	Vocabulary PuzzleMaker CD-ROM Interactive Tutor Self-Assessment CD-ROM Glencoe Skillbuilder Interactive Workbook CD-ROM, Level 1 Audiocassettes* ExamView® Pro Testmaker CD-ROM

*Also available in Spanish.

Chapter 36 Planning Guide

✓ Performance Assessment Activities

Making Maps Provide students with an outline map of the world. Have them label countries discussed in the chapter and create a key using different colors to indicate the European power that ruled each country. Then have students color their maps accordingly, and title it, "Age of Imperialism."

CHAPTER RESOURCES

LITERATURE ABOUT THE PERIOD

Conrad, Joseph. *Heart of Darkness.* In *Joseph Conrad, Tales of Land and Sea.* Hanover House, 1916. Story of one man's journey up the Congo River.

Forster, E.M. *A Passage to India.* Harcourt Brace, 1989. A novel about life in India under British rule.

READINGS FOR THE STUDENT

Clark, Leon E. *Through African Eyes.* Center for International Training & Education, 1981. Collection of material about Africans from before the growth of enslavement to the present.

READINGS FOR THE TEACHER

Editors of Time-Life. *What Life Was Like: In the Jewel in the Crown.* Time-Life, Inc. 1999. A richly illustrated look at British India from 1600–1905.

Hsu, Immanuel C. *The Rise of Modern China.* Oxford Press, 1990. Focuses on major historical events in China from 1600 to present.

KEY TO ABILITY LEVELS

Teaching strategies have been coded for varying learning styles and abilities.

L1 Level 1 activities are **basic** activities and should be within the ability range of all students.

L2 Level 2 activities are **average** activities and should be within the ability range of the average to above-average student.

L3 Level 3 activities are **challenging** activities designed for the ability range of above-average students.

ELL ELL activities should be within the ability range of English Language Learning students.

NATIONAL GEOGRAPHIC Teacher's Corner

INDEX TO NATIONAL GEOGRAPHIC MAGAZINE

The following articles relate to this chapter:

- "Central Asia Unveiled," by Mike Edwards, February 2002.
- "Vanishing Cultures," by Wade Davis, August 1999.

NATIONAL GEOGRAPHIC SOCIETY PRODUCTS AVAILABLE FROM GLENCOE

To order the following, call Glencoe at 1-800-334-7344

- *PictureShow: Story of America Library, Part 2 (CD-ROMs)*

ADDITIONAL NATIONAL GEOGRAPHIC SOCIETY PRODUCTS

To order the following, call National Geographic at 1-800-368-2728:

- *China: Beyond the Clouds (Video)*
- *Great Indian Railway (Video)*
- *National Geographic Atlas of World History (Book)*

Access *National Geographic's* new dynamic MapMachine Web site and other geography resources at:
www.nationalgeographic.com
www.nationalgeographic.com/maps

THE HISTORY CHANNEL. A&E HOME VIDEO. Biography

The following videotape programs are available from Glencoe:

- **Theodore Roosevelt: Roughrider to Rushmore**
  1-56501-806-0
- **The Panama Canal**
  1-56501-243-7
- **Pancho Villa: Outlaw Hero**
  0-7670-0315-2
- **The U.S. in Latin America: Yankee Go Home**
  0-7670-0816-2

To order, call Glencoe at 1-800-334-7344. To find classroom resources to accompany many of these videos, check:

A&E Television: www.aande.com
The History Channel: www.historychannel.com

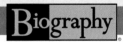

OVERVIEW

Chapter 36 examines the rise of global imperialism during the late 1800s and early 1900s.

- **Section 1** analyzes the economic, religious, and political motivations of imperialism.
- **Section 2** describes European colonization of Africa.
- **Section 3** discusses imperialism in Asian countries.
- **Section 4** explores U.S. intervention in Latin America.
- **Section 5** discusses the effects of imperialism.

CHAPTER OBJECTIVES

After reading Chapter 36, students will be able to:

1. cite causes for the rise of imperialism.
2. discuss the division of Africa by European powers.
3. describe how Asian countries were affected by imperialism.
4. explain U.S. involvement in Latin America.
5. summarize the effects of imperialism.

EXAMINING ARTIFACTS

Ask students what they can infer about the relationship between the British and Indians based on the artifacts. *(that it was unequal; that the Indians served the British)* Have students point to specific details to support their inferences. Then call on them to name one of the things England imported from India. *(tea)* Tell students to write down other reasons Britain wanted India as they read this chapter.

PERFORMANCE ASSESSMENT ✓

Use the Performance Assessment activities on page 578B to help you evaluate students as they complete the chapter.

CHAPTER 36

Rise of Imperialism

1840 A.D.–1916 A.D.

◀ Tea imported into England from India

A British family in India ▼

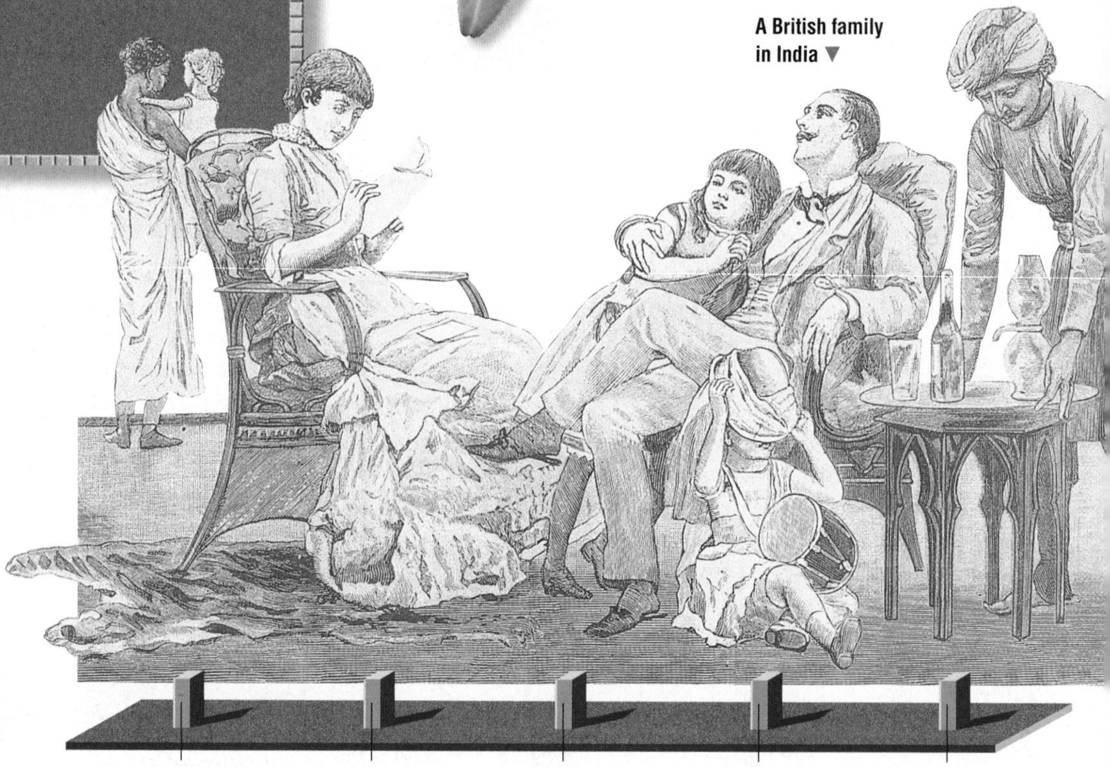

1839	1857	1869	1903	1910
Opium War breaks out in China	Sepoy Mutiny in India	Suez Canal opens	U.S. begins work on Panama Canal	Union of South Africa is formed

TEACHING RESOURCES

TEACHER PLANNING AND SUPPORT

- Reproducible Lesson Plan 36-1, 36-2, 36-3, 36-4, 36-5
- Teaching Strategies for the World History Classroom (Including Block Scheduling Pacing Guides)
- Presentation Plus! CD-ROM

REVIEW AND REINFORCEMENT

- Reading Essentials and Study Guide 36-1, 36-2, 36-3, 36-4, 36-5
- Chapter 36 Vocabulary and Guided Reading Activity
- Vocabulary PuzzleMaker CD-ROM
- Teaching Transparencies 36A & 36B
- Chapter 36 Reteaching Activity
- Chapter 36 Cooperative Learning Activity
- Chapter 36 Activity Book Activity
- Chapter 36 Chart and Graph Skill Activity
- Reading and Study Skills Foldables
- Interactive Tutor Self-Assessment CD-ROM
- Unit 11 MindJogger VideoQuiz

APPLICATION AND HANDS-ON ACTIVITIES

- Daily Questions in Social Studies
- World Games Activity Card 11
- World Crafts Activity Cards 11 & 12
- Student Presentation Builder CD-ROM

Chapter Focus

Read to Discover

- What caused the move toward imperialism.
- How Great Britain and other European powers established colonies in Africa.
- How Asian countries were affected by imperialism.
- Why the United States became involved in Latin America.
- What the effects of imperialism were.

HISTORY Online

Chapter Overview

Visit the *Human Heritage* Web site at **humanheritage.glencoe.com** and click on ***Chapter 36—Chapter Overviews*** to preview this chapter.

Terms to Learn	People to Know	Places to Locate
imperialism	Leopold II	Suez Canal
protectorate	Cecil Rhodes	Indochina
	Matthew Perry	Panama Canal

Why It's Important In the late 1800s, an interest in colonies rose again. Many countries rushed to take over parts of the world that had not been claimed during the Age of Discovery and the expansion of the Americas. New colonial powers were added. Among these new powers were Belgium, Germany, Italy, Japan, and the United States. Those countries in Africa, Asia, and Latin America who were colonized had little say in how their nations developed.

SECTION 1 Growth of Imperialism

There were many reasons for the rise of **imperialism** (im pir' ē uh liz uhm), or the policy of setting up colonies and building empires. One was the Industrial Revolution. Factories in the industrialized countries needed such raw materials as rubber, cotton, oil, tin, and copper. There was also a growing demand for tea, sugar, and cocoa. Both raw materials and food products could be found in areas that were not industrially developed, such as Africa, Asia, and Latin America.

Reading Check What was **imperialism**?

Then, too, industries needed new markets for their products. Factories were turning out more goods than people at home could afford to buy. Many leaders believed new markets could be found in areas that were not industrially developed.

Also, many factory owners had grown rich during the Industrial Revolution. They could not find enough places in their

GEOGRAPHY ACTIVITIES

- Chapter 36 Geography and Map Activity
- Building Geography Skills for Life
- Outline Map Resource Book

INTERDISCIPLINARY CONNECTIONS

- World Music: A Cultural Legacy

ENRICHMENT AND EXTENSION

- World History Primary Source Document Library CD-ROM
- Unit 11 Primary Source Readings
- Chapter 36 Enrichment Activity
- Foods Around the World

ASSESSMENT AND EVALUATION

- Chapter 36 Performance Assessment Activity
- Chapter 36 Section Quizzes 36-1, 36-2, 36-3, 36-4, 36-5
- Chapter 36 Test
- Unit 11 Standardized Test Practice
- Chapter 36 ExamView® Pro Testmaker CD-ROM
- Chapter 36 Digests Audiocassettes Activities and Tests

SPANISH RESOURCES

- Chapter 36 Spanish Chapter Summary and Glossary
- Chapter 36 Spanish Digests Audiocassettes Activities and Tests

HISTORY Online

Chapter Overview introduces students to chapter content and key terms. Have them access ***Chapter 36 Overview*** at **humanheritage.glencoe.com**

FOCUS

Bellringer

Ask students to explain this statement in a paragraph: The sun never sets on the British Empire.

Motivational Activity

Have students share their paragraphs. Then explain that in 1900, the British Empire included one-fifth of the world's land and one-fourth of its population. Tell students that in this chapter they will learn how Great Britain and other world powers established colonies in Africa, Asia, Latin America, and islands in the Pacific.

GUIDE TO READING

Reading Strategy

Ask students to read "Why It's Important" and summarize the chapter's main theme. *(Industrial nations built colonies in Africa, Asia, and Latin America and tried to control development in each of these regions.)*

Vocabulary Precheck

Ask students to define each of the "Terms to Learn." L1 ELL

Use the Vocabulary PuzzleMaker CD-ROM for Chapter 36 to create a crossword puzzle. L1

Assign Chapter 36 Vocabulary and Guided Reading Activity.

Assign Reading Essentials and Study Guide 36-1.

Reading Check Answer **Imperialism** was the policy of setting up colonies and building empires.

TEACH

Guided Practice

L1 **Culture** Have students discuss travel during the late 1800s and early 1900s in relation to their own personal travels. How has traveling to new places changed their views of the world, of other people, and of themselves? ELL

L2 **Geography: The World in Spatial Terms** For an overall introductory view of the depth and spread of imperialism, have students note the nations and areas involved on the map "Imperialism" on page 590. ELL

Use the **Interactive Tutor Self Assessment CD-ROM** to review Section 1.

MAKING CONNECTIONS

➤➤ **History** During the 1890s and 1900s, Germany sought to replace Great Britain as the world's leading sea power and began building a large navy. Great Britain, in turn, enlarged its navy in order to keep ahead of the Germans. This build-up race, along with colonial rivalries among the European powers, led to World War I.

Use the **Vocabulary PuzzleMaker CD-ROM** to create crossword and word search puzzles.

Cocoa Pods

own countries in which to invest. Even when they did invest, they thought the profits were too small. Investments in undeveloped areas, however, generally brought large profits.

Another reason for imperialism was nationalism. Many people thought colonies would add to their country's power. The newly formed countries of Italy and Germany wanted to catch up with Great Britain, France, and other established colonial powers. Japan and the United States wanted to become as important as the colonial powers of western Europe.

Still another reason for imperialism was the belief that western countries had a duty to "civilize" the "backward" peoples of the world. To many westerners, any people whose way of life and religion were different from their own were "backward." These westerners believed they had a mission to spread Christianity and the Industrial Revolution everywhere. The British author Rudyard Kipling (ruhd' yuhrd kip' lēng) called this mission "the white man's burden."

Section 1 Assessment

1. **Define:** imperialism.
2. How did the Industrial Revolution lead to imperialism?
3. How did nationalism lead to imperialism?

Critical Thinking

4. **Demonstrating Reasoned Judgment** If you had lived during the late 1800s, would you have supported or opposed imperialism? Why?

Graphic Organizer Activity

5. Draw this diagram, and use it to show characteristics of imperialist nations.

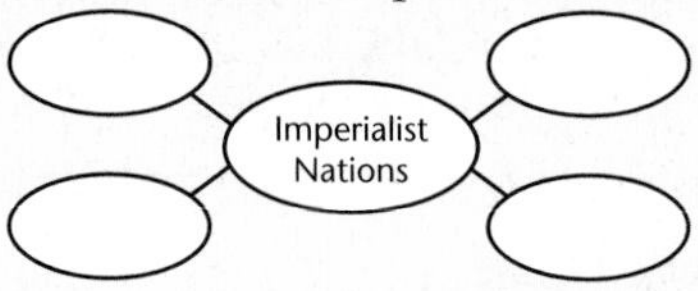

SECTION 2 Africa

Before 1870, European powers had few holdings in Africa. Those they did have were mostly seaports and trading stations along the coast. The only major exceptions were the Cape Colony at Africa's southern tip and Algeria in northern Africa. Great Britain had received the Cape Colony from the Dutch at the Congress of Vienna. Algeria was held by France. Before long, however, most of Africa belonged to European powers.

The Opening of Africa At first, most Europeans stayed along the African coast because they were safer there from tropical diseases and other dangers. Little was known about Africa's interior. Then, missionaries and explorers opened up these areas.

Section 1 Assessment Answers

1. imperialism, establishing colonies and building empires (p. 579)
2. Industrialized countries needed raw materials and food such as tea, sugar, and cocoa, and new markets for their products. These things could be found in areas that were not industrially developed.
3. Many people thought colonies would add to their country's power.
4. Answers will vary, but students should give reasons for their opinions about imperialism.
5. sample characteristics: industrially developed, possessed a class of wealthy factory owners with money to invest, influenced by nationalism, viewed the cultures of undeveloped nations as "backward," felt they had a duty to spread Christianity and the Industrial Revolution

Assign the Chapter 36 **Section 1 Quiz** in the TCR. Testmaker available.

In 1840, a Scottish medical missionary named David Livingstone (liv′ ing stuhn) went to Africa to convert the people to Christianity. During his years in Africa, Dr. Livingstone worked hard to end the Arab trade of enslaved Africans and explored much of the continent's interior. He wrote about his journeys in letters that appeared in newspapers in Great Britain and the United States. These letters aroused a great deal of interest in Africa.

Suddenly, the letters stopped. A New York newspaper decided to find out what had happened to Dr. Livingstone. It assigned reporter Henry Stanley to the story. After two years of searching, Stanley found Dr. Livingstone in a small Arab village on the shores of Lake Tanganyika (tan guhn yē′ kuh). Stanley then became an explorer himself. Between 1874 and 1889, he explored the Congo and wrote about his adventures.

In 1879, Stanley was hired by King Leopold II of Belgium to obtain African lands for him. Stanley signed many treaties with African chiefs in the Congo Basin. Most of the chiefs could not

STANLEY AND LIVINGSTONE This painting shows Henry Stanley (center left) who found David Livingstone (center right) living in the tiny village of Ujiji on Lake Tanganyika. Stanley greeted him with the now famous words, "Dr. Livingstone, I presume?" **Why had Dr. Livingstone gone to Africa?**

L2 **Religion** Have students read more about Dr. David Livingstone and other missionaries who went to Africa. To what areas did they go? What religious groups sent missionaries to these areas? How successful were they in achieving their goals?

L3 **Economics** Discuss the close connection between the Industrial Revolution in Europe and America and the rise of imperialism. Include the idea that the colonies that provided raw materials also became new markets for mass-produced goods. ELL

CAPTION ANSWER

to convert Africans to Christianity

MEETING SPECIAL NEEDS

Organize students with learning problems into five groups, and have each group concentrate on one area of Africa covered in this section: North Africa, West Africa, central Africa, East Africa, and southern Africa. Have the students in each group use the material in the chapter and an encyclopedia to prepare a brief oral or written report on the history of their region of Africa. Then ask one person in each group to present that group's oral report to the other groups.

Refer to ***Inclusion for the Middle School Social Studies Classroom: Strategies and Activities*** for additional resources.

L2 Geography: Places and Regions Ask students to research and report on the economic and geographic importance of the Congo River and the Congo Basin to the rest of Africa. Have them create a poster that shows data about this area, including a map showing its location in the continent.

LINKING PAST TO PRESENT

Among the ceremonies at the opening of the Suez Canal was the premiere performance of the opera *Aida,* composed by Giuseppe Verdi especially for the occasion. *Aida* is among the most popular operas in the world today.

Reading Check Answer

The British made Egypt a **protectorate** because the Egyptians rebelled and because Great Britain wanted control of the Suez Canal.

DID YOU KNOW ??

Boer means "farmer." The average Boer farm was comprised of about 6,000 acres (or 2,400 hectares).

read or write English and did not realize what they were signing away. In return for their lands, many of which were rich in minerals and rubber, the chiefs received cloth, beads, and sometimes guns. The signing of such treaties became a common way of gaining colonial territory.

Leopold II wanted to make a lot of money as quickly as possible. He had his soldiers force the Africans to collect rubber for him. Anyone who resisted was shot. However, missionaries and other Europeans protested so much that the king finally turned the Congo over to the Belgian government. The government did away with forced labor.

In northern Africa, the Suez (sū ez′) Canal was opened in 1869. Built by Egyptian workers and paid for with French funds, it connected the Mediterranean and Red seas. The Suez Canal made possible a shorter all-water route to India and the Far East. In 1875, however, the Egyptian ruler needed money. So, he sold his shares in the canal to Great Britain. Great Britain and France then took over Egypt's finances. This made many Egyptians angry. When they rebelled in 1882, British troops moved in. Egypt became a British **protectorate** (pruh tek′ tuhr it), or a country under the control and protection of a larger, stronger nation.

Then & Now

Trekking The Boers called their northward migration the "Great Trek." The word *trek* comes from Afrikaans, the Dutch-based language spoken by the Boers, and means "to pull a wagon" or "to migrate." Today adventurers use the term *trek* for any ambitious journey, particularly one into the mountains.

Reading Check Why did Great Britain make Egypt a British **protectorate?**

From the Cape to Cairo

Soon after Great Britain made Egypt a protectorate, the British began moving south. After several years of fighting, they conquered the Sudan. There, Great Britain set up a joint government with Egypt.

At the same time, the British began moving north from the Cape Colony. The Boers, or Dutch farmers in South Africa, did not like British rule. They did not want to speak English, and they disagreed with Great Britain's doing away with enslavement. In 1836, many Boers decided to leave the Cape Colony. They traveled northward and finally settled in the grasslands of the interior. There, they set up two independent states, the Transvaal (trans vahl′) and the Orange Free State.

In the late 1800s, gold and diamonds were discovered in the Boer states. Thousands of adventurers began pouring into the area. The Boers were soon outnumbered. Afraid of losing control of their government, the Boers would not allow the newcomers, who were mostly British, to vote. However, the newcomers had to pay heavy taxes.

This angered Cecil Rhodes (rōdz), the prime minister of the Cape Colony. Rhodes had a dream of an English-speaking empire that would stretch from the Cape to Cairo (kī rō), the capital of Egypt. The British already controlled land to the south and west of the Boer states. So, Rhodes built a railway line into land to the north of the Boer states. As soon as the railroad was completed, British settlers began moving into this area, which was called Rhodesia (rō dē′ zhuh).

Charles G. Gordon, Military Governor of the Sudan

COOPERATIVE LEARNING

Have students prepare a news report on the Boer War in the style of a prime-time television program. Organize students into groups—those who will gather information about the war and the issues surrounding it, those who will prepare written copy for the telecast, those who will represent the Boers and the British in interviews, and those who will serve as reporters and anchors for the show.

Linking Across Time

South Africa The labor of black South Africans, such as these 1906 diamond miners (left), helped make South Africa rich. Even so, they lost their rights to the Afrikaners, a white minority who dominated government. The Afrikaners held on to power until 1994, when South Africa held its first all-race election (right) and selected Nelson Mandela as president. **How did South Africa come under British control?**

At this point, Germany, jealous of Great Britain's growing power, offered the Boers its best artillery. The Boers promptly attacked British outposts, and the Boer War began. At first the Boers defeated the British. Then, the British captured the Boer capital. The Boers, however, refused to surrender and carried on guerrilla warfare for more than two years. Finally, the British destroyed Boer farms and imprisoned Boer women and children. When that happened, the Boers gave up. In 1910, the Transvaal and the Orange Free State were joined with the Cape Colony and one other British colony to form the Union of South Africa.

The British gained other African possessions besides Egypt, the Sudan, Rhodesia, and the Union of South Africa. Between 1890 and 1914, Zanzibar (zan′ zuh bahr), Uganda (yū gan′ duh), British East Africa, and Nigeria all came under British control. Except for one German colony, Cecil Rhodes's plan of an English-speaking empire in Africa came true.

Linking Across Time

South Africa came under British control as a result of the Boer War.

LINKING PAST TO PRESENT

Cecil Rhodes came to Africa at the age of 18 and made a fortune in gold and diamonds. He used his wealth to support students by setting up Rhodes scholarships at England's Oxford University. Encourage students to research what requirements must be fulfilled today to obtain a Rhodes scholarship.

MEETING SPECIAL NEEDS

Have students who are visual learners work in pairs to create posters depicting the many opportunities awaiting the bold adventurer in the 1800s. Tell them to be detailed in their designs and write a headline. Posters might show: gold mining in southern Africa; exchanging Western goods for tea and silk with traders in China; or the discovery of minerals and rubber. Display the posters in the classroom.

Refer to ***Inclusion for the Middle School Social Studies Classroom: Strategies and Activities*** for additional resources.

L2 **History** The countries along Africa's northern coast were once known as the Barbary States. From 1550 to 1815, this area of the Mediterranean Sea was notorious for pirate raids on merchant ships. In 1815, the Barbary States promised to stop pirate attacks on U.S. ships. In 1830, France used the raids as an excuse to invade Algeria. Have students create political cartoons illustrating the Barbary States' promise to the United States to stop raids, or France's decision to invade Algeria. ELL

DID YOU KNOW ??

British rule in India was known as the *raj*.

Use the **Interactive Tutor Self Assessment CD-ROM** to review Section 2.

Use the **Vocabulary Puzzle-Maker CD-ROM** to create crossword and word search puzzles.

PRIMARY SOURCES Library

You might assign "British India," from pages 694–695 of the Primary Sources Library.

Painting of King Menelik II

Other European Empires

Leopold's actions in the Congo and the British takeover of Egypt spurred other European powers into action. Over the next few years, they divided the African continent among themselves.

Spain and Portugal kept their original possessions. Angola (an gō' luh), founded in 1648 by the Portuguese, was the oldest colony in Africa. In 1885, Portugal also made Portuguese East Africa, or Mozambique, a protectorate.

The French moved out from Algeria to establish the largest European empire in Africa. This empire included Tunisia, Morocco, French West Africa, French Equatorial Africa, and Madagascar (mad uh gas' kuhr).

The Italians conquered Eritrea (er uh trē' uh), an area on the east coast, and took over part of Somaliland (sō mahl' ē land). However, when they tried to take Ethiopia in 1896, they were defeated by the troops of King Menelik II. In 1911, the Italians acquired two Turkish provinces from the Ottomans. The Italians combined the two and renamed the area Libya. The Germans set up protectorates over Togoland and the Cameroons (kam uh rūnz') in 1884. They later added German Southwest Africa and German East Africa.

By 1914, only two areas in Africa remained independent. One was Ethiopia. The other was Liberia (lī bir' ē uh), which had been founded in the 1830s by former enslaved African Americans from the United States.

Section 2 Assessment

1. **Define:** protectorate.
2. Why did many Boers leave the Cape Colony?
3. What plan did Cecil Rhodes have for Africa? How successful was he in helping Great Britain achieve this plan?

Critical Thinking

4. **Making Inferences** Why do you think the Suez Canal was so valuable to Egypt?

Graphic Organizer Activity

5. Draw this diagram, and use it to show the causes and effects of what is known as the Boer War.

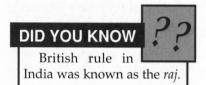

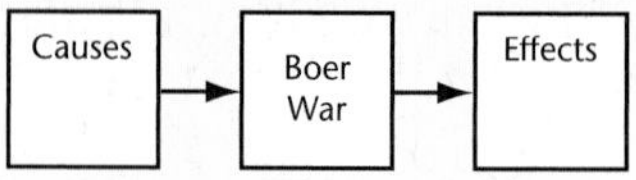

SECTION 3 Asia

The British and the Dutch started trading with Asia in the 1600s. However, Chinese and Japanese rulers allowed only limited contact with the West. So, western European countries turned their attention to India.

Section 2 Assessment Answers

1. protectorate, country under the control and protection of a larger nation (p. 582)
2. because they did not like British rule, abolition and enslavement, and did not want to speak English
3. He wanted an English-speaking empire that would stretch from the Cape to Cairo. Except for one German colony, it was achieved.
4. Answers will vary. Students might indicate that the canal made trade easier by providing a shorter all-water route to India and the Far East.
5. Answers will vary. Causes should reflect rivalries between the Boers and the British over control of southern Africa and imperialist competition between the British and Germans. Effects include British defeat of the Boers and the formation of the Union of South Africa.

Assign the Chapter 36 **Section 2 Quiz** in the TCR. Testmaker available.

India By the middle 1700s, the Mogul Empire of India was breaking up. This allowed Great Britain and France to set up trading stations along the Indian coast. Then, in 1763, France lost the Seven Years' War, also known in the Americas as the French and Indian War. As a result, the French left India, and the British East India Company took over.

The British East India Company stayed in power for almost 100 years. During that time, it brought many changes to India.

Not everyone was happy with British rule, however. Many Indians felt the British were trying to change their culture. In 1857, the **sepoys** (sē′ pois), or Indian soldiers in the British army, mutinied. The immediate cause was a new rifle. Its cartridges were greased, and one end had to be bitten off before loading. The Hindus thought the grease was beef fat. The Muslims thought it was pork fat. Hindus are not allowed by their religion to eat beef, while Muslims are not allowed to eat pork.

Although the Sepoy Mutiny failed, the British government realized that changes were needed. It took control of India away from the British East India Company and gave it to the Crown.

Great Britain wanted to protect its Indian empire from other countries, especially Russia. From 1865 to 1884, most of the central Asian centers of Muslim civilization fell to Russia. To guard India's northwest frontier, the British made Afghanistan (af gan′ uh stan) a protectorate. In Persia, both Great Britain and Russia set up **spheres of influence,** or areas within a country in which another country has special rights.

Reading Check Who were the **sepoys,** and why did they mutiny?

Reading Check What were **spheres of influence?**

THE BRITISH IN INDIA British settlers in India kept many Indian servants. In this painting, Indians unload a newly arrived British family and their luggage. **How did Great Britain try to protect its Indian Empire from Russia?**

L2 **Literature** Have students read writings of Rudyard Kipling, such as *The Jungle Book, Kim,* or "Gunga Din." Have them write a report on the work, concentrating on how Kipling uses India—its culture, people, and geography—in his stories.

Reading Check Answer
The **sepoys** were Indian soldiers in the British army. They mutinied because they thought the British were trying to change their culture and because of a misunderstanding over the grease used on a new kind of rifle cartridge.

MAKING CONNECTIONS

>> **History** Local British garrisons were unprepared for the mutiny of the sepoys. Many British regulars had been sent to duty in the Crimean War before the rebellion began.

Reading Check Answer
Spheres of influence were areas within a country in which another country had special rights.

DID YOU KNOW ??

The British allowed Indian princes to remain in power in many parts of India because it was easier to use them to help run the country than it was to conquer them all.

CAPTION ANSWER

To guard India's northwest frontier, the British made Afghanistan a protectorate and set up a sphere of influence in Persia.

MULTICULTURAL PERSPECTIVES

The incident that led to the Sepoy Rebellion reveals how Great Britain, like many of the imperialist powers in the 1800s, imposed its own culture and values on its colonies. Imperialists were often contemptuous of the sacred beliefs and rituals of the colonial people, often to the point of wiping out other cultures in the name of progress. When Africans and Asians tried to resist imperialist pressures to discard traditional ways of life, as in the Sepoy Rebellion, tension—and sometimes fighting—occurred.

L1 **Economics** Discuss the importance of the Chinese opium trade to the merchants in imperialist countries. For what did the British traders exchange opium? *(tea and silk)* Why did the Chinese government want the trade of opium ended? *(They saw how much damage the drug was doing.)* How did the outcome of the Opium War affect China? *(The Chinese were forced to sign a treaty that opened more ports and gave Hong Kong to Great Britain.)*

MAKING CONNECTIONS

➤➤ **Religion** Confucius said the following about the importance of the family in society: "The superior man spreads his culture to the entire nation by remaining at home . . . . The teaching of filial piety [children's respect for their parents] is a preparation for serving the ruler of his state; the teaching of respect for one's elder brothers is a preparation for serving all the elders of the community; and the teaching of kindness in parents is a training for ruling over people . . . . When individual families have learned kindness, then the whole nation has learned kindness."

CAPTION ANSWER

with the husband's parents

Fun Facts . . .

Migration Many Chinese sought escape from the turmoil caused by the Opium Wars. The 1848 discovery of gold in California triggered a flood of Chinese migrants to the *Gam Saan,* or "Gold Mountain," of America. By 1870, about 63,000 Chinese had migrated to the United States.

China

From the early 1500s, all trade between China and the West was limited to the city of Guangzhou (gwong jō'). The Chinese looked upon westerners as barbarians.

The Chinese people were divided into two classes. The upper class were mostly government officials, scholars, and landowners. They knew how to read and write, and looked down upon people who worked with their hands. The lower class were usually farmers and artisans who did not know how to read and write.

Both classes, however, had certain things in common. They followed the teachings of Confucius and believed that the family was most important. Marriages were arranged to benefit families. When a son married, he and his wife lived with his parents. The Chinese greatly respected their ancestors. On New Year's Day they would burn incense and place an offering of food on the family altar. Then they would tell the ancestors what had happened to the family in the past year.

The Chinese followed their way of life until the 1800s. Then came the Industrial Revolution. Western factory owners and merchants became interested in increasing overseas trade. They were no longer satisfied with the amount of business the Chinese allowed them.

CHINESE SOCIETY Here an upper-class Chinese family is shown receiving gifts for a wedding. **Where will the new husband and wife probably live?**

COOPERATIVE LEARNING

Organize the class into four teams. Then assign each team one of the following questions: How did imperialism affect India? How did imperialism affect China? How did imperialism affect islands in the Pacific and Southeast Asia? How did imperialism affect Japan? Have each team answer its question and select a note taker to record its answers. Encourage students to use their texts and other resources. Have the recorders present their team's findings. Conclude by asking students what similarities and differences they see in the effects of imperialism on these nations or areas.

OPIUM WAR The British and Chinese battled over the selling of opium in China. **From what natural source does opium come?**

About this time, British traders discovered that they could make large profits selling *opium* (ō pē uhm), or a drug made from the dried juice of certain poppies, to the Chinese. The traders took cotton cloth made in Great Britain to India, where they traded it for opium. They then took the opium to China, where it was exchanged for tea and silk to be shipped to Great Britain.

At first, the Chinese government paid little attention to the opium trade. When it saw how much damage the drug was doing, the government declared the trade illegal. When a government official in Guangzhou seized and publicly burned a large shipment of opium, British traders became angry. In 1839, what became known as the Opium War broke out between the British and the Chinese.

Although they greatly outnumbered the British, the Chinese had neither cannon nor steam-driven warships. In 1842, they were defeated and forced to sign a treaty that opened more ports and gave Great Britain the island of Hong Kong. The treaty also gave British citizens in China the **right of extraterritoriality** (rīt of ek struh ter uh tōr ē al' uh tē). This meant that British citizens accused of breaking Chinese laws could be tried only in British courts.

Reading Check How did the **right of extraterritoriality** weaken the power of the Chinese government?

L1 **Geography: Human Systems** On an outline map of the world, have students illustrate the triangular trade that resulted from the opium trade in China. **ELL**

L2 **Critical Thinking** Have students brainstorm a list of laws or rules they do not like to see broken, such as laws against theft or murder, or rules against destroying school property. Ask students how they would feel about students coming into their school, breaking rules, and not being punished for it by school officials. Have them write an explanation of how that situation relates to extraterritoriality, including a statement of their opinion of that practice in China.

LINKING PAST TO PRESENT

Hong Kong was a British colony from 1842 until 1997, when it was returned to Chinese rule. It is still one of the busiest trade and banking centers in Asia.

CAPTION ANSWER

the dried juice of certain poppies

Reading Check Answer

The **right of extraterritoriality** said that British citizens accused of breaking Chinese laws could only be tried in British courts.

MULTICULTURAL PERSPECTIVES

The spirit of revolt, like that of western Europe, also swept through China during the 1800s. The Taiping Rebellion (1851–1864) tore the country apart. A group trying to combine Christian and ancient Chinese beliefs attempted to create a perfect society with an equal division of land among the people. Other goals of the Taipings included ridding China of both the Westerners and the Qing dynasty. Although the rebellion was a failure, it seriously weakened the Qing dynasty and the country. The cost in lives was between 20 million and 30 million. Ironically, the term *taiping* means "great peace."

MAKING CONNECTIONS

➤➤ **History** The true name of the Boxers was the Society of Harmonious Fists. Westerners called its members "Boxers" because they practiced a Chinese form of boxing. Ci Xi promoted the Boxer Rebellion by encouraging anti-foreign groups to plot ways of driving out the imperialists.

CAPTION ANSWER

China was made to pay heavy penalties, and foreign powers gained almost total control of the country.

China lost even more power in the late 1800s. In 1894, Japan and China went to war over Korea. The Japanese won easily and took Chinese territory. Great Britain, France, Germany, and Russia rushed to get *concessions* (kuhn sesh' uhns), or special rights, from the Chinese government. These included the rights to develop mineral resources and build railroads and naval bases. Several countries also got leases on Chinese port cities.

The United States did not want China divided up by foreign powers or kept from trading with American merchants. In 1899, the American government asked countries to approve the Open Door policy. This gave everyone equal trading rights in China.

The Open Door Policy did not please the Chinese because it meant that foreign powers were still trying to control them. So, the Chinese began a movement to drive all foreigners from their country. The movement was called the Boxer Rebellion because it had been started by a Chinese secret society called Boxers. In the spring of 1900, the Boxers began attacking foreigners, including

THE BOXER REBELLION The Boxers were a secret society dedicated to removing all foreign influences from China. British, French, Russian, American, German, and Japanese troops were sent to put down the revolt. In this painting foreign troops attack the rebels in Beijing. **What was the outcome of the Boxer Rebellion?**

EXTENDING THE CONTENT

In signing the Open Door policy, China opened its ports to Western trade. The U.S. business community profited greatly from this agreement. In the 1930s, as tensions leading to World War II escalated, Japan invaded China and threatened to close the open door of trade with the West. The American business community became harsh critics of Japan's aggressive expansionism, adding even more tension to a situation that would soon explode into a world war.

the diplomats in Beijing (bā jing'), the capital of China. The foreign powers joined forces and sent an army to China. In 1901, the rebellion was put down. China had to pay heavy penalties, and foreign powers gained almost total control of the country.

Japan Like China, Japan allowed only limited trade with the West at first. The Japanese government even refused to provide shelter to shipwrecked sailors. In the middle 1800s, however, this changed.

In 1853, the American government sent a naval force under Commodore Matthew Perry to Japan. Perry was able to negotiate a treaty to open up trade and to protect shipwrecked American sailors. Soon after, Japan signed similar treaties with Great Britain, France, Russia, and the Netherlands.

Painting of Matthew Perry

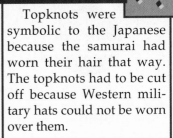

The military strength and industrial accomplishments of the West impressed most Japanese leaders. They felt that in order to survive, Japan must modernize. To this end, in 1868, several Japanese lords overthrew the shogun and restored the power of the emperor. The new emperor moved the capital of Japan from Kyoto (kyō' tō) to Tokyo. He called his rule Meiji (mā' jē), which means "enlightened peace." The changes that came about during this time are known as the Meiji Restoration.

The new government did away with feudalism. Common people were now allowed to take a family name. They also could live and work where they wished. The government ordered all Japanese males to cut off the topknots worn in their hair. Western-style clothing and a new calendar were introduced.

The Meiji government took away the special position of the samurai. Instead, all Japanese men were expected to serve for a certain amount of time in the armed forces. The government also set up a modern army and navy.

In 1889, Japanese leaders wrote Japan's first constitution. Public schools were opened, and education was required for all. Japanese leaders also began a push to industrialize. To help reach this goal, they gave certain privileges and protection to the ***zaibatsu*** (zī' bah tsū'), or the rich and powerful families who controlled many industries.

Reading Check Why did Japanese leaders feel they needed the help of the *zaibatsu?*

By the end of the 1800s, Japan was fully industrialized. However, Japan needed raw materials and markets for its manufactured goods. In addition, because of modern sanitation and medicine, its population was growing rapidly. Japan did not have enough fertile land to grow food for all its people.

To help find answers to these problems, the Japanese began a program of imperialism. Japan gained control of the island of Formosa (for mō' suh), or present-day Taiwan (tī wahn'), and part of Manchuria (man chūr' ē uh) after a war with China. Ten years later, Japan went to war with Russia and got control of the

Independent Practice

L1 History Have students research Matthew Perry's dealings with the Japanese and prepare a television interview with questions and answers for Perry and the Japanese shoguns who signed treaties with him. Have students prepare and present a news interview for U.S. citizens eager to know the outcome of Perry's dealings with the Japanese. Some students can take the role of reporters, and others can represent Perry, his crew, and the Japanese. ELL

L3 Critical Thinking Have students choose a topic dealing with European-Japanese or European-Chinese relations, and create a political cartoon that depicts the situation. In doing so, remind students that their opinion of the relationship could also enter into their cartoon.

Reading Check Answer Japanese leaders felt they needed the help of the *zaibatsu* because these families controlled many of Japan's industries.

DID YOU KNOW ??

Topknots were symbolic to the Japanese because the samurai had worn their hair that way. The topknots had to be cut off because Western military hats could not be worn over them.

SPOTLIGHT ON: PERRY

Matthew Calbraith Perry was born April 10, 1794, in Newport, Rhode Island. He began his naval career early at age 15 as a midshipman on the *Revenge,* under the command of his brother, Oliver Hazard Perry. In his dealings with the Japanese, Matthew Perry arranged for the protection of American seamen and property in Japanese waters. It is said that he impressed the Japanese who were suspicious of other countries, by his forcefulness and insistence on formality. His meetings with the Japanese were conducted with elaborate ceremony, and he and his officers always wore their finest uniforms and were always accompanied by a full honor guard.

DID YOU KNOW ??

In addition to teaching science and other modern subjects, Japanese schools stressed such traditional values as unquestioning obedience to the emperor.

MAKING CONNECTIONS

➤➤ **History** Under Japanese rule, the Koreans lost many of their liberties and began to resist the Japanese. However, the Japanese easily crushed Korean opposition.

L1 **Geography: Places and Regions** Have students study the map "Imperialism" on this page and make charts showing which countries were controlled by Japan and the European countries that are listed in the map legend.

Assign the Chapter 36 **Geography and Map Activity** in the TCR.

MAP STUDY

Answer

Great Britain

MAP STUDY

THE WORLD IN SPATIAL TERMS
By the early 1900s, Europeans had spread their rule throughout the world. **Which country's empire included territories in the greatest number of continents?**

southern half of the island of Sakhalin (sak' uh lēn). It also won a sphere of influence in Korea. Five years later, Japan annexed Korea.

Southeast Asia and the Pacific Europeans first entered Southeast Asia in the 1500s in search of spices. By the 1600s, Portugal, Spain, and the Netherlands all had colonies there. Although there was an active trade with the islands in the area, no one paid much attention to the mainland.

In the late 1800s, the European powers changed their minds. The mainland of Southeast Asia was a source of cash crops, such as coffee and tea. It also had raw materials, such as petroleum, rubber, and tin.

Great Britain and France competed in Southeast Asia. The British took control of Burma, Ceylon, the Malay States, and Singapore. The French set up protectorates in Cochin-China

Imperialism

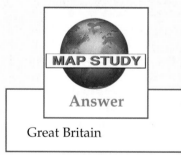

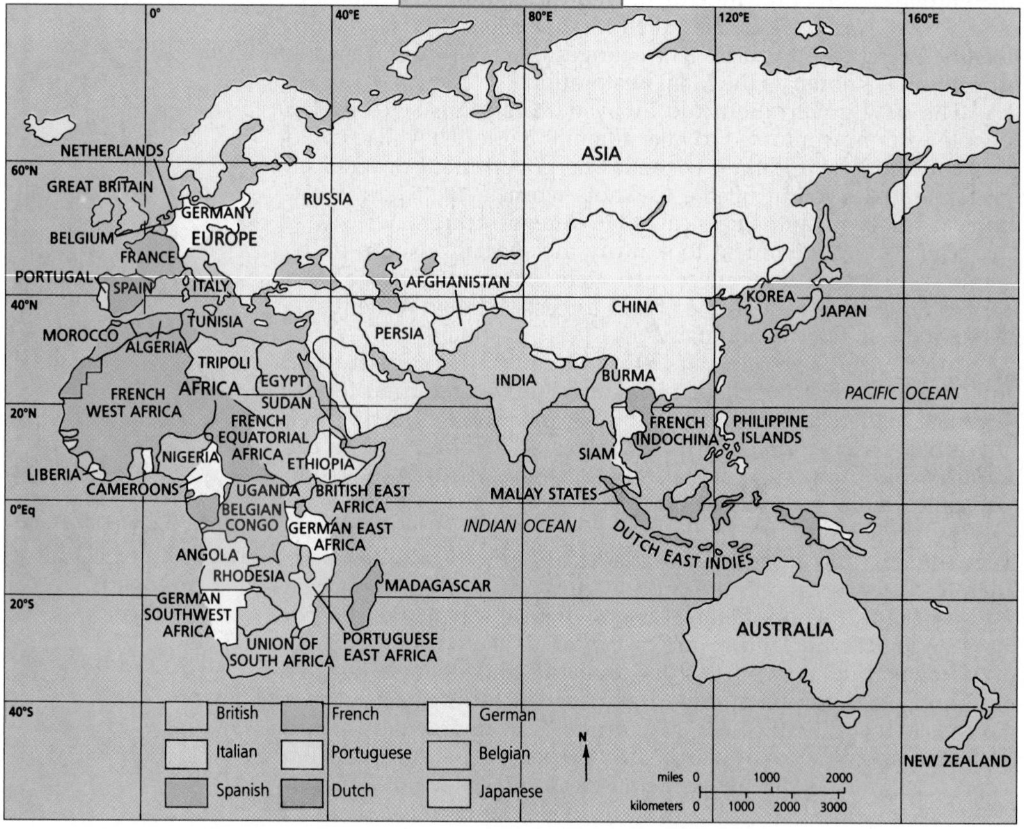

EXTENDING THE CONTENT

Liberia and Ethiopia were the only two countries in Africa that were never colonized. South Africa (1910) and Egypt (1922) gained their independence long before most other African colonies. Between 1951 and 1991, more than 50 African colonies achieved independence. Since the beginning of colonial rule, nationalist groups in Africa had resisted European control, often violently. But following World War II, these relatively small efforts for freedom swelled into powerful mass movements. Africans, many of whom served in the Allied armies, were inspired by the democratic ideals for which the Allies fought in the war—self-rule and freedom from tyranny.

(kō' chuhn chī nuh), Kampuchea, and Annam (a nam'). They then took over Laos (lah' ōs) and combined the four colonies into Indochina. Only Siam, or present-day Thailand, remained independent.

During this period, Great Britain, France, Germany, and the United States were also trying to win control of islands in the Pacific. Some of the islands had rich soil that could be used for sugar and pineapple plantations. Others had minerals. Still others could be used as bases for refueling and repairing ships.

Great Britain, which had the largest navy in the world, already held Australia and New Zealand. Now, it took the Fiji, Solomon, and Gilbert Islands, along with parts of New Guinea (gin' ē) and Borneo (bor' nē ō). France claimed Tahiti, the Marquesas (mahr kā' zuhz), and several other islands. Germany took part of New Guinea and the Marshall, Caroline, and Mariana Islands. Later, Germany divided the Samoan (suh mō' uhn) Islands with the United States. The United States also controlled the Hawaiian and Philippine Islands and Guam (gwahm).

People in History

Liliuokalani
1838–1917

Hawaiian Queen

Born in Honolulu, Liliuokalani came to power in 1891. She tried to restore the power of the monarchy, which had been weakened by the mostly American sugar planters, but was forced to step down in 1895.

Section 3 Assessment

1. **Define:** sepoys, spheres of influence, right of extraterritoriality, *zaibatsu*.
2. Why did the Japanese start a program of imperialism?
3. Why did many European countries in the 1800s want to control territory in Southeast Asia?

Critical Thinking

4. **Identifying Central Issues** What was the central issue in the Boxer Rebellion?

Graphic Organizer Activity

5. Draw this diagram, and use it to show the steps leading to the takeover of India by the British Crown.

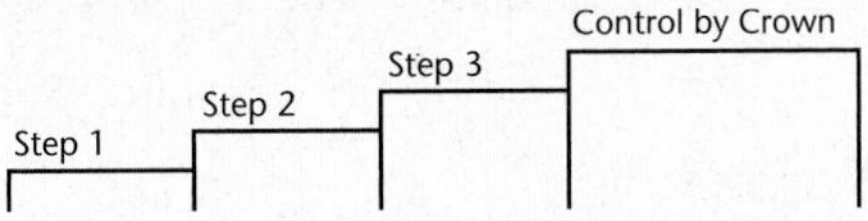

SECTION 4 Latin America

The imperialist powers were also interested in Latin America. The countries there that had gained their independence in the early 1800s faced many problems. Most Latin Americans were poor and had no land of their own. The new leaders had little government experience. There were many revolutions. These shaky conditions seemed to invite outside interference.

GEOGRAPHY AND HISTORY

The Pacific Islands are divided into three groups: Melanesia, Micronesia, and Polynesia. Encourage students to locate these groups in their text Atlas.

MAKING CONNECTIONS

➤➤ **Literature** The influences of various Asian cultures began to find their way into the works of Western writers and artists as a result of the increased contact brought about by imperialism. Joseph Conrad's stories, and Paul Gauguin's paintings reflect the influence of several of the cultures of Southeast Asia and islands in the Pacific.

Use the **Interactive Tutor Self Assessment CD-ROM** to review Section 3.

Use the **Vocabulary PuzzleMaker CD-ROM** to create crossword and word search puzzles.

Section 3 Assessment Answers

1. sepoys, Indian soldiers in the British army (p. 585); spheres of influence, areas within a country in which another country has special rights (p. 585); right of extraterritoriality, right of an accused person to be tried in a court of his or her own nation (p. 587); *zaibatsu*, powerful Japanese families (p. 589)
2. to get raw materials and markets for manufactured goods and food
3. because it was a source of coffee and tea and raw materials
4. foreign influence in China
5. sample steps: British acquisition of India at the end of the French and Indian War, rule of India by the British East India Company, Sepoy Mutiny

Assign the Chapter 36 **Section 3 Quiz** in the TCR. Testmaker available.

L2 Geography: The World in Spatial Terms Ask students to find North America and South America in the text Atlas. Have students write an explanation of how location explains why the United States issued the Monroe Doctrine. ELL

LINKING PAST TO PRESENT

Puerto Rico is now a commonwealth of the United States. Puerto Ricans can enter the United States without a passport. They serve in America's armed forces but do not pay federal taxes and cannot vote in national elections. The U.S. government handles Puerto Rico's foreign affairs. Guam is still a U.S. territory. Cuba became an independent republic in 1902.

CAPTION ANSWER

The United States supported a successful revolution by the people of Panama against Colombia and then signed a treaty with Panama.

THE HISTORY CHANNEL.

The following videotape programs are available from Glencoe to enrich Chapter 36:

- **The Panama Canal**
- **The U.S. in Latin America: Yankee Go Home**

To find classroom resources to accompany these videos, check the following home page:

A&E Television:
www.aande.com

Fun Facts . . .

The Canal and Disease After the Spanish-American War, Colonel William C. Gorgas, a U.S. army physician, wiped out yellow fever in Havana, Cuba. In 1904, Gorgas began an effort to eliminate the disease from the Isthmus of Panama. Scientists had just found that mosquitoes transmit both yellow fever and malaria. By controlling mosquitoes, Gorgas greatly lowered the death toll among workers on the Panama Canal.

To stop this, President James Monroe issued the Monroe Doctrine in 1823. It said that any attempt to gain colonies in Latin America would be considered an unfriendly act toward the United States. Most of the European powers went along with the Monroe Doctrine, largely because the British navy supported the American position. The French made Prince Maximilian of Austria the emperor of Mexico.

By the late 1800s, Spain had colonies in Cuba and Puerto Rico. The Cubans, eager to be independent, had revolted in 1868 and again in 1895. Some Americans, who had large amounts of money invested there, wanted the rebels to win. In 1898, an American battleship, the U.S.S. *Maine,* blew up in the harbor of Havana, Cuba. People in the United States blamed the Spanish. Before long, Congress declared war on Spain.

In less than a year, the United States won the Spanish-American War. The resulting peace treaty gave the United States Puerto Rico, Guam, and the Philippine Islands. Cuba became an American protectorate.

The United States was now a world power. As such, it became even more involved in Latin America.

The United States needed a way to protect its new territories. Its fleet had to be able to sail quickly between American islands in the Caribbean Sea and those in the Pacific Ocean. President

PANAMA CANAL The building of the Panama Canal took over eight years and the labor of more than 40,000 persons. About 5,600 workers died from accidents and disease. Here, the digging of the Gaillard Cut is shown. **How was the United States able to gain rights to the land for a canal?**

COOPERATIVE LEARNING

Organize students into several small groups. Have each group research U.S. relations with the Philippines during one of these time periods: immediately after the Spanish-American War; during World War I; during World War II; during the Cold War; and today. Have each group divide the tasks of gathering data, preparing summaries of the materials, providing a time line to accompany the summaries, and exhibiting the material in a class presentation.

Assign Chapter 36 *Cooperative Learning Activity* in the TCR.

Theodore Roosevelt wanted to build a canal across Panama, a province of Colombia. The United States, however, could not come to terms with Colombia.

In 1903, the United States supported a revolution by people in Panama against Colombia. The revolution was a success. The United States and Panama then signed a treaty in which Panama leased land to the United States to be used for building a canal. In 1914, the Panama Canal was opened. It shortened the route between the two oceans by nearly 7,000 miles, or 11,200 kilometers. The Colombians, however, were angry that the United States had interfered in their affairs.

The United States' interest in Latin America continued. Some countries there had financial and political troubles that led to riots. The United States wanted to protect its business investments. So, between 1912 and 1916, the government sent American soldiers to Nicaragua, the Dominican Republic, and Haiti to restore order.

HISTORY Online

Student Web Activity

Visit the *Human Heritage* Web site at humanheritage.glencoe.com and click on ***Chapter 36—Student Web Activities*** to find out more about U.S. colonies.

Section 4 Assessment

1. Why did President Monroe issue the Monroe Doctrine?
2. Why did the United States want a canal through Panama?

Critical Thinking

3. **Predicting Consequences** What might have happened if most European powers had not gone along with the Monroe Doctrine?

Graphic Organizer Activity

4. Draw this diagram, and use it to show some of the effects of the Spanish-American War.

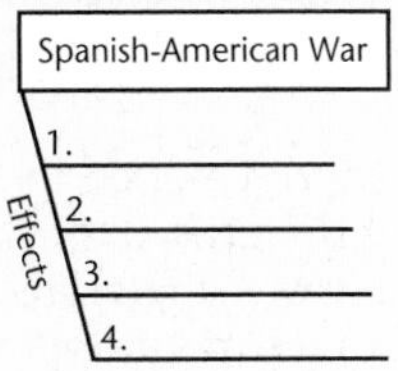

SECTION 5 Effects of Imperialism

By 1914, European colonial powers, Japan, and the United States had brought about 85 percent of the world under their control. This had many benefits. Orderly governments were set up. Many local wars were stopped. Industry, agriculture, and transportation were developed. Hospitals and schools were built, and sanitation was improved. Western ideas about democracy and individual rights spread.

At the same time, however, imperialism brought about major problems. One was bitter feelings between colonists and colonizers. Most Europeans, North Americans, and Japanese thought they were better than the people in the colonies. Colonists were seldom allowed to hold high jobs in government, industry, or the armed forces. Often, they were not even allowed in city areas where Europeans and North Americans lived.

Section 4 Assessment Answers

1. to stop outside interference in Latin American countries
2. to enable its fleet to sail quickly between the Caribbean Sea and the Pacific Ocean
3. Answers will vary, but students could indicate that these nations might have waged war to gain control of certain Latin American countries.
4. sample effects: U.S. acquisition of Puerto Rico, Guam, and the Philippine Islands; establishment of Cuba as a U.S. protectorate; recognition of the U.S. as a world power; construction of Panama Canal

Assign the Chapter 36 **Section 4 Quiz** in the TCR. Testmaker available.

HISTORY Online

Student Web Activity objectives and answers can be found at the ***Chapter 36 Web Activity Lesson Plan*** at humanheritage.glencoe.com

Use the **Interactive Tutor Self Assessment CD-ROM** to review Section 4.

Biography

The following videotape program is available from Glencoe to enrich Chapter 36:

- **Theodore Roosevelt: Roughrider to Rushmore**

To find classroom resources to accompany this video, check the following home page:

A&E Television: www.aande.com

Use the **Vocabulary PuzzleMaker CD-ROM** to create crossword and word search puzzles.

ASSESS

Check for Understanding

Ask students to summarize the main points of the chapter, orally or in writing. Discuss the answers to the Section and Chapter Assessment questions.

Evaluate

Assign the Chapter 36 **Performance Assessment Activity** in the TCR.

Administer the **Chapter 36 Test** in the TCR. Testmaker available.

GLENCOE TECHNOLOGY

MindJogger Videoquiz

Use **MindJogger Videoquiz** to review students' knowledge of the unit.

Available in DVD and VHS

Reteach

Assign the Chapter 36 **Reteaching Activity** in the TCR.

Enrich

Assign the Chapter 36 **Enrichment Activity** in the TCR.

CLOSE

Have students comment on the meaning of the following quotation by Theodore Roosevelt in terms of imperialism: "No nation can claim rights without acknowledging the duties that go with the rights."

Use the **Interactive Tutor Self Assessment CD-ROM** to review Section 5.

HISTORY Online

Self-Check Quiz gives students an interactive chapter tutorial. Have them access ***Chapter 36 Quiz*** at humanheritage.glencoe.com

The colonists resented this. They blamed the colonial powers for the loss of their land and for being forced to work on plantations and in factories. They disliked the colonial powers for trying to change their customs, languages, and religions. These feelings helped nationalism to grow.

There was yet another problem. The scramble for colonies led to a great deal of competition among colonial powers. This, in turn, led to disputes that caused future wars.

Section 5 Assessment

1. What percent of the world was colonized by 1914?
2. What problems did the scramble for empires create for the colonial powers?

Critical Thinking

3. **Identifying Alternatives** If you were a colonist in the early 1900s, would you have tried to get a job in the colonial government or would you have tried to rebel? Explain.

Graphic Organizer Activity

4. Draw this diagram, and use it to weigh the benefits and drawbacks of imperialism.

Benefits	Drawbacks

Chapter Summary & Study Guide

1. Imperialism developed in the 1800s because of the growth of nationalism; the need for raw materials, new markets, and investment opportunities; and the belief among Europeans that they should spread their way of life.
2. By the early 1900s, European nations had carved up Africa, with only Ethiopia and Liberia remaining independent.
3. By the late 1800s, Great Britain controlled India, Russia was moving into central Asia, and foreign powers were competing for control of China.
4. By the early 1900s, Japan had become industrialized and was a powerful imperialist nation.
5. By 1900, Great Britain, France, Germany, and the United States controlled most of Southeast Asia and many islands in the Pacific.
6. In 1823, the United States issued the Monroe Doctrine to keep European nations from expanding their control into Latin America.
7. The United States became an imperialist power after winning Puerto Rico, Guam, and the Philippines from Spain in 1898 and building the Panama Canal in 1903.
8. While imperialism led to the development of orderly governments, industry, and social reforms, it also increased nationalism and dangerous competition for empires.

HISTORY Online

Self-Check Quiz

Visit the *Human Heritage* Web site at humanheritage.glencoe.com and click on ***Chapter 36—Self-Check Quiz*** to assess your understanding of this chapter.

Section 5 Assessment Answers

1. about 85 percent
2. sample problems: bitter feelings between colonists and colonizers, competition for empires, disputes paving the way to future wars
3. Answers will vary, but students should provide reasons for their feelings.
4. Answers will vary but should reflect the points listed in the text. You might ask students to decide whether the benefits of imperialism outweighed the drawbacks or vice versa.

Assign the Chapter 36 **Section 5 Quiz** in the TCR. Testmaker available.

Performance Assessment Activities

Letters to the Editor Ask students to imagine they live in one of these countries after World War I: Italy, Germany, the Soviet Union, France, or Great Britain. Have them write to a newspaper editor expressing their opinions about their country's post-war situation. In their letters, students should describe their identity, such as "I am a young, unmarried woman who wants a university education."

CHAPTER RESOURCES

LITERATURE ABOUT THE PERIOD

Hemingway, Ernest. *The Sun Also Rises.* Scribner's, 1926. A novel about English and American expatriates in France and Spain after World War I.

READINGS FOR THE STUDENT

Frank, Anne. *The Diary of a Young Girl.* Doubleday, 1972. First-person account of a young Jewish girl and her family who spent years during World War II hiding from the Nazis.

Ryan, Cornelius. *The Longest Day.* Simon & Schuster Pocket Books, 1984. Detailed account of D-Day and the Normandy invasion.

READINGS FOR THE TEACHER

Tuchman, Barbara W. *The Guns of August.* Macmillan, 1962. Account of the crucial first six weeks of World War I.

KEY TO ABILITY LEVELS

Teaching strategies have been coded for varying learning styles and abilities.

L1 Level 1 activities are **basic** activities and should be within the ability range of all students.

L2 Level 2 activities are **average** activities and should be within the ability range of the average to above-average student.

L3 Level 3 activities are **challenging** activities designed for the ability range of above-average students.

ELL ELL activities should be within the ability range of English Language Learning students.

NATIONAL GEOGRAPHIC Teacher's Corner

INDEX TO NATIONAL GEOGRAPHIC MAGAZINE

The following articles relate to this chapter:

- "Untold Stories of D-Day," by Thomas B. Allen, June 2002.
- "Russia Rising," by Fen Montaigne, November 2001.
- "The Last Dive," by Priit J. Vesilind, October 1999.
- "The Battle of Midway," by Thomas B. Allen, April 1999.
- "Searching for Ships Lost in the Battle of Midway," by Robert Ballard, April 1999.

ADDITIONAL NATIONAL GEOGRAPHIC SOCIETY PRODUCTS

To order the following, call National Geographic at 1-800-368-2728:

- *PicturePack: World War I Era (Transparencies)*
- *PictureShow: World War I Era (CD-ROM)*
- *PicturePack: World War II Era (Transparencies)*
- *PictureShow: World War II Era (CD-ROM)*
- *Russia's Last Tsar (Video)*
- *20th-Century History Series (3 videos)*

Access *National Geographic's* new dynamic MapMachine Web site and other geography resources at:
www.nationalgeographic.com
www.nationalgeographic.com/maps

THE HISTORY CHANNEL. A&E HOME VIDEO. Biography

The following videotape programs are available from Glencoe:

- **Anne Frank**
  0-7670-1409-X
- **The Decision to Drop the Bomb**
  1-56501-600-9
- **Joseph Stalin**
  1-56501-820-6
- **The Last Days of World War II**
  1-56501-536-3
- **V-J Day: The Day That Changed the World**
  0-7670-0202-4
- **World War II: The War Chronicles**
  1-56501-484-7

To order, call Glencoe at 1-800-334-7344. To find classroom resources to accompany many of these videos, check:
A&E Television: www.aande.com
The History Channel: www.historychannel.com

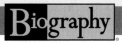

Introducing CHAPTER 37

OVERVIEW

Chapter 37 discusses international affairs during the twentieth century from World War I through World War II.

➤ **Section 1** discusses World War I, focusing on its underlying causes, significant campaigns, and impact.

➤ **Section 2** describes the origins and impact of communism, and traces the rise of dictatorships in Italy and Germany.

➤ **Section 3** analyzes the causes, events, and results of World War II.

CHAPTER OBJECTIVES

After reading Chapter 37, students will be able to:

1. discuss the causes, events, and results of World War I.

2. describe how communism developed in Russia.

3. explain reasons Italy and Germany became dictatorships.

4. trace the course and outcome of World War II.

EXAMINING ARTIFACTS

Ask students what these artifacts tell them about World War I. *(Students might mention the weapons, the faceless soldiers, the involvement of women in war plants, and so on.)* Then refer students to the time line. Have them name other events that shook the first half of the 20th century.

PERFORMANCE ASSESSMENT ✓

Use the Performance Assessment activities on page 602B to help you to evaluate students as they complete the chapter.

CHAPTER 37

Conflict and Change

1900 A.D.–1945 A.D.

▲English poster

◄ Allied soldiers from World War

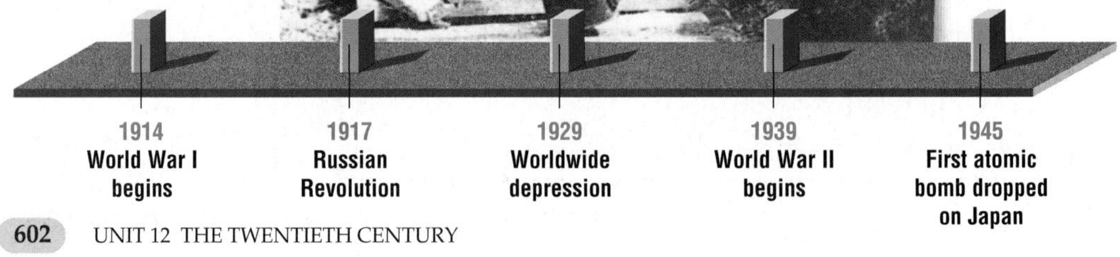

TEACHING RESOURCES

TEACHER PLANNING AND SUPPORT

- Reproducible Lesson Plan 37-1, 37-2, 37-3
- Teaching Strategies for the World History Classroom (Including Block Scheduling Pacing Guides)
- Presentation Plus! CD-ROM

REVIEW AND REINFORCEMENT

- Reading Essentials and Study Guide 37-1, 37-2, 37-3
- Chapter 37 Vocabulary and Guided Reading Activity
- Vocabulary PuzzleMaker CD-ROM
- Teaching Transparencies 37A & 37B
- Chapter 37 Reteaching Activity
- Chapter 37 Cooperative Learning Activity
- Chapter 37 Activity Book Activity
- Chapter 37 Chart and Graph Skill Activity
- Reading and Study Skills Foldables
- Interactive Tutor Self-Assessment CD-ROM
- Unit 12 MindJogger VideoQuiz

APPLICATION AND HANDS-ON ACTIVITIES

- Daily Questions in Social Studies
- Student Presentation Builder CD-ROM

Chapter Focus

Read to Discover

- What the causes, events, and results of World War I were.
- How communism developed in Russia.
- Why Italy and Germany became dictatorships.
- What the causes, events, and results of World War II were.

HISTORY Online

Chapter Overview

Visit the *Human Heritage* Web site at **humanheritage.glencoe.com** and click on ***Chapter 37—Chapter Overviews*** to preview this chapter.

Terms to Learn	People to Know	Places to Locate
mobilize	Franz Ferdinand	Sarajevo
armistice	Woodrow Wilson	Pearl Harbor
soviets	Nicholas II	Hiroshima
dictatorship	Vladimir Lenin	Nagasaki
appeasement	Joseph Stalin	
genocide	Adolf Hitler	
Holocaust	Winston Churchill	

Why It's Important The first half of the 1900s was a period of turmoil throughout the world. In 1914, a war broke out in Europe that turned into World War I. Although it ended in 1918, anger over the peace settlement and poor economic conditions following the war led to World War II. The same period also saw the rise of communism in Russia and neighboring countries.

SECTION 1 World War I

For almost 100 years after Napoleon's defeat, no long, general European war developed. By the early 1900s, however, rivalries among the countries of Europe were causing trouble.

Background

By the early 1900s, tension grew between several countries. France was jealous of Germany because it was industrializing rapidly. Great Britain did not like Germany expanding its navy. Russia involved itself with the problems of the Slavic peoples in Austria-Hungary.

Each European country built up its armed forces and made alliances with other nations. They each promised to help the others in their alliance if they were attacked. Thus, trouble between any two nations of different alliances could draw in many countries. A small war could easily grow into a large one. All that was needed was a spark.

GEOGRAPHY ACTIVITIES

- Chapter 37 Geography and Map Activity
- Outline Map Resource Book

INTERDISCIPLINARY CONNECTIONS

- World Music: A Cultural Legacy
- Unit 12 World Literature Reading 1
- World Art & Architecture Transparency 45, *I Want You for the U.S. Army*

ENRICHMENT AND EXTENSION

- World History Primary Source Document Library CD-ROM
- Chapter 37 Enrichment Activity

ASSESSMENT AND EVALUATION

- Chapter 37 Performance Assessment Activity
- Chapter 37 Section Quizzes 37-1, 37-2, 37-3
- Chapter 37 Test
- Chapter 37 ExamView® Pro Testmaker CD-ROM
- Chapter 37 Digests Audiocassettes Activities and Tests

SPANISH RESOURCES

- Chapter 37 Spanish Chapter Summary and Glossary
- Chapter 37 Spanish Digests Audiocassettes Activities and Tests

HISTORY Online

Chapter Overview introduces students to chapter content and key terms. Have them access ***Chapter 37 Overview*** at humanheritage.glencoe.com

FOCUS

Bellringer

Write the following on the board: List two good things and two bad things about nationalism.

Motivational Activity

Have students share their responses. Point out that in the early 1900s, nationalism created an atmosphere in which a simple incident could have serious consequences. Explain that the direct cause of World War I was the tension created by strong nationalist feelings in Austria-Hungary and Serbia. Tell students they will learn about other causes of conflicts in the first half of the 1900s.

GUIDE TO READING

Reading Strategy

Ask students to read "Why It's Important" and summarize the chapter's main theme. *(This time period was shaped by two world wars and the rise of communism.)*

Vocabulary Precheck

Ask students to define each of the "Terms to Learn." Have a volunteer consult the dictionary for any unfamiliar words. L1 ELL

Use the Vocabulary PuzzleMaker CD-ROM for Chapter 37 to create a crossword puzzle. L1

Assign Chapter 37 Vocabulary and Guided Reading Activity.

Assign Reading Essentials and Study Guide 37-1.

TEACH

Guided Practice

L1 **Geography: The World in Spatial Terms** On an outline map of the world, have students show the locations of the Central and the Allied Powers. Then ask: How did the Central Powers get their name? *(They were located between Allied countries.)* What problem did the Central Powers' location pose? *(They had to fight on two fronts: east and west.)* ELL

Reading Check Answer
Russia began to **mobilize** for war because Austria-Hungary declared war on Serbia, which was an ally of Russia.

Reading Check Answer
World War I was the first war in which **civilians** were attacked.

Reading Check Answer
In **trench warfare,** opposing armies fight from trenches dug in the ground.
To get at the enemy, soldiers had to climb out of trenches and run across open land under heavy **artillery** fire.

The spark for World War I occurred in Sarajevo (sahr uh yē vō), a small town in Austria-Hungary. There, in June 1914, a teenager named Gavrilo Princip shot and killed Archduke Franz Ferdinand, heir to the throne of Austria-Hungary. Princip belonged to a secret nationalist group called the Black Hand. This group wanted the Serbs ruled by Austria-Hungary to be ruled by Serbia (ser′ bē uh).

Austria-Hungary blamed the Serbian government for the Archduke's death and declared war on Serbia. Russia, an ally of Serbia, began to **mobilize,** or call up its troops, to go to Serbia's aid. Germany then showed its support of Austria-Hungary by declaring war on Russia. Shortly after, France and Great Britain entered the war on the side of Russia. So did Japan and, later, Italy and China. The Ottoman Empire, on the other hand, decided to support Germany and Austria-Hungary. Together, Germany, Austria-Hungary, the Ottoman Empire, and Bulgaria were called the Central Powers. Russia, Serbia, France, Great Britain, Japan, Italy, and China were called the Allied Powers.

Reading Check Why did Russia **mobilize** for war?

From 1914 to 1918 World War I, also called the Great War, was different from any earlier war. It was the first war where **civilians** (suh vil′ yuhnz), or people who are not soldiers, were also attacked. The war grew so large that 31 countries, with 65 million soldiers, took part. Although most land fighting took place in Europe, the Middle East, and Africa, naval warfare took place throughout the world.

Reading Check Why was World War I different from other wars for **civilians?**

There were also new, more powerful weapons being used. Machine guns fired bullets one after another at a rapid speed. Huge guns fired shells more than 75 miles, or 120 kilometers, away. Airplanes carried bombs behind enemy lines and dropped them on enemy cities. Submarines attacked ships at sea. Poison gases were used. Tanks and flame throwers were introduced.

Much of the fighting took place on the western front, the zone between France and Germany. There, opposing armies dug themselves into the ground in trenches protected by barbed wire. This kind of fighting is called **trench warfare.** To get at the enemy, each side had to climb out of its trenches and cross open land under **artillery** (ar til′ uhr ē), or mounted gun, fire. The casualties were enormous. One battle alone cost 900,000 lives. In another area, French and German soldiers engaged in trench warfare for ten months.

Reading Check What is **trench warfare?**
Why did **artillery** fire claim so many lives?

On the eastern front, the Russian Empire suffered heavy losses. Some 3.8 million soldiers were killed in just the first ten months of the war. In 1918, after two revolutions, Russia withdrew from the war and signed a separate peace treaty with Germany, having recognized Ukraine as an independent country. The Russians gave up large areas of land previously conquered by them. Located to the

COOPERATIVE LEARNING

Have students research and report on the first six weeks of World War I. Assign each of five groups one of the following: invasion of Belgium, German sweep through France to Paris, retreat of the Allies, Russian mobilization and early victories ending at Tannenberg, and the Battle of the Marne. Students should work in pairs, each student gathering specific information on a specific topic. Then have each group present its report to create a composite picture.

TRENCH WARFARE Much of the fighting of the First World War was carried out from trenches. Men had to charge across "no man's land," the open area in front of the enemy's trenches, in order to attack. Machine guns made these attacks especially dangerous. **Where was the western front located?**

HISTORY Online

Student Web Activity

Visit the *Human Heritage* Web site at **humanheritage.glencoe.com** and click on ***Chapter 37—Student Web Activities*** to find out more about World War I.

west of Russia, these lands included one third of their farmland, one third of their population, and almost all of their resources of coal, iron, and oil.

In the meantime, German submarines tried to stop supply ships to Great Britain and France. In 1917, after the submarines sank American ships with civilians on board, the United States declared war on Germany. Until then, the United States had tried to stay out of the conflict.

The United States sent 2 million fresh troops to Europe to aid the tired Allied forces. The Americans helped to bring a quick end to the war, in favor of the Allied Powers. On November 11, 1918, Germany and its allies agreed to an **armistice** (ar′ muh stis), or a stop in the fighting.

The Great War was over. Over 13 million soldiers and 17 million civilians lost their lives. Another 20 million soldiers had been wounded, and there was billions of dollars in damage to property.

Reading Check How did the arrival of American troops help bring about an **armistice?**

Making the Peace

Woodrow Wilson, the President of the United States, had drawn up a peace plan called the Fourteen Points. Wilson believed that national groups in Europe should have the right to form their own countries. He wanted to reduce **armaments** (ar′ muh muhnts), or equipment for war. Above all,

Reading Check What did Woodrow Wilson want nations to do with their **armaments?**

HISTORY Online

Student Web Activity objectives and answers can be found at the ***Chapter 37 Web Activity Lesson Plan*** at **humanheritage.glencoe.com**

CAPTION ANSWER

between France and Germany

Reading Check Answer

American troops relieved Allied forces, forcing Germany to agree to an **armistice.**

Reading Check Answer

Woodrow Wilson wanted nations to reduce their **armaments.**

EXTENDING THE CONTENT

On the eastern front, Russia was ill-equipped and badly led. Before Lenin's new government signed the Treaty of Brest-Litovsk, more than two million Russians had been killed. In Turkey, the failing Ottoman Empire still controlled the Dardanelles. Mines in the water and on-shore artillery kept the Russians blockaded in their Black Sea ports. At Gallipoli in 1915, an Allied force failed in its attempt to land on the Turkish coast and march to Constantinople. British, New Zealand, Australian, and French troops suffered terrible losses against the Turks and Germans.

L2 **Critical Thinking** Ask students to work in small groups to list three things they would have included in the settlement for World War I. As they read the subsection, "Making the Peace," have students compare their lists with Wilson's Fourteen Points and the Treaty of Versailles.

DID YOU KNOW ??

All the major powers used propaganda during World War I. In August 1918, the United States dropped leaflets behind German lines asking Germans if they were "still willing to die for a hopeless cause."

L3 **Science** Remind students that World War I was the first war to use submarines. Have students research and report on this kind of boat and the scientific principles used to control its buoyancy. Ask students to demonstrate these principles for the class.

CAPTION ANSWER

Germany was blamed for the war, asked to pay for war damages, and lost land in Europe and overseas.

Reading Check Answer

(See page 607 for terms.)

A **mandate** is the right to rule another country.

A nation that follows an **isolationist** policy stays out of world problems and the affairs of other nations.

Then & Now

Remembering Veterans November 11, 1918—the day World War I ended—is a time when members of the armed services are honored in many of the former Allied countries. Once called Armistice Day, since 1954 it has been called Veterans Day in the United States. It is Remembrance Day in Canada and Armistice Day in Britain.

he wanted a world association of nations to keep the peace. The British, French, and Italian leaders, however, had other plans. They wanted repayment for their losses during the war from the defeated countries.

The peace treaty that Germany signed after World War I was called the Treaty of Versailles (vuhr sī'). This treaty put most of the blame for the war and the financial repayment on Germany, for which the Germans were very angry. Under this treaty, Germany lost land in Europe and overseas. Alsace and Lorraine, which Germany had taken from France in 1870, were returned to France. Some of Germany's eastern territory became part of the reestablished nation of Poland. Germany's African colonies were divided between France and Great Britain, while its Pacific colonies were given to Japan.

Under the Treaty of Versailles, Russia lost even more territory than Germany did. Part of the Russian territory was lost to Poland and Romania, and part of it became the new nations of Finland, Estonia, Latvia, and Lithuania. Ukraine's desire for independence, however, was ignored.

The treaty did not deal with the needs of some other countries. India and people in Southeast Asia who had supported the Allied Powers wanted independence from Great Britain and France. Their wishes were ignored. Over the next 30 years, serious troubles developed in all these areas.

The other Central Powers were dealt with in separate treaties. Austria-Hungary was broken up, and four new countries—Austria,

TREATY OF VERSAILLES The Treaty of Versailles was signed in June, 1919, at the palace of Versailles outside Paris. Only the Allied Powers took part in the negotiations. Germany was not allowed to participate. Here, the Allied leaders meet in the Hall of Mirrors. **How was Germany affected by the Treaty of Versailles?**

Reading Check What is a **mandate?** What type of policy does an **isolationist** country follow?

EXTENDING THE CONTENT

The function of aircraft in World War I was at first limited to reconnaissance. Bombs were too heavy to support and were carried instead by dirigibles. Moreover, it was hard to aim heavy rifles or shotguns at anything from these "bucking machines." Roland Garros, a French pilot, was the first to have a machine gun synchronized to shoot through the propeller blades. But in 1915, Garros and his plane went down. The Germans took Garros prisoner, seized the plane, and copied and improved on the technology. Soon air fights, also called dog fights, became a glamorized aspect of war.

Hungary, Czechoslovakia, and Yugoslavia—were created. France received a **mandate** (man'dāt), or right to rule, in Syria and Lebanon. Great Britain received mandates in Iraq and Palestine.

For the most part, President Wilson's peace plan was not followed. However, one point was kept. An organization called the League of Nations was established so the countries of the world could come together to talk over their troubles. Most hoped the League could help prevent future wars. But the League had a serious weakness—it had no army of its own. If a country did not want to obey the League, it could not be forced to do so. The League was also weak because the United States refused to become a member. Many Americans disagreed with the World War I treaties. After 1919, the United States became an **isolationist** country. It decided to stay out of European affairs and world problems.

MAP STUDY

PLACES AND REGIONS The map of Europe changed a great deal after World War I. **Which part of Europe changed the most?**

Europe After World War I

L1 **Geography: The World in Spatial Terms** Ask students to look at the map, "Europe After World War I," and locate the new nations that resulted from the war. ELL

DID YOU KNOW ??

After World War I, Germany's economy was especially hard-hit. High inflation caused the country's paper currency to be worthless and many people used it to light their stoves.

MAP STUDY

Answer

the eastern part

Assign the Chapter 37 **Geography and Map Activity** in the TCR.

MEETING SPECIAL NEEDS

For those students needing extra reinforcement, encourage them to do oral summaries of each section of the chapter. Students may be organized into small groups. Each group would then assign different sections of the chapter to students in the group who would prepare the summaries. Have groups meet again to present the summaries.

Refer to ***Inclusion for the Middle School Social Studies Classroom: Strategies and Activities*** for additional resources.

L3 Critical Thinking Have students discuss the reforms brought about in Russia during the rule of Peter the Great. Ask: What reforms were made in industry, trade, the military, education, and daily life? Ask students to analyze whether each reform made was positive or negative and explain their answers in writing.

Use the **Interactive Tutor Self-Assessment CD-ROM** to review Section 1.

Reading Check Answer
During a **depression,** business experiences a sudden slowdown.

MAKING CONNECTIONS

>> **History** The "Time of Troubles" in Russia included three years of famine, which led to revolt by the peasants as well as invasions by armies from Poland and Sweden. It was during the "Time of Troubles" that a system of secret police was set up in Russia.

Use the **Vocabulary PuzzleMaker CD-ROM** to create crossword and word search puzzles.

Section 1 Assessment

1. **Define:** mobilize, civilians, trench warfare, artillery, armistice, armaments, mandate, isolationist.
2. What made World War I different from earlier wars?
3. Why did the United States refuse to join the League of Nations?

Critical Thinking

4. **Identifying Central Issues** Why do you think many Americans opposed United States membership in the League of Nations?

Graphic Organizer Activity

5. Draw this diagram, and use it to show the new nations created by the treaties ending World War I. (Add more answer circles as needed.)

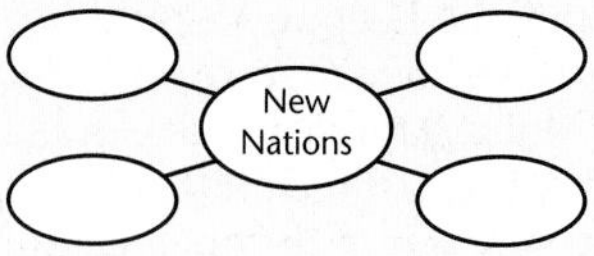

SECTION 2 Between the Wars

The 1920s and 1930s were a difficult time for people everywhere. Most were trying to recover from the damage caused by World War I. Then, in 1929, a **depression,** or a sudden slowdown in business, began. People in many countries started to question their forms of government. In Germany, the people turned to a leader who would soon threaten world peace. People in Russia had overthrown their government and set up the world's first Communist nation.

Reading Check
What happens to business during a **depression?**

Emerging Russia

In Muscovy, the years following the death of Ivan the Terrible in 1584 were called the "Time of Troubles." There was much disorder in the country. The troubles ended in 1613 with the crowning of seventeen-year-old Michael Romanov (rō′ muh nahf) as czar. The Romanov dynasty ruled Russia until 1917.

Painting of Peter the Great

The first great Romanov ruler was a grandson of Michael's, Peter the Great, who came to the throne in 1682. Determined to make Muscovy strong and modern, Peter disguised himself as a sailor and visited the capitals of various European countries. There he learned all he could of western ways.

When Peter returned home, he began reforming the country he named Russia. He started textile factories, built canals, and encouraged mining. He ordered a new capital, St. Petersburg, built on the Baltic Sea. Since St. Petersburg was an ice-free port, the country's trade by water with western Europe continued

Section 1 Assessment Answers

1. mobilize, call up troops (p. 604); civilians, non-soldiers (p. 604); artillery, mounted guns (p. 604); trench warfare, fighting from ditches (p. 604); armistice, end to fighting (p. 605); armaments, war equipment (p. 605); mandate, right to rule (p. 607); isolationist, policy of staying out of world problems (p. 607)
2. 31 countries with 65 million soldiers took part; new weapons; civilians involved
3. because many Americans disagreed with the war treaties and wanted to stay out of world affairs
4. Answers will vary, but many students may point to the technological and global impact of the war.
5. New nations included: Poland, Finland, Estonia, Latvia, Lithuania, Austria, Hungary, Czechoslovakia, and Yugoslavia.

Assign the Chapter 37 **Section 1 Quiz** in the TCR. Testmaker available.

Chapter 38 Planning Guide

Performance Assessment Activities

Time Lines Have students choose a country mentioned in the chapter and create a time line of important events in the country's history between World War II and the present. Tell students to include political, religious, economic, and cultural events. Encourage them to include illustrations or photos on their time lines.

CHAPTER RESOURCES

LITERATURE ABOUT THE PERIOD

Soyinka, Wole. *Aké: The Years of Childhood.* Vintage Books, 1983. Autobiography by Nigerian Nobel Prize-winner.

READINGS FOR THE STUDENT

Bachelis, Faren. *The Central Americans.* Chelsea House, 1990. History and culture of Central Americans and reasons for their flight north.

READINGS FOR THE TEACHER

Cheng, Mien. *Life and Death in Shanghai.* Grove Press, 1987. Personal account of her trials during the Cultural Revolution by an "aristocratic" Chinese woman.

KEY TO ABILITY LEVELS

Teaching strategies have been coded for varying learning styles and abilities.

L1 Level 1 activities are **basic** activities and should be within the ability range of all students.

L2 Level 2 activities are **average** activities and should be within the ability range of the average to above-average student.

L3 Level 3 activities are **challenging** activities designed for the ability range of above-average students.

ELL ELL activities should be within the ability range of English Language Learning students.

NATIONAL GEOGRAPHIC Teacher's Corner

INDEX TO NATIONAL GEOGRAPHIC MAGAZINE

The following articles relate to this chapter:

- "Eyewitness Kosovo," by Alexandra Boulat, February 2000.
- "Kashmir: Trapped in Conflict," by Lewis M. Simmons, September 1999.
- "Cuba," by John J. Putnam, June 1999.
- "Tam Dao—Vietnam's Sanctuary Under Siege," by Michael J. McRae, June 1999.

ADDITIONAL NATIONAL GEOGRAPHIC SOCIETY PRODUCTS

To order the following, call National Geographic at 1-800-368-2728:

- *PicturePack: Civil Rights (Transparencies)*
- *PictureShow: Civil Rights (CD-ROM)*
- *1945-1989: The Cold War (Video)*
- *Capitalism, Socialism, Communism Series: (Video)*

Access *National Geographic's* new dynamic MapMachine Web site and other geography resources at:
www.nationalgeographic.com
www.nationalgeographic.com/maps

THE HISTORY CHANNEL. A&E HOME VIDEO. Biography

The following videotape program is available from Glencoe:

- **Cuba and Castro**
  0-7670-1426-X
- **Democracy Crushed: Tiananmen Square**
  0-7670-1459-6
- **Mahatma Gandhi: Pilgrim of Peace**
  0-7670-0668-2
- **Vietnam: A Soldier's Diary**
  0-7670-0772-7

To order, call Glencoe at 1-800-334-7344. To find classroom resources to accompany many of these videos, check:
A&E Television: www.aande.com
The History Channel: www.historychannel.com

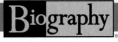

Introducing **CHAPTER 38**

OVERVIEW

Chapter 38 discusses the cold war (1945–1989) and its effect on world affairs.

- **Section 1** traces the growth of tensions between the United States and Soviet Union.
- **Section 2** describes changes in communism as practiced by the Soviet Union and China.
- **Section 3** summarizes the history of developing nations after World War II.

CHAPTER OBJECTIVES

After reading Chapter 38, students will be able to:

1. describe reasons for the cold war and cite examples of cold war crises.

2. discuss political and economic changes in the Soviet Union and China, especially in the 1980s.

3. examine how developing nations in Africa, South Asia, and Latin America have struggled for political and economic independence.

EXAMINING ARTIFACTS

Based on these artifacts, ask students what was one of the biggest popular concerns during the post-World War II era? *(use of nuclear weapons)* What actions did fears of nuclear war cause some people to do? *(take part in protests, build fallout shelters)* Call on students to use the time line to identify some of the crises during the cold war era.

PERFORMANCE ASSESSMENT ✔

Use the Performance Assessment activities on page 624B to help you evaluate students as they complete the chapter.

CHAPTER 38

The Cold War Era

1945 A.D.–1989 A.D.

THERE IS NO SHELTER IN NUCLEAR WAR
I WANT TO GROW UP

▼ Children protesting nuclear buildups

▲ Geiger counter from a 1950s fallout shelter

1948	1950	1959	1960	1989
Berlin airlift	Korean War begins	Cuban Revolution	"Year of Africa"	China crushes student protest in Tiananmen Square

TEACHING RESOURCES

TEACHER PLANNING AND SUPPORT

- Reproducible Lesson Plan 38-1, 38-2, 38-3
- Teaching Strategies for the World History Classroom (Including Block Scheduling Pacing Guides)
- Presentation Plus! CD-ROM
- Chapter 38 Cooperative Learning Activity
- Chapter 38 Activity Book Activity
- Chapter 38 Chart and Graph Skill Activity
- Reading and Study Skills Foldables
- Interactive Tutor Self-Assessment CD-ROM

REVIEW AND REINFORCEMENT

- Reading Essentials and Study Guide 38-1, 38-2, 38-3
- Chapter 38 Vocabulary and Guided Reading Activity
- Vocabulary PuzzleMaker CD-ROM
- Teaching Transparencies 38A & 38B
- Chapter 38 Reteaching Activity

APPLICATION AND HANDS-ON ACTIVITIES

- Daily Questions in Social Studies
- Student Presentation Builder CD-ROM

Chapter Focus

Read to Discover

- How relationships between Western and Communist powers have changed since World War II.
- What changes have occurred in the Soviet Union.
- What life has been like in the People's Republic of China.
- How countries in Africa, South Asia, and Latin America have struggled with political and economic problems.

HISTORY Online

Chapter Overview

Visit the *Human Heritage* Web site at **humanheritage.glencoe.com** and click on ***Chapter 38—Chapter Overviews*** to preview this chapter.

Terms to Learn

cold war
satellite nations
glasnost
perestroika

People to Know

Fidel Castro
Ho Chi Minh
Mao Zedong

Places to Locate

Berlin
Tiananmen Square

Why It's Important Soon after World War II ended, a split occurred between the Soviet Union and other Allied Powers. At issue was the Soviet threat to spread communism beyond its borders. Gradually, a **cold war**, or state of hostility without fighting, developed. Tensions were so high that people feared the outbreak of the world's first all-out nuclear war.

Reading Check Why did a **cold war** develop?

SECTION 1 An Uneasy Peace

After World War II, Europe began its recovery. Tension between the United States and the Soviet Union grew over problems in Berlin, Korea, Cuba, and Vietnam (vē et nahm').

Western Europe When World War II ended, most of Western Europe was in ruins. To help rebuild areas, the United States started a loan program in 1948. It was named the Marshall Plan after George Marshall, the U.S. Secretary of State. Under the Marshall Plan, factories were rebuilt, coal mines were reopened, and roads were repaired or replaced. The economies of Western Europe soon began to grow.

In 1957, six Western European nations formed an economic union called the European Common Market. The six nations were Belgium, France, Italy, Luxembourg (luk' suhm borg), the Netherlands, and West Germany. They agreed to remove all trade barriers among them. This meant that manufacturers could sell their goods in other member nations without paying tariffs.

GEOGRAPHY ACTIVITIES

- Chapter 38 Geography and Map Activity
- Outline Map Resource Book

INTERDISCIPLINARY CONNECTIONS

- World Music: A Cultural Legacy
- World Art & Architecture Transparency 59, *Vietnam Veterans Memorial*

ENRICHMENT AND EXTENSION

- World History Primary Source Document Library CD-ROM
- Chapter 38 Enrichment Activity
- Foods Around the World

ASSESSMENT AND EVALUATION

- Chapter 38 Performance Assessment Activity
- Chapter 38 Section Quizzes 38-1, 38-2, 38-3
- Chapter 38 Test
- Chapter 38 ExamView® Pro Testmaker CD-ROM
- Chapter 38 Digests Audiocassettes Activities and Tests

SPANISH RESOURCES

- Chapter 38 Spanish Chapter Summary and Glossary
- Chapter 38 Spanish Digests Audiocassettes Activities and Tests

HISTORY Online

Chapter Overview introduces students to chapter content and key terms. Have them access ***Chapter 38 Overview*** at **humanheritage.glencoe.com**

FOCUS

Bellringer

Write the following message on the board for students to decode: "Gsv xlow dzi dzh z grnv lu hkrvh zmw xlwvh."

Motivational Activity

Have students share their decoded message. *(If none have solved it, tell them this is an alphabet reversal code that says: "The cold war was a time of spies and codes.")* Tell students that in this chapter they will learn about the cold war.

Reading Check Answer

A **cold war** developed over the Soviet threat to spread communism beyond its borders.

GUIDE TO READING

Reading Strategy

Ask students to read "Why It's Important" and summarize the chapter's main theme. *(Tensions over the spread of communism led to a cold war and fears of all-out nuclear war.)*

Vocabulary Precheck

Ask students to define each of the "Terms to Learn." L1 ELL

Use the Vocabulary PuzzleMaker CD-ROM for Chapter 38 to create a crossword puzzle. L1

Assign Chapter 38 Vocabulary and Guided Reading Activity.

Assign Reading Essentials and Study Guide 38-1.

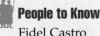

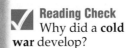

TEACH

Guided Practice

L2 **Critical Thinking** Ask students how a "cold" war might differ from a "hot" war. *(A cold war involves diplomatic relations rather than combat.)*

CAPTION ANSWER

They hoped this would force the western powers to leave the city.

Reading Check Answer **Satellite nations** that fell under Soviet control included Bulgaria, Czechoslovakia, Hungary, Poland, and Romania.

Reading Check Answer The Soviets **blockaded** Berlin because they feared the Allies would unify Germany. The U.S. and Great Britain organized an **airlift** into Berlin.

Economics at a Glance

The European Union
The European Union (EU) formed out of the European Common Market. The 15 countries that belong to the EU practice free trade, meaning that there are no laws that block or limit trade among member nations. The countries of the EU share a common currency called the *euro*. The United Kingdom, Denmark, and Sweden, however, do not use the euro as their currency. Have students use the Internet to find facts about the nations that belong to the EU. Ask students to identify common features among the nations, such as cultural and political similarities. Have students discuss whether a free trade agreement would be effective for countries that do not share similar characteristics.

Fun Facts...

The Iron Curtain In a speech at Fulton, Missouri, in 1946, former British Prime Minister Winston Churchill declared: "From Stettin in the Baltic to Triest in the Adriatic an iron curtain has descended across the continent of Europe." Thereafter, people used the term *iron curtain* to refer to the invisible barrier that split Europe into democratic Western Europe and Soviet-dominated Eastern Europe.

AIRLIFT The children in this photograph watch as an American plane brings food to Berlin during the Soviet blockade. **Why did the Soviet Union block off land and water traffic to the city of Berlin?**

Workers from one nation could take jobs in any other member nation. Between 1957 and 1986, Denmark, Great Britain, Greece, Ireland, Portugal, and Spain also joined the European Common Market. Trade among the nations increased. Today, this economic union is known as the European Union.

The Start of the Cold War Toward the end of World War II, the Soviet Union set up Communist governments in Bulgaria, Czechoslovakia, Hungary, Poland, and Romania. By 1948, these countries were Soviet **satellite nations,** or countries controlled by a stronger neighboring country. Yugoslavia, although Communist, refused to let itself be put under Soviet control.

Reading Check What **satellite nations** fell under Soviet control?

The Soviet leader, Stalin, had originally promised the other Allies that he would allow free elections in these countries. When he broke his promise, the cold war began.

Berlin The first cold war crisis took place over Berlin. In 1948, Great Britain, France, and the United States decided to unite their zones in Germany to encourage peace. The Soviet Union disagreed. It distrusted a united Germany because that nation had invaded the Soviet Union twice in 40 years. In June 1948, the Soviets **blockaded**, or closed off, all land and water traffic into Berlin. They hoped this would force the western powers to leave the city.

Reading Check What was the reason that the Soviets **blockaded** Berlin? What nations organized an **airlift** to break the blockade?

In response, the United States and Great Britain began an **airlift,** or a system of carrying supplies by airplane into Berlin.

EXTENDING THE CONTENT

After World War II, much of Europe was a wasteland. Help came in the form of the Marshall Plan which reconstructed cities of Europe. Many cities were a leveled landscape of gutted buildings, bombed-out bridges, and twisted rail track. As many as 45 million people were homeless. Damage to transportation networks made food distribution impossible. One-fourth of the farmland was out of production. Communication lines were destroyed. The war destroyed almost every major industrial region in the world except those in North America.

Each day planes flew in tons of food, fuel, and raw materials to the city. In May 1949, the Soviets finally lifted their blockade of Berlin. That same year, two separate governments were set up—a democratic one for West Germany and a Communist one for East Germany. East Germany became a Soviet satellite nation.

The Berlin blockade convinced the western powers that the Soviets wanted to control Europe. In 1949, the United States, Great Britain, and France joined with nine other countries to form the North Atlantic Treaty Organization (NATO). All 12 countries agreed to help one another if attacked. Six years later, the Soviet Union and its satellites formed a similar organization called the Warsaw Pact.

Meanwhile, many people in East Germany were unhappy under Communist rule. About three million fled into West Berlin in search of political freedom and better living conditions. Because many of those who fled were well-educated professionals, the East German government wanted to stop these escapes. So in August 1961, it built a wall between East and West Berlin. The Berlin Wall, with Soviet soldiers guarding it, became a symbol of the split between Communist and non-Communist Europe. Many East Berliners continued to try to escape through the wall, risking their lives.

Korea After World War II, Korea was also geographically divided. A Communist government was set up in North Korea and a non-Communist government was organized in South Korea. In 1950, North Korea invaded South Korea in an attempt to take over that country. Both the Soviets and the Chinese sent the North Koreans military aid. The United Nations sent soldiers—mostly Americans— to help South Korea.

General Douglas MacArthur, the United Nations commander, suggested that dropping atomic bombs on Chinese bases and supply lines would gain a quick victory. However, President Harry S Truman refused. Truman did not want the Korean War to turn into World War III. In 1953, North Korea and South Korea signed a truce calling for the two countries, and their governments, to remain separate.

Cuba In 1955 Fidel Castro (fē del' kas trō) launched an unsuccessful revolution in Cuba against dictator Fulgencio Batista (fūl hen' sē ō buh tēs' tuh). In 1959, Castro tried again and finally succeeded—Batista was overthrown.

Castro at first promised free elections and social and economic reforms in Cuba. Many countries, including the United States, supported him. Most of the promises he made, however, were not kept. Cubans who had opposed Castro were jailed or executed. Thousands fled to the United States. Before long, Castro announced that his government would be Communist. He

Photograph of Fidel Castro

Then & Now

NATO Growth Although the Warsaw Pact ended in 1991, NATO continues to grow. In the late 1990s, NATO members voted to invite several former Soviet satellites—the Czech Republic, Hungary, and Poland—to join the organization. In addition, Russia and other members of the former Soviet Union, which dissolved in 1991, were accepted as partner nations.

HISTORY Online

Student Web Activity

Visit the *Human Heritage* Web site at humanheritage.glencoe.com and click on ***Chapter 38—Student Web Activities*** to find out more about the cold war.

Glencoe Literature Library

The following novel from the **Glencoe Literature Library** may be used to enrich this unit:

- *So Far From the Bamboo Grove,* by Yoko Kawashima Watkins. (Exile of Japanese families from Korea during the Korean War.)

HISTORY Online

Student Web Activity objectives and answers can be found at the ***Chapter 38 Web Activity Lesson Plan*** at humanheritage.glencoe.com

L1 **Geography: The World in Spatial Terms** Tell students that Batista was backed by the U.S. government. Next, have students locate the U.S. and Cuba on a map of North America and measure the distance between the two countries. Then ask students why the U.S. would intervene in the affairs of Cuba? *(close location)*

EXTENDING THE CONTENT

The blockade of Berlin cut off all paths of communication. In order to get food, coal, and all other important supplies into Berlin, Western forces approached by air. Between June 1948 and May 1949, British and American air forces carried more than 1.5 million tons of goods into Berlin. One day a single load exceeded 12,000 tons. In this way civilians in both western and eastern sectors were aided. To the relief of British and U.S. pilots, the Soviets did not fire at incoming planes.

MAKING CONNECTIONS

>> **History** In 1960, Cuba negotiated a trade agreement with the Soviet Union that enabled the Soviets to buy Cuban sugar at low prices. Khrushchev promised Soviet protection to Cuba, claiming that the Monroe Doctrine had "outlived its time."

L2 **Culture** Discuss how opposition to U.S. policies in Vietnam led to antiwar protests in the 1960s and 1970s. Ask students to name some things that people protest today.

L2 **Critical Thinking** The increased involvement in Vietnam was justified by those who believed the domino theory—the belief that if one country in a region fell to communism, its neighbors would fall as well. Ask students if they think the domino theory justified the U.S. involvement in Vietnam. Have them summarize their opinions in a written paragraph.

Photograph of Vietnam War Protesters

developed close ties with the Soviet Union, which continued to send him economic aid.

In 1961, Cuban refugees who had been trained in the United States invaded Cuba. Their mission was to force Castro out of power. The invasion, in the area known as the Bay of Pigs, failed. Castro then asked the Soviet Union for more military aid. In 1962, Soviet nuclear missile bases were built on the island. The United States blockaded Cuba and insisted the Soviets remove the missiles. The Soviets finally agreed, and another world war was avoided.

Vietnam

In 1941, Vietnam was a French colony and part of a larger region known as French Indochina. Japan invaded Vietnam in 1941, but pulled out of the country in 1945 at the end of World War II. At that time, the Vietnamese hoped to be independent, but they were invaded again by the French. As a result, Communists and non-Communist Vietnamese nationalists joined together in a guerrilla war against the French. The guerrillas were led by a Communist named Ho Chi Minh (hō chē min'), a Vietnamese nationalist.

In 1954, the French were defeated and the country was temporarily divided into two parts—North and South Vietnam. North Vietnam became a Communist country headed by Ho Chi Minh. South Vietnam became a non-Communist country. A 1956 election meant to unite the two countries was never held. It was protested by the South Vietnamese government who feared it would show Ho's strength.

A war for the control of the country erupted between South Vietnam and North Vietnam. Guerrillas, known as the Vietcong, and the Soviet Union aided North Vietnam. The United States had already been sending military supplies to South Vietnam. It began sending combat troops there in 1965. Altogether, more than 3.3 million Americans fought in the Vietnam War. Eventually 58,000 of them lost their lives, and almost $200 billion was spent.

The Vietnam War deeply divided the American people. Many believed the United States should fight to help South Vietnam and prevent the spread of communism. Many others believed the fight was a civil war that the Vietnamese should settle themselves.

In 1973, an agreement between North Vietnam, South Vietnam, and the United States was reached. American troops pulled out of the country. Then, in 1975, troops from North Vietnam moved into South Vietnam and it came under Communist control.

Satellite view of Venus

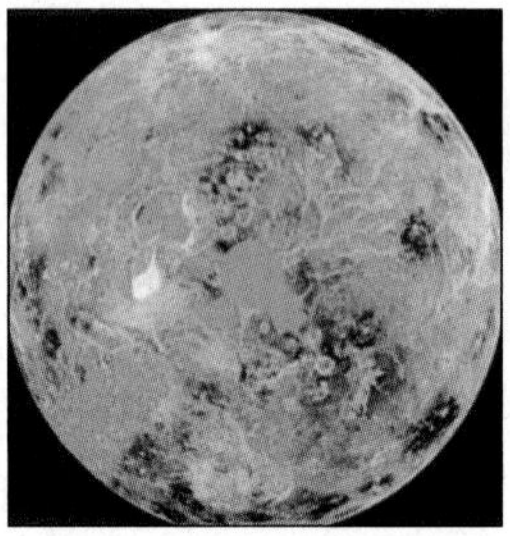

The Space Race

Part of the cold war between the Soviet Union and the United States involved the race to explore space. The Soviets took the first lead. In 1957, they launched *Sputnik I*, the first spacecraft to circle the earth. Four years later, Soviet

MEETING SPECIAL NEEDS

Have auditory learners listen to a record or tape of popular U.S. music from the Vietnam era—such as "The Ballad of the Green Berets" and protest songs such as "Blowin' in the Wind," "Draft Dodger Rag," or "A Hard Rain's Gonna Fall." Use these songs as a lead into a discussion of the fact that the Vietnam War created conflict among Americans since some people were in favor of the war and others opposed the war.

Refer to ***Inclusion for the Middle School Social Studies Classroom: Strategies and Activities*** for additional resources.

astronaut Yuri Gagarin (yū rē guh gahr′ uhn) became the first human being to circle the earth.

Then the United States took the lead. In 1969, American astronaut Neil Armstrong became the first person to walk on the moon. During the 1970s, the first landings on Venus and Mars were made by U.S. unmanned space vehicles. Later, these spacecraft explored Jupiter and Saturn.

Section 1 Assessment

1. **Define:** cold war, satellite nations, blockaded, airlift.
2. Why did Western European nations form the European Common Market?
3. Why did East Germany build the Berlin Wall?
4. Why did Castro have the support of the United States during his revolution? Why did he lose that support?

Critical Thinking

5. **Demonstrating Reasoned Judgment** If you were living during the Vietnam War, would you have supported or opposed the war? Why?

Graphic Organizer Activity

6. Draw this diagram, and use it to summarize the issues during the cold war: Soviet blockade of Berlin, construction of the Berlin Wall, Korean War, Cuban revolution, Vietnamese civil war, launch of *Sputnik I.*

Crisis	Issue Involved

SECTION 2 Communist Powers

After World War II, China became a Communist nation. Later, however, both China and the Soviet Union made changes to the type of communism they practiced.

Revolution in China While the Soviet Union and the United States were competing in the cold war, communism was gaining support in China. The conditions that led to China's acceptance of communism developed over a long time.

Before the 1900s, there had been several revolts over control of the government. All had failed. In 1911, however, a revolt led by Sun Yat-sen (sun′ yaht sen′) overturned the government. He formed the Nationalist party, which wanted China to be a free, democratic republic. He was ousted, and Chinese warlords divided the country.

Glencoe Literature Library

The following novel from the **Glencoe Literature Library** may be used to enrich this chapter:

- *The Clay Marble,* by Minfong Ho. (Cambodian refugees in the 1980s.)

DID YOU KNOW ??

Within a few months after the Soviets launched *Sputnik I,* the U.S. Congress created NASA (National Aeronautics and Space Administration). The first U.S. satellite, *Explorer I,* was launched about four months after *Sputnik I* was launched.

L1 **History** Have students create a time line covering key events in Chinese history from 1919 to 1939. Have them write a summary statement describing the political situation in China in 1911 and in 1989. ELL

Use the **Interactive Tutor Self-Assessment CD-ROM** to review Section 1.

Use the **Vocabulary PuzzleMaker CD-ROM** to create crossword and word search puzzles.

Section 1 Assessment Answers

1. cold war, hostility without combat (p. 625); satellite nations, countries controlled by another (p. 626); blockaded, closed off (p. 626); airlift, supplies flown in (p. 626)
2. to establish an economic union
3. to stop escapes into Western Europe
4. He promised reforms; Cuba became Communist.
5. Answers will vary.
6. Sample causes: Soviet blockade of Berlin—Soviet fears of a united Germany; Berlin Wall—flight of East Germans, especially educated professionals, into West Berlin; Korean War—North Korean invasion of South Korea; Cuban Revolution—rule by dictator Fulgencio Batista; Vietnamese civil war—conflicts over election to unify Vietnam; *Sputnik I*—cold war between the United States and Soviet Union, which launched the space race

Assign the Chapter 38 **Section 1 Quiz** in the TCR. Testmaker available.

CAPTION ANSWER

the Nationalists and the Communists

LINKING PAST TO PRESENT

When the Treaty of Versailles awarded the Shandong Peninsula to the Japanese, Chinese students in Beijing came together for a mass demonstration, urging the Chinese government not to sign the treaty. Similar demonstrations throughout the country culminated in a general strike in Shanghai. Under intense pressure from the students, the government at last yielded to their demands. China's students continue to protest and demonstrate—although not always successfully—as a means of gaining their government's attention.

DID YOU KNOW ??

In 1949, Taiwan was called Formosa.

Then... & Now

Taiwan Taiwan was named Formosa, meaning "beautiful," by Portuguese explorers. In the 1600s, the island was controlled by the Dutch and then the Spanish. Still later it was acquired by China, then Japan, then China again. China, which regards Taiwan as a province, has strongly resisted Taiwanese moves toward independence.

INVASION Japananese troops invaded the streets of Shanghai, China, in 1937. Chinese soldiers united to fight the attack. **What major Chinese parties cooperated in this effort to fight the Japanese?**

After Sun died in 1925, Chiang Kai-shek (chyang kī shek') became the leader of the Nationalist party. He tried to unite China and wipe out the Communists. However, in 1927, the Chinese Communists who opposed the Nationalists began a movement to gain control of the country. Their leader was Mao Zedong (mow' dzuh dung').

The struggle between the two parties was interrupted by the Japanese invasion of China in 1937. The Nationalists joined the Communists to fight the Japanese. After the war, however, the struggle between them continued. In 1949, the Communists gained the support of the peasants with promises of land and forced the Nationalists to leave the Chinese mainland and go to the island of Taiwan (tī wahn'). There, Chiang set up a Nationalist government claiming it ruled China. The Communists set up their own government on mainland China headed by Mao Zedong. They called it the People's Republic of China.

China Under Mao Mao's main goal was to make China a strong, modern country. In 1953, the Chinese began a series of plans to improve the country's economy. By the middle of the 1960s, the Chinese had more food and better health care. Many people had learned how to read and write. Also, under Mao the position of women in China changed. Women were now allowed to choose their own husbands, enter any occupation they chose, and receive equal pay. Men, however, continued to hold the highest positions in government and the best-paying jobs.

COOPERATIVE LEARNING

Organize the class into two groups to report on the influence of Chinese students on the politics of China. Each group should assign its members the tasks of researching, organizing, and reporting on the topic. Have one group examine the political role Chinese students played in the early part of the 1900s. Have the other group research the role Chinese students played in politics during the 1980s. Have each group report its findings to the class. Then discuss how the Chinese student movement between 1900 and 1920 was similar to and different from the Chinese student movement of the 1980s.

Then Mao began to fear that the Chinese had lost their revolutionary spirit. As a result, in 1966 he carried out **purges** (per' juhs), or removals of undesirable members, of the Communist party. He also purged the country's *intellectuals* (in tuh lek' chū uhls), or scholars. This purge was called the Cultural Revolution. Students and young adults known as Red Guards attacked politicians, teachers, and others accused of not supporting communism. The purge soon got out of control, however, and there were battles between Red Guards and other citizens. The Red Guards were later broken up.

Reading Check Who were some of the victims of Mao Zedong's **purges?**

China After Mao After Mao died in 1976, a group led by Deng Xiaoping (duhng' syow ping') came into power in China. Deng cared more about economic growth than about

CHINESE LEADERS From 1928 to 1949, General Chiang Kai-shek (shown left) was a powerful leader in China. In 1949, the Communists, led by Mao Zedong (shown right), overthrew Chiang's government. Mao proclaimed the People's Republic of China on the Chinese mainland, while Chiang set up the Nationalist government on the island of Taiwan. **How did the Communists gain the support of the Chinese peasants?**

Reading Check Answer Victims of **purges** by Mao Zedong included undesirable members of the Communist party and intellectuals.

L2 **Culture** Discuss what it must have been like for the Chinese to go through the dramatic post-war changes in government policies. Ask students to imagine what would happen in the United States if the government started a Cultural Revolution. How do they think Americans would react? Which Americans would be most vulnerable in such a situation?

LINKING PAST TO PRESENT

During the Cultural Revolution, the Chinese educational system was nearly at a standstill, and the door was virtually closed to study at foreign institutions. Today, however, the Chinese constitute a majority of the foreign-student enrollment in U.S. universities.

CAPTION ANSWER

They promised them land.

EXTENDING THE CONTENT

The Cultural Revolution was aimed against the bureaucracy and complacency that Mao Zedong feared had crept into the universities, the government, and the Communist Party. He thought special privileges for the educated elite worked against the ideal of a society in which everyone was equal. He wanted to purge "The Four Olds"—old thoughts, old culture, old customs, and old habits. The Cultural Revolution weakened Mao's leadership position. After Mao's death, Chinese historians began to regard the period as "the ten catastrophic years" and viewed it as a serious setback.

CAPTION ANSWER

They wanted the same control over politics that they had been given over the economy. They demanded democracy.

MAKING CONNECTIONS

>> **History** China exploded its first atomic bomb in 1964. It became the fifth world atomic power, following the United States, the Soviet Union, Britain, and France.

Reading Check Answer

Soviet **hard-liners** were people who stuck to communism regardless of the circumstances.

THE HISTORY CHANNEL®

The following videotape program is available from Glencoe to enrich Chapter 38:

- **Democracy Crushed: Tiananmen Square**

To find classroom resources to accompany this video, check the following home page:

A&E Television: www.aande.com

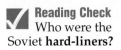

POLITICAL PROTEST As crowds of Chinese demonstrators filled Tiananmen Square in 1989, government officials decided to attack them. **What were the demonstrators protesting against?**

Then & Now

Tibet Human rights are an issue in Tibet, seized by China in 1951. Eight years later, Tibetans waged an unsuccessful rebellion against Chinese control. Since then, the Dalai Lama, the religious leader of Tibet, has led a worldwide movement in support of Tibetan rights from his home in India. In 1989, the Dalai Lama received the Nobel Peace Prize.

revolutionary spirit. He encouraged foreign countries to invest money in China. He let many factory managers decide what goods to produce and what prices to charge. As a result of such changes, economic conditions in China improved greatly.

Political conditions, however, remained the same and many people were unhappy. They wanted the same control over politics that they had been given over the economy. Then, beginning in April of 1989, a demonstration took place in Tiananmen (tyen' ahn men) Square in Beijing. For seven weeks, about one million Chinese people, mostly students, gathered in the square and demanded democracy.

The demonstration was peaceful, but it frightened many Communist leaders. So Deng sent Red Army soldiers into Tiananmen Square to break up the gathering. Between 500 and 1,000 civilians were killed. Other students and labor leaders were imprisoned or executed. Since then, there have been changes in economic balance and trade in China, but not in human rights. Chinese leaders do not acknowledge that the people's human rights are being ignored.

Reading Check

Who were the Soviet **hard-liners?**

Changes in the Soviet Union Two groups of Communists existed in the Soviet Union after Stalin's rule. **Hard-liners,** or people who stick to the rules regardless of the circumstances, made up one group. They wanted to keep the Soviet Union as it

MULTICULTURAL PERSPECTIVES

Zhang Shuyan, a senior researcher in China's State Committee for Reforming the Chinese Written Language, has made a significant study of Chinese names. She found that during the Cultural Revolution, the single most common name was *Red.* Some people born during that time changed their revolutionary names as they entered adulthood. Since the Cultural Revolution, the most common name has been *Hua,* which means "magnificent and prosperous."

was. Reformers made up the other group of Communists. They were interested in economic growth, even if that meant introducing capitalism into the country. Under **capitalism,** most production is privately owned rather than owned by the government. After Stalin died in 1953, there was a Communist struggle for control.

In 1955, a reformer, Nikita Khrushchev (nuh kēt′ uh krūsh chof′), became the leader of the Soviet Union. The following year, he began a program of **de-Stalinization** (dē stahl uh nuh zā′ shuhn), or an attack on the policies established by Stalin. Many labor camps were shut down, and the secret police became less violent. More apartment houses were built, and consumer goods became more available.

In 1964, Leonid Brezhnev (lā uh nid brezh′ nef) became the Soviet ruler. Under Brezhnev, life once again became less free for the Soviet people. In 1985, however, a reformer, Mikhail Gorbachev (mēk′ hī el gōr′ buh chahf), came to power. Gorbachev adopted two policies to try to improve the growth of the economy in the Soviet Union.

Under Gorbachev's policy of ***glasnost*** (glaz nōst), or openness, the Soviet people could say and write what they thought without fear of being punished. Free elections were held in which many non-Communist officials gained office. Under the policy of ***perestroika*** (per uhs troi kuh), which means restructuring, Gorbachev changed the structure of the Soviet government and moved the country's economy toward capitalism.

As the Soviet Union continued moving toward democracy and capitalism, tensions within the country increased. Some people thought Gorbachev was moving too quickly with reform. Others thought he was not moving fast enough. At the same time, many ethnic groups within the country were demanding independence.

Reading Check Who owns production under **capitalism?**

Reading Check What changes took place under **de-Stalinization?**

Reading Check What was the policy of ***glasnost?***

Reading Check What was the economic goal of ***perestroika?***

Reading Check Answer Under **capitalism,** most production is privately owned.

Reading Check Answer Under **de-Stalinization,** labor camps were shut down, the secret police became less violent, new houses were built, and consumer goods became more available.

Reading Check Answer The policy of ***glasnost*** was an openness to speak and write freely.

Reading Check Answer The economic goal of ***perestroika*** was to move the Soviet economy toward capitalism.

Use the **Interactive Tutor Self-Assessment CD-ROM** to review Section 2.

Section 2 Assessment

1. **Define:** purge, hard-liners, capitalism, de-Stalinization, *glasnost, perestroika.*
2. What was Mao Zedong's main goal for China?
3. Why did some people oppose the ideas of *glasnost* and *perestroika?*

Critical Thinking

4. **Predicting Consequences** Based on recent changes, do you think China will become a democracy or remain under strict Communist control? Explain.

Graphic Organizer Activity

5. Draw this diagram, and use it to compare the People's Republic of China under Mao Zedong and Deng Xiaoping.

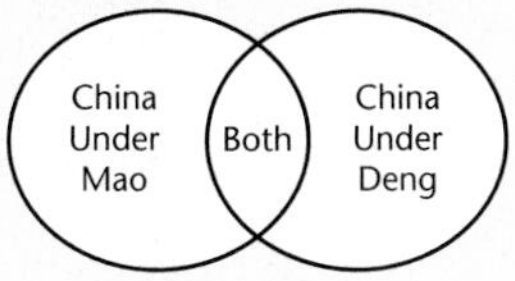

Section 2 Assessment Answers

1. purge, removal of undesirables (p. 631); hard-liners, inflexible people (p. 632); capitalism, privately-owned economy (p. 633); de-Stalinization, attack on Stalin's policies (p. 633), *glasnost,* Soviet openness (p. 633), *perestroika,* Soviet restructuring (p. 633)
2. to rebuild China, making it modern
3. They thought Gorbachev was moving too quickly with reform.
4. Some students might cite the trend of reform, while others might mention ongoing violation of human rights.
5. Diagrams will vary, but students should show the economic reforms initiated by Deng. Both Mao and Deng exercised strict control of government under the Communist Party and use of the Red Army to suppress protests.

Assign the Chapter 38 **Section 2 Quiz** in the TCR. Testmaker available.

L1 **Geography: The World in Spatial Terms** Ask students to list the developing nations discussed in this section. Have them locate the nations on a map of the world and determine where most of the nations are located. *(Africa, Asia, and Latin America)* **ELL**

Reading Check Answer Right after independence, most **developing nations** were poor farming nations with growing populations in need of adequate food, housing, health care, and education.

Reading Check Answer Gandhi used **civil disobedience** to show Indians that they could peacefully protest British laws they considered unjust.

Economics at a Glance

Measuring Development

A standard of living is the material well-being of an individual, group, or nation. In a *developing nation,* there is a relatively low standard of living and less industrial development. Developing nations include Indonesia, Pakistan, and Haiti. A *developed nation,* however, has a relatively high standard of living, with an economy based more on industry than on agriculture. Of the 192 nations in the world, only about 35 are considered developed. Developed nations include the United States, Germany, and Singapore. Have students use the Internet to create a list of developed and developing nations. Then ask students to label the nations on a world map, color-coding the nations according to each one's designation. Have students title the map and write a caption that makes a generalization about the locations of developed and developing nations. Call on students to display and discuss their maps.

SECTION 3 Developing Nations

Most of the countries in South Asia and Africa gained their independence after World War II. The majority of countries in Latin America gained independence in the early 1800s. All of these countries are considered to be **developing nations.** They generally have little industry and most of the people are poor, uneducated, and make their living from the land.

Reading Check What were most **developing nations** like right after independence?

A great number of developing nations also have rapidly growing populations. They cannot produce enough food to feed their people and must buy it elsewhere. As a result, they do not have enough money to provide decent housing, health care, and education for their citizens.

India's Independence

India, originally under British rule, was one of the first colonial countries of Asia in which nationalism grew. At first, several problems in India had to be dealt with. There were two major religions—Hinduism and Islam—many of whose followers did not like each other. The people also spoke hundreds of different languages. However, they had one thing in common—opposition to British rule.

In 1885, a political party called the Indian National Congress was formed. Its members called for more Indian self-government.

About that time, an Indian leader named Mohandas Gandhi (mah hahn' dahs gahn' dē) began a protest movement against British rule. Gandhi was a lawyer and a member of the upper class, but he identified himself with the common people. He went from village to village talking about self-government. The people called him Mahatma (muh haht' muh), which means Great Soul.

Reading Check How did Gandhi use **civil disobedience** to win independence from Great Britain?

Gandhi did not believe in violence. He believed in **civil disobedience,** or refusing to obey laws considered unjust. He convinced millions of Indians to show their resistance to British rule through peaceful demonstrations and boycotts.

In 1947, Great Britain finally granted independence to its Indian colony. Instead of one country, however, two were formed. India, the larger country, had a majority of Hindus. A separate country, Pakistan, was created that had a majority of Muslims.

During the *partition,* or dividing, of India, fighting broke out between Hindus and Muslims. Many Hindus in Pakistan fled to India, while many Muslims in India fled to Pakistan. Of the more than 12 million people who changed homelands, nearly 1 million were killed in the fighting.

COOPERATIVE LEARNING

Organize the class into six groups. Assign three groups to design posters on three of the writers who influenced Gandhi: John Ruskin of England, Henry David Thoreau of the United States, and Leo Tolstoy of Russia. Have a fourth group prepare a poster on Gandhi, emphasizing his belief in nonviolence. Direct the remaining two groups to create posters on two leaders influenced by Gandhi: Nelson Mandela and Dr. Martin Luther King, Jr.

Arrange the posters in a display on the classroom wall. The poster of Gandhi should be in the center. Posters showing writers who influenced Gandhi should be on the left, while the posters of people influenced by Gandhi should be on the right. Have students connect the posters with arrows cut out of construction paper.

Assign Chapter 38 *Cooperative Learning Activity* in the TCR.

INDUSTRIAL INDIA Industry has grown rapidly in India since the nation became independent in 1947. The government has encouraged the establishment of heavy industry in hopes of improving India's economy. Here, workers are employed at an automobile plant. **How do most of India's people make their living?**

In 1971 a civil war broke out between the eastern and western parts of Pakistan. Three years later, Pakistan recognized East Pakistan as the independent nation of Bangladesh.

India Since 1947 After independence, India's leaders worked to set up a stable government. In 1950, a democratic constitution was adopted. Under prime ministers Jawaharlal Nehru (juh wu' har lul nā' rū) and later Indira Gandhi (in dēr' uh gahn' dē), democracy advanced.

Since that time the Indian government has worked to improve people's living conditions. It has encouraged such industries as electric power, iron and steel manufacturing, and textiles. About 70 percent of the Indian people, however, still make their living by farming. Although some have small farms, most work on the estates of large landowners for low pay. Families in Indian villages are generally large although the government has encouraged people to have smaller families.

Many of India's large cities have two sections. One is modern with tall apartment and office buildings. The other section has narrow, twisting, crowded streets. These narrow avenues are lined with two- and three-story, old apartment buildings and hundreds of small businesses.

People in History

Mohandas Gandhi
1869–1948

Indian Leader

Trained as a lawyer, Gandhi practiced law in South Africa where he opposed prejudice against black South Africans. When he returned to India in 1915, he gave up his law practice for a more spiritual life. Using nonviolent resistance, Gandhi led the fight for the independence of India, opposed the caste system, and called for acceptance of all religions.

L1 **Economics** Have students research a major product from one of the developing countries such as coffee or cocoa, and create a flow chart of what happens to this product as it moves from producer to consumer. Have them share their charts with the class.

Biography®

The following videotape program is available from Glencoe to enrich chapter 38:

- **Mahatma Gandhi: Pilgrim of Peace**

To find classroom resources to accompany this video, check the following home page:

A&E Television:
www.aande.com

GEOGRAPHY AND HISTORY

Pakistan consisted of two regions, East Pakistan and West Pakistan, separated by India. Although the people in both regions were Muslims, they spoke different languages and belonged to different ethnic groups. In 1971, a civil war broke out between the two regions. As a result, East Pakistan became the new nation of Bangladesh.

CAPTION ANSWER

by farming

MULTICULTURAL PERSPECTIVES

Indians dress according to their religion, the region in which they live, and how westernized they are. However, Indian men—except in large cities—usually wear a *dhoti,* or a white cotton garment wrapped between the legs. Most Indian women wear a sari. This is a long, straight piece of cotton or silk that is wrapped around the body and then draped over the head.

MAKING CONNECTIONS

➤➤ **History** Two years after Nehru's death, his daughter, Indira Gandhi, was elected prime minister of India. She was instrumental in helping East Pakistan win its independence from West Pakistan.

TECHNOLOGY SKILLS

TEACH

Using an Electronic Spreadsheet

To introduce this lesson, you might write the following information on the board:
Science 88, 90, 85, 98
Social Studies 100, 92, 80, 93
Math 84, 90, 81, 95

Tell students to imagine that these are their report card grades. Then challenge them to figure out their average grade in each subject. Have students use the classroom clock to record the length of time that it takes to complete the assignment.

When students are done, go over the method they used to figure out the averages. Use this discussion as a springboard to assign the skills lesson, which helps students use an electronic spreadsheet to compare birth rates in China, India, and the United States.

Performance Assessment

To encourage self-assessment of using an electronic spreadsheet, have each student complete this individual task management plan.

Self-Management Plan

Name: ____________________
Task: ____________________
Steps to accomplish the task:

Problems to completing the task:

Solutions or attempted solutions:

Signed: ____________________

TECHNOLOGY SKILLS

Using an Electronic Spreadsheet

People use electronic spreadsheets to manage numbers quickly and easily. You can use a spreadsheet any time a problem involves numbers that you can arrange in rows and columns.

Learning the Skill A spreadsheet is an electronic worksheet. All spreadsheets follow a basic design of rows and columns. Each column (vertical) is assigned a letter or a number. Each row (horizontal) is assigned a number. Each point where a column and row intersect is called a cell. The cell's position on the spreadsheet is labeled according to its corresponding column and row—Column A, Row 1 (A1); Column B, Row 2 (B2), and so on.

Spreadsheets use standard formulas to calculate the numbers. You create a mathematical equation that uses these standard formulas, and the computer does the calculations for you.

Skill Practice

Suppose you want to compare the number of births in the three most highly populated nations—China, India, and the United States—over the past five years. Use these steps to create a spreadsheet that will provide this information:

1. **In cells B1, C1, and D1 respectively, type the name of each of the three countries listed above. In cell E1, type the term** *total.*
2. **In cells A2–A6, type each year, starting with the most recent year for which statistics are available.**
3. **In row 2, enter the number of births that occurred in each nation for the year listed in A2. Repeat this process in rows 3 through 6.**
4. **Create a formula to calculate the number of children born for the first year on the spreadsheet. The formula for the equation tells what cells (2B + 2C + 2D) to add together.**
5. **Copy the formula down in the cells for the other four years.**
6. **Use the process in steps 4 and 5 to create and copy a formula to calculate the total births for each of the three countries over a five-year period.**

TEAM TEACHING STRATEGY

Science Work with a science teacher to use the steps in this lesson to create spreadsheets on average yearly precipitation in several developing nations in the regions studied in Chapter 38. (At least one nation should be from a drought-stricken area of Africa, such as Sudan or Chad.) The spreadsheets can be the basis for a science lesson on climate and climate patterns. They can also be used for a social studies lesson linking climate to cash crops, special farming methods, ways of life, and so on. (Suggest that students check electronic encyclopedias and information on the Internet, including online almanacs, for precipitation figures.)

Malaysia Malaysia is another developing Asian country that has gone through revolution and successfully built a cooperative government since World War II. Following riots in 1969 between the Malay and the Chinese, the country has become peaceful. With a prospering economy, it lies in a major shipping crossroads of the Pacific Ocean. Muslims, Christians, Buddhists, and Hindus live together, giving Malaysia its cultural richness. The three major ethnic groups of the country—Malays, Chinese, and Indians—cooperatively share power and resources.

Independence in Africa World War II helped African nationalism grow. During the war, many Africans served in the armies of the European colonial powers. They were sent to fight in many different places around the world. The soldiers saw new sights and learned new skills. When they returned to Africa, they were not content with conditions there and wanted self-rule.

Nationalism grew quickly among educated Africans who worked for independence in different ways. They formed politi-

African Independence

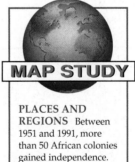

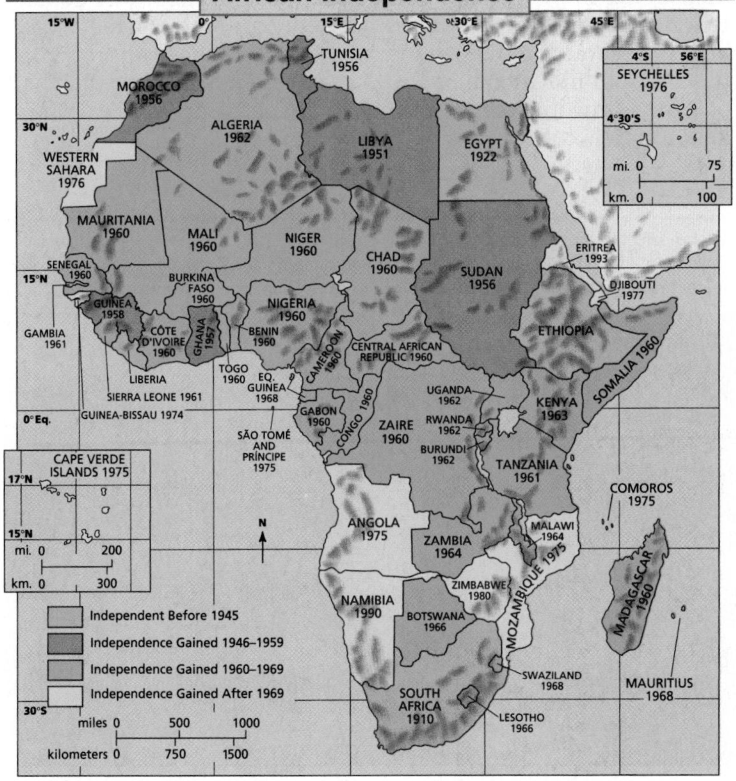

MAP STUDY

PLACES AND REGIONS Between 1951 and 1991, more than 50 African colonies gained independence. **Which colonies gained independence after 1969?**

MULTICULTURAL PERSPECTIVES

There are many results of African influence in American culture. One of these is the celebration of Kwanzaa, the African American celebration of unity that takes place at the end of December. This week-long festival that calls attention to African American achievement and creativity is based on African harvest festivals that are centuries old.

Independent Practice

L1 Geography: Places and Regions Have students write five questions about the map "African Independence" on this page. Then have them gather in small groups and have students quiz each other with their questions. ELL

L2 Government Have students research more about the political history of the two countries showing no dates for independence: Ethiopia and Liberia. Have them write a report explaining what reasons there were for this situation.

MAP STUDY

Answer

Western Sahara, Guinea-Bissau, São Tomé and Príncipe, Angola, Namibia, Zimbabwe, Mozambique, Djibouti, Comoros, and Eritrea

Assign the Chapter 38 **Geography and Map Activity** in the TCR.

NATIONAL GEOGRAPHIC

CD-ROM
Picture Atlas of the World

You and your students can see and read about the physical features of Africa by clicking the "Photos" and "Essay" buttons of individual countries in the region.

Use the **Vocabulary PuzzleMaker CD-ROM** to create crossword and word search puzzles.

L3 Geography: Human Systems Point out to students that the newly independent nations of Africa had great difficulties in forming new governments partly as a result of the way European nations had drawn colonial boundaries in Africa without regard to ethnic differences. Have students compare the map "African Independence" on page 637 with African maps that show ethnic groups. Have students write a brief paragraph that compares the boundaries of the African nations with the boundaries of these groups.

Reading Check Answer

Subsistence farmers produce only enough food for their families. Africa's most important **cash crops** are cacao, coffee, cotton, peanuts, rubber, and tea.

DID YOU KNOW ??

Despite the cold war, both the United States and the Soviet Union supported independence for African nations.

CAPTION ANSWER

lack of education

NATIONAL GEOGRAPHIC

CD-ROM Picture Atlas of the World

Click the "Video" button of Tanzania to view the Masai people and Serengeti National Park.

Then & Now

Meaningful Names Once they won freedom, many African nations took new names with deep historical meaning. Zimbabwe, for example, refers to the 1,000-year-old city of Great Zimbabwe. Massive, protective stone walls gave the city its name, which means "stone enclosure."

cal parties and bargained with government leaders. They also boycotted goods from colonial countries. In some cases, violence broke out.

In 1960, 17 African countries became independent. The year became known as the "Year of Africa." Other African colonies freed themselves from European rule in following years.

At first most newly independent African countries set up democratic governments. Many did not last, however, and today most have one-party governments or are ruled by a military leader.

Many African countries—including Angola, Ethiopia, Mozambique (mō zam beek'), Nigeria, Rwanda (roo ahn' duh), Somalia, Sudan, Zaire (zīhr), and Zimbabwe (zim bahb' wā)—have suffered from civil war since they became independent. When Europeans originally drew colonial boundaries in Africa, they often put groups that had been fighting one another for hundreds of years in the same colony. Fighting often broke out among these groups.

Reading Check What type of farming is done by **subsistence farmers?** What are some of Africa's most important **cash crops?**

Farming About 70 percent of all African workers make their living from farming. In the past, most farmers were **subsistence farmers.** They produced only enough food for their families. Today much of the land is used to grow **cash crops,** or crops that are sold in regional or world markets. In fact, more than half of Africa's income results from selling such crops as cacao (kuh kā' ō), coffee, cotton, peanuts, rubber, and tea.

Rural and Urban Africa Many Africans still live in small rural villages, such as the one in Zaire shown here (left), and hold onto their traditional ways. Africa also has many large, modern cities. **What differences face villagers who move to the city?**

MEETING SPECIAL NEEDS

Organize students with Limited English Proficiency into five groups, one group for each of the five regions of Africa. Have each group create a notebook, one page per country, for each region. Each page should consist of a map and legend, showing the major cities and geographic features. Refer students to an almanac and an atlas for other interesting statistics to include on their pages. Have them draw pictures of or list several influential people (present or past) from each country, write a brief biography, and put them on a separate page. Have students share their notebooks.

Refer to ***Inclusion for the Middle School Social Studies Classroom: Strategies and Activities*** for additional resources.

In recent years, because of poor farming methods, drought, disease, lack of fertilizer, and the increased growth of cash crops, there have been food shortages in Africa. Many African nations must buy food from other countries. Often this food is expensive and not plentiful. African governments have begun to teach farmers better farming methods, but progress is slow. The United States has sent advisers also.

Large parts of Africa, however, are rich in energy resources. Coal, natural gas, oil, and hydroelectric power are plentiful. The continent also has large mineral deposits, such as copper, tin, iron, manganese, gold, and diamonds. To make full use of these resources, however, more money and skilled workers are needed. More roads and railroads are also needed to move the resources to market.

Ways of Life Life has been changing in Africa since the 1960s. Most people still live in rural villages, where they belong to **extended families.** These are made up of parents, children, and other close relatives who live together in one house. Most houses in Africa consist of several buildings surrounded by a wall or fence. Rural village houses are often made of mud, clay, or tall grasses and might not have running water, electricity, or indoor plumbing. Large African cities, however, are modern, active centers of growth and progress.

Reading Check What are **extended families?**

Children in rural areas may receive little or no formal schooling, but they have knowledge of and pride in their group's culture. Many leaders of emerging African nations have encouraged the pride each group within a nation shows in its heritage. Writers, musicians, artists, and scholars of African nations are recognized all over the world for their talent and achievements.

African heritage is also seen in the special body markings and certain colors and kinds of clothing and jewelry African groups display. For example, the Fulani (fū lah' nē) of West Africa wear royal blue, red, and yellow. The Masai (mah' sī) women of Kenya wear huge collars of brightly colored beads.

In recent years, many Africans have left their home villages and moved to the cities in search of jobs and better housing and education. Some high schools and colleges in the cities offer training in higher-level occupations and technology. They hope trained young people will return to the villages to improve their way of life. Lack of education, however, is a serious problem.

Photograph of Housing in Rio de Janeiro, Brazil

Foreign Influence in Latin America Even after gaining independence, most Latin American countries remained under foreign control. Industrial nations such as Great Britain, France, Germany, and the United States organized businesses there. They produced such goods as bananas, sugar, coffee, metals, and oil which were sold in markets overseas.

L2 **Language Arts** Have students research and create a simple outline map that shows the different languages that are spoken in Africa. Ask students to share their maps with the class and discuss the following: do language borders follow political borders? What language is predominant? What language(s) seems to be most widely spread out? If possible, have students learn a word or two in an African language to teach to the class.

Reading Check Answer
Extended families are made up of parents, children, and other close relatives who live together in one house.

Economics at a Glance

Digital Divide

The *digital divide* refers to the unequal use of technology between developed and developing nations. Developed nations use the Internet and other technologies to support their economies. Most developing nations, on the other hand, do not have the financial resources needed to build a technological society, and they do not have populations with a high level of technical skills. Have students research to compare the number of Internet users among nations at www.cia.gov/cia/publications/factbook/index.html Have students choose a developed nation and a developing nation. Students should then click on the "Communications" category and scroll down to "Internet Users." Have them write the number of Internet users in each nation on a sheet of paper. Then have students write one or two sentences that summarize their findings. *(Students should note that the number of Internet users in developed nations is significantly higher than the number of users in developing nations.)*

EXTENDING THE CONTENT

In addition to sculpture and painting, dance is an important traditional African art form. Although it varies from area to area, traditional African dance tends to have at least two characteristics in common. First, it expresses two vital concerns of African life—religion and community relationships. There are dances to celebrate the end of harvest, to mark the beginning of puberty, to honor the village gods, and to wish for a successful hunt. Another characteristic of African dance is that it responds to polyrhythms, or complex combinations of fairly simple but different rhythms played simultaneously.

CAPTION ANSWER

because peasant labor is cheap

L2 **Economics** Remind students that transportation is important to growing economies. Have students create a simple outline of South America and show where the major railway lines run. Ask them to explain, in a paragraph, any obstacles to railways that exist in undeveloped areas.

MAKING CONNECTIONS

>> **History** The United States has tried to improve its relations with Latin America. In 1977, for example, the nation signed a treaty that pledged to return complete control over the Canal Zone to Panama in 1999—an agreement the United States kept.

Reading Check Answer

Haciendas are large Latin American ranches. Most *campesinos* earn a living by working on the *haciendas.*

Biography

The following videotape program is available from Glencoe to enrich Chapter 38:

- **Evita: The Woman Behind the Myth**

To find classroom resources to accompany this video, check the following home page:

A&E Television:
www.aande.com

LATIN AMERICAN FARMING Although Latin America is primarily an agricultural region, wealthy landowners hold much of the land in large ranches. These haciendas are worked by peasants with few modern techniques or tools. Here, a Mexican farmer plows behind a team of oxen. **Why do most hacienda owners have little or no desire to modernize their farms?**

Latin American nations benefited from foreign investments. Wages rose, and there were more jobs. Foreign business interests also built roads, railroads, and ports. They set up telephone systems and electric plants.

Still, there were problems. The economies of most of the countries depended on only one or two products. If the price of these products dropped, their incomes did too. Also, food, clothing, household goods, and other such items had to be brought in from other countries at high cost. In addition, Latin American nationalists who wanted their countries to be free of outside influence resented foreigners.

Domestic Changes in Latin America Since World War II, most Latin American countries have been trying to industrialize. They have greatly increased their production of such goods as steel, chemicals, oil, and automobiles. Argentina, Brazil, and Mexico are now fairly well-industrialized. Yet even they do not produce enough to meet the needs of their growing populations.

Reading Check What are *haciendas?* How do the *campesinos* earn a living?

The Latin American economy depends on farming. Most land is held in ***haciendas*** (ah sē en′ duhz), or large ranches. These are owned by a few very rich families. Most work on the *haciendas* is done by peasants known as ***campesinos*** (kam puh sē′ nos).

COOPERATIVE LEARNING

Have students form five teams, with each team making a poster of a Latin American challenge studied in this section: population growth, urbanization, economic development, the growth of democracy, and Latin America's international and inter-American relationships. Ask students in each group to do research, plan the poster theme, create the art, and present the poster. Tell students to focus on these areas: the background or history of the challenge, a clear statement of the issue and its current status, any key individuals or countries involved with the issue, and possible solutions to the problems. Have students research current material and consolidate information in clearly organized posters.

Chapter Focus

Read to Discover

- How independence came to the nations of Eastern Europe.
- What changes came to Russia after the breakup of the Soviet Union.
- How nations responded to issues of war and peace after the cold war ended.
- What challenges the world faces in the 2000s.

HISTORY Online

Chapter Overview

Visit the *Human Heritage* Web site at **humanheritage.glencoe.com** and click on ***Chapter 39—Chapter Overviews*** to preview this chapter.

Terms to Learn	People to Know	Places to Locate
aggression	Boris Yeltsin	Berlin
coup	Lech Walesa	Chechnya
sovereign	Saddam Hussein	Persian Gulf
secede	Nelson Mandela	Kosovo
autonomous	George W. Bush	Northern Ireland
apartheid	Osama bin Laden	Hong Kong
terrorism		Taiwan
euro		East Timor
		Afghanistan

Why It's Important The 1980s and 1990s saw the end of the cold war and the collapse of the Soviet Union. People looked forward to a new era of peace. However, national and ethnic rivalries soon erupted around the world. Regional conflicts forced leaders to develop new rules for stopping **aggression,** or warlike acts, and intervening in the affairs of other nations.

As the 2000s opened, another threat came from groups that used violence against ordinary citizens to achieve political aims. It had become clear that nations needed to work together to solve these and other problems.

Reading Check What is **aggression**?

SECTION 1 The End of the Cold War

The 1990s saw the collapse of communism in Eastern Europe and the breakup of the Soviet Union. Freed from Communist control, independent nations throughout the region struggled to develop new economic and political systems.

A Spirit of Democracy

The Communist hold on government weakened under Soviet premier Mikhail Gorbachev. Earlier Soviet rulers had refused to publicly discuss problems facing the Soviet

GEOGRAPHY ACTIVITIES

- Chapter 39 Geography and Map Activity
- Outline Map Resource Book

INTERDISCIPLINARY CONNECTIONS

- Unit 12 World Literature Reading 2
- World Music: A Cultural Legacy

ENRICHMENT AND EXTENSION

- World History Primary Source Document Library CD-ROM
- Unit 12 Primary Source Readings
- Chapter 39 Enrichment Activity
- Foods Around the World

ASSESSMENT AND EVALUATION

- Chapter 39 Performance Assessment Activity
- Chapter 39 Section Quizzes 39-1, 39-2, 39-3
- Chapter 39 Test
- Unit 12 Standardized Test Practice
- Chapter 39 ExamView® Pro Testmaker CD-ROM
- Chapter 39 Digests Audiocassettes Activities and Tests

SPANISH RESOURCES

- Chapter 39 Spanish Chapter Summary and Glossary
- Chapter 39 Spanish Digests Audiocassettes Activities and Tests

HISTORY Online

Chapter Overview introduces students to chapter content and key terms. Have them access ***Chapter 39 Overview*** at **humanheritage.glencoe.com**

FOCUS

Bellringer

Have students list challenges facing the world today.

Motivational Activity

Compile students' lists on the board. Then help students to prioritize these challenges, encouraging them to reach a consensus on the top five issues. Tell students that issues such as the ones they have named form the subject of Chapter 39.

GUIDE TO READING

Reading Strategy

Ask students to read "Why It's Important" and summarize the chapter's main theme. *(Following the cold war, nations searched for ways to solve issues that threatened the earth's people.)*

Vocabulary Precheck

Ask students to define each of the "Terms to Learn." Have a volunteer consult the dictionary for any unfamiliar words. L1 ELL

Use the Vocabulary PuzzleMaker CD-ROM for Chapter 39 to create a crossword puzzle. L1

Assign Chapter 39 Vocabulary and Guided Reading Activity.

Assign Reading Essentials and Study Guide 39-1.

Reading Check Answer
Aggression is warlike acts.

HISTORY Online

Student Web Activity objectives and answers can be found at the ***Chapter 39 Web Activity Lesson Plan*** at humanheritage.glencoe.com

TEACH

Guided Practice

L1 **Chronology** Organize the class into small groups, and assign each group a subsection in Section 1. Instruct students to create an illustrated time line of the events discussed in their subsection. Display the time lines on a classroom wall.

Linking Across Time

Germany became reunited on October 3, 1990.

HISTORY Online

Student Web Activity

Visit the *Human Heritage* Web site at humanheritage.glencoe.com and click on ***Chapter 39—Student Web Activities*** to find out more about the fall of the Berlin Wall.

Union. Gorbachev, however, believed the only way to solve these problems was to talk about them freely.

As Gorbachev introduced his new policy of glasnost, or openness, to the Soviet Union, he urged leaders in the Soviet satellites to do the same. He indicated that the Soviet Union would no longer use troops and tanks to support Communist governments, as had been done in Hungary in 1956 and in Czechoslovakia in 1968.

The first successful challenge to Communist rule came in Poland. In January 1989, the Polish government lifted its ban on Solidarity, a labor union that had been calling for reform since 1980. In June, Polish voters elected Solidarity members to two-thirds of the seats in the Polish legislature. For the first time, a Communist government in Eastern Europe had lost power as a result of an election.

Fall of the Berlin Wall In East Germany, Communist leader Erich Honecker ignored the people's call for reform. In 1989, however, Hungary started reforms and opened its borders with Austria. Thousands of East Germans—mostly young people—took this chance to show their rejection of communism by fleeing through Hungary into western Europe. Meanwhile, thousands of other East Germans held protest marches against the government.

In October 1989, Honecker resigned. On November 9, at the stroke of midnight, officials in East Berlin threw open the main gate in the Berlin Wall—a 28-mile-long, steel-and-concrete symbol of the

Linking Across Time

Collapse of Communism The collapse of communism in Eastern Europe was symbolized by the destruction of the Berlin Wall in 1989 (below). Today pieces of the wall can be found on display in the United States (right) and in other places around the world. **When did Germany become reunited?**

SPOTLIGHT ON: POPE JOHN PAUL II

In 1978, the College of Cardinals elected the youngest man to become Pope since 1846 and the first non-Italian in 456 years. The new Pope—Karol Cardinal Wojtyla of Cracow—came from Poland. As a youth, Wojtyla had worked as a laborer, first in a quarry and later in a factory. During World War II, he studied for the priesthood at an illegal underground seminary and risked his life to shelter Jews from the Nazis.

The election of Wojtyla, known as Pope John Paul II, electrified Poland. In 1979, the staunch anti-communist Pope paid a personal visit to his homeland. He went on to become the most widely traveled Pope in history. In 1996, *Time* magazine listed him in its biographical collection entitled *Great People of the 20th Century*.

cold war. A roar went up as people from both East and West Berlin climbed on top of the wall and danced with joy.

The next morning, a gigantic headline in a West Berlin newspaper declared "BERLIN IS BERLIN AGAIN!" That day, soldiers began to knock down the wall. Civilians joined them, whacking away with hammers, axes, and chisels. By December, the entire wall had disappeared.

The Last Satellites East German demands for freedom sparked changes in other Eastern European nations. A week after officials opened the Berlin Wall, Bulgaria's hard-line Communist boss resigned. A little later, popular elections overturned Communist rule in Hungary and Czechoslovakia. When the Communist leader of Romania tried to crush the reform movement, rebels tried him and then executed him for crimes against the people.

As one Communist government after another collapsed in Eastern Europe, Gorbachev astounded the world by refusing to interfere. Throughout 1989, he worked with leaders in Europe and the United States to promote peace in the region.

In early 1990, East Germany held its first democratic election since the rise of Adolf Hitler in the 1930s. On October 3, it was reunited with West Germany. That December, Germans elected Helmut Kohl as the first chancellor of the reunited nation. The cold war, which had begun with the division of Germany after World War II, was over.

Conflict Within the Soviet Union As former Soviet satellites celebrated their independence, trouble brewed within the Soviet Union. The new spirit of openness introduced by Gorbachev allowed **dissent**, or criticism, against the government for the first time since the 1917 Communist takeover.

Although widely popular in Europe and the United States, Gorbachev found himself attacked at home by both hard-liners and reformers. Hard-liners blasted Gorbachev for "giving up" Eastern Europe. They resisted reform, fearing both the loss of their jobs and the weakening of Soviet power. Because the hard-liners included many military leaders, Gorbachev moved carefully to avoid a takeover of the government. The slow pace of change provoked criticism from reformers led by Boris Yeltsin.

Yeltsin's outspoken comments caused a break with Gorbachev, who dismissed him from important positions within the Communist party. Yeltsin responded by taking his case to the Soviet people. In May 1990, he won election as president of Russia, the largest of the 15 Soviet republics. For the first time, a Russian head of state had been elected by the people. Two months later, Yeltsin surprised hard-liners by publicly quitting the Communist party.

Meanwhile, people in the other 14 Soviet republics talked openly of independence. In 1990, the Baltic states of Latvia and Estonia

Fun Facts . . .

East Germany
On October 7, 1989, East Germany celebrated its 40th anniversary. When Gorbachev showed up to speak in East Berlin, thousands of protestors shouted, "Gorbi, help us!" They then started chanting a popular political slogan, "We are the people!"

Reading Check What is **dissent**?

Boris N. Yeltsin

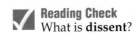

L2 **Government** Guide students in naming the different countries in this section whose Communist regimes ended. ***(Poland, East Germany, Romania, Hungary, Czechoslovakia)*** Then have them create a chart on the board listing each country and the method that it used to achieve independence. Tell students to star those nations that had "peaceful rebellions."

L3 **Current Events** Assign students to research achievements and problems in former Soviet satellites in the 2000s. Have them present their findings in the form of a regional newspaper entitled *Eastern European News.* Headline stories should highlight the most important events or issues in the region. News articles and features should include at least one article on each nation. Encourage students to include visuals similar to those usually found in newspapers, especially political cartoons.

Reading Check Answer
Dissent is criticism, usually against the government.

MEETING SPECIAL NEEDS

Assign gifted students to read and report on literature written by Eastern European authors such as Vaclav Havel, Milovan Dijilas, Milan Kundera, Anna Swir, or other poets, playwrights, novelists, and essayists from this region. Ask these students to select a passage that interests them and read it to the class. Direct students to be prepared to answer questions or to explain difficult portions of the passage.

Refer to ***Inclusion for the Middle School Social Studies Classroom: Strategies and Activities*** for additional resources.

L2 **Geography: Places and Regions** Ask students to compare a political map of the Soviet Union in the 1980s with the map on this page. Ask them to list the changes that took place when the Soviet Union first broke up.

MAP STUDY

Answer

its enormous size and central location

Assign the Chapter 39 **Geography and Map Activity** in the TCR.

Reading Check Answer

Hard-liners attempted a **coup** in 1991 because they wanted to rebuild the Communist state.

NATIONAL GEOGRAPHIC

PICTURE ATLAS OF THE WORLD

You and your students can see and read about the physical features of Russia and Eastern Europe by clicking on the "Photos" and "Essay" button of individual countries. Also, visit the *National Geographic* Web site listed on page 644B to take advantage of the Map-Machine and other map resources.

Commonwealth of Independent States

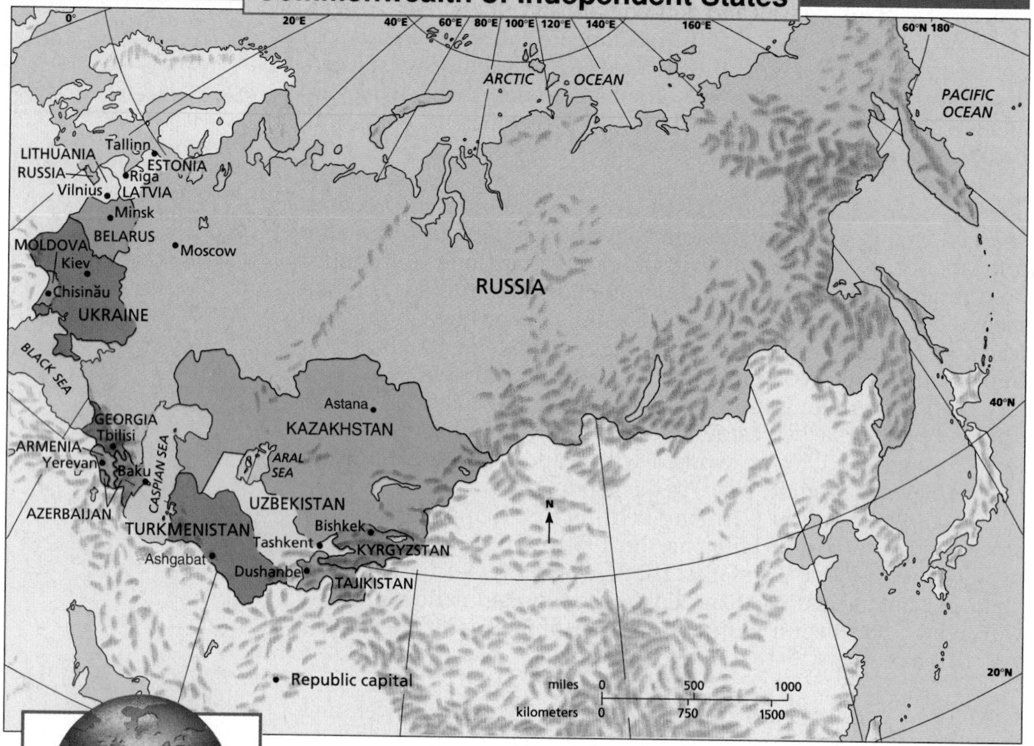

MAP STUDY

PLACES AND REGIONS **What geographic factors made it easier for Russia to have power over the other former Soviet republics?**

proclaimed their freedom. In March 1991, Lithuania—the third Baltic state occupied by Russia at the end of World War II—did the same. Instead of trying to stop the revolt, Gorbachev responded by negotiating Lithuania's independence.

Hard-liners exploded at the breakup of what they called the "Soviet empire." In August 1991, the military and secret police arranged a **coup** (koo), or forced takeover of the government. They placed Gorbachev under house arrest and vowed to rebuild the Communist state.

In a tense, three-day struggle known as the "Second Russian Revolution," Yeltsin stepped in to restore order. He condemned the leaders of the revolt, who then lost the support of the military. On August 24, Gorbachev returned to Moscow. The next day, he shut down the Communist party, thus ending 74 years of Communist rule.

Popular anger at the Communist party and secret police now boiled over. People tore down statues of Communist leaders such as Vladimir Lenin and Joseph Stalin. They rejected names given to cities to honor Communists. Leningrad, for example, returned to its pre-1924 name of St. Petersburg.

Reading Check Why did Communist hard-liners attempt a **coup** in 1991?

COOPERATIVE LEARNING

Organize the class into three groups, assigning each group one of these time spans: 1989–1995, 1995–2000, 2000–present. Instruct each group to research important events in recent Russian history during the time span assigned, starting with the collapse of communism in Soviet satellites and ending with the most important issue or event in the news today. Have students present their findings in the form of a large time line. Students can use connected sheets of computer paper, newsprint, or poster board to construct their time lines. Encourage them to illustrate selected events with copies of photographs or their own drawings.

Independence and Ethnic Rivalries By the end of 1991, all 15 Soviet republics had proclaimed their independence. In December, Gorbachev—a ruler without a country—resigned. Under the leadership of Yeltsin, 11 former Soviet republics formed the Commonwealth of Independent States (CIS)—a loose confederation of **sovereign**, or self-governing, nations.

The growth of independence went hand-in-hand with a spirit of nationalism among the many ethnic and religious groups in Eastern Europe and the former Soviet Union. Starting in 1991, Yugoslavia—a confederation of six individual republics—began to split apart as ethnic rivalries erupted in war. Two years later, Czechoslovakia peacefully split into the Czech Republic and the Republic of Slovakia. That same year, two republics quit the CIS, while Russia acted increasingly on its own.

Within Russia, rebels in the state of Chechnya tried to **secede**, or withdraw, to form their own government. Yeltsin responded by sending in troops and tanks. The drawn-out battle lasted throughout the Yeltsin presidency of the 1990s. The use of force and the failure to resolve the conflict weakened Yeltsin's reputation as a reformer.

Economic Hardships Perhaps no single issue troubled the new governments more than the economy. In the effort to win the cold war, Communist leaders had neglected economic development. As a result, the new governments inherited outdated industries and a shortage of consumer goods, such as household appliances.

For many years, Communist governments had controlled prices, wages, and the production of goods. With the collapse of communism, however, the principle of supply and demand went into effect. In most places, consumer goods remained in short supply throughout the 1990s. This situation created a high demand, which in turn pushed up prices. Because governments no longer employed workers in state-owned businesses, unemployment soared and wages dropped.

Governments moved to **privatize**, or allow the private ownership of, state-owned stores, businesses, and factories. However, few people had enough money or experience to run businesses based on free competition—the cornerstone of capitalism.

By the mid-1990s, about 30 percent of the Russian population had fallen into poverty. Strikes shook Poland as workers demanded wage increases. Throughout the region, interest rates skyrocketed as investment money remained scarce.

Political Challenges At first, citizens expressed a willingness to endure the economic hardships. But as the excitement over independence cooled, the pains of poverty tested people's faith in democracy. Open elections allowed political parties to challenge the supporters of independence. In some nations, including Russia, the

Fun Facts . . .

Fast Food In 1990, McDonald's opened its first restaurant in Moscow. By 1998 there were 15 McDonald's, serving more than a million orders of french fries each month.

Reading Check What are **sovereign** nations? How did Yeltsin respond when Chechnya tried to **secede?**

Chechen rebel

Reading Check What obstacles slowed Russian efforts to **privatize** businesses, shops, and factories?

DID YOU KNOW ??

The Czechs and the Slovaks, though ethnically similar and in close proximity for 1,000 years, were not united politically until the end of World War I.

Reading Check Answer **Sovereign nations** are self-governing nations. When Chechnya tried to **secede,** Yeltsin sent in troops and tanks.

Reading Check Answer Russian efforts to **privatize** were slowed by a lack of money and experience to run businesses based on free competition.

SPOTLIGHT ON: CHECHNYA

The Chechens, a largely Muslim people, have a long history of resistance. They were the most active opponents of czarist Russian occupation of the Caucasus region during the years 1818 to 1917. When the Bolsheviks seized the region in 1918, the anti-communist Chechens immediately rebelled. Soviet troops occupied Chechnya, but they were forced to put down bloody rebellions in 1929 and 1940.

Fed up with resistance, Stalin exiled the entire Chechen nation to Siberia in 1944. In 1957, the remaining Chechens—those who had survived—were allowed to return home. The Soviets, however, treated the Chechen capital of Grozny as enemy territory. When the Soviet Union broke up in 1991, Chechens again declared their independence, triggering battles with Russia that continue today.

DID YOU KNOW ??

In 1986, the Soviet Union launched the history-making space station *Mir* into orbit around the earth. In Russian, the word *mir* means both "peace" and "world." Symbolizing a new era of Russian-American cooperation, an American space shuttle docked with *Mir* in 1995 for the first time. Unable to finance repairs for the space station, the Russians brought down *Mir* in 2001. The fiery remnants of *Mir* crashed into the southern Pacific Ocean.

L2 **Current Events** Assign students to research political elections since the resignation of Boris Yeltsin on December 31, 1999. Have them examine the representation of Communists in the Duma, or Russian parliament, and the party affiliation of the current Russian president. Based on this information, would they say that Russia is more or less democratic today than it was on the day Yeltsin resigned?

CAPTION ANSWER

Political challenges include: rival political parties, Communist efforts to capitalize on economic hardships, and efforts to stabilize the office of the president. Economic challenges include: lack of money and experience to privatize businesses, shortages of consumer goods, high prices, soaring interest rates, and high unemployment.

Lech Walesa, the leader of Solidarity

Fun Facts . . . .

Lech Walesa Lech Walesa first worked as an electrician. He organized the trade union Solidarity and later became Poland's first freely elected President. He won the Nobel Peace Prize in 1983.

Communists reminded people of a time when the government put wages in their pockets and bread on their tables.

In 1994, Hungary elected a number of former Communists to the legislature. In 1995, a former Communist defeated Lech Walesa —the leader of Solidarity—in his bid for reelection as the president of Poland. In 1996, a half dozen candidates in Russia, including a Communist, tried to take the presidency away from Boris Yeltsin.

By the end of the 1990s, however, none of those nations had returned to communism. In 1997, a coalition of groups led by Solidarity overwhelmingly defeated Communist candidates to the legislature. That year, the North Atlantic Treaty Organization (NATO) felt secure enough in the political future of Poland, Hungary, and the Czech Republic to admit all three former Soviet satellites as members.

Suddenly, on December 31, 1999, Russian president Boris Yeltsin resigned. Vladimir Putin was named acting president, later winning the presidency in elections held in 2000. This peaceful transfer of power showed how much the political climate had changed since the days of Communist rule.

Perhaps the most important change in Russia was in the attitudes of young people who grew up during the 1980s and 1990s. They lived at a time when Russians won the right to make their own decisions and to vote freely. As one Russian exchange student in the United States put it: "Let me tell you how Russia has changed. I'm not a Communist. My mother is not a Communist. My father is not a Communist. Do you think I could have said that in the old days?"

POLITICAL CHANGE Teenagers in Russia have more social and political freedom than their parents or grandparents. **What political and economic challenges did Russia face after the fall of communism?**

SPOTLIGHT ON: BORIS YELTSIN

The name Boris means "warrior," and Boris Yeltsin lived up the name at an early age. While still in primary school, he asked to speak to an assembled audience of teachers, parents, and students attending a graduation ceremony. Young Yeltsin took advantage of the opportunity to attack one of the teachers for "cruel, unusual punishment" of students. His outspoken speech earned Yeltsin an expulsion. However, he refused to accept the decision and demanded an appeal. In the end, Yeltsin, the child warrior, won the right to return to the school.

Reading a Demographic Map

In order to show information about where people live on the earth, mapmakers use **demographic maps.** Among other things, these maps can show population density, or the average number of people per square mile, or square kilometer, of land.

Some parts of the world have many people living in each square mile, or square kilometer. People generally live in areas with good physical environments. Other parts of the world have few people, and there are even some areas in which no people live. These are known as *uninhabited* areas.

For example, on the "World Population" map below, the green color indicates areas, such as Southeast Asia, with more than 250 people per square mile, or more than 100 people per square kilometer. This is the highest population density shown. The light brown color indicates areas, such as Antarctica, that are uninhabited.

Map Practice

1. **What color represents 60-125 people per square mile (25-50 per sq. km)?**
2. **What areas in South America have densities of 2-60 people per square mile (1-25 per sq. km)?**

World Population

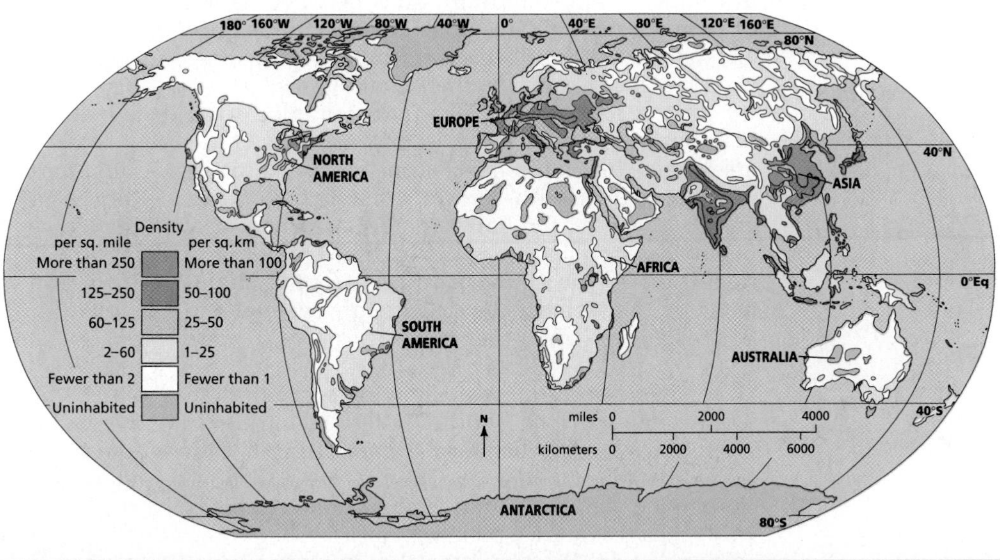

MAP SKILLS

TEACH

Reading a Demographic Map

Direct students to read the instructional part of the feature. Ask: Why do mapmakers use demographic maps? *(to show information about where people live on Earth)* Name one thing that a demographic map can show. *(population density)* What are uninhabited areas? *(places where no people live)*

Next, tell students to study the map. Ask: What color indicates fewer than 2 people per square mile (fewer than 1 per sq. km)? *(white)* What is the approximate population density of the area where you live? *(Answers will vary.)*

After asking these questions, have students work in pairs or in small groups to write questions and answers based on the map in the skill lesson. Call on a spokesperson from each pair or small group to pose their questions to the rest of the class.

Answers to Map Practice

1. pink
2. much of the coastal areas

Use the **Glencoe Skillbuilder Interactive Workbook CD-ROM, Level 1,** to provide instruction and practice in key social studies skills.

SPOTLIGHT ON: WORLD POPULATION

The population of the world is computed only after a careful census has been taken. These counts must be made in a systematic way to record a *de jure* census, which tallies people according to their legal place of residence, or a *de facto* census, which counts them as residing where they spent the night of the day on which the census was taken. In either case, the census distribution is determined by where people sleep, rather than by where they work. Thus, it is a nighttime population count.

DID YOU KNOW ??

Real estate prices vary dramatically in Russia—from as little as $900 to more than $300,000. Unlike prospective home buyers in the United States, the number of Russians obtaining mortgages is very small. In 2002, only 1,200 homes in Russia were bought with a mortgage. Most Russians pay for a house with cash or begin the time-consuming task of building a house for themselves.

Use **Interactive Tutor Self-Assessment CD-ROM** to review Section 1.

LINKING PAST TO PRESENT

UN peacekeeping troops, known as Blue Helmets, were originally formed to maintain peaceful conditions in areas where a cease-fire had been negotiated. Since the end of the cold war, however, Blue Helmets are being sent into situations where violence continues through a cease-fire, or where violence recurs after a cease-fire has been negotiated.

Use the **Vocabulary PuzzleMaker CD-ROM** to create crossword and word search puzzles.

Section 1 Assessment

1. **Define:** aggression, dissent, coup, sovereign, secede, privatize.
2. What changes took place in Eastern Europe as a result of reforms introduced by Mikhail Gorbachev?
3. Why did hard-liners in the Soviet Union try to take control of the government?

Critical Thinking

4. **Making Predictions** Do you think the world has seen the last of communism in Russia? Why or why not?

Graphic Organizer Activity

5. Draw a diagram like this one, and use it to show some of the problems faced by former Soviet satellites.

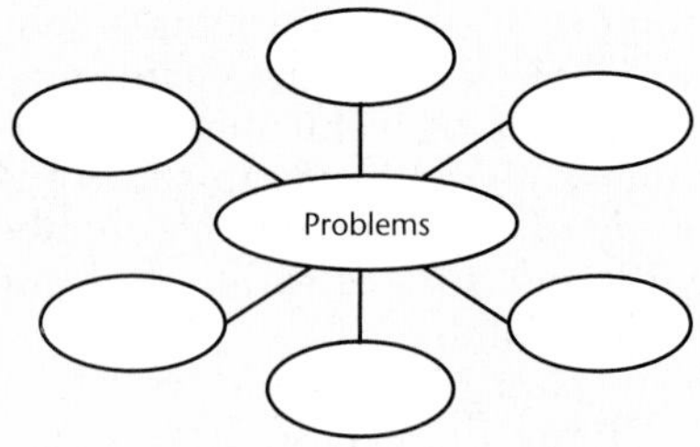

SECTION 2 World Challenges

With the collapse of the Soviet Union, world peace was within reach. There were problems, though, with achieving this peace. During the cold war, the United States and the Soviet Union competed against each other to control events in other nations. After the cold war ended, however, new problems developed. Long-standing issues between nations and groups of people erupted into violence and confusion. World leaders also had to deal with scattered but well-organized groups that used violence to achieve their goals.

In the 1990s, world leaders struggled to find new ways of solving problems to bring about peace. United States leaders looked for the help of other world countries before stepping in to deal with certain problems. However, violence in the Middle East, the Balkans, and elsewhere proved that solving these problems was difficult. At times, global organizations such as the United Nations seemed unable to have any effect on the violence. Peace, though, seemed possible in South Africa, Ireland, and other places.

Iraq One of the most challenging problems after the cold war was dealing with the Middle Eastern country of Iraq. In August 1990, Iraq's leader, dictator Saddam Hussein, ordered the invasion of his oil-rich neighbor Kuwait. He also moved Iraqi troops close to the border of Saudi Arabia. Saudi Arabia is the site of the world's largest known oil reserves.

Section 1 Assessment Answers

1. aggression, warlike acts (p. 645); dissent, criticism (p. 647); coup, takeover (p. 648); sovereign, independent (p. 649); secede, leave (p. 649); privatize, allow private ownership (p. 649)
2. collapse of communism, fall of the Berlin Wall, Eastern European independence
3. because they were angry that Gorbachev let Soviet satellite regimes collapse
4. Answers will vary. Some students might point to the continued presence of the Communist party, while others might point to the rise of a multi-party system and recent elections of non-Communists.
5. Sample problems: ethnic rivalries, soaring prices, high unemployment, low wages, worker strikes, skyrocketing interest rates, political challenges by the Communists.

Assign Chapter 39 **Section 1 Quiz** in the TCR. Testmaker available.

United States leaders were concerned about the safety of the countries in the Middle East. It used the United Nations (UN) as a **forum,** or meeting place. A *coalition,* or a temporary union of nations, was put together to free Kuwait. A coalition army attacked Iraq in January 1991, after Hussein ignored a UN deadline to remove his troops. The United States supported the coalition army. This action was named the Persian Gulf War because of Kuwait's location along the Persian Gulf. By late February, Kuwait had been freed.

Reading Check What is a **forum?**

The Persian Gulf War had mixed results. Although Iraq was forced to leave Kuwait, Hussein was still the country's leader. He continued to abuse the rights of people who did not support him, such as the Kurds. The Kurds are a people living in northern Iraq. Also, UN inspectors were not allowed to check areas in Iraq where they thought dangerous weapons were being stored or built. The inspectors were supposed to make sure Iraq had stopped producing deadly weapons, which included poison gas and bombs that spread dangerous germs that could hurt adults and children.

During the early 2000s, the weapons inspections issue was still a problem. Leaders in the United States believed that as long as Hussein stayed in power, Iraq would develop deadly nuclear weapons. In September 2002, United States President George W. Bush warned that the United States would act on its own if the UN would not enforce tough new weapons inspections demands on Iraq. On October 11, 2002, Congress gave President Bush the authority to use U.S. military force against Iraq if the UN failed to act. In November 2002, the UN approved a plan to send weapons inspectors back into Iraq. Iraq agreed to accept the UN's demands.

GULF WAR As Allied forces put an end to Saddam Hussein's invasion of Kuwait, retreating Iraqi troops set fire to hundreds of oil wells. **What actions did Saddam Hussein take after the Gulf War?**

Fun Facts . . .

Oil Production Kuwait and Saudi Arabia are believed to possess more than 50 percent of the world's known oil reserves. Kuwait has about 20 percent, while Saudi Arabia has 33 percent.

Reading Check Answer
A **forum** is a meeting place.

MAKING CONNECTIONS

➤➤ **History** When the Ayatollah Ruhollah Khomeini came to power in Iran in 1979, he condemned pro-Western and secular Arab leaders as enemies of Islam. Repeatedly, he urged Arab people in other nations to join in a struggle against their leaders. President Saddam Hussein of Iraq, fearful that revolution would sweep into Iraq, invaded Iran in September 1980. The eight-year war that followed is considered to be among the bloodiest in recent history. A UN cease-fire in 1988 ended the war, but by then the two countries had lost about 1 million people and suffered hundreds of billions of dollars in property damage.

CAPTION ANSWER

Hussein continued to abuse the rights of people who did not support him, and he prevented UN weapons inspectors from inspecting areas where they thought dangerous weapons were being built or stored.

DID YOU KNOW ??

Saddam Hussein claimed that his country invaded Kuwait because it was a historic part of Iraq and that Kuwait had unfairly drilled Iraqi oil. Although Iraq was fourth in the world in the production of oil, control of Kuwait would have given Iraq possession of one-fifth of the world's known oil reserves.

EXTENDING THE CONTENT

When the UN imposed a deadline for withdrawal, Hussein vowed not to leave Kuwait until Israel pulled out of its occupied territories and Syria left Lebanon. He also threatened to attack Israel if Iraq were attacked. The day after the UN deadline, the U.S. bombed the Iraqi capital of Baghdad. For the next month, the coalition forces conducted a massive air war aimed at destroying Iraq's war-making ability. Hussein responded by launching missiles at Israel, hoping to draw Israel into the war and split Arab support for the UN coalition. Israel resisted, however, and the U.S. provided Israel with an antimissile defense system.

CAPTION ANSWER

NATO bombed Serbian military targets, forcing the Serbs to allow a peacekeeping force to enter Kosovo.

L1 Geography: The World in Spatial Terms Ask students to locate each of the Balkan nations created by the breakup of Yugoslavia on a wall map of Europe. Then call on a volunteer to slowly read each paragraph aloud in "Balkan Wars." Every time a place name is mentioned, request a volunteer to use a ruler or pointer to locate it on the wall map. Ask: Why do you think most European nations backed NATO involvement in the Bosnia conflict? *(because the region is near their borders; because of memories of other wars that started in the same area)* ELL

Reading Check Answer Kosovo had been an **autonomous,** or self-governing, province in Yugoslavia.

KOSOVO CONFLICT Reports of fighting and hardship for the people of Kosovo spread throughout the world. **How did NATO react to the fighting in Kosovo?**

Balkan Wars Yugoslavia was a war-torn area located in Europe's Balkan Peninsula. Yugoslavia's problems developed in 1980, the year Communist leader Josip Broz Tito died. Since World War II, Tito had held Yugoslavia's six republics together with his iron-fisted rule. When Tito died, however, different ethnic groups struggled for power.

The republic of Serbia tried to rule all of Yugoslavia. Four other republics, though, opposed Serb control and declared their independence. These republics included Slovenia, Croatia, Bosnia-Herzegovina, and Macedonia.

Different groups were struggling for power within each republic in the late 1980s and early 1990s. Fighting in Croatia and Bosnia-Herzegovina was the heaviest. Many people died or fled their homes, becoming refugees. Countries around the world sent food, medical supplies, and warm clothing to help the refugees.

With UN support, NATO carried out air strikes in order to force the different groups to take part in peace talks. The United States supported these peace talks. In 1995, the leaders of Bosnia-Herzegovina, Yugoslavia, and Croatia met in Dayton, Ohio. They signed the Dayton Accords. This peace agreement divided Bosnia into Croat-Muslim and Serb regions. NATO troops stayed in Bosnia to prevent the spread of more violence.

Reading Check What did it mean that Kosovo was an **autonomous** province of Yugoslavia?

Meanwhile, Serb pride was still strong in Yugoslavia. The Serbs decided to try to remove Muslim Albanians from Kosovo. Kosovo had been an **autonomous,** or self-governing, province of Yugoslavia. Albanians formed about 90 percent of Kosovo's

MEETING SPECIAL NEEDS

Many students will benefit from a strong visual and oral presentation that reinforces what they have read. Have small groups of students prepare a brief oral summary of each country in this section. Tell strong visual learners to collect or create images—photographs, illustrations, drawings, posters, collages—of the people, places, and politics they are studying. Have students use a large wall map to trace onto poster board the outline of the region they have chosen. Direct them to paste the images on this outline map. Near the images, have them write a few key words—names, dates, or terms—to help them remember important facts about each country studied.

Refer to ***Inclusion for the Middle School Social Studies Classroom: Strategies and Activities*** for additional resources.

people, and many of them wanted independence. As many Albanian refugees left Kosovo in 1999, NATO bombed Serbian military targets. The Serbs finally allowed a NATO peacekeeping force to enter Kosovo. In the fall of 2000, a new democratic government emerged in Serbia.

Arabs and Israelis The conflict in the Middle East between Arabs and Israelis has deep roots. During World War I, many Arabs sided with Great Britain and France against the Turks of the Ottoman Empire. The Arab countries thought that this would help them gain their independence. By 1947, a number of Arab territories had won their freedom.

At the same time, the situation in Palestine was different. Jews and Arabs lived in Palestine. In 1947, the UN voted to divide Palestine into a Jewish state and an Arab state. The Arabs in Palestine and in neighboring countries did not support this plan. In 1948, when the British withdrew, the Jews established the nation of Israel in their part of Palestine.

Most Arabs opposed the creation of Israel, and five Arab nations waged war on the new nation. The war was difficult for both the Israeli and Arab people. Many lost relatives and friends in the fighting. The war ended with Israel's victory.

Between 1948 and 1993, Arab nations and Israel fought more wars. As a result, Israel won control of some neighboring lands. An Arab group known as the Palestine Liberation Organization (PLO) opposed Israel and wanted an entirely Palestinian state, rather than the state of Israel. The PLO continued to carry out

MIDDLE EAST CONFLICT Attempts to solve the problems between Jews and Palestinians in the Middle East have failed. **When was the nation of Israel established?**

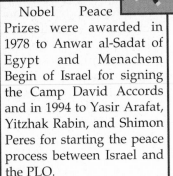

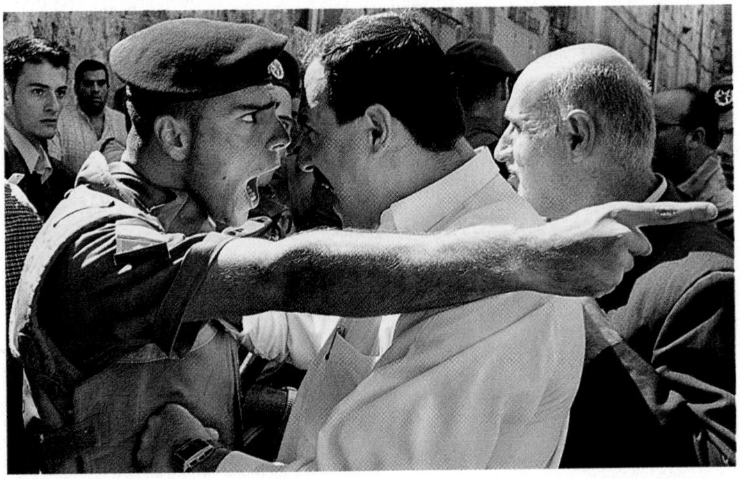

DID YOU KNOW

Nobel Peace Prizes were awarded in 1978 to Anwar al-Sadat of Egypt and Menachem Begin of Israel for signing the Camp David Accords and in 1994 to Yasir Arafat, Yitzhak Rabin, and Shimon Peres for starting the peace process between Israel and the PLO.

CAPTION ANSWER

1948

THE HISTORY CHANNEL.

The following videotape program is available from Glencoe to enrich Chapter 39:

- **Israel: Birth of a Nation**

To find classroom resources to accompany this video, check the following home page:

A&E Television:
www.aande.com

COOPERATIVE LEARNING

Organize students into groups, and ask them to research—in the library or on the Internet—the number of people who follow these religions in the Middle East:

Sunni Islam
Shi'ite Islam
Christianity
Judaism
Other

Direct groups of students to present the information they find in the form of a bar graph. When students have completed their graphs, ask: Which religion has the most members? Which religion has the fewest members? Based upon the information in the graph, which religions do you think would be most likely to come into conflict with each other?

Assign Chapter 39 ***Cooperative Learning Activity*** in the TCR.

DID YOU KNOW

During the post-World War I years, the unifying idea of Pan-Arabism grew. Pan-Arabism was a Middle Eastern political and cultural movement emphasizing ties among all Arab peoples.

L2 **Economics** Have students research the economic differences between Northern Ireland and southern Ireland. In a one-page summary, ask students to describe how the differences have influenced the conflict between the two regions. Students should use facts from their articles to support their summaries.

CAPTION ANSWER

Catholics and Protestants agreed to share power in the government and end the violence that has existed between them.

attacks on Israel. Throughout the 1990s, there were times of peace and times of war.

Although many Arabs and Israelis supported peace efforts, hatred and fears ran deep on both sides. In 2000, violence erupted between the Israelis and Arabs after peace talks failed. Observers believed that ending violence and restoring trust would be necessary before any new peace talks could begin.

Toward Peace in Ireland In the late 1990s, the world saw progress in settling a European conflict that dated back hundreds of years. Historically, Ireland has been controlled by Great Britain. The people of Northern Ireland were mostly Protestants and were satisfied to be ruled by Great Britain. The people of southern Ireland, however, were mostly Catholic and wanted to be independent. In 1922, Catholic southern Ireland finally became self-governing, while the largely Protestant north remained a part of Great Britain.

Beginning in the 1960s, violent fighting broke out between the Catholics and Protestants in British-ruled Northern Ireland. Both groups wanted to control the government. This fighting continued for years.

In 1998, a peace agreement was reached that went into effect the following year. Catholics and Protestants in Northern Ireland agreed to share power in the government. Both groups agreed to end the violence. Continuing distrust between the two sides, however, has made achieving peace very difficult.

NORTHERN IRELAND After nearly 30 years of violence, Gerry Adams (center), a Catholic leader, joins with the people of Belfast in celebrating the peace agreement. **What were the terms of peace agreed upon in 1998?**

MEETING SPECIAL NEEDS

To help visual learners, have students create a time line of key events in the conflict between Protestants and Catholics in Ireland. Students should include events to the present year. Pre-1800 dates may include:

1534 Henry VIII declares himself "King of Ireland"; Irish Catholics resist Protestant rule.

1641 Oliver Cromwell puts down rebellion by Irish Catholics.

1688 Irish Catholics side with James II in the Glorious Revolution; Parliament awards Irish lands to its Protestant supporters.

1778 Irish nationalists rebel against English rule.

1800 Act of Union joins Ireland and England.

Refer to ***Inclusion for the Middle School Social Studies Classroom: Strategies and Activities*** for additional resources.

Changes in China During the 1990s, the future of the world's remaining Communist nations was in doubt. The Soviet Union—formerly a strong Communist country—had collapsed. Without Soviet aid, governments in Cuba and North Korea had severe economic problems. China, however, seemed to be moving toward capitalism.

Chinese leaders in the 1990s set up policies to change the economic system of communism. They began to allow some people to own their own businesses. The Communist party, however, was still in control of the government.

Hong Kong, a busy port on the south China coast, was returned to China in 1997. Until that time, it had been under British rule. Hong Kong had become one of the world's largest financial and trade centers. The Chinese government agreed to allow Hong Kong to keep its capitalist system for 50 years. Many Hong Kong citizens, though, worried about their future under Chinese rule.

Fears over the future of Hong Kong grew worse because of Chinese actions toward Taiwan. Taiwan is an independent country located near China. Non-Communist Chinese leaders have ruled the island since 1949, when the Communists took control of the mainland. China claims Taiwan as its territory. People living on Taiwan, however, do not want to be under Chinese Communist rule. The people are Chinese but have been independent from the mainland for many years. Taiwan also has a free press and democratic elections.

By 2000, the United States had developed a closer trading relationship with China. Charges that the Chinese government did not respect the human rights of its people set off a debate within the United States. Supporters of trade between the two nations claimed that the only way to bring change to China was to speed up the development of capitalism there.

Indonesia For much of the past century, Indonesia has had many problems. Indonesia is made up of more than 17,000 islands. It stretches along the Equator from the Malay Peninsula toward Australia. Indonesia is one of the world's most populated countries. It is also the largest Muslim country and one of the world's leading oil producers.

In 1949, Indonesia won its independence after centuries of Dutch rule. Indonesia's first president tried to unite the country's islands under one government. However, he faced two challenges. Some of the islands wanted greater self-rule, while the Indonesian Communist party wanted to gain control of the country.

In 1965, the communists tried to take over Indonesia's government. Army forces quickly put down the uprising. The government continued to maintain strict control of its people.

This government approved the takeover of East Timor, a nearby island colony that, until 1975, had been Portuguese. The people of East Timor organized an independence movement. Over the next

Port of Hong Kong

Then & Now

Macao On December 20, 1999, Portugal returned Macao—a peninsula and two islands on the south coast of China—to the People's Republic. Founded in 1557, the port was the oldest European outpost in China. As with Hong Kong, Chinese officials promised to respect Macao's way of life for 50 years after the start of Chinese rule.

L2 **Language Arts** Have students use the Internet to find an editorial about the present-day economic relationship between China and the United States. Students should summarize the article in their own words. Ask: Does the author support a closer trade relationship between the United States and China? Should trade be restricted if China refuses to support human rights? What facts does the author use to support his or her position? Then have students discuss their opinions about whether the United States should trade with China. Discuss whether or not the issue of human rights should affect economic agreements between nations.

L2 **Science** Tell students that Indonesia has an estimated 210 endangered plant and animal species—more than any other nation. Assign interested students to compile a list of some of these species. Then, working with a science teacher, introduce the concept of the "web of life." Ask: Suppose people let all 210 of these endangered species disappear. What are the possible consequences?

SPOTLIGHT ON: TAIWAN

Taiwan, originally called Formosa, was "discovered" by Portugal, then controlled by the Dutch and later by Spain. Still later it was acquired by China, then Japan, then China again. Despite its small size, Taiwan has prospered economically. Its major industries include electronics, petroleum refining, chemicals, textiles, iron and steel, and food processing. Militarily, Taiwan ranks above Germany, Italy, Great Britain, and Japan in the number of active troops in its armed forces.

CAPTION ANSWER

Some islands wanted self-rule, while the Indonesian Communist party wanted to control the country.

Reading Check Answer A **referendum** is a popular vote.

Reading Check Answer **Authoritarian rule** developed in many African countries because these countries lacked experience in self-government.

DID YOU KNOW

East Timor lies on the eastern portion of the island of Timor, which is located between the South China Sea and the Indian Ocean. It is about 400 miles northwest of Australia. Many of the refugees who fled East Timor found safety in Australia.

INDONESIA A mosque rises above a modern street in Indonesia. **What were the two problems that Indonesia faced after it won its independence from the Dutch?**

25 years, nearly 200,000 East Timorese died from famine, disease, and fighting.

By the late 1990s, falling oil prices and government corruption had deeply affected Indonesia. As a result of student protests, the strict government was replaced in 1999. The new Indonesian government agreed to hold a **referendum,** or popular vote, for the independence of East Timor. As expected, most East Timorese voted to form their own nation. Fighting broke out among people who did not want East Timor to be separate from Indonesia. In 2002, peace and independence finally came to East Timor.

Reading Check What is a **referendum**?

Meanwhile, Indonesia established a democratic government. In 2001, its new president faced a weakened economy and uprisings in islands that also wanted to separate from Indonesia.

Struggles and Progress in Africa As you know, Africa is made up of many different countries. As the 2000s began, most nations in Africa had been free for less than 50 years. Lack of experience in self-government led to **authoritarian rule**, or government in which one ruler of one political party holds power, for many of these countries. Like other parts of the world, differences that date back hundreds of years also deeply divided some African nations.

Reading Check Why did **authoritarian rule** develop in many African countries?

During the 1990s, Somalia, Rwanda, Sierra Leone, the Democratic Republic of the Congo, and Liberia suffered bloody wars. Many Africans lost their lives, and large numbers of refugees fled to neighboring countries.

MEETING SPECIAL NEEDS

Some students may have difficulty visualizing the locations of the nations discussed in this section. Before students read about each nation, have them locate it on a world map. Students should identify important physical features, such as mountain ranges or rivers, along with the nation's capital and major cities. When important geography information is presented in the text, refer back to the map to discuss it.

Refer to ***Inclusion for the Middle School Social Studies Classroom: Strategies and Activities*** for additional resources.

Even with the conflicts in many places, some experts feel that progress can still be seen. Today there are fewer civil wars in Africa than in the past. Democratic elections have been carried out in some nations. In 2002, African leaders formed the African Union to deal with the problems of the continent.

Perhaps the most remarkable changes, however, have taken place in South Africa. In 1948, South Africa passed into law a system of **apartheid**, or forced separation of races. Apartheid allowed for a small group of whites to have power over the much larger group of black South Africans. To end apartheid, the United States and other nations placed trade restrictions on South Africa in the 1980s.

In 1989, the white South African government led by President F. W. de Klerk gave in to world opinion. It lifted the long-standing ban on the African National Congress (ANC). The ANC was a political group that spoke for most black South Africans. In 1990, Nelson Mandela, the head of the ANC, was released from prison after 27 years. By 1992, most of the laws that made apartheid legal had been thrown out. All South Africans of voting age, regardless of race, won the right to vote.

In 1994, the nation held its first democratic election open to blacks and whites alike. Many stood in lines for hours to exercise their right to vote. The ANC won a majority in the legislature, and Nelson Mandela later became president. During his term of office, Mandela reached out to all black and white South Africans. In 1999, South Africa held its second all-race democratic election.

Reading Check What was **apartheid**?

SOUTH AFRICA Nelson Mandela congratulates Thabo Mbeki on his victory in South Africa's second all-race election. **When was South Africa's first all-race democratic election held?**

People in History

Nelson Mandela
1918–PRESENT

South African Statesman

Born of royal parents, Nelson Mandela experienced apartheid while working in a South African gold mine. He went on to study law and to help form the ANC. Imprisoned in 1964 for his opposition to apartheid, he emerged in 1990 to help F.W. de Klerk end the hated system. In 1993, the two men shared the Nobel Peace Prize.

Reading Check Answer
Apartheid was the forced legal separation of races in South Africa.

L3 Critical Thinking Have students read more about apartheid and how it affected the development of South Africa. Call on them to share their findings with the rest of the class. In a follow-up discussion, compare apartheid with the treatment of African Americans in the first half of the 20th century—a time when Jim Crow laws existed in much of the South.

CAPTION ANSWER

1994

SPOTLIGHT ON: NELSON MANDELA

To extend People in History, provide these additional details on Nelson Mandela:

Nelson Mandela always expected to rule, but not the nation of South Africa. Mandela grew up the son of a Thembu chief and believed he would follow in his father's footsteps. Instead, the injustice of apartheid caused Mandela to join the fight that led to his imprisonment from 1964 to 1990.

When Mandela emerged from prison, his sense of tolerance and justice amazed the world. As South Africa's first black president, Mandela appointed not only his lifetime ANC colleagues to government, but also F.W. de Klerk and Mangosuthus Buthelezi, the Zulu leader who had loudly criticized Mandela for his support for an all-race government. Through Mandela's leadership, South Africa experienced one of the most peaceful political revolutions in modern times.

Use the **Interactive Tutor Self-Assessment CD-ROM** to review Section 2.

L2 **Government** Instruct students to imagine they are part of a UN committee assigned to design a proposal for dealing with global terrorism. Next, organize the class into small groups, and assign each group to represent one of the following nations: United States, Russia, China, South Korea, North Korea, Japan, Iran, Iraq, Afghanistan, Libya, India, Pakistan, Israel, South Africa, Nigeria, Kenya, Mexico, Peru, Nicaragua, and Cuba. Instruct students to research each nation's position on weapons control, the nations with which it is likely to agree or disagree, tradeoffs the nation might be willing to make, and so on.

Appoint some of the students to serve as moderators. Their job is the most difficult—they need to learn something about all the nations, be willing to intervene in conflicts, and suggest possible "win-win" solutions to settle disputes. Allow about a week for research, a day for planning the committee meeting, and two or three days for creating a proposal.

Reading Check Answer
Terrorism is the use of violence to achieve a political goal.

Use the **Vocabulary PuzzleMaker CD-ROM** to create crossword and word search puzzles.

Section 2 Assessment

1. **Define:** forum, autonomous, referendum, authoritarian rule, apartheid.
2. What type of economic system did China move toward in the 1990s?

Critical Thinking

3. **Making Predictions** What role do you think South Africa will play in world affairs during the next 100 years?

Graphic Organizer Activity

4. Draw this chart, and use it to summarize the responses of the world community to these global issues.

Global Issue	World Response
Invasion of Kuwait	
Fighting in Bosnia	
Fighting in Kosovo	
Apartheid in South Africa	

SECTION 3 The World Today

Today, the world faces many challenges that require cooperation among nations. The threat of war and other forms of violence continues to grow. Tensions have developed between industrial and developing nations over the use of limited resources, readily available health care, and other issues. Continued global progress depends on solving these and other problems.

Reading Check What is **terrorism**?

Global Terrorism

The use of violence to reach a political goal—**terrorism**—has become a major global concern. Terrorists—either as individuals or groups—act on their own, usually without formal government support. In 2001, the United States government identified nearly 30 terrorist groups operating in Asia, Europe, the Americas, and Africa.

United States leaders believe that the most dangerous of these terrorists is the Islamic group al-Qaeda (al KY duh), or "the Base." In the late 1990s, al-Qaeda leader Osama bin Laden told Muslims to work toward removing U.S. influence from the Middle East. Bin Laden stated that any action—such as the killing of American citizens—would be acceptable in order to achieve this goal. This view, however, does not follow the beliefs of the religion of Islam.

Al-Qaeda is believed to have been responsible for the bombings of two American embassies in Africa in 1998. The

Section 2 Assessment Answers

1. forum, meeting place (p. 653); autonomous, self-governing (p. 654); referendum, popular vote (p. 658); authoritarian rule, control of government by one person or group (p. 658); apartheid, forced separation of the races (p. 659)
2. capitalism
3. Answers will vary, but many students may suggest that South Africa will take a leading role in helping to spread democracy in the region.
4. Charts will vary but should reflect the trend toward collective action in responding to world crises.

Assign Chapter 39 **Section 2 Quiz** in the TCR. Testmaker is available.

Global Links Progress in the twenty-first century depends upon global cooperation. Issues that affect many, such as water shortages, cannot be solved by one nation alone. Nations must also rely upon each other to share resources.

Few nations can fully meet all the needs of their people without global trade. Some nations have joined together to form trading blocs. Trading blocs are groups of nations that work together to promote trade within the organization. In 1992, for example, 15 western European nations formed the European Union (EU). The EU was based on the earlier Common Market. One of the goals of the EU was the political unity of Europe. It was also designed to help Europe become an economic superpower like the United States.

On January 1, 2002, 12 of the 15 EU members began using a new currency called the **euro**. The euro replaced the individual currencies of these countries. This means that a person can travel among these 12 countries using the same form of money. Many economists believe three other EU nations—Britain, Denmark, and Sweden—will eventually switch to the euro as well.

Reading Check How does the **euro** help create economic ties among the nations of Europe?

Other Trade Agreements Trade agreements were also made between the countries of North America. In 1993, the United States, Canada, and Mexico reduced trade barriers under the North American Free Trade Agreement (NAFTA). In 1995, blocs of nations in South America signed similar trade agreements.

Contact among nations has been further increased by new forms of communications. Satellites have extended the reach of both telephones and the media. People almost everywhere on the earth can now contact each other, either by telephone, fax, or computer. The result has been the rise of what some experts call a *global culture.*

The speed at which goods, ideas, and people move is expected to increase in the years ahead. Cultures around the world will change as they influence each other. The most important force in bringing about the change, say some experts, is teenagers.

There are more than 800 million teens in the world today—the most there have ever been. They travel, watch television, buy things, and most of all, talk. No other global generation has ever known each other better. They, more than any other generation, have the chance to work together to solve some of the earth's most pressing problems.

The Global Culture

Reading Check Answer The **euro** serves as a common currency for some European nations.

L2 **Science** Organize students into groups and have them create an environmental education program for their grade level. Tell students that the course will be taught as a morning lesson one day a week. It will cover approximately eight special topics. Challenge students to select these topics, along with suggestions for projects or field trips related to each topic. You might carry out some of the suggestions as part of the activities surrounding Earth Day, held each April 22. ELL

ASSESS

Check for Understanding

Ask students to summarize the main points of the chapter, orally or in writing. Discuss the answers to the Section and Chapter Assessment questions.

COOPERATIVE LEARNING

Organize the class into five groups, and assign each group to design posters that show how each of the following inventions has helped link the world: communications satellites, telephones, fax machines, computers (the Internet), and jet airplanes. Display the completed posters on a classroom wall, and review them with students. Then hold a class vote ranking these inventions in terms of their importance to promoting a global culture.

GLENCOE TECHNOLOGY

MindJogger Videoquiz

Use **MindJogger Videoquiz** to review students' knowledge of the unit.

Available in DVD and VHS

Evaluate

Assign the Chapter 39 **Performance Assessment Activity** in the TCR.

Administer the **Chapter 39 Test.** Testmaker available.

Reteach

Assign the Chapter 39 **Reteaching Activity** in the TCR.

Enrich

Assign the Chapter 39 **Enrichment Activity** in the TCR.

CLOSE

Have students evaluate this statement: "The world has become a global village, and no country can be an island unto itself."

Use the **Interactive Tutor Self-Assessment CD-ROM** to review Section 3.

HISTORY Online

Self-Check Quiz gives students an interactive chapter tutorial. Have them access ***Chapter 39 Quiz*** at **humanheritage.glencoe.com**

Section 3 Assessment

1. **Define:** terrorism, weapons of mass destruction, communicable diseases, pandemics, greenhouse effect, euro.
2. What serious events occurred in the United States on September 11, 2001?
3. What environmental challenges must be solved in the years ahead?

Critical Thinking

4. **Identifying Alternatives** Do you think the United States should try to reduce the gap between the rich and poor nations in the world? Explain your answer.

Graphic Organizer Activity

5. Draw this diagram, and use it to show the way your own life has been touched by increased contact and communication with other nations.

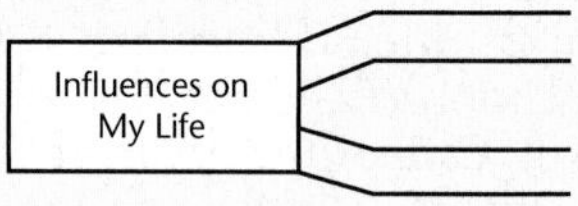

Chapter Summary & Study Guide

1. Between 1989 and 1991, communism collapsed in Eastern Europe and the cold war came to an end.
2. By late 1991, the Soviet Union had formed into 15 independent republics.
3. Differences among people and economic hardships created many challenges for nations formerly under Soviet control.
4. In 1997, NATO offered membership to Poland, Hungary, and the Czech Republic.
5. Following Iraq's invasion of Kuwait, a coalition of nations attacked Iraq.
6. Ethnic conflicts in Bosnia and Kosovo led to NATO air strikes against Serbia.
7. In the Middle East, Israel and several Arab nations took steps toward peace, but conflict remained between Israelis and Palestinians.
8. In 1999, Catholics and Protestants agreed to joint rule of Northern Ireland.
9. Hong Kong was returned to China in 1997.
10. East Timor gained freedom, while a democratic government was established in Indonesia.
11. The September 11, 2001, attacks on the United States encouraged a global struggle against terrorism.
12. Population growth and health and environmental issues challenge the global community.

HISTORY Online

Self-Check Quiz

Visit the *Human Heritage* Web site at **humanheritage.glencoe.com** and click on ***Chapter 39—Self-Check Quiz*** to assess your understanding of this chapter.

Section 3 Assessment Answers

1. terrorism, violence for a political objective (p. 660); weapons of mass destruction, nuclear bombs, poisonous chemicals, and biological weapons that spread disease (p. 663); communicable diseases, passed from one infected person or animal to another (p. 664); pandemics, epidemics spread over a wide area (p. 664); greenhouse effect, buildup of carbon dioxide in the atmosphere (p. 664); euro, common currency for the European Union (p. 665)

2. Planes hijacked by terrorists flew into the World Trade Center towers, the Pentagon, and a field in Pennsylvania, killing thousands.

3. Sample environmental challenges: greenhouse effect, melting of polar ice caps, pollution, overpopulation

4. Students should think in terms of growing global interdependence.

5. Diagrams will vary.

Assign Chapter 39 **Section 3 Quiz** in the TCR. Testmaker available.

CHAPTER 39 Assessment

Using Key Terms

Imagine you are a historian in 2100. You have been asked to write an essay in which you describe the major challenges facing the world as the century opened. Use the following words in your essay.

aggression	secede	privatize
sovereign	forum	autonomous
authoritarian rule	communicable diseases	referendum
terrorism	greenhouse effect	weapons of mass destruction
apartheid	coup	pandemics
euro		
dissent		

Understanding Main Ideas

1. What was the symbolic importance of destroying the Berlin Wall?
2. What problems did Russia face in reforming its government and economy?
3. What were the short-term and long-term outcomes of the Persian Gulf War?
4. What was the role of NATO in Bosnia and Kosovo?
5. What obstacles to peace exist in Africa?
6. What forms of communication link nations in the 2000s?

Critical Thinking

1. Do you agree that trade is linked to the growth of democracy in the People's Republic of China? Why or why not?
2. Do you support the United States giving financial help to peacekeeping forces in places like Bosnia and Kosovo? Explain.
3. How do you think the events of September 11, 2001, changed the world?

Graphic Organizer Activity

Culture Create a diagram like this one, and use it to show some of the causes and effects of increased contact among the diverse cultures of the world.

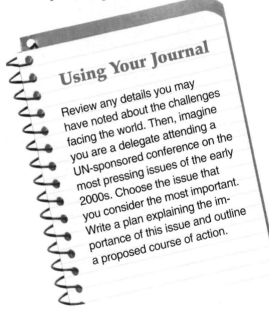

Geography in History

Places and Regions Look at the population map on page 651. Scientists are predicting great increases in the world's population by the year 2050. In what regions would you expect the most growth to take place? Explain.

Using Your Journal

Review any details you may have noted about the challenges facing the world. Then, imagine you are a delegate attending a UN-sponsored conference on the most pressing issues of the early 2000s. Choose the issue that you consider the most important. Write a plan explaining the importance of this issue and outline a proposed course of action.

Bonus Test Question

For Chapter 39 Test

Think about the following challenges facing the world today, rank each, and explain your rankings: controlling weapons of mass destruction, producing enough food, protecting the environment, improving health care. *(Answers will vary.)*

Using Your Journal

Plans will vary, but students should indicate specific ways they would solve the problems. Have volunteers share their plans.

Geography in History

Answers may vary but should indicate areas that are already heavily populated and likely to become more densely populated in the future.

CHAPTER 39 Assessment Answers

Using Key Terms

Essays will vary, but students should use all the key terms in describing major challenges.

Understanding Main Ideas

1. symbolized the collapse of communism in Eastern Europe
2. shortages, high prices, high interest rates, wage disputes, unemployment
3. short term—stopped Iraqi aggression; long term—left Hussein in power, left Iraqi weapons production and related conflicts unresolved
4. forced negotiations, then remained to ensure peace and protect returning refugees
5. lack of experience in self-government, ethnic differences
6. telephones, faxes, and computers

Critical Thinking

1. Answers will vary, but some students may note that new ideas are spread through trade and that these ideas will influence the young people of China.
2. Answers will vary. Some students may argue that the money should be spent to solve problems at home, while others will cite the importance of peace in an interdependent world.
3. Answers will vary. Students may note that there is more global support to end terrorism.

Graphic Organizer Activity

Sample responses: causes—increased global trade, increased speed of travel, a communications revolution; effects—rise of a global culture, chance for people to know each other better, increased cooperation to solve global problems

FOCUS

Objectives

After reading the Around the World for Unit 12, your students will be able to:

1. identify nations affected by the September 11, 2001, terrorist attacks.
2. describe how the fall of the Taliban government affected females living in Afghanistan.
3. explain how the terrorist attacks of September 11, 2001, influenced the relationships between nations.

Bellringer

Have students brainstorm a list of words and images that they think of when they hear about the terrorist attacks of September 11, 2001. Write these words and images on the board.

Motivational Activity

Review the list of words that the students created. Have students categorize each of them as either positive or negative. Discuss the origin of these words and images with students.

TEACH

Geography: Places and Regions Have students examine the map on page 668. Ask students to identify what the shading on the map represents. Discuss how the map's information illustrates why terrorism is a global issue. *(Students should note that the terrorist attacks on September 11, 2001, affected more than 80 countries; thus, terrorism is a global issue.)*

UNIT 12 Around

THE EFFECTS OF SEPTEMBER 11, 2001

The September 11, 2001, terrorist attacks on the United States stunned the world. Countries responded by holding memorial services to remember those who were killed in the attacks. World political leaders gave their support to the United States to help find the people responsible for the attacks. People around the world sent money and donated blood to help the victims of the attacks.

The attacks on the United States had an effect on the global community. Terrorism will continue to be a global issue that challenges countries throughout the world.

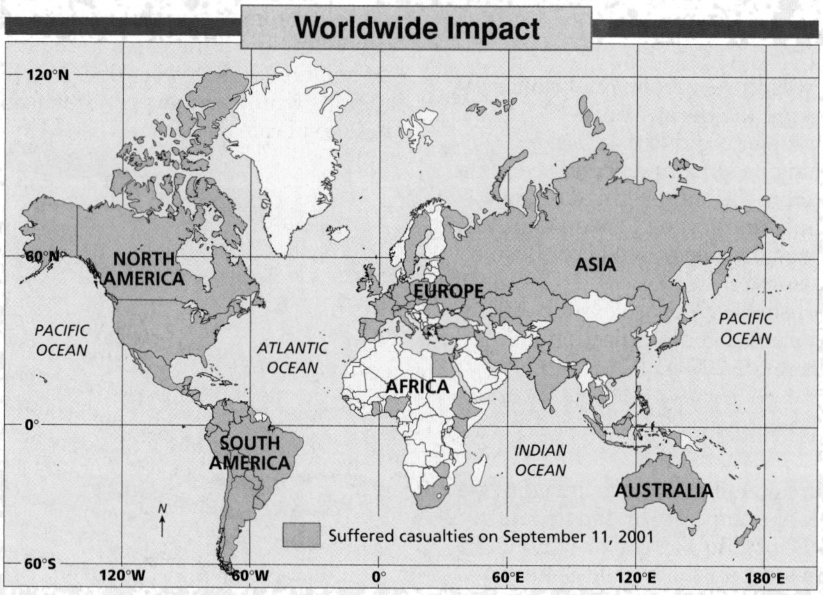

▲ According to the U.S. Department of State, more than 80 countries suffered casualties in the September 11, 2001, terrorist attacks. These countries are shaded on the world map (above).

SPOTLIGHT ON: THE NORTHERN ALLIANCE

At the time of the September 11, 2001, terrorist attacks on the United States, the Northern Alliance was an Afghanistan Islamic rebel faction opposed to Afghanistan's militant Islamic Taliban regime. The alliance was composed of Afghanistan's minorities—Tajiks, Uzbeks, and other groups—while the Taliban primarily consisted of the Pashtun, the country's largest ethnic group. The Taliban took control of Afghanistan's capital, Kabul, in 1996, after which it took control of most of the country. As of September 11, 2001, the Northern Alliance had successfully resisted the Taliban's rule, though alliance members controlled less than 10 percent of the country.

the World

◀ A young girl reads aloud to the class during the first day of 2001 winter classes at the Alfat-Ha school in Kabul, Afghanistan. Before, under the Taliban rule, girls and young women were not allowed to attend classes. After the fall of the Taliban government, however, girls in Afghanistan were allowed to go back to school.

Relations between Russia and the West have improved as a result of the war on terrorism. Russian President Vladimir Putin (left) and British Prime Minister Tony Blair (right) met in December, 2001. ▶

A young man and woman in Prague, the capital of the Czech Republic, remember those who were injured or killed in the attacks. ▶

A Pakistani soldier searches the trunk of a car in Karachi, Pakistan. Governments around the world have begun sharing intelligence information with each other about terrorist groups to prevent more attacks. ▼

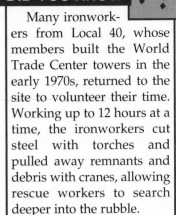

Taking Another Look

1. Why were girls in Afghanistan allowed back to school in the winter of 2001?
2. How have the September 11 attacks on the United States affected relationships among the world's countries?

Hands-On Activity

Writing a Song Write a song that expresses how the September 11 terrorist attacks have affected people throughout the world. 669

ANSWERS TO TAKING ANOTHER LOOK

1. The Taliban government, which did not allow girls to attend school, had collapsed.
2. Students' answers may note that relationships between nations, such as Russia and Great Britain, have improved. Nations have also begun to share intelligence information with each other to prevent further terrorist attacks.

Hand-On Activity

Students' songs may express feelings of sorrow and the desire for peace among nations.

DID YOU KNOW ??

Many ironworkers from Local 40, whose members built the World Trade Center towers in the early 1970s, returned to the site to volunteer their time. Working up to 12 hours at a time, the ironworkers cut steel with torches and pulled away remnants and debris with cranes, allowing rescue workers to search deeper into the rubble.

L2 **Language Arts** Have students interview a family member or an adult about how they first heard about the September 11 attacks and what their initial reaction was. Students should create an audio scrapbook of these memories by having the person describe his or her experiences or feelings on audiotape. Ask volunteers to share their tapes with the class and use them as a springboard to discuss how these acts of terrorism have affected their own lives.

ASSESS

Check for Understanding

Have students answer the questions in Taking Another Look on page 669.

Enrich

Have students use a variety of magazine and newspaper resources to find images of the effects of terrorism, either in the United States or abroad. Have students create a photo essay using these images and sentence captions to tell the story of terrorism today.

CLOSE

Have students summarize in their own words how the September 11, 2001, terrorist attacks affected the global community.

STANDARDIZED TEST PRACTICE

Answers and Analyses

1C History

Page 604 states that World War I was different because civilians were attacked and new weapons were particularly destructive.

THE PRINCETON REVIEW **TEST-TAKING TIP**

This is a good example to illustrate the power of the process of elimination. It is very unlikely that choices A, B, and D were innovations of World War I. Remind students to read the question carefully so they do not misunderstand what type of answer they should look for.

2J History

According to pages 610–611, the Russian people did support the revolution, and the poor did want equality, so choices F and H can be eliminated. Since the government was run by the Communist Party, and was not democratically elected, the best choice is J.

3C History

According to page 614, Hitler *blamed many of Germany's troubles on the Jews and others.* This information best supports choice C.

4J History

According to page 620, President Truman *did not want to invade Japan* and he instead *approved the use of a new weapon—the atomic bomb.* This information best supports choice J.

THE PRINCETON REVIEW

Standardized Test Practice

Directions: Choose the *best* answer to each of the following multiple choice questions. If you have trouble answering a question, use the process of elimination to narrow your choices. Write your answers on a separate piece of paper.

1. Why was World War I different from earlier wars?

- **A** It was the first war fought on European soil.
- **B** It was the first time the United States fought in a war.
- **C** New weapons made it the deadliest war up to that time.
- **D** The war resulted in many political reforms.

Test-Taking Tip: This question asks for a *comparison.* Although the war did result in political reforms (answer D), this fact does not make it *different* from other wars.

2. The Russian Revolution was different from the French and American revolutions in which of the following ways?

- **F** The Russian Revolution was not fought because the poor wanted more equality.
- **G** The Russian Revolution relied on trench warfare.
- **H** The people of Russia did not support the Russian Revolution.
- **J** The goal of the Russian Revolution was not to put a democratically elected government in power.

Test-Taking Tip: This question also asks you to find a *difference* by *comparison.* Ask yourself, how is *communism* different from *democracy?*

3. In which of the following ways did Hitler unite Germany?

- **A** He gave voting rights to all males over the age of 18.
- **B** He enacted a law requiring religion in Germany.
- **C** He united the people of Germany against what he thought was a common enemy.
- **D** He used various tactics from Soviet communism to improve the economy.

Test-Taking Tip: Always read the question and all of the answer choices *carefully.* You may be tempted to choose answer D, since Hitler did promise to improve the economy. However, these tactics were not borrowed from Soviet communism—and they were not his most *significant* unifying action.

4. President Truman avoided sending American troops to invade Japan by

- **F** signing a peace treaty with the emperor of Japan
- **G** convincing other Allied nations to fight in Japan
- **H** limiting the war to a fight for Midway Island
- **J** ordering atomic bombs to be dropped on Hiroshima and Nagasaki

Test-Taking Tip: This question asks you to remember an important event in World War II. President Truman did not limit the fighting just to Midway Island, though an important battle did take place there. Therefore, you can eliminate answer H.

5. The United Nations was formed at the end of World War II. The activities of the United Nations include all of the following EXCEPT

A providing medical care to people in poor countries

B preventing the spread of communism to western nations

C negotiating and keeping peace between nations

D lending money to poor countries

> **Test-Taking Tip:** Think about what you know about the United Nations. It is an organization made up of countries with many different types of governments. Which answer choice best fits this information? Remember, the question is asking for the EXCEPTION.

6. Why is Mohandas Gandhi considered a great leader?

F He convinced the Indian people to boycott British goods.

G He gained the respect of both the upper class and the common people.

H He believed in achieving peace without violence.

J He traveled through India convincing people to support democracy.

> **Test-Taking Tip:** Always read the question and *all* of the answer choices carefully. Even if you do not remember the answer to a fact-based question such as this one, it is usually a good idea to eliminate answers that you know are incorrect and then guess from the remaining choices.

Major Oil Producers in the Middle East

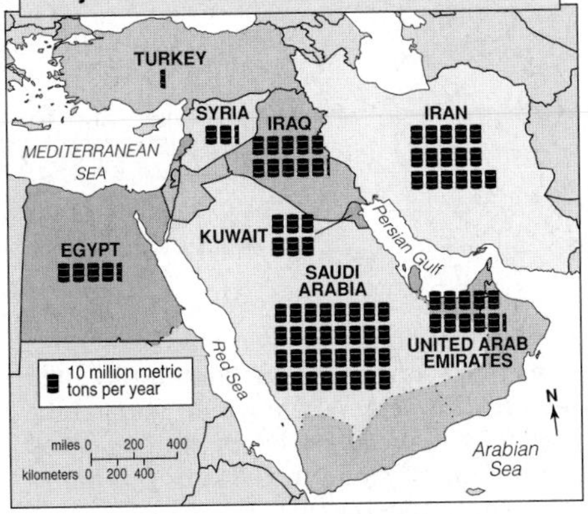

7. According to this map, how much oil does Kuwait produce annually?

A 6 metric tons

B 60 metric tons

C 6 million metric tons

D 60 million metric tons

> **Test-Taking Tip:** Use the map *legend*, or *key*, to understand the symbols used on the map. On this map, each barrel symbolizes a larger number to save space (and make them easier to count!). Make sure you double-check all the answer choices—this type of question can be tricky. However, all the information you need is on the map: you just need to *interpret* it.

STOP

5B History

The UN is discussed on pages 621–622. There it states that the UN's responsibilities *were to prevent war, lend money to poor countries, and provide them with medical care and better education.*

THE PRINCETON REVIEW — TEST-TAKING TIP

Students can often answer EXCEPT and NOT questions by association. Answers A, C, and D are all associated with the activities of the UN.

6H History

Gandhi is discussed on pages 634–635. There it states that he *did not believe in violence. He believed in civil disobedience.* These are the principles for which Gandhi is best known, so therefore, answer H is the best choice.

7J Economics

The map shows 6 barrels next to Kuwait. The legend indicates that each barrel represents 10 million metric tons of oil; therefore, the answer is 60 million metric tons (6×10 million).

THE PRINCETON REVIEW — TEST-TAKING TIP

Students should study all graphics carefully before answering a question. They should pay attention to keys or legends, labels, and titles.

Tested Objectives

Questions	Reading Objective
1, 2	Make comparisons
3	Evaluate information
4, 5	Identify central issues
6	Make inferences and generalizations
7	Analyze information

0:00 OUT OF TIME?

Selections from the Primary Sources Library are designed to supplement unit study by providing additional first-person accounts. If your teaching time is limited, you may use the selections as part of your quarterly or semester reviews.

Introduction

Have volunteers read and discuss the introduction to the Primary Sources Library. Have students complete the activities that follow to familiarize themselves with the types of primary sources.

Oral Histories

Work together with an English or language arts teacher to help students complete the following oral history activity. Provide the following guidelines: Interview a relative or friend who is much older than you. Your aim is to find out how much their lives differed from yours. Devise a list of interview questions, such as: What did you study in school? How did you and your friends spend your free time? What are some of the biggest changes you have seen in your lifetime? What was the most pressing world problem when you were my age?

Ask students to provide a transcript or written record of the interview. If a tape recorder is available, you may want students to record the interview. Have students discuss their findings in class.

PRIMARY SOURCES Library

WORKING WITH PRIMARY SOURCES

Suppose that you have been asked to write a report on changes in your community over the past 25 years. Where would you get the information you need to begin writing? You would draw upon two types of information—primary sources and secondary sources.

Definitions

Primary sources are often first-person accounts by someone who actually saw or lived through what is being described. In other words, if you see a fire or live through a great storm and then write about your experiences, you are creating a primary source. Diaries, journals, photographs, and eyewitness reports are examples of primary sources. **Secondary sources** are secondhand accounts. For instance, if your friend experiences a fire or storm and tells you about it, or if you read about a fire or storm in the newspaper and then you write about it, you are creating a secondary source. Textbooks, biographies, and histories are secondary sources.

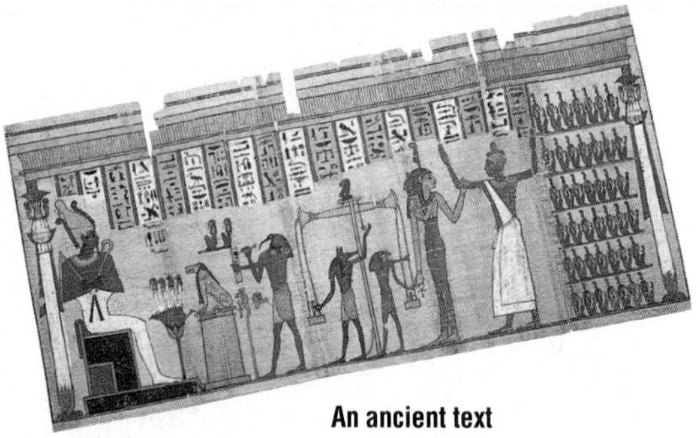

An ancient text

Checking Your Sources

When you read primary or secondary sources, you should analyze them to figure out if they are dependable or reliable. Historians usually prefer primary sources to secondary sources, but both can be reliable or unreliable, depending on the following factors.

Time Span

With primary sources, it is important to consider how long after the event occurred the primary source was written. Generally, the longer the time span between the event and the account, the less reliable the account is. As time passes, people often forget details and fill in gaps with events that never took place. Although we like to think we remember things exactly as they happened, the fact is we often remember them in a way that we wanted them to occur.

Reliability

Another factor to consider when evaluating a primary source is the writer's background and reliability. First, try to determine how this person knows about what he or she is writing. How much does he or she know? Is the writer being truthful? Is the account convincing?

Opinions

When evaluating a primary source, you should also decide whether the account has been influenced by emotion, opinion, or exaggeration. Writers can have reasons to distort the truth to suit their personal purposes. Ask yourself: Why did the person write the account? Do any key

672

TEACHER NOTES

After studying the introduction to the Primary Sources Library, students should be able to meet the following objectives:

- explain the difference between primary sources and secondary sources.
- identify the different types of primary sources.
- understand that primary sources offer a unique view of people and events in a particular era.

Opera glasses, late 1800s

words or expressions reveal the author's emotions or opinions? You may wish to compare the account with one written by another witness to the event. If the two accounts differ, ask yourself why they differ and which is more accurate.

Interpreting Primary Sources

To help you analyze a primary source, use the following steps:

- **Examine the origins of the document.**
  You need to determine if it is a primary source.
- **Find the main ideas.**
  Read the document and summarize the main ideas in your own words. These ideas may be fairly easy to identify in newspapers and journals, for example, but are much more difficult to find in poetry.
- **Reread the document.**
  Difficult ideas are not always easily understood on the first reading.
- **Use a variety of resources.**
  Form the habit of using the dictionary, the encyclopedia, and maps. These resources are tools to help you discover new ideas and knowledge and check the validity of sources.

Classifying Primary Sources

Primary sources fall into different categories:

Printed Publications

Printed publications include books such as autobiographies. Printed publications also include newspapers and magazines.

Personal Records

Personal records are accounts of events kept by an individual who is a participant in or witness to these events. Personal records include diaries, journals, and letters.

Oral Histories

Oral histories are chronicles, memoirs, myths, and legends that are passed along from one generation to another by word of mouth. Interviews are another form of oral history.

Songs and Poems

Songs and poems include works that express the personal thoughts and feelings or political or religious beliefs of the writer, usually using rhyming and rhythmic language.

Artifacts

Artifacts are objects such as tools or ornaments. Artifacts present information about a particular culture or a stage of technological development.

GO TO For additional primary sources, use the **World History Primary Source Document Library CD-ROM.**

TEACHER NOTES

Through the study of the selections in the Primary Sources Library and their accompanying questions and activities, students should be able to:

- find the main idea in the selections.
- analyze information in a variety of written texts in order to make inferences and generalizations.
- provide an interpretation of the material in their own words.

Songs and Poems

Ask students to write a poem about an important event in their lives. Suggest that the poem be in a standard form such as limerick or other specific rhyming scheme.

Personal Records

Tell students that a *journal* is a daily record of events kept by an individual who is a participant or witness to these events. Ask students to keep a journal of interesting events that they observe during a week's time. Encourage them to personalize the events by recording their own opinions or feelings of what they have witnessed.

Artifacts

To help students analyze artifacts, provide the following instructions: Find a primary source from your past—a photograph, a report card, an old newspaper clipping, your first baseball card, and so on. Bring this source into class, and explain why you kept it and what it shows about the time from which the item comes.

Printed Publications

To help students analyze printed publications, instruct them to read the first two paragraphs of the Preamble to the Declaration of Independence (found in the United States history text used in your school). Ask: What is the subject of these paragraphs? What do they tell you about the beliefs of the people who signed this document?

Block Schedule

Team Teaching These selections may be implemented in a team-teaching context, in conjunction with English/Language Arts.

Chapter Links

Use the primary sources selection on pages 674–675 to accompany the study of Unit 1. It provides students with the opportunity to extend their study of the following:

- Chapter 1, Section 5, "Archaeology," pages 25–30.
- Chapter 2, Section 1, "The Paleolithic Age," pages 33–40.

Reinforcing Vocabulary

Review the **Reader's Dictionary** with students to be sure they understand any unfamiliar terms. Call on a volunteer to explain what evidence of *bipedal* hominids Mary Leakey is studying in the photograph on page 675.

Background Information

Artifacts Nearly every family has a collection of artifacts that links it with past generations or with their own history. Have students talk with the oldest friends or relatives that they know and have them find out what unique or special thing they have saved from the past. Tell students to record a description of the object, its approximate age, and reasons the person kept it. If possible, encourage students to photograph or sketch the object. Have students share their findings in a bulletin board display entitled "Pieces of the Past."

PRIMARY SOURCES Library

UNIT 1

AFRICAN ORIGINS

The work of one family—the Leakeys—helped uncover some of the earliest chapters in human history. Louis B. Leakey, born in Kenya in 1903, started the work. He believed that human history began in Africa. He also believed that this history was far older than anyone had ever imagined. His wife, Mary Nicol Leakey, joined him in his work, along with the couple's son, Richard. Together they made some of the most exciting archaeological and anthropological discoveries of the past 100 years.

Reader's Dictionary

petrified ash volcanic dust that has turned into stone
hominid member of a group that includes human beings and early human-like creatures
retained kept
bipedal walking on two feet
tuff pieces of volcanic rock
relief contrast with the surrounding area
haunt to reappear constantly
trek a long journey, usually by foot
perilous dangerous

Printed Publications

Footprints in Time

The death of Louis Leakey in 1972 did not stop Mary and Richard Leakey from digging into the past. In 1978, Mary Leakey discovered a set of ancient footprints south of the Olduvai Gorge in present-day Tanzania. In a 1979 article for *National Geographic*, she describes a trail that carried her back in time.

This article . . . will cause yet another upheaval in the study of human origins. For in the gray, petrified ash . . . we have found hominid footprints that are remarkably similar to those of modern man. . . . Prints that were laid down an incredible 3,600,000 years ago! . . .

Two individuals, one larger, one smaller, had passed this way. . . . We have measured their footprints and the length of their stride. Was the larger one a male, the smaller one a female? Or was one mature, the other young? It is unlikely that we will ever know with certainty. . . .

The closeness of the two sets of prints indicates that their owners were not walking [side by side]. Other clues suggest that the hominids may have passed at different times. For example, the imprints of the smaller individual stand out clearly. The crispness of definition and sharp outlines convince me that they were left on a damp surface that retained the form of the foot.

On the other hand, the prints of the larger are blurred, as if he had shuffled or dragged his feet. In fact, I think that the surface when he passed was loose and dusty, hence the collapsed appearance of his prints. Nonetheless,

674

TEAM TEACHING STRATEGIES

Art Work together with an art teacher to help students illustrate the selection by Mary Leakey. Begin by telling students to imagine they are artists working for *National Geographic* magazine. They have been asked to design a picture showing what the African landscape might have looked like on the day the footprints discovered by Leakey were made some 3,600,000 years ago. Encourage students to do additional research to determine what the region may have been like. To get students started, point out that it was a time of great volcanic activity and that the two walkers probably could see at least one volcano smoldering in the distance.

luck favored us again; the bigger hominid left one absolutely clear print, probably on a patch of once damp ash.

What did these footprints tell us? First, they demonstrate once and for all that at least 3,600,000 years ago, in Pliocene times, what I believe to be man's direct ancestor walked fully upright with a bipedal, freestriding gait. Second, that the form of his foot was exactly the same as ours.

Sometimes, . . . I go out and watch the dust settle over the gray tuff with its eerie record of time long past. The slanting light of evening throws the hominid prints into sharp relief, so sharp that they could have been left this morning.

I cannot help but think about the distant creatures who made them. Where did they come from? Where were they going? We simply do not know. It has been suggested that they were merely crossing this scorched plain toward the greener ridges to the north. Perhaps so.

In any case, those footprints out of the deep past, left by the oldest known hominids, haunt the imagination. Across the gulf of time I can only wish them well on that prehistoric trek. It was, I believe, part of a greater and more perilous journey, one that . . . culminated in the emergence of modern man.

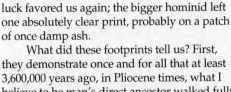

▲ Mary Leakey

Interpreting Primary Sources

1. What effect does Mary Leakey think her article will have?
2. Why does she feel this way?
3. How might a geographer describe the landscape at the time the footprints were made?
4. What does Mary Leakey mean when she says the footprints "haunt the imagination"?
5. What one important thing do you think the footprints revealed?

ACTIVITY

Writing a News Bulletin Write a 30-second news bulletin that a television or radio reporter might have given upon learning of Mary Leakey's discovery.

PRIMARY SOURCES Library

Portfolio Activity Have interested students research information on the Leakey family: Louis Leakey, Mary Leakey, and Richard Leakey. Then have them prepare a poster that illustrates this theme: "The Leakeys: Archaeology's First Family." Suggest that students use back issues of *National Geographic* magazine to find other stories written by or about the Leakeys.

Multiple Learning Styles

Intrapersonal While taking notes is a useful skill for all students, it is especially beneficial for students who have trouble keeping their attention focused on their reading. Inform students that taking notes helps them to identify important facts, organize information, and review for tests. Then direct students to take notes on the selection on pages 674–675. When students have completed the task, review their note-taking procedures and, if necessary, suggest ways to improve them.

ANSWERS TO INTERPRETING PRIMARY SOURCES

1. She thinks it "will cause another upheaval in the study of human origins."
2. She found footprints similar to those made by modern humans, but they were made more than 3,600,000 years ago. (She therefore suggests that humans may be much older than anyone imagined.)
3. Answers will vary, but a geographer would probably focus on the evidence of volcanic activity, particularly the amount of volcanic ash.
4. Students may suggest that Mary Leakey will always wonder who made these footprints, what they looked like, where they were headed, and so on.
5. sample responses: the great age of humans, the origins of early humans in Africa
Activity Bulletins should accurately describe the discovery, and should answer: *who? what? where? when? why?* and *how?*

PRIMARY SOURCES Library

Block Schedule

Team Teaching These selections may be implemented in a team-teaching context, in conjunction with English/Language Arts.

Chapter Links

Use the primary source selections on pages 676–677 to accompany the study of Unit 2. They provide students with the opportunity to extend their study of the following:

- Chapter 3, Section 2, "Later Mesopotamian Empires," pages 61–63.

Reinforcing Vocabulary

Review the **Reader's Dictionary** with students to be sure they understand any unfamiliar terms. Ask students what the word "justice" means to them.

Background Information

Symbols Point out that a *symbol* is a person, place, or object that has meaning in itself and also stands for something other than itself. Symbols communicate meaning even to those who cannot read. Refer students to the artifact from Hammurabi's Code on page 677. Ask: What symbols did the artist use to convey Hammurabi's importance? What did Hammurabi symbolize to the people of his empire?

PRIMARY SOURCES Library

UNIT 2

The Pursuit of Justice

Hammurabi's gift to civilization was his code of laws. Other rulers had enacted laws in the past, but Hammurabi was the first to collect them into a single written code. The code included nearly 300 legal decisions. Some were harsh—even brutal—by today's standards. However, the code made the state responsible for their enforcement. This was a great advance over a system in which people often took justice into their own hands. Under the Hammurabi Code, society began its long journey toward the ideal of "equal justice for all."

Reader's Dictionary

justified proven
commoner someone not of noble birth
thirtyfold thirty times (its value)
render pay
tenfold ten times (its value)
creditor person who has made a loan
interest fee charged on a loan
mina an ancient unit of weight
traffic trade
gored pierced with horns
plumbed tested or examined

Printed Publications

The Hammurabi Code

The Hammurabi Code touched on almost every aspect of life. The purpose of the code, said the prologue, was "to cause justice to prevail in the land, to destroy the wicked and the evil, that the strong may not oppress the weak." Here are some of the laws intended to achieve that goal.

1. If a man . . . bring a charge of murder against another man and has not justified himself, the accuser shall be put to death.

8. If a man has stolen ox or sheep . . . or pig or ship, whether from the temple or from the palace, he shall pay thirtyfold; if he stole from a commoner, he shall render tenfold. If the thief cannot pay, he shall be put to death.

15. If a man has helped a male or female palace slave, or a commoner's slave to escape out of the city gate, he shall be put to death.

21. If a man has broken into a house, he shall be killed . . . and walled in it.

48. If a man has a debt upon him and . . . the grain has not grown for lack of water, in that year he shall make no return of grain to his creditor . . . and he shall not pay interest for that year.

TEAM TEACHING STRATEGIES

Language Arts Work with a language arts teacher to introduce students to the meaning of *colloquial language,* or the everyday language we use in conversation. Then organize students into groups, and assign them to rewrite the laws in Hammurabi's Code so that they would be easy for a third grader to understand. Call on students to share their rewritten laws with the rest of the class.

Artifacts

The Vikings valued captured treasures. However, they also created their own beautiful works of art, including jewelry fashioned from precious metals seized in raids. This brooch shows the complicated designs for which the Vikings became famous.

Songs and Poems

Words of Praise

The Vikings celebrated their conquests in songs and verses written by *skalds*—professional poets hired by kings and nobles throughout Scandinavia.

Cattle die, kinsmen die,
one day you die yourself;
but the words of praise will not perish
when a man wins fair fame.

Interpreting Primary Sources

1. Why did the Vikings raid the villages and towns surrounding the monastery?
2. How did the Vikings avoid capture by the army raised by Abbot Hugo and the king?
3. In addition to Viking raids, what other problems did people living around the monastery face?
4. What do the lines written by a *skald* promise Vikings who win "fair fame"?
5. How did the Vikings use some of their plunder?

ACTIVITY

Writing a Song Imagine you are a *skald*. Write a song about a Viking expedition to explore the waters and lands to the west of Scandinavia.

PRIMARY SOURCES Library

Portfolio Activity After students have studied the monastery records, assign them to write entries that a Viking might have prepared for the same years and same events. Call on volunteers to read their entries aloud. Ask: How did the Viking view of this period in history differ from that of the abbot who kept the monastery records?

Multiple Learning Styles

Verbal/Linguistic Students with language difficulties may have difficulty distinguishing between essential and nonessential details. Explain that one way to identify essential details is to form questions to guide reading. Have students turn the title of this feature, "The Age of Viking Conquest," into a question. Then instruct them to find the essential details in the reading that answer this question.

ANSWERS TO INTERPRETING PRIMARY SOURCES

1. for booty and plunder
2. The Vikings split up and "scattered hither and yon." Then they made their way back to their ships and sailed away.
3. People around the monastery also suffered a famine and a lack of food for their animals.
4. that their great feats will be remembered forever
5. to create jewelry and other works of art
Activity Songs will vary, but details should reflect some of the actual expeditions, such as voyages to Greenland, mentioned on pages 304–308.

PRIMARY SOURCES Library

Block Schedule

Team Teaching These selections may be implemented in a team-teaching context, in conjunction with English/Language Arts.

Chapter Links

Use the primary source selections on pages 686–687 to accompany the study of Unit 7. They provide students with the opportunity to extend their study of the following:

- Chapter 21, Section 1, "Constantinople," pages 317–319.
- Chapter 21, Section 2, "Justinian I," pages 320–324.

Reinforcing Vocabulary

Review the **Reader's Dictionary** with students to be sure they understand any unfamiliar terms. Refer students to the artifact on page 687, and ask: Who is the *sovereign* shown in this detail from a Byzantine altar?

Background Information

Bias Remind students of the importance of detecting bias, or viewpoints that may affect a writer's interpretation of events or people. (You might have students reread the skill lesson on page 170.) Then ask students what bias Anna Commena might have in retelling the story of her father's reign. Why do students think historians might want to check other sources of information about Alexius I?

PRIMARY SOURCES Library

UNIT 7

Byzantine Women

The Byzantines valued intelligence, whether in a man or a woman. An emperor or noble might marry a woman as much for her education or political skills as for her royal birth. As a result, the women who belonged to the royal courts of the Byzantine Empire had a great deal of influence. Rarely did women elsewhere in the world exercise more power than the imperial women of Byzantium.

Reader's Dictionary

concealed kept hidden
confidant close friend
monastery religious community
endowed gifted
aptitude ability
sovereign ruler
reserved kept
ravaged damaged
undaunted fearless

Printed Publications

A Woman on the Throne

In 1081, an able general named Alexius Commenus captured Constantinople. As Emperor Alexius I, he defended the Byzantine Empire against attacks from invaders in both the east and the west. His daughter, Anna Commena, retold the story of his reign in a book called the *Alexiad* (uh lek' sē uhd). She begins her account by describing Alexius's decision to turn the government over to his mother Anna Dalassena. (The story refers to the Byzantine Empire as the Roman Empire.)

It was his desire that his mother should govern rather than himself, but . . . the plan had been concealed for fear that she, if she knew of it, might leave the palace. (Alexius was aware that she considered withdrawal to a monastery.) Nevertheless, in all matters however ordinary he did nothing without her advice: she became his confidant and co-partner in government. Gradually . . . he involved her more and more in state affairs; on occasions he even declared openly that without her brains and good judgement the Empire would not survive. . . .

The truth is that Anna Dalassena was in any case endowed with a fine intellect and possessed besides a really first-class aptitude for government. . . . For my grandmother had an exceptional grasp of public affairs, with a genius for organization and government; she was capable, in fact, of managing not only the

686

TEAM TEACHING STRATEGIES

Language Arts Invite a language arts teacher to explain the meaning of *memoirs*—a biography or historical account of events written from personal experience. Then assign students to imagine they are Empress Theodora. She has decided to compose her memoirs on the reign of her husband, Justinian I. Brainstorm with students a possible title for the book. Then assign students to compose a list of topics that Theodora might include. Have one group of students use this list to compose the memoirs, while another group of students designs the illustrations to accompany the writings.

Roman Empire, but every other empire under the sun as well. . . .

But, as I was saying, once he seized power my father reserved for himself the struggles and hard labour of war, while . . . he made her the sovereign. . . . I can sum up the whole situation thus: he was in theory the emperor, but she had the real power. She was the legislator, the complete organizer and governor. . . .

Such were the events that marked the beginning of the reign. . . . Alexius knew the Empire was almost at its last gasp. The east was being horribly ravaged by the Turks; the west was in bad condition. . . . The emperors before him, having little knowledge of war and military affairs, had reduced Roman prestige to a minimum. Indeed, I have heard it said by men who were soldiers themselves, and by some of the older men, that no other state in living memory had reached such depths of misery. Conditions were desperate then for the emperor. . . . However, being not only a courageous man and undaunted, but having excellent experiences in war, he wanted to restore his Empire. . . .

Artifacts Some empresses were not handed power—they took it. This detail from an altar shows Empress Irene, the Byzantine Empire's first woman ruler. Supported by the generals, she seized the throne from her only son and ruled from 797 to 802. Although she held power for only five years, Irene put in place much-needed financial reforms.

Interpreting Primary Sources

1. Why did Alexius conceal his plans to turn government over to his mother?
2. How did Anna Dalassena help her son to strengthen the Byzantine Empire?
3. What do these two sources of information—the *Alexiad* and the altar artifact—tell you about the role of women in the Byzantine Empire?

ACTIVITY

Writing a News Bulletin Write a short news bulletin announcing Alexius's decision to put his mother in charge of government while he fought invaders along the Byzantine borders.

PRIMARY SOURCES
Library

Portfolio Activity Have students research women rulers in the past 50 years. Direct them to present their findings in short, illustrated biographies. Post these on the bulletin board. Then discuss whether students think they can expect to see a woman president of the United States in their lifetime.

Multiple Learning Styles

Verbal/Linguistic Students with problems decoding unfamiliar words often skip over them. Many times, however, they are successful in comprehending these words based on the context of the sentences. Ask students to scan "A Woman on the Throne" for words with which they are unfamiliar. Then ask them to write these words in their notebooks and to guess their meanings based on context. Have students check their answers in a dictionary, making any necessary corrections.

ANSWERS TO INTERPRETING PRIMARY SOURCES

1. because he feared that she might leave the palace and withdraw to a monastery
2. Answers will vary, but Anna Dalassena ruled the empire while her son fought to restore the empire to its former glory. She passed laws, governed, and did everything that any emperor would do.
3. Answers will vary, but most students will conclude that women played an important role in the government of the Byzantine Empire.
Activity News bulletins will vary but should state the qualifications of Anna Dalassena to rule in Alexius's absence.

PRIMARY SOURCES Library

Block Schedule

Team Teaching These selections may be implemented in a team-teaching context, in conjunction with English/Language Arts.

Chapter Links

Use the primary source selections on pages 688–689 to accompany the study of Unit 8. They provide students with the opportunity to extend their study of the following:

- Chapter 24, Section 2, "The Nobility," pages 369–373.
- Chapter 24, Section 4, "The Manor," pages 375–378.

Reinforcing Vocabulary

Review the **Reader's Dictionary** with students to be sure they understand any unfamiliar terms. Ask students how peasants helped nobles keep their *coffers* filled. *(by tilling the land and providing services that nobles might otherwise have had to buy with money from their treasuries)*

Background Information

Consonance Review with students what *vowels* and *consonants* are. Point out that *consonance* is the repetition of consonant sounds in a line of poetry or a song. Have students find the consonance in the poem on page 689. (For example: "I have no penny," said Piers, "to buy pullets, . . .")

PRIMARY SOURCES Library

UNIT 8

The Medieval Manor

During medieval times, nobody had an easy life. However, nobles and knights enjoyed more benefits than the peasants who worked the land. In exchange for protection, peasants kept a lord's castle well supplied with food, while they themselves lived on little or went hungry.

Reader's Dictionary

alms gifts for the poor
coffers treasury
whence from which
sup eat dinner
pullets young chickens
curds solid substance formed when milk sours; used to make cheese
hovels small, dirty, poorly built houses
charged made responsible for
spare save
meal powder made from grain
porridge hot cereal

Personal Records

A Noble Household

Nobles often threw open their castles to travelers, who sought safety and a place to rest. In this passage, a French traveler describes his stay with a count, a high-ranking noble with close ties to the king.

I shall now tell you several particulars respecting the count and his household. . . . He had, every day, distributed, as alms at his gate, . . . small coin, to all comers. He was liberal and courteous in his gifts, and well knew how to take and how to give back. He loved dogs above all other animals; and during summer and winter amused himself much with hunting. . . . He chose twelve of his most able subjects to receive and administer his finances. . . . He had certain coffers in his apartment, whence he took money to give to different knights, squires, or gentlemen, . . . for none ever left him without a gift. . . . When he quitted his chamber at midnight for supper, twelve servants bore each a lighted torch before him. The hall was full of knights and squires, and there were plenty of tables laid out for any who chose to sup. No one spoke to him at table unless he first began the conversation. He ate heartily . . . [and] had great pleasure in hearing minstrels. . . . In short, . . . though I had before been in several courts, I never was at one which pleased me more. . . .

688

TEAM TEACHING STRATEGIES

Science Work with a science teacher to explain how each of these ideas or inventions helped increase agricultural production during the Middle Ages: the three-field system, heavy iron plows (mounted on wheels), and padded horse collars. Point out to students that each of these developments helped ensure a manor's self-sufficiency. Assign students to create before-and-after posters showing the changes that these inventions brought to agriculture. A possible source of information is *Cathedral, Forge, and Waterwheel: Technology and Invention in the Middle Ages*, by Frances and Joseph Gies, HarperCollins Publishers, 1994.

own carriage full of people behind, this brave little she-dragon of ours flew on. Farther on she met three carts, which being fastened in front of her she pushed on before her without the slightest delay or difficulty; when I add that this pretty little creature can run with equal facility either backwards or forwards, I believe I have given you an account of all her capacities.

Oral Histories

A Horse Race

In 1829, American inventor Peter Cooper tested his new steam-powered locomotive—the *Tom Thumb*—on some track laid down by the Baltimore and Ohio Railroad. The following year, a horse-drawn railcar challenged the *Tom Thumb* to a race. An observer later recalled the scene in a history of railroads compiled by the Baltimore and Ohio Railroad.

The horse was perhaps a quarter of a mile ahead before the engine started. The blower whistled, the steam blew off in vapory clouds, and the pace increased. Then the engine passed the horse, and a great hurrah hailed the victory. But it was not repeated. The engine began to wheeze and pant. Although the steam again did its best, the horse was too far ahead to be overtaken. But the real victory was with Mr. Cooper.

Interpreting Primary Sources

1. What impressed Frances Kemble about the new steam-powered locomotive?
2. What clues in the reading show that she viewed the engine as an "iron horse"?
3. What was the outcome of the race between the horse-drawn railcar and the *Tom Thumb*?
4. What do you think the observer meant by the remark that the "real victory was with Mr. Cooper"?

ACTIVITY

Writing a Diary Entry Imagine you are one of the passengers aboard the Liverpool-Manchester Railway shown in the picture on this page. Describe your trip in the form of a diary entry. Be sure to indicate whether you are a first-class or a second-class passenger and how you feel about your choice of railcar.

Portfolio Activity Assign students to brainstorm headlines that a newspaper might have run about the race between the *Tom Thumb* and a horse. Then have students use these headlines to write a short news article about the event. Point out that reporters try to get all the important facts to the reader as quickly as possible. The first paragraph of the story usually answers almost all of the six question words commonly used by reporters: *Who? What? Where? When? Why? How?*

Multiple Learning Styles

Verbal/Linguistic Some students who have difficulty retaining information or focusing their attention may benefit by audio versions of primary source selections. Request some of your more able readers to record the selections on a tape recorder. Then play the tape for the class as a whole. After every few sentences, turn off the tape recorder and say: "Tell me what you just heard." Repeat this process until the entire selection is read.

ANSWERS TO INTERPRETING PRIMARY SOURCES

1. Answers will vary, but most students will point out the locomotive's great speed, which made Kemble feel like she was "flying."
2. Clues include Kemble's descriptions of locomotive parts. She compares wheels to "feet" and pistons to "legs." She also describes the locomotive as a "snorting little animal" that she felt like patting.
3. In the end, the horse won.
4. Answers will vary, but the race showed the potential of the locomotive, which had initially outrun the horse.
Activity Diary entries will vary but should reflect the different conditions of travel and perhaps some of the enthusiasm that most railroad riders felt at the time.

Block Schedule

Team Teaching These selections may be implemented in a team-teaching context, in conjunction with English/Language Arts.

Chapter Links

Use the primary source selections on pages 694–695 to accompany the study of Unit 11. They provide students with the opportunity to extend their study of the following:

- Chapter 36, Section 3, "Asia," pages 584–591.

Note: You might also use this feature as a bridge into the discussion of Indian independence in Chapter 38, beginning of Section 3, "Developing Nations," pages 634–635.

Reinforcing Vocabulary

Review the **Reader's Dictionary** with students to be sure they understand any unfamiliar terms. How might an opponent of British imperialism have used the postcard on page 695 as evidence of British *despotism?*

Background Information

Persuasion Point out that persuasive writing attempts to sway the reader to think or act in a particular way. Ask students to identify the course of action promoted in this selection. Then ask: Which argument used by the writer do you think is the most persuasive?

UNIT 11

BRITISH INDIA

The British brought many things to India, including a unified government and a railroad system that spanned a subcontinent. They made it possible for Indians to receive a British education and trained Indians as *civil servants*—the name given to people who work for the government. For the most part, however, the British looked down on Indian culture and denied Indians positions of importance. This attitude would be the undoing of British rule in India.

Reader's Dictionary

feeble weak
natives people born and raised in a place; in this case, the people of India
excluded left out
sent out graduated
aught all
material physical
convulsion upheaval
despotism cruel use of power

Printed Publications

Stirrings of Nationalism

An early Indian nationalist named Dadabhai Naoroji admired British self-government. He feared, however, that colonial policies might prevent this system from ever coming to India. In 1880, he described these policies and their effect on India in a strongly worded memo to British officials.

Europeans occupy almost all the higher places in every department of government. . . . While in India they acquire India's money, experience, and wisdom, and when they go they carry both away with them, leaving India so much poorer. . . . Thus India is left without, and cannot have, those elders in wisdom and experience who in every country are the natural guides of the rising generations. . . .

Every European is isolated from the people around him. . . . For any . . . guidance or sympathy with the people, he might just as well be living in the moon. The people know not him, and he knows not nor cares for the people. Some honorable exceptions do now and then make an effort to do some good, . . . but in the very nature of things, these efforts are always feeble . . . and of little permanent effect. . . .

The Europeans are not the natural leaders of the people. They do not belong to the people. They cannot . . . sympathize with their joys or griefs. . . . There may be very few social institutions started by Europeans in which natives, however fit and desirous to join, are not deliberately and insultingly excluded. The Europeans . . . make themselves strangers in every way. . . .

TEAM TEACHING STRATEGIES

Art When students have analyzed the memo written by Naoroji, challenge them to convert his message into the form of a political cartoon. Work with the art teacher to present some of the tools commonly used by cartoonists—caricature, symbols, labels, and so on. When students are done, have them exchange cartoons for editorial review. Ask: What is the main issue addressed by this cartoon? What is the artist's opinion of this issue? What techniques has the artist used to get his or her opinion across?

. . . The thousands [of Indians] that are being sent out by the universities every year find themselves in a most [difficult] position. There is no place for them in their motherland. They may beg in the streets or break stones on the roads, for aught the rulers seem to care. . . .

. . . If the present material and moral destruction of India continues, a great convulsion must inevitably arise by which either India will be more and more crushed under the iron heel of despotism and destruction, or may succeed in shattering the destroying hand and power [that holds it down]. Far, far is it from my earnest prayer and hope that such should be the result of the British rule.

Artifacts Like most visitors to a foreign land, the British sent postcards and bought souvenirs that reminded them of India. The postcard on the left from the 1890s shows a British traveler in India. The photo below shows the Victoria Memorial, built by the British in Calcutta.

Interpreting Primary Sources

1. What things does Naoroji say the British are taking from India?
2. Why does he feel the British are not the "natural leaders" of India?
3. What prediction does he make for the future if Great Britain does not change its policies?
4. What do the postcard and photograph show about the benefits and drawbacks of British rule?

ACTIVITY

Designing a Postcard Design a postcard that an Indian artist might create to capture some aspect of life in British India.

PRIMARY SOURCES Library

Portfolio Activity Assign students to draft a memo that a British official might have sent back to Naoroji. The memo should address or refute his arguments, pointing out the benefits of British rule. (Award extra credit to those students who do additional research on British colonial policy in India.)

Multiple Learning Styles

Visual/Spatial Some students may need concrete examples to understand abstract concepts such as *nationalism.* Ask students to look up a definition of this word in the dictionary. Then brainstorm some of the symbols that stir a sense of nationalism among people in the United States. *(the flag, the national anthem, and so on)* Assign interested students to research some of the national symbols adopted by India upon its independence. For example, what does the Indian flag look like?

ANSWERS TO INTERPRETING PRIMARY SOURCES

1. India's money, wisdom, and experience
2. because they isolate themselves from the people; because they cannot sympathize or understand the concerns of native-born Indians
3. that there will be a "great convulsion," or uprising, in which Indians will either throw off British rule or be subjected to even greater despotism
4. Sample response: Although the British used their wealth to initiate great building projects, they also kept Indians in a position of servitude.

Activity Postcards will vary but should accurately reflect the benefits and drawbacks of imperialism as it existed in India.

PRIMARY SOURCES Library

Block Schedule

Team Teaching These selections may be implemented in a team-teaching context, in conjunction with English/Language Arts.

Chapter Links

Use the primary source selections on pages 696–697 to accompany the study of Unit 12. They provide students with the opportunity to extend their study of the following:

- Chapter 39, Section 2, "World Challenges," pages 652–660.
- Chapter 39, Section 3, "The World Today," pages 660–666.

Note: You might also use this feature to extend information in Chapter 36, Section 2, "Africa," pages 580–584.

Reinforcing Vocabulary

Review the **Reader's Dictionary** with students to be sure they understand any unfamiliar terms. Ask students what type of political *domination* Nelson Mandela spent his life resisting.

Background

Purpose Explain that *purpose* is the intent to explain, persuade, or inform. An author may have more than one purpose. Have students read President Bush's speech to Congress after the attacks on New York City and Washington, D.C. Ask them to identify the purpose of his speech. *(Students may note that he was trying to justify why the United States and other countries should fight terrorism.)*

PRIMARY SOURCES Library

UNIT 12

EQUALITY AND FREEDOM

On June 11, 1964, a South African judge sentenced Nelson Mandela and seven others to life in prison. They opposed apartheid, the system that denied black South Africans their rights. South Africa bowed to world pressure and freed Mandela on February 11, 1990. By the end of the century, a new South African government would be organized based on freedom and equality. On September 11, 2001, terrorists attacked the World Trade Center in New York City and the Pentagon in Washington, D.C., killing thousands of people. In the twenty-first century, the United States and other nations face the challenge of fighting terrorism to preserve freedom.

Reader's Dictionary

domination authority over others
extremism the holding of views that differ a great degree from the majority
perverts to give a wrong meaning to
humanitarian committed to improving the lives of other people
pluralism society with different ethnic and religious groups
tolerance acceptance of and fairness toward people who hold different views
falter to hesitate or be uncertain

Printed Publications

"I Am Prepared to Die"

The following is a portion of a speech that Nelson Mandela delivered in his own defense before being sentenced to life in prison. It is considered one of the great democratic speeches in world history.

During my lifetime I have dedicated myself to this struggle of the African people. I have fought against white domination, and I have fought against black domination. I have cherished the ideal of a democratic and free society in which all persons live together in harmony and with equal opportunities. It is an ideal which I hope to live for and to achieve. But if needs be, it is an ideal for which I am prepared to die.

Printed Publications

Address to Congress

On September 20, 2001, President George W. Bush addressed Congress, nine days after New York City and Washington, D.C., were shaken by suicide aircraft attacks.

On September the eleventh, enemies of freedom committed an act of war against our country. Americans have known wars—but for the past 136 years, they have been wars on foreign soil, except for one Sunday in 1941 [the attack on Pearl Harbor]. Americans have known the casualties of war—but not at the center of a great city on a peaceful morning. Americans

TEAM TEACHING STRATEGIES

Art Invite an art teacher to help students make a collage showing different images that reflect equality and freedom. Students should use the Internet, newspapers, and magazines to find photographs that they feel illustrate the concepts. (Students may want to copy the images shown in newspapers and magazines.) Images may show people voting, demonstrating peacefully, or attending school. After students have organized their photographs and pasted them on poster board, ask volunteers to describe their collages to the class. Be sure that students discuss how the images relate to equality and freedom.

have known surprise attacks—but never before on thousands of civilians. All of this was brought upon us in a single day—and night fell on a different world, a world where freedom itself is under attack. . . .

The terrorists [who carried out the attack] practice a fringe form of Islamic extremism that has been rejected by Muslim scholars and the vast majority of Muslim clerics—a fringe movement that perverts the peaceful teachings of Islam. . . .

This group [al-Qaeda] and its leader, a person named Osama bin Laden, are linked to many other organizations in different countries. . . . The leadership of al-Qaeda has great influence in Afghanistan and supports the Taliban regime in controlling most of that country. . . .

The United States respects the people of Afghanistan—after all, we are currently its largest source of humanitarian aid—but we condemn the Taliban regime.

[The terrorists] hate what we see here in this chamber—a democratically elected government. Their leaders are self-appointed. They hate our freedoms—our freedom of religion, our freedom of speech, our freedom to vote and assemble and disagree with each other. . . .

This is not, however, just America's fight. And what is at stake is not just America's freedom. This is the world's fight. This is civilization's fight. This is the fight of all who believe in progress and pluralism, tolerance, and freedom. . . .

▲ President George W. Bush, center

The civilized world is rallying to America's side. They understand that if this terror goes unpunished, their own cities, their own citizens my be next. Terror, unanswered, can not only bring down buildings, it can threaten the stability of legitimate governments. And we will not allow it. . . .

I ask you to uphold the values of America, and remember why so many have come here. We are in a fight for our principles, and our first responsibility is to live by them. No one should be singled out for unfair treatment or unkind words because of their ethnic background or religious faith. . . .

Great harm has been done to us. We have suffered great loss. And in our grief and anger we have found our mission and our moment. Freedom and fear are at war. The advance of human freedom—the achievement of our time, and the great hope of every time—now depends on us. Our Nation—this generation—will lift a dark threat of violence from our people and our future. We will rally the world to this cause, by our efforts and by our courage. We will not tire, we will not falter, and we will not fail.

Interpreting Primary Sources

1. What kind of government did Nelson Mandela say he wanted in 1964?
2. What was so unusual about the attacks that it made President Bush say that "night fell on a different world"?
3. Why does the President believe other nations should help in the fight against terrorism?

ACTIVITY

Writing a Song Write a song that expresses the views found in President Bush's speech to Congress.

PRIMARY SOURCES
Library

Portfolio Activity Assign students to write an acrostic poem about Nelson Mandela, in which each letter of his name forms the first letter of a line in the poem. (To get students started, you might provide this example for the letter "N": *Never gave up his struggle against apartheid.)*

Multiple Learning Styles

Intrapersonal Have students interview five people to learn how they first heard about the September 11, 2001 terrorist attacks and what their initial reactions were. Students should record their interviews using a tape recorder—after asking the interviewees' permission. Ask volunteers to play their tapes for the class, using the recordings as a springboard to discuss how these acts of terrorism affected people's lives.

ANSWERS TO INTERPRETING PRIMARY SOURCES

1. Nelson Mandela wanted a government free from domination by either whites or blacks and a government in which all persons had equal opportunities.
2. The attacks occurred within the United States and targeted civilians rather than military personnel.
3. President Bush argues that if other countries do not fight terrorism, their own citizens and cities may be the next to be attacked. He also states that terrorism threatens the stability of legitimate governments.
Activity Songs will vary but may include ideas about freedom, tolerance, and world peace.

Reference Atlas

NATIONAL GEOGRAPHIC

ATLAS KEY

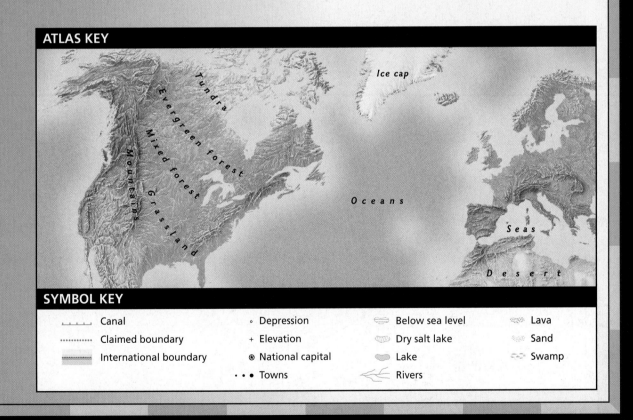

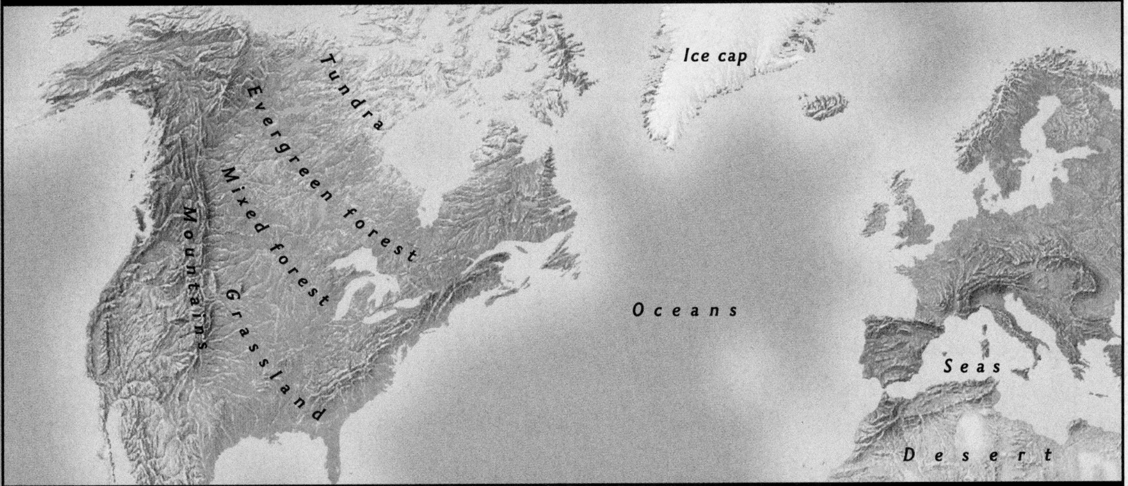

SYMBOL KEY

- Canal
- Claimed boundary
- International boundary
- Depression
- Elevation
- National capital
- Towns
- Below sea level
- Dry salt lake
- Lake
- Rivers
- Lava
- Sand
- Swamp

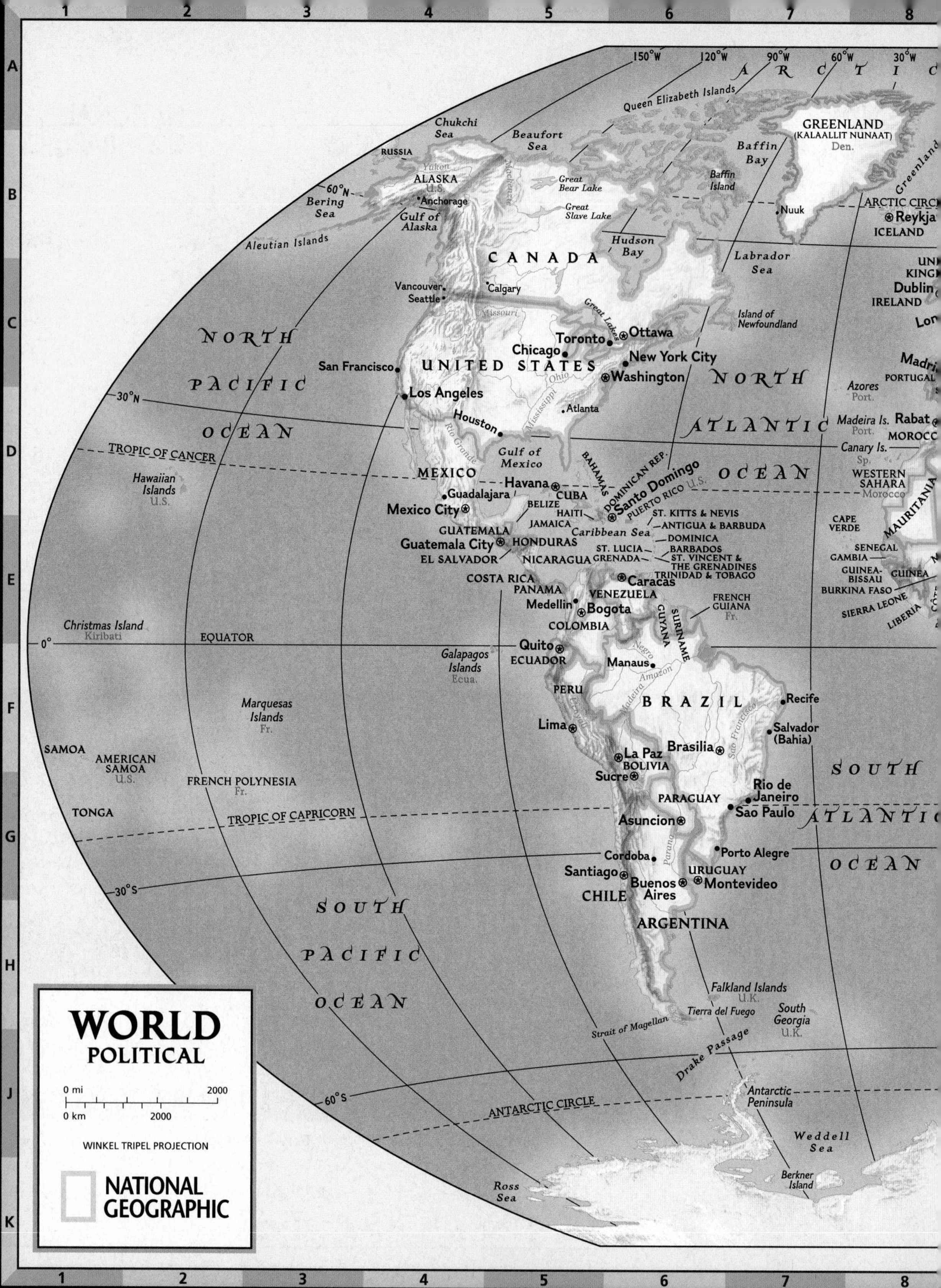
WORLD
POLITICAL
0 mi 2000
0 km 2000
WINKEL TRIPEL PROJECTION
NATIONAL GEOGRAPHIC
150°W
120°W
90°W
60°W
30°W
60°N
30°N
0°
30°S
60°S
ARCTIC
Queen Elizabeth Islands
GREENLAND
(KALAALLIT NUNAAT)
Den.
Baffin Bay
Baffin Island
Nuuk
ARCTIC CIRCLE
Reykja
ICELAND
Chukchi Sea
Beaufort Sea
RUSSIA
Yukon
ALASKA
U.S.
Anchorage
Bering Sea
Gulf of Alaska
Aleutian Islands
Great Bear Lake
Great Slave Lake
Hudson Bay
Labrador Sea
CANADA
Vancouver
Seattle
Calgary
Missouri
Great Lakes
Ottawa
Toronto
Chicago
New York City
Washington
UNITED STATES
Ohio
Mississippi
San Francisco
Los Angeles
Atlanta
Houston
Rio Grande
Gulf of Mexico
Island of Newfoundland
Dublin
IRELAND
Madri
PORTUGAL
Azores
Port.
Madeira Is.
Port.
Rabat
MOROCC
Canary Is.
Sp.
WESTERN SAHARA
Morocco
MAURITANIA
CAPE VERDE
SENEGAL
GAMBIA
GUINEA-BISSAU
GUINEA
BURKINA FASO
SIERRA LEONE
LIBERIA
NORTH PACIFIC OCEAN
NORTH ATLANTIC OCEAN
TROPIC OF CANCER
Hawaiian Islands
U.S.
MEXICO
Guadalajara
Mexico City
Havana
CUBA
BAHAMAS
DOMINICAN REP.
Santo Domingo
PUERTO RICO
U.S.
HAITI
JAMAICA
BELIZE
GUATEMALA
Guatemala City
HONDURAS
EL SALVADOR
NICARAGUA
COSTA RICA
PANAMA
Caribbean Sea
ST. KITTS & NEVIS
ANTIGUA & BARBUDA
DOMINICA
ST. LUCIA
BARBADOS
GRENADA
ST. VINCENT & THE GRENADINES
TRINIDAD & TOBAGO
Caracas
VENEZUELA
Medellín
Bogota
COLOMBIA
GUYANA
SURINAME
FRENCH GUIANA
Fr.
Christmas Island
Kiribati
EQUATOR
Quito
ECUADOR
Galapagos Islands
Ecua.
Manaus
Negro
Amazon
Madeira
PERU
BRAZIL
Recife
Salvador (Bahia)
Lima
Marquesas Islands
Fr.
SAMOA
AMERICAN SAMOA
U.S.
FRENCH POLYNESIA
Fr.
TONGA
La Paz
BOLIVIA
Sucre
Brasilia
Sao Francisco
PARAGUAY
Rio de Janeiro
Sao Paulo
TROPIC OF CAPRICORN
Asuncion
Parana
Cordoba
Porto Alegre
Santiago
URUGUAY
Buenos Aires
Montevideo
CHILE
ARGENTINA
SOUTH ATLANTIC OCEAN
SOUTH PACIFIC OCEAN
Falkland Islands
U.K.
Tierra del Fuego
Strait of Magellan
South Georgia
U.K.
Drake Passage
Antarctic Peninsula
ANTARCTIC CIRCLE
Weddell Sea
Berkner Island
Ross Sea

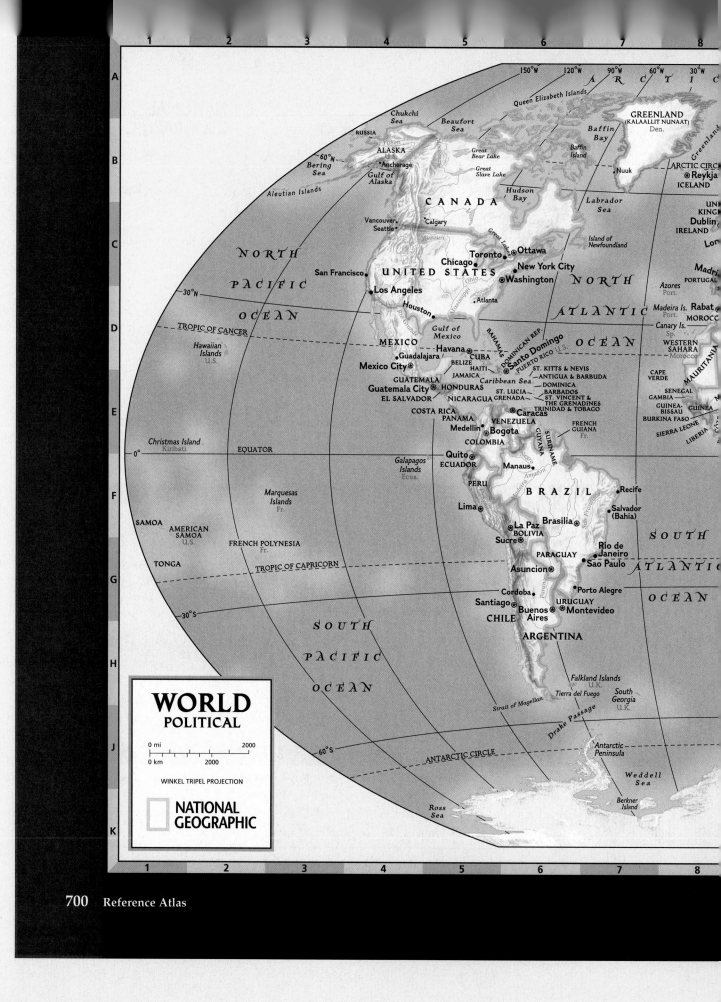

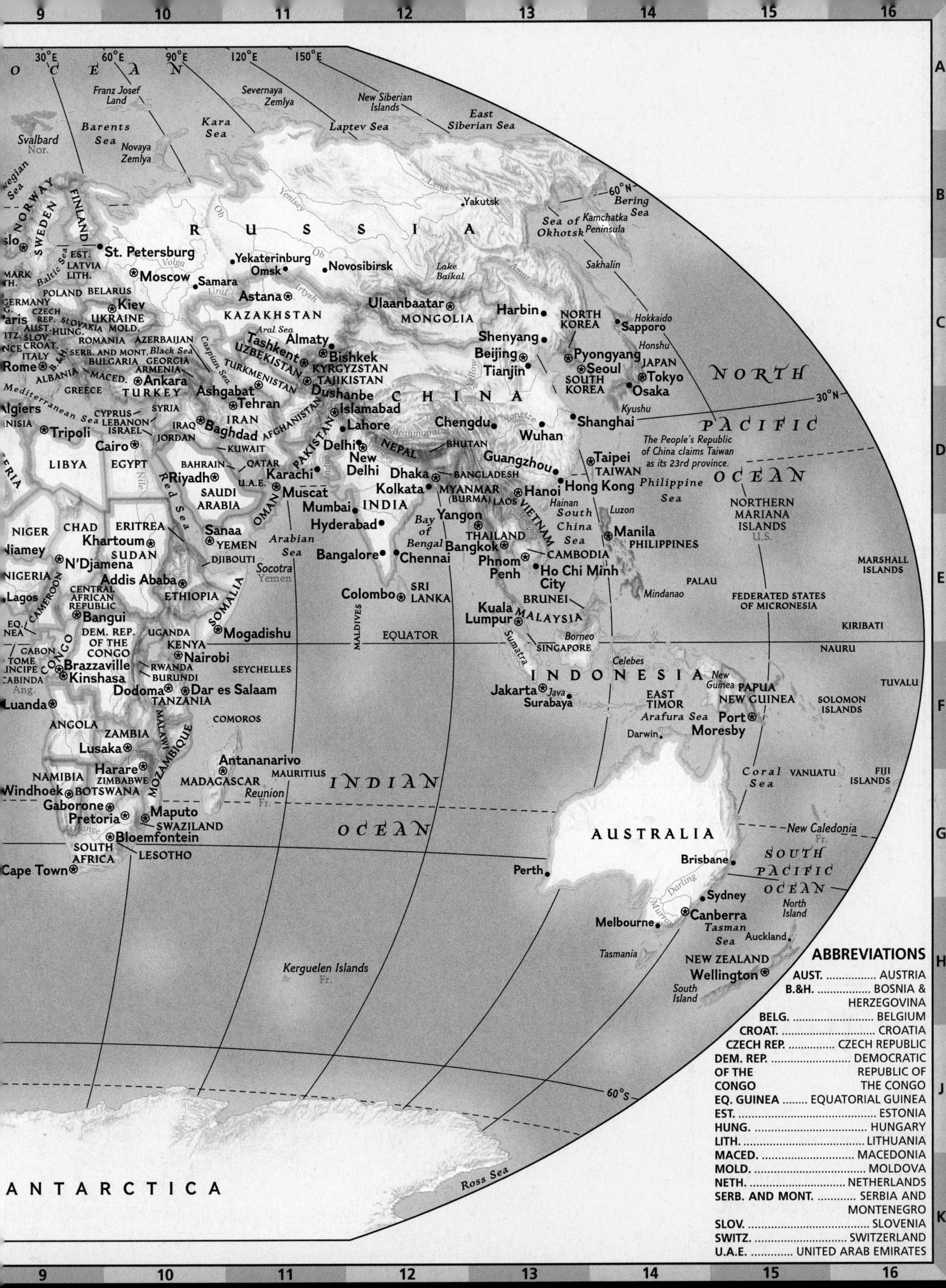

ABBREVIATIONS

AUST.	AUSTRIA
B.&H.	BOSNIA & HERZEGOVINA
BELG.	BELGIUM
CROAT.	CROATIA
CZECH REP.	CZECH REPUBLIC
DEM. REP. OF THE CONGO	DEMOCRATIC REPUBLIC OF THE CONGO
EQ. GUINEA	EQUATORIAL GUINEA
EST.	ESTONIA
HUNG.	HUNGARY
LITH.	LITHUANIA
MACED.	MACEDONIA
MOLD.	MOLDOVA
NETH.	NETHERLANDS
SERB. AND MONT.	SERBIA AND MONTENEGRO
SLOV.	SLOVENIA
SWITZ.	SWITZERLAND
U.A.E.	UNITED ARAB EMIRATES

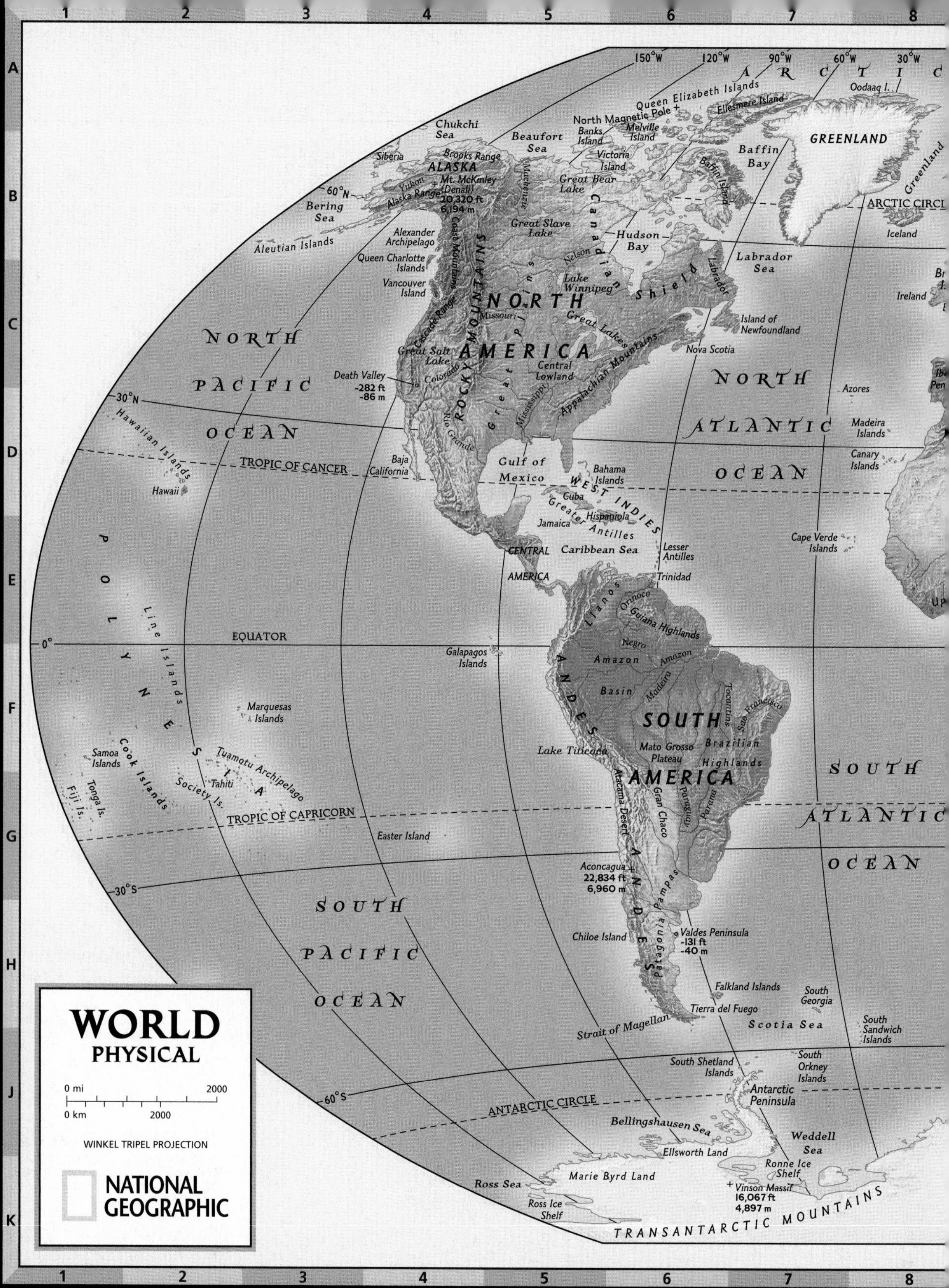
WORLD
PHYSICAL
0 mi 2000
0 km 2000
WINKEL TRIPEL PROJECTION
NATIONAL GEOGRAPHIC
1 2 3 4 5 6 7 8
A B C D E F G H J K
150°W 120°W 90°W 60°W 30°W
ARCTIC
Oodaaq I.
Queen Elizabeth Islands
Ellesmere Island
North Magnetic Pole
Banks Island
Melville Island
Victoria Island
GREENLAND
Greenland
Chukchi Sea
Beaufort Sea
Siberia
Brooks Range
ALASKA
Yukon
Alaska Range
Mt. McKinley (Denali) 20,320 ft 6,194 m
60°N
Bering Sea
Aleutian Islands
Mackenzie
Great Bear Lake
Baffin Bay
Baffin Island
ARCTIC CIRCLE
Iceland
Great Slave Lake
Hudson Bay
Alexander Archipelago
Coast Mountains
Queen Charlotte Islands
Vancouver Island
Nelson
Canadian Shield
Labrador
Labrador Sea
Lake Winnipeg
Ireland
NORTH AMERICA
ROCKY MOUNTAINS
Great Plains
Cascade Range
Missouri
Great Lakes
Island of Newfoundland
Great Salt Lake
Colorado
Central Lowland
Appalachian Mountains
Nova Scotia
NORTH PACIFIC OCEAN
Death Valley -282 ft -86 m
NORTH ATLANTIC OCEAN
Azores
Madeira Islands
Canary Islands
30°N
Hawaiian Islands
Rio Grande
Mississippi
Baja California
Gulf of Mexico
Bahama Islands
TROPIC OF CANCER
Hawaii
WEST INDIES
Cuba
Greater Antilles
Hispaniola
Jamaica
Cape Verde Islands
CENTRAL AMERICA
Caribbean Sea
Lesser Antilles
Trinidad
POLYNESIA
Line Islands
Llanos
Orinoco
Guiana Highlands
0°
EQUATOR
Galapagos Islands
Negro
Amazon Basin
Amazon
Madeira
Tocantins
São Francisco
ANDES
Marquesas Islands
SOUTH AMERICA
Lake Titicaca
Mato Grosso Plateau
Brazilian Highlands
Samoa Islands
Cook Islands
Tuamotu Archipelago
Tahiti
Society Is.
Tonga Is.
Fiji Is.
SOUTH ATLANTIC OCEAN
Atacama Desert
Gran Chaco
Paraguay
Paraná
TROPIC OF CAPRICORN
Easter Island
Aconcagua 22,834 ft 6,960 m
30°S
Pampas
SOUTH PACIFIC OCEAN
Chiloe Island
Valdes Peninsula -131 ft -40 m
Patagonia
Falkland Islands
South Georgia
Tierra del Fuego
Strait of Magellan
Scotia Sea
South Sandwich Islands
South Shetland Islands
South Orkney Islands
60°S
Antarctic Peninsula
ANTARCTIC CIRCLE
Bellingshausen Sea
Weddell Sea
Ellsworth Land
Ronne Ice Shelf
Marie Byrd Land
Ross Sea
Vinson Massif 16,067 ft 4,897 m
Ross Ice Shelf
TRANSANTARCTIC MOUNTAINS

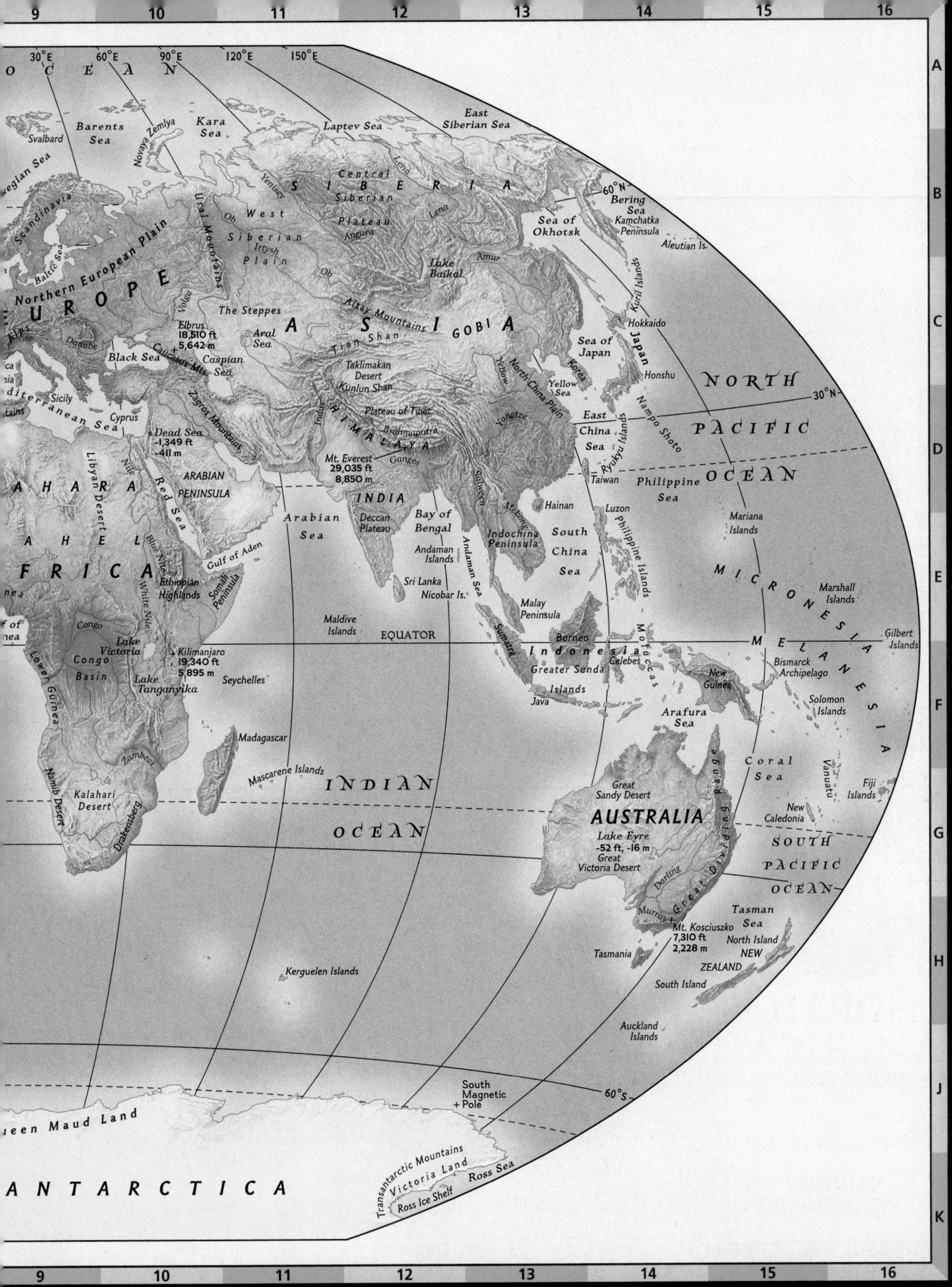
9
10
11
12
13
14
15
16
A
B
C
D
E
F
G
H
J
K
30°E
60°E
90°E
120°E
150°E
OCEAN
Svalbard
Barents Sea
Novaya Zemlya
Kara Sea
Laptev Sea
East Siberian Sea
Norwegian Sea
Scandinavia
Baltic Sea
Northern European Plain
EUROPE
Alps
Danube
Volga
Ural Mountains
Ob
West Siberian Plain
Irtysh
Yenisey
Central Siberian Plateau
SIBERIA
Angara
Lena
60°N
Bering Sea
Kamchatka Peninsula
Aleutian Is.
Sea of Okhotsk
Lake Baikal
Amur
Kuril Islands
Hokkaido
Japan
Honshu
Sea of Japan
Korea
Yellow Sea
Yellow
North China Plain
The Steppes
Elbrus 18,510 ft 5,642 m
Aral Sea
ASIA
Altay Mountains
GOBI
Tian Shan
Taklimakan Desert
Kunlun Shan
Black Sea
Caucasus Mts.
Caspian Sea
Sicily
Mediterranean Sea
Cyprus
Zagros Mountains
Dead Sea -1,349 ft -411 m
Indus
HIMALAYA
Plateau of Tibet
Brahmaputra
Yangtze
Ganges
Mt. Everest 29,035 ft 8,850 m
East China Sea
Ryukyu Islands
Nampo Shoto
NORTH PACIFIC OCEAN
30°N
Taiwan
Philippine Sea
SAHARA
Libyan Desert
Nile
Red Sea
ARABIAN PENINSULA
INDIA
Deccan Plateau
Arabian Sea
Bay of Bengal
Salween
Mekong
Hainan
Luzon
Philippine Islands
Mariana Islands
SAHEL
AFRICA
Blue Nile
White Nile
Ethiopian Highlands
Gulf of Aden
Somali Peninsula
Andaman Islands
Andaman Sea
Indochina Peninsula
South China Sea
Sri Lanka
Nicobar Is.
MICRONESIA
Marshall Islands
Malay Peninsula
Maldive Islands
EQUATOR
Congo
Lake Victoria
Congo Basin
Kilimanjaro 19,340 ft 5,895 m
Lake Tanganyika
Seychelles
Sumatra
Borneo
Indonesia
Celebes
Moluccas
Greater Sunda Islands
Java
New Guinea
Bismarck Archipelago
Solomon Islands
MELANESIA
Gilbert Islands
Lower Guinea
Arafura Sea
Madagascar
Zambezi
Mascarene Islands
INDIAN OCEAN
Coral Sea
Vanuatu
Fiji Islands
Namib Desert
Kalahari Desert
Drakensberg
Great Sandy Desert
AUSTRALIA
Great Dividing Range
New Caledonia
Lake Eyre -52 ft, -16 m
Great Victoria Desert
Darling
SOUTH PACIFIC OCEAN
Murray
Mt. Kosciuszko 7,310 ft 2,228 m
Tasman Sea
North Island
NEW ZEALAND
Tasmania
South Island
Kerguelen Islands
Auckland Islands
South Magnetic Pole
60°S
Queen Maud Land
ANTARCTICA
Transantarctic Mountains
Victoria Land
Ross Ice Shelf
Ross Sea

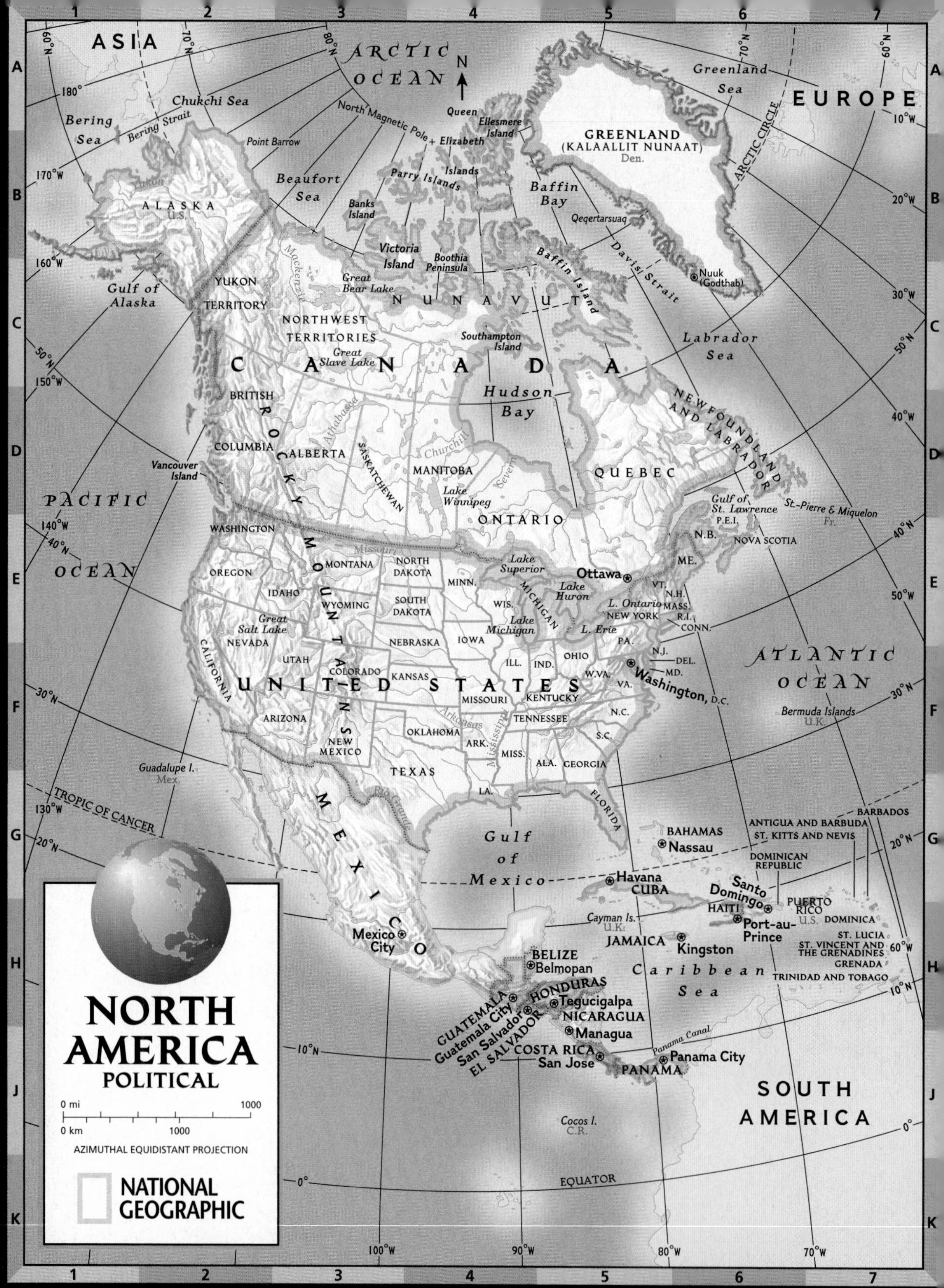
NORTH AMERICA
POLITICAL
0 mi 1000
0 km 1000
AZIMUTHAL EQUIDISTANT PROJECTION
NATIONAL GEOGRAPHIC
ASIA
EUROPE
SOUTH AMERICA
ARCTIC OCEAN
PACIFIC OCEAN
ATLANTIC OCEAN
Chukchi Sea
Bering Sea
Bering Strait
Point Barrow
Beaufort Sea
North Magnetic Pole
Queen Elizabeth Islands
Ellesmere Island
Parry Islands
Banks Island
Victoria Island
Boothia Peninsula
Baffin Bay
Baffin Island
Davis Strait
Qeqertarsuaq
Greenland Sea
GREENLAND (KALAALLIT NUNAAT) Den.
Nuuk (Godthab)
ARCTIC CIRCLE
Labrador Sea
ALASKA U.S.
Yukon
Gulf of Alaska
YUKON TERRITORY
NORTHWEST TERRITORIES
Mackenzie
Great Bear Lake
Great Slave Lake
NUNAVUT
Southampton Island
Hudson Bay
CANADA
BRITISH COLUMBIA
ALBERTA
SASKATCHEWAN
MANITOBA
Athabasca
Churchill
Severn
Lake Winnipeg
ONTARIO
QUEBEC
NEWFOUNDLAND AND LABRADOR
Gulf of St. Lawrence
St.-Pierre & Miquelon Fr.
P.E.I.
N.B.
NOVA SCOTIA
Vancouver Island
ROCKY MOUNTAINS
Ottawa
Lake Superior
Lake Huron
Lake Michigan
L. Ontario
L. Erie
WASHINGTON
OREGON
IDAHO
MONTANA
WYOMING
NORTH DAKOTA
SOUTH DAKOTA
MINN.
WIS.
MICHIGAN
IOWA
NEBRASKA
NEVADA
UTAH
COLORADO
KANSAS
CALIFORNIA
Great Salt Lake
Missouri
ILL.
IND.
OHIO
PA.
NEW YORK
ME.
VT.
N.H.
MASS.
R.I.
CONN.
N.J.
DEL.
MD.
W.VA.
VA.
KENTUCKY
MISSOURI
TENNESSEE
N.C.
S.C.
UNITED STATES
Washington, D.C.
ARIZONA
NEW MEXICO
OKLAHOMA
ARK.
Arkansas
Mississippi
MISS.
ALA.
GEORGIA
TEXAS
LA.
FLORIDA
Rio Grande
Bermuda Islands U.K.
Guadalupe I. Mex.
TROPIC OF CANCER
MEXICO
Mexico City
Gulf of Mexico
BAHAMAS
Nassau
Havana
CUBA
Cayman Is. U.K.
JAMAICA
Kingston
HAITI
Port-au-Prince
DOMINICAN REPUBLIC
Santo Domingo
PUERTO RICO U.S.
ANTIGUA AND BARBUDA
ST. KITTS AND NEVIS
BARBADOS
DOMINICA
ST. LUCIA
ST. VINCENT AND THE GRENADINES
GRENADA
TRINIDAD AND TOBAGO
Caribbean Sea
BELIZE
Belmopan
GUATEMALA
Guatemala City
HONDURAS
Tegucigalpa
EL SALVADOR
San Salvador
NICARAGUA
Managua
COSTA RICA
San Jose
PANAMA
Panama City
Panama Canal
Cocos I. C.R.
EQUATOR
180°
170°W
160°W
150°W
140°W
130°W
100°W
90°W
80°W
70°W
60°W
10°W
20°W
30°W
40°W
50°W
60°N
70°N
80°N
50°N
40°N
30°N
20°N
10°N
0°

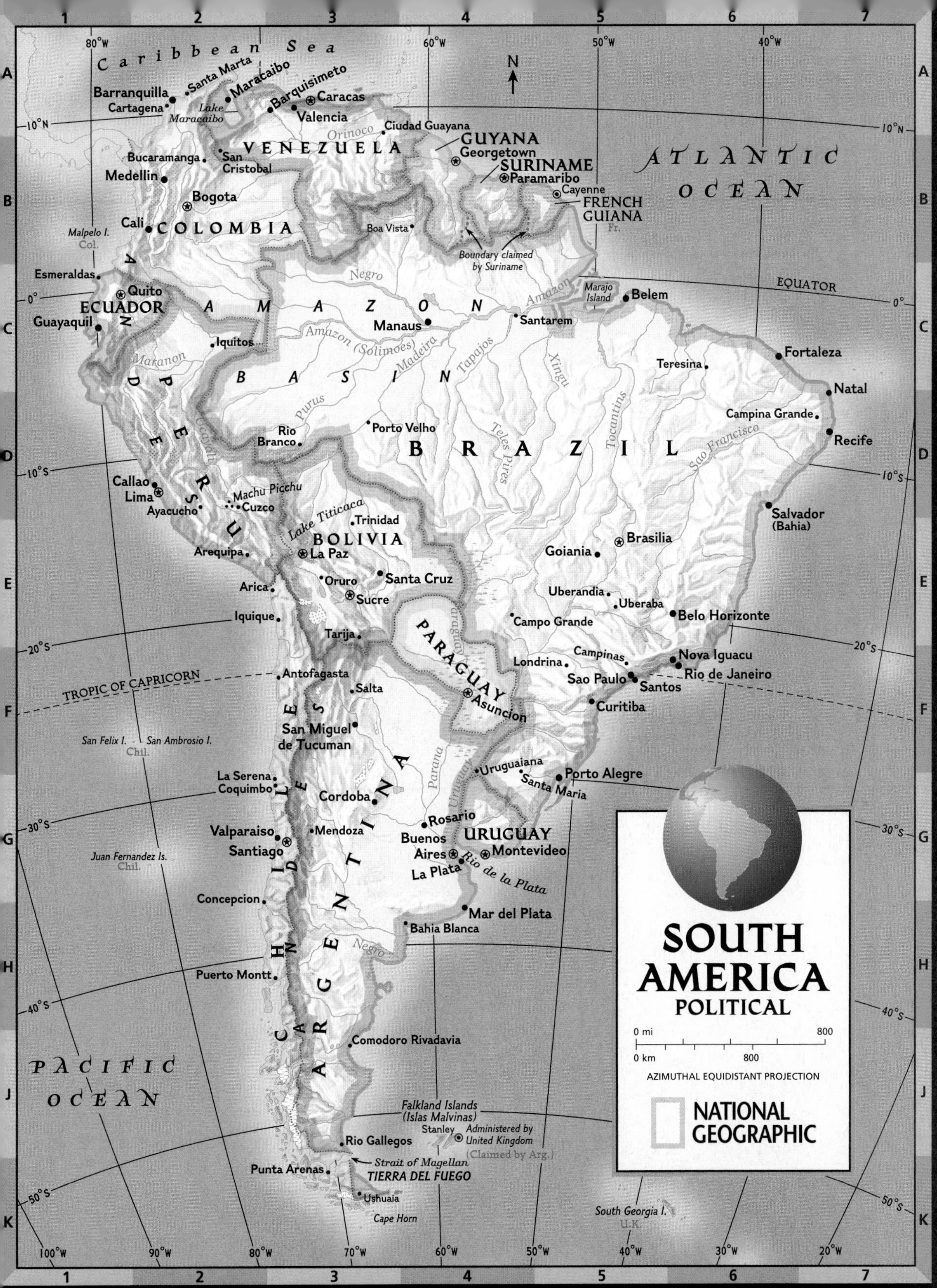
SOUTH AMERICA
POLITICAL
AZIMUTHAL EQUIDISTANT PROJECTION
0 mi 800
0 km 800
NATIONAL GEOGRAPHIC
Caribbean Sea
ATLANTIC OCEAN
PACIFIC OCEAN
VENEZUELA
GUYANA
SURINAME
FRENCH GUIANA
Fr.
COLOMBIA
ECUADOR
PERU
BRAZIL
BOLIVIA
PARAGUAY
CHILE
ARGENTINA
URUGUAY
AMAZON BASIN
ANDES
Barranquilla
Cartagena
Santa Marta
Maracaibo
Lake Maracaibo
Barquisimeto
Caracas
Valencia
Orinoco
Ciudad Guayana
Georgetown
Paramaribo
Cayenne
Bucaramanga
San Cristobal
Medellin
Bogota
Cali
Malpelo I.
Col.
Boa Vista
Boundary claimed by Suriname
Negro
Esmeraldas
Quito
Guayaquil
Marajo Island
Belem
EQUATOR
Manaus
Santarem
Amazon
Amazon (Solimoes)
Iquitos
Maranon
Madeira
Tapajos
Xingu
Teresina
Fortaleza
Natal
Campina Grande
Recife
Purus
Rio Branco
Porto Velho
Teles Pires
Tocantins
Sao Francisco
Ucayali
Callao
Lima
Machu Picchu
Cuzco
Ayacucho
Lake Titicaca
Trinidad
Salvador (Bahia)
Brasilia
Goiania
Arequipa
La Paz
Santa Cruz
Oruro
Sucre
Arica
Uberandia
Uberaba
Belo Horizonte
Iquique
Campo Grande
Paraguay
Tarija
Campinas
Nova Iguacu
Londrina
Rio de Janeiro
Sao Paulo
Santos
Antofagasta
Salta
TROPIC OF CAPRICORN
Asuncion
Curitiba
San Miguel de Tucuman
San Felix I.
San Ambrosio I.
Chil.
Parana
Uruguay
Uruguaiana
Santa Maria
Porto Alegre
La Serena
Coquimbo
Cordoba
Rosario
Valparaiso
Santiago
Mendoza
Buenos Aires
Montevideo
Juan Fernandez Is.
Chil.
La Plata
Rio de la Plata
Concepcion
Mar del Plata
Bahia Blanca
Negro
Puerto Montt
Comodoro Rivadavia
Falkland Islands (Islas Malvinas)
Stanley
Administered by United Kingdom
(Claimed by Arg.)
Rio Gallegos
Strait of Magellan
Punta Arenas
TIERRA DEL FUEGO
Ushuaia
Cape Horn
South Georgia I.
U.K.
80°W
60°W
50°W
40°W
10°N
0°
10°S
20°S
30°S
40°S
50°S
100°W
90°W
70°W
30°W
20°W
1 2 3 4 5 6 7
A B C D E F G H J K

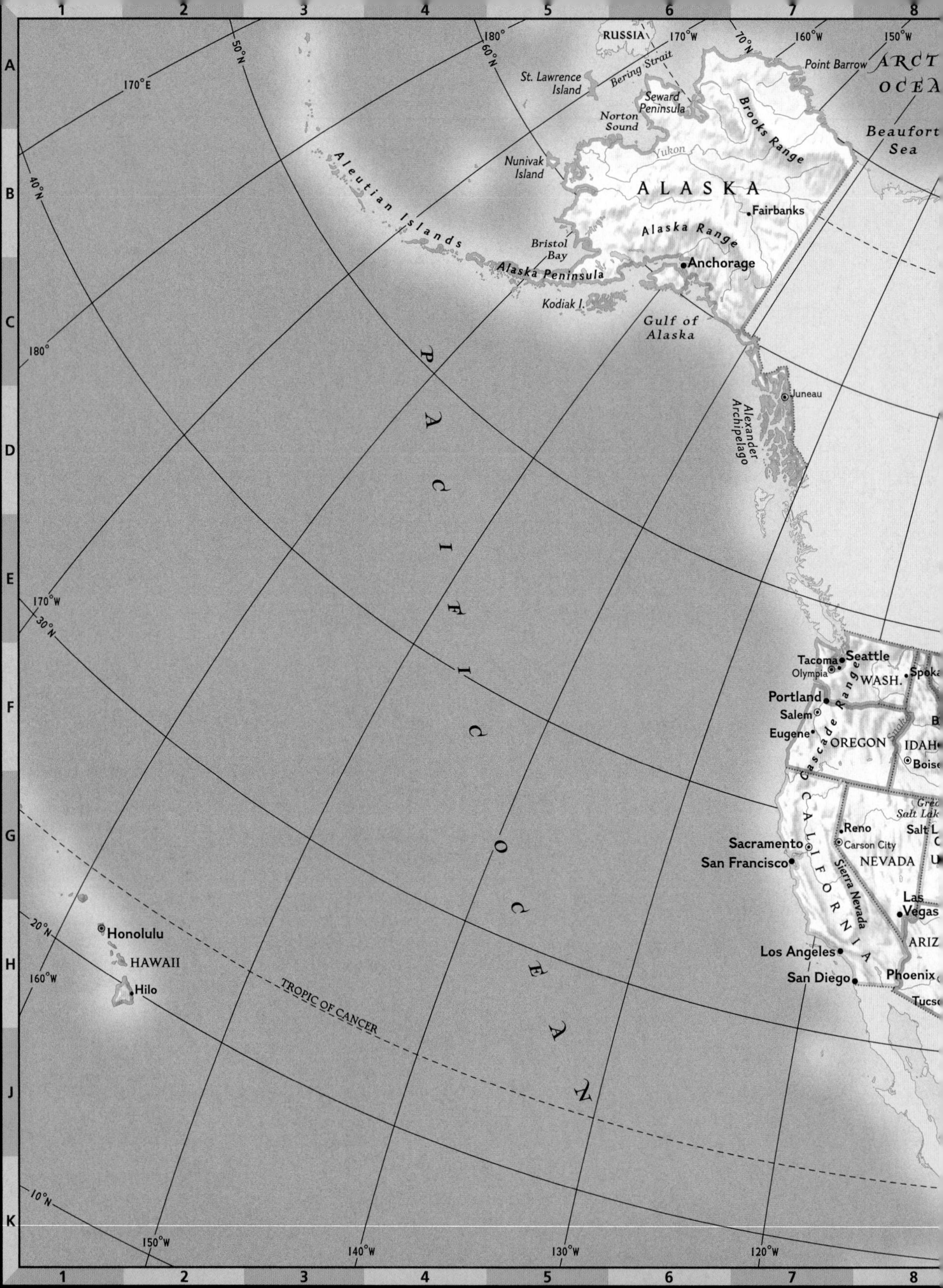
RUSSIA
St. Lawrence Island
Bering Strait
Seward Peninsula
Norton Sound
Point Barrow
Brooks Range
Beaufort Sea
Yukon
Nunivak Island
ALASKA
Fairbanks
Aleutian Islands
Alaska Range
Bristol Bay
Anchorage
Alaska Peninsula
Kodiak I.
Gulf of Alaska
Juneau
Alexander Archipelago
PACIFIC OCEAN
Tacoma
Seattle
Olympia
WASH.
Portland
Salem
Eugene
Cascade Range
OREGON
Boise
Sacramento
San Francisco
Reno
Carson City
NEVADA
CALIFORNIA
Sierra Nevada
Las Vegas
Los Angeles
San Diego
Phoenix
Honolulu
HAWAII
Hilo
TROPIC OF CANCER
170°E
180°
170°W
160°W
150°W
140°W
130°W
120°W
50°N
60°N
70°N
40°N
30°N
20°N
10°N

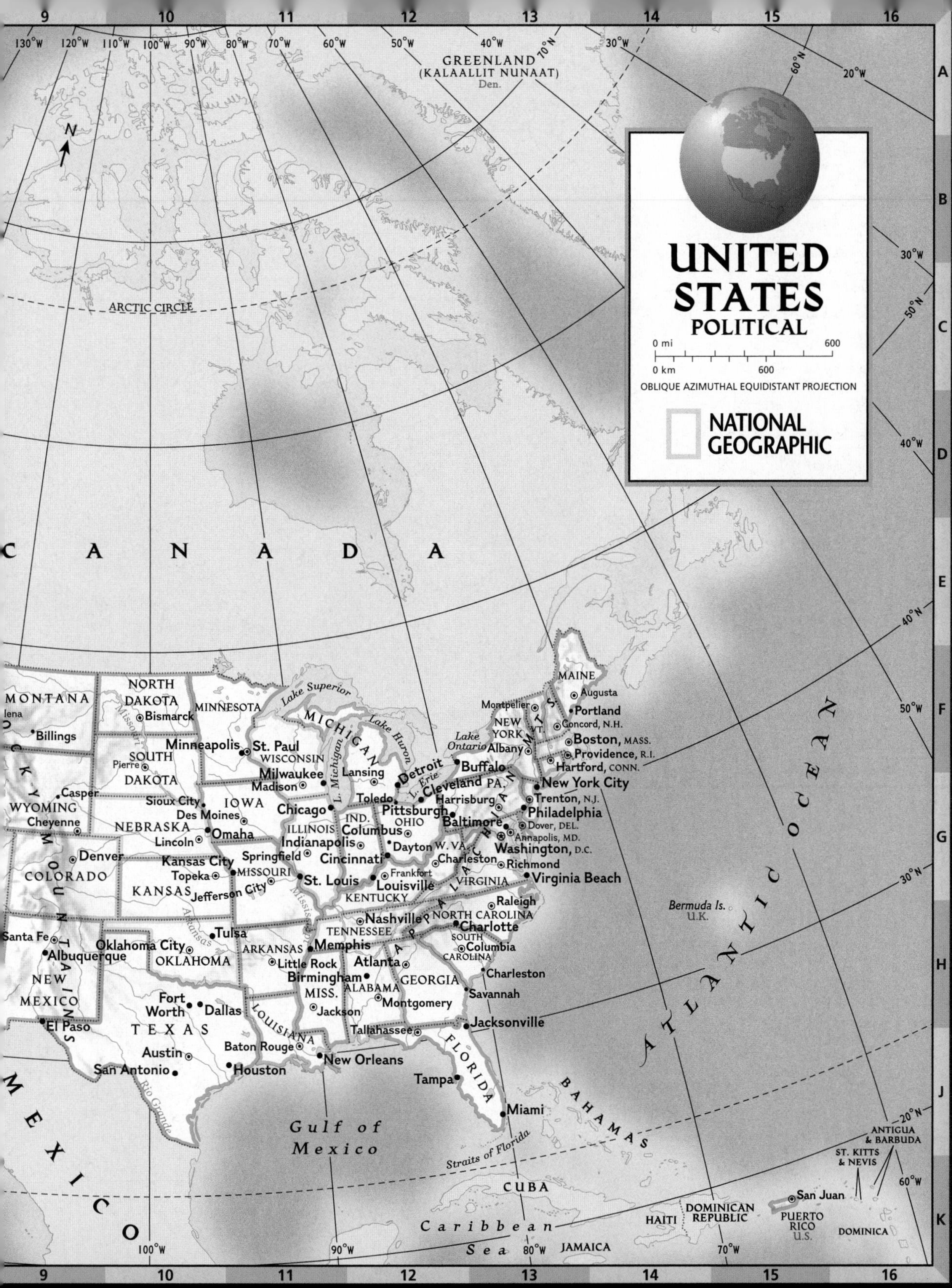
UNITED STATES
POLITICAL
0 mi
600
0 km
600
OBLIQUE AZIMUTHAL EQUIDISTANT PROJECTION
NATIONAL GEOGRAPHIC
GREENLAND
(KALAALLIT NUNAAT)
Den.
ARCTIC CIRCLE
CANADA
ATLANTIC OCEAN
MONTANA
NORTH DAKOTA
Bismarck
MINNESOTA
Billings
SOUTH DAKOTA
Pierre
Minneapolis
St. Paul
WISCONSIN
Lake Superior
MICHIGAN
Lake Huron
L. Michigan
Milwaukee
Madison
Lansing
Detroit
L. Erie
Cleveland
Toledo
Casper
WYOMING
Cheyenne
Sioux City
IOWA
Des Moines
NEBRASKA
Lincoln
Omaha
Chicago
ILLINOIS
IND.
Indianapolis
OHIO
Columbus
Dayton
Cincinnati
Springfield
Denver
COLORADO
Kansas City
Topeka
MISSOURI
KANSAS
Jefferson City
St. Louis
Frankfort
Louisville
KENTUCKY
Pittsburgh
Harrisburg
PA.
Baltimore
Dover, DEL.
Annapolis, MD.
Washington, D.C.
W. VA.
Charleston
Richmond
VIRGINIA
Virginia Beach
Raleigh
NORTH CAROLINA
Nashville
TENNESSEE
Charlotte
SOUTH CAROLINA
Columbia
Charleston
Memphis
ARKANSAS
Little Rock
Atlanta
GEORGIA
Birmingham
ALABAMA
MISS.
Jackson
Montgomery
Savannah
Jacksonville
Tallahassee
FLORIDA
Tampa
Miami
Santa Fe
Albuquerque
NEW MEXICO
Oklahoma City
OKLAHOMA
Tulsa
Fort Worth
Dallas
TEXAS
El Paso
Austin
San Antonio
Houston
Baton Rouge
LOUISIANA
New Orleans
ROCKY MOUNTAINS
APPALACHIAN MTS.
MAINE
Augusta
Portland
Montpelier
NEW YORK
Lake Ontario
Albany
Concord, N.H.
Boston, MASS.
Providence, R.I.
Hartford, CONN.
New York City
Trenton, N.J.
Philadelphia
Buffalo
Bermuda Is.
U.K.
BAHAMAS
Gulf of Mexico
Straits of Florida
CUBA
Caribbean Sea
JAMAICA
HAITI
DOMINICAN REPUBLIC
San Juan
PUERTO RICO
U.S.
DOMINICA
ST. KITTS & NEVIS
ANTIGUA & BARBUDA
MEXICO
Rio Grande
Mississippi
Missouri
Arkansas
9 10 11 12 13 14 15 16
A B C D E F G H J K

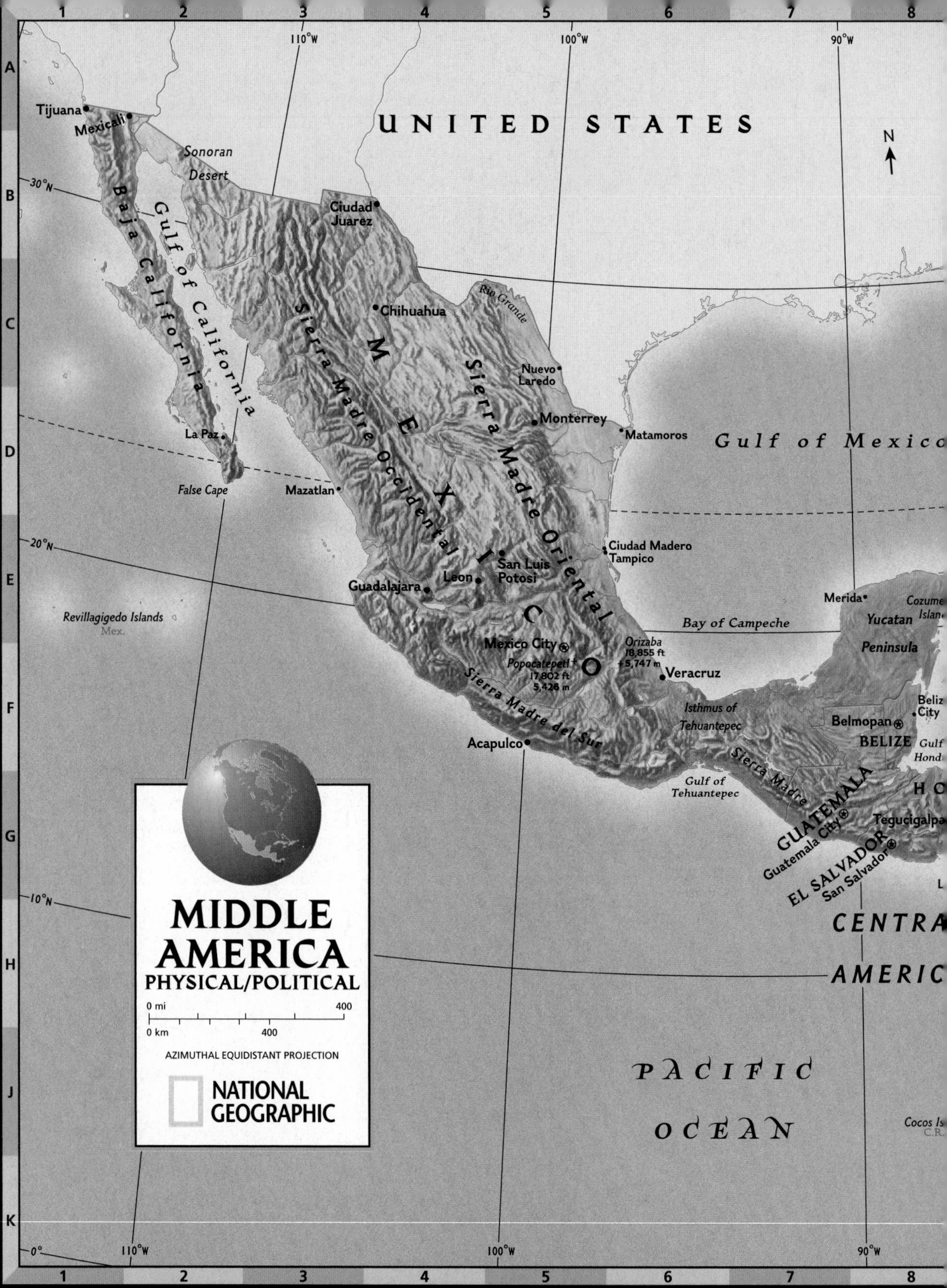
MIDDLE
AMERICA
PHYSICAL/POLITICAL
0 mi
400
0 km
400
AZIMUTHAL EQUIDISTANT PROJECTION
NATIONAL
GEOGRAPHIC
UNITED STATES
MEXICO
Tijuana
Mexicali
Sonoran
Desert
Baja California
Gulf of California
Ciudad
Juarez
Chihuahua
Rio Grande
Sierra Madre Occidental
Sierra Madre Oriental
Nuevo
Laredo
Monterrey
Matamoros
Gulf of Mexico
La Paz
False Cape
Mazatlan
Ciudad Madero
Tampico
San Luis
Potosi
Leon
Guadalajara
Revillagigedo Islands
Mex.
Mexico City
Popocatepetl
17,802 ft
5,426 m
Orizaba
18,855 ft
5,747 m
Veracruz
Bay of Campeche
Merida
Yucatan
Peninsula
Sierra Madre del Sur
Acapulco
Isthmus of
Tehuantepec
Gulf of
Tehuantepec
Sierra Madre
Belmopan
BELIZE
GUATEMALA
Guatemala City
EL SALVADOR
San Salvador
Tegucigalpa
CENTRA
AMERIC
PACIFIC
OCEAN
110°W
100°W
90°W
30°N
20°N
10°N
0°
N
1
2
3
4
5
6
7
8
A
B
C
D
E
F
G
H
J
K

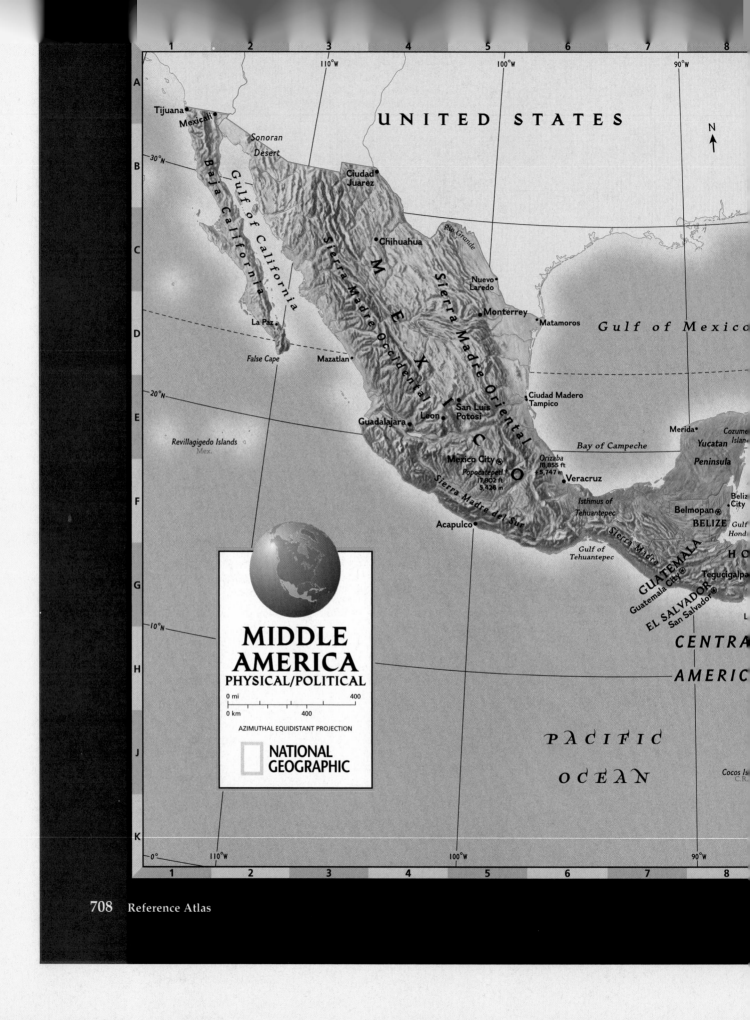

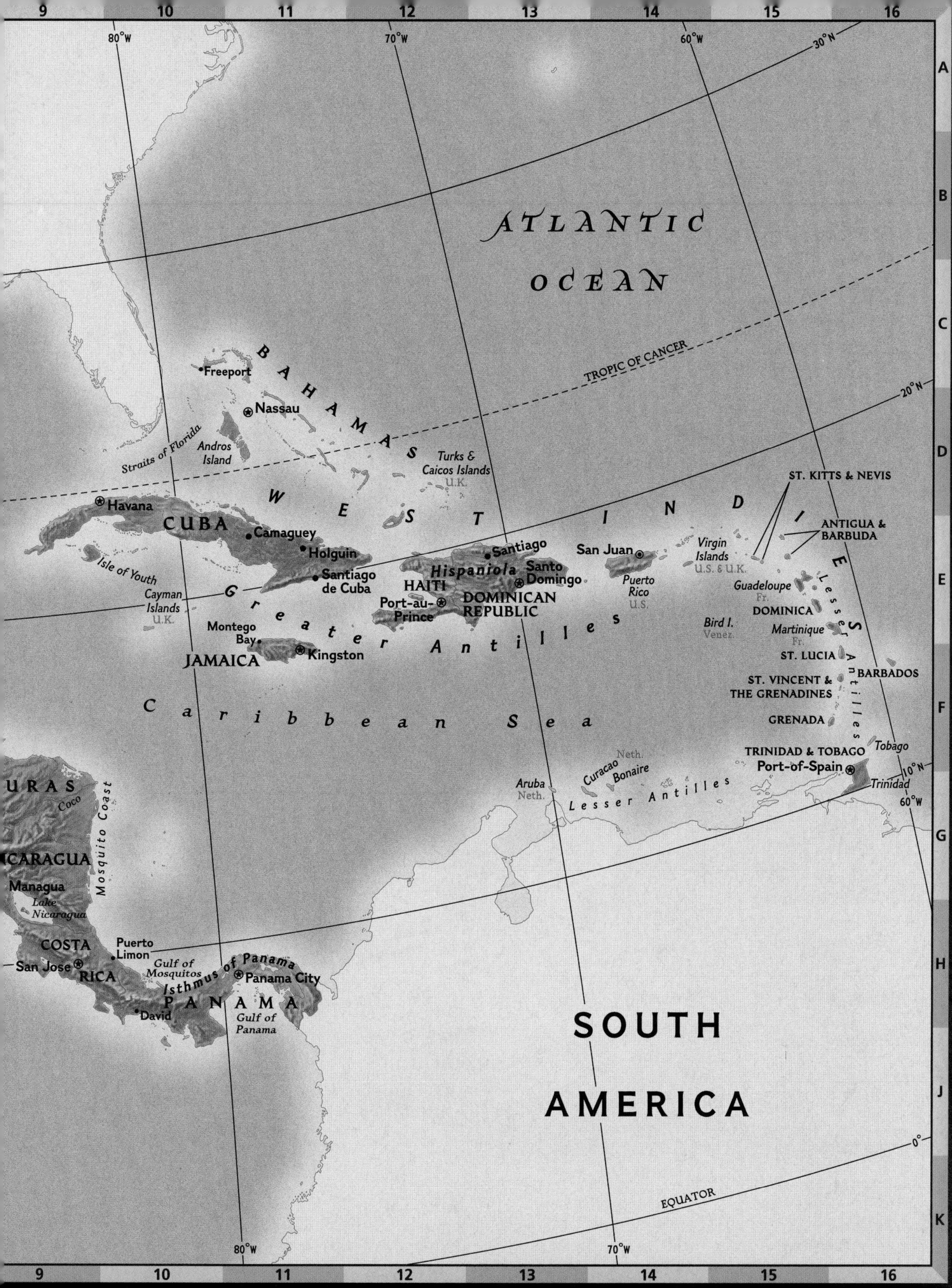
9
10
11
12
13
14
15
16
80°W
70°W
60°W
30°N
20°N
10°N
0°
A
B
C
D
E
F
G
H
J
K
ATLANTIC OCEAN
TROPIC OF CANCER
EQUATOR
BAHAMAS
Freeport
Nassau
Andros Island
Straits of Florida
Turks & Caicos Islands U.K.
WEST INDIES
Havana
CUBA
Camaguey
Holguin
Santiago de Cuba
Isle of Youth
Cayman Islands U.K.
Greater Antilles
Hispaniola
Santiago
HAITI
Port-au-Prince
Santo Domingo
DOMINICAN REPUBLIC
Montego Bay
JAMAICA
Kingston
San Juan
Puerto Rico U.S.
Virgin Islands U.S. & U.K.
ST. KITTS & NEVIS
ANTIGUA & BARBUDA
Guadeloupe Fr.
DOMINICA
Martinique Fr.
Bird I. Venez.
ST. LUCIA
BARBADOS
ST. VINCENT & THE GRENADINES
GRENADA
Lesser Antilles
Caribbean Sea
TRINIDAD & TOBAGO
Port-of-Spain
Tobago
Trinidad
Aruba Neth.
Curacao
Bonaire
Neth.
Lesser Antilles
URAS
Coco
Mosquito Coast
NICARAGUA
Managua
Lake Nicaragua
COSTA RICA
San Jose
Puerto Limon
Gulf of Mosquitos
Isthmus of Panama
Panama City
PANAMA
David
Gulf of Panama
SOUTH AMERICA

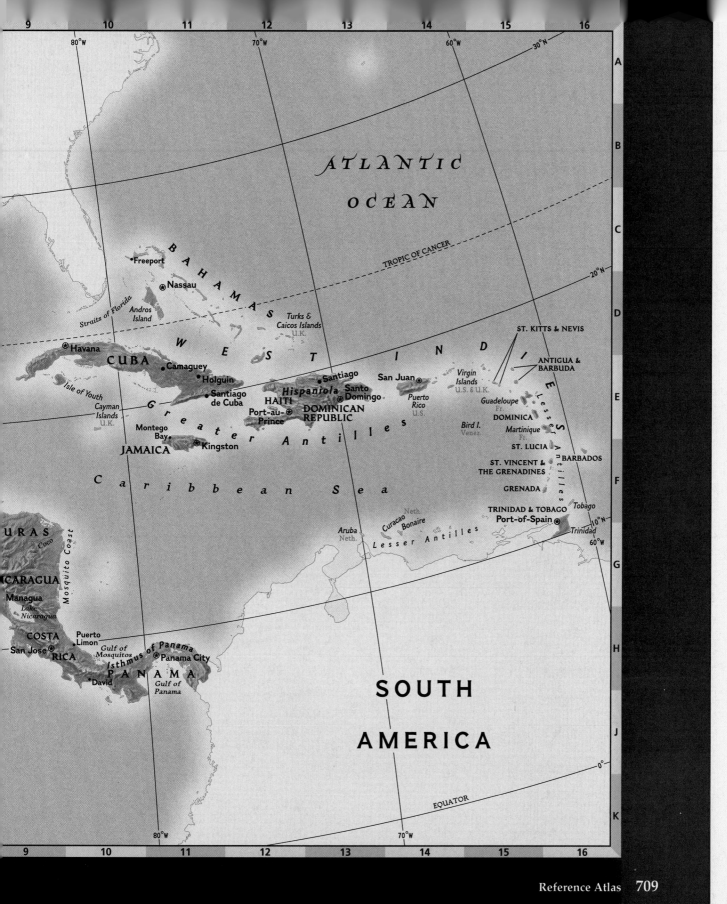

EUROPE
POLITICAL
0 mi 400
0 km 400
AZIMUTHAL EQUIDISTANT PROJECTION
NATIONAL GEOGRAPHIC
1 2 3 4 5 6 7 8
A B C D E F G H J K
60°N
50°N
40°N
30°N
40°W
30°W
20°W
10°W
0°
10°E
70°N
ARCTIC CIRCLE
MERIDIAN OF GREENWICH (LONDON)
N
Akureyri
Reykjavik
ICELAND
Norwegian Sea
Faroe Islands
Den.
Torshavn
Shetland Islands
Lerwick
Orkney Islands
Rockall
U.K.
Isle of Lewis
Inverness
UNITED
SCOTLAND
Aberdeen
Glasgow
Edinburgh
NORTHERN IRELAND
Belfast
IRELAND
Dublin
Cork
Irish Sea
Liverpool
Manchester
KINGDOM
WALES
Birmingham
ENGLAND
Cardiff
London
Celtic Sea
Land's End
Southampton
English Channel
North Sea
Trondheim
Are
Alesund
Sundsvall
Bergen
Stavanger
Oslo
Uppsala
Stockholm
NORWAY
SWEDEN
Skagerrak
Goteborg
Gotland
Arhus
DENMARK
Copenhagen
Malmo
Baltic
Kiel
Hamburg
Gdansk
Bydgoszcz
NETH.
The Hague
Amsterdam
Berlin
GERMANY
POLAND
Brussels
BELGIUM
Bonn
Rhine
Frankfurt
LUX.
Wroclaw
Oder
Prague
CZECH REP.
ATLANTIC OCEAN
Brest
Le Havre
Rennes
Paris
Nantes
Strasbourg
La Rochelle
FRANCE
Munich
Bratislava
Vienna
Zurich
LIECH.
Bern
SWITZERLAND
AUSTRIA
Bay of Biscay
Limoges
Bordeaux
Geneva
Lyon
ALPS
Budapest
SLOVENIA
HUNGARY
Ljubljana
Zagreb
CROATIA
A Coruna
Vigo
Porto
Bilbao
Donostia-San Sebastian
Toulouse
Pyrenees
Milan
Turin
Genoa
Venice
BOSNIA & HERZEGOVINA
Sarajevo
Valladolid
Coimbra
PORTUGAL
ANDORRA
Zaragoza
MONACO
Nice
Marseille
SAN MARINO
Adriatic Sea
Madrid
Lisbon
SPAIN
Barcelona
Corsica
Fr.
ITALY
VATICAN CITY
Rome
Valencia
Palma
Balearic Islands
Sp.
Sardinia
It.
Naples
Cape St. Vincent
Cordoba
Seville
Murcia
Cartagena
Cadiz
GIBRALTAR
U.K.
Malaga
Strait of Gibraltar
Cagliari
Tyrrhenian Sea
Ionian Sea
Mediterranean
Palermo
Sicily
Messina
Catania
AFRICA
Valletta
MALTA

A commonly accepted division between Asia and Europe—here marked by a gray line—is formed by the Ural Mountains, Ural River, Caspian Sea, Caucasus Mountains, and the Black Sea with its outlets, the Bosporus and the Dardanelles.
Europe-Asia boundary
RUSSIA
ASIA
KAZAKHSTAN
URAL MOUNTAINS
Barents Sea
White Sea
Kola Peninsula
Murmansk
Kirovsk
Umba
Kem
Archangel
Severodvinsk
Pechora
Tobseda
Syktyvkar
Perm
Kirov
Ufa
Kazan
Yaroslavl
Nizhniy Novgorod
Tver
Moscow
Samara
Orenburg
Ryazan
Penza
Smolensk
Oral
Ural
Saratov
Volga
Bryansk
Kursk
Volgograd
Astrakhan
Caspian Sea
Stavropol
Groznyy
Caucasus Mountains
GEORGIA
AZERBAIJAN
Baku
FINLAND
LAPLAND
Ivalo
Kiruna
Kemi
Lulea
Oulu
Vaasa
Kuopio
Pori
Tampere
Turku
Helsinki
Lake Onega
Lake Ladoga
St. Petersburg
Tallinn
ESTONIA
Velikiy Novgorod
Riga
LATVIA
Daugavpils
LITHUANIA
Vitsyebsk
Vilnius
Kaunas
Minsk
BELARUS
Homyel
Warsaw
Chernihiv
Sumy
Kiev
Kharkiv
Poltava
Krakow
Lviv
UKRAINE
Vinnytsya
Dniester
Donetsk
Rostov
Dnipropetrovsk
Carpathian Mts.
MOLDOVA
Chisinau
Odesa
Sea of Azov
Kerch
Crimea
Simferopol
Yalta
Sevastopol
ROMANIA
Belgrade
Bucharest
Constanta
Danube
Balkan Mts.
Varna
Black Sea
BULGARIA
Sofia
Skopje
Istanbul
Bosporus
TURKEY
Thessaloniki
Dardanelles
Sea of Marmara
Aegean Sea
GREECE
Athens
Peloponnesus
Rhodes
Crete
Iraklio
Nicosia
CYPRUS
ASIA
30°E
40°E
50°E
70°N
70°E
60°N
80°E
70°E
50°N
60°E
40°N
30°N
30°E
40°E
50°E
9 10 11 12 13 14 15 16
A B C D E F G H J K

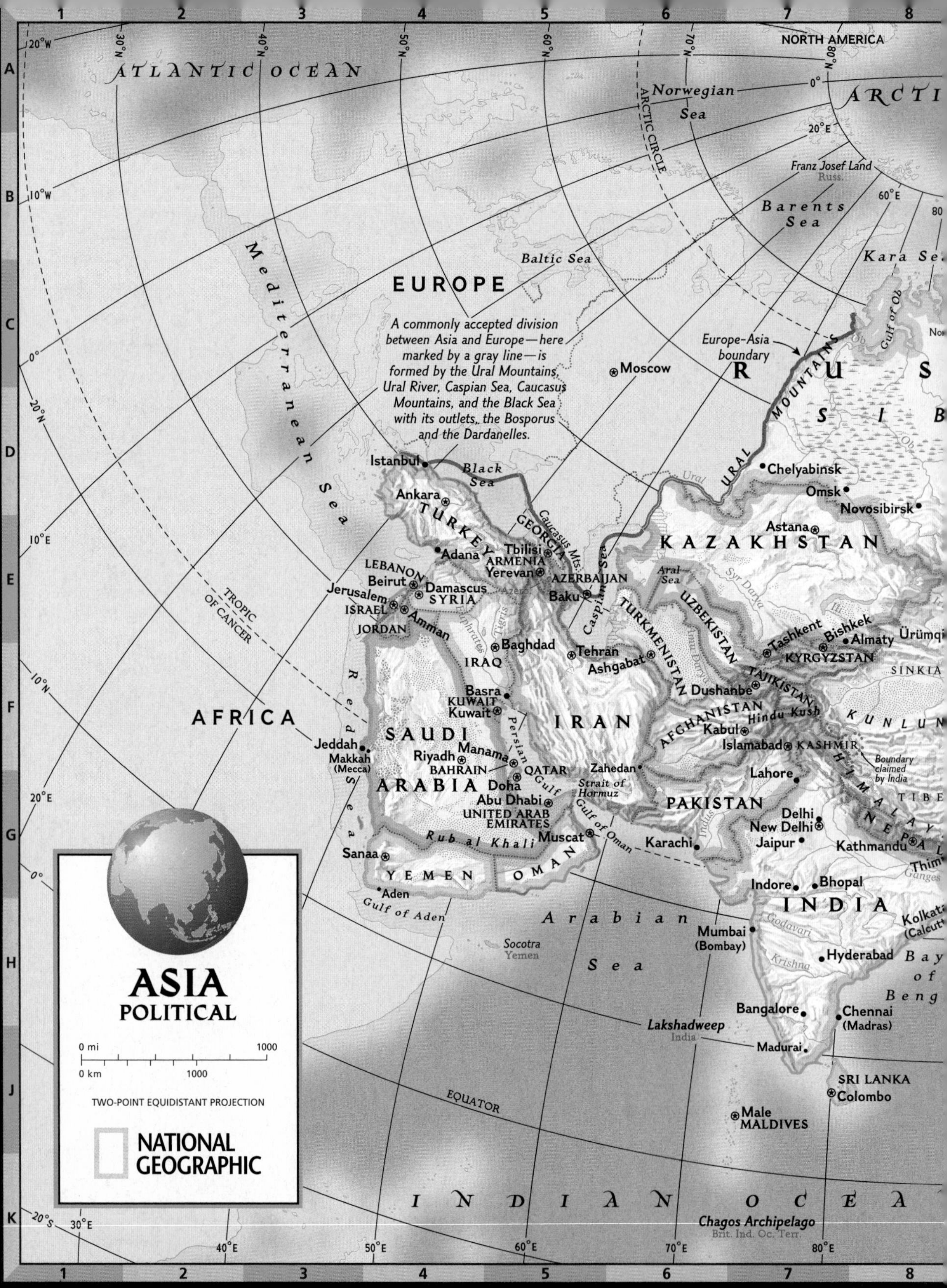
ASIA
POLITICAL
0 mi 1000
0 km 1000
TWO-POINT EQUIDISTANT PROJECTION
NATIONAL GEOGRAPHIC
A commonly accepted division between Asia and Europe—here marked by a gray line—is formed by the Ural Mountains, Ural River, Caspian Sea, Caucasus Mountains, and the Black Sea with its outlets, the Bosporus and the Dardanelles.
Europe-Asia boundary
NORTH AMERICA
ATLANTIC OCEAN
ARCTIC
Norwegian Sea
ARCTIC CIRCLE
Franz Josef Land
Russ.
Barents Sea
Kara Sea
Gulf of Ob
Baltic Sea
EUROPE
Mediterranean Sea
Moscow
URAL MOUNTAINS
RUS
SIB
Ural
Chelyabinsk
Omsk
Novosibirsk
Istanbul
Black Sea
Ankara
TURKEY
Adana
GEORGIA
Caucasus Mts.
Tbilisi
ARMENIA
Yerevan
AZERBAIJAN
Baku
Caspian Sea
KAZAKHSTAN
Astana
Aral Sea
Syr Darya
UZBEKISTAN
TURKMENISTAN
Amu Darya
LEBANON
Beirut
Damascus
SYRIA
Jerusalem
ISRAEL
JORDAN
Amman
Euphrates
Tigris
Baghdad
IRAQ
Tehran
Ashgabat
Tashkent
Bishkek
Almaty
KYRGYZSTAN
Ürümqi
TAJIKISTAN
Dushanbe
SINKIA
TROPIC OF CANCER
Basra
KUWAIT
Kuwait
IRAN
AFGHANISTAN
Kabul
Hindu Kush
KUNLUN
Islamabad
KASHMIR
Boundary claimed by India
AFRICA
Jeddah
Makkah (Mecca)
SAUDI ARABIA
Riyadh
Manama
BAHRAIN
QATAR
Doha
Persian Gulf
Zahedan
Strait of Hormuz
Lahore
HIMALAYA
TIBE
Abu Dhabi
UNITED ARAB EMIRATES
PAKISTAN
Indus
Delhi
New Delhi
Jaipur
NEPAL
Kathmandu
Thim
Ganges
Red Sea
Rub al Khali
Muscat
Gulf of Oman
Karachi
Sanaa
YEMEN
OMAN
Aden
Gulf of Aden
Indore
Bhopal
INDIA
Kolkata (Calcutta)
Arabian Sea
Socotra
Yemen
Mumbai (Bombay)
Godavari
Krishna
Hyderabad
Bay of Beng
Bangalore
Chennai (Madras)
Lakshadweep
India
Madurai
SRI LANKA
Colombo
EQUATOR
Male
MALDIVES
INDIAN OCEA
Chagos Archipelago
Brit. Ind. Oc. Terr.
20°W
10°W
0°
10°E
20°E
30°E
40°E
50°E
60°E
70°E
80°E
30°N
40°N
50°N
60°N
70°N
80°N
20°N
10°N
0°
20°S
1 2 3 4 5 6 7 8
A B C D E F G H J K

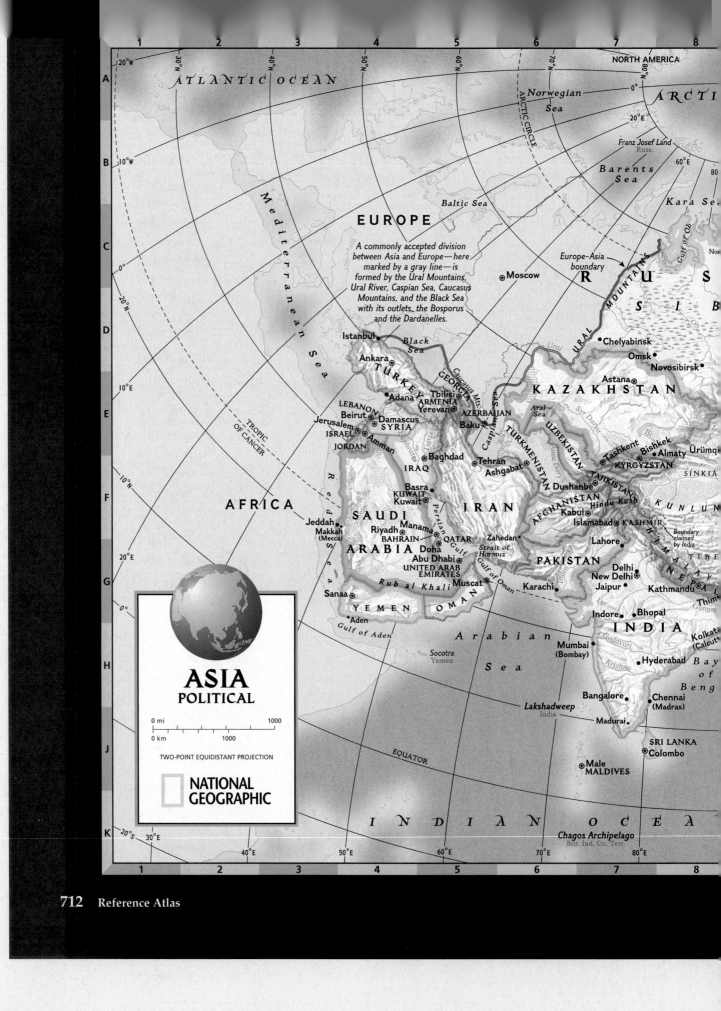

NORTH AMERICA
Bering Strait
Chukchi Sea
North Pole
OCEAN
Wrangel I.
Gulf of Anadyr
Anadyr
Bering Sea
East Siberian Sea
New Siberian Islands
North Land
Laptev Sea
Kolyma Range
Commander Is.
Kamchatka Peninsula
Cherskiy Range
Verkhoyansk Range
Magadan
Lena
Aldan
Sea of Okhotsk
Yakutsk
S I A
E R I A
Sakhalin
Kuril Islands
Amur
Lake Baikal
Hokkaido
Sapporo
Irkutsk
MANCHURIA
Sea of Japan
Vladivostok
Yenisey
Ulaanbaatar
Herlen
Changchun
JAPAN
Tokyo
MONGOLIA
ALTAY MTS.
GOBI
Shenyang
NORTH KOREA
Honshu
Kyoto
Osaka
Pyongyang
Seoul
SOUTH KOREA
Hiroshima
Beijing
Qingdao
Yellow Sea
Kyushu
Shijiazhuang
Xuzhou
East China Sea
Lanzhou
Xi'an
Nanjing
Shanghai
CHINA
Yangtze
Ryukyu Islands
Okinawa
Nanchang
Fuzhou
Chengdu
Changsha
Taipei
TAIWAN
Boundary claimed by China
Guiyang
The People's Republic of China claims Taiwan as its 23rd province.
BHUTAN
BANGLADESH
Dhaka
Kunming
Guangzhou
Hong Kong
Macau
Irrawaddy
Hanoi
Haiphong
Luzon
MYANMAR (BURMA)
LAOS
South China Sea
Hainan
Quezon City
Manila
Samar
Vientiane
Yangon (Rangoon)
Da Nang
Mindoro
PHILIPPINES
Leyte
THAILAND
Panay
Negros
Bangkok
CAMBODIA
VIETNAM
Palawan
Mindanao
Andaman Islands
India
Phnom Penh
Ho Chi Minh City
Gulf of Thailand
Andaman Sea
Bandar Seri Begawan
BRUNEI
SABAH
SARAWAK
MALAYSIA
Nicobar Islands
India
Kuala Lumpur
Medan
SINGAPORE
Borneo
Celebes
Halmahera
Morotai
Moluccas
Buru
Ceram
INDONESIA
Sumatra
Jambi
GREATER SUNDA ISLANDS
Java Sea
Mentawai Islands
Jakarta
Java
Dili
EAST TIMOR
Kupang
Timor Sea
Tanimbar Is.
Aru Is.
Dolak
Kepi
Merauke
New Guinea
Biak
Jayapura
AUSTRALIA
EQUATOR
PACIFIC OCEAN
Philippine Sea
Marcus I.
Jap.
TROPIC OF CANCER
Bonin Is.
Jap.
Volcano Is.
Jap.
Parece Vela
Jap.
80°N
70°N
60°N
50°N
40°N
30°N
20°N
10°N
0°
10°S
20°S
180°
160°E
120°E
100°E
110°E
120°E
130°E
140°E
150°E
160°W
170°W
180°
170°E
160°E
9
10
11
12
13
14
15
16
A
B
C
D
E
F
G
H
J
K

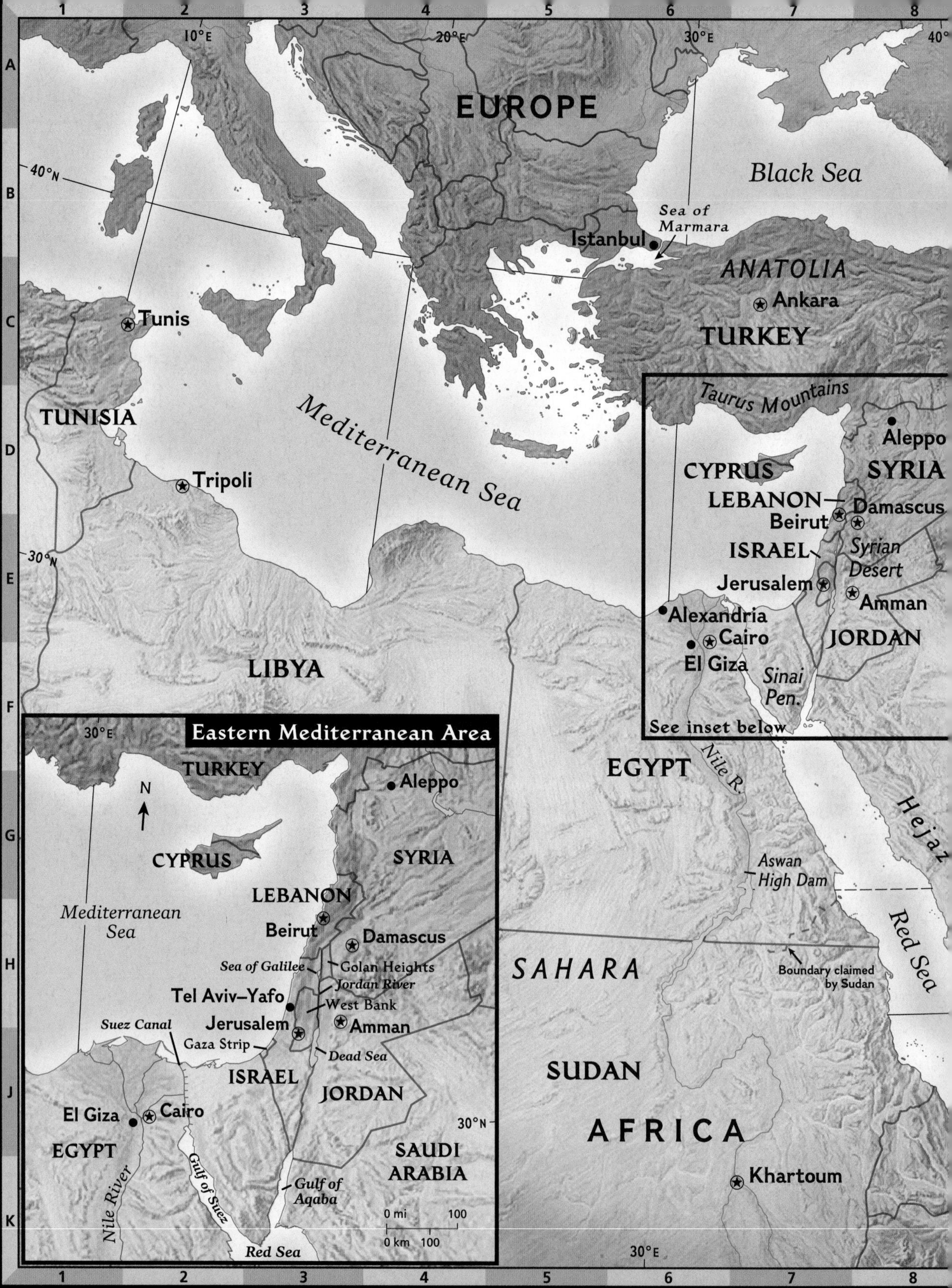
EUROPE
Black Sea
Sea of Marmara
Istanbul
ANATOLIA
Ankara
TURKEY
Tunis
TUNISIA
Mediterranean Sea
Tripoli
LIBYA
Taurus Mountains
Aleppo
CYPRUS
SYRIA
LEBANON
Damascus
Beirut
ISRAEL
Syrian Desert
Jerusalem
Amman
Alexandria
Cairo
JORDAN
El Giza
Sinai Pen.
See inset below
EGYPT
Nile R.
Hejaz
Aswan High Dam
Red Sea
SAHARA
Boundary claimed by Sudan
SUDAN
AFRICA
Khartoum
Eastern Mediterranean Area
TURKEY
Aleppo
CYPRUS
SYRIA
LEBANON
Mediterranean Sea
Beirut
Damascus
Sea of Galilee
Golan Heights
Jordan River
Tel Aviv–Yafo
West Bank
Suez Canal
Jerusalem
Amman
Gaza Strip
Dead Sea
ISRAEL
JORDAN
El Giza
Cairo
EGYPT
SAUDI ARABIA
Nile River
Gulf of Suez
Gulf of Aqaba
Red Sea
0 mi 100
0 km 100
10°E
20°E
30°E
40°E
40°N
30°N
1 2 3 4 5 6 7 8
A B C D E F G H J K

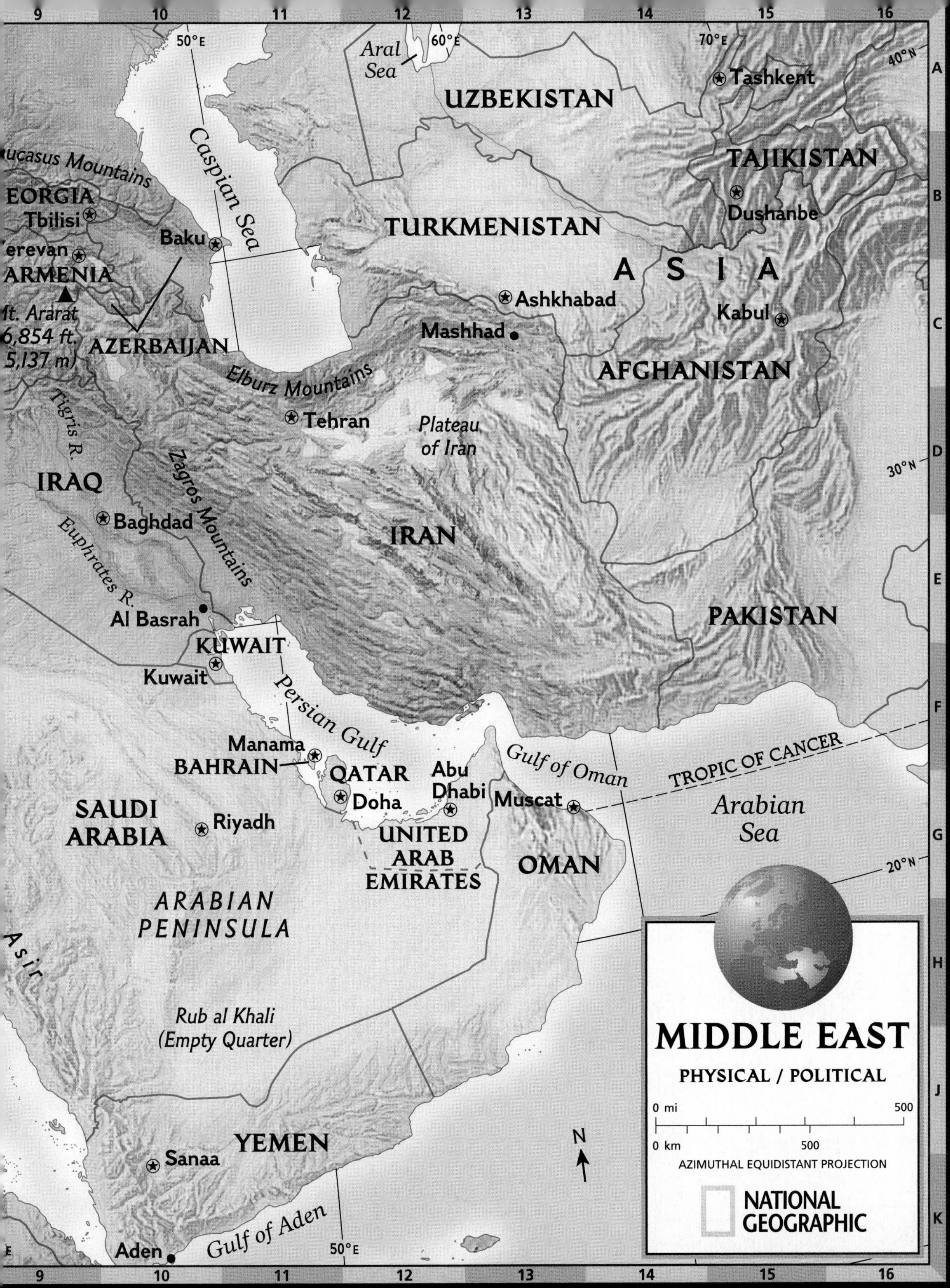

MIDDLE EAST
PHYSICAL / POLITICAL
0 mi 500
0 km 500
AZIMUTHAL EQUIDISTANT PROJECTION
NATIONAL GEOGRAPHIC
ASIA
UZBEKISTAN
Tashkent
TAJIKISTAN
Dushanbe
TURKMENISTAN
Ashkhabad
Mashhad
AFGHANISTAN
Kabul
PAKISTAN
IRAN
Tehran
Plateau of Iran
Elburz Mountains
Zagros Mountains
Caspian Sea
Aral Sea
Caucasus Mountains
GEORGIA
Tbilisi
Yerevan
ARMENIA
Mt. Ararat 16,854 ft. (5,137 m)
Baku
AZERBAIJAN
Tigris R.
Euphrates R.
IRAQ
Baghdad
Al Basrah
KUWAIT
Kuwait
Persian Gulf
Manama
BAHRAIN
QATAR
Doha
Abu Dhabi
UNITED ARAB EMIRATES
Gulf of Oman
Muscat
OMAN
TROPIC OF CANCER
Arabian Sea
SAUDI ARABIA
Riyadh
ARABIAN PENINSULA
Asir
Rub al Khali (Empty Quarter)
YEMEN
Sanaa
Aden
Gulf of Aden
50°E
60°E
70°E
40°N
30°N
20°N
N

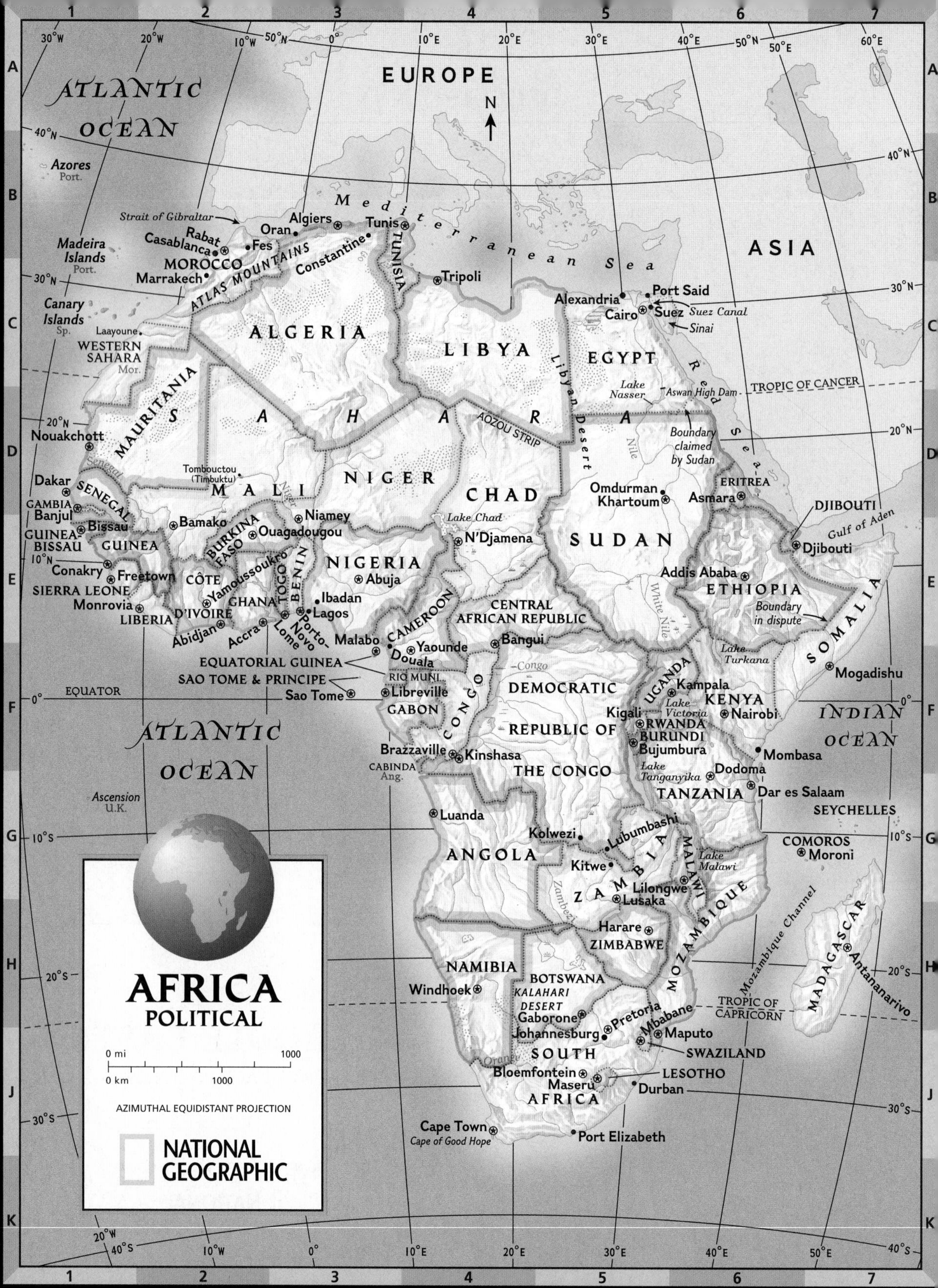
AFRICA
POLITICAL
0 mi 1000
0 km 1000
AZIMUTHAL EQUIDISTANT PROJECTION
NATIONAL GEOGRAPHIC
EUROPE
ASIA
ATLANTIC OCEAN
ATLANTIC OCEAN
INDIAN OCEAN
Mediterranean Sea
Red Sea
Gulf of Aden
Mozambique Channel
Strait of Gibraltar
Suez Canal
Sinai
TROPIC OF CANCER
TROPIC OF CAPRICORN
EQUATOR
Azores
Port.
Madeira Islands
Port.
Canary Islands
Sp.
Ascension
U.K.
WESTERN SAHARA
Mor.
Laayoune
MOROCCO
Rabat
Casablanca
Fes
Marrakech
ATLAS MOUNTAINS
Oran
Algiers
Constantine
Tunis
TUNISIA
ALGERIA
Tripoli
LIBYA
Libyan Desert
SAHARA
AOZOU STRIP
EGYPT
Alexandria
Cairo
Port Said
Suez
Lake Nasser
Aswan High Dam
Boundary claimed by Sudan
Nile
MAURITANIA
Nouakchott
Tombouctou (Timbuktu)
MALI
NIGER
CHAD
Lake Chad
N'Djamena
SUDAN
Omdurman
Khartoum
White Nile
ERITREA
Asmara
DJIBOUTI
Djibouti
ETHIOPIA
Addis Ababa
Boundary in dispute
SOMALIA
Mogadishu
Dakar
SENEGAL
GAMBIA
Banjul
GUINEA-BISSAU
Bissau
GUINEA
Conakry
SIERRA LEONE
Freetown
Monrovia
LIBERIA
Bamako
BURKINA FASO
Ouagadougou
Niamey
CÔTE D'IVOIRE
Yamoussoukro
Abidjan
GHANA
Accra
TOGO
Lome
BENIN
Porto-Novo
NIGERIA
Abuja
Ibadan
Lagos
CAMEROON
Yaounde
Douala
Malabo
EQUATORIAL GUINEA
RIO MUNI
SAO TOME & PRINCIPE
Sao Tome
Libreville
GABON
CONGO
Brazzaville
Kinshasa
CABINDA
Ang.
CENTRAL AFRICAN REPUBLIC
Bangui
Congo
DEMOCRATIC REPUBLIC OF THE CONGO
UGANDA
Kampala
Lake Victoria
KENYA
Nairobi
Lake Turkana
Mombasa
Kigali
RWANDA
BURUNDI
Bujumbura
Lake Tanganyika
Dodoma
TANZANIA
Dar es Salaam
SEYCHELLES
COMOROS
Moroni
Luanda
ANGOLA
Kolwezi
Lubumbashi
Kitwe
ZAMBIA
Zambezi
Lusaka
MALAWI
Lake Malawi
Lilongwe
MOZAMBIQUE
Harare
ZIMBABWE
MADAGASCAR
Antananarivo
NAMIBIA
Windhoek
BOTSWANA
KALAHARI DESERT
Gaborone
Pretoria
Johannesburg
Mbabane
Maputo
SWAZILAND
Orange
SOUTH AFRICA
Bloemfontein
Maseru
LESOTHO
Durban
Cape Town
Cape of Good Hope
Port Elizabeth
N
1 2 3 4 5 6 7
A B C D E F G H J K

ARCTIC OCEAN
PHYSICAL
AZIMUTHAL EQUIDISTANT PROJECTION
NATIONAL GEOGRAPHIC
RUSSIA
Ob
Yenisey
Gulf of Ob
White Sea
FINLAND
SWEDEN
NORWAY
GERMANY
LUX.
BELGIUM
FRANCE
DENMARK
NETH.
North Sea
UNITED KINGDOM
IRELAND
Kara Sea
Novaya Zemlya
Barents Sea
Taymyr Peninsula
Norwegian Sea
Lena
Laptev Sea
North Land
Franz Josef Land
Svalbard
ARCTIC CIRCLE
ICELAND
Greenland Sea
Denmark Strait
New Siberian Islands
ARCTIC OCEAN
North Pole
Oodaaq Island
GREENLAND
Sea of Okhotsk
KAMCHATKA PENINSULA
East Siberian Sea
Lincoln Sea
Queen Elizabeth Islands
Ellesmere Island
Hayes Peninsula
Cape Farewell
Wrangel Island
Baffin Bay
Davis Strait
ATLANTIC OCEAN
Chukchi Sea
Chukchi Peninsula
Devon I.
Somerset I.
Baffin Island
Aleutian Islands
Bering Sea
St. Lawrence Island
Bering Strait
Point Barrow
Melville Island
Seward Peninsula
North Slope
Brooks Range
Beaufort Sea
Banks Island
Prince of Wales I.
Boothia Peninsula
Melville Peninsula
Foxe Basin
Hudson Strait
Victoria Island
Yukon
Nunivak Island
ALASKA
Southampton Island
Mackenzie
PACIFIC OCEAN
Bristol Bay
CANADA
Great Bear Lake
Hudson Bay

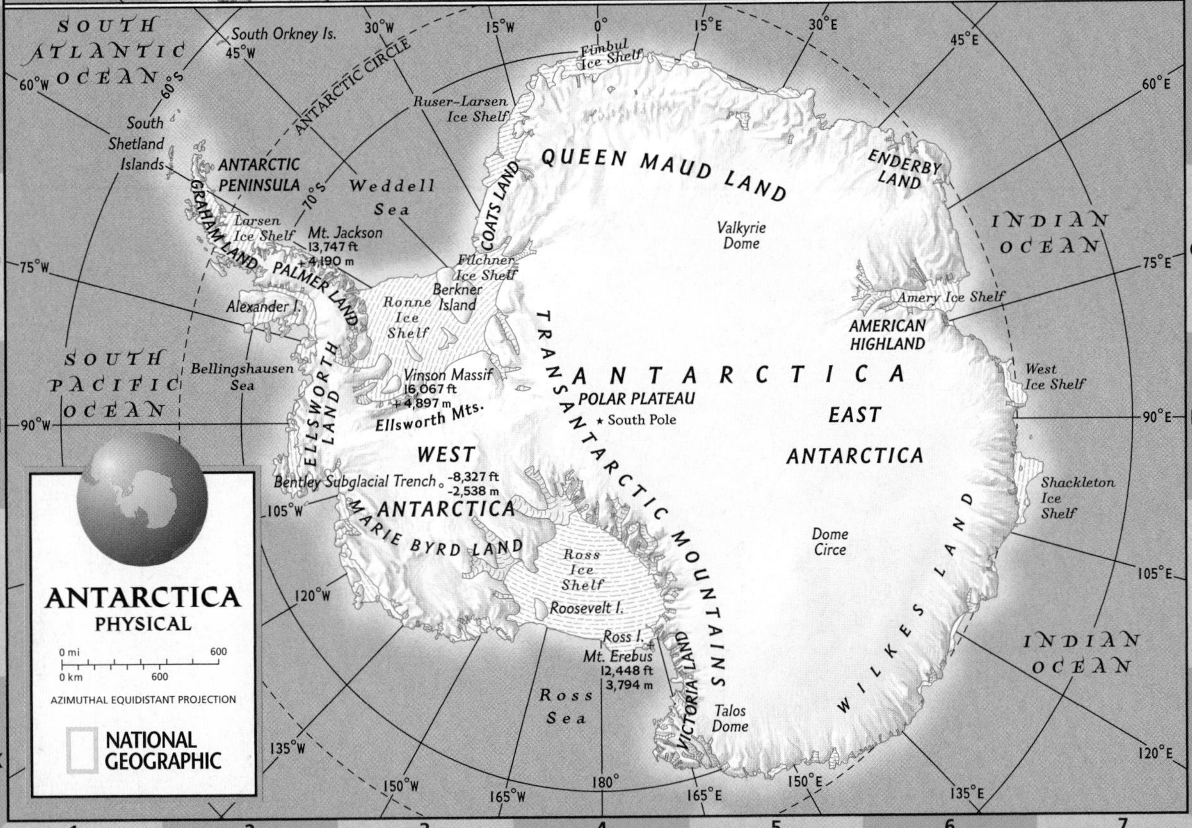

SOUTH ATLANTIC OCEAN
South Orkney Is.
ANTARCTIC CIRCLE
Fimbul Ice Shelf
Ruser-Larsen Ice Shelf
South Shetland Islands
ANTARCTIC PENINSULA
Weddell Sea
QUEEN MAUD LAND
COATS LAND
ENDERBY LAND
GRAHAM LAND
Larsen Ice Shelf
Mt. Jackson 13,747 ft 4,190 m
Valkyrie Dome
INDIAN OCEAN
PALMER LAND
Filchner Ice Shelf
Berkner Island
Alexander I.
Ronne Ice Shelf
Amery Ice Shelf
AMERICAN HIGHLAND
SOUTH PACIFIC OCEAN
Bellingshausen Sea
TRANSANTARCTIC MOUNTAINS
ELLSWORTH LAND
Vinson Massif 16,067 ft 4,897 m
ANTARCTICA
West Ice Shelf
POLAR PLATEAU
South Pole
Ellsworth Mts.
EAST ANTARCTICA
WEST ANTARCTICA
Bentley Subglacial Trench -8,327 ft -2,538 m
Shackleton Ice Shelf
MARIE BYRD LAND
Dome Circe
Ross Ice Shelf
Roosevelt I.
WILKES LAND
Ross I.
Mt. Erebus 12,448 ft 3,794 m
VICTORIA LAND
Ross Sea
Talos Dome
ANTARCTICA
PHYSICAL
AZIMUTHAL EQUIDISTANT PROJECTION
NATIONAL GEOGRAPHIC

RUSSIA
Lake Baikal
Yablonovyy Range
KAMCHATKA PENINSULA
Sea of Okhotsk
Bering Sea
ALEUTIAN ISLA
Sakhalin
Ulaanbaatar
MONGOLIA
ALTAY MOUNTAINS
GOBI
Greater Khingan Range
Manchurian Plain
Amur
Sikhote Alin Range
KURIL ISLANDS
Hokkaido
Beijing
Pyongyang
NORTH KOREA
Seoul
SOUTH KOREA
Sea of Japan
Honshu
JAPAN
Tokyo
Yellow Sea
Yellow
CHINA
Yangtze
Mekong
Kyushu
Shikoku
NAMPO SHOTO
NORTH PACI
East China Sea
RYUKYU ISLANDS
Taipei
TAIWAN
Hawai
INDIA
MYANMAR (BURMA)
Hanoi
Hainan
LAOS
VIETNAM
Vientiane
Yangon (Rangoon)
THAILAND
Bangkok
CAMBODIA
Phnom Penh
Andaman Sea
Luzon
PHILIPPINE ISLANDS
South China Sea
Manila
PHILIPPINES
Philippine Sea
NORTHERN MARIANA ISLANDS U.S.
MARIANA ISLANDS
GUAM U.S.
MICRONESIA
MARSHALL ISLANDS
Ratak Chain
Ralik Chain
Majuro
Palikir
CAROLINE ISLANDS
FEDERATED STATES OF MICRONESIA
PALAU
Koror
Sulu Sea
Mindanao
Bandar Seri Begawan
BRUNEI
Kuala Lumpur
MALAYSIA
SINGAPORE
Borneo
Celebes Sea
Sumatra
INDONESIA
GREATER SUNDA ISLANDS
Java Sea
Celebes
MOLUCCAS
Jakarta
Java
LESSER SUNDA ISLANDS
Dili
EAST TIMOR
Arafura Sea
NEW GUINEA
PAPUA NEW GUINEA
Port Moresby
Tarawa
Gilbert Islands
Yaren
NAURU
KIRIB
Phoenix Is.
MELANESIA
SOLOMON ISLANDS
Solomon Is.
Honiara
Santa Cruz Islands
TUVALU
Funafuti
Toke N.Z.
WALLIS AND FUTUNA IS. Fr.
AMER. S
SAMOA
Apia
CORAL SEA ISLANDS TERRITORY Austral.
VANUATU
Port-Vila
NEW CALEDONIA Fr.
Suva
FIJI ISLANDS
TONGA
Nuku'
TROPIC OF CAPRICORN
Coral Sea
AUSTRALIA
Norfolk Island Austral.
Darling
Great Australian Bight
Lord Howe Island Austral.
Kermadec Islands N.Z.
Canberra
Tasman Sea
NEW ZEALAND
Wellington
INDIAN OCEAN
Tasmania
Chatham Is. N.Z.
105°E
120°E
135°E
150°E
165°E
180°

PACIFIC RIM
PHYSICAL/POLITICAL
0 mi 1500
0 km 1500
MILLER CYLINDRICAL PROJECTION
NATIONAL GEOGRAPHIC
Gulf of Alaska
Kodiak I.
Alexander Archipelago
Queen Charlotte Islands
Vancouver Island
Coast Mountains
ROCKY MOUNTAINS
Cascade Range
GREAT PLAINS
CANADA
CANADIAN SHIELD
Hudson Bay
Ottawa
Great Lakes
Missouri
CENTRAL LOWLAND
APPALACHIAN MTS.
Washington
UNITED STATES
Mississippi
COASTAL PLAIN
ATLANTIC OCEAN
PACIFIC OCEAN
Baja California
Gulf of California
Sierra Madre Occidental
Sierra Madre Oriental
MEXICO
Gulf of Mexico
Nassau
BAHAMAS
Havana
CUBA
TROPIC OF CANCER
Hawaiian Islands
HAWAII
U.S.
Mexico City
BELIZE
HONDURAS
JAMAICA
HAITI
DOMINICAN REPUBLIC
Santo Domingo
GUATEMALA
Guatemala City
San Salvador
EL SALVADOR
Tegucigalpa
NICARAGUA
Managua
Caribbean Sea
Caracas
San Jose
COSTA RICA
Panama City
PANAMA
LLANOS
VENEZ.
Bogota
COLOMBIA
Kiritimati
Line Islands
EQUATOR
Galapagos Islands
Ecua.
Quito
ECUADOR
AMAZON BASIN
BRAZIL
ANDES
PERU
Lima
Marquesas Is.
POLYNESIA
BOLIVIA
La Paz
COOK ISLANDS
N.Z.
Tuamotu Archipelago
Society Is.
FRENCH POLYNESIA
Fr.
Austral Is.
Pitcairn Island U.K.
SOUTH PACIFIC OCEAN
Santiago
CHILE
ARGENTINA
PATAGONIA
Chiloe Island
45°N
30°N
15°N
0°
15°S
30°S
45°S
150°W
135°W
120°W
105°W
90°W
75°W
A B C D E F G H J K
9 10 11 12 13 14 15 16

Glossary

Pronunciations are indicated in parentheses.

A

abbot (ab′ uht) Monastery head. (p. 255)
abdicate (ab′ duh-kāt) Give up the throne. (p. 565)
absolute location (ab sō lūt lō kā shun) Exact location of a place on the Earth's surface. (p. 5)
acropolis (uh krop′ uh lis) Fortified hill in ancient Greek cities. (p. 163)
act of homage (akt of om′ ij) Ceremony in which a vassal promises loyalty to a lord. (p. 368)
ages (ā′ juhs) Time periods. (p. 27)
aggression (uh greh′ shuhn) Warlike acts. (p. 645)
agora (ag′ uh ruh) Ancient Greek marketplace. (p. 163)
airlift (ār′ lift) System of carrying supplies into an isolated area by airplane. (p. 626)
alchemists (al′kuh mists) Scientists who try to turn metals into gold and silver. (p. 343)
alliances (uh lī′ uhn siz) Agreements between people or countries. (p. 195)
amendments (uh mend′ muhntz) Law changes. (p. 513)
ancestors (an′ ses terz) Family members from past generations. (p. 89)
annexation (an ek sā shuhn) Incorporating an area into an existing state. (p. 549)
anointed (uh noin′ tuhd) Blessed with holy oil. (p. 279)
anthropologists (an thruh pol′ uh jists) People who study human beings. (p. 24)
apartheid (uh pahr′ tāt) Separation of the races. (p. 659)
apostles (uh pos′ uhls) Men chosen by Jesus to teach his beliefs to others. (p. 253)
appeasement (uh pēz′ muhnt) Giving in to demands. (p. 615)
apprentice (uh pren′ tis) Person who is learning a craft or trade. (p. 406)
archaeology (ar kē ol′ uh jē) Study of remains of past human cultures. (p. 25)
archaeologists (ar kē ol′ uh jists) People who study ruins and artifacts. (p. 24)
archbishops (arch′ bish uhps) Bishops at the head of churches in large cities. (p. 253)
aristocrats (uh rist′ ō kratz) Members of the upper class. (p. 164)
armada (ar mah′ duh) Fleet of warships. (p. 459)
armaments (ar′ muh muhnts) Military supplies. (p. 605)
armistice (ar′ muh stis) Agreement to stop fighting. (p. 605)
artifacts (ar′ tuh fakts) Products of human skill. (p. 25)
artillery (ar til′ uhr ē) Mounted guns. (p. 604)
artisans (art′ uh zuhnz) Skilled workers. (p. 57)
assembly line (uh sem′ blē līn) Work system in which each worker adds one part to a product until it is assembled. (p. 528)
astrolabe (as′ truh lāb) Navigational instrument used to determine latitude. (p. 467)
astronomers (uh stron′ uh muhrs) People who study the heavenly bodies. (p. 122)
authoritarian rule (aw thōr uh tār′ ē uhn rūl′) Government in which one ruler or political party holds power. (p. 658)
automation (aw tuh mā′ shuhn) Process in which machines replace workers. (p. 527)
autonomous (aw tah′ nuh muhs) Self-governing. (p. 654)

B

bailiff (bā′ lif) Medieval official who saw that peasants did their work. (p. 376)
balance of power (bal′ uhnts of pau′ uhr) Equal strength among countries. (p. 566)
balance of trade (bal′ uhns of trād) Difference between the amount of goods a country brings in and sends out. (p. 492)
bandeirantes (ban duh ran′ tās) Fortune hunters in colonial Brazil. (p. 488)
bands (bandz) Prehistoric groups that gathered food and lived together. (p. 34)
barbaroi (bar′ buh roi) People who did not follow Greek customs. (p. 197)

barter (bar′ ter) To exchange goods without using money. (p. 241)
berserkers (ber zerk′ erz) Viking warriors. (p. 301)
bishop (bish′ uhp) Diocese head. (p. 253)
blitzkrieg (blits′ krēg) Lightning war. (p. 616)
blockaded (blok′ ād uhd) Closed off. (p. 626)
blood feuds (bluhd fyūds) Longstanding quarrels between families. (p. 269)
bourgeoisie (bur zhwah zē) Middle class. (p. 514)
boyars (bō yahrs′) Members of the wealthy class in czarist Russia. (p. 350)
boycott (boi′ kot) Refuse to pay. (p. 509)
bull leaping (būl lēp′ ēng) Minoan bullfighting. (p. 152)
burgesses (ber′ jis ez) Elected representatives in colonial Virginia. (p. 495)
burghers (ber′ guhrz) Freemen or wealthy merchants who lived in medieval towns. (p. 404)
burgs (bergs) Medieval towns. (p. 403)

C

caliph (kā′ lif) Muslim ruler. (p. 336)
campesinos (kam puh sē′ nōz) Latin American farmers and peasants. (p. 640)
canon laws (kan′ uhn lahs) Church laws. (p. 382)
capitalism (ka pih tuhl izm) An economic system where most production is privately owned. (p. 633)
captaincies (kap′ tuhn sēs) Land in Brazil given to Portuguese nobles. (p. 488)
caravans (kar′ uh vans) Groups who traveled together for safety. (p. 121)
caravel (kar′ uh vel) Portuguese ship. (p. 468)
cash crops (kash krops) Crops sold in the market. (p. 638)
castles (kas′ uhlz) Large, fortified houses. (p. 370)
catacombs (kat′ uh kōmz) Underground cemeteries. (p. 214)
cathedrals (kuh thē′ druhlz) Churches headed by bishops. (p. 386)
caudillo (kau dē′ yō) Latin American military dictator. (p. 556)
census (sen′ suhs) Population count. (p. 234)
chancellor (chan′ suh luhr) English university head. (p. 387); Prime minister. (p. 614)
charters (char′ tuhrz) Documents that enabled towns to control their affairs. (p. 405)
chateaux (sha tōz′) French castles. (p. 440)
chieftain (chēf′ tuhn) Clan leader. (p. 267)
churches (cher′ chez) Groups of people who share the same religious beliefs. (p. 252)
circuit judges (ser′ kit juj′ iz) Judges who travel throughout a country. (p. 415)
citadel (sit′ uh duhl) Fortress. (p. 85)
city-states (sit′ ē stāts) Cities and the surrounding territories. (p. 57)
civil disobedience (siv′ uhl dis uh bē′ dē uhns) Refusal to obey government demands. (p. 634)
civilians (suh vil′ yuhnz) Non-soldiers. (p. 604)
civilization (siv′ uh luh zā shuhn) Society with a developed knowledge of farming, trade, government, art, and science. (p. 33)
civil wars (siv′ uhl wōrz) Wars between citizens of one nation. (p. 159)
clans (klans) Groups based on family ties. (p. 267)
classical writings (klas′ i′ kuhl rī tēngs) Ancient Greek and Roman writings. (p. 433)
clergy (kler′ jē) Religious leaders. (p. 367)
climate (klī′ mit) Average weather condition at a place over a period of years. (p. 14)
code of chivalry (kōd of shiv′ uhl rē) Rules knights had to live by. (p. 373)
cold war (kōld wōr) Non-fighting hostility between nations. (p. 625)
collectivization (kuh lek ti vuh zā′ shuhn) Uniting small farms into large ones controlled by the government. (p. 611)
colonies (kol′ uh nēz) Permanent settlements. (p. 105)
colonize (kol′ uh nīz) Permanently settle in an area. (p. 487)
communes (kom′ yūnz) Political groups formed by townspeople in medieval Italy. (p. 405)
communicable diseases (kah mū ni kah bl dis ē zez) Diseases that are passed from an infected person or animal to another person or animal. (p. 664)
compass (kum′ puhs) Instrument used to tell direction. (p. 467)
concentration camps (kon suhn trā shuhn kamps) Prison camps for political enemies. (p. 620)
conquistadores (kon kē stuh dōr′ ēz) Spanish conquerors in the 1500s. (p. 473)
constitution (kon stuh tū′ shuhn) Written laws used to govern a state. (p. 169)
constitutional monarchy (kon stuh tū′ shuh nuhl mon′ uhr kē) Monarchy limited in its powers by a constitution. (p. 518)

consuls (kon′ suhlz) Heads of the ancient Roman Republic. (p. 219)
continental drift (kon tuh nen′ tl drift) Theory that the continents move. (p. 10)
convents (kon′ vents) Communities of nuns. (p. 255)
converted (kuhn ver′ tuhd) Changed. (p. 277)
coracles (kor′ uh kuhls) Small Irish boats. (p. 290)
core (kōr) Central part of the earth. (p. 10)
corregidores (kō rā hē dō′ rās) Spanish royal officials. (p. 423)
cotton gin (kot′ n jin) Cotton-cleaning machine. (p. 527)
counts (kounts) French law court officials. (p. 281)
coup (koo) Forced takeover of government. (p. 648)
cremation ovens (krē mā′ shuhn uh′ vuhns) Furnaces that burn bodies to ashes. (p. 621)
crusades (krū sāds′) Wars fought to regain the Holy Land from Muslims. (p. 388)
crust (krust) Outer layer of the earth. (p. 10)
culture (kuhl′ chuhr) Way of life. (p. 61)
cuneiform (kyū nē′ uh form) Sumerian writing made up of wedge-shaped signs. (p. 58)
czar (zahr) Russian ruler. (p. 355)

D

dauphin (do′ fuhn) Eldest son of the king of France. (p. 417)
defensive league (di fen′ siv lēg) Protective group formed by Greek city-states. (p. 173)
democratic (dem uh krat′ ik) Favoring the equality of all people. (p. 169)
depression (di presh′ uhn) Economic decline. (p. 608)
descendants (di sen′ duhnts) Offspring. (p. 107)
de-Stalinization (dē stahl uh nuh zā′ shuhn) Attack on Stalin's policies. (p. 633)
developing nations (duh vel′ uh pēng nā shuns) Countries advancing in production, technology, and standard of living. (p. 634)
dictator (dik′ tā tuhr) Absolute ruler of a state. (p. 228)
dictatorship (dik tā′ tuhr ship) Government ruled by a dictator. (p. 613)
diet (dī′ uht) Formal assembly. (p. 421)
diocese (dī′ uh sis) Area under the control of a bishop. (p. 253)
direct tax (duh rekt′ taks) Tax paid directly to a government. (p. 509)
dissent (dih sent′) Criticism. (p. 647)
doge (dōj) Ruler of Renaissance Venice. (p. 439)
domesticated (duh mes′ tuh kāt uhd) Tamed. (p. 42)
domestic system (duh mes′ tik sis′ tuhm) Manufacturing done in workers' cottages. (p. 526)
domus (dō′ muhs) Roman house. (p. 236)
dowry (dow′ rē) Wealth brought by a woman when she marries. (p. 322)
dubbing (dub′ ēng) Ceremony in which a squire is made a knight. (p. 374)
dynasty (dī nuh stē) Series of rulers from the same family. (p. 88)

E

earthquake (erth′ kwāk) Shaking or sliding of a portion of the earth's crust. (p. 11)
Eddas (ed′ uhz) Written poems based on stories of Viking gods. (p. 303)
elevation (el uh vā′ shuhn) Altitude. (p. 9)
embalming (em bahm′ ēng) Process used to keep dead bodies from decaying. (p. 73)
emigrated (em′ uh grāt ed) Left one's country. (p. 200)
émigrés (em′ uh grāz) French political exiles. (p. 518)
emirs (i miuhrs′) Muslim army leaders. (p. 393)
emperor (em′ phur uhr) Ruler of an empire. (p. 233)
empire (em′ pīr) Territories governed by a single ruler or nation. (p. 61)
enclosure (en klō′ zuhr) Fencing off common land for individual use. (p. 525)
erosion (i rō′ zuhn) Wearing away by wind, water, and ice. (p. 12)
estates (e stāts′) French social classes. (p. 513)
euro (yur′ ō) Currency used by members of the European Union. (p. 665)
excavate (ek′ skuh vāt) Uncover by digging. (p. 27)
excommunicated (ek skuh myū nuh kā ted) Barred as a member of the Roman Catholic Church. (p. 382)
extended families (ek sten′ duhd fam′ uh lēs) Parents, children, and other relatives living together in one house. (p. 639)

F

factories (fak′ tuhr ēz) Buildings where goods are manufactured. (p. 200)

factory system (fak′ tuh rē sis′ tuhm) Workers and machines in one place to make goods. (p. 527)
fairs (fâuhrz) Medieval gatherings for trade. (p. 402)
fasces (fas′ ēz) Rods tied around an ax. (p. 215)
federal (fed′ uhr uhl) National government. (p. 546)
feudalism (fyū′ dl iz uhm) Medieval political system based on the relation of lords to vassals. (p. 367)
fiefs (fēfs) Pieces of land given to vassals by their lords. (p. 367)
flying shuttle (flī′ ēng shut′ l) Weaving device that carries thread quickly back and forth across the piece being woven. (p. 527)
foreign policy (fōr′ uhn pol′ uh sē) Relations with other countries. (p. 507)
forum (fōr′ uhm) Meeting place. (p. 653)
Forum (fōr′ uhm) Roman public square. (p. 215)
freemen (frē′ muhn) Peasants who paid the lord for the right to farm their own land. (p. 377)
freedmen (frēd′ muhn) Former enslaved people. (p. 234)
friars (frī uhrs) Preachers. (p. 385)

G

galleons (gal′ ē uhns) Spanish ships. (p. 459)
garrison (gar′ uh suhn) Military force stationed in an area. (p. 610)
genocide (jen′ uh sīd) Deliberate destruction of an entire people. (p. 620)
gentiles (jen′ tīls) Non-Jews. (p. 249)
geography (jē ahg ruh fē) Study of the earth and the ways people live and work on it. (p. 5)
glaciers (glā′ shuhrz) Great ice sheets. (p. 13)
gladiatorial games (glad′ ē uh tōr ē uhl gāmz) Roman games in which gladiators fought. (p. 215)
gladiators (glad′ ē ā tuhrz) Fighters in gladiatorial games. (p. 238)
glasnost (glaz nōst) Russian policy allowing openness. (p. 633)
grand jury (grand jūr′ ē) Jury that examines accusations and advises criminal charges. (p. 415)
Greek fire (grēk fīr) Chemical weapon used by the Byzantines. (p. 324)
greenhouse effect (grēn hows uh fekt) Carbon dioxide traps heat from the Earth's surface. (p. 664)
guerrilla warfare (guh ril′ uh wōr′ fār) Hit-and-run fighting. (p. 573)
guilds (gildz) Medieval craft organizations. (p. 406)
guillotine (gil′ uh tēn) Machine that cuts off a victim's head. (p. 518)

H

haciendas (ah sē en′ duhz) Large ranches. (p. 640)
hajj (haj) Muslim journey to Makkah. (p. 336)
hard-liners (hahrd līnuhrz) People who stick to their ideas regardless of circumstances. (p. 632)
heavy industry (hev′ ē in′ duhs trē) Industry that manufactures machines. (p. 611)
helots (hel′ uhtz) Enslaved people owned by city-states. (p. 164)
heresy (her′ uh sē) Religious belief at odds with church doctrine. (p. 253)
heretic (her′ uh tik) Church member who disagrees with official doctrine. (p. 451)
hieroglyphic (hī uhr uh glif′ ik) Egyptian writing system based on pictures. (p. 77)
Holocaust (hol′ uh kahst) Nazi program of genocide against the Jews. (p. 621)
holy of holies (hō′ lē of hō′ lēs) Innermost and most sacred chamber of a temple. (p. 104)
home territory (hōm ter′ uh tōr ē) Area where hunters and food gatherers lived. (p. 35)
hostage (hos′ tij) Person held by another until certain promises are carried out. (p. 193)
humanists (hyū′ muh nists) Philosophers who believe that people are important. (p. 433)
hypothesis (hī poth′ uh sis) Possible explanation for a problem. (p. 188)

I

icons (ī konz) Sacred pictures of Eastern Orthodoxy. (p. 325)
imam (i mam′) Muslim prayer leader. (p. 335)
immigrants (im′ uh gruhnts) People who settle permanently in a different country. (p. 534)
imperialism (im pir′ ē uh liz uhm) Establishing colonies and building empires. (p. 579)
indentured servants (in den′ chuhrd ser′ vuhntz) Settlers who pledged labor for their passage to the Americas. (p. 495)
indulgences (in dul′ juhnt sez) Church pardons that lessen punishment for sins. (p. 450)

industrialized (in dus′ trē uh līzd) Developed industry. (p. 533)

inflation (in flā shuhn) Period when prices go up and money value goes down. (p. 240)

interchangeable parts (in tuhr chān juh buhl parts) Machine parts made to a uniform size so they can be easily replaced. (p. 527)

internal combustion engine (in tuhr′ nuhl kuhm buhs′ chuhn en′ juhn) Engine that is fueled by gasoline. (p. 535)

isolationist (ī sō lā shun ist) A country that stays out of the affairs of other countries. (p. 607)

izbas (iz′ bahs) One-room wooden cabin built by Eastern Slavs. (p. 348)

J

jarls (yahrlz) Viking military leaders. (p. 301)

journeyman (jer′ nē muhn) Person who works under a master for a daily wage. (p. 406)

joust (jowst) Contest on horseback between two knights. (p. 374)

judge (juj) Hebrew tribe leader. (p. 112)

junker (jung′ kuhr) Rich Prussian landowner. (p. 574)

junta (hun′ tuh) Committee organized to take over a government. (p. 553)

juris prudentes (jū′ ruhs prū′ duhntz) Roman lawyers. (p. 236)

K

kaiser (kī′ zuhr) German emperor. (p. 574)

keep (kēp) Strongest part of a castle. (p. 371)

khan (kahn) Mongol leader. (p. 353)

king's peace (kings pēs) Protection extended to any area an Anglo-Saxon king visited. (p. 295)

knight (nīt) Warrior on horseback. (p. 369)

kremlin (krem′ luhn) Russian fortress. (p. 354)

L

labyrinth (lab′ uh rinth) Maze. (p. 153)

ladies (lā′ dēz) Noblewomen. (p. 372)

landforms (land′ forms) Physical features of the earth's surface. (p. 9)

latifundias (lat uh fuhn′ dē uhs) Large Roman estates. (p. 225)

latitude (lat′ uh tūd) Distance north or south of the Equator. (p. 14)

legends (lej′ undz) Folktales or stories passed down from generation to generation. (p. 22)

legionaries (lē′ juh ner ēz) Roman soldiers. (p. 221)

legions (lē juhnz) Divisions of Roman soldiers. (p. 221)

liberals (lib′ uhr uhls) People who favor political reforms. (p. 566)

limited government (lim′ uh tid guv′ uhrn muhnt) Government has only powers given to it by the people. (p. 513)

lords (lordz) Medieval nobles. (p. 283)

M

macadam road (muh kad′ uhm rōd) Road made of layers of crushed rock. (p. 529)

manifest destiny (man′ uh fest des′ tuh nē) Belief that the United States should extend from coast to coast. (p. 548)

mandate (man′ dāt) Authority to govern. (p. 607)

manors (man′ uhrz) Medieval estates with a lord and tenants. (p. 375)

mantle (man′ tl) Part of the earth beneath the crust and above the core. (p. 10)

martial law (mar′ shuhl lah) Rule by the army instead of by civil government. (p. 505)

mass (mas) Worship service. (p. 382)

masters (mas′ tuhrz) Experts. (p. 406)

megaron (meg′ uh ron) Square room in the center of a Mycenaean palace. (p. 155)

mercantilism (mer′ kuhn tēl iz uhm) System in which colonies provide wealth to their parent country. (p. 508)

mercenaries (mer′ suh nār ēz) Men hired to be soldiers for a foreign country. (p. 175)

messiah (muh′ sī′ uh) Savior. (p. 248)

mestizos (me stē′ zōz) People of mixed European and Native American ancestry. (p. 490)

metropolitans (met ruh pol′ uh tuhns) Eastern Orthodox Church officials in charge of large cities. (p. 325)

migrate (mī′ grāt) To move from one place to another. (p. 34)

minerals (min′ uhr uhls) Nonliving substances found beneath the earth's surface. (p. 19)

ministers (min′ uh stuhrz) Protestant religious leaders. (p. 451)

minstrels (min′ struhlz) Medieval traveling poets and singers. (p. 285)

missionary (mish′ uh ner ē) Person who tries to convert nonbelievers. (p. 250)

mobilize (mō′ buh līz) Prepare troops for action. (p. 604)

monarchies (mon′ uhr kēz) Countries ruled by a king or queen. (p. 411)
monasteries (mon′ uh ster ēz) Places where monks live. (p. 255)
monks (mungks) Men who live in a religious community. (p. 255)
monopoly (muh nop′ uh lē) Total control. (p. 508)
monsoons (mon sūnz) Seasonal winds that change direction. (p. 16)
mosaics (mō zā′ iks) Colorful pictures made of stone or glass. (p. 323)
mosque (mosk) Muslim house of worship. (p. 335)
mummy (mum ē) Wrapped body of a preserved dead person. (p. 73)
mundus (muhn′ duhs) Meeting point of the worlds of the living and the dead for the Romans. (p. 216)
municipal (myū nis′ uh puhl) Relating to a city. (p. 215)
mutiny (myūt′ n ē) Revolt against officers. (p. 472)

N

nationalists (nash′ uh nuhl ists) People in favor of national independence. (p. 566)
national workshops (nash′ uh nuhl wuhrk′ shops) Factories run by workers but paid for by the government. (p. 570)
natural resources (nach′ uhr uhl rē′ sōr sez) Materials found in nature. (p. 19)
necropolis (nek rop′ uh luhs) Etruscan cemetery. (p. 214)
nobles (nō′ buhlz) People having high rank in a kingdom. (p. 90)
nomadic (nō mad′ ik) Wandering. (p. 106)
nonrenewable resources (non ri nū′ uh buhl rē sōr sez) Irreplaceable natural resources. (p. 20)
nuns (nunz) Women belonging to a religious order. (p. 255)

O

oath-helpers (ōth help′ erz) Germans who swore an accused person was telling the truth. (p. 269)
ocean current (ō′ shun kur′ uhnt) Water that flows in the ocean in a steady stream. (p. 16)
oligarchy (ol′ uh gahr kē) Government in which a few people rule. (p. 169)
omens (ō′ muhnz) Signs believed to indicate the future. (p. 214)
open-hearth process (ō′ puhn hahrth prah′ ses) Process that uses a special kind of furnace to make steel inexpensively. (p. 529)
oracles (ōr′ uh kuhlz) Greeks through whom the gods spoke. (p. 179)
oracle bones (ōr′ uh kuhl bōnz) Bones used by the Shang to receive messages from ancestors. (p. 90)
orator (ōr′ uh ter) Public speaker. (p. 195)
ordeal (ōr dēl) Painful test used by the Germans to decide innocence or guilt. (p. 269)
orders (ōr′ duhrs) Groups of friars. (p. 386)

P

page (pāj) Person who helped knights care for their horses and armor. (p. 373)
pancratium (pan krā′ shē uhm) Olympic event that combined boxing and wrestling. (p. 183)
pandemics (pan dem′ icks) Epidemics spread over a wide region. (p. 664)
papal line of demarcation (pā′ puhl līn ov dē mahr kā′ shuhn) Line drawn in 1493 dividing Spanish and Portuguese land claims. (p. 473)
papyrus (puh pī′ ruhs) Egyptian paper. (p. 78)
parchment (parch′ muhnt) Material made from thin animal skin used for windows and as paper. (p. 153)
parish (par′ ish) Area assigned to a local church. (p. 253)
patriarchs (pā′ trē arks) Most important bishops in the early Christian church. (p. 253)
patricians (puh trish′ uhnz) Powerful upper-class citizens of ancient Rome. (p. 219)
peninsulares (puh nin sū la′ rās) Colonials born in Spain who later came to the Americas. (p. 490)
pentathlon (pen tath′ luhn) Olympic game made up of five events. (p. 183)
perestroika (pār uhs troi kuh) Russian system of restructuring. (p. 633)
perioeci (pār ē ē′ sī) Merchants and artisans in Spartan villages. (p. 166)
phalanx (fā′ langks) Greek infantry formation. (p. 194)
pharaoh (fār′ ō) Egyptian ruler. (p. 70)
philosophes (fē luh zofs′) French philosophers of the 1700s. (p. 514)
philosophia (fi la sō fē′ ya) The love of wisdom, according to the Greeks. (p. 185)
piazza (pē aht′ suh) Italian city square. (p. 436)
pilgrimage (pil′ gruh mij) Religious journey to a shrine or holy place. (p. 133)
pilgrims (pil′ gruhms) People who travel to a holy place to worship. (p. 332)
pillars of faith (pil′ uhrs of fāth) Five Muslim duties as described in the Quran. (p. 335)

planned communities (pland kuh myū′ nuh tēz) Cities built to a definite plan. (p. 85)
plebeians (pli bē uhnz) Poor and lower-class citizens of ancient Rome. (p. 219)
plebiscite (pleb′ uh sīt) Popular vote. (p. 563)
polar zone (pō′ luhr zōn) Climate zone more than 60° north or south of the Equator. (p. 15)
polis (pah′ lis) Greek city-state. (p. 163)
political parties (puh lit′ uh kuhl par′ tēz) Groups with set ideas about government. (p. 546)
political science (puh lit′ uh kuhl sī′ uhns) Study of government. (p. 187)
popular sovereignty (pop′ yuh luhr sov′ ruhn tē) Idea that government derives its powers from the people. (p. 513)
population (pop ū lā shuhn) Number of living things in a particular area. (p. 42)
population explosion (pop ū lā′ shuhn ek splō′ zhuhn) Sudden growth in the number of people. (p. 136)
precipitation (prē sip uh tā shuhn) Falling moisture such as snow or rain. (p. 16)
prehistory (prē′ his tuh rē) Time before people began to keep written records. (p. 33)
prevailing winds (pri vā′ lēng winds) Winds that blow mostly from one direction. (p. 16)
priest (prēst) Religious leader, usually Roman Catholic or Eastern Orthodox. (p. 253)
priest-king (prēst king) Sumerian governmental and religious leader. (p. 59)
printing press (prin′ tēng pres) Machine for printing books, using movable type. (p. 441)
privatize (prī vuh tīz) Allow ownership by private citizens. (p. 649)
proletariat (pro luh tār′ ē uht) Industrial working class. (p. 568)
prophecy (prof′ uh sē) Statement of what might happen in the future. (p. 179)
prophets (prof′ its) People claiming to have messages from God. (p. 112)
protectorate (pruh tek′ tuhr it) Country that gives up foreign policy to an imperial authority. (p. 582)
provinces (prah′ vins uhs) Political districts. (p. 119)
psalms (sahms) Sacred songs. (p. 112)
publicans (pub′ luh′ kuhnz) Ancient Roman tax collectors. (p. 225)
purges (per′ juhs) Removals of undesirable members. (p. 631)
pyramids (pir′ uh midz) Large Egyptian tombs. (p. 71)

Q

quipus (k′ pūz) Inca counting devices. (p. 142)

R

referendum (ref ah ren′ duhm) Popular vote. (p. 660)
reformation (ref uhr mā′ shuhn) Change. (p. 449)
reform (rē form) Change that leads to improvement. (p. 61)
reign (rān) Period of power. (p. 63)
relative location (rel uhtiv lō kā shun) Location of a place in relation to other places. (p. 6)
relics (rel′ iks) Sacred objects from the past. (p. 319)
relief (ri lēf′) Differences in height between a region's summits and lowlands. (p. 9)
renewable resources (ri nū′ uh buhl rē sōr sez) Replaceable natural resources. (p. 20)
repealed (ri pēld′) Abolished or called back. (p. 507)
representative government (rep ri ent′ uht iv guv′ uhrn muhnt) System of ruling in which officials are elected. (p. 546)
republic (ri pub′ lik) Government in which citizens choose their leaders. (p. 219)
revolution (rev uh lū′ shuhn) Activity designed to overthrow a government. (p. 503)
right of extraterritoriality (rīt ov ek struh ter i tōr ē al′ uh tē) Right of an accused person in a different country to be tried in a court of his or her own nation. (p. 587)
river system (riv′ uhr sis tuhm) River and all streams that flow into it. (p. 14)
rule by divine right (rūl bī duh vīn′ rīt) Rule based on the theory that a monarch's right to rule comes from God. (p. 243)
runes (rūnz) Letters of the Viking alphabet. (p. 303)

S

sabbath (sab′ uhth) Day of the week used for rest and worship. (p. 113)
sans-culottes (san skū′ lahts) French city workers and peasants in the 1700s. (p. 518)
satellite nations (sat′ l īt nā shuhns) Countries controlled by another, stronger country. (p. 626)
scientific method (sī uhn tif′ ik meth′ uhd) Process used by scientists for study. (p. 188)

scorched-earth policy (skōrchd uhrth pahl′ uh sē) Tactic of destruction used by a retreating army. (p. 564)
scribe (skrīb) Sumerian writer. (p. 58)
scriptures (skrip′ churz) Sacred writings. (p. 247)
sea dog (sē dahg) Veteran sea captain in Tudor England. (p. 477)
seceding (si sēd′ ēng) Withdrawing. (p. 551)
seminary (sem′ uh ner ē) School for training priests. (p. 454)
seneschal (sēn′ uh shuhl) Medieval official who looked after the noble's fiefs. (p. 375)
sepoys (sē′ pois) Indian soldiers in the British army. (p. 585)
serfs (serfz) Medieval poor people bound to the land. (p. 285)
shadoof (shuh dūf′) Egyptian machine used to raise water. (p. 68)
sheriff (sher′ if) English government official in charge of a shire. (p. 295)
shires (shīrz) Districts in England. (p. 295)
shrines (shrīns) Sacred places to worship. (p. 154)
silent barter (sī luhnt bahr′ ter) Method of exchanging goods without talking; used in the middle kingdoms of Africa. (p. 132)
slums (slumz) Run-down city areas. (p. 551)
smelting (smel′ tēng) Heating iron or metals to remove impurities. (p. 118)
social justice (sō′ shuhl jus′ tis) Fair treatment of all people in a society. (p. 110)
social order (sō′ shuhl ōr′ der) Social divisions according to wealth and other factors. (p. 213)
social security laws (sō shuhl si kyūr′ uh tē lahz) United States laws that provided for people's welfare. (p. 613)
Socratic method (sō krat′ ik me′ thuhd) Form of questioning developed by Socrates. (p. 186)
soothsayers (sūth′ sā uhrz) People who are believed to be able to fortell the future. (p. 214)
sovereign (sah′ vuh ruhn) Independent and self-governing. (p. 649)
soviets (sō′ vē ets) Communist committees that represent workers and soldiers. (p. 610)
specialization (spesh uh luh zā′ shuhn) Development of occupations. (p. 45)
spheres of influence (sfērs of in′ flū uhns) Areas in one country in which another country has special rights. (p. 585)
spinning jenny (spin′ ēng jen′ ē) Machine for spinning that uses many spindles. (p. 527)
spirits (spēr′ itz) Supernatural beings. (p. 89)
squire (skwīr) Young noble under the care and training of a knight. (p. 373)
stable government (stā′ buhl guv′ uhrn muhnt) Firmly established government. (p. 545)
strike (strīk) Stop work. (p. 569)
subsistence farmers (suhb sis stuhns far muhrs) People who produce only enough food for their own use. (p. 638)
swastika (swos′ tuh kuh) Hooked black cross used as a Nazi symbol. (p. 614)
syllogism (sil′ uh jiz uhm) Form of reasoning developed by Aristotle. (p. 188)

T

tariffs (tar′ ifz) Taxes placed on goods entering one country from another. (p. 235)
tectonic plates (tek ton′ ik plāts) Slow-moving sections of the earth. (p. 10)
temperate zone (tem′ puhr it zōn) Climate zone between 30° and 60° north or south of the Equator. (p. 15)
tenants (ten′ uhnts) People who live and work on someone else's land. (p. 155)
tenements (ten′ uh muhnts) Apartments that meet minimum standards. (p. 551)
terrorism (tār′ ōr izm) Violence to achieve a political goal. (p. 660)
textile (tek′ stuhl) Woven cloth. (p. 526)
theology (thē ol′ uh jē) Study of religion. (p. 320)
theses (thē′ sēz) Statements written by Luther criticizing Church practices. (p. 450)
tithes (tīthz) Payments to the church. (p. 384)
tournaments (tur′ nuh muhnts) Contests to test the skill of knights. (p. 374)
trade unions (trād yū′ nyuhns) Associations of workers. (p. 533)
treaties (trē′ tēz) Formal agreements between nations. (p. 103)
trench warfare (trench wōr′ fāuhr) Warfare in which opposing forces attack from a system of trenches. (p. 604)
trial jury (trī uhl jūr′ ē) Group of people that decides whether a person accused of a crime is innocent or guilty. (p. 415)
tribunes (trib′ yūnz) Roman officials elected to protect the lower class. (p. 220)
triremes (trī′ rēmz) Greek warships. (p. 172)
triumph (trī′ uhmf) Parade to welcome home a Roman hero. (p. 215)

triumvirate (trī um' vuhr it) Group of three people who rule with equal power. (p. 228)
tropical zone (trop' uh kuhl zōn) Climate zone between 30° north and 30° south of the Equator. (p. 15)
tyranny (tir' uh nē) Unjust use of power. (p. 517)

U

unions (yūn' yuhns) Groups of people joined together for a common cause, especially medieval students and teachers. (p. 387)
universal male suffrage (yū nuh ver' suhl māl suhf' rij) Right of all men to vote. (p. 569)
universities (yū ni ver' suh tēs) Institutions of higher learning. (p. 387)
urbanization (uhr buh nuh zā' shuhn) Growth of cities. (p. 551)
utopian socialists (yū tō' pē uhn sō' shuh lists) People who want to set up ideal communities based on economic cooperation. (p. 568)

V

vassal (vas' uhl) Medieval noble who served a lord of higher rank. (p. 368)
veche (ve' chuh) Russian town assembly. (p. 350)
veto (vē' tō) Refuse consent. (p. 219)
viceroy (vīs roi) Ruler of a viceroyalty. (p. 490)
viceroyalties (vīs' roi uhl tēz) Districts in Spain's colonies in the Americas. (p. 490)
vizier (vi zir') Chief adviser to the caliph of the Abbasids. (p. 338)
volcano (vol kā' nō) Opening in the earth's crust through which, when active, steam, ashes, and magma are forced. (p. 11)

W

weapons of mass destruction (we pons ov mas di struk shuhn) Weapons such as nuclear bombs, poisonous chemicals, and biological weapons that spread disease. (p. 663)
wergeld (wuhr' geld) Fine paid by the family of a German who committed a crime. (p. 269)
witan (wi' tuhn) Member of the witenagemot. (p. 295)
witenagemot (wit uhn uh' guh mōt) Anglo-Saxon council that advised the king. (p. 295)

Z

zaibatsu (zī bah tsū) Industrialist families in Japan. (p. 589)
zakah (zuh kah') Muslim charitable giving. (p. 335)
ziggurat (zig' uh rat) Mesopotamian temple. (p. 57)

Index

D

E

F

Spanish Glossary

A

abbot / abad jefe de monasterio. (pág. 255)
abdicate / abdicar dejar al trono. (pág. 565)
absolute location / localización absoluta posición exacta de un lugar en la superficie de la tierra. (pág. 5)
acropolis / acrópolis colina fortificada en las ciudades de la antigua Grecia. (pág. 163)
act of homage / acto de homenaje ceremonia en la cual un vasallo promete lealtad a su señor. (pág. 368)
ages / épocas períodos de tiempo. (pág. 27)
aggression /agresión actos violentos (pág. 645)
agora / ágora plaza pública en las ciudades de la antigua Grecia. (pág. 163)
airlift / puente aéreo sistema de transportar provisiones por avión a un área aislada. (pág. 626)
alchemists / alquimistas científicos que trataron de cambiar los metales a oro y plata. (pág. 343)
alliances / alianzas acuerdos entre pueblos o países. (pág. 195)
amendments / enmiendas cambios de ley. (pág. 513)
ancestors / antepasados miembros de la familia de generaciones pasadas. (pág. 89)
annexation / anexión incorporación de áreas dentro de un estado existente. (pág. 549)
anointed / ungido untado con aceite bendito. (pág. 279)
anthropologists / antropólogos personas que se dedican al estudio de los seres humanos. (pág. 24)
apartheid / *apartheid* separación de las razas. (pág. 659)
apostles / apóstoles hombres escogidos por Jesús para enseñar sus creencias a otros. (pág. 253)
appeasement / apaciguamiento cederse a demandas (pág. 615)
apprentice / aprendiz persona que está aprendiendo una artesanía u oficio. (pág. 406)
archaeology / arqueología estudio de los restos de culturas humanas antiguas. (pág. 25)
archaeologists / arqueólogos personas que se dedican al estudio de ruinas y artefactos. (pág. 24)
archbishops / arzobispos obispos titulares en las iglesias de las grandes ciudades. (pág. 253)
aristocrats / aristócratas miembros de la clase alta. (pág. 164)
armada / armada flota de buques de guerra. (pág. 459)
armaments / armamentos equipo militar. (pág. 605)
armistice / armisticio acuerdo para suspender peleas. (pág. 605)
artifacts / artefactos productos de habilidades humanas. (pág. 25)
artillary / artillería armas montadas. (pág. 604)
artisans / artesanos trabajadores expertos. (pág. 57)
assembly line / línea de montaje sistema de trabajo en el cual cada trabajador agrega una parte a un producto hasta que está ensamblado. (pág. 528)
astrolabe / astrolabio instrumento de navegación usado para determinar la latitud. (pág. 467)
astronomers / astrónomos personas que estudian los cuerpos celestes. (pág. 122)
authoritarian rule / régimen autoritario gobierno en que una persona o partido político tiene todo el poder. (pág. 658)
automation / automatización proceso en el cual las máquinas reemplazan a los trabajadores. (pág. 527)
autonomous / autónomo que se gobierna por sí solo. (pág. 654)

B

bailiff / mayordomo oficial medieval que vigilaba que los campesinos hicieran su trabajo. (pág. 376)
balance of power / equilibrio de poder fuerza igual entre países. (pág. 566)
balance of trade / equilibrio de comercio diferencia entre la cantidad de mercancía que un país exporta a la que importa. (pág. 492)
bandeirantes / **bandeirantes** aventureros de fortuna del Brasil colonial. (pág. 488)
bands / bandas grupos prehistóricos que colectaban comida y vivían juntos. (pág. 34)
barbaroi* / *barbaroi personas que no seguían las costumbres griegas. (pág. 197)
barter / trocar cambiar artículos sin el uso de dinero. (pág. 241)
berserkers* / *berserkers guerreros vikingos. (pág. 301)
bishop / obispo jefe de diócesis. (pág. 253)
blitzkrieg / *blitzkrieg* guerra relámpago. (pág. 616)
blockaded / bloqueado cerrado. (pág. 626)
blood feuds / enemistad hereditaria pleitos antiguos entre familias o clanes. (pág. 269)

bourgeosie / burguesía clase media. (pág. 514)
boyars / boyardos miembros de la clase rica en la Rusia zarista. (pág. 350)
boycott / boicotear rehusar a pagar. (pág. 509)
bull leaping / salto de toros tauromaquia minoica. (pág. 152)
burgesses / diputados representantes elegidos de Virginia en la época colonial. (pág. 495)
burghers / burgueses hombres libres o adinerados que vivían en pueblos medievales. (pág. 404)
burgs / burgos pueblos pequeños medievales. (pág. 403)

C

caliph / califa gobernante musulmán. (pág. 336)
campesinos / **campesinos** paisanos y granjeros latinoamericanos. (pág. 640)
canon laws / leyes canónicas leyes de la iglesia. (pág. 382)
capitalism / capitalismo sistema económico donde la mayoría de la producción es de propiedad privada. (pág. 633)
captaincies / capitanías territorios de Brasil dados a los nobles portugueses. (pág. 488)
caravans / caravanas grupos que viajaban juntos para la seguridad. (pág. 121)
caravel / carabela embarcación portuguesa. (pág. 468)
cash crops / cultivo comercial cosecha vendida en el mercado. (pág. 638)
castles / castillos grandes casas fortificadas. (pág. 370)
catacombs / catacumbas cementerios subterráneos. (pág. 214)
cathedrals / catedrales iglesias dirigidas por obispos. (pág. 386)
caudillo / caudillo dictador militar latinoamericano. (pág. 556)
census / censo escrutinio de la población. (pág. 234)
chancellor / rector director de universidad inglesa. (pág. 387); primer ministro. (pág. 614)
charters / cartas documentos que permitían a las ciudades el control de sus asuntos. (pág. 405)
chateaux* / *chateaux castillos franceses. (pág. 440)
chieftain / cacique jefe de clan. (pág. 267)
churches / iglesias grupos de personas que comparten sus mismas creencias religiosas. (pág. 252)
circuit judges / jueces de distrito jueces que viajan a través de un país. (pág. 415)
citadel / ciudadela fuerte. (pág. 85)
city-states / ciudades estados ciudades y los territorios de sus alrededores. (pág. 57)
civil disobedience / desobediencia civil el negar a obedecer las demandas del gobierno. (pág. 634)
civilians / civiles que no son soldados. (pág. 604)
civilization / civilización sociedad con conocimiento desarrollado de agricultura, comercio, gobierno, arte, y ciencia. (pág. 33)
civil wars / guerras civiles guerras entre los ciudadanos de una nación. (pág. 159)
clans / clanes grupos fundamentados en sus lazos familiares. (pág. 267)
classical writings / obras clásicas escrituras de la antigua Grecia y Roma. (pág. 433)
clergy / clero líderes religiosos. (pág. 367)
climate / clima promedio de las condiciones del tiempo en un lugar a través de un período de años. (pág. 14)
code of chivalry / código de caballerosidad reglamentos que tenían que seguir los caballeros. (pág. 373)
cold war / guerra fría hostilidad entre naciones sin pelear. (pág. 625)
collectivization / colectivización la unión de granjas pequeñas en granjas grandes controladas por el gobierno. (pág. 611)
colonies / colonias poblaciones permanentes. (pág. 105)
colonize / colonizar establecerse permanentemente en un lugar. (pág. 487)
communes / comunes grupos políticos formados por ciudadanos en la Italia medieval. (pág. 405)
communicable diseases / enfermedades contagiosas enfermedades que son transmitidas de una persona o animal infectado a otra persona o animal. (pág. 664)
compass / brújula instrumento usado para determinar direcciones. (pág. 467)
concentration camps / campos de concentración prisiones para enemigos políticos. (pág. 620)
conquistadores / **conquistadores** vencedores españoles en los años 1500. (pág. 473)
constitution / constitución leyes escritas usadas para gobernar un estado. (pág. 169)
constitutional monarchy / monarquía constitucional monarquía limitada en sus poderes por una constitución. (pág. 518)
consuls / cónsules jefes de la antigua República Romana. (pág. 219)

continental drift / deriva continental teoría de que se mueven los continentes. (pág. 10)
convents / conventos comunidades de monjas. (pág. 255)
converted / convertido cambiado. (pág. 277)
coracles / barcos de cuero pequeños barcos irlandeses. (pág. 290)
core / núcleo parte central de la tierra. (pág. 10)
***corregidores* / corregidores** oficiales de la realeza española. (pág. 423)
cotton gin / desmotadora de algodón máquina para limpiar el algodón. (pág. 527)
counts / condes oficiales del tribunal de justicia francés. (pág. 281)
coup / golpe de estado toma del gobierno por la fuerza. (pág. 648)
cremation ovens / hornos de cremación hornos para quemar los cuerpos y quedarlos reducidos en cenizas. (pág. 621)
crusades / cruzadas guerras hechas para recuperar de los musulmanes la Tierra Sagrada. (pág. 388)
crust / corteza terrestre capa exterior de la tierra. (pág. 10)
culture / cultura modo de vida. (pág. 61)
cuneiform / cuneiforme escritura sumeria hecha con signos en forma de cuña. (pág. 58)
czar / zar soberano ruso. (pág. 355)

D

dauphin* / *dauphin hijo mayor del rey de Francia. (pág. 417)
defensive league / liga defensiva grupo protector formado por las ciudades estados griegas. (pág. 173)
democratic / democrático que favorece la igualdad de toda la gente. (pág. 169)
depression / depresión decadencia económica. (pág. 608)
descendants / descendientes progenitura. (pág. 107)
de-Stalinization / de-Stalinización ataque a las políticas de Stalin. (pág. 633)
developing countries / países en desarrollo países progresando en la producción, la tecnología, o la norma de vida. (pág. 634)
dictator / dictador gobernante absoluto de un país. (pág. 228)
dictatorship / dictadura gobierno manejado por un dictador. (pág. 613)
diet / dieta asamblea formal. (pág. 421)
diocese / diócesis área bajo el control de un obispo. (pág. 253)
direct tax / impuesto directo impuesto pagado directamente a un gobierno. (pág. 509)
dissent / disensión crítica. (pág. 647)
doge* / *doge gobernante de la Venecia del Renacimiento. (pág. 439)
domesticated / domesticado sumiso. (pág. 42)
domestic system / sistema doméstico fabricación hecha en las casas de los trabajadores. (pág. 526)
domus* / *domus casa romana. (pág. 236)
dowry / dote riqueza que lleva la mujer cuando se casa. (pág. 322)
dubbing / armar ceremonia en la cual un escudero se hace caballero. (pág. 374)
dynasty / dinastía sucesión de soberanos de la misma familia. (pág. 88)

E

earthquake / terremoto temblor o deriva de una porción de la corteza terrestre. (pág. 11)
Eddas* / *Eddas poemas escritos basados en las historias de los dioses vikingos. (pág. 303)
elevation / elevación altitud. (pág. 9)
embalming / embalsamar proceso usado para mantener los cuerpos muertos sin que se descompusieran. (pág. 73)
emigrated / emigrado haber dejado el país de uno. (pág. 200)
émigrés* /*émigrés exiliados políticos franceses. (pág. 518)
emirs* / *emirs jefes del ejército musulmán. (pág. 393)
emperor / emperador gobernante de un imperio. (pág. 233)
empire / imperio territorios gobernados por un solo gobernante o nación. (pág. 61)
enclosure / cercado encierro de terrenos comunes para uso individual. (pág. 525)
erosion / erosión desgaste de la tierra por el viento, el agua, y el hielo. (pág. 12)
estates / estados clases sociales francesas. (pág. 513)
euro / euro moneda usada por los países miembros de la Unión Europea. (pág. 665)
excavate / excavar dejar al aire libre por medio de remover tierra. (pág. 27)
excommunicated / excomulgado excluido como miembro de la Iglesia Católica. (pág. 382)
extended families / familia extendida padres, hijos, y otros parientes viviendo juntos en un mismo hogar. (pág. 639)

F

factories / fábricas edificios donde artículos son manufacturados. (pág. 200)

factory system / sistema de fábricas trabajadores y maquinarias en un lugar para elaborar la mercancía. (pág. 527)

fairs / ferias recaudaciones medievales para el comercio. (pág. 402)

fasces / fasces varas atadas alrededor de un hacha. (pág. 215)

federal / federal gobierno nacional. (pág. 546)

feudalism / feudalismo sistema político medieval basado en la relación de los señores y sus vasallos. (pág. 367)

fiefs / feudos terrenos dados a los vasallos por sus señores. (pág. 367)

flying shuttle / lanzadera aparato tejedora que lleva el hilo rápidamente hacia adelante y de regreso a través de la pieza que se está tejiendo. (pág. 527)

foreign policy / política exterior relaciones con otros países. (pág. 507)

forum / foro lugar para reuniones. (pág. 653)

Forum / Foro plaza pública romana. (pág. 215)

freemen / hombres libres campesinos que pagaron a su señor por el derecho de sembrar su propia tierra. (pág. 377)

freedmen / libertos antiguos esclavos. (pág. 234)

friars / frailes predicadores. (pág. 385)

G

galleons / galeones barcos españoles. (pág. 459)

garrison / guarnición fuerza militar estacionada en un área. (pág. 610)

genocide / genocidio destrucción deliberada de toda una población. (pág. 620)

gentiles / gentiles que no son judíos. (pág. 249)

geography / geografía estudio de la tierra y las maneras en que viven y trabajan en ella la gente. (pág. 5)

glaciers / glaciares grandes mantos de hielo. (pág. 13)

gladiatorial games / juegos de gladiadores juegos romanos en los cuales luchaban los gladiadores. (pág. 215)

gladiators / gladiadores luchadores en los juegos de gladiadores. (pág. 238)

glasnost* / *glasnost política rusa para permitir franqueza. (pág. 633)

grand jury / gran jurado jurado que examina las acusaciones y aconseja los cargos criminales. (pág. 415)

Greek fire / fuego griego arma química usada por los bizantinos. (pág. 324)

greenhouse effect / efecto invernadero el bióxido de carbono retiene el calor de la superficie de la tierra. (pág. 664)

guerrilla warfare / guerra de guerrillas peleas de asaltar y esconderse. (pág. 573)

guilds / gremios organizaciones medievales de artesanos. (pág. 406)

guillotine / guillotina aparato que quita la cabeza de una víctima. (pág. 518)

H

***haciendas* / haciendas** grandes ranchos. (pág. 640)

hajj* / *hajj jornada musulmana hacia la Meca. (pág. 336)

hard-liners / extremistas personas que se apegan a sus ideas sin preocuparse de las circunstancias. (pág. 632)

heavy industry / industria pesada industria que fabrica la maquinaria. (pág. 611)

helots / ilotas esclavos que eran propiedad de las ciudades estados. (pág. 164)

heresy / herejía creencias religiosas en contra de la doctrina de la iglesia. (pág. 253)

heretic / hereje miembro de la iglesia que no está de acuerdo con la doctrina oficial. (pág. 451)

heiroglyphic / jeroglífico sistema de escritura egipcia basada en figuras. (pág. 77)

Holocaust / Holocausto programa nazi de genocidio en contra de los judíos. (pág. 621)

holy of holies / santo de santo la cámara más profunda y más sagrada de un templo. (pág. 104)

home territory / territorio de hogar lugar donde vivían los cazadores y recolectores de comidas. (pág. 35)

hostage / rehén persona detenida por otra hasta que se cumplan ciertas promesas. (pág. 193)

humanists / humanistas filósofos que creen que la gente es importante. (pág. 433)

hypothesis / hipótesis explicación posible para un problema. (pág. 188)

I

icons / iconos dibujos sagrados del ortodoxo oriental. (pág. 325)

imam / *imam* guía musulmán de oración. (pág. 335)
immigrants / inmigrantes personas que se quedan a vivir permanentemente en un país diferente al suyo. (pág. 534)
imperialism / imperialismo establecer colonias y construir imperios. (pág. 579)
indentured servants / sirvientes escriturados colonos que prometían trabajar a cambio de su viaje a las Américas. (pág. 495)
indulgences / indulgencias perdones de la iglesia que disminuyen el castigo por pecados. (pág. 450)
industrialized / industrializado industria desarrollada. (pág. 533)
inflation / inflación período cuando se suben los precios y se baja el valor de dinero. (pág. 240)
interchangeable parts / partes intercambiables partes maquinarias hechas de un tamaño uniforme para que puedan ser reemplazadas fácilmente. (pág. 527)
internal combustion engine / motor de combustión interna motor que trabaja con gasolina. (pág. 535)
isolationist / aislacionista país que se mantiene afuera de los asuntos de otros países. (pág. 607)
izbas / *izbas* cabañas de un cuarto construidas por los eslavos orientales. (pág. 348)

J

jarls / *jarls* jefes militares vikingos. (pág. 301)
journeyman / oficial persona que trabaja bajo un maestro por un salario diario. (pág. 406)
joust / justa combate en caballo entre dos caballeros. (pág. 374)
judge / juez líder de tribu hebrea. (pág. 112)
junker / ***junker*** terrateniente rico prusiano. (pág. 574)
junta / junta comité organizado para tomar posesión de un gobierno. (pág. 553)
juris prudentes* / *juris prudentes abogados romanos. (pág. 236)

K

kaiser / káiser emperador alemán. (pág. 574)
keep / torre de homenaje la parte más fuerte de un castillo. (pág. 371)
khan / khan líder mongol. (pág. 353)
king's peace / paz del rey protección extendida en cualquier área que visitara un rey anglosajón. (pág. 295)
knight / caballero guerrero a caballo. (pág. 369)
kremlin / kremlin fuerte ruso. (pág. 354)

L

labyrinth / laberinto caminos que entrecruzan, de manera que es difícil orientarse. (pág. 153)
ladies / damas mujeres de la nobleza. (pág. 372)
landforms / formas de tierra características físicas de la superficie de la tierra. (pág. 9)
latifundias / latifundios grandes estados romanos. (pág. 225)
latitude / latitud distancia al Norte o al Sur del ecuador. (pág. 14)
legends / leyendas cuentos o historias populares que se han pasado de generación en generación. (pág. 22)
legionaries / legionarios soldados romanos. (pág. 221)
legions / legiones divisiones de los soldados romanos. (pág. 221)
liberals / liberales personas que están a favor de las reformas políticas. (pág. 566)
limited government / gobierno limitado gobierno que tiene solamente los poderes otorgados por la gente. (pág. 513)
lords / señores nobles medievales. (pág. 283)

M

macadam road / calle de macadán camino hecho de capas de roca triturada. (pág. 529)
manifest destiny / destino manifiesto creencia que los Estados Unidos deberían extenderse de costa a costa. (pág. 548)
mandate / mandato autoridad para gobernar. (pág. 607)
manors / feudos estados medievales con un señor y habitantes. (pág. 375)
mantle / capa terrestre parte de la tierra debajo de la corteza y arriba del núcleo. (pág. 10)
martial law / ley marcial dominio del ejército en lugar de mando del gobierno civil. (pág. 505)
mass / misa servicio de alabanza. (pág. 382)
masters / maestros artesanos expertos. (pág. 406)
megaron / megaron sala cuadrada al centro de un palacio micénico. (pág. 155)
mercantilism / mercantilismo sistema en el cual las colonias proveían de riquezas a su país patrón. (pág. 508)
mercenaries / mercenarios hombres pagados para servir de soldados de parte de un país extranjero. (pág. 175)
messiah / mesías salvador. (pág. 248)

mestizos / **mestizos** personas de ascendencia mixta europea e indígena americana. (pág. 490)
metropolitans / metropolitanos oficiales de la Iglesia Ortodoxo Oriental a cargo de ciudades grandes. (pág. 325)
migrate / migrar trasladarse de un lugar a otro. (pág. 34)
minerals / minerales substancias no vivas encontradas bajo la superficie de la tierra. (pág. 19)
ministers / ministros líderes religiosos protestantes. (pág. 451)
minstrels / trovadores poetas y cantores ambulantes medievales. (pág. 285)
missionary / misionero persona que trata de convertir a los que no creen. (pág. 250)
mobilize / movilizar preparar a las tropas para acción. (pág. 604)
monarchies / monarquías países gobernados por un rey o una reina. (pág. 411)
monasteries / monasterios lugares donde viven monjes. (pág. 255)
monks / monjes hombres que viven en una comunidad religiosa. (pág. 255)
monopoly / monopolio control total. (pág. 508)
monsoons / monzones vientos estacionales que cambian de dirección. (pág. 16)
mosaics / mosaicos dibujos llenos de color hechos de piedra o vidrio. (pág. 323)
mosque / **mezquita** casa de alabanza musulmana. (pág. 335)
mummy / momia cuerpo envuelto y preservado de una persona muerta. (pág. 73)
mundus / *mundus* para los romanos, el lugar donde se reúnen el mundo de los vivos y el mundo de los muertos. (pág. 216)
municipal / municipal tocante a una ciudad. (pág. 215)
mutiny / motín rebelión en contra de los oficiales. (pág. 472)

N

nationalists / nacionalistas personas a favor de la independencia nacional. (pág. 566)
national workshops / talleres nacionales fábricas dirigidas por los obreros pero pagadas por el gobierno. (pág. 570)
natural resources / recursos naturales materiales encontrados en la naturaleza. (pág. 19)
necropolis / necrópolis cementerio etrusco. (pág. 214)
nobles / nobles personas de clase alta en un reino. (pág. 90)
nomadic / nómada ambulante. (pág. 106)
nonrenewable resources / recursos no renovables recursos naturales irreemplazables. (pág. 20)
nuns / monjas mujeres que pertenecen a una orden religiosa. (pág. 255)

O

oath-helpers / colaboradores de juramento alemanes que prestaron juramento de que una persona acusada estaba diciendo la verdad. (pág. 269)
ocean current / corriente oceánica agua que fluye en el océano en un chorro constante. (pág. 16)
oligarchy / oligarquía gobierno en el cual varias personas gobiernan. (pág. 169)
omens / presagios signos que se creen indicar el futuro. (pág. 214)
open-hearth process / proceso de hogar abierto proceso que usa una clase especial de horno para producir económicamente el acero. (pág. 529)
oracles / oráculos griegos por los cuales hablaron los dioses. (pág. 179)
oracle bones / huesos del oráculo huesos usados por el Shang para recibir mensajes de los antepasados. (pág. 90)
orator / orador uno que habla públicamente. (pág. 195)
ordeal / prueba muy dura prueba dolorosa usada por los alemanes para determinar la inocencia o la culpa. (pág. 269)
orders / órdenes grupos de frailes. (pág. 386)

P

page / paje persona que ayudaba a los caballeros en cuidar sus caballos y sus armaduras. (pág. 373)
pancratium / pancracio evento olímpico que combinaba el boxeo y la lucha. (pág. 183)
pandemics / pandemias epidemias que se propagan por una región extensa. (pág. 664)
papal line of demarcation / línea papal de demarcación línea trazada en 1493 dividiendo las tierras demandadas por España y Portugal. (pág. 473)
papyrus / papiro papel egipcio. (pág. 78)
parchment / pergamino material hecho de pieles delgadas de animales usado para ventanas y papel. (pág. 153)

parish / parroquia área designada para una iglesia local. (pág. 253)
patriarchs / patriarcas los obispos más importantes de la iglesia cristiana antigua. (pág. 253)
patriarchs / patricios ciudadanos poderosos de la clase alta de la Roma antigua. (pág. 219)
***peninsulares* / peninsulares** colonos nacidos en España que vinieron luego a las Américas. (pág. 490)
pentathlon / pentatlón juego olímpico con cinco eventos. (pág. 183)
perestroika* / *perestroika sistema ruso de reestructuración. (pág. 633)
perioeci / *perioeci* mercaderes y artesanos de pueblos espartanos. (pág. 166)
phalanx / falange formación de infantería griega. (pág. 194)
pharaoh / faraón gobernante egipcio. (pág. 70)
philosophes* / *philosophes filósofos franceses de los años 1700. (pág. 514)
philosophia* / *philosophia el amor a la sabiduría, según los griegos. (pág. 185)
piazza* / *piazza zócalo italiano. (pág. 436)
pilgrimage / peregrinaje jornada religiosa a un santuario o lugar santo. (pág. 133)
pilgrims / peregrinos personas que viajan a un lugar santo para alabar. (pág. 332)
pillars of faith / pilares de fe cinco deberes musulmanes descritos en el Corán. (pág. 335)
planned communities / comunidades planeadas ciudades construidas según un plan definido. (pág. 85)
plebeians / plebeyos ciudadanos pobres y de baja clase de la Roma antigua. (pág. 219)
plebiscite / plebiscito voto popular. (pág. 563)
polar zone / zona polar zona atmosférica a más de 60° al norte o al sur del ecuador. (pág. 15)
polis / *polis* ciudad estado greco. (pág. 163)
political parties / partidos políticos grupos con ideas establecidas sobre el gobierno. (pág. 546)
political science / ciencia política estudio del gobierno. (pág. 187)
popular sovereignty / soberanía popular la idea de que el gobierno saca sus poderes de la gente. (pág. 513)
population / población número de habitantes que viven en una zona en particular. (pág. 42)
population explosion / explosión demográfica crecimiento inesperado del número de personas. (pág. 136)
precipitation / precipitación humedad cayendo tal como la lluvia o la nieve. (pág. 16)
prehistory / prehistoria la época antes de que las personas empezaron a mantener historias escritas. (pág. 33)
prevailing winds / vientos predominantes vientos que soplan principalmente de una dirección. (pág. 16)
priest / sacerdote líder religioso, generalmente católico romano u ortodoxo oriental. (pág. 253)
priest-king / rey sacerdote líder religioso y gubernamental sumerio. (pág. 59)
printing press / prensa máquina para imprimir libros usando tipos movibles. (pág. 441)
privatize / privatizar permitir que particulares sean dueños de negocios. (pág. 649)
proletariat / proletariado clase industrial trabajadora. (pág. 568)
prophecy / profecía declaración de lo que podría suceder en el futuro. (pág. 179)
prophets / profetas personas que pretenden tener mensajes de Dios. (pág. 112)
protectorate / protectorado país que deja su política exterior a cargo de una autoridad imperial. (pág. 582)
provinces / provincias distritos políticos. (pág. 119)
psalms / salmos cantos sagrados. (pág. 112)
publicans / publicanos colectores de impuestos de la Roma antigua. (pág. 225)
purges / purgas despidos de miembros indeseables. (pág. 631)
pyramids / pirámides grandes tumbas egipcias. (pág. 71)

Q

quipus / quipos artefactos con que contaban los inca. (pág. 142)

R

referendum / referéndum plebiscito o voto popular. (pág. 660)
reformation / reforma cambio. (pág. 449)
reform / reforma cambio que se hace para mejorar. (pág. 61)
reign / reinado período de poder. (pág. 63)
relative location / localización relativa localización de un lugar en relación a otros lugares. (pág. 6)
relics / reliquias objetos sagrados del pasado. (pág. 319)

741

relief / relieve diferencias de altura entre las cimas y las tierras bajas de una región. (pág. 9)
renewable resources / recursos renovables recursos naturales reemplazables. (pág. 20)
repealed / anulado revocado. (pág. 507)
representative government / gobierno representativo sistema de gobierno en el cual los oficiales son elegidos. (pág. 546)
republic / república gobierno en el cual los ciudadanos escogen a sus dirigentes. (pág. 219)
revolution / revolución actividad planeada para derrocar un gobierno. (pág. 503)
right of extraterritoriality / derecho extraterritorial derecho de una persona acusada en diferente país de ser procesado en un tribunal de su propia nación. (pág. 587)
river system / sistema de río un río y todas las corrientes que desembocan en él. (pág. 14)
rule by divine right / dominio por derecho divino mando basado en la teoría de que el derecho de gobernar de un monarca viene de Dios. (pág. 243)
runes / runas letras del alfabeto vikingo. (pág. 303)

S

sabbath / sábado día de la semana usado para descansar y venerar. (pág. 113)
sans-culottes* / *sans-culottes trabajadores municipales y campesinos franceses en los años 1700. (pág. 518)
satellite nations / naciones satélites países controlados por otro país más poderoso. (pág. 626)
scientific method / método científico proceso usado por los científicos para estudiar. (pág. 188)
scorched-earth policy / política de tierra quemada (táctica de avance) táctica de destrucción usada por un ejército al retroceder. (pág. 564)
scribe / escribiente escritor sumerio. (pág. 58)
scriptures / libros sagrados escrituras sagradas. (pág. 247)
sea dog / lobo de mar veterano del mar en Tudor, Inglaterra. (pág. 477)
seceding / separándose retirándose. (pág. 551)
seminary / seminario escuela para el entrenamiento de sacerdotes. (pág. 454)
seneschal / senescal oficial medieval que vigilaba los feudos de un noble. (pág. 375)
sepoys / cipayos soldados indios al servicio del ejército inglés. (pág. 585)
serfs / siervos gente pobre medieval vinculada a la tierra. (pág. 285)
shadoof / cigoñal maquinaria egipcia usada para levantar el agua. (pág. 68)
sheriff / gobernador civil oficial del gobierno inglés a cargo de un condado. (pág. 295)
shires / condados distritos de Inglaterra. (pág. 295)
shrines / capillas lugares sagrados para la veneración. (pág. 154)
silent barter / cambio silencioso método de cambiar artículos sin hablar; usado en los reinos medios de África. (pág. 132)
slums / barrios bajos áreas arruinadas de la ciudad. (pág. 551)
smelting / fundición calentamiento del hierro o de metales para remover impurezas. (pág. 118)
social justice / justicia social tratamiento justo a toda la gente de una sociedad. (pág. 110)
social order / orden social divisiones sociales de acuerdo a la riqueza y otros factores. (pág. 213)
social security laws / leyes de seguridad social leyes de los Estados Unidos proporcionadas para el bienestar de la gente. (pág. 613)
Socratic method / método socrático forma de cuestionamiento desarrollado por Sócrates. (pág. 186)
soothsayers / adivinos gente que se creen habilitados para predecir el futuro. (pág. 214)
sovereign/ soberano país independiente que se gobierna a sí mismo. (pág. 649)
soviets / soviéticos comités comunistas que representan a trabajadores y soldados. (pág. 610)
specialization / especialización desarrollo de profesiones. (pág. 45)
spheres of influence / esferas de influencia áreas en un país en los cuales otro país tiene derechos especiales. (pág. 585)
spinning jenny / máquina de hilar máquina para hilar algodón que utiliza muchos ejes. (pág. 527)
spirits / espíritus seres sobrenaturales. (pág. 89)
squire / escudero noble joven bajo el cuidado y entrenamiento de un caballero. (pág. 373)
stable government / gobierno estable gobierno establecido firmemente. (pág. 545)
strike / huelga paro laboral. (pág. 569)
subsistance farmers / agricultores de subsistencia personas que solamente producen comida suficiente para su propio consumo. (pág. 638)

swastika / esvástica cruz negra ganchuda usada como símbolo nazi. (pág. 614)
syllogism / silogismo forma de razonamiento desarrollado por Aristóteles. (pág. 188)

T

tariffs / tarifas impuestos exigidos para mercancía al entrar de un país a otro. (pág. 235)
tectonic plates / tectónica de placas secciones de la tierra que se mueven lentamente. (pág. 10)
temperate zone / zona templada zona climatológica entre 30° y 60° al norte y al sur del ecuador. (pág. 15)
tenants / arrendatarios personas que viven y trabajan en la tierra de otra persona. (pág. 155)
tenements / casas de vecindad apartamentos que cumplen con los mínimos requisitos para vivir. (pág. 551)
terrorism / terrorismo uso de violencia para llevar a cabo metas políticas. (pág. 660)
textile / textil tela de tejido. (pág. 526)
theology / teología estudio de la religión. (pág. 320)
theses / tesis declaraciones escritas por Lutero criticando las prácticas de la Iglesia. (pág. 450)
tithes / diezmo pagos a la iglesia. (pág. 384)
tournaments / torneos concursos para examinar las destrezas de los caballeros. (pág. 374)
trade unions / gremios asociaciones de trabajadores. (pág. 533)
treaties / tratados acuerdos formales entre naciones. (pág. 103)
trench warfare / guerra de trincheras guerra en la cual fuerzas enemigas atacan desde un sistema de trincheras. (pág. 604)
trial jury / jurado grupo de personas que deciden entre la inocencia o la culpabilidad de una persona acusada de un crimen. (pág. 415)
tribunes / tribunos oficiales romanos elegidos para proteger a las clases bajas. (pág. 220)
triremes / trirremes buques de guerra griegos. (pág. 172)
triumph / triunfo desfile de bienvenida a casa para un héroe romano. (pág. 215)
triumvirate / triunvirato grupo de tres personas que gobiernan con igualdad de poderes. (pág. 228)
tropical zone / zona tropical zona climatológica entre 30° al norte y 30° al sur del ecuador. (pág. 15)
tyranny / tiranía uso injusto de poder. (pág. 517)

U

unions / sindicatos grupos de personas unidas por una causa común, especialmente estudiantes y maestros en la época medieval. (pág. 387)
universal male sufferage / sufragio universal masculino derechos de todo hombre para votar. (pág. 569)
universities / universidades instituciones de la educación superior. (pág. 387)
urbanization / urbanización crecimiento de las ciudades. (pág. 551)
utopian socialists / socialistas utópicos personas que quieren establecer comunidades ideales basadas en la cooperación económica. (pág. 568)

V

vassal / vasallo noble medieval que servía a un señor de rango más alto. (pág. 368)
veche / veche asamblea en un pueblo ruso. (pág. 350)
veto / vetar rehusar permiso. (pág. 219)
viceroy / virrey gobernante de un virreinato. (pág. 490)
viceroyalties / virreinatos distritos de las colonias de España en las Américas. (pág. 490)
vizier / visir primer consejero al califa de los abasidas. (pág. 338)
volcano / volcán una abertura en la corteza terrestre por la cual están forzados vapor, cenizas y magma, cuando está activa. (pág. 11)

W

weapons of mass destruction / armas de destrucción masiva armas como bombas nucleares, sustancias químicas tóxicas y armas biológicas que transmiten enfermedades. (pág. 663)
wergeld / wergeld multa pagada por la familia de un alemán que cometió un crimen. (pág. 269)
witan / *witan* miembro de la *witenagemot*. (pág. 295)
witenagemot / *witenagemot* concilio anglosajón que aconsejaba al rey. (pág. 295)

Z

zaibatsu / zaibatsu familias industriales en el Japón. (pág. 589)
zakah / zakah dádivas caritativas musulmanas. (pág. 335)
ziggurat / *ziggurat* templo mesopotámico. (pág. 57)

Photo Credits

Abbreviation key: **AA** = The Art Archive; **AAA** = Ancient Art & Architecture; **AR** = Art Resource, NY; **BAL** = Bridgeman Art Library; **CB** = Corbis; **CS** = Corbis Sygma; **EL** = Erich Lessing; **MH** = Michael Holford; **LA** = Liaison Agency; **LOC** = Library of Congress; **ME** = Mary Evans Picture Library; **NGS** = National Geographic Society Image Collection; **NWPA** = North Wind Picture Archives; **PR** = Photo Researchers; **RH** = Robert Harding Picture Library; **RS** = Ronald Sheridan; **SM** = Stock Montage; **SPL** = Science Photo Library; **SS** = SuperStock; **TSM** = The Stock Market; **WC** = Woodfin Camp & Associates; **WF** = Werner Forman Archive

Front cover Scala/AR, (bkgrd)Cyberphoto; back cover EL/AR; **iii** RS/AAA; **iv** (t)MH, (b)Walters Art Gallery, Baltimore; **v** WF/AR; **vii** Steve Liss/Timepix; **2** (l)Pat L. Filed/Coleman, (r)Lauros-Giraudon/AR; **4** (t)WF/AR, (b)Tom Till/DRK Photo; **6** RH; **7** David R. Frazier Photolibrary; **8** (l)RS/AAA, (r)Alan Schein/TSM; **12** Mike Maple/WC; **16** Steve McCurry/Magnum; **18** Robert Francis/RH; **20** (l)Conoco, Inc., (r)courtesy Gulf Oil Corp.; **21** Ohio Dept. of Natural Resources/Dept. of Reclamation; **25** (l)Smithsonian Institution, (r)file photo; **26** (l)Kenneth Garrett/NGS, (r)Scala/AR; **28** (l)Gerry Clyde/MH, (r)Ira Block; **32** RS/AAA; **34** Zdenek Buriam; **35** American Museum of Natural History; **36** John Reader/SPL/PR; **37** American Museum of Natural History; **38** (t)Belinda Wright/DRK Photo, (bl)Tom Till/DRK Photo, (br)Peter Skinner/PR; **39** Rene Burri/Magnum; **41** file photo; **42** Zdenek Buriam; **43** Wolfgang Kaehler; **48** David Coulson/Robert Estall Photo Library; **49** (tl)A. DeWildenberg/LA, (tr)Betsy Blass/PR, (c)EL/AR, (b)David Coulson/Robert Estall Photo Library; **52** (l)Ali Meyer/BAL, (r)EL/AR; **54** (l)Scala/AR, (r)MH; **56** (l)MH, (r)John T. Wong/Index Stock Imagery/PNI; **58** Oriental Institute Museum, U. of Chicago/Victor Boswell/NGS; **61** AKG Photo; **63** Hirmer Verlag; **66** (l)Victor Boswell/NGS, (r)Egyptian National Museum, Cairo/SS; **68** Vladimir Bibic; **69** Giraudon/AR; **70** (l)Gianni Dagli Orti/CB, (r)Caroline Penn/CB; **71** Dallas & John Heaton/Corbis Los Angeles; **72** (c)British Museum; **73** Smithsonian Institution; **74** Metropolitan Museum of Art, Rogers Fund and Edward S. Harkness Gift,1929 (29.3.3); **76** SEF/AR; **77** (l)Smithsonian Institution, (r)Egyptian National Museum, Cairo/SS; **79** Courtesy Parke Davis & Co.; **82** (l)Archivo Iconografico, S.A./CB, (r)Angelo Hornak/CB; **85** Vision International; **86** Borromeo/AR; **87** Smithsonian Institution; **88** SM; **90** (l)AA, (r)Wan-Go Weng, Collection of Academia Sinica, Taipei, Taiwan, ROC; **91** (l)Arthur M. Sackler Museum, Harvard University, Bequest of Grenville L. Winthrop/BAL, (r)Ed Lallo/LA; **94** EL/Archaeological Museum, Istanbul, Turkey/AR; **95** (t)Gianni Dagli Orti/CB, (cl)MH, (cr)Metropolitan Museum of Art, Gift of Norbert Schimmel Trust, 1989 (1989.281.12). Photo by Schecter Lee, (b)EL/AR; **98** (l)AA, (r)Gianni Dagli Orti/CB; **100** EL/AR; **102** (l)Louvre, Paris/BAL, (r)Beghin Thierry/LA; **104 106** file photos; **107** Tom Lovell/NGS; **109** NWPA; **110** (l)AKG Photo, (r)file photo; **116** (l)AKG London, (r)Bill Lyons; **118** MH; **121** S. Fiore/SS; **123** (l)American Numismatic Society, (r)US Mint/LA; **124** George Holton/PR; **128** (l)RS/AAA, (r)WF/AR; **130** Timothy Kendall/Museum of Fine Arts, Boston; **131** WF/AR; **132** Geoff Renner/RH; **133** (l)Lee Boltin, (r)AA; **136** Mike St. Maur Sheil/Susan Griggs Agency; **138** O'Neill/AR; **139** (l)Nicholas M. Hellmuth/NGS, (r)SS; **140** Courtesy Department of Library Services, American Museum of Natural History; **144** LA; **145** (tl)file photo, (tr)Asian Art & Archaeology/CB, (c)Seattle Museum of Art/Laurie Platt Winfrey, (b)file photo; **148** (l)Smithsonian Institution, (r)Jack Fields/CB; **150** RS/AAA; **152** C.M. Dixon; **153** Eugene Gilliom; **154** Bettmann/CB; **157** (l)Gianni Dagli Orti/CB, (r)Wolfgang Kaehler; **158** (l)Louvre, Paris/SS, (r)Bettmann/CB; **159** (c)British Museum; **162** (l)AA, (r)Foto Marburg/AR; **166** Bettmann/CB; **167** MH; **168** S. Vidler/SS; **171** MH; **172** Peter Connolly; **174** (l)British Museum/BAL, (r)SS; **175** MH; **178** (l)Araldo de Luca/CB, (r)AAA; **180** (l)ME, (r)Photri; **182** Tom Lovell/NGS; **184** (l)SS, (r)The Purcell Team/CB; **186** Metropolitan Museum of Art, Wolfe Fund,1931, Catharine Lorillard Wolfe Collection (31.45); **187** Vatican Museum; **188** Scala/AR; **192** (l)RH, (r)Fitzwilliam Museum, U. of Cambridge, UK/BAL; **194** file photo; **197** Bettmann/CB; **198** Tom Lovell/NGS; **199** (l)Vanni Archive/CB, (r)Aaron Haupt; **202** Museum of Fine Arts, Boston; **203** (tl)Museum of Fine Arts, Boston, (tr)Giraudon/AR, (bl)courtesy Museum of Fine Arts, Boston, (br)Oriental Institute Museum, U. of Chicago; **206** (l)BAL, (r)Giraudon/AR; **208** (l)Metropolitan Museum of Art, Fletcher Fund, 1924. (24.97.21ab), (r)Archivo Iconografico, S.A./CB; **210** file photo; **212** (l)Scala/AR, (r)Richard Pasley/SS; **213** Archiv/PR; **215** Vatican Museum; **218** (l)Francis G. Mayer/CB, (r)SM; **220** Scala/AR; **221** (l)EL/AR, (r)Mark Richards/PhotoEdit; **222** Smithsonian Institution; **223** Pinacoteca Capitolina, Palazzo Conservatori, Rome/BAL; **225** MH; **226** Stanley Seaberg; **227** Scala/AR; **229** NWPA; **232** (l)MH, (r)EL/AR; **237** 1994 Board of Trustees, National Gallery of Art, Washington/Sir Peter Paul Rubens, *Tiberius and Agrippina*; **238** (l)Nimatallah/AR, (r)Robert Essel/TSM; **243** BAL; **246** (l)Elio Ciol/CB, (r)Scala/AR; **248** (t)MH, (b)Scala/AR; **249** Doug Martin; **252** North Carolina Museum of Art/CB; **254** (l)Galleria dell' Accademia, Florence, Italy/BAL, (r)Miklos Szabo/LA; **255** Giraudon/AR; **258** Nathan Benn/CB; **259** (tl)Gianni Dagli Orti/CB, (tr)Charles & Josette Lenars/CB, (bl br)Nathan Benn/CB; **262** (l)WF/AR, (r)Pierpont Morgan Library/AR; **264** (l)Walters Art Gallery, Baltimore, (r)SS; **266** SM; **267** RS/AAA; **268** (l)NWPA, (r)Kevin Jacobs/Image Works; **274** (l)Scala/AR, (r)Giraudon/AR; **278** file photo; **280** Scala/AR; **282** SM; **283** (l)Archive Photos, (r)Aaron Haupt; **285** file photo; **288** (l)BAL, (r)MH; **291** file photo; **292** Stapleton Collection/BAL; **293** (l)Bettmann/CB, (r)A. Ramey/PhotoEdit; **298** (l)WF/AR, (r)York Archaeological Trust; **300** Lennart Larsen/Frances Lincoln Publishers; **302** (l)(c)British Museum, (r)BAL; **303** Charles & Josette Lenars/CB; **305** (l)(c)British Museum, (r)Randall Hyman/Stock Boston; **307** (l)Tom Lovell/NGS, (r)RS/AAA; **310** Burstein Collection/CB; **311** (t)Borromeo/AR, (c)Scala/AR, (b)Charles & Josette Lenars/CB; **314** (l)Basilica di Sant'Apollinare Nuovo, Ravenna/Explorer, Paris/SS, (r)Scala/AR; **316** (l)WF/British Museum/AR, (r)AAA; **318** (l)Capitoline Museum, Rome/SS, (r) Michael Hampshire/NGS; **319** Dumbarton Oaks; **320** Andre Durenceau/NGS; **321** MH; **325** (l)AA, (r)David Ball/TSM; **326** C.M. Dixon; **330** (l)EL/AR, (r)MH; **333** Robert Azzi/WC; **335** (l)ARAMCO, (r)Pablo Koch/Vision International; **339** (l)AA, (r)Jeff Greenberg/PR; **340** Pablo Koch/Vision International; **342** Freer Gallery of Art, Smithsonian Institution, Washington, D.C. (29.9), *Jug with a bottle neck*, Persia, Seljuk, early 13th century, glazed clay, 18.0x14.8cm; **343** Bodleian Library, Oxford; **346** (l)Christie's Images/SS, (r)Harald Sund/Image Bank; **348** Eugene Gilliom; **349** (t)Scala/AR, (b)Tretyakov Gallery, Moscow; **351** (l)1994 Board of Trustees, National Gallery of Art, Washington, Byzantine 13th century, *Enthroned Madonna and Child*, Gift of Mrs. Otto H. Kahn, (r)Pablo Koch/Vision International; **352** file photo; **353** (l)Statens Historiska Museum, Stockholm, Sweden, (r)Kremlin Museums, Moscow/BAL; **354** file photo; **355** SM; **357** Nationalmuseet, Copenhagen/BAL; **360** Arthur Tilley/FPG; **361** (tl, bc)Dewitt Jones/CB, (tr)George Ranalli/PR, (bl)Tim Davis/PR, (br)Richard A. Cooke/CB; **364** (l)EL/AR, (r)Malcolm Gibson/FPG; **366** Ashmolean Museum/BAL; **366** Pierpont Morgan Library/AR; **370** Scala/AR; **371** Norma Brenneman; **372** (l)Pierpont Morgan Library/AR, (r)Jeff Christensen/LA; **374** BAL; **376** SS; **377** file photo; **380** EL/AR; **382** Don Nieman; **383** Borromeo/AR; **384** (l)MH, (r)Cooper-Hewitt Museum, Smithsonian Institution/AR; **385 387** Bettmann/CB; **389** SM; **390** Lance Nelson/TSM; **392** (l)SM, (r) Robert W. Nicholson/NGS; **393** (t)Library of Istanbul University, (b)file photo; **395** 1994 Board of Trustees, National Gallery of Art, Washington, French 12th century, *Reliquary chasse*, Widener Collection; **398** (l)Archivo Iconografico, S.A./CB, (r)Scala/AR; **402** Giraudon/AR; **404** (t)David Young-Wolfe/PhotoEdit, (b)NWPA; **410** (l)EL/AR, (r)A. Woolfitt/WC/PNI; **412** (t)file photo, (b)Bibliotheque Nationale, Paris/BAL; **414** Tom Lovell/NGS; **416** file photo; **418** Musees Nationaux; **419** SM; **420** Archiv/PR; **421** (l)Biblioteca Trivulziana, Milan/BAL, (r)Bernard Annebicque/CS; **423** BAL; **426** MH; **427** (tl)Victoria & Albert Museum, London/AR, (tr)Tony Stone Images, (cl)Scala/AR, (cr)WF/AR, (b)Michael S. Yamashita/CB; **430** (l)Pepys Library, Magdalene College, Cambridge, (r)Michael Freeman/CB; **432** (l)Scala/AR, (r)Il Museo Leonardo da Vinci; **434** Scala/AR; **435** (l)file photo, (r)Louvre, Paris/AR; **437** (l)Scala/AR, (r)Chuck Savage/TSM; **439** Bodleian Library, Oxford, fol.218r (Venice); **443** (t)file photo, (b)Folger Shakespeare Library; **444** (l)LOC, (r)Folger Shakespeare Library; **445** (l)SM, (r)Folger Shakespeare Library; **448** (l)Sammlungen des Stiftes, Klosterneuburg, Austria/EL/AR, (r)SS; **450** Michael Hampshire/NGS; **452** Museo del Castello Sforzesco, Milan, Italy/BAL; **453** (l)Giraudon/Art Resource, (r)Toyohiro Yamada/FPG; **454** Giraudon/AR; **455** SM; **456** (t)National Portrait Gallery, (b) (c)Reserved to Her Majesty Queen Elizabeth II; **457** (l)MH, (r)Scala/AR; **458** Scala/AR; **459** National Maritime Museum; **460** National Portrait Gallery, London/SS; **461** Victoria & Albert Museum, London/BAL; **466** (l)Victoria & Albert Museum, London/BAL, (r)MH; **468** (l)Archivo Iconografico, S.A./CB, (r)NASA; **469** Bettmann/CB; **470** SM; **471 472** file photos; **474** (l)SM/SS, (r)file photo; **476** Collection of The New-York Historical Society; **480** Philadelphia Museum of Art/CB; **481** (tl)Tanzania National Museum, Dar es Salaam/WF/AR, (tc)RS/AAA, (tr)Hugh Sitton/Tony Stone Images, (bl)David Butz/FPG, (bc br)RS/AAA; **484** (t)Science & Society Picture Library/Science Museum, London, (b)ME; **486** (l)courtesy Pecos National Historic Park, (r)Paul Almasy/CB; **488** Bibliotheque Nationale, Paris; **489** file photo; **490** (c)British Museum; **491** (l) (c)British Museum, (r)Wolfgang Kaehler; **493** Bettmann/CB; **496** Courtesy Enoch Pratt Free Library, reprinted by permission; **497** Culver Pictures/PNI; **502** (t)PR, (b)SM; **506** (l)BAL, (r)National Gallery of Art; **507** (c) Reserved to Her Majesty Queen Elizabeth II; **509** file photo; **510** LOC; **512** Virginia Museum of Fine Arts, Junius Brutus Stearns, *Washington Addressing the Constitutional Convention* (detail), oil on canvas, 37.5' x 54'; **514 515** Giraudon/AR; **516** Aaron Haupt; **517** Huntington Library Art Collections & Botanical Gardens, San Marino, CA/SS; **519** (l)ME, (r)Christie Linford/LA; **522** (l)ME, (r)Bettmann/CB; **525** Bettmann/CB; **528** (l)New York State Historical Association, Cooperstown, NY. Photo by Richard Walker, (r)NWPA; **531** (l)LOC, (r)Greg Girard/TSM; **532** Courtesy Sheffield City Museums; **534** Victoria & Albert Museum, London/AR; **535** file photo; **538** Scala/AR; **539** (tl)Hermitage, St. Petersburg, Russia/BAL, (tr)Bibliotheque Nationale, Paris/BAL, (cl, cr)AAA, (b)Kremlin Museums, Moscow/BAL; **542** (l)Science & Society Picture Library/Science Museum, London, (r)Royal Pavilion Libraries & Museums, Brighton & Hove; **544** (l)Christie's Images, (r)LOC; **547** LOC; **548** George Schneegass/Tom Stack & Assoc.; **550** National Portrait Gallery, Smithsonian Institution/AR; **552** AKG Photo; **554** Organization of American States; **556** Museu Paulista, Universite de Sao Paulo; **557** (l)Flag Research Center, Winchester, MA, (r)Gary A. Conner/PhotoEdit; **560** Peter Harholdt/SS; **562** Leonard de Selva/CB; **563** (t)Jules Talon/FPG, (b)SEF/AR; **566** SM; **568** Bettmann/CB; **569** (l)Tate Gallery, London/AR, (r)Mike King/CB; **570** Giraudon/AR; **573** Archivo Iconografico, S.A./CB; **575** file photo; **578** (t)Hans Georg Roth/CB, (b)E.K. Johnson/ME; **580** David L. Perry; **581** NWPA; **582** Michael Nicholson/CB; **583** (l)NGS, (r)A. Ramey/PhotoEdit; **584** SM; **585** MH; **586** Laurie Platt Winfrey; **587** Metropolitan Museum of Art/Laurie Platt Winfrey; **588 589** LOC; **592** CB; **596** Keren Su/AllStock/PNI; **597** (tl)Lindsay Hebberd/CB, (tr)Julia Waterlow, Eye Ubiquitous/CB, (cl)Ruth Kimpel, (cr)Fred Ward, (b)NGS; **600** NASA; **602** (l)Hulton-Deutsch Collection/CB, (r)Roger-Viollet/LA; **605** Courtesy Director, National Army Museum, London; **606** file photo; **608** Archivo Iconografico, S.A./CB; **609** (t)Archivo Iconografico, S.A./CB, (b)Bettmann/CB; **610** Sovfoto/Eastfoto; **611** Sovfoto/Eastfoto/PNI; **612** (l)Image Bank, (r)courtesy CNN; **613** FPG; **614** Bettmann/CB; **615** FPG; **616** Hulton-Deutsch Collection/CB; **618** U.S. Coast Guard Photo, National Archives; **620** (l)US Air Force Photo/FPG, (r)George Silk/Life Magazine/Time Warner; **621** Bettmann/CB; **624** (l)Photodisc, Inc., (r)Bettmann/CB; **626** UPI/Bettmann/CB; **627** Zadora/Sygma; **628** (t)Dennis Brack/Black Star, (b)Sygma; **630** UPI/Bettmann/CB; **631** (l)Bettmann/CB, (r)Tom Stack/Tom Stack & Assoc.; **632** Peter Turnley/Black Star; **635** (l)Jehangir Gazdar/WC, (r)Topham/Image Works; **636** Ron McMillan/LA; **638** (l)James Sugar/Black Star, (r)Abbas/Magnum; **639** Paulo Fridman/CS; **640** Robert Frerck/Odyssey; **641** (l)Farrell Grehan/FPG, (r)Natsuko Utsumi/LA; **644** (l)Courtesy Apple Computer, Inc., (r)CB; **646** (l)R. Bossu/CS, (r)Lee Snider/ImageWorks; **647** Ivo Lorenc/CS; **649** A. Gyori/CS; **650** (l)Chip Hires/LA, (r)Les Stone/CS; **653** S. Compoint/CS; **654** Alexandra Soulat/Sipa; **655** Amit Shabi/Reuters/STR/Archive Photos; **656** Sion Touhig/CS; **657** Carol Havens/CB; **658** Vince Streano/CB; **659** Jean-Marc Bouju/Wide World Photos; **661** Liz Gilbert/CS; **662** Steve Liss/Timepix; **664** Ch. Simonpietri/CS; **665** Pierre Toutain-Dorbec/CS; **669** (t)AFP/CB, (cl) Richard Lewis/AP/Wide World Photos, (cr) Sean Gallup/Getty Images, (b) Zia Mazhar/AP/Wide World Photos; **672** Louvre, Paris/SS; **673** Courtesy Oakland Museum of California; **675** John Reader/SPL/PR; **677** Gianni Dagli Orti/CB; **679** AA; **681** Cummer Museum of Art & Gardens, Jacksonville, FL/SS; **683** AA; **685** Universitetets Oldsaksamling, Oslo/WF/AR; **687** St. Mark's Cathedral, Venice/WF/AR; **689** Archivo Iconografico, S.A./CB; **691** WF/AR; **693** ME; **695** (l)ME, (r)Earl Kowall/CB; **697** Getty Images.

744